Proceedings of the

FIFTH EUROMICRO WORKSHOP ON PARALLEL AND DISTRIBUTED PROCESSING

— PDP '97 —

Proceedings of the

FIFTH EUROMICRO WORKSHOP ON PARALLEL AND DISTRIBUTED PROCESSING

— PDP '97 —

University of Westminster

January 22–24, 1997   London, United Kingdom

IEEE Computer Society Press
Los Alamitos, California

Washington   •   Brussels   •   Tokyo

IEEE Computer Society Press
10662 Los Vaqueros Circle
P.O. Box 3014
Los Alamitos, CA 90720-1314

IEEE Computer Society Press Order Number PR07770
ISBN 0-8186-7770-8
ISSN 1066-6192

Additional copies may be ordered from:

IEEE Computer Society Press
Customer Service Center
10662 Los Vaqueros Circle
P.O. Box 3014
Los Alamitos, CA 90720-1314
Tel: + 1-714-821-8380
Fax: + 1-714-821-4641
E-mail: cs.books@computer.org

IEEE Computer Society
13, Avenue de l'Aquilon
B-1200 Brussels
BELGIUM
Tel: + 32-2-770-2198
Fax: + 32-2-770-8505
euro.ofc@computer.org

IEEE Computer Society
Ooshima Building
2-19-1 Minami-Aoyama
Minato-ku, Tokyo 107
JAPAN
Tel: + 81-3-3408-3118
Fax: + 81-3-3408-3553
tokyo.ofc@computer.org

Editorial production by Lorretta Palagi
Art production by Alex Torres
Printed in the United States of America by Technical Communication Services

 The Institute of Electrical and Electronics Engineers, Inc.

Contents

Keynote Session 1

Chair: H. P. Zima

> **Speaker:** P. Mehrotra
> *Programming Paradigms for Future Parallel Architectures*

Session 1: Scheduling and Load Balancing

Chair: A. M. Tyrrell

Open Forum Session 1

Chair: B. Di Martino

Session 2: Architectures I

Chair: A. Antola

Session 3: Parallel Applications

Chair: N. Scarabottolo

Session 4: Support Systems for Parallel Applications

Chair: P. Kacsuk

Session 5: Compiler and Run-Time Technology

Chair: P. Milligan

Open Forum Session 2

Chair: B. Di Martino

Session 6: Compiler Technology

Chair: C. A. Thole

Session 7: Architectures II

Chair: E. Pissaloux

Keynote Session 2

Chair: S. C. Winter

Speaker: A. Hey
The Problem of Parallel Program Performance Estimation

Session 8: Parallel Programming Environments

Chair: B. Di Martino

Open Forum Session 3

Chair: B. Di Martino

Session 9: Numerical Algorithms

Chair: G. Sechi

Session 10: Performance Analysis and Evaluation

Chair: S. Smith

Program and Organizing Chairs' Message

Welcome to the Fifth Euromicro Workshop on Parallel and Distributed Processing (PDP'97)! This workshop on parallel and distributed processing is one of the key events in the field and attracts leading researchers and practitioners from industry and academia from all over the world.

Parallel and distributed processing constitute the key elements of high-performance computing. This field is currently undergoing dramatic development, involving major paradigm shifts in areas such as architectures, operating systems, languages, and programming environments. This fifth Euromicro workshop aims at providing a forum for the presentation of original research and the exchange of new ideas at the highest technical level.

The workshop includes two keynote sessions, with invited eminent speakers; 3 sessions for open forum presentations; and 10 sessions of full paper presentations, covering topics in architectures, software engineering, performance evaluation, compiler and run-time technology, and application development for parallel and distributed systems.

More than 100 papers were submitted to the workshop, authored by researchers from 28 different nations. The review process resulted in the selection of 34 papers for full presentation and 35 papers for open forum presentation.

The organisers would like to thank the University of Westminster for its support. We also wish to thank everyone who submitted a paper for consideration and all of the Program Committee members and reviewers for their hard work in evaluating the papers. We are particularly indebted to Chiquita Snippe-Marlisa, Euromicro's administrative manager, who guided us in the organization of this workshop. Special thanks also go to Lorretta Palagi of the IEEE Computer Society Support Staff for her great help and support in producing the proceedings.

Enjoy the workshop!

Hans P. Zima
Program Chair

Beniamino Di Martino
Deputy Program Chair

Stephen C. Winter
Organizing Chair

Program and Organizing Committee

Program Chair

Hans P. Zima

Institute for Software Technology and Parallel Systems
University of Vienna

Deputy Program Chair

Beniamino Di Martino

Institute for Software Technology and Parallel Systems
University of Vienna

Organizing Chair

Stephen C. Winter

Centre for Parallel Computing
University of Westminster

Euromicro Manager

Chiquita Snippe-Marlisa

Program Committee

A. Antola	G. Iannello	N. Scarabottolo
F. Baetke	F. Irigoin	G. Sechi
M. C. Calzarossa	S. Jaehnichen	G. Serazzi
B. Chapman	P. Kacsuk	P. Sguazzero
G. Chiola	P. Mehrotra	H. J. Sips
M. Dal Cin	P. Milligan	C. A. Thole
M. Delves	J. Moscinski	R. Trobec
B. Di Martino	D. Padua	T. Tsuda
T. Fahringer	R. Perrott	A. M. Tyrrell
P. Feautrier	E. Pissaloux	M. Valero
M. Gerndt	I. Plander	S. Winter
J. Gurd	R. Ralha	E. L. Zapata
	J. H. Saltz	H. P. Zima

Session Chairs

A. Antola	G. Sechi
B. Di Martino	S. Smith
P. Kacsuk	C. A. Thole
P. Milligan	A. Tyrrell
E. Pissaloux	S. C. Winter
N. Scarabottolo	H. P. Zima

Referees

Cesare Alippi
Corinne Ancourt
Cosimo Anglano
Anna Antola
F. Arguello
Frank Baetke
Gerardo Bandera
Denis Barthou
Siegfried Benkner
Robert Bennett
Massimo Bernaschi
Jost Bernert
Rudolf Berrendorf
Matthias Besch
Michael D. Beynon
Cart Bik
Polona Blaznik
F. Bodin
Thomas Brandes
Luca Breveglieri
Peter Brezany
Maria Calzarossa
Aleksandar Celic
Barbara Chapman
Giovanni Chiola
Alok Choudhary
Paolo Cremonesi
Fabien Coelho
Patrick Corr
Luc Coyett
Beatrice Creusillet
David Cronk
Danny Crookes
Mario Dal Cin
J. A. Dell
L. M Delves
Luiz De Rose
Ulrich Detert
Beniamino Di Martino
Ramon Doallo
Gabor Dozsa
Pavol Duris
Jose Duato
Daniel Etiemble
Tibor Fadgyas
Thomas Fahringer
Paul Feuatrier
Salvatore Filippone
Rupert Ford
Franco Frattolillo
Andrea Fumagalli
Claudio Gennaro

Michael Gerndt
Ian Glendinning
P. Grassberger
John Gurd
Rudolf G. Hackenberg
Matthew Haines
Ulrich Heinkel
Hermann Hellwagner
Walter Henning
Helmut Hessenauer
Jay Hoeflinger
Jim Humphries
Yuan-Shin Hwang
Giulio Iannello
Francois Irigoin
Stefan Jaehnichen
Pierre Jouvelot
Peter Kacsuk
Nasser Kalantery
Eduard Kelc
Carl Kesselman
Jacek Kitowski
Dusan Krajcovic
Frits Kuijlman
Josep Larriba-Pey
Mario Lauria
Jaejin Lee
Jochen Liedtke
Juan Lopez
Paolo Marenzoni
Luisa Massari
Nicola Mazzocca
Hugh McEvoy
Eduard Mehofer
Piyush Mehrotra
Alessandro Merlo
Hermann Mierendorff
Peter Milligan
Bernd Mohr
Catherine Mongenet
Hans Moritsch
Jacek Moscinski
Andy Nisbet
Klaus Obermayer
Martin Padeffke
David Padua
Yun PaekYunheung Paek
Dietrch Paulus
Mario Pantano
Tomas F. Pena
Ron Perrott
Edwige Pissaloux

Ivan Plander
Norbert Podhorszki
Matteo Pugassi
Zsolt Puskas
Rui Ralha
M. Ranganathan
Marina Ribaudo
Graham Riley
Guy Robinson
Kevin Roe
Emilia Rosti
Stefano Russo
Paul Sage
Joel Saltz
Kamran Sanjari
Iztok Savnik
Nello Scarabottolo
Friedrich Wilhelm Schroeer
Wolfgang Schroeder-Preikschat
Giacomo R. Sechi
Giuseppe Serazzi
Volkmar Sieh
Jurij Silc
Viera Sipkova
Henk J. Sips
Piero Sguazzero
Bostjan Slivnik
S. L. Smith
Angela Sodan
Dietrich Stauffer
Henry Strauss
Daniele Tessera
Clemens-August Thole
Claude Timsit
Roman Trobec
A. M. Tyrrell
Guillermo P. Trabado
Oliver Tschaeche
Patrick Valduriez
Mateo Valero
Arjan J. C. van Gemund
C. van Reeuwijk
Maarten van Steen
Valeria Vittorini
Lionel Waring
Dave Watson
Willy Weisz
Bernd Wender
S C Winter
Klaus Wolf
Shahrzad Zarandi
Hans P. Zima

❖ KEYNOTE SESSION 1 ❖

Programming Paradigms for Future Parallel Architectures

Speaker

P. Mehrotra

Chair

H. P. Zima

❖ SESSION 1 ❖

Scheduling and Load Balancing

Chair

A. M. Tyrrell

Mapping of Coarse-Grained Applications
onto Workstation-Clusters *

Thomas Decker and Ralf Diekmann

Department of Mathematics and Computer Science
University of Paderborn, D-33095 Paderborn, Germany
http://www.uni-paderborn.de/cs/ag-monien.html
e-mail: {*decker, diek*}*@uni-paderborn.de*

Abstract

We present an environment for configuring and co-ordinating coarse grained parallel applications on workstation clusters. The environment named CoPA is based on PVM and allows an automatic distribution of functional modules as they occur in typical CAE-applications. By implementing link-based communication on top of PVM, CoPA is able to perform a "post-game" analysis of the communication load between different modules. Together with the computational load which is also determined automatically by CoPA, all necessary information is available to calculate an optimized mapping for the next run of the application. To optimize the distribution of modules onto workstations CoPA uses state-of-the-art partitioning heuristics as well as Simulated Annealing. Measurements show the large improvements in running time obtained by using optimization heuristics to determine the mapping.

1 Introduction

A balanced distribution of data objects or program modules is one of the most important premises for the efficient use of parallel and distributed systems.

Using massively parallel systems with distributed memory to solve complex problems is a well researched area. Much work has been done on efficiently utilizing multi-processor parallel systems (MPPs). MPPs are usually scalable up to nearly any numbers of processors. The most popular programming model used within such systems is *Single Program, Multiple Data* (SPMD) where every processor executes the same program, but on different data. Here, load balancing is often reduced to the problem of balancing the *data* properly [3].

With the introduction of parallel runtime systems like PVM or MPI, that are independent of the hardware, it is possible to use LAN-connected workstations as parallel systems. The characteristics of such WS-clusters differ significantly from those of MPPs. The single-node performance is nearly the same in both types of systems, but the overhead of initiating communications is much larger in WS-clusters, whereas the available communication throughput is much lower. WS-clusters are usually smaller than MPPs and because of their limited communication performance not scalable to arbitrary sizes.

Therefore, parallel applications which are supposed to run on such systems do not necessarily have to be scalable. It is sufficient, if they are able to use a moderately small number of processors. But because of the limited communication performance of WS-clusters, such applications should be coarse grained. They should produce relatively large computational load but should use only a small amount of communication, where *small* mainly refers to the number of messages (because of the large initiation overheads).

The work described in this paper deals with applications not following the SPMD-approach but consisting of different functional modules which are able to run in parallel. Such applications can be found for example in the area of *Computer Aided Engineering (CAE)*, where virtual laboratories consisting of different "devices" are simulated by a computer [15]. Every device within such a laboratory is simulated by a functional module which repeatedly calculates (sometimes complex) functions from a set of inputs and generates a number of outputs. These outputs are then fed into other modules as inputs. Such applications are characterized by their natural parallelism. They are often coarse grained, but not scalable and thus are particularly suited to be executed on WS-clusters.

The aim of our work is the design of a simple and easy-to-use configuration- and co-ordination environment which allows the user a comfortable definition of complex applications. A once defined configuration of "devices" can be loaded onto arbitrary WS-clusters without any further knowledge about parallel programming, runtime environments, etc. Particularly, the problem of load balancing, i.e. the assignment of modules to workstations to minimize the

---

*Supported by the NRW-MWF-Project "Die Bearbeitung komplexer Entwurfsprozesse der Mechatronik mit Hilfe lokal vernetzter Workstationsysteme", the DFG-Sonderforschungsbereich 376 "Massive Parallelität", EU ESPRIT Long Term Research Project 20244 (ALCOM-IT), and the EC HC&M Project MAP.

5

overall execution time, is done automatically.

The configuration- and co-ordination environment *CoPA* (Coordination of Parallel Applications) requires that all modules which are used within a configuration are available and ready to be started. Each module contains a message passing interface which defines a number of in- and outgoing channels. The interfaces have to be known by CoPA. A configuration is mainly described by a graph connecting the I/O-interfaces of the used modules. The basic runtime environment is PVM [9].

In order to be able to calculate an optimized mapping of modules onto workstations, CoPA needs information about the computational load of nodes and the communication load of edges within the configuration graph. This information is determined by a "post-game" analysis of test-runs of the applications [17]. Such an analysis is of course only advisable if the application is going to run with the same or similar characteristics for some time afterwards. Fortunately, this is the case in the application area CoPA is aiming at. Applications in CAE often perform parameter optimizations which result in doing the same type of calculations for a large number of runs.

The basic load balancing problem for homogeneous workstation clusters using a bus-type interconnection (i.e., Ethernet, Token-Ring, FDDI) can be modelled as a partitioning problem. Here the task is to split a node- and edge-weighted graph into a number of equal-weighted clusters, minimizing the communication weights of edges connecting nodes in different clusters (in order to minimize the communication load on the network). The problem becomes more difficult if heterogeneous WS-clusters are supposed to be used and the difficulties increase even more if the communication network is heterogeneous, too. The latter is the case if machines in different sub-networks are used or if the processors are connected by a communication network instead of a bus.

Another difficuly arises from the fact that workstations may be used by competing applications which leads to a reduction in the computing power available for the CoPA-application. As the partitioning is based only on the characteristics of the application, influences by other applications cannot be considered. One possibility to face this problem is to use CoPA for the generation of an optimal initial placement of the application and, if neccessary, re-balance the load of the workstation by using dynamic load balancing systems like *MIST* [2].

CoPA uses a number of existing partitioning heuristics [5, 13] as well as Simulated Annealing (SA) [3, 4, 14] as more general optimization methods to determine a good distribution of modules over workstations.

The existing research in the area of mapping parallel applications onto WS-clusters mainly deals with the problem of *task-graph scheduling* [11, 12]. Usually, the tasks of such applications are able to run independently of each other and communicate only at the beginning and the end of their execution. Research dealing with applications consisting of parallel running functional modules [10] up to know mainly uses very simple mapping heuristics [1] or is not applicable to the type of long-running jobs we consider. This is mainly due to the type of heuristics used to optimize the mapping. In [17], for example, a "post-game" analysis is used to slightly improve the next execution of an application. To obtain an optimized mapping, a large number of runs is necessary. This is certainly not possible in our type of application.

Thus, CoPA is a novel approach integrating configuration, monitoring, and static load balancing into one environment.

The next section describes the configuration environment CoPA. In section 3 we give the details to the used mapping heuristics and section 4 shows results of simulations on up to eight workstations and on a PowerPC-601 based parallel system *(GC/PP)*.

2 Configuration of Applications

We assume parallel applications to consist of a certain number of autonomous processes which communicate with each other by exchanging messages. Besides the implementation of these processes, the programmer has to solve a *mapping*-problem, which means that he has to place the processes onto the available resources and that he has to organize the communication of the processes. We face both problems with our programming environment *CoPA*. The incorporated mapping and organisation methods qualify CoPA to relieve the programmer from the task of configuring his application.

2.1 The Basic System: PVM

Within CoPA, PVM is used to start the processes on arbitrary hardware components and as a message-passing layer. As PVM only provides the basic functions for parallel programming, more complex tasks like the process mapping are left to the user. Although PVM is capable to place a new process automatically, this is done without any knowledge of the structure of the application which in most cases leads to inefficient mappings of the tasks onto the processors. The specification of the host on which a new process is to be executed by the programmer is again of disadvantage, as the exact hardware configuration on which the application will be executed has to be known at the time of programming. This is not possible in general, because the configuration of the virtual machine changes dynamically (i.e., new hardware components can be added and others be deleted).

Another difficulty which arises from the structure of the PVM-library is the determination of the communication partners of a process. Within PVM, every task is addressed

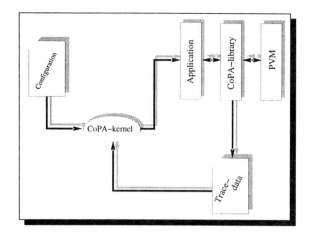

Figure 1: *The CoPA-components and their connections.*

by its uniquely "Task-Identifier (TID)" (which is initially known only to the generator of the process and to the process itself). Consequently, at the time of programming the communication structure of the application has to be known. This restriction aggravates the design of reusable modules, which are to be used within a variety of communication structures or applications.

These configuration problems particularly arise in applications, which are parallelized on the base of functional modules (i.e. each module is designed to fulfil a certain function). From the software engineering point of view, it is desirable for these applications that the basic modules are implemented independently from a concrete application. Only with help of in such a way universally applicable modules, complex applications can be constructed with little effort.

2.2 The Configuration Environment CoPA

With the configuration environment CoPA the programmer is given a tool which on the one hand helps him to build reusable functional modules and on the other hand makes it possible to build and execute complex applications without any expert knowledge in the area of load-balancing and mapping.

Two main concepts allow the strict separation between implementation and usage of the functional modules. First, there is the channel-technique: Every module communicates via a certain number of channels with other processes. The CoPA-library therefore supplies convenient channel oriented send- and receive routines. In order to perform checks of the consistency, it is possible to specify the data types which are allowed to be transmitted through each channel. Additionally, the number of channels can be determined dynamically at runtime. By specifying the semantics of each channel and of course of the module itself, the full functionality of each module can be implemented in advance without any knowledge of the concrete application.

The second concept deals with the configuration of the application. Given the different functional modules, the user has to assemble his application by combining and connecting the modules. This is done with a special configuration language which consists of constructions for the convenient definition of

- the modules to be used with their signature (number of input- and output channels),

- the connection-scheme of the modules

- the hardware characteristics of the hosts which are to be used for the execution.

The CoPA-kernel parses this configuration, calculates a mapping of the processes onto the processors and places the processes. After this start-up phase, the kernel acts as a monitor for the application and thus is responsible for the measurement of the dynamic behaviour of the application and for the termination. This is supported by the runtime system (CoPA-library) which controls the communication of the processes. Figure 1 summarizes these components and their connections. The gathered runtime data is stored and is the base for the calculation of the process-mapping in the next execution of the same application. The methods which are used to obtain the mapping are described more exactly in section 3.

Moreover, a graphical representation of the runtime behaviour is generated with help of the *VCG*-tool ([16]). In this graph, each box (node) stands for one process. The thickness of the boundaries corresponds to the user-time of the process while the mapping which is generated by CoPA is represented by the colours of the boxes (cf. Figure 6). Similarly, the thickness of the connecting edges describes the total number of bytes transmitted through each channel.

2.3 The configuration language

With help of the configuration language, the user supplies information about the application structure and the hardware characteristics which is necessary to obtain a suitable mapping. The former consists of a description of the CoPA-processes as well as of the definition of the connections between them. Figure 2 for example, shows a configuration of a very simple parameter-optimizing application.

2.3.1 Hardware description:

As the communication in the area of workstation clusters is typically realized by bus-orientated media, a detailed description of the connection structure is omitted. In such systems, it is adequate to characterize a communication between two process to be either intern (both processes are on the same processor) or extern (between two processors). The costs for each of the two kinds of communication are determined by two parameters: one for the time needed for starting a message and one for the time it takes

```
/* Linex parameter optimization */

begin  /* hardware */
set placement = all-hs;

set L_ext=0.000001; set L_int=0.0000003;
host(werre, SUN4SOL2, 1.0);

process mopo     is (mopo  [1,1]) arg 1;
process linprep  is (prep  [1,1]);
process linstoch is (stoch [1,1]);

/* data flow : */

connect mopo[0]      -> linprep[0];
connect linprep[0]   -> linstoch[0];
connect linstoch[0]  -> mopo[0];
end;
```

Figure 2: *A simple CoPA-application. The configuration file generates one branch of the Linex-1 application shown in Figure 4.*

to transmit one byte. Consequently, in CoPA the communication performance is characterized by setting four parameters (L_int, o_int, L_ext, o_ext).

The participating hosts (workstations or other processing-resources) are described by entries of the form host (*name*, *architecture*, *performance-rate*). Both the architecture and particularly the relative performance-rate are taken into consideration by the mapping procedure.

2.3.2 Software description:

The second part of a configuration deals with the description of the application. First of all, the different processes have to be declared. This is done by statements of the form:

process *virt_name* is (*process_name* [*i,o*])

This defines the process *virt_name* which has *i* input- and *o* output-channels. *process_name* specifies the filename of the executable code which has to be started. By an optional parameter arg it is possible to define runtime-arguments with which the process should be started. The advantage of using virtual process names is that several copies of the same code can be started without loosing the distinctiveness of the processes.

After specifying the processes, the channels have to be connected via the connect-statement:

connect *source* [*link1*] -> *dest* [*link2*] ;

source and *dest* describe the virtual names of the source- and the destination process respectively. Strictly speaking, link number *link1* of process *source* is connected to link number *link2* of process *dest*.

The configuration in Figure 2 for example generates one branch of the Linex-1-application shown in Figure 4.

2.3.3 Influencing the mapping strategy:

The overall mapping strategy is selected by setting the placement variable. Currently, the following values are accepted:

man: manual placement (according to the place-statements)

sa: placement via Simulated Annealing

global–local: heuristic placement using partitioning algorithms. *global* defines the strategy for generating an initial partitioning. Afterwards this partitioning is improved by exchange heuristics (specified by the parameter *local*) like the *Kernighan-Lin (KL)-* or the *Helpful-Set (HS)*-method ([13]).

If the man-option is used, the placement is described via the place-statement, which takes two arguments:

place (*virt_name*, {*hostname|architecture*}).

In case only the architecture is specified, the process is assigned to one of the matching processors with a round-robin strategy.

3 Mapping
3.1 Application Analysis

A useful side effect of the link-based communication implemented by CoPA is the ability to determine the number and size of messages sent between any pair of modules within an application (cf. Sec. 2). Additionally, CoPA measures the user- and system-time of each module. Together with the knowledge about the interconnection structure, this information forms a node- and edge-weighted graph expressing the characteristics of an application. This graph is the basis for an optimization of the module distribution.

3.2 Mapping by Graph Partitioning

Workstation clusters are usually interconnected by a bus structure (e.g. Ethernet, Token Ring or FDDI) and there are only two types of communication to distinguish: Local communication within a workstation and external communication between processes on different workstations. Therefore, the mapping problem can be reduced to the problem of partitioning the (weighted) application graph into as many equal weighted clusters as there are numbers of processors. The optimization criterion here is to balance the load evenly (according to the speed of the different workstations if heterogeneous clusters are considered) and to minimize the total amount of external communication.

For the graph partitioning problem there exist a number of powerful heuristics (cf. [5] for an overview) which are

```
PROCEDURE SIMULATED_ANNEALING
    start with initial configuration s; k := 0;
    t_k := T_0;  (* initial temperature *)
    REPEAT
        REPEAT
            choose neighbouring configuration s' ∈ R_s;
            calculate ΔC = C(s) − C(s');
            IF (exp (ΔC/t_k) > rand(0, 1)) set s := s';
        UNTIL Equilibrium()
        t_{k+1} := α_k · t_k;  (* temperature reduction *)
        k := k + 1;
    UNTIL Frozen()  (* termination *)
```

Figure 3: The Simulated Annealing Algorithm.

efficiently implemented and available as libraries [7, 13]. These heuristics are able to partition even very large graphs in a short amount of time resulting in very low external communication demands. In CoPA, we use the partitioning library *PARTY* by Preis [13] which also contains some of the functionalities of the *Chaco*-library by Hendrickson and Leland [7]. Besides of very efficient *global* partitioning methods like the *Farhat* algorithm or the *Spectral* method, we are able to use the *KL*- and the *HS*-heuristic as *local* improvement methods [5].

Most of the existing partitioning heuristics perform best on unweighted graphs. They are able to deal with weighted graphs, but if the range of different weights (especially node weights) becomes to large, they run into problems (we will report on some of the problems in Section 4). On the other hand, the proposed applications in CoPA are not very large (normally less than hundred processes). So a more expensive optimization heuristic like Simulated Annealing can still be used to determine a mapping of modules to workstations. In the next section we will see how this is done.

3.3 Mapping by Simulated Annealing

Simulated Annealing (SA) is a very general optimization principle based on the idea of stochastic local search. It operates on *configurations* which in our case are concrete mappings of modules to processors of the workstation cluster. Using a *cost function* C, it assigns a value to each configuration which for example expresses the quality of a mapping (we will see later how C is defined). The space of possible configurations is structured by defining a neighbouring relation, which usually is a simple perturbation transforming one configuration into another. Based on this structure of the solution space, SA performs a stochastic search. Starting from an actual configuration it repeatedly generates randomly chosen neighbouring solutions and calculates their costs (cf. Figure 3). If the search finds a neighbouring solution with lower costs, the actual configuration is replaced by the cheaper one (SA performs a *move*). But if the cost value of the new configuration is higher than the actual one, the move to the new solution

is done with a probability depending on the cost difference of the two configurations and a parameter *temperature*. The control of the temperature, i.e., the choice of T_0, $α_k$, *Equilibrium()* and *Frozen()* is done by a so called *cooling schedule*. This cooling schedule mainly determines the running time of SA and the quality of final solutions found by the search. Within CoPA we use the self adapting cooling schedule first described by Huang et. al. [8]. It adjusts the temperature according to the development of the cost function during the search (i.e., according to the mean value and standard deviation of the cost function). For more detailed descriptions, see [3, 4].

An application within CoPA is described by a graph $G = (V, E, w, c_a, c_g)$ with nodes V, edges $E \subseteq V \times V$, node weights $w: V \to \mathbb{R}$ describing the computational load of modules, and edge weights $c_a, c_g: E \to \mathbb{R}$ describing the number and total size of messages sent over an edge. A mapping onto a WS-cluster with P processors is described by a function $s: V \to \{1, \ldots, P\}$ which assigns each node $v \in V$ to a processor $s(v) \in \{1, \ldots, P\}$. Thus, a configuration is a concrete mapping s. To define the neighbourhood structure, we construct two operators $δ_s$ (swap of the positions of two nodes) and $δ_m$ (movement of one node to a different processor) by:

$$\delta_s(s, i, j) := \begin{cases} s(v) & \forall\, v \neq i, j \\ s(j) & \text{if } v = i \\ s(i) & \text{if } v = j \end{cases} \quad \text{and}$$

$$\delta_m(s, i, p) := \begin{cases} s(v) & \forall\, v \neq i \\ p & \text{if } v = i \end{cases}$$

The neighbourhood space R_s to a configuration s consists of all mappings s' which can be constructed by swapping the position of two nodes in s or by moving one node to another processor, i.e. $R_s := \{s' \mid s' = \delta_s(s, i, j) \lor s' = \delta_m(s, i, p) \text{ for arbitrary } i \neq j \in V, p \in \{1, \ldots, P\}\}$. For the choice of a neighbour s' we randomly select one of the two operators (with a probability of 80% for $δ_s$) and apply it to randomly chosen values of i, j and/or p.

The cost function should be a measure for the quality of a mapping, i.e. "good" mappings should have low costs and "bad" ones should generate high cost function values. Additionally, it is necessary that the cost function is sufficiently smooth. Usually, Simulated Annealing has problems with unsteady functions containing large jumps. To meet these demands we define single processor costs $C_p(s)$ which are caused by mapping s on processor $p \in \{1, \ldots, P\}$. Afterwards, we set the cost value of mapping s to $C(s) = \overline{C_p(s)} + \sigma(C_p(s))$, i.e. to the sum of the average single processor costs and the corresponding standard deviation. For the single processor costs we have:

$$C_p(s) = \sum_{\substack{v \in V, \\ s(v)=p}} \frac{w(v)}{Perf(p)} + \sum_{\substack{e=\{u,v\} \in E, \\ s(u)=s(v)=p}} c_a(e) \cdot (\hat{o} + \hat{L} \cdot c_g(e)) +$$

9

$$\sum_{\substack{e=\{u,v\}\in E,\\ s(u)=p\neq s(v)\vee\\ s(u)\neq p=s(v)}} c_a(e)\cdot(o+L\cdot c_g(e))$$

The first term in the above sum expresses the computational load caused by all modules which are placed onto processor p. The load is weighted by the relative performance $Perf(p)\in[0,1]$ of processor p (cf. Sec. 2). Thus, a placement of heavy modules onto slow workstations produces high costs.

The other two terms express the communication costs. L and o are the latency (time needed to send one byte) and overhead (time needed to initiate a communication) of the interconnection network. $\hat{L}$ and $\hat{o}$ are the corresponding times for processor internal communication. Both values can be assumed to be system specific constants as long as the application does not produce to much communication load.

Such a cost function can certainly not exactly predict the runtime needed by an application. It is not able to express application specific effects like idle times of modules or increasing latency times due to temporary communication hot spots. There are some attempts to take the dynamic behaviour of applications into consideration but up to now they lead to very complex sets of parameters which are difficult to handle [6]. Nevertheless, our cost function allows quantitative statements of the runtime, as can be observed from Figure 5.

4 Results

CoPA was first used in the area of *Computer Aided Engineering (CAE)*. More concrete, CoPA was used to configure simulations of mechatronic systems [15]. For the further evaluation of CoPA we developed a benchmark suite which is on the one hand capable of modelling the typical behaviour of the mechatronic application but on the other hand is flexible enough to simulate applications which are structured differently. Before describing this testbed, we will first give a short description of the "original" mechatronic application.

4.1 Simulating Mechatronical Systems

The characteristic feature of mechatronic systems is the combination of components from various disciplines (mechanics, electrical engineering, hydraulics, electromagnetics, etc.) to build up a module that is efficient and perhaps even equipped with local intelligence. In order to achieve not only optimally designed sub-components but an optimal behaviour of the entire system, it is from the very beginning indispensable to bear in mind a design integrating all components involved.

An important step towards a consistent computer-aided design of mechatronic systems is the standardization of the discipline-related description forms by the state-space representation well-known to the control-engineer. This representation builds up the groundwork of the consistent design environment *CAMeL (Computer-Aided Mechatronic Laboratory)*. CAMeL comprises all tools which are required for the design of complex mechatronic systems. CAMeL is made up of a number of tools for the design of mechatronic systems, among them e.g. the tools for linear identification and optimization (LINEX) and for non-linear simulation (SIMEX). The former is made up of the CAMeL components *LinPrep* (management and linearization), *LinStoch* (stochastic analysis), and *Mopo* (vector optimization). As these modules are realized as independent ADA-tasks, they can easily be adapted to PVM and thus to the CoPA environment [9].

In order to model the typical circling of parameters between these components, our benchmark application is also token-driven. It is made up of several copies of a worker-process which starts its calculation as soon as it receives a message through one of its input-channels. Afterwards, (eventually) new messages are generated and sent out of the output-channels to other worker-processes. The exact behaviour (calculation-time, number and size of generated messages) is described by the runtime-parameters given in the configuration file.

For the remainder of this paper we may concentrate on the constellations shown in Figure 4 and 6. *Linex-1* and *Linex-2* incorporate the typical behaviour of LINEX-applications (i.e., the central position of the *Mopo*-process, the calculation intensity of the *LinPrep*-process, and the intensive communication between the *LinPrep*- and the *LinStoch*-process). In contrast to *Linex-2*, *Linex-1* comprises a very symmetric behaviour.

trees (d) describes a whole divide-and-conquer-like application class. Each application of this class consists of two binary trees of depth d which are connected at the leaves.

4.2 Comparison of Different Mappings
4.2.1 Evaluation of the cost function.

For the use of Simulated Annealing, it is essential that the cost function C reflects the behaviour of the application at runtime. As we would like to minimize the total execution time, we have to check whether C determines high costs for mappings which take a long time to be executed or low costs for efficient mappings respectively.

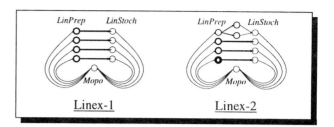

Figure 4: *Typical CAE-applications (the line-size corresponds to the communication or the calculation intensity.)*

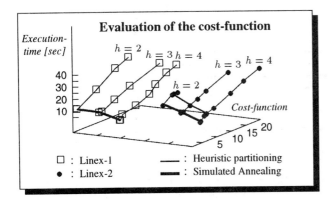

Evaluation of the cost-function

Execution-time [sec]

$h = 2$ $h = 3$ $h = 4$ $h = 3$ $h = 4$

40
30
20
10

$h = 2$

Cost-function

5   10   15   20

□ : Linex-1   —— : Heuristic partitioning
● : Linex-2   ▬▬ : Simulated Annealing

Figure 5: *Measured and calculated costs for mapping* Linex-1 *and* Linex-2 *onto h homogeneous workstations.*

More formally, we claim that for C the following condition holds: For each two mappings s_1 and s_2, we have $C(s_1) \leq C(s_2) \Rightarrow t(s_1) \leq t(s_2)$. In the optimal case, there should be a linear dependance between the cost function and the total execution time ($t(s) = \alpha \cdot C(s)$ for a constant α). Figure 5 shows the relation between the calculated and the measured costs of different mappings for the LINEX-applications.

The runs with high costs correspond to the provisional-results of the SA-algorithm. The costs of the mappings which were generated by the HS-heuristic were also calculated with the cost function C of the annealing algorithm. The final results of both algorithms are connected with a vertical line. Because of the high linearity of the cost function, the most efficient mappings were found by the SA-algorithm. In case of *Linex-2*, the mapping generated by the HS-method are slightly worse than those generated by SA. The reason for this is the fact that by reducing this special mapping problem to a pure partitioning problem, a lot of information which is incorporated in the cost function of SA gets lost.

4.2.2 Evaluation of the mapping strategies.

For the remainder of this section, we will further elaborate the results we obtained by investigating the *trees (d)*-application. Because of the large number of processes (e.g. *trees (d)* consists of 95 processes) and the larger amount of transmitted data this application class is better suited for the evaluation of the mapping techniques. Figure 6 shows a partitioning of *trees (5)* for eight workstations calculated by SA.

Simulated Annealing versus the HS-heuristic: Again, with the *trees*-application we found that the partitionings which were generated by the HS-method were not as balanced as those found by SA and led to longer execution times and thus to a lower speedup (cf. Figure 7). The advantage of HS is its short running time. For example, the partitioning of *trees (5)* with HS took only several seconds, whereas SA needed about 10 minutes. Nevertheless, it depends on the application whether this deficit in parti-

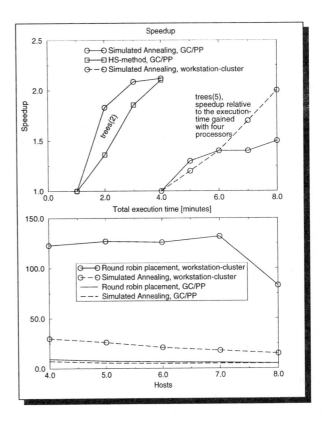

Figure 7: *Measurements of the speedup and the total execution times of the* trees-*application*

tioning quality can be tolerated or not. The loss of quality in case of *trees* (5) was so large that the resulting partitioning exceeded the capacity of both our workstations and the processors of our parallel computer.

Workstation-clusters versus MPPs: With the *trees* (5)-application, runs with a scattered mapping (round-robin) and with mappings generated by SA were started on a workstation-cluster and on the GC/PP. In the former case, the execution times could be reduced significantly (cf. Figure 7). The reason for this is the low bandwidth of the Ethernet which is shared among the participating workstations. Therefore, the extern communication becomes a bottleneck and nearly no speedup is possible if the amount of extern communication isn't reduced by optimization.

Because of the higher bandwidth of the GC/PP, whose nodes are connected with a grid, this architecture is not as sensitive to the amount of the extern communication as the workstation-cluster, and thus no great differences were measured between the scattered and the optimized mapping.

5 Conclusions

With CoPA, we presented an easy-to-use environment for configuring applications which are parallelized on the base of functional modules. By using channel-based communi-

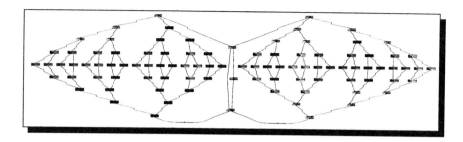

Figure 6: *A partitioning of* trees(5) *for eight workstations calculated by SA.*

cation, CoPA is able to perform a "post-game" analysis of the dynamic behaviour of the application. This knowledge is again used to optimize the mapping of the application in following runs.

The evaluation shows that especially in the area of workstation-clusters this optimization can significantly improve the execution times of coarse-grained applications.

Acknowledgements

Many people helped to make this work possible. We especially thank Peter Klingebiel and Jürgen Seuss for their good co-operation in the application area. Martin Schneider and Markus Fischer did lots of work in implementing large parts of the code. Robert Preis provided the PARTY library and gave lots of hints in using it on weighted graphs. Finally, we thank Reinhard Lüling for many helpful discussions and Joachim Lückel and Burkhard Monien for their encouragement.

References

[1] S.H. Bokhari: On the Mapping Problem. *IEEE TOC* 30(3), pp. 207–214, 1981.

[2] J. Casas, D. L. Clark, P. S. Galbiati, R. Konuru, S. W. Otto, R. M. Prouty, J. Walpole: MIST: PVM with Transparent Migration and Checkpointing, *3rd Annual PVM Users' Group Meeting, Pittsburgh, PA, 1995.*

[3] R. Diekmann, R. Lüling, A. Reinefeld: Distributed Combinatorial Optimization. *Proc. of Sofsem'93,* Hrdonov, Sumava, Czech Republik.

[4] R. Diekmann, R. Lüling, J. Simon: *Problem Independent Distributed Simulated Annealing and its Applications.* Lecture Notes in Economics and Mathematical Systems LNEMS 396, Springer-Verlag, 1993.

[5] R. Diekmann, B. Monien, R. Preis: *Using Helpful Sets to Improve Graph Bisections.* DIMACS Series in Discrete Mathematics and Theoretical Computer Science, Vol. 21, pp. 57-73, AMS, 1995.

[6] E.K. Haddad: Optimal Partitioning of Random Workloads in Homogeneous Multiprocessor and Distributed Systems. *Proc. 2nd IEEE Symp. on Parallel and Distributed Processing (SPDP '90).*

[7] B. Hendrickson, R. Leland: *The Chaco User's Guide.* Techn. Rep. SAND93-2339, Sandia National Laboratories, Nov. 1993.

[8] M.D. Huang, F. Romeo, A. Sangiovanni-Vincentelli: An Efficient General Cooling Schedule for Simulated Annealing. *IEEE Int. Conf. on CAD,* 1986.

[9] P. Klingebiel, R. Diekmann, U. Lefarth, M. Fischer, J. Seuss: CAMeL/PVM, An Open, Distributed CAE Environment for Modelling and Simulating Mechatronic Systems. *Proc. EUROSIM '95,* Vienna, 1995.

[10] J.M. Lépine, F. Rubi: An interface for a mapping software under PVM. *Proc. PVM Users Group Meeting,* Rome, 1994.

[11] T. Lewis, H. El-Rewini: Parallax: A Tool for Parallel Program Scheduling. *IEEE Parallel & Distributed Technology,* pp. 62-72, May 1993.

[12] A.K. Nanda, D. DeGroot, D.L. Stenger: Scheduling Directed Task Graphs on Multiprocessors using Simulated Annealing. *Proc. 12th IEEE Int. Conf. on Distributed Systems,* pp. 20-27, 1992.

[13] R. Preis: *The PARTY Partitioning-Library, User Guide.* Univ. of Paderborn, 1995. (http://hniwww.uni-paderborn.de/graduierte/preis/preis.html)

[14] B. Robic, J. Silc: Algorithm mapping with parallel simulated annealing. *J. of Computers and Artificial Intelligence,* 1995.

[15] R. Rutz, J. Richert: CAMeL: An Open CASCSD Environment. *Proc. IEEE/IFAC Symp. on Computer-Aided System Design (CACSD '94),* 1994.

[16] G. Sander: *Graph Layout through the VCG Tool.* Lecture Notes in Computer Science DIMACS GD'94, Springer-Verlag, pp. 194-205, 1995.

[17] J.C. Yan: New "Post-game Analysis" Heuristics for Mapping Parallel Computations to Hypercubes. *Proc. Int. Conf. on Parallel Processing* (2), 1991.

Task Assignment Heuristic based on the Random Neural Model

Jose Aguilar

Centro de Microcomputacion y Sistemas Distribuidos. CEMISID

Dpto. de Computación. Facultad de Ingeniería. Universidad de los Andes.

Av. Tulio Febres Cordero. 5101 Mérida. Venezuela.

aguilar@ing.ula.ve

Abstract

In this paper we discuss the task assignment problem for distributed systems. The formalization of these problems in terms of a graph theoretic representation of a distributed program. The cost function which needs to be minimized by an assignment of tasks to processors is detailed. Since the task assignment problem is NP-hard, we present a novel heuristic algorithm that we have tested for solving it and compare it to a well-known greedy heuristic, genetic algorithms based heuristic and simulated annealing based heuristic. This novel heuristic use neural networks. Both the resulting performance and the computational cost for these algorithms are evaluated on a large number of randomly generated program graphs of different sizes.

1 Introduction

The problem of assigning each task in a parallel program to some processing unit of the system has major impact on the resulting performance. The problem arises in all areas of parallel and distributed computation, where programs are decomposed into tasks or processes, which must then assigned to processing units for execution.

In certain systems, this assignment is carried out dynamical at run-time: this gives rise to the *Load balancing problem* [9]. However, in many cases, the user or the system will wish to exert explicit control over the assignment of each task – this paper addresses the latter which is known as the *Task Assignment Problem*.

Typically, a distributed program is represented as a collection of tasks, which correspond to nodes in a graph. The arcs of the graph may represent communication between tasks, or precedence relations, or both. Task assignment is then formulated as a problem of partitioning the graph so as to minimize some cost function. Typically, each element (or block) in the partition will represent a set of tasks which will be assigned to the same processor. The cost function may represent a combination of communication costs (which will increase as tasks are dispersed among a larger number of processing units), and computation times (which will typically decrease as the number of tasks included in any block becomes smaller). The assignment is then chosen to minimize this combined cost.

In the general case, since this problem is NP-hard, approximate heuristics are needed because exact solutions would require excessive execution times when the number of tasks in the program and the number of processing units is large.

In the following sections we first introduce task assignment and briefly discuss the related issue of task scheduling. Then, we formalize the task assignment problem and its related cost functions in a graph theoretic framework. Finally, we present our heuristic algorithm to solve the task assignment problem. The approach we propose and evaluate in this paper is a heuristic based on the random neural model of Gelenbe.

2 Problem Definition

Task assignment is simply the choice of a mapping of a set of tasks to a set of processors so as to achieve a pre-defined goal. This goal is usually represented as some cost function which may consider a combination of several criteria: equitable load sharing between the processors, maximization of the degree of parallelism, minimization of the amount (and delay) of communication between the processors, minimization of the execution time of the program, etc. In order to be of use in achieving a satisfactory solution, the cost function must obviously include the constraints and characteristics of the programs involved (such as task execution times, amount of inter-task communication, precedence between tasks), and of the system architecture including the nature and topology of interconnection between processing units, the speed of the processors, memory system properties (shared or private to processors, limits in memory size, etc.).

Usually, the task assignment problem will not consider the actual schedule or order in which the tasks are executed. The Task Scheduling has been actively researched over the years and precisely addresses this specific issue [14]. Thus in the present paper we will not discuss scheduling issues.

In our study, we consider a distributed system architecture which consists of a collection of K processors with distributed memory, i.e. with sufficient memory at each processor so that any one task can be executed. The processors are fully interconnected via a reliable high-speed network. A parallel program which will be executed in this environment is represented by a *Task Graph* [4] which is denoted by:

$$\Pi = (N, A, e, C),$$

where:

- $N = \{1, \ldots, n\}$ is the set of n tasks that compose the program,

- $A = \{a_{ij}\}$ is the incidence matrix which describes the graph,

- e , C are the amount of work related to task execution and to communication between tasks. Thus e_i defines the amount of work — or code to be executed — in task $i = 1 \ldots n$. C_{ij} will denote the amount of information transferred during communication from task i to task j, if $a_{ij} = 1$. Clearly, $a_{ij} \approx 0$ implies that $C_{ij} \approx 0$).

Note that this model may describe precedence between tasks if the graph is directed and acyclic, or it may be used to represent a set of tasks which interact via passage of information when the graph is not directed (in which case we will have $a_{ij} = a_{ji}$ for all i, j).

The task assignment problem at hand is that of assigning the n tasks to K processors. This means that we have to find a partition $(\Pi_1, \ldots, \Pi_K)$ of the set of n tasks in a way which optimizes performance, as expressed by criteria such as:

- The communication between different processors of the system must be kept to a minimum.

- The load of the different processors must be balanced.

- The total effective execution time of the parallel program must be minimized.

The cost function that we will use [2, 4] is:

$$F_C = \sum_{i,j \in D} \tau_{ij} + b \frac{\sum_{z=1}^{K} (N_{G_z} - n/K)^2}{K} \quad (1)$$

where

τ_{ij}	:	communication cost between task i and j
D	:	$\{i \in G_m \ \& \ j \in G_l \ \& \ l \neq m \ \& \ a_{ij} = 1\}$ i predecessor of j, i&j in different partitions
K	:	total number of processors
n	:	total number of program tasks
N_{G_z}	:	number of tasks assigned to processor z (in partition G_z)
b	:	factor of load balancing. In our case, b is in the interval $[0, 2]$.

3 The Heuristic Algorithms used in this Study

Neural networks have been used over the last several years to obtain heuristic solutions to hard optimization problems [15]. The random neural network model has been developed by Gelenbe [11, 12] to represent a dynamic behavior inspired by natural neural systems. This model has a remarkable property called "product form" which allows the direct computation of joint probability distributions of the neurons of the network.

The basic descriptor of a neuron in the random network [11, 12] is the probability of excitation of the M neurons, $q(i), i = 1, \ldots, M$, which satisfy a set of nonlinear equations:

$$q(i) = \frac{\sum_{j=1}^{n} q(j)r(j)P^+(j,i) + \Lambda(i)}{\sum_{j=1}^{n} q(j)r(j)P^-(j,i) + \lambda(i)} \quad (2)$$

Where:

- $\Lambda(i)$ is the rate at which *external excitation signals* arrive to the i-th neuron,

- $\lambda(i)$ is the rate at which *external inhibition signals* arrive to the i-th neuron,

- r(i) is the rate at which neuron i fires when it is excited,

- $P^+(i,j)$ and $P^-(i,j)$, respectively, are the probabilities that neuron i (when is excited) will send an *excitation* or an *inhibition* signal to neuron j.

Notice that this is a "frequency modulated" model, which translates rates of signal emission into excitation probabilities via equation (2). For instance $q(j)r(j)P^+(j,i)$ denotes the rate at which neuron j excites neuron i. Equation (2) can also be viewed as a sigmoidal form which treats excitation (in the numerator) asymmetrically with respect to inhibition (in the denominator).

In order to construct a heuristic for the solution of the task assignment problem, we construct a random neural network composed of $M = nK + K$ neurons, where n is the number of tasks and K is the number of processors. For each (task, processor) pair (i,u) we will have a neuron $\mu(i,u)$ whose role is to *decide* whether task i should be assigned to processor u. We denote by $q(\mu(i,u))$ the probability that $\mu(i,u)$ is excited, and if this probability is close to 1 we will be encouraged to assign i to u. In order to reduce communication times in the assignment, and encourage the placement on the same processor of tasks which communicate with each other, $\mu(i,u)$ will *excite* any neuron $\mu(j,u)$ if $a_{ij} = 1$ or $a_{ji} = 1$, and will tend to *inhibit* $\mu(j,v)$ if $u \neq v$. Similarly, $\mu(i,u)$ will *inhibit* $\mu(j,u)$ if $a_{ij} = 0$, $a_{ji} = 0$.

Neurons $\mu(i,u)$ and $\mu(i,v)$, $u \neq v$, will *strongly inhibit* each other so as to indicate that the same task should not be assigned to different processors. For each processor u we will have a neuron $\pi(u)$ whose role is to let us know whether u is heavily loaded with work or not. If u is very heavily loaded, it will attempt to reduce the load on processor u by *inhibiting* neurons $\mu(i,u)$, and it will attempt to increase the load on processors $v \neq u$ by *exciting* neurons $\pi(u)$. In the same way, $\mu(i,u)$ will *excite* neuron $\pi(u)$ to provide information about processor u's load. The parameters of the random network model expressing these intuitive criteria are chosen as follows:

- $\Lambda(\mu(i,u)) = random$,

- $\Lambda(\pi(u)) = n/K$, to express the desirable equal load sharing property,

- $\lambda(\mu(i,u)) = 0$,

- $\lambda(\pi(u)) = 0$,

- $r(\mu(i,u)) = nK$,

- $r(\pi(u)) = n + K - 1$,

- $r(\mu(i,u))P^+(\mu(i,u),\mu(j,v)) =$
  $\begin{cases} 1, & \text{if } ((a_{ij} = 1 \text{ or } a_{ji} = 1) \text{ and } (u = v)); \\ 0, & \text{otherwise.} \end{cases}$

- $r(\mu(i,u))P^-(\mu(i,u),\mu(j,v)) =$
  $\begin{cases} 1, & \text{if } (u \neq v \text{ and } (a_{ij} = 1 \text{ or } a_{ji} = 1 \text{ or } i = j)) \\ & \text{or } (a_{ij} = 0 \text{ and } a_{ji} = 0); \\ 0, & \text{otherwise.} \end{cases}$

- $r(\mu(i,u))P^+(\mu(i,u),\pi(v)) = \begin{cases} 1, & \text{if } u = v; \\ 0, & \text{otherwise.} \end{cases}$

- $r(\pi(u))P^-(\pi(u),\mu(i,u)) = \begin{cases} 1, & \text{if } q(\pi(u)) \approx 1; \\ 0, & \text{otherwise.} \end{cases}$

- $r(\pi(u))P^+(\pi(u),\pi(v)) = \begin{cases} 1, & \text{if } q(\pi(u)) \approx 1; \\ 0, & \text{otherwise.} \end{cases}$

The equation (2) for this case is:

$$q(\mu(i,u)) = \sum_{\substack{a_{ij} = 1 \, or \\ a_{ji} = 1}} q(\mu(j,u))r(\mu(j,u))P^+(\mu(j,u),\mu(i,u))$$

$$\Bigg/ \Bigg\{ r(\mu(i,u)) +$$

$$\sum_{v \neq u} \sum_{\substack{a_{ij} = 1 \, or \\ a_{ji} = 1 \, or \\ i = j}} q(r(\mu(j,v))P^-(\mu(j,v),\mu(i,u)) +$$

$$\sum_{v} \sum_{\substack{a_{ij} = 0 \, and \\ a_{ji} = 0}} q(r(\mu(j,v))P^-(\mu(j,v),\mu(i,u)) +$$

$$q(\pi(u))r(\pi(u))P^-(\pi(u),\mu(i,u)) \Bigg\}$$

$$q(\pi(u)) = \Bigg\{ \Lambda(\pi(u)) +$$

$$\sum_{j=1}^{n} q(\mu(j,u))r(\mu(j,u))P^+(\mu(j,u),\pi(u)) +$$

$$\sum_{v=1}^{K} q(\pi(v))r(\pi(v))P^+(\pi(v),\pi(u)) \Bigg\} \Bigg/$$

$$\{r(\pi(u))\}$$

4 Performance Comparisons

In this section we summarize the results we have obtained for the heuristic described above, which we compare with each other and with the well-known Kernighan-Lin graph partitioning heuristic [4], a heuristic based on the well-know simulated annealing method [4] and a heuristic based on the random neural model of Gelenbe [11]. Comparisons are carried out for a large number of randomly generated task graphs having a number of nodes which varies widely.

The evaluations are carried out on a large number of randomly generated task graphs having different numbers of nodes n. The task graphs are randomly generated as follows. For a fixed n, and for each node of the graph, we draw at random the number d of neighbors of the node, from a uniform distribution running from 1 to some maximum value d. Each task in the node is assumed to an execution time of 1, and the time for communicating between tasks is also taken to have unit value. Each simulation run then corresponds to the execution of one job (i.e. a single task graph) using only one method for the task assignment (RNA, GA) and one set of parameters.

The results we have obtained are summarized in Figures 1 to 2. These results are obtained for task graphs with $D = 5$, and for both directed acyclic task graphs, and for undirected task graphs. We clearly see that of all the heuristics we have tested, Simulated Annealing provides the best results with respect to minimizing the cost function. The next best results are obtained using the Genetic Algorithm. However it is also quite clear that these two methods are very time consuming in program execution time. On the other hand, the Kernighan-Lin heuristics yields the worst results, though it does run very fast. Interestingly enough, the Random Network Model generally provides results which are substantially better than the Kernighan-Lin heuristic, yet substantially worse than either the Genetic Algorithm and Simulated Annealing. However its run time is comparable to that of the Kernighan-Lin heuristic even for very large task graphs.

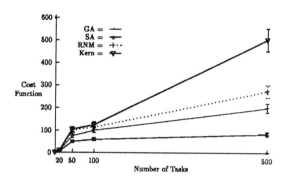

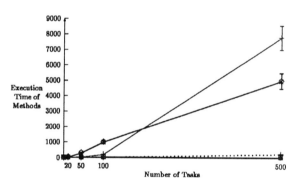

5 Conclusions

The experiments we have run show that the results obtained by each approximate method vary significantly as a function of the size of the graphs considered. However the relative performance of each of the heuristics tested is consistent over different graph sizes.

Simulated Annealing consistently give the best results, but with a substantially larger execution time than the other approaches. The execution time for the Genetic Algorithm heuristic is also very large, and can sometimes be larger than that of Simulated Annealing. This is because the computations for each generation are time consuming.

The Genetic Algorithm and the Random Neural Network based heuristics could be easy to implement on a parallel machine, and this can considerably im-

prove the speed with which these methods obtain a solution.

References

[1] J. Aguilar. *Combinatorial Optimization Methods. A study of graph partitioning problem.* Proc. of the Pan-American Workshop on Applied and Computational Mathematics, PWACM, Caracas, Venezuela, 1993.

[2] J. Aguilar. *Heuristic algorithms for task assignment of parallel programs.* Proc. Intl. Conf. Massively Parallel Processing, Applications and Development, Delft, Holland, 1994.

[3] J. Aguilar. *Resolution du problème de placement de tâches avec de techniques d'optimisation combina-*

toires. Proc. 6éme Rencontres Francophones du par-allelisme, Lyon, France, 1994.

[4] J. Aguilar. *L'Allocation de tâches, l'équilibr age de charge et l'optimisation combinatoire.* PhD thesis, René Descartes Un iversity, Paris, France, 1995.

[5] S. L. B. Kernighan. An efficient algorithm for parti-tioning graphs. *Bell System Technical Journal*, Febru-ary 1970.

[6] H. K. C. Kim. An algorithm for optimal static load balancing in distributed computer systems. *IEEE Trans. on Computers*, 41:381–384, 1992.

[7] F. L. C. Xu. Analysis of the generalized dimension ex-change method for dynamic load balancing. *Journal of Parallel and Distributed Computing*, 16:386–393, 1992.

[8] D. Du. *Allocation de tâches dans les systèmes reconfig-urables de type statique.* PhD thesis, Orsay University, French, 1992.

[9] R. K. E. Gelenbe. *Incremental dynamic load balanc-ing in distributed system.* Proc. Intl. Workshop on Modeling, Analysis and Simulation of Computer and Telecommunication Systems (MASCOTS), Durham, USA, 1994.

[10] P. S. F. Ercal, J. Ramanujam. Task allocation onto a hypercube by recursive mincut bipartitioning. *Journal of Parallel and Distributed Computing*, 10:35–44, 1990.

[11] E. Gelenbe. Random neural networks with positive and negative signals and product form solution. *Neural Computation*, 1(4):502–511, 1989.

[12] E. Gelenbe. Stable random neural networks. *Neural Computation*, 2(2):239–247, 1990.

[13] e. a. M. Schaar. *Load balancing with network coop-eration.* Proc. 11th Conf. on Distributed Computing Systems, Arlington, USA, 1991.

[14] M. W. N. Shirazi. Analysis and evaluation of heuristic methods for static task scheduling. *Journal of Parallel and Distributed Computing*, 10:222–232, 1990.

[15] G. Peretto. *Neural networks and combinatorial prob-lems.* Proc. Intl. Conf. on Neural Networks, Paris, French, 1990.

Task Scheduling for Dynamically Reconfigurable Parallel Machines

Abdelhamid Benaini   David Laiymani

Université de Franche-Comté - LIB
25030 Besançon Cedex
France
phone: (33)-81-66-64-62 - fax: (33)-81-66-64-50
E-mail: (benaini, laiymani)@comte.univ-fcomte.fr

Abstract

This paper presents a compile time scheduling algorithm dedicated to reconfigurable parallel machines i.e. machines in which the interconnection network can be altered during the execution of the same application. We present an heuristic, based on clustering and list scheduling techniques, that schedules a program task graph (DAG) for these machines. We derive upper bounds to the performances of the algorithm and we show that these bounds generalize some well known bounds given in the literature.

1. Introduction

The problem of scheduling a parallel program represented as a directed acyclic task graph (DAG) has been well studied and it is known to be NP-hard [8, 9, 15, 22]. Many heuristic algorithms, which produce sub-optimal solutions, have been proposed. Among them are the *list scheduling* methods [2, 16, 18], the *clustering* techniques [10, 15, 19, 13] and some subsequent improvements of an initial solution [7, 17]. These techniques assume a target parallel machine in which processors are fully or partially connected. However, because of routing costs, the processor network configuration highly influences the quality of any schedule.

The main contribution of this paper is the study of the scheduling problem for reconfigurable parallel machines. These systems provide improvements in computational performances since they allow the architecture to adapt itself to the needs of the application rather than requiring to adapt the application to the architecture [1]. Furthermore they yield a variety of possible topologies (processors graph) for the network and allow any schedule to exploit this topological variety in order to speed up the computations by reducing routing costs [12]. A machine is said *reconfigurable* if its interconnexion network can be altered between different phases of the same algorithm execution. A (p, d)-*reconfigurable*

machine is a reconfigurable machine with p identical processors and d communication links per processor. A possible network topology is any one with a degree less than or equal to d.

Typically a parallel algorithm for a (p, d)-reconfigurable machine is implemented as a series of phases separated by reconfigurations of the interconnection network (multi-phase programming) [20]. Each phase is then executed onto the processor graph that well reflects the needs of the current data transfer pattern [1, 3, 21]. For example, a multi-phase program can be composed of a matrix-vector product running on a ring topology, followed by a norm computation running on a tree topology. We point out that this model can find natural extentions in optical multi-processors since, the communication protocols of these machines seem to be similar to the multi-phase model [5].

Let a parallel program represented as a DAG where vertices represent the different program tasks and arcs indicate communications between tasks. Then, a schedule for a (p, d)-reconfigurable machine (or a multi-phase scheduling) consists in assigning to each task a tuple <phase, processor, starting time>. This assignement must be performed in order to exploit the topological flexibiltiy of reconfigurable machines and so, a topology must be associated to each phase (see figure 3 for an example). The algorithm that we propose computes a combination of tasks schedule with a sequence of topologies, in order to minimize the parallel execution time of the input DAG.

The main difficulties in the multi-phase scheduling problem, is to decompose the initial DAG into a series of phases in a way that

- A maximum of tasks and arcs are assigned to each phase. In this way the inherent parallelism of the DAG will be kept as much as possible and the number of phases is reduced.

- For each phase, communication overheads are minimized by assigning to the same processor tasks which have to exchange costly messages and by minimizing routing costs.

- Furthermore, in the multi-phase model the different re-configurations of the interconnection network may lead some processors to be idle for a certain time. These idle times between the execution of two consecutive phases must be minimized.

Unfortunatetly these goals seem to be conflicting. In order to try to satisfy both of them, we propose a method taking ideas from linear clustering techniques [15, 23] and list scheduling algorithms [2, 16]. The method performs a succession of refinement steps which assign tasks to phases and for each phase, tasks to processors and to starting times.

In section 2 we review some basic concepts and definitions on the architectural environment and on the task model. We also state formally the problem. Section 3 details the algorithm, presents some properties and gives a bound for the performances of the algorithm which generalizes the one given by Gerasoulis et al [10].

2. Problem definitions

2.1. The computational model

The target multiprocessor is a (p, d)-reconfigurable machine with p homogeneous processors and d bidirectional communication links per processor. Each processor is able to perform, in parallel, computations and communications on its d links.

Phases are separated, from one to another, by synchronization-reconfiguration points. So, during the execution of the same multi-phase program, the network is configured at the begining of each phase. Execution of phases is sequential in that computations and communications of the current phase cannot be processed before the end of computations and communications of the previous phase. Reconfiguration overheads are negligible regardless to communications and in the following they are assumed to be null [3].

2.2. The precedence graph

A parallel algorithm is represented as a directed acyclic graph $G = (V, E)$ where $V = \{n_j, j = 1, 2 \ldots v\}$ is the set of tasks. $E = \{e_{i,j} = (n_i, n_j)\}$ is the set of communication arcs which define precedence constraints on V. A weight $c_{i,j}$ represents the communication cost incurred along $e_{i,j} \in E$ which becomes zero if n_i and n_j are mapped to the same processor. The computation cost of task $n_i \in V$ is denoted by τ_i.

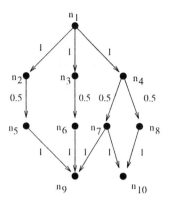

Figure 1. A DAG ($\tau_i = 3$, $i = 1 : 10$)

The *length* of a path is the sum of all tasks computations and arcs communication costs in this path. The *critical path* is the path with the longest length in G. Figure 1 shows a weighted DAG in which a critical path is (n_1, n_2, n_5, n_9) with length 14.5.

The in-degree of a task n_i ($d^-(n_i)$) is the number of in-edges of this task. The in-degree of G is $d^-(G) = max_{n_i \in V} d^- n_i$. For instance in figure 1 we have, $d^-(n_{10}) = 2$ and $d^-(G) = d^-(n_9) = 3$.

A phase $PH = (VP, EP)$ is a sub-set of G such that $VP \subseteq V$ and $EP \subseteq E$ (an arc in EP may have only out-node in VP, see figure 2).

A DAG is then decomposed as a sequence of *disjoint phases* $PH_s, 0 \le s < q$ such that

1. $\bigcup_{s=0}^{q-1} PH_s = G$,

2. the *phases graph* $PG = (GV, GE)$ where $GV = \{PH_s, s = 0, 1, \ldots q - 1\}$ and $GE = \{(PH_s, PH_t) : \exists n_i \in PH_s, n_j \in PH_t, (n_i, n_j) \in E\}$ is acyclic,

3. the execution of each phase must be performed without routing cost on a fixed topology of a (p, d)-reconfigurable machine i.e. an edge in G will correspond to one communication link (at most) of the reconfigurable machine.

Imposing that any edge in G will correspond excatly to one communication link is closely related to the *cardinality* criterion defined by Bokhari in [6]. Clearly, the definition of a phase allows to maximize this criterion and so to build efficient topologies.

Figure 2 shows the different assignment levels that requires a schedule for reconfigurable machines (the schedule presented in this figure is a naive one). The initial level corresponds to the initial DAG. The phase partitionning

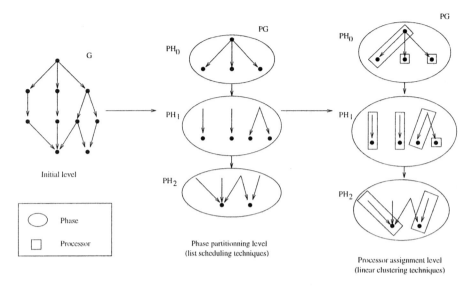

Figure 2. The assignment levels of the multi-phase scheduling

level, corresponds to the decomposition of G in phases. This level defines explicity the phase graph PG. Now, the processor assignment level defines the mapping of tasks to processors for each phase, pointing out in this way, the different topologies.

2.3. Statement of the problem

Given a DAG $G = (V, E)$ and a (p, d)-reconfigurable machine, a *multi-phase* schedule consists in partitionning G into q phases (sub-sets of G), in mapping tasks to phases and processors and in assigning execution starting time to each task. Let $ST(n_i)$ be the starting execution time of n_i and $ET(PH_s)$ be the execution time of a phase PH_s then

$$ET(PH_s) = \max_{n_i \in VP_s} \{ST(n_i) + \tau_i\}$$

As phases are processed sequentially, and as reconfiguration costs are neglected, the parallel execution time of a multi-phase schedule is

$$PT = \max_{n_i \in V}\{ST(n_i) + \tau_i\} = \sum_{s=0}^{q-1} ET(PH_s)$$

Figure 3 points a Gantt chart describing a schedule for the DAG and the phase partitionning of figures 1 and 2. This schedule has a length of 14.5. The topologies associated with the different phases have their degree less than 2 and so can be implemented on a $(4, 2)$-reconfigurable machine. In this figure we have phase $PH_1 = (VP_1, EP_1)$ with $VP_1 = \{n_5, n_6, n_7, n_8\}$ and $EP_1 = \{(n_2, n_5), (n_3, n_6), (n_4, n_7), (n_4, n_8)\}$. Note that arcs $(n_2, n_5), (n_3, n_6)$ and (n_4, n_7) belong to phase PH_1

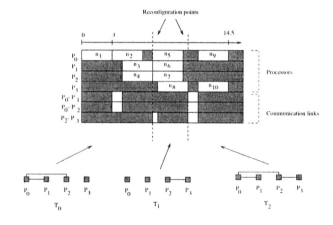

Figure 3. Scheduling results of the DAG of figure 2 on a $(4, 2)$-reconfigurable machine

while n_2, n_3 and n_4 does not belong to this phase (but to phase PH_0).

Formally, the multi-phase scheduling problem consists in partitionning G into q disjoint phases $PH_0, PH_1, \ldots PH_{q-1}$ such that $\sum_{s=0}^{q-1} ET(PH_s)$ is minimized. This scheduling problem is obviously in NP. The proof of its NP-completness follows by a simple reduction from the *Scheduling on a Clique* problem [14, 22].

2.4. Overview and justification of our heuristic

Since the multi-phase scheduling problem is NP-complete we have to develop an heuristic algorithm which produces efficient solutions in polynomial time. The main goals to achieve efficient multi-phase schedules are the following. In a first hand, the decomposition into phases must try to preserve the inherent parallelism of the initial DAG and each phase must contain a maximum number of tasks and edges (regardless to the number of processors and to the degree of the target machine).

On the other hand, reconfigurations which occurs during the execution of a multi-phase algorithm may lead to idle times on processors which must be minimized. For example, let's examine the impact of the first reconfiguration point in figure 3. Because of reconfiguration, it is clear that task n_5 on processor P_0 has to wait for the end of phase PH_0 i.e. the end of tasks n_3 and n_4, before starting computation. This induces an idle time of one onto processor P_0.

Our algorithm builds the different phases one by one. It computes two assignment processes which are an assignment of tasks to phases and an assignment of tasks to processors. Informally, it scans the different tasks of the initial DAG and according to a certain priority function it assigns the choosen task to the current phase (the phase being constructed). While a phase is processed we apply a modified clustering technique [15, 23] in order to assign tasks to processors. In this way we try to well match the physical properties of the target reconfigurable machine. As we will see in the remainder, this construction will clearly define the topologies associated with the different phases.

3. A scheduling algorithm for multi-phase programming

Our approach assignes simultaneously tasks to phases and tasks to processors. So, the algorithm is a succession of refinement steps in order to build phases, one by one, starting by phase PH_0. A typical refinement step is to assign a task to the current phase. Simultaneously to the construction of a phase we apply a linear clustering technique [4] in order to assign tasks to processors. Now let's detail the clustering procedure.

3.1. A modified linear clustering heuristic

Clustering is a mapping of tasks of a DAG onto m clusters (processors). Generally, clustering algorithms are viewed as a succession of refinement steps to group tasks into the same clusters (via some heuristics), in order to zero some communication edges (tasks in the same cluster are executed in the same processor without communication overhead). In the remainder we deal with *linear clustering* where two independant tasks can not be assigned to the same cluster.

The linear clustering procedure is applied during the construction of the different phases. It takes a phase PH_s as input and processes as follows:

1. Initially each node in PH_s forms a cluster.

2. Consider the longest path in the clusterized phase PH_s.

3. Delete on this longest path, the highest cost arc by mapping its end nodes to the same cluster (by respecting the linearity constraint).

4. If it is not possible to delete (zero) an edge on the longest path, then scan arcs according to the highest cost principle and continue refinement until that it was impossible to zero an edge.

The main property of this algorithm is that

Property 1 *The execution time $ET(PH_s)$ of phase PH_s decreases at each clustering refinement step.*

The proof given in [23] can be easily adapted to prove this property. Here, we underline that this clustering algorithm is similar to the one presented by Kim and Brown in [11]. Nevertheless, its application in our scheduling heuristic is quiet different. In figure 4 we illustrate the progression of this procedure for a given phase. In this example $m = 3$ clusters are generated and they are labelled by m_1, m_2, m_3. In the multi-phase scheduling algorithm we will use this technique in order to produce p clusters at most, each of degree less than or equal to d. The degree of a cluster m_i, say $d(m_i)$, is the number of clusters that communicate with m_i. For instance in figure 4 we have $d(m_1) = d(m_2) = d(m_3) = 2$. Remark that the parallel execution time on m processors completely connected, of a clusterized phase PH_s is equal to its the longest path.

21

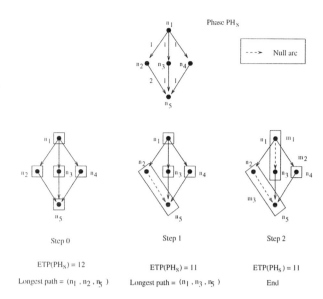

Step 0

Step 1

Step 2

ETP(PH$_s$) = 12

ETP(PH$_s$) = 11

ETP(PH$_s$) = 11

Longest path = (n_1 , n_2 , n_5)

Longest path = (n_1 , n_3 , n_5)

End

Figure 4. Progression of the linear clustering heuristic ($\tau_i = 3$, $i = 1 : 5$)

3.2. The multi-phase scheduling algorithm

Unassigned task which have no predecessor or which have all their predecessors already assigned to a phase are known as ready tasks.

The evaluated finishing time of a task n_k, say $EFT(n_k)$, is equal to the length of the longest path in the clusterized phase PH_s from any entry node to n_k (including τ_k).

$EPT(PH_s)$ is the length of the longest path of phase PH_s. Let $n_1, n_2, \ldots, n_x$ be the set of ready tasks which are candidates to a possible assignment in phase PH_s. We begin by selecting a task for a possible assignment to PH_s. This task, say n_k, is the one satisfying:

$$EPT(PH_s \oplus \{n_k\}) = \min_{i=1..x} EPT(PH_s \cup \{n_i\})$$

where $PH_s \oplus \{n_k\}$ corresponds to the phase PH_s plus task n_k and all its in-edges.

A tie is broken by choosing the task n_k that minimize $EPT(PH_s) - (ST(n_k) + \tau_k)$. This last criterion allows to reduce the waiting time between phase PH_s and PH_{s+1}. Here, it is important to have an accurate evaluation of EPT and ST. As these values are function of longest path, their evaluations assume a sufficient number of processors and communication links. As we will see, this assumption is appropriate since phases are built regardless to the number of processors and to the degree of the target reconfigurable machine.

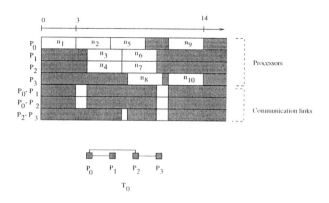

Figure 5. Scheduling of the DAG of figure 2 : results from our algorithm

Now we define when the assignment of a selected task n_k in phase PH_s is accepted. Recall that when a task n_k is selected for a possible assignment to PH_s, the algorithm tries to move n_k into a cluster by applying the linear clustering algorithm onto phase PH_s. This linear clustering procedure generates a number m of clusters $m_1, m_2, \ldots m_m$. The assignment of n_k to PH_s is accepted if and only if:

$$m \leq p \text{ and } d(m_i) \leq d, \ i = 1 : m$$

If these conditions are not satisfied, the algorithm does not assign the selected ready task. It applies the same process with other ready tasks n_k such that $ST(n_k) + \tau_k \leq EPT(PH_s)$ in order to not break the inherent parallelism of the input DAG. When no move are possible the algorithm starts to build phase PH_{s+1}.

The figure 6 illustrates the first steps of the algorithme.

In figure 5 we show scheduling results produced by the algorithm for the DAG of figure 1. It appears that in comparison with the naive scheduling given in figure 3 we reduce the parallel time from 14.5 to 14.

3.3. Properties of the multi-phase scheduling algorithm

Property 2 *The complexity of the multi-phase scheduling algorithm is $O(|V|^2|E|(|V| + |E|))$.*

Indeed, the linear clustering has a complexity of $O(|E|(|V|+|E|))$. As there are at most $|V|$ candidate tasks and $|V|$ tasks to assign, the computational complexity of the multi-phase scheduling algorithm is $O(|V|^2|E|(|V|+|E|))$. Note that the DSC clustering algorithm on an unbounded number of fully connected processors [23] has a complexity of $O((|V| + |E|) \log |V|)$. When processors are limited

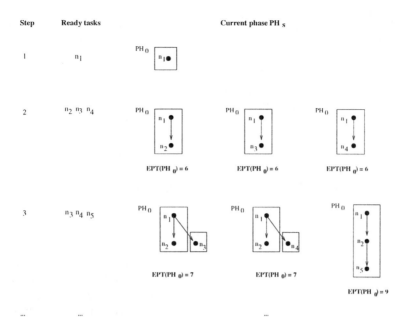

Step	Ready tasks	Current phase PH $_s$

Figure 6. Progression of the multi-phase scheduling algorithm

and partially connected, the list scheduling heuristic proposed in [16] has a complexity of $O(|V|^3 p|E| \log^2 |p|)$. Furthermore, we hope that the complexity of our algorithm can be reduced by a factor of $|V|$ or $|E|$ since the clustering procedure is applied on phases which have a cardinality in tasks and in arcs less than $|V|$ and $|E|$.

Property 3 *Each phase PH_s, $0 \le s < q$ is executed on a (p, d)-reconfigurable machine with no routing cost.*

The proof of this property follows by the construction of the algorithm and it follows that the multi-phase algorithm obtained, runs without any routing.

Now, we propose to evaluate the quality of our scheduling algorithm. Nevertheless, performances of scheduling algorithm are clearly related to the granularity of initial DAG. In order to fit the particularities of multi-phase model, we adapt the granularity definition given in [10] to the multi-phase model as follows. For a task $n_x \in V$ we define

$$g(n_x) = \tau_x / max_j(c_{jx}, c_{xj})$$

Then, the granularity of a DAG G is given by

$$g(G) = min_{n_x \in V}(g(n_x))$$

A DAG is *coarse grain* if $g(G) \ge 1$.

Now, recall that the phase graph obtained by the scheduling method is referenced by PG and its width by $L(PG)$. Let $PT_{opt}(PH_s)$ be the optimal parallel time of phase PH_s.

Clearly, a path in PG is composed of phases and we define the length of a path in PG as the sum of the optimal times of the different phases belonging to this path. Let $PT_{opt}(PG)$ be the length of the longest path in PG. PT_{mps} is the parallel time corresponding to the scheduling results produced by the multi-phase scheduling algorithm.

Theorem 1

If the DAG G satisfies $d^-(G) \le d + 1$ then :

$$PT_{mps} \le (1 + \frac{1}{g(G)})L(PG)PT_{opt}(PG)$$

and for a coarse grain DAG we have

$$PT_{mps} \le 2 \times L(PG) \times PT_{opt}(PG)$$

Otherwise

$$PT_{mps} \le (1 + \frac{1}{g(G)})L(PG)PT_{opt}(PG) + qc_{max}$$

and for coarse grain DAGs we have

$$PT_{mps} \le 2 \times L(PG) \times PT_{opt}(PG) + qc_{max}$$

where $c_{max} = max_{e_{ij} \in E} c_{ij}$.

Proof:

Case 1: It is easy to show [10] that for any phase PH_s, $0 \le s < q$

$$PT_{lc}(PH_s) \leq (1 + \frac{1}{g(G)})PT_{opt}(PH_s) \qquad (1)$$

where $PT_{lc}(PH_s)$ is the parallel time of the scheduling algorithm of phase PH_s. Since

$$PT_{mps} = \sum_{s=0}^{q-1} PT_{lc}(PH_s)$$

we have

$$PT_{mps} \leq (1 + \frac{1}{g(G)}) \times \sum_{s=0}^{q-1} PT_{opt}(PH_s)$$

It is clear, considering the phase graph, that

$$\sum_{s=0}^{q-1} PT_{opt}(PH_s) \leq L(PG) \times PT_{opt}(PG)$$

and

$$PT_{mps} \leq (1 + \frac{1}{g(G)}) \times L(PG) \times PT_{opt}(PG) \qquad (2)$$

Furthermore, if G is a coarse grain DAG i.e. $g(G) \geq 1$ then

$$PT_{mps} \leq 2 \times L(PG) \times PT_{opt}(PG) \qquad (3)$$

Case 2: Assume a task n_y such that $d^-(n_y) > d + 1$. When the linear clustering technique is applied to a such task, it may produce clusters with a degree greater than d. In this case it will not be possible to assign n_x to a phase. So we propose to transform the initial DAG by "breaking" tasks, with a such in-degree, into fictive tasks of null weight as presented in figure 7. The main problem with a such decomposition is that, we may have phases with paths ending by an arc incident to a fictive task (see figure 7). Let c_s be a such arc for phase PH_s. Then equation 1 becomes

$$PH_{lc}(PH_s) \leq (1 + \frac{1}{g(PH_s)})PT_{opt}(PH_s) + c_s$$

Then as for case 1 we get

$$PT_{mps} \leq (1 + \frac{1}{g(G)}) \times (\sum_{s=0}^{q-1} PT_{opt}(PH_s)) + \sum_{s=0}^{q-1} c_s$$

Implying

$$PT_{mps} \leq (1 + \frac{1}{g(G)}) \times \sum_{s=0}^{q-1} PT_{opt}(PH_s) + qc_{max}$$

The remainder of the proof is identical to the one of the first case.

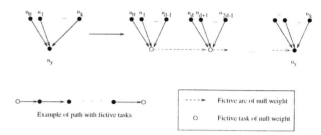

Figure 7. Decomposition of a task n with $d^-(n) > d + 1$

Clearly these bounds are valid for any number of processors. If the number of processors is unbounded and if they are fully connected, it is clear that the algorithm will generate an unique phase. So $L(PG) = 1$ and $PT_{opt}(PG)$ is equal to PT_{opt} the optimal parallel time on an unbounded number of fully connected processors. So for the first case of the theorem we get

$$PT_{mps} \leq (1 + \frac{1}{g(G)})) \times PT_{opt}$$

Furthemore if G is coarse grain we have $PT_{mps} \leq 2PT_{opt}$ which generalizes the result given in [10]. Now for the second case, if the processors are fully connected, it will not be necessary to decompose tasks n_y with $d^-(n_y) > d + 1$. The bound will be then the one of the first case.

Now these bounds can be expressed as functions of PT_{opt}. In this case by a simple modification in the proof we get (for any DAGs)

$$PT_{mps} \leq (1 + \frac{'1}{g(G)})) \times q \times PT_{opt}$$

and if G is coarse grain we have $PT_{mps} \leq 2 \times q \times PT_{opt}$

Again these bounds genaralize the ones given in [10]. And furthermore there are valid for the granularity definition given by Gerasoulis Venugopal in [10].

4. Conclusion

We have presented a scheduling heuristic of a program task graph, dedicated to reconfigurable parallel systems. This method takes into account most of the characteritics of a MIMD reconfigurable parallel machine. Apart unformal methods [3, 21] to our knowledge no scheduling methods of DAGs for reconfigurable parallel machines have been studied.

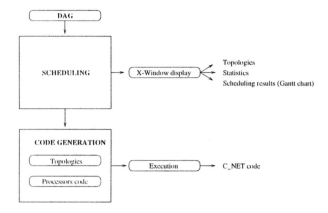

Figure 8. PHARAON (PHAse Reconfigurable Automatic cOde geNerator

The proposed method processes simultaneously the assignment of tasks to phases and of tasks to processors. Actually we work on a method that first entirely decompose the initial DAG into phases and next assign tasks to processors. The fundamental problem here is to characterize a phase in order to obtain an efficient decomposition.

We also think that the extension of the ideas of this paper to iterative graphs [24] would be interesting regardless to the charateristics of the multi-phase model.

Finally, to test our algorithm we are building a prototype named PHARAON (PHAse Reconfigurable Automatic cOde geNerator). This tool produces schedulings for arbitrary DAG and generates code for real reconfigurable architectures using the multi-phase programming paradigm. PHARAON takes a DAG as input and schedules it using the algorithm described in this paper. It also generates the C_NET code [1] corresponding to the definition of the topologies and to the different tasks.

References

[1] J.-M. Adamo and L. Trejo. Programming Environment for Phase-reconfigurable Parallel Programming on Supernode. *JPDC*, 23:278–292, 1994.

[2] M. Al-Mouhamed and A. Al-Maasarani. Performance Evaluation of Scheduling Precedence-Constrained Computations on Message-Passing Systems. *IEEE Trans. Parallel and Distributed Systems*, 5(12):1317–1322, 1994.

[3] A. Benaini and D. Laiymani. Parallel Block Generalized WZ Factorization on a Reconfigurable Machine. In *Proc. of Int. Conf. on Parallel and Distributed Systems - Taiwan*. IEEE Computer Society, December 1994.

[4] A. Benaini and D. Laiymani. Compile-time task scheduling for multi-phase programming. In *EuroPar '96 - Parallel Pro-cessing*, Lecture Notes in Computer Science No 1124, pages 535–538. Springer-Verlag, 1996.

[5] P. Berthomé. *Contribution à l'Algorithmique des Architectures Parallèles : Des Réseaux Point-à-point aux Réseaux Optiques*. PhD thesis, LIP - ENS Lyon, 1995.

[6] S. Bohkari. On the mapping problem. *IEEE Trans. Comput.*, C-30:207–214, Mar. 1981.

[7] V. Chaudhary and J. Aggarwal. A Generalized Scheme for Mapping Parallel Algorithms. *IEEE Trans. Parallel and Distributed Systems*, 4(3):328–345, 1993.

[8] P. Chretienne. Task Scheduling over Distributed Memory Machines. In *Proc. Inter. Workshop Parallel and Distributed Algorithms*. North Holland, 1989.

[9] M. Garey and D. Johnson. *Computers and Intractability : A Guide to the Theory of NP-Completeness*. W.H. Freeman, 1979.

[10] A. Gerasoulis and T. Yang. On the Granularity and Clustering of Directed Acyclic Task Graphs. *IEEE Trans. Parallel and Distributed Systems*, 4(6):686–701, 1993.

[11] S. Kim and J. Brown. A General Approach to Mapping of Parallel Computation upon Multi-processor Architectures. In *Int. Conf. Parallel Processing*, volume 3, pages 1–8, 1988.

[12] I. Lee and D. Smitley. A Synthesis Algorithm for Reconfigurable Interconnection Networks. *IEEE Trans. Comp.*, 37(6):691–699, 1988.

[13] M. Palis, J. Liou, and D. Wei. Task Custering and Scheduling for Distributed Memory Parallel Architectures. *IEEE Trans. on Parallel and Distributed Systems*, 7(1):46–55, 1996.

[14] C. Papadimitriou and M. Yannakakis. Towards an Architecture-Independent Analysis of Parallel Algorithms. *SIAM J. Comput.*, 19(2):322–328, 1990.

[15] V. Sarkar. *Partitionning and Scheduling Parallel Programs for Execution on Multiprocessors*. M.I.T. Press, 1989.

[16] S. Selvakumar and C. S. R. Murthy. Scheduling Precedence Constrained Task Graphs with Non-Negligible Intertask Communication onto Multiprocessors. *IEEE Trans. Parallel and Distributed Systems*, 5(3):328–336, 1994.

[17] B. Shirazi, M. Wang, and G. Pathak. Analysis and evaluation of heuristic methods for static task scheduling. *J. Parallel Distr. Comput.*, 10(3):222–232, 1990.

[18] G. Sih and E. Lee. Scheduling to account for interprocessor communication within interconnection-constrained processor networks. In *Proc. Int. Conf. Parallel Proc.*, 1990.

[19] G. Sih and E. Lee. Declustering : A New Multiprocessor Scheduling Technique. *IEEE Trans. Parallel and Distributed Systems*, 4(6):625–637, 1993.

[20] L. Snyder. Introduction to the Configurable, Highly Parallel Computer. *J. Par. Distr. Comp.*, 15:47–56, 1982.

[21] L. Snyder. The XYZ abstraction levels of Poker-like languages. In *Proc. of the Second Whorshop on Parallel Compilers And Algorithms*, 1989.

[22] B. Veltman, B. Lageweg, and J. Lenkstra. Multiprocessor scheduling with communication delays. *Parallel Computing*, (16):173–182, 1990.

[23] T. Yang. *Scheduling and Code Generation for Parallel Architectures*. PhD thesis, Rutgers University, 1993.

[24] T. Yang, C. Fu, A. Gerasoulis, and V. Sarkar. Mapping Iterative Task Graph on Distributed Memory Machines. In *Int. Conf. on Parallel Processing*, pages 151–158, 1995.

❖ OPEN FORUM SESSION 1 ❖

Chair

B. Di Martino

On the Relative Performance of Diffusion and Dimension Exchange Load Balancing in Hypercubes

Tina A. Murphy
Department of Computer Science
University College Cork
Ireland
sccs6007@bureau.ucc.ie

John G. Vaughan
Department of Computer Science
University College Cork
Ireland
j.vaughan@bureau.ucc.ie

Abstract

The Diffusion and Dimension Exchange synchronous load balancing algorithms are simulated in hypercube multicomputer environments with the objective of minimising the mean systemwide task response time. The influence of algorithm parameter variations on system performance is explored. The relative value of these algorithms is examined, as is their performance with respect to no load balancing. The overriding factor in determining algorithm profitability is found to be the system load level. At low to medium loads, neither algorithm is profitable and, in fact, Dimension Exchange causes system performance to deteriorate. The Diffusion algorithm out-performs Dimension Exchange at all but very high loads.

1. Introduction

Load balancing in distributed memory multicomputer systems can be accomplished in a static, offline manner [7] when the workload is highly repetitive and predictable. However, for problem classes with unpredictable workload distributions, interest has concentrated on dynamic approaches to the problem [1-3, 5, 6, 8-12]. Scalable multicomputer systems tend to restrict interprocessor connectivity so that each processor is directly connected to only a small number of neighbouring processors. Such connection schemes establish a physical environment for load balancing which is different to that hitherto experienced in distributed systems [13]. This environment is typified by the binary hypercube topology [4], for which several load balancing algorithms have been investigated previously [1-3, 5, 8-12, 14]. Algorithms which are suitable for application in such situations belong to the Nearest Neighbour class [12], of which the two best-known subclasses are Diffusion algorithms and Dimension Exchange algorithms.

Diffusion algorithms operate on the principle of reducing the load imbalance between each processor and its neighbours with the aim of diffusing workload through the system and converging towards a systemwide balanced load at each algorithm step. Examples of such algorithms include SID and RID [10], LAL [3, 8], SDM and DASUD [6]. The Dimension Exchange algorithm was originally proposed for hypercubes by Cybenko [1] and extended to other configurations by Xu *et al* [11, 12]. For the hypercube, this algorithm steps through the dimensions and balances load between pairs of processors in each dimension. In a closed system with infinitely divisible loads, this has the effect of achieving perfect balance in one cycle through the dimensions.

The relative performance of Diffusion and Dimension Exchange algorithms was considered from a theoretical standpoint by Cybenko [1] and Xu *et al* [11, 12]. Cybenko [1] examines the reduction in variance of workload due to both algorithms and concludes that 'dimension exchange has uniformly better performance as a load balancing strategy for hypercubes than does diffusion'. This conclusion is reinforced by studies carried out by Xu *et al* [12].

Existing theoretical investigations have, naturally, been subject to certain assumptions regarding workload. Cybenko assumes that all tasks have the same execution time and treats the workload at each processor as a real quantity. Xu *et al* also assume that the workload at a processor is infinitely divisible. In the present work, we are concerned with investigating what happens when tasks are indivisible and have randomly distributed execution times. We limit ourselves to synchronous versions of these algorithms which are

29

executed periodically and simultaneously at each processor. The tasks in our model are independent in that they do not interact with one another, nor do they have predilections for execution on particular processors. Tasks arrive independently at each processor and the time between arrivals is also modelled as a random variate. We use discrete event simulation to investigate the performance of Diffusion and Dimension Exchange algorithms in hypercube multicomputers of various sizes under a range of load levels. We ask five questions regarding these algorithms: First, is Dimension Exchange really better than Diffusion? Second, since the Diffusion algorithm is parameterised, what are its optimal parameter values in practice? Third, what are the best frequencies of execution of the algorithms? Fourth, what is the influence of load level? Fifth, how does system size affect performance? The answers to these questions are somewhat surprising and tend to reverse the prevailing view of the relative values of the Diffusion and Dimension Exchange algorithms.

The remainder of this work is organised as follows: Section 2 presents the Diffusion and Dimension Exchange algorithms as they are implemented here. Section 3 discusses our approach to modelling and simulation of the algorithms and their environments. Our results are detailed in Section 4 and our conclusions are summarised in Section 5.

2. Algorithm Descriptions

The load balancing algorithms considered in this paper are synchronous, periodic and fully decentralised. They aim to balance system load by transferring tasks between neighbouring processors. Tasks are independent and may be migrated at any time between their arrival and completion. The algorithms execute iteratively, apportioning fractions of excess load to underloaded neighbouring processors. Each algorithm has a number of parameters which control its operation.

Load balancing algorithms traditionally comprise five principal policies [13], which are the information, transfer, selection, location and acceptance policies. The *information policy* governs the collection, distribution and use of workload-related information. The *transfer policy* decides whether a task transfer is worthwhile in the current system state. The *selection policy* identifies tasks for migration. The *location policy* selects the destination for a transferred task. The *acceptance policy* determines whether an intended task execution site is bound to accept a proposed task transfer and also controls the number of processors which may be visited by a task in the course of its execution.

In the algorithms examined in this work, load balancing is initiated periodically and synchronously at all processors. The information policy is that each processor notifies its neighbours every time its load changes (due to the arrival, completion or migration of a task). The *load index*, or indication of how busy a processor is, is the total number of tasks instantaneously resident at that processor. Each processor has up-to-date knowledge of the load indices of all of its neighbours at all times. The acceptance policy is also common to both algorithms and forces tasks to be accepted always by their destination processors with the provision that they may be re-migrated before completing their execution. The transfer, selection and location policies for the algorithms are as follows:

2.1. Diffusion

Transfer policy: With the Diffusion algorithm, each processor compares its load with those of each of its neighbours. If an imbalance exists, load balancing is judged to be worthwhile and control passes to the selection policy.

Selection policy: All tasks are equally eligible for transfer. Migrating tasks are taken from the back of the sending processor's execution queue and are placed at the back of the destination processor's execution queue. The basic Diffusion parameter is d, where $0 < d < 1$. An amount of work equal to d times the difference in load index between each pair of neighbouring processors is transferred, provided that this results in the transfer of an integral number of tasks in each case. In the case where the number of tasks recommended for transfer is not an integer the fractional part is truncated since tasks are assumed to be indivisible. The rate of task migration is governed by d: for values of d close to 0, very little migration occurs; on the other hand, as d approaches 1, it is conceivable that the system might be adversely affected by a surfeit of task transfers. In fact, as d becomes larger, a processor may be asked to distribute more tasks than actually exist at that processor. For example, suppose a processor with 12 tasks has two neighbours, each of which has no tasks. Then, for $d = 2/3$, the non-empty processor will be asked to send $2/3(12 - 0) = 8$ tasks to each of its neighbours. Restricting d to be no greater than the reciprocal of the dimension of the hypercube avoids this phenomenon. In our implementation, when this situation arose, we chose to distribute all available tasks in proportion to the relative deficits at the neighbouring processors. This sometimes involved the preemption of the task currently being executed at the sending processor.

Location policy: Tasks are migrated to all neighbouring processors which have been approved as recipients by the transfer and selection policies.

2.2. Dimension Exchange

With the Dimension Exchange algorithm, the hypercube is organised into dimensions and balancing is carried out in one dimension at a time. This permits load balancing activity within a dimension to occur in parallel in 2^{n-1} disjoint subsets, each comprising a processor pair, where n is the dimension of the hypercube. As each dimension is balanced, the load indices are updated, providing accurate information for use in balancing subsequent dimensions. After all dimensions have been balanced, load is evenly distributed throughout the entire hypercube. Within each dimension, the following policies are applied:

Transfer policy: Each processor compares its load with that of its unique partner in that dimension. If an imbalance exists, load balancing is judged to be worthwhile and control passes to the selection policy.

Selection policy: All tasks are equally eligible for transfer. Migrating tasks are taken from the back of the sending processor's execution queue and are placed at the back of the destination processor's execution queue. In a dimension, each processor compares its load with that of its unique partner in that dimension and an amount of work equal to one half of the difference is migrated from the more heavily loaded processor to its partner [1, 12]. As with the Diffusion algorithm, fractional tasks cannot be sent or received and any recommendation by the algorithm to do this is ignored.

Location policy: Tasks which have been approved for migration are sent to the processor's unique partner in the dimension under consideration.

3. Simulation Model

We are concerned with the discrete event simulation of three aspects of a multicomputer system: the execution environment, the work environment and the load balancing algorithm. The execution environment for our investigations comprises a number of homogeneous processors interconnected in the form of a hypercube. Each processor has its own local memory, there is no shared memory and interprocessor communication is via message-passing. The communication links are assumed to be full duplex. Communication delays on the links are not modelled, and neither is any processor

overhead attached to message transmission. Some attention has been paid in the literature to the influence of processor communication port modelling on the Diffusion and Dimension Exchange algorithms [12]. Two models are extant: the one-port model, which allows a process to transmit on only one communication link at a time and the all-port model, which allows simultaneous transmission on all physical links. It is said that the all-port model favours Diffusion since that algorithm has information available for transmission on all links at each step, whereas Dimension Exchange by its very nature transmits on only one link at a time. The way in which port communications are modelled in the present work is as follows: Every time algorithm execution occurs, Diffusion runs at all processors and transmits on all physical links at each processor. Dimension Exchange is stepped through a complete cycle, balancing loads in each dimension and thus also transmitting on all links on every algorithm execution. Thus, in our simulations, the advantage rests with Dimension Exchange since, in a closed system, perfect balance would be achieved in one execution of the algorithm.

The work environment is comprised of tasks arriving in independent streams at each processor. There is no inter-task communication and no precedence constraints are imposed. Task execution times are exponentially distributed with mean $1/\mu$. Interarrival times are also exponential with mean $1/\lambda$ which is changed in the course of the experiments in order to vary the load level $\rho = \lambda/\mu$.

Load balancing algorithm execution incurs no processor overhead. Since there are no interprocessor delays, information updates and task transfers occur instantaneously. In addition, due to the absence of processor overhead for message passing and algorithm execution and due to the approach we have adopted for modelling communications ports, both algorithms instantaneously perform one round of transmissions on all physical links. There is no limit on the number of times a particular task may be migrated due to load balancing activity.

4. Results

This section is organised as a series of experiments which investigate the effects of parameter variations, load level and system size on system performance. The performance metric used here is the mean systemwide task response time, taken as the time elapsed from the arrival of a task to its completion. In the presentation of results, each response time is normalised by dividing it by the corresponding response time value for a system operating under the same load conditions without load balancing. In this way, it is possible to judge rapidly the value of a particular algorithm-parameter combination relative to no load balancing. The following experiments were carried out for hypercubes of 4, 8, 16 and 32 processors operating at load levels of 35%, 50%, 65% and 80%.

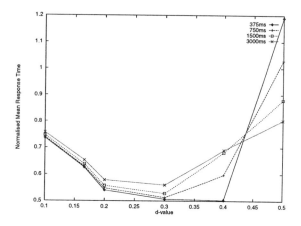

Figure 1. Influence of d-parameter and execution period on response time under the Diffusion algorithm

The first experiment examines the effects of the d-parameter and the execution frequency on the performance of the Diffusion algorithm. Typical results are presented in Figure 1 for a 32-processor hypercube at a load level of 80%. Values of d in the range 0.1 to 0.4 can be seen to improve performance over no load balancing, with a 25% variation in yield over this range. Above $d = 0.4$, response time rapidly deteriorates as increasing d causes a greater degree of useless task transfer. Since performance variation is considerable over a range of valid d-values, it is important to select the d-value most appropriate to a particular situation. In fact, this 'best' d-value depends on system size, as predicted by other authors [1, 11, 12] and this variation has shown up in our experiments. It may also be seen from Figure 1 that the best d-value can depend on how often the algorithm is executed. Thus, for execution periods from 3s down to 750ms, the best value is in the region of 0.3, whereas for more frequent execution at a period of 375ms, the best value appears to be in the region of 0.4. The overall effect of increasing the frequency of algorithm execution is to improve response time, but the improvement below a period of 750ms is not dramatic.

Since the Dimension Exchange algorithm for a binary hypercube is not parameterised, the second ex-

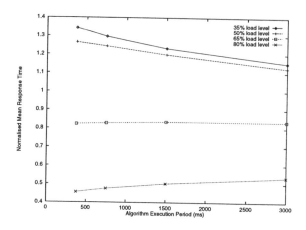

Figure 2. Influence of execution period on response time under the Dimension Exchange algorithm

periment concerns itself with an examination of the effect of execution frequency on the performance of this algorithm. Figure 2, for a 32-processor hypercube, reveals some remarkable results. First, it appears that for load levels of 35% and 50%, Dimension Exchange does not function well under the particular conditions simulated in this work and, in fact, can cause a disimprovement of up to 35% in system performance over no load balancing. However, Dimension Exchange does improve its performance with increasing load level and, whereas the improvement relative to no load balancing for a load level of 65% is only marginal, Dimension Exchange can improve response time for 80% load by up to 35%. The effect of execution period is slight, being almost without variation at the 65% load level with a more pronounced improvement at the 80% load level as the algorithm is executed more frequently. Since Dimension Exchange actually deteriorates performance for load levels of 50% and 35%, executing the algorithm less frequently at these loads causes an improvement in response time which, however, is still worse than that yielded without load balancing.

The effects of load level on the performance of the Diffusion and Dimension Exchange algorithms are investigated in the third experiment. In these tests, the best parameter values as obtained from the two previous experiments were used. For the Diffusion algorithm, Figure 3 shows that performance is always better than without load balancing, although at low loads the improvement is marginal. The effectiveness of Diffusion grows as the load level increases, gradually at first, giving a 7% improvement at 50% load but gain-

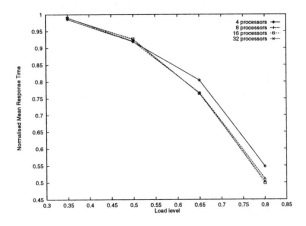

Figure 3. Effect of load level on response time for Diffusion

ing rapidly to yield a 20% to 22% return at 65% load and eventually a 45% to 50% improvement in response time at 80% load. As can be seen in Figure 3, the number of processors in the system has very little effect on the normalised response time.

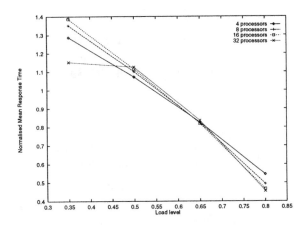

Figure 4. Effect of load level on response time for Dimension Exchange

Figure 4 displays the equivalent results for the Dimension Exchange algorithm. Again, the number of processors in the system makes no appreciable difference to the normalised response time. However, the outstanding feature of this set of plots is that use of the Dimension Exchange algorithm is only profitable above the 55% load level. Thereafter, response time improvement over no load balancing increases to ap-

proximately 20% at the 65% load level and 35% to 45% at the 80% load level.

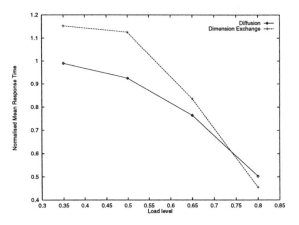

Figure 5. Performance comparison of Diffusion and Dimension Exchange in a 32-processor hypercube

The comparative performance of the Diffusion and Dimension Exchange algorithms is summarised in Figure 5. Here, the system under test is a 5-dimensional binary hypercube which we show as being representative of the results for the lower-dimension hypercubes included in this study. The parameter values used here are those best suited to the particular load levels tested. In contrast to the theoretical predictions [1, 11, 12], it can be seen that Diffusion out-performs Dimension Exchange over a wide range of load levels. Indeed, it is only beyond loads of approximately 73% that Dimension Exchange performs better, and then only slightly so. Dimension Exchange load balancing is a liability to the system until load levels approach 60%, whereas the Diffusion approach is always profitable.

5. Conclusions

We have investigated the performance of two of the principal nearest-neighbour load balancing algorithms in a binary hypercube topology. These algorithms, Diffusion and Dimension Exchange, are executed periodically and synchronously. Both Diffusion and Dimension Exchange have the execution period as a parameter. In general, when the algorithms yield better response time than no load balancing, shortening the period improves the response. However, the relationship is not linear and it is possible to select a period value such that more frequent execution of the algorithm will not give rise to a substantial decrease in response time.

As well as its period of execution, the Diffusion algorithm has a parameter, d, controlling the amount of load imbalance to be redressed at each algorithm step. We found that the performance of Diffusion is greatly dependent on the value of d and that it is important to select the value of d most appropriate to a particular operating environment, since it depends on system size and can even be affected by algorithm execution period.

Our tests have revealed that the value of synchronous load balancing under the particular set of assumptions included in our simulations is greatly dependent on system load. Three remarkable results have been produced: First, neither Diffusion nor Dimension Exchange is particularly effective at load levels below 50%. Second, Dimension Exchange has an adverse effect on system performance for load levels below 55%. Third, Dimension Exchange out-performs Diffusion only at load levels in excess of 75%.

In view of these results, it appears that synchronous load balancing is of limited value in hypercube multicomputers and we conclude that further experimentation is necessary to examine its applicability in other topologies. We also propose to extend our investigations to encompass asynchronous load balancing in this environment.

References

1. Cybenko, G., Dynamic load balancing for distributed memory multiprocessors, *Journal of Parallel and Distributed Computing*, 7:279-301, 1989.

2. Hanxleden, R.V., Scott, L.R., Load balancing on message passing architectures, *Journal of Parallel and Distributed Computing*, 13(3):312-324, November 1991.

3. Hong, J., Tan, X., Chen, M., From local to global: an analysis of nearest neighbour load balancing on hypercube, *ACM Performance Evaluation Review*, 16(1):73-82, May 1988.

4. Hwang, K., *Advanced Computer Architecture - Parallelism, Scalability, Programmability*, McGraw-Hill, Singapore, 1993, ISBN 0-07-113342-9.

5. JáJá, J., Load balancing and routing on the hypercube and related networks, *Journal of Parallel and Distributed Computing*, 14(4):431-435, April 1992.

6. Luque, E., Ripoll, A., Cortés, A., Margalef, T., A distributed diffusion method for dynamic load balancing on parallel computers, *Proceedings of the 3rd Euromicro Workshop on Parallel and Distributed Processing*, pp.43-50, January 1995.

7. Norman, M.G., Thanisch, P., Models of machines and computation for mapping in multicomputers, *ACM Computing Surveys*, 25(3):263-302, September 1993.

8. Qian, X., Yang, Q., Load balancing on generalised hypercube and mesh multiprocessors with LAL, *Proceedings of the 11th International Conference on Distributed Computing Systems*, pp.402-409, May 1991.

9. Shin, K.G., Chang, Y.-C., A coordinated location policy for load sharing in hypercube-connected multicomputers, *IEEE Transactions on Computers*, 44(5):669-682, May 1995.

10. Willebeek-LeMair, M.H., Reeves, A.P., Strategies for dynamic load balancing on highly parallel computers, *IEEE Transactions on Parallel and Distributed Systems*, 4(9):979-993, September 1993.

11. Xu, C.Z., Lau, F.C.M., Analysis of the generalised dimension exchange method for dynamic load balancing, *Journal of Parallel and Distributed Computing*, 16(4):385-393, December 1992.

12. Xu, C.Z., Lau, F.C.M., Monien, B., Lüling, R., Nearest-neighbour algorithms for load balancing in parallel computers, *Concurrency: Practice and Experience*, 7(7):707-736, October 1995.

13. Zhou, S., A trace-driven simulation study of dynamic load balancing, *IEEE Transactions on Software Engineering*, 14(9):1327-1341, September 1988.

14. Zhu, Y., Ahuja, M., Job scheduling on a hypercube, *Proceedings of the 10th International Conference on Distributed Computing Systems*, pp.510-517, May-June 1990.

A Generalized Conflict Relation for Abstract Data Types

SangKeun Lee   SoonYoung Jung   Chong-Sun Hwang

Department of Computer Science & Engineering
Korea University
{lsk,jsy,hwang}@disys.korea.ac.kr

Abstract

This paper proposes preservation as a generalized conflict relation for abstract data types. By explicitly including reverse-operations, preservation can be used independently of execution contexts to which different recovery algorithms and/or object models give rise to. This paper also makes a two-dimension(i.e., execution contexts and operations' specifications) comparison between preservation and other conflict relations. In each execution context, our formal comparison reveals that preservation-based concurrency control achieves more concurrency than commutativity-based one.

1 Introduction

Unlike the conventional database systems where the database operations are composed of Read and Write, object-oriented database systems can increase concurrency by using semantic information of high-level operations on abstract data types. Several protocols based on commutativity of high-level operations, which have much more semantic information than conventional Read or Write operations, have been proposed[1,4,6,15]. Weaker relations than commutativity, such as recoverability[3] and invalidation[13], have also been proposed. By considering only the return values of operations with respect to some particular execution order of operations, weaker relations-based concurrency controls achieve more concurrency than commutativity-based one at the cost of forcing the commit dependency among relevant transactions[3,12,13]. However, most conflict relations may only be used in some particular execution contexts of which differences arise due to different recovery algorithms and/or object models supported in database systems.

This paper proposes a generalized conflict relation called preservation. By explicitly including the reverse-operations, preservation is generalized; that is, it may be used independently of execution contexts, while still being weaker than commutativity. Section 2 describes database model, and defines(or modifies) several conflict relations on the given model. Section 3 proposes preservation as a new conflict relation. Section 4 makes a formal

two-dimensional comparison between preservation and other conflict relations, and Section 5 presents a preservation-based concurrency control. The conclusion is in Section 6.

2 The Database Model and Several Conflict Relations

2.1 Database Model

Transactions in database systems perform operations on instances of abstract data types. A transaction T is modeled by a tuple $(OP_T, <_T)$, where OP_T is a set of abstract operations and $<_T$ is a partial order on them. Concurrent execution of a set of transactions $T_1, T_2, \dots, T_n$ gives rise to a log $E = (OP_E, <_E)$. OP_E is $(\cup_i OP_{Ti})$ and $(\cup_i <_{Ti}) \subseteq <_E$. $<_E$ is a partial order on the operations in OP_E. If $O_i <_E O_j$, we say that O_i executed before O_j. The execution log E is *serializable* if there exists a total order $<_S$, called a serialization order, on the set $\{T_1, T_2, \dots, T_n\}$ such that if an operation O_i in transaction T_i conflicts with O_j in T_j, and if $T_i <_S T_j$, then $O_i <_E O_j$. Execution of operations on different objects give rises to logs E_k for each object k such that the log E is the union of all these logs.

Each object has a type, which defines a possible set of states of the object, and a set of primitive operations that provide the only means to create and manipulate objects of that type. The specification of an operation indicates the set of possible states and the responses that will be produced by that operation when the operation is begun in a certain state. Formally, the specification is a function f such that

$f : S \to S \times V$, where $S = \{s_1, s_2, \dots\}$ is a set of states, and $V = \{v_1, v_2, \dots\}$ is a set of return values.

For a given state $s \in S$, we define two components for the specification of an operation: return(o,s) which is the return value produced by operation o, and state(o,s) which is the state produced after execution of o. The definitions of state(o,s) and return(o,s) can be extended to a sequence of operations O. Thus, state(O,s) is the state produced after execution of operations in O, and return(O,s) is the union of the return values of

35

operations in O. The specification of object defines the set of possible sequences of operations for this object. A sequence of operations h is legal if it pertains to the specification of object. Transactions access and manipulate the objects of the database through operations. A transaction either commits on all objects or aborts on all objects.

The differences of recovery algorithms and/or object models employed in database systems give rise to different execution contexts. The objective of this paper is not to present recovery algorithms or object models(see [1,2,9,15] for more details), but rather to focus on the aspects directly related to concurrency. If an invoked operation's undo-operation(or compensation-operation) is recorded in write-ahead log before the invoked operation is executed, it is called the database systems employ the UIP(Update In Place) model, whereas it is called that the database systems, if an invoked operation is recorded in the invoking transaction's private workspace(intentions list) before executed, employ the DU(Deferred Update) model. In the biversion object model[15], each object x has two states, namely the current state and committed state. In this paper, execution contexts are classified into these three models.

2.2 Several Conflict Relations

The definition of Forward Commutativity(FC)[1], defined on the DU model, is as follows.

Definition 1 Consider two operations o_1 and o_2 executed concurrently by transaction T_1 and T_2 respectively on the same object. Operations o_1 and o_2 "forward commute", and denoted by (o_1 FC o_2), iff
For all state $s \in S$ such that state(o_1,s), return(o_1,s), state(o_2,s), and return(o_2,s) are defined,
state(o_1,state(o_2,s)) = state(o_2,state(o_1,s)), and
return(o_1,s) = return(o_1,state(o_2,s)), and
return(o_2,s) = return(o_2,state(o_1,s)). □

Intuitively, operations o_1 and o_2 forward commute, if both execution "o_1;o_2"(o_1's execution is followed by o_2's execution) and "o_2;o_1" are legal and would have the same effects on the object(the same state) and on the transactions(the same return values).

The definition of Backward Commutativity(BC)[1], defined on the UIP model, is as follows.

Definition 2 Consider two operations o_1 and o_2 such that o_1's execution is immediately followed by the execution of o_2. Operations o_1 and o_2 "backward commute", and denoted by (o_1 BC o_2), iff
For all state $s \in S$ such that state(o_1,s), return(o_1,s), state(o_2,state(o_1,s)), and return(o_2,state(o_1,s)) are defined,
state(o_1,state(o_2,s)) = state(o_2,state(o_1,s)), and
return(o_1,s) = return(o_1,state(o_2,s)), and
return(o_2,s) = return(o_2,state(o_1,s)). □

Intuitively, operations o_1 and o_2 backward commute, if the execution in the reverse order "o_2;o_1" is legal and would have the same effects on the object and on the transactions.

The definition of Forward-Backward Commutativity(FBC)[15], defined on the biversion object model, is as follows.

Definition 3 Consider two operations o_1 and o_2 such that o_1's execution is immediately followed by the execution of o_2. Operations o_1 and o_2 "forward-backward commute", and denoted by (o_1 FBC o_2), iff
For all state $s \in S$ such that state(o_1,s), return(o_1,s), state(o_2,s), state(o_2,state(o_1,s)), and return(o_2,s) = return(o_2,state(o_1,s)) are defined,
state(o_1,state(o_2,s)) = state(o_2,state(o_1,s)), and
return(o_1,s) = return(o_1,state(o_2,s)). □

In the biversion object model, the invoked operation can see both the current and the committed state of the object. With this execution context, it is possible to establish whether return(o_2,s) = return(o_2,state(o_1,s)) condition is satisfied or not.

The definition of recoverability[3], defined independently of execution contexts, is as follows.

Definition 4 Consider two operations o_1 and o_2 such that o_1's execution is immediately followed by the execution of o_2. Operation o_2 is "relatively recoverable" with respect to operation o_1, and denoted by (o_2 RR o_1), iff
For all state $s \in S$ such that return(o_1,s) and state(o_1,s) are defined,
return(o_2,s) = return(o_2,state(o_1,s)). □

Intuitively, recoverability captures what happens when operations are removed from an execution log E. Recoverability is a relation where one operation's return value is not affected by another's concurrent execution.

The definition of invalidation[13], defined on the DU model, is as follows. (" • " in Definition 5 means concatenation of operations.)

Definition 5 Consider two operations o_1 and o_2, arbitrary sequences of operations h_1 and h_2 executed concurrently on the same object. Operation o_1 "invalidates" operation o_2, and denoted by (o_1 IV o_2), iff
For all state $s \in S$ such that $h_1 \bullet o_1 \bullet h_2$ and $h_1 \bullet h_2 \bullet o_2$ are legal,
return(o_2,state(h_2, state(h_1,s))) $\neq$ return(o_2, state(h_2, state(o_1, state(h_1,s)))). □

Invalidation captures what happens when operations are inserted into an execution log E, whereas recoverability captures what happens when operations are removed. In Definition 5, if arbitrary sequences of operations h_1 and h_2 are both empty, the specifications in Definition 5 is equivalent to those in Definition 4. Thus, in the DU model, invalidation is equivalent to recoverabilily.

3 Preservation Relation

3.1 Motivation

Our motivation of a new conflict relation is that, in the UIP or biversion object model, it is very difficult to compare recoverability or invalidation with commutativity, as incorrect state of object or cascading aborts may be induced unless each undo-operation is state-sensitive or concurrent operation-sensitive. Let us consider Account object where deposit(x1) and post(x2) operations are defined. Deposit(x1) returns OK after increments the balance of account by x1, and post(x2) returns OK after interests x2% of balance to the account. Suppose that, in the UIP model, the initial state of Account object is 100, and deposit(100)'s execution is followed by the execution of post(5), both of which return OKs. According to Definition 4 and Definition 5, deposit(100) and post(5) operations are relatively recoverable, and deposit(100) does not invalidate post(5). Thus, these two operations are allowed to execute concurrently and the state of Account object is 210. In the case of deposit(100)'s abort, however, the state of Account would be incorrect 110, after the execution of deposit(100)'s undo-operation, unless it is post(5)-sensitive. Even if this incorrect state of object is detected, cascading abort of causing post(5)'s abort occurs. This phenomenon also occurs in the biversion object model where deposit(100)'s undo-operation present in intentions list executes on the current state of Account object.

With the above motivation, this paper comes up with a new conflict relation, which is a generalized conflict relation in that it can be used in every execution context.

3.2 Reverse-Operations and Preservable Operations

In this paper, an object is extended to contain reverse-operations, along with the type defining the possible state set of object and the (normal) operations accessible to the object. A reverse-operation for an update operation on an object is defined as follows.

Definition 6 Consider one update operation, o, defined on some object. A special operation, denoted by $\bar{o}$, is a "reverse-operation" for o, iff
For all state $s \in S$, state($\bar{o}$, state(o,s)) = s. □

The above Definition 6 states that a reverse-operation $\bar{o}$ for an update operation o obliterates the effects of o on some object. Thus, a reverse-operation for an update operation is equivalent to an undo-operation which has been implicitly employed in the database systems. In the UIP or biversion object model, if a transaction aborts, each reverse-operation for each update operation, present in the write-ahead log(UIP model) or intentions list(biversion object model), should be

executed on the current state of objects in the reverse order during undo process. On the contrary, in the DU model, if a transaction aborts, the update operations present in the intentions list have only to be removed, thus there is no need for explicit reverse-operations. It should be noted that the form of a reverse-operation may be different depending on object designers. For example, one form of reverse-operation for push(x1) operation in Stack object may involve removing the pushed element, x1, from the Stack, and another may involve removing the top element in the Stack.

With the reverse-operations, we define an "immediately preservable" relation as follows.

Definition 7 Consider two operations o_1 and o_2 such that o_1's execution in state s is immediately followed by execution of o_2. An operation o_2 is "immediately preservable" with respect to o_1, and denoted by (o_2 P$_I$ o_1), iff
For all state $s \in S$, there exists $\bar{o_1}$ for an operation o_1 such that,
return(o_2,s) = return(o_2,state(o_1,s)), and
state(o_2,s) = state($\bar{o_1}$,state(o_2,state(o_1,s))). □

Definition 7 contains the condition, which checks if the state of object is preserved correct even after the execution of a reverse-operation for an aborted operation. Thus, if an explicit reverse-operation for push(x1) operation in Stack object involve removing the pushed element, x1, then two push(x1) operations are immediately preservable.

If the fact is taken into account that the form of a reverse-operation may be different depending on object designers, the same two operations may be immediately preservable or may not. For example, two push(x1) operations are not immediately preservable if the reverse-operation for push(x1) involves removing the top element in the stack.

With immediately preservable relation, commutativity relation between two operations is defined as follows.

Definition 8 Two operations o_1 and o_2 "commute", and denoted by (o_1 C o_2), iff
For all states $s \in S$,
state(o_2,state(o_1,s)) = state(o_1,state(o_2,s)), and
(o_2 P$_I$ o_1), and (o_1 P$_I$ o_2). □

So far, (o_2 P$_I$ o_1) was used to denote the fact that o_2 was immediately preservable with respect to o_1, when o_2 was executed after o_1. We extend the concept to include the case where o_2 is preservable to o_1 in spite of intervening operations, which have executed but have not yet committed, between o_1 and o_2.

Definition 9 Consider a sequence of operations $O = \{o_1, \dots ,o_{n-1}\}$, which has executed but not yet committed, and an operation o_n such that for $\forall 1 \leq i < n$, $o_i <_E o_{i+1}$. An operation o_n is "preservable" to o_1, and denoted by (o_n P o_1), iff
For all state $s \in S$ and for any subsequence of O' of O, there exists a collection of each

reverse-operation for each update operation in O', $\overline{O'}$, such that
return(o_n,state(O-O',s)) = return(o_n,state(O,s)),
and state(o_n,state(O-O',s)) =
state($\overline{O'}$,state(o_n,state(O,s))). □

The above Definition 9 states that the preservable relation between two operations, in case there are intervening operations which have executed but have not yet committed, is defined as the relation where the state of object is preserved correct and o_n's return value is not affected even after any subsequence of O' of O is aborted.

Lemma 1 Consider a sequence of operations O = {o_1, ... ,o_{n-1}}, which has executed but not yet committed, and an operation o_n such that for $\forall 1 \leq i < n$, $o_i <_E o_{i+1}$.

For $\forall 1 \leq x < n$, if (o_n P_I o_x) then (o_n P o_1).

Proof) Let F denote the operations that execute between o_n and o_1. The proof is by induction on |F|.
① Induction base : |F| = 1, i.e., F contains only one operation so O = {o_1, o_2}.
Since (o_3 P_I o_2), the state of object will be preserved correct and the return value of o_3 will not be affected even after o_2's abortion. And since (o_3 P_I o_1), (o_3 P o_1).
② Induction hypothesis : |F| = k-1, i.e., F contains k-1 operations so O = {o_1, o_2, ... , o_k}.
For $\forall 1 \leq x \leq k$, we assume that if (o_n P_I o_x) then (o_n P o_1).
③ Induction step : |F| = k, i.e., F contains k operations so O = {o_1, o_2, ... , o_k, o_{k+1}}.
Since (o_n P_I o_{k+1}) and (o_n P_I o_k), we can get (o_n P o_k) by using a reasoning similar to the base case. Further, since ②, for $\forall 1 \leq x \leq k+1$, if ($o_n$ P_I o_x) then (o_n P o_1). □

From the Lemma 1, we know that an operation which is invoked on an object is allowed to execute concurrently when it is immediately preservable to all the operations which have executed but not yet committed on that object.

3.3 Example

It is assumed here that each operation is atomically executed and return values of operations are taken into account in determining a conflict; these considerations increase concurrency between transactions[8,9,12]. With Account object, we show how execution contexts affect the preservation table. Account object provides deposit(x1), withdraw(x2), post(x3) operations, and each reverse-operation for each operation. Each reverse-operation for deposit(x1), withdraw(x2), and post(x3) operation

involves decrementing the balance by x1, incrementing by x2, and decrementing to be $100 \times$ balance/(100+x3) respectively. The preservation for Account object is shown in Table I.

In Table I, the entries denoted by P, P_D, P_U, P_B, and $P_{(B)}$ indicate, respectively, preservation in every models, only in the DU model, UIP, biversion object model, and may be preservable or may not depending on the state of object in the biversion object model. The notation (OP_2,OP_1) used is meant that an operation OP_2 is invoked when OP_1 has executed yet not committed. Consider the pair (withdraw(x2)/OK, deposit(x1')/OK). In the UIP model, this pair is not preservable because the return value OK of withdraw(x2) could be different if previously executed deposit(x1')/OK operation aborted, whereas this pair is preservable in the DU model. On the other hand, in the biversion object model, this pair is preservable if the return value of withdraw(x2) is OK from both the current and the committed state of Account object.

OP₂ requested / OP₁ executed	deposit (x1)/OK	withdraw (x2)/OK	withdraw (x2)/Insufficient	post(x3)/OK
deposit(x1') /OK	P	P_D $P_{(B)}$	P_U P_B	P_D
withdraw (x2')/OK	P	P_U P_B	P_D $P_{(B)}$	P_D
withdraw (x2') /Insufficient	P	P	P	P
post(x3') /OK	P_D	P_D	P_U P_B	P

Table I Preservation for Account

4 Formal Comparison between Preservaton and Other Conflict Relations

In this section, we make a two-dimension comparison between preservation and other conflict relations; one dimension is execution contexts, and the other is the operations' specifications.

The reason for taking execution contexts as one dimension is that it is very difficult to compare the conflict relations each of which is defined in different execution context. For example, the two executions of the same operations, one generated in the DU model on which FC is defined and the other in the UIP model on which BC is defined, are different. That is, the case occurs that the execution recognized as serializable in the UIP model is not necessarily serializable in the DU model[15]. Thus, we take different execution contexts as one dimension for the formal comparison. The operations' specifications indicate both the state of an object and the return values of operations after the execution of concurrent operations. Weaker relations, recoverability and invalidation, considering only the return values of operations achieve more concurrency than commutativity considering both the state of an object and the return values of operations[3,8,10,13]. Thus, we take the operations' specifications as the other dimension for the formal comparison.

With these two dimensions(i.e., execution contexts and operations' specifications), we make a formal comparison between preservation and others, which is shown in Table II. According to the formal comparison, preservation is identical to recoverability and invalidation in the DU model. Preservation, however, is a generalized conflict relation; this is, it can be employed in every execution contexts, while still being weaker than commutativity.

The seemingly overhead of preservation that the reverse-operations should be provided by object designers can be alleviated if the fact is taken into account that undo-operations equivalent to the reverse-operations are inherent in the UIP or biversion object model.

Execution contexts / Operation's specifications	UIP model	DU model	Biversion object model
state of an object & return values of operations	BC	FC	FBC
return values of operations	*Preservation*	*Preservation* Recoverability Invalidation	*Preservation*

Table II Formal comparison between preservation and others

5 Preservation-based Concurrency Control

We now discuss the issues related to a concurrency control based on preservation semantics. Each object scheduler O_k maintains its dependency graph DG_k, which is composed of its commit dependency graph OG_k and its conflict relation graph CG_k. These graphs are defined as the following.

- $OG_k = (N, M)$ is "cOmmit dependency Graph" at object k, where N is the set of nodes corresponding to active transactions that have begun execution but not committed, and M is a set of edges. An edge e belonging to M is a directed edge from T_j to T_i if T_i has executed o_i and T_j has executed o_j such that,

$$o_i <_{Ek} o_j, \neg(o_j \, C \, o_i) \text{ but } (o_j \, P_I \, o_i).$$

- $CG_k = (N, M)$ is "Conflict relation Graph" at object k, where N is the set of nodes corresponding to active transactions that have begun execution but not committed, and M is a set of edges. An edge e belonging to M is a directed edge from T_j to T_i if T_i has executed o_i and T_j has executed o_j such that,

$$o_i <_{Ek} o_j, \text{ and } \neg(o_j \, P_I \, o_i).$$

- $DG_k(= OG_k \cup CG_k)$ is "dependency graph" at object k.

The dependency graph is defined at object k. But, we must ensure that there is no cycle in the dependency graph in the whole database system. To this end, we define the dependency graph in the database system in the following.

- $DG(= \cup DG_k)$ is "dependency graph in the database system".

It is assumed that cycles formed in the DG can be handled using several known techniques of deadlock detection and resolution[10,11]. Each object scheduler O_k controls the concurrent execution of operations using a concurrency control algorithm shown in Figure 1. A concurrency control proposed here is based on a 2 Phase Locking(2PL) scheme, in which concurrency control operates at each invocation of an operation(i.e., pessimistic concurrency scheme).

```
• Input
    o_i : the invoked operation by an active
          transaction T_i
• Algorithm
    conflict := false;
    while (E_k ≠ ∅) and ¬conflict loop
        o_j ⇐ E_k;
        if ¬(o_i P_I o_j) then
            conflict := true;  (T_i→T_j) ⇒ CG_k;
            if Cycle(DG) then Abort(T_i); endif;
        else if ¬(o_i C o_j) then
            (T_i→T_j) ⇒ OG_k;
            if Cycle(DG) then Abort(T_i); endif;
        endif
    endloop
    if conflict then Block(T_i);
            else Execute(o_i);
    endif
```

Figure 1 Concurrency control algorithm

Cascading aborts can be avoided by allowing only preservable operations to execute concurrently. Furthermore, a presented concurrency control algorithm produces a serializable log by scheduling operations such that cycles are not formed in the DG.

Theorem 1 The executions produced by a concurrency control based on preservation are serializable if a log E contains only preservable operations.
(Proof) From a concurrency control algorithm in

Figure 1, all the operations in a log E are preservable, and each object scheduler aborts the transaction that invoked an operation participating in forming a cycle in DG. Therefore, cycles are not formed in DG if a log E contains only preservable operations. □

6 Conclusion

Typed object semantics have been exploited in the scope of weaker relations than commutativity. Examples of these relations are recoverability and invalidation. We showed, however, these two relations are not fitted into some execution contexts, i.e., the UIP and biversion object model. By explicitly including reverse-operations, preservation is better fitted into these models, along with the DU model. Thus, the contribution of this work is to provide a generalized notion of conflict relation in that it can be employed in every execution contexts, while still being weaker than commutativity.

References

[1]   W.   "Commutativity-Based   Concurrency Control for Abstract Data Types," *IEEE Trans. Comput.* Vol.37, No.12, pp. 1488-1505, 1988

[2]   Berstein, P. A., Hadzilacos, V., and Goodman, N. Concurrency Control and Recovery in Database Systems. Addison-Wesley, Reading, Mass., 1987

[3]   Badrinath, B., and Ramamritham, K. "Semantics-Based Concurrency Control : Beyond Commutativity," *ACM Trans. Database Syst.* Vol.17, No.1, pp. 163-199, 1992

[4]   Garcia-Molina, H. "Using semantic Knowledge for Transaction Processing in a Distributed Database," *ACM ' Trans. Database Syst.* Vol.8, No.2 , pp. 186-213, 1983

[5]   Weihl, W. and Liskov, B. H. "Implementation of Resilient, Atomic Data Types," *ACM Trans. Program. Lang. Syst.* Vol.7, No.1, pp. 244-269, 1985

[6]   Weihl, W. "Specification and Implementation of Atomic Data Types," Ph.D. Thesis MIT/LCS/TR-314, MIT, 545 Technology Square, Cambridge, Mass., March 1984

[7]   Skarra, A. H., and Zdonik, S. B. Concurrency Control and objected-oriented databases. In *Object-Oriented Concepts, Databases, and Applications.* Won Kim and F. H. Lochovsky, pp.395-421, ACM Press, New York, 1989

[8]   Schwartz, P. M., and Spector, A. Z. "Synchronizing Shared Abstract Data Types," *ACM Trans. Comput. Syst.* Vol.2, No.3, pp. 223-250, 1984

[9]   Berstein, A. J., and Lewis, P. M. Concurrency in Programming and Database Systems. Jones and Bartlett, Boston

London, 1993

[10]   Mukesh Singhal. Deadlock Detection in Distributed Systems. In *Distributed Computing Systems.* Thomas L., Casavant, and Mukesh Singhal, pp. 52-71, IEEE Computer Society Press, California, 1994

[11]   Knapp, E. "Deadlock Detection in Distributed Databases," *ACM Comput. Surv.* Vol.19, No.4, pp. 303-328, 1987

[12]   Anastassopoulos, P., and Jean Dollimore. A Unified Approach to Distributed Concurrency Control. In *Distributed Computing Systems.* Thomas L., Casavant, and Mukesh Singhal, pp. 545-571, IEEE Computer Society Press, California, 1994

[13]   Herlihy, M. P. "Apologizing versus asking permission : Optimistic concurrency control for abstract data types," *ACM Trans. Database Syst.* Vol.15, No.1, pp. 96-124, 1990

[14]   Herlihy, M. P., and Weihl, W. "Hybrid concurrency control for abstract data types", In *Proceedings of the 7th ACM Symposium on Principles of Database Syst.* pp. 201-210, 1988

[15]   Guerni, M., Ferrié, J., and Pons, J. -F. Concurrency and Recovery for Typed Objects using a New Commutativity Relation. In *Deductive and Object-Oriented Databases.* Lecture Notes in Computer Science 1013. Ling, T. W. et al., pp. 411-428, 1995

A Proposal to Improve Reusability in a Language based on the Occam-CSP Model

F. Araque, M. Capel, J.M. Mantas, A. Palma
Dpto. de Lenguajes y Sistemas Informáticos
E.T.S. Ingeniería Informática
Universidad de Granada
Avda. Andalucía 38, 18071 - Granada
email: mcapel@goliat.ugr.es

Abstract

The need to declare channels as global objects of the applications implemented according to the Distributed Programming Occam-CSP model, limits the desirable reusability of the software-modules of the said applications. The integration of other languages that follow the OO paradigm is not easy either. In this paper, easy solutions are proposed to augment the reusability of languages that follow the existing model based on a class of modules called ODAs and on a previously existing language that implement the above-mentioned modules in a multicomputer based on a Transputer platform.

1. Introduction

It is well known that multicomputers are nowadays the most important technological option to answer the increasing demand of speed and memory of current applications. The absence of a general reference language for programming with this kind of architecture, has been the cause of the overabundance of distributed language proposals in the last fifteen years. Many of these proposals have had a wide distribution, such as PVM [5], but they don't allow the verification of the total correctness of programs. Others, even though carried out by important scientists, e.g. Joyce [6], haven't achieved the necessary diffusion to be implemented in concrete architectures. And classical languages, like Ada [3], are not adequate to be implemented efficiently without severely restricting the language constructions in a distributed system.

None of the aforementioned problems affect the Occam-CSP model of distributed programming. The Occam [2] language is an *almost* complete implementation of the CSP [1] model and has been used as a reference language to develop the SGS-Thomson (formerly called Innos) *Transputer* processor family. The basis for the development of Software Engineering tools, which allows one to derive high quality and secure programs in Occam for multicomputers, has been established based on the formal semantics of the language derived from C.A.R. Hoare's work in the last decade [8].

Traditionally it has been argued that the lack of reusability of the Occam-CSP model is one of the drawbacks which prevents a widespread use of programming following this model. The code of a module or a process, etc. needs to access global channels which communicate processes in the same or in other processors, therefore the reusability of programs developed with the aforementioned model is limited. Nevertheless, this drawback may be resolved by separating the *configuration* of the channels from the programming of the application's modules. This paper proposes a method to overcome this drawback by following this idea.

The integration of Object-Oriented Programming (OOP) concepts with the Occam-CSP model in order to obtain software reusability presents various drawbacks. The Occam-CSP model is mainly static (i.e. all the components should be fixed before program execution), as opposed to the *late binding* of the OOP. Additionally, the communication model of the Occam-CSP is point-to-point synchronous message passing, whereas the OOP employs a *client-server* communication scheme. The parallel granularity unit is at instruction level in Occam, whereas in the case of OO languages it should be at a process or object level. On the other hand, the object-based programming model assumes that aspects referring to the configuration, distribution, mobility, etc, of the objects have to be con-

1066-6192/97 $10.00 © 1997 IEEE

cealed from the user programs. All this seems to point out to the incompatibility of both models.

Our proposal attempts to demonstrate a technique to achieve reusability in distributed applications. This has been developed using a class of modules called ODAs that are used to encapsulate abstract data types, among other information, in SPMD-distributed applications. A language that uses these modules, has been presented in previous papers [11], [12]. In our model, communications are carried out through global channels declared according to the Occam model, while object reusability is achieved using ODA modules, as will be demonstrated. This has been carried out on various platforms, while currently a Telmat TN310 multicomputer with 16 T9000 processors is being used.

In the next section both the distributed programming model based on ODAs and its implementation in an Occam-transputer platform will be explained. In order to solve some of the problems that arise due to the direct implementation in Occam of applications based on ODAs, a previously proposed language [11],[12] that allows ODAs-description is used and the most significant aspects will be revised at the end of section 2.

In the third section, some of the aforementioned language characteristics that improve reusability will be presented.

2. Programming Model: Distributed Active Objects

An ODA module will be implemented as an object whose code is replicated into all the nodes of the multicomputer. The different replicas of the object (see fig. 1) will communicate each other in order to:

- maintain the coherency of the global Abstract Data Type implementation,

- implement the object's operations.

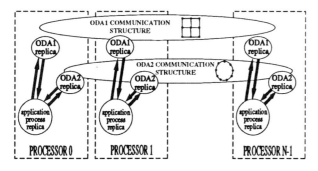

Figure 1

The communication code of the application is encapsulated in the ODAs employing high level constructions of a specific language [12]. By means of messages passed between the replicas of the ODAs, a distributed computation model is achieved in that the application processes only carry out local communication and the ODAs are charged for remote communication. The way in which different ODA-replicas connect and communicate with each other will depend on the represented data type and will reflect the object's own communication structure. The ODA modules are used to implement the code of the operations while also providing their users access to a series of operations which belong to an abstract data type. These operations have a semantic of remote calls which means that one ODA-replica attends operation requests while the clients await a message with results.

2.1. Distributed application building in Occam

In order to implement each ODA-replica in Occam 2, a generic procedure is necessary whose formal parameters are:

- A series of channels for the communication with other ODA-replicas of the same type.

- For each operation, an array of channels for the communication with the application processes.

- Two parameters that will contain the current values of each replica identifier (REP.ID) and the number of replicas (NODES).

In a similar way, the application process is described as an Occam procedure whose formal parameters are the parameters REP.ID, NODES and, for every ODA, a pair of channels for each operation.

The procedures that implement both ODA-replicas and application processes are compiled and linked separately. A complete distributed application is described in a configuration file (see fig. 2), in which the parallel components to be executed in each processor are specified and the channels needed to correctly connect the different processes according to the logical communication structure of the application are declared. The existence of this "configuration phase" is a way to achieve the reusability of components compiled and linked in the distributed applications, or even considering the possibility of having a library of said components.

2.2. ODAs Description Language

To use the ODA modules in the applications in a flexible way, a language to describe these modules has

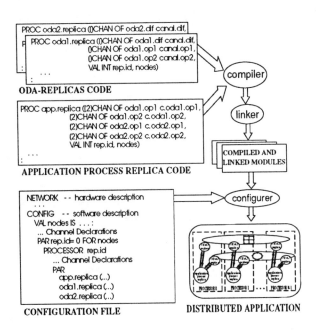

ODA-REPLICAS CODE

```
PROC oda2.replica (()CHAN OF oda2.dif canal.dif,
  PROC oda1.replica (()CHAN OF oda1.dif canal.dif,
                    ()CHAN OF oda1.op1 canal.op1,
                    ()CHAN OF oda1.op2 canal.op2,
                    VAL INT rep.id, nodes)
  : ...
  :
```

APPLICATION PROCESS REPLICA CODE

```
PROC app.replica ([2]CHAN OF oda1.op1 c.oda1.op1,
                  [2]CHAN OF oda1.op2 c.oda1.op2,
                  [2]CHAN OF oda2.op1 c.oda2.op1,
                  [2]CHAN OF oda2.op2 c.oda2.op2,
                  VAL INT rep.id, nodes)
  : ...
```

CONFIGURATION FILE

```
NETWORK  -- hardware description
  ...
CONFIG  -- software description
  VAL nodes IS ... :
    ... Channel Declarations
  PAR rep.id= 0 FOR nodes
    PROCESSOR rep.id
      ... Channel Declarations
      PAR
        app.replica (..)
        oda1.replica (..)
        oda2.replica (..)
```

compiler → linker → COMPILED AND LINKED MODULES → configurer → **DISTRIBUTED APPLICATION**

Figure 2

been proposed, which should allow the programmer of distributed applications freedom from low level details thus improving the programmability and code reusability.

The ODA description language has been shown in previous papers [11],[12]. In the notation of the language the description of an ODA-module is carried out in two separate parts:

1. *Definition.*

   - For every replica, channels that allow communication with other replicas of the same ODA assigned to different processors are declared, making use of the communication channels previously mentioned.

   - The ODA communication structure is described. Specifically, the way in which different ODA-replicas will be connected.

   - The interface for the ODA operations is specified in order to have a similar notation to the remote call channels of Occam 3 [14], conforming more to its semantics.

2. *The implementation.*

   - The ODA-replicas code that implements the operations of the ODA are described.

We distinguish between an *ODA declaration* which makes the definition of an ODA accesible to its users, and *ODA instantation*, where a specific implementation is assigned to the previously declared ODA. Declarations and instantiations are made in a separate module: the application process. We decided that this module will not be reusable, since it seems logical to us that a substitution of the ODA module implies a modification of the user application program code. Reusability is achieved at the ODA level, and the responsibility of generating automatically the configuration file is left to the *configurer* (see fig. 2). Definition and implementation parts of the ODAs remain unlinked until the moment that they are declared and instantiated.

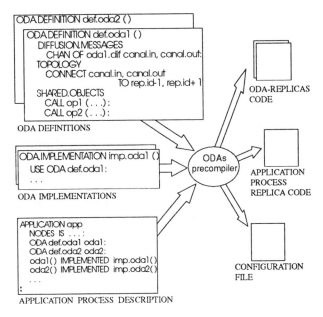

ODA DEFINITIONS

```
ODA.DEFINITION def.oda2 ()
  ODA.DEFINITION def.oda1 ()
    DIFFUSION.MESSAGES
      CHAN OF oda1.dif canal.in, canal.out:
    TOPOLOGY
      CONNECT canal.in, canal.out
                        TO rep.id-1, rep.id+ 1

    SHARED.OBJECTS
      CALL op1 ( . . .):
      CALL op2 ( . . .):
```

ODA IMPLEMENTATIONS

```
ODA.IMPLEMENTATION imp.oda1 ()
  USE ODA def.oda1:
  . . .
```

APPLICATION PROCESS DESCRIPTION

```
APPLICATION app
  NODES IS ... :
  ODA def.oda1 oda1:
  ODA def.oda2 oda2:
  oda1() IMPLEMENTED imp.oda1()
  oda2() IMPLEMENTED imp.oda2()
  . . .
  :
```

ODAs precompiler → ODA-REPLICAS CODE, APPLICATION PROCESS REPLICA CODE, CONFIGURATION FILE

Figure 3

3. Issues of Reusability in the Language

3.1. Use of the same definition with different implementations

After declaring an ODA, a set of operations is offered to its possible users. In the following example, we introduce an ODA definition that represents a distributed integer with two operations: `read` and `write`.

```
ODA.DEFINITION distr.integer ()
PROTOCOL
  integer IS INT:
```

```
DIFFUSION.MESSAGES
  [NODES-1][2] CHAN OF integer integer.diff:
TOPOLOGY -- full connected topology
  DO i=0 FOR NODES-1
    DO j=0 FOR 2
      CONNECT integer.diff[i][j]
              TO ((REP.ID+1)+i)\NODES
SHARED.OBJECTS
  CALL read (RESULT INT data ):
  CALL write (VAL INT data):
```

Any possible implementation for `distr.integer` will include this clause:

```
USE ODA distr.integer:
```

We can have different implementations of ODA-modules that represent a distributed integer. These implementations assume both the same interface and communication structure as if they used the same definition. We would be able to have other implementations that provide different functionability to the ODA operations and that will be used for specific applications. This would allow us to manage a distributed global variable of integer type. Using this implementation (called `ordinary.integer`) the invocation of for example, the *write* operation, would involve updating the locally stored value in any of the replicas while this value is different than the previously stored one. Another possibility would be to have an implementation (called `smallest.integer`) which would cause the update in any of the local replicas where the desired value is lower than the one stored. The interface and communication structure of this new implementation would be the same although the semantics of *write* operation would be slightly different.

In the next application process, two ODAs, e1 and e2, are declared with a `distr.integer` definition. In the instatiation, the `ordinary.integer` implementation is assigned to e1 and the `smallest.integer` implementation to e2:

```
APPLICATION example
NODES IS ...:
ODA distr.integer e1, e2:
DO
  e1() IMPLEMENTED ordinary.integer()
  e2() IMPLEMENTED smallest.integer()
SEQ
  -- Give an initial value to e1
  e1{write}(0)
  -- Give an initial value to e2
  e2{write}(known.value)
  ... etc...
```

The declared ODAs allow us to keep two types of globally distributed variables of integer type, and both can be used in distributed applications according to the required functionability.

3.2. ODAs parameterization

In the ODA module definition heading, formal parameters can be declared. These parameters, together with NODES and REP.ID, allow the "skeleton" description of the distributed object communication structure which will be instantiated in the configuration phase, when these parameters take particular values.

In order to illustrate the application of our scheme, we will show some details about the implementation of an n-way filter algorithm in a multicomputer. We will implement a particular case of the algorithm, in which every leaf node in a tree, defined with a fixed branch degree for all the nodes, takes positive integer values from a file and distributes the said values toward its parent node. Internal nodes in the tree compute the largest values among those obtained from its sons and send the result to its parent node.

In order to encapsulate communication requirements of the algorithm, we have made the following ODA-module definition that represents a type of distributed object with uniform n-ary tree topology. In this definition, the branch degree of each node (n=branch degree), is declared as a formal parameter in the heading.

```
-- Uniform n-ary tree
ODA.DEFINITION n.tree (VAL INT branch.degree)
  PROTOCOL
    n.protoc IS ...:
  DIFFUSION.MESSAGES
    [branch.degree]CHAN OF n.protoc son.c:
    CHAN OF n.protoc parent.c:
    CHAN OF n.protoc before.c, next.c:
  TOPOLOGY
    DO
      IF
        is.internal.node
          DO j=0 FOR branch.degree
            CONNECT son.c[j] TO left.son.node+j
      IF
        NOT is.root.node
          CONNECT parent.c TO parent.node
  SHARED.OBJECTS
    CALL receive.data (RESULT INT data):
    CALL send.data (VAL INT data):
```

44

As can be seen in this definition, an array of channels whose sizes are equal to `branch.degree` parameter (to communicate with the sons of the current node), a channel `parent.c` (to communicate with the parent node) and two other channels, `before.c` and `next.c` (its usefulness will be shown later), are declared. These channels will be mapped onto a uniform n-ary tree topology in the configuration phase.

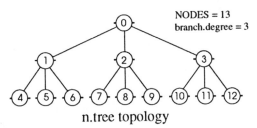

n.tree topology

Figure 4

The `branch.degree` parameter, together with the `NODES` parameter, allow us to define objects with tree topology that can be adapted in a flexible way for multiple distributed applications which request services of an object with this communication structure.

Once the ODA definition has been specified, a compatible implementation which shows the required communication in the filter algorithm, should be defined.

```
ODA.IMPLEMENTATION filter.imp()
 USE ODA n.tree:
 ... etc...
```

3.3. Topologies redefinition

New definitions of the `TOPOLOGY` section can be created starting from previously existing definitions. An easy example showing how this would be possible is the following: suppose we wish to incorporate a graceful termination detection mechanism in the filter processes which will be initiated when any given leaf node receives a particular type of integer data (e.g. any negative integer). In this case, we need a communication structure that will permit the proper termination of the leaf nodes, so that later the internal nodes will also be terminated in an orderly way. This is accomplished by connecting leaf nodes in a ring shape. This can be achieved adapting the `n.tree` definition topology to a new context by assigning `before.c` and `next.c` channels in leaf nodes level (see fig. 5). These channel assignments can be carried out using CONNECT

clauses as can be seen in the `threading.n.tree` ODA definition.

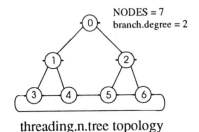

threading.n.tree topology

Figure 5

```
ODA.DEFINITION threading.n.tree
              REDEFINES n.tree
 TOPOLOGY
  DO
   IF
    is.leaf.node
     IF
      (REP.ID<>primer.nodo.hoja) AND
      (REP.ID<>ultimo.nodo.hoja)
        CONNECT before.c,next.c
          TO before.node,next.node
      (REP.ID=first.leaf.node)
        CONNECT before.c,next.c
          TO last.leaf.node,next.node
      (REP.ID=last.leaf.node)
        CONNECT before.c,next.c
          TO before.node,first.leaf.node
```

Using this mechanism, we can create ODA definitions from the previously existing ones in a hierarchical way (see fig. 6). A topology redefinition will not add any new aspect to the ODA module interface, but will only modify the object communication patterns. In this way, reusability of previous definitions will be attained.

We call the set of definitions obtained from a given definition a *family* of ODA definitions. The variations between one definition and another in a family only refer to the communication structure defined to communicate the different replicas of an ODA. The ODA definitions in a family also maintain the same interface. As a general rule, all the definitions in a family can be instantiated with an implementation that is compatible with the communication features that characterize the said family.

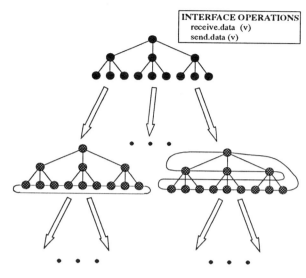

```
┌─────────────────────────┐
│ INTERFACE OPERATIONS     │
│ receive.data  (v)        │
│ send.data  (v)           │
└─────────────────────────┘
```

Figure 6

4. Conclusions

Easy solutions have been established to augment the reusability of software components developed with a language that follows the Occam-CSP model. The said solutions consist essentially of three *features of reusability* that can be applied in the distributed applications development.

1. Reusability based on the definition separated from the interface consisting of replacing the ODA module implementation, so it always maintains the same interface and object communication structure that the said module represents.

2. Reusability based on ODA module parameterization consisting of parameterizing the heading of the definition modules of the ODAs; these parameters will be instantiated in the configuration phase of a given application.

3. Reusability based on the adaptation of the communication structure consisting of a statical redefinition of the ODA communication topology, which will affect the aforementioned communication structure thus allowing the same implementation to remain.

Furthermore, we have given some outlines as to the *ODA description language* that has been previously proposed in the works of our team in order to show practical applications of a concept similar to the distributed abstract data type, which is necessary to obtain the integration between the object-based languages and others that follow the Occam-CSP model.

5. References

1. C.A.R. Hoare. "Communicating Sequential Processes". Communications of the ACM, v.21, n.8, pp.666-677, 1978.

2. Inmos, Lmtd. "Occam Programming Manual". Prentice-Hall, London, 1984.

3. Atkinson, C., Moreton, T. Natali, A. "Ada for distributed systems". Cambridge University Press, 1988.

4. Baumgarten, U. "Distributed systems and Ada-current projects and approaches comparative study's results". Ada Europe international conference, Athens, Greece, May 1991, pp.260-278.

5. Geist, G.A., Sunderam, V.S. "Experiences with Network-Based Concurrent Computing on the PVM System". Concurrency: Practice and Experience, v.4, n.4., pp.293-311, 1992.

6. Brinch-Hansen, P. "The Joyce Language Report". Software Practice and Experience, v.19, n.6, pp.553-578, 1989.

7. Brinch-Hansen, P. "Super-Pascal a publication language for parallel scientific computing". Concurrency: practice and experience, v.6, n.5, pp.461-483, 1994.

8. Hoare, C.A.R. "Communicating Sequential Processes". Prentice-Hall, 1985.

9. Brookes, S.D., Hoare, C.A.R. ,Roscoe, A.W. "A Theory Model for Communicating Processes". Communications of the ACM, v.32, n.3, pp.560-599, 1984.

10. Goldsmith, M.H., Roscoe, A.W., Scott, B.G.O. "A Semantic Model for Occam 2". Transputer Applications and Systems'93. IOS Press, 1993, pp.965-980.

11. Capel, M., Troya, J.M. "An Object Based Tool and Methodological Approach for Distributed Programming". Software Concepts and Tools, v.15, n.4, pp.177-195,1994.

12. Capel, M., Troya, J.M., Palma, A. "Distributed Active Objects: A MethodologicalProposal and Tool for Distributed programming with Transputer Systems".Microprocessing and Microprogramming, v.38, pp.197-204, 1993.

13. Sakdavong, J.C., Bahsoun, J.P., Feraud, L. "Configuration Classes: An Object Oriented Paradigm for Distributed Programming". IWOOOS'95, Lund,Sweden, Aug.1995. IEEE proceedings., pp.200-209.

14. Geoff Barret. "Occam 3 reference manual". Inmos Lmtd, 1992.

A Greedy Approach For Scheduling Directed Cyclic Weighted Task Graphs on Multiple Processors Running Under the Macrodataflow Model of Execution

MA Maiza   T Clarke

Department of Electronics, University of York, Heslington, York YO1 5DD, U.K.
tel: (U.K.) 1904 432419
fax: (U.K.) 1904 432335
e-mail addresses: mm@ohm.york.ac.uk & tim@ohm.york.ac.uk

Abstract

Parallel program tasks to be run on multiple processor systems are frequently represented by Directed Acyclic weighted task Graphs (DAGs). Many algorithms addressing the problem of scheduling DAGs onto parallel architectures have been proposed in the literature. The objective of these scheduling algorithms is usually to allocate tasks onto the processors such that the length of the schedule (latency) is minimised. However, most "real-world" parallel programs contain feedback loops, and the real-time specifications of many of them require not only minimal latency, but also to satisfy a given sampling rate (SR). In such cases, the above algorithms are not valid. In this paper, we propose a new approach for scheduling Directed Cyclic weighted task Graphs (DCGs) running under the Macrodataflow Model of Execution (MDFME) where the objective is to optimise latency and SR. Some experimental results demonstrating the validity of our approach are shown.

1 Introduction

In this paper we study the problem of scheduling Directed Cyclic weighted task Graphs (DCGs) on multiple processor systems running under the Macrodataflow Model of Execution[1] (MDFME) where the main objective is to minimise latency[2] and satisfy a given SR. Many different approaches to the DAG scheduling problem can be found in the literature [2, 3, 4, 5, 6, 7, 8, 9, 10, 11, 12, 13, 1]. None of the approaches tries to optimise latency and satisfy a

given SR simultaneously. Their objective is to allocate tasks onto processors such that latency is minimised. A scheduling algorithm that attempts to minimise a given parallel task graph schedule length can be used in cases where either the associated parallel program is to be run once, or it is to be run iteratively but there is no SR requirement. However, when both latency and SR are to be considered, this scheduling strategy is no longer valid.

Additionally, none of these approaches address the DCG scheduling problem: DAGs have no feedback loops. Parallel programs may contain loops that cannot be eliminated. A linear feedback loop in a task graph may be replaced by an equivalent single graph component through block diagram or signal-flow diagram reduction techniques such as those in [14]. However, these reduction techniques may not hold for the non-linear case. For instance, the feedback loop elimination procedure shown in Figure 1 assumes validity of the distributive law, the multiplicative law and inversion. Such conditions do not necessarily hold for non-linear functions.

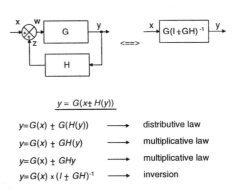

$$y = G(x \pm H(y))$$

$y = G(x) \pm G(H(y))$	$\longrightarrow$	distributive law
$y = G(x) \pm GH(y)$	$\longrightarrow$	multiplicative law
$y = G(x) \pm GHy$	$\longrightarrow$	multiplicative law
$y = G(x) \times (I \pm GH)^{-1}$	$\longrightarrow$	inversion

Figure 1: **Reduction of feedback loops: linearity assumptions.**

---

[1] A task node running under the macrodataflow model of execution must receive all its input data before it can start execution. It executes to completion without interruption, and immediately sends the output data to all its successor tasks [1].

[2] Latency is the total program parallel execution time of an associated task graph.

Here, we propose a new approach for scheduling DCGs running under the MDFME which attempts to optimise simultaneously latency and SR. Scheduling DAGs on parallel processors such that latency is minimised is an NP-complete problem [15, 16]. Very few polynomial time algorithms for some restricted cases have been proposed in the literature [17, 18, 19, 20, 21]. Because DAGs are subsets of DCGs, it follows that the problem of scheduling DCGs is also NP-complete.

This paper is organised as follows: Section 2 introduces the basic concepts of DCGs and states the scheduling goals and the problems arising. Section 3 discusses scheduling strategies for the achievement of the goals and our solutions to the problems. Section 4 shows some experimental results. Section 5 presents conclusions.

2 Scheduling DCGs : Problem Statement

A set of parallel tasks containing loops can be represented by a DCG. A DCG, like a DAG, is a tuple $G = \{V, E, C, T\}$. $V = \{n_i, i = 1 : v\}$ and $T = \{t_i, i = 1 : v\}$ are the set of task nodes and the set of task computation costs respectively, where $t_i \in T$ is the computation time of task node $n_i \in V$ and $v = | V |$ is the number of task nodes. E and C are the set of communication edges and the set of edge communication costs respectively, where $c_{i,j} \in C$ is the communication cost incurred along edge $e_{i,j} = (n_i, n_j) \in E$ (zero if both task nodes are mapped on the same processor) and $e = | E |$ is the number of edges [3].

Given an arbitrary DCG and a multiple processor system, the scheduling problem consists of determining the task to processor assignment and the task execution ordering for each processor, such that some related performance criteria are optimised. Determining such a set of performance criteria is one of the problems for scheduling DCGs corresponding to real-time systems. By definition, in general, a system is said to be real-time when it carries out all its activities respecting timing constraints [22]. From the timing performance requirements viewpoint, achieving steady state system outputs in the shortest possible time is our scheduling objective. Here, both SR and latency play an important part. The satisfaction of a required SR and the minimisation of latency are the main goals. Trying to achieve these two goals presents the following problems.

2.1 SR vs. Latency

One of the problems of scheduling a DCG such that SR and latency are optimised is that these two goals are strongly conflicting: optimising latency implies degrading SR, and vice versa. Figure 2 shows this graphically, where :

- P_i is processor i.

- $AT_x(n_i)$ is the initial arrival time of data signal x at node i.

- T is the sample period, that is, the reciprocal of SR $(T = SR^{-1})$.

- T_{CLOCK} is the system clock period.

- t.u. stands for elemental time units.

- f.u. stands for elemental time units.

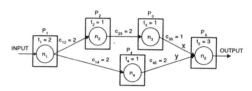

$AT_x(n_5) = t_1 + c_{12} + t_2 + c_{23} + t_3 + c_{35} = 9$ t.u.

$AT_y(n_5) = t_1 + c_{14} + t_4 + c_{45} = 7$ t.u.

latency $= \max(AT_x(n_5), AT_y(n_5)) + t_5 = AT_x(n_5) + t_5 = 12$ t.u.

$T = \max\{t_1, t_2, t_3, t_4, t_5, (AT_x(n_5) - AT_y(n_5))\} + T_{CLOCK} = t_5 + T_{CLOCK} = (3 + T_{CLOCK})$ t.u.

SR $= T^{-1} = (3 + T_{CLOCK})^{-1}$ f.u.

(a)

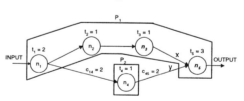

$AT_x(n_5) = t_1 + t_2 + t_3 = 4$ t.u.

$AT_y(n_5) = t_1 + c_{14} + t_4 + c_{45} = 7$ t.u.

latency $= \max(AT_x(n_5), AT_y(n_5)) + t_5 = AT_y(n_5) + t_5 = 10$ t.u.

$T = \max\{(t_1 + t_2 + t_3 + t_5), t_4, (AT_2(n_5) - AT_1(n_5))\} + T_{CLOCK} = (t_1 + t_2 + t_3 + t_5) + T_{CLOCK} = (7 + T_{CLOCK})$ t.u.

SR $= T^{-1} = (7 + T_{CLOCK})^{-1}$ f.u.

(b)

Figure 2: **SR vs. latency trade-off.**

In Figure 2-(a), each task node in the task graph is assigned its own processor. Thus, the best SR is achieved, given by the computation cost of the heaviest of the nodes n_5. Since no communication costs are eliminated, latency is the worst. In Figure 2-(b), a latency minimisation based scheduling algorithm is followed. All the nodes in the longest path are clustered together into the same processor. Thus the best latency is achieved. SR, given by the summation of the computation costs in processor P_1 is now worse.

If the scheduling goal is to achieve steady state system outputs in the shortest possible time, then, if the number of iterations **n** needed to reach such a state is known before running the schedule, it is possible to determine the $[latency, SR]$ pair that will accomplish this. Figure 3 gives an example. The slopes of the plotted lines are the sample periods for the three different conditions. In Case 1, latency is the shortest and SR is low. Time to steady state is hence the highest. Case 3 is the opposite extreme with a long latency and highest SR. The best solution is Case 2 which has neither extreme of latency nor SR but produces the shortest **t_steady_state** for the given **n**.

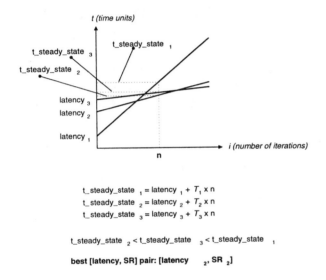

$$\text{t\_steady\_state}_1 = \text{latency}_1 + T_1 \times n$$
$$\text{t\_steady\_state}_2 = \text{latency}_2 + T_2 \times n$$
$$\text{t\_steady\_state}_3 = \text{latency}_3 + T_3 \times n$$

$$\text{t\_steady\_state}_2 < \text{t\_steady\_state}_3 < \text{t\_steady\_state}_1$$

best [latency, SR] pair: [latency $_2$, SR $_2$]

Figure 3: **Determining the best** $[latency, SR]$ **pair when n is known.**

Since **n** is not generally available, we assume, without loss of generality, that the desired SR is externally given. The objective then becomes the minimisation of latency under the satisfaction of a given SR.

2.2 Lack of Synchronism in Directed Weighted Task Graphs

Whenever two input data streams at a task node are not synchronised[3], whether they have the same frequency or not, some loss of data may occur. Figure 4

---
[3]We say that two input data streams at a node are not synchronised if the first time they arrive at the input of the node, they do it at different times. Depending on such a time difference and/or the frequencies of the data streams, some data loss may occur.

is an example of two data streams being fed into output node n_3 at the same SR but with different initial arrival times. Because such a time delay is greater than the input data signals' sample period (T) of 1 t.u. (see Figure 4-(a)), two samples of the data arriving first (in this case x) are lost. As a result, there is a permanent delay of two data samples between x and y. If this data loss cannot be tolerated, the signal generator's SR must be properly set up. T must be set up to $2 + T_{\text{CLOCK}}$ t.u. (see Figure 4-(b)). Since ideally n_3 is capable to work at a T of 1 t.u. , the initial data asynchronism results into a SR degradation. All the different cases of initial data asynchronism and the equations for calculating the corresponding data loss are studied and given in [23].

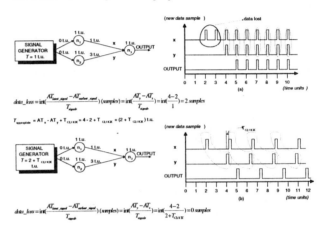

Figure 4: **Asynchronous task graph: (a) inappropriate input SR; (b) appropriate input SR.**

A further problem emerging as a result of the above is that, by analysing only the nodes' computation weight information, it is not possible to determine the appropriate SR at which the system must be set up such that no loss of data occurs. In Figure 4, analysing the nodes' computation weight suggests initially a T of 1 t.u. . However one must also consider communication time delays in order to analyse the data asynchronisms and determine that the graph works properly at a T of $2 + T_{\text{CLOCK}}$ t.u. . The SR determination is then non-trivial.

2.3 Feedback Loops and SR Constraint

In a DCG, it is necessary to set-up some initial data at every feedback loop to make the DCG initiate properly, when external input data are available. These requirements are stated as The Necessary and Sufficient Initial Data Conditions [23].

When a loop in a DCG is run under the classical MDFME from start-off until the end of execution, the SR of every task node within a loop, as well as the

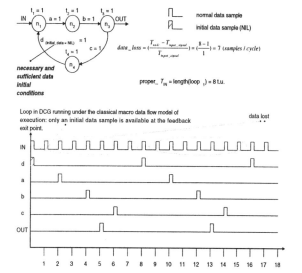

Figure 5: **Feedback loops and SR constraint; loop in DCG running under the classical macrodataflow model of execution from start-off until the end of execution.**

loop's output data rate, will be determined by the length of the loop. This will most probably result in a poor system SR. The system will therefore lose the ability to process all the desired input data. In Figure 5, each individual node in the graph can, in theory, can work at a T of 1t.u. . However, the feedback loop constrains T to 8t.u. . If SR is not properly set up, a new data loss situation arises.

Another problem arised by the existence of feedback loops if that these, especially when they are interconnected among each other, make the determination of SR very complicated and therefore induce long calculation times. Processing times for calculating SR by following the classical approach and our proposed approach are compared in Table 1 and Table 2 (see Section 4).

3 A Greedy Scheduling Approach

Before describing our scheduling approach, the following assumptions are introduced:

a) The multiple processor system on to which the final schedule of a DCG is to be mapped is assumed to be a set of unbounded and fully connected[4] processors. Full connectivity can be easily achieved

---

by following virtual channel routing techniques (for example, see [24]).

b) The target multiple processor system runs under the MDFME.

c) The computation weight of every task node in a given DCG is smaller than the required T. This is assumed so that no task partitioning is necessary.

The approach described here overcomes these problems and also the SR determination complexity problem. The SR vs. latency trade-off cannot be avoided. Some compromise between optimising each must be reached. The strategy here will be to minimise latency for a set SR. With respect to the other problems, we propose solutions which now follow.

3.1 Synchronisation of the Directed Weighted Task Graph

The two problems of asynchronism introduced in Section 2.2 can be solved in a single step by inserting a synchronising communication time delay in the slowest of the input paths of each asynchronous node so that all data arrival times coincide. An example is shown in Figure 6.

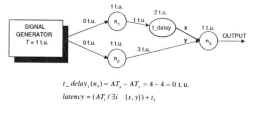

$$t\_delay_y(n_1) = AT_y - AT_x = 4 - 4 = 0 \text{ t.u.}$$

$$latency = (AT_i / \exists i \quad \{x, y\}) + t_3$$

$$T = \max\{t(n_1), t(n_2), t(n_3)\} = \max\{1, 1, 1\} = 1 \text{ t.u.}$$

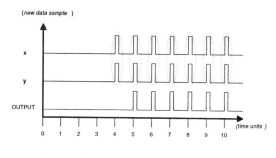

$$data\_loss = \text{int}(\frac{AT_{latest\_signal} - AT_{earliest\_signal}}{T_{signals}}) \, (samples) = \text{int}(\frac{AT_y - AT_x}{T_{signals}}) = \text{int}(\frac{4-4}{1}) = 0 \, samples$$

Figure 6: **Synchronisation of a directed weighted task graph; achievement of best possible SR.**

Once the data are synchronised by communication time delay insertion, SR can be determined by analysing the nodes' computation weight and the feedback loops. For the example above, SR is determined

by the heaviest node's computation cost, which is 1t.u.
. Latency remains unchanged, because the longest arrival time of the data at each node remains also unchanged.

3.2 A Greedy Start-Off Strategy for The DCG

Figure 5 showed the effect of a feedback loop on the SR of a DCG running the feedback part of the loop under the classical MDFME from start-off until the end of execution. When the first input data sample is processed by node n_1, it must then wait for the data to be processed by the rest of the nodes in the loop before the next input sample can be processed. As a result, the SR is significantly slowed down. But why should n_1 wait before processing the next sample ? Can we make the loop work in a greedy manner ? Figure 7 shows an alternative, Greedy Start-Off strategy. In this case, the feedback loop is not initially run under the classical MDFME. Input data are processed as fast as they arrive ($T = 1$t.u.), using repeated injection of initial data at d. Once processed data from d arrives at n_1, the initial data values are no longer injected and the loop starts running under the classical MDFME. The system functional performance at the output is not affected by this if the initial data are properly set up. These could be classical user defined initial conditions data or system performance knowledge based data. SR will no longer be constrained by the length of the loops. Thus, a very significant SR improvement is obtained (see Table 1 and Table 2). Figure 7 shows how the graph in Figure 5 can properly work at a T of 1t.u. following the Greedy Start-Off strategy.

By combining both the data synchronisation and the Greedy Start-Off strategies, the SR of a DCG running under the MDFME will be determined by the computation weight of the heaviest of the nodes. This is the case in Figure 7.

4 Experimental Results

Table 1 and Table 2 show some encouraging results obtained from randomly generated DCGs. These are generated similarly to Yang and Gerasoulis' random DAGs in [1]. First we randomly generate the number of layers in the DCG (range: 50 to 100 layers). Then, in each layer we also randomly place a number of independent nodes (range: 1 to 10 nodes). Next, we randomly connect the edges between tasks at different layers, including feedback connections. Finally, the computation weights for the nodes, as well as the communication costs for transferring the data are randomly set (range: 1 to 9 t.u.).. Any other ranges give

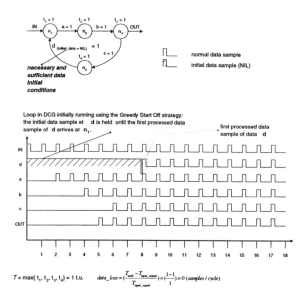

Figure 7: **DCG running under the greedy start-off strategy; a significant SR improvement is obtained (compare to example in Figure 5).**

equivalent results.

The DCGs in Table 1 are not scheduled. An equivalent scheduling would be one where each node in the DCG is mapped to a different processor. The results show that running the DCGs using the classical approach, that is, not taking into account the initial data asynchrony and running the feedback loops under the MDFME from start-off until the end of execution, the SR at which the DCGs can properly work is in all the cases extremely poor. In fact, in some cases, because very long feedback loops and very strong asynchronism are found in the DCGs, the sample period T is even greater than the latency. Running the synchronised DCGs and utilising Greedy Start-Off, the best possible sample period, T, which is the computation of the heaviest of the nodes (9 t.u.) is always obtained. With regard to the SR determination complexity time, using the greedy approach, SR is calculated almost instantly, whereas, for the classical, approach a considerable calculation time is needed. Latency is the same for both approaches. $CPU_{classic}$ and CPU_{greedy} in Table 1 are the actual times needed to calculate the sampling rates using the classical and greedy approaches respectively. An IBM-compatible 486-DX66 is the platform used.

The DCGs in Table 2 are scheduled using a simple linear clustering algorithm [25]. Since better SR is achieved with small clusters, the scheduling strategy is very straightforward. Firstly, the feedforward paths are clustered in order to minimise latency under the SR constraint. Once the feedforward paths are scheduled, and therefore latency is set, the same procedure is run

no. of nodes	no. of connec- tions	latency (t.u.)	T classic (t.u.)	T greedy (t.u.)	CPU classic (sec)	CPU greedy (sec)
191	259	494	305	9	45.9	0.06
127	188	339	383	9	36.4	0.33
131	214	357	430	9	52.1	0.71
129	200	351	320	9	30.7	0.99
160	201	460	229	9	30.4	0.05
149	231	430	467	9	56	0.06
229	378	614	752	9	124.6	0.06
173	333	492	616	9	105.5	0.06
131	192	346	345	9	52.2	0.6
244	390	622	863	9	171.1	0.05

Table 1: **Comparison of SR and time complexity for non-scheduled DCGs between classical approach and greedy approach.**

for the feedback paths. Table 2 shows a representative sample of results taken from a large population (100 DCGs) of random DCGs. The greedy approach always satisfies the required SR, set as $T_{required}$ whereas the classical approach, even under the same schedule (i.e. , same latency, number of processors and processor computation weights), never does. The lack of synchrony in the DCGs and non Greedy Start-Off approach account for this.

no. of no- des	no. of co- nnec- tions	no. of pro- ce- ssors	la- ten- cy (t.u.)	pro- ce- ssor wei- ght	T re- qui- red (t.u.)	T clas- sic (t.u.)	T gree- dy (t.u.)	CPU clas- sic (sec)	CPU gree- dy (sec)
131	179	68	301	24	31	174	30	12.3	0.11
129	172	45	270	39	49	85	48	6.26	0.05
197	308	60	450	45	60	631	57	53.9	0.05
130	173	51	283	32	40	206	40	12.1	0.16
160	232	71	356	23	32	220	31	17	0.05
236	383	100	527	26	37	698	37	74.3	0.06
184	243	62	384	43	61	94	59	9.06	0.38
236	377	114	549	25	32	690	31	74	0.11
233	341	67	468	64	81	427	78	41.6	0.06
161	225	110	383	15	20	415	19	28.6	0.77

Table 2: **Comparison of SR and time complexity for non-scheduled DCGs between classical approach and greedy approach.**

5 Conclusions

In this paper we have presented a greedy approach for scheduling DCGs onto multiple processor systems running under the MDFME where SR and latency must be simultaneously optimised. Lewis and El-Rewini [26] identify DCGs as an important future research area. We show how the data asynchronies and feed-

back loops can constrain the SR of a CTG to very low rates. Our experimental results demonstrate how these constraints can be overcome and the required SRs satisfied by following our DCG synchronisation and Greedy Start-Off strategies. This can be applicable to feedback based systems where satisfying real-time requirements is essential. The work presented in this paper is therefore a suitable stimulus for further developments and demonstrates the first successful approach to scheduling DCGs onto a multiple processor system. The application of this approach to real problems using several different scheduling algorithms and parallel processing systems is our future objective.

References

[1] T. Yang and A. Gerasoulis, "Dsc: Scheduling parallel tasks on an unbounded number of processors," *IEEE Transactions on Parallel and Distributed Systems*, vol. 5, no. 9, pp. 951–967, 1994.

[2] H. El-rewini and H. H. Ali, "Task scheduling in multiprocessor systems," *Computer*, vol. 28, no. 12, pp. 27–37, 1995.

[3] A. Gerasoulis and T. Yang, "A comparison of clustering heuristics for scheduling directed acyclic graphs on multiprocessors," *Journal of Parallel and Distributed Computing*, no. 16, pp. 276–291, 1992.

[4] E. H. Hou, N. Ansari, and H. Ren, "A genetic algorithm for multiprocessor scheduling," *IEEE Transactions on Parallel and Distributed Systems*, vol. 5, no. 2, pp. 113–120, 1994.

[5] S. J. Kim and J. C. Browne, "A general approach for mapping of parallel computations upon multiprocessor architectures," in *Proceedings of the 1988 International Conference on Parallel Processing*, (University Park, PA, USA), p. 18, 1988.

[6] C. L. McCreary, A. A. Khan, J. J. Thompson, and M. E. McArdle, "A comparison of heuristics for scheduling dags on multiprocessors," in *Proceedings of the Eight International Parallel Processing Symposioum*, pp. 446–451, 1994.

[7] T. M. Nabhan and A. Y. Zomaya, "Application of parallel processing to robotic computational tasks," *The International Journal of Robotic Research*, vol. 14, no. 1, pp. 76–86, 1995.

[8] T. M. Nabhan and A. Y. Zomaya, "A parallel simulated annealing algorithm with low communication overhead," *IEEE Transactions on Parallel and Distributed Systems*, vol. 6, no. 12, 1995.

[9] M. A. Palis, J.-C. Liou, and D. S. L. Wei, "Task clustering and scheduling for distributed memory parallel architectures," *IEEE Transactions on Parallel and Distributed Systems*, vol. 7, no. 1, pp. 46–55, 1996.

[10] C. H. Papadimitriou and M. Yannakakis, "Towards an architecture independent analysis of parallel algorithms," *Siam Journal on Computing*, vol. 19, no. 2, pp. 322–328, 1990.

[11] V. Sarkar, *Partitioning and Scheduling Parallel Programs for Multiprocessors*. The MIT Press, 1989.

[12] G. C. Sih, *Multiprocessor Scheduling to Account for Interprocessor Communication*. Phd. thesis, University of California, Barkeley, USA, 1991.

[13] A. Sreenivas, K. N. B. Murthy, and C. S. R. Murthy, "Reverse scheduling - an effective method for scheduling tasks of parallel programs employing a divide and conquer strategy onto multiprocesors," *Microprocessors and Microsystems*, vol. 18, pp. 187–192, May 1994.

[14] F. H. Raven, *Automatic Control Engineering*. McGraw-Hill Book Company, 3 ed., 1978.

[15] H. H. Ali and H. El-Rewini, "On the intractability of task allocation in distributed systems," *Parallel Processing Letters*, vol. 4, no. 1 and 2, pp. 149–157, 1994.

[16] J. P. Ullman, "Np-complete scheduling problems," *Journal of Computer and System Sciences*, no. 10, pp. 384–393, 1975.

[17] H. H. Ali and H. El-Rewini, "An optimal algorithm for interval ordered tasks with communication on n processors," *Journal of Computer and System Sciences*, no. 51, pp. 301–306, 1995.

[18] M. Fjuii, T. Kasami, and K. Ninomiya, "An optimal sequencing of two equivalent processors," *Siam Journal on Computing*, vol. 8, no. 3, 1979.

[19] H. N. Gabow, "An almost linear algorithm for two-processor scheduling," *Journal of the Association of Computer Machinery*, vol. 29, no. 3, pp. 766–780, 1992.

[20] T. C. Hu, "Parallel sequencing and assembly line problems," *Operations Research*, vol. 9, no. 6, pp. 841–848, 1961.

[21] C. H. Papadimitriou and M. Yannakakis, "Scheduling interval ordered tasks," *Siam Journal on Computing*, vol. 8, no. 3, 1979.

[22] J. P. Calvez, *Embedded Real-Time Systems*. John Wiley and Sons, Inc., 1993.

[23] M. A. Maiza and T. Clarke, "Determining sampling rate for computational task graphs running under the macrodataflow model of execution," in *Third International Conference on Electronics, Circuits and Systems, ICECS'96*, (Rodos, Greece), pp. 671–675, 1996.

[24] D. Talia, "Message-routing systems for transputer-based multicomputers," *IEEE Micro*, vol. 13, no. 3, pp. 51–62, 1993.

[25] A. Gerasoulis, S. Venugopal, and T. Yang, "Clustering task graphs for message passing architectures," in *Proceedings of the 4th ACM International Conference on Supercomputing*, pp. 447–456, 1990.

[26] T. Lewis and H. El-Rewini, "Parallax: A tool for parallel program scheduling," *IEEE Parallel and Distributed Technology*, vol. 1, pp. 62–72, May 1993.

On the Evaluation of Efficiency in Heterogeneous Distributed Systems

A. Mazzeo and N. Mazzocca
Dipartimento di Informatica e Sistemistica
Universita' di Napoli
Via Claudio, 21
I-80125 Napoli, Italy
e-mail: [mazzeo,mazzocca]@nadis.dis.unina.it

U. Villano
IRSIP, CNR
Via Claudio, 21
I-80125 Napoli, Italy
e-mail: villano@irsip.na.cnr.it

Abstract

This paper addresses the problem of the performance evaluation of applications running in heterogeneous distributed computing systems by the use of a new efficiency metric (generalized efficiency). After a brief exposition of the generalized efficiency definition and of the main concepts necessary for its evaluation, a case studies is proposed with the aim of clearing up the problems that may be encountered when practical measurements are carried out.

1. Introduction

Efficiency is one of the metrics most commonly used for measuring the performance of a parallel program running on a distributed computing system [1]. The common definition of efficiency is not suitable for heterogeneous systems, which comprise a set of processors of different speed and characteristics [2], [3]. In fact, efficiency is typically defined through the *speedup* $S(N)$. Under the assumption that the N processors making up the distributed system are identical to the one used in the mono-processor environment, the maximum (ideal) value of speedup is N,[1] and efficiency can be defined as the ratio between $S(N)$ and N [5]. For a heterogeneous computing system which, roughly speaking, is made up of variously-assorted "fast" and "slow" processors, the ideal speedup value is not necessarily equal to N. Furthermore, as different processor types are available, it is not completely clear which response times have to be compared in order to evaluate speedup.

To solve the problem of the measurement of efficiency in heterogeneous environments, the Authors have

recently introduced a new metric, *generalized efficiency* [6]. Generalized efficiency addresses in a very simple way the majority of problems linked to efficiency measurement in heterogeneous computing systems and defaults to the "traditional" efficiency if, as a special case, the system is homogeneous. An application of the proposed metric is proposed in this paper, where the stress is on the practical use of generalized efficiency for performance evaluation purposes. In the following Sections, we firstly give a brief exposition of the generalization of the traditional concept of efficiency, introducing the generalized efficiency definition. There then follows a discussion on the problems that may be encountered when practical measurements are carried out. After this, the performance evaluation of 2D-FFT in a heterogeneous cluster of workstations is considered as case study, and the utility of generalized efficiency are discussed.

2. Generalization of the efficiency definition

The efficiency of a distributed computing system for a given problem is typically defined through the *speedup* $S(N)$, the ratio between T_{seq}, the (best) response time for that problem using a single processor, and $T_{par}(N)$, the response time when a distributed computer made up of N processors is used. In theory, if computation were evenly decomposed into N sub-tasks without overhead and N identical processors were used, the parallel version of a program could be completed in a time which is N times lower than the sequential one. Hence efficiency ε can be defined as the ratio between the actually-measured and the theoretical speedup, as follows [5]

$$\varepsilon(N) = \frac{S(N)}{N} \quad . \tag{2.1}$$

Adopting the same rationale as for Eq. (2.1), and defining efficiency through a measure of average

---

[1] Sometimes the speedup $S(N)$ may even be greater than N [4]. This well-known phenomenon (*superlinear speedup*) is neglected in what follows, where, unless otherwise noted, it will be assumed that in any homogeneous system $S_{max}(N)=N$.

processor utilization, it is possible to find a generalization of the efficiency definition suitable also for *heterogeneous* computing systems, where the program tasks are not executed at exactly the same rate by all processors. Doing so, efficiency can be evaluated by taking the ratio of the actually measured speedup $S(N)$ to its ideal maximum value (hereafter denoted by $S^*(N)$):

$$\varepsilon(N) = \frac{S(N)}{S^*(N)} \quad . \tag{2.2}$$

However, the practical use of Eq. (2.2) for efficiency measurements involves the evaluation of $S^*(N)$, which, as mentioned above, is not necessarily equal to N in heterogeneous systems. As a matter of fact, in heterogeneous computing environments the maximum speedup $S^*(N)$ depends on the mapping m of the tasks making up the program to the processors of the distributed system [7]. Two mappings m_1 and m_2 may differ in the code type assigned to every processor (i.e., the type of parallelism embedded in the code: vector, MIMD, SIMD, ...) and/or in the task granularities (the amount of data to be processed).

The latter point is not relevant as far as the computation of the maximum speedup is concerned, since by definition $S^*(N)$ is the speedup that can be achieved assigning optimal data length to every processor. The code type per node defined by m has instead great influence on the maximum speedup value, which is therefore a function both of N and m (i.e., $S^* = S^*(N,m)$). In practice, the dependence of $S^*(N)$ on program mapping is particularly evident only when the application tasks have heterogeneous computational characteristics, i.e., when the blocks of code into which the application is decomposed are substantially different from one another. Most typical examples are programs partitioned by exploiting algorithmic parallelism [8]. In this case, for each particular mapping of tasks to processors there will be a different scenario of elementary execution rates, each one leading (in general) to a different value of the maximum speedup $S^*(N)$. On the other hand, there is a wide class of applications where $S^*(N)$ is rather insensitive to program mapping. This is the case of parallel programs where the component tasks have uniform computational characteristic. Examples are SPMD (same program, multiple data) computations [9], programs obtained by domain decomposition [5], or applications where the same basic computation is performed a huge number of times (e.g., FFT [10]). In this case, execution rates do not actually depend on mapping, and it is possible to define univocally the maximum speedup value $S^*(N)$.

As mentioned above, $S^*(N)$ is the maximum value of speedup that can be obtained for a given problem and computing environment under a certain mapping m. In theory, the maximum value can be obtained by decomposing the problem without introducing overhead and balancing the workload in order to exploit at best the available computing resources. More specifically, the conditions that make it possible for a parallel program to achieve maximum speedup are:

C1) absence of software overhead (partitioning the sequential program does not entail the insertion of additional code, such as data consistency checks, replicated operations, format conversions, ...);

C2) absence of communication overhead (or there is no communication at all, or computation and communication are interleaved in such a way that no performance penalty due to the latency of remote data is introduced);

C3) optimal workload sharing (during program execution no processor is inactive at any time; all processors start executing the program together and terminate at exactly the same time).

Without loss of generality, we can assume that the ideal program P^* fulfilling the above conditions is made up of exactly N tasks, which are allocated one per processor and are started at exactly the same time. Let $TASK^*(i)$ be the name of the task assigned to processor i. For every processor i of the distributed environment it is convenient to define its *relative power index* π_i as the proportionality constant between $T_c(i)$, the time spent by processor i to execute $TASK^*(i)$, and $T_{seq}(i)$, the time that the mono-processor computer would spend to execute the same task:

$$T_{seq}(i) = \pi_i * T_c(i) \quad . \tag{2.3}$$

According to the above definition, every relative power index π_i is given by the ratio of the rates at which $TASK^*(i)$ is executed on processor i and on the sequential processor respectively. Since this task may have different computational characteristics as compared to the other tasks making up the parallel program, only in special cases is the set $\{\pi_i\}$ insensitive to the program mapping m. In general, therefore, the set of power indexes is not unique for a given target application, but depends on its decomposition and the allocation of the resulting tasks to the system processors.

Using the above definitions, and enforcing the conditions **C1**, **C2** and **C3**, it is possible to find [6] that

$$S^*(N) = \sum_{i=1}^{N} \pi_i \quad . \tag{2.4}$$

If $\pi_i = 1 \ \forall i$, this expression returns the usual value $S^*(N) = N$ valid for homogeneous systems. If the system is heterogeneous, it returns values that can be less or greater than N, depending on the relative processor execution rates.

The availability of an expression of $S^*(N)$ valid for any type of distributed system makes it possible to generalize Eq. (2.1), and to define a metric (*generalized efficiency*, ε_g) suitable also for heterogeneous environments, as follows:

$$\varepsilon_g = \frac{S(N)}{S^*(N)} = \frac{S(N)}{\sum\limits_{i=1}^{N} \pi_i} \quad . \tag{2.5}$$

This definition defaults to the usual one for any system composed of identical processing elements, thus providing values less than the limit value of one because of parallel and software overhead and uneven load balancing. If the target computing system is heterogeneous, generalized efficiency is still sensitive to overhead, but the decomposition yielding the highest efficiency value is not the one characterized by even load balancing. In fact, the waste of computing resources is reduced if workload is allocated to each processor in proportion to its relative processing capacity [11].

It should be noted that generalized efficiency is a function of the mapping function m. The actual speedup $S(N)$ is most obviously a function of the task assignment to the target processors. Furthermore, the maximum speedup $S^*(N)$ may also depend on m. Hence their ratio ε_g is actually a function of program mapping, and $\varepsilon_g = \varepsilon_g(m)$. Whenever the maximum speedup is a function of m, i.e., for computationally heterogeneous applications, the particular value $S^*(N)$ to be used for efficiency evaluation is the one corresponding to the mapping actually chosen for program execution. In other words, both the actual and the maximum speedup $S(N)$ and $S^*(N)$ must be evaluated for the same mapping m. It is of paramount importance to point out that the measurement of values of generalized efficiency close to one does not mean that the mapping is optimal, in that it minimizes the program response time. Roughly speaking, generalized efficiency is high when overhead is low and the workload is well shared among processors. This does not necessarily mean that each task has been assigned to the processor most fit to process it.

3. Practical relative power index measurement

Even if generalized efficiency is nothing other than the generalization of the classical concept of efficiency, in practice its use is much more difficult, because it is necessary to measure the relative power index π_i of every involved processor.

π_i has been defined as the ratio of the execution rates on processor i and on the sequential processor of $TASK^*(i)$, the i-th task resulting from the decomposition able to obtain maximum speedup from the distributed computing system. The problem is that the latter is an ideal decomposition, in that the characteristics of $TASK^*(i)$ are unknown and could not even be easily reproduced by any real program. In fact, the only known characteristic of $TASK^*(i)$ is its code-type. As mentioned in the previous Section, the particular value $S^*(N)$ to be used for generalized efficiency evaluation is the one corresponding to the mapping m actually chosen for program execution. Hence each $TASK^*(i)$ is a task with the same code-type of $TASK(i)$, the i-th task allocated to processor number i for the real program execution.

Fortunately in the majority of real cases very accurate efficiency measurements are not necessary, nor even useful. Hence, a reasonable solution for the measurement of the indexes $\{\pi_i\}$ is the use of a set of benchmarks able to mimic as faithfully as possible all known computational characteristics of the ideal tasks $\{TASK^*(i)\}$. If $BENCH(i)$ is the benchmark corresponding to $TASK^*(i)$, and its execution times on the sequential processor and on processor i are denoted by $T_{BENCH(i)}(seq)$ and $T_{BENCH(i)}(i)$ respectively, it follows that

$$\pi_i \cong \frac{T_{BENCH(i)}(seq)}{T_{BENCH(i)}(i)} \quad . \tag{3.1}$$

The design of processor benchmarks and their response time measurement are customary and well-understood activities in high-performance computing [12]. However, the measurement of the indexes π_i also has a very singular characteristic, namely the necessity to reproduce the behaviour of an ideal parallel program. Guidelines to be followed for a successful benchmark construction are ordinately dealt with below.

3.1. Benchmark code-type

In a very general sense, the basic objective of a benchmark should be to measure processor speed on a large set of typical applications [13], [14]. On the other hand, efficiency is to be evaluated for the given problem, and the code-type of the benchmark adopted to measure π_i should reflect the computational requirements of $TASK^*(i)$, which in turn is characterized by the same code-type as $TASK(i)$. Stated another way, the instructions of $BENCH(i)$ should be a well-weighted sample of the operations that are actually executed during the execution of $TASK(i)$, the i-th (real) task making up the parallel program.

If the tasks making up the target program have heterogeneous computational characteristics, the benchmark code-type must be different for each different processor ($BENCH(i) \neq BENCH(j)$ for each $i \neq j$). If, on the other hand, the tasks making up the program are computationally homogeneous, a single benchmark is sufficient for all processors.

3.2. Sequential or parallel benchmarks

The objective of the measurement is to compare the execution rate of every processor i to the rate of the sequential processor. At least in theory, this can be done by means of either a sequential or a parallel benchmark. In the first case, the response times to be compared are found by executing the same sequential program both on the sequential processor and on processor i. Whereas in the second case a parallel program (in theory, the target parallel program) is executed on the whole distributed system twice, using two suitable mappings m_1 and m_2 which assign $BENCH(i)$ to the sequential processor and to processor i respectively.

3.3. Benchmark data set size

Another important issue linked to the measurement of the relative power indexes is the non-linear processor performance in the number of data items to be processed. It is well known that processing time is not always proportional to the size of the input data set. If n is the length of the data sequence and $n_{1/2}$ (*half-performance length*) is the data length required to achieve half the maximum performance [8], only when $n >> n_{1/2}$ is maximum performance achieved. The presence of cache-based CPUs may also introduce analogous timing anomalies, but with the opposite effect.

In practice, the adoption of a value of $S^*(N)$ which is slightly higher than the ideal one has no serious consequence (the limit efficiency value will be slightly lower than one). Whereas, the use of a speedup lower than the ideal one may lead to the detection of efficiency values greater than one whenever an optimal instruction/data length is chosen for (some of) the processors. This should be avoided, as it can suggest incorrect conclusions on system behaviour. A rule of thumb is to choose a data set size that allows maximum processor performance to be obtained for every benchmark. Selecting the highest possible value of π_i for several different data set sizes guarantees that $S^*(N)$ may be overestimated, but never underestimated. As a result, "fake" superunitary speedups can never be obtained.

4. Case study

In this Section we will show a case study where the performance of a distributed system is evaluated through generalized efficiency measurements. The computing environment chosen for the example is a heterogeneous cluster of Sun 4 workstations over an Ethernet connection. In the proposed case study, the parallel program consists of tasks with similar computational requirements. Examples based on heterogeneous tasks are presented in [6].

The application chosen for the following case study is a classical test problem, bi-dimensional (2D) FFT. Generalized efficiency is used to assist the developer in the selection of the best four-processors subset from a heterogeneous cluster of nine Sun 4 workstations. In order to avoid unfair comparisons, the configurations eligible to be chosen are constrained to share the same sum of the relative power indexes of their component processors (i.e., $\sum \pi_i = const$). This guarantees that they have *similar* total processing power. In fact, since by definition the indexes π_i are the FFT execution rates of each processor normalized to the execution rate of the sequential processor, their sum is a rough but effective measure of the asymptotic FFT execution rate for the whole distributed system.

The algorithm adopted here to compute the transform is the so-called *row-column* method. According to this method, the 2D-FFT of an $m * n$ bi-dimensional data matrix is obtained by executing the m (mono-dimensional) transforms of the rows of the matrix, followed by the n transforms of its columns [15]. The $m * m$ data to be transformed are stored in four $m_i * m$ submatrices (with $\sum m_i = m$), each of which is assigned to a different processor. In order to guarantee a fairly balanced workload, the actual amount of data assigned to each processor is determined through the following strategy: the more powerful the processor, the higher the number of rows assigned to it. Since, as mentioned above, the indexes π_i are the (normalized) execution rates of each processor, we will assign to P_i, the i-th processor, a number of rows m_i proportional to π_i. As the matrix is allocated to the processors "slicing" it by rows, every processor can perform the first sequence of 1D-FFT working on its local data, i.e. with no communication. After that, the computed data have to be suitably exchanged in order to transpose the matrix, thus allocating it to the processors by columns. The data transposition is implemented by a global broadcast, in which each processor retains a portion of the locally-allocated data and transmits the remainder to the other processors. After this communication phase, every processor can compute the second sequence of 1D-FFT (on the columns) with no communication. Further details on this algorithm can be found in [16].

As far as benchmarking is concerned, FFT computation is a particularly "benign" application. First of all, the computations carried out are completely data-independent, i.e., they are always the same whatever the input data values. Moreover, 1D-FFT (and hence also 2D-FFT, which is made of two sequences on mono-dimensional transforms) can be obtained by composition of small computational modules (*butterflies*), each of which performs one complex addition, one complex subtraction and one complex multiplication [15]. This means that the code-type is the same for every task resulting from the above described decomposition, even if the amount of data processed in each computing node is variable. Hence the set of indexes $\{\pi_i\}$ is insensitive to program mapping, and a single benchmark is sufficient for all processors.

A further simplification made possible by the FFT peculiarities is that almost every sequential 1D- or 2D-FFT code is perfectly suitable for benchmarking purposes. In other words, for this particular problem there is no significant difference between the adoption of a synthetic code or of a scaled-down version of the real application program. As FFT behaviour is easily predictable, there is also no interest in the adoption of a parallel benchmark. A sequential benchmark well captures the real program behaviour and poses no problem due to the presence of parallel and communication overhead.

The only care to be taken is the choice of a data set size that allows the maximum value of π_i to be obtained for each i. In our particular case, there is no use in adopting benchmarks requiring the processing of too large an amount of data, since all the involved workstations are not provided with vector processors. We have computed the relative power indexes by executing a mono-dimensional FFT code (the FOUR1 routine proposed in Reference 17) on 1024 (complex) data points. The obtained results are proposed in the leftmost column of Table 1, where processor WS2 has been chosen as the reference sequential environment. Incidentally, it is worth pointing out that the *sequential* processor is just a reference, and should not necessarily be one of the four processors used for executing the parallel version of the program.

From the examination of the power indexes in Table 1 it turns out that possible configurations of processors to be compared are (WS3, WS4, WS5, WS6), (WS2, WS3, WS7, WS8), (WS1, WS7, WS8, WS9), all of which have a value of $\sum \pi_i$ equal to 2. The relative power indexes have also been used to find the decomposition of the data matrix, according to the strategy described above. The number of rows allocated to each computing node are

shown in Table 1 for each of the three devised configurations of processors. Sequential (as measured on processor WS2) and parallel response times (obtained by executing the parallel program under PVM [18] in the absence of external load) are shown in Table 2 and 3, respectively, for 256 * 256, 512 * 512 and 1024 * 1024 input data matrices. The non-trivial result emerging from parallel response time figures is that the more heterogeneous the target system, the shorter the response time. Moreover, the optimal hardware configuration appears to be the one consisting of one fast and three (equally) slow processors. In fact, computation times are approximately the same for all configurations due to the chosen workload sharing strategy. Hence the best performance is obtained by assigning a large slice of the matrix to one fast processor and of small portions to the three slow ones, and reducing dramatically the total communication volume.

Table 1. Processor relative power indexes and the three mappings of 2D-FFT over 4 workstations.

processor	rel. pow. index	mapping 1	mapping 2	mapping 3
WS1	1.25			5m/8 rows
WS2	1		m/2 rows	
WS3	0.5	m/4 rows	m/4 rows	
WS4	0.5	m/4 rows		
WS5	0.5	m/4 rows		
WS6	0.5	m/4 rows		
WS7	0.25		m/8 rows	m/8 rows
WS8	0.25		m/8 rows	m/8 rows
WS9	0.25			m/8 rows

Table 3 also presents the generalized efficiency values for each of the three task-to-processor mappings. Efficiency well captures program performance behaviour, since slower response times correspond to higher efficiency, and vice versa (remember that the three considered hardware environments have approximately the same total processing power). It should be noted that it is not correct to deduce that efficiency can always be derived from response times. This may be true only as far as all system configurations share the same total processing power, and very often this is not the case. Furthermore, from the examination of sequential and parallel processing times it is not possible to quantify program overhead. In our example, generalized efficiency makes it possible to detect easily that overhead is dependent on the problem dimension, and that the system (relative) performance is likely to increase as the amount of processed data rises. This well-known phenomenon [19] is due to the growth of computation time as compared to communication time as we move from the 256 * 256 to the 1024 * 1024 data problem.

Table 2. 2D-FFT sequential response time (sec) of workstation WS2.

problem size	T_{seq} (WS2)
256 * 256	1.99
512 * 512	8.77
1024 * 1024	39.93

Table 3. 2D-FFT parallel response time (sec) and generalized efficiency.

Problem size	mapping 1		mapping 2		mapping 3	
	T_{par}	ε_g	T_{par}	ε_g	T_{par}	ε_g
256 * 256	1.36	0.73	1.29	0.77	1.25	0.80
512 * 512	5.72	0.76	5.55	0.79	5.39	0.81
1024 * 1024	25.38	0.79	24.5	0.81	23.98	0.84

5. Conclusions

This paper has addressed the problem of the measurement of efficiency in heterogeneous distributed computing systems by discussing the evaluation of *generalized efficiency* in a case study. Generalized efficiency measurements require the evaluation of the relative processing power of every involved processor in the ideal conditions leading to the maximum speed-up value. In practice, this is obtained by a suitable benchmark code that mimics the actual program behaviour in ideal conditions. The exposition has focused on the problems that may be encountered when practical measurements are carried out, and tried to suggest simple solutions which make it possible to achieve realistic and consistent performance results.

As suggested by its name, generalized efficiency is just the generalization of efficiency to heterogeneous distributed systems, and therefore it has the same virtues and the same drawbacks. Efficiency gives no information on overall response times. However, efficiency measurements of developed software are a very simple way to gain an insight into program performance, because of their ability to point out possible performance bugs by means of a single number. Finding these bugs directly from response times is often possible, but it is also a clumsy and error-prone activity. In this context, a careful use of efficiency figures, especially in union with absolute metrics, often turns out to be a very useful practice.

References

[1] A. H. Karp and H. P. Flatt. Measuring Parallel Processor Performance. *Comm. of the ACM*, 33:539-543, 1990.

[2] A. A. Khokhar, V. K. Prasanna, M. E. Shaaban and C. Wang. Heterogeneous Computing: Challenges and Opportunities. *IEEE Computer*, 26(6):18-27, 1993.

[3] J. B. Andrews and C. D. Polychronopoulos. An Analytical Approach to Performance/Cost Modeling of Parallel Computers. *Journal of Par. and Distr. Computing*, 12:343-356, 1991.

[4] D. P. Helmbold and C. E. McDowell. Modeling Speedup (*n*) Greater than *n*. *IEEE Trans. on Par. Distr. Sys.*, 1:250-256, 1990.

[5] G. Fox, M. Johnson, G. Lyzenga, S. Otto, J. Salmon and D. Walker. *Solving Problems on Concurrent Processors*. Prentice-Hall, Englewood Cliffs, 1988.

[6] A. Mazzeo, N. Mazzocca and U. Villano. Efficiency Measurements in Heterogeneous Distributed Computing Systems: from Theory to Practice. to be published in *Concurrency: Practice and Experience*.

[7] M.-C. Wang, S.-D. Kim, M. A. Nichols, R. F. Freund, H. J. Siegel and W. G. Nation. Augmenting the optimal selection theory for superconcurrency. In *Proc. Workshop on Heterogeneous Processing*, pages 13-22, 1992.

[8] R. W. Hockney and C. R. Jesshope. *Parallel Computers 2*. Adam Hilger, Philadelphia, USA, 1988.

[9] F. Darema *et al.*. A Single-Program, Multiple-Data Computational Model for EPEX/Fortran. *Parallel Computing*, 7:11-24, 1988.

[10] A. Mazzeo and U. Villano. Parallel 1D-FFT Computation on Constant-valence Multicomputers. *Software-Practice and Experience*, 25:681-704, 1995.

[11] S. Selvakumar and C. Siva Ram Murthy. Static task allocation of concurrent programs for distributed computing systems with processor and resource heterogeneity. *Parallel Computing*, 20:835-851, 1994.

[12] R. P. Weicker. An Overview of Common Benchmarks. *IEEE Computer*, 23(12):65-75, 1990.

[13] C. Addison *et al.*. The Genesis distributed-memory benchmarks. Part 1: methodology and general relativity benchmark with results for the SUPRENUM computer. *Concurrency: Practice and Experience*, 5:1-22, 1993.

[14] P. Messina *et al.*. Benchmarking advanced architecture computers. *Concurrency: Practice and Experience*, 2:195-255, 1990.

[15] A. V. Oppenheim and R. W. Schafer. *Digital Signal Processing*. Prentice-Hall, Englewood Cliffs, N.J., 1975.

[16] G. Franceschetti, A. Mazzeo, N. Mazzocca, V. Pascazio and S. Schirinzi. An Efficient Sar Parallel Processor Based on a Two Dimensional Fourier Transform Algorithm. *IEEE Trans. on Aerosp. and Electr. Sys.*, 27:343-353, 1991.

[17] W. H. Press, B. P. Flannery, S. A. Teukolsky and W. T. Vetterling. *Numerical Recipes - The Art of Scientific Computing*. Cambridge University Press, Cambridge 1986.

[18] A. Geist, A. Beguelin, J. Dongarra, W. Jiang, R. Manchek and V. Sunderam. *PVM: Parallel Virtual Machine*. MIT Press, Cambridge, MA, 1994.

[19] J. L. Gustafson, G. R. Montry and R. E. Benner. Development of parallel methods for a 1024-processor hypercube. *Siam J. Sci. Stat. Comput.*, 9:609-638, 1988.

Cache Coherence in Parallel and Distributed File Systems

F. García, J. Carretero, F. Pérez, P. de Miguel and L. Alonso
Universidad Politécnica de Madrid (UPM)
Facultad de Informática
e-28660, Madrid, Spain
E-mail: fgarcia@datsi.fi.upm.es, jcarrete@fi.upm.es

Abstract

Caching improves I/O performance, both for parallel and distributed file systems, but creates a data coherence problem due to the potential existence of multiple copies of the same data. Cache coherence protocols are unpopular in parallel applications because of its overhead. In this paper a new approach to cache coherence, efficient both for parallel and distributed applications, is presented. It uses cache coherence protocols relying on regions with different sizes and shapes. The former model has been implemented in ParFiSys, a parallel and distributed file system developed at the UPM, whose performance results are also presented here to demonstrate its efficiency and scalability.

1. Introduction

The continuous improvement in processors, memories and communications subsystems, has led the I/O subsystems to become a *bottleneck* in many computer systems. This problem slows down many distributed and parallel applications, whose performance may be enhanced using *parallelism* and *caching* in the I/O subsystem. Parallelism in the I/O subsystem is obtained employing multiple independent storage devices, to parallely access different files, and data *declustering*, to parallely access the same file. The former approach has been used in some parallel and distributed file systems (PFS, DFS) described in the bibliography (CFS [13], Vesta [5], *ParFiSys* [3], Galley [12])

Caching improves I/O performance, both for PFS and DFS, by avoiding unnecessary disk traffic, network traffic and servers load, and by allowing prefetching and delayed-write techniques both for PFS [9, 2] and DFS [11, 8]. The use of caching in the clients of a file system introduces the *cache coherence* problem: different caches may hold different copies of the same data in the system. Cache coherence has been unpopular in PFS because of its overhead [10], but it has been usually implemented in DFS where

write sharing is infrequent [11]. DFS coherence models are mostly based on weak [8] or coarse grain models [11]. This solution is not suitable for parallel applications where files are usually written cooperatively.

In this paper a new approach to cache coherence, that solves the problem in an efficient manner both for PFS and DFS, is presented. Cache coherence protocols with different sizes and shapes of granularity are proposed to avoid false sharing. The model has been implemented in *ParFiSys* [2, 3], a parallel and distributed file system developed at the UPM to provide I/O services for the GPMIMD[1]. Performance results are also shown to demonstrate that the cache coherence model is efficient and scalable.

2. Cache coherence protocols

Caching is a technique very used in memory and file systems to improve system performance. Caching is used in PFS and DFS both in clients located at the processor nodes (PN), and file system servers, that execute on I/O nodes (ION). Caching in file system clients reduces the use of critical resources like network, servers and disks improving the overall performance and the scalability of the system.

The main problem with client caching is the write-sharing of a file from different clients, which might lead to an incoherent view of data. Nelson [11] describes two forms of write-sharing: *sequential write-sharing* (SWS), that occurs when a client reads or writes a file that was previously written by another client, and *concurrent write-sharing* (CWS), that occurs when a file is simultaneously open for reading and writing on more than one client. Concurrent write-sharing is rare in DFS [1, 11], but it is very frequent in PFS [10]. Thus, a cache coherence protocol for a high performance environment requires high flexibility to satisfy the I/O patterns from distributed and parallel applications. The problem of write-sharing is solved in the cache coherence model proposed here using two protocols [7]:

---

[1]General Purpose MIMD machine, P-5404, CEE

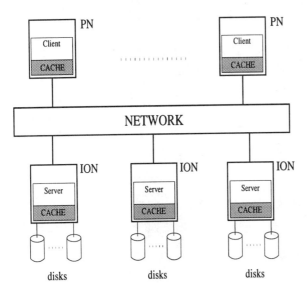

Figure 1. Generic distributed and parallel file system architecture

- *Sequential coherence protocol* (SCP), that solves the SWS problem and detects the CWS on a file.

- *Concurrent coherence protocol* (CCP), that solves the CWS problem after being activated when the SCP detects a CWS situation on a file.

Figure 1 shows the generic distributed and parallel file system architecture to which the protocols proposed in this paper are aimed for. This architecture allows file data distribution across multiple IONs and devices by using *distributed partitions* [3], so that the applications from the PN may access the data in parallel. Caching is intensively used both in clients and servers, including prefetching and delayed-write techniques to improve the I/O performance. A POSIX sharing semantic is assumed, which means that the most up to date version of the data is always obtained by a *read()* call.

2.1. Sequential coherence protocol

This protocol ensures coherence in SWS situations and detects CWS situations on a file. This protocol has a behavior similar to the Sprite protocol [11]: servers tracking *open* and *close* operations to know not only which clients are currently using a file, but whether any of them are potentially writers. When a client opens a file, it must be notified to the server storing the file descriptor. If there is no CWS for the file, the server looks whether another client has updated the file data in its local cache (because of delayed-write policy) and requests it to flush the data. When the server has the most up to date copy of the file, a message is sent to the client

to enable local caching for the file. No more interactions with the server are needed to maintain coherence. When a CWS situation is detected by the server, a message is send to all the clients with the file open to activate the CCP. When the CWS situation disappears, a message is send to all the clients with the file open to deactivate the CCP.

SCP has been optimized to reduce client-server interactions by sending coherence messages to the servers only when a change of the client local state of the file occurs. The local state of a file changes when it is open the first time, when it was open for read and it is open for write, when it is closed for write and it remains open for read, and when it is closed by the last user in the client. SCP has also been optimized to reduce servers load by distributing the protocol overhead among all servers. Each server executes SCP only for the files whose descriptors are stored on it, which alleviates the bottleneck of a centralized service and improves scalability.

2.2. Concurrent coherence protocol

This protocol is activated when a CWS is detected for a file, and it is executed on each access to the file while the CWS situation remains. CWP is based on invalidations, directories and the existence of a exclusive write-shared copy of data. To alleviate false-sharing problems, it would be desirable to allow the parallel applications to adjust their *coherence regions* within the shared files to their I/O patterns. A coherence region is a disjoint subset of the file used as the coherence unit. It has two main features: size and shape. The size of a region may range from the whole file to byte. The shape of a region can be defined according to the most frequent parallel access patterns: sequential and interleaved (see figure 3).

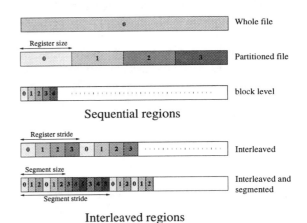

Figure 3. Some Coherence Region Patterns

The users can define the mapping of the regions on a file for parallel applications using the following parameters (see

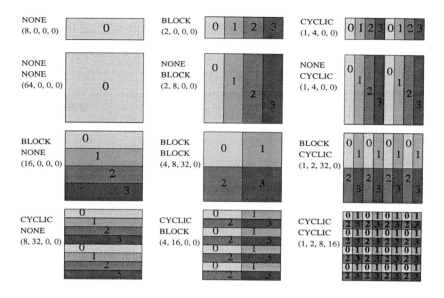

Figure 2. Coherence regions adaptation to HPF

figure 3):

- *Register size*, minimum unit for coherence.

- *Register stride*, width of the register groups into each segment.

- *Segment size*, number of register groups in a segment.

- *Segment stride* distance between two segments.

This model of region is suitable to map very different parallel I/O patterns [10], and it allows to define *optimal regions* on a file. A user defines optimal regions on a file when the number of process of the parallel application is equal to the number of regions and each region is accessed only for a unique process. This kind of regions are the best suited to the access pattern and minimize coherency overhead. As an example, the region coherence model can be applied to the High Performance Fortran [6] distributions, as shown in figure 2. Elements on each dimension of a multidimensional array could be mapped in one PN (NONE), distributed in contiguous segments among the PN's (BLOCK) or distributed in a round-robin fashion among PN's (CYCLIC). The values of the above parameters (register size, register stride, segment size, and segment stride) when four processes access to a file are shown in the figure.

The proposed protocols compel the clients to check the coherence state of the region on every access to it by acquiring the appropriate read or write *tokens*. When a client does not have the appropriate token, a message to the region's manager must be sent to request the desired rights on the region. The server stores a *callback* for each region in a coherence directory to trace the coherence state of the region. If a conflict is detected, the callbacks are revoked. The region's manager guarantees that at any given time there is a single read-write token or any number of read-only tokens. When a write token is revoked in a client, the client must flush any dirty data of the region. If the new token is for read the token in the previous writers is changed from write to read-only. When the appropriate rights on a region are acquired, they remain until explicit revocation.

Two main design criteria were used in *ParFiSys* to define the coherence protocols: callback and directory location and management, and callback revocation policy. Two policies can be used for the first issue: *centralized*, where coherence for all the regions of a file is maintained by the server storing the file descriptor (region manager), and *distributed* (D), where the information of the coherence region is distributed among several servers, each one is in charge of maintaining the coherence of the regions allocated to it. Two approaches can be used to revoke callbacks when a conflict appears: *server driven* (SD) and *client driven* (CD). In SD, the server sends revocation messages to all the clients caching data from the conflictive region. In CD, some clients send revocation messages, on behalf of the servers, to other clients caching data from the conflictive region. Revocation messages can be sent only by the client generating the conflict (CDC), or by several clients (CDD), which cooperate to reduce latency. Several CCP have been implemented in *ParFiSys* by combining different management and revocation policies: C-SD, C-CDC, C-CDD, D-SD, D-CDC, and D-CDD. Table 1 summarizes the number of messages on the server and clients, when m accesses to conflictive regions are done. k is the average number of clients with callbacks for each region, ION is the number of servers in the partition, and l is the *multicast factor*. The distributed

Msgs.	Server	Client
C-SD	$m(2+2K)$	
D-SD	$\frac{m}{ION}(2+2K)$	
C-CDC	$2m$	$2k$
C-CDD	$2m$	$2k/l$
D-CDC	$\frac{2m}{ION}$	$2k$
D-CDD	$\frac{2m}{ION}$	$2k/l$

Table 1. Messages for k callbacks revocation

approach reduces the inherent server load to a centralized server. The client driven approach reduces the server load because the cycles to revoke are executed by the clients, which also improves protocol scalability.

3. Cache coherence services in *ParFiSys*

The cache coherence model previously described has been implemented in *ParFiSys* [2, 3]. To fully exploit all the parallel and distributed features of the I/O hardware, the architecture of *ParFiSys* is clearly divided in two levels: file services, provided by the *ParClient*, and block services, provided by the *ParServer* (see figure 4). Each *ParClient* provides file system services to the applications running in its PN, using a *ParServer* high-performance I/O library to transparently access the I/O servers. Each *ParServer* deals with logical block requests managing them to/from the I/O devices located on its own ION. Both *ParClient* and *ParServer* use caching and aggressive prefetching and *write-before-full* techniques to increase I/O performance.

ParFiSys provides a standard *POSIX interface* where parallel access, data distribution, and data and *metadata* coherence are transparently provided. User can improve the applications performance using the following cache coherence services:

Caching on-off, to activate/deactivate intermediate copies in the file system's block caches for a file, using the following interface:

*set_cache_parameters (char *file_name, int flag_on-off)*

Coherence regions, to dynamically change the granularity (size and shape) of the coherence protocols for a file, using the following interface:

*define_region (char *file_name, int reg_side,*
int reg_stride, int seg_size, int seg_stride)

These services may change dynamically during the file life. The coherence regions of a file may be changed, assuming

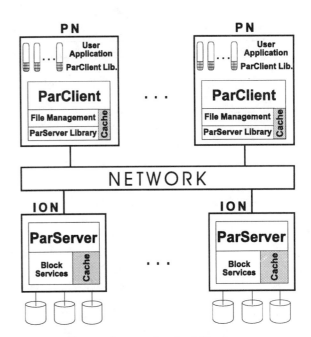

Figure 4. *ParFiSys* **Architecture**

that it is not open.

4. Experimental evaluation

Two benchmarks were defined to evaluate sequential and concurrent coherence protocols: a sequential write benchmark (SWB) to evaluate SCP, and two concurrent write benchmarks (CWB), segmented (SCWB) and interleaved (ICWB), to evaluate CCP. SWB consists of a process that writes a file of 10 MB, declustered across 4 ION-distributed partition with a block size of 8 KB. When the file is completely written, the event is signaled to several processes (1, 2, 4, 8) that read the whole file sequentially. This benchmark evaluates the total execution time for all processes. SCWB uses a parallel program with partitioned access similar to the BLOCK (2,0,0,0) of figure 2. This benchmark divides a file into contiguous segments, one per process, with each segment accessed sequentially by a different process. ICWB uses a parallel program, where each process writes the file in a interleaved fashion, similar to the CYCLIC (1,4,0,0) of the figure 2. The parallel program for each CWB consists of 1, 2, 4, 8 and 10 processes that concurrently write a file of 10 MB, which is declustered across 4 ION with a block size of 8 KB.

The former benchmarks were executed on *ParFiSys* using a Telmat Tnode multicomputer with 10 T800 used like PN and 4 T800 used like ION. Each ION uses one simulated disk with a Bandwidth of 3 MB/s. In all experiments a 1 MB cache per-client and 4 MB cache per-ION were used. The results shown for SWB includes the time of execution and the total number of messages to the servers. The results

Readers	1	2	4	8
Msg. No.				
NO CACHE	2585	3871	6443	11587
WT + VAL	1634	1965	2627	3957
SCP	535	860	1532	2860

Table 2. Absolute Load in SWB

shown for CWB are: aggregate throughput in MBytes per second, and the relative performance compared to a system without coherence.

Figure 5 compares the execution time of SWB using three sceneries in the clients: caching deactivated, caching for read ($WT + VAL$), and sequential coherence protocol. These results indicate that SCP reduces the total time required for SWB compared with no cache and $WT + VAL$. This effect is mainly due to prefetch and delayed-write techniques. Table 2 shows that the total number of messages to the servers generated by SWB is always smaller for SCP.

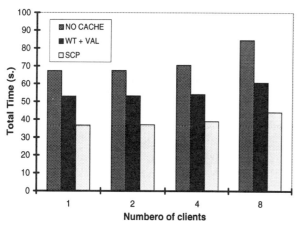

Figure 5. Sequential benchmark

The aggregated bandwidth of CWB for concurrent segmented and interleaved I/O patterns is shown in figure 6. Several cache coherence protocols are evaluated using CWB: cache deactivated, file granularity, block granularity for centralized and distributed protocols, and optimal regions for centralized and distributed protocols. The first relevant result obtained shows that maintaining coherency with file granularity is the worst method, mainly due to false-sharing. Deactivating cache is very similar to the block centralized, because the number of client-server interactions is almost the same. The small difference observed between deactivating cache and block distributed is mainly due to the smaller contention on the servers generated by the coherence

Clients	2	4	8	10
Segmented CWB				
NO CACHE	42.35	38.90	36.47	25.72
WHOLE F.	13.36	6.57	3.64	2.22
BLOCK-C	55.44	52.12	33.41	26.15
BLOCK-D	58.50	54.17	51.10	29.00
OPTR-C	94.94	93.00	94.36	91.2
OPTR-D	94.93	93.32	99.10	93.20
Interleaved CWB				
NO CACHE	47.08	42.49	46.56	28.53
WHOLE F.	12.72	6.47	4.23	2.43
BLOCK-C	55.25	53.32	45.71	28.41
BLOCK-D	57.29	56.22	53.26	49. 41
OPTR-C	92.7	94.36	93.00	85.67
OPTR-D	93.49	94.30	99.10	93.52

Table 3. Relative performance (%) of the segmented and interleaved CWB

protocols. This feature also makes the block distributed protocol more scalable. The best results are obtained with the optimal regions protocols, both centralized and distributed. This behavior is mainly due to the false-sharing elimination, the main problem with whole file granularity, the minimization of the coherence load, the main problem in block granularity protocols, and the local cache utilization, the main problem in cache deactivation. Table 3 shows the relative performance of the former protocols compared with an ideal scenario including client caching without coherence costs. CWB for a segmented and interleaved I/O pattern shows that optimal regions, both centralized and distributed, provide a performance very close to the ideal one. Moreover, they show a good scalability compared with the other protocols, whose performance decrease very quickly as the number of clients increases.

5 Related work

Most existing file systems with cache coherence fail to provide efficient solutions to the problem of cache coherence for parallel applications that concurrently write a file. NFS, very popular in commercial environments, is unable to maintain a consistent view of the file system for parallel applications. AFS [8] does not support concurrent write-sharing due to the session semantic implemented, which makes it not suitable for parallel applications. Sprite [11] ensures concurrent write-sharing coherence by disabling client caches, thus limiting the potential benefits of caching for many parallel applications. There are very few cache co-

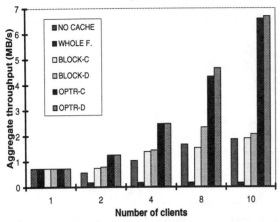 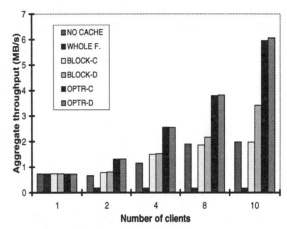

Figure 6. Concurrent segmented and interleaved benchmark

herence solutions in PFS, ENWRICH [14] provides a cache coherence solution, but it is not a general one because client caches are only used for writing.

6. Conclusions and future work

The coherence model shown provides an efficient and general solution to the cache coherence problem both for parallel and distributed file systems without loss of scalability. Data coherence is maintained on user defined *coherence regions* for the conflictive file. The model has been implemented in *ParFiSys*, where services are provided to define the protocol features. The utilization of two protocols, SWP and CWP, allows to afford all the conflictive situations for SWS and CWS patterns, as demonstrated with the evaluation results obtained in *ParFiSys*. The benchmarks used to test the model show considerably better results for our model than for other existing models. Both the aggregated bandwidth and the relative performance obtained are higher when using our model, mainly because false-sharing is reduced, coherence load minimized, and local caches are heavily used. Moreover, the distributed version of the protocols enhances performance and system scalability.

Once demonstrated the flexibility and viability of the proposed model, further work is going on to adapt the *ParFiSys* coherence services to the MPI-IO [4] standard.

References

[1] M. Burrows. *Efficient Data Sharing*. PhD thesis, Computer Laboratory, Universoty of Cambridge, Dec. 1988.

[2] J. Carretero. *Un Sistema de Ficheros con Coherencia de Cache para Multiprocesadores de Propósito General*. PhD thesis, Universidad Politécnica de Madrid, España, July 1995.

[3] J. Carretero, F. Pérez, P. De Miguel, F. García, and L. Alonso. ParFiSys: A Parallel File System for MPP. *ACM SIGOPS*, 30(2):74–80, Apr. 1996.

[4] P. Corbett and et all. MPI-IO: A Parallel File I/O Interface for MPI. Version 0.4. Technical Report NAS2-14303, NASA, Dec. 1995.

[5] P. Corbett, S. Johnson, and D. Feitelson. Overview of the Vesta Parallel File System. *ACM Computer Architecture News*, 21(5):7–15, Dec. 1993.

[6] H. P. F. Forum. *High Performance Fortan Language Specification*. May 1993.

[7] F. García. *Coherencia de Cache en Sistemas de Ficheros para Entornos Distribuidos y Paralelos*. PhD thesis, Universidad Politécnica de Madrid, España, Sept. 1996.

[8] J. Howard and e. al. Scale and Performance in a Distributed File System. *ACM Transactions on Computer Systems*, 6(1):51–81, Feb. 1988.

[9] D. Kotz. *Prefetching and Caching Techniques in File Systems for MIMD Multiprocessors*. PhD thesis, Duke University, USA, Apr. 1991.

[10] D. Kotz and N. Nieuwejaar. File System Workload on a Scientific Multiprocessor. *IEEE Parallel and Distributed Technology. Systems and Aplications*, pages 134–154, Spring 1995.

[11] M. Nelson, B. Welch, and J. Ousterhout. Caching in the Sprite Network File System. *ACM Transactions on Computer Systems*, 6(1):134–154, Feb. 1988.

[12] N. Nieuwejaar and D. Kotz. The galley parallel file system. Technical Report PCS-TR96-286, Darmouth College Computer Science, 1996.

[13] J. Pieper. Parallel I/O Systems for Multicomputers. Technical Report CMU-CS-89-143, Carneghie Mellon University, Computer Science Department, Pittsburgh, USA, 1989.

[14] A. Purakayastha, C. S. Ellis, and D. Kotz. ENWRICH: A Computer-Processor Write Caching Scheme for Parallel File Systems. Technical Report TRCS-1995-22, Department of Computer Science, Duke University, Durhan North Carolina, Oct. 1995.

Intermediate Representations of Concurrent VHDL-based Specifications

J.P. Castellano, Alvaro Suárez, J.C. Bordón
Departamento de Electrónica, Telemática y Automática
Universidad de Las Palmas de G.C.
Campus Universitario de Tafira - Las Palmas de G.C. - 35017
e-mail {francis,alvaro}@cic.teleco.ulpgc.es

Abstract

System level synthesis demands the description of specifications with several concurrent processes. The synthesis from VHDL concurrent specifications is problematic due to the simulation oriented semantics of the assignment to signal and wait statements. An alternative way for modelling concurrent systems is utilize VHDL processes that communicate by means of send and receive synchronous primitives. One of the most important intermediate representations for the synthesis process is the data flow graph utilized in the ASCIS european project. This graph was developed for specifications with only one process. We in this paper present two intermediate representations for concurrent VHDL-based specifications that are based in the ASCIS data flow graph: one supports a modelling style based on the VHDL simulation cycle and the other supports a modelling style based on the send and receive primitives.

1 Introduction

In the last years, the systems complexity has greatly increased according to the technology advances. It has derived the next problems to the system design: 1) The design time is increased. 2) There is an increasing number of design errors.

Design automation from system level specifications is the next step to solve these problems. System level synthesis begins with a system specification (coded in a system level language) and generates a structural description consisting of processors, memories and interconnection networks. System level synthesis demands specifications with several concurrent processes. A widely used system modelling style is based on VHDL concurrent specifications [1][2][3]. It is problematic due to the simulation oriented semantics of the assignment to signal and *wait* statements. The update of the signals is synchronized with the execution of a *wait* statement in all the processes (VHDL simulation cycle). From the point of view of the synthesis this supposes the implementation in hardware of the simulation cycle. This modelling style for the synthesis of concurrent processes is not well suited to many systems, because there is an excessive amount of

synchronization among all the processes that it in many cases is not necessary.

An alternative way for modelling concurrent systems is utilize VHDL processes that communicate by means of *send* and *receive* synchronous primitives. From the synthesis point of view, this model only needs synchronization among the communicating processes.

One of the most important intermediate representations for the synthesis process is the dataflow graph proposed in the ASCIS (Architectural Synthesis for Complex Integrated Systems) european project as an standard representation for the synthesis and verification tools. This graph [4][5] was developed for specifications with only one process. Thus, it does not support:

- The *wait* statement.
- The signal assignment statement semantics.
- The *send/receive* primitives.

As a result, this representation does not support the above modelling styles for synthesis of VHDL-based concurrent specifications.

We in this paper present two intermediate representations for VHDL-based concurrent specifications that are based in the ASCIS graph: one supports specifications based on the simulation cycle (based on the *wait* statement) and the other supports specifications based on the synchronous *send/receive* primitives. We have developed a VHDL compiler for the first approach that generates the data flow graph.

The paper structure is the next: in the section 2, modelling styles are described. The intermediate representations are explained in the section 3. In the section 4, we show the mapping process to the graph for both modelling styles. In the section 5, we present the compiler we have designed to generate the graph for the modelling style based on the *wait* statement. Finally, we present the conclusions and references.

2 Modelling styles

The modelling styles above mentioned are based on VHDL. In this section, we first describe the VHDL subset used in both modelling styles. Next, we present the particular statements of each model.

The definition of the design, objects and data types are common to both modelling styles. The design is composed of an entity and its architecture. The entity specifies the design interface and the architecture specifies the entity functionality. The entity behaviour is specified using a set of communicating processes. This behaviour can be hierarchically expressed using subprograms.

Both modelling styles support the three main VHDL objects: *constants*, *signals* and *variables*.

There are two supported data type classes: scalar and composite. The scalar class is composed of integer and enumerated types. The predefined enumerated types are: *bit*, *boolean* and *character*. The *array* is the only allowed composite type. Moreover, *packages* can be used to group a set of type declarations. For a more detailed modelling description see [6].

2.1 Modelling style based on the *wait* statement

This modelling style uses the next statements for process communication and synchronization:

```
sequential_statement::=
        wait_statement
    | signal_assignment_statement
```

The model supports the syntax and semantics described in [1], but there are some restrictions:

a) We only support the following *wait* statements:

```
[label:] WAIT UNTIL expression ;
[label:] WAIT ON signal_list ;
```

The expression denotes the condition which has to be satisfied for continuing the process or subprogram execution. Signals for communication and synchronization can appear in the expression. The *wait on* statement is sensitive to events on the list signals. The *wait for* statement is not supported because it makes direct reference to the simulation timing notion [7][8].

b) We support the following syntax for the signal assignment statement:

```
[label:] signal <= expression ;
```

The *after* clause is not supported because it makes direct reference to the simulation timing notion and its hardware implementation is not efficient [7][8].

2.2 Modelling style based on *send/receive*

This model uses synchronous *send/receive* primitives for process communication and synchronization. Multiple processes can communicate through a signal, but only one of them can write in it. The meaning of the primitives are:

Send (Signal, Expression)

Assigns the expression value to the signal once all receiver processes are ready (they are executing the corresponding *receive* primitive).

Receive (Signal, Variable)

Assigns the signal value, obtained from the sender, to the variable. The sender and the remain receivers have to be ready (simple or multiway rendezvous).

3 Intermediate representations

In this section we propose the intermediate representations, augmenting the ASCIS data flow graph, for both modelling styles. The main original ASCIS graph advantages are:

- It completely integrates the control flow and the data flow, exposing the maximum parallelism of the specification. Thus, the synthesis tools have a great freedom to make trade-offs between area and time.
- It has a formally defined textual format [4] instead of a binary format. It allows extensions to the graph. Tools can add specific information to the graph without disturbing the compatibility with other tools.
- It semantics is based on token passing. Thus it does not impose restrictions on the hardware timing. However, timing edges can be used to introduce timing restrictions.
- It is not an architecture oriented representation. For instance, we can synthesize a control flow architecture or a data flow architecture.

3.1 ASCIS graph semantics

The ASCIS graph is composed of nodes and directed edges. A node represents an operation and a directed edge represents a value transfer between two nodes. Values are represented as tokens.

Node execution is defined as the process of consuming the node input edges tokens and producing the node output edges tokens. A node can be executed if there are, at least, a token in every input edge. According to this model, various tokens can be queued in an edge. This means, in general, than an edge can not be implemented as a wire. This model can be restricted to allow only a token in every edge.

There are five edge types in the graph:

- *Data edges*: they are used for data transfer.
- *Source edges*: they are used for activating *constant* an *array* nodes.
- *Control edges*: they are used in control flow nodes.
- *Chain edges*: they are used in some nodes (*array*, *update*, *retrieve*, etc.) to establish a sequential execution order.
- *Timing edges*: they are used for specifying timing constraints between nodes.

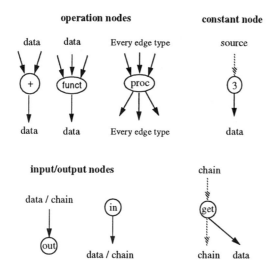

Figure 1.   Basic nodes of the ASCIS graph.

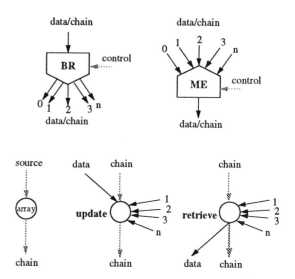

Figure 2.   Nodes for control flow and array operations.

The common nodes to both modelling styles are (figures 1 and 2):

Operation nodes: these nodes realize some kind of processing on data. The function (funct) and procedure (proc) nodes are hierarchical.

Constant nodes: they generate a token with a constant value. They have an input edge of source type to indicate when the token must be generated.

Input/Output nodes: they are used in the subprograms and processes interfaces.

Get node: it is used for reading the signal values. They are chained with chain edges.

Branch and merge (BR and ME) *nodes*: a branch node passes a token from the input edge to one of its output edges, which is selected with the control edge token value. Merge nodes are dual.

Entry and exit (EN and EX) *nodes*: these nodes are functionally similar to the merge and branch nodes, respectively. The only difference between them is that entry node has a special behaviour the first time it is executed because the input edge token passes through the node although the control edge token is not available.

Array operations nodes: there are three types of nodes to operate on arrays: *array*, *retrieve* and *update*.

The *array* node operates as the array declaration and contains information dealing with it. It needs to be activated with a source edge like a constant node. The output edge of chain type allows to chain all the operations realized on the array. The *retrieve* node is used for reading an array value. The *update* node is used for writing a value on the array.

3.2   Wait-based modelling style nodes

The nodes we propose for the wait-based modelling style are (figure 3):

Put node: it is used for writing on signals and is chained with chain edges.

Wait node: the input token waits until the control edge token is true. Then the token passes to the output edge. If the control edge token is false, then it is simply consumed by the *wait* node. It is used in the *wait* statements.

Sync node: the input token waits until a token appears on the control edge. This token appears when all processes

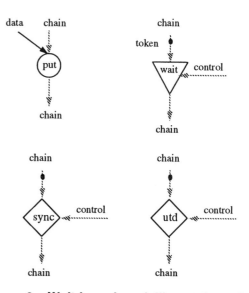

Figure 3.   Wait-based modelling style nodes.

68

are stopped executing a *wait* statement. It is necessary for representing the simulation cycle.

Utd node: the input token waits until a token arrives on the control edge. This token appears when all processes have updated all the signals. It is necessary for avoiding a process to begin a new simulation cycle when the signals have not been updated.

3.3 *Send/receive* modelling style nodes

The nodes we propose for the *send/receive* modelling style are (figure 4):

Send node: it is used for representing the *send* primitives. The token value of the input data edge is written on the signal.

Receive node: it is used for representing the *receive* primitives. The token of the output data edge has the value of the read signal.

Both nodes can be chained with chain edges.

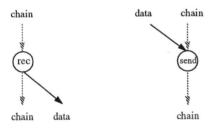

Figure 4. *Send/receive* modelling style nodes.

4 Mapping from modelling styles to graph

In this section we explain the mapping to the data flow graph of both modelling styles. First, we present the mapping of common statements. Then, the mapping for the particular statements of both models are explained.

The mapping for common statements is as follow:

if statement: a pair of *branch-merge* nodes is generated for every involved data flow in the statement.

variable assignment statement: the token value corresponding to the variable is modified.

while statement: a pair of *entry-exit* nodes are generated for every involved data flow.

The statements mapping for the modelling style based on the *wait* statement is as follow:

signal assignment statement: the corresponding *put* node is generated.

wait until statement: a *wait* node is generated for every data flow corresponding to a signal. Besides, a loop is generated to evaluate the *wait* expression (figure 5). This loop has a *sync* node and an *utd* node to take into account the simulation cycle semantics.

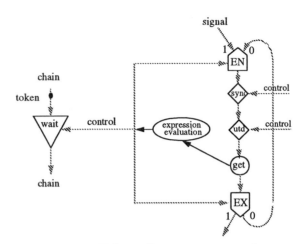

Figure 5. *Wait until* statement mapping

wait on statement: it is analogous to the previous one, but the expression consist of a comparison of the previous and actual values of the signal in order to observe if an event has been occurred (figure 6).

The statements mapping for the modelling style based on *send/receive* is as follow:

send statement: a *send* node has to be generated and it is chained to the involved data flow with the chain edges. The token value of the data edge is taken from the node that produces the expression token (figure 7).

receive statement: a *receive* node has to be generated and it is chained to the data flow with the chain edges. The output data edge must be taken into account in the involved variable data flow (figure 8).

5 Compiler: wait-based modelling style

We have developed a compiler [6] to automate the translation process from the wait-based modelling style to the data flow graph. The compiler phases are:

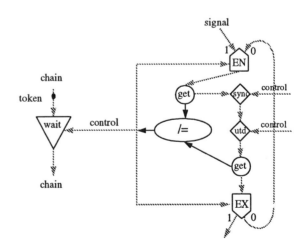

Figure 6. *Wait on* statement mapping.

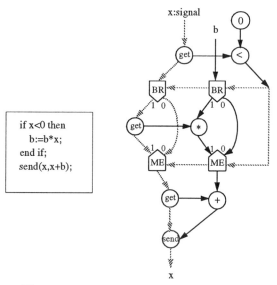

Figure 7. *Send* statement mapping.

Lexical analysis: it recognizes the VHDL specification tokens. We have used the LEX lexical analyser generator [9].

Syntactic analysis: it recognizes the syntax of the VHDL specification. We have generated a LALR(1) grammar in BNF format from the grammar described in [1]. Then, we have used the BISON syntactic analyser generator [10].

Semantic analysis: it mainly realizes type checking and type conversions.

Code generation: it generates the data flow graph using syntax directed translation [11].

5.1 Example

Next we present an example with two processes to show the graph generated by the compiler. The first process multiplies two signals and sends the result to the other. The second process evaluates the power of two of the received data.

```
entity MULT is
    port(   X: in integer;
            Y: in integer;
            O: out integer
        );
end MULT;
architecture BEHAVIOUR of MULT is
signal DATA: integer;
signal request, ack: bit := '0';
begin
    P1: process
        variable mult: integer;
        variable count: integer;
    begin
        mult:=0;
        count:=X;
        while (count>0) loop
            mult:=mult+Y;
            count:=count-1;
        end loop;
        request<='1';
        wait until (ack='1');
        DATA<=mult;
        request<='0';
        wait until (ack='0');
    end process;
    P2: process
        variable mult: integer;
        variable count: integer;
    begin
        wait until (request='1');
        ack<='1';
        wait until (request='0');
        count:=DATA;
        ack<='0';
        wait until (true);
        mult:=0;
        while (count>0) loop
            mult:=mult+DATA;
            count:=count-1;
        end loop;
        O<=mult;
    end process;
end BEHAVIOUR;
```

In figure 9 is shown the graphical representation of the generated data flow graph for the P1 process. The shaded subgraph corresponds to the while loop.

6 Conclusions

System level synthesis demands specifications with several concurrent processes. A widely used system modelling style is based on VHDL concurrent specifications. An alternative way of modelling concurrent systems is utilize VHDL processes that communicate by means of the *send* and *receive* synchronous primitives.

We in this paper have proposed two intermediate representations for VHDL-based concurrent specifications that are based in an extended ASCIS data flow graph: one supports the VHDL simulation cycle for specifications based on the *wait* and signal assignment statements. The other supports specifications based on the synchronous

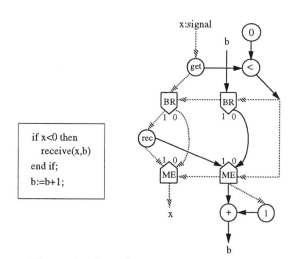

Figure 8. *Receive* statement mapping.

send/receive primitives. Futhermore, we have developed a compiler to automate the translation process from the specifications based on the simulation cycle.

Now, we are developing a compiler for specifications based on the *send/receive* primitives.

References

[1] *IEEE Standard VHDL Language Reference Manual. ANSI/ IEEE Std* 1076-1993.

[2] P. Eles, K. Kuchcinski, Z. Peng, M. Minea. *Synthesis of VHDL subprograms and processes in the CAMAD system.* Proceedings of the Workshop on Design Methodologies for Microelectronics and Signal Processing, Poland, Oct. 1993, pp. 359-366.

[3] P. Eles, K. Kuchcinski, Z. Peng, M. Minea. *Synthesis of VHDL Concurrent Processes.* (c) 1994 ACM 0-89791-687-5/94/0009.

[4] J.T.J. van Eijndhoven, G.G. de Jong, L.Stok. *The ASCIS Data Flow Graph: Semantics and Textual Format.* Eind-hoven University of Technology, 1991.

[5] J.T.J. van Eijndhoven, L. Stok. *A Data Flow Graph Exchange Standard*, EURODAC, 1992,pp. 193-199.

[6] J.C. Bordón. *High Level Synthesis: VHDL Compiler for Generating an Intermediate Representation.* Master´s Thesis. EUITT. University of Las Palmas. January, 1996.

[7] J. Roy, N. Kumar, R. Dutta, R. Vemuri. *DSS: A Distributed High-Level Synthesis System.* IEEE Design & Test of Computers, June 1992, pp. 18-32.

[8] V. Nagasamy, N. Berry, C. Dandelo. *Specification, Planning and Synthesis in a VHDL Design Environment.* IEEE Design & Test of Computers, June 1992, pp. 58-68.

[9] J.R. Levine, T. Mason, D. Brown. *Lex & Yacc.* O'Reilly and Associates, 1992.

[10] C. Donnelly, R. Stallman. *BISON: The Yacc-compatible Parser Generator.* Free Software Foundation, 1991.

[11] A.V. Aho, R. Sethi, J.D. Ullman. *Compilers: Principles, Techniques, and Tools.* Addison Wesley, 1986.

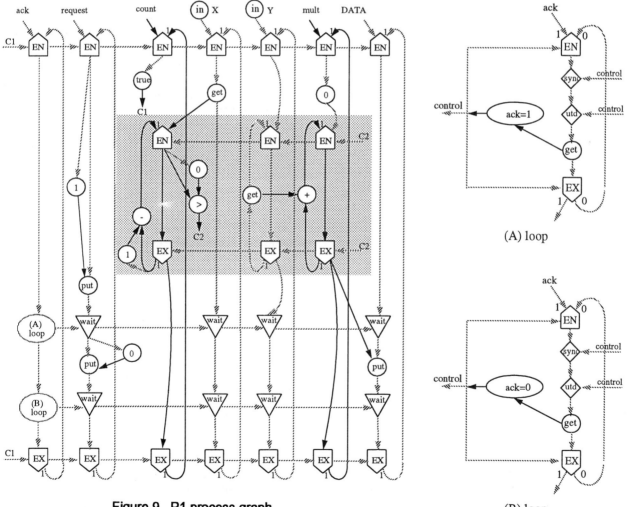

Figure 9. P1 process graph.

(A) loop

(B) loop

Generalised Reduction Operations for HPF

D.C.B. Watson and L.M. Delves
N.A. Software Ltd.
62 Roscoe Street,
Roscoe House,
Liverpool L1 9DW.
U.K.
{ dave,delves } @ nasoftware.co.uk

Abstract

Language extensions to Fortran are proposed which give the programmer the ability to express generalised array operations. The enhancements are discussed in the context of HPF and parallelisation.

1. Introduction

Within the Esprit-funded HPF+ project we are studying language extensions for High Performance Fortran (HPF). The emphasis is on the provision of suitable facilities for expressing more general parallelism than is provided by Fortran90 in conjunction with the data parallel extensions provided by HPF-Version1.1 (HPF1), whilst maintaining the ability to produce efficient code from current compiler technology. A number of language features have been proposed by Vienna [6], and by the HPF Forum as part of the move towards the publishing of a draft for HPF-Version2.0 (HPF2). The features discussed concentrate on allowing programmers to provide a more accurate description of the data distribution needs of their problem, and an ability to describe more general MIMD parallelism than is possible within HPF1. We accept the desirability of such features, and do not try to repeat these aspects. Rather, we discuss here some of the shortfalls in Fortran and propose extensions which we believe enhance the orthogonality of the language and are useful to a parallelising compiler. We focus on the reduction operations defined intrinsically and in HPF_LIBRARY as defined in [4] but hope that it is clear that similar extensions could easily encapsulate other idioms.

In the remainder of this paper we follow [1] and represent keywords as KEYWORD, syntactic terms as *term* and semantic definitions by **defn**. Any notions not defined here can be found in the appropriate standard.

2. Fortran Intrinsics and the HPF Library

The intrinsics in Fortran [1] fall into several classes. We note that some intrinsics operate on all types and/or ranks *e.g.* TRANSPOSE, MERGE and RESHAPE. These intrinsics are really templates for compiler generated operations since it is impossible to precompile such routines. We also note that other classes of operation, in particular the array reduction functions (*e.g.* SUM) and the array location functions (*e.g.* MINLOC), describe practically identical behavior.

HPF1 defines a standard library of procedures which, though nominally not intrinsics, are in practice best implemented closely with the compiler. These procedures encapsulate a range of operations which occur commonly within applications. The most important are a set of array operations which include the following:

XXX_PREFIX : a set of prefix operations, with the particular operation specified by the XXX

XXX_SUFFIX : a matching set of suffix operations.

XXX_SCATTER : a set of scatter operations

The allowed values of XXX include ALL, ANY, COPY, COUNT, IALL, IANY, IPARITY, MAXVAL, MINVAL, PARITY, PRODUCT, SUM. Not all types are allowed for all three groups of procedure.

The resulting library (with other procedures) is prescribed to be made available as a standard Fortran module. This module has the following obvious characteristics:

- It is large since the number of operations specified above must be implemented for all types and ranks.

- There is a lack of orthogonality in the arguments taken by these somewhat similar functions. For example, the COUNT procedures do not have the same interfaces as the SUM procedures.

72

- It can *not* be implemented as an external library within full HPF1.

This last restriction matters little to the user, but a lot to the implementor. It arises because many of the functions must formally be made available for arrays of *any* type and for any conformant array argument. Since the programmer may define arbitrary types there is no way to write this library within Fortran. Similarly, some of the arguments are intended to be conformable which basically allows a scalar to be promoted to an array of a certain shape. Within Fortran a scalar actual argument can not be expanded to conform to an array dummy in a user defined procedure unless it is defined to be *ELEMENTAL*. These restrictions do not apply to intrinsic procedures since a compiler can coerce the arguments appropriately. However, the HPF1 standard [4] explicitly states that HPF_LIBRARY is not intrinsic. This problem can be circumvented to some extent by only providing the procedures for arrays of intrinsic type. This is a restriction on the library specified in [4] since the COPY functions are required for all types.

In addition to the above procedures the HPF_LIBRARY module further increases the number of array reductions (*e.g.* IALL which delivers a bitwise logical AND reduction acoss an array). It is easy to envisage that a user may also wish to further extend such operations with user defined types. Finally, it is cumbersome to remember the full range of such operations despite the fact that there is a clear unifying principle behind the definitions.

The proposals in this paper overcome these problems by encapsulating just those aspects which must be intrinsic, *i.e.* known to the compiler. Indeed, HPF_LIBRARY routines XXX_SCATTER, XXX_PREFIX, XXX_SUFFIX and additional array reduction intrinsics (*e.g.* IANY) (constituting some 41 routines) can be recast as only *three* intrinsics with extensible functionality under this proposal. Similarly seven array reduction intrinsics in Fortran90 are no longer needed. In terms of paper used to describe the functionality alone this seems to us to be a good thing. Since simplicity aids the user we believe programmers would think so too.

3. Generalised Array Reduction

In [5] a case is made for easy identification of reduction operations and the specification of user defined reduction operations. We agree with the aims but believe that the syntax can be more concisely expressed and generally applicable. In particular it is desirable to extend the notion of reduction to arbitrary types and operations. In order to do this we extend the specification of a user defined operator in Fortran. We then define a reduction operator as a restricted form of a user defined operator and use this new operator in conjunction with a new intrinsic to provide the generalised array reduction.

3.1. Operator Specification

User defined elemental subprograms have already been added to Fortran in [2]. We extend the definition of *prefix-spec* for a procedure to include an *op-spec*

prefix-spec	**is**	*type-spec*
	or	RECURSIVE
	or	PURE
	or	ELEMENTAL
	or	*op-spec*
op-spec	**is**	COMMUTATIVE
	or	ASSOCIATIVE

If an *op-spec* is specified, the *prefix-spec* ELEMENTAL is implied (with its constraints)and need not be specified. In addition to the constraints on ELEMENTAL procedures we add

Constraint   *op-spec* shall only be applied to binary functions with argument type defined to be the same as the result type.

Note that the above constraint is a necessary corollary to the mathematical notion of associative and commutative operations. An *op-spec* implies that a processor may compute a sequence of function applications in any order compatible with the property specified. A processor need not prove that the appropriate mathematical property is satisfied.

For example a function with the property of associativity could be declared as

```
integer associative function fass(a,b)
integer a,b
fass = a+b
return
end function fass
```

and a commutative function could be declared as

```
integer commutative function fcom(a,b)
integer a,b
fcom = mod(a-b)
return
end function fcom
```

In Fortran a **defined-binary-op** is defined by a function with a generic interface specifying an operator. We further define a **defined-associative-op** and a **defined-commutative-op** as a **defined-binary-op** with the appropriate *op-spec*. For example we may define an associative operator by

```
interface operator(.assop.)
  associative function fass(a,b)
    integer          :: fass
    integer, intent(in)  ::a,b
  end function fass
end interface
```

or a commutative operator by

```
interface operator(.comop.)
  commutative function fcom(a,b)
    integer             :: fcom
    integer, intent(in) :: a,b
  end function fcom
end interface
```

The intrinsic binary operators which are associative are **intrinsic-associative-op**s and those which are commutative are **intrinsic-commutative-op**s.

3.2. Reduction Operators

In order to implement reductions in parallel we must know that an operation is associative and that it has a unit element. In [5] the identity is specified in a reduction clause attached to every occurrence of a reduction. We use the notion of default initialisation proposed in [2] and extended to intrinsic types in [3] to address this need. Further we permit default initialisation to be applied to optional arguments to provide a default value. We note in this context that the most common use for optional arguments is to allow a procedure to be called with default arguments. This extension removes the need to write the following sort of code which is often seen in libraries:

```
subroutine libsub(a,b,p1,p2,p3)
  real,dimension(:) :: a,b
  real,optional     :: p1,p2,p3
  real              :: c1,c2,c3
  if ( present(p1) )
    c1 = p1
  else
    c1 = 3.0
  endif
    ... etc
end
```

We define a **defined-reduction-op** to be a **defined-associative-op** subject to the following constraints:

Constraint   the function arguments shall have a default initialisation

Constraint   the function arguments shall be optional

The left and right identity elements of the **defined-reduction-op** are identified with the default initialisations of the appropriate arguments. An example of a **defined-reduction-op** is

```
associative function redop(a,b)
integer              :: redop
```

```
integer,optional :: a = 0
integer,optional :: b = 0
fass = a + b
return
end function redop
```

The **intrinsic-associative-op**s are defined to be **intrinsic-reduction-op**s since the compiler can determine the identity elements intrinsically. Note that we do not require that a **reduction-op** is commutative. If such an operator is also commutative it allows the compiler further freedom to order application of the operator in some circumstances.

3.3. Update Operators

In order to enable easy identification of reductions within loops we propose to add a new operator, an update operator. An update operator is automatically defined for every **reduction-op** with associated operator *op* if the type also has a visible assignment operator. This is true for all the intrinsic types and oparators.

update-op **is** *op=*

For example, the following statements are the same:

```
x  = x + y
x += y
```

The update operator is akin to the compound assignment in C (*e.g.* x+=y). Unfortunately this syntax runs into a slight difficulty in Fortran since > is a valid operator and hence >= would be a valid update operator. However, the contexts in which the two are valid are easily distinguishable so we do not believe this is a significant difficulty.

3.4. Generalised Array Reduction

We introduce a new intrinsic REDUCE to perform generalised array reduction. Note that in the following definition we allow an operator to be passed as a function to an intrinsic. We choose to do this to avoid the need to define procedures for each of the intrinsic reduction operators which would be clumsy. The semantics of the generalised array reduction are clearly and concisely expressed irrespective of the operator. All operations have a defined value if the array is zero sized or there are no elements selected according to the mask or, indeed, if the operation is applied to a scalar. We introduce a notion of **reduction-order**. **Reduction-order** is that of array element order unless the **reduction-op** is commutative in which case **reduction-order** can be arbitrarily defined by the processor. This can be very important in a data parallel context when arrays are distributed in a *CYCLIC* fashion since application in array element order imposes extra communication burdens.

```
REDUCE(OP,ARRAY,MASK,DIM)
```

Optional Arguments.   DIM,MASK

Description.   Elements of ARRAY reduced under operation OP along dimension DIM corresponding to the true elements of MASK

Class.   Transformational Function

Arguments.

OP   must be a **reduction-op**

ARRAY   must be of the same type as OP and must be conformable with MASK

DIM (optional)   must be scalar and of type integer with value in the range $1 \geq$ DIM $\leq n$ where n is the rank of MERGE(ARRAY,OP(),MASK)

MASK (optional)   must be of type logical and must be conformable with ARRAY. If MASK is absent it is as if it were present with the value .TRUE.

Result Type, Type Parameter and Shape.   The result type is of the same type as the result of OP

Case (i):   If DIM is absent the result is scalar

Case (ii):   If DIM is present the result is an array of rank $n - 1$. If $n - 1 > 0$ the shape of the result is $(d_1, \ldots, d_{DIM-1}, d_{DIM+1}, \ldots, d_n)$ where $(d_1, \ldots, d_n)$ is the shape of MERGE(ARRAY,OP(),MASK)

Result Value.

Case (i):   If DIM is absent then the result of REDUCE(OP,A,M) is a processor-dependent approximation to RESULT defined informally as

RESULT = OP()
$\forall$ conforming elements a $\in$ A and m $\in$ M
  in reduction order of OP
    RESULT = MERGE(OP(RESULT,a),OP(RESULT),m)

Case (ii):   If DIM is present then the result of REDUCE(OP,A,M,DIM) is defined as

$\forall (i_1, \ldots, i_{DIM-1}, i_{DIM+1}, \ldots, i_n)$ in
$(d_1, \ldots, d_{DIM-1}, d_{DIM+1}, \ldots, d_n)$
RESULT $((i_1, \ldots, i_{DIM-1}, i_{DIM+1}, \ldots, i_n)) =$
  REDUCE(OP, A $((i_1, \ldots, i_{DIM-1}, :, i_{DIM+1}, \ldots, i_n))$,
    M $((i_1, \ldots, i_{DIM-1}, :, i_{DIM+1}, \ldots, i_n)))$

with the obvious changes if either M or A are scalar.

Examples.

Case (i):   REDUCE(+,ARRAY,MASK)   has   the   value   SUM(ARRAY,MASK)

Case (ii):   REDUCE(+,1,MASK)   has   the   value   COUNT(MASK)

Case (iii):   REDUCE(.NEQV.,.FALSE.,MASK)   has   the value PARITY(MASK)

Note that value is specified in terms of a reference model implementation. A processor is expected to provide a semantically equivalent implementation.

3.5. Example Usage

In this section we present an example using generalised array reduction and discuss its advantages. Consider a simplified fragment of code from a real application which iterates over data parallel operations and on each iteration calculates the sum of differences, absolute differences and squared differences of masked array values:

```
DO
    ...
    V1 = SUM(A**2-B**2,MASK=MASK)
    V2 = SUM(ABS(A-B),MASK=MASK)
    V3 = SUM(A-B,MASK=MASK)
ENDDO
```

Most compilers will implement this as three separate reduction operations thus applying the mask three times and loading the arrays several times. We will now express this as a generalised reduction of a user defined type. The type contains the three elemental differences which are required to be calculated

```
MODULE DIFF

    TYPE tD
        REAL :: SD
        REAL :: AD
        REAL :: RD
    END TYPE

    TYPE(tD),PARAMETER :: &
        nD = tD(0.0,0.0,0.0)
```

We now introduce an elemental function *gD* to generate the type *tD* from the basic values and a defined reduction operator *rD* between scalars of type *tD*.

```
    INTERFACE OPERATOR(+)
        MODULE PROCEDURE rD
    END INTERFACE
```

```
   CONTAINS

     ELEMENTAL FUNCTION gD(V1,V2)
       TYPE(tD)          :: gD
       REAL,INTENT(IN) :: V1,V2
       gD % SD = V1**2 - V2**2
       gD % RD =      V1 - V2
       gD % AD = ABS(gD % RD)
     END FUNCTION gD

     ASSOCIATIVE COMMUTATIVE &
     FUNCTION rD(V1,V2)
       TYPE(tD)             :: rD
       TYPE(tD),OPTIONAL :: V1 = nD
       TYPE(tD),OPTIONAL :: V2 = nD
       rD % SD = V1 % SD + v2 % SD
       rD % RD = V1 % RD + v2 % RD
       rD % AD = V1 % AD + v2 % AD
     END FUNCTION rD

   END MODULE
```

Finally, we can rewrite the original problem as

```
   USE DIFF
   TYPE(tD) :: vD

   DO
     ...
     vD = REDUCE(+,gD(A,B),MASK)
   ENDDO
```

Apart from expressing the problem more succinctly (in the original code the simple arrays were actually complex array expressions), there are potential performance benefits from expressing the problem at a higher level of abstraction. Note, there is now only one mask application and one access to each element of the array. Even on a traditional sequential machine this is liable to produce better memory access patterns than the original code. A compiler which can perform inlining can even remove the minimal overhead from the function calls entirely. On a distributed memory parallel machine we have reduced three collective communications to one thus reducing the message passing overhead.

4. Generalised Array Intrinsics

We now briefly consider extending the ideas of the previous section. Firstly we apply them directly to HPF_LIBRARY and then outline more general ways to extend the array processing functionality of Fortran.

4.1. Generalised Array Prefix

We introduce the following new intrinsic to generate all the prefix and suffix functions within HPF_LIBRARY. Note, we do not provide a direct analogue of the functions XXX_SUFFIX since XXX_SUFFIX(1:N) is identical to XXX_PREFIX(N:1:-1). Note also that the order of application of the reduction operator is fixed for the prefix operation so the compiler has no latitude to evaluate in a different order. We believe this specification is neater, more general and easier to remember than the set of definitions in HPF_LIBRARY currently. No extensions beyond those made for the generalised reduction are necessary to add the generalised prefix.

```
PREFIX(OP,ARRAY,MASK,DIM,SEGMENT,EXCLUSIVE)
```

Optional Arguments. DIM,MASK

Description. Computes a segmented scan under operation OP along dimension DIM of array *ARRAY* corresponding to the true elements of MASK

Class. Transformational Function

Arguments.

OP   must be a reduction operator

ARRAY   must be of the same type as OP and must be conformable with MASK

DIM (optional) must be scalar and of type integer with value in the range $1 \geq DIM \leq n$ where n is the rank of MERGE(ARRAY,OP(),MASK)

MASK (optional) must be of type logical and must be conformable with ARRAY. If MASK is absent it is as if it were present with the value .TRUE.

SEGMENT (optional) must be of type logical and must be conformable with MERGE(ARRAY,OP(),MASK).

EXCLUSIVE (optional) must be of type logical and must be scalar. If EXCLUSIVE is absent it is as if it were present with the value .FALSE.

Result Type, Type Parameter and Shape. The result type is of the same type as the result of OP and has the same shape as MERGE(ARRAY,OP(),MASK)

Result Value. For reasons of space we do not give a full definition here. We assume that SEGMENT and EXCLUSIVE are absent. We refer the interested reader to [4]

Case (i): If `DIM` is absent then the result of `PREFIX(OP,A,M)` is a processor-dependent approximation to `RESULT` defined informally as

```
RESULT(1) = OP()
∀ a(i) ∈ A(2:) and m(i) ∈ M(2:)
  in array element order of OP
  RESULT(i) =
    MERGE(OP, RESULT(i-1),a(i)),
           OP(RESULT(i-1)),m(i))
```

Case (ii): If `DIM` is present then the result of `PREFIX(OP,A,M,DIM)` is defined as

$$\forall\ (i_1,\ldots,i_{DIM-1},i_{DIM+1},\ldots,i_n) \text{ in}$$
$$(d_1,\ldots,d_{DIM-1},d_{DIM+1},\ldots,d_n)$$
$$\texttt{RESULT}((i_1,\ldots,i_{DIM-1},i_{DIM+1},\ldots,i_n)) =$$
$$\texttt{PREFIX(OP, A}((i_1,\ldots,i_{DIM-1},:,i_{DIM+1},\ldots,i_n)),$$
$$\texttt{M}((i_1,\ldots,i_{DIM-1},:,i_{DIM+1},\ldots,i_n)))$$

with the obvious changes if either `M` or `A` are scalar.

Examples.

Case (i): `PREFIX(+,ARRAY,MASK)` has the value `SUM_PREFIX(ARRAY,MASK)`

Case (ii): `PREFIX(+,1,MASK(N:1:-1))` has the value `COUNT_SUFFIX(MASK(1:N))`

Case (iii): `PREFIX(.NEQV.,.FALSE.,MASK)` has the value `PARITY_PREFIX(MASK)`

4.2. Extension to Other Operations

We believe other generalised array operations are desirable. In particular the `HPF_LIBRARY XXX_SCATTER` routines are obvious candidates. We consider the location functions (*i.e.* `MAXLOC` and `MINLOC`) and sorting functions (*i.e.* `GRADE_UP` and `GRADE_DOWN`) to also be better treated in this fashion since this avoids the user having to re-invent the wheel for user defined types. Also more general location functions would be useful in many circumstances *e.g.* find the indices of the first element satisfying an arbitrary logical condition rather than simply the maximal or minimal values.

5. Conclusions

We have presented minor syntactic and semantic changes to the current Fortran definition which make the language smaller and more powerful. We believe that these extensions can be made without impacting on the performance of compiled code. Furthermore we enable the programmer to express general classes of idioms and give compilers, particularly parallelising compilers, more information to generate efficient code. We note also that the features presented here supersede current functionalities. However, for backwards compatibility a compiler can easily recognise the current specific forms of intrinsic as shorthand forms of the more general intrinsics and the current `HPF_LIBRARY` can be implemented as simple wrappers around the more general routines proposed should this be desirable as a porting aid.

6. Acknowledgements

This work was supported in part by the CEC within Esprit project HPF+. We are grateful to our colleagues for many useful discussions of this work.

References

[1] Anonymous. *Fortran 90: ISO Standard ISO/IEC DIS 1539*, 1991.

[2] Anonymous. *Part 1 - International Standard Programming Language Fortran, ISO/IEC 1539-1:1996 (Fortran 95)*, February 1996.

[3] L. Delves, D. Lloyd, and D. Watson. Proposals for rationalisation of fortran. HPF+ Working Paper, March 1996.

[4] H. P. F. Forum. *High Performance Fortran Language Specification (Version 1.1)*, November 1994.

[5] R. Schreiber, C. Koelbel, and J. Saltz. Proposed hpf extension for reduction operations in independent loops. hpff-task submission, January 1996.

[6] H. Zima, P. Brezany, B. Chapman, P. Mehrotra, and A. Schwald. Vienna fortran - a language specification. Technical report, Austrian Centre for Parallel Computation, University of Vienna, 1991.

GAMMA: a Low-cost Network of Workstations Based on Active Messages

Giovanni Chiola, Giuseppe Ciaccio
DISI, Universita' di Genova
via Dodecaneso, 35
16146 Genova, Italy
{chiola,ciaccio}@disi.unige.it

Abstract

Networks Of Workstations (NOW) are an emerging architecture capable of supporting parallel processing with significantly low cost/performance ratio. At the moment the implementation of standard high-level communication mechanisms in a NOW does not provide such a satisfactory cost/performance ratio, as modern communication hardware would allow. We show how a standard, Unix-like operating system kernel can be extended with efficient and performant low-level communication primitives based on the Active Message communication paradigm. Higher level standard communication libraries, like MPI, should be implemented on top of such efficient low-level mechanisms. We provide some preliminary results obtained from an experimental prototype called GAMMA (Genoa Active Message MAchine), which is a NOW whose nodes run the operating system Linux 2.0 enhanced with an Active Message communication layer.

1. Introduction

The usual protocol stack which is predominant in the Unix environment for inter-process communication (IPC), namely, the remote procedure call (RPC) level built on top of BSD Sockets or System V Streams built on top of TCP or UDP protocols built on top of the IP protocol now constitutes a de-facto standard that allows inter-operability of different machines. This advantage is payed in terms of efficiency of use of the communication hardware capabilities.

The performance of an Ethernet based LAN exceeded the needs of midrange workstations and "supermini computers" existing fifteen years ago even with the huge overhead of inefficient communication protocol layers. Today, when Ethernet based LANs become the bottleneck of a Network Of Workstations (NOW), the cheapest solution is to switch to faster hardware technologies (such as Fast Ethernet, FDDI, ATM, etc.) rather than producing new, more efficient software.

These economic considerations are correct in most but not all applications. One noteworthy exception is the case of NOWs used as hardware support to parallel processing. We claim that NOWs built out of cheap, fast, off-the-shelf computation and communication hardware components constitute the only hope for parallel processing techniques to spread. As a matter of fact, today no one interested in real applications would see the convenience of moving to parallel processing technologies involving substantially higher costs provided that each year single processors that are much faster and much cheaper than the ones available the year before can be found.

In principle, an efficient and well tuned NOW environment may well provide reasonably good levels of performance, as modern fast LAN devices like Fast Ethernet and ATM are not that much worse than custom, expensive communication networks used a few years ago in massively parallel platforms. The problem of defining a fast NOW-based parallel processing platform is delivering a fraction of the raw performance of communication hardware to the application level much larger than the one typically delivered by usual LAN environments through traditional network protocols.

The best approach to efficient parallel processing in a NOW is to design and implement efficient low-level interprocess communication primitives from scratch, and use these primitives to build higher-level communication mechanisms, like those of MPI[4], which would still enjoy a significant fraction of the raw communication performances.

We have built an extremely cheap NOW prototype

called GAMMA (Genoa Active Message MAchine) equipped with an efficient interprocess communication layer based on the paradigm of Active Messages[6]. GAMMA is a network of 12 Intel Pentium PCs connected by a 100 Mb/s Fast Ethernet LAN. Each workstation runs Linux 2.0 enhanced with a custom device driver and Active Messages communication primitives.

Our result shows that GAMMA can beat very expensive parallel platforms such as the CM-5 in terms of message latency (while of course it cannot compete in terms of communication bandwidth due to the obvious difference in communication hardware complexity and cost). Yet, several parallel processing applications exist that would benefit by the availability of a truly cheap platform offering modest bandwidth, low latency communications.

2. The GAMMA architecture

2.1. Hardware configuration

The current prototype of GAMMA is composed of a set of 12 autonomous workstations connected by means of two independent LANs: one 10 Mb/s Ethernet used with the standard protocol suite to provide network services (such as NFS access to file servers, remote login, etc.) in the Unix environment and one 100 Mb/s, isolated Fast Ethernet dedicated to the implementation of fast inter-processor communication primitives.

Each workstation comprises:

- Intel Pentium 133 MHz CPU

- PCI mother board, 256 KB of 15 ns pipelined secondary cache, PCI Intel Triton chipset

- 32 MB of 60 ns RAM

- 3COM 3C595-TX Fast Etherlink 10/100BASE-T PCI network adapter.

The Fast Ethernet 100 Mb/s LAN consists of a 3COM LinkBuilder FMS 100 repeater hub with 12 RJ-45 ports, to which each Fast Etherlink adapter is connected by a UTP cable.

No communication protocol (except for the IEEE 802.3 which is implemented in firmware inside the PCI cards) is run over the 100 Mb/s LAN.

Each workstation runs the operating system kernel Linux 2.0.0 enhanced with our own communication layer described below.

2.2. The GAMMA Active Message layer

An inter-process communication is accomplished by the sender process invoking an Active Message "send" system call. The goal of this system call is to copy a portion of memory content from the user memory space of the sender process on one node to the user memory space of the receiver on another node.

Sending a message is accomplished by copying the message from user space into the network adapter using no intermediate buffering into kernel space. The overhead is very limited thanks to the low abstraction level of our communication protocol. Messages longer than 110 bytes are split into a sequence of Ethernet frames (each one of length ranging from 60 to 1536 Bytes) that are copied right away to the adapter's transmit FIFO. This poses neither protection problems (as writing to the adapter can only be accomplished through a system call) nor memory access problems (as the transmitting process is running when the transmission function copies from user space to the network adapter).

The Ethernet frames are eventually received by the network adapter on the receiver side. An interrupt handler on the receiving PC is then launched which copies the content of the adapter's input queue to the memory space of the receiver process, again without any intermediate kernel buffering. The frame headers provide the addressing information needed to locate the correct user space buffer where the incoming message is to be stored, as well information needed to correctly rebuild the message from several frames.

Upon completion of the memory-to-memory data transfer, a user defined *receiver handler* is called on the receiver node. The role of a receiver handler is to integrate the incoming message into the data structures of the receiver process and to prepare a user space buffer for the next message to be received. It is worth pointing out that in the Active Message approach each process belonging to a running parallel application has at least two distinct threads, namely:

- the main process thread which performs the computations and sends messages; this thread is subject to the usual schedule policy of the OS kernel;

- one or more receiver threads, corresponding to the execution of the receiver handlers; they are executed right away upon message reception under the control of the device driver's interrupt routine, without involving the OS kernel scheduler.

The receiver threads cooperates with the main process thread by sharing all the global data structures of the program. This multi-threading mechanism avoids the descheduling of the receiver process that is inherent to blocking message reception such as is usually implemented in Unix "sockets", thus substantially reducing latency.

The GAMMA communication protocol provides no message acknowledgement since the high cost in terms of loss of bandwidth and additional latency time is not worth-while in a communication system with extremely low probability of frame corruption. No explicit flow control is provided either, since if the receiver handler invoked upon message receipt completes execution quickly enough, then the fast LAN becomes the bottleneck of the communication system. Indeed flow control should be implemented at the application level in case of long receiver handler code.

However GAMMA implements an error detection feature, by allowing user defined *error handlers* to be called in much the same way as receiver handlers:

- under the control of the network driver's interrupt routine in case of checksum error or frame corruptions when receiving a message;

- under the control of the "send" system call in case of frame loss due to excessive collisions when attempting to send a message.

Receiver and error handlers may be also used to implement connected communication protocols that guarentee message delivery if needed at the application level.

The GAMMA communication layer is embedded into the original Linux kernel in the form of additional system calls and data structures. The additional system calls trap into kernel through a dedicated trap address (unused in the current Linux kernel) which leads to the GAMMA code through a particularly short and optimized code path. The reception software is part of the custom network device driver, and the interrupt routine of the network driver is registered into the Linux kernel as a "fast interrupt", which means that the kernel path from the interrupt request to the driver's interrupt routine is short as well.

2.3. The GAMMA computational model

In what follows, the words "workstation" and "PC" are used as synonyms.

A *physical GAMMA* is the set of M workstations connected to the fast LAN. Each workstation is addressed by the Ethernet address of the corresponding fast network card. A *virtual GAMMA* is a set of $N \leq M$ computation nodes, each one corresponding to a distinct workstation in the physical GAMMA. The nodes are numbered from zero on and this numbering provides the

necessary addressing of nodes at the application level in the most straighforward way. At the kernel level each of these numbers is mapped onto the Ethernet address of the corresponding PC.

A *parallel program* may be thought of as a finite collection of N processes running in parallel, each on a distinct node of a virtual machine. GAMMA supports parallel multitasking, i.e., more than one virtual GAMMA may be spawned at the same time on the same physical GAMMA. Each one runs its own parallel program on behalf of potentially different users.

As a consequence, any workstation may be shared by more than one parallel program at a given time. Each virtual GAMMA and the corresponding running parallel program is identified by a number which is unique in the platform. We call such an identification number a *parallel PID*. Processes belonging to the same running parallel application are characterized by the parallel PID of the application itself. The parallel PID is used to distinguish among processes belonging to different parallel applications at the level of each individual workstation. A maximum of 256 different parallel PIDs may be activated on a physical GAMMA.

Each process has 255 *communication ports* numbered from one on; port number zero is reserved for kernel-level fast communications like those occurring to create a virtual GAMMA and launch a parallel program or to synchronize within a barrier synchronization. Each port is bidirectional, which means that data can be both sent and received through it. The pointer to a user space buffer where incoming messages are stored may be associated to a port in order to use it as input. A user defined receiver handler and a user defined error handler may also be associated to an input port. Each port being used as an output must be mapped to another port of another process belonging either to the same parallel program or to a different one, thus forming an outgoing communication channel. Alternatively, an output port may be bound with N-1 input ports, each belonging to a process on a different node in the same virtual GAMMA, in order to broadcast messages. However in neither cases is the binding accomplished through an explicit connection protocol. Correctness and determinism of the communication topology induced by the port-to-port mapping is up to the programmer.

3. Related Work

Active Messages were originally proposed by researchers at the University of California at Berkeley [6], as a flexible and efficient low-level communication mechanism aimed at reducing communication overhead and allowing communication to overlap computation. The efficiency of the Active Messages communication mechanisms lies in the fact that they do not require message buffering, due to the immediate managing of messages by the user defined handlers.

A well known application of Active Messages as an efficient support to parallel processing is the Active Message Layer introduced by Thinking Machines Co. in the CM-5 platform [1].

The same idea has been followed by the FM project [2], using a fast LAN called Myrinet instead of the Fat Tree interconnection network of the CM-5.

Our modest yet original contribution to the idea of exploiting Active Messages for efficient parallel processing is the application to a cheap platform which exploits only off-the-shelf and cheap hardware devices. In order to experiment this idea we also chose a standard operating system for which source code is freely available, namely Linux.

A somehow similar approach was followed also by researchers at Cornell University in the framework of the U-net project [5]. U-net follows the idea of removing communication support from the OS kernel in order to re-implement it (more efficiently) at the user application level. A pre-defined number of virtual "end points" are multiplexed over the physical adapter. Each end point can be attached to a single user process by means of a system call. This way a virtualization of fast communication devices directly accessible by user processes is obtained which does not require any system call to send messages. An Active Message layer was implemented on top of such virtual fast communication devices. Both an ATM [5] and a Fast Ethernet [7] version of U-net were released.

4. Performance Measurements

We carried out some preliminary performance measures on a GAMMA equipped with a two PCs. A more extensive benchmarking is in progress.

We defined "delay" as the time interval between the instant the sender process invokes the "send" system call and the instant the interrupt routine on the receiver node terminates to copy the message into the user space receive buffer. We used a typical "ping-pong" application to carry out standard round-trip measures. The average message round-trip time divided by two yields the average delay, which of course is a function of the message size. We define *communication latency* as the delay of a zero sized message.

We define the "communication throughput" $T(s)$ as the transfer rate perceived by the application when sending a message of size s: $T(s) = \frac{s}{D(s)}$ where $D(s)$ is

the message delay. We define *communication bandwidth* $B(s)$ according to the formula $B(s) = \frac{s}{D(s)-D(0)}$ where $D(0)$ is the communication latency as defined above.

The IEEE 802.3 standard allows for the frame size to range between 60 and 1536 bytes on the physical channel. With GAMMA, each frame has a 20 byte long header. Sending a message shorter than 40 bytes implies that less than 60 bytes are written to the network adapter, which in this case pads the frame with garbage bytes and transmits 60 bytes on the channel anyway. The header carries information about the size of the significant portion of the frame, so that the receiving CPU may copy only that portion to the user space receiver buffer.

Any message whose size ranges from 40 to 109 bytes results into a single full-sized Ethernet frame. However messages longer than 110 bytes are split into a sequence of frames. We realized that with frame bursts the communication system works as a pipeline, where the receiver CPU gets a previous frame from the RX FIFO queue on the receiver side while the adapters are transmitting the current frame and the sender CPU is writing the next frame in the TX FIFO queue of the sender side. Thanks to such pipeline effect, the fragmentation of medium sized messages into a large number of small frames yields better throughput. The optimal fragmentation of a given message depends on its size, and the optimal fragmentation policy was achieved experimentally. As a consequence of having such a fragmentation policy, the communication delay of messages ranging from 110 to 1516 bytes is no longer a linear function of message size.

The exploitation of cache affects the memory transfer rate. Therefore data were collected in two cases: hot cache, when the send and receive buffers are precharged in cache before invoking the communication system calls; cold cache, when the send and receive buffers are discharged from cache before invoking the communication system calls.

Our average estimates in the case of hot cache are:

- Latency: 18.4 μs

- Maximum Bandwidth: 9.91 MB/s, with messages sized 65536 bytes.

Instead, our estimates in the case of cold cache are:

- Latency: 28.7 μs

- Maximum Bandwidth: 9.83 MB/s, with messages sized 65536 bytes.

Figure 1 depicts the plot of throughput and bandwidth as a function of the message size in the case of

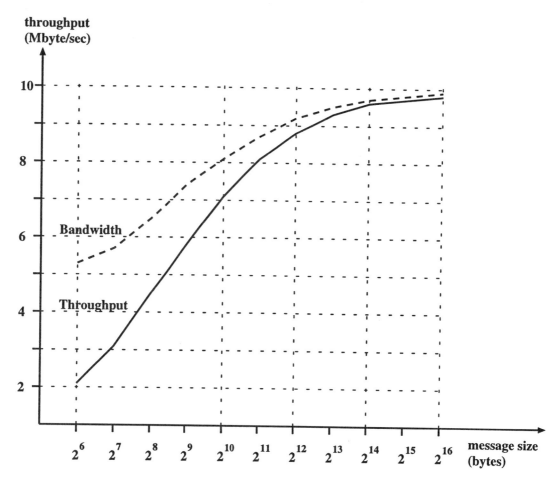

Figure1. Throughput and Bandwidth as a function of message size with hot cache.

Platform	Latency (μs)	Bandwidth (MByte/s)
100 Mb/s LAN, Linux TCP/IP sockets	275.6	3.4
100 Mb/s LAN, PARMA^2 PRP sockets	73.5	6.6
GAMMA cold cache	28.7	9.8
GAMMA hot cache	18.4	9.9
CM-5 CMMD	93.7	8.3
CM-5 CMAML	35.0	
SP2 MPL	44.8	34.9
T3D PVMFAST	30.0	25.1
U-net UAM ATM	35.5	14.8
U-net UAM Fast Ethernet	30.0	12.0

Table1. Ping-pong application: comparison of platforms.

hot cache. We observed that half the bandwidth is exploited already with messages as short as 32 bytes.

Using results provided by our collegues working on the PARMA^2 Project [3, Table 2.1] we can compare the performance of ping-pong on GAMMA with the performance of ping-pong on other platforms. Table 1 reports some of the results obtained by the PARMA^2 group in which the GAMMA results are integrated.

Like PARMA^2, GAMMA cannot compete with real parallel platforms in terms of bandwidth. However, in terms of pure message latency GAMMA provides a dramatic improvement compared to PARMA^2 and is quite competitive even compared to much more expensive parallel platforms. Of course comparing GAMMA performance to the performance of other platforms using MPI or CMMD is not completely fair since only an Active Message layer and not the whole MPI environment runs on GAMMA for the moment. However we do not expect the overhead of the MPI implementation over GAMMA to increase message latency in a substantial way. The comparisons with CM-5 CMAML and the U-net emulation of Active Messages [5] appear instead to be fair. In the case of U-net data are desumed from the cited paper and the hardware platform is constituted by 60 MHz SuperSPARCs connected by 140 MHz ATM.

5. Conclusions and Future Works

Our preliminary experimental results show an improvement of more than 4 times in short message delay as compared to PARMA^2 which in turn had already shown a substantial improvement (one order of magnitude) over the standard implementation of socket based inter-processor communication. These results suggest that with proper kernel support, MPI type communication primitives could show more than one order of magnitude improvement with respect to standard implementations on NOW platforms as currently provided by the best public domain products. Such improvement may suffice to make the use of inexpensive NOW platforms feasible and convenient with respect to expensive "commercial parallel platforms" for a large class of applications and with a fair number of processors.

Of course, our proposed NOW platform lacks one of the main requirements that a massively parallel architecture must consider, namely scalability with respect to the number of processing nodes. If we increase the number of processing nodes in GAMMA sooner or later we will saturate the LAN bandwidth. This problem can be partly alleviated by the adoption of a switched Fast Ethernet, which provides dedicated, full-duplex 100Mb/s connections to each node. The cost of Fast Ethernet switches is now decreasing, and it will soon become an affordable off-the-shelf component, in substitution of traditional repeater hubs.

On the other hand, we think that the cost of the scalability characteristics of "real" parallel platforms such as the CM-5 (with its Fat Tree interconnection network) is hardly justified in the majority of applications where parallel processing would, in principle, make sense. Only very few special applications would really require (and therefore really be worth the current cost of) the scalability characteristics of a "real" parallel platform that a special purpose network can provide with respect to off-the-shelf LAN hardware technology.

This consideration leaves space for a trade-off between the scalability of a parallel machine and the low cost and reasonably good performance of standard LAN hardware provided that the performance of the LAN hardware is not fully wasted by inefficient layers of software.

In conclusion, we think that the preliminary results of our experiment are quite encouraging and that it surely makes sense to propose the inclusion of a small set of communication primitives, implemented according to an accurate, performance-oriented approach into a standard operating system kernel.

References

[1] Connection Machine CM-5 Technical Summary. Technical report, Thinking Machines Corporation, Cambridge, Massachusetts, 1992.

[2] S. Pakin, M. Lauria, and A. Chien. High Performance Messaging on Workstations: Illinois Fast Messages (FM) for Myrinet Computation. In *Proc. Supercomputing '95*, San Diego, California, 1995. ACM Press.

[3] The Computer Engineering Group. *PARMA^2 Project: Parma PARallel MAchine*. Technical report, Dip. Ingegneria dell'Informazione, University of Parma, Oct. 1995.

[4] The Message Passing Interface Forum. MPI: A Message Passing Interface Standard. Technical report, University of Tennessee, Knoxville, Tennessee, 1995.

[5] T. von Eicken, A. Basu, V. Buch, and W. Vogels. U-Net: A User-Level Network Interface for Parallel and Distributed Computing. In *Proc. 15th ACM Symp. on Operating Systems Principles*, Copper Mountain, Colorado, Dec. 1995. ACM Press.

[6] T. von Eicken, D. Culler, S. Goldstein, and K. Schauser. Active Messages: A Mechanism for Integrated Communication and Computation. In *Proc. 19th Int. Symp. on Computer Architecture*, Gold Coast, Australia, May 1992. ACM Press.

[7] M. Welsh, A. Basu, and T. von Eicken. Low-latency Communication over Fast Ethernet. In *Proc. Euro-Par'96*, Lyon, France, Aug. 1996.

Swarm: Parallel Computing Using Lightweight Mobile Processes

Luciano de Errico
l.errico@cpdee.ufmg.br
Departamento de Engenharia Eletronica
Universidade Federal de Minas Gerais - Belo Horizonte (MG) - Brazil

Abstract

A recent trend has been the development of parallel processing environments for physically distributed hardware (e.g. networks of workstations). Existent solutions usually adopt a model where processes are fixed to the nodes and communicate by message-passing or shared-memory. This paper describes Swarm, a parallel architecture based on lightweight processes that can move and execute concurrently on different nodes. Each node is capable of permanently storing arbitrary information and references to other nodes, permitting the creation of persistent and distributed data structures. The main advantage is a flexible programming environment, which combines characteristics of the message-passing and distributed shared-memory approaches. A prototype of the architecture was implemented in a UNIX environment to evaluate the processing model. Preliminary results showed a communication time comparable to remote procedure call (RPC).

1. Introduction

The constant improvement in the cost/performance ratio of workstations, and the availability of high-speed communication networks in recent years, motivated the development of different solutions for parallel processing on physically distributed systems. Some adopt a more direct approach, using message-passing. Others offer more abstract environments, with different levels of support for data sharing and coordination of parallel processes. **Agent-based processing** is one technique that combines many of the advantageous features of these approaches. In this context, an **agent** is a lightweight mobile process that can freely move in the network and execute when it reaches a processing node. This technique completely includes message-passing, adding support for remote execution, and offers a shared data space that naturally maps on the underlying distributed system.

Agent-based processing has already been used in extremely loosely-coupled environments like the Internet (e.g. the Telescript™ package [20]). This paper describes an experimentation with the concept of agent-based processing targeting moderately- and tightly-coupled environments (e.g. LANs and multicomputers). A parallel architecture named Swarm was developed and a corresponding prototype was implemented to evaluate the processing model. Preliminary results showed a communication time which is in the same order of magnitude of remote procedure call (RPC) but is independent of the amount of data transported. This text presents these results, discusses advantages and disadvantages of the model and compares it to other paradigms for parallel processing in distributed systems.

2. Distributed parallel processing

A **distributed parallel processing (DPP)** system is one that permits parallelism within single applications, but executes on a physically distributed environment. The preferred paradigms for DPP have been message-passing and distributed shared-memory. The message-passing approach [9,11] has the advantage of mapping easily on the physical structure of the system (i.e. a number of processing units connected by a communication network). However it imposes a specific programming style, as there is no common address space and the application must be divided into distinct modules that communicate and synchronise by exchanging messages. In practice, this makes passing of complex data structures and migration of processes more difficult, as all information must be transferred to the requesting point instead of just passing a reference.

Shared-memory systems offer a programming interface closer to the one found in conventional computing environments and are, therefore, considered easier to use. However, in multicomputers and distributed systems there is no global memory, but a set of disjoint address spaces, each one belonging to a different autonomous computer. In this case, a software layer must simulate the effect of a distributed shared memory (DSM). Different DSM solutions may adopt different sharing schemes: a global virtual memory with pages distributed among the computers [14]; annotated shared variables, protected by critical regions [4]; or data structures that combine shared access and synchronisation [6,2,3]. Stumm and Zhou [19] analysed several implementations of DSM and concluded that their performance is sensitive to the shared memory access behaviour of the applications, and that no single analysed DSM algorithm is suitable for most applications.

A different approach to DPP is to fix bulky data and move processes or threads. Borrowing a term from the artificial intelligence (AI) area, the mobile process is known as an **agent**. In AI, an agent is a computational entity that can perform a number of actions in the system, on behalf of its user [16]. In the context discussed here, an agent is a process that can move from a computing node to another, carrying its state (program counter, status bits, register contents, and, in some cases, code) and executing when reaching each destination. The immediate advantage of this **agent-based** approach is the elimination of remote data accesses, which becomes relevant if the amount of data to be moved is big or very distributed. A second advantage is increased flexibility, as execution can be moved to a more adequate location, e.g. one that holds the necessary information or is under light loading at the moment. The main disadvantage of this approach is that it can become inefficient if the state of the moving process is large or if the amount of data to be accessed is relatively small. Therefore, two main design issues are the minimisation of the state to be moved and the distribution of the data.

Experiences with lightweight computation migration [12], in the context of operating systems, demonstrate that this new mechanism can outperform remote procedure call (RPC) and message-passing for different applications, and could be an efficient alternative to distributed shared memory (DSM). Supporting this argument, the work with Active Messages [7] proves that remote execution can be implemented in a very efficient way. The Emerald system [13] provides an example of use of mobility in distributed processing. Emerald is an *object-based* system that supports *passive* (data + methods) and *active* objects (data + methods + a process). Active objects can make invocations on other objects, and any object can be moved to make the invocation a local operation.

More recently, mobile processes have been used for processing in the Internet. The General Magic Telescript[TM] system [20,10] is based on agents, described as mobile objects that carry data and procedures. The agent executes at its destination, obtaining data, and returns to its point of origin, delivering the information. Parallel processing is not the main issue here, as the Telescript system focus on flexible and safe distributed processing in the Internet, using remote execution as the basic mechanism.

An alternative agent-based model is used in the Wave system [17,18], which combines agents with a structured and shared data space. Wave manages a persistent data space in the form of a semantic network, where nodes represent concepts or entities and links represent relations. Agents are called **waves** and can move from one node to another, guided by a pattern-matching mechanism. Waves execute when arriving at a node, modifying private (wave owned) data and nodal data. Before leaving a node the wave specifies a combination of links and node identifiers, and each node that satisfies that pattern receives a copy of the original wave. The corresponding language includes primitives to control the *spatial* execution of waves and to modify the persistent data space. A prototype implementation of Wave for UNIX systems, using TCP/IP protocols, has been produced [5,18] and tested in LANs, WANs and in the Internet, proving that the concept is feasible.

3. The Swarm architecture

Swarm [8] is an architecture for distributed parallel processing based on mobile agents. It was conceived as a vehicle for exploratory research into agent-based parallel processing, improving the principles introduced in the Wave system. Differently from Wave, Swarm reduces the level of abstraction to a point where it simplifies the implementation and suits generic processing (either symbolic or numeric). Instead of directly providing a user language layer for interface, the objective was to define a simple and clear **base layer**, for implementation of end-user languages and interfaces, or to provide the basic organisation for a hardware or mixed hardware/software implementation (e.g. for a MIMD parallel computer).

3.1. Execution model

Swarm relies on two elements: **nodes** and **agents**.
- Data is organised using **nodes**. Each **node** is a persistent (i.e. has a lifetime independent from the lifetime of the program that created it) passive object that can store arbitrary data and *links*

(references) to other nodes. Nodes are distributed throughout an abstract environment known as the **nspace.** Links can have a *label* (as a *weight* or a *name*) and, using nodes and links as building blocks, the user can create arbitrary distributed data structures in the nspace.

- Processing is accomplished by **agents**. An **agent** is a volatile active object, a mobile process that carries its own state. Agents are free to move in the nspace and, once at a node, the agent executes its instructions and has read and write access to both its own data and the nodal data. Each agent can dynamically *spawn* new agents and the simultaneous execution of many agents at different nodes provides the parallelism.

Note that Swarm is not *object-oriented* or *object-based*, and nodes do not store any procedure or method to manipulate data. Swarm is *process-oriented*, with agents (mobile processes) that execute a user-defined program. Agents communicate by sharing data stored in the nodes and represent different *threads* of execution in a heavyweight process known as a **task**. Execution starts by creating a task, that *injects* one or more agents in the nspace. When the agent reaches its destination node, it can execute (accessing both nodal and agent data) and then be killed, suspended or spawned. Spawning produces one copy of the agent for each destination node as specified by the executing program. Agents move asynchronously in the nspace and, if more than one agent arrives at the same node, they will queue for execution (in a *monitor*-style synchronisation). A task terminates when no more active agents exist in the nspace or the task is aborted (by the program or the user).

Spawning is the basic primitive for agent mobility in Swarm. Agents can spawn to nodes whose IDs are statically defined by the user or are dynamically collected by the agent during its processing. Each time an agent starts execution in a node, a special structure called *destination list* is emptied. Using direct access, the agent obtains the node ID from the executing program or from data stored in nodes, and appends it to the destination list. Using associative access, the agent can search the nspace for nodes that match a given **key** or search the current node links looking for a particular **link label**. The result is node IDs that can be appended to the destination list, defining the destinations on spawning.

3.2. Organisation

Supporting its agent-based model, Swarm adopts a loosely-coupled organisation named **Swarm Abstract Machine (SAM)**, structured as a collection of **Processing Modules** (PMs) interconnected by an asynchronous communication network (Figure 1.a). Each PM corresponds to a *processor element* of the parallel virtual machine and manages a number of Swarm nodes. A Swarm node is known here as a **data node**. Each data node is uniquely identified by a fixed, system-defined **address** (the node ID), which determines the PM where the node is located. Additionally, a data node has a user-defined **key**, for associative access inside the PM.

Extra structures can be present in the SAM to accommodate special operations. **Service nodes** must be created by the executing task to provide access to services like terminal windows, files or the underlying operating system. A Swarm machine executes tasks started via the **Access Point**, a special PM with a single node (**console node**) that provides console I/O for the task. When there is no task executing, the AP also permits re-configuration of the Swarm machine (by addition or deletion of nodes and PMs). A **root node** is available on each PM, permitting the creation of data nodes when the PM is *empty* (i.e. the PM holds no data nodes). Root nodes are automatically created with the respective PMs, continue to exist as long as the PM exists and cannot be destroyed.

The agent structure and the generic instruction format of the Swarm machine are shown in Figure 1.b. The Swarm architecture adopts a RISC-style instruction set, with additional support for access to built-in structures and coordination of multi-agent execution. The architecture supports 32-bit data and provides load/store, integer arithmetic, comparisons, bitwise boolean, and common control (branches and jumps) operations. Special instructions permit to spawn, stop or suspend agents, to create and destroy nodes, and to manipulate nodal links and PM directories. The agent workspace is used as a bank of registers and data must be moved to it (from nodal workspaces) for manipulation. Parallel applications can be developed directly in this machine language or indirectly, by compilation of a high level language. Agents can be suspended, by program control or by the system (e.g. because it executed a slow I/O operation in a service node). Mutual exclusion is automatic, as only one agent can be active in a specific node at each time. Conditional synchronisation is achieved by suspending agents on a numbered event and re-scheduling them when another agent signalises that event.

The mapping of nodes to PMs facilitates implementation in terms of scheduling, load distribution and task termination detection. The alternative approach, with each node representing a processor element, would be impractical in most of the cases, giving that typical applications are expected to have thousands or more nodes. As node addresses are PM-relative, PMs can be moved around the system (e.g. to improve load balance)

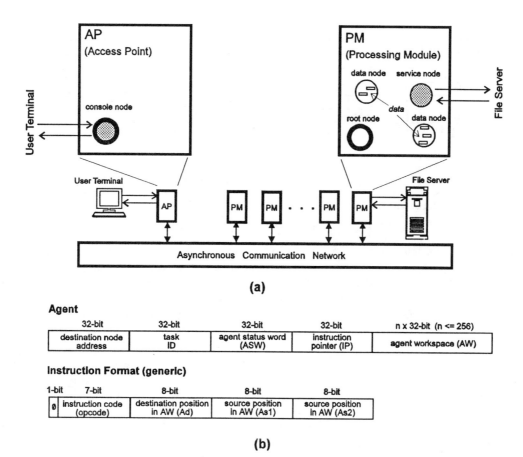

(a)

Agent

32-bit	32-bit	32-bit	32-bit	n x 32-bit (n <= 256)
destination node address	task ID	agent status word (ASW)	instruction pointer (IP)	agent workspace (AW)

Instruction Format (generic)

1-bit	7-bit	8-bit	8-bit	8-bit
0	instruction code (opcode)	destination position in AW (Ad)	source position In AW (As1)	source position in AW (As2)

(b)

Figure 1 - Swarm Abstract Machine: (a) organisation (b) agent structure and generic instruction format

without affecting the links between nodes. The PMs are also responsible for the termination detection of the task. An executing task finishes when all of its agents terminate. Giving the asynchronous model of execution adopted in Swarm, this detection would be an extra burden to the programmer in many applications. The system then provides termination detection by having each PM monitoring its local nodes and, according to a distributed termination detection algorithm, informing the user when no more activity exists.

4. Prototype implementation

For evaluation of the architecture, a prototype implementation of Swarm [8] was constructed in a UNIX environment (written in C language under SunOS v. 4.1.3), running in a single workstation. The asynchronous and non-deterministic nature of the architecture was preserved, as PMs (and the AP) were implemented as individual UNIX processes and agent routing was performed by a Routing Module (RM) connected to all PMs. Agents did not need to carry code, as the user program (in Swarm machine format) was cached in each PM before execution and interpreted

during task execution.

An example application [8] was developed and used for a first evaluation of the prototype. The application consisted in a program for reservation of a path, of specific bandwidth value, between two given nodes in a communication network of arbitrary topology. The program was executed for a network of 10 nodes using two different mappings of nodes to PMs. The main functions of the Swarm prototype were exercised and traced, validating their correct operation. Although absolute performance was not the main consideration when developing the prototype, additional performance tests were executed to determine the execution costs of the main Swarm functions and identify possible points for improvement. Each test program was executed three times in a lightly loaded Sun SPARCStation IPX (Sun 4 architecture, 40 MHz SPARC processor) and the results were averaged. The obtained transfer times for agents of different sizes can be seen in Figure 2, showing that the time required to route an agent was almost independent from the size of the agent workspace (an increase of 4% in time from the minimum to the maximum size). The average transfer time was 1.50 ms/agent. As a comparison, a null RPC executed under similar

agents routed	10,000 agents											
AW size	2				128				256			
module	AP	PM	RM	all	AP	PM	RM	all	AP	PM	RM	all
init	2	2	2	6	2	3	2	7	3	2	2	7
exec	301	262	313	876	302	255	327	884	289	252	368	909
term	0	1	0	1	0	1	1	2	0	0	0	0
TOTAL	303	265	315	883	304	259	330	893	292	254	370	916

AW size = size of the workspace carried by the agent (in number of 32-bit words)
init = task initialisation time (cpu time in ticks, 1 tick = 1/60 second)
exec = task execution time (cpu time in ticks, 1 tick = 1/60 second)
term = task termination time (cpu time in ticks, 1 tick = 1/60 second)
TOTAL = total task time for the module (cpu time in ticks, 1 tick = 1/60 second)

Figure 2 - Results of communication tests

conditions in the same machine produced a round-trip delay of 1.83 ms.

The tests also showed an average instruction execution time of 7.87 μs and a node creation time of 500 μs/node [8]. The average instruction execution time was two orders of magnitude greater than the best execution time of a machine instruction by the physical processor (25 ns for the 40 MHz SPARC processor), showing the impact of interpretation of each virtual machine instruction.. Comparing the figures of average instruction execution time and agent transfer time, a communication/computation ratio of 190 was obtained (1.50 ms/7.87 μs). As the longest program segments between two spawnings in the example application (bandwidth reservation program) have approximately 20 instructions, the program execution time in this example was dominated by communication. Node creation time also revealed to be two orders of magnitude slower than the average execution time for instructions, as consequence of the number of UNIX system calls made to allocate memory for the new node.

5. Discussion

Swarm was conceived as a study in the use of agent-based approaching for the development of a distributed parallel processing (DPP) programming environment. In contrast to most of the existing DPP environments, Swarm does not target the end-user and, thus, does not offer a high-level interface. Instead, the idea behind Swarm is to provide a base layer (with a reduced set of primitive operations and objects) that can be used for further development of user-level languages or interfaces for DPP, or even serve as basis for the design of massively parallel machines.

The two most distinctive aspects of the Swarm architecture are the use of agents and the way its shared data space is structured. Agents provide a more powerful mechanism than common message-passing, as not only

can they carry data but process state as well. The Swarm approach was inherited from the one used in the Wave system and improved for easier implementation. Swarm implements agents in a way that requires minimum storage and results in small overhead both for communication and for processing. Emerald offers a more flexible environment where both processes and data are mobile. It has, however, to rely heavily on compile-time optimisations and its basic mechanisms (like use of synchronous RPCs for interprocess communication) makes the Emerald more suitable for distributed applications than for parallel processing [1]. Swarm can also be compared with the Telescript and Wave environments, which are more heavyweight and adequate for use in loosely-coupled, distributed processing instead of DPP. The abstraction provided by Swarm offers a type of *structured* data space, with nodes, links and PMs, that intentionally exposes some of the underlying structure. This implements a lower-level environment of primitive operations and building blocks than object-based environments [6,2,3], but permits more flexibility, which matches the idea of base layer discussed above.

Although more experimentation is still required, preliminary tests permitted to identify points for improvement. For instance, the average instruction time can be reduced by converting a source program into native code for execution. Direct translation to native code could also improve the agent transfer time, although in this case the overheads introduced by network protocols would still be present. Not surprisingly, communication appears to be a bottleneck, as showed by the execution characteristics of the example program. One option is to adopt more efficient communication mechanisms, like the Active Messages [7,15] which adapts well to the implementation approach used in the Swarm prototype. Optimisations are also necessary in the internal memory allocation routines, in order to reduce the node creation time, and further testing is still necessary to better characterise the operation of the prototype. Nevertheless the results were promising, specially considering that the prototype was non-optmised and adopted code interpretation.

In terms of possible applications, the processing model currently implemented in the Swarm architecture appears to naturally support irregular and distributed data structures where a great number of small sequences of actions should be executed simultaneously at different nodes. These characteristics match applications like relational and network databases, knowledge-based processing and artificial intelligence systems (in special, parallel logic languages or rule-based systems). Scientific and engineering applications that model irregular structures (graph-like) may also benefit from the processing environment offered by Swarm. The intrinsic mobility of agents may be used in distributed simulations or in a support layer for intelligent communication networks and mobile communication networks. Finally, agent-based processing is a promising form of processing for WANs and the Internet, as already in use by some pioneering works. The Swarm architecture may be extended to cover these environments, providing a bridge for parallel processing in parallel machines, LAN networks, and larger domains of internetworked machines.

Acknowledgements

The author would like to acknowledge the CAPES Brazilian agency (grant no. 2533/91-8) for providing a Ph.D. scholarship, Chris Jesshope for his supervision throughout this research, and Paul Connoly and V. Muchnick for the many clarifying discussions.

References

[1] BAL, H.E. (1992) A Comparative Study of Five Parallel Programming Languages. In: *Future Generation Computer Systems*, July, 8(1-3):121-135.

[2] BAL, H.E., KAASHOEK, M.F. and TANENBAUM, A.S. (1992) Orca: A Language for Parallel Programming of Distributed Systems. In: *IEEE Trans. on Software Eng.*, March, 18(3):190-205.

[3] BAL, H.E. and KAASHOEK, M.F. (1993) Object Distribution in Orca using Compile-Time and Run-Time Techniques. In: *SIGPLAN Not.*, October, 28(10):162-177.

[4] BENNET, J.K., CARTER, J.B. and ZWAENEPOEL, W. (1990) Munin: Distributed Shared Memory Based on Type-Specific Memory Coherence. In: *SIGPLAN Not.*, March, 25(3):168-176.

[5] BORST, P.M. (1992) *The First Implementation of the WAVE System for UNIX and TCP/IP Computer Networks* (Tech. Rep. no 18/92), Dept. of Informatics, Univ. of Karlsruhe, Germany.

[6] CARRIERO, N. and GELERNTER, D. (1989) Linda in Context. In: *Comm. of the ACM*, April, 32(4):444-458.

[7] Von EICKEN, T., CULLER, D.E., GOLDSTEIN, S.C. and SCHAUSER, K.E. (1992) Active Messages: A Mechanism for Integrated Communication and Computation. In: *Computer Architecture. News*, May, 20(2):256-266.

[8] ERRICO, L. (1996) *Agent-Based Distributed Parallel Processing*. Ph.D. Thesis, Dept. of Electronic and Electrical Eng., Univ. of Surrey, UK.

[9] GEIST A., BEGUELIN, A., DONGARRA, J., JIANG, W., MANCHEK, R. and SUNDERAM, V. (1994) *PVM: Parallel Virtual Machine - Users' Guide*, MIT Press, Cambridge.

[10] GENERAL MAGIC (1995) *Telescript Programming Guide*, version 1.0 Alpha, General Magic, Sunnyvale.

[11] GROPP, W., LUSK, E. and SKJELLUM, A. (1994) *Using MPI: Portable Parallel Programming with the Message-Passing Interface*, MIT Press, Cambridge.

[12] HSIEH, W.C., WANG, P. and WEIHL, W.E. (1993) Computation Migration: Enhancing Locality for Distributed-Memory Parallel Systems. In: *Proc. 4th ACM SIGPLAN Symp. on Principles and Practice of Parallel Programming* (San Diego, USA, May), ACM, New York, pp. 239-248.

[13] JUL, E., LEVY, H., HUTCHINSON, N. and BLACK, A. (1988) Fine-Grained Mobility in the Emerald System. In: *ACM Trans. on Comp. Systems*, February, 6(1):109-133.

[14] LI, K. (1988) IVY: A Shared Virtual Memory System for Parallel Computing. In: *Proc. Intl. Conf. on Parallel Processing - vol. 2* (Univ. Park, USA, August), Pennsylvania State Univ., Univ. Park, pp. 94-101.

[15] MAINWARING, A. and CULLER, D. (1995) *Active Messages: Organization and Applications Programming Interface* (Tech. Rep.), Computer Science Division, Univ. of California at Berkeley, USA.

[16] RIECKEN, D. (1994) M: An Architecture of Integrated Agents. In: *Comm. of the ACM*, July, 37(7):107-116.

[17] SAPATY, P.S. (1992) *The WAVE Paradigm* (Tech. Rep. No 17/92), Dept. of Informatics, Univ. of Karlsruhe, Germany.

[18] SAPATY, P.S. and BORST, P.M. (1994) *An Overview of the WAVE Language and System for Distributed Processing in Open Networks* (Tech. Rep.), Dept. of Electronic and Electrical Eng., Univ. of Surrey, UK.

[19] STUMM, M. and ZHOU, S. (1990) Algorithms Implementing Distributed Shared Memory. In: *IEEE Computer*, May, 23(5):54-64.

[20] WHITE, J.E. (1994) *Telescript Technology: The Foundation for the Electronic Marketplace*, General Magic, Sunnyvale.

❖ SESSION 2 ❖

Architectures I

Chair

A. Antola

A Traffic-Balanced Interconnection Network for Multicomputers

M. Ould-Khaoua, R. Sotudeh

Electronic & computer Engineering Division
University of Teesside
Middlesbrough TS1 3BA, UK.

L.M. Mackenzie

Department of Computing Science
University of Glasgow
Glasgow G12 8QQ, UK.

Abstract

Router structure greatly influences overall network performance. Two general hardware models for the processor-router interface have been identified in the literature: the Multiple-Accepting Model (MAM) and the Single-Accepting Model (SAM). In the former, a router can remove several messages from the network simultaneously, while in the latter it can remove only one message at a time. The binary n-cube and 2-dimensional mesh are probably the most widely used multicomputer networks to date. The former, where the major traffic bottleneck is at the routers, cannot take advantage of its rich connectivity unless it uses MAM, resulting in an expensive implementation, while the latter benefits little from MAM, since the bottleneck is in the network channels. This paper examines a recently proposed class of multi-dimensional networks, called Distributed Crossbar Switch Hypermeshes (DCSH) which have many desirable topological properties, and shows that the DCSH obtains maximal performance benefit from either the SAM or MAM interface. This is due to the fact that the DCSH can balance more efficiently the traffic between the processors and the network than either the binary n-cube or the 2-dimensional mesh.

Keywords: Interconnection Network, Hypermesh, Mesh, Binary *n*-cube, Latency, Performance Analysis.

1. Introduction

The success of large-scale message-passing multicomputers is highly dependent on the efficiency of their underlying interconnection networks, which are constructed from routers and channels [5, 10, 18]. The routers are responsible for moving data between the processing nodes across the channels. Network performance is influenced by a number of factors, notably *topology, switching method,* and *router interface.*

The network topology defines the way nodes are connected and includes characteristics such as the *degree* and *diameter*: the degree is the maximum number of neighbours connected to a node; the diameter is the largest number of intermediate hops required to cross the network. Ideally, a network topology should have a small degree and a low diameter, and a variety of topologies have been suggested with the aspiration of approaching these goals [4, 7, 16, 21].

In practice, implementation technology places bandwidth constraints on network channels [1, 5]. As a result, a message is broken into several *phits* (i.e. words), each of which is transferred in one cycle. The switching method determines the way by which message phits visit intermediate routers. In *message switching*, a message is buffered at each intermediate router. *Virtual cut-through* [8] and *wormhole routing* [19] allow a message to progress without buffering at an intermediate router if the required channel is not busy. However, in virtual cut-through, an entire message is queued at the router when the channel is busy, while in wormhole routing, it remains spread over multiple channels.

The router interface also affects network performance [1, 17]. Two general hardware models have been identified in the literature which, following the terminology of Abraham & Padmanabhan [1], are referred to as the *multiple-accepting model* (MAM) and *single-accepting model* (SAM). In the former, the router can remove several messages simultaneously from the network while in the latter it can remove only one at a time. In practice, a SAM router would have a single local channel to its local processor while a MAM router would have parallel channels that can transfer several messages simultaneously to the local processor.

SAM is cheaper to implement, and thus has been more widely used in practical systems, including the Cosmic Cube [18], iPSC/2 [13], and Symult 2010 [20].

The binary n-cube (or cube for short) and the 2-dimensional mesh (or mesh for short) have been popular networks for both commercial and experimental multicomputers. For instance, the former is used in the N-cube [12], iPSC/2 [13], and Cosmic Cube [18], while the latter was used in the Symult 2010 [20], Stanford Dash Multiprocessor [10], and iWarp [17].

Common multicomputer network topologies, such as the cube and mesh, can be formally modelled as *graphs* of the form $G(E,V)$, defined over a set of vertices V and a set of edges E. Each vertex typically represents a node, and each edge between two vertices represents a channel connecting the two nodes. A fundamental constraint of the graph model is that each edge joins *exactly* two vertices. If a network channel is permitted to connect any number of nodes, a new general and powerful class of topologies emerges. Using a graph-theoretical framework, members of this class can be modelled as *hypergraphs* [3], which are generalisations of the conventional graph in which individual edges are able to join an arbitrary number of vertices.

The *hypermesh* is a regular k-ary n-dimensional hypergraph which has $N = k^n$ nodes, and is a *Cartesian* n-product of a fundamental *cluster*, consisting of k nodes that are directly connected [20]. A network of this kind has extremely desirable properties [16, 21, 22]. Firstly, its diameter grows much more slowly as the system size is scaled up, compared to most graph networks. Secondly, it can host applications that map naturally on meshes, tori, and cubes. Thirdly, it can realise all SIMD permutations of multi-stage networks. Finally, it is effective at important collective communication, such as broadcast and multicast.

The Distributed Crossbar Switch Hypermesh (DCSH), have be shown to possess several desirable topological and performance advantages over common topologies, including the cube and mesh, taking into account implementation cost in various technologies (e.g. VLSI [5] and multiple-chip technology [1]) [14, 15, 16]. This paper investigates, using realistic queueing models, the impact of the router interface on the performance of the DCSH, cube, and mesh. The results, presented here, show that owing to its topological properties, the DCSH achieves the most effective balance of traffic between the processors and the network.

The rest of the paper is organised as follows. Section 2 describes the DCSH. Section 3 outlines queueing models for the DCSH, cube, and mesh.

Section 4 analyses the impact of the MAM and SAM on the performance of the three networks. Finally, Section 5 draws some conclusion from this comparative study.

2. Distributed Crossbar Switch Hypermesh (DCSH)

There are many possible ways to implement the hypermesh, typical example being the *spanning-bus hypercube*, proposed by Wittie [23], where nodes in a given dimension are connected by means of a shared-bus. Other hypermeshes are based on either crossbar switches [7] or complete-connections [4]. All these implementations, however, suffer from bandwidth limitations as system size scales.

A hypermesh implementation called the Distributed Crossbar Switch Hypermesh (DCSH), has been proposed in [11, 16] as part of the COBRA Project at the University of Glasgow [11]; this project aims to construct a hypermesh-based multicomputer using currently-available electronic technology. Low-dimensional versions of the DCSH (i.e. $n=2$ or 3) can be constructed using a layered implementation that alleviates the most critical bandwidth constraints. Instead of integrating one or more complete nodes on a single chip, the layered implementation separates processing and switching functions into physical layers, thereby increasing the available wiring density and reducing the pin-out requirements. Furthermore, the DCSH has better topological properties and latency characteristics than existing networks [14, 15].

The 1-dimensional DCSH, referred to as a *cluster*, is a hypergraph consisting of k nodes connected by a *distributed crossbar switch*; the multiplexing/demultiplexing functions of the conventional "centralised" crossbar switch are performed in the SEs. Fig. 1 depicts the basic structure of a cluster. Every node possesses a uniquely owned channel that connects it to the other k-1 nodes in the cluster. At each of these k-1 destinations, there is a $(k$-1)-to-1 multiplexer with buffered inputs.

A k-ary n-dimensional DCSH, is a regular hypergraph with $N = k^n$ nodes, formed by taking the *Cartesian* n-product of the cluster topology. This has the effect of imposing the cluster organisation in every dimension, making each node equally a member of n independent orthogonal clusters. When $k = 2$, the DCSH reduces to a cube.

Let dimensions be numbered n-1, ..., 0. A node, v, can then be labelled by an $n \times 1$ address vector with v_i being the node's position in its dimension i cluster. Each node is connected to $n(k$-1) other nodes with

94

which it differs in only one address digit, i.e.
$v = v_{n-1}...v_{i+1}v_iv_{i-1}...v_0$ is connected to
$v' = v_{n-1}...v_{i+1}v'_iv_{i-1}...v_0$ for all $0 \leq i \leq n-1$,
$0 \leq v_i, v'_i \leq k-1$ and $v_i \neq v'_i$.

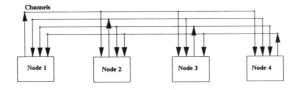

Fig. 1: A DCSH Cluster.

3. Analysis

This section outlines the models for the DCSH, cube, and mesh. Detailed derivations and validation through simulation can be found in [16]. The following assumptions have been made.

a) Messages are transmitted between routers using virtual cut-through.

b) Restricted routing [6], where messages visit network dimensions in a strict order, is used to avoid deadlock situations in the DCSH, cube, and mesh. Using restricted routing results in simpler and faster routers compared to adaptive routing strategies [10, 12, 13]. The results presented here, however, can equally be applied to the other routing schemes.

c) Message destinations are uniformly distributed. This assumption is widely used in the literature as it greatly simplifies the analysis. Although many evaluation studies assume that uniform traffic, it is not always a true reflection of reality. There are, for example, many parallel applications that exhibit communication locality. Nonetheless, there are situations where the assumption is justifiable. For instance, there have recently been several attempts to implement a shared-memory model on multicomputers because it provides a programming model which can be easier to exploit than message-passing [10]. In this model, practices such as memory interleaving and distributed software-tree implementations of barrier-synchronisation tend to spread access uniformly over all nodes [2].

d) A node generates a message independently of any other node with a probability m in a cycle.

e) Messages are B phits long. Each phit requires one cycle transmission time.

f) Message queues are assumed to have infinite

capacity. Simulation experiments show that the assumption of infinite buffering is realistic under uniform traffic [1, 2, 16]. As few as three (or four) message buffers at each queue can provide performance approaching that for infinite buffers. The network operates in traffic regions where channel utilisation is moderate (<80%), so only a few buffers are ever occupied. The performance regions close to 100% utilisation should be avoided in any case as message latency becomes extremely long. Realistic finite-buffer analyses are generally computationally intensive, and infinite-buffer analyses are a reasonable compromise.

g) The router's pipelining time is one cycle (i.e. it takes one cycle to move a phit from one queue to another inside the router). Delays due to the pipelining time have less impact on performance when virtual cut-through is used compared wormhole routing [16].

3.1. The DCSH

Fig. 2 shows the router structure in an *n*-dimensional DCSH. Buffers are provided at both input and output of the router. Messages generated from the local processor are copied into one of the n output queues associated with the required output channel. There is also one $(k-1)$-to-1 multiplexer per dimension. At each data input of multiplexer i $(1 \leq i \leq n)$, there is a queue for messages coming from node j $(1 \leq j \leq n, j \neq i)$ at dimension i. An input queue consists of message buffers each of which has enough storage to temporarily hold an entire message (header plus data phits) if the required channel is busy

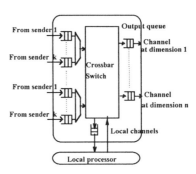

Fig. 2: Router structure with SAM in the DCSH.

The model is derived using G/D/1 queueing theory [9]. The mean waiting time, w, at a G/D/1 queue, with l input streams of rates $r_1,...,r_l$ is given by

$$w = \frac{V}{2E(1-E)} - \frac{1}{2} \qquad (1)$$

where E and V are the expectation and variance of the arrival processes respectively, and are given by

$$E = \sum_{j=1..l} r_j \qquad (2)$$

$$= \sum_{j=1..l} r_j(1-r_j) \qquad (3)$$

The mean message latency, L (cycles), taking into account the mean waiting times at the different queues, can be written as

$$L = (1+w_m)a + (1+w_o)a + (1+w_l) + (B-1) \qquad (4)$$

where a, the average message distance, and is given by

$$a = n\frac{(k-1)}{k} \qquad (5)$$

and w_m, w_o, and w_l are the mean waiting times at the multiplexer, the output queue associated with a network channel, and the output queue associated with a local channel respectively. They are found to be

$$w_m = \frac{\rho B}{(1-\rho)}\frac{(k-2)}{(k-1)} \qquad (6)$$

$$w_o = \frac{(1-1/a)\rho B}{a(1-\rho)} \qquad (7)$$

$$w_l = \frac{(n-1)\rho B}{2a(1-n\rho/a)} \qquad (8)$$

with ρ being the traffic rate on network channels and its given by

$$\rho = \frac{ma}{n}B \qquad (9)$$

3.2 The Cube

As Fig. 3 shows, there is one buffer at each of a cube router as there is only one incoming network channel per dimension.

The latency for the cube is obtained by replacing $k = 2$ in all the above equations yielding

$$L = (1+w_o)a + (1+w_l) + (B-1) \qquad (10)$$

$$a = \frac{n}{2} \qquad (11)$$

$$w_o = \frac{2(n-2)\rho B}{(1-\rho)} \qquad (12)$$

$$w_l = \frac{(n-1)\rho B}{(1-2\rho)} \qquad (13)$$

$$\rho = \frac{m}{2}B \qquad (14)$$

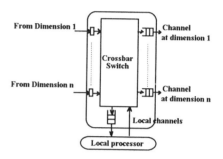

Fig. 3: Router Structure with SAM in the cube.

3.3 The Mesh

The router in the mesh is similar to that in the cube except that there is a network channel in each direction at a given dimension, as depicted by Fig. 4.

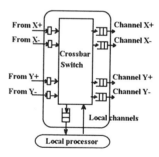

Fig. 4: Router structure with SAM in the mesh.

A model for a k^n node mesh with MAM has been described in [2]. Adding the mean waiting time at the output queue associated with the local channel gives the mean latency as

$$L = (1+w_o)na + (1+w_l) + (B-1) \qquad (15)$$

$$a = \frac{n}{3}(k-\frac{1}{k}) \qquad (16)$$

$$w_o = \frac{\rho}{2(1-\rho)}\frac{(a/n-1)}{a^2/n^2}\frac{(n+1)}{n}B \qquad (17)$$

$$w_l = \frac{(n-1)B\rho}{2d(1-n\rho/a)} \qquad (18)$$

$$\rho = \frac{m}{2n}aB \qquad (19)$$

4 Performance with SAM and MAM

The following discussion compares the effects of the two router hardware models on network performance. For illustration we will use a network size of 4096 nodes and a message length M=128 phits, typical figures for a large system with moderately sized messages, but the results shown are applicable across sizes and message lengths [1, 2, 5]. With this network size, the nodes can be configured as a 64^2, 8^3, 4^6 mesh or DCSH or a 2^{12} node cube. The performance results for n=3 are not presented as the conclusions are similar to those for n=2 and 4.

Fig. 5 (a)-(d) shows latency results for different DCSH configurations. The x-axis in the figures represents the rate at which a node injects messages into the network in messages per cycle. The y-axis gives the mean message latency to cross the network.

The results show that the relative merits of SAM and MAM depend on the dimensionality. As the dimensionality increases, the difference in performance between the two models gets larger. When the dimensionality is low ($n \leq 4$), the difference in the performance is small because the traffic rate on the network channels is comparable to that which enters/exits the network through the local channels. So MAM does not improve performance significantly since the saturation rate of the queue leading to the local processor is comparable to that of a typical output queue associated with a network channel. However, when the dimensionality is high (n=12), as in the cube topology, the difference is large since the traffic rate on output channels becomes lower than the traffic that enters/exits the network. The saturation rate of the output queue leading to the local processor is higher than that associated with a network channel. In the cube, the performance bottleneck is at the network-Processor interface and MAM removes this bottleneck, as has been pointed out in [1].

Fig. 6 shows that the mesh does not benefit from MAM. The bottleneck in the mesh is at its network channels due its simple interconnection pattern. Therefore, even if there existed technology that allowed cheaper implementation of complex routers with MAM, the mesh could not benefit from such technology.

Fig. 7 compares the performance of the 2-

dimensional DCSH to mesh and the cube for both SAM and MAM. The same conclusions are reached for the other DCSH cases. Although the cube has a higher number of channels than the DCSH, it cannot use them efficiently under a SAM regime and both networks saturate at the same traffic load. The cube cannot take advantage of its rich connectivity unless it employs MAM. This will require an expensive router as it has to provide a local channel for each dimension. The mesh has the worst performance since a message has to cross, on average, a large number of intermediate nodes before reaching its destination.

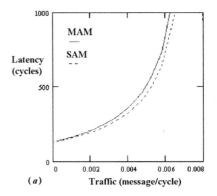

(a)

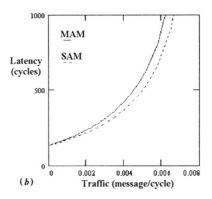

(b)

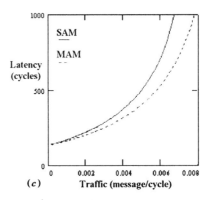

(c)

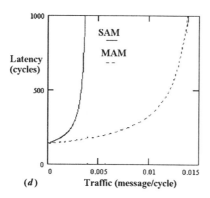

(d)

Fig. 5: Performance of the DCSH for different dimensions. a) *n*=2. b) *n*=4, c) *n*=6. d) *n*=12 (i.e. cube).

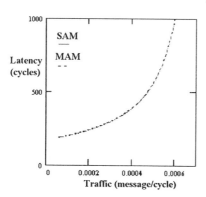

Fig. 6: Performance of the mesh.

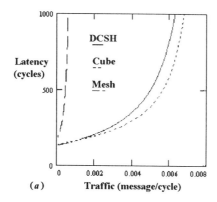

(a)

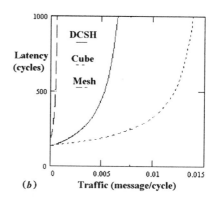

(b)

Fig. 7: Performance of the 2D DCSH, 12D cube, 2D mesh. a) SAM. b) MAM

5 Conclusions

The low-dimensional Distributed Crossbar Switch Hypermesh (DCSH) is a general and powerful structure, that encompasses the topological features of both the mesh and binary *n*-cube. This paper has shown that the DCSH can use routers with the Single-Accepting Model (SAM) that are less expensive to implement, yet still deliver the same performance as with the Multiple-Accepting Model (MAM). Thus the DCSH can efficiently balance the traffic between the processors and the network. The binary *n*-cube, however, has to use a MAM to take advantage of its connectivity. MAM requires costly routers, making the binary *n*-cube's implementation even more expensive than it already is because of its use of a large number of channels. Even if future implementation technology allows cheaper implementation of routers with MAM, the mesh cannot take advantage of such technology as it would not bring any performance benefits due to its inherent simple interconnect topology.

References

[1]   Abraham, S., Issues in the architecture of direct interconnection networks schemes for multiprocessors, Ph.D. thesis, Univ. of Illinois at Urbane-Champaign, 1990.

[2]   A. Agarwal, Limits on interconnection network performance, *IEEE Trans. Par. & Dist. Syst.* 2, 398-412, 1991.

[3]   C. Berge, Graphs and hypergraphs, North-Holland, 1977.

[4]   L.M. Bhuyan & P.D. Agarwal, Generalised

hypercube and hyperbus structures for a computer network, *IEEE Trans. Comp.* C33 (4), 1984, 323-333.

[5] W.J. Dally, Performance analysis of *k*-ary *n*-cubes interconnection networks, *IEEE Trans. Comp.* 39(6), 1990, 775-785.

[6] W.J. Dally, Deadlock-free message routing in multiprocessor interconnection Networks, *IEEE Trans. Comp.*, Vol. C-36(5), 1987, 547-553.

[7] W.K. Giloi & S. Montenegro, Choosing the interconnect of distributed-memory systems by cost and blocking behaviour, *IEEE Parallel Processing Symposium*, 1991, 438-444.

[8] P. Kermani & L. Kleinrock, Virtual cut-through: A new computer communication switching technique, *Computer Networks* 3, 1979, 267-286.

[9] L. Kleinrock, Queueing Systems, Vol. 1, John Wiley, New York, 1975.

[10] D. Lenoski *et al*, The Stanford DASH Multiprocessor, *IEEE Computer*, March 1992, 63-79

[11] L.M. Mackenzie *et al*, The COBRA Project: Alleviating the bandwidth constraints in large multicomputer networks, Tech-Rept R19/91, Comp. Sci. Dept., Glasgow University, Oct. 1991

[12] N-Cube Systems, *N-cube Handbook*, N-Cube, 1986.

[13] S.F. Nugent, The iPSC/2 direct-connect communication technology, *Proc. Conf. on Hypercube Concurrent Computers & Applications*, 1989, 51-60

[14] M. Ould-Khaoua & R. Sotudeh, Comparative Evaluation of Hypermesh and Mesh With Wormhole Routing, *Presented at the Euromico'95*, Como, Italy, Sept. 1995.

[15] M. Ould-Khaoua, L.M. Mackenzie, R. Sotudeh, Comparative Evaluation of Hypermesh and Multi-Stage Interconnection Networks, *The Computer Journal*, 39(3), 1996, 232-240.

[16] M. Ould-Khaoua, Hypergraph-based interconnection networks for large multicomputers, Ph.D. thesis, Comp. Sci. Dept., Glasgow University, 1994.

[17] C. Peterson *et al*, iWarp: a 100-MOPS VLIW microprocessor for multicomputers *IEEE Micro*, Vol. 11, No. 13, 1991, 26-37.

[18] C.L. Seitz, The Cosmic Cube, *Comm. ACM*, Vol 28, Jan. 1985, 22-33.

[19] C.L. Seitz *et al*, The hypercube communication chip, Dept. Comp. Sci., CalTech, Display File5182:DF:85, 1985.

[20] C.L. Seitz *et al*, The architecture and programming of the Ametek Series 2010 multiprocessor, *Proc. 3rd Conf. Hypercube Concurrent Comp. & Appl.*, 1988.

[21] T. Szymanski, Hyper-meshes: Optical Interconnection Networks for Parallel Processing, *J. Parallel & Distributed Computing* 26, January 1995, 1-26.

[22] N. Tanabe *et al*, Base-*m n*-cube: high performance interconnection networks for highly parallel computer PRODIGY, *Int. Conf. Parallel Processing*, 1991, 509-516.

[23] L.D. Wittie, Communication structures for large networks of microcomputers, *IEEE Trans. Comp.* C30 (4), 1981, 264-273.

Process Performance Optimization
in Fault Tolerant Multiprocessor Systems
after a Fault Occurrence

Peter Janík, Margaréta Kotočová
Slovak Technical University
Department of Computer Science and Engineering
Ilkovičova 3, 812 19 Bratislava
Slovak Republic
{janik, kotocova}@elf.stuba.sk

Abstract

In a fault-tolerant multiprocessor system each process in has its copy(ies) allocated on some other processor element(s). After a processor element fault occurrence and its detection, a reconfiguration kernel performs a reconfiguration. Each process that has been running on the faulty processor element is rebuilt and restarted on some other processor element, using its copy. The reconfiguration kernel has to determine which processor element is the most suitable for process rebuilding and restarting.

In this paper we present results of searching for an algorithm of an optimal reconfiguration, in the sense of lowest performance degradation, by means of the Coloured Petri Net (CPN) model. This model has been used to simulate a process run on a multiprocessor system and the reconfiguration of it after a processor fault. Different allocations have been tested to get a behaviour of performance degradation with different process and processor parameters.

Using the simulation results we have designed an algorithm for assigning processors to processes from the faulty processor.

1. Introduction

A fault tolerant multiprocessor system has to proceed in operation despite of fault. If a processor element becomes faulty, reconfiguration will reconfigure the system and each process allocated on the faulty processor element will continue on some other one. Therefore every process has to have at least one copy allocated on some other processor element. The copy will be used to rebuild the process in the reconfiguration after a processor element permanent fault.

The loss of a processor element - after a permanent fault - leads to a performance degradation. The level of degradation is influenced by suitability of process allocation during reconfiguration. Different allocations give different process performance after reconfiguration. A process can be rebuilt and restarted on a processor element it is placed on or its code can be moved to some other processor element that is more suitable for its rebuilding and restarting.

It is very important that processes allocated on a faulty processor element be rebuilt and restarted as fast as possible, especially in real time systems. The decision making has to be very fast and the algorithm very simple.

There are several approaches in the literature dealing with reconfiguration of multiprocessor systems and using the process allocation/reallocation technique for fault tolerance support. In [8] an Evolutionary Strategy is proposed based on the Genetic algorithm for finding process allocation after a processor element fault, running on a dedicated machine. A good solution can be found within minutes if the strategy is running on a single processor, and within seconds when executed on the PVM distributed system.

In [4] and [5] an approach is proposed for process evacuation after a processor element fault using an Evacuation Strategy with Evacuation Points (EP). They use a fault tolerant multitransputer system built on FT nodes with TMR features. After a processor element fault detection the application is evacuated from the faulty module to some spare one. EPs are predefined check points in the application in which the status of the module is checked and in which evacuation can take place. No evaluation of a module suitable for evacuation is performed.

Reference [9] proposes processor assignment using a repartitioning approach. Every application can request spare processors in the start time. After a processor fault occurs, spare processors are used for replacing faulty ones. If there are not enough spare processors, then a repartitioning algorithm takes place. This means that a new initial processor assignment is performed, and applications have to be booted again. No evaluation of processor assignment is executed.

A Fault Tolerant Multi-Transputer Architecture is described in [10]. Every application process has its copy placed on a neighbouring transputer. In the case of a transputer fault copy processes on neighbouring transputers are activated and started. No evaluation of processor suitability is done.

Reference [7] describes an experimental system which can be used to study and compare the behaviour of different process migration strategies for occam programs running on transputer machine.

It can be seen that most approaches do not consider the suitability of processor assignment for processes from a faulty processor. Only one of the previously mentioned approaches takes into account this problem, while the rest neglect it. The method based on the Evacuation Strategy is computationaly intensive and not so suitable for many applications.

In the present study we have attempted to develop a practical approach to reconfiguration in fault tolerant multiprocessor systems and assigning processors to processes from a faulty processor. We have designed an approach for investigating the suitability of different process allocations after reconfiguration and for finding a scheme which would give us some instructions as to how to assign processors to processes from a faulty processor with regard to performance degradation. The approach is based on simulating different process alocations by means of the Coloured Petri Net model. It is a model of a part of a multiprocessor system that will take part in the reconfiguration. One processor element becomes faulty and the reconfiguration takes place in the model. Performance is measured before and after reconfiguration. Different allocations of processes from a faulty processor after the reconfiguration have been tested

here. Simulations have shown that it is possible to find a scheme for assigning processors to processes from a faulty processor with regard to optimal performance degradation. The solution is optimal or close to an optimal one.

In the model presented herein we consider:
- processor element faults only, because a link or a switch fault is simpler to handle [2],
- during reconfiguration no further fault will occur,
- the multiprocessor system uses no spare hardware,
- processes are scheduled on the FIFO (first in - first out) principle,
- process communication is blocking (waiting for acknowledgement).

2. Model of a fault tolerant multiprocessor system

By a multiprocessor system we mean a loosely coupled MIMD multiprocessor system. It consists of processor elements (PEs, processors), communication links (links) and switches. Processes communicate by means of a message passing system. The system is fault tolerant and each process allocated on it (main process) has its copy (copy process) on some other processor. The copy - copy process - can be active (the process is running) or passive (as a stored code, supported by an actual process state updating). After a fault occurrence this copy will be used to rebuild the process and the system will be reconfigured.

A fault tolerant multiprocessor system possesses fault tolerant features - reconfiguration for fault tolerance and a reconfiguration kernel for fault tolerance [1], [2]. The reconfiguration for fault tolerance (*FT-reconfiguration*) helps to retain fault tolerant features of the system after a fault occurrence. It provides the multiprocessor system with a mechanism so that after a fault occurrence of some part of multiprocessor system guarantees that the system will be operational and without cancellation of any

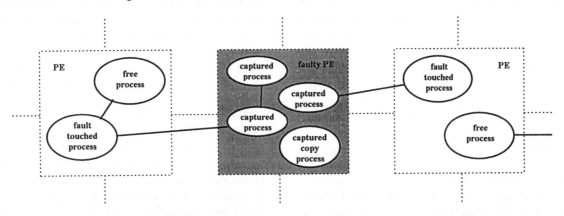

Figure 1. The process attributes after a processor element fault.

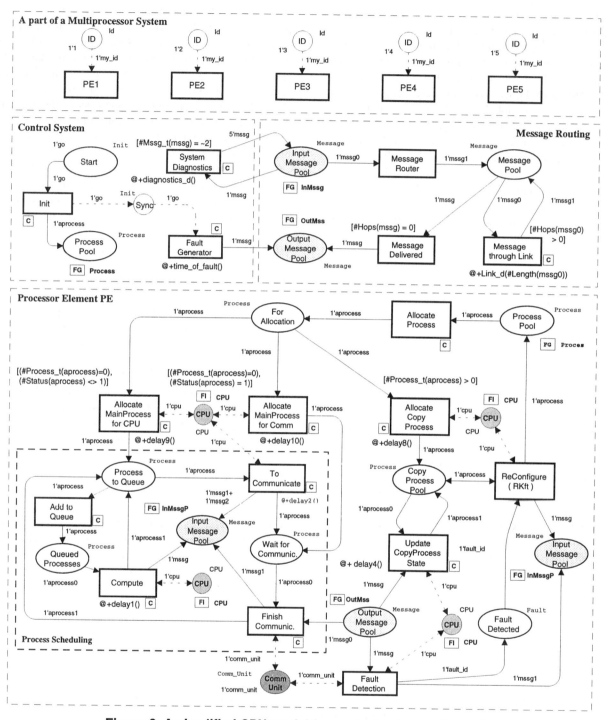

Figure 2. A simplified CPN model for analysis of reconfiguration

process.

Each process of the multiprocessor system, from the moment of a fault occurrence to the end of the reconfiguration process, gets a new attribute (Figure 1).

If a processor element PE has become faulty, then:
- each process allocated on the processor element PE is called a *captured process* (main and copy),

- each process, except captured ones, communicating with any captured process, is called a *fault-touched process*,
- each process, except captured ones, noncommunicating with any captured process, is called a *free process*.

A process communicating with a captured one is process that is either just communicating, either waiting for communication, or will be communicating in the future with the captured process.

The term "captured process" is taken to mean a captured main process unless it is explicitly stated to be a captured copy process.

3. CPN model of a reconfigurable fault tolerant multiprocessor system

The objective of our research is to find an optimal destination PEs for captured processes during reconfiguration with regard to performance degradation. For this purpose we have designed and built the Coloured Petri Net model of a part of a multiprocessor system that will take part in reconfiguration. It models:

- process scheduling for CPU and communication,
- process run and communication,
- a processor element fault,
- reconfiguration of captured processes.

The model has been described in [1] as well. It has been built in the Design/CPN environment (from Metasoft) for Coloured Petri Nets. A simplified version of the model is illustrated in the Figure 2.

The model consists of several parts, namely:

- Processor Element PE,
- Message Routing,
- Control System.

The body of a multiprocessor model is the Processor Element (PE, processor). The model consists of 5 identical PEs (at the top of Figure 2) that will take part in a reconfiguration. They can be placed into different parts of a multiprocessor system by specifying their distances - how many links a message has to route through. There can be up to 30 processes running on the processors, communicating among themselves. Processor elements perform multitasking with constant time slice.

Processes are scheduled for a CPU and communication in the Process Scheduling part of the PE illustrated in Figure 2. A process token from the place *Process to Queue* is added to the queue for CPU in the transition *Add to Queue* and then placed to the place *Queued Processes*. The token waits here for the CPU assignment. When the CPU token is available, the process token is removed from the queue and both tokens are occupied for a constant time slice intervals in the place *Compute*. During that time no other process can use the CPU. After the time slice interval the process token is descheduled and the next process token from the queue can use the CPU. The process token is placed again to the place *Process to Queue*. After several runs on the CPU, a process token requests another process token for communication, and sends that request in the

transition *To Communicate*. It waits while the other side is ready in the place *Wait for Communication*. When the requested process token is in the place *Process to Queue* (on any of 5 PEs) then it is moved to the place *Wait for Communication* through the transition *To Communicate* and the communication takes place. After finishing the communication, both process tokens are placed to the place *Process to Queue* and scheduled for the CPU or communication again.

The communication is performed by routing message tokens through a virtual interconnection network in the Message Routing System. Messages are delayed in he network proportionally to the message length and the number of links it has to route through.

In this manner, allocated processes compete for CPU and communication and create a task.

At a certain time instant, one of the processor elements fails - becomes faulty. The transition *Fault Generator* (Control System) injects a fault to a specified processor. The system diagnostics detects this state in the transition *System Diagnostics* and informs each processor about it. The *Fault Detection* transition informs the processor about this state and fires the *Reconfigure* transition (Reconfiguration Kernel for fault tolerance, RKft) which performs the reconfiguration. The reconfiguration kernel on each non-faulty processor begins the reconfiguration (not shown in the figure). Each captured process is rebuilt by initiating its copy process and a new copy process is created as well. To retain fault tolerant features each captured copy process is replaced by creating new one from its main process that is free or fault-touched. The reconfiguration is performed at a high priority and in parallel with the running of the rest of the system. Only copies of captured processes take part in the reconfiguration. After reconfiguration the system continues with the execution of the task.

This description of the present CPN model is very simplified because of space restrictions. The model is actually more complex, and some of transitions hide a hierarchy submodel.

All the parameters of the model, processes and communication, including process allocation and the reconfiguration scenario, are specified in the input parameter file for the model. That is, the reconfiguration scenario is given in advance, and all of the parameters of the processes and communication are specified before the run is started. By this manner it is possible to modify all parameters that can influence the choice of suitable destination PEs.

The initial process allocation is calculated before the simulation run, using the modified allocation optimization tool based on the Genetic algorithm [6].

We have simulated a model here that is similar to a transputer based multiprocessor by setting parameters in the input parameter file. It is possible, of course, to specify different parameters to make the model similar to other systems.

4. Theory of a process perfomance degradation after reconfiguration

In the present study we have attempted to find some suitable way to measure the performance of the system. References [11] and [12] propose some methods for performance evaluation, but many of them are problem specific. In our case it is useful to measure system performance by performance of the application. Therefore, the approach of process performance evaluation has been chosen, i.e. what the time process needs for executing a certain part of an application task.

The following theory has developed from experiences in many simulations, and has been step-by-step improved. First, we will define some useful terms that will be needed.

If two communicating sites are allocated on the same processor element, this kind of communication is considered *on-chip communication*. Otherwise it is considered *off-chip communication*. The on-chip communication takes 0 time units.

We will suppose:

- every process needs only two resources - a CPU and communication,
- every processor element has enough free communication capacity to carry some extra communication due to reconfiguration,
- processes running on processor elements are allocated with regard to optimization of CPU and communication needs,
- processes are scheduled for CPU on the FIFO principle,
- processes run continuously,
- every process has one copy.

If a process is reconfigured then it is placed on a destination PE. Processes allocated on the destination PE will have to share the PE's resources and the new process will have to compete for them.

A process waits for resources (CPU, communication) and is characterized by the parameters AWT_{CPU} and AWT_{com} - the average waiting time for CPU and communication, respectively.

The time, t^b_i, that the process P_i has spent on a processor element PE until a fault occurrence, is:

$$t^b_i = (AWT^b_{CPUi} + T_{ts}) \cdot \#CPU^b_i + \sum_{j=1}^{n} (AWT^b_{comij} \cdot \#com^b_{ij}) + t^b_{comi} \quad (1)$$

where

- AWT^b_{CPUi} is the average waiting time for CPU of process P_i before a fault occurrence,
- AWT^b_{comij} is the average waiting time for communication of procees P_i to process P_j before a fault occurrence,
- T_{ts} is the time slice period of the CPU,
- $\#CPU^b_i$ is the number of CPU runs of process P_i before a fault occurrence,
- $\#com^b_{ij}$ is the number of communications requested by process P_i to process P_j before a fault occurrence,
- t^b_{comi} is the total time spent by process P_i on communication (data exchange) before a fault occurrence.

The time, t^a_i, that a process P_i has spent on a processor element PE after a fault occurrence, is:

$$t^a_i = (AWT_{CPUi}{}^b + \Delta AWT_{CPUi} + T_{ts}) \cdot \#CPU^a_i + \sum_{j=1}^{n} (AWT_{comij}{}^b + \Delta AWT_{comij}) \cdot \#com^a_{ij} + t^b_{comi} + \Delta t_{comi} \quad (2)$$

where

- ΔAWT_{CPUi} is change of the average waiting time for CPU of process P_i after and before a fault occurrence,
- ΔAWT_{comij} is change of the average waiting time for communication of procees P_i to process P_j after and before a fault occurrence,
- $\#CPU^a_i$ is the number of CPU runs of process P_i after a fault occurrence,
- $\#com^a_{ij}$ is the number of communications requested by process P_i to the process P_j after a fault occurrence,
- Δt_{comi} is change of the total time spent by process P_i on communication (data exchange) after and before a fault occurrence.

If we compare change of process performance of process P_i using the time difference Δt_i for executing the same portion of task by process P_i, then:

$$\#CPU^b_i = \#CPU^a_i \text{ and } \#com^b_{ij} = \#com^a_{ij}$$

for every communicating processes P_i, P_j, and

$$\Delta t_i = t^a_i - t^b_i = \\ = \Delta AWT_{CPUi} \cdot \#CPU^b_i + \\ + \sum_{j=1}^{n} \Delta AWT_{comij} \cdot \#com^b_{ij} + \\ + \Delta t_{comi} \quad (3)$$

This equation says that a process P_i will need more time, the greater is the change of the average waiting time for CPU, the more CPU runs the process has to execute, the greater is the change of the average waiting time for communication, the more communication requests it has, and the greater is the change of communication time to accomplish the same portion of a task.

A matter of interest is how the Equation (3) can be minimized ? It can be done by minimizing the parameters ΔAWT_{CPUi}, ΔAWT_{comij} and Δt_{comi}.

Simulation results have shown that ΔAWT_{CPUi} can be estimated for captured processes as:

$$\Delta AWT_{CPUi} = PE\_AWT_{CPUj} + p_{CPUi} \cdot T_{ts} - AWT_{CPUi}^{\,b} \quad (4)$$

For free or fault-touched process P_j that is placed at the destination PE as:

$$\Delta AWT_{CPUj} = p_{CPUi} \cdot T_{ts} \quad (5)$$

where
- PE_AWT_{CPUj} is the overall average waiting time for CPU at destination PE_i,
- p_{CPUi} is the probability that the process P_i is either waiting for a CPU or running on a CPU.

This means that the ΔAWT_{CPUi} parameter can be minimized by selecting the destination PE which has less the $PE\_AWT\_CPU_i$ parameter.

It is very difficult to minimize the ΔAWT_{comij} parameter. Simulations have shown that it has minimal value, regardless of other processes allocations, on a specific processor. Efforts to identify this processor have been unsuccessful to date. Therefore it is impossible to minimize the ΔAWT_{comij} parameter.

After reconfiguration, an on-chip communication of a captured process will change to an off-chip communication, while some off-chip communication can change to an on-chip one. Therefore the change of the process P_i communication time, Δt_{comi}, will mostly increase due to the amount of its on-chip communications. Minimizing can be achieved by allocating the process as closely as possible to processes with which it mostly communicates.

It is obvious that is not very easy to minimize these parameters. Improving one parameter can make another one larger. An acceptable solution must therefore be some compromise. In section 6. an algorithm is proposed that gives instructions how to assign a destination PE with regard to performance degradation.

5. Simulation results

In the present study we have built a task of 20 processes P_1, P_2, ..., P_{20}, allocated on 5 processor elements PE_1, PE_2, PE_3, PE_4 and PE_5, of the CPN model. The processes vary in CPU and communication parameters - from very low to very high usage of CPU and communication. Each process requests 2 other processes for communication and is requested for communication by 2 processes as well. Four processes are allocated on each processor element.

The question arises as to why there are 5 processors and 20 processes. Several reasons are as follows. First, we wanted to find some approach that could give results in a reasonable time. One simulation run we have used took about 30 minutes on a Sparc 20 workstation and about 45 minutes on a Sparc 10 workstation. Using 20 processes on 5 processors gives 4!=24, the number of all possible allocations of captured processes. Using 6 processors would give 5x4!=120 allocations that would require a period of time 5 times longer to simulate.

The first simulations were run on the model with 6 PEs and 24 processes, i.e. 4 processes on one PE. In the reconfiguration, one processor was not used. Simulations have shown that the performance degradation of this processor was very low (1 - 2 %) compared to other processors. Therefore we judged that it was not necessary to use this processor.

For these reasons we compromised by choosing the usage of 5 processors and 20 processes for simulations. This compromise does not decrease the generality of results.

We modified the task in different sets M_i by changing the communication data length and/or processor elements distance. Each set M_i consists of 5 subsets, M_i^1, M_i^2, M_i^3, M_i^4 and M_i^5, which correspond to the fault of processor elements PE_1, PE_2, PE_3, PE_4 and PE_5, respectively. The set M_i^j includes all possible captured processes allocations A_1, A_2,..., A_{24} during reconfiguration, and consists of simulation records S_k, $M_i^j = \{ S_1, S_2,..., S_{24} \}$. We have obtained over 65 sets M_i^j that represent over 1560 simulation runs.

Process performance has been measured by the time spent by the process on the CPU. If δ_{perfi} denotes the change of the process performance of process P_i after reconfiguration then:

$$\delta_{perfi} = \frac{\dfrac{t_i^b}{t_{CPU}{}^b_i}}{\dfrac{t_i^a}{t_{CPU}{}^a_i}} \cdot 100\% = \frac{t_i^b \cdot t_{CPU}{}^a_i}{t_i^a \cdot t_{CPU}{}^b_i} \cdot 100\% \quad (6)$$

where
- $t_{CPU}{}^b_i$, $t_{CPU}{}^a_i$ is the time that process P_i has spent on the CPU before and after reconfiguration, respectively,
- t_i^b, t_i^a is the measured time interval of process P_i run before and after reconfiguration, respectively.

We have run simulations for 200 000 time units. In the middle of this period one processor element becomes faulty and the reconfiguration takes place. Every captured process is rebuilt and restarted according to the input file. On every non-faulty processor element one captured process is rebuilt and restarted. By this way, every process will theoretically decrease in performance to 80%. Our results show that delta of process performance ranges 69 - 85% in different sets M_i^j and in a particular

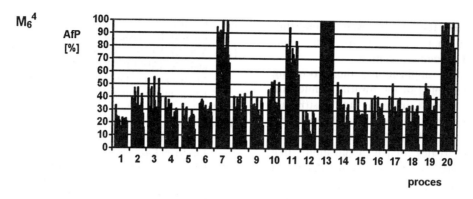

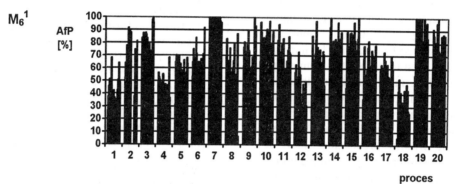

Figure 3. Examples - how can be process performance affected by reconfiguration

set different allocations varied performance degradation in the range from 1.5 to 6.3%.

Every allocation has been evaluated by the worst process performance degradation δ_{perfL} of all processes. Different allocations have been compared using the δ_{perfL} parameter. The best allocation was that with the best value of δ_{perfL}.

Figure 3 depicts two examples how process performance can be affected. The degree to which a process performance cn be affected ranges from a minimum of 0% to a maximum of 100%. In the example M_6^4 the captured processes P_7, P_{13}, P_{11} and P_{20} were affected very highly, while the other processes were affected very little. While in the example M_6^1 the captured processes P_2, P_8, P_{14} and P_{18} are affected to a moderate extent, but free or fault-touched processes P_7 and P_{19} are affected very highly.

In the next section an algorithm is described for assignment of destination PEs for captured processes. This algorithm has been designed using simulation results. It requires process and processor parameters which are necessary for calculating the assignment: AWT_{CPUi}, AWT_{comij}, $\#CPU^b_i$, $\#com^b_{ij}$, $data\_ln^b_{ij}$ - amount of data exchanged between processes P_i and P_j before a fault occurrence, p_{CPUi} and PE_AWT_{CPUj}.

The algorithm has been tested using the above simulation parameters. The assignments we have obtained were either identical to the optimal ones gained

from simulation, or very close to them (maximum difference of about 1% in performance degradation).

6. Algorithm for designation of destination processor element

In this section an algorithm is presented for assigning destination PEs to captured processes. This algorithm takes into account the performance optimization of result allocations, described as follows:

find assignment:

order captured processes according to amount of on-chip communications;
divide available processors into sets $S\_PE\_AWT\_CPU_i$ according to the PE_AWT_CPU parameter;
order sets $S\_PE\_AWT\_CPU_i$;
process captured processes in the order (use the rule - the greatest communication first):
    off-chip communication only;
    on-chip communication;
while a process is not assigned
  { *assign_destination_PE*(<u>process</u>);
  next process; }
return;

106

assign_destination_PE(process):

```
if ( process has any other on-chip communication )
    assign_destination_PE( process' that has the greatest
        on-chip communication with the process );
else
    { start with the set S_PE_AWT_CPU₀ with the lowest
        value PE_AWT_CPU;
    while the set S_PE_AWT_CPUᵢ exists
    {   choose PE that is nearest to the process
            communicating most with process Pᵢ;
        estimate the Δtᵢ parameter for all processes on this
            processor and store the greatest one ( use the
            Equation (3));
        compare the Δt_Pi parameter with the previous PE
            and store better one;
        choose the next set S_PE_AWT_CPUᵢ₊₁;
    }
    assign_destination_PE = PE with the best Δtᵢ
        parameter;
    }
return;
```

The algorithm is a part of the Reconfiguration Kernel for fault tolerance RKft [1], [2] that is replicated on each processor. The algorithm can be performed centrally or distributed on a few processors. As soon as the destination PEs are assigned, the RKft starts reallocation of copy process codes onto the destination PEs, rebuilds and restarts them, and creates new copies as well.

7. Conclusion

We have presented an approach for finding an algorithm for assigning destination processor elements to captured processes after a processor element fault, with regard to process performance degradation, in a fault tolerant multiprocessor system, by means of Coloured Petri Nets. Using the algorithm we have proposed, it is possible to assign a destination processor element to every captured process. The assignment is optimal or close to optimal with regard to process performance degradation after reconfiguration (compared to simulation results).

In future studies the algorithm will be tested on the 64 transputer T.Node machine.

References

[1]   Janík, P., Kotočová, M. Searching for an Optimal Reconfiguration in Fault Tolerant Multiprocessor systems. *Proceedings of International Conference on Parallel and Distributed Processing Techniques and Applications - PDPTA '95*, 835-844, Athens, GA, Nov. 3-4, 1995.

[2]   Janík, P. The Proposal of the Reconfiguration Kernel for Fault Tolerant Multiprocessor Systems. *Proceedings Transputer '94*, 35-42, Slovak Academy of Science, Bratislava, October 1994.

[3]   Janík, P. Reconfiguration of fault tolerant multiprocessor systems. PhD term work. Slovak Technical University, Department of Computer Science and Engineering, Bratislava, Slovakia, January 1993.

[4]   Aghanya, O. A. Towards a Software Framework for supporting Hardware Fault Tolerance. PhD thesis. Department of Computer Science, University of Essex, October 1994.

[5]   Aghanya, O.A., Colley, M.J., Standeven, J. Evacuation: A software strategy to support fault-tolerant transputer systems. *Transputer Application and Systems '93*, 911-922, IOS Press, Amsterdam, 1993.

[6]   Beňušková, L., Fašung, J., Hajdúk J., Vojtek V. Optimization of the Total Communication Cost of Mapping of Processes onto Processors by Means of a Genetic Algorithm. *17th International Conference ITI '95*, 205-210, Pula, Croatia, June 13-16, 1995.

[7]   Candlin, R., Phillips, J.: An Environment for Investigating the Effectivness of Process Migration Strategies on Transputer-based Machines. *Proceedings of the 15th WOTUG Technical Meeting*, 13-23, IOS Press, Amsterdam, 1992.

[8]   Greenwood, G., Gupta, A., Terwilliger, M. Task Redistribution in Faulty Networks Using Evolutionary Strategies. *Proceedings of 1st International Workshop on Parallel Processing*, 249-254, December 1994.

[9]   Vounckx, J., Deconinck, G., Lauwereins R. Reconfiguration of Massively Parallel Systems. *High-Performance Computing and Networking*. International Conference and Exhibition Proceedings, 372-377, Milan, Italy, May 3-5, 1995.

[10] Kumar, R.K., Patnaik, L.M., Sinha, S.K. A fault tolerant multi-transputer architecture. *Microprocessors and Microsystems*, vol. 17, no. 2, 75-81, March 1993.

[11] Puigjaner, R., Potier, D. Modeling Techniques and Tools for Computer Performance Evaluation. Plenum Press, New York, 1989.

[12] Allen, A. O.: *Introduction to Computer Performance Analysis with Mathematica*. AP Professional, Harcourt Brace & Company, Publishers, London, 1994.

Instruction Issue System for Superscalar Processors

I. Urriza, J.I. Garcia and D. Navarro
Dpto. Ingeniería Eléctrica, Electrónica y Comunicaciones, Universidad de Zaragoza
Zaragoza, SPAIN
email: urriza@posta.unizar.es

Abstract

A Superscalar procesor executing a stream of independent instructions, is able to process n instructions per cycle in n functional units. But these high performances decrease if data dependencies among instructions appear, or if a branch or a trap are processed. In this work we propose a new system to issue instructions out of order to multiple functional units, solving data dependencies and implementing branch prediction and precise interruptions handling. The data dependencies are solved renaming the logic registers using a mapping list. A reorder buffer implements "in order completion" of instructions, and stores the necessary information to recover the processor state from a branch missprediction or an interrupt. The system is implemented with random access memories, and no associative search is needed.

1. Introduction

Nowadays the CPUs of the last generation computers have multiple functional units, and are able to issue multiple independent instructions per clock cycle, they are called superscalar processors [2,4,7,10,12,13,16,18,20]. In these CPUs instructions are not executed necessarily in order, an instruction is executed when the processor resources are available. In this way superscalar computers exploits instruction level parallelism to increase the processor throughput.

To execute instructions out of order data dependencies among instructions must be disabled by the scheduling function. If instruction scheduling is performed during compilation is called static scheduling (a well-known technique) otherwise (if it is performed at execution time) is called dynamic scheduling.

Dynamic scheduling detects dependencies in a set of instructions. Instructions with no dependencies are executed by the functional units if they meet the constraints of the issue algorithm (a set of rules which ensures that an instruction can be executed).

Data dependencies among instructions in a code stream, can be classified as follows. [3]

Let Q be the set of instructions indexed by their position:

$$Q = \{q1, q2, ..., qn\}$$

Where qi is the ith instruction. With each member of Q associate two sets,

$$Ri = \{ \text{registers read by } qi \}$$
$$wi = \{\text{register written by } qi \}$$

If qi precedes qj, RAW (read after write), WAR (write after read), and WAW (write after write) data dependencies of qj on qi are defined as follows:

RAW: $Rj \cap Wi \neq \varnothing$
WAR: $Wj \cap Ri \neq \varnothing$
WAW: $Wj \cap Wi \neq \varnothing$

There are other issue problems: branch prediction and fast precise interrupts implementation.

Branches represent around 15% to 30% of executed instructions for many applications. If the instructions after a branch have to wait the branch resolution to be or not tobe executed, the processor losses effectiveness.

Branch prediction may improve performance enabling execution on a predicted path of instructions. If the prediction is not correct, the instructions in the incorrect path have to be invalidated. So quick invalidation capability is very important in modern processors [8].

Interrupts are precise in a processor with out of order execution, if after the execution of the interrupt routine, the state of the processor is rebuilt to its secuential state. This state is that the processor would be, if all preceding instructions to the point of interrupt had been executed in sequence.

In this work we propose an out of order issuing instruction system that supports dependencies resolution, branch prediction, and fast precise interrupts handling. Dependencies are removed renaming the logic registers.

This allows to disable WAW and WAR dependencies.

A reorder buffer [20] stores information about the resources needed to execute instructions. The system state at a given time is stored in a mapping list (current mapping list CML). To restore the execution after an interrupt or a branch, process history is stored into another mapping list (historic mapping list (HML)). Process history is the result state after the last instruction completion. The HML allows to know the processor state from which execution must be restarted after a branch missprediction or an interrupt.

The information to eliminate spurious instructions is stored in the reorder buffer. This information allows to free resources.

In section 2 the elements of microarchitecture are described, section 3 shows how dependencies are eliminated. Precise interruption and fast branch missprediction recovery are described in section 4. Section 5 describes hardware implementation aspects. And in section 6 conclusions and future works are presented.

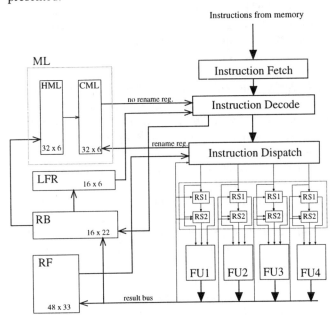

Figure 2.1. Issue unit microarquitecture.

2. Microarchitecture description and processor scheduling.

Our processor is pipelined in five stages (figure 2.1):
Fetch: In this stage the address of the next instruction is computed and 4 instructions are obtained from the cache.

Decode: Necessary resources to execute each instruction are determined.

Dispatch: Decodified instructions to are sent to their respective reservation station. Here, the instruction waits for its source registers before to be executed in the functional unit.[19]

Execute: Each functional unit takes an instruction from one of its reservation station or directly from the dispatch unit and process it out of order.

Completion: An instruction is finished when it leaves the execution stage, and can be completed if all its precedent instructions has been completed and do not generate an interrupt (in order completion). In this stage all resources used by completed instructions that will not be used in the future are freed.

Some modern designs use deeper pipelines to obtain higher clock frequencies. There are works in the literature which supports the use of shorter pipelines that fits better today personal computers need [11,12].

In our system, four are the elements used to eliminate dependencies, implement precise interrupts and fast branch missprediction recovery (figure 2.1). A mapping list (ML) pointing to a register file (RF), a free registers list (LFR) and a reorder buffer (RB). This architecture has four functional units, fed each one by two reservation stations.

Register File (RF): Contains 48 registers, 32 are the architecture registers and 16 are used in renaming. They are 33 bits length and their structure is showed in figure 2.2

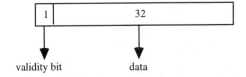

Figure 2.2. Structure of a word in the register file (RF).

Mapping List (ML): Has two 32 words lists (CML and HML) (figure 2.1). They store the physical address where each logic register is located in the register file.

Current Mapping List (CML): Stores the pointers (address) to 32 registers in the register file. These are the working registers for the last decoded instruction.

Historic Mapping List (HML): Stores the pointers to 32 registers in the register file. These are the working registers for the last completed instruction.

Free registers list (LFR): Stores the physical address of the free (unused) registers in the registers file (RF) that can be used to rename a register. It is arranged like a FIFO (figure 2.3).

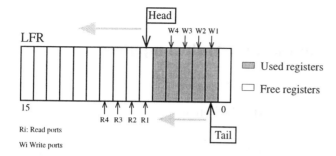

LFR

Ri: Read ports
Wi Write ports

□ Used registers
□ Free registers

Figure 2.3. Structure of the free registers list. *Head* points to the first slot that contains a free register, and *Tail* points to the first address that stores an used register.

Reorder Buffer (RB): Is a first input first output (FIFO) list that holds information in order about decoded instructions. When an instruction is completed, its entry in this list is freed. Each of its words has the structure showed in figure 2.4, where PRF is the absolute address of the register that will be freed when the instruction completes, POR is the address in the register file where the result will be stored, LOR is the logic result register. S is set (1') when the instruction is speculative (instruction after an unresolved branch) and E when the instruction has been executed. All this information is used to implement precise interrupts and branch missprediction recovery.(figure 3.3 and 3.4)

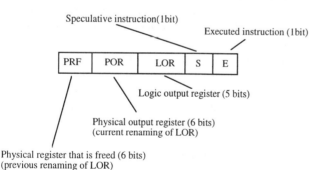

Speculative instruction(1bit)
Executed instruction (1bit)

| PRF | POR | LOR | S | E |

Logic output register (5 bits)

Physical output register (6 bits)
(current renaming of LOR)

Physical register that is freed (6 bits)
(previous renaming of LOR)

Figure 2.4. Structure of a reorder buffer word

The processor scheduling is the following:

Fetch: 4 instructions are loaded from the cache.

Decode: The physical address of each source register is loaded from the current mapping list (CML). The physical address of each output register is loaded from the list of free registers (LFR). The reorder buffer entry for each instruction is computed:

PRF (Physical Register that is Freed): this address is read from the current mapping list (CML).

POR (Physical Output Register): this address is read from the List of free registers (LFR).

LOR (Logic Output Register): is obtained from the instruction opcode

S: is obtained from the branch logic.

E: is reset.

Dispatch: POR addresses are stored at their respective address (LOR) in the CML The data of the source registers is read from the register file and from the result bus Instructions are sent to their respective reservation station.

Execute: Instructions with invalid source registers scan the result bus to get them. Each functional unit get an instruction from its reservation station and execute it.

Completion: The results of executed instructions are stored in the register file, and their respective validity bit is set. The executed bit of the respectives entries in the reorder buffer is set. Until 4 instructions are completed in order, and for each completed instruction:

PRF is stored at the end of LFR

Validity bit in the register file is reset

POR is stored at LOR address in the Historic Mapping List (HML)

3. Elimination of dependencies.

Concurrent execution of instructions is limited by dependencies among instructions. From the set of three possible dependencies described in section one , only RAW dependencies are actually inherents to the program. The others appears when out of order execution is allowed. If we rename the registers, associating dynamically different physical address to a logic register, this problem is solved.[6,7]

We find in the literature several approaches to register renaming, most of them use a renaming buffer . The renaming buffer is a small count addressable memory (CAM) that stores temporally the contents of the renamed registers. When a instruction is completed its result is moved from the renaming buffer to its logic register in the register file. When an instruction needs a source register, looks for it in the rename buffer and in the register file getting the younger instance.

In our system, both renamed and logic registers are found in the same register file and are addressed using a mapping list. Results are written only once in the register file and is not necessary to rewrite them when the instruction completes. The mapping list stores the pointers to the register file. So that, to read the contents of register *Ri* is necessary to read the contents of the entry in the register file pointed by the location *i* of the mapping list .(figure3.1)

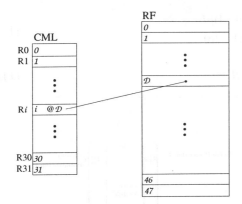

Figure 3.1. Register file mapping.

The register file has 48 words, 32 are used to store logic registers and 16 to store renamed registers. Any word in the register file, can store a logic register, a renamed register or none of them (be free). Initially the first 32 words holds the logic registers, the other 16 are free. When the renaming process begins, any word can hold any register.

The address of a register is assigned at dispatch time following this procedure: If Ri is the output register of the instruction j, then it is renamed and a free address in the register file is reserved to it. This address is written at position i in the current mapping list, so future instructions that use this register as source will take it from the assigned address.

Free registers addresses are found in the free registers list (LFR). Each read to this list gets a free word in the register file.

It is necessary to free renamed registers that will not be used anymore. This happen when all instructions that

have this logic register as source have been completed, and a new instruction writes on it. To ensure it a variant of Smith and Plezscun reorder buffer [14] is used. In our system results are not written in the reorder buffer but in the register file. Reorder buffer only stores the order and the state of instructions.

Decode stage assigns in order an entry in the reorder buffer to each instruction. When an instruction has been executed, information about its state is stored, and the instruction is ready to be completed in order.

When an instruction is completed, previous renaming of the output register is freed (PRF). Next instructions will take as source register the last renaming. Information to free the register is stored in the reorder buffer.

Figure 3.2 describes the completion procedure: the freed register address is written at the top of free register list, the validity bit in its respective entry in the register file is reset, and the address of the output physical register (Rn) is stored in the nth entry of the historic mapping list (this is to recover the correct processor state (section 4)).

We can see its operating with an example:
Let be the following code:

    $i1$ $R2 <- R1 + R3$
    $i2$ $R3 <- R2 + R4$
    $i3$ $R2 <- R5 + R3$
    $i4$ $R5 <- R1 + R6$

These four instructions are processed in parallel, in this stream we find the following dependencies: RAW dependencies appear in $R2$ among $i1$ and $i2$, and in $R3$ among $i2$ and $i3$. WAR dependencies appear in $R2$ among

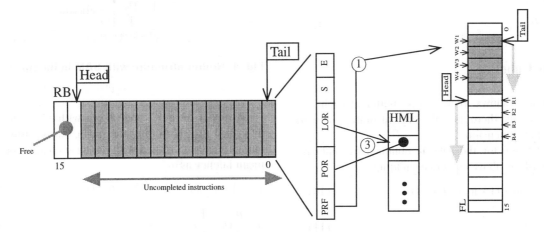

Figure 3.2. Completion procedure
1.- Freed register is stored in the free list
2.- Validity bit in the register file is reset.
3.- Historic mapping list is updated.

111

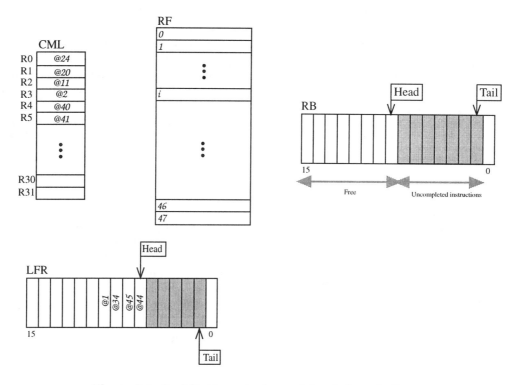

Figure 3.3. Architecture devices state at decode time.

i1 and *i2*, and in *R3* among *i2* and *i3*. WAR dependencies appear in *R2* among *i2* and *i3*, in R3 among *i1* and *i2*, and in *R5* among *i3* and *i4*. And WAW dependencies in *R2* among *i1* and *i3*. We can see how these dependencies are disabled using renaming:

At decode time the microarquitecture devices state is shown in figure 3.3.

The four instruction reach at the same time the decode stage, output registers are renamed and logic registers are translated to physical register. After renaming the code will be:

$$i1 \quad @44 <- @20 + @2$$
$$i2 \quad @45 <- @44 + @40$$
$$i3 \quad @34 <- @41 + @45$$
$$i4 \quad @1 <- @20 + @7$$

Output registers have been renamed, their physical address have been obtained from the list of free registers (LFR) (figure 3.3), and source registers have been obtained from the current mapping list CML. Only RAW dependencies appear in this code, therefore *i1*, *i2* and *i3* must be executed sequentially but *i4* can be executed concurrently with any other. In figure 3.4 devices status after renaming is showed. The mapping list contents have changed, the head pointer in the free list has been changed and four new instructions has been added to the reorder buffer.

4. Implementation of precise interrupts and branch recovery.

Precise interrupts are necessary to process the interruption routine just after the interrupted instruction. When an instruction causes a synchronous interrupt, precedent instructions must be executed and completed, and later instructions must be invalidated before executing the interrupt routine. This is not a trivial problem in pipelines with out of order execution, Sohi gives a review of known solutions in [15].

To solve this problem, the proposed microarchitecture uses a historic mapping list (HML) and a reorder buffer (described in section 2). Reorder buffer stores necessary information to recover the processor state related to the interrupted instruction. This is the state that will see the interrupt routine when it begins its execution. The historic mapping list (HML) stores the contents of the current mapping list (CML) at decode time of the instruction that is going to be completed.

Initially the two mapping lists have the same contents. When an instruction completes, the physical address of its output register is stored in the ith entry of the historic mapping list (let Ri be its output logic register). Therefore, when the next instruction completes, the contents of the historic mapping list are the same as the contents of the current mapping list when the instruction

112

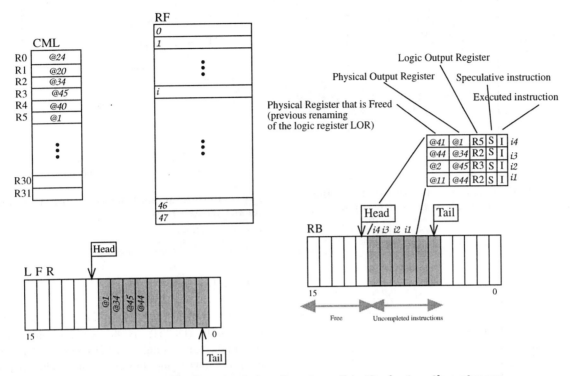

Figure 3.4. Architecture devices after decoding the instruction stream.

was decodified. If this instruction interrupts the processor, it will be only necessary to switch the historic mapping list and the current mapping list to get the correct register mapping.

When a interrupt is detected, the next PC changes to the interrupt routine address, and the instruction processing continues. The processor state is rebuilt and no clock cycle is lost.

To recover the state of the processor, it will be necessary to free the resources used by latter instructions that have to be invalidated. To invalid an instruction means to avoid it to be executed or to write in the register file.

An instruction that must be invalidated, can be at dispatch stage, in a reservation station or in a functional unit. To invalidate those in a reservation station or at dispatch, their validity bit is reset. To invalidate those in a functional unit, their write in the register file or in memory is forbidden.

The used strategy is the following (figure 4.1): All precedent instructions to the interrupted one are completed (figure 4.1 1), and this instruction gets the tail position in reorder buffer. Then mapping lists are switched, validity bits of later instructions in the reservation stations and dispatch stage are reset, and invalid signal (no write) is sent to functional units.(figure 4.1 2).

In the reorder buffer remain the entries related to invalidated instructions These entries contains information about the registers used by the eliminated instructions that have to be freed. These information is processed following a similar procedure to that used to complete instructions: Four entries will be processed in a cock cycle, physical output register (POR) address will be stored in the free registers list, its validity bit in the register file reseted and the historic mapping list is updated (figure 4.1 3).

This procedure is also applied to recover the state of the processor in the case of a misspredicted branch. When instructions after a speculative branch are decodified they are marked as speculatives. If the branch has been misspredicted, the processor changes the program counter to its right value, automatically invalidates all speculative instructions, and goes on processing unspeculative instructions.

Instructions before the branch are executed and completed, when the branch gets the tail position in the reorder buffer, mapping lists are switched and speculative instructions are invalidated.

Only remain to free the resources used by speculative instructions. In the same way as happened with precise interrupts, output registers (POR) are written in the free registers list, their validity bit in the register file is reset, and HML is updated (see section 3).

113

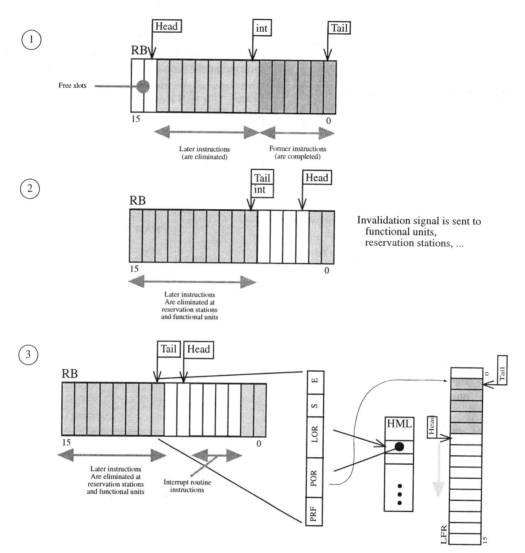

Figure 4.1. Precise interrupts handling:
1.- Former instructions are completed
2.- Interrupted instruction gets the RB tail. Mapping lists are switched. PC is switched to the interrupt routine address. And invalidation signal is sent to functional units reservation stations.
3.- Later instructions are completed and resources are freed.

5. Hardware

Hardware devices used to implement the propose architecture are the following:

Register File (RF):

Stores the 32 logic registers and other 16 renamed registers. Is implemented with a 8 read and 4 write ports RAM. Read ports are used at dispatch stage to read two source registers for each instruction. Four write ports are used to write the results.

The Mapping list (ML) is built up of two 32 slots lists (CML and HML) (figure 2.1).

Are implemented with a RAM with 12 read ports and 4 write ports. Read ports are used at decode, where it is necessary to obtain the physical address of 3 register for each instruction (2 source registers and 1 output register that will be freed when the instruction will be completed). Write ports are used at dispatch to refresh the current mapping list with the new renamed registers. The two lists are identical and interchange their function with the execution of branches and interrupts.

Free registers list (LFR);

Is implemented with a FIFO with four read ports and four write ports. Read ports are used at decode to rename until four output registers, and write ports at complete to free until four registers in a clock cycle. The number of words in this fifo is the same as the reorder buffer (16 words in this implementation) (figure 2.3).

Reorder Buffer (RB):

In this implementation the reorder buffer has 16 entries and works as a FIFO with 4 write ports and 4 read ports. Four write ports are used at the end of decode stage to add information in order from until four instruction per clock cycle. Read ports are used to retire in order until four completed instructions in a clock cycle.

Review of used devices:

	Size (bytes)	Read ports	Write ports
Reg File	48x33	8	4
Mapping List:			
CML	32 x 6	12	4
HML	32 x 6	12	4
List of Free Regs.	16x6 (FIFO)	4	4
Reorder Buffer	16x19 (FIFO)	4	4

6. Conclusions

An issue unit for a four way superscalar processor has been described. This unit uses a renaming technique to avoid simply and effectively instruction dependencies, thereby increasing throughput. The technique uses a mapping list and a register file, and only needs to write the result once in its slot.

Fast precise interrupts are supported by this implementation. A processor state consistent with sequential instruction execution is established in the architected registers, and no clock cycles are lost.

Only RAM memories that are faster and smaller than CAMs are needed, thereby register data can be loaded faster and cycle time can be shortened. The described system is more simple than those based in a renaming buffer contributing to reduce the cycle time

References.

[1] L. Chisvin, R.J. Duckworth. " Content-Addressable and Asociative Memory: Alternatives to Ubiquitous RAM" IEEE COMPUTER, July 1989.

[2] Daniel W. Dobberpuhl "A 200Mhz 64-bit Dual-issue CMOS Microprocessor". IEEE JSSC vol. 27, Nr. 11, Nov. 1992.

[3] H. Dwyer, "A multiple out of order, instruction issuing system for superscalar processors", IBM Technical Report (TR 01.C075) Nov.1991.

[4] "A Tour of the P6 Microarquitectura". Intel . 1994

[5] S.M.S. Jalaleddine, L.G. Johnson, "Associative IC Memories with Relational Search and Nearest-Match Capabilities", IEEE JSSC vol.27 no. 6 june 1992.

[6] M. Jhonson. "Superscalar procesor Design" Prentice Hall, Englewood Cliffs, N.J. 1991

[7] M. Laird et all. "A comparison of several superscalar designs". Dpto. CS Clemson Univerity

[8] J.K.F. Lee, Alan J. Smith. "Branch Prediction Strategies and Branch Target Buffer Design". IEEE Computer. 1984.

[9] "R8000 Microprocessor Chip Set". Product Overview. MIPS August 1994.

[10] "R10000 Microprocessor Chip Set". Product Overview. MIPS October 1994.

[11] "PowerPC 620 Microprocessor". White paper. Motorola. 2.1.95

[12] S. Peter Song, M. Denman, Joe Chang. "The PowerPC 604 RISC Microprocesor". IEEE Micro, Nov. 1994.

[13] Robert P. Colwell, Randy L. Steck. "A 0.6μm BiCMOS Procesor with Dynamic Execution"

[14] J Smith, A.Pleszkun, "Implementation of Precise Interrupts in Pipelined Processors" Proc 12th Ann. Int'l Symp. Computert Architecture, IEEE, 1985.

[15] Gurindar S. Sohi. "Instruction Issue Logic for High-Performance, Interruptible, Multiple Functional Unit, Pipelined Computers". IEEE trans. on Computers. March 1990.

[16] "The SPARC Architecture Manual version 7". Sun Microsystems. Oct 1987.

[17] "The SuperSPARC Microprocessor". Technical White Paper. Sun Microsistems 1992.

[18] "UltraSPARC". Technical White Papers. Sparc TB. September 1994.

[19] R.M. Tomasoulo. "An efficient algorithm for exploiting multiple arquitecture units". IBM Journal of REsearch and Development, 11:25-33,1967.

[20] S. Wallance, N. Dagli, N. Bagherzadeh. "Design and implemetation of a 100 Mhz. Reor der Buffer".

GENERALIZED CUBIC NETWORKS

Kiran R. Desai
Intel Corporation
2200 Mission College Blvd.
Santa Clara, CA-94086
kdesai@mipos2.intel.com

Kanad Ghose
Dept. of Computer Science
State University of New York
Binghamton, NY 13902-6000
ghose@cs.binghamton.edu

Abstract: We introduce a family of cube based hierarchical interconnection networks, called GCNs, which are based on Cartesian graphs, using any network capable of emulating the hypercube as its components. GCNs emulate many interesting properties of the hypercube, albeit using a smaller node degree. We focus on a specific member of the GCN family, based on the HCN interconnection [GhDe 90], dubbed the GC-HCN. The GC-HCN, unlike many cube-like low node degree network, has the ability to embed meshes and tori and lends itself to recursive partitioning to allow sub-network allocations. Furthermore, the diameter of the GC-HCN is about 3/4-ths that of a comparable hypercube, although it uses about half as many links. We also examine GCNs as interconnections within a single VLSI chip or on an MCM. It appears that many varieties of GCNs appear to perform better than the hypercubes in this role.

Keywords: Hypercube interconnection, Algorithm mapping, VLSI interconnections.

1. Introduction

The binary hypercube is a versatile interconnection network and has been used in a wide variety of commercial and experimental distributed memory multiprocessors such as the Cosmic Cube, the Intel "hypercube" systems (iPSC, iPSC/2), the Ametek/Symult S-series, the NCUBE series and the Connection Machines (CM-1, CM-2). The many of the advantages of the hypercube include its low node degree and diameter (both of which equal the logarithm of the number of nodes), the ability to use simple routing algorithms and the ability to permit the embedding of commonly-required interconnection patterns (like meshes, rings, trees, logarithmic graphs). The limitations of the hypercube include its non-planarity (which complicates the layout of hypercubes implemented within VLSI chips), and its inability to grow incrementally.

A variety of hypercube based systems have also been proposed that try to reduce the node degree of the network while maintaining the ability to emulate the connections of the hypercube. The cube connected cycles [PrVu81], shuffle exchange [Le92], binary de Bruijn graph (BDG) [SaPr89], hypernets based on cubelets [HwGh87], hierarchical hypercube [MaBa94], connection cube [Si93] and the HCN [GhDe90] are but a few examples of such networks. Although these networks emulate many properties of the hypercube, most of them fail to embed meshes (which the hypercube allows) or permit recursive partitioning (like the hypercube). Such "space partitionability" is useful for subnetwork allocations in a multiprogrammed system.

In this paper we introduce a family of low node degree interconnection networks, called Generalized Cubic Networks (GCNs), that can efficiently emulate the hypercube connections using a node degree that is lower than in a hypercube interconnection with the same number of nodes. Technically GCNs are instances of Cartesian product graphs [Yo91] and are hierarchical in nature. GCNs use any cube-like network (including the hypercube itself) as a starting point. As an instance of the GCN, we introduce the GC-HCN, which uses the Hierarchical Cubic Network, HCN [GhDe90] as a basis. The GC-HCN emulates all properties of the well-known hypercube and also retains the ability to allow mesh and tori embeddings and space partitioning of the network for subnetwork allocations. The maximum routing distance in the GC-HCN is about three-fourths that of a comparable hypercube i.e., a hypercube with the same number of nodes. All these interesting features of the GC-HCN are provided using almost half as many links as a comparable hypercube.

The advent of single chip multiprocessors, such as the EXECUBE [Ko 94], which pack several complete CPUs with local memory, communication controllers and the necessary interconnection within a single chip demands careful design of the on-chip interconnection. We introduce some potential measures for evaluating such VLSI/MCM interconnections and evaluate GCNs using these measures. We show that many members of the GCN family excel over the hypercube under these measures.

2. Cartesian Product Networks (CPNs) and Generalized Cubic Networks (GCNs)

Consider two basic element graphs, G_1 and G_2. The Cartesian product $G_1 \times G_2$ of two graphs $G_1 = \{V_1, E_1\}$ and $G_2 = \{V_2, E_2\}$ is defined as a network of $|V_1| \times |V_2|$ nodes. Each node is labelled using two digits in a mixed radix system. A node is labelled $r_2 \| r_1$ where r_1 is in radix-$|V_1|$ and r_2 is in radix-$|V_2|$. The connections in the Cartesian product are such that a node $A\|B$ is connected to node $A\|B_c$ such that the edge

$<B,B_c> \in E_1$. The node A||B is also connected to a node A_c||B such that the edge $<A,A_c> \in E_2$. The link between A||B and A||B_c is called a dimension-0 link, while the link between A||B and A_c||B is called a dimension-1 link.

In general, a Cartesian product of n graphs, $G_1, G_2, .., G_n$ has $|V_1|.|V_2|..|V_n|$ nodes labelled using a mixed radix numbering system. Each node is labelled as $r_n||r_{n-1}||..||r_i||..||r_2||r_1$ and r_i is in radix-$|V_i|$, $1 \leq i \leq n$. Each node $A_n||A_{n-1}||..||A_{i+1}||A_i||..||A_1$ is connected to a node $A_n||A_{n-1}||..||A_{i+1}||C_i||..||A_1$, using a dimension-(i-1) link, such that the edge $<A_i,C_i> \in E_i$, $1 \leq i \leq n$. A Cartesian product graph of n graphs is an n-dimensional network: each additional term in the product adds another dimension to the network.

If all the basic element graphs, G_i, are regular with a node degree of p_i, then for every dimension that is added, the node degree increases by p_i, $1 \leq i \leq n$. Thus the degree of a node in G_1 x G_2 x .. x G_n is given as $p_1+p_2+..+p_n$.

2.1 General Routing Algorithm

The routing algorithm for the entire Cartesian product family of networks is very simple because of the recursive manner of construction. A distributed algorithm for routing between two nodes, SRC and DEST uses a destination tag on the message and routes as follows:

```
Route_CPN (SRC, DEST){
   /* SRC in general is the address of the
   node that received a message for routing */
   Let:
   (i_n-1||i_n-2||..||i_k||..||i_0) = address of SRC;
   (j_n-1||..||j_k||..||j_0)= address of DEST;
   k = most significant digit position for
      which i_k ≠ j_k;
      /* dimension ordered routing */
   p = the node in the shortest path from node
      (i_k) to node (j_k) in the basic element
      graph G_k;
   Send the message on the dimension k link
      connected to node:
         (i_n-1||i_n-2||..||i_k+1||p||i_k-1||..||i_0)
}
```

A node $x_{n-1}x_{n-2}..x_1x_0$ is distance $d_{n-1} + d_{n-2} + .. + d_1 + d_0$ away from the node $y_{n-1}y_{n-2}..y_1y_0$ in the n-dimensional CPN, if each node x_i is d_i away from node y_i in the basic element, G_i. Hence the maximum internode distance (diameter) of the n-dimensional CPN is the sum of the network diameters of each basic element graph, G_i. If the diameter of each graph, G_i, is proportional to the logarithm of the number of nodes in G_i, then the diameter of the CPN is proportional to the logarithm of the number of nodes in the CPN. The routing algorithm guarantees a minimal path routing if the routing algorithm used for the basic element provides a minimal path. Although not proved here, we can show that if the routing algorithm for each basic element graph G_i is deadlock-free, then the overall dimension-ordered routing for the CPN is also deadlock-free. The routing algorithm given above can also be adapted to deviate from a dimension-order routing.

2.2 Average Internode Distance

The average internode distance in a Cartesian product graph G of n graphs, $G_1, G_2, .., G_n$ is given by:
$$D(G) = D(G_1) + D(G_2) + ... + D(G_n)$$
where $D(G_i)$ is the average internode distance of graph G_i. The proof of this result, given in [DeGh 96], is excluded here for the sake of brevity.

2.3 Generalized Cubic Networks (GCNs)

An n-dimensional GCN is a Cartesian product graph of n graphs, $G_1, G_2, .., G_n$, where each graph G_i, $1 \leq i \leq n$, is chosen as a well known hypercube emulating network. Examples of cube emulating networks include the shuffle exchange network, the cube connected cycles (CCC), the binary de Bruijn graph (BDG), the hierarchical cubic network (HCN) and the Connection Cube (CC). The well known hypercube can also be trivially considered to be a GCN.

3. GCNs Based on HCNs

In this section we introduce the GC-HCN as the GCN using the HCN [GhDe90] as basic elements. We also establish that the GC-HCN offers some definite implementation advantages over a comparable hypercube network.

3.1 Hierarchical Cubic Networks (HCN) and GC-HCNs

The Hierarchical Cubic Network, HCN, was proposed in [GhDe90] as an alternative to the hypercube specifically from an implementation point of view. The HCN network based on n-cubes, designated as HCN (n, n), uses n+1 links per node to interconnect 2^{2n} nodes and has a maximum routing distance of $n + \lfloor n/2 \rfloor + 1$ [GhDe 95]. It also emulates all the connections of the comparable hypercube of 2^{2n} nodes in constant time. For some types of algorithms like recursive doubling and ascend/descend algorithms, the execution times on HCN and hypercube based systems are virtually identical.

A HCN(n, n) network, which interconnects 2^{2n} nodes is constructed by taking 2^n n-cubes (each called a *cluster*) and establishing the additional connections between node-pairs in different clusters. The unique 2n-bit address of a node is interpreted as (x, y) where x refers to unique n-bit address of a cluster, and y refers to the unique n-bit address of the node within the cluster.

The additional connections between node-pairs in different clusters in a HCN(n,n) network of 2^{2n} nodes:
- (I,J) connects to (J,I) (termed as a *non-diameter link*)
- (I,I) connects to ($\bar{I},\bar{I}$) (termed as a *diameter link*)

for all values of I, J, K, where I,J,K are n-bit numbers. $\bar{I}$ is the bitwise complement of I. Note also that since each cluster is an n-cube, hypercube interconnections within a HCN(n, n) exist between (I,J) connects to (I,K) for all K, such that I J $\oplus$ K I = 1 for all values of I.

The 2-dimensional GC-HCN(m,m,n,n) network is defined as the cartesian product graph, HCN(m,m) x HCN(n,n), of

117

2^{2n+2m} nodes. A node in GC-HCN(m,m,n,n) is labelled as (A,B,C,D) where A and B are m bit numbers and C and D are n bit numbers. The connections in the GC-HCN(m,m,n,n) from a node (A,B,C,D) are:

- (A,B,C,D) connects to (A,B,C,D_h), for all D_h, where $|D \oplus D_h| = 1$.
- (A,B,C,D) connects to (A,B_h,C,D), for all B_h, where $|B \oplus B_h| = 1$.
- (A,B,C,D) connects to (A,B,D,C), if C$\neq$D (called non-diameter link in GC-HCN dimension-0).
- (A,B,C,D) connects to (A,B,$\overline{C}$,$\overline{D}$), if C=D (called diameter link in GC-HCN dimension-0).
- (A,B,C,D) connects to (B,A,C,D), if A$\neq$B (called non-diameter link in GC-HCN dimension-1).
- (A,B,C,D) connects to ($\overline{A}$,$\overline{B}$,C,D), if A=B (called diameter link in GC-HCN dimension-1).

Using the results given in Section 2.2, the average distance for a GC-HCN(m,m,n,n) is equal to the sum of the average distances for the HCN(m,m) and the HCN(n,n). Also, the maximum routing distance in the GC-HCN(m,m,n,n) is given as the sum of the maximum routing distances for the HCN(m,m) and the HCN(n,n), i.e., $(m + \lfloor m/2 \rfloor + 1) + (n + \lfloor n/2 \rfloor + 1)$. The average distances and the maximum routing distance for a GC-HCN(m,m,n,n) network is depicted in Table 1 for different values of m and n. For comparison, the values for a (2m+2n)-cube have also been provided.

		2(m+n)-hypercube			GC-HCN (m,m,n,n)		
m	n	Node Degree	Diameter	Avg. Distance	Node Degree	Diameter	Avg. Distance
3	3	12	12	6	8	10	6.44
3	4	14	14	7	9	12	7.48
4	4	16	16	8	10	14	8.52
4	5	18	18	9	11	15	9.50
5	5	20	20	10	12	16	10.48
5	6	22	22	11	13	18	11.44
6	6	24	24	12	14	20	12.40
6	7	26	26	13	15	21	13.36
7	7	28	28	14	16	22	14.32

Table 1. Diameter and average distances for the GC-HCN and the Hypercube

3.2 Parallel Algorithms on GC-HCNs

In this section, we will propose efficient algorithms for typical parallel applications on the 2-dimensional GC-HCNs. Obvious generalizations are possible for k-dimensional GC-HCNs (see [DeGh 96]).

3.2.1 Recursive Doubling

In parallel algorithms that employ recursive doubling, $N = 2^r$ data values are operated on in pairs at the leaf nodes of a binary tree of depth r. The result from each pair is passed along to the parent node at the next higher level and the algorithm continues till a final value is computed at the root node of the tree in time O(log N). These algorithms (and the required tree interconnection pattern) map on to the GC-HCN

structure in a very natural way. We will establish this by demonstrating the mapping of the MIN algorithm on the GC-HCN.

The MIN algorithm, a specific instance of recursive doubling algorithms, finds the minimum of $N = 2^{2(n+m)}$ data values stored one per node in a GC-HCN(m,m,n,n) by implementing a comparison tree and performing the comparisons in parallel within each level of the tree. A[k] holds the data in node k ($0 \leq k \leq 2^{2n+2m} - 1$). In the first phase of the algorithm the recursive doubling algorithm for the HCN(n,n) is performed to move the minimum of each of the 2^{2m} HCNs at nodes labelled (A,B,0,0) as follows:

- The hypercube recursive doubling algorithm is performed in each of the 2^{2m+n} n-cube clusters to move the local minimum to a node (A,B,C,0) in each n-cube cluster.

- The local minimum from each node (A,B,C,0) is moved to the node (A,B,0,C) using one concurrent routing step across the non-diameter links in dimension-0 of the GC-HCN.

- The hypercube recursive doubling algorithm is then performed in each of the 2^{2m} n-cube clusters identified by an address (A,B,0,C) to move the local minimum to a node (A,B,0,0).

The recursive doubling algorithm for the HCN(m,m) is then performed in the next phase to move the minimum over all the 2^{2n+2m} nodes in node (0,0,0,0). The recursive doubling operation thus takes $(2n+1)+(2m+1) = 2(n+m+1)$ communication and $2(n+m)$ binary comparison steps to find the minimum over all the 2^{2n+2m} nodes of the GC-HCN(m,m,n,n).

The time complexity of this algorithm is O(logN) -- the same as on a comparable hypercube. This shows that for recursive doubling algorithms like MIN (parallel addition, parallel MAX etc.), the 2-dimensional GC-HCN requires only two extra routing steps than in a comparable hypercube.

3.2.2 Ascend/Descend Algorithms

"Ascend/Descend" [PrVu81] algorithms require successive operations on data items that are separated by a distance equal to a power of 2. Bitonic Merge-Sort (BMS), FFT, convolution, matrix multiplication are applications that use algorithms in this general category. Ascend/Descend algorithms map on very efficiently on the GC-HCN and motivate the following theorem:

Theorem 1: The time needed to execute ascend/descend algorithms on the 2-dimensional GC-HCN is equal to the time needed to execute these algorithms on a comparable hypercube plus the time needed to execute four (bidirectional) routing steps on the GC-HCN.

Proof: We will assume 2^{2n+2m} data values, one in each node of a GC-HCN(m,m,n, n). In an ascend type of algorithm using 2^{2n+2m} data values, the successive operations take place on data sets separated by a distance $2^0, 2^1, 2^2, ..., 2^{n-1}, 2^n, ..., 2^{2n+2m-1}$. Let each data item labelled (A,B,C,D) be mapped to a node (A,B,C,D) in the GC-HCN, called the home node for that data item. The first n operations, involving data items separated by a distance of $2^0, 2^1, .., 2^{n-1}$ can be done using the n-cube connections in each HCN(n,n) basic element. In the second part of the algorithm, an exchange operation is performed by simultaneously swapping the data values between nodes (A,B,C,D) and (A,B,D,C) using the non-diameter links of the GC-HCN dimension-0. In essence, this moves data items separated by a distance of 2^k, where $n \leq k \leq 2n-1$, into the same cluster, such that they are separated by a distance of 2^{k-n}. (The exchange step is equivalent to swapping the two least significant n-bits in the 2m+2n-bit address of a node.) Note that no data exchange is needed on a diameter link. The second set of n data operations can now be performed using local movements within a cluster of the HCN (which is a n-cube), as in the first part. Before we start the third part of the operations, an exchange operation is performed by simultaneously swapping the data values between nodes (A,B,C,D) and (A,B,D,C) using the non-diameter links of the GC-HCN dimension-0. All the data items have now reached their home node. Again, a node (A,B,C,D) is also connected to the nodes adjacent in the dimension-2n to dimension-(2n+m-1) links of the hypercube. Hence the next set of m data operations can be performed using the m-cube connections of the HCN(m,m). In the fourth part of the algorithm, an exchange operation is performed by simultaneously swapping the data values between nodes (A,B,C,D) and (B,A,C,D) using the non-diameter links of the GC-HCN dimension-1. In essence, this moves data items separated by a distance of 2^k, where $2n+m \leq k \leq 2n+2m-1$, such that they are adjacent to each other along the m-cube connections of the GC-HCN dimension 1, i.e., HCN(m,m). The fourth set of m operations can be now be performed using the m-cube connections of the HCN(m,m). Finally, a global exchange operation moves all the data items to their home node.

The time needed to execute ascend/descend algorithms on the 2-dimensional GC-HCN is thus equal to the execution time on a comparable hypercube plus the time for the four routing steps needed for the exchange step in each of the four phases of the algorithm.

3.2.3 Hypercube Emulation

Algorithms requiring the hypercube interconnection among processing nodes or for that matter algorithms requiring any interconnection schema emulated by the hypercube (such as meshes, trees, X-trees, butterfly networks etc.) can be implemented very efficiently on the GC-HCN. We state this result formally as the following theorem:

Theorem 2: In data parallel algorithms, a GC-HCN(m,m,n, n) network can emulate a hypercube of the same number of nodes, namely, a (2n+2m)-cube, in $O(1)$ time.

Proof: The proof of Theorem 1 can be adapted to show that a 2-D GC-HCN can emulate all the connections of a comparable hypercube with time complexity O(1).

We also show in [DeGh 96] that torus and meshes of various dimensions can be embedded in the GC-HCN, unlike most other cube-like networks. In fact, the GC-HCN implements algorithms that rely on the existence of mesh and torus interconnections in exactly the same number of steps in a comparable hypercube (See [DeGh 96]).

The time complexities of several parallel algorithms running on the GC-HCN and similar networks as a function of the data set size is depicted in Table 2. The GC-HCN performs identically as the hypercube on all of these algorithms. Further, as established in some of the previous sections, the absolute running time of several algorithms on the GC-HCN are identical, for all intent and purpose, to that for the hypercube. In addition, it should be noted that the diameter links of the form $<(A,A,C,D),(\bar{A},\bar{A},C,D)>$ and $<(A,B,C,C),(A,B,\bar{C},\bar{C})>$ are not used in any of the algorithms studied in the above sections.

The GC-HCN thus performs the recursive doubling, ascend/descend and the mesh/torus algorithms in execution times that are virtually identical to that of the execution times on a comparable hypercube. Since these form the basis for many parallel algorithms, the hypercube emulation mode may not be necessary on the GC-HCN. The GC-HCN provides these interesting properties by using almost half as many links as the comparable hypercube.

Network	Vector sum	Matrix Multiplication	N X N convolution with M X M window	Bitonic sort
2-D GC-HCN	log N	log N	M^2 + log N	$\log^2 N$
HCN	log N	log N	M^2 + log N	$\log^2 N$
Hypercube	log N	log N	M^2 + log N	$\log^2 N$
Hypernet	log N	log N	M^2 + log N	$\log^2 N$
2-D Mesh	$N^{0.5}$	N	M^2	N
Binary Tree	log N	N^2	N^2	N

Table 2. Time-Complexities of Some Parallel Algorithms

3.3 Partitionings in the GC-HCN

Efficient partitioning of a network supports multiprogramming such that different programs can be assigned separate partitions of the network. The GC-HCN(m,m,n,n) is formed from 2^{2m} copies of the HCN(n,n). Each HCN(n,n) is formed by connecting 2^n n-cube clusters. Hence the GC-HCN can be partitioned into 2^{2m+n} n-cubes. Similarly, it can also be partitioned into 2^{m+2n} m-cubes. The Cartesian product of an m-cube and an n-cube is an (m+n)-cube. Hence the GC-HCN(m,m,n,n) can also be partitioned into 2^{m+n} (m+n)-cubes. In addition, the GC-HCN(m,m,n,n) can be recursively partitioned into a small number of partitions such that the *hypercube emulation can be efficiently performed in each partition*, as shown in [DeGh 96].

4. Other GCN Interconnections

A k-dimensional GCN network can be constructed by taking the Cartesian product of k cube emulating networks. The

Cartesian product graphs (n–cube $\times$ 2^m node shuffle exchange), (2^p node BDG $\times$ 2^q node SE $\times$ 2^r node BDG) are all examples of GCNs. If all the basic elements, BE, involved in the cartesian product are the same then we will call it a GC-BE. The (2^m node SE $\times$ 2^n node SE) will be referred to as a 2-dimensional GC-SE. The (2^m node BDG $\times$ 2^n node BDG) will be referred to as a 2-dimensional GC-BDG.

The topological properties of the various 2-dimensional GCNs are summarized Table 3. Figure 1 shows the product of the network diameter and the node degree as a measure of the *network cost* as defined in [BhAg84] for different network sizes of the GCNs. The graphs show that the GC-HCNs are preferred over the other networks compared under this metric.

2-D GCN	#Nodes	Nodedegree	Diameter
GC-HCN	2^{2m+2n}	$m+n+2$	$(m + \lfloor m/2 \rfloor + 1) + (n + \lfloor n/2 \rfloor + 1)$
GC-CC	$2^{2m+2n+2}$	$m+n+2$	$2.(m+n+2)$
GC-SE	2^{2m+2n}	6	$2.(2m+2n-1)$
GC-BDG	2^{2m+2n}	8	$2.(m+n)$
Hypercube	2^{2m+2n}	$2.(m+n)$	$2.(m+n)$

Table 3. Topological properties of various GCNs

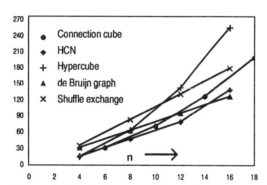

Figure 1. (Node degree x diameter) product of 2^n node 2-D GCNs for various basic elements

The parallel algorithms on any cube emulating network can be adapted for execution on the k-dimensional GCN in a manner similar to the techniques presented in section 5.2 for the GC-HCNs. The recursive doubling and ascend/descend algorithms on the GC-SE network can be performed one dimension at a time in a manner similar to the algorithms on the GC-HCN. The recursive doubling algorithm on a 2-dimensional GC-SE graph of $2^{2(n+k)}$ nodes requires $2(k+n-2)$ additional routing steps than the implementation on the 2-D GC-HCN network. The ascend/descend algorithm requires $2(n+k-2)$ additional bidirectional routing steps than the implementation on the comparable GC-HCN. *In a manner similar to the proof for Theorem 2, it can be shown that the Cartesian product graph of any number of cube-emulating networks can efficiently emulate a comparable hypercube.*

5. VLSI/MCM Implementation of GCNs

With increasing levels of device integration several complete processing nodes and their interconnection can be put into a single VLSI chip. The EXECUBE architecture [Ko94], is an example where 8 complete CPUs, each with 64KB of local memory were integrated into a single chip together with the necessary interconnections. As device densities continue to grow, the number of computing nodes that can be put into a single chip will go well beyond these current numbers. A typical VLSI layout for computing nodes and their interconnections is in the form of a two dimensional array of the nodes (CPU + local memory + I/O), with spacings (called *wiring channels*) left between adjacent rows and adjacent columns for the wiring needed by the interconnection, as shown in Figure 2. A wiring channel consists of *tracks* running across its length with each track being shared by non-overlapping interconnection links among the nodes, as depicted in Figure 3. The total die area for the chip (minus the area of the pad drivers) is thus determined by the area occupied by the nodes and the wiring channels. It is thus imperative to minimize the total areal requirement of the wiring channels, but without sacrificing connectivity and performance. A desirable interconnection for VLSI implementation of single chip multiprocessors should thus use an interconnection whose wiring channel area on a per node basis is small but which still provides sufficient performance. Performance in this respect not just refers to the raw bisection bandwidth, but also to the ability to subsume interconnection patterns demanded by typical parallel applications. Similar considerations apply in the choice of the interconnect for constructing multi-CPU systems on a multi-chip module (MCM) or a wafer scale (WSI) implementation.

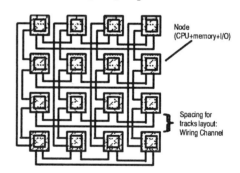

Figure 2. A 2-D layout for a 4-cube (i.e., 2-cube x 2-cube)

We primarily focus on two dimensional GCNs i.e., GCNs as products of two graphs. Our main reason for doing so are as follows:

1. Given a fixed number of nodes, an increase in the number of dimensions in the GCNs does not produce a commensurate decrease in the network diameter.

2. Each additional dimension results in additional swapping steps in the GCNs for hypercube emulation.

3. The number of switches needed in an all-port router for a k-dimensional network with r links per dimension is roughly

proportional to $(kr+1)^2$. This strongly discourages the use of higher dimensional networks for on-chip interconnections.

We now propose some metrics that tie the areal requirement with the network performance and evaluate them for some GCN networks.

5.1 Track Requirements of Basic Elements

The wiring channel area per node is dependent on the width (i.e., the spacing between layouts of adjacent nodes) of each wiring channel. The width of a wiring channel is determined by the maximum number of tracks that have to be laid out within the wiring channel. The number of tracks required for a linear layout of a basic element thus decides the wiring channel width for the 2(or n)-dimensional GCN. In general, if a link is w bits wide, the corresponding track will require at least w metal lines. In the analysis that follows, we count the number of tracks required for a linear layout of many of the basic elements studied in this paper. Assuming that w is fixed, the number of tracks decides the wiring channel width.

The track requirements for a linear layout for the hypercube, shuffle exchange and the binary de Bruijn graph (BDG) has been discussed in [ChAgBu93] and is as follows:

$\#Tracks(2n\text{-cube}) = 2^{2n} - 2n$
$\#Tracks(2^{2n} \text{ node shuffle exchange}) = (^{2n}C_n)/2 + 2$
$\#Tracks(2^{2n} \text{ node BDG}) \geq {}^{2n}C_n + 2$

We now establish the track requirements for a linear layout of the HCN. There are 2^n n-cube clusters in a HCN that are interconnected using diameter and non-diameter links. The 2^n n-cubes are placed sequentially alongside each other sharing the 2^n-n tracks required to lay out each n-cube.
$\#Tracks_{cluster} (HCN) = 2^n - n = T1 \text{ (say)}$
The non-diameter links can be considered to form a complete connection of 2^n nodes. In [ChAgBu93] it has been shown that the number of tracks required for a linear layout of a complete connection of 2^n nodes is $(2^{2n} - 1)/3 - 1$. Thus,

$\#Tracks_{non-diameter-links} (HCN) = (2^{2n}-1)/3 - 1 = T2 \text{ (say)}$
There are a total of 2^{n-1} diameter links in a HCN(n,n). Thus,

$\#Tracks_{diameter-links} (HCN) = 2^{n-1} = T3 \text{ (say)}$

Therefore, the total number of tracks for HCN(n,n)
$= T1 + T2 + T3 = 2^n + 2^{n-1} + (2^{2n}-1)/3 - n - 1.$

Clearly the number of tracks for a HCN(n,n) is about one-third the number of tracks required for the linear layout of a comparable hypercube, for large values of n. Figure 3 shows the linear layout for the HCN(2,2).

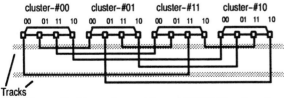

Figure 3. Linear Layout for a HCN(2,2) network

5.2 Area Efficiency and System Cost for GCNs

The efficiency of the VLSI/WSI layout for a network has been defined in terms of the number of tracks for a linear layout and the number of links of the network , in [ChAgBu93] as

Track Efficiency = Number of Links / Total Number of Tracks

A comparison of the Track Efficiency of various basic elements is shown in Figure 4 for system sizes of 2^n nodes, for $1 < n < 10$.

The two dimensional GCNs can be laid out in a regular manner in a VLSI layout with connections in dimension i spanning across tracks in dimension i in space. The area requirements of the layout depends on the number of nodes in each dimension, the track width of the basic element, and the area of the node and communication controllers. Let W_{node} be the width of a node along with communication controllers in both dimensions, and let T_{BE} be the track requirement of a basic element, BE. Let α be the ratio of the physical track width to the width W_{node}. For an N x N system, the VLSI area requirement on a per node basis is:

$VLSI\_AREA_{NxN-system} = W_{node}.(\alpha.T_{BE} + 1) . W_{node}.(\alpha.T_{BE} + 1)$

We now define the Network Cost of the on-chip interconnections as the product of the area required and the network diameter. (This was defined as the *cost of ownership* of a VLSI/WSI network in [ChAgBu93].) The inclusion of the network diameter in the network cost reflects an aspect of network performance that is not captured in a pure areal measure. Thus:

Network_Cost = Area_Estimate X Network_Diameter

The contributions to the overall die area for a single chip multiprocessor, excluding the I/O pad drivers, come from the following components associated with each node: the CPU, the local memory of the CPU, the communication controller(s) and the average inter-node wiring area for a single node. The area requirements of the communications controller is decided by several factors:

a. *The node degree*: for a node of degree k, if an all-port router is used, the router will require two (k+1) by (k+1) switches, since input-output from the node itself will require an extra set of connections. The area requirement for the router and control logic is thus $C1.(k+1)^2$, where C1 is a constant. The size of the buffers within the router will be approximately proportional to the number of inputs (and/or outputs) to the routing switch and will be given by $C2.(k+1)$, where C2 is a constant.

b. *The width of each link*: if each link consists of w wires, i.e., the width of each link is w, then the area requirements of the switches and buffers for w-bit wide links will be proportional to w.

The overall area required by the communications controller within a node is thus given by:

$$T_{comm} = w.C1.(k+1)^2 + w.C2.(k+1)$$

On a per node basis, if the total area required by the communication controller is fixed at a fraction A of the area required by the CPU and local memory, then interconnection topologies that have a lower node degree can use more wires per link. What this effectively does is to increase the bandwidth per link (i.e., the link capacity).

In this case, the VLSI area requirement of a 2^n x 2^n node GCN with a basic element of node degree, d, on a per node basis is:

$$NORM\_VLSI\_AREA_{NxN-system} = [(\alpha.T_{BE}.((n+1)(n+2)/(d+1)(d+2)) + 1).W_{node}]^2$$

This equation assumes that the constants C1 and C2 in the equation for T_{comm} (above) are equal. (In the EXECUBE prototype [Ko 94], the area between the routing mechanism and the link buffers is split about 40-60. Assuming C1 and C2 to be equal is thus not a significant departure from at least one real example. Refer to [DeGh 96] for results using other values of C1 and C2. The increase in capacity of a link translates into reducing the end to end packet transmission time. Hence, the network cost of a VLSI/WSI network has been redefined on a per node basis as:

$$NORM\_Network\_Cost = NORM\_VLSI\_AREA_{NxN-system} \times Network\_Diameter \times [(d+1)(d+2)/(n+1)(n+2)]$$

Note that in this scenario, the width of the wiring channel is a function of the specific topology.

Another scenario arises when the total area devoted to the wiring channels have to be constrained. Equivalently, the peak capacity of all links across the cross section of the wiring channel is bounded in this case, similar to a limitation of the bisection width. For this case, networks that have a lower track width can now use more wires per link, thereby increasing the capacity of each link. Assuming that the area requirement of the node does not increase with the increase in the number of bit-drivers for the wider links, the area requirement for all the networks can be considered to be equal. An appropriate cost measure for an N x N system in this scenario is:

$$FIXED\_BISECT\_Network\_Cost = Network\_Diameter \times (T_{BE} / N)$$

Some remarks on the impact of the number of metal layers and crossovers must now be made. In general, the impact of increasing the number of metal layers is to simply scale up the link capacity. Crossovers, on the other hand, in general, translate into an increase in the track widths. For the network sizes that are realistic for single chip multiprocessors, the number of crossovers play a secondary role, since with the use of 4 or more metal layers crossovers can be made virtually transparent.

Figure 5 depicts the normalized network costs required for various GCN systems using single port routers. Figure 6 depicts the normalized network costs for GCN systems using all-port routers. The network costs under the fixed bisection (or total die area) are shown in Figure 7.

Figures 5 and 6 show that GC-HCNs are preferred over all the other GCNs (including the hypercube) up to systems with 2^{12} nodes. Since system sizes of more than a few hundred to at best a few thousand nodes are impractical on a single chip, the GC-HCN clearly outperforms the other networks in this useful range. Note that the graphs for the GC-BDG and the GC-SE have a negative slope at the beginning of the cost graphs. This is a consequence of the interplay between the various factors in the cost function.

Figure 7 shows that under the fixed bisection width constraints the GC-HCN fares competitively with the GC-SE and GC-BDG. For large system sizes, the GC-HCN costs significantly less than the hypercubes.

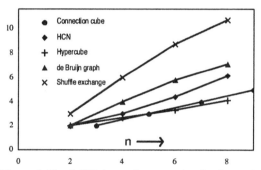

Figure 4. Track Efficiency for some basic elements of 2^n nodes.

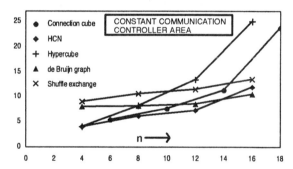

Figure 5. Normalized network cost of 2^n node 2-D GCNs for some basic elements with a single-ported router

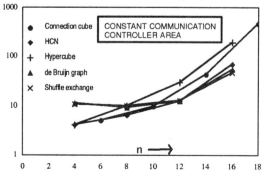

Figure 6. Normalized network cost of 2^n node 2-D GCNs for various basic elements for all-ported systems

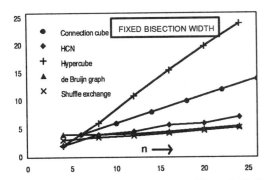

Figure 7. Normalized network cost: 2^n node 2-D GCNs for some basic elements for fixed bisection widths

6. Assessments and Conclusions

We introduced a family of cube based interconnection networks, called GCNs, which are based on Cartesian graphs. The GCNs are hierarchical in nature and use any network capable of emulating the hypercube as the basis. A key element of the GCNs is the ability to emulate many interesting properties of the hypercube, albeit using a smaller node degree. We introduced a specific GCN network called the GC-HCN which uses the HCN introduced in [GhDe90] as a basis. The resulting network not only emulates the connections of a comparable hypercube but unlike many cube-like low node degree networks, such as the ones described in Section 4, has the ability to embed meshes and tori and lends itself to recursive partitioning to allow sub-network allocations for multiprogrammed systems. Being recursively partitioned, each of these partitions of the GC-HCN have the ability to efficiently emulate the hypercube and embed meshes and tori. The network diameter of the GC-HCN is about 3/4-ths that of a comparable hypercube. We also showed that the GC-HCN outperforms all the other GCNs using the standard (diameter * node degree) product. All these properties of the GC-HCN are provided using almost half as many links as a comparable hypercube.

We also examined GCNs as VLSI interconnections, i.e., as interconnections within a single VLSI chip or on an MCM. In particular we looked at the area requirement for the wiring channels and the total die area under a variety of constraints. We also defined some possible measures of evaluating VLSI interconnections. It appears that many varieties of GCNs such as GC-BDG, GC-SE and GC-HCN appear to perform better than the hypercubes. However, given the fact that the GC-HCN is recursively partitionable to allow hypercube emulations and mesh/torus embeddings, the GC-HCN appears to be the network of choice for VLSI interconnections among other members of the GCN family.

References

[BhAg84] L. N. Bhuyan, and D. P. Agrawal, , "Generalized Hypercube and Hyperbus Structures for a Computer Network," IEEE Trans. on Computers, Vol. C-33, No. 1, April 1984, pp. 323-333.

[ChAgBu93] C. Chen., D. P. Agrawal., J. Burke., "dBCube: A New Class of Hierarchical Multiprocessor Interconnection Networks with Area Efficient Layout," IEEE Trans. on Parallel and Distr. Systems, pp. 1332-1344, Dec. 1993.

[DeGh 96] K. R. Desai and K. Ghose, "Generalized Cubic Interconnections", Technical Report CS-TR 96-14, Dept. of CS, SUNY-Binghamton, 1996.

[GaPr93] E. Ganesan., D. K. Pradhan., "The Hyper-deBruijn Networks: Scalable Versatile Architecture," IEEE Trans. on Parallel and Distr. Systems, vol. 4, no. 9, pp. 962-978, Sep. 1993.

[GhDe95] K. Ghose., K. R. Desai., "Hierarchical Cubic Networks," IEEE Trans. on Parallel and Distr. Systems, Vol 6, No. 4, Apr. 1995.

[GhDe90] K. Ghose and K. R. Desai, "The Design and Evaluation of Hierarchical Cubic Networks", Proc. Int'l. Conf. on Parallel Processing, 1990, Vol.I, pp. 355-362.

[HwGh87] K. Hwang, K. and J. Ghosh, "Hypernet: A Communication Efficient Architecture for Constructing Massively Parallel Computers," IEEE Trans. on Computers, Vol. C-36, No. 12, Dec 1987, pp 1450-1466.

[Ko94] P. M. Kogge., "EXECUBE - A New Architecture for Scalable MPPs" Proc. Int'l. Conf. on Parallel Processing, Vol. I, Aug. 1994, pp. 77-84.

[Lei92] F. T. Leighton., *Introduction to Parallel Algorithms And Architectures: Arrays-trees-hypercubes*, Morgan Kaufmann Publishers, 1992.

[MaBa94] Q. M. Malluhi and M. A. Bayoumi, "The Hierarchical Hypercube: A New Interconnection Topology for Massively Parallel Systems," IEEE Trans. on Parallel and Distr. Systems, Vol 5, No. 1, Jan. 1994.

[PrVu81] F. P. Preparata and J. Vuillemin, "The Cube-Connected Cycles: A Versatile Network for Parallel Computation," Comm. ACM, Vol. 24, No. 5, May 1981, pp. 300-309.

[SaPr89] M. R. Samatham., D. K. Pradhan., "The De Bruijn Multiprocessor Network: A Versatile Parallel Processing and Sorting Network for VLSI," IEEE Trans. on Computers, Vol. 38, No. 4, pp. 567-581, Apr. 1989.

[Si91] N. Singhvi., "The Connection Cubes: Symmetric Low Diameter Interconnection Networks with Low Node Degree" Proc. IEEE Int'l Parallel Processing Symp., Apr. 1993, pp. 260-267.

[SuBa77] H. Sullivan and T. R. Bashkow, "A Large Scale Homogeneous, Fully Distributed Parallel Machine, I," Proc. Fourth Symp. Comp. Architecture, March 1977, pp. 105-117.

[Yo91] A. Youssef., "Cartesian Product Networks," Proc. Int'l Conf. on Parallel Processing, pp. 684-685, Aug. 1991.

[ZhLoRa92] X. Zhong., V. Lo., S. Rajopadhye., "Optimal Implementation of Parallel Divide-and-Conquer Algorithms on de Bruijn Networks", Proc. of IEEE Symp on the Frontiers of Massively Parallel Computation, pp. 583-585, Oct. 1992.

❖ SESSION 3 ❖

Parallel Applications

Chair

N. Scarabottolo

An optimization of data movement operations : application to the tree-embedding problem

Jaafar Gaber and Bernard Toursel
L.I.F.L., Université des Sciences et Technologies de Lille1
59655 Villeneuve d'Ascq cedex -France-
e-mail: {gaber, toursel}@lifl.lifl.fr

Abstract

The goal of this paper is to present dynamic tree embedding algorithms with experimental results. This paper begins by presenting an optimization of data movement operations previously described for synchronous parallel machines in [1]. The data movement technique and the optimization are used for dynamically embedding arbitrary M-node trees in either a N-PEs hypercube or N-PEs q-dimensional mesh. The paper seeks to optimize the load of the embedding algorithms in order to satisfy the demands of load balancing. A randomized algorithm which achieves $O(M/N)$ load with high probability is presented. Experimental results obtained by the implementation of these tree embeddings, to validate our framework, on the two-dimensional mesh of the massively parallel computer MasPar MP-1 with 16,384 processors, are also given.

Keywords: *data movement technique, Dynamic embedding, arbitrary trees, randomized algorithm, interconnection networks*

1 Introduction

Parallel computers can be classified basically into two models of parallel computation [2, 3, 4]. One model is the PRAM model, which is a synchronous parallel system based on a shared memory which can be accessed by all processors in constant time. The second model is the distributed memory model, in which communication is performed through a fixed interconnection network [2]. Examples of the second model include hypercube-based computers and mesh-connected computer. Most algorithms designed for this model are mainly concerned with solving the routing and collision avoidance problem when data movement operations are needed.

In parallel processing, the problem of the implementation of tree-structured computations on a network of processors, the simulation of the tree-connected architecture by another and the problem of finding efficient representations for tree data structures are modeled as a graph embedding problems [2, 5, 6].

In general, an embedding of a guest graph G into a host graph H is a mapping of nodes of G into the nodes of H and a mapping of each edge of G to a path of H. The quality of an embedding is guided by some constraints that may differ from application to application [5]. Two common measures of quality of an embedding are the *load* and the *dilation*. The load of an embedding is the maximum number of nodes of the guest graph that are embedded in any single node of the host graph. The dilation which measures the communication delay is the maximum distance between the images of any pair of nodes in the host graph that are adjacent in the guest graph. The dilation is an important issue when the embedding is a one-to one mapping (or an injective mapping) and when we are allowed to "stretch" the edges of the guest graph on a path of the host graph. It is especially the case of the simulation of one architecture by another as founded in [2, 7, 8, 5, 6, 9, 10, 11]. When we consider many-to-one embedding, the load become the important issue [2].

Embeddings can be constructed as *Static* embeddings or *dynamic* embeddings. We have a static embedding when the whole information about the structure of the guest graph is known in advance. In a Dynamic embedding, the tree may grow or shrink in a manner that may be impossible to predict beforehand. Note that tree-structured computations are often dynamic in many applications. The dynamic embedding problem is harder than the static one ; if we are al-

127

lowed to see the entire tree before embedding it, then deterministic embedding algorithms can achieve constant dilation, load and congestion. F.T.LEIGHTON shows in [2] that any dynamic embedding algorithm that simultaneously optimizes maximum load and dilation must be randomized.

For SIMD computers, the data movement technique will be used to carry out communications among nodes. Note that this useful technique provides communications between all the PEs of the distributed architecture and all communications arrive at their targets simultaneously which cannot be achieved by any tree-embedding. Our main interest is therefore to balance the load and we don't acre about dilation. So our approach here is different from the previous works.

The rest of the paper is organized as follows. In section 2, we present the data movement operations. In section 3, we show that under some assumptions, the data movement operations may be reduced by a constant factor without otherwise altering the result. In section 4, we show how to use the data movement technique and the optimization to embed arbitrary trees in the hypercube and the q-dimensional mesh. Also, we analyze a randomized algorithm and provide experimental results on a 128×128 mesh which confirm the predicted analysis.

2 Basic Data movement operations

D.NASSIMI and S.SAHNI have introduced in [1] two important operations for moving and copying data among processors in synchronous parallel computers, the *random-access read* (RAR) and *random-access write* (RAW).

An SIMD computer consists of N processing elements (PEs). The PEs are indexed 0 through $N-1$ and may be referenced as $PE(i)$. Each PE has a some local memory. The PEs are connected together via an interconnection network. Different interconnection networks lead to different SIMD architectures. In this paper we shall consider two architectures, the q-dimensional mesh-connected computer (MCC) and the q-dimensional hypercube configured computer. [1].

The data stored in each memory is a record $G(i)$ having one key $h(i)$, a destination field $d(i)$, and one or more data fields $df(i)$ (i.e., $G(i) = (h(i), d(i), df(i))$). In a RAR operation, each record $G(i)$ is to read the data field of the record $G(j)$, where $d(i) = h(j)$. In RAW operation, each record $G(i)$ is to copy one of its

data fields to the corresponding data field of record $G(j)$, where $d(i) = h(j)$. In [1] it was shown that both of these operations can be implemented by a constant factor of well-defined steps. These are described below.

1. *Sort* : following a Sort, the records $G(i)$ will have been rearranged such that $h(i) \leq h(i+1)$, $0 \leq i < N-1$.

2. *Rank* : the rank of a selected record is the number of selected records in PEs with a smaller index. For example, the ranks of the flagged records (with an asterisk over a key value) $(-, 2, -, 2^*, 3^*, 4, 4^*, 7^*)$ are $(-, -, -, 0, 1, -, 2, 3)$.

3. *Concentrate* : assumes that the records have been ranked so that $h(i) = r(i)$. A Concentrate results in records $G(i)$ being moved to $PE(r(i))$. For example assume that $G(O : 7) = (A, -, -, B, -, C, -, D)$. Following a Concentrate, $G(O : 7) = (A, B, C, D, -, -, -, -)$

4. *Distribute* : Let $h(i)$ be a destination of the record $G(i)$ initially in $PE(i)$. The purpose of Distribute is to route $G(i)$ to $PE(h(i))$. Note that a Distribute is the inverse of a Concentrate. Suppose that $G(O : 7) = (A, B, C, -, -, -, -, -)$ and that $h(0) = 1$, $h(1) = 5$ and $h(2) = 6$. Following a Distribute, $G(O : 7) = (-, A, -, -, -, B, C, -)$

5. *Generalize* : a Generalize copies records $G(i)$ into PEs $h(i-1) + 1$ through $h(i)$ (for convenience, $h(-1) = 0$). Let $G(O : 7) = (A, B, C, -, -, -, -, -)$ and $h(0) = 1$, $h(1) = 5$ and $h(2) = 6$. Following a Generalize, $G(O : 7) = (A, A, B, B, B, B, C, -)$

Let N be the number of PEs in the q-dimensional mesh and the hypercube (note that $N = n^q = 2^p$ in the q-dimensional $n \times n \times ... \times n$ MCC). The complexity of Rank, Concentrate and distribute is $O(qn)$ on a q-dimensional $n \times n \times ... \times n$ mesh and $O(log N)$ on a N-PEs hypercube [1].

For example, consider $N = 8$. Moving a given record in PE(110) to the PE(011) ($h(110) = 011$) and a record in PE(011) to the PE(001) ($h(011) = 001$) is carried out by the following algorithm. At first, ranks are computed (ranks here are 0 and 1 resp. for the two records) by the procedure *Rank*. The records are next concentrated using the ranks just computed by the procedure *Concentrate* (concentrated in the example resp. in PE(0) and PE(1)). Finally, the concentrated records are distributed according $h(i)$ by *Distribute*.

3 Optimization of data movement operations

In order to get the right data to the right destination, certain well-defined steps should be performed. First, records are sorted into nondecreasing order of their destinations. The next step is to rank the records. We next concentrate the data using the ranks just computed. Finally, the concentration is followed by a distribute step according to the destination.

In the example shown in Fig.1, we have $N = 8$ PEs and records that have to be moved to the $d(i)$th PEs. We suppose that records are already sorted so we do not use Sort. In this example, we can simply route each record to its destination with only the procedure Concentrate. Note that no two records will ever collide at a node. In reverse order, we use the Distribute algorithm which is the inverse of the Concentrate.

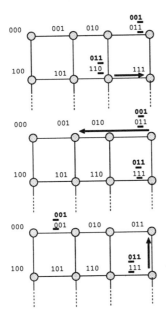

Figure 1: Concentration is carried out by first moving all records to PEs such that the PE index and $d(i)$ (in boldface) agree in bit 0. The next routing ensures that PE indices and $d(i)$ agree in bits 0 and 1 and so on until records have been routed to correct PEs.

Suppose at the start of some iteration b during a concentration step, we have two records originating respectively from the $PE(i)$ and the $PE(j)$ and their destinations are respectively $R(i)$ and $R(j)$. during this iteration, these records will be collide in $PE(\ell)$ only if [12]

$$\ell = (i_{k-1:b+1}, R(i)_{b:0}) = (j_{k-1:b+1}, R(j)_{b:0})$$

which implies $|i - j| < 2^{b+1}$ and $|R(i) - R(j)| \geq 2^{b+1}$. Hence the ranking are such $|i - j| \geq |R(i) - R(j)|$, no two records will ever collide [12]. An exemple of the situation where two records can collide, let concentrate two records from $PE(110)$ and $PE(111)$ respectively to $PE(011)$ and $PE(101)$. These two records will collide in $PE(111)$ since that during the first iteration, the record in $PE(111)$ will get destroyed (overwritten) by the incoming record from $PE(110)$.

For the distribute operation, the proof is similar; two records will collide if only

$$\ell = (R(i)_{k-1:b}, i_{b-1:0}) = (R(j)_{k-1:b}, j_{b-1:0})$$

which implies $|R(i) - R(j)| < 2^b$ and $|i - j| \geq 2^b$. Or we have $|i - j| \leq |R(i) - R(j)|$ as the records are concentrated.

As a consequence of this analysis, under the assumption that the distance between the origins of two messages (resp.destinations) is greater than the destinations (resp.origins), the routing algorithm has to use just two steps, Sort + Concentrate (resp. Distribute), instead of four steps, Sort+Rank+Concentrate+Distribute. The running time of the routing algorithm is decreased by a constant factor without otherwise altering the result.

We ran, on the SIMD massively parallel computer MasPar's MP-1 (with 16384 PEs), a parallel implementation of an algorithm wherein a complete binary tree grow during the course of the computation. Fig.2 show experimental results when the optimization is (resp. is not) used on the 2D-mesh. Note that in a complete binary tree, the distance between two nodes is greater than the distance between their parent nodes as it will be shown in the next section.

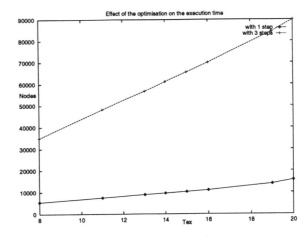

Figure 2: Effect of the optimization on the execution time.

4 Application to the Tree-embedding problem

We focus now on embedding arbitrary trees into a q-dimensional mesh or an hypercube. We cite these two architectures since they are well known and that the data movement technique is developed for both them.

Embedding binary trees onto different architectures has been widely studied as in the hypercube [2],[5],[6],[13], [14], the grid [9], [10], [15], [11], the star graphs [16], the hexagonal array [17], and the pyramid networks [18]. The embedding algorithms that we will describe here will work for every (binary or not) tree. We will show that these embedding algorithms embed any M-node tree in N-PEs hypercube or N-PEs q-dimensional mesh with load $O(M/N)$, which is optimal for all M since the load of any embedding is always at least $\Omega(M/N)$ [2].

4.1 Definitions

The data movement technique without optimization is well suited for randomized routing (i.e. moving data from one set of PEs to any another predetermined set of PEs) as is the case when data is stored in a random fashion in memories. However, when embedding trees in a mesh or a hypercube, each node of the trees is assigned a PE according to some mapping function. As a consequence, data is stored in memories according to some logical pattern. By being more careful in our embedding, we will be able to benefit in the optimization described in the previous section.

Given an arbitrary tree T (binary or not) with M nodes. We consider here the two following mapping :

- an *irregular mapping* : the node v with index i is stored in processor $PE(i \bmod N)$. An index i of each node of the tree is obtained by traversing T in Breadth First manner (counting from left to right).

- a *regular mapping* : the positions of the nodes of the tree are computed as follows. A node of T in $PE(i)$ has d children that are in $PE((di + 1) \bmod N)$, $PE((di + 2) \bmod N)$, ..., $PE((di + d) \bmod N)$. Once a node of the tree is embedded, it cannot be moved.

In what follow, we will examine the load of the embedding algorithms and the effects of the two mapping functions on tree-operations; In reality, to be able to manipulate the tree, we need basic tree operations which provide communication between children and parent nodes, namely *Child→Parent*, *Children→Parent*, *Parent→Child* and *Parent→Children*. These operations will be implemented with the data movement operations.

4.2 irregular embedding

Consider the embedding which use the irregular mapping function. Note that the load of this embedding is $\lceil M/N \rceil$ which is optimal. Moreover, as a consequence of the preceding analysis, when T is a complete binary tree for example, to perform an operation like *Child→Parent*, only the procedure Concentrate has to be used, since we have the inequality $|i-j| > |\lfloor (i-1)/2 \rfloor - \lfloor (j-1)/2 \rfloor|$ (when a node v is located in $PE(i)$, his parent node is in $PE(\lfloor (i-1)/2 \rfloor)$). Note that we do not need the procedure Sort since the children nodes indices are higher than parents nodes indices.

This result is not immediate for arbitrary trees. The situation whereis we need to perform all the data movement procedures occur when the distance between two nodes is less than the distance between their parent nodes. Let $R(j)$ and $R(l)$ be the parent nodes respectively of j and l. Suppose that $|R(j) - R(l)| > |j - l|$ and $j > l$. Each node k in $[R(l)..R(j)]$ has his right and left child (if any) in $[l..j]$. if $R(j) - R(l) > j - l$ then we have some w nodes k, where $w = (R(j) - R(l)) - (j - l)$, that they have not any child (note that indices of PEs are naturals).

In the case where each node of $[R(l)..R(j)]$ has at least one child, we are be able to benefit in the optimization. Otherwise, a test should be carried out to foreknow that conflicts could be arise. Of course, this test increase the running time. The complexity of this operation is the same as that of procedure Rank. By using the regular mapping function, we do not need any test.

4.3 regular embedding

In this mapping, the position of the nodes of the tree are computed as follows. For simplicity, we will assume that the tree T is an arbitrary binary tree. A node of T in $PE(i)$ has two children that are in $PE(2i + 1)$ and $PE(2i + 2)$. Once a node of the tree is embedded, it cannot be moved. Such logical node storage patterns lead to use the optimization; the distance between any nodes is essentially higher than the distance between the corresponding parent nodes. Unfortunately, this simple algorithm just described does not obtain very good load. We destroy this negative aspects associated with regularity by using a randomized algorithm similar to the very interesting *flip-bit algorithm* described by F.T.LEIGHTON in [2]; *the flip-bit algorithm* embed an arbitrary M-node binary tree in an N-node hypercube with dilation 1 and load $O(M/N + \log N)$. This algorithm is also used in [2] for embedding an arbitrary M-node binary tree in the hypercube with dilatation $O(1)$ and load $O(M/N + 1)$; the embedding is a composition of an embedding of the M-node binary tree in an N-node hypercube of cliques and the embedding of a hypercube of cliques in a hypercube [2].

Note that our algorithm here embed M-node arbitrary tree (binary or not) in a hypercube or in a q-dimensional mesh.

4.4 probabilistic analysis

The embedding algorithm operates as follows. Each tree node v is assigned a random value $a(v) \in [0,1[$. Let $b(v) = a(v) \times 2$ (since T is a binary tree), $b(v) \in [0,2[$ and that is equally likely to be in $[0,1[$ or $[1,2[$. The children of v are embedded according this value. Suppose v is embedded in processor i. If $b(v) \in [0,1[$ then the left child of v (if it exists) is embedded in processor $2i+1$ and the right child (if it exists) in processor $2i+2$. If $b(v) \in [1,2[$ then the children are embedded in reverse fashion. By using a Markov process to model the embedding algorithm, we will show that the algorithm embeds any M-node tree with load $O(M/N)$ with high probability.

At the start, the root of the tree is mapped to a processor chosen with a probability $1/N$. The initial state is $P(0) = (p_i)_0$, where $p_i = 1/N$ for $0 \leq i \leq N$. The choice of children's processors (processors on which children are mapped to) at the state k depends only on the father's processor i.e. depend only on the state $k-1$. We have thus a Markov's chain for which the transition matrix is $A = (a_{ij})_{0 \leq i,j \leq N}$ where there exist j_1, j_2 such that $a_{ij_1} = a_{ij_2} = 1/2$ and $a_{ij} = 0$ for all $j \neq j_1, j_2$, $i = 1, ..., N$

At the state k, we have

$$P(k) = A^k P(0) = AP(k-1), \ \forall k \geq 1$$

As a consequence of the form of the matrix A, we have

$$P(k) = (p_k)_k = P(0), \ \forall k \geq 1$$

Thus, the probability that a processor j is chosen at any step is $1/N$ (cf the example below).

Let $X_i = 1$ (resp. $X_i = 0$) if the node i is (resp. is not) in the processor j. X_i is a Bernoulli random variable (a bernoulli random variable is a $0-1$ random variable, more precisely, X_i is a bernoulli random variable if and only if $Prob[X_i = 0] + Prob[X_i = 1] = 1$).

Since we have $Prob[X_i = 1] = 1/N$ (and $Prob[X_i = 0] = (N-1)/N$), X_i follows a Bernoulli law i.e. $X_i \sim \mathcal{B}(1; 1/N)$.

Let X denote the number of the nodes that are mapped to a processor i. We have thus

$$E(X) = E(\sum_{i=1}^{M} X_i) = M \times 1/N$$

which means that the average number of nodes $E(X)$ mapped to a processor i is M/N (note that $E(X_i) = 1/N$).

We have now showing as desired that the embedding algorithm embed any M-node tree in N-PEs with load $O(M/N)$, which is optimal for all M since the load of any embedding is always at least $\Omega(M/N)$.

Example : For example, consider the behavior of the randomized algorithm on $N = 4$ processors. We will assume for simplicity that the tree is an arbitrary binary tree. Let $p(A/B)$ denote the probability that a processor A is to be able to be reached by the child of the node embedded in the processor B. For example, $p(1/0) = p(2/0) = 0.5$, since children of node i are in $(2*i+1) mod\, 4$ and $(2*i+2) mod\, 4$. Thus, we have the following transition matrix 4×4

$$\begin{pmatrix} p(0) \\ p(1) \\ p(2) \\ p(3) \end{pmatrix}_{k+1} = \begin{pmatrix} 0 & 0.5 & 0 & 0.5 \\ 0.5 & 0 & 0.5 & 0 \\ 0.5 & 0 & 0.5 & 0 \\ 0 & 0.5 & 0 & 0.5 \end{pmatrix} \begin{pmatrix} p(0) \\ p(1) \\ p(2) \\ p(3) \end{pmatrix}_{k}$$

Sine at the start

$$P(0) = \begin{pmatrix} 1/4 \\ 1/4 \\ 1/4 \\ 1/4 \end{pmatrix}_0$$

We have $P(k+1) = AP(k) = P(0), \forall k \geq 1$ and $E(X) = M/4$. we can conclude that the load is distributed evenly throughout the processors.

We ran a parallel implementation of an algorithm wherein an arbitrary tree grows during the course of the computation (as in branch-and-bound serach, divide-and-conquer or game tree evaluation), on a 128×128 mesh. The following table gives the experimental results in terms of load when the randomized algorithm is (resp. is not) used to balance load.

Number of nodes	load without randomized algorithm	load with randomized algorithm	ideal load
3123	93.00	1.17	1
55791	219.00	4.59	3.41
65135	4.00	4.00	3.98
99325	16.00	6.82	6.06
204383	64.00	13.43	12.47
731923	64.00	45.86	44.67
1640123	256.00	102.59	100.11

This table gives the execution time of an algorithm wherein an arbitrary binary tree grows on a 128×128 mesh of the MasPar. The randomized algorithm is used to balance load.

Number of nodes	load without random.	execut. time	load with random.	execut. time
12641	16.00	12.820	5.00	12.680
15771	2.00	10.107	1.80	11.628
18555	34.00	13.289	6.00	12.776
20697	25.00	13.103	6.00	12.775
85845	57.00	14.017	14.00	13.005
122095	40.00	13.849	19.00	13.501
424039	144.00	24.095	40.00	21.609
1044231	178.00	25.040	71.30	24.22

5   Conclusion

In this paper, tree embedding algorithms on mesh and hypercube are presented. We have validated our approach of embedding on the 2D-mesh of the massively parallel machine MasPar. Our framework is based on the data movement techinque. An optimization of this technique and a randomized algorithm are also presented with experimental results. We expect that our randomized algorithm which is not related to any topologies can be useful for balancing load in other networks.

Acknowledgment

We are grateful to Said Elhamine and Vincent Lesage for their helpful suggestions and discussions. We thank also J.C. Routier and E. Wegrzynowski for their helpful comments and discussions.

References

[1] D.Nassimi and S.Sahni. Data broadcasting in simd computers. *IEEE Transactions on Computers*, C-30(2):101–107, February 1981.

[2] F. Thomson Leighton. *Introduction to parallel algorithms and architectures*. Morgan Kaufmann Publishers Inc., 1992.

[3] F. Thomson Leighton. *Introduction aux algorithmes et architectures parallèles*. trad. Pierre Fraigniaud et Eric Fleury, International Thomson publishing France, M.K. Publishers Inc., 1995.

[4] H. M. Alnuweiri and V. K. Prasanna. Efficient parallel computations on the reduced mesh of trees organization. *Journal of Parallel and Distributed Computing*, 20(2):121–135, February 1904.

[5] P.Kulasinghe and S.Bettayeb. Embeddings binary trees into crossed cubes. *IEEE Transactions on Computers*, 44(7):923–929, July 1995.

[6] A.S.Wagner. Embeddigs all binary trees in the hypercube. *Journal of Parallel and Distributed Computing*, 18(1), May 1993.

[7] A.M.Gibons and M.S.Paterson. Dense edge-disjoint embedding of complete binary trees in interconnection networks. *CS-RR-208*, February 1992.

[8] A.M.Gibons and R.Ziani. The balanced binary tree technique on mesh connected computer. *Information Processing Letters*, 37(2):101–109, January 1991.

[9] M. JIBER and A. BELLAACHIA. Embedding quadtree structures on x-mesh networks. *Proc. 10th Annual International Symposium on High Performance Computers, Ottawa, Canada (5-7), June, 1996.*

[10] M.-C. HEYDEMANN, J. OPATRNY, and D. SOTTEAU. Embedding of complete binary trees into extended grids with edge congestion 1. *Research Report no. , LRI, Université de Paris Sud, Centre d'Orsay, France, 1996.*

[11] J.Gaber, B.Toursel, G.Goncalves, and T.Hsu. Embedding trees in massively parallel computers. *Euromicro Journal of Systems Architecture*, 42(3):165–170, October 1996.

[12] D.Nassimi and S.Sahni. Parallel permutation and sorting algorithms and a new generalized connection network. *Journal of the ACM*, 29(3):642–667, July 1982.

[13] A.S.Wagner. Embeddig the complete tree in the hypercube. *Journal of Parallel and Distributed Computing*, 20(2):241–247, Feb 1994.

[14] V. HEUN and E.W. MAYR. Efficient dynamic embedding of arbitrary binary trees into hypercubes. *In Proc. of the 3rd IRREGULAR'96, Lecture Notes in Computer Science 1117, Springer-Verlag*, pages 287–298, 1996.

[15] E.Horowitz and A.Zorat. The binary tree as an interconnection network. *Proc. of the 1980 conf. on networks*, April 1980.

[16] Heydemann M.C., J.Opatrny, and D.Sotteau. Embedding of complete binary trees into star graphs with congestion 1. *Research Report no. 906, L.R.I., Université de Paris Sud, Centre d'Orsay, France*, May 1994.

[17] D.Gordon, I.Coren, and G.M.Silberman. Embedding tree structures in vlsi hexagonal arrays. *IEEE Transactions on Computers*, January 1984.

[18] A.Dingle and I.H.Sudborough. Simulation of binary trees and x-trees on pyramid networks. *Journal of Parallel and Distributed Computing*, 19(2), October 1993.

Dynamic Load Balancing for Parallel Traffic Simulation

Andrej Tibaut[⊗], Dipl. Eng. Comp. Sc.

University of Maribor, Faculty of Civil Engineering, Smetanova 17, 2000 Maribor, Slovenia,
tel: +386 62 2294382, fax: +386 62 224 179
andrej.tibaut@uni-mb.si

Abstract

In this paper, we describe implementation of the Parallel Traffic Simulator which applies parallel algorithms and computer graphics in the field of traffic simulation. It simulates traffic behaviour at the individual vehicle level. Parallel environment used consists of a set of workstations connected in a network. Networked workstations make up a loosely coupled parallel computer architecture with distributed memory. PVM network programming environment is used to implement message passing between workstations.

Simulation of traffic is an example of computation with changing load balance. Data parallel approach with initial static data decomposition distributes road network and initial positions of vehicles across participating workstations. However, as the simulation progresses, vehicles may concentrate only on some workstations which leads to system imbalance. Therefore we have developed a dynamic load-balancing algorithm.

Key words: parallel computing, parallel algorithm, dynamic load-balancing, PVM

1. Introduction

Much work has been done in the recent years in parallel computing. Parallel computing has brought substantial benefits to the areas where scientific problems are so complex that solving them requires extraordinary powerful computers (quantum chemistry, astrophysics, meteorology, computational fluid dynamics and turbulence). Of course, another application areas grab results from parallel computing as well. Simulation of traffic at the individual vehicle level is an interesting problem domain where complexity is measured in terms of large data sets that are often too large for a single processor to hold in memory at once. On a single processor it is impossible to control a movement of a very large number of vehicles along roads without making a sacrifice of simulation performance. This implies that by harnessing additional processors in parallel and decomposing the problem domain into sub-domains we can speed-up the simulation. Researchers at University of Edinburgh have proved the benefits of parallel computing. Their traffic simulation can move 200,000 vehicles spread over 7,000 roads at real time rates [1]. Data decomposition is the next important issue when designing parallel algorithms. Using data parallel approach, parallel algorithm initially distributes data across processors and makes them responsible for them. Thus, parallel algorithm for traffic simulation needs to parallelise data such as road network geometry, road network topology and initial positions of vehicles. In [1] each processor is *statically* assigned a queue, the parallel item of data, which is associated with all the lanes that comprise one direction of the road link. The relation processor-queue remains unchanged during the simulation run. As the number of vehicles on the particular processor vary between simulation frames this can result in situations where some processors have only a few or even none vehicles to control (all vehicles are outside the processor's region). If such situation occurs load imbalance increases and usage ratio of the processor falls. Dynamic nature of traffic has motivated us to investigate dynamic load-balancing; dynamic redistribution of intersections, roads and vehicles during the simulation.

Our parallel computing environment is a multicomputer; set of UNIX based workstations on a local area network.

[⊗] work done whilst at School of Computing and Information Technology (CIT), Griffith University, Nathan, Queensland 4111, Australia, under supervison of dr. Rok Sosič. This research was funded in part by the Slovene Science Fundation and Izobraževalna fundacija Pomurja.

134

The remainder of this paper is structured as follows: We first give an overview of essential requirements in designing traffic simulation. Subsequently, we describe parallel algorithms and compare them with the parallel environment, parallel algorithm and load-balancing used in our project. Implementation details of the parallel algorithm and dynamic load-balancing are given in following sections. Finally, we draw some conclusions and give directions for further work.

2. Traffic simulation

Traffic simulation has been in existence for many

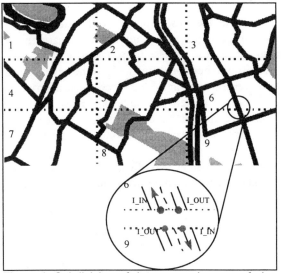

Figure 1: Subdivision of data space in case of nine networked workstations with an example of a road link split

years. They all had to use simplified models of traffic flow in order to produce results within practical timescales. A typical assumption is to represent traffic flow in a particular road as a single quantity. Such models are generally called *macroscopic* models, simulation being called macroscopic simulation. Unfortunately, such models do not properly represent real traffic behaviour in congested situations, and do not reproduce the fluctuating nature of real world situations [1]. Models that model traffic at the individual vehicle level being called *microscopic* models. Microscopic simulation enables more accurate study of congestion formation and dispersion and emphasizes the insight into the nature of road traffic flow. During each time step, the vehicles are moved towards its destinations, and from road to road if necessary, as in real-life.

3. Parallel traffic simulation

The parallel environment used for our project consisted of networked workstations connected by an Ethernet. Our parallel environment can be thought of as a MIMD system. The system consists of a set of computers connected in a network, each executing its own copy of the simulation program and having its own data subset on which to operate. One of the computers, called host, directs the simulation. It dispatches data and control to other workstations which are called nodes. Host process runs on a single workstation from which we can control the simulation. It provides user interface and displays the road network with current positions of vehicles. The application provides a separate load-balancing window. The window shows current distribution of roads on nodes by displaying the parts of the road network in different colors; all roads with the same color correspond to a single node.

3.1. Network data

In order to simulate the movement of vehicles we need road network data. We describe underlying road network with intersections (nodes) and roads (links). In terms of geometry we use two graphical primitives (point and line) to describe the topology of a graph. The simplest intersection has two roads (entry and exit road); two directed links having one node in common. Each intersection-to-intersection connection is either one- or two-way road. Additional data associated with roads (maximum speed allowed, road width, parkdistance, roadlength, etc.) intersections (traffic lights, giveway roads, etc.) and polygons (shaded areas on the map which are not important for simulation - buildings, grass, etc.) complete the topology of the road network. Given the described data we can transform them into the parallel form.

3.2 Parallelising the data

Generally, we achieve the concurrency of a computation with:
- *functional parallelism* (pipelining) where a computation is divided into a number of steps that are executed concurrently;
- *data space parallelism* where a computation associated with a program load is initially distributed over the participating processors in either of two ways:
  - *image space parallelism* (often referred to as *image space partitioning* or *screen subdivision*) where areas of pixels are assigned to each processor.
  - object space parallelism (often referred to as object partitioning)

Algorithm for object space parallelism divides the input data, which can be 2D (set of polygons) or 3D (volumes, voxels) objects in some arbitrary manner into data subsets or subvolumes, respectively, and distributes them to multiple processors. Each processor processes these parallel items of data separately and locally, and finally redistributes and composites them into a final image. The total number of data subsets can be expressed as P x G, where P is the number of nodes and G is the number of data subsets per node (*granularity ratio*). G must be chosen properly so as to minimise overhead in data partitioning phase and maximize load balance.

The first task in the design of a parallel algorithm is to build a parallel data framework for simulation process. We have implemented object space partitioning technique where parallel items of data, regions, have to be computed first in order to partition road network geometry into that regions. Given a road network an algorithm divides the simulation area extent (rectangular area of an underlying road network that is used for simulation) into disjoint square regions. The size of these regions is adjusted according to the number of nodes we use (Figure 1). The regions form an equal lattice along each dimension. Each node controls one region. This reduces the amount of computation when partitioning the data but potentially increases the load imbalance. Next task is to classify each road and polygon (from underlying road network) according to the regions they overlap and send them to the nodes assigned to those regions. If road overlaps with two or more regions it will be split into two or more road segments, respectively. Each of these road segments belongs to a separate region and, therefore, is associated with a separate node.

Alternative approaches to partitioning of the data would be:

- An algorithm with G>1. Increasing the number of regions (tasks) per node results in more work involved in partitioning the data and more communication between nodes, but load is better balanced [4].
- Road network geometry partitioning where an algorithm assigns the first N roads encountered as the first road subset. Using this approach implies each road subset to be a collection of roads which do not necessary lie within square region.

3.3 Parallel algorithm

The parallel algorithm for traffic simulation has two parts: *host process* and *node process*. Host process starts a simulation by loading road network geometry, data for simulation in microscopic form and parameters for parallel environment. It then initializes the parallel environment and subdivides a simulation area extent into 2D square regions. Regions are then mapped onto nodes:

each node is assigned one region together with network data context associated with that region (roads, polygons, intersections, statecycles and initial positions of vehicles). Then all nodes allocate the data, for which they are responsible, in a local memory. When they finish, they notify the host, which sends them a message to start the simulation. During the simulation run host sends messages to nodes at regular intervals in order to provide the movement of vehicles and an update of vehicles positions in simulation window. It also triggers the execution of a load-balancing code in nodes, if necessary, and gathers statistic on current number of vehicles per node.

Node process does the actual simulation work. It acts as a slave to the host process. Node executes a non-blocking loop (asynchronous communication) while waiting for a new request from a sender which can be either host or other node. Request is a message associated with a specific task in node. When request arrives into node's receive buffer, the node processes it and starts with an execution of the corresponding sequential code. When the requested task is completed, notification is sent back to the sender.

Node's tasks can be classified, according to the flow of the parallel algorithm, into three groups: *data partitioning tasks* (initialize node, set node number, set mapview, set window size, set vehicle size, etc.), *simulation tasks* (simulation report, update data, update display, exchange vehicles, transmit intersection info, transmit vehicles info, report positions of vehicles, give vehicle, etc.), *load-balancing tasks* (report load-balancing, move data, receive intersection, receive road, receive vehicle, receive statecycle, direct intersection, merge entryroad, merge exitroad, etc.). The intention is to minimize the communication overhead as it is known that sending messages is expensive and slows the performance of the parallel algorithm.

Node associated with its respective simulation region controls and moves vehicles within that region towards their destinations. A single vehicle whether remains within the boundaries of region A or leaves the region on the map associated with node A and continues in the neighbouring region associated with node B. In the latter case nodes communicate by sending messages.

3.4 Load-balancing

In distributed system with set of nodes capable to work in parallel we want to optimize the nodes' usage while ensuring even amount of load, and therefore computation, for all nodes. Load-balancing is not an intrinsic part of the parallel algorithm, but an extension.

In the parallel traffic simulation we can achieve load-balancing with static distribution or dynamic redistribution of simulation load. Vehicles are referred to as simulation load. Vehicles may concentrate the computation on few nodes only while consequently other nodes show low usage ratio or even latency intervals. To avoid this, we have implemented *dynamic load-balancing* approach which uses the heuristics based upon node's local information to determine the part of the entire road network that will be moved to another node.

Our algorithm uses simple criteria for evaluation of load imbalance, *number of vehicles per node*. The algorithm checks the number of vehicles on each participating node and finds out the nodes with the maximum, and the minimum number of vehicles. Maximum number of vehicles tells the load-balancing algorithm about the node (source) from which the reasonable amount of load has to be transferred to the node (destination) with the minimum number of vehicles.

Load-balancing forces nodes to more autonomous

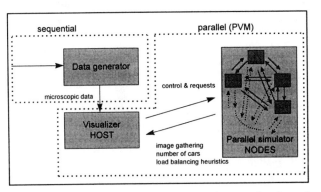

Figure 2: Architecture and communication mechanism of the Parallel Traffic Simulator

behaviour by having decision making capabilities that we have built in nodes, *the agent* [3]. Through these decision making capabilities nodes are able to share the load and co-ordinate their activities by means of communication. An *agent* is the function in node that responds to the message from host to node controlling the maximum number of vehicles. An agent locally and independently, without any prior knowledge, decides which intersection will be moved to the destination node. After the communication task that follows is completed the destination node takes over the control of the new intersection in its list. During the communication task the algorithm transfers all data that define the intersection including all entry and exit roads. We will describe both host-agent and node-agent in more details later in this report.

The essence of our load-balancing algorithm is disassociation of image space and nodes' responsibility. The early distribution of data between nodes makes the correlation between the road network primitives (data space), their positions on the screen (image space) and the (static) distribution of responsibility for these primitives

which remains unchanged until load-balancing starts. More precisely, a road that fall in the upper left region, when dividing the simulation area into disjoint regions and making nodes responsible for all actions that affect their respective regions, resides in that region but the responsibility for it changes depending on the load-balancing flow. Thus, nodes' responsibility changes dynamically. We are currently exploring load-balancing heuristics that can take the complexity of dynamic nature of traffic into account when deciding about which intersection to move to ensure equal loads on all nodes. Proper heuristics makes it possible to achieve good load-balancing without excess communication.

4. Implementation of the Parallel Traffic Simulator

Parallel Computing Unit, at Griffith University, School of Computing and Information Technology, in collaboration with IBM, has built a simple parallel computer to demonstrate the concepts of parallel computing to the general public. Originally, the parallel system consisted of 10 personal computers; one is called the host and the other 9 are called nodes, because they do the actual work in parallel. The problem is one of modelling Brisbane's traffic. The movement of vehicles is simulated, as well as the behaviour of traffic lights and uncontrolled intersections. In order to simulate all of Brisbane's traffic at the individual vehicle level, it would be normally be necessary to use a very fast computer system [2].

Two versions of the Parallel Traffic Simulator have been implemented: one on groups of PCs and another on groups of networked workstations Silicon Graphics Indy. The programming model used is a host/node model. Both implementations make use of X-Windows and PVM. Figure 2 shows the three major software components of our implementation.

4.1 Networked workstations

A group of nine workstations Silicon Graphics Indy connected by an Ethernet has been used for this implementation. Each of these workstations is equipped with processor R4600SC/133MHz, rated at 73.7 SPECfp92, with 32 Mbytes of physical memory.

Networked workstations make up a loosely coupled parallel computer architecture which in our case uses PVM (Parallel Virtual Machine), a parallel program development environment, to implement message-passing for communication and synchronization between nodes. Real time simulation is generally not achievable in such an environment, but with minor changes the code can be ported to a massively parallel supercomputer.

The latest extension of the Parallel Traffic Simulator concerns study and implementation of the adaptive load-balancing algorithm.

4.2 PVM 3.0

PVM ([5]) is a software system that permits a network of heterogeneous UNIX computers to be used as a single parallel computer. Thus large computational problems can be solved by using the aggregate power of many computers. Under PVM collection of networked workstations appear as one large distributed-memory computer (virtual machine). Applications written in C, can be parallelized by using message-passing PVM constructs common to most distributed-memory computers.

To run a program under PVM the user first executes the daemon process on the local host computer which in turn starts up daemon processes on all other node computers. The user's application (the node program) which should reside on each node can then be invoked on each node by a local host program (the host program) via the daemon processes.

4.3 Data generator

Data generator is sequential process in the pre-processing phase where several programs are used to prepare data in a microscopic form suitable for use by Parallel Traffic Simulator.

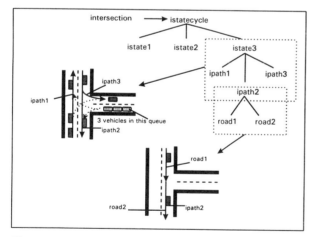

Figure 3: Structure of microscopic data for use by Parallel Traffic Simulator

Intersection is a point (junction) in a road network graph consisting of pairs of entry- and exit-roads. *Istate-cycle* has at least one *istate* and each of them has one or more *ipaths*. Istatecycle is essentially a traffic light. Each Istate opens its corresponding paths (ipath) for a specified time (green light interval - vehicles using this paths are allowed to move forward) and closes the previous ones

(red light interval - vehicles on this path are requested to stop and wait for the next green light interval). Figure 3 shows the hierarchical structure of microscopic data and an example of an intersection with the active state istate3. Exploded situation shows intersection with three open paths (ipath1, ipath2, ipath3). This data, once in microscopic form, is then mapped into the parallel data structures on the host at program start-up. The data generation process needs typically to be performed once only to set up file with microscopic data for a given road network.

Figure 3 shows an extract of the road network traffic with the lanes outlined. Dashed lines with arrows and shaded show the lanes where the vehicles must stop and wait until green light goes on. Vehicles on each link (entry- and exit-road) compose a *queue of vehicles*. A *queue of vehicles* is the most variable data structure in nodes. When moving from one link to another (at junctions), vehicle is removed from one queue and inserted into another. When the node process starts it sets-up these queues and fill them with data received from host.

4.4 Host process

According to the approach we settled on for our parallel algorithm the host process first reads data needed for the initialization of parallel environment. It then reads topology data for the given road network and builds its internal dynamic representation (frame). At the beginning majority of code here deals with intersection as it is the key structure and as such most complex of all. Data decomposition phase starts with the splitting of the previously created dynamic frame into the portions (subframes) used for the simulation according to the number of nodes in simulation. Then, clipping algorithms place intersections, roads and polygons within the boundaries of their corresponding nodes. Host then spawns node processes and sends initialization data to them. They remain idle until subframes to them. Now that host has successfully distributed data among nodes it can initialize X-Windows based application user interface. We use primitives from the X-Widgets library for user interface. Then host sends its first message (SCM_FULLDISPLAY) to all nodes. If we use standalone workstations as nodes then they are capable to display their parts of simulation on their local displays. Although we can optionally switch off displays rather then spend processing time for displaying simulation on nodes.

4.5 Node process

Host process launches node processes using PVM daemons in nodes. First, node process does initialization and receives basic information from the host that should be present before the simulation can be started. It then starts the simulation server which is an asynchronous message handler (non-blocking message polling loop) that allows node responding to both X and PVM events. PVM events start new tasks in node and may be generated either by host (i.e. loadbalancing report message) or by another nodes (i.e. receive car message). When a requested task has been completed, notification will be sent back to the sender.

4.6 Load-balancing algorithm

The algorithm, roughly described in previous sections, can be divided into four steps. The code for the first two steps reside on host, step 3 and 4 execute on node. In this context we introduced two individual agents: host-agent (step 1, step 2) and node-agent (step 3, step 4). Load-balancing is the interplay between these two agents. Host-agent receives request for balancing the simulation load at regular intervals. It then requests positions of vehicles from nodes by sending message SCM_REPORT_LOADBALANCING to them. Immediately afterwards it calls the function where it gathers road co-ordinates from nodes and redisplays roads with node specific colours. The idea for host-agent is to find two nodes: the node with the maximum number of vehicles and the node with the minimum number of vehicles. If these two values diverge much from the calculated average value we can designate the simulation load as not well balanced. In this case the node with the maximum number of vehicles receives the message LB_LOADBALANCING_MOVE. Host-agent does not know what node-agent is actually going do to contribute to good load-balancing.

Now, node-agent can start with step 3 of the algorithm. Node-agent expects from host-agent two integers which conform to the unique identifier of a node with the lowest workload during the current frame. In this step node-agent chooses single intersection among all intersections on the node. The simplest method for selection of intersection is the one based on random function. However, such approach reveals potential drawback of our algorithm. It does not guarantee that the selected intersection has the highest number of vehicles on its entry- and exitroads. It may even have none of them. If such situation occurs and intersection migrates to destination node, load distribution remains unchanged, but communication overhead increases. Finally, in step 4 node deploys PVM-routines to transfer the data structures associated with selected intersection to the destination node. Vehicles are transferred as well.

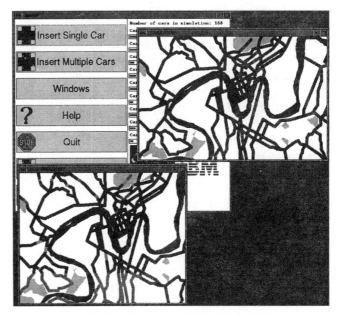

Figure 4: GUI of the Parallel Traffic Simulator

4.7 Visualizer

The Visualizer is a part of the application user interface designed in the X Window System programming environment that gives us the possibility to present a similar application user interface across all X-Windows based workstations. The Visualizer has three parts (Figure 4.): user menu based upon the X Toolkit library (Xt Intrinsics and Athena widgets), simulation window (parallel traffic simulator using road network in Brisbane) and load-balancing window.

User menu provides simulation control to the user and draws the graphs showing the current relative count of vehicles on each node. Simulation window simplifies the insight into simulation and load-balancing window enables better study of a load-balancing algorithm.

5. Future work

The main goal was to study and to implement the adaptive load-balancing for a traffic simulator. To illustrate the efficiency of such adaptive load-balancing approach we need to complete the tests that would show detailed performance and benefits of this method.

To evaluate the performance of the load-balancing algorithm we plan to compare the following three approaches:

- simulation without load-balancing,
- random load-balancing - node-agent selects intersection randomly, fragmentation of intersections could be high,
- local load-balancing - in order to decrease the fragmentation of intersections in node, node-agent

tends to select the intersection which is close to the one previously selected

The efficiency of the load-balancing algorithm described above closely depends on the following components:

- host-agent algorithm (step 1: an algorithm for evaluation of load imbalance heuristics, step 2: an algorithm for determination of source and destination node),
- node-agent algorithm (step 3: an algorithm for selection of intersection, step 4: an algorithm for transfer of selected intersection)

We plan to refine these algorithms as they can significantly improve load-balancing policy.

References

[1] "PARAMICS - Moving Vehicles on the Connection Machine", *Proceedings of Supercomputing '94, Washington D.C.*, November 1994

[2] "A Demonstration Parallel Computer" - Project Information, *http://www.cit.gu.edu.au:80/~davida/demonstrator.html*

[3] Schaerf A., Shoham Y., Tennenholtz M., "Adaptive Load-balancing: A study in Multi-Agent Learning", *Journal of Artificial Intelligence Research*, May 1995

[4] Whitman S., "Dynamic Load-balancing for Parallel Polygon Rendering", *IEEE Computer Graphics and Applications*, Vol. 14, July 1994, pp. 41-48

[5] G. Geist, V.Sunderam, "Network-based Concurrent Computing on the PVM System", *Concurrency: Practice and Experience*, Vol. 4, June 1992, pp. 293-312

[6] M. J. Quinn, "Parallel Computing - Theory and Practice", McGraw-Hill, 1994.

[7] B. H. McCormick and T. A. DeFanti and M. D. Brown, "Visualization in Scientific Computing", *Computer Graphics*, Nov. 1987, Vol. 21, No. 6,

[8] "PVM 3.0 USER'S GUIDE AND REFERENCE MANUAL", Oak Ridge National Laboratory Oak Ridge, Tennessee 37831 (pvm@msr.epm.ornl.gov)

Design and Implementation of Parallel Software
for Terrain Characterisation
on Irregularly Sampled Data

Andrea Clematis, Michela Spagnuolo

Istituto per la Matematica Applicata
Consiglio Nazionale delle Ricerche
Via De Marini, 6 - 16149 Genova, Italy
clematis@ima.ge.cnr.it
michi@ima-ge.cnr.it

Abstract

Spatial data handling and processing may require a high computational cost for significative applications. In this context, as a first experience, we have parallelised a class of algorithms for the characterisation of terrain represented by regularly sampled data. Very good performances have been obtained using the local area network. In this paper we consider the case of topographic characterisation of terrain represented by irregularly sampled data, which are coded as a triangulated irregular network. Irregular data present specific problems that are addressed in this paper. A parallelisation strategy has been defined that has been used to implement a parallel version of the terrain characterisation on the local area network. This strategy as well as performances are presented in the paper.

1. Introduction

Spatial data handling and processing offers a variety of problems and applications which are worth to be considered in a parallel computing context. The huge amount of data and the complexity of the relationships used to completely code natural phenomena make it necessary to develop approaches and methods to speed up computation and retrieval of information. Many applications have been presented in the last few years on these topics, with large attention devoted to the problem of distributed data bases and real-time processing.

Our specific interest is on topographic characterisation of terrain, which is an important aspect of spatial data handling aiming at the extraction of surface specific points and lines, e.g. peaks, pits, ravines and so on. Even if efficient algorithms are used to perform the recognition of topographic features, the computational cost is usually high, due to the number of points stored in digital terrain models. This has led us to considering the problem of parallelising such algorithms in a manner which is suitable and affordable to the users of Geographical Information Systems (GIS), thus assuming as constraints the following requirements:

- the parallelisation should not be based on any specific parallel hardware, which is likely to be unavailable to traditional GIS users;

- the parallelisation should allow large re-use of sequential code;

- the parallelisation should be simple, efficient and based on standard tools (portability);

- the parallel algorithm is candidate to be used within applications with soft real-time requirements, and with response time which may range from seconds to minutes, hence it makes sense to parallelise algorithms whose execution time is normally in the range from 5 to 20 seconds.

Following the previously listed guidelines, the choice of a network based approach to parallel processing is quite straightforward, while the use of standard tools such as Linda [5] and PVM gives us the possibility both to re-use sequential code and to develop portable libraries for feature extraction.

The parallelisation of topographic characterisation has been firstly considered for terrain represented by digital models with regular topology, i.e. regular grids, where the domain properties easily yield to a parallelisation strategy based on domain decomposition [1]. In particular, we have considered three different algorithms for terrain characterisation as test cases for the parallelisation: the well-known algorithm of Peucker and Douglas [2]; the techniques proposed by Skidmore [3] which improves the algorithm of Peucker and Douglas; an original method for terrain characterisation, which classifies each point on the grid according to a curvature value [4]. The proposed strategy for the parallelisation relies on the property of locality of the previously listed algorithms, that is, the computations used to process each point of the terrain model involve only a local neighbourhood of the point. The defined approach, however, can be generally applied to a whole class of methods for terrain analysis, which are based on a local (or semi-local) neighbourhood processing.

As a second step, the parallelisation of algorithms for the characterisation of terrain defined over irregularly spaced data has been addressed. In this case, the domain decomposition technique deserves more attention since its topology is not regular. First of all, an extension of the Peucker and Douglas algorithm has been devised, which can be applied to TINs. Then the characterisation kernel algorithm has been parallelised and performance data have been collected. As a further improvement the pre-processing phase of the characterisation algorithm has been parallelised.

In the reminder of the paper, the main properties of the characterisation algorithms for regular and irregular digital terrain models will be outlined; then, the parallelisation strategy for TIN based algorithms will be described and finally the results in terms of speed up and efficiency will be discussed.

2. Topographic feature extraction

Topographic feature extraction is a process aimed at the identification of characteristic points and lines on a digital terrain model (DTM), i.e. points having a morphological significance on the terrain, such as peaks, pits, passes, ridges and ravine lines, or drainage networks. This problem has been mainly addressed for DTM defined as regular grids, that is, terrain represented by a two-dimensional matrix $T(i,j)$ where the index pair (i,j) identifies a location in the real world and the value stored is the elevation of the terrain at that position. The ease of storing and retrieving data in grid form is possibly the main reason for the widespread use of such DTM and for the development of the majority of spatial analysis tools for this kind of models.

As a representative of this class of terrain characterisation methods, we have chosen to describe

and use the algorithm defined by Peucker and Douglas [2] which is particularly suitable to be paralleled in a distributed schema of computation. The authors suggest that, when a surface is topographically well-behaved, (i.e. on the discrete surface there are not sharp variations in height between a point and its neighbours) every point on the surface can be classified by analysing the differences in elevation between the point and its neighbours, considered either in clockwise or counter-clockwise sequence around the point. Due to the regular topology of grid models, the neighbourhood of a point is defined by the fixed number of points corresponding to the "natural" neighbours of the point on the grid (usually four or eight, see Figure 1(a) and 1(b), respectively).

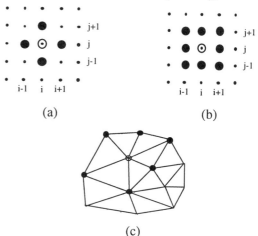

Figure 1: The 4-neighbourhood on a grid (a) and the 8-neighbourhood (b); the neighbourhood of a point on a triangulation (c).

The size of the neighbourhood, or window, used works as a filter for the feature to be detected in the sense that the distance from the point to its neighbours determines the frequency of relief which can be detected [1]. The classification procedure is then based on the following quantities. More precisely, let n be the number of neighbours of a point; Δ_+ (resp. Δ_-) the sum of all positive (resp. negative) differences in height between a point and its neighbours; N_c the number of sign changes in the difference vector and let L_c be the number of points between two sign changes. Then, the classification scheme defined by Peucker and Douglas is summarised in Table 1(ts, tr, tss and tf are thresholds), while the complete classification scheme can be found in [4], where several algorithms are presented to implement the classification procedure.

142

Peak:	$\Delta_+ = 0$, $\Delta_- > tp$, $N_c = 0$;
Pit:	$\Delta_+ > tp$, $\Delta_- = 0$, $N_c = 0$;
Ridge:	$\Delta_- - \Delta_+ > tr$, $L_c \neq n/2$, $N = 2$
Flat:	$\Delta_+ + \Delta_- < tf$
Pass:	$\Delta_+ + \Delta_- > tps$, $N_c = 4$;
Ravine:	$\Delta_+ - \Delta_- > tr$, $L_c \neq n/2$, $N_c = 2$
Slope:	$|\Delta_+ - \Delta_-| < ts$, $\Delta_+ + \Delta_- > tss$, $L_c = n/2$ $N_c = 2$

Table 1: Classification scheme by Peucker and Douglas

It is interesting to point out that the majority of algorithms developed for regular DTM, have the common characteristic of using the *moving window* technique, that is, each point on the grid is processed by doing some computation on its neighbours defined by a window which is moved on the grid. As for the Peucker and Douglas method, the result of the computation generally depends only on these neighbours and not on the result of the processing on some other point of the grid. In other words, the computation is local. The locality of computation together with the similar processing technique have suggested the definition of a parallelisation strategy into which an entire class of "equivalent" algorithms could be easily embedded [1].

The next step of our study on this topics is to extend the parallelisation strategy to DTM whose supporting topology is irregular, as for example triangulation. Triangulation models are defined over samples which are irregularly distributed over the terrain and consist of triangular facets having the vertices at the terrain samples. In a triangulation, the neighbourhood of a point is defined by all its edge-adjacent points, thus having a variable number of neighbours (see Figure 1(c)).

The approach of Peucker and Douglas has been adapted to the TIN context, preserving the property of locality of computation, and replacing the concept of neighbourhood on the grid with that of neighbourhood on the TIN: thus, while in the case of grids the neighbourhood of a point will contain a fixed number of points, in the TIN context, the neighbourhood of a point will contain a variable number of points. The vector of elevation differences will consequently have a variable dimension and the classification criteria have to be considered under this change. More precisely, it is possible to keep unchanged the procedures for all

topographic labels except for ridges and ravines which are replaced by the concept of mountain and valley respectively. This is due to the fact that, while the grid defines fixed directions along which the surface is examined, on a triangulation the terrain is analysed without reference to any preferred direction. Thus, using combinatorial criteria on the elevation differences is not enough to detect directional critical points, such as ridges and ravines.

The method defined on the TIN still have the locality property of computation as the traditional Peucker and Douglas method, thus allowing us to proceed with the parallelisation, as explained in the following section.

3. A Parallel Algorithm for TIN

The parallelisation for regular grids characterisation algorithms was based on a simple but effective strategy [1].

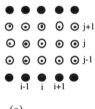

(a)

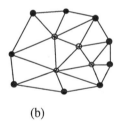

(b)

Figure 2: An extended subdomain on a grid (a); an extended subdomain on a triangulation (b).

A row based approach was adopted to divide the domain, as exemplified in Figure2a. Each subdomain is a group of adjacent rows, and has an overlap area, that generally corresponds to the rows immediately above and below the subdomain. The subdomain plus the adjacent area is identified as an *extended subdomain*, and can be handled independently. Subdomain size is then defined in such a way that makes it easy to obtain a load balanced computation on an heterogeneous workstation network. More details can be found in [1]. The master/worker paradigm was adopted to implement the algorithm.

The parallelisation of irregular domain algorithms presents some more difficulties. The idea of dividing the original domain into independent subdomains and then handling extended subdomains in parallel is still the base of the parallelisation strategy. The main steps which have been recognised in parallelising TIN based algorithms are summarised in Figure 3, where the high level flow chart of the parallel process are shown.

The first step is to acquire the data describing the TIN model.

TIN, are normally implemented using dynamic data structures. Thus to partition a TIN over a distributed memory virtual machine we should translate references maintained through pointers into memory independent or symbolic references. This could lead to heavily code rewriting, and hence to an high cost of the parallelisation process. To simplify the development and to avoid problems in this first version of the parallel algorithm we maintained the TIN dynamic data structure only in the master process, which uses static array to distribute data to slaves processes. Actually slaves processes are only interested in neighbourhood relationships, or more precisely for each point it sufficient to know the number of its direct neighbours, and for each neighbours its elevation quote. To record relevant data the master use a *neighbours list*. Each item of this list is represented by a vertex, its elevation, the number of its neighbours, and the elevation of each neighbour. This list is implemented using an array, which is then partitioned among processes. Associating to each point the elevation data of its neighbours we provide all the information which are necessary for the classification algorithm. In this case an extended subdomain corresponds to a sublist, and each subdomain contains all the information necessary during the classification phase. A parallel version of the algorithm is then obtained applying the sequential classification scheme in parallel on extended subdomains.

Unfortunately the number of neighbours is variable for TIN, hence the definition of extended subdomains needs a pre-processing in order to identify the neighbours for each point of the domain and for border points in particular(Figure 2b). This is a costly activity and itself a good candidate for parallelisation. However its parallelisation has to be considered carefully because it may produce a partition of the data set in subdomains with different sizes and lead to an unbalanced computation. For this reason we do not consider its parallelisation in our first approach.

To obtain a load balanced computation we adopted at this stage a strategy similar to that previously adopted for regular grid domain. Whose main points are summarised in the following..

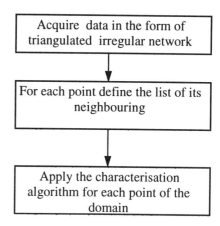

Figure 3: High level flow chart of the characterisation software

The used farmer-worker programming paradigm provides a simple but effective means of load balancing and it is especially well suited to an heterogeneous network. A fundamental problem is to determine an appropriate granularity for subdomains in order to obtain efficient parallel algorithms. Looking for appropriate subdomain granularity we have considered two different points of view, in order to be able to fit into the optimisation strategy both application dependent parameters and heterogeneous network parameters. An upper limit for domain decomposition is derived from application dependent parameters, while heterogeneous network parameters suggest a lower limit for the same aim. If the upper and lower limits define a non empty set, a heuristic is used to select a convenient (possibly optimal) value in the set. Otherwise (if the lower limit is greater than the upper limit) we have to increase the problem size, to use available resources efficiently, or decrease the number of nodes used, in order to avoid the situation where parallel overheads dominate and reduce absolute performance.

4. Experimental Results for the First Version

A network based version of the parallel algorithm has been developed. This first version is based on a master slave approach, which permits a better load balancing among the heterogeneous nodes of the network. The Linda library has been used to manage parallelism. The present situation of our workstation network is characterised by the availability of highly different nodes in terms of performances. This makes difficult to exploit all the available nodes in an efficient way. The preference is naturally for more perfomant machines while little or no advantage is obtained adding low performance nodes. Table 2 summarises relative performances values of 4 machines with different architectures. The value of the most powerful workstation is equal 1, while other values are a fraction of it. These values have been obtained by running the sequential algorithm, on a 264 K points input, on the different machines.

CPU type -RAM	Relative Performance
sparc 20 -32 Mb	1
sparc 10 - 32 Mb	0,76
sparc 10 - 24 Mb	0,65
sparc 1-4/40 - 36Mb	0,16
Total	2,57

Table 2: Relative performance values for four nodes of the network. The last row is the total available performance.

In Figure 4 execution times for a 264 K points, and for a 352 K points test cases are shown. The best values have been obtained for a subdomain size of around 10 K points for each subdomain. This size is small enough to reduce the use of virtual memory, and at the same time does not introduce a too high communication overhead.

It is interesting to evaluate efficiency values with respect to the number of workstation and with respect to the available performance. Table 3 summarises such data for the 352 K points test case.

Number of workstation (N)	Available performance (P)	Efficiency wrt N	Efficiency wrt P
2	1,76	0,66	0,75
3	2,41	0,56	0,70
4	2,57	0,47	0,73

Table 3: Efficiency with respect to the number of workstation and the available performance

It is interesting to notice that despite one of the workstation has around an order of magnitude of performance less then the best one, it could be still useful to add it to the network if the domain size is big enough.

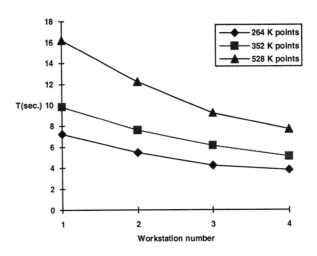

Figure 4: execution times for three test cases

5. Extending the Parallel Algorithm

The results presented in the previous section refer to the parallelisation of the last step of the flow chart depicted in Figure 3. This step represents only a fraction of the whole computation, its cost has been estimated to be around one third of the total cost .

We may notice the following:

- Triangulated irregular network is constructed off-line for the considered applications, hence its parallelisation is not a primary goal in this case. However there exist previous experiences about parallelising triangulation algorithms for MIMD and SIMD architectures. [6]

- Data acquisition is a suitable candidate for parallelisation, but the problem is related to parallel I/O handling, and we do not address it here.

- The construction of neighbouring list is then the best candidate for parallelisation

In order to parallelise the neighbouring list construction we have to divide the original data domain. Providing a suitable solution of this task, permits to extend the parallel part of the program thus reducing the sequential fraction and improving global performances.

A memory independent representation is used to record a TIN on mass-storage, and starting from this representation it is possible to define a structure that can be suitably partitioned over a distributed memory architecture.

The TIN is represented by two tables: the list of vertex coordinates and the list of triangles. Each triangle is defined by the list of its vertices and by the adjacency relationships with other triangles in the list. The subdomains are defined partitioning the whole domain along the x-axis, using fixed size intervals. Each subdomain contains all the points that have x-coordinate within a given interval, i.e. $x_{i-1} \leq x \leq x_i$. An extended subdomain is obtained collecting all the points that have a neighbouring relationship with one of the point of the original subdomain.

To construct extended subdomain it is sufficient to read the input, that is the vertex and triangle tables, and for each triangle to put it and its vertices in the relevant extended subdomains. A triangle belong to an extended subdomain if one of its vertex belong to the subdomain. Normally a triangle either belongs to one or two extended subdomains (border triangle). In pathological situation a triangle may belong to three extended subdomains. The master builds up extended subdomain in a linear time in the number of triangle, while neighbouring list and characterisation are computed by workers on extended subdomains.

This new version of the parallel algorithm has lead to improved performance of the whole process, not only of the true characterisation algorithms thus providing a significative practical result.

6. Conclusions

In this paper we have discussed a parallelisation approach for terrain characterisation algorithm on TIN. The proposed approach has been experimented using the local area network. Early results seems to provide good results and point out that the use of parallelism could provide an effective strategy to achieve the computing power which is required by many GIS applications. Further development will consider the use of massively parallel machines, as well as the integration of parallel characterisation algorithms in true systems.

References

[1]   Clematis,A., Falcidieno,B., Spagnuolo,M., *Parallel Processing on Heterogeneous Networks for GIS Applications*, Int. J. Geographical Information Systems - Special Issue on Parallel Processing in GIS, 1996, vol. 10, no. 6, 747-767

[2]   Peucker,T.K., Douglas, D.H., *Detection of surface-specific points by local parallel processing of discrete terrain elevation data*, Computer Graphics and Image Processing, 4, pp. 375-387, 1975

[3]   Skidmore, A.K., *Terrain position as mapped from a gridded digital elevation model*, International Journal of Geographical Information Systems, Vol. 4, n°1, pp. 33-49, 1990

[4]   Falcidieno, B., Pienovi,C., Spagnuolo,M., *Geometric reasoning on topographic surfaces*, Proceedings of the Fourth European Conference and Exhibition on Geographical Information Systems, pp. 494-502, 1993.

[5]   SCA- Scientific Computing Associate - Inc. *C-Linda User Guide and Reference Manual* 1995

[6]   Magillo P., Puppo E., *Algorithms for parallel terrain modelling and visualization*, In Parallel Processing Algorithms for GIS, R.G. Healey et al. Eds., Taylor & Francis 1996

❖ SESSION 4 ❖

Support Systems for Parallel Applications

Chair

P. Kacsuk

Parallel simulation of 1D probabilistic cellular automata on Associative String Processing machine (ASTRA)

Géza Ódor
Research Institute for Materials Science
P.O.Box 49 H-1525 Budapest, Hungary
odor@ra.atki.kfki.hu

György Vesztergombi
Research Institute for Particle Physics
P.O.Box 49 H-1525 Budapest, Hungary
veszter@rmki.kfki.hu

Francois Rohrbach
CERN
Genève 23, CH-1211, Switzerland
F.Rohrbach@cern.ch

Abstract

Simulation algorithms on stochastic, one-dimensional cellular automata – as simple models of complex, dynamical phase transitions – have been implemented for the prototype of the Associative String Processor with 8K processors. For testing the algorithms and the random generator designed for this machine time dependent simulations for different universality classes of phase transitions have been performed. The critical points and exponent δ of the Rule-18 and the Grassberger-B CA were determined with great accuracy. As a relevant result for physics the damage spreading transitions of these models have been investigated. Timing data are compared with other up to date computer's results and show that this kind of simulations are efficient on this architecture.

1 Introduction

The associative string processing (ASP) ASTRA machine has been built as the outcome of the Massively Parallel Processing Collaboration [18] as a prototype and test-bed for real applications. Existing machines with 4 and 8K processors are real examples of massively parallel machines. The processors (APE-s) have very simple structure: 64-bit memory register, 1-bit adder CPU and a few flag bits for special purposes. The communication is also as simple as possible; basically a couple of string buses connecting the APE-s to the central controller, plus a one-bit inter APE communication channel, but the special associative functions make it a quite flexible architecture. The basic designing idea was to integrate as many as possible of these simple APE strings on a simple chip, making it an effective tool for processing large quantity of data in real time. This architecture, and the basic operations (convolution type) for which it was designed make it applicable for simulating cellular automata (CA) among others.

Physicists became interested in CA, invented by von Neumann, when they discovered, that CA with some external noise (stochastic CA (SCA)) can be regarded as models of statistical physical systems [20]. Since the detailed balance condition is not necessarily satisfied during the evolution, the systems are not converging to a thermodynamic equilibrium. Therefore SCA in general provide a model for non-equilibrium systems. This area of statistical physics is far less known than the equilibrium physics and therefore much interest is paid for it currently. It turned out that this field covers a very rich area of phenomena ranging from physical and chemical reactions to biological and economical models. One can model with it complex systems of many variables, which can be humans (e.g voter models or disease spreading), animals (e.g. races of populations), economical units (e.g. crashes of stock exchange), vehicles (e.g. traffic models), elementary particles and many other things.

Our interest now is concentrated on the exploration of phase transitions and critical phenomena. They are connected to many other new topics like self organised criticality, chaotic systems, fractals etc. The advantage here is that even one-dimensional systems may exhibit phase transitions and different critical universality classes. Therefore these low dimensional "toy models" serve as learning base of more complex systems. Furthermore in many cases the real physical space is low dimensional.

In this study we want to show that new and well accepted simulation methods can be implemented effectively on the

149

ASP by mapping one cell variable per APE. We shall investigate the critical phase transition of different one-dimensional SCA. In order to make the simulations of the stochastic CA feasible on the ASP we needed fast, on-processor random number generator (RG). Since the memories of APE-s are very limited we implemented a lagged Fibonacci RG with limited (18-bit) resolution. That means that although the RG cycle is large, the accuracy of the probability that we can achieve is 2^{-18}, which is enough, since usually the maximum accuracy what we need is $4-5$ digits. The algorithm of this RG will be shown in section 2. To illustrate the way of ASP programming in section 3 we shall show some tricks of the algorithm (thresholding etc.). In section 4 we introduce time dependent simulations to measure time dependence survival probability and critical exponents. Two SCA possessing different set of critical exponents (universality classes) have been chosen to test the algorithms and the random generator. The critical exponents, that we have determined with great accuracy are all in accordance with previous results. Finally in section 5 we apply the method to measure damage spreading and investigate the relation of damage spreading transition to the parity conserving phase transition as well. Timing results will be compared with serial and other parallel machine's data.

2 The random number generator

As it was mentioned in the Introduction the APE-s are very simple processing elements, built up from a one-bit adder, a 64-bit memory register, where each bit in the registers can be selected in parallel for all APE by the central controller. There is a 6-bit "activity register" a carry, an activity, and tagging flags in each APE, see Figure 1. The detailed description can be found in [14]. The APEs are content addressable via the 32-bit data bus, the 6-bit activity bus and the comparators with ternary logic (1,0,dont'care). The flow of instructions roughly starts as follows. Partition of the string, according to some architecture (e.g. subdivision to substrings etc.) fitting the best to our data structure. Partition of the local memories of APE-s simultaneously. Each operation is built of two main parts:

- Selection of operands
    - by selection of bits within the memory registers of all APEs,
    - by content addressing ("Tagging") of APEs (this involves logical function of data and activity register bits)
    - and by an activation of some neighbourhoods of the selected APEs.

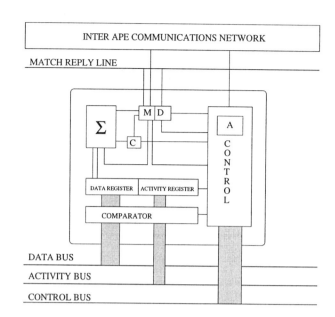

Figure 1. Associative Processing Element

- The execution of the logical functions on the operands and storing them to the selected places

The horizontal and vertical repartitioning of the string-memory can be repeated any time during the program flow.

Owing to the bit-addition capabilities of APE-s, a natural choice for random generator was a "lagged Fibonacci" generator :

$$x_i = (x_{i-l} \pm x_{i-k} \pm c) \, mod \, 2^b, \qquad (1)$$

where the lags are in practice (l, k) : $(17, 5)$; $(55, 24)$; $(24, 10)$ ..., and the carry c comes from a previous generation step. We choose (l, k) : $(17, 5)$, which is used in the Connection Machine 5 for parallel random number generation too. This type of generator has a very long cycle in general [13, 15].

Generating "good" random numbers is not an easy task, one can never be sure of the true randomness of a very long sequence and as digital computers have been developed more and more generators failed on more and more demanding statistical tests [13]. In fact the growing number of scientific papers and disputes aiming to increase the quality of random generators shows that it is far from being solved.

We have tested our generator by checking the results on CA simulations. The 64-bit long x_i random numbers are loaded along the 64-bit segmented ASP string, so that each APE contains one bit of x_i, $i \in (1..18)$. Therefore the bits of different random numbers make up a random integer word of size 18 in each APE. The advantage of this kind of representation that it does not take too much register space (since we don't need too high resolution) but still we have a long period (determined by the length (64) of x_i. Furthermore we

150

can execute the additions in bit parallel with the "look-ahead carry algorithm", which avoids carry propagation. To build random words for all APE-s we update the 18 bits sequentially within 18 simple operation cycles.

3 ASP algorithmic tricks

The random number integers should be compared to some threshold value in order to make a decision. For this purpose the global "SerialShiftRegister" of the controller (LAC) was used. We load the $pt \in [0, 2^{18})$ integer threshold in it at the initialisation, which is the rescaled $p \in [0, 1)$ value. Then we use the test-and-rotate command of the LAC to apply parallel thresholding for all APEs simultaneously from the most significant bit to the least significant bit. The generator works in a constant number of steps, the thresholding requires 18×2 steps.

The CA automaton rule is easily parallelizable. We demonstrate it on the stochastic Rule 18. This is a rule, according to the state of $s(i, t) \in (0, 1)$ variable at time t and space i is determined by $s(i - 1, t - 1)$, $s(i, t - 1)$ and $s(i + 1, t - 1)$. For the deterministic Rule 18 we get a 1 at time t if just one of the neighbours of $s(i, t - 1)$ was 1 and $s(i, t - 1)$ was in 0 state. The possible cases look like :

```
t-1:  100 001 000 111 011 110 010 101
t:     1   1   0   0   0   0   0   0
```

The nearest neighbour communication can be done in parallel for all APEs by the "TagShift" operation within 2 CPU clocks. The rule can be applied in 4 clock units by the "Tag-Byte" and "BitWrite" instructions.

To make the CA random, we dilute the 1-s with probability p acceptance rule. That means the comparison of the 1-s with the threshold value (pt) in 18×2 steps.

Altogether we can see that running the SCA simulation can be done within a few clock cycles independently of the size.

To process the information carried by the states one would need in general data concentration. The calculation of some statistical measure requires $O(\log(\text{system size}))$ time theoretically, limited by the inter APE communications. We have chosen a simpler variable for our demonstration. We measure the time necessary for falling in the absorbing state. This can be checked by the global "Match-Reply" capability of the ASP, and we only have to count the elapsed time steps during a run.

This SCA can have two different type of steady states – separated by a phase transition – by varying the acceptance probability. For small p values the system always evolves to the "absorbing state" built up from 0-s only and from which there is no return according to the rule. For $p > p_c(\sim 0.809)$ a chaotic steady state of finite concentration emerges. At the

critical point the survival probability shows a power-law behaviour characterised by some universal critical exponent.

4 Time dependent Monte Carlo simulation

Time dependent Monte Carlo simulation (TDS) suggested by [8] have become a very precise and effective tool in statistical physics. We start the system from a single active state and follow its statistical properties for a few thousand time steps. In this case we don't let the maximum size of the active cluster to over-grow the computer memory, therefore no finite size effects can come in. We have to take into account finite time corrections and statistical errors only. In this case mapping of the cellular space onto processors is not very effective since at the phase transition point to the absorbing state the system is very sparse, plus we started from a single active seed. List oriented algorithms exploit the processor power much better. Still we have chosen to start our simulation works on the ASTRA machine with a one cell-to one APE mapping TDS becase there are well established results to check the programming and the random number generator. Also this mapping can algorithmically be very effective for slightly more complex time dependent simulations, example for damage spreading or persistence measurements.

In general one can calculate the following quantities ;

- survival probability $p_s(t)$
- concentration $c(t)$
- average mean square distance of spreading from the center $R^2(t)$

The evolution runs are averaged over N_s independent runs for each different value of p in the vicinity of p_c (but for $R^2(t)$ only over the surviving runs). At the critical point we expect these quantities to behave in accordance with the power law as $t \to \infty$, i.e.

$$p_s(t) \propto t^{-\delta} , \qquad (2)$$

$$c(t) \propto t^{\eta} , \qquad (3)$$

$$R^2(t) \propto t^z . \qquad (4)$$

For our test purposes we realized the measurement of the survival probability, which results in the exponent δ.

We have chosen for the first test a well known SCA, the stochastic Rule 18 model [1, 19] possessing universality of the Directed Percolation (DP) or Reggeon Field Theory[10, 3, 2]. Since the definition of this model has been given already in section 3, we just present the results here.

We followed the time evolution of this system for $t = 8192$ time steps and averaged over $N_s = 10^5$ independent samples for each p control parameter. To estimate the critical exponents we determined the local slope:

$$-\delta_p(t) = \frac{\ln \left[p_s(t)/p_s(t/m) \right]}{\ln(m)} \qquad (5)$$

using $m = 8$. In the case of power-law behaviour we should see a straight line as $1/t \to 0$, when $p = p_c$. The off-critical curves should possess curvature. Curves corresponding to $p > p_c$ should veer upward, curves with $p < p_c$ should veer down. The Figure 2, shows our result for this quantity as

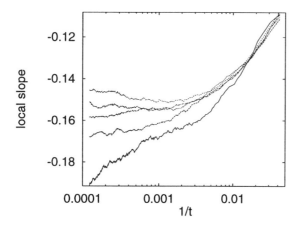

Figure 2. TDS results for the slope $\delta_p(t)$ at the critical point. Parameters corresponding to curves from the bottom to top $p = 0.809, 0.8092, 0.80948, 0.80949, 0.8095$.

function of $1/t$. As we can see, the value $p = 0.80948(1)$ results in the most power-law like behaviour therefore the critical point is there in agreement with former results of the Rule 18 SCA [1, 19]. For the critical exponent δ we can read of ~ 0.16. This value agrees with the most precise series expansion estimate for the directed percolation [12] : $\delta_{DP} = 0.1597(3)$.

The other model, which is an exception from the robust class of DP is Grassbergers's B model. This model belongs to the so called "Parity Conserving" (PC) universality [4, 9, 11, 16], because the number of particles is conserved modulo 2, i.e. the elementary reactions are :

- $X \to 3X$ reproduction

- $2X \to 0$ annihilation,

while in case of the DP we have $X \to 2X$ for the reproduction. It is realized by the following SCA (we show the configurations at $t - 1$ and the probability of getting 1 at time t)

```
t-1: 100 001 101 110 011 111 000 010
  t:   1   1   1   p   p   0   0   0
```

The time evolution pattern for small p is a regular chessboard (with double degeneracy), while for $p > p_c$ it is chaotic. If we consider differences from the alternating ground state pattern as kinks : 00 or 11, the dynamics of these kinks is described by the processes above. These kinks can be regarded either as particles or "Bloch walls of a spin system". They can also be mapped to surface growing problem with a roughening transition.

Again we have performed simulations to measure exponent δ and the critical point. As the Figure 3 shows the results are in good agreement with that of [4]. The exponent δ

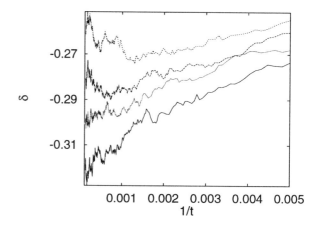

Figure 3. TDS results for $\delta(t)$ for nearly critical point values of $p = 0.535, 0.538, 0.54, 0.545$. The statistical averaging was done over 10000 independent samples

is around $0.29(1)$, which agrees well with the PC universality class value [11] $\delta_{PC} = 0.285(2)$.

5 Damage spreading calculations

Damage spreading simulations have become an important tool for exploring time-dependent phenomena in statistical physics[5]. By applying it to spin systems or stochastic cellular automata (SCA) one follows the evolution of a single difference (damage) between two replicas, driven by the same random sequence. The initial damage may grow or shrink depending on control parameters (temperature etc.) of the model. If there is a phase transition between such regimes one can measure dynamical critical exponents very precisely[6]. Grassberger conjectured that [7] damage spreading transitions separating chaotic and non-chaotic phases always belong to the DP universality class except they coincide with some ordinary phase transition point of different universality class. Examples for this hypothesis are the Ising model with different dynamics. In case of absorbing phase transitions there have been a few exception from the DP universality class up to now. One of them is the PC transition and therefore we thought it would be interesting to investigate the damage spreading properties for models exhibiting this kind of phase transition. One candidate for this would be the Grassberger B SCA, which is chaotic for $p = 1$ and ordered in the $p = 0$ limiting cases therefore there must be a damage spreading transition in between.

The replica systems are started from random initial conditions in this case and therefore the full capacity of the parallel machine is used now at the beginning. We applied periodic boundary conditions. We followed the extinction of the damage in case of Grassberger's model B. Similarly to the simple TDS case near the transition point the damage survival probability curves veer up or down showing that the initial damage survives or heals in the long time limit. As figure 4 shows the two regime is separated by a straight line

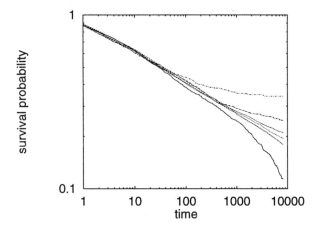

Figure 4. Log-log plots of the survival probability curves for different values of $p = 0.62, 0.63, 0.632, 0.634, 0.64, 0.65$**. The statistical averaging was done over 10000 independent samples**

meaning power-like behaviour of the extinction. Therefore the damage spreading critical point is at $p = 0.632(1)$ not coinciding with the ordinary phase transition point ($p_C = 0.54$) of kinks. This means that the system at the ordinary critical point is insensitive to perturbations like random mixing because they die out exponentially in time. The slope of the straight line determines the exponent δ, which is $0.160(1)$ indicating DP universality class in agreement with Grassberger's hypothesis although the parity of the damages is conserved modulo 2. More discussion on this topic is in preparation [17]. In conclusion, the active phase is divided up by the damage spreading critical point similarly to the case of the Domany-Kinzel SCA [7].

As for the timing we achieved 2×10^{-7} sec / cell up-

date speed at the critical point. This is about one fifth of the speed that we measured on FUJITSU AP-1000 supercomputer built up from 64 Supersparc processors where we applied task parallelism. That means that each processor runs the same program with different numbers to increase the statistics. That means that the 8K ASTRA was about thirteen times faster than a single Supersparc CPU.

6 Conclusions

Efficient program have been developed and tested for the massively parallel ASTRA machine. The realization of the fast on-processor random generator made it possible to use the architecture for simulation of statistical physical systems. The generator and the algorithm were tested by different cellular automaton simulations. Critical points and exponents were determined by great accuracy and the timing results were compared with sequential and other parallel machines data. Since the hardware elements of the machine represent the late 80-ies we can give a performance scaling to show the effectiveness of the architecture. By assuming 200 MHz clock speed instead of the present 20 MHz and 10^6 number of processors contrary the present 8192 we could achieve a speed-up factor of ~ 1000 because of the linear scaling of the algorithm we presented (the first initialisation of the random generator is the only sequential communication along the string). The algorithms can easily be developed further for other dynamical simulations like damage spreading or persistence exponent measurements. We have performed damage spreading studies resulting in relevant physical results.

We thank John Lancaster for the help he gave concerning ASTRA machine.

References

[1] N. Boccara and M. Roger. *Instabilities and Nonequilibrium Structures IV*. Kluwer Academic, The Netherlands, 1993.

[2] J. L. Cardy and R. L. Sugar. *J. Phys. A: Math. Gen.*, 13:L423, 1980.

[3] P. Grassberger. *Z. Phys. B*, 47:365, 1982.

[4] P. Grassberger. *J. Phys. A : Math. Gen.*, 22:L1103, 1989.

[5] P. Grassberger. *J. Phys. A : Math. Gen.*, 28:L67, 1995.

[6] P. Grassberger. *Physica A*, 214:547, 1995.

[7] P. Grassberger. *J. Stat. Phys*, 79:13, 1995.

[8] P. Grassberger and A. de la Torre. *Ann. of Phys*, 122:373, 1979.

[9] A. T. H. Takayasu. *Phys. Rev. Lett*, 68:3060, 1992.

[10] H. K. Janssen. *Z. Phys. B*, 42:151, 1981.

[11] I. Jensen. *Phys. Rev. E*, 50:3623, 1994.

[12] I. Jensen and R. Dickman. *J. Stat. Phys.*, 71:89, 1989.

[13] T. A.-N. K. Kankaala and I. Vattulainen. *Phys. Rev. E*, 48:R4211, 1993.

[14] R. M. Lea. Asp: a cost effective parallel microcomputer. *IEEE Micro*, October 1988.

[15] M. Luscher. *DESY preprint*, 93(133), 1993.

[16] N. Menyhárd. *J. Phys. A : Math. Gen.*, 27:6139, 1994.

[17] G. Ódor. in preparation.

[18] F. Rohrbach. The mppc project : final report. *CERN preprint*, 93(7), 1993.

[19] G. Szabó and G. Ódor. *Phys. Rev. E*, 49:2764, 1994.

[20] S. Wolfram. *Rev. Mod. Phys.*, 55:601, 1983.

The COupled COmmunications LIBrary

Erik Brakkee, Klaus Wolf, Dac Phuoc Ho, Anton Schüller
GMD Forschungszentrum Informationstechnik
Schloss Birlinghoven
D-53754 Sankt Augustin
Germany
erik.brakkee@gmd.de

Abstract

This paper describes the basic concepts behind the COupled COmmunications LIBrary (COCOLIB), which is being developed in the European Esprit project CISPAR [2]. The purpose of the library is to enable the coupling of industrial simulation codes on parallel computers. The industrial simulation codes themselves are parallel codes as well. The MPI [5, 3] message passing standard will be used for the implementation of COCOLIB because MPI provides facilities to keep the communication of COCOLIB separate from that of the codes it is linked with, and to keep the communication within the individual applications separate as well. We describe the main tasks of COCOLIB and the guidelines behind the development. We show that a general class of coupling algorithms can be easily realized using the present design, while keeping algorithmic details completely outside of COCOLIB. We conclude with some remarks on how to achieve coupling standards.

1. Introduction

Now, after significant progress in both software and hardware technology, it is possible to carry out multiphysics simulations. Examples are simulations in the areas of fluid-structure interaction, magneto-hydro-dynamics, acoustics, vibrations of structures due to electromagnetic forces, and sono-chemistry.

One way to do this is to solve the partial differential equations describing the different physical phenomena within one code. However, a drawback of this approach is that either a completely new code must be written, or that existing codes must be combined in one (see e.g. [7]). An advantage of the first approach is that the runtime performance of such a code can be very good because the numerical methods for the different physical phenomena (e.g. fluid flow, structural deformation) can be completely tuned to one another. However, the time needed to develop such a code from scratch will be very large since the years of experience in all involved disciplines are not directly re-used.

The second approach combines the experience in the involved disciplines but may pose severe technical problems because of name conflicts and because the parallelization of the individual codes is not easily extended to the multiphysics code.

The aim of the European project CISPAR (Coupling of Industrial Simulation codes on PARallel computers) [2] is to combine the advantages of both and eliminate the disadvantages as much as possible. To realize this, the individual codes will be coupled with each other on a parallel computer using a coupled communications library (COCOLIB) that will be developed based on the MPI [5, 3] message passing standard. This ensures that the full functionality of the individual codes will be available within the coupled simulation. Also, existing pre- and postprocessors will remain applicable, so that a coupled simulation will require minimal training for end users. Finally, the use of a communications library to couple the codes allows a working prototype to be built quickly.

COCOLIB will be the main result of the CISPAR project. The purpose of COCOLIB is to define an open interface to make it relatively easy to couple existing simulation codes to others. Either in-house codes or codes provided by independent software vendors can be used. Industrial end users in medical engineering (Sulzer Innotec), ship certification (Germanischer LLoyd), automotive (Mercedes-Benz) and aircraft simulation (Aerospatiale) have identified important coupled problems, that will be computed during the CISPAR project with the help of COCOLIB. For this purpose, the end users have selected the structural mechanics codes PAM/CRASH/PAM-SOLID (Engineering Systems International) and PERMAS (INTES GmbH), and the fluid dynamics code STAR-CD (Computational Dynamics/Imperial College). These independent software vendors cooperate in CISPAR with the GMD and the end users in the development of COCOLIB. The project is managed by PALLAS.

2. Coupling algorithms supported

We want to obtain the solution to multi-physics problems by coupling the different physical problems in different three-dimensional regions of space. The boundaries between the different physical regimes (e.g. flow and structure) are formed by two-dimensional contact surfaces. The coupling algorithms that COCOLIB will support are based on exchanging coupling quantities through these surfaces. This means that from each of the regions, boundary conditions are determined on the contact surface such that the physical problem on the other side can be solved.

The simplest example of such an algorithm in the literature is the so-called Neumann-Dirichlet domain decomposition algorithm. Examples of this method are found in e.g. [4, 1, 9]. The Neumann-Dirichlet algorithm aims to solve the equation

$$\mathcal{L}v = f \qquad (1)$$

on Ω with appropriate boundary conditions on the boundary $\partial\Omega$. Ω is decomposed in two non-overlapping subdomains Ω_1 and Ω_2, see Figure 1. The common boundary Γ between Ω_1 and Ω_2 is called the coupling interface. In three dimensions this will be a coupling surface.

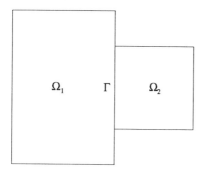

Figure 1. A non-overlapping domain decomposition.

It can be shown that, for second order elliptic operators $\mathcal{L}v = -\nabla \cdot a(x,y)\nabla v$, eq. (1) is satisfied on the whole domain if (1) holds for the subdomains and if both v and its normal derivative $a\partial v/\partial n$ are continuous across the interface Γ, where n is the unit outward normal of subdomain Ω_1 on Γ. This leads to the following algorithm. Given the

k-th iterate v^k, solve

$$\begin{cases} \mathcal{L}v_1^{k+1} = f & \text{on } \Omega_1 \\ a_1\frac{\partial v_1^{k+1}}{\partial n} = a_2\frac{\partial v_2^k}{\partial n} & \text{on } \Gamma \\ v_1^{k+1} = g & \text{on } \partial\Omega_1 \setminus \Gamma_1, \end{cases} \qquad (2)$$

and

$$\begin{cases} \mathcal{L}v_2^{k+1} = f & \text{on } \Omega_2 \\ v_2^{k+1} = v_1^{k+1} & \text{on } \Gamma \\ v_2^{k+1} = g & \text{on } \partial\Omega_2 \setminus \Gamma_2, \end{cases} \qquad (3)$$

where $a_1 = a|_{\Omega_1}$, and $a_2 = a|_{\Omega_2}$. The quantities v and $\frac{\partial v}{\partial n}$ are called coupling quantities, and their values are called coupling values. On convergence of the Neumann-Dirichlet iteration, the solution to (1) is obtained.

We will use this basic principle of exchanging coupling values through a coupling interface also for the multi-physics problems. For this purpose, we extend this Neumann-Dirichlet method by allowing different governing equations on the each of the subdomains (i.e. $\mathcal{L}_1$ on Ω_1 and $\mathcal{L}_2$ on Ω_2), and by adjusting the types of coupling quantities (v and $\partial v/\partial n$) accordingly. In addition, we will also apply the method to in-stationary problems. Specifically, the CISPAR project will take fluid-structure interactions as examples, where the different physical phenomena will be solved by separately developed fluids and structures codes. COCOLIB will assist in the exchange of coupling values through the contact surface.

3. COCOLIB tasks

The exchange of coupling values is a non-trivial task. This is because each of the codes uses independent mesh generation, so that the grids at the interfaces do not match, see Figure 2. Furthermore, each of the codes may be a parallel code, so that the coupling surface itself is distributed over different processes. The main problem is here for COCOLIB to determine how these surfaces fit together (the so-called neighborhood computation), see e.g. [6, 7]. This information is then used to establish the interprocessor communication and to assist the codes in the interpolation of coupling values between the different grids. In addition, COCOLIB will offer simple built-in interpolations so that the interpolation aspects can be totally hidden from the codes if desired.

The coupling may be further complicated by the movement of the contact surface itself. For example, with fluid-structure interactions, the fluid exerts a force on the structure, which may deform under that force. This means that the grid points of the contact surface can be a coupling quantity as well. In summary the following changes of the contact surface can occur:

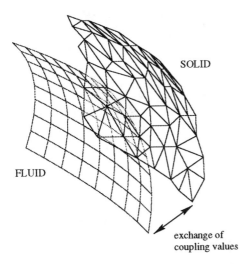

Figure 2. Exchange of coupling values through non-matching grids. The distance between the surface grids is exaggerated.

- mesh deformation, where one mesh deforms (e.g. the solid), and the mesh on the other side (e.g. of the fluid) must deform with it.

- mesh sliding, where the meshes move with respect to each other without deforming,

- remeshing, where a completely new mesh is generated for the same geometry on one or both sides, or when an old mesh is refined.

- load balancing by a code, where the distribution of the coupling surface over the processes of a code changes.

Also, some combinations of these 4 types of mesh changes are possible. COCOLIB will provide the basic functionality for exchanging coupling values through coupling surfaces for parallel codes. The communication and interpolation of coupling values will be handled transparently, also in the case of the mesh changes mentioned above.

In addition to this basic functionality, which supports the general coupling algorithm for exchanging coupling values through a coupling surface, COCOLIB will eventually support specific coupling algorithms. These so-called coupling standards will make it even easier to couple new simulation codes with others through COCOLIB. This paper only describes the algorithm-independent basic COCOLIB library. Section 6 shows that this basic functionality already allows us to realize coupling algorithms with relative ease. Some remarks on coupling standards are also made in Section 6.

4. The COCOLIB design

The execution model will be as follows. The coupled computation will make use of a control process, which sets up the communication between the processes, and monitors the coupled computation (possibly with a graphical user interface attached to it). This monitoring function provides more robustness to the coupled computation. For example, if one application unexpectedly terminates (e.g. unrecoverable error), then the control process will detect this and send an error message to the other codes. The control process can also be used to manage some collective communication tasks. Possibly, a debug mode can be provided in which the control process monitors the parallel computation and gives warnings for possible dead-lock situations. The control process can be compared to a PVM [8] console, which also does not participate in the computations but (interactively) controls the computation.

To achieve scalability, most communication through CO-COLIB will be as directly as possible between the individual processes of different codes (e.g. exchange of coupling values), without the control process being involved, see Figure 3. To perform this communication, each process that calls COCOLIB subroutines is linked with COCOLIB and thus has its own COCOLIB layer (CCL layer). The actual information needed to perform communication using the underlying MPI system is stored in these COCOLIB layers. Specifically, this means that the coupling surface is also distributed among different processes. The difficult task of keeping this information consistent will be carried out by COCOLIB.

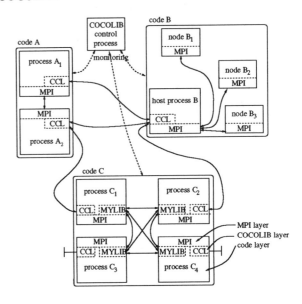

Figure 3. Coupling through a parallel communications library: process view.

In addition to communication through the CCL layers using COCOLIB calls, it is of course still possible to perform communication directly through MPI. In Figure 3 for example, codes A and B perform their internal parallelization directly through MPI. Code C performs its code-internal communication using a separate library 'MYLIB' which in turn also uses MPI. Also COCOLIB will offer possibilities for the processes of different codes to communicate directly with each other through MPI (subroutine CCL_Comm_extract). The MPI contexts (see further on) allow this without any conflicts with communication through the CCL layers.

Not every process of a code may share a part of the coupling surface with a process of another code. Therefore, these processes do not have to perform COCOLIB communication calls for these parts, see for example processes C_3 and C_4 in Figure 3. Other COCOLIB calls are still possible. Alternatively, it is possible that some processes of a code do not want to call COCOLIB subroutines at all, see for example processes B_1, B_2, and B_3. Therefore, it is allowed that only general subsets of the processes of a code perform COCOLIB calls. The processes in this subset are called the COCOLIB processes.

This mechanism of communication between subgroups of the processes of different codes makes COCOLIB independent of the parallelization strategy used by a code. In particular, both host-node and SPMD parallelizations are supported. Compare for instance Figure 3 again, where codes B and C use host-node and SPMD parallelizations respectively.

This concept of two subgroups of processes performing communication is directly supported by MPI through the inter-communicator concept, shown in Figure 4. An inter-communicator is used for communicating between two arbitrary non-overlapping subgroups of processes (of the total group of processes). An inter-communicator is a handle to an MPI internal storage structure which contains a local group (to which the process where the structure resides belongs), and a remote group (the other group).

In MPI calls, the actual (remote) process is indicated by its rank, also indicated in Figure 4.[1] Communication using an inter-communicator is always between processes of different groups. For communicating within a certain subgroup, MPI offers intra-communicators. In a sense, an intra-communicator may be considered an inter-communicator where the local and remote groups coincide.[2]

Each MPI communicator indicates a communication domain. Communication in different communication domains is guaranteed not to interfere with each other. This is real-

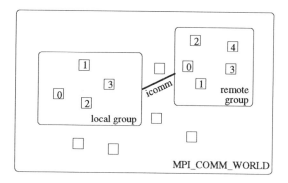

Figure 4. An MPI inter-communicator is used for communicating between different subgroups of processes

ized through so-called communication contexts. This communication context is added automatically to any message sent using this communicator, and is recognized by MPI itself. This is an important difference with other message passing methods such as PVM, where a message tag had to be added explicitly to any outgoing message by the sender, and had to be distinguished explicitly by the receiver.

This context or communication domain is an important MPI concept which allows for the development of parallel libraries. The MPI contexts partition message space. In particular, code-internal communication is automatically separate from library-internal communication, and from communication between processes of different codes.

COCOLIB extensively uses MPI inter-communicators. To ensure that COCOLIB-internal communication does not interfere with communication by a code, we have chosen to hide these MPI inter-communicators behind CCL (CO-COLIB) inter-communicators in COCOLIB subroutines. Each CCL inter-communicator is associated with a pair of codes, and refers to an MPI inter-communicator used internally by COCOLIB, in combination with information about the coupling surface between the codes.

This direct mapping of COCOLIB onto MPI ensures efficiency. Also, some MPI concepts will be visible through the COCOLIB interface. This enables us to avoid duplication of MPI functionality as much as possible. Furthermore, there is a subroutine CCL_Comm_extract, which provides the caller with a duplicate of the MPI inter-communicator used internally by COCOLIB (that is, with a different context). In this way, the processes of the two codes can also perform direct communication with one another through MPI, without interfering with COCOLIB-internal communication. In addition, there is a COCOLIB subroutine CCL_Comm_dup similar to MPI_Comm_dup, which creates a duplicate of a CCL inter-communicator with a new context. This can be used if more than one independent communication domain

---

[1]In COCOLIB calls, process ranks are not needed since it is a CO-COLIB task to figure out the processes to which messages should be sent.

[2]It is an MPI-2 task to ensure that this correspondence between inter- and intra-communicators holds. This is not yet the case with MPI-1.

is wanted between the same two codes. It can be of use for example with the coupling of two multi-grid codes where separate communication is desired on each grid-level.

The above points make the current COCOLIB design very efficient, general, and extendible.

5. Coupled computation using COCOLIB

Figure 5 shows the control flow of the coupled computation. The coupled computation is divided into the startup, coupling definition, coupled computation, and termination phases which are explained below.

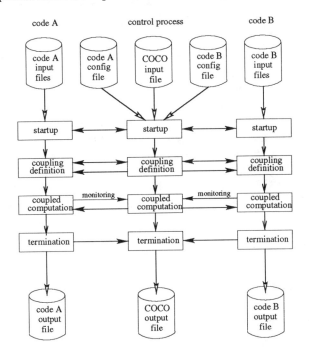

Figure 5. Control flow in the coupled computation for an example of two codes. More than two codes are also allowed.

5.1. Startup

At startup of the coupled computation, the control process and each of the involved codes reads its input files, that are specified by the end user. The control process reads the COCOLIB input file which contains a definition of the coupling types to be exchanged between each pair of codes. These coupling types are checked by the control process against the code configuration files which contain the definitions of coupling types a code can handle. For instance, if the user specifies that code A is to compute forces at the coupling surface for code B, then the configuration files for

codes A and B should mention that code A is able to compute forces, and code B is able to use forces as boundary conditions, respectively.

Directly after startup the codes must call subroutine CCL_Init to enroll in the coupled computation, and subroutine CCL_Comm_init to specify those processes that will perform further COCOLIB calls (the COCOLIB processes). After these calls, CCL inter-communicators with the other involved codes are made available. Also, an MPI communicator CCL_MPI_COMM_CODE is available that contains all processes of the current code. This communicator must be used instead of MPI_COMM_WORLD to perform code-internal communication. The latter is needed because MPI-1 will be used initially. With MPI-2 on the other hand, the control process could spawn each of the codes directly, in which case MPI_COMM_WORLD would automatically be local to each code and contain all its processes.

5.2. Coupling definition

During the coupling definition phase each of the CO-COLIB processes of a code specifies its interfaces to CO-COLIB, and the initial neighborhood computation takes place. This establishes the communication paths for the coupling values to be exchanged through the coupling surface.

The interface parts are defined using subroutines CCL_Vertex_spec and CCL_Topol_spec, which specify the vertices and topology of an interface part respectively.

Subroutine CCL_Vertex_spec announces a new interface part, and returns an interface handle to this part. Interface handles are used in COCOLIB calls for referencing interface parts. Figure 6 shows several interface handles. Interface handles are local to a process, which means:

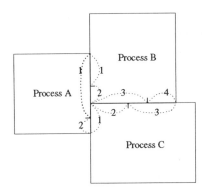

Figure 6. Interface handles (2-D example, the actual computations will be 3-D).

1. Different parts of the coupling interface of a process

159

have distinct interface handles. This allows the interface handle to be used to reference interface parts.

2. The actual integer value of interface handles may be used for other parts of the coupling interface on other processes. This allows local numbering $1, 2, 3, \ldots$ to be used on all processes and simplifies coding for the application codes.

3. One interface part announced by a process may correspond to more than one other interface part announced by processes of other codes. This ensures that grid generation (and domain decomposition) of the different codes may be done completely independent of one another.

Subroutine CCL_Topol_spec is used to specify the topology of interface parts defined using CCL_Vertex_spec. Specification of the topology is necessary for neighborhood computation and thus enables interpolation between several coupling interfaces. Assuming the coordinates of the vertices p_i ($i = 1, \ldots n_v$) are known, the topology is described by specifying the number of elements *nelem* and the element type *itype*, together with for each element the indices of the vertices that determine the element, see Table 1. By

ielem	p_1	$\ldots$	p_m
1	$p_{1,1}$	$\ldots$	$p_{1,n}$
		$\ldots$	
nelem	$p_{nelem,1}$	$\ldots$	$p_{nelem,n}$

Table 1. Topology specification for an interface with only a single element type.

allowing the element type to differ for each element, one can define interfaces with mixed types of elements.

Each code is free to use its own element types. This is already indicated in Figure 2, where the fluid uses quadrilateral elements and the solid uses triangular elements. Figure 7 shows some element types that will possibly be supported by COCOLIB.

In addition to the definition of the coupling surface itself, as done by CCL_Vertex_spec and CCL_Topol_spec, the coupling types and their locations must also be defined, and the initial neighborhood computation must take place. This is done by subroutines CCL_Type_info and CCL_Commit, respectively. Subroutine CCL_Type_info retrieves the coupling types to be exchanged with another code. Subroutine CCL_Commit performs the initial neighborhood computation. CCL_Commit also requires a CCL inter-communicator so that also the neighborhood computation takes place in a separate communication context.

Separate communication contexts in the neighborhood computation are useful. Consider again the example of the

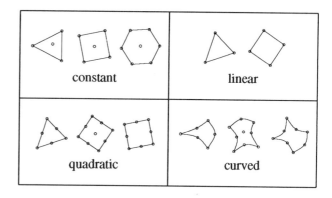

Figure 7. Different types of surface elements may be used to describe the coupling surface in 3-D.

coupling of two multi-grid codes. In this case, having a separate communication context for each grid-level ensures that neighborhood computation is performed independently on each grid-level. This avoids the problem of matching a fine grid of one code with a coarse grid of another, which would make no sense for this type of coupling.

The CCL inter-communicators are also used in the coupled computation phases to perform COCOLIB communication.

5.3. Coupled computation

During the coupled computation phase, information is exchanged through the coupling interfaces. The coupling interface may change dynamically in several ways, and this may require subsequent neighborhood computation. COCOLIB will keep this neighborhood information up-to-date automatically.

Subroutines CCL_Put_vert and CCL_Put_elem for specifying computed coupling values for an interface part in vertex-wise or element-wise manner. The vertex-wise specification can be used to specify values at the same locations as specified in the call to CCL_Vertex_spec. Element-wise specification can be used to specify values at so-called derived vertices, whose location were not specified using CCL_Vertex_spec, but can be computed using the other vertices. An example of where this is needed is for instance with cell-centred finite-volume discretization, where it may be easier for a code to compute values at the center than at the corners of the grid cell. The center vertex is here computed as the arithmetic average of the corner points.

The specified coupling values for the different coupling types are stored by COCOLIB and can be sent using CCL_Send. This subroutine requires a CCL inter-communicator argument to indicate the communication domain. All information previously specified is then sent for all interfaces attached to this inter-communicator. The subroutines CCL_Recv, CCL_Get_vert, and CCL_Get_elem are needed to receive and extract the information from COCOLIB respectively. For optimal efficiency, a subroutine CCL_Exchange is also provided which has the combined functionality of CCL_Send and CCL_Recv.

5.4. Termination

The coupled computation is terminated by calling subroutine CCL_Finalize. This subroutine cleans up all COCOLIB state. After this call, control returns to the caller who is not allowed to call any further COCOLIB subroutines, including CCL_Init.

6. An example coupling algorithm

This section shows how one of the most commonly used coupling algorithms can be easily implemented using basic COCOLIB subroutines without requiring any extensions of COCOLIB. The coupling example is a time-dependent fluid-structure interaction with an exchange of coupling values (bi-directional communication!) at common points in time $t_0, t_1, \ldots, t_n$.

At each time point t_i the coupling values computed from the flow field $f(t_i)$ and the solution of the structures problem $s(t_i)$ are exchanged and these values are imposed as boundary conditions for the fluids and structures code to compute the solution at the next coupling time t_{i+1}.

To determine the next coupling time t_{i+1}, a simple collective CCL_Reduce call may be used. The functionality of this subroutine is similar to MPI_Allreduce and its purpose is to compute a maximum, minimum, or any other type of associative operation from values specified by the processes participating in the collective call. The result is returned to all involved processes.

The pseudo code is given in Figure 8. In the pseudocode, only one coupling time step is computed in advance. This may be costly since CCL_Reduce is a collective operation, and may have synchronizing effects. To minimize these communication costs, more than one coupling time can be determined in advance, which is completely analogous to the MPI_Allreduce function which also accepts arrays of arguments.

Another use of the CCL_Reduce function is to determine convergence or divergence of the coupled computation. Assuming that the coupled computation has converged if all codes have converged, we can solve this problem as follows. Define the constants CONVERGED = 0, NOT_YET_CONVERGED = 1, DIVERGED = 2. If now each code specifies their convergence state to CCL_Reduce and uses the MAX operation, the result will be DIVERGED if at least one of the codes has diverged, NOT_YET_CONVERGED if at least one of the codes has not yet converged, and CONVERGED only if all codes have converged.

A generalization of the pseudo-code of Figure 8 is obtained by generalizing coupling time to coupling step. In this case, t_i does not have to be a real number but may be an arbitrary data structure consisting of integers, reals and strings. This generalization is achieved using the powerful derived data-type concept of MPI in combination with the ability to define new reduction operations in MPI. Since the CCL_Reduce call accepts arbitrary MPI data types as arguments, this MPI flexibility is also immediately available in COCOLIB.

Some requirements are put on the code owners for the described coupled computation to work:

- Both codes should have identical views on what a coupling step is.

- Both codes should use the same reduction operation (max, min) in the COCO_Reduce call.

- Each code should specify the same number of coupling steps in the COCO_Reduce call.

- Each code must be able to compute the coupling quantities required by the other code.

- Each code must provide the coupling values at the required coupling times.

Alternatively, these requirements may be considered a 'coupling standard'. For example, in the above case this coupling standard would include definition of what a coupling step is, the type of reduction operation to perform, and a prescription of the implementation in terms of pseudo-code. Only with these requirements, we can obtain the 'plug in' effect where each new code can 'join COCOLIB' just by fulfilling the coupling standard and without knowing anything about the other codes involved in the computation. Note that the above coupling standard does not actually require any additional coding inside of COCOLIB nor by the code owners.

7. Conclusions

This document described the basic concepts behind the COupled COmmunications LIBrary for coupling industrial simulation codes on parallel computers. We showed that by mapping COCOLIB onto MPI we can get an efficient, general, and extendible library. This was realized through the use of so-called CCL inter-communicators, which are handles to MPI inter-communicators with additional information about the coupling surface connections.

```
Fluid's code                            Structure's code

time = t(0)                             time = t(0)
i = 0                                   i = 0
while ( time < tend )                   while ( t < tend )

           // compute coupling values to be exchanged //
                           ....

                  // exchange coupling values //
    COCO_Iface_exchange(...)                COCO_Iface_exchange(...)

    // both fluid's en solid's code compute their next desired   //
    // coupling time t_next                                      //
    t_next = ...                            t_next = ...

             // compute the next coupling time t(i+1) //
    CCL_Reduce(t_next, t(i+1), MIN)     CCL_Reduce(t_next, t(i+1), MIN)

       // compute the solutions at the next coupling time  t(i+1) //
    ......                                  .....

    time = t(i+1)                           time = t(i+1)
    i = i + 1                               i = i + 1
end                                     end
```

Figure 8. Pseudo code for an example coupling algorithm. Only the arguments to CCL_Reduce that are essential to the example are shown.

The obtained COCOLIB interface is algorithm-independent. It was shown that an important general class of coupling algorithms can be easily implemented in this way using COCOLIB, requiring no additions to the library and with simple coding for the application codes. This was possible because some MPI aspects are visible in the COCOLIB interface, so that many advanced MPI features are automatically available in COCOLIB as well.

One of the ideals of the CISPAR project is to obtain a 'plug-in' effect using coupling standards, meaning that each new code can just 'join' COCOLIB by fulfilling a coupling standard without needing to know anything about other codes. It has been shown that a coupling standard will consist of requirements on the algorithm used and coding style. Possibly some additions to the basic COCOLIB must be made to support more specific coupling algorithms.

References

[1] C. Börgers. The Neumann-Dirichlet domain decomposition method with inexact solvers on the subdomains. *Numer. Math.*, 55:123–136, 1989.

[2] CISPAR – open interface for Coupling of Industrial Simulation Codes on PARallel computers, ESPRIT Project 20161. See also http://www.pallas.de.

[3] M. P. I. Forum. MPI: a message-passing interface standard. *Journal of Supercomputer Applications*, 8(3/4), 1994. special issue on MPI.

[4] D. Funaro, A. Quarteroni, and P. Zanolli. An iterative procedure with interface relaxation for domain decomposition methods. *SIAM Journal of Numerical Analysis*, 25:1213–1236, 1988.

[5] W. Gropp, E. Lusk, and A. Skjellum. *Using MPI; portable parallel programming with the message-passing interface.* Scientific and engineering computation. MIT Press, Cambridge, Mass., 1994.

[6] R. Löhner. Some useful data structures for the generation of unstructured grids. *Applied Numerical Mathematics*, 4:123–135, 1988.

[7] R. Löhner, C. Yang, J. Cebral, J. D. Baum, H. Luo, D. Pelessone, and C. Charman. Fluid-structure interaction using a loose coupling algorithm and adaptive unstructured grids. AIAA Paper 95-2259, 1995.

[8] V. Sunderam, G. Geist, J. Dongarra, and R. Manchek. The PVM concurrent computing system: Evolution, experiences and trends. *Parallel Computing*, 20:531–545, 1994.

[9] R. v. d. Wijngaart. *Composite-grid techniques and adaptive mesh refinement in computational fluid dynamics.* PhD thesis, Stanford University, 1990.

ParaDict, a Data Parallel Library for Dictionaries*

Joaquim Gabarró   Jordi Petit i Silvestre
Universitat Politècnica de Catalunya
Departament de Llenguatges i Sistemes Informàtics
C/ Pau Gargallo, 5
08028 Barcelona, Spain
{gabarro, jpetit}@lsi.upc.es

Abstract

ParaDict , a data parallel library for dictionaries having two different interfaces is presented. The first interface is written in C* for data parallel users and the second interface in C, for users that want to use a parallel library but not to write parallel programs. We have seen that C* is an adequate tool to code theoretical PRAM algorithms into readable programs. These programs were ran on a CM 200 with better times than other existing implementations. They also have much better asymptotic behaviour when compared to a sequential implementation on a workstation. Finally, the relationship between data parallelism and vectorization is explored, transforming C* code into C code plus compiler directives and running the result on a Convex C3480 machine. Even if (almost all) the loops were vectorized, the performances were modest. All these facts allow us to look at the development of other parallel libraries with moderate optimism.

1. Data parallel libraries

Sequential abstract data types are well known from theory and practice and complete libraries exist for them. For instance, the well known LEDA library developed by K. Melhorn and S. Näher [12] written in C++ is widely used (even on introductory courses). It belongs to the so called SP/SL model:

SP/SL model: A Sequential Program calls a Sequential Library. In this case, the program and the library are both written in a sequential language.

The situation is quite different on massive parallelism. We have a very sophisticated theory on parallel data structures (cf. J. JáJá [11]) but very few practical work. Therefore, it was really tempting to explore the "practical" issues of this theory writing (a small part of) a library in a data parallel language. We choose C* [18] as a high level data parallel language since using it we can code data parallel algorithms with reasonable time and effort getting clear and readable programs. These programs were ran in a SIMD Connection Machine 200 [10].

What kind of users could be interested in such a library? Data parallel programmers could find it interesting, but this community is rather small and we would like to recover sequential programmers. Therefore we introduce the following two models (and interfaces):

PP/PL model: A Parallel Program calls a Parallel Library. This approach is addressed to data parallel programmers. This means in practice a C* program calling functions written in C*. Thanks to data parallelism, the use of this interface is almost identical to that used in sequential environments.

SP/PL model: A Sequential Program calls a Parallel Library. Addressed to sequential programmers. Since C* contains C as a subset, programmers can write C code and call operations of a parallel library. This library starts transforming sequential data into parallel data and runs data parallel procedures in the parallel system. Depending on the problems this approach can be interesting.

In this paper, we consider the design, implementation and evaluation of a parallel library for handling dictionaries (ParaDict). This is a theoretically well known domain: taking only the research based on dynamic data structures on PRAMs we have among others, the work of W. Paul, U. Vishkin and H. Wagener based on 2-3 trees [14] (on which our implementation is based), the work of L. Higham and E. Schenks on B-trees [9] the work of J. Gabarró, C. Martínez and X. Messeguer based on Skip Lists [7] or the work

---
*This work has been partially supported by ESPRIT LTR Project no. 20244 — ALCOM-IT.

of J. Gabarró and X. Messeguer based on AVL trees [8]. However, less implementations have been realized. We know the works done by M. Gastaldo *et al.* [5] and by X. Messeguer [13]. We shall compare their results with ParaDict.

The remaining of this paper is organised as follows. By the means of a toy example, we first develop the use of the previous parallel interface models. Then we show how, inspired by the LEDA sequential library, we have designed ParaDict's interfaces. After that, we comment our implementation using 2-3 trees and we present some experimental results aiming to evaluate it. Finally we show how we have ported the C* programs to a vectorial machine. We close the paper with some concluding remarks.

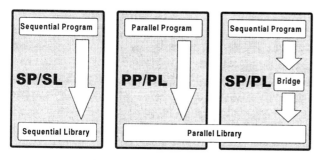

Figure 1. Library models.

2. PP/PL and SP/PL models: a toy example

Let us develop a little bit more these three models with a toy example based on sorting integers. Figure 1 sketches the three approaches. In the SP/SL model the sequential program can use the procedure

```
void Sort (int a[], int n) {
    Sequential sorting code
}
```

In this case, the sequential program calls `Sort(a,n)` where `a` is a sequential array. For the PP/PL model, the main data parallel program calls `Sort(&a)` where `a` is a parallel variable having a shape decided at run-time (using the `current` keyword) in order to have a neutral data distribution [6]:

```
void Sort (int:current *a) {
    [Rank(*a)]*a=*a;
}
```

In the SP/PL approach, the sequential programmer calls `Sort(a,n)` where `a` is a sequential array variable:

```
void Sort (int a[], int n) {
    shape [n]s;
    with (s) everywhere {
```

```
        int:current pa;
        pa=write_to_pvar(a);      /* FE->CM */
        [Rank(pa)]pa=pa;
        read_from_pvar(a,pa);     /* CM->FE */
    }  }
```

this procedure uses the C* primitives `write_to_pvar` and `read_from_pvar` connecting sequential and parallel variables. Remark that the core of the data parallel sorting algorithm (`[Rank(pa)]pa=pa`) can be the same in the PP/PL and in the SP/PL models. Moreover the SP/SL and SP/PL headers (`Sort(int a[], int n)`) also coincide.

To construct the SP/PL library from the PP/PL case, we just need to add a *bridge* level (see figure 1) made of two steps that wrap the parallel program: the first (`write_to_pvar`) spreads the sequential array to the parallel subsystem, the second (`read_from_pvar`) gathers the result to the front end.

Of course, it can be argued that the introduction of the bridge level can produce a decrease of the performances of programs, mainly due to the overload of connecting parallel and sequential variables. We have found, however, that this approach is useful for some kinds of problems. For instance, figure 2 compares the running time of the previous programs. Thus, it can be seen which is exactly the time consumed by the bridge and that (even with it) the SP/PL model is faster than the SP/SL (which uses `qsort` from `stdlib.h`). This will happen, in general, when dealing with big problems, with large amounts of data or long execution times.

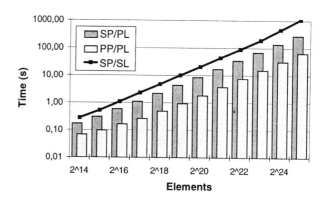

Figure 2. Running time for sorting vectors in dependence of the model: SP/SL (Sun Sparc 10), SP/PL and PP/PL (both with a CM 200 with 16K processors).

3. The design of ParaDict's library interface

The library we present, ParaDict, implements the operations to efficiently handle dictionaries on parallel computers using a data parallel approach. Concretely, we offer two different implementations (a prototype kind, and a 2-3 tree based kind) with two different interfaces: a parallel one and a sequential one. The former interface is written in C* and it is aimed for parallel programs (PP/PL model); the latter is written in C and it is designed to be used within sequential programs (SP/PL model). Both interfaces contain the same operations which are based on the sequential implementation of dictionaries in LEDA [12]. We think that this is a good starting point, due to the relevance of the LEDA library in sequential computing. Refer to [17] for a complete description of ParaDict's interfaces.

Parallel interface. In order to use parallelism, LEDA headers have to be enhaced. The way to do it in C* is easy: where LEDA expects a single key, value or item, ParaDict expects a parallel variable of them. In C*, a parallel variable can be seen as a usual array where each component has a (virtual) processor associated to it. All our functions maintain the meaning of the context, so the inactive positions will not be treated. For instance, let us consider the operation that, given a key in a dictionary returns its associated value. The name of this method in LEDA is Access and its header in C++ syntax is

```
TVal d.Access (TKey key)
```

where TKey is the type of the keys, TVal is the type of the values and d is a dictionary object. The header for the same operation in the PP/PL interface of ParaDict is

```
TVal:current Access (TDict *d,
                     TKey:current keys)
```

where TDict is now the dictionary ADT. The meaning for the parallel version is the extension of the sequential one: for each active key, its associated value in the dictionary is returned. The following headers list the main functions of ParaDict's *parallel interface:*

```
TItem:current Insert (TDict *d,
                      TKey:current keys,
                      TInf:current infs)
TItem:current Lookup (TDict *d,
                      TKey:current keys)
void DelItems (TDict *d,
              TItem:current items)
void Change (TDict *d,
            TItem:current items,
            TInf:current infs)
bool:current IsNil (TDict *d,
                   TItem:current items)
TKey:current Keys (TDict *d,
                  TItem:current items)
TInf:current Infs (TDict *d,
                  TItem:current items)
```

Sequential interface. The same operations than before are available, but in order to follow Ansi C, some of the parameters have been changed and some have been added. In fact, since all these functions work with open arrays, the user has to supply an integer k representing their size. For convenience, a new parameter called mask simulating the setting of the context in C* has also been added. This can be seen in the SP/PL version of the Access procedure:

```
void Access_ (TDict *d, int k, bool mask[],
              TKey keys[],TVal vals[])
```

The following headers list the main functions of ParaDict's *sequential interface:*

```
void Insert_ (TDict *d, int k, bool mask[],
              TKey keys[],
              TInf infs[],
              TItem items[]);
void Lookup_ (TDict *d, int k, bool mask[],
              TKey keys[],
              TItem items[]);
void IsNil_ (TDict *d, int k, bool mask[],
             TItem items[],
             bool arenil[]);
void DelItems_ (TDict *d,int k,bool mask[],
                TItem items[]);
void Change_ (TDict *d, int k, bool mask[],
              TItem items[], TInf infs[]);
void Keys_ (TDict *d, int k, bool mask[],
            TItem items[],
            TKey keys[]);
void Infs_ (TDict *d, int k, bool mask[],
            TItem items[],
            TInf infs[]);
```

Lacks and drawbacks. The most important of them is the lack of genericity or polymorphism. Once the types TKey and TVal have been defined, dictionaries parametrized with them have to be used. Another important restriction is that, for the current implementations, the TKey type has to be arithmetic. It is hard to correct these drawbacks in a coherent form without changing the language in which the code of library is written, C*. A more object oriented, yet data parallel language could be of interest.

4. C* implementation

To implement ParaDict we choose the algorithms given by W. Paul, U. Vishkin and H. Wagener [14] based on 2-3 trees (a class of search trees where all leaves have the same depth and internal nodes have two or three sons). These algorithms on a EREW (exclusive read, exclusive write) have time

$$T(n, k) = \mathcal{O}(\log n + \log k)$$

where k is the number of keys to search, insert or delete and n is the number of leaves in the tree.

We found them interesting because a 2-3 tree is an irregular structure and because the algorithms involve many interesting programming points. To give a flavour of them, we briefly describe some procedures of the main algorithms (search, insertion and deletion). The complete documented implementation can be found in [15].

Search. The basic data structure we need (besides the tree) is the "packet". Each key [i] keys to search, belongs to a packet [j] pckts. A packet has the following structure:

```
typedef struct {
  char   state; // Active,Passive or Located
  TItem  node;
  nat    firstP,lastP;
  TKey   firstK,lastK;
  TCell  cell;
} TPacket;
```

The fields firstP and lastP are pointers to the first and last key that a packet contains. firstK and lastK are these keys. The field node is a pointer to the node where the packet is located and cell is a copy of it (it contains the keys and pointers to the sons and parent). These redundances avoid concurrent reads.

The function Locate creates a set with a unique packet that contains all the keys to search (InitPackets) and, from the root to the leaves, splits and routes down this set of packets (RoutePackets). When all the packets become inactive, the located leaves are notified to each member of every packet with a segmented copy scan operation.

```
TItem:current Locate (TDict *d,
    TKey:current keys)
{
  TPacket:current pckts;
  bool:current b;

  InitPackets(d,&pckts,keys);
  while (|= (pckts.state==Active))
    where (pckts.state==Active)
      RoutePackets  (d,&pckts,keys);
  b=pckts.state==Located;
  return scan(pckts.node,0,
    CMC_combiner_copy,CMC_upward,
    CMC_start_bit, &b ,CMC_inclusive);
}
```

In procedure RoutePackets, Direction returns the values DirL, DirR, DirM, Stop or Split allowing the packets to move down one step (to the left, right or middle son), to split if they collide with a key in the tree and, finally, to stop when they arrive to a leaf.

```
void RoutePackets (TDict *d,
    TPacket:current *pckts,
    TKey:current keys)
{
  char:current dir = Direction(*pckts);

  where (dir==DirL) {
    pckts->node=pckts->cell.Lp;
    pckts->cell=[pckts->cell.Lp]*d->cells;
  } else where (dir==DirM) {
    pckts->node=pckts->cell.Mp;
    pckts->cell=[pckts->cell.Mp]*d->cells;
  } else where (dir==DirR) {
    pckts->node=pckts->cell.Rp;
    pckts->cell=[pckts->cell.Rp]*d->cells;
  } else where (dir==Stop) {
    pckts->state=Located;
  } else /* where (dir==Split) */ {
    SplitPackets(d,pckts,keys);
} }
```

Procedure SplitPackets handles the packets that have to be splitted. Using a dichotomic scheme, new packets are created, and their fields are correctly updated.

```
void SplitPackets (TDict *d,
    TPacket:current *pckts,
    TKey:current keys)
{
  TItem:current mid;

  mid=1+(pckts->firstP+pckts->lastP)/2;
  [mid]*pckts=*pckts;
  [mid]pckts->firstP=mid;
  [mid]pckts->firstK=[mid]keys;
  pckts->lastP=mid-1;
  pckts->lastK=[mid-1]keys;
}
```

Insertion. Parallel insertions use a *divide and conquer* scheme. They are done using a *bottom-up* tree reconstruction using *pipelines*, with several hanging requests at diferent levels of the tree, forming waves. Basicly, a hanging request contains a source subtree to hang to a destination node. This is the data structure which leads the algorithm:

```
typedef struct {
  bool   active;
  TItem  source,destination;
  TPos   pos;
} THang;
```

While there exist active requests, the main insertion routine alternates two calls to LeavesUp with one call to HangsUp. LeavesUp is used to launch hanging requests at the base of the tree; it uses an implicit divide and conquer. When possible, HangsUp hangs the hanging requests, otherwise it splits the nodes and lifts up these requests to the upper level of the tree. In order to not have interferences between the levels they modify, waves of requests must be separeted at least by two levels.

```
InitHangs (leaves,&hangs,&nodes);
LeavesUp (d,leaves,&nodes,...,&hangs);
while (|= hangs.act) {
  HangsUp(d,&hangs);
  HangsUp(d,&hangs);
  LeavesUp (d,leaves,&nodes,...,&hangs);
}
```

Deletion. The deletion algorithm works in a similar way: the TEraser auxiliary data structure is used to direct the divide and conquer and pipeline processes. Again, waves must be separated by two levels:

```
typedef struct {
  char state;
  TItem source;
} TEraser;

DelItems2 (TDict *d, TItem:current items) {
  TEraser:current erasers;

  InitErasers(&erasers,items);
  while (|= (erasers.state!=Passive)) {
    RemoveLeaves(d,&erasers);
    ArrangeLevels(d,&erasers);
    ArrangeLevels(d,&erasers);
  } }
```

We found that programming all these techniques was not obvious and quite challenging for a C* programmer. Against our first impression, we found C* well adapted.

5. Experimental results

In order to evaluate the performance of some usual operations of our library, we have measured and analyzed their running time on a CM 200. Experiments have been repeated enough times; results shown below are their mean. The variances were not substantial.

Evaluation of the Lookup and Insert operations. The experimental results obtained for searching or inserting k keys in a dictionary storing n elements are shown in figure 5. For comparison with a well-known workstation, we also show the times needed for the equivalent sequential insertions. We conclude that, with our machines, even if the sequential implementation is faster than the parallel one for reasonable values of k, the time increase is smoother, making clear the scalability of our parallel library.

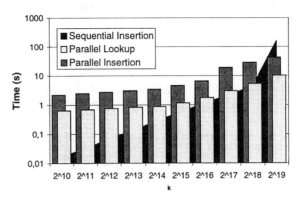

Figure 3. Running time for searching / inserting k keys in a dictionary of size n=150000 on a CM 200 with 16K processors. In the background, insertions on a Sun Sparc 10.

Comparisons with other implementations. Figure 5 compares results from [13] with ours. Since the experimental conditions where the same, we can affirm that ParaDict's implementation with 2-3 trees is slightly more efficient than X. Messeguer's implementation based on skip lists. Moreover, it saves space and can store much more elements.

The comparison of our results against the ones given in [5] by M. Gastaldo, shows that our implementation is 5 times faster. For instance, an insertion of 500000 elements can be done in 43 seconds (7 if the dictionary is empty) on a Connection Machine with 16K processors with ParaDict, whereas on a MasPar-1 with 1K processors it takes 240 seconds. However, we have to cautious about this kind of information, because we are not only comparing the algorithms but the parallel machines involved in the measurements.

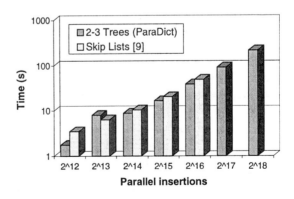

Figure 4. Running times for inserting k elements in a dictionary of size 150000 when using 2-3 trees (ParaDict) or skip lists [13] on a CM 200 with 2K processors.

6. C#, vectorization using data parallelism

There is a lot of resemblance between the data parallel and vectorial programming models: both consist of applying the same operation to different data. For this reason, we found interesting to port our parallel programs written in C* to a vectorial computer (a Convex C3480, a machine with registers of 128 elements and 8 banks of memory). We achieved it by defining a set of transformations to convert C* code to C code augmented by compiler directives (which have the #pragma _CNX form) [4]. In the following, this language is called C#. In this paper, we describe only some of these transformations. The complete set we used can be found in [16].

Send operation. The first transformation we show is for the *send* operation, which in C* is written as:

```
int:current dst,src,indx;
[indx]dst=src;
```

where indx is supposed to be a permutation. Its correct transformation to a C# efficient program is the following:

```
int src[],dst[],indx[];
for (i=0; i<n; i++) indx2[i]=indx[i];
for (i=0; i<n; i++) src2[i]=src[i];
#pragma _CNX force_vector
for (i=0; i<n; i++) dst[indx2[i]]=src2[i];
```

Auxiliary copies have to be generated, because these vectors could be the same. The compiler directive has to be given, since the compiler cannot recognize indx2 as a permutation. This operation (or its dual, the *get* operation) can be efficiently executed if the processor has *scatter* (or *gather*) instructions, which is the case on the Convex.

Parallel prefix. This second operation is related to another important operation in data parallel programming. Given an operator $\oplus$ and a vector $a = [a_0, \ldots, a_{n-1}]$, we define $/\!\!/_{\oplus} a = [b_0, \ldots, b_{n-1}]$ where $b_i = \bigoplus_{j=0}^{i} a_j$. In C* this function is called scan and belongs to the standard communication library. A naive implementation would be:

```
for (b[0]=a[0], i=1; i<n; i++)
    b[i]=b[i-1]+a[i];
```

but the vectorizing compiler could not solve the recurrence and would leave this loop scalar. However, implementing the classic PRAM algorithm [11] as:

```
for (i=0; i<n; i++) b[i]=a[i];
for (j=1,p=pow2(j-1); j<=log2(n); j++) {
  for (i=p/2; i<n; i++) aux[i]=b[i];
  for (i=p; i<n; i++) b[i]=aux[i-p]+aux[i];
}
```

the compiler can stripmine the i loops. We have found that on the Convex machine, the second implementation is 2.5 times faster than the first one when $n > 4096$. This result is negative, since according to Amdahl's law, this low speedup will have effect on all the algorithms that contain it.

Conditioning. Let us now consider the conditioning instruction where (cond) S. We code the active context with an unidimentional array. As the contexts have a block structure, we need a stack. This approach has been already considered by L. Bougé and J. Levaire [3] to give an operational semantics to a basic data parallel language, $\mathcal{L}$. The corresponding transformation is:

```
for (i=0; i<n; i++) if (cond[i]) S(i);
```

As the Convex C3480 and CM 200 machines have a similar masking behaviour the transformation is efficient. Both have also the same drawback: the execution time does not decrease when only few unmasked elements of a vector are processed. The instruction where (cond) S1 else S2 can be rewritten as t=cond; where (t) S1; where (!t) S2, and the preceding technique applies.

Example: Radix sort. Sorting is also a usual operation on data parallel machines. Radix sort is a good candidate because it is easily implemented on the CM 200 machine and it will be interesting to see what kind of C vectorizable code we will obtain. First of all, recall the RadixSort procedure written in C* as:

```
void RadixSort (nat:current *a, nat n)
{
 nat:current enu;
 nat d,k,D=boolsizeof(nat:current);

 for (d=0,k=1; d<D; d++,k<<=1) {
   where (*a & k)
     enu=(n-1) - enumerate(0,CMC_downward,
       CMC_exclusive,CMC_none,CMC_no_field);
   else
     enu=enumerate(0,CMC_upward,
       CMC_exclusive,CMC_none,CMC_no_field);
   [enu]*a=*a;
} }
```

Its transformation is the following:

```
void RadixSort (nat a[], nat n) {
  nat enu[MAX],aux[MAX];
  nat i,d,k,e,D=sizeof(int)*8;

  for (d=0,k=1; d<D; d++,k<<=1) {
    for (e=n-1,i=n-1; i>=0; i--)
      if (a[i]&k) enu[i]=e--;
```

168

```
    for (e=0,i=0; i<n; i++)
        if (!(a[i]&k)) enu[i]=e++;
    for (i=0; i<n; i++) aux[i]=a[i];
    for (i=0; i<n; i++) a[enu[i]]=aux[i];
} }
```

Note that the transformation into C# give us a code where only the more external loop remains sequential. The other loops corresponding to enumerations, copy and send operations have been vectorized by the Convex C compiler.

Segmented scans. Segmented scans have been extensively studied by G. Blelloch in [1, 2]. Assume we have an array v and another array f of flags. Each flag specifies the start of a new segment. For instance, if we consider the following array $v = [1\ 1\ 1\ 7\ 1\ 4\ 1\ 5\ 6\ 8\ 4]$ and $f = [1\ 0\ 0\ 1\ 0\ 1\ 0\ 0\ 0\ 1\ 0]$ the segmented array is represented as $s = [1\ 1\ 1\ |\ 7\ 1\ |\ 4\ 1\ 5\ 6\ |\ 8\ 4]$ and the segmented prefix sum will be $/\!/_+ s = [1\ 2\ 3\ |\ 7\ 8\ |\ 4\ 5\ 10\ 16\ |\ 8\ 12]$. The segmented version of an $\oplus$ operation can be implemented as $(v_a, f_a) \otimes (v_b, f_b) = (v_r, f_r)$ where $v_r = v_b$ if f_b holds, $v_r = v_a \oplus v_b$ if $\neg f_b$ holds and $f_r = f_a \vee f_b$. In C# we get the following code:

```
for (j=1,k=log2(n); j<=k; j++) {
    p=pow2(j-1);
    for (i=p/2; i<n; i++) {
        v2[i]=v[i]; f2[i]=f[i];
    }
    for (i=p; i<n; i++) if (!f2[i]) {
        v[i]=v2[i-p]+v2[i];
        f[i]=f2[i-p];
    }
} }
```

A first judgement. We presented a way to transform *directly* data parallel programs written in C* into C# programs. Therefore it is possible to transform data parallelism into hightly vectorizable code and we have a connection between these two approaches to parallelism. However, as we have seen in the parallel prefix transformation, the speedup is not so important. Therefore, transformations seem to be good but the speedup seems to be bad. To get a better inside into the behaviour of C# we developed a vectorial version of ParaDict. Next section explores the results.

7. C# vectorial dictionaries

Applying these kinds of transformations to a subset of ParaDict, we have obtained its vectorial implementation (with the SP/PL interface). Even if almost every loop was made vectorial by the optimizing compiler, the performances achieved at run-time were very poor: table 7 reports it. The speedup of the vectorial implementation with respect to the sequential one is 5 for the building operation and 2 for

the search operation. Vectorizing the insertion operation is self-defeating.

Operation	CM 16K	Convex	
(Measures in seconds)	Par	Sca	Vec
Build with 2^{20} leaves	7.118	26.723	7.658
Search 2^{16} keys	1.776	6.624	3.340
Insert 2^{14} keys	—	2.407	40.309

Table 1. Some measures characterizing the behaviour of the different implementations. Searches and insertions are made on a tree with 150000 leaves.

We conjecture that the reason for these modest improvements (when they exist) is again the highly irregular structure we are dealing with, and the bottleneck it creates accessing the limited set of memory banks.

8. Conclusions

In parallelism, there seems to be a gap between theory and practice. In many cases it is quite difficult to measure the effort necessary to transform an informal algorithm into readable code. We got a pleasant surprise with C*, because sophisticated algorithms were easily coded. As in the sequential case, the program development by stepwise refinement has been extensively used to get readable programs.

Moreover it has been possible to define two complete and useful interfaces: a sequential and a parallel one. This is important because they reflect two different views of parallelism. The sequential interface is planned to be used by sequential programmers using data parallelism in a hidden way. The data parallel interface is to be used by programmers having a knowledge of data parallelism. Both classes of programmers coexists today. People coming from computer science uses friendly data parallel environments, but most of the people coming from other disciplines prefers a sequential environment. However both classes of programmers can take advantatge of data parallel libraries. More important, only one kind of data parallel program has to be developped. These parallel programs can be used from a sequential environment just adding a *bridge level*, always easy to build. We claim that the whole approach will remain true for other applications.

Experimental results left open many questions. Whereas our dictionary implementation (a highly irregular and dynamic object) performs better than previous implementations, parallel results are not so good in relation to their sequential counterpart. However, in many cases these comparisons are not so clear and, in our case, involve rather old

SIMD machines against new and powerful sequential computers. It is unclear what happens with more modern parallel machines. Moreover, in the near future, compilers for data parallel languages on MIMD machines could become more popular. If this happens, data parallel programming could become every day programming, but care has to be taken when dealing with irregular data structures as ours.

Many questions remain open about the distinction between *high* and *low level* approaches to programming in parallel. Programming with a sequential languages plus a message passing library (e.g. PVM) is for us a low level approach. We also consider a low level activity to write (directly) good sequential vectorizable programs. From the other side we consider C* programs as high level. Transformations from C* to C# connects high and low levels, but the results were poor. We guess the same will happen if we try a transformation from data parallel programs to sequential programs + message passing. In both cases the problem seems to be the *fine grain* and the *irregularity* of the application, but this is just a feeling without any theoretical proof. In any case, we think that data parallel languages will continue to be an interesting and elegant high level counterpart to other low level approaches.

Further information

Further information regarding ParaDict can be found on the World Wide Web at the address

http://www-lsi.upc.es/ParaDict

Acknowledgements

The implementation and evaluation of our programs has been done at the Centre Europeu de Paral·lelisme de Barcelona (CEPBA, now C^4) and at the Parallelldatorcentrum (PDC) of the Kungl Tekniska Högskolan (Sweden). We acknowledge X. Messeguer for help and letting us use its code.

References

[1] G. Blelloch. Scans as primitive parallel operations. *IEEE Trans. Comp.*, 38(11):1526–1538, 1989.

[2] G. Blelloch. *Vector Models for Data-Parallel Computing.* MIT, 1990.

[3] L. Bougé and L. Levaire. Control structures for data-parallel SIMD language: Semantics and implementation. *Future Generation Computer Systems*, (8):363–378, 1992.

[4] Convex Computer Corporation. *Convex C Optimization Guide*, 1991.

[5] T. Duboux, A. Ferreira, and M. Gastaldo. MIMD dictionary machines from theory to practice. In *Conpar92-VappV*, LNCS 634, pages 545–550. Springer-Verlag, 1992. Look

also M. Gastaldo PhD thesis: Contribution a l'algorithmique parallele des structures de données discretes: machines dictionnaire et algorithmes pour les graphes, ENS-Lyon, 1993.

[6] I. Foster. *Designing and Building Parallel Programs*. Addison Wesley, 1995.

[7] J. Gabarró, C. Martínez, and X. Messeguer. A design of a parallel dictionary using skip lists. *TCS*, (158):1–33, 1996.

[8] J. Gabarró and X. Messeguer. Massively parallel and distributed dictionaries on AVL and Brother trees. In *Parallel and Distributed Computing Systems*, pages 14–17. ISCA, 1996.

[9] L. Higham and E. Schenks. Maintaining B-trees on an EREW PRAM. *JPDC*, (22):329–335, 1994.

[10] W. D. Hillis. *The Connection Machine*. MIT, 1987.

[11] J. JáJá. *An Introduction to Parallel Algoritms*. Addison Wesley, 1992.

[12] K. Mehlhorn and S. Näher. LEDA: A platform for combinatorial and geometric computing. *CACM*, 38(1):96–102, 1995.

[13] X. Messeguer. A sequential and parallel implementation of skip lists. Technical Report LSI-94-41-R, LSI-UPC, Nov. 1994.

[14] W. Paul, U. Vishkin, and H. Wagener. Parallel dictionaries on 2-3-trees. In *10th ICALP*, LNCS 154, pages 397–609. Springer-Verlag, 1983. Look also: Parallel computation on 2-3-trees, RAIRO, 397–404, 1984.

[15] J. Petit. ParaDict. A data parallel implementation of dictionaries with 2-3 trees. Technical report, LSI-UPC, Sept. 1996. LSI-96-7-T.

[16] J. Petit. Llibreria de diccionaris paral·lels: disseny, implementació, avaluació, Jan. 1996. FIB-UPC Computing Project.

[17] J. Petit. ParaDict's User Guide. Technical report, LSI-UPC, May 1996. LSI-96-4-T.

[18] Thinking Machines Corporation. *C* Programming Guide*, 1991.

❖ SESSION 5 ❖

Compiler and Run-Time Technology

Chair

P. Milligan

Symbolic Expression Evaluation to Support Parallelizing Compilers

Thomas Fahringer
Institute for Software Technology and Parallel Systems
University of Vienna
Liechtensteinstrasse 22, A-1090 Vienna, Austria
e-mail: tf@par.univie.ac.at

Abstract

Symbolic analysis is of paramount importance to further advance the state-of-the-art of parallelizing compilers. The quality of various compiler analyses and optimizing code transformations depend on the ability to evaluate symbolic expressions for equality and inequality ($=, <, >$) relationships. This paper describes a powerful algorithm that computes lower and/or upper bounds of wide classes of linear and non-linear symbolic expressions given a set of constraints on loop variables and loop invariants. The algorithm is used to compare symbolic expressions, examine non-linear array index functions for data dependences, and simplify systems of constraints. Among others the algorithm supports dependence analysis, detecting zero-trip-loops, dead code elimination, and performance prediction. We have implemented the algorithm and use it as part of a parallelizing compiler and a static performance estimator.

1 Introduction

Many parallelizing compilers fail to effectively parallelize programs caused by the deficit of the compiler to analyze complex – in particular non-linear – loop bounds, conditionals, and array index functions. Non-linear symbolic expressions are commonly caused by induction variable substitution, linearizing arrays, parameterizing data parallel programs with symbolic number of processors and/or problem size, and so forth. Numerous researchers [7, 2, 9, 8] have reported on the occurrence of non-linear symbolic expressions in practical codes and the need of effective techniques to analyze such programs. Non-linear symbolic expressions seriously hamper crucial compiler analysis including testing for data dependences, optimizing communication, simplifying code, dead code elimination, performance prediction, detecting zero-trip-loops, etc.

Consider the loop nest in Example 1.1 which contains linearized and indirect array referencing and is very similar to a code excerpt as found in the TRFD code of the Perfect

Benchmarks [3]. In loop $L1$ array IA is initialized with a non-linear array index function $(I*(I-1))/2$, which is then used in $S4$ to read $X(IJ, KL)$ and write $X(KL, IJ)$ with $IJ = (I*(I-1))/2 + J$ and $KL = (K*(K-1))/2 + L$, respectively. In order to examine whether loop $L5$ can be executed in parallel, we must determine whether statement $S4$ implies a true dependence (array elements are written before they are read) with respect to $L5$. Conventional dependence tests cannot examine non-linear array index functions and therefore assume a data dependence that sequentializes loop $L5$. This paper describes an algorithm that can compare non-linear array index functions such as KL and IJ, and consequently determines the absence of a true dependence, which enables the underlying compiler to parallelize loop $L5$.

Example 1.1

```
L1:  DO I=1,N
S1:      IA(I)=(I*(I-1))/2
     ENDDO
        ...
L2:  DO I=1,N
L3:      DO J=1,I
S2:          IJ=IA(I)+J
            ...
L4:          DO K=1,I
                ...
L5:              DO L=1,J-1
S3:                  KL=IA(K)+L
                    ...
S4:                  X(KL,IJ)=X(IJ,KL)+VAL
                 ENDDO
             ENDDO
         ENDDO
     ENDDO
```

For the loop nest in Example 1.2 a compiler may determine whether the condition of statement S1 ever evaluates to TRUE. If not then we can simply eliminate the entire conditional statement (dead code elimination). Detecting zero-trip-loops [8] is a similar problem which tries to determine whether the loop body of a given loop nest is ever executed. Other related problems require loop iteration or statement execution counts which are key figures to estimate a program's performance [7, 4]. All of these problems can be formulated as a set of linear and non-linear constraints $\mathcal{I}$ defined over loop *variables* and *parameters* (loop invariants), which are commonly derived from loop bounds and conditional statements. For instance, $\mathcal{I}$ is given by $\{1 \leq I1 \leq N, N/(2*I1) \leq I2 \leq N, I1*I2 \leq N\}$ based on Example 1.2. Most analyses based on systems of constraints are significantly alleviated if $\mathcal{I}$ is simplified by eliminating redundant constraints and detecting contradictions.

Example 1.2

```
    DO I1=1,N
      DO I2=N/(2*I1),N
S1:      IF (I1*I2 ≤ N) THEN
            A(I1,I2) = ...
         ENDIF
         ...
      ENDDO
    ENDDO
```

This paper describes an algorithm that computes lower and/or upper bounds of wide classes of linear and non-linear symbolic expressions given a set of constraints defined over loop variables and loop invariants. The algorithm is based on substituting variables and parameters by their associated lower and upper bound expressions. Rewrite rules for lower and upper bound functions and simplification techniques are applied until the symbolic expression consists only of constants, $-\infty$ or ∞. Among others this algorithm can be used to compare symbolic expressions for equality and inequality ($=, <, >$) relationships, examine non-linear array index functions for data dependences, and detect redundant inequalities in a set of constraints.

We have implemented the algorithm and use it as part of P^3T [5, 4], a performance estimator for parallel programs, and *VFCS* [1], a parallelizing compiler for data parallel programs on distributed memory parallel architectures. Experiments will be shown that demonstrate the usefulness of our approach.

This paper is organized as follows: In Section 2 we present our algorithm for computing lower and upper bounds of symbolic expressions and how this algorithm is used to compare symbolic expressions and examine data dependences of non linear array index functions. Section 3 shows how to simplify a set of symbolic constraints. Related work is discussed in Section 4. Section 5 gives a detailed example of how to detect redundant inequalities in a set of symbolic constraints. Conclusions and final remarks are given in Section 6.

2 Evaluating Symbolic Expressions

In this section we present our algorithm which compares symbolic expressions for equality or inequality relationships. The following notations and definitions are used in the remainder of this paper:

- Let $\mathcal{I}$ be a set of non-linear and linear constraints defined over loop *variables* and *parameters* (loop invariants) which are derived from the loop bounds and conditional statements of a program. $\mathcal{V}$ is the set of variables and $\mathcal{P}$ the set of parameters appearing in $\mathcal{I}$.

- $low(E)$ and $up(E)$ are two functions, which define the minimum and maximum value of a symbolic expression E for all values of variables and parameters appearing in E. These two functions (up and low) will be referred to as δ-*functions*. $\delta(E)$ which is either $low(E)$ or $up(E)$ is denoted as δ-*expression*. Note that E may again contain δ-expressions.

- A *symbolic (integer-valued) expression* E may consist of arbitrary division, multiplication, subtraction, addition, exponentiation, maximum, minimum, and δ-functions. Its operands can be variables, parameters, integer constants and infinity symbols ($\infty, -\infty$).

2.1 Algorithm

Figure 1 shows algorithm EXPR_BOUND which tries to compute the lower and/or upper bound of a symbolic expression E defined in $\mathcal{V} \cup \mathcal{P}$. The input to EXPR_BOUND is E, $\mathcal{B}$, and $\mathcal{Q}$. $\mathcal{B}$ is the set of known upper and lower bound expressions (constraints) for each variable and parameter. These constraints are derived from $\mathcal{I}$, the set of constraints of the underlying problem.

Assume that the cardinality of $\mathcal{V}$ and $\mathcal{P}$ respectively is n and m, then $\mathcal{Q}=\{(v_1;v_1^l,v_1^u),...,(v_n;v_n^l,v_n^u), (p_1;p_1^l,p_1^u),...,(p_m;v_m^l,v_m^u)\}$. $(v_i;v_i^l,v_i^u)$ – where $1 \leq i \leq n$ – specifies a variable $v_i \in \mathcal{V}$ with its associated maximum lower bound v_i^l and minimum upper bound v_i^u. $(p_j;p_j^l,p_j^u)$ – where $1 \leq j \leq m$ – specifies a parameter $p_j \in \mathcal{P}$ with its associated maximum lower bound p_j^l and minimum upper bound p_j^u. The algorithm maintains the maximum lower and minimum upper bound for each variable and parameter in $\mathcal{Q}$. If a new lower bound for a variable is deduced by the algorithm that is larger than the current maximum lower bound as stored in $\mathcal{Q}$, then $\mathcal{Q}$ is updated accordingly. Similar accounts for the minimum upper bound.

Let us continue Example 1.1 of Section 1. The set of constraints $\mathcal{I}$ for this problem is derived from the corresponding loop nest. $\mathcal{I} = \{1 \leq I \leq N, 1 \leq J \leq I, 1 \leq K \leq I, 1 \leq L \leq J-1\}$. This yields the following sets of variables, parameters, lower and upper bounds:

$\mathcal{V} = \{I, J, K, L\}, \mathcal{P} = \{N\}, LB_I = \{1, J, K\}, UB_I = \{N\},$
$LB_J = \{1, L-1\}, UB_J = \{I\}, LB_K = \{1\}, UB_K = \{I\},$
$LB_L = \{1\}, UB_L = \{J-1\}, LB_N = \{I\}, UB_N = \{\infty\},$

$$\mathcal{B} = \bigcup_{q \in \{I,J,K,L,N\}} LB_q \cup UB_q$$

EXPR_BOUND($E,\mathcal{B},\mathcal{Q}$)

- **INPUT:**

  E: δ-expression defined in $\mathcal{V} \cup \mathcal{P}$

  $\mathcal{B}$: Set of lower and upper bound expressions for variables and parameters defined in $\mathcal{V} \cup \mathcal{P}$.

- **INPUT-OUTPUT:**

  – $\mathcal{Q}$: Set of single lower and upper bound for each variable and parameter updated by EXPR_BOUND.

- **OUTPUT:**

  – Bound for E which is a constant, ∞, or -∞.

- **ALGORITHM:**

  $\mathcal{V}$ = Set of variables appearing in E.
  $\mathcal{P}$ = Set of parameters appearing in E.
  $E_{orig} = E$
  REPEAT
      $E = E_{orig}$
      $\mathcal{Q}_{old} = \mathcal{Q}$
      WHILE variables appear in E DO
          S1: Choose a δ-expression in E for rewriting
          S2: Rewrite δ-expression of S1 in E
          S3: Simplify E
          S4: Update $\mathcal{Q}$
      ENDWHILE
      WHILE parameters appear in E DO
          S5: Choose a δ-expression in E for rewriting
          S6: Rewrite δ-expression of S5 in E
          S7: Simplify E
          S8: Update $\mathcal{Q}$
      ENDWHILE
  UNTIL $\mathcal{Q} \equiv \mathcal{Q}_{old}$
  S9: Determine Bound for E

Figure 1. A Demand driven algorithm to compute the lower and/or upper bound of a symbolic expression defined in $\mathcal{V} \cup \mathcal{P}$.

Initially all lower and upper bounds in $\mathcal{Q}$ are set to $-\infty$ and ∞, respectively.

The algorithm traverses E and replaces all δ-expressions of E using bound expressions in $\mathcal{B}$ and $\mathcal{Q}$, and rewrite-rules of Table 1 until E is a constant, $-\infty$, or ∞. During a single iteration of the REPEAT loop, the bounds in $\mathcal{Q}$ may become tighter as compared to the previous loop iteration. Tighter bounds in $\mathcal{Q}$ may induce tighter and consequently more precise bounds for E as well. Therefore, the algorithm iterates as long as $\mathcal{Q}$ changes between any pair of consecutive REPEAT loop iterations. At the end of a specific iteration, E might be a constant or an infinity symbol which cannot be changed by additional iterations of the algorithm as no variables or parameters are available for substitution. For this reason E is set to the original expression at the beginning of each iteration of the REPEAT loop.

2.2 Rewrite δ-Expressions

Rewriting $\delta(x)$ describes the process of applying a rewrite rule (see Table 1) to $\delta(x)$. For instance, a δ-expression $low(x + y)$ is rewritten as $low(x) + low(y)$ according to rule 7: $low(x + y) \rightarrow low(x) + low(y)$. This means that $low(x + y)$ is textually *replaced* (semantically equivalent) by $low(x) + low(y)$. Rewrite rules can be applied to either a single variable, parameter or a symbolic expression. If x in $\delta(x)$ is a variable or a parameter then we frequently use the term *substituting* instead of rewriting.

Continuing Example 1.1 of the previous section, where we try to prove that $IJ \geq KL$ in statement S4: X(KL,IJ)=X(IJ,KL)+VAL for all loop iterations of $L5$ which implies that $L5$ can be executed in parallel. Note that this may still imply an anti dependence (array elements are read before written). If array X is block distributed then statement $S4$ still causes communication, however, all communication can be hoisted outside of $L5$ through communication vectorization and aggregation [1].

As IJ $= \frac{I*(I-1)}{2} + J$ and KL $= \frac{K*(K-1)}{2} + L$ according to statements $S1$, $S2$ and $S3$ of Example 1.1, we have to show that $\frac{I*(I-1)}{2}+J \geq \frac{K*(K-1)}{2}+L \iff \frac{I*(I-1)}{2}+J-\frac{K*(K-1)}{2}-L \geq 0$. The set of constraints $\mathcal{I}$ for this problem is given in Section 2.1. In order to prove the absence of a true dependence we have to show that low($\frac{I*(I-1)}{2} + J - \frac{K*(K-1)}{2} - L$) ≥ 0:

$$low(\frac{I*(I-1)}{2} + J - \frac{K*(K-1)}{2} - L)$$
$$\rightarrow \quad low(\frac{I*(I-1)}{2}) + low(J) - up(\frac{K*(K-1)}{2}) - up(L) \quad (1)$$

Which is based on rewrite rules (7) and (8) of Table 1. Note that Table 1 displays primarily rewrite rules for *low* functions. Rewrite rules for *up* functions are similar. Rewrite rules for expressions containing infinity symbols have not been included, since they are easy to determine.

The aim of rewriting δ-expressions is to reduce all subexpressions, variables, and parameters of E until E is a constant or an infinity symbol, which is then returned as the result of the algorithm. In order to find the correct rewrite rule to be applied to a multiplication, division or exponentiation expression, the algorithm may have to determine the value ranges (signs) for the associated sub-expressions. This is done by recursively calling EXPR_BOUND.

It may actually occur that variables are induced again by replacing parameters, as the bounds of parameters (in $\mathcal{B}$) may contain variables. In this case we recursively call the algorithm for the variable bounds required.

In order to guarantee that EXPR_BOUND terminates we use the following *termination condition (TC)*: If the algorithm is trying to rewrite *low(expr)* in a recursive call of EXPR_BOUND while trying to rewrite *low(expr)* in a previous recursion, then *low(expr)* is replaced by $-\infty$. The same accounts for *up(expr)*, which is replaced by ∞. Furthermore, if there are no lower or upper bounds given for a variable or a parameter, then the associated lower and upper bound is assumed to be $-\infty$ and ∞, respectively.

Whenever EXPR_BOUND deduces a new possible tighter lower or upper bound for a variable, it is stored (statement S4 and S8) in Q, which is a global data structure across all recursive calls to EXPR_BOUND.

Some of the rewrite rules for δ-functions may contain δ-functions applied to x^- (all negative integers of x) or x^+ (all positive integers of x). If the algorithm is unable to apply rewrite rules to such expressions because there is no information available for the value range (sign) of x^+ and x^-, then the following rules – which guarantee conservative and therefore correct bounds – are used:

$$
\begin{aligned}
low(x^-) &\rightarrow -\infty \\
low(x^+) &\rightarrow 1 \\
up(x^-) &\rightarrow -1 \\
up(x^+) &\rightarrow \infty
\end{aligned}
$$

2.3 Rewrite Policies

In statement S1 of Figure 1 it is first tried to find subexpressions of E for rewriting that contain variables. Each variable corresponds to a loop variable with a unique loop nest level. Those δ-expressions $\delta(expr)$ that contain the variable with highest loop nest level (loop variable appearing in innermost loop) have to be rewritten first; the one with second innermost loop variable second, ..., the one with outermost loop variable will be rewritten at the very end. If there are several δ expressions which contain a variable with highest loop nest level then choose any of these δ expressions for rewriting.

If there are no more variables in E then rewrite (statements S5 and S6) those δ-expressions in E first that contain parameters which depend (their lower or upper bounds contain other parameters) on other parameters.

Substituting variables – with their lower or upper bounds – before parameters enables us in many cases to find tighter bounds for δ-expressions. Each variable is in fact a loop variable in the underlying problem. Loop variables may directly or indirectly depend on constants or parameters (loop invariants). Overly conservative expression bounds may be computed if we reduce all variables to constants, $-\infty$, and ∞ without ever trying to simplify intermediate expressions. See also Section 2.4.

Continuing rewriting (1) of the previous section, we determine:

$$
low(\frac{I*(I-1)}{2}) + low(J) - up(\frac{K*(K-1)}{2}) - up(L)
$$

$$
\rightarrow \quad low(\frac{I*(I-1)}{2}) + low(J) - up(\frac{K*(K-1)}{2}) - up(J\text{-}1) \quad (2)
$$

$$
\rightarrow \quad low(\frac{I*(I-1)}{2}) - up(\frac{K*(K-1)}{2}) + 1 \quad (3)
$$

$$
\rightarrow \quad low(\frac{I*(I-1)}{2}) - up(\frac{I*(I-1)}{2}) + 1 \quad (4)
$$

First we have to rewrite the term that contains the innermost loop variable L which is $up(L)$. By replacing L with its upper bound $(J-1)$ we obtain (2). Simplifying (2) yields (3), which is explained in the next section. Thereafter, we search again for the term with the highest loop nest level. Only I and K appear in (3). K is substituted next as it has a higher loop nest level than I, which results in (4).

2.4 Simplify Expressions

In statement S3 and S7 we try to simplify E by first saving the outermost δ-function of E in δ_c, then replacing all $\delta(expr)$ in E by $expr$ which yields E', and then simplify E' using standard symbolic expression simplification. Finally, E is replaced by $\delta_c(E')$ which is the new simplified E. Note that $\delta_c(E')$ is guaranteed (proof in [6]) to represent either the same or a tighter bound for E. E.g. let $E = \mathbf{low}(\frac{up(n^2)+up(n)}{low(n)} - 1)$, then the algorithm first saves the outermost δ-function of E – which is $\mathbf{low}$ – in δ_c. Replacing all $\delta(expr)$ in E by $expr$ yields $E' = \frac{n^2+n}{n} - 1$, which can be further simplified to $E' = n$. We then re-apply δ_c to E' which yields $low(n)$, the new simplified E. If we would have tried to reduce all variables and parameters to constants and infinity symbols, then we may get very conservative bounds. Consider an example where $E = low(n) - up(n) + 1$, $low(n) = 1$, and $up(n) = \infty$. If we simplify E according to the method described above, then we obtain $n - n + 1$ which is further reduced to 1. On the other hand, we may reduce E as follows: $low(n) - up(n) + 1 \rightarrow 1 - \infty + 1 \rightarrow -\infty$. Clearly, the first result represents a much tighter bound for E than the second result.

Continuing Example 1.1, we can simplify (4) as follows:

$$
low(\frac{I*(I-1)}{2}) - up(\frac{I*(I-1)}{2}) + 1
$$

$$
\rightarrow \quad \frac{I*(I-1)}{2} - \frac{I*(I-1)}{2} + 1
$$

$$
\rightarrow \quad 1 \quad (5)
$$

2.5 Determine Result

Finally, in statement S9 we reach a point where E is an expression consisting only of constants and infinity symbols. If E is a constant, $-\infty$ or ∞ then E is returned as the result. In all other cases the algorithm makes a worst-case assumption and respectively returns ∞ or $-\infty$ depending on whether the algorithm has been called for an upper or lower bound.

In continuation of Example 1.1 we determine that (5) has already been simplified to an integer constant, which is the lower bound of $low(\frac{I*(I-1)}{2} + J - \frac{K*(K-1)}{2} - L)$. This enables us to conclude the following: As $low(\frac{I*(I-1)}{2} + J - \frac{K*(K-1)}{2} - L) \geq 1$ and therefore $IJ \geq KL$, we can safely parallelize loop $L5$ of Example 1.1. Conventional dependence analysis techniques assume a true dependence

$$up(x) \rightarrow min(up(UB_1(x)), \ldots, up(UB_u(x))) \qquad \text{: if } x \text{ is a symbolic variable with u upper bounds} \qquad (1)$$

$$up(c) \rightarrow c \qquad \text{: if } c \text{ is an integer constant} \qquad (2)$$

$$low(x) \rightarrow max(low(LB_1(x)), \ldots, low(LB_l(x))) \qquad \text{: if } x \text{ is a symbolic variable with } l \text{ lower bounds} \qquad (3)$$

$$low(c) \rightarrow c \qquad \text{: if } c \text{ is an integer constant} \qquad (4)$$

$$low(-x) \rightarrow -up(x) \qquad (5)$$

$$up(-x) \rightarrow -low(x) \qquad (6)$$

$$low(x + y) \rightarrow low(x) + low(y) \qquad (7)$$

$$low(x - y) \rightarrow low(x) - up(y) \qquad (8)$$

$$low(x * y) \rightarrow \begin{cases} low(x) * up(y) & : \text{ if } x \leq 0 \text{ and } y > 0 \\ up(x) * low(y) & : \text{ if } x \geq 0 \text{ and } y < 0 \\ low(x) * low(y) & : \text{ if } x, y \geq 0 \\ up(x) * up(y) & : \text{ if } x, y < 0 \\ min(low(x) * up(y), up(x) * low(y), low(x) * low(y), up(x) * up(y)) & : \text{ otherwise} \end{cases} \qquad (9)$$

$$low(\frac{x}{y}) \rightarrow \begin{cases} \frac{up(x)}{up(y)} & : \text{ if } x \geq 0 \text{ and } y < 0 \\ \frac{up(x)}{low(y)} & : \text{ if } x, y < 0 \\ \frac{low(x)}{up(y)} & : \text{ if } x \geq 0 \text{ and } y > 0 \\ \frac{low(x)}{low(y)} & : \text{ if } x < 0 \text{ and } y > 0 \\ min(\frac{up(x^-)}{low(y)}, \frac{low(x)}{low(y^+)}, \frac{up(x)}{up(y^-)}, \frac{low(x^+)}{up(y)}) & : \text{ otherwise} \end{cases} \qquad (10)$$

$$low(x^c) \rightarrow \begin{cases} (low(x))^c & : \text{ if } (x \geq 0 \text{ and } c \geq 0) \text{ or} \\ & : \qquad (x \leq 0 \text{ and } c \geq 0 \text{ and } c \text{ odd}) \text{ or} \\ & : \qquad (x < 0 \text{ and } c < 0 \text{ and } c \text{ even}) \\ (up(x))^c & : \text{ if } (x > 0 \text{ and } c < 0) \text{ or} \\ & : \qquad (x \leq 0 \text{ and } c \geq 0 \text{ and } c \text{ even}) \text{ or} \\ & : \qquad (x < 0 \text{ and } c < 0 \text{ and } c \text{ odd}) \\ min((low(x))^c, (up(x))^c, (low(x_0^+))^c) & : \text{ otherwise} \end{cases} \qquad (11)$$

Table 1. Rewrite rules for simplifying expressions containing low and up functions. x and y are symbolic integer-valued expressions. x^- and x^+ respectively refer to the set of negative and positive integer values (neither contains 0) of x. x_0^+ is defined by x^+ including also 0. c is an integer constant.

for statement $S4$ in this code and consequently serialize loop $L5$ as they fail to evaluate non-linear array index functions.

3 Simplification of Systems of Constraints

The complexity of many compiler analyses as well as the associated results which are based on a set of constraints $\mathcal{I}$ can be considerably reduced, if tautologies, contradictions, equalities and redundant constraints can be detected and eliminated. Simplifying a set of constraints has been shown [7, 8] to be critical in order to alleviate performance as well as compiler analysis. We have developed and implemented the following simplification techniques:

- Tautology inequalities (e.g. $2 > 0$, $n \leq n$, and $n \leq n * n$) in $\mathcal{I}$ are detected and removed by using standard symbolic expression simplification and algorithm EXPR_BOUND.

- Search for two inequalities $I_1, I_2 \in \mathcal{I}$ which induce an equality. E.g. let I_1 be $2 * i * j - n \leq 0$ and I_2 is $2 * i * j - n \geq 0$, which implies $I_3 : 2 * i * j - n = 0$. If so, then we search for a variable v with a coefficient as simple as possible (e.g. constant) in the resulting equality, solve it for v and substitute in $\mathcal{I}$ for all occurrences of v. Once we have successfully substituted an equality I_3 – deduced from two inequalities I_1 and I_2 – we can delete I_1, I_2, and I_3 in $\mathcal{I}$.

- Examine whether two inequalities of $\mathcal{I}$ contradict each other (e.g. $2 * i * j + m > 0$ and $2 * i * j + m + 3 \leq 0$), which means that $\mathcal{I}$ has no solution. If contradictions are detected many compiler analyses can be immediately terminated.

- Try to detect and eliminate redundant inequalities in $\mathcal{I}$. This is in particular important for inequalities involving variables, as the number of inequalities in $\mathcal{I}$ is in many cases directly proportional to the complexity of finding a solution to $\mathcal{I}$.

The following theorem states a condition which allows us to eliminate redundant inequalities in a set of constraints.

THEOREM: Let E_1, E_2 be two symbolic expressions defined in $\mathcal{V} \cup \mathcal{P}$, and $q \in \mathcal{V} \cup \mathcal{P}$. I_1, I_2 are two inequalities of $\mathcal{I}$ such that I_1 is defined by E_1 REL q and I_2 by E_2 REL q. REL is an inequality relationship in $\{\leq, <\}$. Then I_2 can be eliminated from $\mathcal{I}$, if at least one of the following two conditions is satisfied.

1. $low(E_1 - E_2) \geq 0$ for all values of variables and parameters appearing in E_1 and E_2

2. $up(E_2 - E_1) \leq 0$ for all values of variables and parameters appearing in E_1 and E_2.

This theorem has been proved in [6]. The theorem for inequality relationships $>$ and $\geq$ is similar. Algorithm EXPR_BOUND can therefore also be used to detect and eliminate redundant inequalities.

4 Related Work

Blume [2] developed an algorithm to compare two expressions based on symbolic ranges. A range $[a : b]$ for a variable x defines a single lower and upper bound on x, which can also be written as $a \leq x \leq y$. The main difference between our algorithm and the one of Blume is that Blume's techniques are based on manipulation of symbolic expressions containing variable ranges, whereas our method applies δ-functions to symbolic expressions. Although Blume's algorithm is quite general, we encountered sufficient problems to justify the development of our own method for comparing symbolic expressions:

- Blume assumes for the range $[a : b]$ of a variable v that $a \leq b$. This restriction makes it difficult for some important compiler analyses to apply his algorithm. For instance, in order to compute loop iteration counts [5, 7] or detect zero-trip-loops [8], we must allow loop variables whose lower bounds can be larger than their upper bounds for some loop iterations. Our algorithm EXPR_BOUND has been designed to handle such cases.

- Blume does not discuss how to handle multiple lower and upper bounds for a variable v, which is a critical issue for symbolic sum algorithms [7] or dead code elimination. Again, our approach models such cases.

- Our rewrite rules for simplifying expressions are less conservative than those of Blume, which means that our approach may obtain tighter bounds for expressions.

For instance, Blume's rewrite rules [2] for multiplication of a variable range [a:b] with a constant c – if the sign for c is unknown – is $[-\infty:\infty]$. Our rewrite rules for multiplication operations (Table 1) do not contain any $-\infty$ or ∞. If we apply Blume's rewrite rule to the expression $x*y$ where $0 \leq x \leq y$ and the sign of y is unknown, then $x*y \rightarrow [0 : y]*y \rightarrow [-\infty : \infty]$. Applying rewrite rule (9) of Table 1 to $low(x*y)$ yields the following substitution: $low(x*y) \rightarrow min(low(x)*up(y), up(x)* low(y), low(x) * low(y), up(x) * up(y)) \rightarrow min(low(x) * up(y), up(y) * low(x), low(x) * low(y), up(x) * up(y))$ by substituting $up(y)$ for up(x), and $low(x)$ for $low(y)$. In our algorithm according to Section 2.2, we assume $up(y)$ is equal to ∞ as there is no upper bound information available for y. Consequently the previous expression can be rewritten as $min(0*\infty, \infty*0, 0*0, \infty*\infty) \rightarrow min(0, 0, 0, \infty) \rightarrow 0$. Therefore, our method deduces the tightest lower bound possible based on the constraints given, whereas Blume's approach derives a worst case answer $-\infty \leq x * y$.

- Our approach for obtaining a replacement order for variables in expressions is similar effective as Blume's technique – which requires a dependence graph of variable bounds and topological sorting of strongly-connected components in this graph – but much cheaper in terms of complexity.

Other related work has been done by M. Haghighat and C. Polychronopoulos [8]. They describe techniques to prove that a symbolic expression is strictly increasing or decreasing, which enables them to analyze codes for data dependences. P. Tu and D. Padua [9] present an algorithm to determine the relationship between two symbolic expressions which is based on gated static single assignment form.

5 Experiments

In this section we continue Example 1.2 of Section 1 which demonstrates how algorithm EXPR_BOUND can be used to eliminate a redundant constraint on a variable and as a consequence simplifies other compiler analyses significantly. Consider the following set of inequalities as obtained from the code of Example 1.2.

$$\mathcal{I} = \{1 \leq i_1 \leq n, \tfrac{n}{2*i_1} \leq i_2 \leq n, i_1 * i_2 \leq n\}$$

This yields the following sets of variables, parameters, lower and upper bounds:
$\mathcal{V} = \{i_1, i_2\}$, $\mathcal{P} = \{n\}$, $LB_{i_1} = \{1, \tfrac{n}{2*i_2}\}$, $UB_{i_1} = \{n, \tfrac{n}{i_2}\}$,
$LB_{i_2} = \{\tfrac{n}{2*i_1}\}$, $UB_{i_2} = \{n, \tfrac{n}{i_1}\}$, $LB_n = \{i_1, i_2, i_1 * i_2\}$,
$UB_n = \{2*i_1*i_2\}$, $\mathcal{B} = LB_n \cup UB_n \cup \bigcup_{1 \leq j \leq 2} LB_{i_j} \cup \bigcup_{1 \leq j \leq 2} UB_{i_j}$

where LB_r and UB_r are respectively the sets of lower and upper bounds for a variable or parameter r which

Rec	Step	E	Q	Comments
1	1	$low(n - \frac{n}{i_2})$		
	2	$\to low(n) - up(\frac{n}{i_2})$		rule (8)
2	1	$low(i_2)$		
	2	$\to low(\frac{n}{2*i_1})$		rule (3)
3	1	$low(i_1)$		
	2	$\to max(low(\frac{n}{2*i_2}),1)$	$(i_1;1,\infty)$	rule (3)
			$(i_2;-\infty,\infty)$	TC for $low(i_2)$
4	1	$up(i_2)$		
	2	$\to min(up(n),up(\frac{n}{i_1}))$		rule (3)
5	1	$low(n)$		
	2	$\to max(low(i_1),low(i_2),low(i_1*i_2))$		rule (3)
	3	$\to max(1,low(i_2),min(low(i_1)*up(i_2),$	$(n;1,\infty)$	
		$up(i_1)*low(i_2),low(i_1)*low(i_2),up(i_1)*up(i_2))$		rule (9)
6	1	$up(i_1)$		
	2	$\to min(up(n),up(\frac{n}{i_2}))$		rule (1)
	3	$\to min(up(n),\infty)$		TC for $up(\frac{n}{i_2})$
	4	$\to up(n)$	$(i_1;1,n)$	
5	4	$\to max(1,-\infty,min(1*\infty,up(n)*-\infty,1*-\infty,up(n)*\infty))$		TC for $up(n)$
	5	$\to max(1,-\infty,min(\infty,-\infty,-\infty,\infty))$		simplify
	6	$\to max(1,-\infty,-\infty)$		simplify
	7	$\to 1$		simplify
4	3	$\to min(up(n),\frac{up(n)}{low(i_1)})$		rule (10)
	4	$\to min(up(n),\frac{up(n)}{1})$		substitute $low(i_1)$
	5	$\to up(n)$	$(i_2;-\infty,n)$	
3	3	$\to max(min(\frac{up(n^-)}{low(2*i_2)},\frac{low(n)}{low(2*i_2^+)},\frac{up(n)}{up(2*i_2^-)},\frac{low(n)}{up(2*i_2)}),1)$		rule (10)
	4	$\to max(min(\frac{low(n)}{2},\frac{up(n)}{2*(-1)},\frac{low(n)}{2*up(n)}),1)$		substitute
	5	$\to max(-\frac{up(n)}{2},1)$		simplify
	6	$\to 1$		simplify
2	3	$\frac{low(n)}{2*up(i_1)}$		rule (10)
	4	$\frac{low(n)}{2*up(n)}$		substitute $up(i_1)$
	5	$\to \frac{1}{2}$		simplify
	6	$\to 1$	$(i_2;1,n)$	i_2 integer
1	3	$\to low(n) - \frac{up(n)}{low(i_2)}$		rule (10)
	4	$\to low(n) - \frac{up(n)}{1}$		substitute $low(i_2)$
	5	$\to low(n) - up(n)$		simplify
	6	$\to 0$		proved $n \geq \frac{n}{i_2}$

Table 2. Using EXPR_BOUND to prove that $n \geq \frac{n}{i_2}$:

are derived from $\mathcal{I}$. An interesting question arises whether one of the two upper bounds for i_1 in $\mathcal{I}$ is redundant. If we can show that $low(n - \frac{n}{i_2}) \geq 0$ for all possible values of variables and parameters in $\mathcal{V} \cup \mathcal{P}$ according to the theorem on page 6, then $i_2 \leq n$ is redundant in $\mathcal{I}$. For this purpose we invoke EXPR_BOUND(E=low(n-$\frac{n}{i_2}$),B,Q=$\{i_1;-\infty,\infty),(i_2,-\infty,\infty),(n,-\infty,\infty)\}$). Table 2 shows the most interesting steps for each recursion of EXPR_BOUND. Note that there are no rule numbers for up functions as they are not shown in Table 1.

In what follows we will describe the most important recursions of EXPR_BOUND as shown in Table 2 in more detail. *Rec* specifies the current recursion of the algorithm, and *Step* the processing step within the recursion. E is the current symbolic expression as processed by EXPR_BOUND. *TC* refers to the termination condition of EXPR_BOUND. The current contents of $\mathcal{Q}$ at a specific table entry is the union of the most recent table entries for each different variable and parameter. E.g. $\mathcal{Q} = \{(i_1;1,n),(i_2;1,n),(n;1,\infty)\}$ at recursion 2 step 6.

An item $i.j$ of the following itemized list corresponds to recursion i, step j of algorithm EXPR_BOUND. We will specify the corresponding statements of the algorithm according to Figure 1 where appropriate.

1.2 In order to identify the rewrite rule to apply to $up(\frac{n}{i_2})$, the value range for i_2 needs to be known. Therefore, the algorithm is recursively (recursion 2) called for $E = low(i_2)$ to find out whether i_2 can ever be negative.

3.2 Allows to immediately deduce $low(i_1) \geq 1$, which is added into $\mathcal{Q}$. Then the algorithm is evaluating $low(\frac{n}{2*i_2})$ to investigate whether this expression is larger than 1. In order to determine the correct rewrite rule to apply to $low(\frac{n}{2*i_2})$, we need to determine the value range for i_2. As recursion 2 already tried to deduce $low(i_2)$, we add $-\infty \leq i_2$ into Q based on the termination condition (see Section 2.2) of EXPR_BOUND. Then the algorithm is recursively called for $E = up(i_2)$ to determine whether i_2 can ever be positive.

5.3 As the maximum function for $low(n)$ contains 1, we can immediately add $1 \leq n$ into Q. In order to further substitute the minimum function we need to know the sign for $up(i_1)$.

6.3 As in recursion 1 step 2 the algorithm already tried to evaluate $up(\frac{n}{i_2})$, we substitute $up(\frac{n}{i_2})$ by ∞ according to the termination condition of EXPR_BOUND. After step 4 of this recursion the algorithm returns to recursion 5.

2.5 The expression of recursion 2 step 4 has been simplified according to statement S7, which yields $\frac{1}{2}$. This means that $low(i_2) \geq \frac{1}{2}$, and consequently, $low(i_2) \geq 1$ as $low(i_2)$ must be an integer.

1.5 Simplifies $low(n) - up(n)$ according to statement S7, which yields $n - n$ and finally 0.

1.6 Proves that $n \geq \frac{n}{i_2}$ for all values of i_1, i_2, and n. Therefore, the inequality $i_2 \leq n$ is redundant in $\mathcal{I}$ according to the theorem of page 6.

Other important compiler analyses such as detecting zero-trip-loops, dead code elimination, and performance prediction commonly examine whether $\mathcal{I}$ has a solution at all. If $\mathcal{I}$ contains program unknowns (parameters) then these analyses may yield guarded solutions. In [7] we have described a symbolic sum algorithm that computes the number of solutions of a set of linear and non-linear constraints which are defined over variables and parameters. For instance, by detecting and eliminating the redundant inequality $i_2 \leq n$ in $\mathcal{I}$, the number of guarded solutions to $\mathcal{I}$ as determined by our symbolic sum algorithm is reduced by 50 %.

Please note that Table 2 shows an overly conservative application of our algorithm for the sake of illustrating the most interesting aspects of EXPR_BOUND. The actual implementation of EXPR_BOUND detects at the beginning of the first recursion that $i_1, i_2, n \geq 1$ by simply checking the lower bound expressions of $\mathcal{B}$ and initializes Q with this information. Based on Q the following rewrite rules are applied: $low(n - \frac{n}{i_2}) \rightarrow low(n) - up(\frac{n}{i_2}) \rightarrow low(n) - \frac{up(n)}{low(i_2)} \rightarrow low(n) - \frac{up(n)}{1} \rightarrow low(n) - up(n) \rightarrow 0$. Therefore, our implementation of EXPR_BOUND can prove in 5 steps that $n \geq \frac{n}{i_2}$ under the constraints of $\mathcal{I}$.

6 Conclusions

Numerous researchers have shown the importance of symbolic compiler analysis [8, 2, 7, 9] for optimizing and predicting performance of parallel programs. A crucial problem of many symbolic compiler analyses is to determine the relationship between symbolic expressions.

We have described a demand driven algorithm that computes the upper and/or lower bound of linear and non-linear symbolic expressions. This algorithm is used to examine non-linear array index functions for data dependences, compare symbolic expressions, and simplify systems of constraints. Previous methods are based on algorithms that are either restricted to a smaller class of symbolic expressions, are more expensive in terms of complexity, or produce less accurate results (tighter bounds).

We have demonstrated the effectiveness of our techniques by proofing the absence of a data dependence in a loop with non-linear array references that enables the compiler to parallelize this loop. Conventional dependence analysis would have serialized this loop. We also showed how to use our algorithm to detect redundant inequalities in a set of non-linear constraints, which as a result significantly reduces the complexity of other important compiler and performance analysis.

References

[1] S. Benkner, S. Andel, R. Blasko, P. Brezany, A. Celic, B. Chapman, M. Egg, T. Fahringer, J. Hulman, Y. Hou, E. Kelc, E. Mehofer, H. Moritsch, M. Paul, K. Sanjari, V. Sipkova, B. Velkov, B. Wender, and H. Zima. *Vienna Fortran Compilation System - Version 2.0 - User's Guide*, October 1995.

[2] W. Blume. *Symbolic Analysis Techniques for Effective Automatic Parallelization*. PhD thesis, Center for Supercomputing Research and Development, University of Illinois at Urbana-Champaign, June 1995.

[3] M. Berry. et al. The PERFECT club benchmarks: Effective performance evaluation of supercomputers. *International Journal of Supercomputing Applications*, pages 3(3): 5–40, 1989.

[4] T. Fahringer. Estimating and Optimizing Performance for Parallel Programs. *IEEE Computer*, 28(11):47 – 56, November 1995.

[5] T. Fahringer. *Automatic Performance Prediction of Parallel Programs*. Kluwer Academic Publishers, Boston, USA, ISBN 0-7923-9708-8, March 1996.

[6] T. Fahringer. Symbolic Expression Evaluation. Technical report, Institute for Software Technology and Parallel Systems, Univ. of Vienna, Oct 1996.

[7] T. Fahringer. Toward Symbolic Performance Prediction of Parallel Programs. In *IEEE Proc. of the 1996 International Parallel Processing Symposium*, pages 474–478, Honolulu, Hawaii, April 1996.

[8] M. Haghighat and C. Polychronopoulos. Symbolic Analysis for Parallelizing Compilers. CSRD Report No. 1355, CSRD, University of Illinois at Urbana-Champaign, IL, 1994.

[9] P. Tu and D. Padua. Gated SSA-Based Demand-Driven Symbolic Analysis for Parallelizing Compilers. In *9th ACM International Conference on Supercomputing*, Barcelona, Spain, July 1995.

Storage Management in Parallel Programs

Vincent Lefebvre
Laboratoire PRiSM
Université de Versailles
45, avenue des Etats-Unis, 78 035 Versailles Cédex, France
Vincent.Lefebvre@prism.uvsq.fr

Paul Feautrier
Laboratoire PRiSM
Université de Versailles
45, avenue des Etats-Unis, 78 035 Versailles Cédex, France
Paul.Feautrier@prism.uvsq.fr

Abstract

We have been interested in this article on the data stuctures generation as part of the polyedric technique designed in PAF (Paralléliseur Automatique pour Fortran). The removal of dependences which are not data flows in a program is generally realized by a total memory expansion of data structures. We present a new technique which allows to reduce the memory cost by expanding carefully selected parts of code only. It consists in limiting the memory expansion process in accordance with contraints imposed by the schedule determined for the parallel program.

1 Introduction

The polyedric method, an automatic parallelization technique, uses explicit schedules. A schedule has to satisfy constraints which are given by dataflow analysis. The goal is to determine the execution date of each operation of the source program. Operations which have the same execution date are gathered in wavefronts, which can be executed in parallel. Dependences which don't belong to the dataflow are called false dependences. A partial removal of false dependences, is the price to pay to preserve the correctness of the parallel program. It is realized by data expansion. One generally builds a single assignment form for the source program. Total data expansion has a high memory cost. For instance, in matrix multiplication, the single assignment form has a data space of $O(n^3)$ memory words, instead of $O(n^2)$ in the classical version. This paper presents a new technique which limits memory expansion in accor-

dance with contraints imposed by the schedule of the parallel program. We will first restate several classical techniques of program semantic analysis (array dataflow analysis) and transformations (scheduling, existing memory management techniques). Finally, we will present our optimized storage technique for parallel programs.

2 Semantic Analysis of Static Control Programs

2.1 Static Control Programs

We focuse on automatic parallelization of static control programs. For Static control programs, one may describe the set of operations which are going to be executed in a given program run. Let be E the operations set of a program. Static control programs are built from assignment statements and DO loops. The only data structures are arrays of arbitrary dimensions. Loop bounds and array subscripts are affine functions in the loop counters and integral structure parameters. An operation is one execution of a statement. It may be named $\langle R, \vec{x} \rangle$ where R is a statement and $\vec{x}$ the iteration vector built from the surrounding loop counters (from the outside to the inside). The iteration domain $\mathcal{D}(R)$ of a statement R, is the set of instances of R and can be described by the conjunction of all inequalities for the surrounding loops. It gives values that the iteration vector $\vec{x}$ can have. We will take as a running example the sequential program of figure (1).

```
        PROGRAM scalar
        INTEGER s,i,j,n
        DO i = 1,n
{S1}        s = 0
            DO j = 1,n
{S2}            s = s + 1
            ENDDO
        ENDDO
        END
```

Figure 1. The source program

2.2   Sequential Execution Order

Let us introduce the following notations.

- The k-th entry of vector $\vec{x}$ is denoted by $\vec{x}[k]$.

- The subvector built from component k to l is written as: $\vec{x}[k..l]$.

- The expression $R \lhd S$ indicates that statement R is before statement S in the program text.

- N_{RS} is the number of loops surrounding both R and S.

The fact that operation $\langle R, \vec{x} \rangle$ is executed before operation $\langle S, \vec{y} \rangle$ is written: $\langle R, \vec{x} \rangle \prec \langle S, \vec{y} \rangle$. It is shown in [5] that:

$$\langle R, \vec{x} \rangle \prec \langle S, \vec{y} \rangle \equiv$$
$$\vec{x}[1..N_{RS}] \ll \vec{y}[1..N_{RS}] \vee (\vec{x}[1..N_{RS}] = \vec{y}[1..N_{RS}] \wedge R \lhd S) \quad (1)$$

The sequential order can be split with respect to depths:

$$\langle R, \vec{x} \rangle \prec \langle S, \vec{y} \rangle \equiv \bigvee_{p=0}^{N_{RS}} \langle R, \vec{x} \rangle \prec_p \langle S, \vec{y} \rangle \quad (2)$$

where

$$0 \leq p < N_{RS} :$$
$$\langle R, \vec{x} \rangle \prec_p \langle S, \vec{y} \rangle \Leftrightarrow (\vec{x}[1..p] = \vec{y}[1..p]) \wedge (\vec{x}[p+1] < \vec{y}[p+1]) \quad (3)$$

$$\langle R, \vec{x} \rangle \prec_{N_{RS}} \langle S, \vec{y} \rangle \Leftrightarrow \vec{x}[1..N_{RS}] = \vec{y}[1..N_{RS}] \wedge R \lhd S \quad (4)$$

2.3   Dependences

Two operations $\langle R, \vec{x} \rangle$ and $\langle S, \vec{y} \rangle$ are independent if their order of execution can be reversed without changing the global effect on the program store. If not, the operations are said to be dependent. The goal of automatic parallelization is to build a parallel program which exactly gives the same results as the sequential program. $\mathcal{R}(R, \vec{x})$ is the set of memory cells which are read by $\langle R, \vec{x} \rangle$ and $\mathcal{M}(R, \vec{x})$, is the set of memory cells which are modified by $\langle R, \vec{x} \rangle$. Supposing for instance that $\langle R, \vec{x} \rangle \prec \langle S, \vec{y} \rangle$, one can distinguish three kinds of dependences:

- **flow dependence** ($\mathcal{M}(R, \vec{x}) \cap \mathcal{R}(S, \vec{y}) \neq \emptyset$, written $\langle R, \vec{x} \rangle \delta \langle S, \vec{y} \rangle$);

- **anti-dependence** ($\mathcal{R}(R, \vec{x}) \cap \mathcal{M}(S, \vec{y}) \neq \emptyset$, written $\langle R, \vec{x} \rangle \bar{\delta} \langle S, \vec{y} \rangle$);

- **output dependence** ($\mathcal{M}(R, \vec{x}) \cap \mathcal{M}(S, \vec{y}) \neq \emptyset$, written $\langle R, \vec{x} \rangle \delta^o \langle S, \vec{y} \rangle$).

One may be more precise and associate a dependence to a depth p. For instance, if one writes $\langle R, \vec{x} \rangle \delta_p \langle S, \vec{y} \rangle$, it indicates that $\mathcal{M}(R, \vec{x}) \cap \mathcal{R}(S, \vec{y}) \neq \emptyset \wedge \langle R, \vec{x} \rangle \prec_p \langle S, \vec{y} \rangle$.

2.4   Array Dataflow Analysis

The sole real dependences inherent to the algorithm are direct flow dependences from a definition to a use of the same memory cell (data flows). All others dependences which are called false dependences, are due to memory reuse and can be deleted by data expansion. Direct flow dependences are detected by dataflow analysis technique. If a memory cell c is read in an operation $\langle S, \vec{y} \rangle$, dataflow analysis determines the latest writing into c, which is given by the *source* function [5]:

$$source(c, \langle S, \vec{y} \rangle) = \max_{\prec} \{ \langle R, \vec{x} \rangle \in E \mid \langle R, \vec{x} \rangle \delta (S, \vec{y}) \} \quad (5)$$

The result of the analysis is a quasi-affine tree or quast, i.e. a many-level conditionnal in which predicates are tests for the positiveness of affine forms in the loop counters and structure parameters and leaves are either operation names, or $\perp$. $\perp$ indicates that the array cell under study is not modified. For our example, we have:

$$source(s, \langle S2, i, j \rangle) = \begin{cases} \textbf{If } j \geq 2 \\ \textbf{Then } \langle S2, i, j - 1 \rangle \\ \textbf{Else } \langle S1, i \rangle \end{cases} \quad (6)$$

3   Program Transformations

3.1   Parallelization by Scheduling

From constraints given by dataflow analysis, one deduces a schedule which gives a logical execution time to each operation of the source program. It must also respect the constraints implied by the *source* functions. If $\theta(S, \vec{y})$ is the schedule of $\langle S, \vec{y} \rangle$, one must have:

$$\forall \langle S, \vec{y} \rangle \in E, \forall c \in \mathcal{R}(S, \vec{y}) : \theta(source(c, \langle S, \vec{y} \rangle)) \ll \theta(S, \vec{y}) \quad (7)$$

For complexity reasons, finding the exact solution of (7) is not practicable. One limits oneself to affine one-dimensionnal ([6]) or multidimensionnal schedules ([7]). In the case of our example, one must have:

$$(\textbf{if } (j \geq 2) \textbf{ then } \theta(S2, i, j - 1) \textbf{ else } \theta(S1, i)) \ll \theta(S2, i, j) \quad (8)$$

One may show that $\theta(R, i) = 0$ and $\theta(S, i, j) = j$ is the best schedule for our example, i.e gives the largest operations fronts. From a schedule given by θ, one deduces operations fronts:

$$\mathcal{F}(\vec{t}) = \{ \langle R, \vec{x} \rangle \in E \mid \theta(R, \vec{x}) = \vec{t} \} \quad (9)$$

There is no dataflow between operations of a given front. Hence, all such operations can be executed in parallel. The parallel program must enumerate all lexicographical executions dates :

$$\{\vec{t} \mid \begin{array}{l} \vec{t} \in \tau \\ \text{execute in parallel operations in } \mathcal{F}(\vec{t}) \\ \text{synchronize} \end{array} \tag{10}$$
$$\}$$

The set τ is the lexicographical enumeration of each possible execution date.

3.2 Changing Data Structures

However, using any execution order which satisfies (7) for constructing a parallel program will give an incorrect result, because output dependences, anti-dependences and spurious flow dependences (flow dependences which are not dataflows) have not been taken into account. One can get rid of these false dependences by data expansion. Several techniques have been proposed in the litterature.

3.2.1 Total Memory Expansion

The easiest solution consists in translating the source program in single assignment form. This transformation is independent from scheduling but needs results given by dataflow analysis. Generally, total memory expansion is realized before the parallelization.

There is a strong relation between output dependences and anti-dependences. Consider two operations $\langle S, \vec{y} \rangle$, $\langle T, \vec{z} \rangle$, and c a cell memory, such as $c \in \mathcal{R}(S, \vec{y})$ and $c \in \mathcal{M}(T, \vec{z})$. In a correct program, each variable must be set before being read. So, there is necessarily an operation $\langle R, \vec{x} \rangle$ which sets c and which is executed before $\langle S, \vec{y} \rangle$: $\langle R, \vec{x} \rangle \prec \langle S, \vec{y} \rangle \prec \langle T, \vec{z} \rangle$. There is also a output dependence between $\langle R, \vec{x} \rangle$ and $\langle T, \vec{z} \rangle$. From this, one may deduce that if all output dependences are deleted, then anti-dependences and spurious flow dependences also disappear. Total memory expansion consists in assigning one distinct memory cell to each operation. The following algorithm presented in [3] establishes the single assignment form of a static control program:

1. **Renaming :** for each statement R, with $\vec{x}$ as iteration vector, associate a specific data structure InsR:

$$R : a[\vec{f}(\vec{x})] = \ldots \rightarrow \text{InsR}[\vec{f}(\vec{x})] = \ldots$$

2. **Expanding:** for each instruction R, replace the subscript function $\vec{f}(\vec{x})$ in InsR by $\vec{x}$ in left hand-sides:

$$R : \text{InsR}[\vec{f}(\vec{x})] = \ldots \rightarrow \text{InsR}[\vec{x}] = \ldots$$

3. **Reconstructing the dataflow:** replace all read reference by its new representation as given by the source

function. The value produced by $\langle R, \vec{x} \rangle$ is stored in InsR$[\vec{x}]$. So if one finds the following source function for a memory cell c in an operation $\langle S, \vec{y} \rangle$: $source(c, \langle S, \vec{y} \rangle) \equiv \langle S, \vec{x} \rangle$, then c must be replaced by InsR$[\vec{x}]$ in the single assignment program.

Renaming deletes all output dependences which appear between two operations instances of two different instructions. Expanding deletes output dependences which appear between two operations instances of the same instruction. The single assignment form version of our running example is given in fig. (2). It is clear that the memory cost is high. Starting from a scalar s, one gets an array of n elements and another one with n^2 elements.

A first intuitive approach can easily show that deleting all false dependences is not necessary. During an execution of a parallel program in single assignment form, a memory cell InsR$[\vec{x}]$ is empty until the execution of $\langle R, \vec{x} \rangle$ at $\theta(R, \vec{x})$. Moreover in many cases, a value stored in a memory cell can become useless in memory after a limited delay. Consider InsS2[i,j] in our running example:

- In the parallel program scheduled by θ, this memory cell is empty until the execution of $\langle S2, i, j \rangle$ at $\theta(S2, i, j) = j$.

- The value produced by $\langle S2, i, j \rangle$ is read by $\langle S2, i, j+1 \rangle$ at $\theta(S2, i, j+1) = j+1$. After this time, the value is useless but still resides in memory.

```
           PROGRAM scalar
           INTEGER i, j, n, InsS1[n], InsS2[n,n]
           DO i = 1,n
{S1}           InsS1[i] = 0
               DO j = 1,n
{S2}               InsS2 [i,j] = if (j >= 2) then InsS2 [i,j-1]
                                 else InsS1 [i] + 1
               ENDDO
           ENDDO
           END
```

Figure 2. The `scalar` program in single assignment form

3.2.2 Previous Techniques to Reduce Memory Cost

Some methods try to eliminate false dependences with a reduced memory cost. Wolfe in [11] defines the method of array contraction for vector architectures. After scalar expansion and loop interchange, he performs array contraction because the vector instructions only concern the innermost loop of each loop nest. Maydan and Lam in [8], Li and Lee in [9] define a method which optimize array privatization after a renaming phase. Privatization is equivalent to expansion. They don't delete an output dependence between operations instances of a same instruction R, if it is masked by a dataflow. Darte, Vivien, Calland and Robert in [1] intoduce two graph transformations to eliminate anti and output dependences by renaming. They give an unified framework for such transformation and prove that the problem of determining a minimal process of renaming is NP-complete. Values Lifetime Analysis is a technique which comes from the "systolic" community. It takes into account single assignment form programs and try to generate output and antidependences without changing the dataflow([2],[10]).

4 Minimal Memory Expansion With Respect to a Schedule

Our method tries to maintain as many false dependences as possible from the original program to the parallel one. One takes into account the original data structures, the results given by data dependences and data flow analysis, the schedule function. One generates a program with new data structures which is still sequential but can be parallelized according to the scheme (10).

4.1 Neutral Dependences

Consider an operation $\langle R, \vec{x} \rangle$ instance of an assignment statement R. Let $\mathcal{U}(R, \vec{x})$ be the set of operations such that there is a dataflow from $\langle R, \vec{x} \rangle$ to each operation $\langle S, \vec{y} \rangle$ of $\mathcal{U}(R, \vec{x})$:

$$\mathcal{U}(R, \vec{x}) = \{(S, \vec{y}) \in E \mid source(c, \langle S, \vec{y} \rangle) \equiv \langle R, \vec{x} \rangle\} \quad (11)$$

Let be $\mathcal{V}(R, \vec{x})$ the value produced by $\langle R, \vec{x} \rangle$, $\mathcal{V}(R, \vec{x})$ must absolutely reside in memory for $\vec{t} \in [\theta(R, \vec{x}), \max_{\mathcal{U}(R, \vec{x})} \theta(S, \vec{y})]$. Before and after these dates this value is useless in memory. Suppose that one has an output dependence at depth p between $\langle R, \vec{x} \rangle$ and an operation $\langle T, \vec{z} \rangle$ (written $R \delta^o_p T$) in the sequential program. If $\theta(T, \vec{z}) \gg \max_{\mathcal{U}(R, \vec{x})} \theta(S, \vec{y})$, it is clear that this output dependence can be maintained in the parallel program, because $\mathcal{V}(R, \vec{x})$ is useless in memory at $\theta(T, \vec{z})$. To improve this idea, we will develop the concept of neutral dependences.

Definition 1. *An output dependence is neutral for a schedule θ, which satifies (7), iff keeping this dependence doesn't change the sequential dataflow in the parallel program obtained from θ by scheme (10).*

An output dependence can be maintained in a parallel program iff it is neutral. In this case, the results of the parallel program are still valid. The following proposition gives specific conditions that an output dependence must verify to be neutral.

Proposition 1. *A output dependence $R \delta^o_p T$ (R and T are two statements) is neutral for θ iff:*

$$\mathcal{M}(R, \vec{x}) = \mathcal{M}(T, \vec{z}) \wedge \langle R, \vec{x} \rangle \prec_p \langle T, \vec{z} \rangle \Rightarrow \theta(R, \vec{x}) \ll \theta(T, \vec{z}) \quad (12)$$

and

$$\theta(T, \vec{z}) \gg \max_{\mathcal{U}(R, \vec{x})} (\theta(S, \vec{y})) \quad (13)$$

(12) ensures that the execution order between $\langle R, \vec{x} \rangle$ and $\langle T, \vec{z} \rangle$ is the same in the sequential and parallel programs. (13) verifies that dataflow between $\langle R, \vec{x} \rangle$ and operations in $\mathcal{U}(R, \vec{x})$ won't be affected by $\langle T, \vec{z} \rangle$. This condition ensures that $\mathcal{V}(R, \vec{x})$ is present in memory when $\vec{t} \in [\theta(R, \vec{x}), \max_{\mathcal{U}(R, \vec{x})} (\theta(S, \vec{y}))]$, even if the output dependence is not removed in the parallel program.

We can extend this definition to anti-dependences and flow dependences which are not dataflows. For these kinds of dependences it is just necessary to verify that execution order of operations in dependance is the same in the sequential and parallel programs.

Definition 2. *An anti-dependence between two instructions S and T is neutral for a schedule function θ which satisfies (7) iff the execution order of these operations is the same in the sequential and parallel programs.*

The definition is the same for a spurious flow dependence.

Proposition 2. *A anti-dependence $S \overline{\delta_p} T$ is neutral according to θ iff:*

$$\mathcal{R}(S, \vec{y}) \cap \mathcal{M}(T, \vec{z}) \neq \emptyset \wedge \langle S, \vec{y} \rangle \prec_p \langle T, \vec{z} \rangle \Rightarrow \theta(S, \vec{y}) \ll \theta(T, \vec{z}) \quad (14)$$

(14) ensures that if this dependence is not deleted, it will still be verified in the parallel program.

Proposition 3. *A spurious flow dependence $R \delta_p T$ is neutral for θ iff:*

$$\mathcal{M}(R, \vec{x}) \cap \mathcal{R}(S, \vec{y}) \neq \emptyset \wedge \langle R, \vec{x} \rangle \prec_p \langle S, \vec{y} \rangle \Rightarrow \theta(R, \vec{x}) \ll \theta(S, \vec{y}) \quad (15)$$

4.2 Tests of Neutrality

4.2.1 Neutral Output Dependences

Let's consider:

$$\begin{aligned} R: & \quad a[\vec{f}(\vec{x})] = ... \\ T: & \quad a[\vec{g}(\vec{z})] = ... \end{aligned}$$

Consider the output dependences between operations instances of R and T at depth p. A dependence $R \delta^o_p T$, is characterized by the following conditions:

- $\langle R, \vec{x} \rangle$ and $\langle T, \vec{z} \rangle$ must exist: $\vec{x} \in \mathcal{D}(R)$, $\vec{z} \in \mathcal{D}(T)$;
- Access conflict: $\vec{f}(\vec{x}) = \vec{g}(\vec{z})$;
- Sequencing Predicate at depth p: $\langle R, \vec{x} \rangle \prec_p \langle T, \vec{z} \rangle$

184

Therefore, there is a dependence iff, system $Q_{RT}^p(\vec{x}, \vec{z})$,

$$Q_{RT}^p(\vec{x}, \vec{z}) = \{ \quad \begin{aligned} &\vec{x} \in \mathcal{D}(R) \wedge \\ &\vec{z} \in \mathcal{D}(T) \wedge \\ &\vec{f}(\vec{x}) = \vec{g}(\vec{z}) \wedge \\ &\langle R, \vec{x} \rangle \prec_p \langle T, \vec{z} \rangle \} \end{aligned} \qquad (16)$$

has a solution. To verify (12), one must have a dependence in the sequential program, which must still be verified in the parallel program. Therefore, in the parallel program, we must have: $\theta(R, \vec{x}) \ll \theta(T, \vec{z})$. If this execution order is not respected for only one of the operations instances of R and T linked by this dependence, the condition (12) is not verified. So we simply consider that (12) is verified if for no operation of R and T in dependence, one has $\theta(T, \vec{z}) \ll \theta(R, \vec{x})$ that is to say if the system $N_{RT}^p(\vec{x}, \vec{z})$,

$$N_{RT}^p(\vec{x}, \vec{z}) = \{ \quad \begin{aligned} &\vec{x} \in \mathcal{D}(R) \wedge \\ &\vec{z} \in \mathcal{D}(T) \wedge \\ &\vec{f}(\vec{x}) = \vec{g}(\vec{z}) \wedge \\ &\langle R, \vec{x} \rangle \prec_p \langle T, \vec{z} \rangle \wedge \\ &\theta(T, \vec{z}) \ll \theta(R, \vec{x}) \} \end{aligned} \qquad (17)$$

has no solution. $Q_{RT}^p(\vec{x}, \vec{z})$ is a $\mathbb{Z}$-polyhedron. $\theta(R, \vec{x})$ and $\theta(T, \vec{z})$ are vectors of affine functions in the loop counters. Hence $N_{RT}^p(\vec{x}, \vec{z})$ is a disjunction of $\mathbb{Z}$-polyhedra which must all be empty. So verifying the emptiness of $N_{R,T}^p(\vec{x}, \vec{z})$ can be easily done by the PIP (Parametric Integer Programing) tool (see [4] for more explanations). Remember that in our example, we have chosen the schedule function $\theta(R, i) = 0$ and $\theta(S, i, j) = j$. Let's verify (12) for program scalar. For the $R \delta_0^o R$ dependence, one has **if** $1 \leq i \leq n$ **then** $N_{RR}^0(i) \neq \emptyset \Rightarrow$ this dependence is not neutral. For others dependences, one can find that (12) is verified for $R \delta_0^o S$, $R \delta_1^o S$ and $S \delta_1^o S$ dependences and not verified by $S \delta_0^o R$ and $S \delta_0^o S$ dependences (hence these dependences are not neutral).

Theorem 1. *The condition (13) is verified for a given output dependence iff all anti-dependences generated by this dependence, are neutral.*

Proof: consider the operations of $\mathcal{U}(R, \vec{x})$. If there is an output dependence between $\langle R, \vec{x} \rangle$ and an operation $\langle T, \vec{z} \rangle$ at depth p, there is also an anti-dependence between any operation $\langle S, \vec{y} \rangle \in \mathcal{U}(R, \vec{x})$ and $\langle T, \vec{z} \rangle$ at depth p':

$$\prec: \quad \begin{aligned} \langle R, \vec{x} \rangle : &\quad c = \ldots \\ \langle S, \vec{y} \rangle : &\quad \ldots = \ldots c \ldots \\ \langle T, \vec{z} \rangle : &\quad c = \ldots \end{aligned}$$

If every dependence $S \overline{\delta_{p'}} T$ is neutral, it ensures that $\theta(S, \vec{y}) \ll \theta(T, \vec{z})$ (according to (14)). Therefore $\theta(T, \vec{z}) \gg \theta(S, \vec{y}), \forall \langle S, \vec{y} \rangle \in \mathcal{U}(R, \vec{x})$, hence $\theta(T, \vec{z}) \gg \max_{\mathcal{U}(R, \vec{x})} \theta(S, \vec{y})$. So (13) is verified.

4.2.2 Neutral Anti-dependences

Consider:

$$\begin{aligned} S: &\quad \ldots = \ldots a[\vec{h}(\vec{y})] \ldots \\ T: &\quad a[\vec{g}(\vec{z})] = \ldots \end{aligned}$$

One must determine if the $S \overline{\delta_p} T$ dependence is neutral, that is to say verify (14). To determine if (14) is respected, one has to verify that the execution order between $\langle S, \vec{y} \rangle$ and $\langle T, \vec{z} \rangle$ stays the same in the parallel program for the operations instances of S and T which are linked by this dependence. Also the dependence $S \overline{\delta_p} T$ is neutral iff the system $N_{ST}^p(\vec{y}, \vec{z})$

$$N_{ST}^p(\vec{y}, \vec{z}) = \{ \quad \begin{aligned} &\vec{y} \in \mathcal{D}(S) \wedge \\ &\vec{z} \in \mathcal{D}(T) \wedge \\ &\vec{h}(\vec{y}) = \vec{g}(\vec{z}) \wedge \\ &\langle S, \vec{y} \rangle \prec_p \langle T, \vec{z} \rangle \wedge \\ &\theta(T, \vec{z}) \ll \theta(S, \vec{y}) \} \end{aligned} \qquad (18)$$

has no solution.

When one knows that an anti-dependence is not neutral, one knows that for the associated output dependence the condition (13) is invalidated and the dependence is not neutral. Suppose, one has the following situation: $c = \mathcal{M}(R, \vec{x}) = \mathcal{M}(T, \vec{z})$ and $\langle R, \vec{x} \rangle \equiv source(c, \langle S, \vec{y} \rangle)$. If the $S \overline{\delta_p} T$ dependence is not neutral, then the operation $\langle T, \vec{z} \rangle$ kills the value produced by $\langle R, \vec{x} \rangle$ and stored in c before it is read by $\langle S, \vec{y} \rangle$ in the parallel program. This situation would have occurred if the output dependence between $\langle R, \vec{x} \rangle$ and $\langle T, \vec{z} \rangle$ was not deleted. So the output dependence between $\langle R, \vec{x} \rangle$ and $\langle T, \vec{z} \rangle$ is not neutral. We know the depths p and p' of $S \overline{\delta_p} T$ and $R \delta_{p'} S$ dependences. We must determine the depth p'' of $R \delta_{p''}^o T$ dependence. With the $S \overline{\delta_p} T$ dependence, we have: $\langle S, \vec{y} \rangle \prec_p \langle T, \vec{z} \rangle \Leftrightarrow (\vec{y}[1..p] = \vec{z}[1..p]) \wedge (\vec{y}[p+1] < \vec{z}[p+1])$. With the $R \delta_{p'} S$ dependence, we have: $\langle R, \vec{x} \rangle \prec_{p'} \langle S, \vec{y} \rangle \Leftrightarrow (\vec{x}[1..p'] = \vec{y}[1..p']) \wedge (\vec{x}[p'+1] < \vec{y}[p'+1])$. We must consider, three cases:

1. $p = p'$: $(\vec{x}[1..p] = \vec{z}[1..p]) \wedge (\vec{x}[p+1] < \vec{z}[p+1]) \Rightarrow \langle R, \vec{x} \rangle \prec_p \langle T, \vec{z} \rangle \Rightarrow p'' = p$

2. $p < p'$: $(\vec{x}[1..p] = \vec{z}[1..p]) \wedge (\vec{x}[p+1] < \vec{z}[p+1]) \wedge (\vec{x}[p+1] < \vec{z}[p+1]) \Rightarrow \langle R, \vec{x} \rangle \prec_p \langle T, \vec{z} \rangle \Rightarrow p'' = p$

3. $p > p'$: $(\vec{x}[1..p'] = \vec{z}[1..p']) \wedge (\vec{x}[p'+1] < \vec{z}[p'+1]) \wedge (\vec{x}[p'+1] < \vec{z}[p'+1]) \Rightarrow \langle R, \vec{x} \rangle \prec_{p'} \langle T, \vec{z} \rangle \Rightarrow p'' = p'$

So, if the $S \overline{\delta_p} T$ dependence is not neutral, then the $R \delta_{min(p,p')}^o T$ dependence is not neutral either. In our running example, consider the $S \overline{\delta_0} S$ dependence, we have:

$$source(s, \langle S2, i, j \rangle) = \begin{cases} \textbf{If } j \geq 2 \\ \textbf{Then } \langle S2, i, j-1 \rangle \\ \textbf{Else } \langle S1, i \rangle \end{cases}$$

The first leaf of the source function concerns a instance of $S2$, so one must determinate if the $S2 \overline{\delta_0} S2$ dependence is neutral. One finds that $N_{S2S2}^0(i, j) \neq \emptyset \Rightarrow$ so this dependence is not neutral, and $S2 \delta_0^o S2$ dependence is not neutral either. The second leaf of the source function concerns an instance of $S1$, hence the dependence $S1 \delta_0^o S2$ is not neutral. For others anti-dependences, one finds that dependence $S2 \overline{\delta_1} S2$ is neutral and that $S2 \overline{\delta_0} S1$ is not neutral. As a consequence the dependences $S2 \delta_0^o S2$ and $S1 \delta_0^o S1$ are not neutral.

Finally, we have for the output dependences in our running example: $S1\,\delta_0^\circ\,S1$, $S2\,\delta_0^\circ\,S2$ $S2\,\delta_0^\circ\,S1$ and $S1\,\delta_0^\circ\,S2$ which are not neutral; $S1\,\delta_1^\circ\,S2$ and $S2\,\delta_1^\circ\,S2$ which are neutral.

4.2.3 Neutral Spurious Flow Dependences

Theorem 2. *It is useless to verify if a flow dependence, which is not a dataflow, is neutral.*

Proof : consider the following operations:

$$\prec:\quad \langle R,\vec{x}\rangle:\quad c = ...$$
$$\langle T,\vec{z}\rangle:\quad c = ...$$
$$\langle S,\vec{y}\rangle:\quad ... = ...c...$$

Suppose that $\langle S,\vec{y}\rangle \in \mathcal{U}(T,\vec{z})$. Dependence $R\,\delta_p\,S$ is not a dataflow, because the value stored in c by $\langle R,\vec{x}\rangle$ is killed by $\langle T,\vec{z}\rangle$ before the reading of c by $\langle S,\vec{y}\rangle$. In the parallel program, one has $\theta(T,\vec{z}) \ll \theta(S,\vec{y})$ according to (7). We must consider two cases:

1. If the output dependence between R and T is not neutral, then it must be removed in the parallel program and the flow dependence has disappeared.

2. If this output dependence is neutral, one has also $\theta(R,\vec{x}) \ll \theta(T,\vec{z}) \Rightarrow \theta(R,\vec{x}) \ll \theta(S,\vec{y})$ hence (15) is verified and it means that the dependence $R\,\delta_p\,S$ is neutral.

4.3 Exploitation of Results

The examination of neutrality of output dependences will help us to decide if we must add a dimension or new elements in a specific dimension (*minimal expanding*) or if we must proceed or not in renaming a data structure used by two different instructions (*minimal renaming*). We have developped the following algorithm which gives an optimized storage for data of a parallel static control program:

1. **Minimal expansion for each statement** R: if a is the data structure in the left hand side of R, one must find the minimal shape that a can have in R. The goal is to eliminate all output dependences $R\,\delta^\circ\,R$ which are not neutral. If an output dependence at depth p between operations instances of R is not neutral, one must expand a according to $\vec{x}[p+1]$:

   - one adds one dimension to a. The size of this dimension is the number of iterations of the loop $p+1$ which surrounds R;
   - This new dimension must be indexed by the counter of this loop in left hand side of R.

   $$R: a[\vec{f}(\vec{x})] = ... \rightarrow a[\vec{f}(\vec{x}), \vec{x}[p+1]] = ...$$

In our running example, for $S1$, the dependence $S1\,\delta_0^\circ\,S1$ is not neutral hence

$$S1 : (s = ... \rightarrow s[i] = ...)$$

The scalar s is now an array of n elements because there are n iterations in the loop i. In $S2$, the dependence $S2\,\delta_0^\circ\,S2$ is not neutral so it must be deleted, the dependence $S2\,\delta_1^\circ\,S2$ is neutral, so it can be maintained:

$$S2 : (s = ... \rightarrow s[i] = ...)$$

With these new subscript functions, we are sure that every output dependences which only concern operations instances of a single statement R and which are not neutral, are deleted.

2. **Correcting the dependence graph:** the minimal expansion can suppress some output dependences which appear between operations instances of different instructions. Consider our previous statements R and T ($R \neq T$). Suppose that in the next steps ot this algorithm, one doesn't proceed in renaming the array a shared by the statements. After minimal expansion, one gets two data structures which can be different. If there is no renaming, the data struture shared by R and T must be in fact the rectangular hull of the union of the two data structures defined by minimal expansion of R and T. Imagine that there is an output dependence $R\,\delta^\circ T$ at depth p in the original program with $p \in N_{RT}$. If, for instance, one had expanded a in R according to $\vec{x}[p+1]$, it adds the following constraint in $Q_{RT}^p(\vec{x},\vec{z})$ which is $\vec{x}[p+1] = \vec{z}[p+1]$. One knows that $\langle R,\vec{x}\rangle \prec_p \langle T,\vec{z}\rangle \Rightarrow \vec{x}[p+1] < \vec{z}[p+1]$. Hence, now $Q_{RT}^p(\vec{x},\vec{z})$ has no solution and the output dependence has disappeared. In our running example, minimal expansion deletes the dependences $S2\,\delta_0^\circ\,S1$ and $S1\,\delta_0^\circ\,S2$.

3. **Minimal renaming**: we must take into account all residual output dependences between R and T, $\forall p \in N_{RT}$. If only one of these dependences is not neutral, we must rename a in T, because all these kind of dependences must be deleted. If all dependences are neutral, the data structure may remain the same in the two statements. Finding the minimal number of data structures to rename is a NP-complete problem, as it shown in [1]. We suggest the following heuristics: one builds a graph for each data structure a which appears at least once in a left hand side of a statement in the original program. Each vertex represents a statement where a is the left hand side. There is an edge from a vertex R to another one T iff there is a residual $R\,\delta_p^\circ\,T$ dependence which is not neutral ($\forall p \in N_{RT}$). Then one can apply on this graph a greedy coloring algorithm. Finally it is clear that vertices that have the same colour

can share the same data structure. In our example, the residual output dependence between R and S is $R\,\delta_1^o\,S$ which is neutral. So it is unnecessary to rename s in S. The final shape of each data structure shared by many statements must be the rectangular hull of the union of all shapes built form minimal expansion. The program is reconstructed with the new data structures and their subscripts functions.

Finally, one gets the program of figure (3). The removal of the conditional expression is due to the fact, that s has not been renamed.

```
        PROGRAM scalar
        INTEGER i, j, n, s[n]
        DO i = 1,n
{S1}        s[i] = 0
            DO j = 1,n
{S2}            s[i] = s[i] + 1
            ENDDO
        ENDDO
        END
```

Figure 3. The `scalar` program in single assignment form

The array (4) gives an overview on the shape of different data structures generated for the scalar program by the different techniques referenced in this article: in the source program (1), in the single assignment program (2), in the program generated by the Chamsky's method (3), by Dror and Lam's method (4) and by our technique (5).

(1)	(2)	(3)	(4)	(5)
s	InsS1[n]	InsS1[n]	InsS1[n]	s[n]
	InsS2[n,n]	InsS2[n,2]	InsS2[n]	

Figure 4. Data structures generated by different methods

The program has now the appropriate data structures and can be parallelized with the model given by (10).

5   Conclusion

Notice that if one builds a schedule function equivalent to the sequential execution order, one finds that all dependences are neutral, so there is no expanding and no renaming and we keep the scalar s. We have then obtained a very satisfying result: inherently sequential programs are fixed points for our parallelization method. Our method effectively reduces the memory cost in the data expansion process for static control programs. Our performances are strongly linked to the parallelism degree (size of operations

fronts) given by the schedule. Hence one can go further and improves our results by adjusting the scheduling to the architecture. Consider for instance, that the target architecture is a pipeline processor Cray. In this case, the real size of a front is limited to 64 which is the size of a vector register. One can easily adjust the schedule function such as no front has more than 64 operations. In the case of our running example, the memory requirement is reduced to an array of 64 elements. The interest of our method is that it can have result on one hand on the expansion and on the other hand on renaming. All previous methods focused on only one of these two topics. The technique has been implemented in Lisp within the PAF project. This methods takes the place of single assignment form translation.

To conclude one gives our results obtained with the `cholesky` program:

- Original version:

```
        program choles
        integer i, j, k
        real x
        real a(10,10), p(10)
        do i=1,n
S1          x = a(i,i)
            do k = 1, i-1
S2              x = x - a(i,k)**2
            end do
S3          p(i) = 1.0/sqrt(x)
            do j = i+1, n
S4              x = a(i,j)
                do k=1,i-1
S5                  x = x - a(j,k) * a(i,k)
                end do
S6              a(j,i) = x * p(i)
            end do
        end do
        end
```

- Single assignment form version:

```
        PROGRAM choles
            real a(10,10)
            real insS1(n)
            real insS2(n,n-1)
            real insS3(n)
            real insS4(n,n-1)
            real insS5(n,n-1,n-1)
            real insS6(n,n-1)
            integer n,i,j,k
            DO i = 1,n,1
S1              insS1(i) = a(i,i)
                DO k = 1,i-1,1
S2                  insS2(i,k) = if (k-2 >= 0)
                                    then insS2(i,k-1)
                                    else insS1(i)
                                      - ins6(k,i) ** 2
                END DO
S3              insS3(i) = 1./sqrt(if (k-2 >= 0)
                                    then insS2(i,j-1)
                                    else insS1(i))
                DO j = i+1,n,n
S4                  insS4(i,j) = a(i,j)
                    DO k = 1,i-1,1
S5                      insS5(i,j,k) = if (k-2 >=0)
                                        then insS5(i,j,k-1)
                                        else insS4(i,j)
                                          - insS6(k,j) * insS6(k,i)
                    END DO
S6                  insS6(i,j) = if(i-2 >= 0)
```

```
                              then insS5(i,j,j-1)
                              else insS4(i,j)
                                   * insS3(i)
            END DO
          END DO
      END
```

- Version with minimal data expansion:

```
      PROGRAM choles
          integer i,j,k,n
          real x(n)
          real a(10,10)
          real p(10)
          real sqrt
          real insS4(n,n-1)
          DO i = 1,n,1
S1            x(i) = a(i,i)
              DO k = 1,i-1,1
S2                x(i) = x(i) - a(k,i) ** 2
              END DO
S3            p(i) = 1./sqrt(x(i))
              DO j = i+1,n,1
S4                insS4(i,j) = a(i,j)
                  DO k = 1,i-1,1
S5                    insS4(i,j) = insS4(i,j) -
                                  a(k,j) * a(k,i)
                  END DO
S6                a(j,i)= insS4(i,j) * p(i)
              END DO
          END DO
      END
```

References

[1] P.Y Calland, A. Darte, Y. Robert, F. Vivien. *On the removal of anti and output dependences.* Technical report RR96-04, laboratoire LIP - école normale supérieure de Lyon - Feb 1996.

[2] Zbigniew Chamski. *Environnement logiciel de programmation d'un accélérateur de calcul parallèle.* Thèse de l'université de Rennes I - chapitre IV - 1993, numéro d'ordre 957.

[3] P. Feautrier. *Array expansion.* ACM Int. Conf on Supercomputing, pages 429-441, 1988.

[4] P. feautrier. Parametric integer programing. *RAIRO Recherche opérationnelle*, 22:243-268, Sept 1988

[5] P. Feautrier. *Dataflow Analysis of Array and Scalar References.* Int. J. of Parallel Programming, 20(1):23-53, February 1991.

[6] P. Feautrier. *Some efficients solutions to the affine scheduling problem, I, one dimensionnal time.* Int J. of Parallel Programming, 21(5):313-348, October 1992.

[7] P. Feautrier. *Some efficient solutions to the affine scheduling problem part II : multidimensional time.* Int J. of Parallel Programming, 21(6):389-420, December 92.

[8] D. E. Maydan, S. P. Amarasinghe, M. S. Lam. *Array Data-Flow Analysis and its Use in Array Privatization.* In Proc. of ACM Conf. on Principles of Programming Languages, pages 2-15, January 1993.

[9] Z. Li, G. and G. Lee. *Symbolic array dataflow analysis for array privatization and program parallelization.* In Supercomputing 95, 1995

[10] S. Rajopadhye and D. Wilde. *Memory Reuse Analysis in the Polyhedral Model.* In Bougé, Fraignaud, Mignotte and Robert, editors, Euro-Par'96 Parallel Processing, Vol I, pages 389-397. Springer-Verlag, LNCS 1123, August 1996.

[11] M. Wolfe. *Optimizing Supercompilers for Supercomputers.* Pitman 1989.

A General but Simple Technique to Handle Asynchronous Data-Parallel Control Structures

Emmanuel Melin, Bruno Raffin, Xavier Rebeuf and Bernard Virot
LIFO - IIIA Université d'Orléans
4, rue Léonard De Vinci - BP 6759 F-45067 Orléans Cedex 02 - FRANCE
Bernard.Virot@lifo.univ-orleans.fr

Abstract

Nowadays, most of distributed architectures are easily scalable MIMD (Multiple Instruction streams, Multiple Data streams) parallel computers or networks of workstations. The challenge consists in taking advantage of the power of these architectures. It has been shown that data-parallel languages offer both a programming model easy to understand and several execution models which are able to exploit these distributed architectures. The compilation process has nevertheless to fill the gap between the synchronous and centralized programmer's point of view and an asynchronous and distributed execution model. An important problem is to reduce the number and the complexity of synchronizations between processors. This leads to complex program transformations, such as absorption techniques, in conditioning control structures, loops or routines. We propose a simple general technique based on structural clocks that permits the use of one-sided wait instructions instead of global synchronizations. Hence, no program transformation is needed and synchronization requirements are reduced. In particular, management of recursive routines is greatly facilitated. To illustrate these techniques, we propose an application to Strassen's algorithm for matrix product.

Keywords: *Design of Parallel Programming Languages; Data-Parallel Programming Model; Desynchronization; Asynchronous Execution Model; Partial Synchronization; Structural Clock; Data-Parallel Routine; Strassen's Algorithm.*

1. Introduction

The data-parallel programming model allows to take advantage of the scalability of recent distributed architectures, such as MIMD computers or networks of workstations, by expressing the parallelism through a sequential composition of actions applied to parallel data. Indices (virtual processors) to which actions are applied are active while the others are idle. From the programmer's point of view data-parallelism involves a single program, the control is centralized and very close to a sequential one. This model is structured and scalable. It inherits its qualities from classical sequential programming. The difficulty is then transferred to the compiler which has to efficiently run a data-parallel program on loosely synchronized architectures, while preserving the initial semantics of the synchronous and centralized programming model. Therefore data-parallel compilers have to realize complex optimizations up to manage data distribution and time desynchronizations between indices, especially regarding loops or routines.

In [6], Hatcher and Quinn propose a systematic approach to desynchronize data-parallel programs. Starting from the initial synchronous interpretation, considering every sequential composition as a global synchronization, the problem consists in removing unnecessary synchronizations. They keep synchronizations surrounding every communication phase to ensure that *potentially* exchanged data are the same as data that would be exchanged in the synchronous interpretation. With this approach, synchronizations are global to avoid handling dynamical sets of indices. Global synchronizations nested within control structures require a program transformation involving a mechanism of synchronization absorption [3, 6]. Nested synchronizations, which could only be accessed by active indices, are extracted from control structures in such a way that inactive indices are also engaged. The management of loops needs auxiliary variables to force indices which have terminated a loop to be engaged into the synchronizations for all the iterations. A similar program transformation is applied to routine calls to ensure that all indices will perform it.

In previous papers [4, 5], we have introduced a small asynchronous data-parallel language called $\mathcal{SCL}$ (which stands for Structural Clock Language). This language is designed to manage asynchronous data-parallel control structures (conditioning and loop). We use the program structure, a shared static information, to generate *structural clocks*. Each index owns a structural clock encoding its position in the program structure. Therefore, by the means of a partial order on structural clocks, each index knows its relative position towards the positions of other indices. This knowledge allows to locally decide if an index has to wait for another one. In this way we reduce the coupling between indices. This framework allows us to introduce partial synchronizations, thereby avoiding absorption machineries for conditioning control structures or loops.

In this paper we show that it is possible to reuse our approach to handle asynchronous, and possibly recursive, data-parallel routines. We propose a semantics of parameter-passing. We use structural clocks to obtain a simple management of recursion. In contrast with the approach of Hatcher and Quinn [6], there is no need for program transformation linked to routines.

We first provide an informal description of the $\mathcal{SCL}$ language and we present the structural clock construction. Next, we introduce asynchronous and recursive routine calls. Finally, we present an application of asynchronous routines through a matrix product algorithm using the Strassen's method inspired by McColl in the BSP framework [9].

2. The $\mathcal{SCL}$ language: syntax and informal description

In this section, we first briefly present the data-parallel programming model. Next, we define a suitable execution model and we give an informal description of the $\mathcal{SCL}$ language.

2.1. The data-parallel programming model

In the data-parallel programming model, basic objects are arrays with parallel access, called vectors. They are denoted with uppercase initial letters. The component of the parallel variable X located at index u is denoted by $X|_u$. Expressions are evaluated by applying operators componentwise to parallel values. Two kinds of actions can be applied to these objects: *componentwise* operations or *communications*. A program is a sequential composition of such actions. Each action is associated with the set of array indices at which it is applied. An index at which an action is applied is said to be *active* for this action. Legal expressions are usual *pure* expressions, i.e. without side effects, like the definition of *pure* functions in HPF [1]. The value of a pure expression at each index u only depends of the values of variable components at index u. We make use of a special

vector constant called $This$. The value of its component at each index u is the value u itself: $This|_u = u$.

2.2. An execution model based on a twin memory management

We briefly recall the execution model previously defined for the $\mathcal{D}$ language [8]. It allows to reduce data-dependencies and is fully reusable in our framework. It is based on a simple array of asynchronous virtual processors. Each index u owns a *private memory* containing the components of all vector variables at u, and a *public memory* containing a copy of the private memory of the same index. Updating of public memories are explicitly executed through a specific instruction (dump). Private memories are dedicated to local computations. Public memories are reserved for communications. This mechanism allows to express more asynchronism, as local transitions between two dump instructions are temporarily masked for other indices.

2.3. Basic statements

We give an informal description of the $\mathcal{SCL}$ language.

- skip **statement.** This instruction does nothing and just terminates.

- dump. Each index executing this instruction locally copies its private memory in its public one.

- **Assignment:** $X := E$. Each index u executing this instruction updates its component $X|_u$ of its *private* memory with the local value $E|_u$. As E is a *pure* expression, $E|_u$ is evaluated in the *private* memory of the index u.

- **Communication:** get X from A into Y. Each index u executing this instruction, evaluates the address $A|_u$ using its own private memory. Next, the component $Y|_u$ is updated, in the private memory of u, with the remote value $X|_{A|_u}$. The expression $X|_{A|_u}$ is evaluated using the public memory of the index $A|_u$.

2.4. Control structures

We turn now to the control structures available in $\mathcal{SCL}$.

- **Sequencing:** $S; T$. As soon as an index u ends the execution of S, it starts the execution of T. This statement does not involve any implicit synchronization.

- **Concurrent conditioning:** where B do S elsewhere T end. This statement is an asynchronous double-branched conditioning construct. All active indices are divided into two disjoint sets depending on the current value of the pure expression B. An active index u which evaluates the expression $B|_u$ to true (respectively false) executes the program S (respectively T). This statement does not involve any implicit synchronization.

Remarks:

- The where/elsewhere construct is a concurrent version of the if/else of MPL [2] or where/elsewhere of HYPERC [7].

- It makes explicit in the syntax the absence of dependence between two sets of indices. The programmer has to guarantee this independence. In turn, a synchronization mechanism may take advantage of this information.

- **Iteration:** loopwhere B do S end. Each currently active index u repeats the computation of the block S while the pure expression $B|_u$ evaluates to *true*. When an index terminates the loop, it goes on executing the instructions that directly follow the loop without any implicit synchronization.

  Remark: This is an asynchronous version of the while of MPL [2] or whilesomewhere of HYPERC [7].

2.5. Routine calls

Now, we extend our language with routine calls. A routine call has the following syntax: call $Routine\_name(variable\_list)$. An index active for this instruction executes the program associated with the routine $Routine\_name$, with its arguments instantiated by the variable list $variable\_list$. A routine declaration consists in a routine name $Routine\_name$, several arguments typed by attributes, a list of local variables $variable\_list$, a SCL program S and a routine end:

$Routine\_name(\ attribute : argument\_list;$
$\qquad\qquad\qquad attribute : argument\_list)$
$local\_variable\_list;$
$S;$
$end\{Routine\_name\};$

Each argument is preceded by an attribute that specifies the way data exchanges are authorized. The attribute *in* corresponds to a call by value. If a parameter holds this attribute, then its final values (in public and private memories), at the end of the execution of the routine call, are **not** propagated outside this routine. The attribute *in-out* corresponds to a call by address. If a parameter holds this attribute, then its final values (in public and private memories), at the end of the execution of the routine call, are propagated to the calling program.

Such a specification of routines involves, for each index, a stack of public memories and a stack of private memories. An index beginning a routine call pushes a new instance of its private memory on the stack. It pops this instance at the end of the routine.

In a similar way, an index pushes a corresponding instance of its public memory on the stack at the beginning of the execution of a routine call. However, before popping such a stack level, an index must ensures that no other index may later reference data stored there. Hence, an index u pops the public memory when all indices have step over the routine call. For sake of simplicity, in the following, we only update the public memory in the main program. This restriction avoids to handle stacks of public memories.

Example: The SCL language allows public memory clashes between communications and updatings, thereby yielding non-determinism. Let us give a simple example. In the left hand side program, the first branch of the where/elsewhere construct only modifies A in private memory and the call to $Assign$ in the second branch references the value of A in public memory. Therefore, the two branches are *independent*. In the right hand side program, the first branch updates the public copy of A while the second branch references this value. Hence, the two branches are not *independent*.

$Assign$(in X; in-out: Y)   get X from 1 into Y ;   end; $\{Assign\}$
 	
 $\{Mainprogram\}$
 where $(This < 2)$ do
   $A := 1;$
 	
 elsewhere
   $Assign(A, B);$
 end;
	$Assign$(in X; in-out: Y)
	   get X from 1 into Y ;
	 end; $\{Assign\}$
	
	 $\{Mainprogram\}$
	 where $(This < 2)$ do
	   $A := 1;$
	   dump;
	 elsewhere
	   $Assign(A, B);$
	 end;

2.6. Waiting mechanism

In order to ensure determinism, the programmer has to manage the consistency of public memories references by serializing instructions which interfere with these memories. With this aim in view, classical approaches [6] use a global synchronization mechanism. We suggest to substitute global synchronizations for a wait notion. We introduce the waiting statement wait A, where A is a pure expression. The intuitive idea is the following. This instruction delays the index u which is executing it, until the target index $A|_u$ has stepped over all the instructions referencing public memories (dump,get) and preceding the wait instruction. Note that $A|_u$ might never reach some preceding instruction referencing the public memory due to loops and conditioning structures. So, an index u can step over the wait point as soon as $A|_u$ executes a different branch from u in a where/elsewhere structure, or as soon as $A|_u$ has terminated the current loopwhere executed by u. Therefore, we see that only dump, get, where/elsewhere and loopwhere instructions play a rôle in the wait management. We qualify them as *meaningful* instructions. Note that routine calls do not interfere with the public memories and do not modify index activity. Therefore, they are not meaningful statements. To sum up, the instruction wait A can terminate if and only if the two following conditions **C1** and **C2** are satisfied.

- **C1:** The index $A|_u$ has evaluated the boolean conditions of all enclosing where and loopwhere constructs.

- **C2:** If the index $A|_u$ enters the innermost instruction block inside which u is waiting, it must have stepped over all *meaningful* statements coming before the wait instruction.

We can now formalize the semantics of the $\mathcal{SCL}$ waiting instruction:

- **Waiting point:** wait A. An index terminates this instruction if the conditions **C1** and **C2** are satisfied.

Partial synchronization. The wait_all instruction is a generalization of the wait statement. An index terminates this instruction when it has performed a wait for all other indices.

Remarks:

- An index u may step over a wait A instruction even if the index $A|_u$ needs to execute non-meaningful statements before to reach the waiting point.

- A wait instruction can be seen as a one-sided point to point synchronization.

- A wait_all can be viewed as a partial synchronization as some indices may not execute it.

- Note that with our approach, routine calls are non-meaningful statements. Therefore they do not bound asynchronism.

Determinism: Two simple programming rules are sufficient to avoid non determinism.

- It is impossible to impose an ordering on the execution of the instructions of the two branches of a where/elsewhere construct. To avoid this source of non-determinism, it is sufficient to forbid the presence of get X from A into Y instructions in one branch, if the variable X is modified and copied (dump) in public memory in the other branch.

- Moreover, to avoid clashes between dump and get instructions, it is sufficient to introduce a wait_all before each dump and a wait A before each get X from A into Y. The wait_all instruction ensures that other indices have passed all previous get instructions before to execute the dump. In the same way, the wait A instruction ensures that the target index at the address $A|_u$ has executed all previous dump instructions.

Remark: Although the preceding rules are sufficient to ensure determinism, it is often possible to reduce synchronization requirements by a more careful analysis of data dependences (Cf. 3)

2.7. Structural clock presentation

For the sake of completeness, we recall now the construction of structural clocks . Each index owns a structural clock that encodes its current position during program execution, with regard to the meaningful statements. An index position is defined by the meaningful control structures it is nested in and by the last meaningful instruction executed in the innermost one. To record an index position we just need to know the number of meaningful statements already executed in each instruction block of each nesting level. Therefore, a structural clock encodes index positions by a list. Each term of the list corresponds to a nesting level. The *Structural Clock t_u* of an index u is so expressed by a list of pairs. Each pair (l, c) is composed of a label l and an instruction counter c. The counter c represents the number of meaningful instructions already executed in the corresponding instruction block level. The label l is used to distinguish which branch of a where/elsewhere statement an index is inside. Lists are built by popping or pushing pairs on their right hand side.

- **The get and dump instructions**

  When an index u executes a get or a dump instruction its clock $t_u = t(l, c)$ becomes $t_u = t(l, c + 1)$.

- **The where structure**

  After evaluating the condition B of a where/elsewhere statement, if $B|_u$ is true (resp. false) the clock $t_u = t$ becomes $t_u = t(1, 0)$ (resp. $t_u = t(2, 0)$). When the index u exits a where or elsewhere branch, the clock $t_u = t(l, c)(m, d)$ becomes $t_u = t(l, c + 1)$.

- **The loopwhere structure**

  In a loopwhere, an index which does not compute an iteration directly exits the loop. Therefore, it turns out that we do not have to consider each iteration as a new nesting level in the structural clock list. We only push a new term on the list at the first loop iteration and next, we count instructions already executed in the loopwhere body.

When the index u enters for the first time a loopwhere instruction, if the condition $B|_u$ evaluates to true, then its clock $t_u = t$ becomes $t_u = t(1,0)$. Otherwise its clock $t_u = t(l,c)$ becomes $t_u = t(l,c+1)$. If it has already executed at least one loop iteration, then if $B|_u = true$, its clock $t_u = t$ remains unchanged, otherwise $t_u = t(l,c)(1,d)$ becomes $t_u = t(l,c+1)$.

Remark: At the beginning of the execution, each index initializes its structural clock to $(0,0)$.

Structural clock ordering. We define a partial order on structural clocks. To order two structural clocks, we compare the local counters corresponding to the common instruction block of the innermost nested level. We so define this partial ordering as a lexicographical order based on partially ordered pairs:

A index u is said to be later than an other index v (denoted by $t_u \prec t_v$) if one of the following conditions holds:

- *there exists t not empty such that $t_v = t_u\, t$;*
- *there exists t^1, t^2, t^3, c_u, c_v and l such that $t_u = t^1(l,c_u)t^2$, $t_v = t^1(l,c_v)t^3$ and $c_u < c_v$.*

The former condition above formalizes the intuitive idea that the index v is inside the first meaningful control structure that follows the instruction currently executed by u. Note that there is no meaningful instruction between this instruction and the control structure. The latter one expresses that, with regard to the block encoded by $t^1(l,...)$, the index u is later than v.

2.8. Handling wait statements using structural clocks

Structural clocks yield a general mechanism to handle wait statements. The conditions **C1** and **C2** above are captured by the following rule:

Consider an index u with structural clock t_u that asks for a wait *A. This index can terminate the wait instruction if the index $v = A|_u$ with a structural clock t_v satisfies $t_v \prec t_u$.*

Remark: We can easily prove that any $\mathcal{SCL}$ program is deadlock free using the following property: an index owning a minimal clock is never blocked (if it has not finished the program execution, otherwise all indices have finished).

3. Example of recursive program: the Strassen's algorithm

We turn now to an example (Fig. 1). This $\mathcal{SCL}$ program illustrates the use of recursion in our asynchronous model. It can be viewed as an improvement of a BSP program initially proposed by Mc Coll for Strassen's Algorithm [9].

Let A and B be two $n \times n$ matrices and consider the problem of computing the product $C = A.B$. A classical recursive algorithm consists in regarding each matrix as four $n/2 \times n/2$ sub-matrices. The computation of C is then given by the computation of the four sub-matrices C_{ij} $(i,j \in \{1,2\})$ where $Cij = A_{i1}.B_{1j}+A_{i2}.B_{2j}$. This yields eight sub-matrix products that are treated recursively by the same method. The Strassen's algorithm consists in reducing these eight sub-matrix products to seven, by using shrewd matrix additions and subtractions.

We consider matrices A, B and C whose size are $n = 4^k.7^k$. These matrices can be seen as 4^{2k} sub-matrices of 7^{2k} elements. The underlying geometry of indices corresponds to a two dimensional array $[1..7^k, 1..7^k]$. Each index is identified with one of the 7^{2k} element position within each sub-matrix. An index initially holds all the 4^{2k} elements which are in that position within their sub-matrix.

We now describe the algorithm starting from this configuration (Fig. 1). The Strassen's algorithm is programmed in $\mathcal{SCL}$ by using four routines $Stras\_par1$, $Stras\_par2$, $Communication$ and $Strassen\_local$. The parallel routine $Stras\_par1$ initiates the algorithm, halting each chain of recursive calls when the level of recursion reaches $2k$. Each step of the recursion consists in computing seven matrices $L[K]$ and $R[K]$ $(1 \le K \le 7)$ by additions and subtractions of the four sub-matrices of A and B. Then, we proceed to the next recursion level by computing the seven matrix products $L[K].R[K]$. All the indices are engaged during these steps. We obtain 7^{2k} recursion leaves that are numbered from 1 to 7^{2k}. When a leaf number Q is reached, the two matrices to be multiplied are of size 7^k. Each index owns exactly one element of each matrix. To record locally these values we use two arrays $Tmp1[Q]$ and $Tmp2[Q]$.

When the execution of $Stras\_par1$ terminates, the parallel routine $Communication$ starts. Each index gathers the data stored in the memories of other indices, in the components of $Tmp1$ and $Tmp2$ that corresponds to its index number. These data are transferred in the matrices $A1$ and $B1$. So, the matrix product linked to each leaf can be computed locally, in parallel on all indices, using $Strassen\_local$, a sequential version of the Strassen's algorithm. This yields a matrix $C1$ for each index.

```
Stras_par1( in-out:Tmp1, Tmp2;in:A,B;in-out:Q; in:N)
L,R:array[1..7] of array[1..4^k, 1..4^k] of real;
I,J,K:integer;
where N ≥ 2 do
   forwhere I := 1 to N/2 do
      forwhere J := 1 to N/2 do
         L[1][I,J] := A[I,J];
         L[2][I,J] := A[I,J + N/2];
         L[3][I,J] := A[I + N/2,J]
                     +A[I + N/2,J + N/2];
         L[4][I,J] := A[I,J] − A[I + N/2,J];
         L[5][I,J] := L[3][I,J] − A[I,J];
         L[6][I,J] := A[I,J + N/2] − L[5][I,J];
         L[7][I,J] := A[I + N/2; J + N/2];
         R[1][I,J] := B[I,J];
         R[2][I,J] := B[I + N/2,J];
         R[3][I,J] := B[I,J + N/2] − B[I,J];
         R[4][I,J] := B[I + N/2,J + N/2]
                     −B[I,J + N/2];
         R[5][I,J] := R[4][I,J] + B[I,J];
         R[6][I,J] := B[I + N/2,J + N/2];
         R[7][I,J] := B[I + N/2,J] − R[5][I,J];
      end;
   end;
   forwhere K := 1 to 7 do
      call Stras_par1(Tmp1,Tmp2,L[K],R[K],
                      Q,N/2);
   end;
elsewhere (N=1)
   Tmp1[Q] := A[1,1];
   Tmp2[Q] := B[1,1];
   Q := Q + 1;
end;
end{Stras_par1};
```

```
Communication( in: Tmp1,Tmp2;
                    in-out: A1, B1 )
I,J:integer;
forwhere I := 1 to 7^k do
   forwhere J := 1 to 7^k do
      wait (I,J);
      get Tmp1[This] from (I,J) into A1[I,J];
      get Tmp2[This] from (I,J) into B1[I,J];
   end;
end;
end{Communication};
```

```
Stras_par2( in-out:C; in: C1;in-out:Q;in:N)
M:array[1..7] of array[1..4^k, 1..4^k] of real;
T:array[1..2] of array[1..4^k, 1..4^k] of real;
I,J,K:integer;
where N ≥ 2 do
   forwhere K := 1 to 7 do
      call Stras_par2(M[K],C1,Q,N/2);
   end;
   forwhere I := 1 to N/2 do
      forwhere J := 1 to N/2 do
         T[1][I,J] := M[1][I,J] + M[5][I,J];
         T[2][I,J] := T[1][I,J] + M[4][I,J];
         C[I,J] := M[1][I,J] + M[2][I,J];
         C[I,J + N/2] := T[1][I,J]
                        +M[3][I,J] + M[6][I,J];
         C[I + N/2,J] := T[2][I,J] + M[7][I,J];
         C[I + N/2,J + N/2] := T[2][I,J]
                        +M[3][I,J];
      end;
   end;
elsewhere (N=1)
   wait Q;
   get C1[This_x,This_y] from Q into C[1,1];
   Q := Q + 1;
end;
end{Stras_par2};
```

```
{Main program}
A,B,C:array[1..4^k, 1..4^k] of real;
A1,B1,C1:array[1..7^k, 1..7^k] of real;
Tmp1,Tmp2:array[1..7^k] of real;
Q:real;

Q := 1;
call Stras_par1(Tmp1,Tmp2,A,B,Q,4^k);
dump;
call Communication(Tmp1,Tmp2,A1,B1);
call Strassen_local(A1,B1,C1);
dump;
Q := 1;
call Stras_par2(C,C1,Q,4^k);
```

Figure 1. This SCL program illustrates the use of recursion in our asynchronous model.

In a last part a new recursion is initiated with $Stras\_par2$. Computations are performed during the back-track on the recursion tree. First of all, the results of the local matrix products are distributed among the indices. For a leaf number Q, each index (i,j) gets $C1[i,j]$ from the index Q. Each time a recursion level is finished, we obtain a matrix product $M[K] = L[K].R[K]$. From the seven matrices $M[K]$, the matrices $T[1]$, $T[2]$ and then the matrix C are locally computed by each index.

Two addressing systems are used. The parallel constants $1 \le This\_x \le 7^k$ and $1 \le This\_y \le 7^k$ appoint respectively the line number and the column number of each index. The parallel constant $1 \le This \le 7^{2k}$ provides a linear coordinate. We also use an instruction forwhere that merely corresponds to the loopwhere instruction with an iteration counter.

```
forwhere J := 1 to N do          J := 1;
     S                    ≡       loopwhere (J <= N) do
end                                    S;
                                       J := J + 1
                                  end
```

Communications are performed through global variables by using public memories. The program uses two dump instructions executed by all indices. They are necessary to copy the variables $Tmp1$, $Tmp2$, and then $C1$ in public memories.

Remarks:

- In section 2.6 we proposed an approach to systematic $\mathcal{SCL}$ programming, by putting a wait_all before each dump and a wait A before each get X from A into Y. Nevertheless, careful analysis of data dependences can yield interesting optimizations. We use this technique for our program.

    - A wait_all instruction is useless before the first dump since no get precedes it.

    - Only one wait is required before the get instructions of the routine $Communication$ because the two get instructions are contiguous and access the same target index.

    - The get instructions of the routine $Communication$ and the second dump are not separated by a wait_all. Therefore, such a get can be executed after the dump. The acceded data in $Tmp1$ and $Tmp2$ are nevertheless not erroneous since no modification of these data occurs after the first dump.

- This program may be written differently removing all wait instructions and putting a wait_all after each dump instruction. Such a program would have been close to

the original BSP one [9]. The interest of our approach is to allow more asynchronism by interleaving point to point synchronizations and computations.

4. Conclusion

In this paper, we have proposed a structured approach mixing data-parallelism and task parallelism. In contrast to classical synchronous data parallelism, asynchronism allows us to introduce task parallelism through the where/elsewhere construct. Our approach relies on the structural clock mechanism to manage synchronizations. The structural clocks record index positions with regard to the program structure. The waiting algorithm then uses an ordering on structural clocks to compare index positions. Structural clocks yield safe synchronizations as they manage waiting instructions without deadlock.

The structural clock mechanism requires additional computations and data exchanges. The size of structural clocks, and so the complexity of the comparison algorithm, depends on the program. It is equal to the deepest nesting of control structures and routine calls. The amount of additional exchanged data evolves at most linearly with the number of indices, as each index owns exactly one structural clock.

Loosely synchronized programs are obtained without the machinery needed by other desynchronization methods [6, 3]. Moreover, these methods generally use global synchronization barriers whereas the wait instruction authorizes one-sided and partial synchronizations.

We have shown that it is possible to extend the $\mathcal{SCL}$ language with recursive routines. In a restricted framework where communications are authorized only on global variables, we had shown that neither routines nor recursion reduce asynchronism.

The potentialities of our language and of structural clocks are exemplified through Strassen's Algorithm. Using $\mathcal{SCL}$ programming, the involved harness of synchronizations and communications is expressed in a very simple and intuitive way.

Note that communications on local variables and in arguments would require stacks of public memories. If routine calls are not surrounded by wait instructions, informations on index positions are then necessary to ensure consistency of public memories. Structural clocks can be used to provide these informations and so to handle such routines without additional synchronizations.

Our approach is general enough to be extended easily to more complex languages. It relies on a clear theoretical model which provides well-founded program transformations [10].

References

[1] C.H.Koelbel, D.B.Loveman, R.S.Schreiber, G. Jr., and M.E.Zosel. *The High Performance Fortran Handbook*. The MIT Press, 1994.

[2] Digital Equipment Corporation. *DECmpp Programming Langage, Reference Manual*, 1992.

[3] G.Utard and G.Hains. Deadlock-free absorption of barrier synchronisations. *Information Processing Letters*, 56:221–227, 1995.

[4] Y. L. Guyadec, E. Melin, B. Raffin, X. Rebeuf, and B. Virot. A Loosely Synchronized Execution Model for a Simple Data-Parallel Language. In L. Bougé, P. Fraigniaud, A. Mignotte, and Y. Robert, editors, *EuroPar'96 Parallel Processing*, number 1123 in LNCS. Springer-Verlag, 1996.

[5] Y. L. Guyadec, E. Melin, B. Raffin, X. Rebeuf, and B. Virot. Structural Clocks for a Loosely Synchronized Data-Parallel Language. In *MPCS'96* . EUROMICRO and Istituto di Ricerca su Sistemi Informatici Parallele, may 1996. *(Preliminary Proceedings)*.

[6] P. J. Hatcher and M. J. Quinn. *Data–Parallel Programming on MIMD Computers*. The MIT Press, 1991.

[7] Hyperparallel Technologies. *HyperC Documentation*, 1993.

[8] Y. Le Guyadec. Désynchronisation des programmes data-parallèles: une approche sémantique. *TSI*, 14(5):619–638, 1995.

[9] W. F. McColl. A BSP Realisation of Strassen's Algorithm. Oxford University Computing Laboratory, May 1995.

[10] E. Melin, B. Raffin, X. Rebeuf, and B. Virot. A Loosely Synchronized Execution Model for a Simple Data-Parallel Language.
Technical Report RR96-11, LIFO, Orléans, France, October 1996. http://web.univ-orleans.fr/~virot.

❖ OPEN FORUM SESSION 2 ❖

Chair

B. Di Martino

A Parallel Test-Pattern Generator Based on Spectral Techniques

Consolación Gil
Dept. de Informática y Sistemas.
Universidad de Murcia.
Murcia, SPAIN
cgil@dif.um.es

Julio Ortega
Dept. de Electrónica y Tecnología de
Computadores. Universidad de Granada
Granada, SPAIN
julio@casip.ugr.es

Abstract

This communication presents a parallel procedure to determine the patterns for testing digital circuits. The procedure represents a new approach to speed-up the test-pattern generation using multicomputers. It is based on an algorithm which mixes both the Boolean difference and the Digital spectral techniques, and so is different from other methods proposed up to now that deal with the parallelization of test generation algorithms, such as PODEM, that carry out an implicit enumeration of the input pattern space. The procedure here proposed is able to reach efficiencies close to one without using complicated procedures for load balancing, thus allowing good scalability.

1. Introduction

The procedures of generating patterns for testing digital circuits look for the set of assignments to the circuit inputs that allow us to distinguish between a faulty and a fault-free circuit [1]. Among all the types of faults proposed to model a defect in a circuit, the most effective, and so the most frequently used, is the single stuck-at fault that fixes the faulty line to the logical value 0 (stuck-at 0 fault) or 1 (stuck-at 1 fault). To solve the test problem requires a large amount of design time. Although, by using techniques such as LSSD [2], the problem can be reduced to the generation of tests for combinational circuits; indeed in this case the problem is NP-complete. There has been a lot of research work trying to develop more efficient algorithms to search for test patterns through the space of all input combinations. Nevertheless, the increase in the circuit sizes and complexities has been faster than the improvements achieved with the new serial procedures. So, it would be very useful to provide parallel procedures which allow us to speed up test generation by using multiprocessors. This tendency is also common in other problems dealing with computer-aided design of VLSI circuits, and is becoming more and more attractive due to the increase in the availability of parallel processing machines.

Previous research into algorithms to generate test patterns for stuck-at faults in combinational circuits has followed two main approaches [3]. The first one, and the most widely used, includes the algorithms that perform an implicit enumeration of the input patterns through a search of the solution space. This search may consist of assignments to all the lines in the circuits, as D-algorithm [1] does; to all the primary inputs, as PODEM [1,4] does; or to all the primary inputs plus some selected internal lines, as for example SOCRATES [1] does. These algorithms use local information about the circuit in order to determine the assignment to its lines, so directing the search in the space of possible solutions. Sometimes the algorithm makes an incorrect assignment and it has to go back to the last point where an assignment was made and try an alternative. This is called backtracking, and thanks to this property, these algorithms may enumerate a large enough part of the solution space to find a pattern for a given fault. Nevertheless, as test generation is an NP-complete problem, an algorithm cannot guarantee that, for some circuit, it will not need to search an exponentially large part of the space for a particular fault.

These faults are called hard-to-detect faults. The parallel test pattern generators reported to date are based on these algorithms, mainly in PODEM and its derivatives. The techniques that have been mainly used to parallelize these test algorithms are the following [1]:

- **Fault partitioning**: The set of faults is divided among the multiple processors and then, each processor generates the patterns for each fault of its list.

- **Search-Space partitioning**: The space of possible assignments to the inputs, to the lines, or both, is divided among the processors. Thus, the processors work together searching for a pattern for each fault This approach is a parallel implementation of the branch-and-bound method, which involves concurrent evaluation of subproblems.

- **Algorithmic Partitioning**: The sequential test generation algorithm is divided into independent subtasks that can be executed in parallel on separate processors.

The problem with fault partitioning when using an implicit enumeration algorithm is that the amount of space to search could vary greatly depending whether or not the fault is hard-to-detect [1]. So it is necessary to use an efficient dynamic scheme to balance the sets of faults assigned to the processors. Such a load balancing procedure consumes computer resources and could imply negative effects on the scalability of the parallel procedure.

With respect to the Search-Space partitioning, perhaps PODEM [4] is the algorithm that has been most frequently parallelized using this technique [5-7]. PODEM explores the solution space structured as a binary tree, so that the determination of disjoint subspaces to be evaluated by different processors is relatively easy. Nevertheless, as in the fault partitioning case, here it is also necessary to implement a load balancing method which divides the search space into parts that imply similar amounts of work. As it is difficult to determine the magnitude of the search space before the execution of the procedure, the load should be dynamically balanced, thus causing some overhead. Moreover, the speedup obtained for a given fault depends on the size of the tree been searched by the serial PODEM. If a fault is easy to detect, the parallel algorithm cannot provide much speedup because the part of the tree to be searched is small and cannot support much concurrency; only if the fault is hard to detect (HTD) is it possible to obtain good speedups.

The problem with algorithmic partitioning is that the speedup which it is possible to get is limited by the degree to which the serial test pattern generator can be usefully split.

The second kind of serial procedures for test pattern generation, called **algebraic procedures** [3], are those based on the Boolean difference or a variation of it. They differ from algorithms such as PODEM in that they use a mathematical formulation of the test problem. The first implementations of these methods were very slow. Nevertheless, in these methods the difference between hard-to-detect faults and easy-to-detect faults disappears because faults usually require similar computing times. Recently several Boolean methods have been reported [3]. To the best of our knowledge, the parallelization of these algorithms has not been considered.

Here we propose a parallel procedure based on a new test generation algorithm which can be considered as belonging to the algebraic techniques. The algorithm allows us to speed-up test generation by carrying out the corresponding operations in the Reed-Muller spectral domain. By doing this it is possible not only to quickly obtain the equation that the patterns for a given fault must

verify, but also to formulate it in such a way that it allows us to determine one of its solutions (i.e., a test pattern) in an easy way. In essence, our parallel procedure distributes the lines of the circuit among the processors in the computer and then each processor sequentially applies the new test generation algorithm to its set of lines. Thus, this parallel procedure falls into the category of fault partitioning. However, due to the characteristics of the serial algorithm we have previously developed, the drawbacks shown by fault partitioning when an implicit enumeration algorithm is parallelized are not so important here. This is so because the test generation algorithm does not have to perform a search in spaces whose sizes are not known, but carries out some specific operations with a computational cost that can be easily estimated according to the position of the line in the circuit.

The communication has been structured into six sections. Following this introduction, Section 2 gives a brief description of the new test-pattern generation algorithm we propose. The opportunities for parallelism of this algorithm and the alternative we have implemented are presented in Section 3, while the experimental results obtained and the comparisons of our parallel procedure with other proposed methods are provided in Section 4. Section 5 gives some conclusions and finally, the references are given.

2. A new algebraic algorithm for test pattern generation

In this section we describe a new procedure [10] to find the test patterns for the stuck line faults of a given combinational circuit. As indicated above this method can be classified as an algebraic or Boolean test generation technique which uses a mathematical formulation of the test generation problem, thus being different from techniques based on an implicit enumeration of the input patterns such as PODEM, SOCRATES, etc.

Given a circuit with n inputs, $y = (y_0,...,y_{n-1})$ and w lines, $i = 0,..., w$-1, the function implemented by the line i is noted as $f_i(y) = f_i(y_0,...,y_{n-1})$. The function synthesized by a given output of the circuit is indicated as $\mathcal{F}(y) = \mathcal{F}(y_0,...,y_{n-1})$. For any internal line i, it is also possible to describe $\mathcal{F}(y)$ as a function of both, the inputs, y and f_i, $\mathcal{F}(y) = \mathcal{F}_i(f_i, y_0,...,y_{n-1})$[3]. If the line i presents a stuck-at α fault, then $f_i(y) = \alpha$ for all values of $y = (y_0,...,y_{n-1})$, and the set of input patterns that will allow to detect this fault are those that verify

$$f_i(y_0,...,y_{n-1}) = \overline{\alpha} \qquad (1)$$

and

$$\mathcal{F}_i(\alpha, y_0, \ldots, y_{n-1}) \oplus \mathcal{F}_i(\overline{\alpha}, y_0, \ldots, y_{n-1}) = 1 \quad (2)$$

By solving the system of equations (1) and (2), the set of test pattern for the stuck-at α fault in the line i can be determined. All Boolean test procedures use these equations or an alternative formulation to generate the test pattern for a fault. In the procedure here presented, the equations (1) and (2) are written in terms of the Reed-Muller spectrum [8].

Any function can be univocally expressed, in terms of the Reed-Muller coefficients, as

$$\mathcal{F}(y) = \oplus_i g_i (y_0^{i_0} y_1^{i_1} \ldots y_{n-1}^{i_{n-1}}), \quad (i = 0, 1, \ldots, 2^n - 1) \quad (3)$$

where $i = i_0 + i_1 2 + \ldots + i_{n-1} 2^{n-1}$; $y_i^0 = 1$ and $y_i^1 = y_i$; and $\gamma_i \in \{0, 1\}$. The set of coefficients γ_i, $i = 1, \ldots, 2^n-1$, are called Reed-Muller coefficients, and they provide an univocal representation of a logic function as, for example, the minterms do. Considering (3) it is possible to write the function $\mathcal{F}_i(f_i, y_0, \ldots, y_{n-1})$ as

$$\mathcal{F}_i(f_i, y_0, \ldots, y_{n-1}) = f_i(y) \, g_i(y) \oplus h_i(y) \quad (4)$$

where $g_i(y)$ and $h_i(y)$ are two functions that must be calculated to allow the equality (4) to be verified. By substituting the right hand term of (4), (2) is transformed into

$$(\alpha \, g_i(y) \oplus h_i(y)) \oplus (\overline{\alpha} \, g_i(y) \oplus h_i(y)) = g_i = 1 \quad (5)$$

and by considering that (1) is equivalent to

$$f_i(y_0, \ldots, y_{n-1}) \oplus \alpha = 1 \quad (6)$$

the Boolean equation that the test patterns for a stuck-at α in the line i must satisfy, is given by

$$(f_i(y) \oplus \alpha) \, g_i(y) = 1 \quad (7)$$

This way, the procedure we propose to determine a test pattern for a stuck-at fault in the line i implies to obtain the f_i and g_i functions, to reach equation (7) and to calculate one of its solutions [10]. The f_i functions can be calculated for all the lines of the circuit beginning from the inputs and proceeding through the internal lines until a given output is reached. In a similar way, the g_i functions can be obtained beginning from the outputs and finishing at the inputs of the circuit. The operations used in these processes depend on the particular logic gate.

The obtention of the g_i functions in only one pass through the circuit is not possible if there are fanout points in the circuit, because at these points the operation that transform several g_i functions into only one g_i is not defined. Nevertheless, in these cases it is possible to obtain the g_i's by using an alternative procedure. From expression (4) it is verified that

$$\mathcal{F}_i(f_i = 1, y_0, \ldots, y_{n-1}) = g_i(y) \oplus h_i(y) \quad (8)$$

and

$$\mathcal{F}_i(f_i = 0, y_0, \ldots, y_{n-1}) = h_i(y) \quad (9)$$

Thus

$$\mathcal{F}_i(f_i = 1, y_0, \ldots, y_{n-1}) \oplus \mathcal{F}_i(f_i = 0, y_0, \ldots, y_{n-1}) = g_i(y) \quad (10)$$

In this way, it is possible to obtain the g_i function for a line i by determining the functions $\mathcal{F}_i$ with the line i fixed at 0 and at 1 and computing the EXOR of both functions. In this case the obtention of the g_i function for each line i is independent of the others.

All the operations involved in the determination of the f_i and g_i functions are carried out by using the Reed-Muller descriptions of the functions, thus allowing us to compute them in a fast way, and to obtain the equation expressed in such a way that makes it easy to determine one solution for each equation [8].

Table 1 gives some experimental results obtained with this new procedure implemented in the computer Power Challenge XL of Sillicon Graphics. As benchmark circuits, we have used some circuits of the ISCAS85 and ISCAS89 sets plus the ALU 74181 (which is termed ALU in the Tables). In Table 1 **N_fault** is the number of faults in the circuit, **T_fault** is the average time per fault in seconds, **L_tes** is the number of test patterns in the test set, and **Cover** is the percentage of faults detected by the procedure. The meaning of **V_cut** needs further explanation. As the test-pattern generation is an NP-complete problem, this implies that any general test algorithm that can be applied to any circuit would need an exponential amount of time, memory, or both, in some cases. In the procedure here presented this fact implies that, for some lines in some circuits, the number of Reed-Muller coefficients needed to describe the test equation could be higher that the available memory. So, just as in the PODEM-like methods a limit in the number of backtracks is imposed, here a limit in the number of coefficients in the f_i and g_i functions is imposed. This limit is V_cut.

The results of our method are similar to those of PODEM with respect to time needed for a given fault coverage. Nevertheless, the number of test patterns obtained by the proposed method for a 100% coverage is less than that obtained with PODEM.

Circuit	N_fault	T_fault	L_test	V_cut	Cover
ALU	384	0.005	70	70	100%
c432	864	0.15	125	100	95%
c499	998	0.15	300	100	99%
c880	1760	0.11	350	100	100%
c1355	2710	0.25	375	30	98%
c1908	3816	0.26	411	30	98%
c3540	7080	0.26	400	20	97%
c6288	12576	0,18	305	2	96%
s349	680	0.005	76	100	100%
s382	764	0.007	106	100	100%
s386	772	0.002	114	100	100%
s400	800	0.02	110	100	100%
s444	888	0.02	94	200	100%
s510	1020	0.004	99	500	100%

Table 1. Some experimental results with the serial procedure here proposed

3. The Parallel Procedure PARALGI

From the alternatives to parallelize the previous serial procedure we decided to use a fault partitioning scheme. As has been explained in Section 1, this alternative requires us to use a procedure that provides a balanced workload distribution among the processors. Moreover, when the test-generator to be parallelized is based on an implicit enumeration procedure as PODEM, that load balancing procedure must be dynamic because prior to the execution it is difficult to make a good enough evaluation of the workload associated with each fault. This procedure should also be carefully designed to avoid a possible high overhead that might seriously affect the efficiency and scalability of the parallel procedure.

In the spectral procedure here presented, it is relatively easy to predict the amount of work associated with the computation of the f_i and g_i functions for a given line, according to its situation in the structure of the circuit with respect to the outputs. Given a line i in the circuit, the volume of work to determine the f_i and g_i functions mainly depends on the level where this line is situated in the circuit. The nearer the line i is to the outputs, the easier it is to compute the g_i function, and viceversa with the f_i function. So, the lines of the circuit can be quickly divided among the processors.

Figure 1 gives a diagram for the parallel procedure here proposed. It is called PARALGI. In the figure, the procedure **distribute_lines** allows the distribution of the workload among the processors and is concurrently executed in all the processors. Each processor determines the f_i functions for all the lines of the circuit by using the **compute_all_f**. In this way, the processors do some

redundant work, and this will imply a reduction in the speedup that can be achieved. Nevertheless, the time needed to compute the f_i functions is several orders of magnitude less than the time required to compute the g_i functions. As the determination of the f_i's represents a small part of the work to be done, it is better to repeat the obtention of the f_i functions in every processor thus avoiding the communication and synchronization overheads due to the interchanges of the f_i's among the processors, when they use them to compute the g_i's.

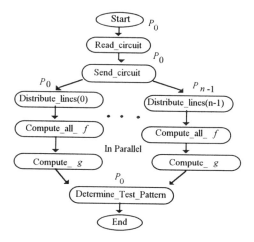

Figure 1. Diagram for the procedure PARALGI.

4. Experimental results and comparisons with other parallel methods

The parallel algorithm PARALGI has been implemented in C and it has been executed in the multicomputer iPSC/860.

Circt	V_cut	S_2	S_4	S_8	S_16	S_32	Cover
ALU	70	1.70	4.00	8.00	16.00	30.00	100%
c432	100	1.66	3.37	6.94	15.62	35.70	95%
c499	100	1.82	3.70	7.50	14.28	30.40	98%
c880	100	1.93	3.65	7.05	13.86	26.80	99%
c1355	30	1.92	3.82	7.03	13.33	27.27	97%
c1908	30	1.90	3.50	6.94	12.63	24.01	97%
c3540	20	1.64	2.79	5.39	10.54	21.51	96%
s382	100	2.08	4.16	8.33	16.27	31.20	100%
s386	100	2.09	4.60	8.33	16.27	31.20	100%
s400	100	1.80	3.00	5.00	9.00	15.00	100%
s444	200	2.09	4.60	7.60	15.33	23.00	100%
s510	500	1.93	2.14	7.25	14.50	29.00	100%

Table 2: Some experimental results with procedure PARALGI

Table 2 gives the results obtained for a representative set of circuits selected from the ISCAS85 and ISCAS89 benchmark circuits. In the table, S_n means the speedup achieved with n processors.

Figure 2 shows, for some example circuits, the evolution of the speedup when the number of processors is increased. It reveals that, at least up to the maximum number of processors used, the speedup is not saturated. As it can be also seen, the efficiencies are close to one in every case.

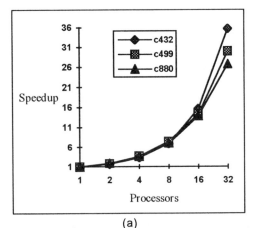

(a)

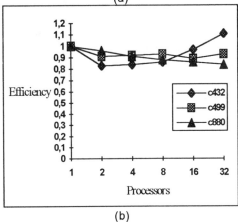

(b)

Figure 2. Speedups (a) and efficiencies (b) for some circuits of the ISCAS sets.

Table 3 compares the performances of our parallel algorithm with the speedup results provided in [5] for the hard-to-detect (HTD) faults (columns **HTD Sp** in the Table 3) with 4, 8 and 16 processors. The procedure of [5] uses search-space partitioning to parallelize PODEM together with a dynamic load balancing scheme. The results in [5] correspond to two different heuristics used to guide the search: SCOAP heuristic (**HTD Sp(S)** column in Table 3) and RANDOM heuristic (**HTD Sp(R)** column in Table 3). The speedups obtained with our algorithm, which considers all the faults, are better than the results of

[5] with the SCOAP heuristic but are worse than those obtained with the RANDOM heuristics. Although the Speedup results of [5] correspond only to the HTD faults, this paper also gives some data that allows us to estimate the speedups if all the faults were considered (**Overall Sp(S)** and **Overall Sp(R)** columns in Table 3).

Thus, If all the faults are considered, as in PARALGI, the speedup values in [5] will decrease. For example, if we take the results of [5] for the c3540 circuit and the SCOAP heuristic, the uniprocessor time/fault is t_{se}=290 ms for the easy-to-detect faults (N_e=3092) and t_{sh}=8796 ms for the hard-to-detect faults (N_h=289) and a bactrack limit of 375. The total amount of time for the serial algorithm is $T_s = t_{se}N_e + t_{sh}N_h$=3438.7 s. The time/fault for the hard-to-detect faults is t_{ph}=640 ms when using the parallel algorithm with 16 processors. Thus, the parallel time is approximately $T_p = t_{se}N_e + t_{ph}N_h$ =1081.64 s., and the speedup is $S = T_s/T_p$=3.18 instead of t_{sh}/t_{ph}=13.7 if only the HTD faults are considered. This is because in the easy-to-detect faults, which usually represents a large part of the whole set of faults, the parallel procedure is not able to reach an important speed-up. This reduction in the speedup is a sample of the Amdahl's law. This is not a problem for our procedure because it can speedup all the faults of the circuit in the same way.

Circt	Proc	HTD Sp (S)	Overall Sp(S)	HTD Sp(R)	Overall Sp(R)	PLGI Sp
c432	4	2.5	1.0	5.4	1.6	3.3
	8	5.8	1.2	10.6	2.3	6.9
	16	11.6	1.5	15.6	3.4	15.6
c499	4	2.6	1.0	5.2	1.3	3.7
	8	5.5	1.1	11.9	1.8	7.5
	16	9.0	1.4	19.9	2.6	13.8
c1355	4	2.5	1.2	6.6	1.5	3.8
	8	5.1	1.8	12.0	1.9	7.0
	16	7.5	2.6	17.6	2.5	13.3
c1908	4	2.6	1.0	8.9	1.5	3.5
	8	7.3	1.1	20.9	2.1	6.9
	16	12.3	1.4	34.0	3.2	12.6
c3540	4	3.2	1.4	3.0	1.4	2.7
	8	7.2	2.0	7.1	2.3	5.3
	16	13.7	3.1	11.8	3.5	10.5

Table 3. Results of PARALGI compared with results obtained from [5]

Another important aspect to consider is the scalability of the parallel algorithms. The scalability can be measured by using the **isoefficiency function** [11] that plots the rate of growth of the size of the problem with respect to the number of processors for a given value of the efficiency. Figure 3 gives the isoefficiency function of the procedure here proposed. The curve has been obtained for an efficiency equal to 0.7 and considering the number of lines of the circuit as the parameter which indicates the volume of the problem. As can be seen the curve is $O(\log(N))$, when N is the number of processors. The paper [6] indicates that in a fully connected multicomputer the isoefficiency function of a good load balancing scheme is $O(N\log(N))$. Our procedure does not use a dynamic scheme for distributing the work because the computational cost to determine the patterns for a given fault can easily be estimated by considering the position in the circuit of the affected line. This allows us to carry out an efficient static partition of the circuit lines.

To complete our comparison with [5], as it is indicated in [6], the isoefficiency function for the procedure of [5] is $O(N^2\log(N))$, because it uses a load balancing scheme with a centralized scheduler. The same happens with the procedure described in [7]. This is very illustrative because [7] uses, as in our procedure, a fault partitioning technique to parallelize the algorithm PODEM, but it needs to implement a load balancing schema to get good speedups. In our method this is not necessary and so it presents good scalability.

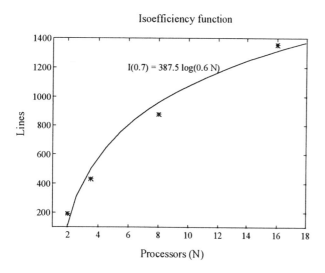

Figure 3. Isoefficiency function for PARALGI with the circuits ALU 74181, c432, c880 and c1355.

5. Conclusions

We have presented a parallel procedure to speed-up test pattern generation for digital circuits. It is based on a new test algorithm which operates in the Reed-Muller spectral domain. This accelerates the computation of the test equations and facilitates their solution in order to determine the test patterns. As the amount of work involved in each fault is relatively easy to estimate, it is

possible to implement an efficient static procedure to distribute the lines among the processors. The values obtained for the speedup show efficiencies close to one for our algorithm and good values for scalability.

When all the faults (not only the HTD faults) are considered, PARALGI shows better speedups than other parallel procedures. As our serial procedure requires similar amounts of time than the other serial procedures, such as PODEM, the speedups we have obtained represent a reduction in the time to generate the test patterns with respect to those parallel procedures.

References

[1] R.H. Klenke, R.D. Williams, J.H. Aylor. Parallel-Processing Techniques for Automatic Test Pattern Generation. *IEEE Computer*, 71-84, January 1992.

[2] S. Dasgupta, P. Goel, R.G. Walther, T.W. Williams. A variation of LSSD and its Implication on Design and Test Pattern Generation in VLSI. *Proc. of the International Test Conference*, 63-66, 1982.

[3] R.T. Stanion, D. Bhattacharya, C. Sechen. An Efficient Method for Generating Exhaustive Test Sets. *IEEE Trans. on CAD*, 14(12):1516-1525, December 1995.

[4] P. Goel. An Implicit Enumeration Algorithm to Generate Tests for Combinational Circuits. *IEEE Trans. on Computers*, (30):215-222, March 1981.

[5] S. Patil, P. Banerjee. A Parallel Branch and Bound Algorithm for Test Generation. *IEEE Trans. on CAD*, 9(3):313-322, March 1990.

[6] S. Arvindam, V. Kumar, V.N. Rao, V. Singh. Automatic Test Pattern Generation on Multiprocessors: a Summary of Results. *Lecture Notes in Artificial Intelligence*, (444):41-51, 1990.

[7] A. Motohara, K. Nishimura, H. Fujiwara, I. Shirakawa. A Parallel Scheme for Test Pattern Generation. *In Proc. Intl. Conference on Computer-Aided Design*, 156-159, 1986.

[8] J. Ortega, A. Lloris, A. Prieto, F. Pelayo. Test-Pattern Generation Based on Reed-Muller Coeficientes. *IEEE Trans. on Computers*, 42(8):968-980, August 1993.

[9] S. Smith, B. Underwood, M.R. Mercer. An Analysis of several approaches to Circuit Partitioning for Parallel Logic Simulation. *Proc. IEEE Int. Conference Computer Design: VLSI in Computers and Processors*, 664-667 1987.

[10] C. Gil. Procedimientos Paralelos basados en los Coeficientes de Reed-Muller para la Generación de Patrones de Test en Circuitos Digitales. Ph.D.dissertation, University of Granada, 1996.

[11] V. Kumar, A. Grama, V.N. Rao. Scalable Load Balancing Techniques for Parallel Computers. *Journal of Distributed and Parallel Computing*, (22):60-79, 1994.

I/O Management for Hierarchically Structured Array Architectures

Uwe Eckhardt *
Dresden University of Technology
Institute of Circuits and Systems
Mommsenstr. 13, 01069 Dresden, Germany
eckhardt@iee.et.tu-dresden.de

Abstract

This paper is concerned with the I/O-management of multiple partitioned massively parallel array architectures. Formulas are given for the computation of an I/O data layout which is adjusted to the access pattern of the array. We assign in each partition to each boundary processing element an input and/or output stream. The length of these streams is given by the length of the time period from the first input operation at one of the processors of the partition until to the last output operation. We tackle the problem for the combination of sequential and parallel scheduling schemes and for hierarchically structured array architectures. Hence, we consider the derivation of the input/output streams for the components of different system levels (processors, boards of processors etc.). The presented automatical generation of these I/O-streams represents an essential step for the design of peripheral circuitry (I/O subsystems) and control software of the array architecture.

1. Introduction

The application of massively parallel array architectures for the processing of systems of uniform recurrent equations (URE's) [8] requires the knowledge about the time instance and the locus, i.e. the processor element and the I/O-channel, at which a data item has to be transferred to the array. Furthermore, the data items transmitted from a locus at the array at a given time instance to the peripheral circuitry have to be detected as instances of a variable. The concern of this paper is to give a mathematical description of this behaviour. The automatic derivation of these I/O-streams represents an essential step for the computation of an I/O data layout which is adjusted to the access pattern of the array and hence, for the design of peripheral circuitry especially of the I/O subsystems in massively parallel architectures [4].

Supported by Deutsche Forschungsgemeinschaft SFB 358/A1

Existing treatises [5, 6] of the I/O-problem of systolic arrays are devoted to non partitioned and arbitrarily shaped convex index spaces with a purely parallel scheduling, where in [5] a constructive method including the optimization has been given. Our contribution to the I/O-problem consists of the following points: (i) We consider partitioned algorithms and arrays. (ii) We give an approach for hierarchically structured array architectures [3]. (iii) We consider a simultaneous parallel and sequential scheduling of operations in the array caused by the combination of LPGS- and LSGP-partitioning [3]. (iv) Functions for the automatic derivation of the input/output streams are given.

The arrays are supposed to be synthesized by means of Lamports hyperplane method [9]. The remainder of this paper is organized as follows: Section 2 gives basic definitions of Systems of Uniform Recurrent Equations (URE'S), of the mapping onto systolic arrays, and of the partitioning. Section 3 is devoted to the derivation of the loci of the I/O-tasks. Section 4 presents the generation of I/O-streams for purely LPGS-partitioned arrays. The extension to LSGP-partitioned LPGS-partitions of URE's is given in section 5. Finally, Section 6 is concerned with the I/O-streams for $q-$fold nested partitions of URE's.

2. Basic definitions

We introduce the definitions of the considered system of uniform recurrence equations (URE's), of the mapping onto massively parallel processor arrays, and of the partitioning.

Definition 1 (System of URE's) *A system of uniform recurrence equations (URE's) on a linearly bounded lattice is a set of equations*

$$y_j[\mathbf{i}] = F(x_1[\mathbf{i} - \mathbf{d}_{x,1}], \ldots, x_l[\mathbf{i} - \mathbf{d}_{x,l}], y_1[\mathbf{i} - \mathbf{d}_{y,1}],$$
$$\ldots, y_m[\mathbf{i} - \mathbf{d}_{y,m}]), j = 1, \ldots, m \quad (1)$$

where the index space $\mathcal{I}$ of these equations is a linearly bounded lattice

$$\mathcal{I} = \{\mathbf{i} \mid \mathbf{i} = \mathbf{B}\mathbf{z} + \mathbf{b}_0 \ \wedge \ \mathbf{A}\mathbf{i} \geq \mathbf{a}_0\}, \quad (2)$$

$\mathbf{i} \in \mathcal{I}$ are index points and $\mathbf{i}, \mathbf{z}, \mathbf{b}_0 \in \mathcal{Z}^n, \mathbf{a}_0 \in \mathcal{Q}^m, \mathbf{G}^* \in \mathcal{Z}^{n \times n}, rank\, \mathbf{G}^* = n, \mathbf{A} \in \mathcal{Q}^{m \times n}$. The data dependence vectors $\mathbf{d}_{i,j} \in \mathcal{D}$ are constant, where $\mathcal{D}$ is the set of all data dependence vectors in (1).

The set of all data dependence vectors $\mathcal{D} = \{\mathbf{d}\}$ together with the algorithm's index space $\mathcal{I}$ form the data dependence graph $\langle \mathcal{I}, \mathcal{D} \rangle$. We assume that the data dependence graph is connected. Otherwise the graph can be subdivided into independent partitions according to the independent partitioning scheme [2, 12]. Each partition forms an independent design problem. The subgraphs differ only by the translation $\mathbf{b}_0$.

Example: The multiplication $\mathbf{C} = \mathbf{A}\mathbf{B}$ of two square matrices of order four is given by:

$$c[\mathbf{i}] = c[\mathbf{i} - (0\ 0\ 1)^t] + a[\mathbf{i} - (0\ 1\ 0)^t] * b[\mathbf{i} - (1\ 0\ 0)^t]$$

$$\mathbf{i} \in \mathcal{I} = \{\mathbf{i} = (i\ j\ k)^t \mid \mathbf{i} = \mathbf{I}\mathbf{z},$$

$$\left(\begin{array}{c} \mathbf{I} \\ -\mathbf{I} \end{array} \right) \mathbf{i} \geq (0\ 0\ 0\ -3\ -3\ -3)^t \},$$

where $\mathbf{I}$ is the identity matrix of order three. •

The synthesis of a computing system for such an algorithm includes first of all two tasks: to assign to each index point a processing time (scheduling) and a locus of processing (allocation). We apply Lamports hyperplane method [9]. The scheduling of the computation tasks $\mathbf{i} \in \mathcal{I}$ is defined by scalar product with the scheduling vector τ, and the allocation to processors is defined by a linear projection with a projection vector $\mathbf{u}$.

Definition 2 (Mapping of URE's onto arrays) *The mapping M of the algorithm onto the systolic array is of the following form:*

$$M : \mathcal{I} \to \mathcal{J} \subseteq \mathcal{T} \times \mathcal{P}$$

$$M : \mathcal{D} \to \mathcal{C} \subseteq \mathcal{T}_v \times \mathcal{V}, \tag{3}$$

where $\mathcal{J}$ is the time processor space, $\mathcal{T} = \{t | t = \tau \mathbf{i}\}$ is the set of time instances at which the iterations $\mathbf{i}$ are processed, and $\mathcal{P} = \{\mathbf{p} | \mathbf{p} = \mathbf{S}\mathbf{i}\}$ is the processor space, where $\mathbf{S}\mathbf{u} = 0, \mathbf{S} \in \mathcal{Z}^{n-1 \times n}, rank\, \mathbf{S} = n - 1$. $\mathcal{C}$ is the set of interconnection primitives, where $\mathcal{V} = \{\mathbf{v} | \mathbf{v} = \mathbf{S}\mathbf{d}\}$ is the set of interconnections which have to be realized in the array, and $\mathcal{T}_v = \{t_v | t_v = \tau \mathbf{d}\}$ is the set of time delays associated with the interconnections. The constraints $\forall \mathbf{d} \in \mathcal{D} : \tau \mathbf{d} > 0$ (causality) and $\tau \mathbf{u} \neq 0$ have to be satisfied. The resulting array architecture is called full size array.

Obviously, the processor space is a linearly bounded lattice. This commonly used mapping leads to a direct dependence of the array architecture on the size of the algorithm. In general, resource constraints like processor count and I/O-demand cannot be taken into account. Partitioning techniques [10, 13, 1, 11, 3] establish the tool for the transformation of the full size array into a structure which is adjusted to the given constraints.

Definition 3 (Partitioning) *The partitioning of the index space $\mathcal{I}$ of a system of URE's is given by the partitions $\mathcal{I}_\pi(\mathbf{i}')$ in the index space and the set $\mathcal{I}'_\pi$.*

$$\mathcal{I}_\pi(\mathbf{i}') = \{\mathbf{i} \mid \mathbf{i} = \mathbf{i}' + \mathbf{G}^* \kappa^*, \mathbf{i} \in \mathcal{I}, 0 \leq \kappa_z < \vartheta_z,$$

$$z = 1, \ldots, n - 1\}, \tag{4}$$

$\kappa_z, \vartheta_z \in \mathcal{Z}, \kappa^* \in \mathcal{Z}^n, \mathbf{G}^* = [\mathbf{G}, \mathbf{u}] = [\mathbf{g}_1 \ldots \mathbf{g}_{n-1}\ \mathbf{u}]$ and $\mathbf{G}$ is an integral basis of the hyperplane $\tau \mathbf{i} = 0$ and $\mathbf{i}' = \mathbf{G}\kappa, \kappa \in \mathcal{Z}^{n-1}$. The set $\mathcal{I}'_\pi$ of (reference) vectors $\mathbf{i}'$ is given by

$$\mathcal{I}'_\pi = \{\mathbf{i}' \mid \mathbf{i}' = \mathbf{i}_{zero} + \mathbf{G}\Theta\mathbf{c}, \mathbf{L}\mathbf{c} \geq \mathbf{1}, \mathbf{c} \in \mathcal{Z}^{n-1},$$

$$\mathbf{i}_{zero} = \mathbf{G}\kappa, \kappa \in \mathcal{Z}^{n-1}\} \tag{5}$$

with $\Theta = diag(\vartheta_i)$ and the polyhedron $\mathbf{L}\mathbf{c} \geq \mathbf{1}$ is given by the successive projection of the convex hull of

$$\left(\begin{array}{cc} \mathbf{A}\mathbf{G}^* & \mathbf{A}\mathbf{G}\Theta \\ \mathbf{I} & 0 \\ -\mathbf{I} & 0 \end{array} \right) \left(\begin{array}{c} \kappa_1 \\ \vdots \\ \kappa_n \\ \mathbf{c} \end{array} \right) \geq \left(\begin{array}{c} \mathbf{a}_0 - \mathbf{A}\mathbf{i}_{zero} \\ 0 \\ -(\vartheta - 1) \end{array} \right) \tag{6}$$

along the κ_j-axes, $j = 1, \ldots, n$, i.e. by Fourier-Motzkin elimination, where $\vartheta - 1 = \left(\begin{array}{ccc} \vartheta_1 - 1 & \ldots & \vartheta_{n-1} - 1 \end{array} \right)^t$, and $\mathbf{I} \in \mathcal{Z}^{(n-1) \times (n-1)}$ is the identity matrix.

Hence, the processors space $\mathcal{P}$ is subdivided into partitions

$$\mathcal{P}_\pi(\mathbf{p}') = \{\mathbf{p} \mid \mathbf{p} = \mathbf{p}' + \mathbf{N}\kappa, \mathbf{p} \in \mathcal{P}, 0 \leq \kappa_z < \vartheta_z,$$

$$z = 1, \ldots, n - 1\} \tag{7}$$

with $\mathbf{N} = [\mathbf{n}_j = \mathbf{S}\mathbf{g}_j]$, and $\mathbf{p}' \in \mathcal{P}'_\pi$,

$$\mathcal{P}'_\pi = \{\mathbf{p}' | \mathbf{p}' = \mathbf{S}\mathbf{i}_{zero} + \mathbf{N}\Theta\mathbf{c} \wedge \mathbf{L}\mathbf{c} \geq \mathbf{1}\}. \tag{8}$$

There exist two scheduling schemes [7] for partitioned URE's: (i) all tasks of a partition are scheduled in parallel and the partitions are scheduled sequentially (LPGS-scheme) and (ii) all tasks of a partition are scheduled sequentially on one processor of the partition and the partitions are scheduled in parallel (LSGP-scheme).

It has been pointed out in [3], that a multiple application of this partitioning can be used for: (i) the adaptation of a full size array to a given fixed size as well as to a given I/O-behaviour by combining together the LPGS- and the LSGP-scheduling scheme, and (ii) for the mapping of URE's onto hierarchically structured computing systems.

Definition 4 (Nested Partitioning) *The nested partitioning scheme is a q-fold application of the partitioning (4) is defined by:*

$$\mathcal{I}_\pi^{(q)} = \{\mathbf{i}^{(q)} \mid \mathbf{i}^{(q)} = \mathbf{i}^{(q+1)} + \kappa_n \mathbf{u}$$

$$+ \mathbf{G} \sum_{j=1}^{q} \left(\prod_{l=0}^{j-1} \mathbf{\Theta}^{(l)} \right) \boldsymbol{\kappa}^{(j)}, \ \mathbf{i}^{(q)} \in \mathcal{I}\} \qquad (9)$$

with $0 \leq \kappa_z^{(j)} < \vartheta_z^{(j)}$, $z = 1, \ldots, n-1 \wedge \mathbf{\Theta}^{(j)} = diag(\vartheta_z^{(j)})$, $\mathbf{\Theta}^{(0)} = \mathbf{I}$. The set $\mathcal{I}_\pi^{(q+1)} = \{\mathbf{i}^{(q+1)}\}$ is given according to (5), where ϑ in the vector on the right hand side in (6) has to be replaced by $\vartheta^{(q)} = \left(\prod_{l=0}^{q-1} \vartheta_1^{(l)} \cdots \prod_{l=0}^{q-1} \vartheta_{n-1}^{(l)} \right)^t$.

3. I/O-processors of a partition

We assume, that input tasks from the peripheral circuitry to the array take place only at *input processors* $\mathbf{p}_{in}^* \in \mathcal{P}_\pi$ with $\mathbf{p}_{in}^* - \mathbf{v} \notin \mathcal{P}_\pi$, and output tasks from the array to the peripheral system take place only at *output processors* $\mathbf{p}_{out}^* \in \mathcal{P}_\pi$ with $\mathbf{p}_{out}^* + \mathbf{v} \notin \mathcal{P}_\pi$. We denote the set of all input processors in a partition (7) by $\mathcal{P}_{in}^*$, and the set of all output processors by $\mathcal{P}_{out}^*$. The I/O-processors w.r.t. a data dependence vector $\mathbf{d}$ and hence, w.r.t. an interconnection $\mathbf{S}\mathbf{d} = \mathbf{v} = \mathbf{N}\boldsymbol{\lambda}$, $\boldsymbol{\lambda} \in \mathcal{Z}^{n-1}$ are given by:

$$\mathcal{P}_{in}^* = \begin{cases} \mathcal{P}_\pi & \text{if } \exists \lambda_i : |\lambda_i| \geq \vartheta_i \\ \mathcal{P}_\pi & \text{if } \forall \lambda_i : \lambda_i = 0 \\ \mathcal{P}_\pi \setminus \tilde{\mathcal{P}}_{in} & \text{otherwise}, \end{cases} \qquad (10)$$

$$\tilde{\mathcal{P}}_{in} = \left\{ \mathbf{p} \mid \mathbf{p} = \mathbf{N}\tilde{\boldsymbol{\kappa}}, \ \begin{matrix} \lambda_i \leq \tilde{\kappa}_i < \vartheta_i & \text{if } 0 \leq \lambda_i < \vartheta_i \\ 0 \leq \tilde{\kappa}_i < \vartheta_i + \lambda_i & \text{if } 0 \leq -\lambda_i < \vartheta_i \end{matrix} \right\},$$

and

$$\mathcal{P}_{out}^* = \begin{cases} \mathcal{P}_\pi & \text{if } \exists \lambda_i : |\lambda_i| \geq \vartheta_i \\ \mathcal{P}_\pi & \text{if } \forall \lambda_i : \lambda_i = 0 \\ \mathcal{P}_\pi \setminus \tilde{\mathcal{P}}_{out} & \text{otherwise} \end{cases} \qquad (11)$$

$$\tilde{\mathcal{P}}_{out} = \left\{ \mathbf{p} \mid \mathbf{p} = \mathbf{N}\tilde{\boldsymbol{\kappa}}, \ \begin{matrix} 0 \leq \tilde{\kappa}_i < \vartheta_i - \lambda_i & \text{if } 0 \leq \lambda_i < \vartheta_i \\ -\lambda_i \leq \tilde{\kappa}_i < \vartheta_i & \text{if } 0 \leq -\lambda_i < \vartheta_i \end{matrix} \right\}.$$

4. Generation of I/O-streams for LPGS-partitioned URE's

We have to compute the first and the last time instance, defined by κ_n, at which a valid data item has to be transferred to/from the I/O-processor. We denote these time instances by $\kappa_{n,in/out}^{\min}$ and $\kappa_{n,in/out}^{\max}$ respectively. We assume that the considered data dependence vector is associated with a variable $x[f(\mathbf{i})]$, where $f(\mathbf{i}) = \mathbf{F}\mathbf{i} + \mathbf{f}$, $\mathbf{F} \in$

$\mathcal{Z}^{m \times n}$, $\mathbf{f} \in \mathcal{Z}^m$ is an affine index function. The components of the input stream of an input processor $\mathbf{p}_{in}^* \in \mathcal{P}_\pi$ are given by:

$$Inp\left(\mathbf{p}_{in}^*, t(\kappa_n)\right) = x[f(\mathbf{i}_{zero} + \mathbf{i}' + \mathbf{G}\mathbf{N}^{-1}\mathbf{p}_{in}^* + \kappa_n\mathbf{u})], \qquad (12)$$

where $\kappa_{n,in}^{\min} \leq \kappa_n \leq \kappa_{n,in}^{\max}$, and the components of the output stream of an output processor are given by:

$$Out\left(\mathbf{p}_{out}^*, t(\kappa_n)\right) = x[f(\mathbf{i}_{zero} + \mathbf{i}' + \mathbf{G}\mathbf{N}^{-1}\mathbf{p}_{out}^* + \kappa_n\mathbf{u})], \qquad (13)$$

where $\kappa_{n,out}^{\min} \leq \kappa_n \leq \kappa_{n,out}^{\max}$. The variable κ_n represents the hyperplane $\tau i = const.$, and the variable $t(\kappa_n)$ is the time instance relative to the begin of the scheduling period of the partition.

Example: Fig. (1a) and (1b) illustrate the problem for two data dependence vectors $\mathbf{d}_a = (0\ 1)^t$ and $\mathbf{d}_b = (-1\ 1)^t$ for the LPGS-partition at $\mathbf{i}' = (1\ 0)^t$

$$\mathcal{I}_\pi(\mathbf{i}') = \{\mathbf{i} | \mathbf{i} = \mathbf{i}_{zero} + (1\ 0)^t + (1\ 0)^t \kappa_1 + (1\ 1)^t \kappa_2\},$$

where $0 \leq \kappa_1 < 4$. The grey shadings emphasize the index points at which I/O-tasks occur. The limits $\kappa_{n,in/out}^{\min(\max)}$ for the example in Fig.(1) are given in table (1). •

We subdivide the set of data dependence vectors into two subsets $\mathcal{D}^0 = \{\mathbf{d} | \mathbf{S}\mathbf{d} = 0, \mathbf{d} \in \mathcal{D}\}$ and $\mathcal{D}^{\neq 0} = \mathcal{D} \setminus \mathcal{D}^0$. In the following, we refer to the variables introduced in Fig.(1). We turn to the computation of the limits $\kappa_{n,in/out}^{\min(\max)}$ for $\mathbf{d} \in \mathcal{D}^{\neq 0}$. The problem can be stated as follows:

$$\mathbf{i}^+ = \mathbf{i}^* + \alpha\mathbf{d} \leftrightarrow \begin{pmatrix} \boldsymbol{\kappa}^* \\ \kappa_n^* \end{pmatrix} = \begin{pmatrix} \boldsymbol{\kappa}^+ \\ \kappa_n^+ \end{pmatrix} - \alpha\mathbf{G}^{*-1}\mathbf{d}, \quad (14)$$

where $\kappa^{*(+)} = (\kappa_1^{*(+)} \ldots \kappa_{n-1}^{*(+)})^t$. We denote the inverse of $\mathbf{G}^*$ by $\mathbf{G}^{*-1} = \begin{pmatrix} \mathbf{\Gamma} \\ \gamma \end{pmatrix}$, where γ is the last row vector of $\mathbf{G}^{*-1}$. Hence, we obtain the following integer linear programs for the computation of the limits $\kappa_{n,in/out}^{\min(\max)}$.

Objective Function:

$$\kappa_n^* = \begin{pmatrix} \kappa_n^+ & \alpha \end{pmatrix} \begin{pmatrix} 1 \\ -\gamma\mathbf{d} \end{pmatrix} \rightarrow \begin{matrix} \min \\ (\max) \end{matrix}$$

Restrictions:

i) $\quad \kappa_n^+ - \alpha\mathbf{\Gamma}\mathbf{d} = \kappa_n^*$

ii) $\quad \begin{pmatrix} \mathbf{I} \\ -\mathbf{I} \end{pmatrix} \boldsymbol{\kappa}^* \geq \begin{pmatrix} 0 \\ -(\vartheta - 1) \end{pmatrix}$

iii) $\quad \begin{pmatrix} \mathbf{I} \\ -\mathbf{I} \end{pmatrix} \boldsymbol{\kappa}^+ \geq \begin{pmatrix} 0 \\ -(\vartheta - 1) \end{pmatrix}$

iv) $\quad \mathbf{A}\mathbf{G}^* \begin{pmatrix} \boldsymbol{\kappa}^+ \\ \kappa_n^+ \end{pmatrix} \geq \mathbf{a}_0 - \mathbf{A}(\mathbf{i}_{zero} + \mathbf{i}')$

v) $\quad \alpha \begin{matrix} \geq \\ (\leq) \end{matrix} 0$

The settings for the computation of the different limits are:

$$\kappa_n^* \to min \ \land \ \alpha \geq 0 \quad \kappa_{n,in}^{\min} \quad \text{first input at } \mathbf{p}^* = Si^*,$$
$$\kappa_n^* \to max \ \land \ \alpha \geq 0 \quad \kappa_{n,in}^{\max} \quad \text{last input at } \mathbf{p}^* = Si^*,$$
$$\kappa_n^* \to min \ \land \ \alpha \leq 0 \quad \kappa_{n,out}^{\min} \quad \text{first output at } \mathbf{p}^* = Si^*,$$
$$\kappa_n^* \to max \ \land \ \alpha \leq 0 \quad \kappa_{n,out}^{\max} \quad \text{last output at } \mathbf{p}^* = Si^*.$$

Note, that it is possible, that the solution set is empty for an I/O-processor. This case occurs if there is no computation allocated on the processing element in the partition. We

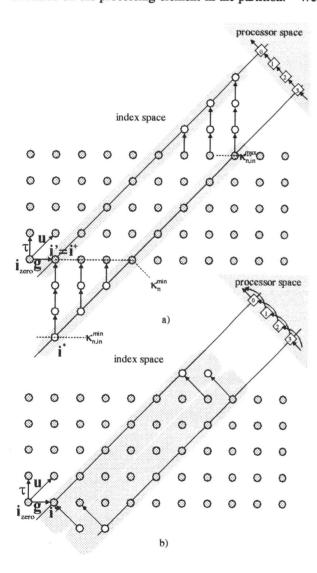

Figure 1. *Extension of an LPGS-partition for I/O-management*

unify the length of the I/O-streams of all $\mathbf{p}_{in}^* \in \mathcal{P}_{in}^*$ and $\mathbf{p}_{out}^* \in \mathcal{P}_{out}^*$ to the length of the whole scheduling sequence of the partition by adding of *idle signs* $*$. The begin of the

	$\mathbf{p}_{in}^*$	$\kappa_{n,in}^{\min}$	$\kappa_{n,in}^{\max}$	$\mathbf{p}_{out}^*$	$\kappa_{n,out}^{\min}$	$\kappa_{n,out}^{\max}$
$\mathbf{d}_a$	3	-3	4	0	0	7
$\mathbf{d}_b$	3	-1	4	0	0	5
	2	-1	4	1	0	5

Table 1. *Limits to example Fig.(1)*

scheduling sequence is given by:

$$\tilde{\kappa}_{n,in}^{\min} = \min_{\forall \mathbf{d} \in \mathcal{D}^{\neq 0} \land \forall \mathbf{p}_{in}^* \in \mathcal{P}_{in}^*} \kappa_{n,in}^{\min}(\mathbf{p}_{in}^*, \mathbf{d}), \quad (15)$$

and the termination of the scheduling sequence is given by:

$$\tilde{\kappa}_{n,out}^{\max} = \max_{\forall \mathbf{d} \in \mathcal{D}^{\neq 0} \land \forall \mathbf{p}_{out}^* \in \mathcal{P}_{out}^*} \kappa_{n,out}^{\max}(\mathbf{p}_{out}^*, \mathbf{d}). \quad (16)$$

The next step is to include also the interconnections $\mathbf{d} \in \mathcal{D}^0$. Here, it is obviously not possible to use the associated interconnections to transfer the variables from and/or to the inner processors. A simple solution to this problem is to use interconnections which are associated with data dependence vectors which are not mapped onto the zero vector. This proposal has the advantage, that we obtain a homogeneous I/O-behaviour also for the input and output phases.

A minimal time demand for the input phase results if we distribute the input tasks for the $\mathbf{d} \in \mathcal{D}^0$ onto the interconnections associated with the $\mathbf{d} \in \mathcal{D}^{\neq 0}$, such that:

$$\min_{\forall \mathbf{d}_j \in \mathcal{D}^{\neq 0}} \left(\tilde{\kappa}_{n,in}^{z\,min}(j) - \varepsilon_j \big(\kappa_n^{min} - \tilde{\kappa}_{n,in}^{z\,min}(j) \big) \right) \to max.$$

$$\text{and} \quad \sum_{j=1}^{|\mathcal{D}^{\neq 0}|} \varepsilon_j = |\mathcal{D}^0| \quad (17)$$

holds, where κ_n^{min} represents the first computation in the partition, if the I/O-problem is omitted (see Fig.(1)). The variable $\tilde{\kappa}_{n,in}^{z\,min} = \min_{\forall \mathbf{p}^* \in \mathcal{P}_{in}^*} \kappa_{n,in}^{min}(\mathbf{p}^*)$ tags the first time instance at which one of the variables which are associated with the data dependence vector $\mathbf{d}$ has to be put into an input processor $\mathbf{p}^* \in \mathcal{P}_{in}^*$. Note, that this procedure can be used to send control data for initialization purposes to the processors.

5. Generation of I/O-streams for LSGP-partitioned LPGS-partitions of URE's

The basic idea of combining together the LPGS- and LSGP-partitioning scheme [3] can be stated as follows: Find a partitioning $(\{\vartheta_j\}, \mathbf{G})$ which can be decomposed into $\{\vartheta_j = \vartheta_j^{LSGP} \vartheta_j^{LPGS}\}$, such that the mean value $\Omega / \det \Theta^{LSGP}$ of the I/O-demand Ω is adjusted to the given

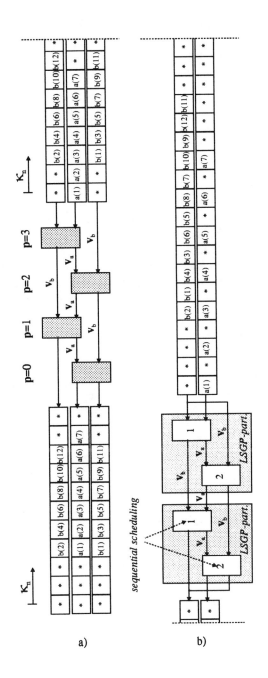

a)   b)

Figure 2. *I/O-streams at the fixed fize array and at the nested partitioned array*

notation for a partition in the index space:

$$\mathcal{I}_\pi = \{\mathbf{i} \mid \mathbf{i} = \mathbf{i}' + \kappa_n \mathbf{u} +$$

$$\mathbf{G}\left(\mathbf{\Theta}^{LSGP}\boldsymbol{\kappa}^{LPGS} + \boldsymbol{\kappa}^{LSGP}\right) \wedge \mathbf{i} \in \mathcal{I}\} \qquad (18)$$

with $\mathbf{\Theta}^{LSGP} = diag(\vartheta_j^{LSGP}), 0 \le \kappa_j^{LSGP} < \vartheta_j^{LSGP}, 0 \le \kappa_j^{LPGS} < \vartheta_j^{LPGS}, j = 1, \ldots, n-1$.

The set $\mathcal{I}'_\pi = \{\mathbf{i}'\}$ is given according to equations (5) and (6), where $\mathbf{\Theta} = \mathbf{\Theta}^{LPGS}\mathbf{\Theta}^{LSGP}$.

Hence, the computation tasks, which belong to an LSGP-partition are given by:

$$\mathcal{I}_\pi^{LSGP} = \{\mathbf{i}|\mathbf{i} = \mathbf{i}_{ref} + \mathbf{G}\boldsymbol{\kappa}^{LSGP} + \kappa_n \mathbf{u} \wedge \mathbf{i} \in \mathcal{I}\}, \quad (19)$$

where $\mathbf{i}_{ref} = \mathbf{i}_{zero} + \mathbf{i}' + \mathbf{G}\mathbf{\Theta}^{LSGP}\boldsymbol{\kappa}^{LPGS}$. Hence, an LSGP-partition in the processor space is given by:

$$\mathcal{P}_\pi^{LSGP} = \{\mathbf{p}|\mathbf{p} = \mathbf{p}_{ref} + \mathbf{N}\boldsymbol{\kappa}^{LSGP} \wedge \mathbf{p} \in \mathcal{P}\}, \quad (20)$$

where $\mathbf{p}_{ref} = \mathbf{S}\mathbf{i}_{ref}$. The computation tasks, which are allocated on an LSGP-partition are scheduled sequentially on one processor of the partition. Hence, we have to take into account the sequentialized computations by a modification of the κ_n-axis. We suppose, that we consider an (extented) LPGS-partition of size $0 \le \kappa_j^{LPGS} < \vartheta_j^{LSGP}\vartheta_j^{LPGS}$. We obtain the limits $\kappa_{n,in/out}^{min(max)}$ as described in the previous section. Now, we take into account the sequential scheduling of the tasks in the LSGP-partitions by stretching the κ_n-axis as follows:

$$\hat{\kappa}_{n,in}^{min} \le \hat{\kappa}_n < \hat{\kappa}_{n,out}^{max}, \qquad (21)$$

$$\hat{\kappa}_{n,in}^{min} = \tilde{\kappa}_{n,in}^{min},$$

$$\hat{\kappa}_{n,out}^{max} = (\tilde{\kappa}_{n,out}^{max} - \tilde{\kappa}_{n,in}^{min} + 1)\det\mathbf{\Theta}^{LSGP} + \tilde{\kappa}_{n,in}^{min},$$

where $\tilde{\kappa}_{n,in}^{min}$ is given by (15), and $\tilde{\kappa}_{n,out}^{max}$ is given by (16). The $\hat{\kappa}_n-$axis is the stretched κ_n-axis. Hence, an instance of κ_n is mapped onto an interval of the $\hat{\kappa}_n-$axis:

$$\hat{\kappa}_n = \tilde{\kappa}_{n,in}^{min} + (\kappa_n - \tilde{\kappa}_{n,in}^{min})\det\mathbf{\Theta}^{LSGP} + r$$

$$0 \le r < \det\mathbf{\Theta}^{LSGP}. \qquad (22)$$

The inverse mapping of (22) is :

$$\kappa_n = \tilde{\kappa}_{n,in}^{min} + \left\lfloor \frac{\hat{\kappa}_n - \tilde{\kappa}_{n,in}^{min}}{\det\mathbf{\Theta}^{LSGP}} \right\rfloor \qquad (23)$$

We assume that all processors $\mathbf{p} \in \mathcal{P}_\pi^{LSGP}$ of an LSGP-partition (20) are mapped onto $\mathbf{p}_{ref}$. A processor $\mathbf{p}_{ref}$ of an LSGP-partitioned LPGS-partition is called an I/O-processor $\mathbf{p}_{ref,in/out}^*$, if one of the processors which are mapped onto

limit Ω^* of the I/O-capacity, and $\mathbf{\Theta}^{LPGS}$ represents the layout of the given target machine. Fig.(2b) depicts an example in the processor space with $\vartheta_1^{LPGS} = \vartheta_1^{LSGP} = 2$. The mean value of the I/O-demand has been decreased from 6 (Fig.2a) to 3 tasks per clock cycle. For the sake of a simple illustration of the discussed I/O-problem, we choose for the example (Fig.2b) only two processors for the LPGS-partition. The formalization of this idea yields the following

$\mathbf{p}_{ref}$ is an I/O-processor in the extented LPGS-partition. We define that the I/O-stream of a processing element without input (output) tasks and which is mapped onto $\mathbf{p}^*_{ref,in/out}$ consists entirely of idle signs. So, all $\mathbf{p} \in \mathcal{P}^{LSGP}_\pi$ have to perform an input (output) task at time instance κ_n before the sequential scheduling has been introduced. Now, the input (output) task of a processor $\mathbf{p} \in \mathcal{P}^{LSGP}_\pi$ is performed at one of the time instances in the interval according to (22). We derive the I/O-stream of $\mathbf{p}^*_{ref,in/out}$ by defining that for all $\mathbf{p} \in \mathcal{P}^{LSGP}_\pi$ holds, that the data item which has to be transferred at κ_n on $\mathbf{p}$ is on the I/O-stream of $\mathbf{p}$ in the entire interval (22) and the function which defines the sequential scheduling generates from all these I/O-streams the I/O-stream of $\mathbf{p}^*_{ref,in/out}$.

The scheduling of the computation tasks of an LSGP-partition is a bijective mapping $\{\kappa^{LSGP}\} \to \{t^{LSGP}\} = \{0, \ldots, \det \Theta^{LSGP} - 1\}$. We denote the scheduling function by $\sigma(\kappa^{LSGP}) = t^{LSGP}$. We obtain the input/(output)-stream for a processor $\mathbf{p}^*_{ref,in,(out)}$ by:

$$Inp\left(\mathbf{p}^*_{ref,in}, \hat{\kappa}_n\right) = Inp\left(\mathbf{p}(\kappa^{LSGP}), t(\kappa_n)\right), \quad (24)$$

$$Out\left(\mathbf{p}^*_{ref,out}, \hat{\kappa}_n\right) = Out\left(\mathbf{p}(\kappa^{LSGP}), t(\kappa_n)\right), \quad (25)$$

$$\mathbf{p}(\kappa^{LSGP}) = \mathbf{p}_{ref} + N\kappa^{LSGP},$$

$$\kappa^{LSGP} = \sigma^{-1}\left((\hat{\kappa}_n - \tilde{\kappa}^{\min}_{n,in}) \bmod \det \Theta^{LSGP}\right),$$

$$t(\kappa_n) = t\left(\left\lfloor \frac{\hat{\kappa}_n - \tilde{\kappa}^{\min}_{n,in}}{\det \Theta^{LSGP}} \right\rfloor + \tilde{\kappa}^{\min}_{n,in}\right),$$

The bounds of $\hat{\kappa}_n$ are given by (21). Fig.(2a) shows the I/O-streams before and Fig.(2b) after an LSGP-partitioning of the LPGS-partition in Fig.(1), where $\vartheta^{LSGP} = 2$.

6. Extension to $q-$fold partitioned URE's

We consider an array architecture with an hierarchy of $h_{\max}$ levels. The adjustment of the parameters at each level requires a combined partitioning (LSGP,LPGS) at each level. Hence, we have a $2h_{\max}-$fold nested partitioning. According to [3], we define that all LSGP-paramaters in (9) are represented by the odd indices q and the LPGS-parameters by the even indices q. To obtain the I/O-streams for level h, we assume that first level h is an extented LPGS-partition of size $0 \le \kappa^h_j < \prod^{2h}_{l=1} \vartheta^l_j$ for the computation of $\mathcal{P}^*_{in,(out)}$.

The κ_n-axis has to be stretched as follows:

$$\hat{\kappa}^{\min}_{n,in} = \tilde{\kappa}^{\min}_{n,in} \le \hat{\kappa}_n < \hat{\kappa}^{\max}_{n,out} \quad (26)$$

$$\hat{\kappa}^{\max}_{n,out} = (\tilde{\kappa}^{\max}_{n,out} - \tilde{\kappa}^{\min}_{n,in} + 1) \det\left(\prod^{h_{\max}}_{l=1} \Theta^{(2l-1)}_j\right) + \tilde{\kappa}^{\min}_{n,in},$$

where $\tilde{\kappa}^{\min}_{n,in}$ is given by (15), and $\tilde{\kappa}^{\max}_{n,out}$ is given by (16). The $\hat{\kappa}_n-$axis is the stretched κ_n-axis.

The I/O-streams $Inp\left(\mathbf{p}^{*,(h)}_{ref,in}\right)$, $Out\left(\mathbf{p}^{*,(h)}_{ref,out}\right)$ at level h are given by (24) and (25) respectively, where $\det \Theta^{LSGP}$ has to be replaced by $\det\left(\prod^{h_{\max}}_{l=1} \Theta^{(2l-1)}_j\right)$.

7. Conclusion

A mathematical framework has been given for the generation of I/O-streams for in general hierarchically structured systolic array architectures for the processing of systems of URE's. We considered a combination of sequential and parallel scheduling at each level of the system. The results represent a basis for the automatic synthesis of the peripheral programs for the controlling of the array architecture by computing the I/O access pattern of the array.

References

[1] J. Bu. *Systematic design of regular VLSI processor arrays*. PhD thesis, Delft University of Technology, 1990.

[2] E. D'Hollander. Partitioning and labeling of loops by unimodular transformations. *IEEE Trans. on PDS*, 3(4), July 1992.

[3] U. Eckhardt. Nested partitioning. Technical Report SFB 358-A1-2/96, Deutsche Forschungsgemeinschaft, TU Dresden, 1996.

[4] D. Feitelson, P. Corbett, S. Baylor, and Y. Hsu. Parallel I/O subsystems in massively parallel supercomputers. *IEEE Parallel & Distributed Technology*, Fall 1995.

[5] D. Fimmel and R. Merker. Propagation of I/O-variables in massively parallel processor arrays. In *Proc. 4th Euromicro Workshop on Parallel and Distributed Processing*, 1996.

[6] H. Jagadish, S. Rao, and T. Kailath. Array architectures for iterative algorithms. *Proc. of the IEEE*, 75(9), Sept. 1987.

[7] K. Jainandunsing. Optimal partitioning scheme for wavefront/systolic array processors. In *Proc. IEEE Symp. on Circuits and Systems*, 1986.

[8] R. Karp, R. Miller, and S. Winograd. The organization of computations for uniform recurrence equations. *Journal of the ACM*, 14(3), July 1967.

[9] L. Lamport. Parallel execution of DO loops. *Communications of the ACM*, 17(2), Feb. 1974.

[10] D. Moldovan and J. Fortes. Partitioning and mapping of algorithms into fixed-size systolic arrays. *IEEE Trans. Computers*, C35(1), Jan. 1986.

[11] H. Nelis and E. Deprettere. Automatic design and partitioning of systolic/wavefront arrays for VLSI. *Circuits systems signal processing*, 7(2), 1988.

[12] J.-K. Peir and R. Cytron. Minimum distance: A method for partitioning recurrences for multiprocessors. *IEEE Trans. on Computers*, 38(8), Aug. 1989.

[13] J. Teich and L. Thiele. Partitioning of processor arrays: a piecewise regular approach. *INTEGRATION, the VLSI journal*, 14, 1993.

Distributed Algorithm Development with PVM-Prolog

José C. Cunha, Rui F. P. Marques
Universidade Nova de Lisboa
Departamento de Informática
2825 Monte de Caparica
Portugal
$(jcc|rfm)@di.fct.unl.pt$

Abstract

The design of parallel and distributed algorithms poses many difficulties. This has motivated proposals of high-level languages for parallel program composition, their physical distribution in multiprocessor architectures, specification of communication and synchronization, and failure handling. In this paper, we describe an approach for prototyping parallel and distributed programs, that is based on a logic programming system called PVM-Prolog. PVM-Prolog is a programming interface from Prolog to the PVM system, offering all PVM functionalities to the logic programmer such as process spawning and control, virtual machine management, and failure handling. We describe the PVM-Prolog model and illustrate its application.

Keywords: Distributed algorithms, logic programming, PVM.

1. Introduction

Explicit specification of parallelism and distribution at the user level is required by many applications. In order to overcome the difficulties in designing parallel and distributed processing systems, there is a demand for advanced programming environments providing an integrated view of the specification and execution stages, including debugging, performance evaluation and program visualization [5]. Therefore it is important to use very high-level notations for parallel program decomposition and communication which could also be integrated with low-level run-time tools. A compromise must be achieved between the required user transparency degrees, and the need of providing control of low-level execution, e.g. for performance tuning.

Among the high-level notations, logic programming models offer many interesting characteristics, namely clarity and ease of programming, and facility for developing rapid prototypes. On the other hand, classical logic languages such as Prolog, pose several difficulties concerning efficient implementations and support for large scale program development. The past decade has shown many relevant proposals to use logic languages for parallel and distributed programming, in search for an adequate model to express interactions among multiple autonomous components of an application. However, high-level logic concurrency definitions are difficult to conciliate with the requirements for efficient implementations and low-level control of the execution environment.

As a solution to these problems, we have proposed PVM-Prolog [1] [2] [3], a Prolog interface to the PVM environment [4]. PVM-Prolog allows programming using the Prolog style, and some degree of control of the system level abstractions. As it is an intermediate layer, it has simple concurrency semantics which are in fact inherited from the ones of PVM, suitably adapted to a logic framework. On the other hand this layer provides the basic platform upon which one can implement more high-level language models, or applications. Also for several Artificial Intelligence applications there is the requirement to model a system through a collection of cooperating agents. Current research in this area is studying the reasoning and behavioral models for such agents, and modified Prolog interpreters can be used for this purpose. The interactions between agents can be tested under real distributed settings by using PVM-Prolog as the implementation layer to support inter-agent communication, agent distribution, as well as concurrency within each agent. We must stress the fact that PVM-Prolog is a low-level programming layer that can typically be used to build the above mentioned high-level abstractions.

By expressing parallelism, distribution, communication schemes, and virtual machine management in PVM-Prolog, the user is freed from certain low-level details, and can concentrate mainly on the logical organization of the applications. In a first stage of application development it is easy to obtain a rapid prototype that can be used to test and debug logical correctness, and to experiment with alternative configurations of the parallel PVM virtual machine towards better performance. These requirements can also partially be met by other low-level distributed Prolog systems such as SICStus Prolog and IC-Prolog II which support TCP/IP socket based communication [11, 12]. However, the PVM-Prolog system is more easy to install and to use, and it is easily portable to a large number of hardware platforms.

At this point we have developed a fully operational PVM-Prolog implementation[1], and we are currently developing tools such as a high-level distributed debugger, and a monitoring system.

This paper illustrates the PVM-Prolog programming model through a few simple examples involving both parallel and distributed processing issues. In section 2 we describe the fundamental concepts of the PVM-Prolog model. In section 3 we give some simple examples. Finally we conclude by briefly discussing ongoing work.

2. The PVM-Prolog Programming Model

The PVM-Prolog system consists of two distinct components: the virtual machine (PPVM) and the process engine (PE). The process engine is the building block that represents the computing entities in a particular PVM-Prolog application. It supports a specific core inference engine for Prolog, or for a different language, as the PPVM interface allows the control and communication in programs composed of heterogeneous multilingual components. The virtual machine (PPVM - Parallel Prolog Virtual Machine) provides primitives for the activation and control of process engines, interprocess communication and synchronization, and management of the execution environment.

2.1. The PPVM interface

All of the PVM functionalities are accessible at the Prolog level, through a raw interface to PVM, called PPVM0 that is implemented as a set of Prolog built-in predicates. Messages are interpreted as Prolog terms,

and extensions to PVM pack and unpack functions are provided in order to convert term representations in hybrid heterogeneous applications. C data types such as character strings, arrays, and structures are converted, respectively, to Prolog atoms, lists, and compound terms, and vice-versa. All of the interface predicates exhibit a strict deterministic behavior, i.e. they all fail on backtracking.

On top of PPVM0, an upper layer – PPVM1 – offers a higher-level semantics for process control and communication as described in [1] [2] [3].

Task identification, entry and exit to PVM-Prolog PVM-Prolog processes correspond to PVM tasks.[2]

The `pvm_mytid( -tid )` predicate allows a PVM task to determine its own unique PVM *Task Identifier*, and if the process is not already a PVM task, it becomes so. The `pvm_exit` predicate detaches a process from the PVM environment.

Task creation and destruction `pvm_spawn` creates new PVM-Prolog tasks.[3] Here we assume an homogeneous PVM-Prolog system with the Prolog engine defined by default[4].

```
pvm_spawn( +progname, +goal,
           +opt_list, +where,
           +ntasks, -tid_list,
           +StacksSize, +HeapSize )
```

`ntasks` are created to solve the given `goal` in the presence of the specified program. `progname` is the name of the file containing the Prolog program. The task identifiers of these processes are returned in `tid_list`. A PVM task is spawned for executing an instance of the NanoProlog engine which will consult the specified Prolog file. Then the specified `goal` is activated. The new process is completely detached from its parent, and all its interactions with other processes must be explicitly programmed. All known PVM options are available in `opt_list` concerning the specification of a specific machine, or architecture type for running the newly created process.

A task can invoke `pvm_kill` to terminate another task. `pvm_exit` allows a task to exit from PVM.

---

[2] In predicate definitions we use the convention of putting a + for input arguments, - for output and ? for input/output ones. Square brackets ([]) denote optional parts on predicate names, compacting the definition of similar predicates.

[3] The raw interface provides a more basic form for this predicate, supporting the spawning of different types of process engines.

[4] Our current prototype relies upon the WAM model as the process engine, based upon a system called NanoProlog, developed at our Department by A. M. Dias [7].

---

[1] The system is available by contacting the authors.

Communication At PPVM1 level, a reasonable transparency is preserved concerning communication management. We have hiden all PVM buffer manipulation primitives [4] because all Prolog representations are based on terms. However, at the PPVM0 level, one must use PPVM0 predicates for packing and unpacking terms so that conversions between Prolog and C can be performed under program control.

`pvm_send( +tid, +msgtag, +term )` sends messages to another task, while `pvm_mcast( +tid_list, +msgtag, +term )` multicasts messages to several recipients given by `tid_list`.

`pvm_recv( ?tid, ?msgtag, -msg )` performs a blocking receive, while `pvm_nrecv` performs a non-blocking receive and fails if there's no pending message at invocation time. The message tag (`msgtag`) may be a positive integer, such that only messages with that tag will be accepted, or it can be an uninstantiated variable if we want to accept any incoming message. The tid may also be an uninstantiated variable, if messages are to be accepted from any sender.

Management of the PVM configuration Some control and status information may be obtained concerning the configuration of the PVM host machines and tasks by invoking the following predicates.

`pvm_mstat( +host, -mstat )` provides information about host status by returning `mstat` instantiated to the host status (ok, down, unknown). `pvm_config( -nhost, -narch, -hostlist )` reports on the global configuration of the PVM virtual machine, namely, number of hosts, number of distinct architecture types, and a list of terms, one for each host, with information on its characteristics.

`pvm_tasks( +which, -ntasks, -tasklist )` requests PVM task status information through the `which` numeric parameter: all tasks in the PVM environment; all the tasks in the given host; or just the task identified by tid.

Dynamic configuration of the virtual machine is possible through insertion and removal of hosts:

`pvm_addhosts( +hostlist, -infolist )` gives a list of hosts to be included into the environment and `infolist` is a list returning the success codes of this operation, for each machine. `pvm_delhosts( +hostlist, -infolist )` deletes the given hosts from the PVMenvironment.

Task Groups PVM-Prolog also gives access to PVM grouping mechanisms by providing predicates for joining and leaving groups, as well as communication and synchronization operations [1] [4].

2.2. A Multithreaded Prolog Engine

It is possible to run a PVM-Prolog application consisting of multiple distinct Prolog engines, i.e. single or multi-threaded, or even supporting internal forms of implicit parallelism. They all use the same PPVM interface for communication and process control.

We have extended a core inference engine for sequential Prolog in order to support multiple threads of control, by managing multiple goal execution contexts. Threads are useful when there is a need for internal concurrency to an agent. In a multi-agent system, each agent may be required to react to some event when it is executing some other computation. Threads also allow to exploit concurrency with smaller overhead than conventional, heavy-weighted, processes.

Threads A Prolog process is a place for the concurrent execution of multiple threads, each solving its own goal, and sharing the same logic program (set of Prolog clauses). Each thread has an unique *Thread Identifier*. Within each process threads execute one at a time. When a process starts, an initial thread with identifier 0 is created, which will usually, in an interactive process, run the Prolog interpreter. Threads are dynamically created and terminated as follows.

`t_create(+Goal,+Stacks,+Priority,-ThID)` creates a new thread, by specifying the goal for the new thread to solve, and a thread identifier is returned in ThID. The new thread is put into the ready state, and the invoking thread proceeds with its execution. `t_kill(+ThID)` allows a thread to terminate the execution of another (or even itself!). There is no variable sharing among individually created threads from a given clause. Furthermore `t_create` is always successful; any failure in the child thread must be explicitly handled by the program. `t_mytid(-ThID)` enables a thread to determine its own identifier.

Threads with the same priority are scheduled in a round robin fashion. The currently running thread may yield the control to another ready thread by calling `t_switch`, or else run until either it blocks, or until it invokes a control predicate and some higher priority thread becomes ready, or until it its timeslice period expires. Each priority has an associated FIFO scheduling queue, and higher priority threads always preempt lower priority ones (at the mentioned preemption points.)

Thread Communication Thread communication and synchronization within a process is based on *Term Queues*, where threads may *put* and *get* terms, in FIFO order, by using the following predicates.

`queue_put( +Queue, +Term )` puts a `Term` into Queue in a nonblocking way. `queue_get( +Queue, -Term )` consumes a term from `Queue`, instantiating `Term` to it. If the queue is empty, the thread blocks. If `queue_nget` (non-blocking) is used, the predicate fails when the queue is empty, otherwise it behaves like `queue_get`. A thread can also test if a queue is empty without blocking, by calling `queue_empty` or can non-deterministically select a term in a list of term queues by invoking the predicate `queue_[n]select` (see [1]).

As there is no variable sharing between threads, once a term is passed onto another thread, all its uninstantiated variables are "freshened" (replaced by newly created ones). No automatic backtracking coordination is implied concerning thread communication through term queues.

Binding Messages and queues Signals and messages can be explicitly received by a PVM-Prolog program, through a mechanism for automatic handling of signal and messages. A message sent to a PVM-Prolog process may be automatically saved in a term queue, with `msg_bind(+FromTID,+Tag,+Queue,-BID)`. The given queue is bound to the event corresponding to the arrival of any message coming from the specified process with the given tag. In case these two arguments are uninstantiated, then any messages can be caught by this mechanism. Messages are automatically put into the queue as they arrive, and they are simply consumed by invoking `queue_get`.

3. Examples

In this section we present a few simple examples which illustrate the PVM-Prolog model.

3.1. A multithreaded remote query evaluator

We describe how to spawn remote "goal servers." Each goal server corresponds to a rule data base (Prolog program). It executes remote queries and delivers answers to a client program. For simplicity, only a single client is assumed, but it is easy to change the program to handle multiple clients.

The server is created with the command:

```
start_server( ProgName, TID ) :-
        pvm_spawn( goal_server,
                   server(ProgName),
                   [], [], 1, [TID] ).
```

`ProgName` is the file containing the data base. The server's `TID` (task id) is later used by a client to start new goals:

```
start_goal( TID, Goal, Tag, Number ) :-
        pvm_send( TID, 1, Goal/Tag/Number ).
```

The term that is sent in this message carries information for the server process: `Goal`, the goal that must be evaluated, `Number` the number of solutions to be obtained, possible values being `one` or `all`, and `Tag`, the message tag that is used later to get the answers from the server:

```
get_answer( TID, Tag, Answer ) :-
        pvm_recv( TID, Tag, Answer ).
```

The server process waits for the arrival of new goals, and executes them, using `t_create` to ensure that multiple queries are evaluated concurrently.

```
server(ProgName) :-
    [ProgName],
    msg_bind(AnyTask,1,goalqueue,_),!,
    repeat,
      queue_get( goalqueue, Goal/Tag/Number ),
      t_create( answers( Goal, Tag, Number ) ).
    fail.
```

The **answers** predicate computes one or all answers, sending them to the server. After producing all the answers, a `fail` atom is sent, meaning no more answers.

```
answers( Goal, Tag, Only1 ) :-
        Goal, deliver_answer(Goal, Tag),
        Only1=one.
answers( Goal, Tag, _ )       :-
        deliver_answer( fail, Tag ).
deliver_answer( Answer, Tag ) :-
        pvm_parent(PTID),
        pvm_send(PTID, Tag, Answer).
```

3.2. PVM controlling predicates

The PVM-Prolog interpreter can be used as an interactive shell to PVM, through the direct use of interface predicates. More powerful control predicates are easily implemented, e.g. `pvm_reset`, a predicate that kills all user processes in the current environment (except the killer process).

```
pvm_reset :-
    pvm_tasks(0, L, _),
    member(taskinfo(TID,_,_,_), L),
    not pvm_mytid(TID),
    pvm_kill(TID),
    fail.
pvm_reset.
```

214

4. Conclusions

We have described a programming interface supporting several forms of explicit parallelism and distribution of programs in a PVM environment.

Multiple applications of the PVM-Prolog model are being exploited in the scope of several research projects in which we are participating: as the implementation language to build a parallelised Prolog interpreter for non-monotonic reasoning with explicit negation [8] [9], with application to the domain of model-based diagnosis [10]; to implement shell and controller processes that are able to activate and manage the software components of a distributed processing system, as well as to build specialized intelligent interfaces that must access services which are implemented in distinct languages; as the distribution and communication control platform that supports cooperation among multiple multiprocessing sites, each supporting a specific computation model [6].

Acknowledgments

This research was supported in part by Programa Ciência, project PRO-LOPPE (PRAXIS/3/3.1/TIT/24/94) and DEC EERP PADIPRO, (P-005).

References

[1] R. Marques, J.C. Cunha. *PVM-Prolog: Parallel Logic Programming in the PVM System.* Procs. of the 1995 PVM User's Group Meeting, Pittsburgh, May 1995.

[2] R. Marques, J.C. Cunha. *Using PVM with a Logic Programming Interface.* Procs. of the Second Euro PVM User's Group Meeting, Lyon, September 1995.

[3] J.C. Cunha, R. Marques. *PVM-Prolog: A Prolog Interface to PVM.* In Proceedings of the 1st Austrian-Hungarian Workshop on Distributed and Parallel Systems, DAPSYS'96, Miskolc, Hungary, October 1996.

[4] A, Beguelin, J.J. Dongarra, G.A. Geist, R. Manchek, V.S. Sunderam. *A User's Guide to PVM Parallel Virtual Machine.* Technical Report, ORNL/TM-118266, Oak Ridge National Laboratory, 1991.

[5] S. Winter, P. Kacsuk. *Software Engineering for Parallel Processing.* Proc. of the 8th Symp. on Microcomputer and Microprocessor Applications, Budapest, 1994, pp. 285-293.

[6] P. Kacsuk. *LOGFLOW: Prolog on Massively Parallel Machines.* Invited Paper in the Proc. of the 6th Conf. on Artificial Intelligence and Information-Control Systems of Robots, 1994, pp. 71-80.

[7] A.M. Dias. *Implementation of Contextual Logic Programming System.* M.Sc. Dissertation, IST-UTL, 1990.

[8] L.M. Pereira, J.J. Alferes. *Well founded semantics for Logic Programs with Explicit Negation.* In B. Neumann (ed.), European Conf. on AI, pp. 102-106, J. Wiley & Sons, 1992.

[9] L.M. Pereira, J.C. Cunha, L. Damas. *Parallel Logic Programming with Extensions.* Proc. GULP PRODE'95, Joint Conf. on Declarative Programming, Italy, September 1995.

[10] I.A. Mora, J.J. Alferes. *Modelling Diagnosis Systems with Logic Programming.* Procs. of 7th Portuguese AI Conf., LNAI, Springer-Verlag, Funchal, Oct . 1995.

[11] M. Carlsson, J. Widen. *SICStus Prolog User Manual.* Research Report, Kista, Sweden, 1988.

[12] D. Chu. *I.C.Prolog II: A Language for Implementing Multi-Agent Systems.* Proceedings of the Special Interest Group on Cooperating Knowledge Based Systems, Keele, September 1992.

Language and Library Support for Practical PRAM Programming*

Christoph W. Keßler

FB 4 Informatik, Universität Trier
D-54286 Trier, Germany
kessler@psi.uni-trier.de

Jesper Larsson Träff†

Max–Planck–Institut für Informatik
D-66123 Saarbrücken, Germany
traff@mpi-sb.mpg.de

Abstract *We investigate the well-known PRAM model of parallel computation as a* practical *parallel programming model. The two components of this project are a general-purpose PRAM programming language called Fork95, and a library, called PAD, of efficient, basic parallel algorithms and data structures. We outline the primary features of Fork95 as they apply to the implementation of PAD. We give a brief overview of PAD and sketch the implementation of library routines for prefix-sums and bucket sorting. Both language and library can be used with the SB-PRAM, an emulation of the PRAM in hardware.*

1 Introduction

We describe a project investigating the PRAM (see e.g. [8]) as a *practical programming model*. The components of the project are a general-purpose programming language for PRAMs, called *Fork95*, and a library of basic *PRAM Algorithms and Data structures*, called *PAD*. The central theme of the project is efficiency: The programming language must be adequate for the implementation of parallel algorithms as found in the literature, and efficiently compilable to the target machine; the library should include the most efficient algorithms (in terms of parallel work, as well as constants), and support easy implementation of more involved algorithms. Although not dependent on a particular physical realization of the PRAM model, this work is immediately applicable to the SB-PRAM [1], a physical realization of a Priority CRCW PRAM built by W. J. Paul's group at the University of Saarbrücken. A 128 PE prototype is operational; the full 4096 PE version is under construction.

This paper reports on work in progress. A very brief outline was given in [12]. Fork95 is described in detail in[1] [10, 11], PAD[2] in [18, 19].

---

*This work was partially supported by ESPRIT LTR Project no. 20244 - ALCOM-IT

†This author was supported by DFG, SFB 124-D6, VLSI Entwurfsmethoden und Parallelität.

[1] These reports are available at the Fork95 homepage at http://www.informatik.uni-trier.de/~kessler/fork95.html or ftp://ftp.informatik.uni-trier.de/pub/users/Kessler. The Fork95 kit contains the compiler, documentation, a simulator for the SB-PRAM, and small example programs.

[2] Documentation and a first release of PAD is available at http://www.mpi-sb.mpg.de/guide/activities/alcom-it/PAD.

2 Fork95 features used in PAD

Fork95 is a language for explicit programming of synchronous shared memory computers (PRAMs) in the SPMD (Single Program, Multiple Data) paradigm. Hence concepts like processors, processor ID's, shared memory, and synchronicity are explicit to the programmer. In contrast to the unlimited number of processors often assumed in the PRAM literature, Fork95 supports only a fixed number of processors, as determined by the underlying hardware. Fork95 offers means for deviating from strictly synchronous execution, in particular asynchronous program regions where exact statement-level synchrony is not enforced. Fork95 grew out of a proposal [5] for a strictly synchronous PRAM programming language, but has been based on the C programming language, from which it inherits features like pointers, dynamic arrays, etc. Carefully chosen defaults permit inclusion of existing C sources without any syntactical change. The asynchronous mode of computation (the default mode) allows to save synchronization points and enables more freedom of choice for the programming model.

For efficiency reasons the significant run time overhead of virtual processor emulation has been abandoned by restricting the number of processes to the hardware resources, resulting in a very lean code generation and run time system. To compensate for this conceptual drawback, the library routines of PAD can be called by any number of processors and with data instances of arbitrary size. Additionally, "parallel iterators" are provided for common data types such as arrays, lists, trees etc., which helps the programmer to schedule the processors evenly over data instances larger than the number of processors.

Fork95 supports many parallel programming paradigms, such as data parallelism, strictly synchronous execution, farming, asynchronous sequential processes including parallel critical sections, pipelining, parallel divide-and-conquer, and parallel prefix computation [10].

2.1 Shared and private variables

The entire shared memory of the PRAM is partitioned into private address subspaces (one for each processor) and a shared address subspace, as configured by the programmer. Accordingly, variables are classified either as private (declared with the storage class qualifier `pr`, this is the default) or as shared (`sh`), where "shared" always relates to the group of processors (see Subsection 2.5) that defined that variable. Private variables and objects exist once for each processor.

The usage of pointers in Fork95 is as flexible as in C, since all private address subspaces have been embedded into the global shared memory. In particular, one does not have to distinguish between pointers to shared and pointers to private objects, in contrast to some other parallel programming languages, for example C* (see eg. [17]). The following program fragment

```
pr int prvar, *prptr;
sh int shvar, *shptr;
prptr = &shvar;
```

causes a private pointer variable `prptr` of each processor to point to the shared variable `shvar`.

Fork95 maintains three kinds of heaps: a global, permanent shared heap, an automatic shared heap for each group of processors, and a private heap for each processor. Space on the private heaps is allocated and freed by `malloc()` and `free()` as in C. Objects allocated on the automatic shared heap by `shalloc()` exist as long as the group of processors that executed `shalloc()`. Permanent shared objects allocated on the permanent shared heap by `shmalloc()` exist until they are explicitly freed by `shfree()`.

Fork95 makes no assumption about concurrent read/write operations, but inherits the conflict resolution mechanism of the target machine. In case of the SB-PRAM both simultaneous read and write operations are allowed. In case of simultaneous writing to the same memory cell, the lowest numbered processor wins, and its value gets stored. Assume all processors execute the following statement simultaneously:

```
shptr = &prvar;  /* concurrent write */
```

This makes the shared pointer variable `shptr` point to the private variable `prvar` of the processor with the lowest processor ID. In this deterministic way, private objects can be made globally accessible.

Processors in Fork95 are identified by their processor ID, which is accessible as a special private variable `$`, initially set to the physical processor ID. At any point during execution of a Fork95 program the processors form groups (see Section 2.5); a special variable `@` shared by all processors belonging to the same group holds the current group ID. `$` and `@` are automatically saved and restored at group–splitting operations.

2.2 Synchronous and asynchronous mode

Fork95 offers two different programming modes that are statically associated with source code regions: synchronous and asynchronous mode. In synchronous mode, processors work strictly synchronous:

> **Synchronicity Invariant (SI):** All processors belonging to the same (active) group have their program counters equal at each time step.

In asynchronous mode, the SI is not enforced.

Functions are classified as either synchronous (declared with type qualifier `sync`) or asynchronous (`async`, this is the default). A synchronous function is executed in synchronous mode, except from blocks starting with a `farm` statement

```
farm <stmt>
```

which enters asynchronous mode and re-installs synchronous mode after execution of <stmt> by an exact barrier synchronization.

An asynchronous function is executed in asynchronous mode, except from the body of a `join` statement which enters synchronous mode, beginning with an exact barrier synchronization. The `join` statement

```
join( <lower>, <upper>, <groupspace> )
    <stmt> [ else <otherstmt> ]
```

(cf. [11]) offers a means for several asynchronously operating processors to meet at this program point, form a new group, and execute <stmt> in synchronous mode. The first two parameters may be used to install a lower resp. upper bound on the number of collected processors. Statement <stmt> is executed by at most one group of processors at any time, and can thus be viewed as a *synchronous parallel critical section*. A shorthand for a common special case of `join` is

```
start <stmt>
```

which collects *all* available processors to enter the synchronous region <stmt>.

Synchronous functions can only be called from synchronous regions. Calling asynchronous functions is possible from asynchronous and synchronous regions, where a synchronous caller causes the compiler to insert an implicit `farm` around the call, maintaining asynchronous execution mode for the callee.

The importance of being synchronous. In synchronous mode, shared variables need not be protected by locks because they are accessed in a deterministic way: the programmer is guaranteed a fixed execution time for each statement which is the same for all processors. Thus no special care has to be taken to avoid race conditions. This is due to the absence of virtual processing in Fork95. For instance, in

```
sync void foo( sh int x, a )
{... if ($<10)  a = x;  else  y = a; ...}
```

all processors of the `else` part must, by the semantics of synchronous mode, read the *same* value of `a`. To guarantee this in the presence of virtual processing would require a group lock for each shared variable.

217

Due to the presence of pointers and weak typing in C, a lock would be required for each shared memory cell!

The importance of being asynchronous. In asynchronous program regions there are no implicit synchronization points. Maintaining the SI requires a significant overhead also for the cases where each group consists of only one processor, or when the SI is not required for consistency because of the absence of data dependencies. Marking such regions as asynchronous can lead to substantial savings. Considerate usage of `farm` and asynchronous functions can result in significant performance improvements (see Sect. 3.2).

2.3 Explicit Parallelism

A Fork95 program is executed by all started PRAM processors in SPMD mode. Thus, parallelism is statically present from the beginning of program execution, rather than being spawned dynamically from a sequential thread of control.

As mentioned Fork95 does not support virtual processing. The PAD library compensates for this inconvenience by having its routines be implicitly parametrized by the number of executing processors. A *work-time* framework [2, 8] is thus convenient for describing the performance of the routines in the library. A library routine implementing an algorithm with running time t (assuming an unbounded number of processors) while performing w operations in total to do its job, runs in time $O(t + w/p)$ when called by a group of p synchronously operating processors. We will say that a routine which runs in $O(n/p)$ time on a data instance of size n takes *(pseudo)constant time* (this is indeed so when $p \geq n$). — In order to make a program independent of the number of processors, PAD provides parallel iterators on common data structures. The number of calling processors is determined by the routines themselves by the Fork95 routine `groupsize()`, and needs not be supplied by the caller.

For instance, a dataparallel loop over n array elements using p processors with ID's $\$ = 0, 1, \ldots, p-1$

```
sh int p=groupsize(); /*get # procs in my group*/
pr int i;
for (i=$; i<n; i+=p)  a[i] = b[i] + c[i];
```

could also be written using a PAD macro
```
par_array(i,n)  a[i] = b[i] + c[i];
```
which causes the private variable i of the processor with ID $\$$ to step through the values $\$$, $\$+p$, $\$+2p$, ..., up to n. This takes (pseudo)constant time and works both in synchronous and asynchronous mode.

2.4 Multiprefix operations

Multiprefix operations are essential parallel programming primitives, which can be provided at practically no extra cost in massively parallel shared memory emulations (theoretically, ie. with no asymptotic loss in efficiency, as well as in the number of extra gates needed). The SB-PRAM offers highly efficient multiprefix instructions which execute in only two CPU cycles, independent of the number of processors.

The atomic multiprefix operators of Fork95 are inherited from the SB-PRAM, but should be thought of as part of the language. The expression

```
prvar = mpadd( &shvar, <exp> )
```

atomically adds the (private) integer value of `<exp>` to the shared integer variable `shvar` and returns the old value of `shvar` (as it was immediately before the addition). The operators `mpmax` (multiprefix maximum), `mpand` and `mpor` (multiprefix bitwise AND resp. OR) work analogously. The Fork95 run-time library offers routines for various kinds of locks, semaphores, barriers, self-balancing parallel loops, and parallel queues. All these are based on multiprefix operators.

The multiprefix operators also work if executed by several processors at the same time and even with different shared integer variables `shvar`. Among the processors participating in an `mpadd` instruction on the same shared integer variable `shvar` at the same time, the processor with the ith-largest physical processor ID (contributing an expression `<exp>` evaluating to a private integer value e_i) receives the (private) value $s_0 + e_0 + e_1 + \ldots + e_{i-1}$, where s_0 denotes the previous value of `shvar`. Immediately after the execution of this `mpadd` instruction, `shvar` contains, as a side effect, the global sum $s_0 + \sum_j e_j$ of all participating expressions. Thus, the multiprefix operators provide fast reduction operators for integer arrays which can be used in synchronous as well as in asynchronous mode.

An immediate application of the `mpadd` operator is a PAD library routine to compute, in constant time, the prefix sums over an array of n integers:

```
sync void prefix_add( sh int x[], sh int n,
                      sh int y[], sh int offset)
{ sh int sum = offset;
  pr int i, s;
  par_array(i,n) {   /* n/p segments of size p */
    s = x[i];
    y[i] = mpadd( &sum, x[i]);
    y[i] += s;                              } }
```

For an input array x of size n, `prefix_add()` computes in array y the prefix sums of the input array, offset by `offset`. Ie., y[i] is assigned x[0]+...+x[i]. The actual number of calling processors is implicitly determined by the parallel iterator `par_array()`.

The fact that multiprefix operators can be executed with different shared variables `shvar`, provides for easy implementation of even more powerful primitives. For instance, "colored prefix summation" in which each element of the input array has an associated color (an integer between 0 and $c - 1 \leq n$) and prefix sums are to be computed colorwise, can also be done in constant, ie. $O(n/p)$ time:

```
sync void colorprefix( sh int x[], sh int n,
       sh int color[], sh int c, sh int ccount[])
{ pr int i, s;
  par_array(i,c) ccount[i] = 0;
  /* ccount[i] will count elements of color[i] */
  par_array(i,n) {
    s = x[i];
    x[i] = mpadd(&ccount[color[i]],x[i]);
    x[i] += s;                              } }
```

Upon return from this routine, x[i] holds the sum of all elements up to and including i of the same color as x[i] (ie. color[i]), and ccount[i] holds the sum of all elements with color color[i]. We give a surprising application of this primitive in Section 3.2.

2.5 The group concept

In synchronous mode, the processors are partitioned into independent, synchronous groups. Shared variables and objects exist once for the group that created them; global shared variables are visible to all processors. Processors within an (active) group maintain the SI, but there is no enforced synchrony among processors belonging to different groups. Such processors, although synchronous at the instruction level (as guaranteed by the hardware), may be executing different instructions of the program at the same time.

Splitting the current group of processors into subgroups can be done explicitly by the fork statement

```
fork (<exp1>; @=<exp2>; $=<exp3>)  <stmt>
```

which evaluates the shared expression <exp1> to an integer g and splits the current leaf group in g subgroups, with local group ID's @ numbered $0,1,...,g-1$. Each processor decides by the value of <exp2> which of the new subgroups it will join, i.e. all processors for which the private expression <exp2> evaluates to the same value i join group i with @ $= i$. The assignment to the group-relative processor ID $ permits local renumbering of $ inside each new subgroup. The SI is only maintained within subgroups. The parent group is restored (by exact barrier synchronization) when all subgroups have finished their execution of <stmt>.

As long as control flow depends only on "shared" conditions that evaluate to the same value on each processor, the SI is preserved without changes. If control flow diverges, due to "private" conditions in if or loop statements, the active group is deactivated and split into new subgroups, in order to preserve the SI within the subgroups. These are active until control flow reunifies again. Then, after exact barrier synchronization, the SI holds again for the parent group which is reactivated. Thus, at any point during program execution, the groups form a tree-like hierarchy, with the root group consisting of all started processors, and the leaf groups being the currently active

ones, for which the SI currently holds. Subgroup creation can be directly used for parallel Divide&Conquer implementations, as eg. in PAD's quicksort routine.

In asynchronous mode, there is no (implicit) splitting of groups required as no statement-level synchrony is to maintain.

3 The PAD library structure

The PAD library of parallel algorithms provides support for implementation of parallel algorithms as found in the current theoretical literature by making basic PRAM algorithms and computational paradigms, like prefix sums, sorting, list ranking, tree computations etc. available. PAD provides a set of abstract parallel data types like arrays, lists, trees, graphs, dictionaries. However, the user of the library is responsible for ensuring correct use of operations on data objects, since Fork95 does not support abstract data types as such (see Section 4). PAD contains type definitions for some common parallel data types, and is organized as a set of routines which operate on objects of these types. Computational paradigms, e.g. prefix sums over arrays of arbitrary base type with a given associative function are provided for by library routines with function parameters. The standard operations have often certain "canonical" instances, e.g. prefix sums for integer arrays. Library routines for both general and special cases are normally available.

3.1 The prefix library

The prefix library contains basic operations for the array data type, mainly of the "prefix-sums" kind. Operations like computation of all prefix sums, total sum, prefix sums by groups etc. for arrays over arbitrary base types with a user specified associative function are available. For instance, "prefix sums" of an array x of n objects of type struct x_object, with a function f implementing an associative function f on the set of struct x_object, can be computed by

```
Prefix( x, n, sizeof(struct x_object), PR3 f);
```

Here f is a (user-defined) Fork95 function which implements the assignment $x = f(y, z)$ when called with pointers to objects x, y and z. The macro PR3 performs the necessary type casting. The recursive routine takes $O(\log n + n/p)$ time, in contrast to the constant time routine prefix_add() for integer arrays.

3.2 The merge library

The merge library contains operations for parallel searching and merging of ordered arrays, and sorting of arrays. The *merge* routine implements the CREW algorithm in [4], which runs work-optimally in $O((m + n)/p + \log(m + n))$ time, m and n being the lengths of the input arrays. The implementation is very efficient when compared to a "reasonable" sequential merge routine. The running time of the parallel algorithm with one processor (almost) equals the running time of the sequential implementation, and the parallel algorithm gives very close to perfect speed-up [19]. This can be partly ascribed to the use of asynchronous mode. The algorithm partitions the input arrays into p pairs of subsequences of size at most $\lceil (m+n)/p \rceil$, which are then merged together, one pair for each processor. Obviously the concurrent mergings are independent and therefore executed in asynchronous mode, which reduces running time considerably, up to a factor 2. A trick in [4] makes it easy to implement a work-optimal parallel *merge sort* algorithm, which runs in $O(\log^2 n + n \log n/p)$ time, using the abovementioned general merge routine. Speed-up of up to 41 with 128 processors has been achieved for arrays of only 8K integers, see Tab. 1.

With `colorprefix()` we can implement a parallel *bucket sort* which sorts n integers in the interval $0, \ldots n - 1$ in (pseudo)constant time. The routine is surprisingly short and simple: `colorprefix()` computes for each input element `x[i]` the number of elements before `x[i]` that are equal to `x[i]`, if we simply use, as the color of element `x[i]`, `x[i]` itself. This yields the *rank* of each element `x[i]`. A prefix sums computation over the `rank` array suffices to determine, for each element `x[i]`, how many elements in array `x` are strictly smaller than `x[i]`. The final position `rank[i]` of `x[i]` in the output is the rank of `x[i]` plus the number of strictly smaller elements:

```
sync void smallperm( sh int keys[], n, rank[])
{ sh int *count = (int *) shalloc(n*sizeof(int));
  pr int i;
  par_array(i,n)  rank[i] = 1;
  colorprefix( rank, n, keys, n, count);
  preprefix_add( count, n, count, 0);
  par_array(i,n)
    rank[i] = rank[i] - 1 + count[keys[i]];      }
```

`preprefix_add( count, ...)` stores in `count[i]` the prefix sum `count[0]+...+count[i-1]`; it is implemented similar to `prefix_add()` in Section 2.4. Bucket sorting just calls `smallperm()` and permutes the input according to the computed `rank` array.

Proposition 1 *On the SB-PRAM (or other parallel shared memory machine with constant time multiprefix addition) prefix sums, colored prefix sums with n colors, and bucket sorting of integer arrays with n elements in the range $0, \ldots, n-1$ can be done in (pseudo)constant, i.e. $O(n/p)$, time with p processors. The constant hidden in the O-notation is very modest.*

Some results. Tab. 1 gives the results of sorting integer arrays using PAD's quicksort, mergesort and smallsort routines as described above. Timings are given in SB-PRAM clock cycles (using the simulator for the machine, which explains the small input sizes). The parallel routines are compared to a

n=2737	mergesort	SU	quicksort	SU	smallsort	SU
Seq	2807273		3106589		1068453	
8	567288	5	1002876	3	134639	8
16	317314	9	678262	5	67949	16
32	207650	14	484662	6	34409	31
64	146534	19	292538	11	17639	61
128	113508	25	140578	22	9449	113
n=8211						
Seq.	9829269		10829273		3203313	
8	1828718	5	4741482	2	401399	8
16	972582	11	2411150	4	201329	16
32	604776	16	1223450	9	101099	32
64	364248	27	696608	16	51179	63
128	241906	41	433704	25	26219	122

Table 1: Sorting results. SU = absolute speed-up.

reasonable corresponding sequential implementation. Bucket sorting is very efficient and gives speed-up very close to p. Small deviations (eg. 113 instead of 128) are due to allocation of the auxiliary arrays. Mergesort is somewhat more efficient than quicksort, both in absolute terms and wrt. speed-up.

3.3 Parallel lists

A *parallel list* data type gives direct access to the elements of an ordinary linked list, and is represented as an array of pointers to the elements of the list. The primary operation on parallel lists is *ranking*, i.e. the operation of determining for each element of the list its distance from the end of the list [8]. A parallel list contains in addition to element pointers the necessary fields for the list ranking operations. Currently a simple, non-optimal list ranking operation based on pointer jumping is implemented in PAD, as well as two work-optimal algorithms from the literature [3, 13]. At present, pointer jumping is at least twice as fast as the best of the work-optimal algorithms [13] for lists of up to 50K elements. Other operations on lists include reversal, catenation, permutation into rank order, and others. A parallel iterator `par_list(elt,i,n,list)` is available for processing the elements of a parallel list in "virtual" parallel.

3.4 Trees and Graphs

Trees are represented in PAD by an array of edges and an array of nodes, where edges directed from the same node form a segment of the edge array. An edge is represented by pointers to its tail and head nodes, and to its reverse edge. A "next edge" pointer is used to represent Euler tours. PAD offers routines which allow a single processor to access and manipulate nodes and edges, as well as collective, parallel operations on trees. Parallel operations on trees include computing an Euler tour, rooting a tree, computing pre- and postorder traversal number, level numbers etc.

PAD also supports least common ancestor preprocessing and querying. The currently implemented routines are based on the reduction to the range query problem, which is part of the prefix library.

220

In the current implementation, preprocessing takes $O(\log n + n \log n/p)$ time (non-optimal), and processors can then answer least common ancestor queries in constant time. Other parallel operations on trees include routines for generic tree contraction

A data type for directed graphs similar to the tree data type is defined. Parallel operations include finding the connected components of a graph, and computing a (minimum) spanning tree

3.5 Parallel dictionaries

Currently PAD contains one non-trivial parallel dictionary data structure based on 2-3 trees [15]. Dictionaries can be defined over base types ordered by an integer key. A parallel dictionary constructor makes it possible to build a dictionary from an ordered array of dictionary items. Dictionary operations include (parallel) searching and parallel (pipelined) insertion and deletion. Dictionaries can also maintain the value of some associative function, and provide a generic search function. [18] gives the full implementation.

4 Status, conclusion, and future work

A compiler for Fork95, together with the system software required, is available for the SB-PRAM. Due to the powerful multiprefix instructions of the SB-PRAM, the overheads for locking/unlocking, barrier synchronization and group splitting are very modest.

PAD complements some inconveniences in Fork95. On the other hand, PAD's implementation exemplifies the usability and expressivity of Fork95 for larger scale parallel programming. A first version of PAD, as outlined in Section 3, is available from October 1996. It will be extended with more advanced graph and combinatorial algorithms, e.g. graph decompositions and maximum flow algorithms. An important test for both language and library design will be the ease with which such more involved algorithms can be implemented.

Further developments of Fork95 are foreseen, possibly by including new language constructs, possibly in the direction of making (parts of) the language useful for other machine models or PRAM variants. A Fork95++ based on C++ would make a safer and more elegant library interface possible.

5 Related work

Other PRAM–oriented languages NESL [2] is a functional dataparallel language partly based on ML. Its main data structure is the (multidimensional) list. Elementwise operations on lists are converted to vector instructions (by *flattening*) and executed on SIMD machines. In contrast, the MIMD-oriented Fork95 also allows for asynchronous and task parallelism, low-level PRAM programming and direct access to shared memory locations. — Dataparallel variants of Modula [9, 16] support a subset of Fork95's functionality. The main constructs to express parallelism are synchronous and asynchronous parallel loops. However no strict synchronicity is supported, and there is no group concept. [9] compiles to a PRAM simulator while [16] offers back-ends for several existing machines. 11 [14], a similar approach, uses Pascal as base language. Further dataparallel languages in this tradition (see e.g. [17]) are C^*, *Dataparallel C* [6], and dataparallel Fortran dialects such as *HPF*. The latter ones are mainly targeted towards distributed memory machines and require data layout directives to perform efficiently. Exact synchronicity is not supported as it is not available on the target architectures considered.

Other PRAM-oriented parallel libraries A large number of PRAM-inspired algorithms has already been implemented in NESL [2]. [7] reports on concrete implementations on a MasPar for many of the same algorithms as those in PAD.

References

[1] F. Abolhassan, R. Drefenstedt, J. Keller, W.J. Paul, and D. Scheerer. On the physical design of PRAMs. *The Computer Journal*, 36(8):756–762, 1993.

[2] G.E. Blelloch. Programming parallel algorithms. *Communications of the ACM*, 39(3):85–97, 1996.

[3] R. Cole and U. Vishkin. Deterministic coin tossing with applications to optimal parallel list ranking. *Information and Control*, 70:32–53, 1986.

[4] T. Hagerup and C. Rüb. Optimal merging and sorting on the EREW PRAM. *Inform. Processing Letters*, 33:181–185, 1989.

[5] T. Hagerup, A. Schmitt, and H. Seidl. FORK: A high-level language for PRAMs. *Future Generation Computer Systems*, 8:379–393, 1992.

[6] P.J. Hatcher and M.J. Quinn. *Data-Parallel Programming*. MIT Press, 1991.

[7] T.-S. Hsu, V. Ramachandran, and N. Dean. Implementation of parallel graph algorithms on a massively parallel SIMD computer with virtual processing. In *9th International Parallel Processing Symposium*, pp 106–112, 1995.

[8] J. JáJá. *An Introduction to Parallel Algorithms*. Addison-Wesley, 1992.

[9] S. Juvaste. The Programming Language pm2 for PRAM. Technical Report B-1992-1, Dept. of Computer Science, University of Joensuu, Finland, 1992.

[10] C.W. Keßler and H. Seidl. Integrating Synchronous and Asynchronous Paradigms: The Fork95 Parallel Programming Language. Tech. Report 95-05, FB 4 Informatik, Univ. Trier, 1995.

[11] C.W. Keßler and H. Seidl. Language Support for Synchronous Parallel Critical Sections. Tech. Report 95-23, FB 4 Informatik, Univ. Trier, 1995.

[12] C.W. Kessler and J.L. Träff. A library of basic PRAM algorithms and its implementation in FORK. In *8th Annual ACM Symposium on Parallel Algorithms and Architechtures (SPAA)*, pp 193–195, 1996. Research Summary.

[13] C.P. Kruskal, L. Rudolph, and M. Snir. The power of parallel prefix. *IEEE Trans. on Computers*, C-34(10):965–968, 1985.

[14] C. León, F. Sande, C. Rodriguez, and F. Garcia. A PRAM Oriented Language. In *EUROMICRO PDP'95 Workshop on Parallel and Distributed Processing*, pp 182–191, 1995.

[15] W. Paul, U. Vishkin, and H. Wagener. Parallel dictionaries on 2-3 trees. In *Proc. 10th ICALP*, Springer LNCS 154, 1983.

[16] M. Philippsen and W.F. Tichy. Compiling for Massively Parallel Machines. In *Code Generation – Concepts, Tools, Techniques*, pp 92–111. Springer, 1991.

[17] M.J. Quinn. *Parallel Computing, Theory and Practice*, 2nd edition. McGraw-Hill, 1994.

[18] J.L. Träff. Explicit implementation of a parallel dictionary. Tech. Report SFB 124-D6 10/95, Univ. Saarbrücken, SFB 124 VLSI Entwurfsmethoden und Parallelität, 1995. 53 pp.

[19] J.L. Träff. Parallel searching, merging and sorting. Tech. Report SFB 124-D6 1/96, Univ. Saarbrücken, SFB 124 VLSI Entwurfsmethoden und Parallelität, 1996. 45 pp.

Implementation and Optimisation of a Parallel Database System

A. Esposito ([O]), G. Matarese ([+]), A. Viola ([+]) and M. Magliulo ([*])

([O]) Scientific Department, Italian Air Force Academy - Via Domitiana - 80078 Pozzuoli - Italy;
([+]) Parallel Information Systems Research Institute, Italian Research Council - Via P. Castellino 111 - 80131 Napoli - Italy
([*]) Department of Computer Science and Systems, University of Naples - Via Claudio 21 - 80125 Napoli - Italy

Abstract

This paper describes a parallel DBMS designed in order to experiment the efficacy of a small-grained parallelisation in a distributed environment. After a description of the design criteria and the prototype's architecture, the realisation of some subsystems is presented. The prototype allows to exploit intra-operation parallelism and has been tested by preliminary performance tests on join query, because the join stresses a DBMS more than the other kinds of queries. At present, the system is under tuning in order to give better performance. An heuristic algorithm has been realised to find a splitting strategy of the query on several nodes with limited storage capacity. The experiments demonstrate that the proposed algorithm is effective in reducing execution time when the parallelism is high.

1. Introduction

Workload within databases used in management information systems is continuously increasing in terms of on-line users and amount of involved data. Moreover, the increase in information to be managed has led to an explosion of related activities (update transactions, query-only retrievals, information analyses and manipulations). For a definite number of users, high performance systems are required, in case of:

- a high transaction rate (tps, transaction-per-second, in hundreds),
- a complex database architecture (high number of accesses per transaction),
- a sophisticated control system on data to guarantee transaction correctness.

By their characteristic sequential conventional systems are not particularly suited for database applications. For this reason, in order to obtain a high transaction rate, high performance allowed by parallel environments is required [2]. In general, parallelism can be performed by replication or by partitioning. In the former case, on each node there is an identical copy of entities constituting the processing: *replication* is useful mainly in order to obtain a fault-tolerant system. General-purpose parallel systems perform partitioning that can be applied usually to the algorithms or to the data.

Within the *data partitioning*, each node works on an independent partition of the overall data set. In this case, each node executes the same operation set on different data, so allowing with an appropriate file management system the parallel execution of I/O operation on different files. With reference to massively parallel systems, data partitioning is very useful within database environment, since allows high performance improvements, and it can be performed together with a third parallelism modality, the *function parallelism*, utilised for parallel execution of different system functionalities (data access, lock management, I/O operations, update, etc.).

From the data management point of view, the possible implementations can be classified as *shared-everything* if each processor can see the entire database with shared main memory, *shared-disks* if only mass storage is shared or *shared-nothing* if each processor acts as a server for its own data. Shared-nothing implementations with replication of functions allow the increase of parallelism in direct proportion to the growing capacity of the database if the workload is uniformly distributed among all the database stores [7]. Moreover, shared-nothing systems transfer only control messages and filtered data, whereas raw data exchange between processors and memory within shared resource systems involves a huge communication overhead [3].

In the implementation of a relational DBMS, parallelism can be exploited at different levels. Query processing requires a co-ordinate set of relational operators, which can be represented as the nodes of a tree describing the data flow among these operators. This structure is suitable to exploit the intrinsic parallelism among operators (*inter-operation* parallelism). Moreover, owing to the distribution of data on several disks attached to different processors (data partitioning), each operator can be parallelised (*intra-operation* parallelism). Intra-operation parallelism allows to use specialised algorithms with better performance.

The main commercial products such as Oracle Parallel Server are based on shared-memory architecture and inter-operation parallelism. This paper describes a research project aimed at the realisation of a distributed DBMS, based on shared-nothing architecture with inter-operation and intra-operation parallelism. In Section 2, we present an overview of the environment. Section 3 describes the approaches followed in designing the parallel DBMS. In Section 4, we report the results of computational experiments to verify the implementation. Section 5 presents and analyses an optimisation technique to reduce the query processing time with storage capacity constraints.

2. The environment

The hardware platform is constituted by several machines with system-call compatible operating systems. One of the purposes of our project is to obtain a software system which could be easily ported on the different available machines (IBM SP2, Meiko CS-2 and Relational Data Cache, Convex Metaseries, SUN and IBM clustered workstations). In this way, we do not implement a machine dedicated to data base management: the PDBMS is an application running on several nodes available inside the system together with applications of different kind. Our system is largely configurable, in order to optimise the use of available resources. The set of nodes for PDBMS can be subdivided into *client nodes* running user programs, *storage nodes* assigned to data access and filtering operations (selections and projections) and *operator nodes* running processes required for query execution (basically joins and data aggregations). In the proottype currently under implementation, the client nodes share via NFS a file system containing database catalog. At the installation, nodes are described in a configuration file containing information about resource availability and other parameters useful to system tuning.

Data are distributed on several disks attached to different storage nodes. So, besides intrinsic parallelism among operators, each operator can be efficiently parallelised. On all storage and operator nodes, during the bootstrap phase one dispatcher and a number of operator processes are created. A group of such operator

processes, running on different nodes, realises the parallel implementation of one of the nodes in the query tree when the query is executed.

Many algorithms have been developed, optimised on a specific architecture topology [5] or independent from the underlying architecture [12]. In [6] a survey of efficient algorithms and software architectures of database query execution engines for executing complex queries over large databases is included.

In this first phase we are testing the join query, because the join stresses the performance of a relationa DBMS more than other kinds of queries. We have chosen to implement both a broadcast-based nested loop algorithm and a hash-partitioned algorithm. In order to exploit also inter-operation parallelism, the scheduling algorithms simultaneously execute possible independent subqueries. The dispatcher processes carry out the assignment of processes to operator nodes during the set-up phase of the execution, according to a suitable protocol [4]. Each user program must be linked to a library containing the functionalities of the application program interface, which allows the user program to submit DDL and DML commands to the DBMS. Data communications among modules are performed by using PVM 3.3 communication primitives.

3. Design criteria

The context of the PDBMS has two external systems: the final user and the operating system (UNIX) plus the communication software (PVM), as shown in fig. 1.

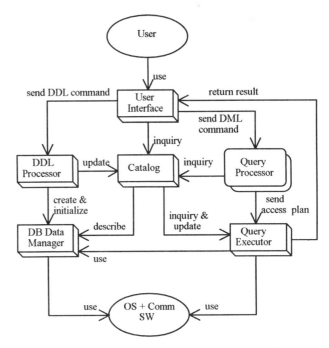

Fig. 1: PDBMS Schema

The main subsystems constituting the PDBMS are: Query Processor, Query Executor and Data Manager. The Query Processor, constituted by scanner, parser and optimiser according to the schema shown in fig. 2, manages the translation of the SQL query in internal format and the definition of the query tree, which describes the access plan. The access plan is treated by the Query Executor whose behaviour reflects the intra-operation parallelism principle. Depending on the resource allocation (contents of the cache memory in each node and functional specialisation of the nodes) and depending on the actual availability of the processes, the Query Executor through the scheduler activates the suitable operators for the algorithms.

Query scheduling and execution control can be based on two different approaches: *control-flow* and *data-flow*. In the former case, a single process controls all processes involved in execution, taking care of their initialisation, synchronisation and termination. In the latter case, the control function is distributed among processes, which trigger each other, according to their processing state and to the availability of their input data. The data-flow approach is particularly suitable for massively parallel processing, because it decreases the weight of control communication messages and avoids that a single process has to control many other process by means of complex synchronisation mechanisms [13].

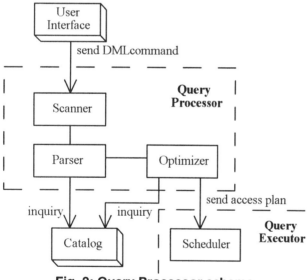

Fig. 2: Query Processor schema

The relational tables are horizontally fragmented on the disks of the different nodes (declustering technique), according to the hash criteria. The typical fragmentation techniques are:

- *hash partitioning*: a tuple is inserted into a particular fragment according to the result of a hash function applied to a key attribute;

- *round-robin*: tuples are distributed among the fragments in a circular fashion;
- *range partitioning*: tuples are distributed according to the range of a key attribute.

4. Parallel database system : first version

Initially, programming effort has been concentrated on Query Executor and Data Manager subsystems, by implementing code for the management of distributed files, for the operators and heir communications and for the scheduler of the access plan. Practical join scheduling algorithms tend to increase the number of joins which may be performed on the involved nodes. In [10] bounds on the resource requirements under a variety of assumptions regarding the page connectivity graph are presented. The PDBMS first version includes only hash partitioned relations without optimisation [4].

The software has been installed in a cluster of IBM R/6000 model 530H workstations, connected by Ethernet, and in the Convex Metaseries, constituted by a cluster of HP model 730 nodes, connected by FDDI. The software system has been tested by preliminary performance tests, on a table hash partitioned among the nodes and made up of 80,000 tuples, each of 100 bytes of information data. In table 1, the results for a simple query on a single condition with 50% selectivity are shown. The tests are performed by varying the number of nodes among which the table is partitioned. The values are times in seconds, measured by means of UNIX primitives and averaged on several tests, without output times from the nodes.

Nodes	R/6000 cluster		Convex Metaseries	
	Time	Speedup	Time	Speedup
1	25.20	1.00	24.32	1.00
2	12.61	2.00	12.28	1.98
3	8.67	2.91	8.34	2.92
4	7.00	3.60	6.16	3.94

Table 1

As we can see, the speedup increases with good scalability. The result transmission is about 10.5 seconds for the cluster of workstations and 2.2 seconds for the Convex, which has a higher bandwidth and an optimised version of PVM.

5. Optimisation

The optimisation technique that we have implemented, consists in two phases. In the first phase we make up an heuristic optimisation algorithm (named *Kruskal algorithm*) that determines a join operation order to reduce the query processing time[8]. This order is a sub-optimal solution of the problem, so in the performance evaluation we compare it with the optimal solution calculated by an exhaustive algorithm (that we have implemented). In the second phase we study the query execution problem on a multiprocessor hardware platform. We have realised a custom algorithm to find a splitting strategy of the query processing on several processing nodes considering that each node has a limited storage capacity[1].

Finally, we analyse the performance of optimisation strategy about processing times of two optimisation phases and for discovering the quality of selected solution of the problem. The target of the first phase is to minimise the communication time needed to transfer data between several processing nodes. The join execution technique is hash-partitioned join [9], as shown in fig. 3.

To perform a join operation we must split the join relations among nodes and hence there is a meaningful information exchange. The basic idea of our optimisation strategy is to share the relation as little as possible [6]. The results of the first phase are an optimal or sub-optimal solution for a portion of optimisation problem, that is to produce the execution order of join operations.

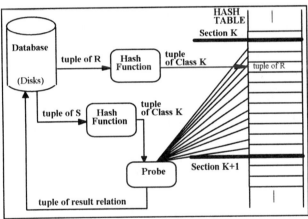

Fig. 3: Hash Join technique.

To evaluate the difference between Kruskal and exhaustive algorithms we have found the minimum, maximum and average value of relative error. The performance analysis consists of testing the two algorithms submitting to both ones a meaningful number of query with the join conditions ranged from 3 and 20. The experimental results are shown in table 2. These values prove the reliability of the heuristic algorithm. In fact the average error of Kruskal algorithm is reduced and hence the first phase of the optimisation problem provides an approximate solution that is not far from optimum. In addition, the processing time of Kruskal algorithm is very small (few milliseconds) respect the execution time of exhaustive algorithm (some minutes).

The target of the second phase is to find an access plan that satisfy two conditions:

1. the intra-operation parallelism is maximum,
2. the minimum required central memory is available for each join operation.

Average	**2.8%**
Maximum	16.3%
Minimum	0%

Table 2: Relative Error.

With the first condition we get a *maximum parallelism access plan* [11], but if the memory requirements of this plan are greater than available memory we can reduce the memory requirements increasing the step in the plan. In this way (second condition) we make up an *optimum access plan* that reduce the page faults when the memory is insufficient with respect the demand [10,12].

To execute a join with an hash join technique we need to execute three different tasks:

· *Scan*: to read one table from the disks
· *Build*: to build the hash table for one of the two join relations
· *Probe*: to seek the tuples which satisfies the join condition

The join operation tree, when the query is represented by a binary tree, can be used to identify the tasks that it is possible to carry out in parallel. Among possible topologies (left deep query tree, right deep query tree and bushy query tree) we have chosen the bushy query tree and available parallelism can be obtained as in following example.

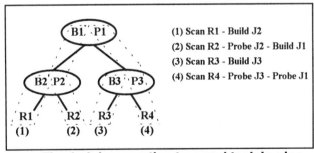

Fig. 4: Join operation tree and task in pipe

Fig. 4 shows that is possible to execute some tasks in pipe, but it underlines, also, that is necessary to respect the precedence constraints in elementary tasks scheduling. In fact, to perform probe operations, the hash table regarding one of the two relations should be load in the memory. After satisfying this constraint, it is possible to perform more probe operations in pipe. This method makes possible to start comparison operation, regarding the next join, before previous probe is concluded. For instance, the probe P1 performs the comparison between the hash table built by Build B1 and the Probe P3 result while the Probe P3 produces the result. Also the Scan-Build operation can be performed in pipe in this way: one tuple of the relation is read from the disk, on one of its attribute an hash function is applied, then the tuple is assigned to one processing node while the scan of a new tuple is performed from the disk.

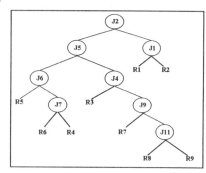

Fig. 5. Join operations tree example.

The maximum parallelism access plan is obtained detecting the tasks that can be scheduled in pipe, saving the precedence constraints between tasks and trying to compute as many as possible pipes of task in parallel. This access plan is built with a minimum number of sequential steps, but if the central memory constraints need an hash table high paging, the increasing of the execution sequentiality is preferred to reduce the single operations response times. For instance for the join operation tree in fig. 5, it is possible to have a maximum parallelism access plan with four steps or an optimum access plan, that doesn't overtake the logic memory constraint of 400, with seven steps (fig. 6).

Maximum parallelism access plan

1) Scan 6 - Build 7(15.0) , Scan 5 - Build 6(250.0) , Scan 3 - Build 4(285.0) , Scan 7 - Build 9(105.0) , Scan 1 - Build 1(40.0) , Scan 8 - Build 11(30.0)
2) Scan 4 - Probe 7 - Probe 6(63.0) - Build 5
3) Scan 9 -Probe 11 -Probe 9 -Probe 4-Probe 5(34.1) - Build 2
4) Scan 2 - Probe 1 - Probe 2 spool(11.6)

Maximum memory =400

1) Scan 6 - Build 7(15.0) , Scan 5 -Build 6(250.0) , Scan 7 - Build 9(105.0)
2) Scan 4 - Probe 7 - Probe 6 spool(63.0)
3) Scan 8 - Build 11(30.0) , Scan 1 - Build 1(40.0)
4) Scan 9 - Probe 11 - Probe 9 spool(47.2)
5) Scan 3 - Build 4(285.0) , Build 5
6) Probe 4 - Probe 5 spool(34.1) - Build 2
7) Scan 2 - Probe 1 - Probe 2 spool(11.6)

Fig. 6: Access plans examples.

Memory requirements of a step can be calculated by adding the memory associated to operations involved in the step (memory requirements of an operation is in the brackets near the name of operation in fig. 6) If the

availability of memory is too low the disk spool of the last pipe probe result is needed. Second access plan is obtained from the first one reducing the number of Probe operation performed in pipe.

Here, we present the behaviour of execution time of the two optimisation phase respect the number of join conditions and relations. Obviously, the execution time of the first phase increases with number of join conditions, while in second phase time depends on relations' number. In fact, in the first phase, Kruskal algorithm must find the optimal join order among all join conditions ; on the contrary, the start point of the second phase is the order of *join operations*. To find execution times we used four processors SUN Sparc Viking and the behaviour of times is shown in fig. 7.

First Optimisation Phase   Second Optimisation Phase

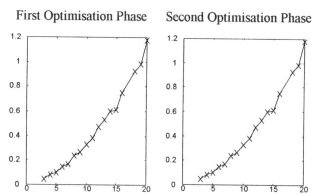

Number of join conditions   Number of join relations

Fig. 7: Execution time of optimisation phases.

Now, we compare the execution time of a query using the maximum parallelism access plan and the optimum access plan. The parallel algorithm for query execution is control flow, so there is a master process for spawning the slave processes (that perform tasks of access plan) on the processors of parallel machine and waits an ending signal by slaves. The execution strategy uses the access plan and permits the parallel processing of all tasks in the same step of the plan. The query executor performance that use optimum access plan is compared with ones that use the maximum parallelism access plan. The execution time of a query with six joins and seven relations on four processors is shown in the table 3, with memory constraints of 55 MB. The optimum access plan provides the best results when the dimension of a relation is greater than 16 Megabytes (4 MB for each node), otherwise the execution times of the two access plans are comparable.

We have tested the parallel algorithm by varying the number of processing nodes. Table 4 shows the values for a query with six joins and seven relations, measured by means of Unix primitives and averaged on several tests.

Dimension of Relations for each node [MB]	Exec. Time [s] Max. Parall. Access plan	Exec. Time [s] Optimum access plan
1	34.07	33.27
2	37.23	36.08
3	47.37	46.55
4	59.96	57.04
5	79.02	69.04
6	120.31	77.09
7	168.12	93.81
8	239.77	108.71

Table 3: Execution times with four nodes.

Number of Processors	Size of a Relations for each node [MB]	Execution Times [s]	Speed-up
1	8	128.26	1,00
2	4	64.70	1.98
3	2.7	47.15	2.72
4	2	38.64	3.31
5	1.6	35.39	3.62

Table 4: Speed-up.

The speed-up regularly increases when we reduce noticeable the size of relations, but if the reduction in Kilobytes is only few hundreds (400KB from four to five processors) the execution time decreases very little and the system is no more scalable. On the contrary, relations with constant dimension for each node show good scalability, as we can see in table 5 for a query with 3 join operations and 4 relations of 3MB dimension. The performance is acceptable for a number of processors less than seven. For seven and eight processors we have a considerable reduction of scale-up due to an high increasing of inter-process communications and synchronisation.

Number of Processors	Execution Times [s]	Scale-up
1	29.71	1
2	31.29	0.9495
3	31.52	0.9425
4	32.24	0.9215
5	32.43	0.9159
6	32.89	0.9033
7	36.57	0.8124
8	37.69	0.8038

Table 5: Scale-up.

Concluding remarks

In this paper we have described a PDBMS prototype. We presented a representative sample of results, indicating that the system is portable and scalable. Query processing has been optimised with a practical algorithm which produces results close to optimal values from the exhaustive algorithm. Our current activity is centred to improve the prototype and perform other benchmarks in order to better validate design criteria.

References

[1] D. J. De Witt. , D. Schneider "A Performance Evaluation of Four Parallel Join Algorithms in a Shared-Noting Multiprocessor Environment". *Proc. SIGMOD Conference*, Portland, 1989.

[2] D. J. DeWitt and J. Gray "Parallel Database Systems: The Future of High Performance Database Systems" *Commun. ACM*, v. 35, no 6 (June 1992) pp. 85-98

[3] A. Esposito, G. Gullo and I. Marra "Benchmarking a Parallel Data Base Environment" *Euromicro Wshop on Parallel and Distributed Processing*, Gran Canaria, Jan. 1993, pp. 247-252

[4] A. Esposito, G. Gullo, R. Vaccaro and A. Viola "A Data Flow Query Execution Algorithm for a Parallel Database System on General-Purpose Machines" *Convegno Sistemi Evoluti per Basi di Dati*, Ravello (I), July 1995

[5] O. Frieder "Multiprocessor Algorithms for Relational-Database Operators on Hypercube Systems" *IEEE Computer*, v. 23, no. 11 (Nov. 1990) pp. 13-28

[6] G. Graefe "Query Evaluation Techniques" *ACM Comp. Surveys*, v. 25, n. 2 (June 1993), pp. 73-170

[7] D. K. Hsiao "A Parallel, Scalable, Microprocessor-Based Computer for Performance Gains and Capacity Growth" *IEEE Micro*, (Dec. 1991) pp. 44-60

[8] M. Jark , J. Koch. "Query Optimization in Database System". *ACM Computing Surveys*, Vol.16, No.2, June 1984.

[9] P. Mishra e M. H. Eich. "Join Processing in Relational Database". *ACM Computing Surveys*, Vol.24, No.1, March 1992.

[10] M. C. Murphy and D. Rotem "Multiprocessor Join Scheduling" *IEEE Trans. Knowledge & Data Eng.*, v. 5, n. 2 (Apr. 1993), pp. 322-328

[11] D. Schneider, D. J. De Witt."Design Tradeoffs of Alternative Query Tree Representation for Multiprocessor Database Machines". *Technical Report 869, Computer Science Department - University of Wisconsin*, Aug. 1989.

[12] D. Schneider and D. J. DeWitt "Tradeoffs in Processing Complex Join Queries via Hashing in Multiprocessor Database Machines" *Proc. 16th Intl. Conf. on Very Large Data Bases*, Melbourne, Aug. 1990

[13] W. Teew and H. Blanken "Control versus Data Flow in Parallel-Database Machines" *IEEE Trans. Parallel & Distr. Systems*, v. 4, no. 11 (Nov. 1993)

Programming Concurrent Backward Error Recovery: General Methodologies and Practical Approaches

A. Clematis[1], V. Gianuzzi[2] and A.M. Tyrrell[3]
1 - IMA-CNR, via DeMarini, 16149 Genova, Italy
2 - DISI University of Genova, via Dodecaneo 35, 16146 Genova, Italy
3 - Department of Electronics, University of York, Heslington, York Y01 5DD, UK

Abstract

In this paper we propose the use of a hierarchical software architecture to program fault tolerance in control applications. In our approach, a multilevel architecture is define, with the use of a different fault tolerant mechanism at each level. Each level of the hierarchy is also specialised towards a specific goal, such as data protection, filtering of residual software errors, and so on. In the same way, the design of atomic action boundaries is organised using the same hierarchy of functionality. This largely reduces the complexity of the necessary analysis since it is only necessary to ensure the consistency with an unusually small number of actions and communications. The work considers both the design and implementation problems of such work when applied to concurrent systems.

1. Introduction

A distributed processing system, comprising a set of discrete processing units, offers the user not only the prospect of increased efficiency and throughput through parallelism, but its inherent redundancy might also be exploited to enhance reliability. To do so requires a properly designed fault tolerance infrastructure which maintains the integrity of the system under fault conditions. This paper describes how backward error recovery techniques can be incorporated into concurrent systems to provide fault tolerance software structures across a distributed system to ensure safe operations in the presence of faults.

Notwithstanding the use of standards and guidelines in the design of software-based real-time systems for safety-critical applications, and the concomitant adoption of formal methods, it is probable that faults will still be introduced into a design either explicitly as part of a particular component or implicitly through the omission of a particular feature. It is unrealistic to expect all software design faults to be detected during design and testing, and latent faults may persist into system use.

Fault tolerance [1] is often incorporated into a design as a ruggedisation process to protect a process or set of processes regarded as critical to safe system operation. The fault tolerance mechanisms are required to recognise faults by the errors they cause and to prevent error migration from the faulty process to elsewhere in the system, so that error recovery is localised. The extent of the error recovery operation can be limited if a boundary can be identified within the state-space of the distributed system across which error propagation by interprocess communication is impossible; it must include all processes which interact with the function being protected and exclude all processes that do not interact with it. In other words, the state-space of the system has to be partitioned into a hierarchy of atomic actions [2]. It is then possible to introduce a distributed error detection and recovery mechanism around the atomic action [2] which ensures that all the processes affected by the fault co-operate in recovery. This localisation of fault tolerance simplifies the design and can help to meet timing constraints in real-time systems [3].

2. Error recovery using software

A generalised backward error recovery mechanism could be considered as a set of recovery procedures, each of which is executed in-turn and subjected to an acceptance test to check for data 'correctness'. There are two problems that must be addressed to develop fault tolerant software: (i) what kind of recovery program structure to adopt, and (ii) how to design the fault tolerant software application.

2.1 Programming structure for fault tolerance

The Recovery Block (RB) [4] is a construct based on checkpointing. Several alternate try blocks, all implementing the same functionality, are combined to achieve one fault tolerant execution. At block entry, the status of the program is saved and the first alternate is executed. Then, before block exit, the computed results are checked by means of an acceptance test. If this test fails, the computation is rolled back to resume block entry status, and an alternate try block is executed. Otherwise, the recorded status is discarded, and each process continues its execution separately.

N-Version Programming (NVP) [5] uses diversity to mask software faults. Several independently designed versions of the same software are executed, and their computed results are compared to one another by some hardware or software adjudicator unit. The result computed by a majority of them is then accepted. Usually, in order to achieve a fast response time, such versions are executed in parallel, on different machines. In this case, no checkpointing or rollback is required, but different initial status copies have to be created.

Recovery Block and N-Version Programming are usually applied in sequential programs. When considering concurrent programs, if these mechanisms are applied without coordination, the domino effect can occur, because errors may be exported to other processes by means of communication. A fault in a process, for which a rollback is needed, can then provoke a rollback in another process, because of a communication between them, and this in turn may affect the whole set of processes, causing the computation to restart from the initial status. Thus, the above mechanisms have to be suitably extended to apply to concurrent environments.

When applied to a concurrent systems, consisting of a set of interacting processes it is general for the fault tolerant procedure to include a co-ordinated set of recoverable blocks, with one recoverable block in each interacting process, allowing distributed error detection and recovery. The mechanism is bounded by an entry line, an exit line and two side walls which completely enclose the set of interacting processes which are party to the mechanism, and across which interprocess interactions are prohibited. The structure is indicated diagrammatically in Figure 1.

The entry line defines the start of the backward error recovery mechanism and consists of a co-ordinated set of recovery points for the participating processes. The exit line comprises a co-ordinated set of acceptability tests. Only if all participating processes pass their respective acceptability tests is the mechanism deemed successful and all processes exit, in synchronism, from the action. If any acceptability test is failed, recovery is initiated and processing "passed" to another set of recoverable processes. Thus all processes in the recovery mechanism co-operate in error detection.

The Conversation [4] scheme follows such guidelines: it is a checkpoint and rollback strategy where a group of processes may interact in a safe way; it is conceptually a concurrent extension of the RB scheme. A checkpoint is taken when each process enters a Conversation. This process may communicate only with processes already entered in the Conversation to ensure that no information smuggling (that is, spreading of not yet validated data) can take place. When all processes have completed their operations, a global acceptance test takes place; in case of failure, all processes roll back and execute their next alternates. If the acceptance test is satisfied, all processes may discard their checkpoints and proceed, exiting synchronously from the Conversation.

The Conversation scheme guarantees that no subsequent error will ever force processes to roll back to some point prior to a successful acceptance test; hence no domino effect will ever occur. Several implementation variants to the above scheme have been proposed in the literature, to extend and adapt the Conversation scheme to various environments and programming styles.

To an external observer the activity of a process is defined by its sequence of external interactions; any internal actions (of which there may be many) can not affect the external observer, at least until the next external interaction. This allows the concept of an atomic action to be derived [2]: the activity of a set of processes is defined as an atomic action if there are no interactions between that set of processes and the rest of the system for the duration of that activity. The extension to hierarchically

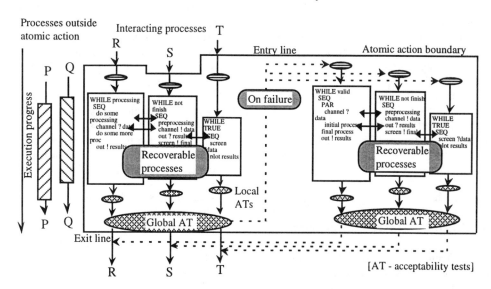

Figure 1. The structure of a fault tolerant mechanism involving processes R, S, and T.

229

nested atomic actions is straightforward. These concepts are used in a number of design techniques for the construction of fault tolerant procedures [2].

2.2 Design Aspects

The process of identifying the error recovery procedures within a parallel system design brings into clear focus the structure of interprocess interactions and thus the route by which errors might propagate under fault conditions. All common mechanisms for providing fault tolerance in parallel systems, such as forward error recovery, N-version programming, conversations, consensus recovery blocks and distributed recovery blocks, have to cope with error confinement and achieve this by imposing logic structures 'around' atomic actions. The structure considered in this paper will fit into the backward error recovery class of fault-tolerant mechanisms.

Any attempt to incorporate an entry line and an exit line at arbitrary locations in a concurrent system is unlikely to lead to a properly formed recovery mechanism [2]. It is necessary to identify a boundary within the state space of the complete set of processes across which error propagation by communication is prevented. Clearly, this boundary will be the boundary of an recovery procedure, since such a boundary of necessity prohibits the passing of information to any process not involved in the recovery procedure and similarly embraces all interacting processes within the recovery procedure. Recovery mechanisms can be nested systematically in the same hierarchical fashion as atomic actions. If this duality is not imposed, then should the system attempt to backtrack and recover in response to a fault, progressive collapse by the domino effect [4] can occur.

In the literature, strategies for implementing fault tolerance in parallel systems [6, 7] and for handling problems which occur if the chosen mechanism is incorrectly located, have received more detailed attention than the fundamental problem of placing the mechanisms correctly [2]. Correctly placed mechanisms, coincident with atomic action boundaries, avoid error propagation problems. Ideally, a design method would incorporate the requisite, appropriately placed, recovery procedures and the associated fault tolerance infrastructure into a system with a minimal amount of re-analysis and re-design, and an eventual goal is to define such a design method. However, the techniques are still insufficiently mature for this to be achieved and the normal design practice in which fault tolerance mechanisms are superimposed upon selected atomic actions and the new designs subjected to re-analysis is considered here.

3. Further Implementation Problems

Different papers discuss the possibility of an effective use of backward error recovery, however different authors agree on the fact that there are some problems in using Conversations.

Problem 1: The implementation of backward error recovery strategy normally assumes that the behaviour of a program is entirely determined only by the input vector and some transformational function on it. That is, given an input vector I, the program must produce a unique result f(I) applying the function f to the input vector. However, this type of behaviour is not applicable to many cases of practical interest, eg all control programs. The software component of many critical systems is a concurrent program consisting of a set of data, which represent the state of the system, and a set of processes, which cooperate to reach a common goal. Such systems can be described as concurrent distributed computations, possibly with real-time requirements. Their behaviour is determined by a distributed input vector and by a distributed internal system state. In order to improve the reliability of a reactive program, data representing the state of the system must be protected, and to ensure the reliability of concurrent processes. Thus, software fault tolerance must be achieved by suitably partitioning the system, and by applying different methodologies to each part.

Problem 2: Another important problem is specifically related to the implementation of Conversations; Conversations can be executed concurrently, but processes participating in them should execute in a mutual exclusive way to avoid information smuggling and to warranty a correct and consistent execution. Moreover, Conversations introduce the need of additional synchronisation among processes. Constraints on scheduling of Conversation must then be introduced also to avoid the danger of a particular form of deadlock due to the presence of so called deserter processes. This double level of concurrency, among processes and among Conversations, in a single layer of software can lead to programs which are difficult to understand and to manage, and require the use of costly scheduling algorithms.

Problem 3: The use of language diversity is likely to be very important, in fact reliability is better achieved if the different versions of code are developed using different programming languages. This significantly increases error independence among versions. In the case of concurrent programs, each language assumes a particular style (eg shared memory, or message passing, or client-server approach) and integrating them as alternative versions is a very complex task.

Problem 4: Finally, ensuring reliable process interaction through software fault tolerance is only half of the story. As mentioned in the introduction we have also to ensure data consistency, protection and availability. These requirements can be satisfied using a transaction based scheme to implement access to system state data. The problem which remains to be solved is how to combine the use of software fault tolerance, which improves process reliability, with transactions, which ensure data reliability.

4. Design of concurrent backward error recovery

Substantial work has been performed on the ability to model systems, and to reason about their behaviour, using state space representations such as Petri nets or GMB [2]. In the Petri net approach, each process state can be associated with a Petri net place, and each state transition with a Petri net transition. Process execution is simulated by allowing marking tokens to flow through the Petri net. From the formulation of a reachability graph, the behaviour of the Petri net, and therefore of the modelled system, can be analysed.

Experience with occam as a design language for loosely-coupled real-time concurrent systems has led to Petri net methods for identifying atomic actions. By only permitting synchronous, atomic, communications, occam forces communicating processes into mutual synchronisation at communication points. This not only imposes a strict discipline on the designer (because errors in the synchronisation logic can lead to deadlock) but also leads to a system more amenable to analysis. The system is designed using the requirement specification and modelled as a Petri net. Examination of the state reachability graph permits the designer to identify the boundaries of atomic actions. Inspection determines which atomic action boundary encloses which system function, and an appropriate error detection and recovery mechanism to protect any chosen system function can then be incorporated at the level of the atomic action without disturbing the constituent processes or their inter-process actions.

Although the method is effective, it requires:

a) translation of an existing textual occam design into a graphical Petri net

b) translation between the graphical Petri net and set theory or matrix-based methods for reachability analysis.

c) translation of the identified atomic action entry and exit points back to the original occam design.

which are made more difficult because:

d) for all but the simplest examples, there is a computational explosion which could restrict the analysis.

Although automated tools exist for these translation processes, often error-prone manual methods are still involved. For Petri-net based methods the designer must be satisfied that the translation steps (a) - (c) do not themselves introduce errors.

Occam has a mathematical basis in the theory of Communicating Sequential Processes (CSP). CSP permits a fundamental description of a concurrent processing system in terms of the component processes, the interactions between the processes, and interactions with the real-world environment. Since a CSP description is directly amenable to mathematical analysis, it is possible to decide behavioural properties, such as the presence of reachability pathologies, without the need for error-prone translation into a complementary representation. The ability to reason about timeliness in recent extensions to CSP should further promote its use in the design of time-critical and safety critical systems.

The trace of a CSP process is a record of the sequence of events in which a process could engage and indicates directly a possible execution behaviour of that process. During the design phase it would be advantageous to determine all the possible traces which a process might produce. This procedure is termed trace evaluation in [2]. For all but the simplest process there will be a number of possible traces; for a set of concurrently executing processes the overall trace set will be all permitted interleavings of the traces of the component processes. If the processes interact only by synchronous communications, then the processes are brought into synchronism for the communication event. The communication event will be in the alphabet of both the communicating processes and will constrain the set of all possible traces.

5. Implementation of concurrent programs with backward error recovery

So far we have discussed general methodologies for the design and implementation of concurrent fault tolerant software. The key points of that discussion are: there exists a number of programming structures for fault tolerance; each structure could be better employed in well defined situation; it is advisable to use formal methods in order to identify atomic actions within the software; and the applications of interest are often control applications, which are organised as endless control loops with an internal hierarchical structure.

Hereafter, we propose the use of a hierarchical software architecture to program fault tolerance in control applications. In our approach, a multilevel architecture is defined, with the use of a different fault tolerant mechanism at each level. Each level of the hierarchy is also specialised towards a specific goal, such as data protection, filtering of residual software errors, and so on. In the same way, the design of atomic action boundaries is organised using the same hierarchy of functionality. At each level a Petri-net approach is employed independently. This largely reduce the complexity of the necessary analysis since it is only necessary to ensure the consistency with an unusually small number of actions and communications.

Let us start from Problem 1; Looking at the model of reactive system presented above, the existence in the program of a two-level hierarchy is evident. The control loop, together with the identifiers of the processes which constitute each action, is at the upper level, and will be denoted as being at the *control manager* level. At the lower level, the code of each process is specified, together with their data sets. We will refer to this as the *process* level. In order to increase the reliability of the system, it is possible to apply, at each separate level, the most suitable fault tolerant mechanism, avoiding at the same time interferences between different mechanisms. A first step is to establish what parts of the system require the use of software fault tolerance. The control manager level is a simple structure, the correctness of which can be thoroughly validated and/or tested. We also remark that the two mechanisms of RB and NVP cannot be easily applied to it. With respect to the RB scheme, the complexity of the acceptance test, which must verify that the event has really occurred and that no conflict arise among actions, is as complex as the alternate is. Moreover, since the choice of the event is non deterministically performed, the NVP method cannot be applied, since the result of each version might not be uniquely determined. Hence, no fault tolerance mechanism can be applied to this level. On the contrary, good candidates for the use of software fault tolerance are the actions, that is, their constituent processes. Since actions do not communicate with one another, they can be considered as atomic and independent entities, sharing the system state in mutual exclusion. If we do not consider the presence of this shared system state, the behaviour of an action is completely functional. Then, to increase reliability, we can apply Recovery Block or N-Version Programming techniques, or some simplified version of Conversation. This represents a solution for Problem 1.

We have still to face the problem of the shared system state. The system state is originally partitioned among processes which participate in the different actions. Each process holds part of the state, hence if we replicate the actions (then the processes), we must also replicate the system state. The problem of maintaining its consistency can then become a very complex and costly task. An additional problem is that knowledge of the system state is also required for the action manager level, in order to test the occurrence of the events and to select the action which must be activated. Hence, the same processes participating in actions, should also participate to an agreement protocol for the event choice. All these problems can be avoided if the system state is separated from processes. In this way the system state can be subdivided into a set of objects which must be suitably distributed. Accesses to an object are of read and write type and can be disciplined using a transaction based methodology. In this way we introduce a third level in the hierarchy; referred to as the *object* level. This represents a possible solution to Problem 4.

The resulting hierarchy can be summarised as:

Object level: a set of distributed objects which keep the system state;

Process level: the set of processes implementing the actions. Since shared data (the system state) are not kept in processes which implement the actions, each action can be implemented by a set of processes which do not participate in other actions. That is, they may be considered as process instances which have a life-time limited to a single action.

Control Manager level: the execution of the control loop can be assigned to a centralised process or to a group of distributed processes which access the system state and decide which action must be activated.

Each level is characterised by the possibility of applying a specific fault tolerance methodology as summarised in Table 1.

Level	Features and FT techniques
Control Manager	high level specification; no redundancy
Processes	replication and diversity
Objects	transactions

Table 1: Fault tolerance hierarchy

To increase the reliability of each action, some alternative actions must be provided, together with an acceptance test or an adjudicator to validate the final results. Then, a set of alternative actions can be compared to the alternates of a Conversation, possibly written in different languages.

To protect the system state the condition that the actions are executed as transactions with respect to the updates on the distributed objects is enforced. With respect to the non fault tolerant scheme, the selection of the enabled actions to be activated is no longer necessary, since possible conflicting actions are serialised by the transaction manager. As a consequence, the process interactions are free from domino effect and the information smuggling is avoided.

In this way problem 2 is avoided, in fact the double level of concurrency within a software layer no longer exists. If conversations are used, each action corresponds to a conversation and vice versa. Hence the concurrency relationship among conversations corresponds to the concurrency relationship among actions, and it is managed by the transaction manager.

With the proposed hierarchical structure also problem 3, that is the use of different languages to implement versions, is solved since the interface between versions and system state values is provided by the transaction system itself.

6. Combining the design strategy and the software architecture

We have so far presented two different methodologies for the proper and efficient design and implementation of fault tolerant control applications; The first is a hierarchical architecture that permits a modular and multilevel approach to the implementation of a complex fault tolerant software system. The second is a design methodology, based on Petri net analysis, that helps identify concurrent actions and to define consistent recovery lines in multiprocesses interactions. The next step is the coordinated use of the two methodologies. This largely depend on the type of application considered.

In practical situations we may distinguish two basic starting points:

1. It is necessary to add up fault tolerance to a flat, or low modularised, existing application, largely reusing existing code; and
2. A new fault tolerant application is designed from scratch using a hierarchical approach.

In the first case it is necessary to start with a bottom up approach, at least in the first phase of the transformation process. The goal of the bottom up analysis is to understand the concurrent structure of the application in order to properly identify shared objects, concurrent processes, and alternative actions. This will permit a first design of a possible set of atomic actions and recovery lines. Petri-nets are fundamental in carring out this first step, since it permits identification in an automatic way the items (object, processes, actions) that will be used to build up the hierarchical architecture. It is worthwhile to point out that the Petri net analysis can be carried out in a simplified form, with a low computational cost, since it is not interesting to detect all possible interactions, but only if an object is shared, two processes are concurrent or two actions are alternative. After the bottom up phase a modularisation phase may take place which lead to a first hierarchical structure. This structure is then analysed using Petri nets so that possible inconsistency between the fault tolerant architecture and the original concurrent structure are detected. The above analysis is repeated till a consistent and satisfactory structure is obtained.

The second case is a typical top down approach, in which the application hierarchical design is implemented giving rise to a modular program. The hierarchical approach greatly reduces the number of interactions among entities belonging to different levels, since atomic action boundaries can be set before the implementation.

These two approaches, bottom-up and top-down, that apparently have no similarities, can be combined in order to reduce the efforts needed to implement fault tolerance.

Recalling the problems listed in section 3, a suitable solution for the first problem is to manage the state vector variable as a data base, completely separated from the control processes. The top-down approach can be conveniently applied to isolate and to separately design the actions needed to deal with control subproblems, when possible. On the other hand, other system components could not allow an a-priori partitioning, for example because they are part of already existing code, then only a-posterior partitioning is possible.

Thus, different fault tolerance mechanisms can be applied to these entities, also depending on their criticality: transactions on data representing the permanent state vector, conversations on processes interacting in a highly critical action, checkpoints-rollback for operational phases where no software replication is needed, and software-implemented hardware fault tolerance is sufficient.

Transaction management traditionally includes support for atomicity, and Petri net based analysis allows the partitioning of the process code for the non software replicated parts of the system.

Conversation implementation is a more difficult task, since information smuggling is possible, if some process is involved in more than one conversation. Moreover, to solve problem 2, each conversation alternate could be implemented by different processes, possibly written in different programming languages. In this case, complex interactions can exist among conversations, and Petri nets can be again useful, from a different point of view.

If Petri net analysis is applied on the graph representing process interactions, it is possible to point out those conversation which cannot have information smuggling with other enabled actions. For those conversations it is not strictly necessary to require atomicity. In the other cases the obtained information may provide hints for changes and optimisation

7. Conclusions

This paper has investigated the design and implementation of fault tolerant structures and techniques within a concurrent programming environment. There are a number of problems identified for the design of such systems, and indeed their implementation. A number of novel ideas have been proposed to solve these problems and help in the design of dependable concurrent computer systems.

Acknowledgements

This work is supported by the British Council and MURST in Italy.

References

[1] P.A. Lee, and T. Anderson, "Fault Tolerance: Principles and Practice" Springer Verlag, 1991.
[2] A.M. Tyrrell, and G.F. Carpenter, "CSP Methods for Identifying Atomic Actions in the Design of Fault Tolerant Concurrent Systems", IEEE Transactions on Software Engineering, Vol 21, No 7, pp 629-639, June 1995.
[3] T. Anderson, and J.C. Knight, "A framework for software fault tolerance in real-time systems", IEEE Transactions on Software Engineering, Vol 9, No 12, pp 355 - 364, May 1983.
[4] B. Randell, "System Structure for Software Fault Tolerance", IEEE Transactions on Software Engineering, Vol. 1, pp. 220 - 232, June 1975.
[5] A. Avizienis, "The N-version approach to fault-tolerant software", IEEE Transactions on Software Engineering, Vol 11, No 12, pp 1491 - 1501, Dec 1985.
[6] K.H. Kim, and S.M. Yang, "Performance impact of look-ahead execution the conversation scheme", IEEE Transactions on Computers, Vol 38, No 8, pp 118 - 1202, August 1989.
[7] R.H. Campbell, T. Anderson, and B. Randell, "Practical Fault Tolerant Software for Asynchronous Systems", Proc. SAFECOM'83, Cambridge, pp 59 - 65, 1983.

Simulating the Universe

F.R.Pearce, P.A.Thomas, R.M.Hutchings
Astronomy Centre,
University of Sussex
Falmer, Brighton, U.K.
frazerp@central.susx.ac.uk

H.M.P.Couchman
Astronomy Department
University of Western Ontario
Ontario, Canada
couchman@coho.astro.uwo.ca

A.R.Jenkins,C.S.Frenk
University of Durham Astronomy Department
Science Laboratories
South Rd, Durham, U.K.

S.D.M.White, J.M.Colberg
Max Planck Institut für Astrophysik
Garching, Germany

Abstract

We present an astrophysics N-body code that incorporates smoothed particle hydrodynamics (SPH) to model the gas phase. This code is written in CRAFT and runs in parallel on a Cray T3D. It uses a dynamic mesh adaptation strategy to reduce the total amount of CPU required per step and both fine and coarse grained load balancing techniques.

The collisionless variant of the code has already completed several 16.7 million particle simulations whilst the full SPH code has completed several 4.2 million particle runs. These are currently the largest astrophysical simulations of their kind in the world.

1. Introduction

Cosmological simulations are one of the most ambitious applications for the worlds most powerful supercomputers. The aim is to model a large fraction of the Universe throughout most of its history. A typical simulation has a volume of nearly 10 percent of the Universe and spans 10 billion years in time. Rather than microsceonds, a typical timestep jumps ten million years and we employ a mass unit of around 10^{40}kg.

A simulation starts with of order 10 million mass points distributed nearly uniformly within a cubical box. As time advances these mass points are followed as they move under the influence of gravity (and short range gas forces if gas is present). As gravity is an attractive force, structure evolves within our simulation volume. Static load balancing techniques do not work well because the locations at which structure develops are not known beforehand. This causes severe problems even for dynamic load balancing strategies. In this paper we hope to briefly outline our approach to solving this problem; the use of an adaptive grid refinement strategy to simultaneously reduce the total amount of computational work and to break the problem up into many smaller parts which can be distributed using a task farm approach. We begin with some background to the cosmological N-body problem.

Since the pioneering work of von Hoerner [17] and Aarseth [1] N-body simulation has advanced a long way. The early codes used a direct summation (particle-particle or PP) approach, laboriously but accurately calculating the force by standing on each particle and adding up the contribution from all the others in turn. The computing time required for this method scales as N^2, making it a very expensive way of solving the general N-body problem for even moderate N.

To circumvent this problem two main alternative methods have been used. The first, grid based codes, will be discussed here. The parallelisation of treecodes has been discussed elsewhere [5]. Grid based codes, in particular particle-particle, particle-mesh (P^3M) codes, have been applied to a variety of problems, ranging from large scale structure formation and cosmology to galaxy mergers and galaxy formation [6, 8, 14, 15]. Several authors [9, 16] have incorporated smoothed particle hydrodynamics (SPH) to follow the gas [12]. Grid based codes are very efficient in their use of memory but in general are very expensive when the amount of clustering becomes high. The use of adaptive refinement to increase the grid resolution in selected regions has somewhat alleviated this problem and the latest workstations can run simulations with $N \sim 7$ million particles in a reasonable amount of time [2].

Recently the British supercomputing community invested in a Cray T3D which was installed in Edinburgh. This is a massively parallel machine which now has 512 processors. These processors are linked together with high speed interconnections so that inter processor communication is very fast. Each processor has its own local memory and is essentially a workstation in its own right. The idea behind a parallel system is that if a problem can be split into N equal sized pieces that can be done independently then if these pieces are farmed out one to each processor the problem can be done N times faster. In practice, the pieces are not independent and require some communication between processors, so the actual speed up is less than the ideal amount.

In this paper we present the first parallel adaptive particle-particle, particle mesh plus smoothed particle hydrodynamics algorithm (parallel Hydra). In section 2 we describe how Hydra works on a workstation. In section 3 we deal with the problems of a parallel version of this code, for which we use CRAFT, a parallel fortran variant provided by Cray. In section 4 we look at the code's performance, in particular the load balance and speed, on a Cray T3D in both clustered and unclustered environments.

2. Hydra

Hydra [4] is the endpoint of several stages of code development which we briefly describe below before giving a more detailed description of Hydra itself.

Once N, the number of particles being modeled, reaches a few thousand the computational cost of the PP method becomes prohibitive and so people began to look for a better method. The simplest of these was the particle-mesh or PM approach. This involves placing a grid over the particles and then smoothing out the particle properties onto this grid. This reduces the mass distribution to a matrix which allows Poisson's equation to be Fourier transformed and solved for the gravitational potential. Interpolation can then be used to derive the forces at the particle positions. The computational cost of the PM method scales as $N \log N$.

The main drawback of this approach is that it smoothes out structures on small scales. This is in fact a difficulty for all fixed grid codes in 3 dimensions, because the computational storage scales as L_{mesh}^3 which limits $L \leq 512$ for even the best equipped machines (L_{mesh} is the size of the grid in each dimension). The two big advantages of this scheme are that it is extremely fast, because fast Fourier transform (FFT) algorithms are very efficient and that it is automatically periodic, a very desirable feature if you are modeling large sections of the Universe.

The next advance was to couple together the PP and PM methods to produce the particle-particle, particle-mesh (P^3M) scheme [7]. This method employs the PM method on large scales and then adds a short range PP component to the force on small scales. The time for this method scales as $N \log N + N_n^2$ where N_n is a measure of the mean number of particles that participate in the PP part of the calculation. This produced a scheme with potentially much better spatial resolution than the PM method and much greater speed than the PP method. The difficulty occurs when heavy clustering is present so that the number of neighbours rises and the N_n^2 nature of the PP calculation begins to dominate the CPU time.

The automatic placement of higher resolution sections of grid within the original framework [3] solved this problem. Here, 'hotspots' are identified where the computational work is going to be high so that a finer grid can be placed in this region. Then the range of the PP interaction is reduced (typically this is of order the grid spacing) and so is the number of neighbours.

Finally, smoothed particle hydrodynamics was incorporated into the adaptive P^3M code to form Hydra. The workstation version of which is available to the community from either of the following web sites;

http://coho.astro.uwo.ca/pub/hydra/hydra.html

http://star.maps.susx.ac.uk/~frp/hydra/hydra.html

2.1. Force matching

The main difficulty in a P^3M code is matching the PP contribution to the force onto the PM part. This is done by calculating the theoretical force curve for the FFT grid and subtracting the contribution within the PP search radius. As is shown in Fig 1, the long range force that results from the FFT is the r^{-2} of gravity but at short range it falls off below this. The further out you choose to calculate the PP force the closer the PM force is to the r^{-2} relation and the smaller the error. Hydra sets the PP search length automatically from a supplied error parameter. For a typical error parameter of 7.7 Hydra searches out for PP neighbours up to 2.16 times the grid spacing.

Refinements are handled in a similar fashion. Here you must match the force contributions from two FFT's and then graft on the PP forces which now have a much shorter range. This operation is recursive and you may have several layers of refinement stacked one inside the other.

2.2. Placing refinements

Refinements are regions where a higher resolution grid will be placed. They are positioned by placing a grid into the computational volume and counting the number of particles within each grid cell. If the number of particles within any cell exceeds a threshold then that cell is flagged as being in need of refinement. Once all the cells above the threshold have been flagged a pattern recognising routine is used

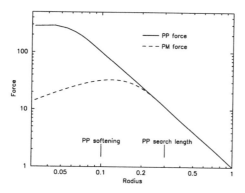

Figure 1. Matching the PP force onto the PM force. Hydra chooses the PP search length automatically.

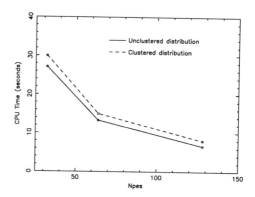

Figure 2. PM speed in seconds for both clustered and unclustered positions.

to group together contiguous cubic regions, expanding and translating them to maximise the work saving.

3. Parallel Hydra

Hydra breaks down into 3 distinct parts, the long and short range force calculations and placing the refinements. We look at parallelising each of these in turn.

The P^3M method does not lend itself easily to parallelisation because although the PM part can be done efficiently [10], and there are parallel PP schemes [11] it is difficult to produce a combined method that makes efficient use of memory and has a good communication strategy. To allow us to circumvent these problems we utilise the shared memory facility of CRAFT for our scheme. We are currently working to develop a message passing version.

3.1. Long range force calculation (PM)

The long range force calculation involves smoothing the particle masses onto a grid and then a fast Fourier transform of this grid. This is followed by a convolution, a second FFT and then interpolating the forces back onto the grid points. We can consider each of these operations separately when we try to parallelise them.

Smoothing onto a grid is a well studied and difficult problem to parallelise efficiently [10, 13].

The ability of CRAFT to make the distributed memory of a MPP machine look like shared memory makes the task of parallelising the code much easier. We employ a fixed distribution of the particles and grids among the processors, so each processor stores and operates upon N/N_{pes} particles and holds L/N_{pes} sheets of the PM mesh.

Once the particle positions become clustered this method would appear to lead to a large amount of contention (when two or more processors try to update the same grid point).

In practice little degradation in speed is observed (see Fig 2) even under very high levels of clustering. With this distribution of the particles the load balance is very nearly perfect as each processor needs to do exactly the same number of operations.

Parallel fast Fourier transforms are now readily available for the T3D. We built our parallel 3-dimensional FFT from many 1-dimensional ones. As the grid to be transformed is arranged in sheets, two dimensions can be transformed entirely locally and require no off-processor information. In the final dimension a small local array is loaded with the off-processor values, transformed and then the transformed values are written back off-processor. This method for implementing a parallel FFT is well known and scales beautifully (see Fig 2).

Now you need to convolve the Fourier transformed density field with a Green's function generated from the appropriate force law (see Fig 1). Each sheet of the convolution is independent of the others so the convolution routine can be parallelised by doing the calculation one sheet at a time.

Interpolation of the force back onto the particles is automatically load balanced as we have chosen to keep the same number of particles on each node. No blocking problems occur because we are only reading information about the force values at the nearest grid points, not trying to write to them. The only worry here is that as time goes on the communication overhead grows because the particle you are considering has wandered into another processor's grid space and so all the force value requests are off-processor. This is not a problem for CRAFT as local array accesses and remote array accesses take approximately the same time.

3.2. Short range force

The short range forces come in two parts, the direct summation over nearby particles for gravity and the more complicated two stage process for the gas of firstly averaging the

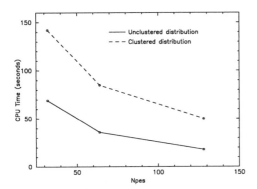

Figure 3. PP speed in seconds for both clustered and unclustered positions.

local properties and then applying them.

The short range PP part of the gravity calculation is parallelised by getting each processor to do the calculation one box at a time. At the start of the step temporary arrays are loaded with the properties of the particles in the 26 surrounding boxes. This scheme doesn't make use of data locality, in fact in general the current box will not contain particles whose properties are stored locally.

The reason for using this approach is load balancing. Almost all the time spent at this stage is taken up doing the few large clumps (because the work goes as N_n^2). By scattering the work in such a fine grained manner much better load balancing is achieved than if the volume was divided amongst the processors in sheets or blocks. This approach is quite effective, as Fig 3 shows.

Parallelising the SPH part of the calculation is not very difficult because you essentially get it for free. The SPH formalism sits well within P^3M because the PP part of the algorithm automatically finds the nearest neighbours (actually this is only strictly true in the denser regions). So once you have parallelised the PP algorithm you just have to do the same thing for the gaseous component.

3.3. Placing refinements

Placing refinements in parallel is very difficult. This is because you want total freedom as to their position and size so any blocking strategy you employ to divide up the computational volume between the processors can lead to boundary problems.

Refinements are placed by examining the numbers of particles in each of the PP boxes. Peaks in the density field can be located by getting each processor to search a section of the array containing the number of particles in each PP box for values above a threshold. Once it finds a box above the threshold it then walks uphill through the array until it finds a local maxima. This walk may take it off-processor.

Each new peak is tagged with a unique number along with the route to the top. This is done in a self-consistent way by using a shared counter visible to all the processors.

Once the positions of the peaks have been found all subsequent operations are carried out on a single processor but as these involve at most a few thousand refinements this procedure doesn't incur a significant overhead.

To further reduce the amount of time spent placing refinements we only replace the top level refinements every 10 steps. This doesn't lead to problems because the refinement positions do not change rapidly. Further levels of refinements are placed every step. With this restriction the time taken to place refinements is less than 2 percent of the total even in very difficult highly clustered positions.

3.4. Parallel refinements

For each refinement the same sequence of operations must be carried out as those done at the top-level. The only extra complication is that the Fourier transforms are now no longer periodic, nor is the convolution. Parallel isolated FFT's and convolutions are very similar to the wrapped ones.

An extra, and problematic concern is that you now no longer know *a priori* either what size grids you are going to have or the number of particles involved.

3.5. Load balancing

Load balancing is crucial for an efficient parallel code. If all the work is being done by a single processor while all the others stand idle then the load balance is very bad. The ideal is to have all of the processors working all of the time. There are two main types of load balancing, fine and coarse grained, both of which are used by Hydra but Hydra also has an extra type of load balancing that is implicit in the workstation method. This is because we try to balance the amount of work spent in the long range force calculation (PM) against the work spent on the short range force calculation (PP). This is done by placing refinements. Placing a refinement increases the PM work and decreases the PP work, whilst hopefully decreasing the total work.

Fine grained load balancing usually takes place at the very bottom level of the code and refers to the way in which small units of work are distributed amongst the processors. For it to work efficiently you need a great deal of these 'work units' with $N_{unit} \gg N_{pes}$.

The two main areas where we use this type of load balancing are the PM routine and the PP routine. In the PM routine there are two units of work, a particle or a grid point. An equal number of both of these units are distributed to each processor which efficiently balances the work because the amount of work associated with each unit is the same. In the PP routine the unit of work is a PP cell. These are distributed to the processors on a 'first come, first served' basis by using a shared counter. This ensures that despite the fact that some of the cells take much longer than others to complete there is very little lag time at the end of a step.

Coarse grained load balancing usually takes place at a much higher level. Large sections of work are distributed to each processor, perhaps many subroutines at once.

Within Hydra we use this type of load balancing because it is much more efficient to do small refinements entirely on a single processor. Once a series of temporary arrays are loaded all accesses are local. We complete the top level in parallel using the whole machine, then we complete all refinements above a certain size, again using the whole machine and then we employ a task farm approach to complete the small refinements one to a processor. Typically there are 10 big refinements and 1000 small refinements for 4 million particles.

4. Performance

4.1. Testing

One of the major advantages of using CRAFT is that the parallel code is immediately portable to a workstation. Throughout the code development the output was tested against the original code, tests of which have been published [4]. Once the parallel code was completed we made 3 test runs, each a complete simulation using the new code on a workstation and the T3D and the original workstation code. All three runs produced equivalent results. All of our algorithm development and testing takes place on workstations using the production parallel code.

4.2. Speed

Hydra is extremely fast when the particles are unclustered, running at around 12 Mflops/processor even under CRAFT. This is because the mean number of neighbours for which you need to do PP work is small and so the code sees the full $N \log N$ speed of the Fourier transform. Fig 4 shows the timings for the full routine. This combines the PP and PM timings from Figs 2 & 3 with an overhead from placing the refinements and building lists. The refinement placing and list building overhead is much smaller in the unclustered case.

Once structure has formed Hydra is still fast but the increase in the mean number of neighbours increases the amount of work significantly. The amount of communication required for the parallel code also rises sharply because under CRAFT the PP calculation is very expensive.

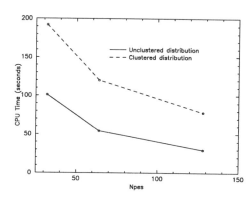

Figure 4. Full routine speed in seconds for both clustered and unclustered positions. The raw speed is very high and almost unaffected by clustering. The scaling properties are also excellent.

4.3. Load Balance

Initially the load balance is very good because there is very little PP work and the PM section is well balanced. Once clustering develops we encounter three problems. Firstly, some of the PP cells take a long time to complete and so even with the very fine grained balancing employed by the PP routine there is an imbalance while one processor finishes a particularly difficult cell. Secondly, the big refinements that are done across the full machine are really too small to be done in this way. The maximum number of processors that should be used for the FFT routine is L_{mesh}, the size of the PM grid. In practice, $L_{mesh} = 64$ for these refinements and the time taken does not scale well if more than 32 processors are used. CRAFT does not have a facility that would allow you to assign a subset of the processors to such a task, you are limited to either using all the processors or one processor. Finally, a refinement cannot be started before its parent has been completed. This means that the small refinements cannot be completed as a single task farm but must be done one level at a time. Unfortunately, the time then scales as the number of refinement levels multiplied by the time taken by the biggest refinement at that level. This leads to a load imbalance while one processor finishes off the most difficult refinement at each level.

5. Conclusions

A parallel adaptive grid code based on Couchman's [3] algorithm has been implemented on the Cray T3D using CRAFT. Identical code can be run on a workstation by using a preprocessor directive. This makes testing of the code very easy as local workstations can be used. We have also incorporated SPH into our code following the prescription

238

of [4].

The code has been used successfully to run 16.8 million particle dark matter and 4.2 million particle mixed dark matter and gas cosmological simulations.

References

[1] S. J. Aarseth. A direct summation n-body method. *MNRAS*, 126:223, 1963.

[2] S. Cole. Adding long-wavelength power to n-body simulations. Preprint, 1996.

[3] H. M. P. Couchman. Mesh-refined p3m - a fast adaptive n-body algorithm. *ApJ*, 368:L23, 1991.

[4] H. M. P. Couchman, P. A. Thomas, and F. R. Pearce. Hydra: An adaptive-mesh implementation of p3m-sph. *ApJ*, 452:797, 1995.

[5] J. Dubinski. A parallel treecode. Preprint, 1996.

[6] G. Efstathiou, M. Davis, C. S. Frenk, and S. D. M. White. Numerical techniques for large cosmological n-body simulations. *ApJS*, 57:241, 1985.

[7] G. Efstathiou and J. W. Eastwood. On the clustering of particles in an expanding universe. *MNRAS*, 194:503, 1991.

[8] G. Efstathiou, C. S. Frenk, S. D. M. White, and M. Davis. Gravitational clustering from scale-free initial conditions. *MNRAS*, 235:715, 1988.

[9] A. E. Evrard. Formation and evolution of x-ray clusters - a hydrodynamic simulation of the intracluster medium. *ApJ*, 363:349, 1990.

[10] R. Ferrell and E. Bertschinger. Particle-mesh methods on the connection machine. *Int. Jour. Mod. Phys.C*, 5:933, 1994.

[11] R. Ferrell and E. Bertschinger. A parallel processing algorithm for computing short-range forces with inhomogeneous particle distributions. In *Proceedings of the 1995 Society for Computer Simulation Multiconference*, 1995.

[12] J. J. Monaghan. Smoothed particle hydrodynamics. *ARA&A*, 30:543, 1992.

[13] F. R. Pearce, H. M. P. Couchman, A. R. Jenkins, and P. A. Thomas. Hydra - resolving a parallel nightmare. In *Dynamic Load Balancing on MPP Systems*, 1995.

[14] F. R. Pearce, P. A. Thomas, and H. M. P. Couchman. Mergers of collisionless systems. *MNRAS*, 264:497, 1993.

[15] F. R. Pearce, P. A. Thomas, and H. M. P. Couchman. Head-on mergers of systems containing gas. *MNRAS*, 268:953, 1994.

[16] P. A. Thomas and H. M. P. Couchman. Simulating the formation of a cluster of galaxies. *MNRAS*, 257:11, 1992.

[17] S. von Hoerner. Direct summation methods. *Zeit. Ap.*, 184:50, 1960.

Parallel Simulation for Queueing Networks on Multiprocessor Systems

F. de la Puente[1], J. D. Sandoval[1], P. Hernandez[1], F. Herrera[2]
[1]C.M.A., E.T.S.I.T., Univ. L.P.G.C., Spain
[2]Facultad de Informática, Univ. L.L., Spain
FAX : 34-28-451243 TEL :34-28-451235
email : fpuente@cma.ulpgc.es

Abstract

It is generally a good idea to leave all the hard work for computers instead of doing it ourselves. Therefore, we have developed a graphical environment for system simulation which makes the simulation work easier. It has been designed for working under Windows NT in multiprocessor environments. It lets us design queueing networks by simply placing and connecting the basic elements, setting for each one the necessary parameters to correctly define its behaviour. This is enough to provide the program all the information required for it to simulate the system. We based our implementation on the Chandy-Misra paradigm, introducing some modifications for avoiding the memory management problems which arise in parallel simulations. This way, we can run parallel simulations reliably and, by using multiprocessor systems, reduce the simulation times.

1. Introduction

Sequential computers can only execute one instruction at a time. Although, parallel computers can execute several instructions at the same time by having many processors working together. This makes it possible to obtain a higher processing speed. But, in order to use multiprocessor computers, we have to consider the simulation as composed of actions that "can be done at the same time". The actions, also called tasks or processes, can be executed in a fairly independent way over one or several processors. In case all tasks are independent it is enough to associate a processing resource to every one of them to obtain a reduction of the execution time: N independent tasks will execute N times faster over N processors than over only one processor. Unfortunately, in real applications, tasks generally show dependencies, because some actions must finish in order to start another ones. Dependencies, therefore, penalise the processing resources assignment to tasks and some resources must stay inoperative or waiting part of the time.

We will deal only with parallel computers with shared memory, where all data of an application is located on one common memory space. This way, a task executing over one processor P1 has the physical possibility to access the data of another task executing over another processor P2. This is a very useful property as soon as it lets us pass information from one processor to another through shared variables. In a parallel machine with distributed memory, this is not possible and we need to add an external interconnection network so they can share data by passing messages. There are already some architectures for which the shared memory access time is similar to that associated to the interprocessor communication through the network.. This simulation system can also be adapted to this architectures with only a few implementation changes.

The most important contribution to parallel simulation was the statement of the Chandy-Misra Paradigm [1], which gives the clues for maintaining the precedence order of different processes in a parallel simulation system. We have based this simulation on this paradigm and have adapted it to meet the requirements for real systems (limited available memory).

Actually, most of the work on parallel simulation is being implemented using object oriented programming languages, like C++. The primal idea is that both the data and the functions which interact with the data become one unique entity. A class is a description of the variables and functions of similar objects while an object is an instance built up according to the description given for its class. With this description we can create many objects and have then working simultaneously on our system. Inheritance is one of the main characteristic which distinguishes object oriented languages from other languages. It lets us inherit the characteristics and behaviour of one or many other classes when creating new ones, letting programmers reuse and extend the existent code. This way, we may easily come up with a full hierarchy of classes reducing the programming effort. We have developed our own library of classes for parallel simulation of queuing networks. This library has been developed for Windows NT but it can be adapted with very little effort to other operating systems. The most important feature is that every node object we create has it's own execution process. This way, we have simulation objects that can work in parallel to carry out our simulations.

This approach provides a simple way to access parallel simulation without the need to learn special simulation languages or anything. For that purpose, we provide a graphic environment to set all the parameter of the nodes for the simulation, leaving all the parallelization work to the simulator. Therefore, all we have to do is provide an adequate description of the queueing network model of the system to simulate and put the simulator to work.

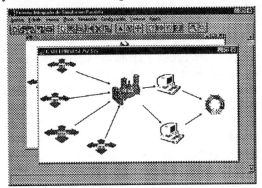

Fig. 1 Graphic environment for system simulation

2. Queueing Networks Parallel Simulation

2.1 Queuing networks

A queuing network is a system in which there are users trying to make use of some resources that can only be used by one user at a time. A user can represent anything we want. They are created at the sources and destroyed at the sinks. Once they are created they pass through stations where they can make use of the processing resources, although sometimes they have to be queued until they can access one of them. When a user has finished its processing at a given station, it is passed to another node, until they get to a sink, where they are destroyed.

In any queuing network we can find three main types of object:

- **Source:** A source does not receive any user from other objects.
- **Station:** A station receives, processes and sends users.
- **Sink:** A sink does not send any user to other objects.

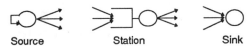

| Source | Station | Sink |

Fig. 2 Types of nodes in queuing networks

Combining this three types of elements we can modelize nearly any possible system.

2.2 Chandy-Misra paradigm for parallel simulation

It can be said that a simulation protocol is correct if all events occurring at a logical process are executed in nondecreasing timespamp order. To guaranty this we need to follow a few synchronisation rules. This is the only way to ensure that the results obtained with the parallel simulator are the same as if we were executing it on a sequential simulator. In order to do so we use the Chandy-Misra paradigm [1] which guarantees that the system satisfy the causality constraint. The Chandy-Misra protocol follows two waiting rules to satisfy the causality constraint. We first describe the assumptions of a Chandy-Misra simulation.

- *The FIFO message sending assumption:* Communication between two processors preserve the first-in-first-out (FIFO) property (i.e., the messages are received in the order they are sent).

- *The static topology assumption:* The network topology is static (i.e., the communication channels between processes do not change during simulation). If process p_i may send a message to process p_j, then a communication link is directed from p_i to p_j. This link is called an input channel (output channel) p_j (p_i).

The original Chandy-Misra protocol further assumes that the buffer capacity of a process to store the incoming messages is limited. The purpose of this restriction was to limit the memory usage of a Chandy-Misra simulation. However, it has been proved [2], [3] that in general limiting the input buffer capacities of processes does not limit the total memory usage for a Chandy-Misra simulation. In 3.2 we propose a different system for controlling the memory usage.

The concept *lookahead* is of great importance in the Chandy-Misra protocol. Lookahead is the ability of a process to predict its future behaviour. In a queueing network simulation, lookahead exists if each job at process p_i requires a minimum service time ε_i. Knowledge that each future job at process p_i requires at least ε_i allows a process to predict that a job that arrives immediately will not depart for at least ε_i time units. For our purpose, we will always consider that all processes have a constant lookahead. Studies [4], [5] have indicated that the larger the lookahead values, the better the performance of a Chandy-Misra simulation becomes.

Two waiting rules ensure the correctnes of the Chandy-Misra protocol.

- *The input waiting rule:* Before process p_i executes an event e, p_i must receive from each of its input channels an event (including e), and e must have the smallest timestamp among the events in the input channels.

- *The output waiting rule:* Consider an event e' created at process p_i and scheduled for process p_j. Event e' is sent to p_j after p_i has started executing event e, where e'.ts ≤ e.ts + ε_i. If several events satisfy this inequality, then they are sent to p_j in nondecreasing timestamp order.

Following this two waiting rules it is guaranted that the event execution order at a given process is equivalent to that obtained by a sequential simulator, and therefore, the global simulation results are correct.

2.3 Solving deadlocks in Chandy-Misra parallel simulations

In a Chandy-Misra simulation, deadlock may occur in a feedback loop. Consider the feedback network in Figure 3. The initial events are generated by the source process p_0. At the beginning, p_0 sends an event e to process p_1. According to the input waiting rule, p_1 cannot handle e before it receives a message from p_4. Unfortunately, p_4 will not produce any output message before p_1 produces the first message. Thus, processes p_1, p_2, p_3 and p_4 fall into a deadlock situation.

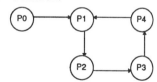

Fig. 3 Deadlock situation

Two approaches have been proposed to resolve the deadlock situation:

- **Deadlock avoidance using null messages:** Null messages provide only timing information which is used to reduce the overhead of the input waiting rule as well as to avoid deadlock [6]. For example, after a process p_i has executed event e, it may send a null message e', where e'.ts = e.ts + ε_i, to the output channel connected to p_j. When p_j receives e', it knows that it will never receive any message with timestamp less than e'.ts from p_i. In Figure 3, suppose that process p_i ($1 \le i \le 4$) has a constant lookahead value ε_i and its local clock $ck_i = 0$ initially. At the beginning of the execution, p_i sends a null message with timestamp $ck_i + \varepsilon_i$ to the output channel. When the destination p_j receives the null message, p_j is essentially promised by p_i that it will not send a message to p_j carrying a timestamp smaller than ε_i, and ck_j is incremented from 0 to ε_i. Then p_j sends a null message with timestamp $ck_j + \varepsilon_j = \varepsilon_i + \varepsilon_j$ to its output channel. After the null messages have circulated in the loop several times, p_1 eventually receives a null message with timestamp larger than e.ts. According to the input waiting rule, p_1 executed e and the deadlock is avoided.

- **Deadlock recovery:** In this case no null messages are sent. A separate mechanism is used to detect when the simulation is deadlocked, and another mechanism is used to break the deadlock. Deadlock detection mechanisms are described in [7], [8], [9]. In the deadlock recovery mechanism, all processes cooperate to find the events with the smallest timestamp in the system. These events can be safely executed, and the deadlock situation is thus recovered.

Both approaches lead to a high computational overhead, reducing the advantage taken of the processing capability of parallel computers. As we will show in 3.1, we propose a third alternative for avoiding deadlocks in parallel simulations.

3. Multithread simulator implementation

In order to provide a high level of modularity for the simulator we have developed a parallel simulation class library in C++ which is the core of this simulator. In 3.3 we give a brief description of the most important classes. Besides the class library, we use a small program which is in charge of creating and stablishing the parameters for all the objects in the simulation from the description found at the specification file.

Although, this parallel simulation class library is not our main contribution to parallel simulation. On the contrary, the main features of this simulator are the deadlock avoidance system and the memory management. The deadlock avoidance system intends to solves the deadlock problems in the Chandy-Misra simulations introducing only an acceptable computing overhead. Also, we have studied in detail the memory management problem in parallel simulations to develop a particular memory management model which avoids the memory overloads associated to parallel simulations not reducing the performance of the simulator.

3.1 Deadlock avoidance system

As we said before, there are two main alternatives for solving deadlocks in a Chandy-Misra simulation: using null messages or using a deadlock recovery system. Both choices present an overhead which cannot be ignored. We have selected the first alternative, although we made some changes on it. We have said that after a process p has executed an event e, it sends a null message e', where e'.ts = e.ts + ε(e), to each one of its output channels. When processes p_i connected to the output channel of p receive e' they are told that they will not receive any other message from p with timestamp smaller than e'.ts. This information is used to reduce the overhead of the input waiting rule as well as to avoid deadlocks. If each time a process p executes an output event it also has to send null messages to all the other processes connected to its output channel we will end up with the system saturated with null messages. This, more than activating the simulation, it slows it down. If, on the contrary, we just send null messages when we are not able to produce an output event according to Chandy-Misra waiting rules, then we reduce the overhead of null messages without avoiding deadlocks. It is clear that, with this method, processes have to wait more for their inputs. While processes are waiting they are in a "sleeping" state and they release their processing resources so that they can be used by other processes meanwhile. This means that all processors are always used as much as possible.

3.2 Memory management for Chandy-Misra parallel simulations

In this parallel simulation there is a process for each one of the nodes of the system we want to study. This processes are executed in parallel with the only synchronisation of that provided by the Chandy-Misra waiting rules. This brings up problems which are not found in sequential simulations. This problems can be classified into two main types.

We will consider first the situation shown in Figure 4. It can be seen that the output time of the two sources is very different. Although, we should recall that the time required to process a user at a given thread doesn't depend on this parameter. Therefore, both sources, as independent processes, will create nearly the same amount of users. In a sequential simulation, although, source S1 would create 1000 times more users than S2. Therefore, we see that the user generation in the sources in parallel simulations is not balanced. Given that the input waiting rule prevents the process from handling an input until all the input channels have at least a user with timestamp greater than its own, users received from source S2 have to be wait much more to be processed than those of source S1. Therefore, the input buffer with users from S2 soon saturate of users waiting to be processed while the other has only a few users in it. In a sequential simulation this never happens, but in parallel implementations it becomes an important problem leading the simulation to a deadlock caused by a lack of memory.

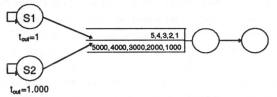

Fig. 4 Example of a situation with two sources with very different output times

The solution we have found for this memory problem is to synchronise all the sources in the system. With this we ensure that the global generation rate of users in the whole system is identical to that of a sequential simulator. This way we can avoid situations such as the one shown in Figure 5. To synchronise effectively all the sources we have use a single process to handle all the execution of the sources in the system, making sure that in the global generation sequence is always non-decreasing in timestamp order. This means that at any time there can only be one source executing and this has to be the one generating the smallest timestamp. We must say that this doesn't make the simulator sequential because generally the number of sources in real system is much smaller than the rest of elements in the system, and the loss of parallelism is not excessively high.

Another problem we find in the implementation of the parallel simulator is due to a lack of synchronisation between sources and all the other processes in the simulator. If the generation speed at the sources is higher than the processing speed in the rest of the system, stations would see how they input buffers grow without being able to process them that fast. We have to consider that for each new user created we need a certain amount of memory to store its own data and if the number of users in the systems is too large we might end up in a deadlock situation due to a lack of memory. It is also possible, although less dangerous, that the generation rate at the sources is less than the processing rate at the rest of the processes in the system. In this case, we will not get out of memory but the performance of the parallel simulator decreases due to the continuous changes between the slept and active states at the station processes instead of working at a fairly constant speed.

We could think that all process can work together to maintain a correct generation rate, but the computational cost for this is too high to be considered. We have used a global semaphore in order to control the amount of user circulating through the system at any time during the simulation. Semaphores are tool provided by multiprocess operating systems to synchronise the execution of processes. Our semaphore is a long integer which is decremented each time a user is created and incremented each time a user is destroyed. If the semaphore's value is zero and a source intends to decrement it, the process of the source is stalled until its value is greater than zero. Therefore, if we initially set the semaphore's value with N then we will have there is never more than N users in the system and the memory usage is always limited beforehand.

4. Implementation of the Simulation Elements

4.1 Source Objects:

A source, from its definition, doesn't have any input, so we can bypass the input waiting rule. Therefore, a source only has to schedule output events in nondecreasing timestamp order. That is, if the source schedules e_1 earlier than e_2, then $e_1.ts \leq e_2.ts$. For that purpose, we calculate the output timestamp as the sum of the previous output timestamp and the time to output variable ($t_{out} \geq 0$) $e_{i+1}.ts = e_i.ts + t_{out}$. According to our deadlock avoidance system, a source will only send a null message in case the established maximum number of active users is reached. This is the only possible case where a deadlock can be found if we don't use null messages.

Sources are the key for the memory management system. First, we limit the total generation of events in the sources by using a semaphore. If a source requests the

access to the semaphore when its value is zero the generation process is suspended until the resource is released. Therefore, we have to request the semaphore whenever we want to generate an output event in a source and release that semaphore when it is destroyed in a sink. To set the value of the maximum number of users produced that we want in the system at the same time we need to initialise the semaphore's with that value. Also, as we said before, we need to synchronise all the sources so that the generation sequence is the same as in a sequential simulation. We do this by using only one thread to execute all generation events of all sources, making sure that all generation events are executed in non-decreasing timestamp order. This is enough to keep the memory requirements to practically the same as in a sequential simulation.

4.2 Station Objects:

A general station object must have always an input queue and a server. We have implemented this two elements as independent classes. This modular design lets us change the behaviour of this elements simply by changing the corresponding object.

We have implemented queue objects prepared to work on multithread environments. We use an input buffer for each input channel to store the incoming users until they can enter the queue. The size of this buffers is assumed to be infinite so that no overflow may happen. In the queue we have all the users with timestamp smaller than the time set in the local clock of the station, just like in a real station. Fig. 5 shows a block diagram of the structure of a general input queue.

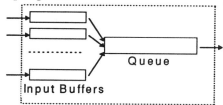

Fig. 5 General diagram of an input queue object

We use critical sections to control the access to the station's data. Critical sections are, as well as semaphores, synchronising mechanisms available in multithread operating systems. They restrict the access to sections of code which should not be executed by more than one thread at a time.

The server block represents all the processing resources that are available at that station. It works just the same as in a sequential simulator because the imput and the output order is always the same as in a sequential simulator.

A station's thread have to stop its execution until everyone of its input lines have received a user with timestamp greater or equal to the time set in the station's local clock. Only if we are dealing with FIFO queues of infinite size and no pre-emptive we only need to have all input lines not empty to continue executing without any risk of breaking the causality constrain. In case we can go on with the execution of the station's thread, then we will have to decide which will be first, an input to the server or an output. If the server is busy we will have to produce an output. otherwise, we need to see when is the next input and when the next output and choose the first event. The local clock will then be substituted by the time of the event produced.

4.3 Sink Objects:

The sink object is in charge of destroying all the users that it receives, releasing the memory used so that other users can be created. This is done by releasing the generation semaphore.

It is important to state that, for the simulation results, it is irrelevant the order in which the user are destroyed in the sinks. Therefore, we can bypass the input and output waiting rules for this objects. We take advantage of this fact executing the sinks code over the thread corresponding to the element which is sending the user to the sink. This is made simply by placing all the functionality of the sink objects in the input function (which is executed by the thread which calls it).

5. Summary

This paper shows the principals of our parallel simulation system. On one hand we have built an object oriented parallel simulator which provides a powerful tool for simulating queuing networks. On the other hand, we provide a graphic environment for designing and simulating systems easily.

We provide a graphic environment prepared to work under Windows NT with which we can design and simulate queuing networks with nearly no effort. In order to simulate a system, we create a model with the graphic environment, set all the parameters of the system, save the design and run the simulator. This means that we don't need to write a specification file using some simulation language or specific code in order to simulate a given

system. This helps us speeding up the global process of simulating system and makes it easier to handle.

The simulation code has been programmed with C++. We have created a library of classes which can be used directly or can also be used as a base for creating new classes. In order to simulate a system, we just create the objects for each node and put them to work. This simulator runs under Windows NT, but the code has been designed so that it can be easily adapted to other operating systems.

We have based this simulation system on the Chandy-Misra Paradigm which assures the complete satisfaction of the causality constrain. We have develop those ideas to create a set of general system simulation rules. This implementation has been produced so that the only memory deadlocks are the same as those we would find in a sequential simulation. For that purpose we have developed new memory management ideas so that we can overcome most of the problems related to the asynchronous parallel execution.

References

[1] K. M. Chandy and J. Misra, "Distributed simulation: A case study in design and verification of distributed programs," IEEE Trans. Software Eng. , vol. SE-5, pp. 440-452, Sept. 1979

[2] Y.-B. Lin and B. R. Preiss, "Optimal memory management for time warp parallel simulation," ACM Trans. Model. Comput. Simulation, vol. 1, pp. 283-307, Oct. 1991

[3] D. Jefferson, "Virtual time II: The cancelback protocol for storage management in time warp," Proc. 9th Annu. ACM Symp. Princip. Distrib. Comput., Aug. 1990, pp. 75-90

[4] R. M. Fujimoto, "Lookahead in parallel discrete event simulation," Proc. Int. Conf. Parallel Process., vol. III, 1988, pp. 34-41

[5] B. R. Preiss, W. M. Loucks, "Impact of lookahead on the performance of conservative distributed simulation," Proc. SCS Europ. Multiconf. Simulation Method., Lang., Architect., 1990, pp. 204-209

[6] K. M. Chandy and J. Misra, "Asynchronous distributed simulation via a sequence of parallel computations," Commun. ACM, vol. 24, pp. 198-206, Apr. 1981

[7] E. W. Dijkstra, C. S. Scholten, "Termination detection for diffusing computations," Inform. Process. Lett., vol. 11, no. 3, pp. 1-4, 1980

[8] L. Liu and C. Tropper, "Local deadlock detection in distributed simulations," in Proc. 1990 SCS Multiconf. Distrib. Simulation, Jan. 1990, pp. 64-69.

[9] J. Misra, "Distributed discrete-event simulation," Comput. Surveys, vol. 18, pp. 39-65, Mar. 1986

[10] Yung-Chang Wong, Shu-Yuen Hwang, Jason Yi-Bing Lin, "A Parallelism Analyzer for Conservative Parallel Simulation," IEEE Transactions on Parallel and Distributed Systems, vol. 6, No. 6, Jun. 1995

Evaluation of a Visual-Tracking Adaptive Robot Control Algorithm

Christos Ginis, Dewi I. Jones
School of Electronic Engineering and Computer System
University of Wales, Bangor
cginis@sees.bangor.ac.uk

Eduardo Zavalla
Instituto de Automatica, Universidad Nacional de San Juan
Argentina

Abstract

The paper considers parallel computation of a visual-tracking adaptive robot control algorithm. The algorithm is represented as a complex directed acyclic graph and a static scheduling technique, implemented as a set of Matlab functions forming part of a Matlab 'Scheduling Toolbox', is applied to generate a schedule and place these tasks onto a network of transputers. The measured execution times are presented and the results analysed.

1. Introduction

1.1. Motivation

Visual information is an extremely powerful form of sensory capability and its use for robot control is the subject of much current research. One use of visual information is to provide a tracking input to a camera carried on the end-effector of a robot manipulator, the goal being to maintain the object of interest in the centre of the camera's field of view by controlling the robot's joints. This problem has been considered by several workers including Nasisi et al [1] who propose an adaptive control scheme for this purpose. The advantages of their algorithm are that it compensates for uncertainties in the robot dynamics and the boundedness of the control errors has been proved by stability analysis. The resulting controller is based on inverse dynamics and requires a non-linear robot model to be embedded in the control law. Combined with the adaptive update law, this places a high computational demand on the digital control processor. In this paper the use of parallel processing for computing the control scheme described by Nasisi et al [1] for a 2 link manipulator is considered. The goal is to minimise the execution time of the algorithm, so that the digital controller can sustain a high sample rate and thereby achieve good dynamic tracking performance. The approach adopted here has been used previously in the case of adaptive impedance control, requiring a very short sample time [2]. The paper also illustrates the use of the Matlab 'Multiprocessor Scheduling Toolbox' [3] which is being developed as a tool, aimed particularly at control engineers, to simplify the parallel implementation of control algorithms.

1.2. Overview of the paper

The next section describes the computational structure of the visual control algorithm and shows how it was partitioned into tasks for parallel evaluation. Section 3 describes how one static multiprocessor scheduling technique, originally proposed by Kim and Browne [4], was implemented as part of a Matlab scheduling toolbox and applied to this case. Section 5 analyses the effect of communication time on the parallel execution time using a simple multiprocessor model presented by Stone and described in [5]. Experimental results are presented in section 6. Finally, section 7 discusses these results and presents some conclusions.

2. Parallel representation of the vision control algorithm

This paper considers a parallel implementation of the adaptive controller presented in [1] which uses visual feedback for robots with a camera-in-hand configuration. The mathematical description of the visual tracking algorithm is lengthy and is not of immediate interest here. Essentially the computation consists of evaluating several trigonometric functions and many floating point expressions within the limited sampling period of a digital control system, typically a few hundred microseconds in this application. There are no conditional branches or iterative loops and the algorithm is evaluated afresh at each sample time with new input data obtained from sensors located on the robot manipulator.

246

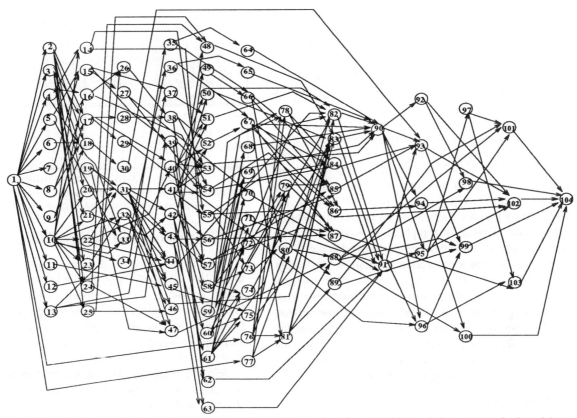

Figure 1. Directed Acyclic Graph representation of the adaptive-tracking vision control algorithm

The algorithm can be partitioned into tasks for parallel execution and represented as a directed acyclic graph (DAG). Each node in the graph represents a task and is weighted with an execution time. Each directed arc represents a precedence relationship and is weighted with a communication time. The multiprocessor is commonly abstracted as an undirected graph, where the nodes represent processors and the edges represent bidirectional communication channels.

Figure 1 is a task graph representation of the adaptive-tracking algorithm for the case of a manipulator with 2 degrees of freedom. It consists of 104 tasks with sizes varying from $3\mu s$ to $40\mu s$ averaging at $10\mu s$. With such a great number of tasks the visual representation of Fig.1 is of limited use but it does serve to illustrate the high connectivity and the flow of data from input to output. Fig. 1 shows the logical interconnections between tasks but omits information about task sizes and communication times along edges.

Nonlinear robotic algorithms have stimulated several examples of the use of multiple processors as a means of achieving satisfactory sample rates. Early work was restricted to evaluating simple robotic algorithms where adaptation was not considered but advances in nonlinear control theory now require that more complex structures be considered for parallel evaluation.

Minimising execution time requires careful scheduling to identify and place parallel and sequentially dependent tasks on to the available processors. This must be done without violating any precedence constraints which may exist between tasks or any other constraints imposed by the characteristics of the target multiprocessor architecture. It is well known that the general scheduling problem belongs to the NP-complete category [6] and therefore, to obtain a good (though sub-optimal) schedule, a heuristic approach must be used.

Scheduling methods can be classified as being static or dynamic. In general, static scheduling techniques are appropriate for applications with a constant task set while dynamic scheduling is selected if there is a variable task set or a task set with unpredictable behaviour. A more complete guide to scheduling methods can be found in [7]. Static scheduling is suited to this application because the task set is constant and because a low scheduling overhead is essential. Further, given the relatively small sizes of many of these tasks, communication times are expected to be a major influence on the overall parallel execution time. This was an important factor in the selection of a scheduling method.

3. Scheduling method and toolbox application

Kim and Browne's [4] algorithm takes communications overhead into account directly and can be described in terms of the following stages:

- *Linear Clustering.*
- *Iterative Refinement.*
- *Virtual Architecture Graph (VAG).*
- *Physical Architecture Graph (PAG).*

The first stage of the technique consists of repeated application of a critical path algorithm which separates the task graph into a set of sub-graphs (called clusters) which contain nodes that must be computed sequentially. The separation is done by cutting out of the task graph the cluster representing the 'longest' route from the beginning node to the end node. The 'longest' route is actually defined by an objective function, equation (1), which is a weighted sum of inter-node communication time as well as node computation times. Cutting out this route yields a number of sub-graphs and the critical path algorithm is recursively applied to each of these until only linear clusters are left.

$$\sum_{i=1}^{l-1}[w_1 T_{comp_i} + (1-w_1)(w_2 T_{comm_{i(j+1)}} +$$

$$(1\text{-}w_2)\sum_{j \in N_{adj_{j \neq i}}^{i+1}} T_c omm_{(i+1)j})] \quad + \quad w_1 T_{comp_i} (1)$$

where:

T_{comp_k} is the computation time of node n_k

$T_{comm_{st}}$ is the communication time of node n_s with node n_t

N_{adj}^t denotes the set of nodes adjacent to n_t

w_1 is a weighting function on computation and communication.

w_2 is a weighting function on nearest-neighbour and next-neighbour communications

The second stage tries to identify highly communicating linear clusters. This stage consists of identifying edges which have been cut during the linear clustering process which, if reconnected, will reduce the overall execution time. Merging these clusters may result in a loss of parallelism but the reduction in communications overhead is beneficial in reducing the overall execution time.

The third stage represents the clusters that remain after iterative refinement as an undirected graph, called the Virtual Architecture Graph (VAG). Each node in this graph represents a cluster whereas each edge represents communication requirements between clusters. It is assumed that there is no limit on the number of nodes in the VAG.

The final stage applies the maximum spanning tree al-

gorithm on the VAG to derive what is termed its Dominant Request Tree (DRT). The principle of the last step of mapping is to seek a graph isomorphism between the DRT and the Physical Architecture Graph (PAG) which represents the topology of the practical multiprocessor. In the case of transputers, which are (within-limits) re-configurable, the PAG can adopt the topology of the VAG. The method has been implemented as a set of Matlab functions (Table 1) which form a prototype Matlab static scheduling toolbox. Identifying linear clusters in the task graph uses the **lin-clust()** function which in turn calls a number of lower level functions, including **lgpth()** to compute the longest path and **dfs()** to search the task graph. The clusters realised after applying **linclust()** are used as input to the iterative refinement stage which, at present, is performed manually but aided by

Function	Action
linclust()	perform linear clustering
lgpth()	find longest path
refine()	iterative refine linear clusters
dfs()	perform depth first search
merge()	merge clusters with nodes or clusters with clusters
label()	label edges for iterative refinement
vag()	produce adjacency matrix for cluster interaction
mst()	maximum spanning tree
dfihs()	schedule based on DFIHS
cpmisf()	schedule based on CPMISF
cp()	schedule using critical path analysis
lb()	lower bound function
generate()	generate nodes for use with CPMISF and DFIHS
spth()	find shortest path
gc()	Gantt chart representation of schedule
atgg()	task graph generator
minst()	find minimum spanning tree

Table 1. Toolbox functions and action

the use of **refine() label()**, and **merge()** . The first two are used to compute and label edges according to equation (2).

$$level_{edge}(e_{ij}) = wcomp_j + (1-w)comm_{ij} + level_{node}(n_j)$$
(2)

where:

$$level_{node}(n_j) = \max_{n_k \in D_j} (level_{edge}(e_{jk}))$$

and:

w is a weighting factor

$comp_j$ is the computation time of n_j

$comm_{ij}$ is the communication time from node i to node j.

The **merge()** function reconnects highly interacting clusters. This procedure continues iteratively until no further reduction in execution time is obtained.

The third stage uses **vag()** to produce an adjacency matrix that represents the dependencies between the refined clusters. In the final stage, **mst()** is used to produce the DRT of the VAG and a list containing edge communication times in a descending order of priority. This is used to assist the mapping process wherever a direct graph isomorphism does not exist between the DRT and the physical processor arrangement.

In general, the toolbox is designed using a set of lower level building block functions implemented either in C, using Matlab's mex file interface, or as M-files. Table 1 presents the functions that have been implemented as part of the toolbox, which includes four complete scheduling methods, namely Kasahara and Narita's CPMISF and DFIHS [8] methods, Hu's critical path scheduling method [8] and Kim and Browne's linear clustering algorithm. More on the Toolbox can be found in [2].

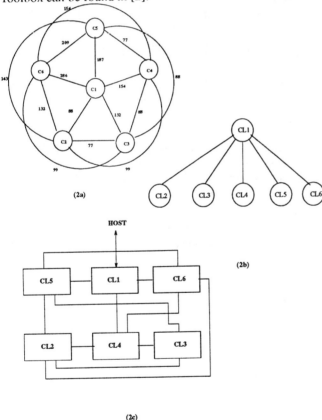

(2a)

(2b)

(2c)

Figure 2. (2a)The Virtual Architecture Graph. processor arrangement

(2b) The Dominant Request Tree (2c) The physical

4. Application of the linear clustering technique

Applying the **linclust()** toolbox function to the visual tracking algorithm identified 41 clusters. However, repeated application of iterative refinement reduces the number of clusters to 6, represented in Table 2. The virtual architecture for the final six clusters can be seen in Fig.2(a) and subsequent application of **mst()** produces the DRT of Fig.2(b).

Clusters	Nodes
CL1	1 2 6 19 31 41 55 73 82 90 95 97 101 104
CL2	3 21 29 42 60 71 91 93 94 100 102
CL3	4 5 33 34 35 36 66 67 80 81 84 88 89 99
CL4	7 9 13 16 17 26 37 38 39 40 52 53 54 58 62 63 76 78 86 92 98
CL5	14 23 24 25 28 32 43 46 47 48 51 57 61 64 65 74 77 79 83 85
CL6	8 10 11 12 15 18 20 22 27 30 44 45 49 50 56 59 68 69 70 72 75 87 96 103

Table 2. Clusters remaining after iterative refinement

The scheduling software therefore predicts that, due to communications overhead, using more than 6 processors actually increases the total execution time. Using the **gc()** function a Gantt chart representation of the schedule is produced and presented in Fig.3, where a schedule length of $220\mu s$ is predicted. It is of interest to note the wide range of execution times shown in the Gantt chart and the substantial proportion of time for which some processors are idle.

The mapping procedure was repeated for the cases of 2 and 4 processors, respectively, in the PAG. This can be done on the basis of the VAG already described because Kim and Browne's method assumes that an infinite number of processors is available for the VAG - the actual number of processors available is not taken into account prior to the stage of mapping from VAG to PAG. To remain consistent with the principles of their method, which groups nodes to minimise communications costs, highly interactive clusters were placed onto the same processors when 2 and 4 processors were used. The execution times predicted were $371\mu s$ and $272\mu s$ for 2 and 4 processors, respectively, indicating that 6 processors should yield a near-minimum execution time.

The limited number of links (four per transputer) prevents the DRT of Fig(2b) being realised directly. Use is therefore made of the priority list produced by the **mst()** function which finally leads to the physical processor arrangement of Fig.2(c).

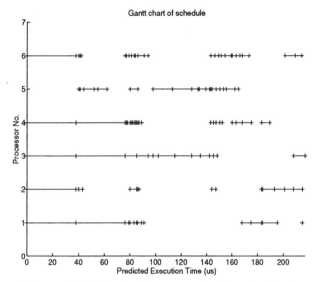

Figure 3. Gantt chart representation of schedule.

5. Effect of communications overhead

The impact of communications overhead can be estimated using a simple mathematical model. In general, the principle source of overhead in static scheduling algorithms is the interprocessor communication which is necessary because of interacting tasks placed on different processors. A measure of the performance of a multiprocessing system is the $\frac{R}{C}$ ratio which determines the granularity of tasks. The effect of varying the $\frac{R}{C}$ ratio will influence the parallel execution time and this can be illustrated by reference to Stone's multiprocessor model [5]. The parallel execution time of M identical tasks on N fully connected multiprocessors is given by the relation :

$$E_p = Rmax(k_i) + \frac{C}{2N} \sum_{i=1}^{N} k_i(M - k_i) \qquad (3)$$

where C is the communication time between processors, R is the run time of a task and k_i is the number of tasks assigned to the ith processor. Moreover, if tasks are scheduled onto processors using *load balancing* which assumes the even distribution of M tasks across the N processors then $k_i = \frac{M}{N}$. Furthermore, the sequential execution time of the M tasks is simply:

$$E_s = MR \qquad (4)$$

Substituting (4) into equation (3) an expression for the parallel/sequential execution time ratio is given by:

$$\frac{E_p}{E_s} = \frac{1}{N} + \frac{M}{2N}(1 - \frac{1}{N})\frac{C}{R} \qquad (5)$$

The first term on the right hand side of equation (5) is the ideal parallel execution time and the second term is the overhead component. It clearly indicates that the influence

on the overhead increases as the $\frac{R}{C}$ ratio falls thus indicating the desirability of coarse granularity.

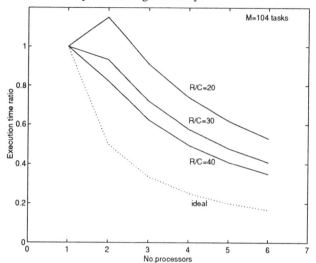

Figure 4. Variation of the R/C ratio based on Stone's multiprocessor model

This model must be used with caution, because there are significant differences between its underlying assumptions and the situation in practice. Nevertheless, the variation of parallel execution with $\frac{R}{C}$ ratio is expected to have the form shown in Fig.4.

6 Results

The experimental work was conducted on a Transtech Parastation consisting of several INMOS T805-20 32 bit transputers hosted on a SparcStation IPC. This can be classified as a loosely-coupled MIMD architecture where each processor possesses local memory and communication is by means of message passing via an interconnection network. Physically this is done by means of 20Mbits/s duplex serial links (4 per transputer) which are either connected directly between processors or via a programmable switch. The code is written in occam 2.

The measured execution times for 1,2,4 and 6 processors are presented in Fig.5 which also includes the execution times predicted using the **gc()** function and the ideal execution time, ie. the execution time expected if communication between processors is negligible. Using two transputers decreases the total execution time from the single transputer case, but only slightly, from $682\mu s$ to $646\ \mu s$. Using 4 processors yields a substantial decrease in execution time but, contrary to prediction, it increases again when 6 processors are used.

Fig.6 shows the measured execution times of Fig.5 normalised to the single processor execution time. There is a similarity can be identified between the form of this graph and the $\frac{R}{C} = 30$ case of Fig.4, which correctly predicts the

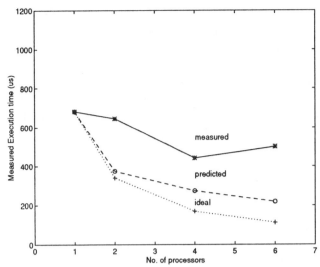

Figure 5. Real, predicted and ideal execution times for 1,2,4,6 transputers

limited decrease in execution time using 2 processors and the more substantial decrease using 4. However Stone's model predicts that a further decrease in execution time will be observed as the number of processors is increased from 4 to 6 which does not occur in practice. This is because the network of six processors requires through-routing of data via intermediate processors, adding again to the complexity of the support software and making the communication times longer. This effect is not included in Stone's model.

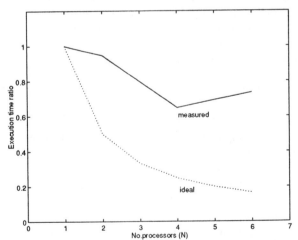

Figure 6. Normalised measured execution time variation for 1,2,4 and 6 processors

7. Conclusions

The results show that the method has proved effective in producing a schedule for a complex task graph in the difficult case where the communication times dominate. The measured execution times are greater than predicted and there are two major reasons for this:

- There is a mismatch between the granularity required to exploit the algorithm's parallelism and the characteristics of the transputer.
- The scheduling technique does not take account of limited connectivity, particularly the need for message through-routing as the network grows.

Caution is needed when using Stone's model because, despite the apparent agreement with the experimental results, the model assumptions and underlying causes of the overhead differ significantly.

- The task graph's connectivity is much less than the full connectivity assumed in the model and also imposes sequential relationships on the tasks, in contrast to the model's independent tasks;
- The model assumes equal task sizes whereas there is a considerable size variation in practice;
- The Communication via intermediate processors due to the hardware constraints of the transputer are not accounted for.

The model may be used, with care, to deduce broad performance features but cannot be used to predict quantative parallel execution times. Research is being performed to develop an improved mathematical model which takes message through-routing into account and is a closer match to the particular characteristics of the target processor.

Further, some of the factors that effect the performance of Kim and Browne's scheduling method are being investigated, particularly , the effect of the choice of the weight w_1 and w_2 in equation (1) and how rules can be included within the method to take into account processors' limited connectivity.

The use of the 'Multiprocessor Scheduling Toolbox' has also been illustrated. Despite being an early prototype, it was a valuable aid to deriving a good schedule for a complex task graph. Work is concentrating on extending and refining the toolbox by including more scheduling techniques and seeking methods to automate the iterative refinement stage which is one of current weaknesses.

In practice, it is necessary to consider the case of a robot with 3 links and experience shows [2] that this is a very much larger problem which provides more scope for exploiting parallelism and has a granularity which is more suited to transputer implementation. This problem will be considered in a future investigation.

Finally the use of enhanced hardware through-routing [9] is being considered as a means of reducing the communication boundedness of the computation.

8. Acknowledgement

This work was supported by a collaborative grant awarded by the British Council and Fundacion Antorchas, Argentina. Mr Ginis holds a scholarship of the University of Wales, Bangor.

References

[1] O.H.Nasisi, R.Carelli, and B.Kuchen, "Tracking Adaptive Control of Robots with Visual Feedback," *13th World Congress IFAC, San Fransisco USA*, June 1996.

[2] C.Ginis, R.Carelli, D.I.Jones, and E.Zavalla, "Parallel computation of a control algorithm for a robot manipulator.," *Control Engineering Practice*, vol. 4, pp. 179–186, Feb. 1996.

[3] D.I.Jones and C.Ginis, "Development of a multiprocessor scheduling toolbox," *Proc. Third IFAC/IFIP workshop on Algorithms and Architectures for Real-Time Control, Ostend*, pp. 247–252, 1995.

[4] S.J.Kim and J.C.Browne, "A general approach to mapping of parallel computations upon multiprocessor architectures," *IEEE Conf. on Parallel Processing*, pp. 1–8, 1988.

[5] H.S.Stone, *High Performance Computer Architecture (2nd ed.)*. Addison Wesley, 1987.

[6] M. Garey and D. Johnson, *Computers and Intractability - A Guide to the Theory of NP-Completeness*. New York: W.H.Freeman and Company, 1979.

[7] B.A.Shirazi, A.R.Hurson, and K.M.Kavi, *Scheduling and Load Balancing in Parallel and Distributed Systems*. IEEE Computer Society Press, 1995.

[8] H.Kasahara and S.Narita, "Practical multiprocessor scheduling algorithms for efficient parallel processing.," *IEEE Trans. on Computers*, vol. C-33, pp. 1023–1029, Nov. 1984.

[9] M.P.Craven, K. Curtis, S. Wilde, B. O'Neil, and J.W.Ellis, "Conflict-free hardware routing for communication bound applications," *Parallel Processing Developments*, no. WoTUG-19, 1996.

Arena – a Run-Time Operating System for Parallel Applications

K.R. Mayes and J. Bridgland
Centre for Novel Computing,
Department of Computer Science,
University of Manchester,
Oxford Road, Manchester, UK
ken@cs.man.ac.uk
bridglaj@cs.man.ac.uk

Abstract

This paper presents the case for a run-time operating system to provide predictable and controllable resource management for parallel applications. Developments in compilers for parallel applications, which depend on analysis of program behaviour, require corresponding developments in predictable and controllable operating system-level resource management. A customisable system, Arena, is described which provides operating system-level resource management at user-level, where it is accessible to application and run-time system developers. This resource management is accessed via libraries, and effectively becomes part of the application run-time system. In such a system the application gets only the resource management that it needs. A low-policy hardware-dependent executive provides a low-level interface presenting an abstraction of processor hardware to the hardware-independent resource managers. The use of Arena on a Sparc-based distributed store multicomputer is described, and three parallel application areas being investigated on Arena are briefly discussed.

1. Introduction

This paper discusses using a *run-time operating system* to achieve optimal performance for parallel applications.

A variety of run-time systems exist which provide, for example, a message-passing interface or a virtual shared memory interface to parallel applications. This paper is not about the debate between advocates of different abstract machine paradigms, but is about how these machines should be implemented on high performance architectures. The point is that these run-time systems rely on the native operating system to provide resources such as servers and communication primitives. Indeed, the purpose of such run-time systems is to map the parallel machine required by the application on to the machine actually provided by the operating system. Inefficiencies arise where there are incompatibilities between these two levels of machine, and where compromises have to be made in the run-time system implementation. That is, policy embedded by the designer of the operating system interface may have to be avoided by reimplementation at the run-time library level. Furthermore, general-purpose operating systems may introduce unpredictability into the execution of an application. The system may determine when housekeeping daemons run, for example, or when deferred I/O processing occurs, without reference to the requirements of the application.

Developments in compilers for parallel applications, which depend on analysis of program behaviour, require corresponding developments in predictable and controllable operating system-level resource management.

One way around these problems is to link the application with only that resource management it requires, load this object onto the *bare hardware*, and let it run. This is the situation found in many real-time applications. Mukherjee and co-workers described such real-time systems using the term 'operating software' in order to emphasise the intimate connection between real-time application and real-time operating system [20]. However, it is unreasonable to expect parallel application developers to write their own low-level, hardware-specific code.

This paper describes a solution to this problem – to provide a generic 'hardware' interface which can reside on the nodes of the parallel machine and which can host the run-time operating system. Arena is a system being developed which takes this approach [16]. It emphasises individual application performance (though it is designed to allow multiple applications to run 'concurrently' if required).

2. Background

It has been argued (e.g. [12]) that operating systems for multicomputers should present an abstraction, a 'single system image', to hide the physical machine architecture from users. However, not all users of parallel architectures require such abstractions.

For example, Bryant and co-workers described their experience with Fortran users of the IBM RP3 system [5]. These users regarded the operating system "as an adversary bent on denying them direct access to the hardware". Similarly, developers of data management and persistent object stores need sophisticated use of caching, and allowing the application access to file-caching policies has been found to improve performance [6]. Many existing parallel language implementations multiplex their own process structure onto a smaller set of operating system-provided processes, where the operating system-provided process may run a user-level scheduler. There are many problems associated with building a language on a conventional operating system platform due to mismatches between operating system process model and the requirements of the language [22].

The problem then, for high performance systems, is how to empower the application writer and language developer so that they can safely access the hardware mechanisms, and control the policy of resource management which is traditionally locked into the operating system kernel.

The key here is to separate operating system policy from mechanism. The desirability of separating policy from mechanism has been recognised for some time, and was a motivating force in the design of the Hydra operating system [26]. A trend in operating system work has been to move policy out of the supervisor-mode kernel and into the realm of the user. That is, to put policy at *user-level*. The implication is that these policy routines can be provided by the *users* of the computer system themselves, rather than by the systems programmers who created the operating system kernel. These routines, perhaps generated by language system implementors, will become encapsulated into libraries and accessed by applications in association with the language run-time libraries.

3. Arena

Moving all policy into user-level resource manager libraries effectively extends the run-time system into the operating system. Figure 1 shows schematic diagrams comparing a conventional monolithic operating system with the approach taken in Arena. All the hardware-dependent code for manipulating the hardware resides in a 'nanokernel', or run-time executive, which is accessed by a generic low-level interface. Having a general low-level interface facilitates system portability. Arena has been implemented on the EDS

[25] Sparc and PC-AT Intel 3/486 architectures.

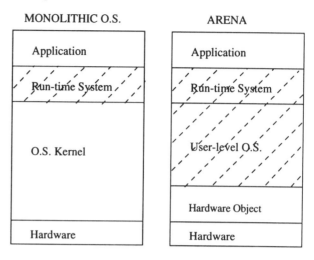

Figure 1. A schematic comparison of approaches to operating systems. Library-based components are shaded.

3.1. Arena structure

The basic structure of Arena is shown in Figure 2. There are basically two components. One component consists of *hardware-independent* resource manager libraries for linking to application. These represent a run-time operating system. The other component is the *hardware-dependent* code. The run-time operating system gains access to hardware-dependent code via an abstract interface. This interface is called the Hardware Object (HWO) interface. The main principle in this division is to distinguish between policy and mechanism. The HWO is intended to give access to the mechanisms provided by the hardware. The resource manager libraries determine the policy in the use of these mechanisms.

3.2. Hardware Object

The HWO is essentially a run-time executive which provides a primitive machine interface to the resource managers. This interface presents a generalised view of processor hardware, so that porting of the system to various hardware platforms is facilitated [23]. The HWO interface provides a set of *downcalls* which is used by the hardware-independent, user-level, manager code. There are, at present, 34 primitives in the HWO interface (Figure 2), not including any device-specific interface primitives. This structure represents an instance of the system that would reside on each node of a distributed-store machine. Note that the trap interface is internal to the HWO.

This HWO interface is accessed via a library. The HWO code is implemented at user-level whenever possible. However, for protection, and access to supervisor-mode instructions/registers, some library routines consist of a stub which traps to supervisor and accesses the code conventionally via the trap table.

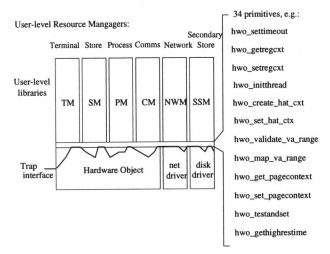

Figure 2. Structure of the Arena system.

The HWO interface gives an abstraction of processor and store which can be implemented on any processor with memory management hardware. The HWO deals mainly with low-level concerns such as general *register contexts* and *address translation*. By providing interface primitives for manipulating register contexts separately from address translation, the HWO interface allows the policy of associating threads of control with address spaces to be determined at user-level. The HWO also provides the concept of a *va_range*, a range of virtual addresses which can be validly accessed in a particular hardware address translation context. The HWO also supports the concept of a *page context* for user-level handling of page faults, for example in the implementation of virtual shared memory (VSM). The *page context* is analogous to the *register context*. Both are hardware-dependent data types enabling the user-level to save and restore aspects of the hardware state, in a hardware-independent manner. The HWO internals are protected from user-level access by page access rights. The HWO imposes protection between applications by forbidding access to hardware address translation contexts which are not owned by an application.

Interfaces to devices such as disks and networks are an extension of the HWO interface. The reasoning here is that different systems will have different devices which may, in turn, require different interfaces. Typical disk (secondary store) interfaces are *hwo_ssm_open()* to establish rights to access certain disk blocks and *hwo_ssm_io()* to read or write

to a disk block. A message is sent to a network device via a call to *hwo_cio_netsend()*.

3.3. User-level managers

Arena resource management components are decoupled, interacting via well-defined interfaces, and implemented in C++. Resource manager base classes are defined for Process Manager (PM), Store Manager (SM), Secondary Store Manager (SSM), Communication Manager (CM), Network Manager (NWM) and Terminal Manager (TM). Only those managers required by an application need be used. For example, a single-node application needs no NWM, whereas only applications doing disk I/O will need an SSM.

The interface provided by each of these managers has three components:

1. A set of operations used by application code. These operations are at the level of a typical microkernel interface. They serve to map conventional concepts on to the low-level HWO interface. The PM provides operations for manipulating and switching *threads* and *address spaces*. Threads in Arena are entirely user-level constructs. The HWO has no concept of a *thread*. The HWO only provides the concept of a *register context*. The SM operations allow *regions* to be created and mapped. The CM provides message passing via the familiar *port* abstraction.

2. A set of operations used by other managers. These operations allow managers to interact. For example, the PM provides interfaces for the SSM to stop and resume threads which are involved disk I/O. The SM operations allow managers to allocate regions: the PM requires regions for thread stacks; the SSM requires regions for buffer caches. The PM uses an SM operation to obtain a new address space. The NWM provides operations to allow other managers to exchange messages, upwards and downwards, with the network device interface of the HWO.

3. A set of operations used by the HWO. Such operations allow the manager to do deferred handling of events at user-level. These routines are executed by distinct *event threads* (see section 3.4).

Arena is a customisable system. Resource manager subclasses allow instantiation of a resource manager for particular policies. An application links to the managers providing the required resource management policies. For example, different PMs exist for cooperative, priority-based and round-robin scheduling of threads. Different SSMs can be selected for particular caching policies. Relinking to the application and other manager libraries is facilitated by using base-class pointers.

3.4. Arena event handling

Hardware events, such as disk and network interrupts, and page faults, can be handled at user-level. The mechanism is shown in Figure 3. Events can be handled by application-specific event threads. These threads are scheduled by the user-level PM scheduler code. Thus the application can determine both when and how events are handled.

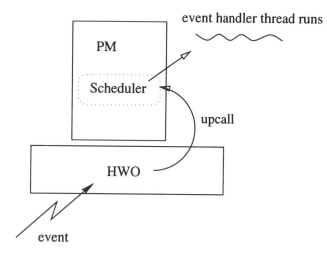

Figure 3. User-level event handling. Deferred handling of events can occur under control of the application.

As will be discussed in section 5.3, the use of user-level code to handle page faults allows the implementation of application-specific VSM policies on parallel architectures.

4. Parallel Arena

Arena is specifically intended to run in parallel on both shared memory and distributed memory architectures (i.e both multiprocessors and multicomputers). The conventional approach to operating system architecture is different on these two types of hardware platform. With multiprocessors, there is generally a single kernel instance running on all processors, and shared data structures are protected by locks. Arena has been implemented for execution on multiprocessor platforms, although this aspect is not emphasised, and has not yet been tested.

Arena does however already run on a distributed store multicomputer. The EDS machine [25] has nodes connected by an internal deltanet. Each node consists of two Sparc processors sharing 64 Mb of store. Only one of these Sparcs receives the network interrupts, and at present Arena runs only on that processor on each node. When running an application, each multicomputer node has its own local HWO

and instances of resource managers. Such replication serves to maximise local activity and minimise global activity. No attempt is made to share HWO data structures across distributed store, so there is no contention for HWO resources between nodes.

Where an application is distributed, a set of the resource manager objects for that application occurs on each node on which the application is running. Communication between nodal components of the application resource management occurs via the NWM object instances, mediated via the HWO and network driver, on each node (Figure 4). Network performance in Arena, for user-level to user-level transfer of data, was measured to be faster than a microkernel running on the EDS machine [15]. Both systems used user-level message buffers in the transfer, with no intermediate copying.

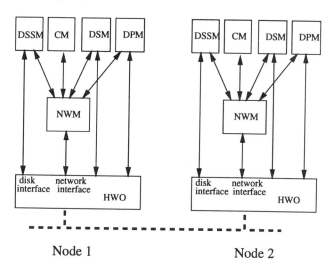

Figure 4. Resource management for a distributed application.

5. Target application areas

In order to demonstrate the usefulness of the Arena approach, several applications are being investigated.

5.1. Requiem database

The Requiem relational database [21] has been ported to Arena. It runs on both EDS and PC platforms. The database is the target application for work on secondary storage management [4]. Requiem runs on a Unix system call interface. This is provided on Arena by using a library of Unix system calls, implemented at user-level on top of the SSM interface. Although Requiem is not a parallel database, it is being used to investigate distributed file system implementation on the EDS machine. The Arena secondary store is implemented on the EDS machine using RAM disks. The EDS machine does not have physical disks attached to its nodes. Thus the effects of caching on secondary store performance with physical disks are being investigated on a PC-compatible Intel 386 machine. This allows comparisons between performances of database transactions on Requiem running on Linux and on Arena. Initial results indicate that performance of the two systems is similar using a flush-back policy. However with a more realistic write-through policy, Arena out-performs Linux by a factor of 1.6.

5.2. UFO language

Arena is intended to support parallel languages. Investigations into running the parallel UFO language [24] on Arena are in progress. Current work is using a distributed PM and CM to investigate a multi-nodal implementation on the EDS machine. The distributed PM allows remote creation of threads. Arena permits the run-time system implementor to rewrite the existing, more general-purpose, CM to achieve performance enhancements, where the developer has knowledge of language run-time system behaviour. More 'kernelised' general-purpose systems would not facilitate this.

5.3. Virtual shared memory for Fortran

Work has been done on parallel Fortran using user-level VSM on a microkernel-based system running on an EDS machine [9]. It is intended to use the accessibility of the mechanisms provided by Arena to implement the primitives of a VSM framework [10] which will be incorporated into a Fortran compiler.

As mentioned in Section 3.4, the Arena page fault handling thread can implement VSM. VSM implementation is based is the transferring of a virtual page between nodes, over a network, in response to a page fault in a virtually-shared region. This mechanism has been implemented and early results indicate that Arena is appreciably faster than a microkernel on EDS (by a factor of 6). However, this initial Arena implementation does not include the directory processing carried out by the microkernel.

6. Related work

There are two ways in which user-level policy can be implemented: by providing a user-level *server process* or by providing a *library* of routines. Existing microkernels such as Mach and Chorus support user-provision of store, file and network management by user-level servers (e.g. [7] [11]). Microkernel systems can locate code in servers, and use an

IPC mechanism to bind applications to that code. Although this allows some redefinition of management code outside the kernel, it requires process management and IPC support in the kernel. It has been argued that such systems provide insufficient flexibility for library and language implementors [18] [13].

Work on Psyche [14] and on scheduler activations [1] take thread scheduling out of the kernel by enabling the kernel to make 'upcalls' to the user level. Threads on Arena exist only at user-level. There are no kernel threads, and no permanent kernel state for user-level threads [17]. This means that all scheduling policy decisions are in the user-level PM, in the realm of the application.

More recent systems, which are similar to Arena in emphasising user-level application-specific resource management, are PANDA [2] and Exokernel [8]. This latter paper coined the term 'library operating system' to describe such systems.

An alternative approach to application-orientated resource management is to allow the operating system kernel to be tailored [19] [3].

7. Discussion

Users of high performance parallel computers may wish to develop and link their applications directly on some node of the target machine (though this would seem to be unnecessary with a cross-compiler). For this application development, the machine may be required to provide a familiar general-purpose operating system environment. However, it seems unreasonable to force the application to *execute* using general-purpose resource management facilities. It is suggested here that high performance applications should be loaded onto parallel machines and execute with appropriate resource management policies. That is, that the operating system should conform to the application.

8. Acknowledgements

The authors would like to thank Professor Brian Warboys, Rupert Ford, Andy Nisbet and other members of the CNC. Stuart Quick was responsible for the hardware object implementations. Daniel Pollard of the UFO group is investigating UFO on Arena. This work is supported by EPSRC grants grants GR/J 84045, 93315512 and 91309499.

References

[1] T. Anderson, B. Bershad, E. Lazowska, and H. Levy. Scheduler activations: Effective kernel support for the user-level management of parallelism. *tocs*, 10(1):53–79, 1992.

[2] H. Assenmacher, T. Breitbach, P. Buhler, V. Hubsch, H. Peine, and R. Schwarz. Meeting the application in user space. In *Proceeding of the 6th ACM SIGOPS European Workshop*, pages 82–87, September 1994.

[3] B. Bershad, S. Savage, P. Pardyak, E. Sirer, M. Fiuczynski, D. Becker, C. Chambers, and S. Eggers. Extensibility, safety and performance int the spin operating system. In *Proceeding of 15th ACM Symposium on Operating System Principles*, pages 267–284, 1995.

[4] J. Bridgland. Secondary store management in a customisable operating system. 1996. In Preparation.

[5] R. Bryant, H. Chang, and B. Rosenburg. Experience developing the rp3 operating system. In *Proceedings of Usenix Association Distributed and Multiprocessor Systems*, pages 1–18, Summer 1995.

[6] P. Cao, E. Felten, and K. Li. Application-controlled file caching policies. In *Proceedings of Usenix Association Conference*, pages 171–182, June 1994.

[7] R. Draves. A revised ipc interface. In *Proceedings of Usenix Mach Symposium*, pages 101–121, 1990.

[8] D. Engler, M. Kaashoek, and J. O'Toole. Exokernel: An operating system architecture for application-level resource management. In *Proceeding of 15th ACM Symposium on Operating System Principles*, pages 251–266, 1995.

[9] R. Ford, A. Nisbet, and J. Bull. User-level vsm optimization and its application. *Proceedings of 2nd International Workshop on Applied Parallel Computing. Lecture Notes in Computer Science*, 1041:223–232, 1995.

[10] R. Ford, A. Nisbet, and M. O'Boyle. A new hybrid coherence mechanism: compilation and application. 1996. In Preparation.

[11] M. Guillemont, J. Lipkis, D. Orr, and M. Rozzier. A second-generation micro-kernel based unix; lessons in performance and compatibility. In *Proceedings of Usenix Association Conference*, pages 13–21, Winter 1991.

[12] B. Herrmann, M. Ortega, and L. Philippe. Unix on a multi-computer: The benefits of the chorus architecture. Technical Report CS/TR-91-46, Chorus Systems, 1991.

[13] E. Lazowska. System support for high performance multi-processing. In *Proceeding of the Usenix Association Symposium on Experiences with Distributed and Multiprocessor Systems*, pages 1–11, March 1992.

[14] B. Marsh, M. Scott, T. LeBlanc, and E. Markatos. First-class user-level threads. In *Proceeding of 13th ACM Symposium on Operating System Principles*, pages 110–121, 1991.

[15] K. Mayes, J. Bridgland, S. Quick, and A. Nisbet. Network performance in arena. *Proceedings of High Performance Computing and Networking, Europe. Lecture Notes in Computer Science*, 1067:1007–1008, 1996.

[16] K. Mayes, S. Quick, J. Bridgland, and A. Nisbet. Language- and application-oriented resource management for parallel architectures. In *Proceeding of the 6th ACM SIGOPS European Workshop*, pages 172–177, September 1994.

[17] K. Mayes, S. Quick, and B. Warboys. User-level threads on a general hardware interface. *ACM SIGOPS Operating Systems Review*, 29(4):57–62, 1995.

[18] T. L. M.L. Scott and and B. Marsh. Multi-model parallel programming in psyche. In *Proceedings of the 2nd ACM SIGPLAN Symposium on Principles and Practice of Parallel Programming*, pages 70–78, March 1990.

[19] B. Mukherjee and K. Schwan. Experimentation with a reconfigurable microkernel. In *Proceedings of the Usenix Association Symposium on Microkernels and other Kernel Architectures*, pages 45–60, September 1993.

[20] B. Mukherjee, K. Schwan, and P. Gopinath. A survey of multiprocessor operating system kernels. Technical report, Georgia Institute of Technology, College of Computing, 1993.

[21] M. Papazoglou and W. Valder. *Relational Database Management – A Systems Programming Approach*. Prentice Hall, 1989.

[22] D. Pierson. Integrating parallel lisp with modern unix-based operating systems. *Lecture Notes in Computer Science*, 441:312–315, 1989.

[23] S. Quick. *A generalised hardware interface for operating systems*. PhD thesis, Department of Computer Science, 1996.

[24] J. Sargeant. Uniting functional and object-oriented programming. *International Symposium on Object Technologies for Advanced Software. Lecture Notes in Computer Science*, 742:1–26, 1993.

[25] M. Ward and P. Townsend. Eds hardware architecture. *Lecture Notes in Computer Science*, 457:816–827, 1990.

[26] W. Wulf, E. Cohen, W. Corwin, A. Jones, R. Levin, C. Pierson, and F. Pollack. Hydra: The kernel of a multiprocessor operating system. *cacm*, 17(6):337–345, 1974.

Multiple Tuple Spaces onto Massively Parallel Architectures: a Hierarchical Approach

Antonio Corradi
DEIS - Università di Bologna
2, Viale Risorgimento - 40136 Bologna - ITALY

Letizia Leonardi, Franco Zambonelli
DSI - Università di Modena
213/b, Via Campi - 41100 Modena - ITALY

E-mails: {acorradi, lleonardi, fzambonelli}@deis.unibo.it

Abstract

The paper proposes a tuple space implementation model suited for massively parallel architectures. The model achieves scalability by organising the system in a hierarchical way and by encouraging the presence of multiple tuple spaces with a constrained scope. The effectiveness of the model is evaluated onto a transputer-based architecture.

1. Introduction

The shared memory abstraction is a widely spread and accepted concept [1]. Among a variety of different shared memory models that have been proposed in the past, the simplicity and the generality of the **tuple space model** made it a **general coordination model** for parallel programming [2].

In spite of its power, the globality of the tuple space model makes its implementation in large parallel system difficult. Because any centralised approach introduces a bottleneck that limits the **scalability** of a system, the tuple space must be distributed among different nodes, each one with its local memory and autonomous execution capacity, and the different parts of the memory are made transparently available to every node of the system. However, scalability problems may still arise: if the number of participating processors is too large, the tuple space may exhibit unacceptable latency time in accessing remote data.

The paper faces the above problems and proposes an implementation model of the tuple space abstraction for massively parallel architectures. The proposed model exploits **tuple replication** to grant limited latency times and separates the resources devoted to the implementation of the tuple space from the resources used by the application processes to avoid overhead. In addition, the model achieves scalability and locality by enforcing the presence of **multiple tuple spaces** with a well defined scope. The proposed model distributes multiple tuple spaces across a tree of nodes. Tuples are replicated in the tree with a given depth that depends on the scope of the tuples space they belong to. The paper shows that this solutions avoids bottlenecks in the hierarchy and achieves tuple access times proportional to the **degree of locality** of the access itself and **logarithmically bounded** with respect to the system size.

The paper is organised as follows. Section 2 presents the tuple space model and its implementation issues. The hierarchical model is described in section 3 and analysed in section 4. Section 5 describes the transputer implementation of the model and section 6 evaluates its performances.

2. The Tuple Space Model

In the tuple space model [3], the elementary unity of access to the memory is the **tuple**, an ordered set of typed fields (defining the tuple structure) with either a defined value or an undefined value. An additional field, a defined string, is usually adopted to classify tuples by type, i.e., by their structure. Two tuples are said to **"match"** if they belong to the same type and the values of their defined fields are the same. The result of the match is the unification of the two matching tuples w.r.t. their defined values.

The operation for interacting with the tuple space are **Out, In** and **Read**. The Out operation stores a tuple in the tuple space. The Read operation searches in the tuple space for a tuple matching with a "request tuple". In case one match occurs, the unified tuple returns to the calling process. The In operation is similar to the Read operation, but the matching tuple is removed from the tuple space and is no longer available to other matching operations. In case of possible multiple matches (one In operation that matches with several tuples or one tuple that makes several Ins match with itself) the choice is non-deterministic.

We emphasise the duality of the In and Read operations with the Out one. When one In or Read

259

operation does not produce any match, it is necessary to store the "request tuple" in the tuple space, so to test the future match possibilities (with incoming tuples produced by successive Out operations). Conversely, when an Out operation produces a tuple, it is necessary to test the presence of "request" tuples with which to match. In the following we indicate the tuples produced by In, Read, Out operations as In-tuples, Read-tuples and Out-tuples, respectively.

2.1 Implementing Distributed Tuple Spaces

The implementation of a distributed tuple space requires the definition of **policies** to **distribute** tuples onto the system nodes and eventually **replicate** them onto different nodes. We stress the separation between distribution policies and matching mechanisms: the matching search can occur locally to a node, on the basis of the tuples locally assigned to it, without any knowledge neither of the global distribution. The paper focuses on distribution policies.

The simplest **distribution policy** is based on a **hash** solution. A tuple is allocated in one of the nodes of the system on the basis of a hash function applied the type field of the tuple. The problem of this solution is that it can be difficult to achieve a homogeneous distribution of tuples; moreover, the solution does not exploit any locality principle. **Full replication** techniques can exploit locality. On the one hand, Out-tuples can be fully replicated in every node of the system while In and Read-tuples are not replicated and can locally search for potential matches. On the other hand, the dual solution stores Out-tuples only on one node while In and Read-tuples are globally replicated on every node of the system, so to globally search for a match [4]. Both these solutions, even if they are simple, are not effective for large systems: they are based on a global replication strategy and, thus, need non-scalable global coherence protocol. **Partial replication** techniques may limit the replication degree of tuples and can provide better scalability: in this case, tuples are replicated only partially in the system, assuming that the replication space of the Out-tuples forms a **non-null intersection** with the replication space of the In-tuples. An interesting example is the one of the Linda Machine [5]: the system is shaped after a 2-D mesh topology and tuples are replicated either by row or by columns depending on their type. The problem of partial replication techniques is their strict architecture-dependence: the replication strategy must take into account the topology of the communication system, that influence the implementation costs of both replication strategy and coherence protocols.

2.2 Multiple Tuple Spaces

The global model implied by the tuple space abstraction introduce scalability problems. In addition, the unstructured globality of the tuple space model does not fit with modern parallel programming styles that, instead, tend to structure and limit the interactions between the components of parallel applications. In most parallel applications, the interactions between processes can be described by a limited set of communication patterns (such as pipelines, farms, trees) [6, 7]. The result is a **structured application** and the scope of the references, both references to other processes and to shared variables, is confined within the parallel structure that use it, in a way similar to the local variables of a sequential procedure. Similar considerations have been recently applied to distributed logic programming [8] and toward extensions of the PRAM model [9].

With reference to the tuple space model, the above considerations encourage extensions toward the presence of multiple tuple spaces [10]: application processes can structure their accesses to several tuple spaces by making use of them as confined interaction spaces. In particular, in a multiple tuple space model, one identifier is associated to a tuple space: the In, Read and Out operations must specify the identifier of the referred tuple space and the matching mechanism is restricted to act within the specified tuple space.

From an implementation point of view, multiple tuple space models can provide better scalability only by tuple distribution policies able to physically exploit the logical locality enforced by the model. In other words, the presence of multiple and well-confined tuple spaces should induce locality at the architectural level. The presence of multiple tuple space does not grant any benefits when tuples are still globally distributed on the system - for example by means of a hash function - without any distribution strategy that take into account their scope.

3. The Tree Structured Tuple Space Model

Our tuple space implementation model follows a **partial replication** policy, as seen in section 2.1: the main points of the scheme are to make the replication degree of tuples (and the costs of the introduced coherence protocols) grow slowly with the system size and to facilitate the implementation of a multiple space model by **physically exploiting the logical locality** enforced by the model. In addition, the model clearly splits the nodes devoted to the execution of application processes (called execution nodes) from the nodes devoted to the implementation of the tuple space (called memory nodes):

this avoids any overhead of the memory activities on applications and grants more predictable performances.

More in detail, the system is shaped after a tree whose leaves are the execution nodes (figure 1). Each execution node is connected to a memory node of the immediately higher level. Each memory node is connected, in its turn, with one memory node of the higher level and some node (L-1, if L is the connectivity degree of a node) of the lower level, that can be memory nodes or execution nodes. The root memory nodes has no higher memory nodes to connect to.

3.1 Tuple Distribution Strategy

Let us temporarily disregard the presence of multiple tuple spaces and consider the tree as a global and unique tuple space.

The adopted tuple distribution strategy is based on a replication scheme that follows the vertical direction of the tree. Tuples (both In-tuples, Read-tuples and Out-tuples) are replicated along the whole path that starts from the execution node that generated it and goes up to the root. This replication scheme grants the property of non-null intersection: every tuple shares with every other one the nodes included in the path from the lowest common ancestor to the root. At least, two tuples share only the root. Since the height of the tree grows logarithmically with the system size, the replication degree of tuples (and so the cost of the coherence protocol) also follows this trend, making the model well-scalable.

When a tuple enters the tuple space, it climbs the tree by replicating itself in every node it crosses, after verifying the possibilities of match in those nodes. Replication stops if a match is found (figure 1): this optimises the replication degree since, in a couple of matching tuples, only one of them (the first that joins the tuple space) is replicated up to the root while the replication of the other is blocked at the lowest common ancestor. When a match occurs, the unified tuple must be yielded to the execution node that requested it.

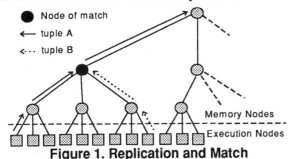

● Node of match
← tuple A
←··· tuple B

Memory Nodes
Execution Nodes

Figure 1. Replication and Match
the tuple A enter the tuple space and it is replicated up to the root when the tuple B enter the tuple space match with A and stops to replicate itself

3.2 Multiple Tuple Spaces in the Tree

Introducing multiple tuple spaces in our hierarchical model is simple and quite intuitive. Each memory node of the tree identifies a sub-tree of which it is the root: each one of these sub-trees can be considered as one tuple space in itself, independently on the fact that it is part of a deeper tree. Thus, several logically separated tuple spaces can coexist within the same physical tree of memory nodes.

With regard to the tuple distribution strategy, each tuple will be assigned a given tuple space, extending along a sub-tree of memory nodes, and it will be replicated only in a sub-tree corresponding to its scope. At one extreme, a tuple can belong to the minimal tuple space composed of one memory node only. At the other extreme, a tuple can be replicated along the whole tree, thus belonging to the global tuple space that every execution node can access to.

The main point of this solution for accommodating multiple tuple space in a system is that the locality of references within a tuple space reflects in the physical locality of the nodes of the tuple space: the enforcement of the locality principle is then encouraged not only by the programming model but even by the implementation.

4. Matching and Coherence Protocols

Replicating data introduces the problem of coherence and the need of protocols that grant it. In a tuple space, we argue that coherence can be guaranteed if:
1) any given Out-tuple is extracted by only one In-tuple operation;
2) any given In (Read) operation extracts (read) only one Out-tuple;

These relations are independent and so are the protocols to guarantee them: we can guarantee one of them without guaranteeing the other one. The choice of one coherence protocol does not influence the another one: only efficiency can be influenced.

4.1 Two vertical dual protocols

With reference to our hierarchical model, two dual protocols can be adopted to grant the **first coherence condition** within a tuple space (i.e., a sub-tree). We call it respectively UP-DOWN and DOWN-UP.

Let us suppose that, on a node, an In-tuple belonging to a given sub-tree matches with an Out-tuple belonging to the same sub-tree. By recalling that all tuples are stored in the lower levels of the sub-tree down to the path to the respective leaves that generated them, the Out-tuple can be assigned to the matching In-tuple - and extracted from the tuple space - only if no other In-tuple has already matched - and extracted - a different replica of the same

Out-tuple. The **UP-DOWN protocol** (figure 2), before assigning an Out-tuple to a given In-tuple, explores the sub-tree from the matching node down to the path that generated it, by extracting the Out-tuple from every node. If the Out-tuple is not found in one of these nodes, this means it has been already extracted from another matching In-tuple. In this case, a *NOT-OK* message is returned up to the matching node to notify the unavailability of the Out-tuple and the matching In-tuple must be stored and replicated up in the sub-tree, waiting for another match. If and only if the Out-tuple extraction process proceed down to the leaf, it succeeds. An *OK* message is returned up to the matching node and the Out-tuple is assigned to the In-tuple, because no other In-tuple will be given possibility to extract the same tuple from the leaf level.

When the matching protocol succeeds at a given level of the sub-tree, the Out-tuple must be necessarily extracted also from the upper level. Even if the protocol grants that the tuple will no longer assigned to any other In-tuple, because it is no more present in the lower level, its presence in the sub-tree could cause a waste of memory resources. However, the extraction process of the Out-tuple from the upper level of the sub-tree can occur in parallel with the UP-DOWN protocol and does not cause any additional access cost.

The **DOWN-UP protocol** (figure 2) is the dual of the above described one. In this case, a match occurred on a given node is validated only if the Out-tuple extraction process succeed up to the root of the sub-tree. We recall that if an In-tuple joins the tuple space before the matching Out-tuple, the Out-tuple will not be replicated up to the root: in this case, the protocol can then immediately validate the match. As in the UP-DOWN protocol, the Out-tuple must be extracted from the whole sub-tree, but the extraction from the lower lever can proceed in parallel with the protocol execution.

The **second coherence condition** states that one In-tuple must extract only one Out-tuple. In other words, if a replica of the same In-tuple on different nodes matches with different Out-tuples, only one of these Out tuple must be extracted from the sub-tree. Note that this coherence condition must be honoured by Read-tuples too. Again, two dual protocols can be identified: an UP-DOWN protocol and a DOWN-UP one.

In the UP-DOWN protocol, once a match has been validated by the first coherence protocol, the In-tuple descends the tree following its replication path by extracting itself from every node. If this and only if extraction process succeeds, the unified tuple generated from the match must join the execution node from where the In-tuple was generated. Instead, if the In-tuple replica

is not found on a node, another Out-tuple has already matched with a replica of it at a lower level of the tree and the unified tuple is not returned down to the execution node. In case of In-operations, the matched Out-tuple must no more be extracted: it is "outed" again in the sub-tree and made available to other Ins. In parallel with this protocol, the In-tuple is extracted from the upper level of the tree.

The dual scheme (DOWN-UP protocol) is not viable. The attempt of extracting the In-tuple up to the root, in fact, forces the protocol to span down to the tree before finally certifying the match and returning the unified tuple up to the execution node.

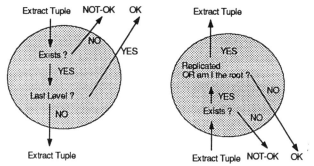

Figure 2. Coherence protocols on a node:
UP-DOWN (left) and DOWN-UP protocol (right)

4.2 Costs of the Protocols

The cost C of complete matching process (a successful one) can model the access time to the memory for retrieving information. Given a tuple space identified by a sub-tree of height D (i.e., the number of levels including the root of the sub-tree and the execution nodes) and by the supposing a In-Out match occurs on a memory node at a distance d from the execution nodes, these costs are:

- $C_{In-Out} = O(d)$ by adopting the UP-DOWN or by adopting the DOWN-UP one in the case the Out-tuple joins the tuple-space before the In-tuple;

- $C_{In-Out} = O(D)$ by adopting the DOWN-UP protocol in the case the In-tuple join the tuple space before the Out-tuple.

In fact, the protocols act across the vertical direction of the sub-tree, extending their action along d levels in the first two cases, along the whole height of the sub-tree in the latter. Since the height D of the sub-tree is proportional to the logarithm of the number of execution nodes that can have access to the given tuple space, and since $d \leq D$, the application cost of the protocols grows slowly with the size of the tuple space, making them scalable.

A more concrete analysis should also take into account the limits of the memory, communication and execution capability of each memory node. In fact, when the number of tuples becomes high, the management of the memory can require a high number of execution, memory and communication resources, making the tuple space access time grows. Because of the hierarchical structure of our model, this can become a problem in large sized systems: the higher the level of the tree, the less the physical resources available to the management of the tuple space.

Let us suppose that, in the unity of time, the tuple space has to manage, in its whole, M matches caused, for sake of simplicity, by M Out operations and by M corresponding In operations. In the case all tuples belong to a single, global tuple space, about half of the tuples joining the tree will be replicated up to the root (as explained in section 3.2). Let us suppose the other half stops their replication path, because of a match, at a distance $d \geq l$ from the execution nodes. By recalling that every tuple flowing across a node issues in it a matching mechanism, and by considering also the matching mechanisms issued by the coherence protocols, the total execution load at the level l of the tree can be expressed as: $C_{TOT}(l) = kMC + hMCp(l)$ where C is the cost, in terms of execution resources, of a matching mechanism, k and h are terms that depends on the adopted coherence protocol and $p(l)$ is the probability that a match occurs at the level $d \geq l$ in the tree. The load C_{TOT} is shared, at the higher levels of the tree, among a lowering level of memory nodes. Since M is likely to grow with the system size (the bigger the system the more the processes accessing the tuple space), the higher levels of the tree, in a large system, may not have enough resources to manage the C_{TOT} load, introducing a bottleneck in the system. A high degree of locality in applications can force a high probability $p(l)$ of producing matches at the lower levels of the tree. However, the first term in C_{TOT} is constant and represents a load that is present at any level of the tree, independently of the application characteristics.

When tuples are partitioned in multiple tuple spaces with a scope limited to given sub-trees, the load at a given level l of the tree is no more caused by all the tuples accessing the tree, but only by those tuples belonging to a tuple space whose sub-tree extends its height at the level l. In this case, the load at a the level l the tree can be expressed as $C_{TOT}(l) = q(l)(kMC + hMCp(l))$ where $q(l)$ represents the percentage of tuples replicated at the level l.

The presence of multiple tuple spaces with a well-defined scope makes any constant term in the load at a given level of the tree disappears. The load imposed on the memory nodes is made application dependent and the performance of our model are made dependent on the distribution $q(l)$ of tuples across multiple tuple spaces.

Since the tree structure of our model makes the number of memory resources exponentially diminish with the height of the tree, the only solution that grants a balanced distribution of the load among the memory nodes is the one that makes the number of tuples replicated at a given level of the tree exponentially diminish with the height of the tree, i.e., $q(l) \propto exp(-l)$. However, in many practical cases, less restrictive assumptions on the distribution of tuples can grant good performances in terms of memory access time, as the following section shows.

5. The Transputer Implementation

The project of the memory node support for implementing the tuple space model for a transputer-based architecture (a Meiko CS-1) separates mechanisms (tuples storing, matching and tuples extraction) from policies (tuples distribution and replication, coherence protocols). Two different layers have been identified: the **tuple layer** and the **distribution layer** (see figure 3). This separation permits to change the distribution policy (and the tuple space model) without influencing mechanisms and, viceversa.

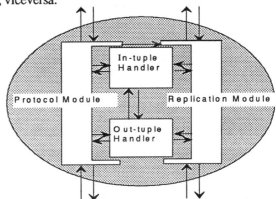

Figure 3. Modular layout of a memory node

At the tuple layer, the node support has been designed to allow a great degree of concurrency in actions, in particular for concurrently processing the In and the Out-tuples. Two modules implements these functions on a node: the *Out-tuple Handler* is dedicated to Out-tuples storage and extraction; the *In-tuple Handler* manages In and Read-tuples, stored in the node while waiting for matching Out-tuples. The arrival of a In-tuple onto a node is managed by the above handlers by following the below steps: 1) the Out-tuple handler checks for the possible matches with already stored Out-tuples beginning to the same tuple space; 2) if at least one match occurs, the matching Out-tuple it is extracted and the control is passed to the distribution layer, in charge of managing the coherence protocols; 3) if no match is possible, the Out-tuple handler passes the control of the tuple to the In-tuple handler, that provides to store it in the node. The replication module in the distribution layer will eventually decide to further replicate the tuple in the higher level. Any Out-tuples incoming on a node follows a complementary scheme.

At the distribution layer, the replication and the coherence module are in charge of managing tuple replication and of implementing the coherence protocols, respectively. The *replication module* on one node, receives the replication messages from the nodes of the lower level and then provides to pass the tuple to the corresponding handler. Depending on the result produced by the above handler, the replication modules decides whether to activate the coherence protocol (if a match has occurred) or to send a replication message to the higher level node (if no match has occurred). The *protocol module* can receive both protocol issuing messages from the replication modules of its node (when, as seen above, a match has occurred in the node) and messages from the protocol modules of the memory nodes it is connected with, being involved in the protocol session started because of a match occurred in another node.

6. Evaluation

To evaluate the performance of the presented implementation we have measured the time needed by a process to retrieve information from the memory with one In-operation, in the case the Out-tuple is already stored somewhere in the tree. We refer to a system composed of a four layers memory tree and 81 execution nodes.

When the tuple space is global (table 1), i.e., $q(l) = constant$, all tuples are replicated up to the root. In this case, if processes intensively access to the tuple space, the higher levels of the tree becomes the bottleneck and the access times to the memory, far from being proportional to the depth at which the match occurs, tends to exponentially grow with it. The growth in the access times is less significant when the assignment of tuples to multiple tuple spaces linearly decreases the number of tuples replicated up to a given level, i.e., when $q(l) \propto l$. In this case, only when the processes intensively access to the tuple space the access times increase significantly. When tuples are distributed among multiple tuple spaces so to make the number of tuples replicated at a given level of the tree exponentially decreases with the height of the tree, i.e., $q(l) \propto exp(-l)$, the access times to the memory is directly proportional to the depth of the tree at which a match occurs, without significant deviations even in very high traffic condition.

The above experiments have been performed with different sizes of the system: the main result is that the

access times do not show any dependence on the global system size but only on the depth at which a match occurs and on the distribution of the tuples in the system.

Level of the Tree	Level 2		Level 3		Level 4 (root)	
Distribution	LI	HI	LI	HI	LI	HI
$q(l) \propto constant$	2.4	5	4.5	15	7.9	34
$q(l) \propto l$	2.4	3.6	4.5	8.6	7.2	18
$q(l) \propto exp(-l)$	2.4	3.3	4.5	6.8	6.5	10.4

Table 1. Tuple access times (ms)
with different distribution of tuples and different intensity of the accesses to the tuple space (High and Low Intensity)

7. Conclusions and Future Work

The paper presents a tuple space implementation model that distributes multiple tuple spaces with a limited scope across a tree of nodes. The model achieves logarithmic scalability and allows applications to exploit locality in the accesses to a tuple space. The experience on a transputer-based architectures confirms the effectiveness of the model.

We are currently porting the presented model on a network of workstations by maintaining its hierarchical structure at the logical level.

References

1. B. Nitzberg, V. Lo, 'Distributed Shared Memory: A Survey of Issues and Algorithms', Computer, Aug. 1991.
2. D. Gelernter, N. Carriero, 'Coordination Languages and Their Significance'; Comm. of the ACM, Feb. 1992.
3. N. Carriero, D. Gelernter, 'LINDA in Context', Comm. of the ACM, April 1989.
4. N. Carriero, D. Gelernter, 'The S/Nets's LINDA Kernel', ACM Trans. on Computer Systems, May 1985.
5. S. Ahuja et al., 'Matching Language and Hardware for Parallel Computation in the LINDA Machine', IEEE Trans. on Computers, Aug. 1988.
6. B. Bacci et al., 'P3L: a Structured High-Level Parallel Language and its Structured Support', Concurrency: Practice and Experience", May 1995.
7. J. Darlington et al., 'Parallel Skeletons for Structured Compositions', ACM Symp. on Principle and Practice of Parallel Programming, Santa Barbara (CA), July 1995.
8. E. Denti et al., "An Extensible Framework for the Development of Coordinated Applications", Proc. of Coordination '96, Cesena (I), April 1996.
9. T. Heywood, S. Ranka, 'A Practical Model of Parallel Computation', J. of Parallel and Distributed Computing, Nov. 1992.
10. D. Gelernter, 'Multiple Tuple Spaces in Linda', Proc. of PARLE '89, June 1989.

A Static Mapping System for Logically Shared Memory Parallel Programs

C. Andras Moritz and L.-E. Thorelli

Department of Teleinformatics, Royal Institute of Technology, S-164 40 Kista, Sweden

e-mail:{andras,le}@it.kth.se

Abstract

A general model for parallel programs, the LSM (Logically Shared Memory) model, is outlined. It is based on parallel objects exchanging information by operations on shared variables subject to synchronization constraints in dataflow style. An experimental system EMAPPER for static mapping of LSM programs on multiprocessors is described. It uses a cost model suitable for (almost) acyclical programs of objects connected by data dependency. The mapping is performed in three phases, shared variable pre-assignment, clustering, and processor assignment. Experiments are reported, and generalizations of the mapper are discussed.

Keywords: cost models, static mapping, logically (virtually) shared memory multiprocessing models.

1. Introduction

The falling price/performance ratio of multiprocessor based systems has led to the usage of such systems in traditional application areas as banking systems and real-time systems, and new application areas are emerging. One of the most important problems to resolve in parallel and distributed systems is the development of suitable methods and tools for an efficient distribution or mapping of the parallel program to the available multiprocessor.

A mapping is static when the distribution of the objects is determined before program execution begins and the system does not modify the distribution during the program execution. The mapping decisions are made at compile-time using apriori knowledge of the system. Static schemes apply in systems where information such as a data dependency graph, or equivalent, is available before program execution. Static schemes can be very efficient for some type of parallel applications, in particular for real-time industrial systems where predictable performance is important. For more insight into the mapping and scheduling problem the reader is referred to M. G. Norman's and P. Thanisch's survey [6] and a recent book edited by B. A. Shirazi et al. [7].

The optimality of a mapping is measured relative to a cost model, i. e. a set of rules used to express the execution times from computation, communication-synchronization times and other costs. A cost model reflects the characteristics of the parallel program model and also the multiprocessor hardware and the kind of performance goal(s) to be achieved. Unfortunately, different programming models and variations in hardware implementation makes it difficult to define a general cost model for parallel systems.

The motivation behind this work is to study the static mapping problem of LSM programs. The EDA [4,8] programming model, as an example of an LSM model, is shortly outlined. An LSM program is based on parallel objects exchanging information by operations on shared variables subject to synchronization constraints. In this work we suggest mapping automatically the shared variables to processor nodes as a part of the mapping process. In this first approach we restrict the class of LSM programs used with the mapper to those with only data-dependency synchronization and (almost) acyclical communication graphs. EMAPPER is the software tool implemented for static mapping of this special class of LSM programs. It is based primarily on communication cost optimizations. The chosen program class and the assumed hardware platform and execution model allows us to neglect implementation aspects such as the overhead resulting from context-switching and a more detailed analysis of synchronization situations. We also assume that each processor has sufficient work to do (this can be true if the granularity is fine enough), so that it will not experience any idle time until all its work is finished. Experiments are described which show the performance improvements which can be achieved by EMAPPER.

At the end we point out some important aspects in an LSM cost model and discuss further improvement of the mapper to broaden the class of LSM programs that can be reliably mapped statically.

2. The LSM program model

An LSM program is composed of executing entities, here called objects, and shared variables. An object has local variables accessible only to itself, and pointers to shared variables necessary for exchanging information with other objects. Shared variables are used both for asynchronous and synchronous communication between objects. Accesses to shared variables are subject to synchronization constraints, e. g., a message cannot be read before it has been written. Naturally, due to the possible physically distributed shared memory, some shared variable accesses can be remote memory accesses.

The multiprocessor hardware is assumed to be a multiprocessor with processor elements (PE) interconnected through a network. The LSM model is general. It incorporates other models such as message passing, shared memory, virtually shared memory, and mixed models with both shared memory and message passing, and even distributed systems.

The structure of an LSM program can in general be represented by a directed graph as follows:

Nodes: Objects O
    Shared variables V
Edges: Read access edges $Er \subset V x O$
    Write access edges $Ew \subset O x V$

An edge $(v, o) \in Er$ represents one or more read accesses by the object o to the variable v, and an edge in Ew similarly represents write accesses. We refer to this graph as the LSM directed communication graph. It is sometimes convenient to use undirected edges, representing any kind of access. In this case the graph is called an LSM undirected communication graph, or simply an LSM communication graph.

Figure 1 shows a simple application program consisting of three objects executing in parallel. Object $O1$ communicates with object $O2$ executing operations to variable $V2$ and to variable $V3$. Object $O2$ executes operations on $V3$ and $V2$. Object $O3$ executes operations involving shared variables $V1$ and $V3$.

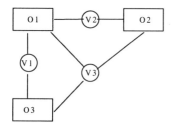

Figure 1 Example of an LSM Communication Graph.

The LSM mapping problem. Given an LSM program graph $<O \cup V, Er \cup Ew >$ and a computer system with a set of processor elements P. A mapping is then a pair $<\mu, \psi >$ where

$$\mu : V \rightarrow P \qquad \psi : O \rightarrow P$$

The LSM mapping problem consists of finding an optimal, i.e. least-cost mapping. Here cost is defined by a cost model for the assumed program and computer system classes.

The EDA model. EDA is an LSM programming model developed at the Royal Institute of Technology, Stockholm. The name EDA is an acronym for Extended Dataflow Architecture, or Extended Dataflow Actors [4, 8]. Shared variables are of three types in EDA: *I, S* and *X*. They have different semantics covering different synchronization situations. I-data is used to enforce data-dependency between objects. Reading an empty I-data variable will lead to suspension of the object, thus reading I-data is potentially very time-consuming. X-data is used for mutual synchronization: writes and reads must be performed in strictly alternating order. S-data is intended for stream type communication. S writes are asynchronous, while S reads can cause synchronization delays when reading from an empty stream. The semantics of these operations clearly suggest variations in synchronization and communication costs depending on the variable type used.

Currently there are different EDA implementations on uniprocessors and on parallel and distributed systems [8, 1].

Classes of LSM programs. Since the primary goal of this research is the *static* mapping of LSM programs, studying the classes of LSM programs which can be successfully mapped statically is necessary. Our classification is primarily based on the following factors: shared memory access types, communication graphs and communication restrictions.

A) Classification based on shared memory access type:
We separate the following program classes:
- programs with only data-dependency allowed (corresponding to I variables in EDA)
- programs with stream-like communication also allowed (both I and S variables allowed in EDA programs)
- programs with complex synchronization allowed (i.e. I, S, X variables in EDA)

X variables or similar constructs are necessary in programs where complex synchronization constructions need to be implemented : e.g. rendezvous, monitors. The use of X variables introduce synchronization conditions (time conditions) which need to be taken in consideration in the scheduler to avoid blocking situations.

B) Classification based on the program's communication graph/pattern:
- Acyclical graph i.e. DAG (also incorporates special graph cases as chains and   trees)
- Cyclical graphs: Cyclical graph type I: read/write allowed to the same variable from the same object; Cyclical graph type II: cycles allowed between objects connected through a   shared variable; Cyclical graph type III: any kind of cycles between arbitrary objects allowed

C) Classification based on communication restrictions introduced:

The communication restrictions are used for capturing communication models frequently used in real-world applications. Two important models are task-based communication and process-based communication. Task-based communication is restricted to the beginning and end of object's execution, whereas process-based communication is allowed to occur at any time during the object's execution.

D) Classification based on program granularity:

The granularity is defined as the ratio between the number of objects and the number of PEs of the target computer system. We define an LSM program as coarse grained if the number of objects is lower than the number of PEs. In a medium grained program the number of objects is a few times larger than the number of PEs. A fine grained program has many more objects than PEs.

3. The EMAPPER

EMAPPER is a software tool for static mapping of a class of LSM programs.

Cost model.   The objects of the program perform computations and shared-variable accesses as determined by the script of the object, a sequence of basic blocks and shared variable accesses. Each basic block bb has an associated computation time $T_{comp}(bb)$, independent of the mapping. A shared variable operation svo has a communication time $T_{comm}(svo)$, and a synchronization time $T_{synch}(svo)$.

The cost model implemented in EMAPPER can be described shortly as follows:
- Computations: $T_{comp}(bb) = \gamma(bb)$, the execution time of the basic block.
- Communication time: The communication time depends on the mapping, whether or not the object communicating through a shared variable has been assigned to the same processor as the variable itself:
$$\psi(o) = \mu(v) \Rightarrow T_{comm}(svo)=0$$
Otherwise $T_{comm}(svo)$ is assumed a constant depending on the kind of operation   (Fetch/Store and type of shared variable I/X/S, in the case of EDA):
$$\psi(o) \neq \mu(v) \Rightarrow T_{comm}(svo)= f_c(svo) >0$$

The communication time for shared variable operations that can be overlapped with computations (e.g. IStore in case of EDA) has $f_c(svo) = 0$.
- Synchronization cost: A simplified model is used. Data-dependencies can cause context-switching but no processor blocking time is assumed. No static scheduling is necessary as we assume that each processor has sufficient work to do so it will not experience any idle time until all its objects have finished executing. $T_{synch}(svo)= f_s(svo) >0$ where f_s depends on the kind of operation and type of the shared variable, but not on the mapping.
- The total cost attached to shared variable operations svo:
$$T_{mem}(svo)= T_{comm}(svo) + T_{synch}(svo)$$
- Execution costs:
$$T_{o\_exec}(o)= \sum_{bb \in scr(o)} T_{comp}(bb) + \sum_{svo \in scr(o)} T_{mem}(svo)$$
$$T_{exec}(p) = \sum_{\{o | \psi(o)=p\}} T_{o\_exec}(o)$$
- Cost function:
Example of a cost function is the *parallel execution time (PET)* defined as the maximum processor execution time.
$$PET = \max_{p \in P} (T_{exec}(p))$$

Assumed program class. Based on the program classification presented in the previous section the following restrictions are made for the class of programs mapped with EMAPPER:

A) Shared memory access type: programs with only data-dependency allowed;

B) Communication graph: acyclical graphs (DAGs) and cyclical graphs of type I allowed;

C) Communication restrictions: both task-based and process based communication models allowed;

D) Based on program granularity: medium and fine grained programs allowed.

Without these restrictions our cost model would not be realistic.

4. Algorithms

Shared variable pre-assignment. The shared variable assignment described in this work is the problem of assigning shared memory variables into object nodes, minimizing the cost of communication.

For object o and shared variable v we denote the total communication cost by $c(o,v)$. Let $\mu 1 : V \to O$ denote an assignment. We define the cost of $\mu 1$ as follows (where a non-existing edge (o,v) has zero cost):

$$C(\mu 1) = \sum_{v \in V} \sum_{o \in O} \{c(o,v)|\mu 1(v) \neq o\}$$

The following rule is used.

SVP: Assign each shared variable to an object with maximum access cost.

Theorem 1: The SVP rule gives an assignment with minimal cost.

Proof: If there exists a v such that $\mu 1(v) = o$ and $c(o,v) < c(o',v)$ for some o, o', it is possible to reduce the cost by $c(o',v) - c(o,v) > 0$, by changing the assignment of v to o'.

Clustering. A cluster is a set of objects that execute on the same processor. The goal of clustering is to group objects with high intercommunication costs relative to computational costs into the same cluster. Clustering will reduce communication costs. All inter-cluster shared variable accesses are assumed to have zero communication cost.

The execution cost of cluster c is

$$Tcl(c) = \sum_{o \in c} (e(o) + \sum_{v} \{c(o,v)|\mu 1(v) \notin c\})$$

where $e(o)$ denotes the combined execution and synchronization costs for object o, i. e. those costs which are not affected by mapping.

The clustering algorithm *CL* performs a sequence of join steps, starting from unit sets containing a single object:

> Join step. Given clusters c_1, c_2.
> If $max\{Tcl(c_1), Tcl(c_2)\} \geq Tcl(c_1 \cup c_2)$, then the clusters are joined, otherwise they are kept disjoint.

We define the *object graph* as the DAG obtained from the directed communication graph by collapsing each shared variable v into the object $\mu 1(v)$.

The sequence of join steps is defined as follows. The initial unit clusters are sorted topologically according to the object graph, producing the sequence $c_1, c_2, ..., c_n$, where the indegree of c_1 is zero.

> For $j = 2, ... , n$: Let i be the smallest integer $< j$ such that there is an edge from c_i to c_j. Try to join c_j into c_i, if such an i exists.

The algorithm is fast but not optimal. The reason is the fixed clustering sequence and absence of backtracking. Other clustering algorithms can be easily obtained from adaptation of heuristic clustering algorithms used for message-passing systems, e.g. the

critical path algorithms. Critical path algorithms [3, 2] are generally slower because of quadratic complexities.

Processor assignment. The last phase in the mapping process involves the distribution of the clusters to processors. In this phase clusters are assigned to the available processors trying to keep the parallel execution time minimal. Shared variables are also implicitly mapped to PEs.

The following algorithm assigns clusters to processors, thus finally defining the mapping $<\mu, \psi>$.

PA: Sort the clusters in descending Tcl order, resulting in $c^1, c^2, ..., c^m$.
> For $j = 1, ... , m$:
> Find a processor p with minimum $Load(p)$.
> Set $\psi(o)$ to p for all $o \in c^j$
> Where

$$Load(p) = \sum_{o} \{(e(o) +$$

$$\sum_{v} \{c(o,v)|\psi(\mu 1(v)) \text{ undefined or} \neq p\})|\psi(o) = p\}$$

μ is defined by $\mu(v) = \psi(\mu 1(v))$, i. e., $\mu = \mu 1 \circ \psi$.

PA is not optimal i. e. does not always give the assignment with minimum parallel execution time. One can argue that one deficiency of this mapping algorithm is the fact that we do not use topological sort information of clusters in the algorithm. It is also important to note that in the case of more general LSM programs a topological ordering of all objects is not always possible.

5. Experiments

The goal of the experiments was to study the efficiency of the LSM mapping model proposed and implemented in EMAPPER. The influence of each step in the mapper is analyzed and compared for different scenarios.

The parameters we vary are the number of processor elements, the costs attached to shared variable accesses and the sequence of algorithms used. Results for a set of representative program graphs are derived in form of speedup diagrams.

Notations and definitions
- *CL* = clustering algorithm of section 4
- *noCL* = no clustering i. e. each object mapped separately
- *SVP* = shared variable pre-assignment of section 4
- *Ra* = randomly allocated shared variables
- *Pa* = processor assignment algorithm of section 4

$$R^{csc} = \sum \ (\ T_{comp} + T_{synch} \ ) / \sum \ T_{comm}$$ is the ratio of

computation and synchronization costs to communication costs in the program.

Speedup SVP is the speedup obtained by utilizing *SVP* instead of *Ra*.

Speedup CL is the speedup obtained by applying *CL* instead of *noCL*.

Speedup SVP+CL is the speedup obtained by applying *SVP+CL* instead of *Ra+noCL*.

Applications types. The mapper was tested for several programs. The programs used in the experiments are generated, chosen to reflect the characteristics of the intended program class as described in section 3. A summary of the test programs are presented in Table 1.

APPL	Nr of objects	Nr of Shared Variables	Com. graph	Shared memory access types
Appl1	31	1-2 /object	acyclic	only data-dependency
Appl2	61	1-2/object	acyclic	only data-dependency
Appl3	90	1-3/object	acyclic	only data-dependency
Appl4	15	1 /object	tree	only data-dependency

Table 1 Characteristics of programs used in experiments

In the experiments the R^{csc} ratio was varied, reflecting the different communication to computation cost scenarios.

Diagrams. The diagrams show the impact of shared variable pre-assignment, clustering and the combined effect of the algorithms on speedup. A sample of speedup diagrams is presented for Appl3 and Appl4.

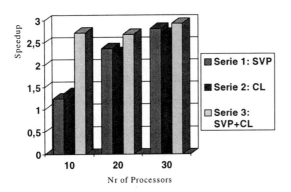

Figure 2 Speedups Appl3: R^{csc}=0,4

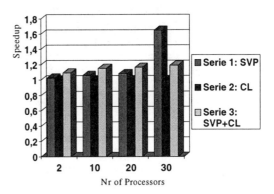

Figure 3 Speedups Appl3: R^{csc}=2

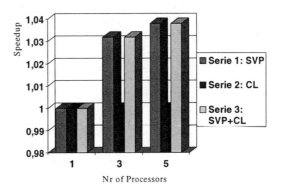

Figure 4 Speedups Appl4: R^{csc}=4

The main observations can be summarized as follows:
- the clustering step has good impact for all applications with large communication latencies but negligible effect when the communication costs are low;
- shared variable pre-assignment causes good speedup improvements in most of the cases;
- the combined speedup improvement of clustering and shared variable pre-assignment is significant in all cases.

6. Conclusions and further work

We have presented an approach to static mapping of parallel programs composed of objects and shared variables (LSM programs), using a cost model reflecting different synchronization and communication costs for different kinds of shared variable accesses in a dataflow style.

Mapping is performed in three steps, shared variable pre-assignment, clustering, and processor allocation. We described the EMAPPER implementation of this approach and an evaluation of it.

The evaluation has shown that automatic assignment of shared variables as a part of the static mapping process contributes significantly to speed improvement. Porting of an LSM program to different platforms (with different communication costs) can be done in an efficient way as the shared variable assignment and clustering step will optimize the program execution for the new platform.

Our work considered a restricted class of programs and cost model. More general LSM programs require refinements in both the cost model and in the mapping methods used. Synchronization events should be considered in more detail. Every shared memory operation is causing a synchronization event. The cost of the shared memory operation is determined by the necessary synchronization costs until the successful synchronization situation is reached. This overhead is heavily dependent on the implementation, e. g. the use of caching and/or prefetching. Special mapping and scheduling strategies will be required to minimize synchronization events with object-blocking operations and estimate blocking times.

Taking in consideration these factors the LSM mapping problem should be refined as follows: determine the *place of execution* and the *release time* of each basic block and shared variable operation from every object as well as *the place* of the shared variables in such a way to obtain a least-cost mapping. This is the direction of our future research on mapping and scheduling of parallel programs.

REFERENCES

[1] H. Ahmed, L.-E. Thorelli, V. Vlassov, *"mEDA: a parallel programming environment"*, Proc. 21st EuroMicro Conf., IEEE Comp. Soc. Press, 253-260, 1995

[2] Marios D. Diakaiakos, Anne Rogers, Ken Steiglitz, *A comparison study of heuristics for mapping parallel algorithms to message-passing multiprocessors*, Princeton University, 1993

[3] A. Gersoulis, S. Venupogal, T. Yang, *A comparison of clustering heuristics for scheduling DAGs on Multiprocessors, Journal of Parallel and Distributed Computing*, 16;276-291, 1992

[4] J. Milewski, H. Wu, L.-E. Thorelli, *"Sharing data in an actor model"*, Proc. 1992 Int. Conf. On Parallel and Distributed Systems, Taiwan, 245-250, 1992

[5] D.M. Nicol and D.R. O'Halloran, *Improved algorithms for mapping pipelined and parallel computations*, IEEE Transactions on Computers, Vol. 40, 1992

[6] Michael G. Norman, Peter Thanisch, *Models of machines for mapping in multicomputers*, ACM Computing Surveys, Vol. 25, No 3, September 1993

[7] Behrooz A. Shirazi, Ali R. Hurson, Krishna M. Kavi, *Scheduling and Load Balancing in Parallel and Distributed Systems*, IEEE Computer Society Press, ISBN 0-8186-6587-4, 1995

[8] L.-E. Thorelli, *"The EDA multiprocessing model"*, TRITA-IT R94:28, KTH, Stockholm 1994

❖ SESSION 6 ❖

Compiler Technology

Chair

C. A. Thole

Code Generation in **Bouclettes**

Pierre BOULET
Laboratoire de l'Informatique du Parallélisme
École Normale Supérieure de Lyon
46, allée d'Italie, 69364 Lyon Cedex 07, France
Pierre.Boulet@lip.ens-lyon.fr

Michèle DION*
DER/IMA/MMN
1, avenue du General de Gaulle
92141 Clamart Cedex
Michele.Dion@der.edfgdf.fr

Abstract

Bouclettes is a source to source loop nest parallelizer. It takes as an input **Fortran** *uniform, perfectly nested loops and gives as an output an equivalent* **High Performance Fortran** *program with data distribution directives and parallel (*$HPF!$ *INDEPENDENT) loops.*

This paper explains how the HPF program is built from a "shifted linear schedule" and a data allocation. We focus on the problems we had to solve to generate the **High Performance Fortran** *code. We detail the code generation phase and prove that our rewriting algorithm is correct.*

1. Introduction

1.1. What is Bouclettes?

Bouclettes is a source to source loop nest parallelizer. It takes some **Fortran 77** loops (perfectly nested with uniform data dependences loops) as input and returns an equivalent parallel program in HPF (High Performance Fortran).

Bouclettes has been written to validate some scheduling and mapping techniques based on the hyperplane method. These techniques are briefly sketched in section 2. The goal persued when building **Bouclettes** was to have a completely automatic parallelization tool. This goal has been reached and the input of the user is only required to choose the parallelization methodologies to be applied.

We have chosen HPF as the output language because we believe it can become a standard for parallel programming. Furthermore, data parallelism is a programming paradigm that provides a simple way of describing data distributions and of managing the communications induced by the computations. It thus relieves the programmer (or the parallelization tool) of generating the low-level communications.

A general presentation of **Bouclettes** can be found in [1].

---

*was at the LIP, ENS Lyon when writing this paper

This paper is organized as follows: after the introduction, we recall in section 2 how the parallelism is extracted from the input program; and in the following two sections, we explain how the code is rewritten in HPF. We first describe the issues of rewriting a program scheduled with a linear schedule in section 3, and then propose a technique to rewrite a program scheduled with a shifted linear schedule in section 4. Finally we conclude in section 5.

A detailed example is presented in an extended version of this paper (see research report [3]). And some experimental results testing the generated HPF code on some HPF compilers are presented in [2].

1.2. Related work

Automatic parallelization has been studied by many researchers and some tools for automatic parallelization have been written: SUIF [9], at Stanford University, California, PIPS [13] at the École Nationale Supérieure des Mines de Paris, France, the Omega Library [12] at the University of Maryland, Maryland, LooPo [10] at the University of Passau, Germany, and PAF [14] at the University of Versailles, France, among others.

The particularities of **Bouclettes** in regards of these other tools are the methodologies employed and the output language. Indeed, **Bouclettes** focuses on a more restricted class of programs that enable us to use some techniques whose optimality has been proven to derive a schedule where most of the other tools use heuristics. Further more **Bouclettes** generates complete HPF code with data placement directives which is not always done by the other tools.

2. Data analysis and parallelism extraction

The parallelization process can be decomposed into several inter-dependent tasks. See figure 1.

The dependence analysis consists in building a graph representing the constraints on the execution order of the in-

1066-6192/97 $10.00 © 1997 IEEE

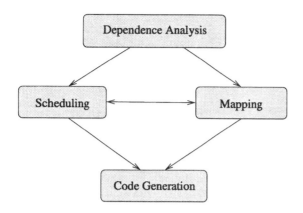

Figure 1. The parallelization stages

stances of the statements. The scheduling uses the dependences to build a function that associates an execution time to an instance of a statement. The mapping stage maps the data arrays and the instances of the statements to a virtual mesh of processors. The two previous stages (the scheduling and the mapping) are inter-dependent: we want the global transformation of the original loop nest to respect data dependences. The last stage is the code generation. We generate here code with parallel loops (`INDEPENDENT` loops) and a data allocation (`DISTRIBUTE` and `ALIGN` directives).

The **Bouclettes** system is organized as a succession of stages:

1. the input program is analyzed and translated into an internal representation,

2. this representation is used to compute the data dependences, in our case, data dependences are uniform, so a simple custom dependence analyzer is enough to get the exact data dependences,

3. from these data dependences, a linear or shifted linear schedule is computed,

4. the schedule and the internal representation are used to compute a mapping compatible with the schedule,

5. finally, the **HPF** code is generated following the previously computed transformation.

We detail below the analysis and parallelism extraction phases.

2.1. Dependence analysis

The dependence analysis consists in finding the constraints on the execution order of the iterations of the statements. The dependence analysis is quite simple in the re-

stricted context we have here. It basically consists in finding all the data dependences between the inner statements. The three kinds of dependences (direct, anti and output dependences) can be computed in the same way: the dependence vectors are differences between two data access functions that address the same array and reciprocally, all the differences between two data access functions that address the same array are dependence vectors.

2.2. Scheduling

Darte and Robert have presented techniques to compute schedules for a given uniform loop nest [5, 7]. These techniques are part of the theoretical basis of **Bouclettes**.

Currently, the user has the choice between the linear schedule and the shifted linear schedule. A schedule is a function that associates to each computation point (each iteration of a statement) the time when it is computed in the parallel program.

the linear schedule is a linear function that associates a time t to an iteration point $\vec{i}$ ($\vec{i} = (i, j, k)$ if the loop nest is three dimensional) as follows:

$$t = \left\lfloor \frac{p}{q} \pi . \vec{i} \right\rfloor$$

where p, q are mutually prime integers and π is a vector of integers of dimension d (the depth of the loop nest) whose components are relatively prime.

the shifted linear schedule is an extension of the linear schedule where each statement of the loop nest body has its own scheduling function. All these functions share the same linear part and some (possibly different) shifting constant are added for each statement. The time t for statement k is computed as follows:

$$t = \left\lfloor \frac{p}{q} \pi . \vec{i} + \frac{c_k}{q} \right\rfloor$$

where p, q, c_k are integers and π is a vector of integers of dimension d (the depth of the loop nest) whose components are relatively prime.

The computation of these schedules is done by techniques which guarantee that the result is optimal in the considered class of schedules. Here "optimal" means that the total latency is minimized.

2.3. Mapping

Darte and Robert have presented a technique to build a mapping of data and computation on a virtual processors grid [6]. That is the technique used in **Bouclettes**.

A mapping function is a function that associates to each computation point the processor which will do the computation and to each array element the processor whose memory it will be stored in.

Based on the computation of the so called "communication graph", a structure that represents all the communications that can occur in the given loop nest, a projection M and some shifting constants are computed. The base idea is to project the arrays (and the computations) on a virtual processor grid of dimension $d-1$. Then, the arrays and the computations are aligned (by the shifting constants) to suppress some computations.

More precisely, M, the projection matrix, is a $(d-1) \times d$ full ranked matrix of integers and the constants α_x are dimension $d-1$ vectors of integers. To each array or statement x is then associated an allocation function defined by:

$$\text{alloc}_x(\vec{i}) = M\vec{i} + \alpha_x$$

As the considered loop nests are uniform, choosing a different matrix for different arrays or statements would not improve the mapping. The schedule has to be taken into account to choose the matrix M. Effectively, the transformed loop nest will have as iteration domain the image of the initial iteration domain by the transformation:

$$\vec{i} \mapsto \begin{bmatrix} \pi \\ M \end{bmatrix} \vec{i}$$

It is mandatory to have this iteration domain mapped onto $\mathbb{Z}^d$, as otherwise we would need rationally indexed processors. As the choice of M does not have a high impact on the number of communications that remain, $\begin{bmatrix} \pi \\ M \end{bmatrix}$ is just computed as the unimodular completion of vector π.

Once M has been computed, the alignment constants are determined in order to minimize the number of computations. Here the user can choose if he wants to respect the owner computes rule (as in HPF) or not. If he chooses not to respect this rule, some temporary arrays may be generated in the next stage to take it into account.

3. Coding the linear schedule

We show here how to generate HPF code for a linear schedule.

3.1. Loop rewriting

Bouclettes uses techniques presented by Collard, Feautrier and Risset in [4] to rewrite the loops after reindexation. Reindexation yields a new iteration space, which is a convex integer polyhedron defined by a set of affine constraints. Rewriting the nested loop needs to scan all the

integer points of this convex and the algorithm relies on a parameterized version of the Dual Simplex, **PIP** (see [8]).

Consider the initial perfect loop nest (see program 1), where $\vec{z}$ is a vector of structure parameters (see [4]):

Program 1 Initial perfect loop nest

```
do  i_1=i_1^l(z),  i_1^u(z)
    do  i_2=i_2^l(i_1,z),  i_2^u(i_1,z)
        ...
        do  i_d=i_d^l(i_1,...,i_{d-1},z),  i_d^u(i_1,...,i_{d-1},z)
            S_1(i_1,i_2,...,i_d,z)
            ...
            S_k(i_1,i_2,...,i_d,z)
        enddo
    ...
    enddo
enddo
```

We rewrite the loop nest after an unimodular linear transformation U. The vector coordinates $\vec{i} = (i_1, \ldots, i_d)^T$ and $\vec{j} = (j_1, \ldots, j_d)^T$, respectively in the old and new basis, are related by:

$$\vec{j} = U\vec{i}$$

where U is a $d \times d$ unimodular matrix $(\det(U) = \pm 1)$. Since we are dealing with perfect loop nests, the iteration spaces are finite convex polyhedra of $\mathbb{Z}^d$ that can be defined by a set of inequalities such as:

$$D(\vec{z}) = \{\vec{i} \,|\, \vec{i} \in \mathbb{Z}^d, C\vec{i} + C'\vec{z} + \vec{b} \geq 0\}$$

where C, C' are constraint matrices and $\vec{b}$ is a constant vector. In the new iteration space, the polyhedra can be defined as :

$$D(\vec{z}) = \{\vec{j} \,|\, \vec{j} \in \mathbb{Z}^d, CU^{-1}\vec{j} + C'\vec{z} + \vec{b} \geq 0\}.$$

Collard, Feautrier and Risset have proved that the initial loop nest (program 1) can be rewritten in the new iteration space in the form given in program 2 where the loop bounds j_n^l and j_n^u, $1 \leq n \leq d$ are simple enough (for an HPF compiler) expressions of the structure parameters and of the surrounding indices $j_1, \ldots, j_{n-1}$. For a perfect loop nest of depth d, the new loop bounds are obtained after $2d$ successive calls to **PIP**.

3.2. When the OCR is not respected

HPF compilers respect the *owner computes rule* (OCR): each processor computes its own data only. In the mapping process of **Bouclettes**, the user can choose not to respect the OCR. Let us consider an array element $a(\vec{i}+c_a)$ computed in a statement $S(\vec{i})$. The mapping process can return allocation functions such that: $(M(\vec{i}+c_a)+\alpha_a) \neq M\vec{i}+\alpha_S$. To make both the allocation functions and the OCR compatible, we

Program 2 Rewritten perfect loop nest

```
do j₁=j₁ˡ(z⃗),  j₁ᵘ(z⃗)
   do j₂=j₂ˡ(j₁,z⃗),  j₂ᵘ(j₁,z⃗)
      ...
         do j_d=j_dˡ(j₁,...,j_{d-1},z⃗),  j_dᵘ(j₁,...,j_{d-1},z⃗)
            S₁(U⁻¹j⃗,z⃗)
            ...
            S_k(U⁻¹j⃗,z⃗)
         enddo
   ...
   enddo
enddo
```

need to add "temporary" arrays during the code generation stage.

Hence, the loop nest of program 3, where *expr* is an expression of other array elements of the program is transformed by adding temporary arrays into the loop nest of program 4.

Program 3 Initial loop nest which does not verify the OCR

```
real a(n,n)

do i⃗
      S(i⃗)    a(i⃗ + c_a) = expr
enddo
```

Program 4 Loop nest which verifies the OCR after the addition of temporary arrays

```
real a(n,n)
real a_tmp(n,n)

do i⃗
      S₁(i⃗)    a_tmp(i⃗ + c_a) = expr
      S₂(i⃗)    a(i⃗ + c_a) = a_tmp(i⃗ + c_a)
enddo
```

The new allocation functions are deduced from the initial functions to respect the OCR:

$$
\begin{aligned}
\text{alloc}_a(\vec{i}) &= M\vec{i} + \alpha_a \\
\text{alloc}_{S_1}(\vec{i}) &= M\vec{i} + \alpha_s \\
\text{alloc}_{a_{tmp}}(\vec{i}) &= M\vec{i} + \alpha_S - Mc_a \\
\text{alloc}_{S_2}(\vec{i}) &= M\vec{i} + Mc_a + \alpha_a.
\end{aligned}
$$

3.3. Array alignment

In HPF, the programmer can specify the data mapping at two levels. First the arrays are aligned with respect to one another with the directive ALIGN. Then, the aligned data are distributed to the processors with the directive DISTRIBUTE [11].

The general alignment statement is:

```
!HPF$ ALIGN array WITH target
```

This specifies to the compiler that the array should be aligned with the target. The target can be either another array of the program or a TEMPLATE (a virtual array). An example of alignement statement is:

```
!HPF$ ALIGN A(i,j) WITH B(j+1,i+1)
```

The general distribution statement is:

```
!HPF$ PROCESSORS proc
!HPF$ DISTRIBUTE arrays [ONTO proc]
```

The programmer can also specify the way to distribute the arrays on the processors (BLOCK, CYCLIC or CYCLIC(n)). **Bouclettes** can generate any type of distribution. The best one would certainly be a CYCLIC(n) one where the size of the block would depend on the target machine. As in current **HPF** compilers, only BLOCK distributions are implemented, we have chosen to make **Bouclettes** generate BLOCK distributions.

According to the projection matrix M, we adopt two different strategies in the code generation to align the data:

- if the projection is along one axis of the iteration, we are able to align directly the arrays as we explain in the following,

- otherwise, we need to "redistribute" the arrays before aligning them (see Section 3.4).

When the projection is along one direction of the iteration space D. Let a_k, $(1 \leq k \leq n)$ be the arrays of a loop nest of depth d. Let $\text{alloc}_{a_k}(\vec{i}) = M\vec{i} + \alpha_{a_k}$ be the allocation function for array a_k. Let π be the linear scheduling vector for the loop nest. Let $\vec{i} \in D$ and $\vec{j} = \vec{i} + \left(\begin{smallmatrix} \pi \\ M \end{smallmatrix}\right)^{-1} \left(\begin{smallmatrix} 0 \\ \alpha_{a_k} \end{smallmatrix}\right)$. We have

$$
M\vec{j} = M\vec{i} + M \left(\begin{array}{c} \pi \\ M \end{array}\right)^{-1} \left(\begin{array}{c} 0 \\ \alpha_{a_k} \end{array}\right).
$$

Let $\left(\begin{smallmatrix} \pi \\ M \end{smallmatrix}\right)^{-1} = (X_1\ X_2)$, we have

$$
\left(\begin{array}{c} \pi \\ M \end{array}\right)(X_1\ X_2) = \left(\begin{array}{cc} \pi X_1 & \pi X_2 \\ M X_1 & M X_2 \end{array}\right) = Id.
$$

Hence, $M X_2 = Id$ and

$$
M\vec{j} = M\vec{i} + M(X_1 X_2) \left(\begin{array}{c} 0 \\ \alpha_{a_k} \end{array}\right)
$$

$$
M\vec{j} = M\vec{i} + \alpha_{a_k}
$$

Let $p = M\vec{i} + \alpha_{a_k}$ (the processor p receives the value $a_k(\vec{i})$). p and the image of $\vec{j}$ by M correspond to the same point in the virtual processor space. To align all arrays a_k with respect to one another, one possibility is to declare a template Temp of dimension d and to align each array with the following directive:

```
!HPF$ ALIGN a_k(⃗i) WITH Temp(⃗i + (π/M)^{-1} (0 / α_{a_k}))
```

The distribution of the aligned data onto the processors is then specified with the directive:

```
!HPF$ DISTRIBUTE Temp
     (BLOCK,...,BLOCK,*,BLOCK,...,BLOCK)
```

The "*" corresponds to the direction of the projection. Let us notice that this is possible only because the projection is parallel to one direction of the iteration space.

3.4. Array rotation

When this projection is not along one axis, we need to "redistribute" the arrays to write the HPF directives.

Let $U = (\frac{\pi}{M})$. For each array a_k of the loop nest, we define the new array $a_{k,\text{rot}}$ such that $a_{k,\text{rot}}(\vec{i}) = a_k(U^{-1}(\vec{i}))$.

We compute the new allocation function for array $a_{k,\text{rot}}$ from the allocation function for array a_k. Let $\text{alloc}_{a_k}(\vec{i}) = M\vec{i} + \alpha_{a_k}$, we choose $\text{alloc}_{a_{k,\text{rot}}}(\vec{i}) = MU^{-1}\vec{i} + \alpha_{a_k}$ ($a_{k,\text{rot}}(\vec{i})$ and $a_k(U^{-1}(\vec{i}))$ are in the memory of the same processor).

As in Section 3.3, let $U^{-1} = (X_1 \ X_2)$. Hence, we have $MU^{-1} = (MX_1 \ MX_2)$ and

$$UU^{-1} = \begin{pmatrix} \pi X_1 & \pi X_2 \\ MX_1 & MX_2 \end{pmatrix} = \text{Id}.$$

Hence,

$$MU^{-1} = \begin{pmatrix} 0 & \\ \cdot & \\ \cdot & \text{Id} \\ 0 & \end{pmatrix}.$$

The projection matrix for the new "rotated" arrays defines a projection parallel to the first dimension of the processor space.

Besides, after rewriting, the access to array a_k in the new loop nest is $a_k(U^{-1}\vec{j} + c_{a_k})$. We have

$$a_k(U^{-1}\vec{j} + c_{a_k}) = a_{k,\text{rot}}(U(U^{-1}\vec{j} + c_{a_k}))$$
$$= a_{k,\text{rot}}(\vec{j} + Uc_{a_k}).$$

If we replace in the new loop nest, all the occurrences of array a_k by the corresponding occurrences of array $a_{k,\text{rot}}$, we obtain again a rewritten loop nest with uniform access to arrays.

3.5. Summary

To summarize our approach, the strategy to generate the code after a linear scheduling is:

1. verify if the data and computation mapping is compatible with the OCR, if not insert temporary arrays,

2. rewrite the loop nest,

3. verify if the projection matrix corresponds to a projection along one dimension of the iteration space, if not replace the initial arrays by rotated arrays, generate the parallel loops at the beginning and at the end of the program to respectively initialize with the correct values the rotated arrays and to copy the values of the rotated arrays into the initial arrays,

4. generate the alignment directives to align each array of the loop nest with respect to a template,

5. generate the distribute directive to map the template to virtual processors.

4. Coding shifted linear schedules

The aim of this section is to show how coding shifted linear schedules boils down to coding linear schedules.

4.1. From linear scheduling to shifted linear scheduling

As explained before, we have rewritten the initial loop nest taking into account only the linear part of the schedule. This transformed loop nest looks like program 5.

Program 5 A loop nest after the linear transformation

```
      do t=t^l, t^u
$HPF! INDEPENDENT
        do pr_1=pr_1^l(t), pr_1^u(t)
        ...
$HPF! INDEPENDENT
          do pr_{d-1}=pr_{d-1}^l(t), pr_{d-1}^u(t)
            S_1(t,pr_1,...,pr_{d-1})
            ...
            S_k(t,pr_1,...,pr_{d-1})
          enddo
        ...
      enddo
    enddo
```

Let us consider the following schedule:

$$\text{schedule}(\vec{i}) = \left\lfloor \frac{1}{q}(p\pi\vec{i} + c) \right\rfloor \quad (1)$$

for a given statement.

The previous transformations uses $t = \pi\vec{i}$. So the execution time following the shifted linear schedule (equation 1) can be rewritten as

$$\text{exe}(t) = \left\lfloor \frac{1}{q}(pt + c) \right\rfloor. \quad (2)$$

277

In the above transformed code, the processors on which the computations are executed depend only on the execution time t (and on the parameters of the program). So, if we can "inverse" the exe function, we will be able to rewrite the loop nest with a new time variable corresponding to the time given by the schedule.

We now show that this inverse is:

$$\text{lin}(T) = \left\lceil \frac{1}{p}(qT - c) \right\rceil. \tag{3}$$

We have to prove the following proposition.

Proposition 1.

$$\forall t \in \mathbb{Z}, (t \in [\text{lin}(T), \text{lin}(T+1)[\Leftrightarrow \text{exe}(t) = T)$$

Proof. Let $t \in \mathbb{Z}$ such that: $\text{lin}(T) \leq t < \text{lin}(T+1)$ We can successively deduce:

$$\left\lceil \frac{1}{p}(qT - c) \right\rceil \leq t < \left\lceil \frac{1}{p}(q(T+1) - c) \right\rceil \tag{4}$$

and

$$\frac{1}{q}\left(p \left\lceil \frac{1}{p}(qT - c) \right\rceil + c \right) \leq \frac{1}{q}(pt + c)$$
$$< \frac{1}{q}\left(p \left\lceil \frac{1}{p}(q(T+1) - c) \right\rceil + c \right). \tag{5}$$

Let $f(T) = \frac{1}{q}\left(p \left\lceil \frac{1}{p}(qT - c) \right\rceil + c \right)$, we then have:

$$f(T) \leq \frac{1}{q}(pt + c) < f(T+1).$$

There always exist α and β such that

$$qT - c = p\alpha + \beta, 0 \leq \beta < p, \alpha \in \mathbb{Z} \tag{6}$$

Let us compute $f(T)$:

$$f(T) = \frac{1}{q}\left(p \left\lceil \frac{1}{p}(qT - c) \right\rceil + c \right)$$
$$= \frac{1}{q}\left(p \left\lceil \alpha + \frac{\beta}{p} \right\rceil + c \right)$$
$$= \frac{1}{q}\left((p\alpha + c) + p \left\lceil \frac{\beta}{p} \right\rceil \right)$$
$$= \frac{1}{q}\left((qT - \beta) + p \left\lceil \frac{\beta}{p} \right\rceil \right)$$
$$= T + \frac{1}{q}\left(p \left\lceil \frac{\beta}{p} \right\rceil - \beta \right).$$

If we proved that $\lfloor f(T) \rfloor = T$, we would obtain

$$T \leq \left\lfloor \frac{1}{q}(pt + c) \right\rfloor < T + 1$$

which is equivalent to $\text{exe}(t) = T$, thereby establishing the proof.

Let us discuss the value of

$$\lfloor f(T) \rfloor = \left\lfloor T + \frac{1}{q}\left(p \left\lceil \frac{\beta}{p} \right\rceil - \beta \right) \right\rfloor$$

as a function of β.

- If $\beta = 0$ then $f(T) = T$ and $\lfloor f(T) \rfloor = T$.

- Otherwise $0 < \beta < p$ and so $\left\lceil \frac{\beta}{p} \right\rceil = 1$. We would like to have $\frac{1}{q}(p - \beta) < 1$. This is equivalent to prove

$$1 < \frac{q + \beta}{p}. \tag{7}$$

  - If $p < q$ then equation 7 is verified.
  - Else, as $p \wedge q = 1, p > q$. Remember the hypothesis (equation 4):

$$\left\lceil \frac{1}{p}(qT - c) \right\rceil \leq t < \left\lceil \frac{1}{p}(q(T+1) - c) \right\rceil.$$

This implies that

$$\left\lceil \frac{1}{p}(qT - c) \right\rceil < \left\lceil \frac{1}{p}(q(T+1) - c) \right\rceil.$$

Introducing α and β (equation 6) in this equation leads to

$$\left\lceil \alpha + \frac{\beta}{p} \right\rceil < \left\lceil \alpha + \frac{\beta + q}{p} \right\rceil.$$

As α is an integer, we have

$$\left\lceil \frac{\beta}{p} \right\rceil < \left\lceil \frac{\beta + q}{p} \right\rceil.$$

As $\left\lceil \frac{\beta}{p} \right\rceil = 1$, we have

$$1 < \left\lceil \frac{\beta + q}{p} \right\rceil$$

which implies equation 7.

We have proven that in all cases, $\lfloor f(T) \rfloor = T$, which implies $\text{exe}(t) = T$ and

$$\forall t \in \mathbb{Z}, (t \in [\text{lin}(T), \text{lin}(T+1)[\Rightarrow \text{exe}(t) = T).$$

We now have to prove the opposite.
It is immediate to see that

$$\bigcup_{T \in \mathbb{Z}} [\text{lin}(T), \text{lin}(T+1)[= \mathbb{Z}.$$

So, let $t \in \mathbb{Z}$ and $T = \text{exe}(t)$. The previous equation implies that $\exists T', \text{lin}(T') \leq t < \text{lin}(T'+1)$. We have just proven that this implies that $\text{exe}(t) = T'$. We can now conclude that $T' = T$ and that

$$\forall t \in \mathbb{Z}, (T = \text{exe}(t) \Rightarrow t \in [\text{lin}(T), \text{lin}(T+1)[).$$

$\square$

4.2. The formal transformation

We show here how to transform the code obtained with the linear schedule to the one we want for the shifted linear one.

4.2.1 The time boundaries

After the linear transformation, the time t varies from t^l to t^u. We have to find the boundaries of the final time T which corresponds to the interval $[t^l, t^u]$. We take as execution time:

$$\text{exe}_s(t^l) \le T \le \text{exe}_s(t^u) \qquad (8)$$

where $\text{exe}_s(t) = \left\lfloor \frac{1}{q}(pt + c_s) \right\rfloor$.

Using proposition 1, for statement S_s, considering $\text{lin}_s(t) = \left\lceil \frac{1}{p}(qt - c_s) \right\rceil$, we have the code of program 6:

Program 6 Code for statement S_s with shifted linear schedule

```
        do  T=exe_s(t^l),  exe_s(t^u)
$HPF!  INDEPENDENT
            do  t=lin_s(T),  lin_s(T+1) - 1
$HPF!  INDEPENDENT
                do  pr_1=pr_1^l(t),  pr_1^u(t)
                ...
$HPF!  INDEPENDENT
                    do  pr_{d-1}=pr_{d-1}^l(t),  pr_{d-1}^u(t)
                        S_s(t,pr_1,...,pr_{d-1})
                    enddo
                ...
                enddo
            enddo
        enddo
```

Let us verify that this transformation is the one we were looking for: does the T loop index defined above corresponds to the schedule? Consider index point $\vec{i}$. Statement $S_s(\vec{i})$ should be executed at time $T = \text{exe}_s(\pi\vec{i})$. Proposition 1 proves that $\pi\vec{i}$ is in the definition interval of t. So statement $S_s(\vec{i})$ is indeed executed at the required time on the processors computed in the mapping phase.

4.2.2 When there are several instructions

It would be interesting here to have a construct to express control parallelism in HPF. For the moment —the current specification is HPF 1 and can be found in [11]— such a construct does not exist, but at the time of writing, it is discussed into the HPF Forum to consider its inclusion in the HPF 2 specification.

Indeed, we would like to execute in parallel all the statements that have the same schedule. As it is not currently

possible, we just execute them sequentially —it is likely that they would be sequentialized by the compiler anyway.

The last problem we have to solve is how to deal with different shifting constants for different statements. It is not very difficult:

- first, let the sequential time T go from the lower bound of the time given by the smallest constant to the upper bound of the time given by the largest constant: T varies from T^l to T^u defined as

$$T^l = \left\lfloor \frac{1}{q}\left(pt^l + \min_s c_s\right) \right\rfloor$$

$$T^u = \left\lfloor \frac{1}{q}\left(pt^u + \max_s c_s\right) \right\rfloor$$

- and then verify for each instruction that the corresponding linear time t does not exceed its definition interval $[t^l, t^u]$. This can be done by letting t vary from $\max(t^l, \text{lin}_s(T))$ to $\min(t^u, \text{lin}_s(T+1) - 1)$.

Note: this style of program writing is correct because in Fortran, *if a* do *loop has its lower bound greater than its upper bound, its body is not executed.*

4.2.3 Some last optimizations

To avoid as much as possible the computation of min and max functions, we can distinguish three stages in the execution of the parallelized program:

1. The initial stage when at each time some statements may not execute: we compute the lower bound as $\max(t^l, \text{lin}_s(T))$ but let the upper bound without the min: $\text{lin}_s(T+1) - 1$. This is for values of T varying

$$\text{from} \quad \left\lfloor \frac{1}{q}(pt^l + \min_s c_s) \right\rfloor$$

$$\text{to} \quad \left\lceil \frac{1}{q}(pt^l + \max_s c_s) \right\rceil - 1.$$

2. The steady-state phase when all statements always execute: there are no min and no max. This is for values of T varying

$$\text{from} \quad \left\lceil \frac{1}{q}(pt^l + \max_s c_s) \right\rceil$$

$$\text{to} \quad \left\lfloor \frac{1}{q}(pt^u + \min_s c_s) \right\rfloor - 1.$$

3. The final stage when some statements may have finished to execute: we let the lower bound without the max: $\text{lin}_s(T)$ and compute the upper bound as

$\min(\text{lin}_s(T+1) - 1)$. This is for values of T varying

$$\text{from} \quad \left\lfloor \frac{1}{q}(pt^u + \min_s c_s) \right\rfloor$$

$$\text{to} \quad \left\lfloor \frac{1}{q}(pt^u + \max_s c_s) \right\rfloor .$$

We suppose here that n the size parameter of the program is large enough.

We have also worked on the symbolic simplification of loop bounds. The module that work on symbolic expressions puts affine expressions in a "normalized form" (each symbolic constant appears only once) then the floor and ceil functions are deleted if the expression on which they apply is an integer expression and the number of division is reduced by factorizing the common denominators of fractions. This leads to more readable code and less expensive computations to determine loop bounds.

A third optimization addresses the case of non executed loops because their lower bounds is greater than their upper bound. If it is always the case for a loop, this loop is discarded. And if a loop has the same lower and upper bounds, the do statement is replaced by an assignment of the common bounds value to the loop index. These simplifications give a more readable form for a human being, which is also easier to analyze for a compiler program.

5. Conclusion

We have presented in this paper the problems to solve for code generation in the **Bouclettes** tool and the solutions that have been implemented. We have chosen HPF as output language and this choice has proven critical for the code generation. Indeed, the use of HPF has relieved us from generating all the low level communications in the output parallel program. On the other hand, some complications arise from some current limitations of HPF:

- the fact that HPF respects the owner computes rule has forced us to generate some temporary arrays when the mapping is not compatible with this rule. It should be pointed out that the user can select an option in **Bouclettes** that forces the mapping to respect the owner computes rule.

- the data distributions allowed in HPF are not always powerful enough to express the mapping. We have then developed a redistribution scheme to deal with all our mappings.

- the pure data parallelism of HPF does not allow control parallelism that would be necessary to express all the parallelism exposed by some shifted linear schedules.

References

[1] P. Boulet. Bouclettes: a fortran loop parallelizer. In H. Liddell, A. Colbrook, B. Hertzberger, and P. Sloot, editors, *High-Performance Computing and Networking*, volume 1067 of *Lecture Notes in Computer Science*, pages 784–791, Brussels, Belgium, Apr. 1996. Springer Verlag.

[2] P. Boulet and T. Brandes. Evaluation of automatic parallelization strategies for hpf compilers. In H. Liddell, A. Colbrook, B. Hertzberger, and P. Sloot, editors, *High-Performance Computing and Networking*, volume 1067 of *Lecture Notes in Computer Science*, pages 778–783, Brussels, Belgium, Apr. 1996. Springer Verlag.

[3] P. Boulet and M. Dion. Code generation in bouclettes. Research Report 95-43, Laboratoire de l'Informatique du Parallélisme, Nov 1995.

[4] J.-F. Collard, P. Feautrier, and T. Risset. Construction of do loops from systems of affine constraints. Technical Report 93-15, Laboratoire de l'Informatique du Parallélisme, may 1993.

[5] A. Darte, L. Khachiyan, and Y. Robert. Linear scheduling is nearly optimal. *Parallel Processing Letters*, 1(2):73–81, 1991.

[6] A. Darte and Y. Robert. The alignment problem for perfect uniform loop nest: Np-completeness and heuristics. In J. Dongarra and B. T. eds, editors, *Environments and Tools for Parallel Scientific Computing II*, SIAM Press, pages 33–42, 1994.

[7] A. Darte and Y. Robert. Constructive methods for scheduling uniform loop nests. *IEEE Trans. Parallel Distributed Systems*, 5(8):814–822, 1994.

[8] P. Feautrier. Parametric integer programming. *RAIRO Recherche Opérationnelle*, 22:243–268, Sept. 1988.

[9] S. C. Group. Suif compiler system. World Wide Web document, URL: http://suif.stanford.edu/suif/suif.html.

[10] T. group of Pr. Lengauer. The loopo project. World Wide Web document, URL: http://brahms.fmi.uni-passau.de/cl/loopo/index.html.

[11] C. H. Koelbel, D. B. Loveman, R. S. Schreiber, G. L. S. Jr., and M. E. Zosel. *The High Performance Fortran Handbook*. The MIT Press, 1994.

[12] W. Pugh and the Omega Team. The omega project. World Wide Web document, URL: http://www.cs.umd.edu/projects/omega/index.html.

[13] P. Team. Pips (interprocedural parallelizer for scientific programs). World Wide Web document, URL: http://www.cri.ensmp.fr/~pips/index.html.

[14] P. S. Team. Systematic construction of parallel and distributed programs. World Wide Web document, URL: http://www.prism.uvsq.fr/english/parallel/paf/autom_us.html.

A Rigorous Approach to the Decomposition of Data (Structures)

H.H. ten Cate, M.R. Roest and E.A.H. Vollebregt
Delft University of Technology,
Faculty of Technical Mathematics and Informatics,
P.O. Box 5031, 2600 GA Delft, The Netherlands,
tencate@pa.twi.tudelft.nl

Abstract

Domain decomposition is a well known technique in parallel computing. It requires the decomposition of a problem domain into sub-domains. This involves also a decomposition of the data structures for the problem into substructures, one for each sub-domain. If the data structures are complex, then the decomposition of the data structures may be a complicated task.

This paper will show how the problem of decomposition of data structures is significantly reduced by first describing the decomposition of objects on a high level of abstraction and then working down to code level in a rigorous way. It will be shown that the high level decomposition abstracts from the precise form of the data structures, in which the objects are represented. This allows for the construction of one generic mechanism for decomposition of data structures.

1 Introduction

Much of the simulation software that is in daily use for many applications makes use of complex data structures, often involving indirect addressing. When porting such software to parallel computers, the problem arises of decomposing these data structures so that every processor can keep the part of a data structure that is relevant for it in its local memory. Most present day parallelising compilers are unable to deal with complex data structures and they certainly fail on the use of indirect addressing.

At present a lot of research is going on to tackle difficulties caused by indirect addressing. One strategy is to resolve the situation at runtime, such as is developed in the framework of the *inspector-executor paradigm* [5]. This solution may incur a significant overhead at runtime, especially in situations where more information could have been fed to the compiler.

In another strategy that information is indeed passed through the compiler. For example very often the partitioning technique is known at compile-time, therefore programming languages are extended such that these techniques can be specified and exploited [3] by the compiler. In the current paper it will be shown that even more information can be fed to a compiler. That information concerns the representation of data. It appears that a specification of the partitioning and distribution of data is much simpler at a higher level of abstraction than at programming level. With help of the knowledge about the representation of the data such a specification of data partitioning and distribution can be transformed into a program decomposing low level data structures.

Throughout the paper, the discussion of the concepts will be done using an example in which a partial differential equation (PDE) is to be solved on an arbitrarily shaped domain. The discretisation method can be a finite element or finite volume or finite difference method. These methods start by representing the domain by a mesh and discretising all data on the mesh into mesh functions. Complex data structures arise in such applications if the domain has a highly irregular shape and if some of the data is defined only in a small number of mesh-points (as with special boundary conditions). This supplies an excellent example of the application of the ideas that are presented in the paper.

The problem of decomposing complex data structures is much alleviated if it is tackled as early as possible in a software design. On a high level of abstraction, at the level of the PDE, thus before any specific structuring of the data has been chosen, the decomposition of the domain where the PDE is defined fully specifies the decomposition of the data that is defined on that domain. Starting from such a high abstraction level and going down to code level through data-reification steps, it is possible to specify how the data structures in the code must be decomposed. This will be shown in two steps. First in Section 2 it will be presented how decomposition of a problem on a high level of abstraction is worked down to the level just above the point where data structures are introduced. Then, in Section 3, the consequences for data structures will be introduced by means of an example.

Not surprisingly, it turns out that the decomposition of data structures can be specified in terms of a specification of the decomposition of the domain and an abstraction function that specifies how a data structure implements a mesh-function (the abstract data-type). Having noted this, it is possible to find a consistent decomposition of the different data structures in a program, as will be shown in Section 4. Along the way, this paper will show the general principles underlying the decomposition of any data structure resulting in a generic formulation.

Starting from the generic formulation it is possible for a sophisticated programming system to generate data distribution software semi-automatically. Input for such a system would be a high level definition of the data objects, a description of their reification and a specification of the decomposition of the high level objects. In Section 5 automatic generation will be discussed and compared with what is now possible in HP-Fortran.

2 From the mathematical problem to its discretised decomposed version

In the following, it will be shown how domain decomposition on an abstract level results in problem decomposition on lower levels of abstraction. In the subsequent sections the same line of working will be extended all the way down to code level, where different representations of data exist.

To illustrate the concepts we will assume that domain partitioning is applied for the numerical solution of a partial differential equation (PDE) $\mathcal{L}u = f$ on Ω subject to some boundary conditions, where Ω is the domain on which the unknown u must be computed. Further $u, f : \Omega \rightarrow \mathbb{R}$. The solution of the PDE is to be obtained using a finite difference, finite element or finite volume approximation of the problem. Therefore, the domain Ω is discretised resulting in a mesh. At the same time the functions u and f are represented by discrete functions $U, F : Mesh \rightarrow \mathbb{R}$. Apart from the discretization of the domain the PDE is discretised too. Further explanation is omitted since the current paper concentrates on the representation of data.

Applying domain decomposition means that the mesh is decomposed into possibly overlapping sub-

meshes $Mesh_p$, such that:

$$Mesh = \bigcup_{p \in \mathcal{P}} Mesh_p$$

In general the local coordinates of a sub mesh start at $(1,1)$. Thus there may be some coordinate transformation $CoordTrans$ on each sub-mesh, such that:

$$CoordTrans : \mathcal{P} \rightarrow \{Mesh'_p \rightarrow Mesh\}$$

which means that $CoordTrans(p)$ is the coordinate transformation on sub-mesh $p \in \mathcal{P}$. The decomposition of the mesh also leads to a decomposition of mesh functions U and F into sub-mesh functions U'_p, F'_p, defined on $Mesh'_p$, where:

$$\forall p \in \mathcal{P} \; \forall (m_p, n_p) \in Mesh'_p :$$
$$U'_p(m_p, n_p) = U(CoordTrans(p)(m_p, n_p)) \qquad (1)$$

and likewise for F'_p. Equality (1) specifies the relation between he mesh function U and its decomposed representation U' (which is the composition of U'_p). That data-reification can be formalised in an abstraction function, which maps the set containing the representations U' on the set containing all mesh functions U, see [2]. In the current paper we will consider the data-reification for the mesh functions U, F, and the decomposed mesh functions U' and F' into pointer structures. But first an illustration of the concepts will be presented.

3 An example to introduce rigorous data decomposition

To illustrate the concepts behind the generic mechanism for decomposition of data structures we first consider the example mesh in Figure 1. On this mesh water levels must be computed starting from an initial estimate. The computation can be done using a software package running on a workstation. The software implements the initial estimate as a one dimensional array based on the numbering in Figure 2. To improve the performance, the package must be modified such that it can run in parallel on a workstation cluster.

One aspect of the modification is that the initial estimate (a mesh function) must be distributed over the, say, two workstations. For that the grid in Figure 1 is partitioned (by software or by hand) in two strips. That partitioning implies the distribution of the one dimensional array implementing the initial estimate for the water levels. In the following a relation between the global one dimensional array and the distributed one dimensional sub arrays will be derived.

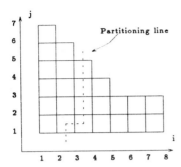

Figure 1. An irregular mesh in a coordinate system. The dashed line splits the mesh in two sub meshes.

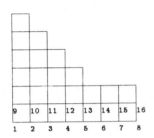

Figure 2. A numbering of the nodes in the example mesh of Figure 1.

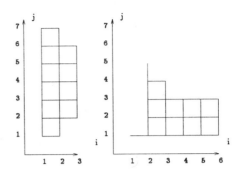

Figure 3. The sub meshes of Figure 1 in local coordinate systems.

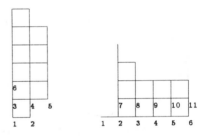

Figure 4. Local numbering of nodes in the meshes of Figure 3.

Conceptually the water levels are specified by a mesh function: $wl : Coords \rightarrow \mathbb{R}^+$. $Coords$ is the set of nodes in Figure 1. A node appears at the intersection of the grid lines. To implement the water levels in the one dimensional array the nodes in the mesh of Figure 1 are lexicographically numbered, starting with increasing i, see Figure 2. The numbering is specified in a table, i.e. a mapping: $numb : Coords \rightarrow \mathbb{N}$ with definition $(1,1) \mapsto 1, (2,1) \mapsto 2, (8,1) \mapsto 8, (1,2) \mapsto 9$ and so on. With help of the table $numb$ the relation between the water levels mesh function wl and the water levels array $wlarr$ can be specified: $wl(i,j) = wlarr(numb(i,j))$ where $(i,j) \in Coords$, e.g. $wl(1,2) = wlarr(9)$.

The distributed mesh functions $wl1$ and $wl2$ are defined similar to wl: $wl1 : Coords1 \rightarrow \mathbb{R}^+$ and $wl2 : Coords2 \rightarrow \mathbb{R}^+$, where $Coords1$ and $Coords2$ are the set of nodes in the left and right mesh of Figure 3, respectively. Both $wl1$ and $wl2$ can be implemented in two one dimensional arrays, $wlarr1$ and $wlarr2$, where the indices are again obtained by a numbering, say

$numb1 : Coords1 \rightarrow \mathbb{N}$, and $numb2 : Coords2 \rightarrow \mathbb{N}$. With help of these two mappings the relation between $wl1$ and $wlarr1$, and between $wl2$ and $wlarr2$ can be given, e.g. $wl1(i,j) = wlarr1(numb1(i,j))$ where $(i,j) \in Coords1$.

The relation between $wlarr$ on the one hand and $wlarr1$ and $wlarr2$ on the other hand can be found in comparing the numbers of a node in Figure 2 with that of the same node Figure 4:

$$
\begin{aligned}
wlarr1(1) &= wlarr(1) \\
wlarr1(2) &= wlarr(2) \\
wlarr1(3) &= wlarr(9) \\
wlarr1(4) &= wlarr(10) \\
&\vdots \\
wlarr2(1) &= wlarr(3) \\
wlarr2(2) &= wlarr(4) \\
&\vdots \\
wlarr2(6) &= wlarr(8)
\end{aligned}
$$

$$wlarr2(7) = wlarr(12)$$
$$wlarr2(8) = wlarr(13)$$
$$\vdots$$

The jumps in the indices of $wlarr$ (e.g. in the second and third line) seem to complicate the programming of distribution software. However an investigation of the relations between the mesh functions and the array opens the way to a generic mechanism for decomposition of data structures.

The theory starts with the relation between the water levels mesh function (wl) and the two distributed mesh functions ($wl1$ and $wl2$). That relation has already been given in relation (1) where $\mathcal{P} = \{1, 2\}$ and where U, U_1, U_2 are replaced by wl, $wl1$ and $wl2$. The coordinate transformation $CoordTrans(1)$ is in this case: $CoordTrans(1) : Coords1 \rightarrow Coords$ with definition $CoordTrans(1)(i, j) = (i, j)$. Similar $CoordTrans(2) : Coords2 \rightarrow Coords$ with definition $CoordTrans(2)(i, j) = (i + 2, j)$.

Further for each coordinate a number exists. Consider local coordinate $(2, 2)$ in sub mesh 2 and global coordinate $CoordTrans(2)(2, 2) = (4, 2)$, then $numb2(2, 2) = 7$ and $numb(4, 2) = 12$, i.e. the (local) index 7 of $wlarr2$ corresponds to (global) index 12 of $wlarr$. Such a correspondence exists for all global and local indices.

Let g be a global and and l be a local index of $wlarr2$ then the correspondence is:

$$
\begin{aligned}
g &= numb \circ CoordTrans(2) \circ numb2^{-1}(l) \\
&= numb(CoordTrans(2)(numb2^{-1}(l))). \quad (2)
\end{aligned}
$$

Here $numb2^{-1}(l)$ gives the local coordinates in sub mesh 2. Subsequently $CoordTrans$ gives the global coordinates and finally $numb$ gives the number, i.e. the global index. Working this out in relation (1) gives the relation between a local sub array and the global array. For $wlarr2$ that is:

$$
\begin{aligned}
wlarr2(l) &= \\
wlarr&(numb \circ CoordTrans(2) \circ numb2^{-1}(l)).
\end{aligned}
$$

Indeed it follows that $wlarr1(4) = wlarr(10)$. In fact the relation formalises the hand work, i.e. the comparison of a node number in Figure 2 with the number of the same node in Figure 4.

In the subsequent section the concepts which are explained here will be generalised. Relation 2 will appear as a mapping, $GlobNr$, and Relation (10) will be a generic form of the relation above between $wlarr2$ and $wlarr$. But before that, some remarks should be made. An observant reader could have wondered why the mesh function wl has been partitioned in stead of

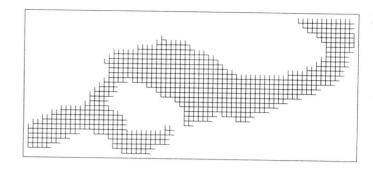

Figure 5. Typical irregularly bounded mesh for the application TRIWAQ

the array $wlarr$. The answer is that a partitioning of the array is in fact a row-wise partitioning of the mesh. The column-wise partitioning used here is better, since it will minimise communication.

Further this section assumes that the partitioning is known, and that the local and global numbering are also known. In some cases that is not necessary. If the partitioning results in parts which have the same structure as the original domain then the local numbering can be generated from the global numbering method and $CoordTrans$, which specifies the local nodes.

4 Representation of the Mesh Functions

In this section, a common type of representation for a mesh function will be discussed. In this case the mesh is represented as a set of mesh rows, where every mesh row comprises a set of mesh points. This type of representation is typical for the case where mesh functions are not defined on a rectangular structured mesh, but only on structured mesh with irregularly shape, such as in Figure 5. Essentially, the data structure is a pointer structure: i.e. a set of pointers that all point to a collection of mesh nodes. The representation of the mesh function is based upon that mesh representation. A typical appearance of the pointer structure in a Fortran implementation is:

```
FOR r=1,R DO FOR i=1,I(r) DO
  Uvalues(ritomn(r)+i) = Uvalues(ritomn(r)+i)
        + Uvalues(ritomn(r)+i-1)
ENDO ENDO
```

where $ritomn(r) + 1$ denotes the first computational point in row r.

Similar structures appear in the representation of mesh functions on the boundary of the mesh, like those which specify boundary conditions. These structures also appear in the representation of a list of finite elements, in which per element the local element numbers are related to the global element numbers. Further such structures appear as storage schemes for sparse matrices.

Based on the discussion of the representation of a mesh function as a pointer structure, a general scheme for the construction of per sub-domain (local) data structures from the (global) data structures for the complete domain and for the construction of conversion software from global to local data is proposed at the end of this section.

4.1 Representation of a mesh function as a pointer structure

A storage scheme which reduces the use of memory for mesh functions defined on a structured mesh such as presented in Figure 5 is based upon the representation of the mesh as a set of mesh rows[1]. A mesh row is a subset of *Mesh* (see Section 2), such that the n-coordinate is constant and that the m-coordinates are consecutive. That is: each point (m,n) of the mesh is represented by the tuple (r,i) where $r \in \mathcal{R} \subset \mathbb{N}$ is the number of the row in which the point is located and $i \in \mathcal{I}_r \subset \mathbb{N}$ is the number of the mesh point within its row. This representation can be described by the bijective function *ritomn*:

$$ritomn : \{(r,i) \mid r \in \mathcal{R}, i \in \mathcal{I}_r\} \mapsto Mesh$$

The introduction of the new representation of the mesh constitutes a reification step, which is the same for U and F. The step can formally be identified by an *abstraction function* [1, 4]. Call this abstraction function *PTRtoMESHFUNC* then we have that:

$$U \equiv PTRtoMESHFUNC(U^S) \tag{3}$$

which states that "the pointer" U^S has been chosen to represent U.

In Section 2 it has been defined that $U \in \{Mesh \to \mathbb{R}\}$, in the same way $U^S \in \{\mathcal{S} \to \mathbb{R}\}$, where $\mathcal{S} = \{(r,i) \mid r \in \mathcal{R}, i \in \mathcal{I}_r\}$ is the pointer index-set of the array. Further the relation between the pointer indices and the nodes in Mesh is defined by the function *ritomn*, which leads to the definition of *PTRtoMESH-FUNC*:

---

[1] In fact the mesh used in this section is a grid, a restricted appearance of a mesh.

Definition 1 *Conversion of a pointer structure to a mesh function*

$$PTRtoMESHFUNC : \{\{\{(r,i) \mid r \in \mathcal{R}, i \in \mathcal{I}_r\} \to \mathbb{R}\} \to \{MESH \to \mathbb{R}\}\}$$
$$\forall U^S \in \{\{(r,i) \mid r \in \mathcal{R}, i \in \mathcal{I}_r\} \to \mathbb{R}\} \ \forall (m,n) \in Mesh$$
$$PTRtoMESHFUNC(U^S)(m,n) = U^S(ritomn^{-1}(m,n))$$

Applying a similar reification step to the decomposed mesh functions U'_p for each $p \in \mathcal{P}$ leads to a similar treatment:

$$U'_p \equiv PTRtoMESHFUNC_p(U'^S_p) \tag{4}$$

where $PTRtoMESHFUNC_p$ differs from $PTRto MESHFUNC$ in *ritomn*, which is now $ritomn_p : Mesh_p \mapsto \mathcal{S}_p$. The last definition can be different for each $p \in \mathcal{P}$. It appears that it is not necessary to work out the functions *ritomn* explicitly. In a coming article this will be shown.

Substituting equalities (3) and (4) in Relation (1), subsequently evaluating the abstraction functions, then modifying the index variables and finally replacing the quantified variables (m_p, n_p) by (r_p, i_p) gives the representation of the abstract Relation (1).

$$\forall p \in \mathcal{P} \ \forall r_p \in \mathcal{R}_p \forall i_p \in \mathcal{I}_{r,p} :$$

$$U^S_p(r_p, i_p) = U^S(ritomn^{-1}(CoordTrans(ritomn_p(r_p,i_p)))) \tag{5}$$

Expression (5) can be simplified by introducing the functions $GlobNr_p$, defined as:

$$GlobNr_p : \{(r_p, i_p) \mid r_p \in \mathcal{R}_p, i_p \in \mathcal{I}_{pr_p}\} \to \{(r,i) \mid r \in \mathcal{R}, i \in \mathcal{I}_r\}$$
$$GlobNr_p(r_p, i_p) = ritomn^{-1}(CoordTrans(p)(ritomn_p(r_p,i_p))) \tag{6}$$

The components of this vector function will be denoted by the subscripts 1 and 2 to refer to the first and second element of a tuple, omitting the subscript p. Then, Relation (5) becomes:

$$\forall p \in \mathcal{P} \ \forall r_p \in \mathcal{R}_p, i_p \in \mathcal{I}_{r_p,p} :$$

$$U^S_p(r_p, i_p) = U^S(GlobNr_1(r_p,i_p), GlobNr_2(r_p,i_p)) \tag{7}$$

Since the cardinality of the set $\mathcal{I}_r$ depends on r a storage in a two-dimensional array spoils memory. For that reason often another data-reification step is carried out. The pointer structure U^S is represented in a one-dimensional array. In SPMD semi-Fortran code Relation (7) is then written as:

```
FOR rp=1,Rp DO
 FOR ip=1,Irp DO
 DatArP( PoiArP(rp)+ip) =
 DatAr(PoiAr(GlobNr_1(rp,ip))+GlobNr_2(rp,ip))
 ENDO
ENDO
```

Since there often exist other mesh functions which are defined on $Mesh$, e.g. F, it is worthwhile first to compute $GlobNr$ and then to evaluate the upper Fortran code for each mesh function. Since mesh functions defined on a boundary of $Mesh$ are stored in specific data structures, they require a treatment on their own. Nevertheless the treatment is similar to the discussion in this section and fits in a generic scheme which is presented below.

4.2 Generalisation

From the previous two subsections, it can be seen that in general, a representation of mesh functions can be described in the following way. Let a mesh function be represented in such a way, that the data for mesh point (m, n) is stored at a location indicated by the tuple $\vec{i} \in \mathcal{I} \subset \mathbb{R}^n$ for some n, thus $F \in \{Mesh \to \mathbb{R}\}$ and $F^R \in \{\mathcal{I} \to \mathbb{R}\}$. Let the relation between (m, n) and $\vec{i}$ be defined by a bijective vector function (the arrow will be omitted in the notation of vector functions):

$$repr : Mesh \to \mathcal{I}$$

such that an abstraction function can be defined specifying the relation between F and F^R. Let F_p, F_p^R, $repr_p$ be defined in a similar way but then for sub-mesh $p \in \mathcal{P}$, then Relation (1) becomes:

$$\forall p \in \mathcal{P} \; \forall \vec{i}_p \in \mathcal{I}_p :$$

$$F_p^R(\vec{i}_p) = F^R(repr(CoordTrans(p)(repr_p^{-1}(\vec{i}_p)))) \quad (8)$$

Introducing the vector functions $GlobNr_p(\vec{i}) \; \forall p \in \mathcal{P}$:

$$GlobNr_p(\vec{i}_p) : \mathcal{I}_p \to \mathcal{I}$$
$$GlobNr_p(\vec{i}_p) = repr(CoordTrans(p)(repr_p^{-1}(\vec{i}_p))) \quad (9)$$

then Relation (8) can be written as:

$$\forall p \in \mathcal{P} \; \forall \vec{i}_p \in \mathcal{I}_p : F_p^R(\vec{i}_p) = F^R(GlobNr_p(\vec{i}_p)) \quad (10)$$

This relation defines the relationship between any representation of a data field on the decomposed problem and that of the data field on the non-decomposed problem. Note that this relationship is defined in essentially two parts: the coordinate transformation $CoordTrans$ and the representation functions $repr$ and $repr_p$. Hence, if the representation of mesh functions

in F^R is specified by means of an abstraction function then $repr$ has been defined, from which $repr_p$ can be derived. The representation F^R will be chosen such that it is a data-structure in a programming language. This means that $GlobNr$ has a similar data-structure (compare their domain and range) and that Relation (10) can easily be programmed in the programming language.

The generation of the source code to fill the programming variable $GlobNr$ depends on the availability of $repr$ and $CoordTrans$ as tables at runtime or the availability of their function definition at compile time. For each situation it is simple to generate the source code.

Further it is worthwhile noting that the range of the mesh functions does not have to be $\mathbb{R}$. A generalisation to any type of range, e.g. I or $\mathbb{R}^n$, is possible. The only requirement is that equality is defined for the objects in the range such that Relation (10) is valid. Subsequently source code can simply be generated starting from Relation (10) and replacing the equality by a copy instruction.

So the conclusion of this section is that if data representations are specified by abstraction functions, and if copy instructions are known for all data-structures then source code for the decomposition of data can be generated (semi-) automatically from Definition (9) and Relation (10).

5 Towards automatic decomposition of arbitrary data structures

Above it has been shown that the relationship between the data structures for a decomposed problem and those of the original non-decomposed problem can be written in a general form on an abstract level. From this abstract formulation, it can be seen that, once it is known how each element in a data structure is related to the mesh (i.e. once $repr$ is known) then the construction of the data structures for the distributed problem follows immediately. Hence, much of this can be automated.

In the field of parallelising compilers, part of this is already common practice. For instance, in the HPFortran language [6] it is possible to *align* arrays with a so called *Template*, which is a restricted form of the *Mesh* that is used in the discussion above. This alignment is similar to the *repr* function. The decompositions that are allowed for *Templates* and the possible forms of alignment are such that an explicit expression $GlobNr$ is possible. This expression is then used to convert local addresses to global addresses and back.

However, the requirements that are posed in HPFortran on decompositions and alignments are still rather restrictive. For instance, many scientific codes codes make extensive use of indirect addressing. Certainly in the field of finite element computations on unstructured meshes, indirect addressing is hardly avoidable. Parallelising compilers are as yet unable to deal with such a situation.

The formulation of the problem in Definition (9) and Relation (10) gives a good starting point for automating the decomposition of data structures. If the programmer provides the function *repr*, the functions *repr_p* and the function *CoordTrans* in some form (e.g. a table), then the function *GlobNr* can be determined (Definition (9)), either in terms of an expression or in terms of a lookup-table. After that, the construction of data structures per sub-domain and the generation of conversion software (Relation (10)) is trivial.

In the examples of the previous section, it has been assumed that the data per sub-domain is structured in exactly the same way as for the complete domain (*repr_p* has been defined similar to *repr*). This is because the software that is available for computations on the complete domain can then be used to implement the computations on the sub-domains. Still, it is not strictly necessary to use the same representation both on the global and on the sub-domains.

Thus, if a programming system is available that can interpret a fairly general description of data-types, then it does not only allow a decomposition of the related data structures in the way described above, but also opens the way to automated modification of data structures. In fact, the decomposition described above can be understood as a modification of a data structure from one data structure to a decomposed data structure.

Obviously, the applicability of such a system depends on the ability of the programmer to express the way in which the data is structured. This will usually require the construction of a sequence of reification steps such as illustrated in Section 4.1. This shows how a formal approach to software (reverse-)engineering opens possibilities for automation that save a lot of tiresome programming work.

6   Conclusions and Future Work

It has been shown that a rigorous description of the way in which data is structured opens the way to automated modification of data structures. This is an important issue in the field of parallel computing. To make effective use of distributed memory parallel computers, it is necessary to decompose data structures such that every processor can keep the part that it needs in its local memory. The decomposition of the data structures should be done automatically, if possible.

The description of decomposition of data (structures) at a high level appears in general to be much more simple than at the programming level (especially in case of pointer structures). Decomposition is in principle a coordinates transformation. Based on the high level description and a rigorous description of data representations source code for the decomposition can be generated (semi-) automatically.

Experience with automatic decomposition of data structures has been obtained in the Parallel02 project [8], a cooperation of the Dutch National Institute for Coastal and Marine Management (RIKZ) and the Parallel Algorithms group at Delft University of Technology. The project aims at the parallelisation of a large code that is used for the simulation of flow and transport in coastal zones. A *partitioner* has been developed that uses a description of the data structures in the code and constructs the data structures per sub-domain automatically [7]. An important feature of this partitioner is that indirect addressing tables can be included in the description of the data structures, which sets it apart from most other parallelisation tools.

In the future, more research needs to be done to develop an expressive language for the description of data-reifications by means of abstraction functions and a tool for manipulations of such descriptions. Further a library of abstraction functions should be developed. Finally the theory presented in the current paper must be applied to data structures, which have different characteristics then those presented here. Experience has already been gained in semi-automatic code generation for simulation of PDE's with help of a formula manipulation language. The current theory will be implemented in that system. All this will form an important contribution to the process of providing support for programming on a higher level than is presently common.

Acknowledgement

This work was supported by the Dutch National Institute for Coastal and Marine Management (RIKZ).

References

[1] H.H. ten Cate. Applying abstraction and formal specification in numerical software design. *Computers and Mathematics Applications*, 29(12):81–102, 1995.

[2] H.H. ten Cate, M.R.T. Roest, and E.A.H. Vollebregt. Towards tool support for recording development steps for CFD packages. In J. van Katwijk, J. J. Gerbrands, M. R. van Steen, and J. F. M. Tonino, editors, *Proc. First Annual Conference of the ASCI*, pages 165–174, Delft, May 1995. Advanced School for Computing and Imaging, ASCI.

[3] B. Chapman, H. Zima, and P. Mehrotra. Extending HPF for advanced data-parallel applications. *IEEE Parallel & Distributed Technology*, pages 59–70, Fall 1994.

[4] T. Clement. The role of data reification in program refinement. *Computer Journal*, 35:451–459, 1992.

[5] R. Das, R. Ponnusamy, J. Saltz, and D. Mavriplis. Distributed memory compiler methods for irregular problems - data copy reuse and runtime partitioning. In J. Saltz and P. Mehrota, editors, *Languages, Compilers and Run-Time Environments for Distributed Memory Machines*, pages 185–219. Elseviers Science Publishers, Amsterdam, 1992.

[6] High Performance Fortran Forum. High Performance Fortran Language Specification, Version 1.0. Draft, January 1993.

[7] M.R.T. Roest. *Partitioning in Parallel Processing*. PhD thesis, Delft University of Technology, 1997.

[8] M.R.T. Roest, E.A.H. Vollebregt, H.H. ten Cate, and H.X. Lin. Structured parallelisation of the flow simulation package TRIWAQ. In B. Herzberger and G. Serazzi, editors, *High-Performance Computing and Networking, Proc. Int. Conf. and Exhibition, Milan, 1995*, pages 136–141. Springer Verlag, 1995.

Compiling High Performance Fortran for Shared Memory and Shared Virtual Memory Systems

Thomas Brandes

German National Research Center for Information Technology (GMD)
Schloß Birlinghoven, D-53754 St. Augustin, Germany
e-mail: brandes@gmd.de

Abstract

High Performance Fortran (HPF) is the de facto standard language for writing data parallel programs. This language is intended to be efficient for shared and distributed memory systems. Currently, the HPF compilers rely on the message passing programming model for the target platforms. Though this model can be easily and efficiently emulated on shared memory systems, it is not quite clear how to take advantage of the capabilities of a shared memory or shared virtual memory architecture for the HPF compilation.

This paper discusses an HPF execution model for shared and shared virtual memory architectures and describes its implementation within an HPF compiler. The essential idea is to share only selected arrays between the processors and to use the data distribution directives for the load distribution as opposed to allocating parts of arrays as local to each processor. Using this method, the HPF compilation techniques for shared and distributed memory are very similar and can therefore be combined into one compilation system.

Our experiments demonstrate the effectiveness of the chosen approach but also a weakness. On the one hand, certain programs will be more efficient if shared or shared virtual memory support is available. But on the other hand, the use of shared arrays can also result in a dramatical loss of performance.

1. Introduction

High Performance Fortran (HPF) is the de facto standard language for writing data parallel programs for shared and distributed memory parallel architectures [8, 9]. Since HPF provides a global address space at the user level, HPF programs are much easier to write than conventional message-passing programs.

Until recently, large-scale parallel machines have only distributed address spaces (e.g. Intel Paragon, Thinking Machines CM-5, IBM SP-2). HPF compilers have to emulate the global address space by software and have to generate explicit message passing code. Examples of such compilers are the Portland HPF compiler [12], the DEC HPF compiler [6], and the NA Software HPF mapper [10].

Shared Memory (SM) multiprocessors provide the global address space on a physically shared memory where each access to it has nearly the same costs. As for performance reasons the local cache of one processor must be utilized, the caches of all processors must be kept coherent. So when data is shared between different processors, the hardware guarantees that an update of a line in cache will make copies of it invalid on all other processors. Examples of such architectures are the Silicon Graphics POWER Series (TM) or the SUN multiprocessor systems.

Shared Virtual Memory (SVM) architectures provide a global address space on distributed hardware with no physically shared memory. SVM promises the benefit of the ease of programming with the scalability of message-passing multiprocessors. The global address space can be built either on top of coherent hardware caches or on top of the virtual memory paging mechanism within the operating systems. A cache miss or a page fault will implicitly cause communication if the cache line or the page is on another processor. The Advanced Shared Virtual Memory system (ASVM) on the Intel Paragon is an example of a system that maintains coherence automatically. In this case, the unit of coherence is a page [15].

Compiling programs for shared memory architectures is relatively easy, since the global address space no longer has to be emulated by the compiler and so it is not necessary to explicitly manage communication for non-local data. But interprocessor communication, though hidden, is still quite expensive and this approach will only be efficient if data locality is exploited.

There are many language proposals for SM and SVM systems, but we use HPF for the following reasons. The main reason is obviously the fact that HPF is a quasi standard and may allow to have one version of a program to run on all architectures. We also want to reduce interprocessor communication which is still quite expensive for non-local memory access. HPF provides locality by the distribution directives so that page-level locality can be exploited. Furthermore, we do not have to focus on the extraction of parallelism in sequential programs and can take advantage of the data parallelism supported in HPF.

After a short discussion about languages for shared memory systems, an HPF execution model that is suitable for shared and shared virtual memory systems is presented. This model has been implemented within the HPF compilation system ADAPTOR [4]. Although ADAPTOR was intended to generate message passing programs, it employs the same technology to generate programs for shared address space machines. Only some additional techniques are required. The results on some architectures with global address spaces prove the effectiveness of the chosen approach and identify the problems.

2. Languages for Shared Memory Systems

Many compilers for SM architectures are able to identify loops in serial code that are safe to execute in parallel. Therefore the serial language can be directly used for the parallel execution. However, the parallelization is usually driven by directives and can be tuned by additional assertions. An example of such a language is MIPSpro Power Fortran 77 [13].

There are also many language proposals for SM or SVM architectures. Usually, these languages allow the definition of parallel loops, parallel sections, and explicit synchronization between different iterations and sections. Unfortunately, there is no official standard for such a language.

As a pure shared memory programming model might be inefficient on shared virtual memory architectures, some other languages additionally allow explicit load distribution. This gives the user the possibility for increasing data locality. This was an explicit design goal of SVM Fortran [7].

When comparing HPF with the typical SM languages, the following differences can be identified:

- An efficient HPF program requires directives for data distribution.

- The basic HPF has no load distribution directives although they are being considered as an approved extension within HPF 2.0 [9]. But in any case, dynamic scheduling of loop iterations cannot be specified.

- HPF has no features for explicit synchronization (e.g. semaphores, critical sections).

- An HPF program should not rely on storage or sequence association for distributed data.

Experiences so far have shown that porting serial applications to HPF requires major code restructuring while using SM languages and automatic parallelization allows a simpler migration to a shared memory architecture. But as HPF is standardized, it is worthwhile to investigate how HPF programs can be compiled more efficiently on shared and shared virtual memory systems.

3. Execution Model for HPF on Shared Memory Systems

3.1. Basic Execution Model

The first general decision was to start with the same HPF execution model that is used for distributed memory systems. Here, an HPF compiler translates the data parallel program to an equivalent SPMD program (single program, multiple data) that runs on all available nodes. It distributes the arrays of the source program onto the node processors where the parallel loops and array operations are restricted to the local part owned by the processor (see Figure 1). Communication statements for exchanging nonlocal data will be generated automatically. The control flow and statements with scalar code are replicated on all nodes. The global address space is not used except for the communication if the message passing interface uses this facility for the sake of efficiency.

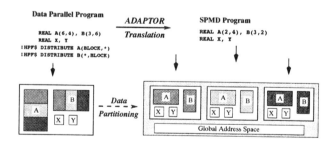

Figure 1. MIMD partitioning within HPF compilers.

We based this decision on the fact that operations on local data are faster than operations on shared data (see also results in Section 5.1). The partitioning done by the HPF compiler provides contiguous accessing of the local parts of the array which enhances spatial locality. It minimizes false sharing since data from different processors will not be in the same cache line or on the same page.

The replication of flow of control and scalar data avoids implicit broadcasts on SVM systems which would be necessary if only one processor executed the serial parts.

In the case of structured communication, this approach might also be faster since the synchronization is directly coupled with the data movement. The compiler can generate closed formulas for the data that has to be sent and to be received.

Only in the case of nonstructured communication, this approach requires complex and expensive runtime support. Unstructured communication requires complex ownership computations and additional communication to set up communication schedules (*inspector phase*). This schedule specifies which data each processor has to send and to receive (*executor phase*). This functionality must be available in the runtime system and usually has a very high overhead.

In the case of unstructured communication, a parallel program will benefit from shared arrays that are the essential extension of this basic execution model.

3.2. Shared Arrays

In the extended execution model for SM and SVM architectures, an array can be shared among all the processors. The array is not distributed onto the different processors within the local address spaces but is kept within the global address space. This facility of a shared array can be embedded in HPF in the following way:

- The SHARED directive specifies that an array should be embedded within the global address space.

- The SHARED attribute can be combined with all the other mapping directives. Since shared arrays have only one incarnation, no mapping that implies replication is allowed. The mapping directives will only be used to drive the load distribution.

- Replicated arrays, scalars, and templates cannot be shared.

- For shared arrays within a COMMON block, the same rules apply as if they were distributed.

- Shared arrays can be used within all data parallel operations just like distributed ones.

HPF provides the SEQUENCE directive to declare an object to be sequential so that it can be storage associated or sequence associated. Although for shared arrays the order of array elements might not be changed and sequence association is guaranteed, we propose to distinguish between sequential and shared arrays for the following reasons:

- In HPF 2.0 [9], a sequential array may not be explicitly mapped.

- Shared arrays should not be storage associated with other data via an EQUIVALENCE statement.

- Ignoring the SHARED directive should not result in an invalid program.

3.3. Compiling HPF with Shared Arrays

A shared array will not imply any changes regarding the execution of statements and parallel loops. In other words, the HPF mapping directives are used in the same way as for distributed arrays to determine where the statements or the iterations of the parallel loops are executed.

The addressing of the shared array remains completely unchanged as if it was not partitioned at all. So a shared array will imply changes in the following situations:

- Indirect addressing of a shared array no longer requires complex runtime support. In the following example, the arrays A and IND are distributed and aligned. Each processor will need some values of the array B or write some values to it. If the array B is shared and available in the global address space, no communication has to be inserted by the compiler.

```
        REAL A(N), B(M)
        INTEGER IND(N)
!HPF$ DISTRIBUTE (BLOCK) :: A
!HPF$ DISTRIBUTE (BLOCK), SHARED :: B
!HPF$ ALIGN IND(I) WITH A(I)
        ...
        A = B(IND)
        B(IND) = A
```

- For INDEPENDENT DO loops an HPF compiler tries to extract all the necessary communication and to place it before and/or after the loop. If this is not possible, the execution must remain serial to make sure that the exchanging of data is still possible.

```
!HPF$ SHARED :: A, B
        ...
!HPF$ INDEPENDENT
        DO I = 1, N
           A(f(I)) = B(g(I))
        END DO
```

Shared arrays in an independent loop require no communication to be generated by the compiler. Every processor can update the values of the shared array A and read the values of the shared array B. Possible communication is left to the operating system and/or to the hardware.

- Any remapping of shared arrays only implies changes regarding the load distribution. Data movements are not necessary.

```
        REAL A(N,N)
!HPF$ DISTRIBUTE (BLOCK,*) :: A
!HPF$ SHARED, DYNAMIC      :: A
        ...
!HPF$ REDISTRIBUTE (*,BLOCK) :: A
```

- Remapping of shared arrays at subroutine boundaries is not necessary if the actual and dummy argument both have the SHARED attribute.

```
        REAL A(N,N)
!HPF$ DISTRIBUTE (BLOCK,*), SHARED :: A
        ...
        CALL SUB (A,N)

        SUBROUTINE SUB (B,N)
        REAL B(N,N)
!HPF$ DISTRIBUTE (*,BLOCK), SHARED :: B
```

- I/O statements are usually executed by only one selected processor. If a distributed array is involved in I/O, communication becomes necessary to collect or to spread the data to or from the I/O-processor. This is no longer necessary for shared arrays since the processor responsible for I/O can access all the data directly.

3.4. Shared and Distributed Arrays

An assignment of a distributed array to a shared array implies that the distributed data is copied into the global address space. Though this operation may be rather expensive and should be avoided, it might be useful if the corresponding data is indirectly accessed afterwards.

A distributed array passed to a subroutine where the corresponding dummy argument has the SHARED attribute implies data movement. The compiler has to generate code that copies the data in the global address space on entry and restores the global data into the local parts on exit. Also global data can be localized during the lifetime of the subroutine by the opposite way.

As the data movement involved might be expensive, we provide the possibility for a dummy argument to specify whether it may be shared or not. Just as the INHERITED attribute, the compiler should generate code that can deal with both kind of arrays without any remapping.

```
        SUBROUTINE SUB (B,N)
        REAL B(N,N)
!HPF$ DISTRIBUTE (*,BLOCK), ?SHARED :: B
```

Attention: If an array may be shared or not, the compiler cannot assume the SHARED attribute during the compilation.

3.5. Synchronization

One big penalty of the shared arrays is the necessity for adding explicit synchronization. The compiler has to make sure that the correct values are always used. For parallel loops working on shared arrays, a compiler will probably employ barrier synchronization. But also explicit point-to-point synchronization can be utilized.

```
        REAL A(N), B(N)
!HPF$ DISTRIBUTE (BLOCK) :: A, B
        A(N) = B(1)
        B(1) = C
```

The first assignment is executed by the owner of A(N) and the second one by the owner of B(1). If the arrays are distributed, there will be an implicit synchronization as the owner of B(1) will send the old value before updating it. If the arrays are shared, an explicit synchronization must be added, otherwise the owner of A(N) could already read the new value of B(1).

Hint: Other shared memory programming models only have to insert barrier synchronization before and after a parallel loop as the serial part is executed by a single processor. This is not the case for the execution model presented here where the owner is always responsible for the updates.

4. Implementation of Shared Arrays within ADAPTOR

4.1. The ADAPTOR Tool

ADAPTOR (Automatic Data Parallelism Translator) is a public domain HPF compilation system developed at GMD for compiling data parallel HPF programs to equivalent message passing programs [4].

The latest release of ADAPTOR supports nearly the full HPF 2.0 base language. Fortran 90 derived types and pointers have still a lot of limitations. Furthermore, block-cyclic distributions cannot be utilized. Some of the Fortran and HPF intrinsics and library procedures are not efficiently implemented. Read accesses within PURE routines are restricted to local data.

On the other hand, ADAPTOR already supports some of the approved extensions of HPF 2.0, like general block distributions, dynamic redistributions, the SHADOW and RANGE directive, the ON HOME and RESIDENT directive, as well as extrinsic HPF_LOCAL, HPF_SERIAL and F77_LOCAL routines.

The functionality of the system is still increasing. It is also part of an HPF programming environment [2] and serves for the investigation of new language features supporting sparse data structures [3].

4.2. Design Issues for Shared Arrays

The following properties of ADAPTOR made it very easy to extend this HPF compilation system to support shared arrays in the proposed way (see Section 3):

- Nearly all the transformations and optimizations during the translation take the global view of the data within the parallel program. These phases of the compilation remain unchanged for shared arrays.

- During the translation shared arrays will be considered as arrays that will not require communication in certain operations. This property is hidden in a single predicate (boolean function) implemented within the translation system.

- The SPMD program generated by ADAPTOR is a FORTRAN 77 program where dynamic and distributed arrays become pseudo dynamic arrays. The data will be allocated on the heap and a small static array is indexed out of bounds to access this heap memory. The same technique is used for shared arrays in the global address space. This results in the same addressing schemes for distributed and shared arrays.

In fact, the extension of ADAPTOR to compile for shared memory systems resulted in a more convenient design of the whole system. The redesign takes into account that we can also take advantage of other new features like active messages or one-sided communication.

4.3. Array Descriptors and Run Time Support

For procedure calls, ADAPTOR passes an array via a descriptor or handle as is typically done in HPF implementations. These descriptors are also used within the runtime system. The descriptors now have an additional entry to indicate that an array is shared between the processors.

The shared attribute in the descriptor tells the runtime system whether a global or a local addressing scheme is used for the operations on this array.

Using this way, all functionality of the run time system provided for distributed arrays can be used in the same way for shared arrays. This includes the many routines for copying, packing and unpacking of array sections as well as sending and receiving of shared array data. Global reductions on shared arrays will use the same global communication routines like the reductions on distributed arrays. Furthermore, pipelining and tiling techniques also work for shared arrays.

4.4. Availability

The source files of ADAPTOR, documentation files in PostScript and a number of example programs are available via `ftp` [1]. ADAPTOR supports shared arrays as presented in this paper.

Currently, the functionality of shared arrays can be used on all machines that support the System V shared memory segments (e.g. SUN, SGI Power multiprocessor systems).

On the Intel Paragon, shared arrays are supported within the Advanced Shared Virtual Memory system (ASVM) [15]. The pagefault times are quite high due to the memory management overhead on the Intel Paragon. Pagefaults requiring communication with other processors typically take 1.5 ms up to 2.5 ms.

4.5. Optimizations

The current implementation has identified some topics that will be taken into account in the next releases of ADAPTOR. This includes the removal of unnecessary synchronization.

Currently, the user himself decides whether an array is shared or not. This way, he will be responsible for any redistribution. In an advanced compilation system this should be decided by the compiler, also for portability reasons. The development of good strategies and heuristics is still necessary.

5. Results

The following results have been measured on a SUN multiprocessor system, on a SGI Power Challenge SC900 multiprocessor system, two typical SM architectures, and on an Intel Paragon that stands for an SVM architecture.

5.1. Structured Reading and Writing

At first we take a look at the penalties of shared arrays in the case of local computations where no communication is necessary. We compare the memory transfer rate of distributed arrays with the one of shared arrays.

```
      PARAMETER (N=8192)
      DOUBLE PRECISION X(N), Y(N), S(N)
!HPF$ DISTRIBUTE (BLOCK) :: X, Y, S
!HPF$ SHARED :: S
      X = Y      ! local assignment
      X = S      ! reading a shared array
      S = Y      ! writing into a shared array
```

Table 1, 2, and 3 show the bandwidths (in million words per second) of copying contiguous sections of distributed and shared arrays.

	1	2	3	4
X = Y	3.3	6.4	9.1	12.3
X = S	3.1	6.2	8.9	11.9
S = Y	2.3	2.1	1.9	1.8

Table 1. Memory bandwidth on a SUN multiprocessor system (in MW/s).

The reading of shared arrays is nearly as efficient as reading distributed arrays. But writing into a shared array is less efficient and does not really scale.

	1	2	4	8
X = Y	37.0	73.9	147.7	294.4
X = S	36.9	73.8	147.2	295.1
S = Y	35.0	27.4	34.2	49.5

Table 2. Memory bandwidth on SGI Power Challenge multiprocessor system (in MW/s).

Also writing into a shared array on a shared virtual memory system does not scale well (see Table 3). It should also be mentioned that the shared write operation considered here shows best case behavior as all processors write on different pages.

	1	2	4	8	16
X = Y	9.2	18.4	37.0	74.4	148.5
X = S	9.2	18.4	36.8	73.8	147.5
S = Y	9.1	7.2	7.0	9.8	14.8

Table 3. Memory bandwidth on Intel Paragon XP/S (in MW/s).

5.2. Unstructured Reading and Writing

Now we take a look at the benefits of shared arrays for unstructured communication in case of unstructured reads and unstructured writes. For comparison, we also consider the case where the inspector phase is not necessary because the communication schedule is already available.

```
      DOUBLE PRECISION X(N), Y(N), S(N)
      INTEGER IND(N)
!HPF$ DISTRIBUTE (BLOCK) :: X, Y, S, IND
!HPF$ SHARED :: S
      X = Y(IND) ! distributed read
      X = Y(IND) ! same, but reusing schedule
      X = S(IND) ! shared read
      X(IND) = Y ! distributed write
      X(IND) = Y ! same, but reusing schedule
      S(IND) = Y ! shared write
```

Table 4 and 5 verify that HPF programs benefit enormously if the indirectly accessed array is shared. On the one hand, the shared arrays avoid the high overhead of the inspector phase. But also packing and unpacking of the exchanged data is no longer necessary and results in higher bandwidths.

	1	2	4	8
X = Y(IND), insp./ex.	0.3	0.6	1.2	2.1
X = Y(IND), ex. only	2.7	4.3	7.5	12.2
X = S(IND), shared	9.3	18.5	37.1	73.9

Table 4. Unstructured reading on SGI multiprocessor systems (in MW/s).

	1	2	4	8	16
X = Y(IND), insp./ex.	0.1	0.3	0.4	0.7	1.3
X = Y(IND), ex. only	0.9	1.7	2.8	4.5	6.0
X = S(IND), shared	5.3	7.4	9.5	15.7	28.8

Table 5. Unstructured reading on Intel Paragon XP/S (in MW/s).

Tables 6 and 7 show that writing arbitrarily into a shared array is very inefficient.

	1	2	4	8
X(IND) = Y, insp./ex.	0.3	0.6	1.2	2.1
X(IND) = Y, ex. only	2.7	3.8	6.8	13.0
S(IND) = Y, shared	10.4	3.1	2.9	4.5

Table 6. Unstructured writing on SGI multiprocessor systems (in MW/s).

The memory bandwidth for writing into a shared array was only about 0.005 MW/s on the shared virtual memory system for more than four processors (see Table 7). Shared writing implies a lot of communication caused by writing on the same page. For writing it is necessary to be the owner of the cache line or of the page (*strong consistency*). Therefore the cache line or page will move every time (ping pong effect). Writing into a shared array should be avoided unless sufficient locality is guaranteed.

5.3. Results for an Application Kernel

For testing the benefits of shared arrays, we used a benchmark solver based on a conjugate gradient method with diagonal scaling. This solver is part of an industrial fluid dynamics package, developed especially for comput-

294

	1	2	4	8	16
X(IND) = Y, insp./ex.	0.1	0.2	0.4	0.7	1.1
X(IND) = Y, ex. only	1.1	1.6	2.7	4.5	5.9
S(IND) = Y, shared	7.6	0.1	0.0	0.0	0.0

Table 7. Unstructured writing on Intel Paragon XP/S (in MW/s).

ing compressible and incompressible turbulent fluid flow as encountered in engineering environments.

The solver is an iterative one that works on unstructured grids. The unstructured grids are represented by one-dimensional arrays to reduce the memory requirements. The relation between the grid points is given by an integer array that will be used for indirect addressing within all programs. The solver has been rewritten to HPF.

Within every iteration step, the loop consuming the most execution time is the the loop containing the indirect addressing.

```
      REAL, DIMENSION (nnintc) :: direc1, direc2
      INTEGER, DIMENSION (6,nnintc) :: lcc
!HPF$ DISTRIBUTE (BLOCK) :: direc1
!!HPF$ ALIGN WITH direc1 :: direc2,
!HPF$ ALIGN lcc(i,j) with direc1(j)
      ...
      DO WHILE (.NOT. converged)
        ...
        FORALL (nc = 1:nnintc)
   &      direc2(nc) = f (direc1(nc),
   &        direc1(lcc(1,nc)), direc1(lcc(4,nc)),
   &        direc1(lcc(5,nc)), direc1(lcc(3,nc)),
   &        direc1(lcc(2,nc)), direc1(lcc(6,nc)) )
        ...
        direc1 = g (direct2)
        ...
      END DO
```

Three versions of the solver have been compared:

- *NORMAL* is the HPF version with an inspector and executor phase. The communication schedule is computed in every iteration step.

- *REUSE* is the same code but where the inspector phase is executed only once. This is legal as the integer array `lcc` does not change during the iterations.

- *SHARED* is the HPF code using a shared array that provides a global copy of the data for unstructured reading.

Two data sets have been considered: tjunc (13845 cells, 338 iterations), and pent (108000 cells, 546 iterations).

Table 8 shows the results to demonstrate the benefits of shared arrays on a SUN multiprocessor system. The execution times are rather bad for the first version that will be generated by a straightforward compilation. If the compiler is able to recognize that the communication pattern can be

reused, the execution times are much better. When using shared arrays the performance is obviously the best and that without powerful optimization techniques.

tjunc 13845	NP 1	NP 2	NP 3
NORMAL	320.9	212.9	175.8
REUSE	110.5	73.6	65.1
SHARED	61.2	44.6	41.6

Table 8. Results for the benchmark kernel on the SUN MP system (walltime in seconds).

On the Intel Paragon we measured both data sets. For small numbers of processors, the use of shared arrays is more efficient. But this approach does not scale well due to the structured writing into the shared array. As the shared array is not big enough, the processors might write data onto common pages.

tjunc, 13845	NP 2	NP 4	NP 8	NP 16	NP 32
NORMAL	101.4	51.7	27.1	14.9	9.4
REUSE	30.0	15.7	8.6	5.0	3.4
SHARED	28.3	19.2	15.9	20.1	26.2
pent 108000	NP 2	NP 4	NP 8	NP 16	NP 32
NORMAL	–	–	328.1	163.6	86.6
REUSE	409.4	205.1	103.4	52.9	26.6
SHARED	296.3	155.3	93.0	62.2	52.7

Table 9. Results for the benchmark kernel on the Intel Paragon XP/S (walltime in seconds).

6. Related Work

Lam et al. have presented a set of unified compilation techniques that exemplify the convergence in compilers for shared and distributed address space machines [14]. Their results are based on experimental measurements with the SUIF (Stanford University Intermediate Format) parallelizing compiler.

Boyle and Bodin have developed a new compiler method that reduces the number of executed barriers on a shared virtual memory architecture using dependence and scheduling information [11]. Their ideas are very promising and will be considered for our implementations.

Brezany, Gerndt and Sipkova have provided SVM support in the Vienna Fortran Compilation System for the iPSC/2 using the Koan system [5]. They have the same approach and also exploit the strength of both, message passing and shared memory communication. Although they provide an optimization technique that eliminates redundant redistributions between shared and distributed arrays, they restrict the use of shared arrays to forall loops.

7. Conclusions

The experience with ADAPTOR has shown that an HPF compiler supporting the message passing model can be extended to take benefit of a global address space. Data parallel operations and the runtime system can be implemented in the same way for shared and distributed data. Since library routines on distributed arrays are used in the same way as for shared arrays, the approach chosen avoids expensive redistributions.

Shared-memory support is extremely useful for unstructured reading. Where communication cannot be extracted at compile time, if offers a higher potential for parallel execution.

Unstructured writing into shared arrays can become very inefficient and does not scale. False sharing of data causes a dramatic loss of performance. The SVM approach seems to be unsuitable for writing into shared arrays, unless there is sufficient data locality. Any load distribution that is not aligned to page boundaries decreases the performance. This situation would become better if the SVM system supported *weak consistency*. This concept allows the processors to write into different copies of the same page that will be merged at the next synchronization point into a valid one. HPF compilers could utilize this property for generating more efficient code.

Acknowledgements

I would like to warmly thank Michael Gerndt (ZAM, Forschungszentrum Jülich, Germany) for valuable discussions and many technical hints. Thanks to the ZAM for providing access to the Intel Paragon XP/S and the necessary customer support as well as to the RRZ at the University of Cologne for providing access to the SGI Power Challenge SC900.

References

[1] T. Brandes. ADAPTOR Installation Guide (Version 5.0). Technical documentation, GMD, January 1997. Available via anonymous ftp from ftp.gmd.de as gmd/adaptor/docs/iguide.ps.

[2] T. Brandes, S. Chaumette, M. C. Counilh, A. Darte, J. C. Mignot, F. Desprez, and J. Roman. HPFIT: A Set of Integrated Tools for the Parallelization of Applications Using High Performance Fortran, Part 1: HPFIT and the TransTOOL Environment. In *Proceedings of Third Workshop on Environments and Tools for Parallel Scientific Computing, SIAM*, August 1996. to be published.

[3] T. Brandes, S. Chaumette, M. C. Counilh, A. Darte, J. C. Mignot, F. Desprez, and J. Roman. HPFIT: A Set of Integrated Tools for the Parallelization of Applications Using High Performance Fortran, Part 2: Data-Structures Visualization and HPF Support for Irregular Data Structures With Hierarchical Scheme. In *Proceedings of Third Workshop on Environments and Tools for Parallel Scientific Computing, SIAM*, August 1996. to be published.

[4] T. Brandes and F. Zimmermann. ADAPTOR - A Transformation Tool for HPF Programs. In K.M. Decker and R.M. Rehmann, editors, *Programming Environments for Massively Parallel Distributed Systems*, pages 91–96. Birkhäuser Verlag, April 1994.

[5] P. Brezany, M. Gerndt, and V. Sipkova. SVM Support in the Vienna Fortran Compilaton System. Interner Bericht KFA-ZAM-IB-9401, Research Center Jülich, January 1994.

[6] Digital Equipment Corporation. Digital High Performance Fortran 90 HPF and PSE Manual. Manual, DEC, Maynard, Massachuesetts, 1995.

[7] M. Gerndt and R. Berrendorf. SVM-Fortran, Reference Manual, Version 1.4. Interner Bericht KFA-ZAM-IB-9510, Research Center Jülich, May 1995.

[8] High Performance Fortran Forum. High Performance Fortran Language Specification. Version 1.1, Department of Computer Science, Rice University, November 1994.

[9] High Performance Fortran Forum. High Performance Fortran Language Specification. Version 2.0.δ, Department of Computer Science, Rice University, October 1996.

[10] NA Software. NA Software HPF Mapper, Users Guide version 1.0. Manual, NAS, February 1995.

[11] M. O'Boyle and F. Bodin. Compiler reduction of synchronisation in shared virtual memory systems. In *1995 International Conference on Supercomputing*, pages 318–327. ACM Press, July 1995.

[12] Portland Group, Inc. PGHPF User's Guide. Manual, PGI, November 1994.

[13] Silicon Graphics, Inc. MIPSpro (TM) Power Fortran 77 Programmer's Guide. Document 007-2363-002, SGI, 1996.

[14] C.-W. Tseng, J. Anderson, S. Amarasinghe, and M. Lam. Unified compilation techniques for shared and distributed address space machines. In *1995 International Conference on Supercomputing*, pages 67–76. ACM Press, July 1995.

[15] S. Zeisset. Evaluation and Enhancement on the Paragon Multiprocessor's Shared Virtual Memory System. Master's thesis, Technical University of Munich, 1993.

A Portable Collective Communication Library using Communication Schedules*

Tim Rühl   Henri E. Bal

Dept. of Mathematics and Computer Science

Vrije Universiteit, Amsterdam, The Netherlands

Abstract

We describe a flexible and efficient implementation of a portable collective communication library based on communication schedules. With communication schedules the communication pattern of an operation is expressed before it is actually executed. We provide a simple set of functions to create such a communication schedule and to check whether the communication pattern is correct. Analyzing this communication schedule provides information that can be used at run-time to reduce the number of acknowledgment messages and to eliminate the overhead of context switching during data forwarding.

1. Introduction

Efficient communication is crucial for the performance of most parallel applications. Unfortunately, a highly tuned parallel programming system for a specific architecture may be hard to port to other architectures. We have implemented a virtual machine called *Panda* [17] that achieves both portability and efficiency. Panda provides threads and communication to higher software layers in a machine and operating system independent way. To obtain efficiency, Panda is designed as a flexible system consisting of building blocks that can be adapted to the characteristics of the underlying machine and operating system.

We have used Panda to implement Orca [2], a task-parallel programming language for distributed systems. Orca provides an object-based distributed shared memory model. Processes communicate and synchronize by performing user-defined operations on shared data-objects. Recent research on data-parallel extensions to Orca [5] has shown the need for collective communication operations. Also, our research on atomic functions [18], a model in which processes can execute atomic operations on *multiple* objects, has shown that compile-time information can aid the runtime system to generate optimized communication patterns.

Based on these research results we have developed an abstraction, called *communication schedules*, that provides a flexible way to express arbitrary collective communication operations. Furthermore, the information in a communication schedule can be used for run-time optimizations. In this paper, we describe this mechanism and assess the performance improvements of the optimizations on top of Panda.

The rest of this paper is organized as follows. Sections 2 and 3 describe Panda and collective communication. Section 4 describes the design and implementation of communication schedules. Section 5 explains how collective communication operations are implemented. Section 6 describes two optimizations that can be applied to communication schedules. Section 7 gives performance measurements. Section 8 relates our work to other research, and in Section 9 we draw conclusions.

2. Collective communication

Collective communication is communication that involves a group of processes. A collective communication operation is executed by having all processes in the group call the communication routine, with matching arguments. Collective communication operations are inherent in many message-passing algorithms and are also

---
[1]This research is supported by a PIONIER grant from the Netherlands Organization for Scientific Research (N.W.O)

Operation	Before	After
broadcast	x at P_k, k given	x at all processors
gather	x_j at P_j	x at P_k, k given
allgather	x_j at P_j	x at all processors
scatter	x at P_k, k given	x_j at P_j
reduce	x_j at P_j	$\oplus_{j=0}^{p-1} x_j$ at P_k, k given
allreduce	x_j at P_j	$\oplus_{j=0}^{p-1} x_j$ at all processors

Table 1. Summary of some collective communication operations.

often used as target primitives in the translation of data parallel programming languages.

The MPI [10] message-passing standard defines a set of core library routines that are efficiently implementable on a wide range of computers. Table 1 gives a summary of some of the collective communication operations defined by the MPI standard (see also [3]). There are p processors, labeled $P_0...P_{p-1}$. Before an operation starts, a processor can have all (x) or part (x_j) of the data. The operation $\oplus$ represents an associative and commutative combine operation. MPI also defines a *barrier* operation, which causes a caller to block until all processors have called it.

3. Panda

Panda is a virtual machine that hides the operating system and machine specifics. It provides a standard interface for threads and communication that can be used by higher software layers so that these layers are easy to port. Panda has been used to implement the Orca RTS, a subset of PVM, and SR [1, 17].

The Panda thread interface resembles the Pthreads [11] interface. It provides primitives to create and destroy a thread and a yield call to force an explicit thread switch. Two mechanisms are provided for synchronization between threads: mutexes and condition variables.

Figure 1 gives an overview of the Panda system. It consists of an internal system layer that provides threads and two low-level communication primitives: unicast and multicast. On top of that the interface layer defines multiple communication modules. Since all communication modules are implemented on top of the system interface, porting Panda involves porting only the system layer. Most operating system and machine specifics are hidden in the system layer. Two properties, however, cannot be hidden without causing too much overhead:

- whether the low-level communication primitives are reliable or unreliable;

- whether the underlying system imposes a fixed upper bound on the packet size or not.

Instead of implementing a communication module for the worst case scenario (unreliable communication with a fixed upper bound on the packet size), we have multiple implementations that are tailored to these two properties. When Panda is configured for a system, the appropriate module implementations are selected. Since a communication module has a fixed interface and fixed semantics, higher software layers will not notice the difference.

The system layer uses an *upcall* mechanism to deliver packets to a communication module. When a packet arrives at a processor, the system layer determines which communication module must handle this packet and calls a registered function. After all packets of a message have arrived, the communication module also makes an upcall to deliver the complete message to the application. Since the implementation of the system layer may use the thread that makes the upcall to handle further communication, the application program may not block in the upcall function waiting for another message [6]. This contract between Panda and the application makes it possible to implement communication efficiently on a large number of architectures.

For our implementation of communication schedules we use two communication modules: reliable point-to-point message passing and reliable group communication. With message passing, the sender can either wait until the message has been delivered at the destination processor (synchronous send) or it can continue immediately (asynchronous send). With asynchronous send, an upcall is made at the sending processor

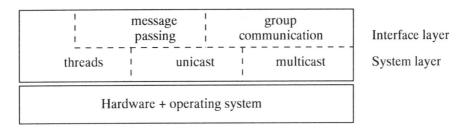

Figure 1. Structure of the Panda system.

when the message is known to have been delivered at the destination processor.

The implementation of reliable message passing on unreliable communication is based on a stop-and-wait protocol. Every Panda system layer packet[1] is confirmed by an explicit acknowledgment message from the receiver to the sender. If no acknowledgment arrives, the packet is retransmitted. For efficiency, however, the message passing module provides three modes for the last acknowledgment (see Figure 2):

a) **explicit acknowledgment**: an explicit acknowledgment message is sent immediately when the last packet arrives. When the acknowledgment message is received, the send is known to be delivered (dashed arrow in Figure 2a). This is the default mode.

b) **piggybacked acknowledgment**: an acknowledgment is piggybacked on the first packet that is sent from the receiver to the sender (dashed arrow). If no such packet is sent soon enough, an explicit acknowledgment is sent. Both the sender and receiver have to set a timer in this mode: the sender to retransmit the packet and the receiver to send an explicit acknowledgment.

c) **implicit acknowledgment**: no acknowledgment message is scheduled at the receiver, but the sender knows that it will receive a message that is causally related. When this reply message arrives, the application has to make a call to the message passing module to confirm that the message is delivered at the destination. Only the sender has to set a timer to retransmit a packet.

Group communication in Panda provides reliable totally-ordered multicast, which guarantees that all multicast messages arrive in the same order at all destinations [13]. If two processes simultaneously multicast a message, either all receivers get the first message first or they all get the second message first. The sender can wait until the message has been delivered locally (synchronous send) or it can continue immediately (asynchronous send).

Panda has been ported to several operating systems (including Amoeba [20], Solaris, Linux, and Parix) and machines (including the CM-5, Parsytec GCEL, Parsytec PowerXplorer, CS-2, IBM SP-2, and a Myrinet cluster).

4. Communication schedules

Using Panda's communication modules, it is not very hard to implement collective communication operations. The optimal communication pattern, however, strongly depends on the characteristics of the underlying system [7, 15]. For a portable collective communication library it is thus important that the communication pattern of an operation can be adapted easily. We therefore designed an abstraction called a *communication schedule*, that allows us to express this communication pattern in terms of communication and handler functions.

A communication schedule consists of a number of phases. In each phase, each processor is allowed to perform one action (a send or a receive). Figure 3 shows the communication schedule for a barrier operation on four processors. The schedule consists of six phases. As can be seen, not all processors have to perform an action in a phase. The barrier implementation uses a spanning binomial tree with the root at processor 0 to synchronize. When all processors have arrived at the barrier, processor 0 sends a broadcast message.

A communication schedule is initialized on all processors by registering all actions. Each action

---

[1]A system layer packet may be larger than the packet size provided by the underlying hardware. On Solaris, for example, a 8 KB UDP packet is sent over an Ethernet.

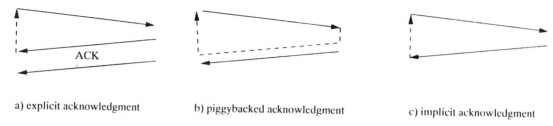

a) explicit acknowledgment   b) piggybacked acknowledgment   c) implicit acknowledgment

Figure 2. Different acknowledgment schemes for message passing.

consists of the type of action (send or receive) and which part of the data it uses. The data that the communication schedule operates on is given in terms of blocks of data. When a communication schedule is executed, it gets as argument a block descriptor with the pointers to the data and the size of each block.

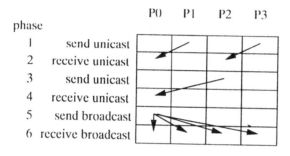

Figure 3. Communication schedule for a barrier on 4 processors.

The following functions are defined to insert the corresponding action in a communication schedule:

send unicast send the data part with a point-to-point message to a specific processor.

receive unicast receive a point-to-point message from a specific processor sent in a specific phase. A receive handler function is registered.

send broadcast send the data part with a broadcast message to all processors.

receive broadcast receive a broadcast message from a specific processor sent in a specific phase. A receive handler function is registered.

With each receive action a receive handler function is registered that gets the received mes-

sage and the data part as arguments. The implementation of collective communication operations uses three receive handler functions: *copy* to copy the whole message to the data part; *copy part* to copy part of the message to the data part; and *ignore* to discard the message. The *ignore* handler is used to specify that a message is only used for synchronization, like in the barrier implementation.

After all actions are registered for a communication schedule, some consistency checks can be performed. Our current implementation checks whether each unicast message is received by one and only one other processor. Also, each broadcast message should be received by all processors. Finally, a check is made whether all receives happen in a later phase than the corresponding send. This ensures that no deadlock can occur due to circular dependencies.

After the communication schedule is checked for consistency, we can use the information that it presents to optimize the execution of a communication schedule. In Section 6, we will discuss two optimizations that make use of this information: implicit acknowledgments and continuation functions. The first optimization reduces the number of acknowledgment messages and the second eliminates context switching during data forwarding.

5. Using communication schedules

In Section 4 we described an implementation of the barrier operation. We can use the same communication pattern to implement the (all)gather and (all)reduce operations. The allgather and allreduce implementations collect the final result on processor 0, and then broadcast this result to all other processors. The normal gather and reduce operations get as argument a processor identifier, the *root*, that has to receive the final result. Since the communication pattern

300

depends on the root, a communication schedule is generated per root processor. We exploit our implicit acknowledgment optimization by sending an empty broadcast at the end.

The broadcast and scatter operations are implemented with a broadcast. The only difference is the message handler function; the broadcast implementation copies all data, while the scatter implementation copies only the relevant part of the data. Again we have a communication schedule per root processor.

A large number of variations are possible for each operation. The barrier implementation, for example, could send a unicast message from every processor directly to processor 0. Whether this is more efficient depends on the underlying system and on the number of processors. More than one communication schedule can be used to implement an operation, as long as a deterministic selection is made based on the arguments of the collective operation invocation.

6. Optimizations

In this section, we show that the communication schedule not only provides flexibility, but also contains information that can be used to reduce the number of acknowledgment messages and to eliminate the overhead of context switching during data forwarding.

6.1. Implicit acknowledgments

The Panda message passing layer provides different acknowledgment schemes to reduce acknowledgment communication (see Figure 2). We would like to exploit this property to reduce the number of acknowledgment messages in collective communication operations. Figure 3 shows, however, that the use of the piggybacked acknowledgment mode does not gain anything in this case. Since the message passing layer will not send a message to a sender in the spanning tree, it has to send an explicit acknowledgment anyway.

Figure 4 again gives the communication pattern of a barrier, but in this figure it is emphasized that the final broadcast message can function as an implicit acknowledgment for all messages in the spanning binomial tree. To determine which unicast messages are implicitly acknowledged, the communication pattern of the

schedule is *simulated*. For each phase the simulation determines the vector time [14] of every action. On every send action, the sender's element of the vector time is set to the current phase index (see Figure 3). On a receive action, a new vector time is computed in which every element is set to the maximum of the local vector time and the vector time associated with the send.

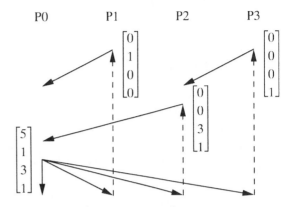

Figure 4. Implicit acknowledgments in the barrier communication schedule.

Figure 4 shows the vector timestamp for each send operation. All processors start with vector time $(0, 0, 0, 0)$. When processor 0 performs the first receive action (matching a send from processor 1), it sets its vector timestamp to $(0, 1, 0, 0)$. After the second receive action it gets timestamp $(0, 1, 3, 1)$. Finally, when it broadcasts the final message, it sets its own index to 5, the current phase index.

On a receive action the vector timestamp of the associated send gives all actions that causally precede this message. In particular, the receiver's element specifies that all unicast messages sent before or at this phase are implicitly acknowledged by this message. For example, when processor 3 in Figure 4 receives the final broadcast message with vector time $(5, 1, 3, 1)$, this implicitly acknowledges the unicast, since it is sent in phase 1. This information is stored in the communication schedule, so that the best mode in which a unicast message can be sent is known during the execution of the schedule. In the example in Figure 4, all unicast messages are sent in implicit acknowledgment mode and all are acknowledged when the broadcast arrives.

After all precomputations on the communication schedule have been performed, only the part of the schedule that describes the local actions has to be preserved (i.e., in the order of the number of phases). All other information can be discarded to reduce memory consumption.

6.2. Continuation functions

One way to implement the execution of communication schedules is to use the user thread that calls the operation for executing the actions. To receive a message the user thread blocks on a condition variable until the message arrives. When a processor receives a message, the upcall handler has to wake up the user thread, so it takes one context switch for every message. In Figure 5a we show this execution behavior for the barrier implementation on processor 2. When the message from processor 3 arrives, the handler function wakes up the user thread. After the message from processor 3 is received, the user thread sends a message to processor 0 and blocks until it receives the broadcast message.

A more efficient way is to let the upcall handler perform all the actions that are caused by the receipt of a message. To do this, the user thread leaves some state information, a *continuation* [8], for the upcall thread to continue the execution. Since the upcall thread may not block, it has to send messages asynchronously. After executing the asynchronous send it leaves state information for the next continuation. Only when the communication schedule is finished is the user thread signaled. Figure 5b again shows the behavior for the barrier implementation on processor 2. In this case, however, the handler function that handles the message from processor 3 calls a continuation function that performs all actions up to and including the send to processor 0.

Implementing continuations by hand is hard and error prone. Most systems that provide continuations (such as functional languages) depend on compiler support. An exception is the work presented in [6], where hand coded continuations are added to the Orca runtime systems to execute operations on shared objects from within the upcall handler. In our system, the communication schedule contains most of the state that has to be preserved. The only functions that need to be written as continuation function are inside the core library for the execution of communication schedules. This implies that all operations implemented on top of communication schedules, including our collective communication library, benefit from it without any additional coding.

7. Performance

To determine the performance improvement caused by our optimizations, we wrote three versions of the communication schedule execution code. The first implementation performs none of our optimizations, the second uses only the implicit acknowledgment, and the third applies both optimizations, implicit acknowledgments and continuation functions. For this experiment we used the barrier implementation discussed in Section 4. The measurements were done on a cluster of workstations running the Amoeba [20] operating system. The system consists of 64 Micro-SPARC processors running at 50 MHz. The processors contain 32 MB of local memory and are connected by a 10 Mbit/sec switched Ethernet (using a Kalpana Ethernet switch).

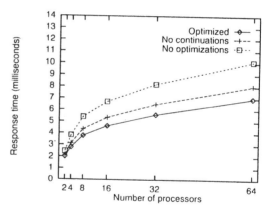

Figure 6. Performance of the barrier.

Figure 6 shows the results of these three implementations. The performance gain of the implicit acknowledgment optimization ranges from 13 to 20 percent. Applying both optimizations gives a performance gain from 18 to 31 percent. The reduction of acknowledgment messages that need to be sent equals the number of processors minus one, since all messages in the spanning tree use the implicit acknowledgment mode. The number of context switches along the longest chain of messages in the non-optimized version equals $\lfloor \log(number\ of\ processors) \rfloor$. Our performance measurements show that a context switch from the message handler function to

302

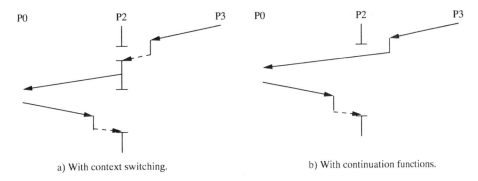

a) With context switching.

b) With continuation functions.

Figure 5. Execution on processor 2 of the barrier implementation.

the user thread that executes the communication schedule takes $250\mu s$ on Amoeba.

8. Related work

Islam and Campbell [12] describe a system that employs the communication pattern of the whole application to reduce the number of messages needed for reliability. A communication pattern is specified as a sequence or iterations of basic patterns, such as sendrecv, multicast, reduce, and exchange. Our communication schedules only support unicast and multicast, and can be applied to part of the execution of an application.

iCC [16] is a high performance collective communication library developed for the Intel family of parallel supercomputers with reliable communication. It is implemented on two sets of building blocks: short vector primitives (broadcast, combine-to-one, scatter, and gather) and long vector primitives (scatter, gather, bucket collect, and bucket distributed combine). The implementation of operations use *hybrid* collective communications algorithms: for short and long vectors, the short and long vector algorithms must be respectively employed. The building blocks in iCC are higher-level than our unicast and broadcast primitives. Each building block can be optimized, but no optimizations can be performed over multiple blocks. Our work is also targeted at a wider range of architectures.

Parachute [9] is a protocol compiler that uses a pattern description of the whole application to determine the most optimal communication strategy. Its primary focus is on reducing protocol overhead, such as buffer management. The prototype compiler only accepts data-parallel programs and generates a tailored protocol library

that can be linked with the application. Our protocol is intended to be used in both task-parallel and data-parallel applications, and focuses only on those parts of the execution that can be expressed in advance.

CHAOS [19] is a run-time support system for adaptive irregular problems, i.e., applications in which data arrays are accessed via indirection arrays and in which the data access pattern changes during the computation. A preprocessing state computes a communication schedule that describes the data access pattern. During execution, the runtime system analyses this data access pattern and generates optimized communication calls. CHAOS primarily deals with reducing data movement between machines. In our system, the communication pattern is fixed, and we use the communication schedule to reduce the overhead of communication at run-time.

Ben Hassen [4] describes an earlier implementation of collective communication operations on the same hardware system we use. The protocol can use multiple binomial spanning trees (forests) to implement one operation. The performance of the barrier operation on top of Amoeba's unreliable FLIP protocol is better than ours (up to 40%). There is also a more recent implementation on top of Panda, but no performance figures are available yet.

9. Conclusions

In this paper, we have described the design and implementation of a collective communication library on top of an existing portability layer, Panda. The collective communication operations are constructed using an abstraction called communication schedules. By using this abstraction we were able to localize two important optimizations, implicit acknowledgments and continuation functions, in the core functions of our implementation. This makes it easy to design new communication patterns for the collective communication operations while preserving the benefits of these optimizations.

Acknowledgments

We would like to thank Saniya Ben Hassen and Raoul Bhoedjang for making valuable comments on draft versions of this paper.

References

[1] G. R. Andrews and R. A. Olsson. *The SR Programming Language*. Benjamin/Cummings, Redwood City, CA, 1993.

[2] H. Bal, M. Kaashoek, and A. Tanenbaum. Orca: A language for parallel programming of distributed system. *IEEE Transactions on Software Engineering*, 18(3):190–205, Mar. 1992.

[3] M. Barnett, S. Gupta, D. G. Payne, L. Shuler, R. van de Geijn, and J. Watts. Interprocessor collective communication library (InterCom). In *Proceedings of the Scalable High Performance Computing Conference*, pages 357–364, Knoxville, Tennessee, May 23–25 1994. IEEE.

[4] S. Ben Hassen. Implementation of nonblocking collective communication on a large-scale switched network. In *Proceedings of the 1st Annual Conference of the Advanced School for Computing and Imaging*, pages 1–10, Heijen, The Netherlands, May 16–18 1995.

[5] S. Ben Hassen and H. Bal. Integrating task and data parallelism using shared objects. In *Proceedings of the 10th ACM International Conference on Supercomputing*, Philadelphia, PA, May 25-28 1996.

[6] R. Bhoedjang and K. Langendoen. Friendly and efficient message handling. In *Proceedings of the 29th Hawaii International Conference on System Sciences*, pages 121–130, Wailea, Maui, Hawaii, Jan. 3–6 1996.

[7] D. Culler, R. Karp, D. Patterson, A. Sahay, K. E. Schauser, E. Santos, R. Subramonian, and T. von Eicken. LogP: Towards a realistic model of parallel computation. In *Proceedings of the 4th ACM SIGPLAN Symposium on Principles & Practice of Parallel Programming*, pages 1–12, San Diego, CA, May 19–22 1993. ACM.

[8] R. Draves, B. Bershad, R. Rashid, and R. Dean. Using continuations to implement thread management and communication in operating systems. In *Proceedings of the 13th ACM Symposium on Operating Systems Principles*, pages 122–136, Pacific Grove, California, Oct. 1991. SIGOPS Notices 25(5).

[9] E. W. Felten. *Protocol Compilation: High-Performance Communication for Parallel Programs*. PhD thesis, Univ. of Washington, 1993.

[10] M. P. I. Forum. *MPI: A Message-Passing Interface Standard*, June 12 1995.

[11] IEEE. *Threads Extensions for Portable Operating Systems (Draft 6)*, p1003.4a/d6 edition, Feb. 1992.

[12] N. Islam and R. H. Campbell. Techniques for global optimization of message passing communication on unreliable networks. In *Proceedings of the 15th International Conference on Distributed Computing Systems*, pages 246–253, Vancouver, Canada, May 30– June 2 1995.

[13] M. Kaashoek. *Group Communication in Distributed Computer Systems*. PhD thesis, Vrije Universiteit, Amsterdam, 1992.

[14] F. Mattern. Virtual time and global states of distributed systems. In M. Cosnard et al., editors, *Proceedings of the Workshop on Parallel and Distributed Algorithms*, pages 215–226, North-Holland, 1989. Elsevier.

[15] P. K. McKinley, Y.-J. Tsai, and D. F. Robinson. Collective communication trees in wormhole-routed massively parallel computers. *IEEE Computer*, 28(12):39–50, Dec. 1995.

[16] P. Mitra, D. G. Payne, L. Shuler, R. van de Geijn, and J. Watts. Fast collective communication libraries, please. Technical Report CS-TR-95-22, Univ. of Texas at Austin, June 6 1995.

[17] T. Rühl, H. Bal, R. Bhoedjang, K. Langendoen, and G. Benson. Experience with a portability layer for implementing parallel programming systems. In *Proceedings of the International Conference on Parallel and Distributed Processing Techniques and Applications*, pages 1477–1488, Sunnyvale, CA, Aug. 9-11 1996.

[18] T. Rühl and H. E. Bal. Optimizing atomic functions using compile-time information. In W. Giloi, S. Jähnichen, and B. Shriver, editors, *Progrmming Models for Massively Parallel Computers*, pages 68–75, Berlin, Germany, Oct. 9–12 1995. IEEE.

[19] S. D. Sharma, R. Ponnusamy, B. Moon, Y. shin Hwang, R. Das, and J. Saltz. Run-time and compile-time support for adaptive irregular problems. In *Supercomputing '94*, pages 97–106, Washington, DC, Nov. 1994.

[20] A. Tanenbaum, R. van Renesse, H. van Staveren, G. Sharp, S. Mullender, A. Jansen, and G. van Rossum. Experiences with the Amoeba distributed operating system. *Communications of the ACM*, 33(2):46–63, Dec. 1990.

❖ SESSION 7 ❖

Architectures II

Chair

E. Pissaloux

A Generalisation of Router Chip Design

Pauline Catriona Haddow
The Norwegian University for Science and Technology
Department of Computer Systems
7030 Trondheim, Norway
pauline@idt.ntnu.no

Abstract

To improve performance in parallel computers, the challenge is to reduce the communication bottleneck by decreasing latency and increasing throughput. There is currently much research into finding solutions to the bottleneck problem where the focus is on increasing throughput. However, many of these proposed solutions lead to an increase in complexity at the network level. This gives rise not only to an increase in latency but also an increase in costs. Traditional performance models have not, in general, focused on the cost issue. Most performance models are developed for a particular or restricted set of network designs and performance criteria and therefore can be said to be static in nature. New design ideas will often result in the development of a new model. Therefore, to create a detailed model applicable to both existing and future networks a more flexible model structure is required. This paper presents a model based on a generic router for cost versus performance analysis at the network level for a range of router designs.

1 Introduction

In a message-passing multicomputer each node contains an autonomous processor and local memory that is physically separate and logically private from the memories of the other nodes. Interprocessor communication occurs by routing messages explicitly through a message-passing network. An interface is required to control the flow of information between the processor and the interconnection network. The complexity of this interface depends on the quality of service offered by the computer system, the topology of the interconnection network and the division of work between the interface and the compute processor itself. This interface is termed a router.

In this paper a performance and cost model, based on the design of a generic router, is presented. Section 2 explains the need for a more flexible model of router design for per-

formance analysis purposes. Section 3 describes the architecture of a generic router. An overview of the model is provided in section 4. In section 5 the set of router modules is introduced. Section 6 discusses the effects of design issues on the modules and discusses, in more depth, a selection of the modules. To illustrate use of the model, a model of the Torus Routing Chip is developed in section 7. Ongoing and future work is presented in section 8 and finally a summary is given in section 9.

2 Background and motivation

Design of a hardware router involves decisions regarding many interdependent design issues, selection and design of the required components, and design of their interconnection.

Evaluation of interconnection network performance using existing or proposed router designs involves development of specific models to meet the evaluation criteria and the type of router to be modelled. Due to the complexity in router design, these models involve simplifying assumptions for non relevant router components. This results in a restricted use of a model to the evaluation criteria in the specification. It also makes direct comparison of results from one model to another rather ambiguous.

One such assumption, often seen in the literature, is to assume a fixed delay through a router independent of its complexity [1]. However, it is shown by Chien [2] that router complexity has a significant effect on the delay encountered by a message traversing a router and, as such, is an important factor for performance analysis purposes.

Chien [2] developed a parameterised cost model, based on a specific technology, for a generic router architecture. However, although this generic architecture allows a number of routing algorithms to be compared, the focus on routing algorithm analysis removes the requirement to model other components in the router which have no effect on this analysis.

The choice of routing algorithm is one of many design issues. Chien[2] states that no single router architecture is suitable for comparison of all routing algorithms. Even more so, no single architecture allows comparison of a number of design issues.

A flexible model is therefore, required which offers cost and performance analysis of a wide range of routers with respect to various designs issues. This is the goal of this research.

3 The router architecture

A router may be considered as consisting of three logical parts, as shown in figure 1. The central part implements the functionality of the router — switching, routing and flow control. The switching method describes the physical path setup i.e. end-to-end or node-to-node, the routing algorithm decides which node is the next node i.e. which outgoing link to choose and the flow control checks the availability of the required buffers. The router applies this functionality to traffic entering and leaving at the two outer parts — the processor and the network interface.

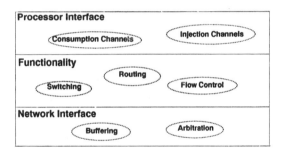

Figure 1. A functional router description

The structure of a router can be described as a collection of components working together to meet these functional requirements. For a specific router, the selection of the required components, the complexity of the individual components and the method of connected them is dependent on the design choices made. Complexity in router design arises from the variety of design issues and their interdependencies.

4 Overview of the model

The goal of the model is to provide a flexible router framework for modelling a wide range of router designs. Figure 2 illustrates the four key parts of the model - a set of generic modules, technology data, a set of parameters and performance analysis equations.

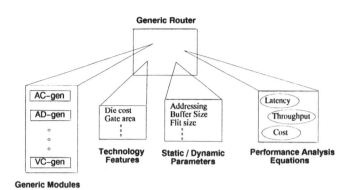

Figure 2. Network model

It is chosen to model the generic router as an interconnection of a set of modules. The set of modules chosen are a restricted subset of the generic modules available in the model. To limit the number of modules required, a module is not necessarily a single router component but may be made up of a number of components.

The modules are generic in that each module is not restricted to a particular implementation. Each module provides a frame into which a specific design, selected from the available module design set, is included. The framework includes a list of parameters effecting the design of the particular module and mathematical expressions which, when executed, provide performance data from the module to the generic router.

To provide flexibility in the model, many router features — referred to as decision issues, are provided as parameters to the model. Static parameters provide information regarding design choices made and dynamic parameters allow traffic patterns to be fed into the model.

Performance analysis equations consist of expressions for the three key performance features: latency, throughput and cost. Mathematical expressions to support these features depend on the number of parameters given to the model and as such, a selection of expressions are available to support different router issues. Technology data, expressing technology features, also provides the model with the ability to conduct cost analysis.

5 Identifying a set of router modules

A survey of a number of router designs was undertaken to build up the set of router modules— [4, 7, 6, 8, 5, 3]. These routers were chosen to represent both deterministic and adaptive, synchronous and asynchronous designs. It is assumed, that only point-to-point communication takes place in the network and therefore all multi-cast and broadcast features of these routers are ignored, at present. The resulting set of modules is shown in table 1 and the relationship between this set of modules and the functionality of the router, discussed in section 3, is shown in table 2.

Symbol	Module
AC	Address Comparator
AD	Address Decrementer
AR	Arbiter
AX	Address Converter
B	Data buffer
CB	Crossbar
CC	Consumption Channel
CS	Control Code Manager
CU	Channel Update
HU	Header Update
IJ	Injection Channel
MB	Message Build
MS	Message Split
MX	Multiplexor
RD	Routing Decision
SC	Signal Converter
SM	Signal Manager
SY	Synchroniser
VC	Virtual Channel Controller

Table 1. The set of router modules

The operation of many of the generic modules are self evident from their names and therefore a further description is not included in this paper e.g. address decrementer, address converter and data buffer.

The name address comparator has been chosen to represent both a zero checker and an address comparator due to the similarity of implementation.

Queueing in the router occurs both at the processor and the router interface, as described in section 3. However, it has been chosen to create separate modules for the network interface queues, the queues to the processor (consumption) and the queues from the processor (injection). This decision provides additional module structures at the interface where communication functionality, not currently implemented at the network level, may be implemented. As such, these modules may offer more than just the existing queueing function.

Function	Components
Processor Interface	IJ, CC
Switching	AR, CB, MX
Routing	AC, AD, AX, CU, HU, RD
Flow control	CS, MB, MS, VC, SM
Network Interface	B, SC, SY

Table 2. Functionality of the router modules

Switching in the router is often achieved by a crossbar **CB** and controlled by it's associated arbiter. A Crossbar module refers to the case of an $n \times n$ crossbar unit. However, if the switching functionality is distributed over the router to the extent that several $n \times 1$ units are required, then multiplexor modules are used instead of crossbar modules.

There are three levels of arbitration which may exist within a router. The first two levels, the **AR** module (crossbar arbiter), and **VC** module (virtual channel controller), allocate resources within a router. The third component, the **SM** module (signal manager), controls allocation of the external channel to the neighbouring node. There are two main reasons for separating the two internal arbitration functions. The first being their physical separation in most current routers. The second, is the difference in size of the arbitration units. The arbiter (**AR**) arbitrates between requests for output channels on a packet basis whereas the virtual channel controller (**VC**) may arbitrate either on a packet or flit basis.

Other more specialised modules include message split and message build which refer to the additional hardware required for the case where the control and data paths through a router are separated. Header update and channel update refer to hardware required to support adaptive routing and circuit switching respectively.

The virtual channel controller module includes both queueing and control logic to support all the virtual channels on a physical channel. As such, the buffering module is only required in routers where there are no virtual channels or there exists intermediate buffering within the router.

The two main methods of control implementation are request/acknowledgement lines and control codes. Being two quite different control mechanisms, it is chosen to implement these as two different modules — **SM** and **CS** respectively.

6 Design issue effects on router modules

As stated earlier, router design involves a large number of design issue decisions, some of which are interdependent.

Different design issues effect different components and traffic characteristics effect the components which exhibit decision or queueing features. Thus a generic router requires not only a set of modules to select from, but also a set of implementations (design set), for each module.

There are two types of design decisions — those affecting the router module itself (router parameters) and those affecting individual modules (module parameters). The router parameters e.g. switching technique, affect the performance expressions built into the model. and the number of instances of a given module required in the design. Module parameters on the other hand affect the design and number of instances required of a given module.

A full discussion of all the modules listed in table 1 is not possible within the space provided and therefore, taking the Torus Routing Chip [5] as an example, all further discussions refer to the models used in the description of the TRC. This set of modules includes the address comparator, address decrementer, arbiter, crossbar, routing decision unit, signal converter, signal manager and virtual channel controller.

6.1 Address comparator (AC)

The address comparator module represents either a zero checker — where relative addressing is implemented, or an address checker — for absolute addressing. It is often placed at the input to a router where it checks if the incoming message is destined for the local processor or not. The complexity of an AC depends on the length of the word to be compared. In this case, it is the length of the address or in other words the flit size.

In general, the number of AC modules required depends on the number of input channels to the router as a separate logic path is provided for each input. However, in the case of virtual channel deadlock avoidance, either the virtual channels on a particular physical channel follow the same logic path or a separate logic path is available for each virtual channel. As such, in the later case, the number of AC modules required is determined by the multiplication of the number of physical channels with the number of virtual channels per physical channel. Otherwise, the number of modules required is equal to the number of physical channels.

6.2 Address decrementer (AD)

An address decrementer is used in deterministic routers with relative addressing to decrement the relative address. Implementation of an AD is often achieved by some form of adder. The size of the adder is dependent on the flit size, where a flit holds the relative address in the current direction. As such, the design of the decrementer AD is parameterised by the flit size. The number of decrementers required

is equivalent to the number of ACs i.e. the number of data paths in the router.

6.3 Arbiter (AR)

The purpose of an arbiter is to make a decision about the assignment of a shared resource. This decision is based on both the arbitration policy or method and the routing algorithm. The arbitration policy describes the priority of the competing inputs and the routing algorithm limits the choice of outputs for a given input. The delay through the arbiter is due to both the amount of traffic competing, the ease of winning (arbitration method) and the choice of outputs (routing algorithm). The complexity of the implementation is also dependent on whether control of the router is synchronous or asynchronous.

As such, the design of the arbitration unit is dependent on the arbitration policy; the number of channels to be arbitrated between; asynchronous or synchronous control; traffic in the network and the routing algorithm.

In theory, a single arbiter could be used to control the switching unit. However in practice, due to bottlenecks resulting in a central control unit, a form of distributed arbitration is usually implemented. One such form is where there exists one arbiter unit for each switching unit. Another form, as in the case described in section 6.4, the arbiter is further distributed and a small arbitration unit exists at each crossing point of the crossbar i.e. n^2 arbitration units. This is the case for the Torus Routing Chip.

6.4 Crossbar (CB)

As stated earlier, a crossbar unit handles part or all of the switching functionality of a router with the aid of an arbiter — see section 6.3. In general, for an $n \times n$ crossbar where there are n inputs and n outputs, 2n buses are required for the input and output data and n^2 crossing points for switching between these buses. Therefore, implementation is dependent on the number of inputs to the crossbar, equivalent to the number of data paths traversing it, and the size of the arbiter itself.

The number of crossbars required depends on the distribution of the crossbar in the router but will always be less than the number of data paths through the router.

6.5 Routing decision (RD)

The routing decision module includes a routing table which implements the routing algorithm. For deterministic routing, generation of the output channel is based on information regarding the input channel and the destination address. However in adaptive routing there are a choice of outputs for each input. The number of choices depends on the amount of adaptivity in the routing algorithm. The more adaptivity, the more complex the routing module. Traffic information supplied by the other routers is used to update each router's routing table such that a best output channel is selected based on the updated information. As such, complexity is determined by the routing algorithm and the number of outputs, or in other words the network degree. The number of routing modules is equivalent to the number of routing paths.

6.6 Signal converter (SC)

The signal converter handles convertion between two different signalling conventions. In the case of the TRC, 2-phase signalling is used between neighbouring routers and 4-phase signalling within the router. The complexity of the module is therefore dependent on the number of signal lines to be converted and the technology of implementation. The number of units required equals the number of output channels.

6.7 Signal manager (SM)

Control of the flow of data between two neighbouring routers may be achieved by request/acknowledgement lines or control codes. A sender must have control of the channel, the receiver must be ready to receive and in the case of virtual channels, a virtual channel must have won use of the channel before a request can be raised and data sent.

Generation of request/acknowledge signals is under the control of the signal manager (SM). There are two main signalling conventions in use. Either a single req/ack line may be used where the acknowledgement cancels the request or two separate lines are used where a request is acknowledged when both lines are equal. If virtual channels are implemented then the number of signal lines required is multiplied by the number of virtual channels per physical channel.

The complexity of the signal manager is thus dependent on the number of signal lines per physical channel which is in turn dependent on the number of virtual channels and the signalling convention. The number of units required is equal to the number of output channels.

6.8 Virtual channel controller (VC)

The Virtual channel controller includes both queueing for and multiplexing between the virtual channels of a physical channel. In the case of virtual channels it is more common to use output buffering than input buffering so that data destined for a particular virtual channel is not blocked behind data for other virtual channels on the same or different physical channels.

The parameters to this component are therefore the number of virtual channels per physical channel, the amount of output buffering provided and the arbitration method to arbitrate between the virtual channel queues. The VC module controls all the virtual channels for a single physical channel and therefore the number of VC modules required depends on the number of physical output channels of the router.

6.9 Summary of design issues

The effect of design issues on the design (d), number of (n), or performance (v) of a sub-set of the router modules is summarised in table 3.

	Modules							
Design Issues	AC	AD	AR	CB	RD	SC	SM	VC
Addressing	d							
Arbitration method			d					d
Buffer Size								d
Control			d			d	d	
Flit size(bits)	d	d						
Network Degree	n	n	d	dn	d	n	n	n
Number of VCs	n	n	d	dn	d	d	d	d
Queueing								d
Routing Algorithm			d		d			
Technology	d	d	d	d	d	d	d	
Network Traffic	f	f	v	f	fv	f	f	v

Table 3. Relationship between modules and their design issues

It should be noted that although traffic is not, in general, regarded as a model parameter but a model stimulator, it is included here as a parameter since traffic is fed into the implemented model as a dynamic parameter. Traffic does not directly effect either the design or the number of modules but the performance of a given design. The table shows the effect of network traffic as either fixed **f** or variable performance **v**. This implies that the performance of the **f** modules are unaffected whereas the performance of the modules with **v** vary with the amount of traffic in the network.

As would be expected, the choice of implementation technology effects the design of all modules. Symbol variants used in the table include **dn** and **fv**. **dn** refers to the discussion in section 6.4 and 6.8 regarding the extent of data path partitioning, which can give rise to either an increase in design complexity per unit or an increase in the number of units. In the case of deterministic routing, performance is independent of traffic **f**, and in adaptive routing performance is dependent on traffic **v** thus giving rise to the symbol **fv**.

7 Use of the model

Generating a router configuration requires four key components as shown in figure 3. A design file is created where the required modules are selected and their interconnection described. Default parameters may be chosen or actual parameters given to the design by updating the data files.

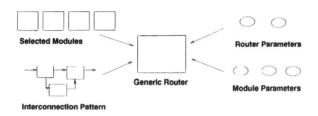

Figure 3. Choosing a router configuration

As an example, we will continue our discussion focusing on the Torus Routing Chip [5]. As described earlier, the list of required modules are: an address comparator, address decrementer, crossbar, arbiter, virtual channel controller, signal converter, signal managers and a routing decision module. This selection is specified in the design file along with the required interconnections.

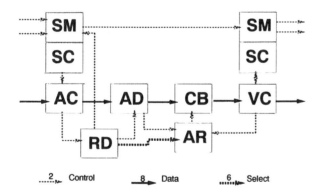

Figure 4. Torus Routing Chip - data and signal path

Figure 4 illustrates the interconnections required in the design file for a single path in the TRC. For each instance of a module, all incoming and outgoing signal and data connections are specified in respect to the adjoining module(s). An outgoing connection can be to a single or multiple destinations.

The next stage is to update the parameters for the design choices. Table 4 lists the relevant parameters for the

TRC. These parameters have been chosen to represent TRC routers in a 4×4 mesh topology using a 10 flit packet.

Addressing :	relative
Arbitration - arbiter :	priority chain
Arbitration - VC :	fair
Buffer Size :	4 flits (32 bits)
Flit Size :	8 bits
Network Degree :	4
Network Diameter :	6
Number of VCs :	2
Packet size :	10 flits
Queueing :	output queueing
Routing Algorithm :	dimension order routing
Switching Technique :	virtual-cut-through
Control :	asynchronous, req/ack
Implementation technology :	3μ CMOS

Table 4. Torus Routing Chip (TRC) design parameters

As stated earlier, these parameters are used to select the actual designs from the set of designs available. If we take for example the address decrementer, then assuming the design set shown in figure 5, the parameter list will result in the selection of the design AD_dsg_A_8. This is an 8 bit asynchronous arbiter. As there is only one technology available then the technology choice has no effect. At present, only one instance of a module will be automatically chosen by the parameter list, thus leaving the designer to specify the number of instances required. However the relevant parameters, in this case Network Degree and Number of Virtual Channels, are present to allow this feature to be added at a later date.

The router parameters, on the other hand, select the performance equation, in this case expressions for virtual-cut-through routing, and specify the packet size, header size and network diameter. Lastly traffic is added to simulate a loaded network.

8 Ongoing and future work

The model is currently in the implementation phase. The generic router and associated generic modules are implemented in the Performance Description Language (PDL) [9]. PDL is designed specifically for generic performance modelling enabling design instances to be compiled and analysed, thus suitable for this type of work.

The individual modules are being implemented in synthesisable VHDL code. Synthesisable VHDL code is chosen since the code may be synthesised into more than one

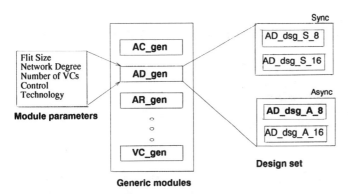

Figure 5. Relationship between parameter choice and module design

technology and may easily be adapted to reflect simple design changes. Therefore, it provides flexibility in design, a goal of this work.

Each net-list generated from synthesis of VHDL code is then converted into a PDL-compatible net-list. These net-lists will provide a library of component designs available to the PDL model.

9 Summary

This paper has described work which establishes a connection between conflicting design issues and the complexity of the routers final implementation. It therefore provides a base for modelling a wider variety of routers than current network level models provide and provides sufficient detail for performance cost trade-offs to be applied.

It is not assumed that the set of modules provided is the exhaustive set for all current and future routers. However, as the model assumes a router is built from a subset of the set of modules, a new router feature may be modelled by adding a new module to the module set. Also, as each individual component is parameterised by its respective design issues, these parameters can be varied to reflect changing design ideas. However, if a suitable design is not available in the design set then the respective VHDL code will have to be adjusted, synthesised and converted before the design will be available.

The range of available technologies are currently limited but may easily be expanded by including further data files for new technologies or updating existing data files to reflect advances in existing technologies. However, different technologies will often give rise to different net-lists and, similar to the above, new designs will require to be added to the library through synthesis and conversion of the VHDL code.

10 Acknowledgements

I would like to thank Lasse Natvig for his continuing support and advise in this ongoing project.

References

[1] A. Agarwal. Limits on Interconnection Network Performance. *IEEE Trans. on Parallel and Distributed Systems*, 2(4), Oct. 1991.

[2] A. A. Chien. A Cost and Speed Model for K-ary N-cube Wormhole Routers. In *Proc. of Hot Interconnects '93*, Aug. 1993. Dept. CS, University of Illinois at Urbana-Champaign.

[3] A. A. Chien and J. H. Kim. Planar-Adaptive Routing: Low Cost Adaptive Networks for Multiprocessors. In *19th Intern. Sympos. on Computer Architecture*, 1992. Dept. CS, University of Illinois at Urbana-Champaign.

[4] W. J. Dally and L. R. Dennison. The Reliable Router: A Reliable and High Performance Communication Substrate for Parallel Computers. In *Proceedings of the 1st International Parallel Computer Routing and Communication Workshop*, 1994. AI lab, MIT.

[5] W. J. Dally and C. L. Seitz. The Torus Routing Chip. *Distributed Computing*, 1:187–196, Jan 1986.

[6] W. J. Dally and P. Song. Design of a Self-Timed VLSI Multicomputer Communications Controller. *Proceedings of the Intern. Conf. on Computer Design*, (IEEE CS Press, 2473):230–234, 1987.

[7] J. M. Hsu and P. Banerjee. Hardware Support for Message Routing in a Distributed Memory Multicomputer. In *1990 International Conference on Parallel Processing*. University of Illinois at Urbana-Champaign, 1990.

[8] P. R. Nuth and W. J. Dally. The J-machine Network. In *IEEE International Conference on Computer Design: VLSI in Computers and Processors*, Oct. 1992.

[9] B. Vemuri, R. Mandayam, and V. Meduri. Performance Modelling using PDL. *IEEE Computer*, pages 44–53, April 1996.

PROTECTED, LOW-LATENCY MESSAGE PASSING IN THE SNOW PROTOTYPE*

Kanad Ghose, Arun K. Jayendran and Brian T. Stein
Department of Computer Science
State University of New York
Binghamton, NY 13902-6000
{ghose, jayen, brian}@cs.binghamton.edu

Abstract: Several attempts have been made recently to tightly couple stock, volume produced workstations to allow them to be used as a low to medium end parallel machine. This paper describes the implementation of low latency message passing and barrier synchronization in an experimental system called *SNOW* (hardware-supported Shared Memory on a Network Of Workstations). *SNOW* uses a custom network interface card (NIC), with field-programmable gate array devices to tightly couple standard SPARC 20 multiprocessing workstations running Solaris. The programmable nature of the NIC allows for experimentation with the degree of coupling, providing support for fast message-passing, barrier synchronization and coherent distributed shared memory. An end-to-end communication latency of about 7 μseconds is achieved over fully protected virtual channels between processes running in adjacent nodes by using fast authentication checks, zero and single copy message interfaces, fixed-size messages. and modifications to the Solaris kernel to allow an ultra light weight system call.

Keywords: Workstation cluster, low latency message passing, distributed memory multiprocessors, barrier synchronization.

1. INTRODUCTION

The development of integrated components to support high data rate communication ushers in the possibility of tightly coupling workstations to build a cost-effective parallel system. Several projects have been initiated to explore this possibility such as COW [Hill 95], NOW [ACPN 95], SHRIMP [BDF+ 95], MINI [MBH 95], Telegraphos [Kate 94] and Flash [HGD+ 94]. At least one vendor now offers a tightly coupled system of workstations based on a custom switch (and customized software) to support a distributed memory parallel programming model IBM SP/2 [IBM 93].

To tightly couple stock workstations in the same fashion as multiprocessor systems requires a high interconnect bandwidth as well as a low end-to-end latency. To obtain this low latency requires an appropriate hardware interface and modifications to the operating systems to allow users to have a direct but protected access to the network interface. Traditional means for accessing the network from user level do not provide the latency required for tightly coupled parallel applications.

A tightly coupled network of workstations, NOW [Patterson 94], also called a workstation cluster, used as a parallel machine has several advantages. First, the solution is cost-effective, primarily because workstations are produced in volume. Second, each workstation in the cluster can still be used for general purpose computing in a standard OS environment. Third, the system as a whole features distributed I/O capability. Finally, as noted in [ACPN 95], RAM in remote workstations can be used to hold pages swapped out from the local RAM of a workstation – a fact that can potentially speed up performance compared to what is realized by conventional swapping between RAM and disks.

One of the goals of the SNOW (hardware-supported Shared Memory on a Network Of Workstations) project [GhSu 95] is to design and implement a family of tightly coupled network of stock workstations for experimenting with workstation clusters in a cost effective fashion with minimum alterations to the native OS. As an aspect of these studies, field programmable gate array devices (FPGAs) are used to allow a variety of hardware artifacts to be included within the network interface. Thus, hardware includes support for fast message-passing using virtual channels, barrier synchronization and support for implementing coherent, distributed shared memory across the workstation cluster.. Reflective memory is implemented as a variation of page-level coherent shared memory.

The current SNOW prototype incorporates eight Sun SPARC 20 multiprocessor workstations, connected in a ring. SNOW uses a custom network interface card (NIC), sitting on the I/O bus (SBUS). The communication hardware on the card has an effective data rate of 212 Mbits/sec, with 8b/10b encoding, with serial transmitters and receivers driven by custom protocol hardware designed around Xilinx FPGAs. A star topology will be implemented as the second member of the SNOW family in the near future.

2. THE NETWORK INTERFACE HARDWARE

The main components of the NIC, depicted in Figure 1, support message-passing, barrier synchronization and coherent, page-level distributed shared memory in SNOW. A simple flow control strategy is used: each node has a limit on the number of outstanding messages it can have; a message is considered as outstanding till it comes back to the sending node, at which point it is dropped from the network.

* The construction of the SNOW prototype is supported in part by the NSF through award No. STI-9413854.

1066-6192/97 $10.00 © 1997 IEEE

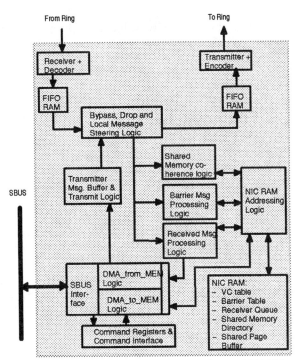

From Ring   To Ring

Figure 1. The Network Interface Card of SNOW

2.1 The NIC Interface

The NIC interfaces to the software components (trusted code for sends, receives and barriers, kernel code etc.) through eight 32-bit registers in the SBUS address space. For the message-passing and barrier synchronization mechanisms, we use the following interface registers on the NIC:

- A command register (NIC_CMD_REG) is written to for the NIC hardware to interpret, with access protected through a software lock.

- A register for the descriptor (a physical address pointer to a message in a buffer for a virtual channel) of an outgoing message to be sent (NIC_SEND_REG).

- An address register (NIC_ADDR_CNT_REG) contains the starting address of a location within the workstation's RAM, as well as a word count, indicating the location that will be targeted by a DMA transfer initiated by the software components.

- A latch data/address register (NIC_LATCH_REG) is used by the commands that read and write latches internal to the NIC.

Additional interface registers are used for implementing the shared memory environment but are not described here.

The software components which interact with the NIC can issue various commands to the NIC, including such functions as: initialization, DMA transfers, reading/writing of internal NIC latches, and other functions for supporting shared memory and barriers.

2.2 NIC Support for Fast Virtual Channels and Barriers

The NIC incorporates the following information in the 1 Mbyte of SRAM (hereafter called the NIC RAM) shown in Figure 1:

Virtual-channel table: This is a table that stores a pointer to the next 64-byte free slot within the 4K memory buffer for a receive channel. Appropriate routing and higher level flow control information is also maintained within each entry.

Barrier table: Entries maintain the 'state' of a given barrier, including the number of processes at the barrier and whether an interrupt is to be triggered at completion.

Received message queue: This is a queue that holds locally destined messages that have not yet been DMAed into the workstation's RAM.

Queue of outgoing message descriptors: The execution of a *send* primitive in the applications eventually results in depositing a message descriptor on this queue. The NIC uses the descriptor to DMA in the actual message from the workstation RAM for transmission.

All other functional blocks depicted in Figure 1 are implemented on the Xilinx FPGAs and miscellaneous glue logic.

The NIC implements the following functions in hardware to support message-passing and barrier synchronization:

Command Interpretation: The interface between the OS and the NIC is in the form of command registers implemented on the NIC. The OS can access these registers using the standard SBUS interface.

Network functions: The NIC implements the normal network transmission and receptions for the unidirectional ring network. It also implements a low-level flow control protocol and data CRC checks. Locally-sourced packets are given a preference during transmission over packets that came in from the preceding node in the ring. The NIC is also responsible for dropping a locally-originated packet off the ring, when the packet has made a complete traversal of the ring.

Packet sending: The NIC interprets the message descriptor passed to it and uses DMA to get the message with the pre-generated header and sends it out on the network.

Packet receiving: Without any CPU involvement, the NIC extracts the virtual channel ID from the received packet and then copies the packet to the appropriate slot in workstation (WS) RAM.

Barrier initialization: The process initializing a barrier variable makes a function call which initializes the value of the barrier variable and sends an initialization message to all the other nodes.

Barrier synchronization: The process reporting to a barrier makes a function call which decrements the value of the barrier variable on the local NIC and sends a report message to all other nodes, so that the barrier variable is updated in all the nodes. The process then goes to sleep, and is awakened when the NIC generates an interrupt, indicating the barrier has reached zero.

3. LOW LATENCY, PROTECTED MESSAGE PASSING IN SNOW

The message-passing model supported in SNOW is comprised of a number of concurrent SNOW processes that interact via message-passing. (Solaris sees SNOW processes as typical user-level processes.) There are a variety of low-latency message-passing primitives for hardware supported virtual channels and barrier synchronization. These primitives are part of a message passing library.

Obvious optimizations are made by the library primitives when the logical communication is between processes on the same node. The following discussion applies to communications across remote nodes.

In general, *protected* low-latency mechanisms for message passing must meet the following conditions:

1. A virtual channel and its associated buffer must be protected from unwarranted access by other processes, even though the hardware network interface is shared by many processes. Additionally, a process should be prevented from sending or receiving messages on VCs that it is not authorized to use.

2. Applications must have access to the NIC and VC buffers, with minimum intervention by the OS.

3. Copying of messages between buffers must be minimized to keep the overall latencies low.

4. Message buffers must be locked into memory to avoid being swapped-out.

To put the second and third requirement in perspective, in the Intel Touchstone system, the overall latency of message based communications (a send-receive pair) is about 35 msecs., of which only 2 to 3 msecs. are spent within the network hardware and on the wire. Therefore, the key to low latency message-passing mechanism lies in reducing software overhead. Several attempts have been made in this direction, such as [DrPe 93], [BDF+ 95], [MBH 95], [vBB+ 95].

3.1 Implementing protected virtual channels

There are two aspects of protection in a message-passing environment. First, a process should not be allowed to access a channel buffer not belonging to itself. Second, a process must not be able to send or receive on any channel that it has not opened. Since SNOW relies on the use of system assigned virtual channel IDs (called VCIDs) to identify communication channels, this requirement boils down to making VCIDs unforgeable.

SNOW meets the first requirement by mapping the channel buffers into the address space of the owning process and using the memory protection hardware already in place to prevent unauthorized access. The second requirement is met by keeping a table (the *VC table*, which holds the VCIDs

usable by a process) and the buffers associated with the channels named by the VCIDs, within the address space of the process. The VC table is write-protected from the process so that malicious processes cannot forge entries in this table. A SNOW process is only allowed to send or receive on channels listed in this table. Authentication of processes is performed as part of the send/receive primitives.

3.2 Reducing OS interference

The role of the operating system must be minimized when SNOW processes interact with the shared NIC. The following are possible solutions to let a SNOW process write a message descriptor to the NIC without generating an interrupt:

a.) Implement the send primitives as system calls that invoke the kernel to perform the write to the NIC. This is the traditional implementation in most message-passing systems.

b.) Memory map the *device drivers* for the NIC to the address space of applications and use an exception handler to allow the access to the NIC interface to proceed when an exception is raised on an attempt to access the NIC from the application when it executes the driver code.

c.) Implement the virtual channel buffers in the NIC and memory map these buffers to the address space of processes. This is the best solution, since it also offers the possibility of avoiding message copying, but requires the RAM buffers on the NIC to be directly placed on the memory bus – a facility that does not exist in the current prototype. (The second generation of SNOW, which uses a memory-bus (MBUS) based NIC will use this approach.)

The approach taken in SNOW comes closest to (b), but differs in several important ways. First, kernel modifications are made to virtually eliminate the normal delay of vectoring to the exception handler. Second, in SNOW the entire set of message-passing (and barrier synchronization) primitives are memory-mapped to the application's address space. Fast authentication checks are performed *without the intervention* of the OS within these primitives. In fact, unlike (b), the NIC devices drivers are not directly accessible to the applications, ruling out any malicious use of the device driver code. The system-supplied SNOW library primitives are pre-loaded (at boot-time) into locked page-frames (in main memory). A SNOW program is dynamically linked to these primitives with execute-only privileges.

The protection mechanism described above alludes to some of the steps taken to reduce the overhead of message-passing in SNOW. The following is a summary of the approach taken in SNOW to implement protected, low latency, virtual channels:

(i) The virtual channel buffers are memory-mapped into the address space of an individual process; existing protection hardware validates accesses to these buffers.

(ii) Authentication checks when a send or receive primitive is executed are implemented directly by the linked-in, system supplied code for send and receive routines by looking up the VC table in user-space.

(iii) The write to the NIC needed for depositing a message descriptor is implemented by system supplied trusted code (which is mapped in execute-only mode into the user's address space). The Solaris first-level interrupt handler is modified to allow writes to the NIC to be implemented quickly on behalf of this trusted code.

(iv) Buffer management overhead is drastically reduced and packetization overhead is avoided by keeping the size of the messages fixed.

In the next few sections, the implementation of the various message-passing routines and primitives in SNOW are discussed.

3.3 The SNOW daemons

All virtual channels in SNOW are unidirectional, where each buffer is associated with the two end points of a channel. VC buffers in SNOW are page-sized. SNOW relies on the memory protection hardware already in place in the host workstations to implement protected buffers for virtual channels.

At system boot time, within each node, a SNOW daemon process is started. Reserved communication channels are set up to allow SNOW daemons at each node to communicate with daemons at other nodes. Requests by applications to open or close virtual channels (or set up/de-allocate barrier synchronizers) are handled by the SNOW daemons.

At boot time, a pool of page frames are locked into core to serve as virtual channel buffers for SNOW processes within the node. Also, at boot time, a set of globally unique virtual channel IDs (global VCIDs) are also pre-assigned to the SNOW daemons at each node to allow each daemon to dispense global VCIDs to local applications without the need for any negotiations when these applications request a VC to be opened.

3.4 Process initialization

A SNOW application/process is statically bound to the system-supplied library of SNOW primitives at link time. When a SNOW process is started up, it makes a system call to the routine:

snow_init(sid)

where sid is the globally unique logical ID (*SNOW pid*) of the process. The SNOW pid is a concatenation of the unique ID of the host node (where this process is running), and the logical ID assigned to the process by the application programmer (i.e., sid = node_ID || logical_ID). In response, the SNOW daemon allocates a set of memory-locked (i.e., non-swappable) page frames from the pool of pre-allocated, non-swappable page frames for use as virtual channel buffers by the process. This guarantees each SNOW process the availability of a minimum set of VC buffers. As a part of the process initialization, these page frames are memory mapped into the address space of the SNOW process. VC buffers are thus allocated without the need for any system calls for buffer allocations.

One of the structures set up during process initialization is the VC table. Fields in each entry in the VC table are initialized with the virtual addresses of the mapped page frames for the VC buffers, but each entry is marked as invalid, since channels have yet to be set up. This page is, however, write protected to prevent malicious users from altering or forging entries in the VC table. A pointer to the VC table is returned as the result of the call to snow_init.

3.5 Buffers and queues

The various buffers and queues used in SNOW are shown in Figure 2 are maintained in a locked page frame and mapped into the caller's address space. Each SNOW process has its own set of memory-locked VC buffers. Each page frame representing a buffer has a header and a section where a FIFO queue of 64-byte message slots are maintained. The pointers to these queues are maintained within the header. Each SNOW node also maintains two global queues within the NIC. These are the raw hardware queues, NIC_GRQ and NIC_GRCVQ, that contain descriptors of messages to be transmitted and 64-byte messages received off the network for local processes, respectively. These raw hardware queues are implemented in NIC RAM. The message descriptors in the NIC_GRQ are essentially physical address pointers into the message buffers for sending channels. The NIC uses a descriptor to DMA out the actual message for transmission.

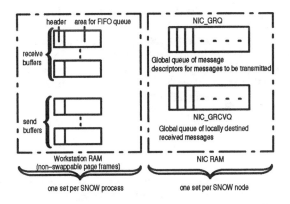

Figure 2. Data Structures Related to Message Passing

3.6 Virtual channel setup in SNOW

All virtual channels in SNOW are unidirectional, where each buffer is associated with the two end points of a channel. To simplify and speed up buffer management, message sizes are fixed. The message size in the prototype is 64 bytes, conforming to the maximum size of a SBUS burst. A SNOW process requests a VC to be opened by calling:

snow_open(src_sid, dest_sid, direction, &buf)

where src_sid is the SNOW pid of the process that initiates the open and dest_sid is the SNOW pid of the process that will be receiving messages. The parameter direction indicates whether the caller is opening the channel for sending or receiving messages, while buf holds the virtual address of a page already mapped to the caller's address space through a snow_init call. The effect of this call is to set up virtual-channel table entries within the NICs at each end, in the global virtual-channel table at each end (by the SNOW daemons), and within the VC tables for the end-point processes. The opening of a channel by a SNOW process results in the allocation of such a global VCID, as well as a *local* VCID for the channel. The index of the VC table entry set up for the channel in the VC table of the calling process is the local VCID for the channel. and this is returned as a result of the call to snow_open. The VC table entry marks the associated buffer (i.e., page frame) as valid and also notes the direction for the VC being set up.

A SNOW process attaches itself to a channel that was already opened by its communicating partner by using:

snow_attach(src_sid, dest_sid, direction)

This call returns the local VCID for the channel if it was already set up as a result of the open, otherwise it returns an error code.

3.7 Sending messages

Processes that have snow_open-ed virtual channels use snow_send call to send a 64-byte message (4-byte header and 60-byte body) using the VCID and appropriate buffer information. This is a non-blocking primitive:

snow_send(VCID, &msg, flag)

where VCID refers to the channel being used, &msg is a pointer to the structure containing the message and flag indicates if the receiver needs to be interrupted when the message is DMAed into the receiver's buffer. SNOW also supports a blocking primitive (snow_sendb) that blocks the caller until the actual message is DMAed into the NIC – this primitive is not discussed in this paper.

The snow_send primitive implements the following steps:

1) The VC table of the sender is checked to see if the specified channel is valid and if it is set up to send.

2) A header is added to the message – the header has the global VCID, which was picked up from the process-local VC table in the previous step, as well as the specified flag.

3) A software lock (send_lock) is set to guarantee exclusive access to the NIC_SEND_REG. This may introduce spin-waiting before a process can possess the lock.

4) The message descriptor is written to the NIC_SEND_REG register as follows. The attempt to write to the shared NIC interface from the system-supplied snow_send routine, executing under the purview of the user, triggers an interrupt. The Solaris interrupt handler is modified to check for this interrupt before it checks for interrupts from other potential sources, allowing almost immediate vectoring to the handler for this exception. The handler ascertains that the trap originated from the *known physical address* of the trusted library code and then performs the write to the NIC on behalf of the snow process and ultimately returns control to it.

The NIC hardware, in response to the writing of the descriptor into the NIC_SEND_REG, copies the message descriptor into its global transmit request queue, NIC_GRQ (Section 3.5), and resets the send_lock.

3.8 Receiving messages

Applications use the following primitive to receive a message on a specified channel. These primitives have the following forms:

snow_receive(VCID, &msg);
snow_breceive(VCID, &msg); /* blocking receive */

The following primitives implement a zero-copy receive:

snow_ncprcv(VCID, &slot);
snow_bncprcv(VCID, &slot); /* blocking receive */

All of the receive accept a local VCID and a pointer to the message (&slot), thereby allowing the message to be consumed in-place. An associated primitive:

snow_free_slot(VCID, slot);

is used to free up the slot once the message has been consumed. Note that these in-place consumptions are possible since SNOW maps message buffers into the address space of the applications, making them completely visible. Many concurrent applications can effectively make use of the in-place consumption by accessing the message using its pointer into the received-message queue.

A straightforward approach for implementing the receive primitives is to allow the NIC to access the buffers for the individual channels, using a lock in the RAM of the workstation (WS RAM) to guarantee exclusive access to the pointers for the queue set up in the buffer. In fact, most implementations of fast network interfaces follow this approach. The main drawback of this approach is in the form of extensive traffic on the SBUS, as listed below:

- lock traffic - at least one read-modify-write cycle, (lock in WS RAM)
- actual DMA out of NIC into buffer in WS RAM
- update of tail pointer in buffer
- unlock traffic (one write from NIC)

A similar amount of traffic is generated by the applications when they read the receive buffer, leading to an unacceptably high communication latency. A more fundamental problem that precludes the above implementation is the inability of a SBUS device - such as the NIC - to *directly* generate an atomic read-modify-write (RMW) cycle on the memory bus (MBUS) to gain access to the lock in the WS RAM. Implementing the lock on the NIC card avoids the problem for the NIC, but results in a further increase in the latency of the communication primitives.

The approach taken in SNOW does not require any mutual exclusion facility invocable from the NIC and at the same time guarantees that applications and the NIC can manipulate the receive buffers without mutual interference. This is made possible by ensuring that the following two requirements are met:

R1. Applications should only read buffer slots that contain valid messages.

R2. The NIC should not overwrite buffer locations that contain valid messages that the application has not read.

R1 is met by using a single valid bit to indicate whether the buffer slot contains a valid message. A receive primitive reads the buffer slots in FIFO order and checks if the item read is valid. The application-level primitives return an indication of failure when the slot read does not indicate a valid message. After a message slot has been read (or consumed), it is marked as invalid.

To meet the second requirement listed above, R2, the NIC writes messages in a FIFO order into the receive buffers for a range of buffer slot addresses. The limits of this range, for each VC buffer, is maintained within the VC entry in the NIC RAM as two pointers, `NIC_NEXT_SLOT` and `NIC_HI`. `NIC_NEXT_SLOT` points to the next available free slot within the buffer, while `NIC_HI` indicates the extent to which the `NIC_NEXT_SLOT` pointer can be incremented without intruding into regions where unconsumed messages reside. Likewise, the application uses a pointer (*next_msg*) to point to the next slot that it has to read. This pointer is maintained within the header region of a VC buffer.

When messages are added by the NIC into the buffer, the NIC simply DMAs the message from the receive queue within the NIC to the appropriate slot in the buffer (which are mapped as non-swappable into the WS RAM). When an incoming message has to be DMAed and when `NIC_NEXT_SLOT` equals `NIC_HI`, the NIC reads in the value of *next_msg* from the WS RAM. Two cases now arise:

Case 1: If `NIC_HI` does not equal next_msg, the buffer still has available slots to hold the incoming message. `NIC_HI` is updated to the value of (*next_msg* – 1) (taking into account that the buffer is circular) and the message is DMAed into the buffer slot pointed to by `NIC_NEXT_SLOT`.

Case 2: If `NIC_HI` equals *next_msg*, there is no space left in the VC buffer. In this case the NIC generates an interrupt. This interrupt is handled by the SNOW daemon. The daemon copies the incoming message into an overflow buffer (with high and low watermarks) and a signal is sent to the sending node's daemon to throttle the sender. The incoming messages in the overflow buffer are eventually DMAed into the VC buffer when the receiving process consumes part of the messages already sitting in the VC buffer.

In the normal course of operations, the NIC can thus DMA incoming messages into the VC buffer by only consulting pointers maintained locally within the NIC RAM. Occasionally, when the NIC finds `NIC_NEXT_SLOT` to be equal to `NIC_HI`, the NIC has to perform a read of the WS RAM to get the most recent value of *next_msg* to update `NIC_HI`, before DMAing the incoming message. Finally, the NIC is compelled to generate an interrupt only when the receiving VC buffer is full – a situation that should not arise, or at best, arise only very rarely.

We now describe the actions carried out by the **snow_receive** primitive. (The actions carried out by the other receiving primitives are similar.)

a) An authentication check is performed, as in the case of **snow_send**, by looking up the process local VC table. The function returns with an error code if this check fails.

b) The head pointer (*next_msg*) to the receive queue is used to read the message tag from the slot that it's pointing to. If the message slot is tagged invalid, **snow_send** returns as error code.

c) The (valid) message is copied into the user-space message structure using the pointer supplied in the call.

d) The buffer slot from which the message was just copied is marked as invalid.

e) The head pointer (*next_msg*) to the message FIFO is updated.

The implementation of **snow_ncprcvs** are slightly different.

4. BARRIER SYNCHRONIZATION MECHANISMS IN SNOW

Parallel applications in both the message-passing model and the shared memory model can benefit from the use of a low-latency barrier synchronization mechanism. SNOW provides hardware assistance within the NIC for implementing barrier synchronization. The following SNOW primitives are related to barrier synchronization:

    snow_open_barrier (N, sbid, flag);
    snow_attach_barrier (sbid);
    snow_report (BID);
    snow_status_barrier (BID);
    snow_set_barrier (N);

The function **snow_open_barrier** allows the creation of a barrier, identified through a programmer-assigned logical id (sbid), and initializes the barrier synchronization tables on the NIC with the appropriate values for that entry (e.g. should an interrupt be generated on completion). Note that this call initializes this entry within NIC RAM *at all nodes* to N, the count of the participating processes. A process-local barrier table is set up in the same page frame as the virtual-channel table, allowing fast authentication checks when the barrier synchronizer is used. A system-assigned barrier id (BID) is returned as the result of the call to **snow_open_barrier**.

Also, as part of **snow_open_barrier**, a local WS shared-RAM location is allocated and initialized. The address of this location is entered in the local barrier table for the process, as well as the barrier table in NIC RAM. This RAM location is a flag that indicates if the barrier synchronization is completed. The function **snow_attach_barrier**, allows participating processes to register with an already set up barrier.

The function **snow_report** is invoked when a process participating in a barrier synchronization arrives at a barrier. This call performs an authentication check using the data in the process-local barrier table. If the authentication test passes, a `NIC_report_barrier` command is issued to

319

the NIC, with the global BID (obtained from the process-local barrier table) as the argument. The write to the NIC is performed as in the case of a snow_send, as described earlier. The NIC reacts to the `NIC_report_barrier` command by decrementing the barrier counter within the barrier table in NIC RAM and sending out a special message (that includes the global BID) to all nodes to decrement the remote copies of the barrier counter. When the counter reaches zero, the NIC hardware clears the shared flag in the local RAM to indicate that synchronization has completed. All NICs that receive the special report message and decrement the counter to zero react in a similar fashion.

PRIMITIVE/ OPERATION	OVERALL LATENCY (micro-seconds)	COMPONENTS (micro-seconds)			
		SOFTWARE	SBUS	NIC	WIRE
send	2.88	1.5	0.88	0.5	N.A.
receive	0.38	0.38	N.A.	N.A.	N.A.
ncprcv	0.16	0.16	N.A.	N.A.	N.A.
NIC to receive buffer	1.74	N.A.	0.64	1.1	N.A.
send-receive communication: end-to-end delay for a 64B message	7.3	1.88	1.52	1.6	2.2

Table I. Best-case Latencies for **Protected** Message-passing in the SNOW Prototype

The function snow_status_barrier is invoked to read the value of the shared-memory flag for the specified barrier. An authentication check is performed before this read is allowed; if the check passes, the flag is read. Processes typically use the snow_status_barrier primitive to implement either a busy-waiting barrier or a sleep-waiting barrier.

The function snow_set_barrier re-initializes the value of the barrier counter at every node. An authentication check ensures that the calling process was the one that opened the specified barrier.

The performance gains with the NIC-assisted barrier synchronizers are significant, compared to naive software implementations (where processes broadcast their reports to each other), as well as efficient software implementations like the Butterfly Barrier.

5. PRELIMINARY PERFORMANCE RESULTS

Table I summarizes the best-case latencies for the send and receive primitives individually (for communication between adjacent ring segments in the prototype). The table shows the contributions to the latency from various components, of a send-receive pair for the 8-node prototype. The timings are for SPARC-20s, using 50 MHz., 4-way superscalar CPUs and 212 Mbits/sec. transceivers. Recall that the message size is fixed at 64 bytes.

The delay of the snow_send primitive is from the moment the function is invoked to the time when the first bit of the message is just about to be transmitted on the wire. The delay

of the snow_receive and snow_ncprcv primitives are from the point of the invocation of the functions to the point when the call terminates, assuming that the message is in the buffer. Since the overall end-to-end latency depends on the NIC-to-receive-buffer transfer time, a separate entry for this part of the latency is shown in the table. Calculation of overall latency takes into account the fact that the message has just arrived into the raw receive queue within the NIC and has to be decoded and DMAed.

Knowing that the latency of the NIC in decoding an incoming message in the raw receive queue and routing it to the transmit queue at the next node on the ring is roughly 0.3 μsecs., one may compute the latency of a send-receive pair on two machines that are 7 hops away from each other (the worst-case hop-count in our 8-node prototype) as follows:

$$(1.88 + 1.52 + 1.6 + (0.3 + 2.2)*7) \text{ } \mu secs. = 22.5 \text{ } \mu secs.$$

The timings given in Table I indicate that the various techniques employed in SNOW to cut down on the message latencies are quite effective.

6. RELATED WORK

The Stanford FLASH project [HGD+94] uses the programmable MAGIC chip to provide a flexible communication mechanism. However, the use of a custom chip rather than an FPGA device (as in SNOW) places significant limitations on such flexibility. Our use of readily available components on our NIC also reduces the design time and development costs significantly. The Wisconsin COW (Cluster of Workstations) also uses FPGA based logic to snoop on the memory bus of dual-CPU SPARC 20 workstations to implement a cache coherent workstation cluster. The communication interface for COW is not on the card that includes the snooping logic. The Telegraphos project at the University of Crete is another project that uses custom communication chips for tightly coupling workstations in a message-passing architecture, together with support for remote memory accesses. Telegraphos does not incorporate caches to reduce remote memory access times. The SHRIMP project at Princeton [BDF+ 95] represents one of the pioneering efforts for implementing tightly coupled workstations in a message passing framework. SHRIMP II implements distributed shared memory in software on top of the fast message-passing hardware. Our work also differs from the efforts in [ACPN 95], [IBM 93] and [MBH 95] in its use of hardware support within the network interface for implementing a coherent cache based shared memory environment across the workstation cluster. Further, few of these projects, incorporate a programmable network interface hardware, leaving out the possibility of fine tuning and experimentation. The S3.mp project [MAB+ 95] represents an attempt to use custom high speed interconnects to implement a directory based distributed shared memory system using SPARC boards. S3.mp does not incorporate support for barrier synchronization; nor does it allow experimentation with the nature and degree of hardware support for tight coupling. The various custom components raises questions about the cost-effectiveness of the S3.mp system. The ParaStation/ParaPC project uses a custom, toroidal interconnection and network interface to connect DEC workstations and PCs as a cluster, achieving an impressive 2.5 micro-second latency but only on an unprotected network interface. With protected interfaces, the message latencies are likely to be higher. SNOW, unlike ParaStation/ParaPC also provides hardware support for a distributed shared memory environment.

Several efforts have been undertaken to reduce the message-passing overhead in standard networked environments for TCP/IP. In the Jetstream project [EWL+ 94] developed at HP Bristol, applications can reserve buffer pools on the Afterburner board [DWB+ 93]. Afterburner uses FIFO ports on the network interface, and independent transmit, receive engines and a variety of other interesting features. The limitation of the Jetstream effort is that all protocols which can access Afterburner buffers directly must be through kernel services. This type of restriction is overcome in U-Net [vBB+ 95], where protocols which can manipulate buffers that are shared with the workstations network interface. Unfortunately, U-Net does not have sufficient hardware support to tightly couple workstations effectively. Techniques for avoiding buffer copying and buffer management overhead to reduce message-passing and I/O latencies, respectively, have been described in [DrPe 93] and [ThKh 95]. SNOW takes these approaches further and augments the performance with hardware support within the NIC.

7. CONCLUSIONS

This paper described the implementation of protected low-latency message-passing in SNOW. SNOW uses fixed-sized messages, zero-copy and single copy message interfaces, fast authentication checks and an ultra-lightweight system call to reduce message latencies. We are currently experimenting with optimizations to further reduce the latencies reported in this paper. The low latencies result from the software components as well as from the hardware support provided in the NIC. The NIC also provides support for barrier synchronization which is essential in a parallel programming environment. SNOW implements a page-level cached and coherent distributed shared memory, using hardware support in the NIC, as described in [GhSu 95]. In addition, the use of FPGAs in the NIC makes SNOW an interesting test-bed for experimenting with the nature and degree of hardware support for tight coupling. The second generation of SNOW will employ memory-mapped virtual channel buffers and a switched-star topology, perhaps using the Myricom chipsets.

References

[ACPN 95] Anderson, T.E. et al., "A Case for NOW (Network of Workstations)" IEEE Micro, Vol. 15, No. 1, pp. 54–64.

[BDF+ 95] Blumrich, M. A., "Virtual Memory-Mapped Network Interfaces", IEEE Micro, Vol. 15, No. 1, pp. 21–28.

[Chandra 95] Chandra, Subhachandra, "An implementation of fast message passing and software based distributed shared memory for the SNOW prototype", Master's Thesis, Dept. of Computer Science, SUNY-Binghamton, August 1995.

[DWB+ 93] Dalton, C., Watson, G., Banks, D., Calamvokis, C., Edwards, A. and Lumley, J., "Afterburner", IEEE Network Magazine, Vol 7, No. 4., July 1993, pp. 36–43.

[DrPe 93] Druschel, P. and Peterson, L., "Fbufs: A High-Bandwidth Cross-Domain Transfer Facility", in Proc. of the 14th SOSP, December 1993, pp. 189–202.

[EWL+ 94] Edwards, A,. Watson, G., Lumley, J., Banks, D., Calamvokis, C. and Dalton, C, "User-space protocols deliver high performance to applications on a low-cost Gb/s LAN", in Proc. of SIGCOMM-94, Aug 1994, pp. 2–13.

[GhSu 95] Ghose, K. and Subhachandra, C., "SNOW: Hardware Supported Shared Memory Over a Network of Workstations", in Proc. Workshop on Challenges for Parallel Processing, Int'l. Conf. on Parallel Processing, August 1995, pp. 148–154.

[HGD+] Heinlein John J. et al., "Integration of Message Passing and Shared Memory in the Stanford FLASH Multiprocessor", Proc. of the 6th Int'l Conference on Architectural Support for Programming Languages and Operating Systems, Oct. 94.

[Hill 95] Hill, Mark, Web page on the Wisconsin COW, at http://www.cs.wisc.edu/~wwt/cow/html.

[IBM 93] IBM Corporation, SP/2 Product Overview, 1992.

[Kate 94] Katevenis, M., "Telegraphos: High Speed Communication Architecture for Parallel and Distributed Computer Systems", Technical Report Number FORTH-ICS/TR-123, Inst. of Computer Science, Univ. of Crete, 1994.

[ThKh 95] Thadani, M. and Khalidi, Y. A., "An Efficient Zero-Copy I/O Framework for UNIX", Sun Labs draft technical report, January, 1995.

[Mason 94] Mason, Susan A., SBus Handbook, SunSoft Press, 1994.

[MBH 95] Minnich, R. et al., "The Memory-Integrated Network Interface", IEEE Micro, Vol. 15, No. 1, pp. 11–20.

[NAB+ 95] Nowatzyk, A., Abhay, G., Browne, M., Kelly, M., Parkin, E., Radke, B. and Vishin, S., "The S3.mp Scalable Shared Memory Multiprocessor", in Proc. ICPP, Vol. I, 1995.

[Patterson 94] Patterson, David A., (editor & organizer), Record of The First Network of Workstations Workshop, held in conjunction with ASPLOS-VI, 1994

[vBB+ 95] vonEicken, T., Basu, A., Buch, V. and Vogels, W., "U-net: A User-Level Network Interface for Parallel and Distributed Computing". in Proc. of 15th Operating System Principles, 1995.

[WBT 96] Warschko, T.M., Blum, J. M. and Tichy, W. F., "The ParaPC/ParaStation Project: Efficient Parallel Processing by Clustering Workstations", Technical Report 13/96, Dept. of Informatics, Karlsruhe University.

Massively Parallel Architectures and Systolic Communication

Michael Sampels
Universität Oldenburg
Fachbereich 10
26111 Oldenburg, Germany
sampels@informatik.uni-oldenburg.de

Abstract

In the theory of distributed architectures, the class of vertex-transitive graphs is suitable for the description of the regularly structured architecture of a massively parallel computer. It is shown that the concept of systolic dissemination of information can easily be carried on these graphs and that it corresponds to the subclass of Cayley graphs. The technique of bitelegraph-mode communication is introduced, and a family of vertex-transitive graphs which are extremal with regard to the number of nodes of an abelian Cayley digraph for a given systolic broadcast time t is constructed. It turns out that it is worthwhile developing the layout of a distributed system in direct correspondence with a basic algorithm working on it.

Keywords: *massively parallel architectures, systolic algorithms, broadcasting*

1 Introduction

The analysis of different interconnection networks for the use as distributed architectures of supercomputers has been a main topic of research in computer science for the last years. This research roughly focuses on three aims:

1. How can a network A be efficiently simulated on a network B? This question arises when one wants to run a program written for the architecture A on a given architecture B without changing the code. A parallel computer for a general purpose should be built in such a way that the different architectures required by the applications can be effectively supplied. A large number of simulation strategies can be found in [18].

2. How can distributed operating system algorithms, e.g. broadcasting, gossiping, or accumulation algorithms, be efficiently implemented on a specific network? An overview is given in [11] and some exemplary more recent references in this area are [12, 13, 15, 16]. The literature on this topic is widely spread and the results cannot be compared directly because of the various underlying models of basic communication and the miscellaneous complexity measures.

3. What are good interconnection networks regarding graph theoretic quality measures as e.g. diameter and connectivity? The articles [2, 8] are illustrative of this domain.

The split of the research in the two latter aspects is rather artificial and it is yielded by the fact that many authors concentrate their research on known and practically approved architectures as e.g. hypercubes, butterfly networks, or cube-connected cycles, whereas other authors do not think of graphs as abstractions of interconnection networks first. This split is not productive concerning the question which one really wants to answer: How can an interconnection network be constructed that allows efficient implementations of distributed operating system algorithms? It should be a promising approach to develop the interconnection networks together with suited communication algorithms working on them. The complexities of these algorithms seem to be a more practical and useful quality measure of the constructed topology than the graph theoretic measures mentioned above. However, this requires a proper definition of an appropriate measure of complexity.

In this article, we first introduce the class of vertex-transitive graphs using the terminology and some basic ideas of [4], and we explain why they make a good model for network topologies. Then, we describe the concept of systolic communication, which was first in-

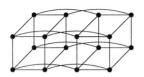 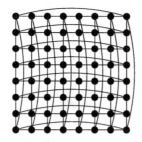

Figure 1. Two vertex-symmetric interconnection networks: binary hypercube of dimension 4 and 8×8-torus

Figure 2. The binary hypercube H_3 on the left and its image by the automorphism $\alpha = x \mapsto \mathrm{xor}_{111}(\mathrm{xor}_{100}(x))$ on the right. α maps vertex 100 to 111.

troduced in [19] and further extended in [14], and we explain the correspondence to Cayley graphs, which are a subclass of vertex-transitive graphs. The measure of complexity is defined with respect to the bitelegraph-mode of communication. We address the problem of constructing an extremal graph providing a broadcast scheme that establishes a broadcast time t, and we show that the systolic model enables us to construct a family of extremal abelian Cayley graphs. Brief prospects for future research are given in the final section.

2 Vertex-Transitive Graphs as Models for Interconnection Networks

Looking at different network topologies one can obtain that most of them are symmetrical, i.e. viewed from any vertex, they look the same (see Fig. 1). This fact is not only due to the easy way of building hardware out of equal components, it also allows a facile implementation of distributed operating system algorithms, because every processor can run the same basic algorithm. This concept is explained in detail in [3].

The idea of treating symmetrical interconnection networks like hypercubes or cube-connected cycles from an algebraic point of view was first presented in [1]. This approach yields a common superclass for various known topologies, the class of vertex-transitive graphs. From this viewpoint, one can now use algebraic methods for their examination and also for their construction.

Definition 1 Let $G = (V, E)$ be a directed graph with vertices V and edges $E \subseteq V \times V$. A mapping $\alpha : V \to V$ is a graph automorphism, if α is bijective and for every edge $(v, w) \in E$ holds $\{\alpha(v), \alpha(w)\} \in E$. $A(G)$ denotes the set of all automorphisms of the graph, which obviously forms a group by concatenation of automorphisms. G is called vertex-transitive, if

$A(G)$ acts transitively on V, i.e. for every pair of vertices (v, w) there is an automorphism $\alpha \in A(G)$ with $\alpha(v) = w$.

Example 2 The binary hypercube of dimension m, denoted by H_m, is the graph whose nodes are all binary strings of length m and whose edges connect those binary strings which differ in exactly one position. Formally, we write $H_m = (V, E)$ with $V = \{a_1 a_2 \dots a_m \mid a_i \in \{0, 1\}\}$ and $E = \bigcup_{i=1,\dots,m} E_i$ with $E_i = \{(v, w) \mid v, w \in V, \pi_i(v) \neq \pi_i(w), \bigwedge_{j \neq i} \pi_j(v) = \pi_j(w)\}$. $\pi_i(v)$ denotes the projection of the ith component of v.

The mapping $\mathrm{xor}_p : V \to V$, which maps a vertex v to its binary exclusive-or composition with the pattern $p \in V$, is obviously bijective on V. It preserves adjacency, because only if two vertices differ in exactly one component, their exclusive-or compositions with p do also. For any two vertices v, w we can get an automorphism α with $\alpha(v) = w$ by $\alpha = x \mapsto \mathrm{xor}_w(\mathrm{xor}_v(x))$. Thus, $A(H_m) \supseteq \{\mathrm{xor}_v \mid v \in V\}$ acts transitively on V, and H_m is a vertex-transitive graph. As an example, Fig. 2 shows a graph automorphism on H_3 that maps vertex 100 to 111. It should be remarked that the whole automorphism group of the hypercube contains much more automorphisms than those given above. The efficient computing of automorphism groups of graphs is described in [20].

The prior definition only describes the class of vertex-transitive graphs. In order to analyze different regularly structured network topologies, it is useful to have a constructive method for the generation of vertex-transitive graphs. Cayley graphs [4] form a proper subclass of vertex-transitive graphs, which can easily be generated by group arithmetics.

Definition 3 Let Γ be a group and S be a generating set of Γ with $1_\Gamma \notin S$. The Cayley graph $G_S(\Gamma)$ is defined as the graph with vertex set $V = \Gamma$ and edge set $E = \{(g, h) \mid g^{-1} h \in S\}$.

Corollary 4 If the generating set S is symmetrical, i.e. $s \in S \Rightarrow s^{-1} \in S$, the Cayley graph $G_S(\Gamma)$ contains with $(v, w) \in E$ also $(w, v) \in E$, and the edges can be regarded as bidirectional links.

Example 5 Let $\Gamma = Z_2^3$ be the three-dimensional vector space over the additive group of two elements, and $S = \{(1, 0, 0), (0, 1, 0), (0, 0, 1)\}$ be a generating set of Γ. S is symmetrical and we get as $G_S(\Gamma)$ the hypercube of Fig. 2. The automorphism there can be expressed as the group operation of the element $(0, 1, 1)$.

Corollary 6 Cayley graphs are vertex-transitive.

Proof. Let $G_S(\Gamma)$ be a Cayley graph (Γ, E) of some group Γ generated by S. For each g in Γ we may define a permutation $\bar{g}$ of $V = \Gamma$ by the rule $\bar{g}(h) = gh$ ($h \in \Gamma$). This permutation is an automorphism of $G_S(\Gamma)$, because

$$(h, k) \in E \;\Rightarrow\; h^{-1}k \in S$$
$$\Rightarrow\; (gh)^{-1}gk \in S$$
$$\Rightarrow\; (\bar{g}(h), \bar{g}(k)) \in E \; .$$

$\square$

As in Ex. 2, the whole automorphism group of a Cayley graph can contain strictly more elements than those automorphisms induced by the elements of the group. Indeed, every group automorphism α of Γ, which stabilizes the generators S setwise, i.e. $\bigwedge_{s \in S} \alpha(s) \in S$, is also a graph automorphism fixing the vertex 1_Γ. After a few preliminary remarks, we can obtain a general result in Lem. 9.

Definition 7 Let Δ be a group acting on a set of vertices V. The stabilizer of a vertex v contains the group elements which fix v. We denote $\mathrm{Stab}_\Delta(v) = \{d \in \Delta \mid d(v) = v\}$. A group Δ acts regularly on V, if Δ acts transitively on V and the stabilizer of each vertex $v \in V$ is trivial ($\mathrm{Stab}_\Delta(v) = \{1_\Delta\}$).

Corollary 8 Suppose Δ is a group acting regularly on $V = \{v_1, v_2, \ldots, v_n\}$. Then, for $1 \le i \le n$ there is a unique $d_i \in \Delta$ such that $d_i(v_1) = v_i$. The order of Δ is n.

Proof. Let us assume that there are two elements $d_i, \tilde{d}_i \in \Delta$ with $d_i(v_1) = \tilde{d}_i(v_1) = v_i$. Then, $d_i \circ \tilde{d}_i^{-1}(v_1) = v_1 \Rightarrow d_i \circ \tilde{d}_i^{-1} = 1_\Delta$, as $d_i \circ \tilde{d}_i^{-1} \in \Delta$ and Δ acts regularly on V. It follows $d_i = \tilde{d}_i$. $\Delta = \{d_1, d_2, \ldots, d_n\}$, because for any two vertices $v_i, v_j \in V$ v_i is mapped on v_j via $d_i^{-1} \circ d_j$. Thus, $|\Delta| = |V| = n$. $\square$

Lemma 9 Let $G = (V, E)$ be a connected graph. A subgroup Δ of $A(G)$ acts regularly on V, if and only if G is isomorphic to a Cayley graph $G_S(\Gamma)$, for some set S generating Δ.

Proof. Suppose $V = \{v_1, v_2, \ldots, v_n\}$, and Δ is a subgroup of $A(G)$ acting regularly on V. Then, for $1 \le i \le n$ there is by Cor. 8 a unique $d_i \in \Delta$ such that $d_i(v_1) = v_i$. Let $S = \{d_i \in \Delta \mid (v_1, d_i(v_1)) \in E\}$. It can be checked easily that S is a generating set satisfying the conditions required by Def. 3 and generating the Cayley graph $G_S(\Delta)$ and that the bijection $v_i \leftrightarrow d_i$ is a graph isomorphism of G with $G_S(\Delta)$. Conversely, if $G = G_S(\Delta)$ then the group Γ of the induced automorphisms defined in the proof of Cor. 6 acts regularly on V, and Γ is isomorphic to Δ. $\square$

The essence of Lem. 9 is that the restriction of the investigations into vertex-transitive graphs to Cayley graphs is reasonable, because a regular acting subgroup of the automorphism group of a network permits a natural and easy communication scheme as shown in the following section. In this paper we only concern ourselves with abelian Cayley graphs, i.e. Cayley graphs of abelian groups. They are a generalization of Cayley graphs of cyclical groups, in computer science normally called loop networks [5, 10], and have been well examined with respect to the degree/diameter problem [9]. Some improved results can be found in [27], and case studies are carried out in [26].

Cayley graphs of more general types of groups are studied in [25], where a table of the largest known networks for small given systolic broadcast complexities and small given degree is compiled. With the analysis of abelian Cayley graphs, a general lower bound on the largest number of nodes for given systolic broadcast complexity and given degree can be derived.

It should be remarked that vertex-transitive graphs do exist which are not Cayley graphs, as e.g. the Petersen graph in Fig. 3. An distributed architecture founded on this graph is described and analyzed in [24]. Every vertex-transitive graph can be represented as a group-coset graph. This concept is a generalization of the Cayley graph principle, and the interested reader is referred to [29] or [27].

3 Systolic Communication

The concept of systolic or periodic communication was presented first in [19]. Since then, it has been refined and investigated by Hromkovič and Labahn in several articles, e.g. [14, 17]. The central idea of its development is the following: For a long time the emphasis of the research in communication algorithms has

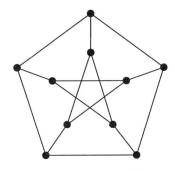

Figure 3. The Petersen graph

been on good or even optimal total time behavior of communication schemes disregarding the complexity and the difficulty of the communication schedule they involve. To be more practical and to focus on the feasibility of implementation, one should first concern a model of a "regular" communication mode and then treat questions about optimal schemes. Def. 10 leads to a general view of a communication scheme, which is afterwards refined to known measures of communication complexity.

Definition 10 A communication round in a network modeled as a graph G is a factor F of G. A factor of a graph is a subgraph containing all vertices of the graph.

The meaning of a communication round F is that for any edge $(v, w) \in E(F)$ v sends a message to w. This message dissemination can be regarded as information propagation: After a communication round F a vertex w knows the information of its predecessors v with $(v, w) \in E(F)$. In order to restrict the model or to describe a concrete system behavior, some conditions are demanded for the communication rounds. The so called telephone-mode is defined for graphs with bidirectional links and represented by the rule that the edges used in a single communication round must form a matching in the underlying undirected graph, i.e. $(v_1, w_1), (v_2, w_2) \in E(F) \Rightarrow (w_1, v_1) \in E(F) \land \{v_1, w_1\} \cap \{v_2, w_2\} \in \{\{v_1, w_1\}, \emptyset\}$. Respectively, the telegraph-mode of communication is expressed by the claim that $(v_1, w_1), (v_2, w_2) \in E(F) \Rightarrow (v_1, w_1) = (v_2, w_2) \lor \{v_1, w_1\} \cap \{v_2, w_2\} = \emptyset$. We will further concentrate on the restriction that a vertex can do at most one send and one receive operation per communication round and call this mode bitelegraph-mode. This mode seems to be at least as reasonable for computer architectures as the telegraph- or telephone-mode. Other constraints, e.g. to the maximum degree of F, are also conceivable.

Definition 11 A communication round that respects the bitelegraph-mode of communication in a graph G is a factor F of G with a set of edges E that contains every vertex at most once as source and at most once as target, i.e. $(v_1, w_1), (v_2, w_2) \in E(F) \Rightarrow (v_1, w_1) = (v_2, w_2) \lor (v_1 \neq v_2 \land w_1 \neq w_2)$.

A communication algorithm can now be described as a finite sequence of communication rounds which all fulfill the rule of the same mode. Liestman and Richards demanded in [19] that the sequence must be a partition of the edges into color classes, each color representing a matching in the graph. This led to the idea of representing an endless but regular scheduling of communication by the switching of colors. A more general definition is the following.

Definition 12 A communication scheme of length n is a finite sequence of communication rounds $\langle F_i \rangle_{i=1..n}$. An infinite communication scheme is an infinite sequence of communication rounds $\langle F_i \rangle_{i=1..\infty}$. An infinite communication scheme is called systolic, if there exists a constant p with $\bigwedge_{i=1..p-1} \bigwedge_j F_i = F_{i+pj}$. The minimal valid value of p is the period length of the communication scheme. A communication scheme that can be described by a sequence $\mathcal{F} = F_1, F_2, \ldots, F_p$, which is repeated regularly, is called a systolic communication scheme.

The articles about systolic communication schemes, e.g. [14, 17], focus mainly on the question which delay must be accepted when changing from an ordinary communication scheme to a systolic one with a given maximum period length p, both solving the same specific problem. However, we will continue with investigations into which graphs are well suited for systolic communication in the bitelegraph-mode. This requires a measure of complexity which is introduced in the following section.

4 Broadcast Trees and Upper Bounds

The broadcast problem is along with the gossiping problem one of the most intensively investigated areas in the study of distributed system algorithms. A survey is given by [11], and the problem of constructing good networks with algebraic methods providing efficient broadcasting schemes is treated in [7]. Results of experimental comparisons between ordinary networks and optimized graphs are carried out in [26]. They show that the theoretical improvements are indeed worthwhile in practice.

First, we present the broadcast problem from a graph-theoretical point of view, and then, we describe the relation with the algebraic techniques described above.

Definition 13 A directed broadcast tree of level i BT^i is recursively defined as follows: BT^0 is the trivial graph with one vertex and no edges. BT^{i+1} is constructed from the broadcast tree BT^i by joining every vertex of BT^i with a copy of itself by a directed edge. If $BT^i = (V = \{v_1, \ldots, v_n\}, E)$ then $BT^{i+1} = (\{V \cup \{v_1', \ldots, v_n'\}, E \cup \{(v_1, v_1'), \ldots, (v_n, v_n')\})$. The vertices of $BT^i \setminus BT^{i-1}$ have level i, the vertex of BT^0 has level 0.

A directed broadcast tree represents a communication scheme which represents an upper bound on the maximal possible flow of information during a broadcast algorithm in an arbitrary graph under the telegraph-, the telephone-, and the bitelegraph-mode of communication. The communication scheme $\langle F_i \rangle_{i=1\ldots t}$ with $F_i = (V(BT^t), \{(v, w) \mid (v, w) \in E(BT^t), v$ has level $i-1, w$ has level $i\}$ establishes the propagation of a piece of information from the root to all vertices of the tree within t communication rounds. At first, the vertex of level 0 contains a piece of information which is sent to the node of level 1 in the first communication round. In the ith round, every vertex sends the information to one of its neighbors, one copy of itself in the definition above. If we know that the network is of bounded outdegree δ, we can cut this directed broadcast tree with respect to δ as follows.

Definition 14 A directed broadcast tree of level i and bounded outdegree δ BT_δ^i is recursively defined as follows: BT_δ^0 is the trivial graph with one vertex and no edges. BT_δ^{i+1} is constructed from BT_δ^i by joining only those vertices of BT_δ^i with outdegree $< \delta$ with copies of themselves by directed edges.

With the two latter definition, the determination of the complexity of an broadcast algorithm in a given graph can now be formulated as a graph embedding problem. If a graph G allows a broadcast from a vertex v in t communication rounds, there must be a graph monomorphism from a subtree BT^t onto G which is surjective on the vertices of G. The subtree must contain the vertex of level 0, and the graph monomorphism must map this vertex to v. For a graph G that allows a broadcast time $\leq t$ from every vertex there must exist such graph monomorphisms for every vertex of G. Clearly, it is enough to check this property for the representatives of the orbits of the automorphism group $A(G)$ on $V(G)$.

Corollary 15 A graph which allows a broadcast in at most t time units can contain at most 2^t vertices. The

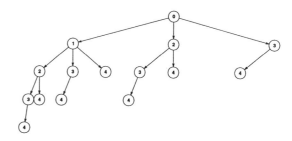

Figure 4. The directed broadcast tree BT_3^4 with the labels of the nodes

maximal order of a graph with bounded outdegree δ which allows a broadcast in at most t time units can be described recursively by the following formula: $N(t) = 2^t$ for $0 \leq t \leq \delta$ and $N(t) = 2N(t-1) - N(t-\delta-1)$ for $t > \delta$.

Proof. The first fact can be proven by induction over the recursive construction rule of directed broadcast trees. To obtain the second result, we see that in a directed broadcast tree BT_δ^t only those vertices can inform a new vertex whose outdegree has not reached δ yet. This are the vertices which have been informed during the last δ rounds. For $t > \delta$, the number of vertices with outdegree δ in the directed broadcast tree BT_δ^{t-1} is $N(t-\delta-1)$. □

Example 16 For a graph with maximal outdegree 3 that allows a broadcast within 4 time steps, 15 is an upper bound for its order. The broadcast tree BT_3^4 is presented in Fig. 4.

The proof techniques being used to show that a graph is optimal for a specific broadcast time t and a number of vertices n are complicated [11]. And, as the resulting graphs need not to be vertex-transitive, even not to be regular, the research in this area is rather artificial. A more natural question is which vertex-transitive graphs offer a good broadcast behavior. As motivated in Sect. 3, we even focus on looking for vertex-transitive graphs with a systolic communication scheme. The bitelegraph-mode suggests to examine schemes with period δ on δ-regular graphs. Since we are interested in vertex-transitive graphs, we obtain from Lem. 9 that the study of Cayley graphs is sufficient as follows.

We describe the communication rounds as color classes of the graph satisfying the bitelegraph-mode. The group of color preserving graph automorphisms $C(G)$ should act transitively on the vertices, in order to get a systematic hardware realization. Since the edges leaving a vertex v must have different colors in the bitelegraph-mode, $Stab_{C(G)}(v)$ is trivial. Thus, the whole automorphism group $A(G)$ contains a subgroup acting regularly on the vertices.

We consider the question which abelian Cayley graph of outdegree δ is maximal and grants a systolic communication scheme which allows a broadcast in t rounds. An upper bound for the maximum number of vertices of a graph that allows a systolic broadcast scheme which completes within a given number of rounds t can be given with an optimal communication scheme of maximal length t in the directed broadcast tree BT_δ^t. Considering the restrictions on the communication rounds demanded by the bitelegraph-mode (see Def. 11), we obtain the result that there even exists a systolic communication scheme of period length δ which has optimal complexity. In the following definition, we construct a corresponding scheme, which can be represented by a graph coloring.

Definition 17 A systolic coloring of a directed broadcast tree with bounded degree δ BT_δ^i is given by the rule that an edge connecting a vertex of level $j-1$ with a vertex of level j is colored with $j \bmod \delta$.

Corollary 18 A color class of the systolic coloring of BT_δ^i fulfills the conditions of the bitelegraph-mode.

Proof. Every vertex of BT_δ^i has at most indegree 1 and the δ outgoing edges have different colors, because by Def. 14 a vertex of level $j-1$ is connected by at most δ outgoing edges with vertices of level $j, \ldots, j+\delta-1$. $\square$

Again, the question of the systolic broadcast complexity can be formulated as a graph embedding problem. For a colored graph $G = (V, E)$ with bounded degree δ which allows a δ-periodic systolic broadcast in t rounds starting at a vertex v, there must exist a color preserving graph monomorphism from a subtree containing the vertex of level 0 of the colored directed broadcast tree with bounded degree δ BT_δ^i which is surjective onto G and maps this vertex to v. If we demand that G is vertex-transitive, it is useful in striving for a natural communication scheme, which means symmetrical and therefore easy to implement, to demand that the coloring of G is preserved by a subgroup Δ of $A(G)$ which acts transitively on V.

5 Optimal Family of Abelian Cayley Graphs

In the following, we analyze the question how an optimal family of abelian Cayley graphs can be constructed regarding their systolic broadcast complexity. We focus on the construction of an abelian Cayley

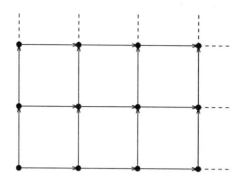

Figure 5. The Cayley graph of the free abelian group Φ_2

graph of outdegree δ, i.e. with a generating set S and $|S| = \delta$. In order to get an upper bound on the number of nodes that a corresponding graph can be composed of, we look at the free abelian group Φ_δ generated by the δ abstract generators $S = \{s_1, s_2, \ldots, s_\delta\}$ (see for instance Fig. 5).

Lemma 19 Let Φ_δ be the free abelian group generated by the abstract generators $S = \{s_1, s_2, \ldots, s_\delta\}$, and let BT_δ^t be the directed broadcast tree with bounded outdegree δ with a systolic coloring according to Def. 17. There exists a color preserving monomorphism from a subtree ST of BT_δ^t containing the vertex of level 0 into the Cayley graph $G_S(\Phi_\delta)$ and ST has $(m+2)^n \cdot (m+1)^{\delta-n}$ nodes (with $t = m\delta + n, 0 \le n < \delta$). There is no bigger subtree.

Proof. Let Red be the graph which is constructed from BT_δ^t with a systolic coloring according to Def. 17 by identification of vertices satisfying the following rule: $v \sim v'$ iff $\bigwedge_i c_i(v) = c_i(v')$, where $c_i(v)$ is the number of edges of color i from the root to v. Let ST be an arbitrary spanning tree of Red, which is obviously a subtree of BT_δ^t. As ST is a tree, these vertices can be represented uniquely by the sequences of colors on the path from the root sorted in increasing order, as $0 \ldots 0 1 \ldots 1 \ldots (\delta-1) \ldots (\delta-1)$. It follows from Def. 17 that a color i appears at most $m+1$ resp. m times depending on whether $i \le n$ or $i > n$ with $t = m\delta + n, 0 \le n < \delta$. If we identify a color i with an abstract generator s_{i+1} we get due to the commutative structure of the free abelian group a natural mapping from ST into Φ_δ and an induced monomorphism on its Cayley graph $G_S(\Phi_\delta)$. There are only $(m+2)^n \cdot (m+1)^{\delta-n}$ different nodes with a distance of at most t from the root in the Cayley graph, therefore there is no bigger embeddable subtree. $\square$

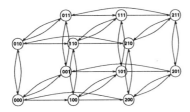

Figure 6. The abelian Cayley graph $G_S(\Psi_3^4)$ **with** $\Psi_3^4 = Z_3 \times Z_2 \times Z_2$ **generated by** $S = \{(1,0,0),(0,1,0),(0,0,1)\}$ **which has a systolic broadcast time** 4.

This upper bound can be reached, and with the following lemma, we give a method for the construction of a finite abelian group and a set of generators, such that ST can be embedded, and there is an bijection between the nodes of the Cayley graph and ST.

Theorem 20 Let $t = m\delta + n$ with $0 \le n < \delta$, and let

$$\Psi_\delta^t = \Phi_\delta / [s_1^{m+1}, \dots, s_n^{m+1}, s_{n+1}^m, \dots, s_\delta^m = 1]$$
$$S = \{s_1, \dots, s_\delta\} \ .$$

There exists a colored subtree ST of a colored directed broadcast tree BT_δ^t with a surjective color preserving graph monomorphism from ST onto $G_S(\Psi_\delta^t)$.

Proof. If we take $G_S(\Psi_\delta^t)$ with only the edges on the paths of length $\le t$ from the identity, it is obvious that this graph exactly corresponds to the fragment of the Cayley graph of the free abelian group in the proof of Lem. 19, and the result follows directly. □

Corollary 21 The abelian Cayley graph $G_S(\Psi_\delta^t)$ has a systolic broadcast time t with a period length δ. This is optimal for an abelian Cayley graph. The communication scheme in bitelegraph-mode is systolic with a period length δ and consists of the factors $F_i = \{(g,h) \in (\Psi_\delta^t)^2 \mid g^{-1}h = s_i\}$.

Example 22 Fig. 6 shows the optimal abelian Cayley graph of outdegree 3 which provides a systolic broadcast time 4. We use a representation as direct product of cyclic groups.

Lemma 23 Let $t = m\delta + n$ with $0 \le n < \delta$. A lower bound for the order of the maximum graph of maximum outdegree δ which allows a δ-systolic broadcast complexity of t is given by $(m+2)^n \cdot (m+1)^{\delta-1}$.

Proof. With Theorem 20, a constructive method is given to compose a graph with the above properties. □

6 Future Work

In this article, we showed that vertex-transitive graphs are a suitable model for network topologies and that the analysis of systolic dissemination of information corresponds to the family of Cayley graphs, which are a subclass of vertex-transitive graphs. We finally constructed an optimal family of abelian Cayley graphs regarding their systolic broadcast complexity, and obtained a lower bound for the order of a maximal graph. It was shown in [25] that it is fruitful to examine also Cayley graphs of non-abelian groups in connection with systolic algorithms. Optimizations founded on the abstract presentations of the groups have already delivered new results [27], and the used methods will be extended further. Beyond the study of the bitelegraph-mode of communication other restrictions to the communication rounds are conceivable, and other routing techniques, as e.g. standard wormhole routing methods [21, 23] and more advanced strategies [6, 22, 28], have to be studied.

References

[1] S. B. Akers and B. Krishnamurthy. A group theoretic model for symmetric interconnection networks. In *Proceedings of the International Conference on Parallel Processing*, pages 216–223, 1986.

[2] B. Alspach. Cayley graphs with optimal fault tolerance. *IEEE Transactions on Computers*, 41(10):1337–1339, Oct. 1992.

[3] B. W. Arden and K. W. Tang. Representations and routing for Cayley graphs. *IEEE Transactions on Communications*, 39(11):1533–1537, Nov. 1991.

[4] N. Biggs. *Algebraic Graph Theory*. Cambridge University Press, 2nd edition, 1993.

[5] S. Cheng and X.-D. Jia. Undirected loop networks. *Networks*, 23:257–260, 1993.

[6] R. Cypher, F. Meyer auf der Heide, C. Scheideler, and B. Vöcking. Universal algorithms for store-and-forward and wormhole routing. In *Proceedings of the 26th STOC*, 1996.

[7] M. J. Dinneen, M. R. Fellows, and V. Faber. Algebraic constructions of efficient broadcast networks. In H. F. Mattson, T. Mora, and T. R. N. Rao, editors, *Applied Algebra, Algebraic Algorithms and Error-Correcting Codes*, LNCS 539, pages 152–158. Springer-Verlag, 1991.

[8] M. J. Dinneen and P. R. Hafner. New results for the degree/diameter problem. *Networks*, 24:359–367, 1994.

[9] R. Dougherty and V. Faber. The degree-diameter problem for several varieties of Cayley graphs, I: The abelian case. Technical report, Los Alamos National Laboratory, Dec. 1994.

[10] P. Erdős and D. F. Hsu. Distributed loop network with minimum transmission delay. *Theoretical Computer Science*, 100:223–241, 1992.

[11] S. M. Hedetniemi, S. T. Hedetniemi, and A. L. Liestman. A survey of gossiping and broadcasting in communication networks. *Networks*, 18:319–349, 1988.

[12] C.-T. Ho and M.-Y. Kao. Optimal broadcast in all-port wormhole-routed hypercubes. *IEEE Transactions on Parallel and Distributed Systems*, 6(2):200–204, Feb. 1995.

[13] J. Hromkovič, R. Klasing, E. A. Stöhr, and H. Wagener. Gossiping in vertex-disjoint paths mode in d-dimensional grids and planar graphs. In T. Lengauer, editor, *Algorithms — ESA '93*, LNCS 726, pages 200–211. Springer-Verlag, 1993.

[14] J. Hromkovič, R. Klasing, W. Unger, H. Wagener, and D. Pardubskà. The complexity of systolic dissemination of information in interconnection networks. In M. Cosnard, A. Ferreira, and J. Peters, editors, *Parallel and Distributed Computing*, LNCS 805, pages 235–249. Springer-Verlag, 1994.

[15] R. Klasing. *On the Complexity of Broadcast and Gossip in Different Communication Modes*. Shaker Verlag, 1996.

[16] R. Klasing, B. Monien, R. Peine, and E. Stöhr. Broadcasting in butterfly and DeBruijn networks. In A. Finkel and M. Jantzen, editors, *Theoretical Aspects of Computer Science — STACS 92*, LNCS 577, pages 351–362. Springer-Verlag, 1992.

[17] R. Labahn and A. Raspaud. Periodic gossiping in back-to-back trees. Technical report, Universität Rostock, Fachbereich Mathematik, 1994.

[18] F. T. Leighton. *Parallel Algorithms and Architectures*. Morgan Kaufmann Publishers, San Mateo, California, 1992.

[19] A. L. Liestman and D. Richards. Network communication in edge-colored graphs: Gossiping. *IEEE Transactions on Parallel and Distributed Systems*, 4(4):438–445, Apr. 1993.

[20] B. D. McKay. Embedding one interconnection network in another. *Congressus Numerantium*, 30:45–87, 1981.

[21] P. K. McKinley, Y.-j. Tsai, and D. F. Robinson. A survey of collective communication in wormhole-routed massively parallel computers. Technical Report MSU-CPS-94-35, Michigan State University, June 1994.

[22] F. Meyer auf der Heide and B. Vöcking. A packet routing protocol for arbitrary networks. In *Proceedings of the 12th STACS*, pages 291–302, 1995.

[23] L. M. Ni and L. M. N. McKinley. A survey of wormhole routing techniques in direct networks. *IEEE Computer*, 26:62–76, Feb. 1993.

[24] S. R. Öhring and S. K. Das. The folded Petersen network: A new versatile multiprocessor interconnection topology. In J. van Leeuwen, editor, *Graph-Theoretic Concepts in Computer Science*, LNCS 790, pages 301–314. Springer-Verlag, 1993.

[25] M. Sampels. Algebraic constructions of efficient systolic architectures. In *Proceedings of the 2nd International Conference on Massively Parallel Computing Systems (MPCS '96)*. IEEE, 1996.

[26] M. Sampels. Cayley graphs as interconnection networks: A case study. In *Proceedings of the 7th International Workshop on Parallel Processing by Cellular Automata and Arrays (PARCELLA '96)*, pages 67–76, Berlin, 1996. Akademie-Verlag.

[27] M. Sampels and S. Schöf. Massively parallel architectures for parallel discrete event simulation. In *Proceedings of the 8nd European Simulation Symposium (ESS '96)*, volume 2, pages 374–378. SCS, 1996.

[28] C. Scheideler and B. Vöcking. Universal continuous routing strategies. In *Proceedings of the 8th SPAA*. ACM, 1996.

[29] H. P. Yap. *Some topics in graph theory*. London Mathematical Society Lecture Note Series 108. Cambridge University Press, 1986.

❖ KEYNOTE SESSION 2 ❖

The Problem of Parallel Program Performance Estimation

Speaker

A. Hey

Chair

S. C. Winter

❖ SESSION 8 ❖

Parallel Programming Environments

Chair

B. Di Martino

Designing Distributed Object Systems with PARSE

Anna Liu[1] and Ian Gorton[2]

[1]School of Computer Science and Engineering,
University of New South Wales, Kensington NSW 2052, Australia
[2]CSIRO Division of Information Technology, Locked Bag 17, North Ryde NSW 2113, Australia
contact email: annaliu@cse.unsw.edu.au

Abstract

With the emergence of distributed object technology, such as CORBA, IBM's SOM/DSOM, Microsoft's COM/OLE, and Java, distributed object technology is becoming more commonplace. However, most object-oriented design methods do not focus on producing high performance, concurrent, distributed and verifiable object-oriented systems. The PARSE software design method provides a hierarchical, object-based approach to the development of parallel and distributed software systems. In PARSE, deadlock avoidance in the software development process can be carried out via the explicit use of design heuristics involving client-server modelling. A graphical design notation known as process graphs is firstly used to capture the structural and dynamic properties of the required distributed software system. Then, the process graph designs can be analyzed and transformed into client-server behaviour graphs, for the purpose of design verification. This paper briefly presents the PARSE design notation. Next, the design and construction of a cooperative graph editor utilizing the PARSE methodology will be presented. Finally, experience of an implementation involving the Common Object Request Broker Architecture (CORBA) will be discussed.

1. Introduction

The recent emergence of so-called *middle-ware* technology has created a strong interest in the high-performance software community in building distributed object systems. Available middle-ware products include the Object Management Group's CORBA, IBM's SOM/DSOM, and Microsoft's COM/OLE [1]. These systems enable the construction of extensible software with reusable, distributed components. As a result, distributed solutions to solve problems in various domains including cooperative work environments, distributed databases, and distributed real-time control applications are emerging.

However, most object-oriented design techniques are somewhat inadequate for distributed system design [2], despite the fact that the distributed software engineer faces various complex issues relating to the partitioning and distribution of software components. Although middle-ware technology provides an abstraction for the underlying communication required by the distributed components (thus simplifying the implementation process), issues such as synchronization, deadlock avoidance, and dynamic process creation and deletion still need to be considered during the design stage.

The PARSE project aims to develop a distributed software engineering methodology that guides the software engineer from design to verification and through to software implementation. It provides an explicit representation of the parallelism and distribution in a system. It also enables the designer to verify their design at an early stage of the engineering process, hence reducing resource overheads incurred in discovering deadlock at the later testing stage [3].

In this paper, we will examine the use of the PARSE design method in the area of cooperative applications. This type of application presents new requirements, and challenging design and development issues that are common to distributed systems. These requirements include complex coordination and consistency issues, dynamic creation and deletion of various system components, and complex real-time interactions between various entities in the system. In addition, a prototype implementation using CORBA is discussed and simple mapping rules from PARSE design features to CORBA features are presented.

This paper focuses on the PARSE design method and the design verification method. For details on the other aspects of the PARSE methodology, please refer to [4][5].

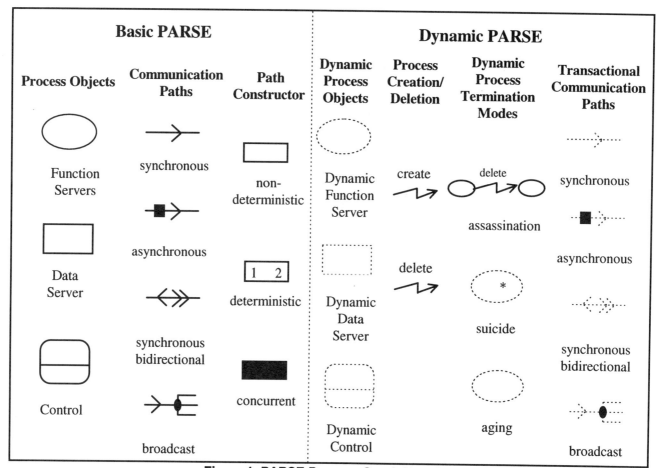

Figure 1. PARSE Process Graph Notation

2. The PARSE design methodology

The PARSE software design methodology provides a hierarchical, object-based approach to the development of parallel and distributed software systems. A system is decomposed into a set of concurrently executing *process objects* which communicate via message passing. These process objects can also be hierarchically decomposed in order to handle complexity in design. A graphical design notation known as process graphs is firstly used to capture the structural and dynamic properties of the required distributed software system.

Figure 1 shows the basic design components present in the PARSE process graph notation.

A typical design process involves the following steps:

- identify the various process objects in the system.
- classify the process objects to be one of: active control object, passive function object, and passive data server.
- specify the interaction between the process objects using the 4 different types of communication paths:

synchronous, asynchronous, bi-directional (request-reply), and broadcast.
- for each process object, indicate the order of handling of all incoming messages to that process object.
- use dynamic PARSE notations for systems with dynamic process creation and deletion features.

Further, in the PARSE methodology deadlock avoidance in the software development process is carried out via the explicit use of design heuristics involving client-server modelling. Once the structural and dynamic properties of the required distributed software system has been captured using the process graphs, the designs can then be transformed into client-server behaviour graphs [6], which serve the purpose of design verification.

Figure 2 illustrates the client-server behaviour graph components, proposed by Birkinshaw and Croll [6].

The transformation from PARSE designs to client-server behaviour graph is relatively simple:

- for each process object in the PARSE design, determine its functional behaviour, that is, whether it acts as a client, a server, or both client-server in the system.

336

- the direction of a communication path between two process objects is indicated on the client-server behaviour graph. In the case of bi-directional (request-reply communication) path, use the request message direction.
- ignore all dynamic process creations and deletions, we assume all process objects do not exit the system unexpectedly.
- ignore path constructors.
- start this transformation from bottom up, that is, start with the lowest level PARSE designs first. Then at each level, analyze the overall behaviour of that

particular module, and simplify it to be a composite client, composite server, composite client-server, or a perfect client-server node in the client-server behaviour graph. Continue this until reaching the top-level PARSE design diagram.

The resultant client-server behaviour graphs are directed graphs which show the client-to-server dependencies. A topological sort on the client-server ordering would reveal any client-server cycles. An absence of cycles is sufficient to indicate structural deadlock freedom [6]. The use of this design heuristic thus indicates potential problem areas in a system at an early stage of the software design process.

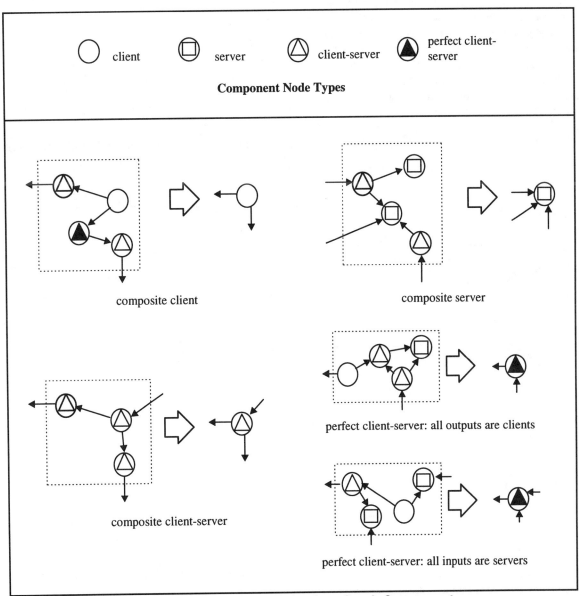

Figure 2. Client-Server Behaviour Graph Components

337

3.   Case study: a cooperative graph editor

The case study is a cooperative graph editor. This editor caters for several users, working at different workstations, and cooperating in constructing the one diagram. The diagram under construction is composed of a number of primitive graphical elements, where each element has attributes that are subjected to edits. In this editing system, each user is informed in real time of the actions of the others. For example, if an attribute of a particular graphical element has been modified by a user, all other users in the system would be notified of this change immediately. In the Computer Supported Cooperative Work (CSCW) vocabulary, such a tool may be classified as synchronous groupware, which has the features of WYSIWIS (What You See Is What I See).

Users may start an editing session by firstly sending a login request to the cooperative editor. The user may then use the services provided by the editor to obtain a lock on a desired graphical element, and make edits to it. Each change performed to the graphical element is then broadcast to all users in the system. There is also a data control area where the consistent copy of the graph under construction is kept. Figure 3 shows the top-level PARSE design diagram of this editing system.

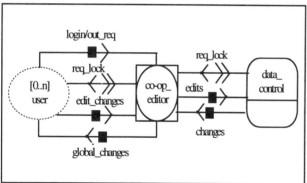

Figure 3. Top Level PARSE Diagram - Collaborative Editing System[1]

Figure 4 shows an instance of the decomposed *user* process object. Each composite object is instantiated when a user joins the editing session.

The *user* process object consists of two main function process objects. The *request_module* initiates the lock on graph element requested, and subsequently allows edits to the locked element. It also informs the *co-op_editor* of its own existence via the *login_request* at the beginning of a session. *Display_module* is responsible for the display of changes in the graph under construction through the use of

local_cached_graph. Notice that the path constructor on *local_cached_graph* specifies that this data server handles the incoming *global_changes* to the graph first, before it replies to the *display_module* for its request for the current graph. This is to ensure that the most recent version of graph under construction is displayed.

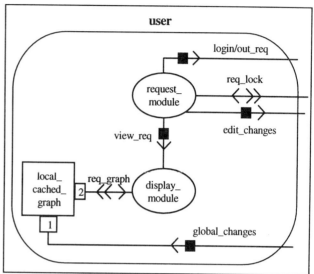

Figure 4. PARSE Process Graph - Decomposed User Process Object

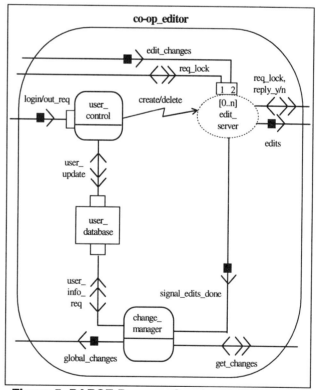

Figure 5. PARSE Process Graph - Multithreaded Co-op Editor

---

[1] The symbol circle enclosed by a rectangle denotes a 'multithreaded server object' [7].

338

Figure 5 shows the decomposition of *co-op_editor*. The *user-control* process object is responsible for handling *login* requests from new users, and *logout* requests from existing users. Upon receiving a *login* request, it makes an update to the *user_database*, and creates a dynamic function process *edit_server* to handle edit requests for this particular *user*. Note how the *edit_server* process object is of a dynamic nature. It is created in order to provide services for users who enter and exit the system at run-time. In the implementation stage, the *edit_server* process object may be created and distributed across a network, or alternatively, a multithreaded implementation strategy may be adopted. The replicated *edit_server* process objects thus handles all editing related communication, and leaves the main control process object, ie. *user_control*, to just monitor the structural change of the system.

Further, a deterministic path constructor has been used to enforce the editing protocol. The user first needs to select a graphical element for editing by passing a message *req_lock* to the *edit_server*. Then, the change to that particular graph element is processed via *edit_server*. The smaller number on the deterministic path constructor indicates that its corresponding message path has a higher processing priority.

Figure 6 shows the decomposition of *data_control*. The *lock_control* object receives lock requests on various graph elements from different *edit_servers* acting on behalf of different users. It ensures that each graph element can be locked by at most one user at a time. The process object *edit_control* makes edits to the master copy of the graph under construction stored in *graph_database*. It also releases the lock on the graph element once edits are completed.

Deadlock freedom verification

The above PARSE process graph designs can be systematically transformed into client-server behaviour graphs for verification of deadlock freedom [6].

Notice how the *user* module can be reduced to a perfect-client-server, this breaks the cycle between *co-op_editor* and *user*. Hence, it can be concluded that this cooperative editor is free from structural deadlocks. If however a potential structural deadlock had been detected in the design, revisions could be performed in order to eliminate any possible deadlock arising from client-server dependency cycles.

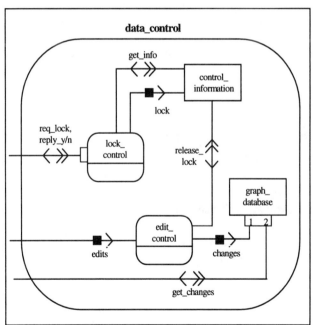

Figure 6. PARSE Process Graph - Decomposition of 'Data Control'

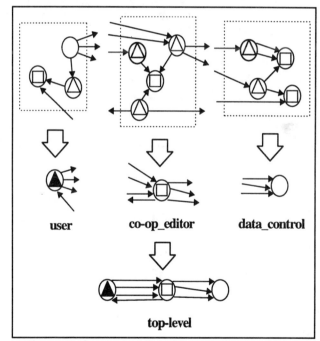

Figure 7. Structural Deadlock Detection Using Client-Server Modelling

The *change_manager* is responsible for broadcasting the *global_changes* to all *users* in the system. Once an edit has been carried out, the *change_manager* obtains the change specification, requests the current user information from *user_database*, and notifies all *local_cached_graph* of the changes.

4. Prototype implementation on CORBA

A prototype of the collaborative editing system has been implemented using the Common Object Request Broker Architecture (CORBA) standard [8]. Specifically, the CORBA implementation we have used is Orbix [9] from Iona Technology. CORBA aims to specify an environment that supports the development and execution of distributed object systems. The Object Request Broker (ORB) enables objects to transparently make and receive requests and responses in a distributed environment, suitable for the construction of distributed object system on both homogeneous and heterogeneous networks. Figure 8 illustrates how the Object Request Broker (ORB) supports transparent object invocations.

The ORB is responsible for the interaction between a client and a server. A client object can make a request for a service to be provided by a server object. The client has an object reference for the server object and activates operations for the object. This reference is opaque, and the client does not need to know the location of the server implementation, nor any other implementation details. it only needs to know the specification of the operation request, which is specified using the platform independent Interface Definition Language (IDL).

The provision of a standardised interface definition language IDL ensures inter-operability between different object systems, as well as portability across different platforms. Currently, CORBA has standard mappings from OMG IDL to C, C++ and SmallTalk, and Orbix provides automatic code generation to target languages including: C, C++, SmallTalk, and Java.

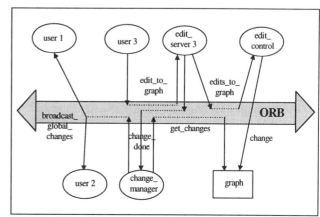

Figure 8. ORB Support Transparent Remote Object Interactions

CORBA also supports the dynamic creation of object instances via the Basic Object Adaptor (BOA) mechanism. Besides simple instantiation of a class statically, objects

PARSE Features	CORBA Features
Process Objects • function process object • control process object • data server process object • dynamic process object creation • hierarchical, composite process objects	**IDL Object Interface Definition** • IDL interface definition • IDL interface definition with *readonly* attributes for storing control states • various abstract data types: structs, arrays, user defined types, etc. • created at run-time via Basic Object Adaptor (BOA) • IDL Module definition
Communication Paths • synchronous • asynchronous • bi-directional • broadcast	**Inter-object Operations via ORB** • default • *one-way* object invocation or multi-threaded implementation • simulate using 2 operation calls in opposite directions or return value from a normal operation call • simulate using multiple *one-way* object invocations
Path Constructors • non-deterministic • deterministic • concurrent (only apply to objects that can be decomposed)	**Object Invocation Ordering** • default • explicit ordering required in object implementation • different lower-level objects handle different invocations

Table 1. Corresponding Features Between PARSE and CORBA

can be created dynamically using BOA, where objects are registered at run-time, and activated when it is firstly invoked. The BOA mechanism is a useful feature of CORBA that supports the construction of distributed object applications where objects need to be created at run-time.

Table 1 shows the simple mapping from PARSE design features to CORBA implementation features.

Experience shows that, by following the mapping rules in Table 1, PARSE designs can be easily translated into a CORBA implementation written in C++. In the prototype, we have implemented the *user* process object using the BOA implementation approach. Hence whenever a person begins an editing session, an *user* process object is created at run-time. Similarly, the dynamic *edit_server* is also implemented using the BOA mechanism. On the other hand, static process objects such as the *user_manager* are created statically, since they are required to provide service to users at all times. The appendix shows a sample OMG IDL code for the *co-op_editor* module. The IDL thus constructed can be translated by Orbix to produce high performance, distributed and object-oriented code.

5.   Summary and further work

In this paper, we have illustrated the use of the PARSE design method in a cooperative application environment. We have employed a simple client-server modelling approach to verify design deadlock freedom. We have also shown that PARSE designs can be transformed in a straightforward manner and implemented on the CORBA framework.

There still remains much future work to be done in relating the PARSE approach to distributed object system design. We are currently adding formal semantics to the basic building blocks of the PARSE process graph. We are also examining the integration of conventional object-oriented design methods and architectures with PARSE descriptions, to provide a comprehensive set of compatible views of a system design.

Acknowledgments

The authors gratefully acknowledges C.I.Birkinshaw and P.R.Croll (Sheffield University, UK) for their work on the client-server behaviour graphs in relation to verification of deadlock freedom of PARSE designs.

References

[1] El-Rewini, H., Hamilton, S., et.al. (1995) Object Technology: A Virtual Roundtable, *IEEE Computer*, Vol.28, No.10, 48-57.

[2] Kramer, J. (1994) Distributed Software Engineering, *Proc. 16th Int'l Conf. Software Engineering*, IEEE Computer Society Press, Calif., 253-63.

[3] Carter, F. and Fekete, A. (1996) Cerberus - A Tool For Debugging Distributed Algorithms, *Proc. 1st IFIP TC10 Int'l Workshop on Parallel and Distributed Software Engineering*, Chapman and Hall, 110-21.

[4] Gorton, I., Gray, J.P. and Jelly, I.E. (1995) Object-based Modelling of Parallel Programs, *IEEE Parallel and Distributed Technology*, Vol.3, No.2, Summer, 52-63.

[5] Gorton, I., Jelly, I.E., Gray, J. and Chan, T.S. (1996) Reliable Parallel Software Construction Using PARSE, *Concurrency: Practice and Experience*, Vol.8, No.2, March, 125-46.

[6] Birkinshaw, C.I. and Croll, P.R. (1995) Modelling the Client-Server Behaviour of Parallel Real-Time Systems Using Petri Nets, *Proc. 28th Ann. Hawaii Int'l Conf. System Sciences, Parallel Software Engineering Minitrack, Vol.2: Software Technology*, IEEE Computer Society Press, Calif., 339-48.

[7] Liu, A. and Gorton, I. (1996) Modelling Dynamic Distributed System Structures in PARSE, *Proc. 4th Euromicro Workshop on Parallel and Distributed Processing*, IEEE Computer Society Press, Calif., 352-9.

[8] Object management Group, (1995) The Common Object Request Broker: Architecture and Specification, Revision 2.0, OMG.

[9] Iona Technologies Ltd, (1995) Orbix 2 - Distributed Object technology, Programming and Reference Guide, Release 2.0, Iona Technologies Ltd.

Appendix:
Sample OMG IDL For co-op_editor

```
// editor.idl
// CORBA IDL definition of the co-op_editor module.
// The interface as seen by user process objects are defined
here.

module CoOpEditor {

    struct UserEntry {
        string user_name;
        short user_id;
    };

    interface user_database {
        oneway void new_user_entry();
        oneway void delete_user_entry(in short user_id);
    };

    interface user_control {
        oneway void create_user_session();
        oneway void delete_user_session
                        (in short user_id);
    };

    interface edit_server {
        boolean req_lock(in short user_id,
                        in short graph_elem_id);
        oneway void edits(in short user_id,
                        in string new_attributes,
                        in short graph_elem_id);
    };

    interface change_manager {
        oneway void edits_done();
        // this invokes the change_manager to broadcast
          global changes.
    };

}; //end module
```

Execution Replay for TreadMarks

Michiel Ronsse
Department of Electronics
and Information Systems
Universiteit Gent
Sint-Pietersnieuwstraat 41
B-9000 Gent, Belgium
ronsse@elis.rug.ac.be

Willy Zwaenepoel
Department of Computer Science
Rice University
6100 S. Main Street
Houston, TX 77251-1892
USA
willy@cs.rice.edu

Abstract

As most parallel programs are non-deterministic, the execution path of a parallel program can vary from one execution to another. When such a program contains an error, we can no longer guarantee that consecutive runs with the same input will result in the same error. As a consequence, cyclic debugging techniques as such become unusable. However, if we can force re-executions to be 'equivalent' to the faulty one, we can still use those techniques. This can be accomplished using a replay method. Such a method traces a particular program execution. Using those traces, the method forces subsequent executions to be equivalent to the traced one. This paper presents an implementation of a recently introduced method (ROLT) for TreadMarks, a DSM (Distributed Shared Memory) system.

1. Introduction

A parallel program consists of a set of separate tasks that can be executed in parallel by different processors. The debugging of these programs is a time-consuming task because it is likely that a parallel program contains many errors due to the complex nature of parallel programs. Another, even more important, reason is the non-deterministic nature of most parallel programs. Because we cannot guarantee that subsequent executions of the program with the same input will result in the same program flow, we cannot use cyclic debugging techniques as such. These are commonly used techniques to detect errors in sequential programs, based on the fact that re-executions of a sequential program will result in the same program flow if we supply the same input.[1] During those re-executions we can analyse the program ex-

---

[1] We assume that during replay the user input, file input, system calls, ... return the same result.

ecution by setting breakpoints, watching variables, ... until we find the error.

2. Replay methods

As parallel programs can be non-deterministic, cyclic debugging techniques as such become unusable: re-executions will not result in the same program flow. Therefore it is possible that the re-execution of a faulty program will show no error, or that another error will occur. However, if we can force re-executions to be 'equivalent' to the execution that contains an error, we can still use cyclic debugging techniques. This can be accomplished using a replay method. Therefore we trace the ongoing program execution (record phase) by instrumenting the program, the libraries, the operating system or by using hardware probes. We only trace the information that is needed to force the following runs to be 'equivalent' to the traced one. As these forced re-executions (replay phase) will be deterministic we can use intrusive debugging techniques (breakpoints, collecting data for performance debugging, ...). To be practical, it is important that the tracing produces small trace files and has a small overhead, circumventing the probe effect [1]. If the overhead is low enough the tracing can be left on all the time, i.e. not only during the debugging phase.

There are two possible approaches to force executions of a parallel program that uses the shared memory paradigm to be 'equivalent' to a traced execution. The first is to force the processors to read the same shared variable values as during the traced execution by logging the original value. The second is to force the processors to access the shared variables in the same order as during the traced execution, forcing the variables to undergo the operations in the same order as during the record phase. As the first approach isn't feasible because it leads to huge trace files, we use the second approach.

Instant Replay [5] introduced a widely accepted replay

method. It records the order of coarse grained accesses by the different processors to the shared objects. Netzer [7] introduced a new method based on vector clocks producing smaller trace files w.r.t. Instant Replay. This method makes it possible to obtain large reductions of the trace files. In contrast with Instant Replay this method was presented considering fine-grained operations: the order of individual memory accesses is replayed.

Our method, ROLT (Reconstruction Of Lamport Timestamps) [6], has the advantage that it produces smaller trace files and is much less intrusive than Netzer's. In [6] the ROLT method was shown to be better – less operations need to be logged – than [7]. Originally, the ROLT method was implemented for operations with large granularity (monitor operations) and in [9] the method was tested for individual memory accesses. This was done by simulating the ROLT method with a multiprocessor simulator.

To enforce a faithful replay, we have to trace the accesses to all shared resources (memory, disks, screen, network, ...) during the record phase. This forces us to intervene at every access to a shared resource, introducing an intolerable computational overhead. Therefore, we use a different approach. During the record phase, we trace the order of the synchronisation operations. This will lead to the same execution path during replay as long as the program is data race free. A data race is an unsynchronised access to a shared object by two processors when at least one processor modifies the resource. This is most of the time the outcome of a lack of synchronisation or the wrong synchronisation. As there is no synchronisation, no information will be stored during the record phase. Therefore, the replay method will be unable to force the accesses to occur in the same order as in the record phase. However, existing data race detection schemed can be used during the replay phase, as is explained in [8].

The ROLT method uses Lamport clocks [4] to attach logical timestamps to synchronisation operations (see Fig. 1.a). Logical timestamps may not reflect the actual real-time order of the operations. However it is required that operations on the same synchronisation variable (called object from now on) have consistent timestamps, that is, that the timestamps of all operations on the same object reflect their execution order. Each processor updates its own clock using a deterministic algorithm. A possible algorithm is incrementing the clock by one every time a processor executes a synchronisation operation. At some operations on the objects the Lamport clock must be additionally incremented in order to maintain consistency. To accomplish this we attach to every object the Lamport clock of the latest operation. When the Lamport clock of the processor is smaller than the timestamp attached to the object, the processor clock is adjusted: the new value is the timestamp of the object incremented by one. In contrast with the increment caused by the deterministic algorithm, this is a non-deterministic increment (called

an update form now on).

During replay, the timestamps of the original execution are used to add sufficient synchronisation for a correct replay: operations with a lower timestamp are executed first. To be able to do this, the same Lamport timestamps as in the original execution must be attached to the corresponding operations. This can be done by logging only when the clock is updated: the deterministic increments do not need to be logged since they can be re-computed during replay (see Fig. 1.b).

3. TreadMarks

TreadMarks[2] is a Distributed Shared Memory system: it enables programmers to use a shared memory paradigm to program a network of workstations (Fig. 2). Using multiple-

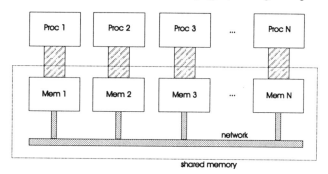

Figure 2. A DSM system allows the use of shared variables on a system without shared memory.

writer protocols and lazy release consistency [3], a good performance is obtained. As this paper discusses an implementation of ROLT for TreadMarks enforcing 'equivalent' executions on the highest abstraction level (the shared memory level), we will only discuss TreadMarks topics that are relevant to the implementation of ROLT. TreadMarks offers the programmer two type of synchronisation:

locks: there are two types of operation possible on locks: `lock_acquire` and `lock_release`. The first one blocks the calling processor until the lock is free, the last one releases the lock. These operations are strictly bracketing: only the processor that acquires a lock can release it;

barriers: all processors must arrive at the barrier before anybody can proceed.

TreadMarks uses messages to exchange information between the different workstations. These messages are exchanged to grab locks, pass barriers, move shared variables, ... across the network.

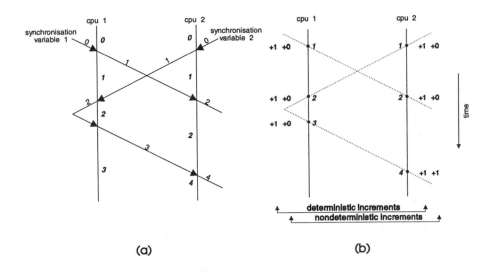

Figure 1. Updating the Lamport clocks. Operations on the same object are connected by arrows, pointing from the operation that occurred first to the next operation on that object.

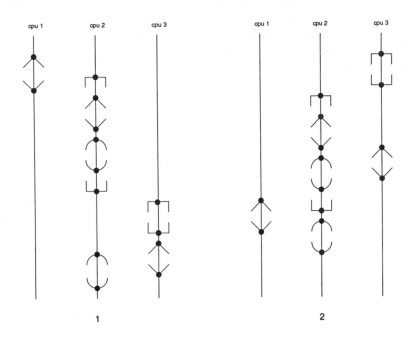

Figure 3. Two different executions of the same non-deterministic TreadMarks program: a dot represents a synchronisation operation, a convex symbol a `lock_acquire` **and a concave symbol a** `lock_release`. **Operations on the same lock are denoted by the same symbol.**

4. Implementation

In our implementation, we used 32-bit Lamport clocks. As mentioned before, we only log the non-deterministic increments of the Lamport clocks. This means that we have to log a pair of timestamps for each non-deterministic increment: the value before and after the update. However, it is sufficient to log the increments; most of the time it will be much smaller than the Lamport timestamps itself. If the increment is smaller than 255 we use 8 bits to write it to the log file. If the increment is larger than 254, we use 40 bits: the value 255 (8-bit) followed by the increment (32-bit). This is a very simple compression algorithm, allowing the Lamport clocks to be coded and decoded very fast. More powerful algorithms could introduce a better compression, in return for a (de)coding that takes much longer. As we have to limit the perturbation introduced by the replay method, such an algorithm is less useful. During the record phase, the Lamport clocks are collected in a buffer. When the buffer is full, they are encoded and written to disk.

As mentioned before, each processor has a Lamport clock, and when a processor performs a synchronisation operation, the Lamport clock has to be incremented. We have to consider three different cases:

lock_acquire: when a lock is requested, an acquire message is sent. When the lock is granted, the timestamp of the lock is piggybacked on the return message. The processor then compares his clock with the timestamp he received, calculates the maximum and adds one. This value becomes the new Lamport clock of the processor, and it is also attached to the lock. We log if there is a non-deterministic increment; this only happens if the timestamp of the lock is larger than the clock of the processor.

lock_release: as the lock operations are bracketing, one could argue that we don't have to trace the lock_release operations because the processor performing the lock_release is the one that performed the last lock_acquire, making the occurrence of lock_release deterministic. However, this can lead to deadlock during the replay phase if we nest different lock_acquire - lock_release-pairs (Fig. 4). To alleviate this problem, we have to update the Lamport clock of the processor and the one attached to the lock when we perform a lock_clear. As the Lamport clock of the processor is at least as large as the timestamp attached to the object, we don't have to compare the two values. We simply increment the Lamport clock of the processor with one, and attach this value to the object. As this is a deterministic increment, we never have to log it. An example is given in fig 5.

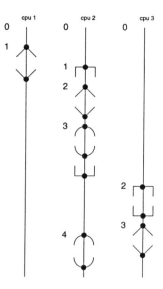

Figure 4. A record method that leads to deadlock during the replay phase: the first operation of the third cpu needs to be executed after the sixth operation of the second cpu, while replay will force the fourth operation of the second cpu to be executed after the first operation of the third cpu.

barriers: at a barrier, the Lamport clocks of all processors are piggybacked on the request message, compared, and the maximum value is piggybacked on the return message. Each processor updates his own Lamport clock based on the value returned and logs if necessary. For at least one of the processors the update will be deterministic (the processor that had the maximum value), the other updates will be non-deterministic and must be logged.

4.1. Replay phase

During the replay phase, all operations with a timestamp smaller than x must be executed before we can execute an operation with timestamp x. Comparing the timestamps would be too time-consuming, because they would have to reside in shared memory. Hence, they would have to be moved between the processes on the different workstation all the time. Therefore, another approach is used: each processor is forced to perform $x - y$ non-instrumented barrier operations between two operations with timestamps x and y. Notice that the synchronisation added during the replay phase is too strong (Fig. 5): e.g. the second operation of the third cpu is forced to appear after the seventh operation of the second cpu, while there is no reason to do this.

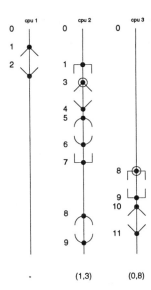

Figure 5. A record method that leads to a correct, deadlock-free replay phase. A circle around an operation denotes a non-deterministic increment; the numbers below the graph are the numbers to be logged (before encoding).

5. Experimental Evaluation

This paragraph contains an experimental evaluation of the ROLT replay method. We used a parallel Tread-Marks program that performs 2 `barrier` (one at the start and one at the end), 1681 `lock_acquire` and 1681 `lock_release` operations. All test were performed on a network of 8 Sun workstations.

5.1. Size of the traces

5.1.1. Original method

An important property of a replay method is the size of the trace files it produces. Without compression, the maximum possible size of the trace files is 13512 bytes for our test program. This occurs when we have to log at all `lock_acquire` and `barrier` operations. Using the compression algorithm described above, this corresponds with a file size between 3378 and 16890 bytes, depending on the values to be logged.

Fig. 6 (delta=0) shows the size of the trace files in function of the numbers of processors. A few things can be noticed:

- the size of the trace files is substantially smaller than 16890, caused by the fact that we don't have to log at

all operations and that the encoding algorithm yields a good compression;

- if we use more processors, the trace files get larger. This is caused by the fact that the total number of lock operations is the same for all executions: if we use more processors, each processor will execute less lock operations. Therefore, the chance that the clock of the processor is larger than the timestamp of the object diminishes, resulting in an increased number of non-deterministic increments.

5.1.2. Optimised method

We can reduce the size of the trace files by reducing the number of non-deterministic increments. We can't do anything about the non-deterministic increments at a barrier, but we can reduce the number of updates caused by `lock_acquire`. As mentioned before, a non-deterministic increment occurs when the timestamp of the lock is larger than the clock of the processor. However, we can increment the clock of the processor with a value larger than one, before we compare the clock and the timestamp. This will diminishes the chance that the timestamp is larger than the clock, resulting in an increased chance that the increment will be deterministic. As the additional increment (we will call this 'delta') is deterministic, we don't have to log it. However, as the timestamp of the object gets larger after the operation, it is possible that the next operation on the object will result in a non-deterministic increment.

Nevertheless, experiments (Fig. 6) show that the additional increment reduces the size of the log files. In this figure, the size of the trace files is plotted in function of the number of processors. We notice a few things:

1. there is almost no difference between delta=0 and delta=1, delta=2 and delta=3, ...;

2. for all values of delta, the trace files get larger if we use more processors;

3. if we make delta larger, the size of the trace files drops (as expected);

4. the size of the trace files for 2 processors drops substantially when delta $\geq$ 2, for 3 processors when delta $\geq$ 4, for 4 processors when delta $\geq$ 6, ...

This can be explained as follows: when the Tread-Marks program is symmetric (all processors execute the same code) and the load on all machines is approximately the same, we'll end up with an execution as depicted in Fig. 7: between two successive locks by a processor, all other processors grab the lock once. If we have p processors, this means that $p - 1$ processors will execute one lock_acquire (resulting in an increment of the timestamp of the object with one, supposing this update is deterministic) and one lock_release (a deterministic increment with one). This results in a total increment for the timestamp of a lock with $2 \times (p - 1)$ between a lock_release and a lock_acquire. Therefore, incrementing the Lamport clock of the processor with $2 \times (p-1)$ before the lock_acquire will make the clock of the processor equal to the timestamp attached to the objected, resulting in a deterministic increment. Fig. 7 shows this for 3 processors and delta= $2 \times (3 - 1) = 4$. As the figure shows, the optimised method can't do anything about the non-deterministic update at the first operation performed by a processor (startup effect). However, after the first operation, the ideal sequence of Lamport clocks can usually be maintained for a long time, resulting in a drastic decrease of the size of the trace files.

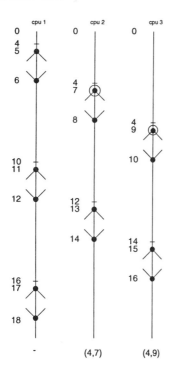

Figure 7. Using the optimised method decreases the number of non-deterministic updates. (A small horizontal line represents the additional increment before the lock_acquire)

Both the test results and the optimisation are targeted at programs using locks, and no or a limited number of barriers. However, tracing a program using barriers and no locks, will result in no trace information to be logged at all. This is desirable because such programs are deterministic. The

ROLT method won't log anything because at all barrier operations, all processors will have an equal Lamport clock. This has as a consequence that all processors will have the maximum, resulting in a deterministic increment for all processors. If the program uses both locks and barriers, we still can use the optimisation. However, the barrier will disturb the ideal sequence of timestamps, because it synchronises the Lamport clocks of the processors. Therefore, the startup effect will occur after each barrier operation. The ideal sequence will be regained at the next operation in return for a non-deterministic increment.

5.2. Overhead

Another important property of a replay method is the overhead introduced, especially during the record phase. If this phase is to intrusive, the program execution will be perturbated, possibly masking errors. The overhead during the replay phase is less important as we will probably use an interactive debugger or another intrusive tool to check the program. We have to compare four different execution times, being the execution time using:

1. the original TreadMarks library;

2. the instrumented library with record & replay switched off: the library works the same way as the original, except that each message is four bytes longer and that the mode (record, replay or nothing) is checked at each operation. Comparing this time with 1 will give us an idea about the cost of exchanging the Lamport clocks between the different computers and the time needed to check the mode (*send*);

3. the instrumented library, record phase: comparing this time with the time in 2 will give us an idea about the time it takes to calculate the new Lamport clocks (*calc*) and to write to disk (*disk*). It is interesting to make a distinction between these two because, supposing the buffer is large enough to hold all the Lamport clocks, *calc* will be distributed over the total program run and *disk* will occur when the program finishes. In TreadMarks a processor notifies his arrival at the end of the program using a special barrier operation (Tmk_exit). As *disk* occurs after this barrier, it won't perturbate the program execution (see Fig. 8). Therefore, we measured the overhead for two different cases:

   (a) writing to disk;

   (b) writing to /dev/null.

If we write the log files to /dev/null instead of to disk, *disk* will be nearly zero and we will measure *calc*. This will give us an idea about the minimal program

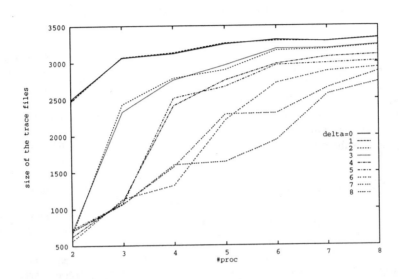

Figure 6. Optimised method: size of the trace files (in bytes) in function of the number of processors, for different values of delta.

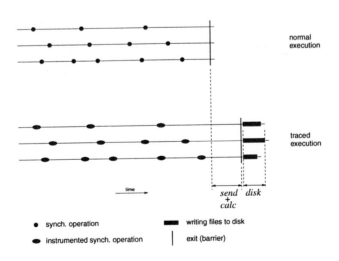

Figure 8. The total overhead is the sum of the overhead introduced by sending additional information and calculating the new Lamport clocks (*send + calc*), and the overhead introduced while writing to disk (*disk*).

library	mode	avg (s)	min-max (s)	*send* (s)	*calc* (s)	*file* (s)
original	-	43.9439	42.9-46.1	-	-	-
instrumented	normal	43.9675	42.7-47.7	0.0236	-	-
	record to /dev/null	44.0625	42.8-47.8	0.0236	0.0950	-
	record to file	44.1976	42.8-47.5	0.0236	0.0950	0.1351

Table 1. The overhead caused by the replay method.

perturbation caused by the record mechanism: when the buffer is large enough to hold all clocks;

4. the instrumented library, replay phase: as the Lamport clocks are re-executed during the replay phase and additional synchronisation is added, comparing this time with 3 will give us information about the cost of the extra synchronisation.

As the overhead is very small, the test program was changed in order to perform meaningful tests. The main loop of the program is executed ten times longer than the original, and all non-synchronisation operations are removed from the loop. Table 1 shows that the overhead is very small. Writing the buffers to file causes the largest overhead. As mentioned before, when we make the buffers large enough to hold all logged timestamps, this won't perturbate the program execution.

6. Conclusions

This paper showed that it is necessary to use a replay method if one wishes to use cyclic debugging techniques for the debugging of non-deterministic parallel programs. An efficient implementation of the ROLT method for TreadMarks was proposed and experiments showed that the method generates small trace files, and that the overhead introduced is small.

Acknowledgements

Michiel Ronsse is supported by a grant from the 'Flemish institute for the promotion of the scientific technological research in the industry (IWT)'. The work described in this paper was performed at Rice University, Houston (TX), where the author spent two months in the Department of Computer Science. He would like to thank Willy Zwaenepoel and Jan Van Campenhout for their support and advice.

References

[1] J. Gait. A probe effect in concurrent programs. *Software - Practice and Experience*, 16(3):225–233, March 1986.

[2] P. Keleher, A. L. Cox, S. Dwarkadas, and W. Zwaenepoel. Treadmarks: Distributed Shared Memory on standard workstations and operating systems. Department of Computer Science, Rice University, Houston (TX).

[3] P. Keleher, A. L. Cox, and W. Zwaenepoel. Lazy Release Consistency for Software Distributed Shared Memory. In *Proceedings of the 19th International Symposium of Computer Architecture*, pages 13–21, May 1992.

[4] L. Lamport. Time, clocks, and the ordering of events in a distributed system. *Communications of the ACM*, 21(7):558–565, July 1978.

[5] T. LeBlanc and J. Mellor-Crummey. Debugging parallel programs with Instant Replay. *IEEE Transactions on Computers*, C-36(4):471–482, April 1987.

[6] L. Levrouw, K. Audenaert, and J. Van Campenhout. A new trace and replay system for shared memory programs based on Lamport Clocks. In *Proceedings of the Second Euromicro Workshop on Parallel and Distributed Processing*, pages 471–478. IEEE Computer Society Press, January 1994.

[7] R. Netzer. Optimal tracing and replay for debugging shared-memory parallel programs. In *Proceedings ACM/ONR Workshop on Parallel and Distributed Debugging*, pages 1–11, May 1993.

[8] D. Perkovic and P. Keleher. Online Data-Race Detection via Coherency Guarantees. 1996. To appear in *Second Symposium on Operating Systems Design and Implementation (OSDI '96)*.

[9] M. Ronsse, L. Levrouw, and K. Bastiaens. Efficient coding of execution-traces of parallel programs. In J. P. Veen, editor, *Proceedings of the ProRISC/IEEE Benelux Workshop on Circuits, Systems and Signal Processing*, pages 251–258. STW, Utrecht, Mar. 1995.

Detecting Deadlock with Client-Server Analysis[1]

Innes Jelly[1], Mauro Mastroianni[2], Stefano Russo[2], Carlo Savy[2], Peter Croll[3]

[1] Computing Research Centre, Sheffield Hallam University,
Napier Street, Sheffield S11 8HD, UK
[2] Dipartimento di Informatica e Sistemistica, Università di Napoli,
Via Claudio 21, 80125 Napoli, Italy
[3]Department of Computer Science, University of Sheffield,
Portobello Road, Sheffield S1 4DP, UK

Abstract. *Client-server behaviour modelling is a heuristic technique to design a parallel software system so as to prevent the occurrence of deadlock. A client-server graph (a kind of directed graph used to express client/server relationships between processes) is a useful design aid for the application of this technique. In this paper, we use client-server graphs as a means to detect potential deadlocks in a parallel system designed with the PARSE process graph notation. The new proposed method consists into translating a given process graph into a client-server graph, and then adopting an ad hoc algorithm to detect cycles within it. This avoids visual inspection, and automatically reveals to the designer all process interactions in a PARSE design which could lead to deadlock situations.*

1. Introduction

The avoidance of deadlock is a fundamental requirement for the development of concurrent software systems. Two approaches are possible: to construct software in such a manner as to rule out the possibility of deadlock situations arising, or to carry out a post hoc verification procedure to determine if deadlock exists. There are a number of formal techniques and tools to support the latter approach, and informal heuristics to guide the designer in the former.

Client-server behaviour modelling has been shown to be a useful technique for *deadlock prevention* [1]. By constraining processes to act in a passive (server) or active (client) mode and restricting the permitted communication paths between them, deadlock freedom can be guaranteed as long as no client-server cycles exist within the graph. In this approach the designer is required to follow a set of rules which dictate the communication strategy between processes [2].

In this paper we show how client-server models can form the basis for a new method of *deadlock detection*. In this situation the designer is not constrained to develop software under strict client-server rules, but can employ the client-server concept to provide post design checks for potential deadlocks. The method involves the translation of the design into a simple client-server notation; this representation is then subjected to cycle detection analysis. The technique can be used in association with different design notations - in this paper we demonstrate its application to designs originally developed in PARSE process graph notation.

The use of PARSE process graphs to develop parallel and distributed software systems has been well established in a number of different application areas, eg [3], [4]. Previous work has demonstrated that it is possible to verify PARSE process graph designs by means of translation into Petri net formalism [5], [6]. However the use of Petri net verification presents a number of problems to the parallel software engineer. Not only is it computationally expensive for nets of realistic complexity, but the developer needs to be experienced in the analysis techniques involved. In addition when designs are translated from process based models, much of the structuring of the original design may be lost, and it becomes difficult to relate the analysis information back to the software design.

The use of client-server analysis with PARSE process graphs offers an alternative approach to design verification. We document the translation from PARSE process graphs into a client-server graph and describe the analysis methods involved. A new two stage algorithm is presented: first, redundant nodes in the client-server graph are eliminated, and this is followed by a cycle

[1] This work has been supported in part by funds from BC and CNR, and from the University of Naples under the International Collaborations Programme.

identification routine. The presence of cycles indicates the potential for deadlock and pinpoints the aspects of the design that are at fault. The effect of this algorithm is to provide deadlock analysis which is computationally more efficient than standard methods, and provides the designer with the information required to correct the design.

The paper is structured as follows: Section 2 outlines the principles of client-server behaviour modelling. Section 3 demonstrates the use of PARSE in relation to a distributed security system. In Section 4 the client-server analysis of the distributed security system is discussed, and we demonstrate how the analysis techniques reveal a number of potential deadlocks within the system.

2. Client-Server Behaviour Modelling

Directed graphs can be used to express the client-server relationships with nodes representing processes and arcs the communication paths. Each process can be represented as one of three node types, according to its behaviour. We use the notation defined in [2] to indicate the node types within client-server graphs - Figure 3 demonstrates the use of this notation.

Server nodes: These nodes can only output as a response to an input, i.e. they can never initiate an output. On the graph, servers are shown as only having arcs which converge on the node.

Client-Server nodes: This node type can both receive inputs and generate outputs. The outputs may be either in response to an external input or any independent action initiated by the client-server node itself.

Client nodes: Finally, client nodes are the opposite of server nodes, i.e. they cannot receive inputs except in response to an output generated by the client. For clients, all arcs on the graph diverge from the client nodes.

There are a number of additional necessary conditions that must be met if client-server analysis is to be used [1]. A server must guarantee to accept a client request within a finite time. The client then awaits a response, optionally carrying out additional but terminating computation, but not attempting further communication. The server guarantees to respond to the client within a bounded time, and will not accept additional client requests until the first has been serviced. In order to service the request, however, the server can act as a client to another server, in which case it behaves as a client-server.

For systems expressed in terms of these client, server, and client-server nodes, verifying the absence of cycles is sufficient to prove deadlock freedom [1], based on Hoare's notion of subordination [7].

3. PARSE Design for a Distributed Security System

3.1 PARSE Process Graphs

PARSE process graphs allow developers to describe the system in terms of a hierarchy of interacting components [8]. The process graph notation provides a simple approach to the expression of key aspects within parallel software design. It is object based, and encourages the production of reusable design classes by clear interface provision. Process objects interact by message passing on designated communication paths. Process objects belong to one of three classes: *function* and *data servers*, and *control process objects*. Function and data servers represent the passive objects in the system, and frequently describe general purpose components in the system, indicating the potential for reuse. Control process objects are responsible for coordinating and managing activity within the system and are normally application specific. Communication paths are divided into four classes indicating the manner of operation: *synchronous, asynchronous, broadcast* and *bi-directional synchronous*, the latter describing a coupled request-reply communication. In addition information about the dynamic behaviour of the system is captured with the graphical notation by the introduction of path constructors which describe the order of handling of incoming messages by process objects. Support is provided within the notation for replication of process objects and communication paths, and timing requirements for message passing can also be directly represented.

3.2 The Security System Design

The software to control a distributed security system has been developed using the PARSE method, and process graph descriptions produced [9]. The system controls access to a number of office premises; it permits authorised personnel to enter and leave, and keeps a record of all entries and exits for security and safety reasons. At each door two card readers are installed and entries and exits are checked by means of photoelectric cells at each door. Card readers and photocells are managed by a local controller connected to a central system which maintains information about the level of authorisation for each employee. The system also controls an alarm system to warn against access violations and includes procedures in the event of fire and other emergencies. There is a separate

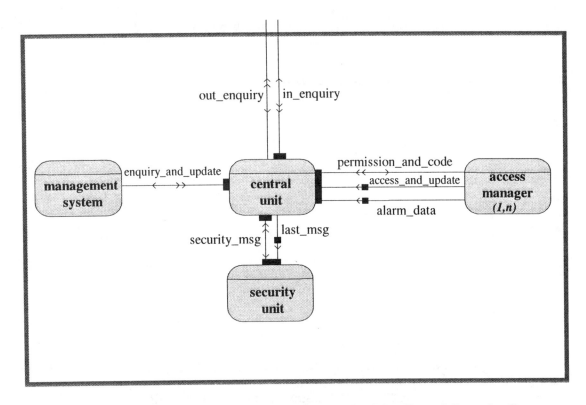

Figure 1: Top level PARSE process graph for the Distributed Security System

procedure for permitting workers from other sites and visitors to enter the premises.

Figure 1 shows the top level PARSE process graph for the software. This is replicated at each site. Figure 2 represents the decomposition of central unit process object in the second level design. The full design involves three levels and 25 process objects.

The top level comprises four process objects of the control class, indicating that there are active objects, and together coordinate the system's activities. Central unit is the basic object and contains, amongst other things, the system database and the application . It is responsible for communication with central units of the other plants of the company. This is accomplished by means of the two paths in_enquiry and out_enquiry.

The central unit also processes enquiries coming from the management system where an operator generates reports and issues queries and update requests.

The paths between the central unit and the access manager objects carry the messages for the accesses of the employees and visitors in the premises, namely the query from the access manager to check for the user's access permissions, and the database updates or the alarm messages. In these cases, the central unit acts as a *server*.

The connections with the security unit is provided in order to manage the various alarms which are generated by the access manager and routed to the alarm unit. Security_msg carries the enquiries made by security unit and the replies sent by central unit. For example, these enquiries will request display of the alarms occurred in a given interval time. On path last_msg flow the actual alarm activation signals coming from access manager.

In the second level process graph (Figure 2) central unit is decomposed into five concurrent process objects. Alarms filer and accesses filer are data servers, representing the stores of persistent information in the system. Check permission and alarm manager are function servers. Logic and database is another control process object and it is further decomposed.

Note that the incoming messages to alarms filer and accesses filer are handled by the non deterministic path constructor - the empty box attached to the process object symbol.

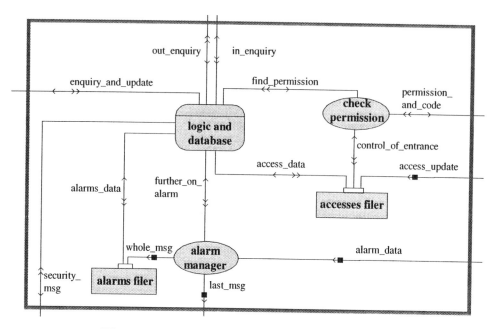

Figure 2: Decomposition of Central Unit

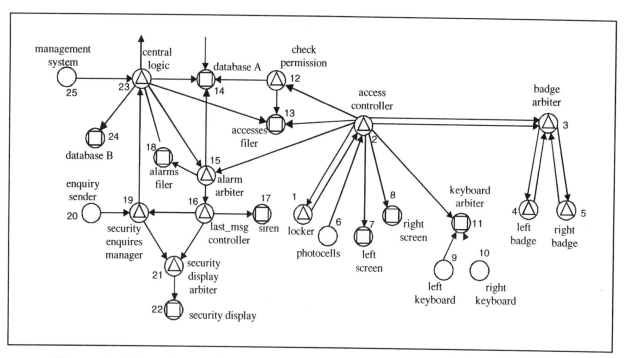

Figure 3: Client-Server Behaviour Graph for the Distributed Security System

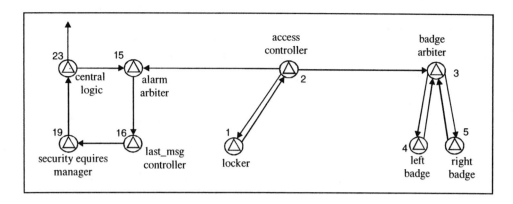

Figure 4: Client-Server Behaviour Graph of the Security System, after the First Phase

4. Client Server Analysis of the Security System

4.1 Client-Server Representation of PARSE Process Graph

Figure 3 shows the client-server graph which has been derived from the PARSE process graph of the security system. All objects are primitive objects, that is they are in their lowest level of decomposition.

To model each PARSE process object with a of C/S object, its input and output paths have been inspected. Objects having only paths coming outside them are *clients*. In the same way, objects which have only paths coming inside them are *servers*. Obviously, a data server can only be a server. Finally, objects that are neither clients nor servers are *client-server*.

Notice that the asynchronous paths (indicated with a little black square as `access_update` path shows in Figure 2) are considered in the C/S behaviour model as well. In fact, in real applications, buffers do not have infinite length and have to be considered.

4.2 Analysis of Client-Server Graphs

In order to check for client-server cycles within the graph a two phase algorithm is applied. In the first stage the graph is successively reduced until the remaining nodes are those within which cycles exist. At this stage, if nodes (and hence cycles) are still present on the graph, the second stage of the algorithm identifies where in the graph the cycles can be found.

4.2.1 Phase One - Graph Pruning

As only the presence of client-server nodes can lead to cycles, all client and server nodes are eliminated from the graph. This is an iterative process as the removal of the original client and server nodes may result in nodes which were formally of client-

server type becoming clients or servers. Equally possible, some client-server nodes are left without connections and can thus be eliminated. During this phase, any duplicated connections between nodes are simplified to a single arc. The first phase can therefore be described as follows:

> Replace duplicated connections between nodes with a single connection
> Repeat
> > Remove all client and server nodes with all associated connections
> > Remove all unconnected client-server nodes
> > Transform client-server nodes into client or server nodes if possible
> Until the graph contains only client-server nodes

The algorithm eliminates in an iterative manner all nodes which cannot form cycles. It produces a simplified graph which forms the basis for the cycle detection phase. Note that the remaining client-server nodes must *necessarily* contain at least one cycle.

Figure 4 shows the result of applying the first phase of the algorithm to the client-server graph of the security system.

The resulting client-server graph is in this instance simple enough for the developer to pinpoint immediately where the cycles exist. However not all graphs produced during the first phase of the analysis will be as straightforward to interpret, and a cycle detection routine is required for the more general case.

4.2.2 Phase Two - Cycles Detection

This part of the analysis involves consideration of each node in the simplified client-server graph. Each node is successively eliminated and its connections replaced by other paths which describe the same communication possibilities. Figure 5 shows how the original connections eliminated with their original node can be transformed. The new arcs are labeled

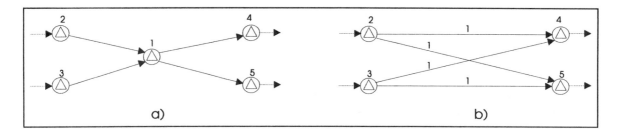

Figure 5: Removal of an Object and Creation of New Paths

with the identification of the node they replaces - in this instance node 1. As the algorithm proceeds, nodes are eliminated and arcs may receive multiple labels.

The algorithm is completed when all nodes are processed. During the elimination of the nodes, cycles are detected when an arc begins and ends at the same node.

In the proceeding of the steps that detect the cycle, some unusual situations can be met. The following second phase of the algorithm take into account these conditions and solves the net finding out the cycles:

Repeat
    Consider an object.
    If there are arcs which start and end from and to the considered object then these arcs have to be removed and a cycle is detected.
    Create as many arcs as many combinations among the input lines and output lines exist and label the arcs with the objects' number through which the arcs pass. If a new arc needs to be labeled with at least a couple of equal numbers, then do not create this arc. Eliminate the old lines.
    Eliminate the considered object along with the eventual lines that are still attached to it (these lines will be only input lines or only output lines).
Until all objects are removed.

After the execution of the second phase, the algorithm find out the three client-servers cycles existing in the C/S behaviour graph.

4.3 Analysis Results

In the case of the security system, the client-server analysis revealed cycles within the design and hence the potential for deadlock. Two of these cycles involved a classic case of direct communication between two processes (ie nodes 3 and 4, and nodes 3 and 5). This alerts the designer to ensure that correct sequencing of messages flow between the pairs of processes is required - no non deterministic exchanges

are permitted. The other cycle, among objects 15-16-19-23, which the method revealed, is more subtle, involving communication patterns between more than two processes. The cycle is not immediately detectable by a first sight of figure 3. In reworking the design to avoid deadlock, the developer will have to consider introducing a "cycle breaker" in the form of a client or server node. Obviously, the fact that a cycle exists here does not necessarily means that there will be a deadlock: it depends on the dynamic behaviour of the objects included in the cycle.

5. Conclusions

In this paper, we have described a method to detect the potential deadlock situations in a parallel software system designed with PARSE process graph notation. The method is based on the use of client-server behaviour graphs.

In client-server behaviour modelling, the absence of deadlock is guaranteed in the parallel system provided process interactions are designed according to some restricted patterns. Our post design method aims at checking this behaviour in a given process graph by translating it into a client-server graph and then using an ad hoc detection algorithm.

The proposed method supports the development of reliable software. It is more efficient than a general state space exploration approach and offers clear information to the developers on how to correct design errors. The method is easily automatable and forms the basis for an additional verification tool to be incorporated within a support framework for the PARSE methodology.

Acknowledgments

We would like to thank Carl Birkinshaw for his help in the use of client-server modelling methods.

References

[1] P Welch, G Justo and C Willcock, *"High -Level Paradigms for Deadlock-Free High-Performance Systems"*, Transputer Applications and Systems '93 Vol.2 - IOS Press (1993)

[2] C I Birkinshaw and P R Croll *"Modelling Client-Server Behaviour of Parallel Real-Time Systems Using Petri Nets"*, Proc HICSS-28, Hawaiian International Conference on System Sciences, Vol 2 (Software Technology Track), IEEE CS Press (1995)

[3] A Crookell and I E Jelly *"Development of an Industrial Real-time System using High Level Design Techniques"*, Proc Euromicro Workshop on Real-Time Systems, June 1996, L'Aquila, Italy, IEEE CS Press (1996)

[4] A Y Liu, T S Chan and I Gorton, *"Designing Distributed Multimedia Systems Using PARSE"*, Proc IFIP Workshop on Software Engineering for Parallel and Distributed Systems, April 1996, Berlin, Germany, Chapman and Hall (1996)

[5] I Gorton, I E Jelly, J P Gray and T Soon Chan *"Reliable Parallel Software Construction using PARSE"*, Concurrency: Practice and Experience Journal, March 1996

[6] S Russo, C Savy, I E Jelly and P Collingwood *"Petri net modelling of PARSE designs"*, Proc of EuroPar 96, August 1996, Lyon, France, LNCS 1123, Springer Verlag (1996)

[7] C A R Hoare *"Communicating Sequential Processes"*, Prentice-Hall International (1985)

[8] I Gorton, J P Gray and I E Jelly *"Object Based Modelling of Parallel Programs"* IEEE Parallel and Distributed Technology Journal, Vol 3, No. 2 (1995)

[9] M Mastroianni *"A Corporate Security System: A Case Study for the PARSE Methodology"*, Degree Dissertation in Computer Engineering, University of Naples, June 1996

GRADE: A Graphical Programming Environment for PVM Applications

Gábor Dózsa,   Péter Kacsuk,   Tibor Fadgyas

KFKI-MSZKI
Research Institute for Measurement and Computing Techniques
of the Hungarian Academy of Sciences
P.O.Box 49, H-1525 Budapest, Hungary
e-mail: {dozsa,kacsuk,fadgyas}@sunserv.kfki.hu

Abstract

The PVM system – which is one of the most popular message-passing interface currently – represents a low-level tool that enables to write parallel programs but misses the high-level support which could make this work acceptable easy and efficient. To provide high-level graphical support for PVM based program development, a complex programming environment (GRADE) is being developed. GRADE provides tools to construct, execute, debug and visualise message-passing parallel programs. GRADE offers the programmer the same graphical user interface during the whole development process. This paper deals with the graphical program editor and the post-mortem visualising tool in details.

1. Introduction

A number of MP interfaces are available today, but one of the most popular is the PVM software package. PVM stands for Parallel Virtual Machine[7]. PVM permits a user to configure his own virtual computer by hooking together a heterogeneous collection of UNIX based machines, on which the user has a valid login and are accessible over some network. The user views PVM as a loosely coupled distributed memory computer programmed in C or FORTRAN with message-passing extensions. PVM may be configured to contain various machine architectures including sequential processors, vector processors, multicomputers, etc. PVM provides a low-level interface that enables to write and execute parallel applications but misses high-level supports which could make this work acceptable easy and efficient. In the framework of SEPP [14] and HPCTI

Copernicus projects, a complex programming environment (GRADE) is being developed to assist the development of parallel programs based on the message-passing paradigm.

GRADE stands for GRaphical Design Environment and currently consists of the following tools as main components:

- GRED: A graphical editor to write parallel applications

- GRP2C: A precompiler to produce the C code of the graphical program. This C code contains the necessary PVM function calls.

- DDBG: A distributed debugger [3]

- Tape/PVM: A monitoring tool to generate trace file during execution of the PVM application [11] (developed independently at LMC-IMAG, Grenoble, France).

- PROVE: A visualisation tool to analyse and interpret the Tape/PVM trace file information and present them to the programmer graphically.

The scheme of the program development cycle in GRADE is depicted in Fig. 1. Different software tools that comprise the system are denoted by rectangles (GRED, DDBG, etc.) Ovals represent data files used by GRADE. As a first step the user applies the GRED graphical editor to design and construct the parallel program written in a special graphical programming language called GRAPNEL. The GRED editor creates the so-called GRP file from the GRAPNEL program. The GRP file contains all the information necessary to restore the program graph for further editing and

358

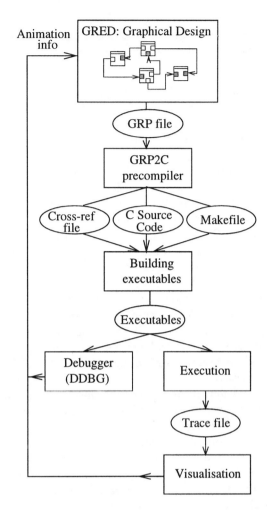

Figure 1. Program Development in GRADE.

2. The GRED editor

In GRADE, parallel programs can be constructed according to the syntax and semantics of GRAPNEL [9] language by using the GRED editor. GRED is built on the top of the UNIX X-Window system. The code is written in C++ and the Interviews 3.1 library is applied to program the X interface.

As the first step in the development cycle, the programmer must write the code of the parallel application. We state that at this phase graphics are needed to provide high-level support and abstraction mechanism. In the design and implementation of parallel programs the user is often encouraged to specify computational issues by drawing graphs and to take these drawings into consideration when he wants to track the run-time behaviour of the application. A good example of such a computational issue can be the process communication graph. It's no use making these drawings with paper and pencil when it is possible to draw them by using a comfortable and intelligent graphical program editor. However, there are program parts which nobody wants to draw, e.g. sequential functions or procedures that have nothing to do with message-passing or multiprocessing at all. It is only the outline of the parallel code which is worth being described by graphics; the low level details are more concise and more comfortable to be defined in ordinary textual way. That is the main idea behind the GRAPNEL language. Processes, communication operations and communication connections must be described graphically, while low-level code of the processes can be written in C (or in FORTRAN in the future). A graphical outline of the application can facilitate the work of the programmer in the design phase as well as in the debugging and performance tuning phases. In the design phase, structured code can be written – or better to say, can be drawn – above the level of individual processes (i.e. above the level of C 'main' functions) by grouping processes which can be viewed as one unit into one node, or by using predefined communication topology templates. During the debugging or performance tuning phase, the programmer has the global view of message-passing related part of the application, where the errors or the bottlenecks can be spotted much faster then having and observing only the textual code of several processes using ordinary text editors and debuggers.

Due to the lack of space, we just summarize here the main ideas behind the graphical language and the functionalities of the GRED editor. The exact definition of the language elements can be found in [9].

to compile the GRAPNEL program into a C+PVM code. The latter is the task of the GR2PC precompiler which additionally creates other auxiliary files including makefiles used by the UNIX make utility for building the executables. The executable code is loaded to the processors and is executed either in debugging mode or trace mode. In debugging mode, the DDBG distributed debugger controls the execution of the program by providing commands to create breakpoints, step-by-step execution, animation, etc. In trace mode, a trace file is generated containing all the trace events defined by the user. These events are visualized by the PROVE graphical visualization tool assisting the user in spotting performance bottlenecks in the GRAPNEL programs.

In the current paper we describe the GRED graphical editor and the PROVE visualisation tool. Other components of the system are just mentioned briefly and references are given to their detailed descriptions.

2.1. The GRAPNEL Programming Model

The GRAPNEL programming model is entirely based on the message-passing paradigm. The programmer can define processes performing computations independently and interacting only by sending and receiving messages. A process can be either a single unit, or a member of a process group. A process group is an ordered collection of processes. Both processes and process groups are defined graphically as boxes. Process groups can be used in two important ways. Firstly, they can be used to specify the scope of a collective communication operation, such as multicast (i.e. a message can be received by all members of a group). Secondly, they can be used as an abstraction mechanism to support structured design at the level of processes, i.e. processes can be put into a group to be managed together as one unit. Since process groups can be nested, they support hierarchical design. Communications among processes are either point-to-point or group communications and they always takes place via communication ports. Ports can belong either to processes or process groups and they are connected by channels. To ensure that the form of the transmitted data matches at both the sender and receiver sides, each port has its own protocol. Inside the processes, send and receive operations are represented graphically, and they are joined with the port symbols on which the communication operations are to take place. The user can define the data to be sent or received by simple listing the names of the program variables where the data should be stored or should come from.

In GRAPNEL programs, three hierarchical design levels are distinguished. At the top level the outline of the whole application is described graphically with respect to communication connections among the processes, while at lowest level the textual code fragments are given (remember, that GRAPNEL is a hybrid language). At the middle level the send and receive operations are defined inside the code of a process graphically. Accordingly, GRED provides three different types of window to support the program development in GRAPNEL.

1. *Application window* It is for constructing the application level of the program (i.e. to create the process communication graph).

2. *Process window* This window aids to define or modify the graphical structure of individual processes with respect to the communication operations.

3. *Text window* It is used to write or modify the tex-

tual contents of the graphical icons. At the moment, it is simple a text editor.

A sample GRADE session is depicted in Figure 2 to illustrate these windows in practice. Their main features are summarized as follows.

2.2. Application Window

The window offers several functionalities to manipulate processes and communication connections (i.e. the communication graph) graphically. The programmer can create new processes as icons, name them, delete them or move them to new positions in the window. A process appears as a rectangle symbol with caption (i.e. the name of the process) at this level. The user can create new communication ports as well, which are represented by a square symbol clung to the border of process symbols. A communication channel can be created by joining two ports. Ports are arranged around the processes automatically to ensure the best possible layout of the communication channels (i.e. to minimize channels' crossings).

The locations of the processes in the application window are controlled explicitly by the programmer. We have considered the possibility of implementing different graph layout algorithms to generate nice layout for the process communication graph automatically. However, we have decided to neglect such algorithms because considering a number of parallel applications we found that if there are large number of processes in the application then the processes are always arranged with small number of particular topologies, like process farm, ring, mesh, hypercube, etc. Therefore, GRAP-NEL provides graphical process topology templates instead of general graph layout algorithms. The process group abstraction mechanism also aids to reduce the complexity of the graph by allowing the user to construct structured hierarchical communication graphs. Although the concepts of groups and templates have been elaborated in the GRAPNEL language [9], the current version of the editor does not support them yet. The editor will have been equipped with these facilities by the end of the SEPP project.

2.3. The Process Window

In this window, the message-passing related part of the process's control flow is constructed graphically. The point is that communication operations (i.e. send, receive) must appear graphically in the process's code. In this way, the underlying message-passing library, which means the PVM system currently, can be hidden from the programmer, i.e he/she does not have to know the syntax of PVM functions such 'packing' or 'unpacking' routines, buffer management, etc. Actually, no PVM functions are written in the GRAPNEL code at all. They are generated by the GRP2C precompiler automatically based on the graphical language elements and the textual code belonging to those graphical elements, e.g. name of the program variables where the data to be received should be stored. This technique also allows that all message transfers can be animated graphically in debugging and visualising phase which can ease significantly the identification of message-passing related bugs in the program. However, only those segments of the control flow must appear graphically which contain send or receive actions. The textual block symbol is defined for denoting an arbitrary large and sophisticated textual code fragment that does not contain any send or receive action, so which can be defined textually at a lower level (i.e. text code level).

The layout of the control flow graph is fully supervised by the editor. The programmer is not permitted to draw control lines himself or to change the locations of program items "by hand". Instead, he can choose a control line segment and the editor will split this segment and place the new program item here automatically. This mechanism ensures that only syntactically correct control flows can be drawn.

The exact list of the graphical program elements available to construct the code of a process can be found in [9].

The process window provides cut-copy-paste functionalities to assists the programmer in editing the graphical code. Graphical symbols can be selected and cut from the code or copied to new location. If the control flow graph tends to be too large (i.e. the whole graph does not fit the window) the programmer can use the scroll and zoom facilities to focus on the currently interesting part of the graph. Moreover, the so called graphical block symbol can be applied as an abstraction mechanism to construct layered graphical control flow (i.e. subgraphs of the control flow can be put into a graphical block so they will appear as a single icon in the process window).

2.4. The Text Editor Window

Each GRAPNEL program item defined in the process window (e.g. text block) – except for the graphical block – possesses an appropriate piece of C code fragment. The programmer can write such a textual code fragment by opening a textual window for that graphical symbol. The textual window is a simple text editor currently. The text editor that is invoked by

GRED to edit these text parts of the program can be defined by the user through UNIX environment variables (i.e. without recompiling the system). As a result, the programmer may use his favorite text editor (e.g. emacs, vi, etc.) in GRED. An example for a textual window (Worker11:Init) is depicted in Figure 2.

3. Compiling the GRAPNEL programs

The programmer can save the code of his application into the so called GRP file. It is a text file, which contains all the information necessary to restore the graphical program in the GRED editor, or to produce the executables. The executables are generated in two steps. In the first step, the pure C code of the GRAPNEL program is generated by the GRP2C precompiler. Afterwards, a standard C compiler is invoked to produce the executable binaries from the C code. Both steps can be performed from the application window of the editor. Detailed description of the GRP2C precompiler can be found in [5].

After building the executables, the programmer can start the PVM daemons on the hosts and execute his parallel program through the menu system of GRADE.

4. Animation and debugging of GRAPNEL programs

GRED provides a high level interface for on-line debugging of GRAPNEL programs. The programmer can debug the application in exactly the same environment where it was constructed. Moreover, in the design of GRAPNEL language we particularly focused on the debugging aspects (i.e. the graphical outline of the program is extremely useful to locate communication related errors). For this purpose GRADE uses the services provided by the DDBG (Distributed DeBuGger [3]), which applies a process-level debugger to supervise tasks of PVM applications at its lowest level. DDBG defines a set of C functions that can be embedded into other systems in the same way as it has happened in case of GRADE. The architecture of DDBG is described in [3].

GRADE offers an user-friendly interface that allows to invoke debugging commands with reference to the graphical entities that are displayed in the user windows. The information on specific debugging commands is directly related to the GRAPNEL source program, e.g. by highlighting corresponding entities in the graphical representation, and their corresponding lines of source code in the textual program representation. More about this topic can be read in [5].

Application Level

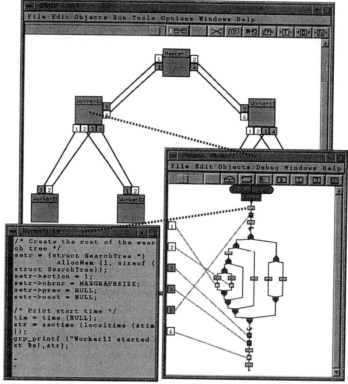

Text Code Level   **Process Level**

Figure 2. A Sample GRADE Session

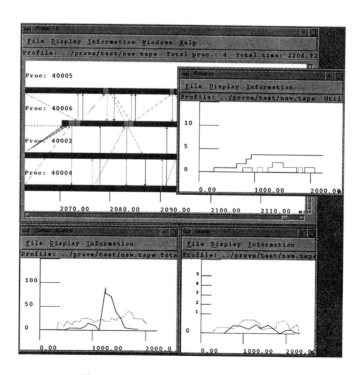

Figure 3. A Sample PROVE Session

5. The Tape/PVM Monitoring Tool

Tape/PVM is a tool to generate event traces of PVM applications for post-mortem performance analysis. Though Tape/PVM is integrated into the GRADE environment, it has been developed independently from the SEPP/HPCTI project, at LMC-IMAG, Grenoble, France.

Tape/PVM generates events at user application level by intercepting the original PVM library calls. A preprocessor is provided to instrument the user source code (C or FORTRAN) automatically, i.e. to exchange every PVM library call for the corresponding Tape/PVM call. Tape/PVM allows selective tracing; i.e. the user can specify before executing the instrumented code what kind of PVM calls he wants to be monitored. Moreover, the programmer can define additional events (i.e. user defined events) beside the PVM related ones.

6. Visualisation by PROVE

6.1. Generals

PROVE is a performance visualisation tool. It is an adaptation of the PACVIS [6] system for distributed memory computers[1]. PROVE is a post-mortem tool which reads the information from a tracefile that was generated during the application run by the help of the TAPE/PVM monitoring system. The TAPE/PVM system generates an event (i.e. a record in the trace file) whenever a PVM function call occurs. Additionally, the GRADE system also defines its own events related to the entering into sequential or communication blocks.

PROVE uses the X11 facilities and the OSF/Motif widget set for displaying the required information. All required default values and constants (colors, default sizes, button names etc.) can be customized via X11 application resources. The most important features can also be selected by command line arguments. Fig. 3 depicts a sample PROVE session.

PROVE has several windows that display two-dimensional graphs (where the horizontal axis is always the time axis):

1. **Behavior Window:** Displays the processes, their different states, interactions, start (spawn) and terminate events, communication events and ports, user marks, etc.

---

[1]PACVIS supports the shared memory model.

2. **Processor Window:** Displays the utilization of the processors (i.e. PVM hosts) during the runtime of the application program.

3. **Communication Window:** Displays the communication among the **processes**, especially the rates and the amount of data transferred between the processes.

4. **Hosts Window:** Displays the communication among the **hosts**, especially the rates and the amount of data transferred between the host computers (processors).

6.2. The Behavior Window of PROVE

The **Behavior Window** is the central window of the PROVE tool and it is created on the startup of the program. The behavior graph is a two-dimensional representation of the program run. The horizontal axis represents the execution time while the executed processes are arranged along the vertical axis. Each process is represented by a horizontal line that shows the time during which the process was executed by a processor. The thick horizontal lines have several sections coloured differently showing the stages of the process (e.g. computation, communication, etc.). The number of processes and the total program runtime are displayed at the top of the window.

By default, only the process lines are displayed. However, some additional amount of information can be selected:

- **Start:** shows the new process creation. An arrow (black) starts from the parent process to the child process.

- **Stop:** shows when a process kills another process. A black arrow starts from the killer process to the victim process.

- **Wait:** the wait (blocked receive) dependencies are displayed by red arrows between the waiting process and the process waited for.

- **Send:** the data delivery is displayed by green arrows between the sender and receiver processes.

- **Ports:** as an additional information to the send/receive arrows the port numbers are also displayed. A port number appears inside a small rectangle attached to the horizontal bar of the sending/receiving process.

- **Mark:** the time marks created by the user are shown by blue vertical lines in the graph.

All these layers of information can be independently switched on and off and arbitrarily combined. The user can select/deselect specific communication events because they are assigned to different PVM message tags. Additionally, moving the mouse pointer within the graph lets the user zoom (i.e. enlarge) rectangular subsections of the graph.

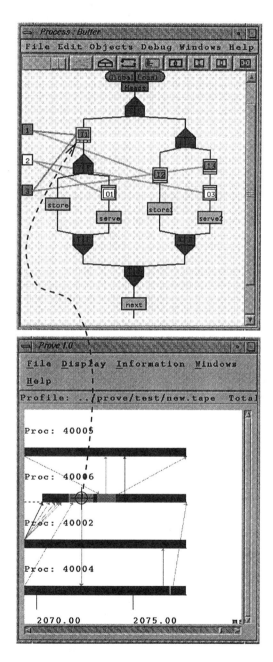

Figure 4. Animation by GRED and PROVE

6.3. The Animation Feature of PROVE

Although PROVE can be used as a stand alone visualizing tool for analyzing communications, performance issues, its animation feature requires the GRED editor. Typically, the user controls the whole application development (e.g. editing, compiling, running, debugging, visualizing, ... etc.) from the GRED's main window. So, when the user investigates the previous run of the application by PROVE, most of the cases the application is loaded into the GRED editor as well.

To understand the application behavior in the PROVE's **Behavior Window** at a specific time interval, the user frequently needs to identify which code fragment was executed at that time. By the help of the animation feature a single mouse click in the **Behavior Window** causes the relevant source code block to be highlighted in the GRED's **Process Window**. (See Fig. 4.)

The user is supposed to position the cursor to the level of the process in focus and to the relevant section of the process's horizontal bar and then to make a click with the right mouse button. From the position of the cursor in the **Behavior Window** PROVE finds the actual process (based on the vertical coordinate) and the actual block in the process (based on the time coordinate). First PROVE identifies the reference code of the block that was executed at that time, then sends an animation message which comprises the name of the process and the reference number of the active block. As a reaction to the message, the GRED editor opens a process window (if it was not already open) displaying the process and highlights the icon belonging to the specified reference code.

By the help of this feature the user can easily identify the relevant source code objects meanwhile he/she investigates the program behavior by PROVE. According to our experience it significantly reduces the time spent on debugging or performance tuning.

7. Related Works

A number of other visual parallel programming language and environment have been developed (e.g. HENCE [2],CODE [12], PSEE [10], Paralex [1], TRAPPER [13]). Most of them are based upon the idea that nodes represent computation, and arcs represent interactions (of some form) among nodes. The problem with the HENCE, CODE, Paralex and PSEE approaches is that they force computations to be split into separate nodes when communications occur or when branching decisions control communications (i.e. some kind of dataflow approach). This can result in complicated, awkward and large graphs. This problem does not arise in TRAPPER, which system is very close to GRADE concerning both purpose and functionality. However, the TRAPPER model is static as it has originally been designed for transputer systems and it does not offer an integrated debugger for on-line debugging and animating in the same graphical environment that was used to design the code.

In GRADE, all communication activities can be defined graphically without any restriction concerning their locations. Dynamic process creation and predefined topology templates are going to be implemented based on the definition of GRAPNEL language. Furthermore, the programmer can design and debug his/her parallel application by using the same graphical user interface and abstraction mechanism. Program tuning is supported by PROVE visualisation tool which cooperates with the same graphical user interface as well.

8. Conclusions

The more people encounter the possibility to exploit the available computational power of heterogeneous networks of computer, the more vital is the demand for high-level tools to assists the development of message-passing-based parallel applications. GRADE provides a complex programming environment where the user can develop his parallel program by using high level tools and abstractions without worrying about the low-level details of message-passing primitives.

The first evaluation of the GRADE environment revealed the modifications and extensions that are necessary to make it really comfortable and useful for parallel program development. We plan to implement a replay mechanism and to integrate a simulation tool ([4]). FORTRAN is to be supported to write the textual program parts of the application as well as MPI [8] for low level message-passing interface. Furthermore, the GRED editor will be equipped with dynamic features and predefined communication topology templates.

9. Acknowledgment

This work is partly funded by the Commission of European Communities Contract Num: CIPA-C193-0251, CP-93-5383 and by the Hungarian National Committee for Technological Development (OMFB) in the framework of Austrian-Hungarian inter governmental cooperation under Project Num: B.52.

References

[1] O. Babaoglu, L. Alvisi, A. Amoroso, and R. Davoli. Paralex: An environment for parallel programming in distributed systems. In *Proc. of ACM International Conference on Supercomputing*, 1992.

[2] A. Beguelin, J. Dongarra, G. Geist, and V. Sunderam. Visualization and debugging in a heterogeneous environment. *IEEE Computer*, 26(6), June 1993.

[3] J. C. Cunha, J. Lourenco, and T. Antao. A debugging engine for parallel and distributed environment. In *Proc. of 1st Austrian-Hungarian Workshop on Distributed and Parallel Systems, Miskolc, Hungary, October 2-4*, pages 111–118, 1996.

[4] T. Delaitre, G. Justo, F. Spies, and S. Winter. Simulation modelling of parallel systems. In *Proc. of 1st Austrian-Hungarian Workshop on Distributed and Parallel Systems, Miskolc, Hungary, October 2-4*, pages 25–32, 1996.

[5] G. Dózsa, P. Kacsuk, and T. Fadgyas. Development of graphical parallel programs in pvm environments. In *Proc. of 1st Austrian-Hungarian Workshop on Distributed and Parallel Systems, Miskolc, Hungary, October 2-4*, pages 625–643, 1996.

[6] T. Fadgyas and W. Schreiner. Visualization of parallel programs: The pacvis visualization tool. In *Proc. of the 2nd Austrian-Hungarian Workshop on Transputer Applications, Budapest*, pages 43–61, 1994.

[7] A. Geist, A. Beguelin, J. Dongarra, W. Jiang, R. Manchek, and V. S. Sunderam. *Parallel Virtual Machine – A Users' Guide and Tutorial for Networked Parallel Computing*. MIT Press, London, 1994.

[8] W. Gropp, E. Lusk, and A. Skjellum. *Using MPI : Portable Parallel Programming with the Message-Passing Interface*. MIT Press, London, 1994.

[9] P. Kacsuk, G. Dózsa, and T. Fadgyas. Designing parallel programs by the graphical language grapnel. *Microprocessing and Microprogramming*, 41:625–643, 1996.

[10] E. Luque, R. Suppi, and J. Sorribes. Overview and new trend on psee (parallel system evaluation. *IEEE Software*, 1992.

[11] E. Maillet. Issues in performance tracing with tape/pvm. In *Proc. of EuroPVM'95, Lyon*, pages 143–148, 1995.

[12] P. Newton and J. Browne. The code 2.0 graphical parallel programming language. In *Proc. of ACM International Conference on Supercomputing*, 1992.

[13] C. Scheidler and L. Schafers. Trapper: A graphical programming environment for industrial high-performance applications. In *Proc. of PARLE'93: Parallel Architectures and Languages Europe, Munich, Germany*, 1993.

[14] S. Winter and P. Kacsuk. Software engineering for parallel processing. In *Proc. of 8th Symp. on Microcomputer and Microprocessor Applications, Budapest*, pages 285–293, 1994.

❖ OPEN FORUM SESSION 3 ❖

Chair

B. Di Martino

A High-Level Programming Environment for Distributed Memory Architectures[*]

W. K. Giloi and A. Schramm

RWCP Massively Parallel Systems GMD Laboratory
at the GMD Research Institute for Computer Architecture and Software Technology

Abstract

The ultimate solution to the programming difficulties of parallel computers will be abstract, application-oriented programming paradigms, supported by parallelizing compilers that hide the low-level issues of optimal data distribution, communication, and thread coordination from the user. The Promoter programming system described in the paper presents such a high-level model. Promoter reconciles easiness and expressiveness by the concept of high-level data parallelism, leading to a system of distributed types with parallel operations. The model enables the user to describe the logical spatial structure of a wide spectrum of numerical and non-numerical application in a simple, uniform algebraic formalism that enables the compiler to efficiently map the problem onto the target platform. A first version has been implemented as C++ extension.

Key words: Message-passing architectures, programming models, high-level data parallelism, application-oriented topologies, distributed types, abstract communication and coordination, parallelizing compiler, optimized mapping

1. Introduction

Scalable, distributed memory parallel architectures have the potential of providing any desired performance at maximum cost-effectiveness. However, these advantages will only then be generally utilized if the programming difficulties with such machines are overcome. Existing parallel programming models such as *message-passing* or *shared memory* reflect the manner in which the machine works rather than the nature of the application.

Specifically, message-passing programming is considered difficult, for it burdens the programmer with the tasks of data distribution, inter thread communication, and coordination of thread execution. Some computer architecture schools see the solution to the programming problem on distributed memory machines in the provision of a global address space that allows the use of the shared memory paradigm. Ingenious software or hardware solutions—e.g., the *virtual shared memory architecture* [1] or *the distributed shared memory architecture* [2]— have been developed to make a distributed memory architecture look like a shared memory machine. However, the price for the seeming programming convenience is a significant increase in software overhead or hardware cost, respectively. Moreover, if performance is an issue (which it almost always is), shared memory programming is not really much easier than message passing. Because of the large variation in latency between local and remote data accesses, data distribution remains as optimization issue, and the replacement of sequential consistency by more efficient weaker consistency models mandates data access synchronization. Yet there is even a more serious argument against the global address space solution: Pointers as technique to construct spatial structures—though a most flexible approach—fail entirely to express any high-level structural information.

A step in the right direction has been the creation of *data parallel languages* and compilers for them, the best-known example being High Performance Fortran (HPF) [3]. HPF provides the user with control over data alignment yet hides the concrete communication activities from the programmer. Parallel processing takes the form of *loop parallelization*. However, because of the rigid array structures, irregular structures can be expressed only through indirect indexing, an approach that degrades the array from a structure-preserving concept to a mere memory heap, that is, to the level of pointers.

In our opinion, what is needed are high-level programming models and parallelizing compilers that allow the user to formulate a parallel program in terms of application-specific concepts, while low-level issues such as optimal data distribution and coordination of the parallel threads is handled by the compiler. Specifically, the model must provide expressive means for defining explicitly all kinds of application-specific data structures,

[*] This work was supported by the Real World Computing Partnership, Japan

array-like or hierarchical, static or dynamic, regular or irregular.

Such a high-level programming environment is *Promoter* (<u>pro</u>gramming <u>mo</u>del <u>t</u>o <u>e</u>nable <u>r</u>eal-world computing). Promoter allows the user to program in an application-oriented abstract formalism rather than for a particular architecture. The wide semantic gap between the abstract formalism and the executing platform is closed by the compiler, and the issues of data distribution, communication, and coordination are hidden.

The paper is organized as follows. Chapter 2 gives an overview over the Promoter programming model. Chapter 3 illustrates by examples what new language types are needed and how they are used. Chapter 4 describes briefly the specific features of the Promoter programming environment. The paper ends with a conclusion.

2. The Promoter programming model

2.1 Objectives of the Promoter development

Promoter [4,5,6] is a programming environment designed to
- enable its user to program massively parallel applications at a high level of abstraction
- for a large variety of applications and solution algorithms
- in a machine independent manner.

The underlying abstract machine must be sufficiently flexible to deal with not just arrays but also hierarchic and other structures such as trees, graphs, etc. In most numeric applications spatial structures are motivated geometrically (e.g., PDE solving), whereas in non-numeric applications spatial structures typically are hierarchic; and there may be structures that combine both aspects (e.g., in multi-level methods). While regular spatial structures are defined by construction rules, there may be no rules in the case of a highly irregular structure, leaving the enumeration of its constituents as the only recourse.

The universality of the Promoter programming environment may result in many differing parallel program threads, as opposed to the SPMD (<u>s</u>ingle *program* - <u>m</u>ultiple <u>d</u>ata) execution model in simple data parallelism. On the other hand, we want to stay away from the MIMD model of unrestricted asynchronous execution, since at the current state of the art neither a human programmer nor a compiler is able to individually coordinate a large multitude of totally asynchronous threads. This dichotomy is resolved by restricting MIMD so that the individual scheduling of threads is replaced by some global coordination such that *local autonomy of thread execution* is maintained. We call this the *GC-MIMD* (<u>g</u>lobally <u>c</u>oordinated <u>MIMD</u>) execution mode.

2.2 High-level data parallelism

In contrast to the common understanding of data parallelism (e.g., as in HPF), we exploit in Promoter a more universal, polymorphic form of parallelism which we call *high-level data parallelism*, for homogeneity of data domains and temporal coordination may exist only at a sufficiently high level of abstraction. In this model, parallel algorithms are described by their temporal and spatial structures under the following assumptions:
- there is always *some* form of temporal coherence and coordination, however loose;
- within each unit of temporal coherence there exists spatial homogeneity of the individual parallel operations;
- at lower levels of abstraction there may be spatial heterogeneity and/or temporal incoherence.

In the high-level data parallelism paradigm, programs are written at a level at which the data types look homogeneous, whereas local differences in thread execution may evolve at run time. That is, we have a global uniformity "in the large", from which deviations may be given on a finer time scale. Although the nominally same method is called in the points of a domain or subdomain, there may be local differences at run time in the method body. This is obtained by local control flow autonomy and object-oriented polymorphism.

In the Promoter language, the individual threads that are handled by one global control flow appear as object-parallel statements and expressions. Hence, thread execution is subjected to some *coordination scheme* in which the individual thread executions proceed collectively yet with meaningful variations of synchronization requirements, e.g., as in lock-step, wave front, or other synchronization patterns. The global control flow may consist of any combination of parallel atomic steps on distributed variables such as loops, operations on non-distributed variables, reduction expressions, etc.

2.3 Topologies

The application-specific *domain of computation* consists of a set of spatially distributed discrete points. We call the spatial distribution a *topology*. All data are arranged in the form of such a (virtual) topology. In each point of the topology, a *program thread* is to be executed. The embedding of these threads in a common control flow ensures a coordinated program behavior in all data points. This model implies the following characteristics. (i) *Spatial homogeneity* allows the use of distributed types (variables and functions) defined on the topology of the application. (ii) Data structure objects are not restricted to arrays but may readily be trees or other hierarchic structures. (iii) Parallel computation means to process all the elements of the potentially large data structures in one step.

2.4 The structured universe

Promoter satisfies the requirements postulated above by its novel *structured universe* approach [6]. In this approach, domains of computation are created as finite, possibly irregular and dynamic substructures of a regular, static, possibly infinite universe.

A universe is an index domain with group property. There are two ends of the spectrum: Abelian groups for arrays and free groups for trees. Other structures may have commutativity properties somewhere between these extremes, and they may combine geometric and hierarchical aspects (e.g., multi-level grids). The generators of such groups formalize the notion of a nearest neighbor relationship. Actual application-specific *topologies* may be arbitrary data clusters embedded in the (static) universe. That is, topologies are substructures that inherit the geometric properties of their universe.

The index space of a distributed variable, say x, is split into the subdomain containing the interesting, i.e., non-zero element values, the *support* of x, and the (generally infinite) uninteresting rest. The support must be finite, otherwise it can be any subset of the index domain. This constitutes a polymorphism of spatial structure. Whatever the support of a distributed value, it is always a subset of the universe that inherits its geometric structure. Hence, distributed types offer the geometric expressiveness of indexable structures for problem-specific index domains. Because of the polymorphism of supports, distributed types provide the same flexibility as pointers and recursive types, albeit by different means. Figure 1 shows an example of the embedding of an irregular two-dimensional finite element mesh into a three-dimensional index space.

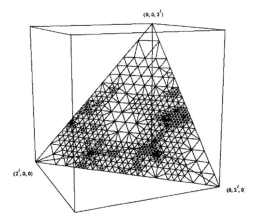

Figure 2 Embedding of a two-dimensional finite element mesh in a three-dimensional universe

Because of their Cartesian-product nature, distributed types do not impose any hierarchy on the data points. Arbitrarily different data hierarchies, partitions, and coverings can be formulated as collections of subsets of the universe. The interpretation of spatial structures is an issue of the individual operation and not of the type itself. The group structure of the type itself (given by its universe) merely provides the geometric framework for expressing topologies. Topologies may be dynamic and combine regular and irregular aspects (e.g., multi-level linear solver for a dynamically adaptive discretization of an irregular domain). Topologies must be *explicitly* described, yet at a *problem-specific level*.

2.5 Abstract domain topologies

The set of data points of a domain is represented in the object-oriented Promoter programming model by a *data structure object* **O** with topology **T**, and computations on it are represented by methods (functions) replicated over **T**. A class of data structure objects and the methods applicable to them form a *distributed type*. Hence, a distributed type expresses the topology (logical spatial structure) of the application, thus enabling the compiler to optimally map the topology onto a given target platform.

Topologies are subsets of $\mathbf{Z}^n$, with $\mathbf{Z}$ being the set of integer numbers or, more generally speaking, subsets of a finitely generated group. They are viewed geometrically, thus appealing to the user's imagination, yet described algebraically by index expressions. Index expressions belong to the algebraic structure of groups.

Topologies may be regular or irregular, dense or sparse, static or dynamic. Irregular topologies are obtained by adding constraints to the index expressions (simple examples are given below). The methods for specifying dynamic topologies are discussed in Section 3.2.

2.6 The view of communication

Communication is viewed in each data point as the observation of the states of some other points. States reside in distributed variables; hence, "observation of state" means a call (by value) of elements of distributed variables. This frees the programmer from having to call communication constructs. Each element of a distributed object resides in a logical address space of its own. Pointers exist only in the scope of a thread (since the language is an extension of C++) but are not provided as vehicle of communication between threads. This approach offers the simplicity of the shared memory model, yet it is free of side-effects and, thus, safer.

Data domains and communication patterns are both expressed by the same concept, viz. the specification of topologies. Communication topologies are relations in which the pairs denote communicating points. A data topology and the communication topology defined on it jointly form a directed graph whose nodes are the data points and whose edges are the communication relation. Any application-specific data structure–e.g. grids or trees– is represented by such a graph. The flexibility of the underlying graph structure is the key to Promoter's flexibility in expressing application-specific data structures. Moreover, it readily allows the specification of different communication topologies on the same data topology, thus providing an easy way of formulating multi-grid methods.

2.7 Thread coordination

In contrast to the common message-passing model, thread coordination is separated from communication. In Promoter, the user implicitly specifies thread coordination simply by choosing the appropriate *coordination scheme*, which is then automatically carried out by the system. Examples of coordination schemes are:

- lock-step synchronization
- wave fronts
- asynchronous iterations
- chaotic iteration

Figure 2 illustrates as a case in point the coordination scheme of *asynchronous iteration*.

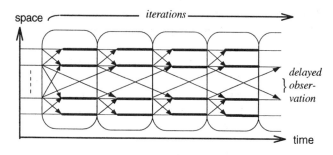

Figure 2 Asynchronous iteration [6]

Asynchronous iteration plays an important role in applications where non-determinism is allowed such that the observed states in an iteration step may be values of a previous step rather than the actual ones, without jeopardizing the convergence of the iteration (though convergence may be slower). This case permits a high degree of autonomy of the individual parallel operations ("free wheeling"), which can be exploited for *latency hiding* through the overlapping of computation and communication. Our application studies show that these four coordination schemes seem to suffice. Expressing the temporal structures of parallel programs by a coordination scheme extends the applicability of the model even to

applications that are usually not associated with data parallelism as, for example, discrete-event simulation.

3. New language types

3.1 General remarks

Realizing the Promoter model in the form of a high-level programming language requires novel language concepts such as topologies, distributed variables, and a generalized form of functional replication. Promoter has been implemented in the form of extensions to the object-oriented language C++, an approach that avoids the acceptance problems usually encountered with a new language design. It is here not the place for a complete, formal specification of the Promoter language (the reader may please refer to [7]). Rather, we shall just try to briefly convey some of the flavor of the language by example.

3.2 Specifying data topologies

The declaration of a data topology for a distributed type has the form:

T <X> tx

where X is called the *element type*. Element types may be any type C++ provides. Hence, a distributed type consist of a *data domain* (the topology) and an element type, its state space being the Cartesian power of the state space of its component type over the index space of its topology.

A topology is defined by an index space in conjunction with an (optional) set of constraints. An index space is described as the Cartesian product of a number of integer intervals, according to the dimensionality of the domain. The following is a simple example for the declaration of a two-dimensional static topology.

```
topology T(m,n)
  1:m, 1:n
  { i,j | i+j mod2 = 0   // constraint
  }
```

Without the constraints, the declaration would define a two-dimensional rectangular array. By the constraints some of the points of the rectangular domain are selected while others are "culled off." In the example above, the result is the white field of an mxn checkerboard. Figure 3 shows the declaration of a band matrix. More complex topologies may be formed as unions of already defined simpler topologies.

We introduced in Section 2.4 the support of distributed types as arbitrary, finite subsets of their index domains. Supports are statically declared or dynamically constructed as unions of one or more regular subdomains of their index domains. They may be static (generated at compile time) or dynamic (constructed at run time). The latter case usually involves the use of parameterized index expressions evaluated at run time.

```
declaration:   topology tridiag
               1:8, 1:8
               {$i, $j |: abs(i-j)<=1
               };
```

geometry:

● ● ○ ○ ○ ○ ○ ○
● ● ● ○ ○ ○ ○ ○
○ ● ● ● ○ ○ ○ ○
○ ○ ● ● ● ○ ○ ○
○ ○ ○ ● ● ● ○ ○
○ ○ ○ ○ ● ● ● ○
○ ○ ○ ○ ○ ● ● ●
○ ○ ○ ○ ○ ○ ● ●

Figure 3 Simple topology declaration with constraints for a diagonal matrix

The structured universe concept covers the entire spectrum between fully regular and totally irregular structures. One extreme is a support formed by the "union" of one single regular block; the other extreme is a union of "subdomains" that are just single points. Between these extremes, any degree of regularity or irregularity is possible, determined by the shape and size of the regular constituents. By specifying the regular subdomains and their unions, the user has complete control over the support of the distributed objects and the level of granularity of their representation.

Distributed types with a dynamic topology are denoted by the keyword **dynamic**, which indicates that the so declared object, say x, has a topology that is a dynamically selected subset of the originally declared topology. The topology of x can be modified by constructs such as:

x.new(...), x.union(...), x.delete (...)

These constructs create, enlarge or diminish, respectively, or delete the dynamic topology of x according to the *selection* specified in the parentheses.

3.3 Specifying communication topologies

The Promoter communication scheme of simply denoting elements of distributed variables as communication partners, without any need for explicit synchronization, reduces the task of the user to the declaration of a *communication topology*. Communication topologies are created by a specific language construct called *communication product* that has the form of a generalized vector-matrix multiplication. This approach allows for the modeling of sparseness, irregularity, and dynamic communication structures.

For example, a vector of values observed from some other points can be obtained by a simple "inner product" where the vector-operand is a distributed variable and the

matrix is a Boolean *connectivity matrix* that selects the values to be read. The result is the vector of selected values. However, communication matrices may as well be numeric. Communications may be many-to-one, in which case the result is obtained by reduction operations. E.g., in the simulation of a neural network the weighted inputs of a neuron may be obtained by one single inner product expression. In general, communication are functions on distributed variables that move the elements of their argument to some other place in its index domain or to a place in another index domain. The result is again a distributed value that may serve as input argument in a parallel operation. Figure 4 illustrates the *communication product* philosophy of Promoter.

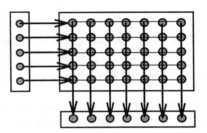

Figure 3 Illustration of the communication product (vector-matrix case)

3.4 Specifying distributed types

A distributed variable (object) is a topology of data points such that each value has the same element type. The programmer may specify any element type provided by the host language (C++). As usual in data parallel programming, we obtain parallelism by *function lifting*, i.e., by constructing new functions that consist of multiple applications of a function (method) of one of the types of the host language, the replication space of function lifting being the topology.

The properties of distributed types can be summarized as follows:

- they reconcile the different notions of indexable point sets and recursive types; thus unifying geometric and algebraic models;
- they are polymorphic, thus providing a powerful scheme for formalizing sparseness, irregularity, and dynamic spatial structures.

3.5 An application example

As a simple example we show the Promoter program text for a step of a Jacobi relaxation algorithm.

```
topology Grid: 1:M, 1:N ();
topology NN: Grid, Grid  // short for:
nearest neighbor
```

```
{ $i, $j, i, j+1;
  $i, $j, i, j-1;
  $i, $j, I+1, j;
  $i, $j, i-1, j;
// this is equivalent to: $i, $j, $k, $l |:
abs(i-k) + abs(j-l) = 1
};
Grid<double> g;
do {
    g_old = g;
    g = 0.25 * NN!g + b;
    }
while (reduce(abs(g-g_old), + )) > eps);
```

4. Promoter programming environment

4.1 Parallelizing compiler

The specification of data and communication topologies in conjunction with the selected coordination scheme enables the Promoter compiler to insert the appropriate message passing constructs (send, receive) into the code. A much less trivial task for the compiler is to optimally partition the set of data points of a program into entities that are then mapped onto the nodes of the target platform. The condition for an optimized mapping is twofold: (i) the computational load should be approximately the same on all nodes and (ii) the data movement called for by the *observation of state* approach should be minimized.

Mapping is an NP-complete optimization problem [8]. Consequently, one must resort to appropriate heuristics. Dynamic data structures may have to be re-mapped during program execution; thus, the speed of the mapping algorithm is very important. Several mapping heuristics were tested as to their suitability, such as the *Kernighan-Lin algorithm* [9] and *Recursive Spectral Bisection* [10]. In addition, a new mapping algorithm has been developed for Promoter, called *balanced hypersphere tessellation* (BHT) [11]. BHT is a generalization of vector quantization and proved to work well for the partitioning of irregular domains of arbitrary dimensions.

To assist the compiler in the task of minimizing communication cost, a weight is assigned to each partitioning according to the frequency of its execution. Currently, the programmer must provide this information by annotations. Mapping in Promoter also comprises the automatic, communication-driven alignment of not necessarily rectangular domains at compile time, in order to exploit the existing regularities.

4.2 Runtime system

The Promoter runtime system implements a template class for distributed objects and a set of template functions on distributed objects. The templates provide a "generic" interface in the sense that operations on distributed objects are implemented on the same framework for different topologies, different mapping strategies, and different element types. E.g., there are functions for assignment, function call, point-to-point communication, and collective communication (reduction, expansion, cross product, and communication product).

Specialization is supported by container classes (e.g. topology and mapping) of distributed objects. Objects of container classes can be shared by different distributed objects. Communication and computation can be overlapped. All this supports the compiler in performing application-specific optimizations.

The runtime system provides portability between different platforms. Promoter has been implemented on two existing parallel computers, the experimental MANNA supercomputer developed at GMD FIRST [12] and a commercial product, the IBM SP-2. There exist also an implementation for the standard message-passing library MPI. This allows for running Promoter on workstation clusters. There exists even an implementation for single-processor SUN workstations. Though there is no parallel computing on the single workstation, there still is the benefit of easier programming. The variety of Promoter implementations for workstations, clusters of workstations, and parallel computers reflects the fact that Promoter enables its user to formulate potentially parallel application algorithms in a highly abstract form, leaving it to the system to execute in parallel to the degree allowed by the executing platform.

4.3 Performance

To demonstrate the efficiency of Promoter code, we compare some common benchmarks programmed in Promoter with those programmed in Fortran under PVM. The executing platform is the MANNA supercomputer. Note that PVM on MANNA is not a port but a (highly optimized) implementation that takes advantage of the very low communication latency of MANNA [12].

The benchmarks are: 128*128 matrix multiplication, 512*512 Jacobi relaxation, and 1000*1000 conjugate gradient method. Tpro is the time for the Promoter version and Tpvm the time for the PVM version (in seconds). Table 1 lists the execution times as function of the number of processors (4, 8, or 16). We recognize that for these applications Promoter programs and PVM message-passing programs have almost the same performance. In both cases we obtain a nearly linear speed-up.

374

Benchmark	Execution Time Tpro/Tpvm (sec.)		
	4P	8 P	16 P
Matrix Mult. 128*128	.291/.246	.155/.137	.088/.083
Relaxation 512*512	.280/.261	.137/.132	.075/.072
Conj. grad. 1000*1000	8.23/8.21	4.12/4.11	2.36/2.34

Table 1 Benchmark comparison Promoter - PVM

5. Conclusion and future work

The Master Plan for the Real World Computing Program [14] postulates in 1992 that "flexible execution models, which can be bases of general-purpose architectures, should have the ability to fill the gaps between the language models and hardware." These systems should "provide the programmers (with) a high level of abstract(ion) of a general-purpose parallel system in order to make the parallel programming easier." And: "the elimination of synchronization overhead, access control and communication overhead will become more serious issues. The language for the massively parallel system must be able to describe the coordinated operations of a number of processes." Promoter satisfies these demands.

These goals have been reached through the unique structured universe approach. A first version of the Promoter programming system has been implemented on several platforms, and application experiences have been gained. They prove that Promoter is applicable to a wide spectrum of applications. Examples were taken from: computational fluid dynamics, finite element methods, particle simulation. molecular biology, quantum chromodynamics, continuous system and discrete event simulation, and neural network simulation. Rather than listing here all the application studies performed, we ask the interested reader to kindly look up our home page:

http://www.first.gmd.de/org/promot.html

While the Promoter concepts seem to satisfy the demands for high-level parallel programming, there is still room for improving their implementation. Here are some of the issues for future work.

- Refinement of the approach to mapping. While the BHT algorithm seems to be quite promising, it is not clear at this point whether it will work in all possible cases. The ultimate solution may be to have a choice of algorithms and a knowledge-based system that selects the right one for a given application. It is also envisioned to employ a rule-based system to generate the communication weights automatically.

- The issue of a symbolic evaluation of topology-defining expressions as a first step for optimal load balancing is to be further pursed. It is conceivable that such expressions are partially evaluated already at compile time.

- The problem of aggregation, that is, the condensation of the many parallel threads in each node into one maximally efficient "operating system process" must be attacked.

References

[1]   Li K.: Shared Virtual Memory on Loosely Coupled Multiprocessors, Ph.D.thesis, Yale University 1986

[2]   Lenoski D. et al.: The Stanford DASH Multiprocessor, COMPUTER (March 1992), 63-79

[3]   High Performance Fortran Forum: High Performance Fortran Language Specification, Version 1.0, Rice University, Houston, TX (May 1993)

[4]   Giloi W.K., Schramm A.: PROMOTER, An Application-Oriented Programming Model for Massive Parallelism, in Giloi W.K., Jaehnichen S., Shriver B.D.(eds.): *Programming Models for Massively Parallel Computers*, IEEE-CS Press order no. 4900-02 (Sept. 1993)

[5]   Giloi, W.K., Kessler, M., Schramm, A.: "PROMOTER: A High Level, Object-Parallel Programming Language, Proc. Internat. Conf. on High Performance Computing, McGraw-Hill Publishing Co., New Delhi, India 1995

[6]   Schramm A.: PROMOTER: A Programming Model for Massive Parallelism, to be published

[7]   Enskonatus P., Kessler M., Schramm A.: PROMOTER Language Definition, GMD FIRST Tech. Report 1996

[8]   Garey M., Johnson D., Stockmeyer L.: Some simplified NP-complete graph problems, Theoretical Computer Science, no.1, 237-267, 1976

[9]   Kernighan B.W., Lin S.: An Efficient Heuristic Procedure for Partitioning Graphs, The Bell System Technical Journal, Feb. 1970, 291-307

[10] Pothen A., Simon H.D., Liou K.P.: Partitioning Sparse Matrices With Eigenvectors of Graphs, SIAM J. Matrix Anal. 11 (1990), 430-452

[11] Besch M., Pohl H.W.: Topographic Data Mapping by Balanced Hypersphere Tessellation, to be published

[12] Giloi W.K., Bruening U., Schroeder-Preikschat W.: MANNA: Prototype of a Distributed Memory Architecture With Maximized Sustained Performance, Proc. Euromicro PDP96 Workshop 1996, IEEE-CS Press

[13] Anonymous: The Master Plan for the Real-World Computing Program (DRAFT of May 1992)

Evaluating the Impact of Coherence Protocols on Parallel Logic Programming Systems

Vítor Santos Costa,* Ricardo Bianchini, and Inês de Castro Dutra

Department of Systems Engineering and Computer Science
Federal University of Rio de Janeiro
Rio de Janeiro, Brazil
e-mail: {vitor,ricardo,ines}@cos.ufrj.br

Abstract

In this paper we use execution-driven simulation of a scalable multiprocessor to evaluate the performance of the Andorra-I parallel logic programming system under invalidate and update-based protocols. We study a well-known invalidate protocol and two different update-based protocols. Our results show that for our sample logic programs the update-based protocols outperform their invalidate-based counterparts. The detailed analysis of these results shows that update-based protocols outperform invalidate-based protocols regardless of the type of parallelism exhibited by the benchmarks. The reasons for this behaviour are explained in detail. We conclude that parallel logic programming systems can benefit from update-based protocols and that multiprocessors designed for running these systems efficiently should adopt some form of update or hybrid protocol.

1. Introduction

One of the most important advantages of logic programming is the availability of several forms of implicit parallelism that can be naturally exploited on shared-memory multiprocessors. These forms include: or-parallelism, independent and-parallelism, dependent and-parallelism, data-parallelism, and combined and–or parallelism [4]. All the systems implementing these forms of parallelism have been able to obtain good performance on bus-based machines, such as the Sequent Symmetry multiprocessors.

As modern architectures are developed and the gap between CPU and memory speeds widens, the issue arises of whether the current parallel logic programming systems can

also perform well on the new, scalable, architectures. In modern multiprocessors, performance depends heavily on the miss rates and may be limited by the communication overhead that is involved in the sharing of writable data.

Sharing in parallel logic programming systems occurs under several circumstances. The use of logical variables for communication in dependent and-parallel applications, for instance, is an example of producer–consumer sharing of data.

A second major form of sharing, migratory sharing, arises from synchronisation between processors. Synchronisation occurs in tasks such as fetching work from other processors, and on being the leftmost goal or branch to execute cuts or side-effects.

The sharing of writable data structures introduces the problem of coherence between the processors' caches. Most parallel machines have used a write invalidate (WI) protocol [5] in order to keep caches coherent. Write update (WU) protocols [8] are the main alternative to invalidate-based protocols.

WI protocols have been more popular than WU protocols because of the extra traffic updates introduce. Quite often the updates sent will not be used by their recipients. This introduces extra, useless, traffic that consumes bandwidth and can actually degrade performance. However, the nature of sharing in parallel logic programming systems suggests that update-based protocols might be more appropriate than their invalidate-based counterparts. In order to confirm this hypothesis, in this paper we evaluate the performance of update and invalidate-based protocols for parallel logic programming systems.

We use execution-driven simulation of a scalable multiprocessor running the Andorra-I system [11]. The system was developed at the University of Bristol by Beaumont, Dutra, Santos Costa, Yang, and Warren [11]. Andorra-I is an ideal subject for our experiments because it supports two rather different forms of parallelism in logic pro-

---
*On leave from the Universidade do Porto, Portugal. Research supported by the Brazilian Research Council, CNPq, under grant 300953/95-0

grams, and-parallelism and or-parallelism. We use a detailed on-line, execution-driven simulator that simulates a 24-node, DASH-like [7], directly-connected multiprocessor. The simulator was developed at the University of Rochester and uses the MINT front-end [14] (developed by Veenstra and Fowler) to simulate the MIPS architecture, and a back-end [1] (developed by Bianchini, Kontothanassis, and Veenstra) to simulate the memory and interconnection systems. We study a well-known invalidate protocol and two different update-based protocols. More details about the simulator and the Andorra-I system can be found elsewhere [10].

Our approach contrasts with previous studies of the performance of coherence protocols for parallel logic programming systems. Tick and Hermenegildo [13] studied caching behaviour of independent and-parallelism in bus-based multiprocessors. Other researchers have studied the performance of parallel logic programming systems on scalable architectures, such as the DDM [9], but did not evaluate the impact of different coherence protocols. Our goal in this study is to evaluate the performance implications of different protocols for parallel logic programming systems on scalable multiprocessors, while categorising cache misses and update messages in the system.

The paper is organised as follows. Section 2 presents speedup results for the or-parallel, and-parallel, and combined parallel benchmarks ran in Andorra-I under WI and WU protocols. Section 3 evaluates the performance of a hybrid protocol for the same benchmarks. Finally, Section 4 draws our conclusions and suggests future work.

2. Performance Under WI and WU Protocols

In this section we present speedup results for Andorra-I under both kinds of protocol, WI and WU. We experimented with applications representing predominantly and-parallelism, or-parallelism, and both and- and or-parallelism. The benchmarks represent real applications used by companies or in academia. More details about the applications can be found elsewhere [4]. We tried to select applications with good parallelism, whilst avoiding applications with too much parallelism that would scale well regardless of architecture.

2.1. And-Parallel Applications

As an example and-parallel application, we used the clustering algorithm for network management from British Telecom.

Figure 1 shows the speedups for both protocols. The application has excellent and-parallelism, resulting in almost linear speedups for the perfect curve. This curve is obtained for an ideal shared-memory machine, where data

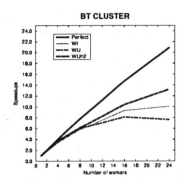

Figure 1. Speedups for bt-cluster

items can always be found in cache, and gives an idea of the maximum available parallelism in the application. The Wuh2 curve will be discussed later.

Performance for a realistic machine is acceptable. The invalidate protocol (WI curve) starts with an efficiency of 87% for 2 processors. Efficiency smoothly decreases as the number of processors increases, but is still over 50% for 16 processors. The update protocol (WU curve) has a very interesting behaviour. It starts with excellent efficiency of about 90% up to four processors. Then performance starts degrading, and after 16 processors there is a smooth slowdown. We discuss this problem in detail in the next section.

2.2. Or-Parallel Applications

As our or-parallel application we use an example from the natural language question-answering system chat-80.

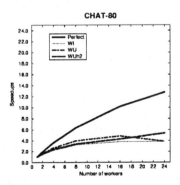

Figure 2. Speedups for chat-80

Figure 2 shows the speedups for both protocols, from 1 to 24 processors. The perfect curve gives almost linear speedup up to 4 processors, after which the speedup starts to level off. These speedups are very similar to the ones obtained under the Sequent Symmetry architecture [4]. The main difference is that the speedup on the Symmetry levels-off at a maximum speedup of 10. This comparison shows that the Symmetry behaves almost as if memory accesses were free of cost, which for state-of-the-art processor and memory speeds is unrealistic.

A comparison between the perfect and realistic curves proves this point. On this small-scale benchmark, the invalidate protocol manages to obtain a maximum speedup of 4. Up to 16 workers, performance for the update protocol is from 20% to 27% better for this benchmark, obtaining a maximum speedup of 4.9 for 16 workers. It is very interesting to notice that, as the number of workers increases up to 24, performance for the update protocol quickly deteriorates, whereas the invalidate protocol manages to sustain performance.

2.3. And/Or-Parallel Applications

We used a program to generate naval flight allocations, based on a system developed by Software Sciences and the University of Leeds for the Royal Navy.

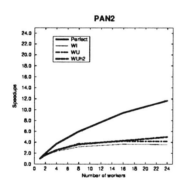

Figure 3. Speedups for pan2

Figure 3 shows the speedups for pan2. The perfect speedups are acceptable. The application performs well up to 8 workers, and then parallelism starts to level off. The performance of pan2 on the Symmetry is slightly worse than perfect [4].

The performance on a realistic machine demonstrates effects similar to the previous applications. Andorra-I on a modern machine cannot match speedups it would obtain under a machine with one-cycle memory access time. The invalidate protocol starts with an efficiency of about 80% for two workers. Efficiency then decreases quickly, but the machine is able to improve speedups up to 16 workers. The update protocol starts with an advantage of 5% for two workers over invalidate. This advantage improves up to 8 workers, and then starts decreasing.

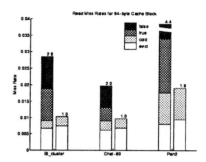

Figure 4. Read miss rate under WI (left) vs. WU (right), 16 processors.

2.4. Analysis of Results

According to the results shown in the previous section, the WU protocol invariably performs better than the WI protocol for small numbers of processors. As we increase the number of processors, performance of the WU protocol starts to degrade. Figures 4, 5, and 6 help to understand this phenomenon. Figure 4 shows the shared read miss rates for the three applications, with WI as the left bar and WU as the right one. The percentage at the top of each column represents the percent of all shared reads that result in a miss. For WI, within a column, misses are classified according to the algorithm described in [3], as extended in [1]. A **cold start miss** happens on the first reference to a block by a processor. A **true sharing miss** happens when a processor references a word belonging in a block it had previously cached but has been invalidated, due to a write by some other processor to the same word. A **false sharing miss** occurs in roughly the same circumstances as a true sharing miss, except that the word written by the other processor is not the same as the word missed on. An **eviction (replacement) miss** happens when a processor replaces one of its cache blocks with another one mapping to the same cache line and later needs to reload the block replaced. Note that the WU protocol does not have sharing misses.

As expected, WU always results in lower read miss rates, even though WI usually exhibits lower replacement miss rates as invalidations effectively free up cache space. The reason is that for WI most misses are sharing misses (from 55%, in chat-80, to 70%, in bt-cluster). This is sufficient to compensate for the increase in eviction misses from WU, which increases up to 17% for bt-cluster. Ultimately, by avoiding sharing misses, WU more than halves the total miss rate for the benchmark set.

Note that for all applications Andorra-I demonstrates a very high percentage of false sharing misses, ranging from 24% of total misses in pan2 to 34% in bt-cluster. False sharing mainly hurts performance under the WI pro-

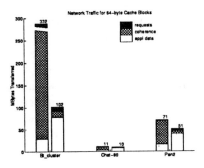

Figure 5. MBytes transferred under WU (left) vs. WI (right), 16 processors.

tocol, by increasing the miss rate. False sharing may arise from shared variables in the schedulers, or from two logical variables that were created in sequence, say, within the same compound term.

Although WU produces lower miss rates than WI, it is at the cost of a large increase in network traffic. This increase can cause several forms of performance degradation due to an increase in network and memory congestion. Figure 5 shows this difference for 16 processors. Basically, WU causes an increase in network traffic with respect to WI that ranges from a factor of 3 in bt-cluster to 40% in pan2 and 11% in chat-80.

It is important to note that most of the traffic generated by the WU protocol is coherence-related, i.e. update messages. However, as previous studies have shown [2], most of these updates are useless, at least for scientific applications. In order to determine whether the same is true for Andorra-I, we classify updates as either *useful*, which are needed for correct execution of the program, or *useless*. The latter category of updates is classified according to the algorithm described in [1].

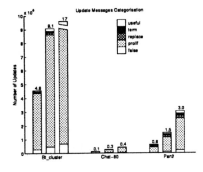

Figure 6. Categorisation of updates, 4 (left), 8 (center), and 16 (right) processors.

True sharing updates are updates where the receiving

processor references the word modified by the update message before another update message to the same word is received. **False sharing updates** are updates where the receiving processor does not reference the word modified by the update message before it is overwritten by a subsequent update, but references some other word in the same cache block. **Proliferation updates** are updates where the receiving processor does not reference the word modified by the update message before it is overwritten, and it does not reference any other word in that cache block either. **Replacement updates** are updates where the receiving processor does not reference the updated word until the block is replaced in its cache. A **termination update** is a proliferation update happening at the end of the program.

We can observe from figure 6 that for 16 processors more than 90% of the update messages are indeed useless, with the actual percentage of useful updates varying from only 2.5% in the bt-cluster application, to 4.4% in chat-80, and 6% in pan2. The main culprits are by far the proliferation updates, which grow quickly with the number of processors and eventually become 77% of the useless updates in chat-80, 81% in pan2, and 93% in bt-cluster for 16 processors. A high rate of proliferation updates is typical of migratory sharing of data such as in shared counters, or shared work queues: data structures that are updated very often during execution, and which are indeed very common in both and- and or-schedulers and in memory allocation within a team.

The second most important category of useless updates in all applications is false updates. For 16 processors they are 4% of the total number of useless updates in bt-cluster, 7.5% in pan2, and 16% in chat-80. These updates are the direct consequence of the widespread false sharing in the system. bt-cluster is an interesting example where processors do falsely share data, but not simultaneously.

This excessive increase in useless update traffic for large numbers of processors degrades WU performance significantly by increasing memory access times due to network and memory congestion. These results suggest that reducing the number of useless updates should improve WU performance and therefore improve its scalability.

3. A Hybrid Protocol for Andorra-I

In order to reduce the number of update messages of the WU protocol, we experimented with protocols that aim at reducing update traffic. The best performance was under a dynamic hybrid protocol (WUh2) [6] based on the coherence protocols of the bus-based multiprocessors using the DEC Alpha AXP21064 [12]. In these multiprocessors, each node makes a local decision to invalidate or update a cache block when it sees an update transaction on the bus. We associate a counter with each cache block and invalidate the block when the counter reaches the threshold. References to a cache block reset the counter to zero. We used counters with a threshold of 2 updates.

Figures 1, 2, and 3 show speedup curves for the WUh2 protocol. The application `bt-cluster` that contains only dependent and-parallelism (figure 1) has its speedups enormously improved with the hybrid protocol. Speedups for 24 processors increased from 8 with the WU protocol to 13.4 with the WUh2 protocol. Moreover, the knee of the speedup curve, which is reached for 16 workers with WU, is not reached with WUh2 up to 24 processors.

The `chat-80` benchmark (figure 2) performs well under the hybrid protocol. This protocol achieves the best performance overall, being comparable to the WU protocol for smaller numbers of processors, while maintaining rising speedups for the largest number of processors.

Finally, we would expect the `pan2` application (figure 3) to also improve speedups with a change of protocol, as it contains a reasonable amount of and-parallelism. This is indeed the case, although the difference is not as impressive as for `bt-cluster`. WUh2 performs closely to WU up to 16 processors, and then obtains slightly better performance for 24 processors. WUh2 also has better performance than WI for all numbers of processors.

3.1. Analysis of Results

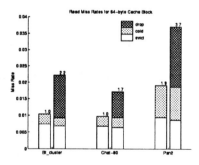

Figure 7. Read miss rate under WU (left) vs. WUh2 (right), 16 processors.

Figure 7 compares the shared read miss rate for WU (left) and WUh2 (right). The cache miss categorisation now includes an extra class, `drop` misses, to account for cache misses resulting from excessively eager self-invalidations. The results show that the price to pay for WUh2 is a significant number of drop misses: 46% of total misses with `chat-80`, 50% for `pan2`, and 58% of total misses for `bt-cluster`. As a result, the read miss rate about doubles in comparison to WU for all applications. In the case of

`bt-cluster` the total shared read miss rate is still significantly lower than for WI, 2.2% versus 2.8%. The difference is smaller in `chat-80` and `pan2`. For `chat-80` it is 1.7% versus 2.0%, and for `pan2` it is 3.7% versus 4.4%.

Figure 8 shows the network traffic for all applications under the WU (right) and WUh2 (left) protocols for 16 processors. In all cases there is an increase in application data transfer. The increase is most substantial in `bt-cluster`, where application data transfer more than doubles.

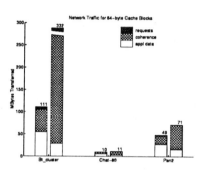

Figure 8. MBytes transferred under WUh2 (left) vs. WU (right), 16 processors.

However, in `bt-cluster` the major effect is the decrease in coherence traffic. The `pan2` benchmark also benefits from the same effect, but in `chat-80` the reduction in coherence traffic is less significant as a percentage of the total traffic. This behaviour of `chat-80` is due to the fact that data sharing is not widespread in or-parallel execution; the vast majority of update operations have a single recipient for all numbers of processors.

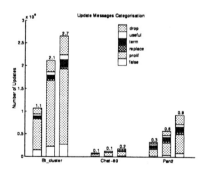

Figure 9. Categorisation of updates, WUh2, 4 (left), 8 (center), and 16 (right) processors.

In figure 9 we present the categorisation of update messages for the WUh2 protocol. The categorisation of updates shown in the figure includes an additional category, `drop` updates, to account for the updates that cause blocks to be invalidated. A comparison between figures 9 and 6 shows that the total number of update messages in WUh2 versus WU at 16 processors has been reduced by a factor of 2 for chat-80, 3 for pan2, and 6 for bt-cluster. This is a direct result of the fact that WUh2 has been very effective at reducing the number of proliferation messages: for 16 processors, the proliferation updates dropped by 90% in bt-cluster, by 82% in pan2, and by 69% in chat-80.

In summary, WUh2 seems to be the most appropriate coherence protocol, as it consistently achieves better scalability than the other protocols, and performs acceptably for small numbers of processors.

4. Conclusions and Future Work

The main conclusion of our work is that parallel logic programming systems that aim at good performance on scalable machines will benefit from some form of update-based protocol. In our benchmarks this was clear both for applications with dependent and-parallelism and or-parallelism. The trend towards faster CPUs, larger caches, and more available bandwidth also favours update-based protocols.

Our results have given a better perspective into the performance of the current version of Andorra-I and how it can be improved. A major result from our analysis is that migratory sharing in the system, not data sharing in the applications, is the most significant form of sharing in Andorra-I. We have also noticed that a substantial part of this sharing is false, and it must come from accesses to static scheduler data structures. We confirmed these results by performing an in-depth analysis of the caching behaviour of the system's shared data structures [10]. This result suggests that to obtain better scalability in Andorra-I the key effort should be on improving scheduling and synchronisation. This is good news, as reducing sharing in the applications would require work from Andorra-I users. We have noticed that the system can be easily improved by reducing false sharing in the schedulers' data structures. More distributed algorithms for fetching work and synchronisation within and between teams will require substantial changes to the Andorra-I's schedulers and to the system's memory management. We are currently investigating new scheduling algorithms for Andorra-I.

In the near future, we will be performing a similar analysis for other parallel logic programming systems. Besides confirming the generality of our claims, such an analysis will give us further insight into the current performance and scalability of parallel logic programming systems.

Acknowledgements The authors would like to thank Leonidas Kontothanassis and Jack Veenstra for their help with the simulation infrastructure used in this paper. The authors would also like to thank Rong Yang, Tony Beaumont, D. H. D. Warren for their work in Andorra-I. Vítor Santos Costa would like to thank the University of Porto and the PROLOPPE project for their support.

References

[1] R. Bianchini and L. I. Kontothanassis. Algorithms for categorizing multiprocessor communication under invalidate and update-based coherence protocols. In *Proceedings of the 28th Annual Simulation Symposium*, April 1995.

[2] R. Bianchini, T. J. LeBlanc, and J. E. Veenstra. Categorizing network traffic in update-based protocols on scalable multiprocessors. In *Proceedings of the IPPS'96*, April 1996.

[3] M. Dubois, J. Skeppstedt, L. Ricciulli, K. Ramamurthy, and P. Stenstrom. The detection and elimination of useless misses in multiprocessors. In *Proceedings of the 20th ISCA*, pages 88–97, May 1993.

[4] I. Dutra. *Distributing And- and Or-Work in the Andorra-I Parallel Logic Programming System*. PhD thesis, University of Bristol, Department of Computer Science, February 1995.

[5] J. R. Goodman. Using cache memory to reduce processor-memory traffic. In *Proceedings of the 10th International Symposium on Computer Architecture*, pages 124–131, 1983.

[6] A. R. Karlin, M. S. Manasse, L. Rudolph, and D. D. Sleator. Competitive snoopy caching. *Algorithmica*, 3:79–119, 1988.

[7] D. Lenoski, J. Laudon, K. Gharachorloo, A. Gupta, and J. Hennessy. The directory-based cache coherence protocol for the DASH multiprocessor. *Proceedings of the 17th ISCA*, pages 148–159, May 1990.

[8] E. M. McCreight. The Dragon Computer System, an Early Overview. In *NATO Advanced Study Institute on Microarchitecture of VLSI Computers*, July 1984.

[9] S. Raina, D. H. D. Warren, and J. Cownie. Parallel Prolog on a Scalable Multiprocessor. In P. Kacsuk and M. J. Wise, editors, *Implementations of Distributed Prolog*, pages 27–44. Wiley, 1992.

[10] V. Santos Costa, R. Bianchini, and I. Dutra. Analysing the Caching Behaviour of Parallel Logic Programming Systems. ES-390/96, COPPE/Sistemas, Universidade Federal do Rio de Janeiro, May 1996.

[11] V. Santos Costa, D. H. D. Warren, and R. Yang. Andorra-I: A Parallel Prolog System that Transparently Exploits both And- and Or-Parallelism. In *Third ACM SIGPLAN Symposium on Principles & Practice of Parallel Programming*, pages 83–93. ACM press, April 1991. SIGPLAN Notices vol 26(7), July 1991.

[12] C. P. Thacker, D. G. Conroy, and L. C. Stewart. The alpha demonstration unit: A high-performance multiprocessor for software and chip development. *Digital Technical Journal*, 4(4):51–65, 1992.

[13] E. Tick. *Memory Performance of Prolog Architectures*. Kluwer Academic Publishers, Norwell, MA 02061, 1987.

[14] J. E. Veenstra and R. J. Fowler. Mint: A front end for efficient simulation of shared-memory multiprocessors. In *Proceedings of the 2nd International Workshop on Modeling, Analysis and Simulation of Computer and Telecommunication Systems (MASCOTS '94)*, 1994.

Branching Transactions in a Shared-Memory Parallel Database System

Albert Burger
Department of Computing and Electrical Engineering,
Heriot-Watt University, Edinburgh, Scotland *

Abstract

In order to exploit parallel computers, database management systems must achieve a high level of concurrency when executing transactions. In a high contention environment, however, parallelism is severely limited due to transaction blocking.

In [3] a new transaction model, Branching Transactions, was proposed together with an appropriate concurrency control algorithm (based on multi-version two-phase locking) which, in case of data conflicts, avoids unnecessary transaction blockings and restarts by executing alternative paths of transactions in parallel.

In this paper, we describe a branching transaction system running on a shared-memory parallel computer. A new concurrency control algorithm, which is able to dynamically switch between branching and non-branching modes at run-time, is introduced and a two-layer approach for the implementation of our new algorithm on top of an existing (non-branching) two-phase locking module is proposed. Furthermore, a simulation study comparing the flat transaction model using strict two-phase locking with our new approach is discussed for a shared-memory parallel computer environment.

1. Introduction

In recent years, multi-processor systems based on fast and inexpensive micro-processors have become widely available. The costs for shared-memory parallel computers, also known as SMP (Symmetric Multi-Processor) systems, in particular, have dropped significantly within the last ten years, and will drop even further as the commodity PC market is now also producing such systems. The total performance/price ratio of these systems is usually higher than that of traditional mainframe computers.

Performance improvements of database systems through the use of increasingly powerful parallel computer hardware can, however, be hindered by data contention (delays of transactions due to lock conflicts) [4]. The component of a database management system dealing with synchronization of access to shared data, and therefore responsible for issues of data contention, is the *concurrency control manager*. All existing algorithms — with the exception of Speculative Concurrency Control (SCC)[1] — resolve conflicts either by *blocking* or *restarting* transactions at the time of conflict (pessimistic algorithms) or when a transaction tries to commit (optimistic algorithms). Common to both groups, the decision made at the time of conflict may not be the right one. In a pessimistic algorithm, for example, the roll-back of a transaction is frequently caused by a situation that *might* have led to a deadlock; or a transaction is blocked because it *might* have violated serializability. In an optimistic algorithm, a conflict that was ignored during the execution may require the restart of a transaction. The key problem is that at the time of conflict we usually don't know which is the right decision to make. In [3], an approach was proposed where a transaction, instead of making a particular decision, follows up alternative paths of execution concurrently. Once it is known which was the right path to pursue, all others can be aborted.

The remainder of the paper is organized as follows: Section 2 gives a brief introduction to the branching transaction model; Section 3 describes the new multi-version two-phase locking algorithm for branching transactions and how it could be implemented on top of an existing (non-branching) two-phase locking module using a two-layer approach; Section 4 presents

---

*This paper is based on research work which was partially carried out by the author while at the Department of Computer Science, Edinburgh University.

[1] SCC is rooted in the same basic idea as branching transactions, but applies a rather different synchronization mechanism and is primarily geared towards real-time scheduling. For more details, see [1].

the results of our performance study; Section 5 gives a conclusion and summary of future work.

2. The Branching Transaction Model

Assume the following situation: transaction T_1 has to read database items x and y during its execution, transactions T_2 and T_3 update x and y, respectively, and at the time T_1 is issuing its Read requests, T_2 and T_3 have already updated the data items, but have not yet committed.

Since it is not known whether T_2 and T_3 will eventually commit or abort, it is also not clear whether T_1 should read the new versions of x and y. In this situation, under the branching transaction model, the system pursues alternative paths of execution of a transaction until it is known which one is correct. In other words, at the time of conflict a transaction branches into two or more alternative copies of itself which then continue to execute in parallel. Branching of transactions leads to a transaction tree structure, where each node in the tree represents some part of execution of the transaction; we refer to these transaction parts as *branching transaction components* (BTCs). The development of this transaction tree for T_1 of above example is shown in Figure 1

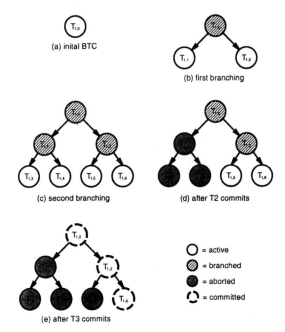

(a) inital BTC

(b) first branching

(c) second branching

(d) after T2 commits

(e) after T3 commits

O = active
◨ = branched
● = aborted
◌ = committed

Figure 1. Transaction Component State Changes within a Branching Transaction

Initially T_1 begins execution as $BTC_{1,0}$ (Figure 1, part a). When $BTC_{1,0}$ tries to read x it branches into

$BTC_{1,1}$ and $BTC_{1,2}$ (Figure 1, part b); $BTC_{1,1}$ reads the original value of x, $BTC_{1,2}$ reads the version of x created by T_2. These new BTCs branch even further when they try to read item y: $BTC_{1,1}$ becomes $BTC_{1,3}$ and $BTC_{1,4}$, $BTC_{1,2}$ becomes $BTC_{1,5}$ and $BTC_{1,6}$ (Figure 1, part c). The resulting 4 BTCs reflect the 4 possible scenarios of T_2 and T_3's future development: both abort, only T_2 commits, only T_3 commits, or both commit. Once T_2 actually commits, the left subtree can be aborted (Figure 1, part d), since $T_{1,1}$ was run under the (wrong) assumption that T_2 will abort. Similarly, $BTC_{1,5}$ is aborted once T_3 commits. At the end only the path which was executed under the correct assumptions remains (Figure 1, part e). In spite of data conflicts with other transactions, T_1 was executed without any delays due to blocking or restarts.

Any two transaction components of the same transaction tree can be executed in parallel, unless there exists a path in the tree between them. Any two components from different paths execute in isolation: they do not read any updates made by the other and are allowed to update the same data items independently. Concurrency control between BTCs from different transactions is discussed next.

3. Hybrid Dynamic Locking Algorithm

To avoid non-serializable transaction schedules, some form of concurrency control must be applied. Building on our original branching transaction multi-version two-phase locking (BT-MV-2PL) [3][2] algorithm, in this section, we introduce a new (hybrid) concurrency control algorithm, referred to as HBT-MV-2PL, which is able dynamically to switch between branching and non-branching modes at run-time. This allows us to pursue branching as long as sufficient resources are available and to switch dynamically to a more resource conservative approach — "normal" (non-branching) two-phase locking — if the system becomes overloaded.

The new algorithm uses the following lock types: VRL (Version Read Lock), VWL (Version Write Lock), CRL (Certified Read Lock), CWL (Certified Write Lock) and TCRL (Tentative Certified Read Lock). There exists one committed and zero or more uncommitted versions of each data item in the database. CRLs, CWLs and TCRLs are set on committed data item versions only. VRLs and VWLs are only used for uncommitted data item versions.

During the execution of a transaction, the mode of concurrency control may dynamically change between

<hr>

[2]In [3], we also discuss issues of branching restriction policies and logging and recovery; issues not covered here.

2PL and BT-MV-2PL. Depending on which mode is active at the time of request, Read and Write requests must be handled in different ways. The algorithm works as follows:

- **Read Request** under **2PL:** the BTC must first obtain a CRL on the requested item. It then reads the committed version of the item.

- **Write Request** under **2PL:** the BTC must first obtain a CWL on the requested item. It then overwrites the existing committed version of the item[3].

- **Read Request** under **BT-MV-2PL:** if no uncommitted versions exist, the BTC simply reads the committed version and a TCRL is set. If uncommitted versions exist, branching takes place; one new BTC for each existing version that has not been created by another BTC of the same transaction (which is branching). The new BTCs read the corresponding versions; accordingly VRLs are set on the relevant uncommitted data item versions and a TCRL is set on the committed version.

- **Write Request** under **BT-MV-2PL:** the BTC simply creates a new version of the corresponding data item and is automatically granted a VWL for it.

Before a BTC can be committed, it must be certified. Certification is governed by the following rules: 1) a BTC must wait until all versions it has read have become committed, and 2) all Write locks (VWL) must be certified, i.e. they must be upgraded to CWLs. VRLs are automatically converted to CRLs once the corresponding writer BTCs have committed. TCRL must explicitly be upgraded to CRL before the corresponding BTC can be certified.

VRL and VWL requests are never rejected; they do not conflict with any other locks; there exists, however, by definition always only one VWL per uncommitted version. Since version locks (VRL and VWL) only exist on uncommitted data and certified locks (CRL and CWL) are only requested for committed data, there can be no conflict between these two groups. CRLs are compatible with TCRLs and other CRLs. TCRLs are compatible with all other locks, except CWLs. CWLs are incompatible with TCRLs, CRLs and other CWLs.

---

[3]It does not actually overwrite the committed version, since we apply a deferred-update recovery policy, but the old committed version is not accessible to any other BTC any longer, unless it is recovered due to a failure of the BTC which has "overwritten" it.

If a lock request is made for which there exists an incompatible lock already, the requesting BTC is blocked. Some deadlock detection/resolution or deadlock prevention policy must be applied.

The relationship between CWLs and TCRLs is somewhat different from all other lock conflicts: depending on the circumstances, a CWL may pre-empt a TCRL and abort the corresponding BTC. We allow this if the BTC which is holding that TCRL has a "sibling" BTC that read the version of the item which was created by the BTC which is requesting the CWL; this sibling allows the possibility that the corresponding transaction can eventually commit (without a restart) in spite of the abort of the branches which contain the BTC with the pre-empted TCRL. Table 1 shows the lock compatibility matrix for HBT-MV-2PL.

HBT-MV-2PL	Lock Held				
Lock Req.	VRL	VWL	TCRL	CRL	CWL
VRL	yes	yes	yes	yes	yes
VWL	yes	yes	yes	yes	yes
TCRL	yes	yes	yes	yes	no
CRL	yes	yes	yes	yes	no
CWL	yes	yes	no	no	no

Table 1. Lock Compatibility Matrix for HBT-MV-2PL

A transaction can be committed once all BTCs of at least one branch are certifie d. The correctness of this algorithm is formally proved in [2].

HBT-MV-2PL Layered Approach Implementing a branching transaction scheduler from scratch is not an easy task. To be able to make use of existing DBMS components, we suggest a two-layer approach for the development of an HBT-MV-2PL concurrency control manager, where the lower layer captures general (non-branching) 2-phase locking, and the higher layer provides full HBT-MV-2PL functionality. Separating the scheduler in these two components supports the possibility of reusing existing 2PL scheduler code.

In addition to the usual Read and Write lock, and Commit and Abort requests, a 2PL module used in our two layer model would also need to support the following features:

Read/upgrade: a Read lock request which is granted if no Write locks exist for that item at that time (blocked Write lock requests may exist). If the lock cannot be granted, the requesting BTC must be aborted. This request is needed to upgrade TCRLs to CRLs.

Read/set: Sets a Read lock for a given BTC. This is needed to upgrade a VRL to a CRL.

Write/upgrade: A Write lock request which, if it cannot be granted, is queued in front of other blocked requests; except for other blocked upgrade requests. Upgrade requests from VWL to CWL should be handled with higher priority than regular lock requests.

A Write request to the HBT layer can directly be passed as a Write request to the 2PL layer, if the current CCM mode is 2PL. Otherwise, in BT-MV-2PL mode, a VWL entry is made in the HBT lock table. Under 2PL and MV-2PL mode, Read requests are passed directly to the 2PL layer. A Read request under BT-MV-2PL mode is entirely handled by the HBT-MV-2PL layer: it decides whether branching needs to be performed and sets TCRLs and VRLs accordingly.

When certification of a BTC is requested, the HBT-MV-2PL layer first waits until all VRLs for that BTC have been upgraded to CRLs. It then tries to upgrade all of this BTC's TCRLs by making Read/upgrade requests to the 2PL layer. Finally, it tries to upgrade the BTC's VWLs. For each VWL it must first determine if there are any conflicting TCRLs and whether they can be preempted. If no conflicting TCRLs remain, a Write/upgrade request is made to the 2PL layer.

To commit a BTC, the HBT-MV-2PL layer must upgrade all VRLs which have read data which was written by the committing BTC. It does so by sending Read/set requests to the 2PL layer for the appropriate items. All locks held by the committing BTC are then released in the HBT lock table. A commit message is sent to the 2PL layer to release the BTC's locks there as well.

Abort processing also effects both layers. Hence, in addition to aborting the BTC within the HBT-MV-2PL layer, an Abort request is also sent to the 2PL layer.

4. Performance Evaluation of Branching Transactions in Shared-Memory Parallel Database System

In this section we compare the performance of our new hybrid algorithm (HBT-MV-2PL) with "normal" (non-branching) two-phase locking, assuming an underlying SMP hardware architecture.

4.1. Simulation Model

The system is modeled as a closed queueing network with *NumTerm* terminals. After the completion of a

transaction is reported to a terminal, there is a random delay — drawn from an exponential distribution with mean *ThinkTime* — before the next transaction is started. These and other simulation parameters are summarized in Table 2. Unless stated otherwise, the values of these parameters are as indicated in this table.

The deadlock handling algorithm used in this study is Cautious Waiting [5]. Under this policy a transaction is aborted if it gets blocked by another transaction which itself is already blocked. This prevents any cyclic wait-for dependencies and deadlocks can, therefore, not occur. In the case of branching transactions, a BTC is aborted if it gets blocked by another BTC which belongs to a transaction which has all of its own BTCs either blocked, aborted or branched.

Each experiment was replicated (using different random number streams) until a confidence level of 90% for a confidence interval of ±10% of the output variable was reached.

Parameter	Meaning	Value
NumTerm	number of terminals	50
ThinkTime	think time of a user before submitting a new transaction	2.5 sec
TransSize	average size of a transaction	10 pages
WriteProb	probability that a DB access a write operation	0.5
PageCPU	CPU time to process one page	10 ms
DBSize	size of the database in pages	1000
NumCPU	number of CPUs in system	5
NumDisks	number of disks in system	4
PageIO	page transfer time between disk and main memory	35 ms
UndoCPU	CPU time to undo an update	1 ms
CacheHit	probability of a DB cache hit	0.7

Table 2. Simulation Input Parameters

4.2. Simulation Results

Transaction Workload This first experiment measures response times for an increasing workload, where the workload was increased be reducing the *Thinktime* from 4.5 seconds to 0.5 seconds. Results are shown for 10% and 50% Write operations.

Figure 2 shows a clear performance advantage for HBT-MV2PL over 2PL in case of 50% Write operations. When only 10% of a transaction's operations were updates, no performance difference could be observed, except for high workloads, where HBT-MV2PL was again better than 2PL.

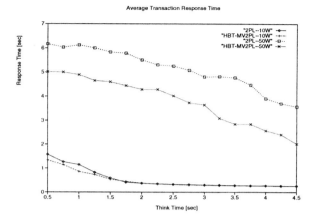

Figure 2. Response Time vs. Workload

It is not surprising that virtually no difference in performance between 2PL and HBT-MV2PL was found in lower workloads with 10% Write operations. Since 90% of operations are Reads, which do not conflict with each other, there is only little data contention, and performance is mostly determined by the availability of hardware resources. The Read/Write ratio of transaction operations is obviously an important factor for the relative performance of HBT-MV2PL. The next experiment looks at this aspect in more detail.

Read/Write Ratio In this experiment the workload was fixed (*ThinkTime* = 2.5sec) and the percentage of Write operations varied from 0% to 100%. Results are shown in Figure 3.

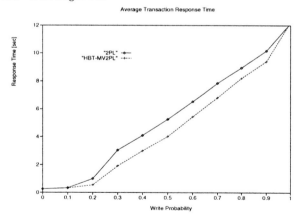

Figure 3. Response Time vs. Write Probability

As expected, there is no difference in performance between 2PL and HBT-MV2PL for a read-only environment since no data access conflicts occur. Under both algorithms each Read-lock request is granted immediately; since no Write operations are executed, no exclusive Write-locks ever exist on any data item. Fur-

thermore, no branching takes place, since no temporary, uncommitted versions of data items are ever created.

As the Write probability increases, HBT-MV2PL gains a performance advantage over 2PL. The improvement, however, is getting less once the probability of a Write operation exceeds 0.5, and is entirely lost in a Write-only environment.

To understand this behavior it is important to point out that Write operations are modeled as so-called "blind writes", i.e. the item which is updated is not read before-hand. This means that in the Write-only case, no Reads are executed at all. Since branching transactions only branch on Read operations, no branching takes place at all for 100% Write, and hence, no improvement of performance can be achieved.

Since the biggest performance improvements are achieved for the 50/50 Read/Write ratio, one would also expect to find most branching activity in this area. This is indeed the case as can be seen from Figure 4. Furthermore, as one would expect, more branching takes place for higher workloads, since Read/Write conflicts are more likely with more transactions in the system.

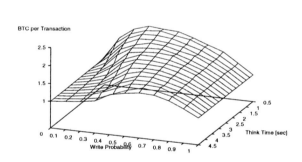

Figure 4. Average Number of BTCs per Transaction

Number of CPUs Since branching transactions compute several alternatives of transactions in parallel and all but one are eventually discarded, we expected a significantly higher utilization of CPUs when branching transactions are used. As a consequence, it was also expected that non-branching two-phase locking would outperform HBT-MV2PL in experiments with only one or two CPUs in the system.

To test this hypothesis, an experiment was carried out under which the number of available CPUs was varied from 1 to 10. All other parameters were fixed

(*ThinkTime* is 2.5 seconds, *WriteProb* is 0.5). The results are shown in Figure 5.

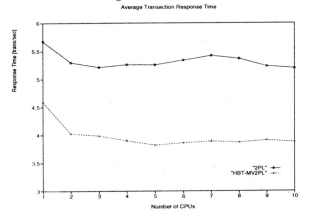

Figure 5. Response Time vs. Number of CPUs

Contrary to our expectations, even when CPU resources were sparse, branching transactions achieved a performance advantage over the non-branching approach. The explanation for this result lies in a wrong assumption that was made for the original hypothesis: under the same level of data contention, the branching transaction model leads to a significantly higher CPU utilization due to its branching activities, and hence, CPU shortage is a much more severe problem for branching transactions. This turns out not to be the case, i.e. even though the CPU utilization is somewhat lower for the non-branching case, the difference is not significant enough to offset the performance advantage of branching transactions. While a higher level of data contention leads to more branching activities, it is also true that, in the case of (non-branching) two-phase locking, the number of transaction restarts increases.

Branching Control Policies and Deadlock Handling For all experiments carried out the maximum number of BTCs allowed per transaction was 5. Increasing this number did not lead to any performance advantages. Lifting *all* branching restrictions did not lead to an explosion of the number of average BTCs, but stayed about the same as reported earlier. This may not be that surprising, considering the fact that a (non-branching) system may suffer from data contention, even though the average queue length for a page lock is no more than 1. A further consideration is the effect of an increasing number of transaction aborts which is likely to limit the amount of branching that takes place. As described earlier, the deadlock handling mechanism used in this study is "Cautious Waiting", a mechanism which is more likely to cause transaction aborts than a wait-for-graph based approach. It would

be of interest to carry out a comprehensive study of the effects of various deadlock handling algorithms on the performance of branching transactions.

5. Conclusion

With an increasing availability of parallel computers, in particular SMP systems, the performance bottleneck in a parallel DBMS is likely to shift from resource to data contention (for some application types: OLTP). Branching transactions offer a new way of exploiting parallel hardware to address the issue of data contention.

In this paper, we introduced a new concurrency control algorithm which can dynamically switch between branching and non-branching modes at run-time, and therefore, exploit the parallelism of branching transactions without ever overloading the system. A two-layer approach for such an algorithm was proposed to be able to reuse existing two-phase locking software when developing a branching transaction system.

A performance study of branching transactions in a shared-memory parallel hardware environment confirmed that performance improvements can be achieved without the need of excessive branching. It also emerged, however, that the choice of deadlock handling may be an important factor in the performance of a branching transaction system, and that further studies in this area are required.

References

[1] A. Bestavros and S. Broudakis. Value-cognizant Speculative Concurrency Control for Real-Time Databases. *Information Systems*, 21(1):75–101, 1996.

[2] A. Burger. *Branching Transactions: A Transaction Model for Parallel Database Systems*. PhD thesis, The University of Edinburgh, Scotland, 1996.

[3] A. Burger and P. Thanisch. Branching Transactions: A Transaction Model for Parallel Databases. In *Proceedings of the 12th British National Conference on Databases*, pages 122–136, July 1994.

[4] P. Franaszek and J. Robinson. Limitations of Concurrency in Transaction Processing. *ACM Transactions on Database Systems*, 10(1):1–28, March 1985.

[5] M. Hsu and B. Zhang. Performance Evaluation of Cautious Waiting. *ACM Transactions on Database Systems*, 17(3):477–512, September 1992.

Adding Persistency Support to DO-OPEN

Lorenzo Mezzalira [1], Andrea Omodeo [2], Matteo Pugassi [1], Nello Scarabottolo [3]

1 Dipartimento di Elettronica e Informazione, Politecnico di Milano
piazza L. da Vinci 32, I20133 Milano, Italy

2 ENEL, Centro Ricerca di Automatica
via Volta 1, I20093 Cologno Monzese (MI), Italy

3 Dipartimento di Scienze dell'Ingegneria, Università degli Studi di Modena
via Campi 213, I41100 Modena, Italy

Abstract

In this paper, we discuss the concept of object persistency (i.e., the capability of an object to keep track of its state changes across different executions of the same Object-Oriented program) when applied to distributed systems.

In particular, we show why different kinds of persistency may become useful in real industrial applications, and we present the implementation strategy we adopted for our DO-OPEN environment (a distributed Object-Oriented programming environment prototype for C++ programs we built on top of the PVM communication library for networked UNIX systems).

1. Introduction

The work here described is the evolution of a prototype Distributed Object-Oriented Programming ENvironment (DO-OPEN) developed by the authors under research contract CRA 71/94 and presented in [1].

The rationale behind the design of such a prototype was the need of an industry-oriented tool for supporting development of compute-intensive applications (e.g., simulation of large electric power generation and distribution plants) coupling:

- the availability of huge amounts of "wasted" processing power in networked PCs and workstations;
- the advantages of the Object-Oriented programming approach in terms of team work support and software reusability;

- the vitality of *de facto* standards in the arena of Object-Oriented programming (i.e., the C++ programming language [2][3]) and distributed computing (i.e., the PVM [4][5][6] runtime support).

The DO-OPEN prototype described in [1] proposed a solution to the very basic problem of distributing C++ based Object-Oriented applications upon a network of UNIX workstations, adopting PVM to allow the construction of a Parallel Virtual Machine. This solution — summarized in section 3 — proved to be very efficient and almost transparent to the structure of sequential C++ code (i.e., C++ code written for a single machine). However, several features of a complete Object-Oriented environment were left in this first prototype, and postponed after the demonstration of the feasibility of a simple, C++ based environment on top of PVM.

Among these features, we started considering *persistency* as a key aspect in the industrial environment we were looking for. The rest of the paper is organized as follows:

- section 2 discusses persistency, and how it has been introduced in other works related to this subject;
- section 3 briefly recalls the main characteristics of DO-OPEN;
- section 4 discusses how persistency has been added to DO-OPEN;
- section 5 details the structure of persistent DO-OPEN;
- section 6 shows the guidelines of an example.

2. Object persistency

In Object-Oriented programming, an object is defined *persistent* if it has the property of keeping track of its

This work has been supported by ENEL, the Italian Power Company, under research contract R23VC0003.

388

states across multiple executions of the same instance. This means that, at every activation, an object can use some form of "object memory" to reload its previous state, thus modifying its behavior depending on previous activation results.

The importance of persistency is manifold:

- by keeping track of previous history, it is possible to define data structures which span over the life of programs (this means, e.g., the ability to manage databases where data are stored inside C++ objects);
- persistent objects are a way to add checkpointing features to a program, both for enabling transaction processing and for adding fault tolerance to the resulting system. The programmer can force a *save* operation when the program is in a known good state, so this state can be recovered in case of a hardware/software failure;
- in industrial control applications, persistency is a *must* to allow the controller to correctly resume its control activities after being switched off (e.g., as a consequence of a power failure).

The importance of persistency is well proved by the attention it received from several works, related to DO-OPEN, present in the literature ([4], [5], [6], [7], [8], [9], [10], [11], [12], [13], [14], [15], [16], [17], [18], [19]).

For instance, the Arjuna system — described in [7][8] — automatically adds persistency to *every* remote class, whose state is continuously mirrored to disk storage (in some sense, the "real" object state is kept by Arjuna in secondary storage, while the main memory just holds its temporary, evolving copy).

On the contrary, the Mentat system — described in [9][10][11] — distinguishes between *regular* classes (which can be freely instantiated by the system wherever possible) and *persistent* classes (needing coherent activation and state tracking in secondary storage).

The higher degree of freedom foreseen by the Mentat approach suggested us to consider persistency in DO-OPEN as an *optional* attribute of a class; in fact, this allows:

1. to limit the state saving and loading overhead to the objects actually requiring historical memory;
2. to ease parallel activation and concurrent use of objects whose lifetime does not encompass several program activations.

Like Arjuna and Mentat we decided to hide persistency handling details in order to ease system usage, instead of forcing the programmer to deeply understand implementation details as in the CORBA approach — described in [19], [20], [21] and [22] — The proposed implementation of DO-OPEN persistency is described in section 4, after a brief discussion of the basic DO-OPEN characteristics.

3. Main characteristics of DO-OPEN

As already said, DO-OPEN (short for Distributed Object-Oriented Programming ENvironment) is a system aimed at the seamless realization of Object-Oriented applications on a PVM [4][5][6] virtual machine.

The key aspects of DO-OPEN are related to its implementation on top of a virtual machine like the one supplied by PVM itself:

- capability to run on any platform where the virtual machine is available, thus allowing the usage of heterogeneous parallel machines;
- use of standard C++ syntax, thus allowing porting of existing C++ applications and/or prototyping on normal C++ systems.

In DO-OPEN, three types of objects exist:

1. *standard C++* objects, that belong to a given task and cannot be used by other tasks running on the virtual machine;
2. *public* remote objects, whose methods can be invoked over the network (thus implying shared use of them by other tasks);
3. *private* objects (anonymous), accessible only by the tasks that receive the object handle from the object owner.

Every DO-OPEN object is a separate PVM task, so the programming model is suitable for what is usually called "coarse grain" parallelism. Multiple client tasks can invoke methods on the same object, which becomes a shared data structure. Currently, the method scheduler executes method invocations on a sequential, first-in first-out basis; a future version may include the capability of concurrently executing methods based on user-specified rules.

The system has the capability of running activities in parallel (i.e. the local code and one or more remote object methods) by declaring a special form of variables identified by the `future` *keyword*. A future variable can be used to receive the result of a remote method: the called method and the client can evolve in parallel until the method result is actually needed by the client.

Distributed classes are declared in a manner very similar to C++, with few limitations. The distributed environment requires the reinforcement of what is already considered "good" Object Oriented programming: functions that directly access data of other classes are strictly banned. If a C++ program already follows these guidelines, its conversion to DO-OPEN can be straightforward.

By using these features, a programmer can invoke methods simultaneously running on separate objects, possibly allocated on independent computers of the same

Parallel Virtual Machine. Some demo applications have already been written using DO-OPEN, deriving them from "normal" C++ applications.

From the implementation point of view, in DO-OPEN, the remotization of objects is obtained by generating a local class which "mirrors" the behavior of the real one. The real class is kept in a separate, "wrapper" task which answers to the network messages coming from the "mirror" objects. This structure is similar to what is used on some other distributed object systems, like Arjuna ([7], [8]) Mentat ([9], [10], [11]) and CORBA ([20], [21], [22]), where the communication details are hidden to the programmer.

Methods of the "mirror" class directly translate in the primitives needed to pack and send the parameters to the remote server. The programmer is required to write the procedures for sending any data type which is not directly supported by the system (e.g. C++ base types and mirror objects themselves). The mirror class then returns control to the caller, formatting the return data in a way that is suitable for *future* synchronization.

Obviously, many mirror objects can connect to the public server of a remote object, which becomes a shared resource.

4. Persistency in DO-OPEN

As already said, persistency in DO-OPEN is an *optional* attribute, set by prefixing a class declaration with the `persistent` keyword. The persistency attribute, together with the presence in DO-OPEN of public (named) objects and private (anonymous) ones, results in a richer object taxonomy:
- public and persistent
- public and non persistent
- private and persistent
- private and non persistent

It is our opinion that this variety of object types provides a wide coverage of normal user needs for persistent objects.

In fact, public (persistent or non persistent) objects easily model resources concurrently accessed by different tasks that provide atomic methods or that are internally capable of handling concurrency (e.g., printer drivers, database managers, and so on).

Private persistent objects provide a mechanism for handling complex systems, requiring accesses from different tasks in a sequential manner. For these objects, persistency is a way to keep track of the state from the previous instance to the current one, leaving all concurrency control to the DO-OPEN run-time support.

Private non persistent objects easily model stateless resources, that can be freely instantiated by each task (e.g., mathematical libraries or data crunching codes).

It is important to note that — in DO-OPEN — the `persistent` keyword prefixed to a class definition does not mean that every object of such a class will be persistent: only at the real object instantiation, it is possible to specify if the object instance has to be persistent and how.

In fact, we distinguished among different persistency policies for the two phases of the object life affected by persistency:
- start-up of an object instance (which is automatically performed by a connection to a remote object not yet activated);
- shutdown of an object.

The different persistency conditions that can be specified for object start-up and shutdown are:
- DO_NO_LOAD
- DO_SOFT_LOAD
- DO_HARD_LOAD
- DO_NO_SAVE
- DO_SAVE

The user can combine the previous object attributes in order to obtain the desired behavior from the newly instantiated object.

The DO_xx_LOAD group of attributes control the object start up phase, providing an exact control on the object state situation after the connection to the remote server.

The DO_NO_LOAD starts the object without trying to reload the state from the file system, obtaining a standard C++ object that is initialized by the constructor only.

Using the DO_SOFT_LOAD the user requires the runtime support to create the object with its constructor and, after, to try and load a previously saved state from mass storage.

The difference between the DO_SOFT_LOAD and the DO_HARD_LOAD is the action executed in case of a failure in the load attempt: the SOFT version continues the start up job reporting the error to the user (i.e. the client object), the HARD version aborts the job destroying the newly created object.

The DO_xx_SAVE attributes control the last phase of the life of an object, just before the destructor invocation.

The user can choose between two different options: DO_NO_SAVE that inhibits the autosave feature of a persistent object loosing the state, or DO_SAVE that enables the automatic save of the object state after the disconnection of the last client.

The absence of a DO_HARD_SAVE operating mode is due to the fact that, in DO-OPEN, a public object does not know the number of client objects connected to itself. Since a shutdown is automatically performed after the disconnection of the last client object, there is no possibility to report saving failures, because no other object in the system is caring about the activities of the object shutting down.

Two other attribute values exist, in order to ease the instantiation of standard persistent objects:

- DO_PERSISTENT
      (DO_SOFT_LOAD and DO_SAVE)
- DO_HARD_PERSISTENT
      (DO_HARD_LOAD and DO_SAVE)

Note that the general, automatic object naming support implemented in DO-OPEN ensures a coherent behavior of the activations of persistent objects (e.g., checking that subsequent users of a public object agree with the persistency mode set up by the first user during start-up).

During execution, a persistent object user can also issue a save state command that is transmitted to the remote object, which is the only one in charge of saving itself. It is DO-OPEN philosophy to leave to the user the task of performing real jobs: only the communication phases and the concurrency constraints are in charge of the run-time system. So the user — that knows the implementation details of the remote class — must provide the handling code of the save state message. He/she is in charge of contacting the object saver in order to obtain a *Save IDentifier* (SID) that will be used to save the state of the object itself and of all the other objects it contains. This save phase is propagated in a top-down manner from object to object until all the object states have been sent to the object saver. This hierarchical procedure ensures that all the vital parts of an object are saved in a consistent manner.

The restore phase is handled in the same way, thus ensuring that all objects receive their previous state without errors.

It must be noted that, differently from the CORBA approach, in DO-OPEN all the persistency management is provided by the runtime support, thus freeing the programmer from this tedious task.

5. Implementation details

In DO-OPEN, persistency support has been highly integrated with the existing runtime support. Before explaining how object persistency has been realized it is necessary to briefly outline the DO-OPEN runtime, which is extensively described in [1].

As with many other distributed object systems, what appears to the application programmer as a remote object is made up of two parts: a *local* one, linked to the calling program, and a *remote* one, which in our case is enclosed

in a PVM task. The first one, which we call *stub*, is a C++ object whose methods are declared to reproduce the behavior of the real class.

Every time the client program calls a method of the stub object, the supplied parameters are packed in a PVM message and sent to the remote object. The stub class definition is derived from the definition of the object to be remotized, by using a custom parser which adds a few keywords to standard C++.

Using C++ inheritance, the methods of the stub class are in part derived from the description supplied by the programmer, and in part inherited from a base class, which supplies basic DO-OPEN behavior (for instance keeping track of a stub-remote connection and managing the assignment and copy constructors for the stub).

Adding persistency support to the existing system required small modifications to the parser, which builds slightly changed versions of the stub and remote objects when the `persistent` keyword is specified in the object declaration. On the local side, the stub for a persistent class is derived from a different C++ base class, which contains additional methods required to force the remote object to save or restore its state.

On the remote side, methods are added to help the job of saving/restoring the state, but the ultimate decision of what to save and in which order to save it are left to the programmer, who is the only one knowing the behavior of the object, and who is required to supply a couple of methods. Helper functions are set up to save primitive types and to contact the "Object Saver".

The Object Saver is a PVM task available to DO-OPEN objects which need to save/restore their state. The Object Saver stores objects on persistent storage (the file system of the machine where it is running) as a tree of directories (one for each persistent class) and files.

Communications between DO-OPEN tasks are XDR-encoded using PVM primitives, and we decided to save objects to disk exactly on the same format. This guarantees that an object saved by a program running on a given machine can be restored on a different one.

The problem of saving objects having other objects as part of their state has been solved by introducing the concept of *save sessions*. When a persistent object is required to save its state (the method `save_to()` is called), the object contacts the Object Saver and a new save identifier (SID) is generated and returned to the object.

The object can then save its state using this SID, and then pass the same SID when it calls the `save_to()` method of the classes it encloses. This guarantees that the whole object state is recorded in an atomic session. This will also help to support inheritance between DO-OPEN classes, which will be the next step in the DO-OPEN project.

The choice of using a single Object Saver task has been taken in order to simplify the housekeeping needed on stored files, but nothing prevents from building a network of Object Savers available to remotized objects. The Object Saver state is always stored on disk, and the action of overwriting a stored image with a more recent version is atomic, ensuring that no damage can result from a Saver failure.

If the only need for persistency is to store and recover objects, the programmer is not even required to know about the Object Saver or its implementation. However, the Saver task exposes some programming interfaces that can be interesting for a distributed system.

The main feature allows the programmer to classify saved objets as programming scenarios. A program can save its state (by coordinately saving each of its objects) under a scenario and then try to change some of its runtime parameters to follow a certain execution path. If, during a certain time in the future, execution seems to reach a dead point, the program can save the "dead" state and restore the last known good one.

This feature is simply obtained by saving the objects in a directory tree under a user-defined root. If no root is specified, a default one is used. The programmer can select the current scenario by calling a specific function or using an external Object Saver control utility.

6. An example

The persistency modes defined in DO-OPEN have been tested on a case study, constituted by the simulator of an automated chrome-plating factory, constituted by the following main elements.

- **Input belt**, transferring single pieces to be processed inside the plant. Note that the various pieces can require different processing inside the plating plant: this corresponds to couple each piece with a corresponding *plating recipe*.
- **Cranes** (2), dedicated to move pieces around the plant.
- **Tanks** (n), containing different chemical solutions, and dedicated to different plating steps. Each tank can contain a single piece at the time, and is characterized by its own processing capability (thus, it may be required by a given piece according to the piece plating recipe).
- **Output belt**, transferring processed pieces outside the plant towards the storing area.
- **Operator console**, showing the state of the plant.

Mapping the above plant upon the O-O model supported by DO-OPEN — i.e., consisting of *passive* objects — resulted in the following set of **classes** and of main *methods*.

InBelt

PiecePresent	detects arrival and type of a new piece
GetPiece	picks a piece from the belt

Crane

GoTo	moves the crane
TransportPiece	transports a piece from input belt or tank to tank or output belt
GetState	gets state (e.g., idle/busy)

Tank

PlungePiece	signals insertion of a piece
ExtractPiece	signals extraction of a piece
GetState	gets state (e.g., empty/full)

OutBelt

PutPiece	stores a processed piece

Console

ShowTankInfo	shows state of a tank
ShowCraneInfo	shows state of a crane
ShowPieceInfo	shows state of a piece
Configure	configures display
GetUserInput	detects user commands

In addition to the above set, two additional classes have been defined:

WorkPiece

PlungeIntoTank	signals insertion into tank
ExtractFromTank	signals extraction from tank
GetNextProcess	asks for next recipe step
GetState	gets state (e.g., present position)

Scheduler

Start	starts plant activities

The overall plant is controlled by the Scheduler, which waits for tanks signaling the end of their job, looks for cranes free to move pieces, monitors pieces recipes and, when plant resources are available, looks for new pieces arrival.

Persistency has been added to take into account possible power failures of the plant, and to differentiate the behavior of the system during warm boot. As a consequence, the various plant classes have been defined in the following way:

- HARD persistency has been used for the Scheduler (which has to know the plant layout) and for each Workpiece (which must remember its recipe and the plating step(s) it already passed);
- SOFT persistency has been assigned to Tank objects: in fact, a tank should know its own state (e.g., usage of its chemical solution, maintenance information, etc.) but it can also be activated from scratch by refilling it before usage.

- NO persistency is required for Cranes and for Belts (the position and the state can be detected through suitable sensors at each power on).

The simulation code obtained with DO-OPEN allowed us to evaluate different scheduling algorithms, distributions of computing nodes inside the plant, and to estimate several possible situations arising in case of power failures.

7. Concluding remarks

Persistency is considered a very attractive characteristic for dealing with flexible, distributed Object-Oriented applications. The DO-OPEN approach emphasizes programmer's freedom by defining:

- a *persistent* attribute, optionally given to classes whose objects may require persistency;
- several persistency policies, which can be requested when an object is actually instantiated by another object.

8. Acknowledgments

Thanks are due to Dario Lucarella of the Information Technology Department of ENEL, for having promoted and advised the DO-OPEN research project.

9. References

[1] A. Omodeo, M. Pugassi, N. Scarabottolo: "DO-OPEN: a Distributed Object-Oriented Programming Environment", 4th Euromicro Workshop on Parallel and Distributed Processing, Jan 1996.

[2] B. Stroustrup: "The C++ Programming Language", 2nd ed., *Addison-Wesley*, 1991.

[3] ANSI Committee X3J16: "Working Paper for Draft Proposed International Standard for Information Systems: Programming Language C++", Apr. 1995.

[4] V. S. Sunderam "PVM: a Framework for Distributed Computing", *Concurrency: Practice and Experience*, Vol. 2, no. 4, Dec. 1990.

[5] A. Geist, A. Beguelin, J. Dongarra, W. Jiang, R. Mancheck, V. Sunderam: "PVM - A Users' Guide and Tutorial for Networked Parallel Computing", *MIT Press*, 1994.

[6] A. Beguelin, J. Dongarra, A. Geist, R. Mancheck, V. Sunderam: "Recent Enhancements to PVM", 1994, available via anonymous ftp from netlib2.cs.utk.edu in /pvm3.

[7] S. J. Caughey and S. K. Shrivastava: "Implementing Fault-Tolerant Object Systems on Distributed Memory Multiprocessors", *Proc. of the Second IEEE International Workshop on Object Orientation in Operating Systems*, Sep. 1992.

[8] G. D. Parrington: "Reliable Distributed Programming in C++: the Arjuna Approach", *Second USENIX C++ Conference*, Apr. 1990.

[9] A. S. Grimshaw: "The Mentat Run-Time System: Support for Medium Grain Parallel Computation", *Proceedings of the 5th Distributed Memory Computing Conference*, Apr. 1990.

[10] A. S. Grimshaw: "Easy to use Object-Oriented Parallel Programming with Mentat", *IEEE Computer*, May 1993.

[11] A. S. Grimshaw: "Mentat Programming Language (MPL) Reference Manual", *University of Virginia, Computer Science TR. 91-32*, 1991.

[12] M. Albano, R. Morrison: "Persistent Object Systems: Implementation and Use", Sprinter-Verlag, 1992.

[13] M.P. Atkinson, R. Morrison: "Orthogonally Persistent Object Systems", *VLDB Journal*, Vol. 4, Mar. 1995.

[14] M.P. Atkinson, P.J. Bailey, K.J. Chisholm, W.P. Cockshott, R. Morrison: "An Approach to Persistent Programming", *Computer Journal*, Vol. 26, n. 4 1983.

[15] E. Fong, D. Yang: "Interoperability Experiments with CORBA and Persistent Object Base Systems", *U.S. Department of Commerce, National Institute of Standards and Technology, Computer System Laboratory*, Gaithersburg, MD 20899, 1995.

[16] P. Laurent, N. Silverio: "Persistence in C++", *Journal of Object-Oriented Programming*, Oct. 1993.

[17] R. Morrison, R.C.H. Connor, Q.I. Cutts, G.N.C. Kirby: "Persistent Possibilities for Software Environments", *The Intersection between Databases and Software Engineering*, IEEE Computer Society Press, 1994.

[18] M. Sequeira, J.A. Marques: "Can C++ be used for programming distributed and persistent objects?", *Proc. 1991 Int'l Workshop on Object-Orientation in Operating Systems*, Palo Alto, CA, Oct. 1991.

[19] Object Management Group: "Persistence Service", *OMG Document 94.10.17*, 1994.

[20] Object Management Group: "Common Object Request Broker: Architecture and Specification, Revision 2.0", *OMG Document 96.03.04*, 1996.

[21] Object Management Group: "C++ Language Mapping Request for Proposal", *OMG Document 92.12.11*, 1992.

[22] S. Vinoski: "Distributed Object Computing with CORBA", *C++ Magazine*, Jul./Aug. 1993.

PARALLEL ALGORITHMS FOR POLYADIC PROBLEMS

Rodríguez C., González D., Almeida F., Roda J., García F.
Dpto. Estadística, Investigación Operativa y Computación,
Universidad de La Laguna, Tenerife, Spain
casiano@ull.es

Abstract

We broach the optimal parallelization of biadic dynamic programming problems using the simplest topologies, pipeline and ring networks. A general parallel approach is presented and applied very efficiently to three problems: the two-dimensional cutting stock problem, the integral knapsack problem and the multiplication parenthesization problem. These three examples can be viewed as instances of a same paradigm to obtain optimal parallel algorithms for biadic problems. Experimental results both for transputer networks and for local area networks using PVM are presented. The experience proves that the parallel technique can be easily and efficiently implemented.

1. Introduction

Dynamic programming is an important problem-solving technique that has been widely used in various fields such as control theory, operations research, biology, and computer science [6]. Sequential computation for dynamic programming has been studied extensively. General discrete Dynamic Programming programs viewed as multistage finite automatons with a certain cost structure superimposed are presented in [15, 18]. Hybrid dynamic programming/branch and bound approaches as a way to reduce storage and to improve the efficiency of the programs are introduced in [13, 14, 20, 25].

Many authors describe parallel algorithms for specific Dynamic Programming problems. Parallel dynamic programming algorithms for 0/1, two-dimensional and integer knapsack problems have been proposed for different architectures in [2, 3, 5, 8, 9, 24, 25, 29]. A general model for parallel Dynamic programming for multistage processes has been presented in [28]. However, there are problems which does not fit the multistage model so, the parallel model described in [28] can not be applied, these type of problems are usually referred as polyadic problems.

A generic instance of a biadic dynamic programming problem can be stated as the following recurrent computation in the set of states Q of the problem:

$$G(q) = min \{\mu(G(q'),G(q'')) \, / \, \lambda(q',q'') = q\} \; (I)$$

where q, q' and q'' are states, λ is the combination or transition function and μ is an arbitrary cost function. The problem to solve is to find

$$G^* = min \{G(q) \, / \, q \text{ in } Q_F\} \; (II)$$

where Q_F is a subset of distinguished final states.

This is a biadic problem because it involves two recursive terms. Specific biadic relations such as shortest paths, optimal binary search tree, optimal chained matrix multiplication parenthesizations etc. have been approached for systolic arrays [19, 27], general sharedmemory multiprocessors [10] for PRAM models in [11, 17] and for a ring of processors in [22].

We broach the parallelization using the simplest topologies, pipeline and ring networks, of three biadic problems: the two-dimensional cutting stock problem, the integral knapsack problem and the multiplication parenthesization. The same parallel technique is applied efficiently to the three problems. These three examples can be viewed as instances of a same paradigm to obtain optimal parallel algorithms for biadic problems.

In section 2 we describe the general parallel method used for the three problems. Sections 3, 4 and 5 describe the problems considered and their parallel algorithms respectively.

For each problem we present the experimental results both on a LAN using PVM and on a transputer network using Inmos languages. The LAN is an heterogeneous system consisting of 31 SUN workstations (IPX, SPARC-5, SPARC-10 and SPARC-20) connected via an ethernet network. The transputer network consists of a reconfigurable array of 32 T805 transputers (links operating at 10Mb/s) hosted on a PC. Each PVM program was executed 10 times for each problem. To avoid conflicts with the LAN users and to grant a low load of the LAN, all the experiments were accomplished during the night. The execution was performed only when the load was lower than a certain threshold. All the tables show the best time obtained from these 10 experiments. The sequential time for the PVM corresponds to an IPX SUN. All the times are expressed in seconds.

Along the paper, all the code segments describing algorithms are expressed in a Superpascal [7] or occam [16] like style.

2. The General Method

Since we are dealing with a biadic problem, the value G^* of equation (II) must be computed, according to the values $G(q)$ of equation (I). The general strategy is to find an ordered partition $\Pi = \{Q_0, ..., Q_n\}$ of Q such that the dependence graph given by λ always goes in increasing order of the partition indices, that is:

For all q_i in Q_i and q_j in Q_j, the state $q_r = \lambda(q_i, q_j)$ belongs to a set Q_r with index $i \leq r$ and $j \leq r$.

This fact allows to solve the problem using a pipeline with as many processors as sets Q_j in the partition Π by allocating the computation of the optimal values $G(q)$ with q in Q_j to processor j. When computing $G(q)$, processor j receives and echoes the optimal values $G(q')$ with q' in Q_i, $i < j$. As soon as $G(q)$ is computed it is immediately sent to the neighbour in the right. When the number n of sets in the partition exceeds the number p of processors the set Π is partitioned into subsets of bands $B(k)$, $1 \leq k \leq n/p$ in such a way that Q_j belongs to $B(k)$ if and only if, $j / p = k$ [23]. Implementation is achieved on a one way ring topology where the first and last processors are connected through the root processor. Besides its participation in synchronizations, the root processor also administrates a queue where messages are stored. A straightforward implementation of this idea will lead to an inefficient behaviour of the parallel algorithm. The values produced when computing the band $B(i)$ are turning around the ring for all bands $B(k)$, $k > i$. This produces an unnecessary replication of values that have been already received. This phenomenon can be easily avoided by discarding during the computation of band $B(k+1)$ the values produced during the computation of band $B(k)$.

3. The Two-dimensional Cutting Stock problem (CSP)

The *two-dimensional cutting stock problem* (CSP) [12] can be stated as follows:

Consider a supply of stock rectangles of width W and length L, and a demand for N_i rectangles of width w_i and length l_i, $i = 1, ..., n$. A two-dimensional problem is to cut the stock rectangles into the smaller demand rectangles using as few stock rectangles as possible.

Problems resembling the one just described turn out to be surprisingly common in applications. Among obvious examples of this are the production of glass, metal sheets, newspapers design among many others. Inexpensive cutting methods appear frequently to have one common characteristic: a cut in a piece of material must begin on one side of the material and traverse the material in a straight line to the other side. This is the kind of cut made by many types of machinery and used in many industries. One example is the guillotine cutter used in cutting paper sheets, and for this reason this type of cut is called a guillotine cut. Restricting the admissible cuts in a two-dimensional cutting pattern to guillotine cuts severely limits the permissible patterns.

The problem is to maximize $p_1z_1 + p_2z_2 + ... + p_nz_n$ where p_i is a profit associated to rectangle i and z_i are non-negative integers such that the rectangle (L, W) can be divided into z_i rectangles of size (l_i, w_i). A two dimensional rectangle function $F(x, y)$ can be defined that gives the maximum total profit obtainable for any stock rectangle of size (x, y) using all n rectangles. $F(x, y)$ can be computed using the recurrence [12]:

$F(x, y) = max \{F_0(x, y), F(x_0, y) + F(x - x_0, y), F(x, y_0) + F(x, y - y_0)\}, 0 \leq x_0 < x/2, 0 \leq y_0 < y/2. F_0(x, y) = max\{0, p_i / l_i \leq x \text{ and } w_i \leq y\}.$

The sequential algorithm for this problem following this recurrence function runs in time $O(LW(L + W) + n) = O(LW(L+W))$ [12].

Since for this problem the transition function is given by $\lambda((i, k), (i, j - k)) = (i, j)$ for all k in $[0, j/2]$ and

$\lambda((k, j), (i - k, j)) = (i, j)$ for all k in $[0, i/2]$. an obvious choice for the set of states is to take $Q_j = \{(i, j) / 1 \leq i \leq W\}$ as the column j, $1 \leq j \leq L$. Following the general scheme described in section 2 the parallel algorithm in figure 1 can be obtained. Figure 1 shows the code for processor with identifier *name*. The code segments of lines 12-15, 17-28 run in parallel. Using the loop of lines 13-14 the processor updates $F[i][j]$ in term of the optimal values corresponding to its own column. At the same time the values corresponding to the former band starting from its neighbour in the right and ending in the processor in the left in the ring are received using lines 21-27. Its own last value emitted in the former stage is discarded in line 18. Now all the values required to perform the second type of dependencies have been arrived and are used in lines 30-31.

Theorem: The parallel algorithm of figure 1 is optimal and its complexity is $O(LW(L+W)/p + L)$.

proof: See [4].

3.1. Experimental results

Tables 1 and 2 show the experimental results obtained for the execution of this algorithm on the transputer network and on the local area network respectively. We have

```
1:    for k := 0 to num_objects do – Initialization code
2:        F[w[k]][l[k]] = p[k];
3:    bands := (L + 1) / num_processors;
4:    – omited code for the first band
5:    for b := 1 to bands do
6:    begin
7:        j := (num_processors * b) + name; – current column
8:        last_column := (j = L );
9:        for i := 2 to W do
10:       begin
11:          cobegin
12:          begin
13:              for k := 0 to (i/2) do – compute in column
14:                  F[i][j] := max(F[i][j], F[k][j] + F[i - k][j]);
15:          end
16: ||
17:          begin
18:              in ? CASE value; dummy;
19:              – take out of the circulation the value
20:              – produced in former band
21:              for k := 1 to num_processors do – receive and send
22:              begin
23:                  received := old_j + k;
24:                  in ? CASE value; F[i][received];
25:                  if NOT last_column then
26:                      out ! value; F[i][received];
27:              end;
28:          end;
29:          coend;
30:          for k := 0 to (j/2) do – compute in row
31:              F[i][j] := max(F[i][j], F[i][j - k] + F[i][k]);
32:          if NOT last_column then
33:              out ! value; F[i][j]; – Sends current value
34:          old_j := j;
35:      end;
36: End
```

Figure 1. Parallel algorithm for the CSP. Code for processor name.

```
1: for object := 1 to n do
2:    if F[w[object]] < p[object] then
3:        F[w[object]] := p[object];
4: bands := (M + 1) / num_processors
5: – omited code for the first band
6: for b := 1 to bands do
7: begin
8:    j := (num_processors * b) + name; – current column
9:    last_column := (j = M );
10:   in ? CASE value; dummy; – take out of the circulation
11:   – the value produced in former band
12:   for k := 1 to num_processors do – receive and send
13:   begin
14:       received := old_j + k;
15:       in ? CASE value; F[received]
16:       if NOT last_column then
17:           out ! value; F[received];
18:   end;
19:   for k := 0 to (j/2) do – compute in column
20:       F[j] := max(F[j], F[k] + F[j - k]);
21:   if NOT last_column then
22:       out ! value; F[j]; – Sends current value
23:   old_j := j;
24: end;
```

Figure 2. Parallel algorithm for the IKP. Code for processor *name*.

developed six series of experiments where the demand rectangles have been randomly generated. Columns are labeled with the number of processors and rows with the problem. Problem *AxBxC* is a problem with $n = A * 100$ demand rectangles, an stock rectangle with length $L = B * 100$ and width $W = C * 100$. For this algorithm the factor $O(L)$ due to communications in the complexity of the algorithm dominates the computation. On the transputer network the larger is the quotient W/L the greater is the speedup of the algorithm since the overlapping between computation and communication is greater (lines 12-15 and 17-28 of algorithm in figure 2). An maximum speedup of 10 is obtained for problem 10x1x9 with 32 processors. On table II the columns holding '-' means that the running time increase with the number of processors. On the local area network the sequential algorithm reflects the effect of the memory access dependence on sizes of rows and columns, leading in some cases to a false superlinearity of the parallel algorithm. The best parallel results are obtained for small width of the stock rectangle ($W = 100$) on the contrary of the behaviour observed on the transputer network. In this case an small W implies a reduced number of communications.

4. The Integral Knapsack Problem (IKP)

The *integral knapsack problem* (IKP) can be formulated as follows:

Given a set Q of n different objects $Q = \{1,2,...,n\}$ and a knapsack of capacity M, where the object i has *weight* w_i and profit p_i, find a combination of nonnegative integers $x_1,...,x_n$ such that the total weight fits the knapsack, $w_1x_1 +...+w_nx_n \leq M$, and the total profit, $p_1x_1 +...+p_nx_n$, is maximized.

Knapsack problems arise as subproblems of many combinatorial problems. These combinatorial problems model many industrial situations such as cargo loading, capital budgeting, cutting stock and project selection [21].
A biadic dynamic programming formulation for this problem has been proposed in [25]. The recurrent formula for this problem is:

$$F_j = \max\{F_k + F_{j-k} / k = 1...j/2\} j = 1, ..., M$$

F_j gives the total profit for an integral knapsack problem of capacity j considering all the objects. The former recursive equation drives to a $O(M^2 + n)$ sequential algorithm.

For this problem

$$\lambda(k, j - k) = j \text{ for all } k \text{ in } [1, j/2]$$

and a feasible partition of the set of states is obtained taken $Q_j = \{j\}$, $1 \leq j \leq n$. Following the general method described in section 2 a parallel algorithm can be straightforwardly obtained (figure 2).

Theorem: The parallel algorithm of figure 2 is optimal and its complexity is $O(M^2/p+p)$.

proof: See [4].

4.1. Experimental Results

To contrast the performance of this algorithm we have developed nine series of experiements where randomized knapsack problems where generated. The number of objects (*400, 800* and *1600*) and the capacity of the knapsack (*800, 3200* and *12800*) were fixed. In each table row labeled kxc contains the times in seconds for the problem with the number of objects $n = k * 100$ and capacity $M = c * 100$. Tables 3 and 4 reflect that the behaviour of the algorithm is quite independent on the number of objects. A maximum speedup of 10 is obtained for problems with capacity 12800 and 32 processors on the transputer network, a maximum speedup of 2.5 is obtained for the largest problems.

5. The Multiplication Parenthesization problem (MPP)

Consider the problem of the evaluation of the products of n matrices $M_1 \times M_2 \times ... \times M_n$, where each M_i is a matrix with r_{i-1} rows and r_i columns. The order in which the matrices are multiplied together can have a significant effect on the total number of operations required to evaluate M, no matter what matrix multiplication algorithm is used. Trying all possible orderings in which to evaluate the product of n matrices is an exponential process [1], which is impractical when n is large. However, dynamic programming provides an $O(n^3)$ algorithm. Let $c(i, j)$ the minimum cost of computing $M_i \times M_{i+1} \times ...x M_j$ for $1 \leq i \leq j \leq n$. It can be easily stated that, $c(i, j) = 0$ if $i = j$,
$$c(i, j) = min\{c(i, k)+c(k+1, j) + r_{i-1}r_kr_j\}, i \leq k < j$$

Many problems in computer science can be solved by the use of this biadic recurrence equation. These include shortest paths, optimal parenthesization, matching problems, optimal triangulation of a polygon and optimal binary search trees among others [1, 11].

The transition function is defined for this problem as:
$\lambda((i, k), (k+1,j)) = (i, j)$ for all k in $[i, j)$ and the partition of the set of states can be obtained by simply considering $Q_j = \{(i, j) / 1 \leq i \leq j\}$ as the column j, $1 \leq j \leq n$ as depicts the algorithm in figure 3.

Theorem: The parallel algorithm of figure 3 is optimal and its complexity is $O(n^3/p)$.

proof: See [4].

5.1. Experimental Results

Tables 5 and 6 show the experimental results obtained both for the transputer network and for the local area network respectively. Five series of experiments have been developed where dimensions of the matrices have been randomly generated. Columns are labeled with the number

	1	2	4	8	16	31
10x9x1	254.56	249.51	126.35	123.06	93.53	87.93
20x9x1	254.57	249.55	126.41	123.18	93.77	88.38
10x5x5	712.15	557.62	283.54	237.43	172.46	156.20
20x5x5	712.16	557.66	283.6	237.56	172.70	156.66
10x1x9	245.56	151.19	78.85	48.00	31.58	25.23
20x1x9	245.57	151.23	78.91	48.13	31.82	25.69

Table 1. CSP: Time in Seconds for the transputer network.

	1	2	4	8	16	31
10x9x1	24.28	7.83	9.49	19.85	–	–
20x9x1	24.28	7.92	10.01	21.32	–	–
10x5x5	42.53	41.21	42.62	97.34	–	–
20x5x5	43.03	41.28	42.63	96.09	–	–
10x1x9	5.98	35.53	51.84	122.57	–	–
20x1x9	6.06	35.38	51.86	118.61	–	–

Table 2. CSP: Time in Seconds for the local area network.

	1	2	4	8	16	31
4x8	0.66	0.96	0.53	0.30	0.20	0.15
4x32	10.44	14.44	7.38	3.79	2.05	1.21
4x128	166.77	228.19	114.72	57.72	29.45	15.49
8x8	0.66	0.96	0.53	0.30	0.20	0.15
8x32	10.44	14.44	7.38	3.79	2.05	1.21
8x128	166.77	228.20	114.73	57.72	29.45	15.49
16x8	0.66	0.96	0.53	0.30	0.20	0.15
16x32	10.44	14.45	7.38	3.79	2.06	1.22
16x128	166.78	228.20	114.72	57.72	29.45	15.49

Table 3. IKP: Time in Seconds for the transputer network.

	1	2	4	8	16	31
4x8	0.10	0.85	0.70	0.70	0.80	0.85
4x32	1.71	4.24	2.84	2.40	2.32	2.30
4x128	26.64	61.94	30.39	18.50	12.10	9.49
8x8	0.10	0.68	0.66	0.68	0.86	0.85
8x32	1.72	4.18	2.84	2.37	2.44	2.27
8x128	26.76	60.67	30.48	18.29	12.16	9.94
16x8	0.10	0.69	0.71	0.67	0.82	0.88
16x32	1.71	4.50	2.88	2.43	2.40	2.29
16x128	26.62	56.29	30.20	18.40	12.11	9.96

Table 4. IKP: Time in Seconds for the local area network.

	1	2	4	8	16	31
100	2.64	1.84	1.14	0.79	0.62	0.53
200	21.01	13.96	7.46	4.62	3.17	2.43
300	70.68	45.29	23.33	13.7	8.72	6.18
400	167.26	108.28	57.71	30.22	18.37	12.28
500	326.36	210.11	108.21	56.34	33.15	21.21

Table 5. MPP: Time in Seconds for the transputer network.

	1	2	4	8	16	31
100	0.23	1.03	0.74	1.15	4.20	30.88
200	1.81	5.23	2.57	2.11	4.78	42.03
300	6.27	17.24	7.43	5.31	7.70	52.02
400	15.24	20.53	16.84	11.41	11.48	61.25
500	30.44	25.29	19.18	13.43	21.74	66.56

Table 6. MPP: Time in Seconds for the local area network.

```
1: for b := 0 to bands
2: begin
3:      j := (num_processors * b) + name; – current column
4:      last_column := (j = (num_matrices - 1));
5:      c[j][j] := 0;
6:      if last_column then
7:         out ! value; c[j][j];
8:      for m := 1 to j do
9:      begin
10:        i := j - m;
11:        c[i][j] := INFINITE;
12:        for k := i to j - 1 do – receive, send and compute
13:        begin
14:           in ? CASE value; c[i][k];
15:           if NOT last_column then
16:              out ! value; c[i][k];
17:           c[i][j] := min { c[i][j],
                    c[i][k] + c[k+1][j] + r[i] * r[k+1] * r[j+1]};
18:        end
19:        if NOT last_column then
20:           out ! value; c[i][j]; – send current value
21:     end;
22: end;
```

Figure 3. Parallel algorithm for the MPP. Code for processor *name*.

of processors and rows with the number of matrices in the problem. The speedup on the transputer network increases with the size of the problem and with the number of processors. A maximum speedup of 15 is obtained for problem 500 with 32 processors on the transputer network and a maximum speedup of 2.25 is obtained for the local area network with 8 processors.

6. Conclusions

A general parallel dynamic programming procedure that can be applied to biadic problems is presented. The proposed scheme admit easy and efficient implementations as confirm the computational experiments. These computational experiments agree with the theoretical results: the parallel approach proves to be optimal.

The computational results show the good scalability for the transputer network. For the local area network, the factor due to communications dominates the computation. The best results are obtained for the larger problems.

These three problems constitutes a same paradigm to obtain optimal parallel algorithms for biadic problems.

References

[1] Aho A., Hopcroft J., Ullman J.. *The Design and Analysis of Computer Algorithms*. Addison Wesley. 1974.

[2] Almeida F., Morales D., Roda J.L., Rodríguez C., García F.. *The Single Resource Allocation Problem: Parallel Algorithms on Distributed Systems*. Proceedings of the 19th Technical Conference of the World

399

Occam and Transputer User Group (WOTUG). Nottingham. 1996.

[3] Almeida F., García F., Morales D., Rodríguez C.. *A parallel algorithm for the integer knapsack problem for pipeline networks.* Journal of Parallel Algorithms and Applications. 6 (3/4). 1994.

[4] Almeida F. *Models in Parallel Dynamic Programming for the Discrete Case.* PhDegree. DEIOC. University of La Laguna. September 1996.

[5] Andonov, Raimbault, Quinton. *Dynamic Programming Parallel Implementations for the Knapsack Problem.* Technical Report 740. IRISA. June 1993.

[6] Bellman R.. *Dynamic Programming.* Princeton U. P.. 1957.

[7] Brinch Hansen P.. *The Programming Language Super-Pascal.* Soft.-Pract. Exp.. 24. 1994.

[8] Chen G., Chern M., Jang J.. *Pipeline Architectures for Dynamic Programming Algorithms.* Parallel Computing. 13, 111-117. 1990.

[9] Chen G., Jang J.. *An Improved Parallel Algorithm for 0/1 Knapsack Problems.* Parallel Computing. 18. 811-821. 1992.

[10] Edmonds P., Chu E., George A.. *Dynamic Programming on a Shared Memory Multiprocessor.* Parallel Computing. 19, 9-22. 1993.

[11] Gibbons A., Rytter W., *Efficient Parallel Algorithms.* Cambridge University Press. 1988.

[12] Gilmore P., Gomory R.. Multistage cutting stock problems of two or more dimensions. Operations Research. 13. 94-120. 1965.

[13] Helman P.. *A common Schema for Dynamic Programming and Branch and Bound Algorithms.* Journals of the Association for Computing Machinery. Vol. 36. 1, 97-128. 1989.

[14] Ibaraki T. *Branch and Bound procedure and the State-Space representation of Combinatorial Optimization Problems.* Inf. and Control. Vol. 36, 1-27. 1978

[15] Ibaraki T.. *Enumerative Approaches to Combinatorial Optimization*, Part II. Annals of Operations Research. Vol. 11, 1-4. 1988.

[16] INMOS Limited. *Occam2 Reference Manual.* Prentice Hall. Series in Computer Science. C.A.R. Hoare Series Editor. 1988.

[17] JáJá J. *An Introduction to Parallel Algorithms. Addison Wesley.* 1992.

[18] Karp R., Held M.. *Finite-State Processes and Dynamic Programming.* SIAM J. Appl. Math. 15, 693-768. 1967.

[19] Louka B., Tchuente M.. *Dynamic Programming on 2D Systolic Arrays.* Parallel Processing. 265-275. 1988.

[20] Marsten R., Morin T.. *A hybrid approach to discrete mathematical programming.* Mathematical programming. 14, 21-40. 1978.

[21] Martello S., Toth P. *Knapsack Problems. Algorithms and Computer Implementations.* John Wiley and Sons. 1990.

[22] Miguet S., Robert Y. *Dynamic Programming on a Ring of Processors.* Hypercube and Distributed Computers. Elsevier Science Publishers. 1989.

[23] Moldovan D., Fortes J.. *Partitioning and Mapping Algorithms into fixed size Systolic arrays*, IEEE Trans. Comput. C-35 (1), 1-12. 1986.

[24] Morales D., Roda J., Almeida F., Rodríguez C., García F.. *Integral Knapsack Problems: Parallel Algorithms and their Implementations on Distributed Systems.* Proceedings of the 1995 International Conference on Supercomputing. 218-226. ACM Press. 1995.

[25] Morales D., Roda J., Rodríguez C., Almeida F., García F.. *A parallel algorithm for the Integer Knapsack Problem.* Concurrency: Practice and Experience. Vol 8(4), 251-260. 1996.

[26] Morin T., Marsten R.. *Branch-and-Bound Strategies for Dynamic Programming.* Operations Research. Vol. 24. 4, 611-627. 1976.

[27] Myoupo J.. *Mapping Dynamic Programming onto Modular Linear Systolic Arrays.* Distributed Computing. 6, 165-179. 1993.

[28] Rodriguez C., Roda J., Garcia F., Almeida F., Gonzalez D.. *Paradigms for Parallel Dynamic Programming.* Proceedings of the 22nd Euromicro Conference. Beyond 2000: Hardware and Software Strategies. IEEE. Prague. September 1996. (to appear).

[29] Ulm D., Wang P.. *Solving a two-dimensional Knapsack Problem on SIMD Computers.* International Conference on Parallel Processing. 1992.

EDPEPPS*: An Environment for the Design and Performance Evaluation of Portable Parallel Software

T. Delaitre, G.R. Justo, F. Spies, S. Winter
University of Westminster
Centre for Parallel Computing
12-14 Clipstone street, London W1M 8JS

E-mail: {delaitt,justog,spiesf,wintersc}@wmin.ac.uk

Abstract

This paper describes the architecture of a development environment for computer-aided parallel software engineering. The environment comprises tools for program design, simulation, and visualisation. The toolset supports an interactive, performance-oriented software development life-cycle, and the user interface makes extensive use of graphics and animation.

1. Introduction

The recent rapid growth of parallel cluster computing has signalled the urgent need for tools to support a parallel program design life-cycle. Concurrent programs are certainly no less complex than serial ones, but whereas serial programmers can rely on a simple and stable programming model (the von Neumann machine), parallel programmers must cope with two additional issues: platform configuration; and mapping (of the concurrent program onto the parallel platform). In high-performance computing, many assumptions made by serial software engineers no longer hold. For example, in serial life-cycle models, performance engineering is a relatively low-priority activity. Yet in high-performance computing, one of the major areas in which parallel processing is currently being applied, performance is clearly the dominant issue.

In response to this problem, many researchers have developed tools and methodologies for parallel programming [1]. Typical first-generation tools, developed largely by hardware vendors, and based on proprietary hardware, are suitable for raw programming, but are not sophisticated enough for large-scale project use. The most recent approaches aim to provide a complete tool-based environment for computer aided parallel software engineering. For example, the SEPP project [2] has developed an overall architecture based on five principal tool types: Static Design Tools; Dynamic Support Tools; Behaviour Analysis Tools; Simulation Tools; and Visualisation Tools.

One of the earliest toolsets for parallel programming was the Transim/Gecko toolset, developed under the Parsifal project at the University of Westminster [3]. This toolset combines simulation of occam-like programs on transputer-based multiprocessors with an animation-based representation of the resulting trace. The tools have been placed in many research establishments, where they have been used with good effect in the design process. The approach has been the model for several simulation-based tool environment projects. The HAMLET Application Development System [4], is an environment for developing real-time applications for parallel architectures based on the transputer (primarily) and the PowerPC. The philosophy is essentially that of Transim/Gecko, but with increased sophistication. The environment combines graphical design tools, DES, for both software and hardware configurations, a simulation tool, HASTE, for predicting execution patterns, and a visualisation tool , TATOO, for examining execution traces. The system assumes contextual support from target tools such as debuggers, profilers and monitors, which run on the target system. The CAPSE (Computer Aided Parallel Software Engineering) environment [5] assists the development of performance-oriented SPMD (Single Program Multiple Data) programs by integrating tools for performance prediction, and analytical or simulation based performance analysis in the detailed specification and coding phase. The goal of the ALPES project [6] is to

*This project is funded by an EPSRC PSTPA programme, Grant Number : GR/K40468, and also by EC Contract Num: CIPA-C193-0251, CP-93-5383

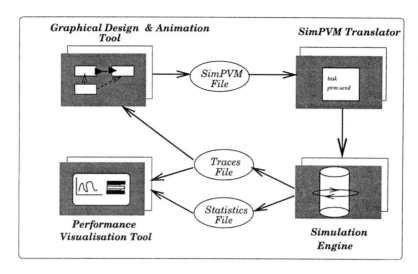

Figure 1. The EDPEPPS Architecture.

develop an environment for the performance evaluation of parallel programs on parallel machines. A parallel program is modeled as a valued task graph from which a parallel synthetic program is derived. This synthetic program can be modified in order to emulate different parameters of parallel machines like, for example, the computation/communication ratio. The synthetic program is executed. Traces are generated and treated. The presentation of performance information is done through a visualization tool.

The importance of visualisation as a design aid can hardly be overestimated. Currently, the ability to design complex computational systems is limited only by the imaginations of programmers and designers. Visualisations with high information content will increase the imaginative powers of the users, enabling them to develop increasingly sophisticated, and effective programs. A key feature of a visualisation facility is the ability to relate clearly cause and effect in a program, relating trends seen in actual (or simulated) behaviour to source code.

The aim of the EDPEPPS (Environment for Design and Performance Evaluation of Portable Parallel Software) project is to create a tool-based environment which will enable program designers to rapidly synthesize and evaluate methods for optimising the performance of concurrent software executing on a parallel platform. EDPEPPS is based on a rapid prototyping philosophy, in which the designer synthesizes a model of the intended software, which may then be simulated, and the performance subsequently analysed using visualisation.

In the next section, the main overall features and philosophy of the EDPEPPS environment are de-

scribed. The following sections deal with the individual tools, and their respective interfaces in some detail.

2. Overview of EDPEPPS

The EDPEPPS toolset is based on three principal tools: a graphical design tool (PVMGraph); a simulation facility; and a visualisation tool. Figure 1 illustrates the simple cyclic relationship between the three tools. Interfaces between the tools are defined: SimPVM, which represents the graphical program in a purely textual form; and two simulation output files, a trace file and a statistics file, which encapsulate the simulated program behaviour. EDPEPPS is based on an MPMD (Multiple Process Multiple Data) process model, and views the message-passing layer of a distributed operating system as the fundamental (parallel) execution platform. In the current phase of development, the message-passing and concurrency model is PVM [7], which is widely used and supported, and assumes a C+PVM parallel programming style.

The philosophy of EDPEPPS emphasizes the role of modelling and simulation as a solution to the parallel program design problem. Simulation is a well-known approach within traditional engineering disciplines (eg. VLSI design) and is invariably used to optimise the performance of the engineered product. For serial software engineers, however, the dominant design issue has been correctness, rather than performance, and the role of simulation as a software engineering tool has been relatively unknown. Based on models of a concurrent program, and the parallel execution platform, a simulation will yield approximate, but nevertheless highly useful information to the designer, facilitating the delivery of acceptable performance in the resulting system. As the design proceeds, the accuracy of the simulation model can be expected to improve, as measurements are gathered from the run-time system, giving more reliable information to designers and managers alike.

Simulation of the PVM platform in EDPEPPS is built using SES/Workbench^{TM} [8]. The Workbench has sophisticated built-in graphical input and visualisation facilities, which allow the rapid development of discrete-event simulations. The EDPEPPS simulation has four layers: the application layer; the message-passing layer; the operating system layer; and the hardware layer. By comparison, Transim was based on occam and the transputer – a two-level model. Simulations themselves can consume large amounts of computing power, and a related project at the University of Westminster is directed at the problem of optimising the performance of parallel discrete-event simulations [9].

Visualisation in EDPEPPS is derived from concepts pioneered in Gecko, in which graphical program representations are animated – thus "bringing the program to life". This not only maintains the necessary strong relationship between program and trace, but allows the designer to remain in the same visual environment for both the creative and analytic phases of the design process. The visualisation environment also makes extensive use of generic tools (ParaGraph for instance), in order to track a range of issues which originate within the platform, strictly below the 'visible' programming level.

3. Graphical Design of Parallel Programs

There are compelling reasons to represent (program) designs graphically. One of them is to expose the software structure as the description of the constituent software components and their patterns of interconnection, which provides a clear and concise level at which to specify and design systems. In terms of message passing parallel programs, their structures are naturally graphical as parallel activities can be represented by the nodes of a graph and message flow can be denoted by the arcs. This explains the popularity of graphical representations for parallel systems (for a survey refer to [10]). Furthermore, a clear description of a parallel program is important during the mapping and load balancing which are essential activities in the development of a parallel program.

Most of the graphical representations for parallel programs can be classified into two main groups: one concentrates on an abstract view of the design and specification, the other one concentrates on the details of the algorithm or behaviour of the task components. Examples of the first group are presented in [11, 12]. They represent the components of a design such as the modules (usually tasks or processes) and their relationships (port and message flow) but they do not describe the behaviour (or algorithm) of each task. At the other extreme, the representations in the second group [13, 14] enable us to describe the details of the behaviour of each task in a similar way to a flowchart. The advantage of the representations in the first group is to show the software structure but little can be done in terms of design analysis and evaluation as the behaviour of the tasks is hidden. In the representations of the second group, although the behaviour of each task is described, there is no clear relationship between the behaviour of each tasks and the structure of the whole program.

The graphical representation we are developing for EDPEPPS tries to balance the aspects of design structure and the behaviour description of the components into a single graphical representation. The principle is that the design of a parallel program consists of nodes (tasks) and arcs (message flow) but the graph must be enriched with special *allegories* (symbols) which correspond to important aspects of the behaviour of the tasks. Since EDPEPPS aims at PVM programs, these aspects refers to the operations of PVM. In this way, for most of the PVM operations we define special symbols.

A PVM program design consists basically of a collection of *processes* (*tasks*) which interact by message passing. A task is the basic component of the design. The *interaction* between tasks is carried out by calling PVM operations. A task is denoted by a *box* with its name, and each operation has its own symbol. In order to simplify the graphical representation, however, we assume at this stage[1] that the actions are divided into two groups: *inputs* and *outputs*. An *input* means that the task will receive some data if that interaction happens. An *output* means that the task will send some data. A triangle pointing to inside the box means an input. A triangle pointing to outside the box denotes an output. To identify to which operation the action corresponds the user must select one PVM operation when the action symbol is inserted. Figure 2 illustrates certain symbols of our graphical representation.

Some special PVM operations may correspond to more than one input or output at the same time. A **pvm_reduce**, for example, performs global operations over all the tasks in a group. All group members call **pvm_reduce** with their local data, and the result of

---

[1]In later versions, each operation will have its unique graphical symbol.

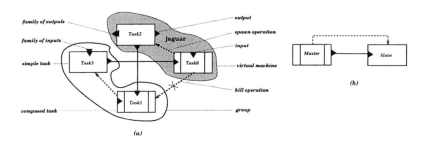

Figure 2. EDPEPPS graphical objects.

the reduction operation appears on the task specified as *root*. For the *root* task, a **pvm_reduce** corresponds to a "special input" as it receives several messages. This kind of input is defined as a *family of inputs* and is represented by two input symbols as illustrated in Figure 2. Similarly, **pvm_mcast**, **pvm_bcast** and **pvm_scatter** generate *families of outputs* which are also illustrated in Figure 2.

A task may contain sub-tasks forming a hierarchical structure. This type of task, called *composed task*, is represented with double boxes as shown in Figure 2. A task becomes a composed task when it calls the PVM **pvm_spawn** operation.

It is worth pointing out that the notion of composed task in PVM does not involve the idea of encapsulation (abstraction) as in Conic [11], for example, where the sub-tasks cannot interact directly with other tasks outside the composed task, except via the ports of the composed task. In PVM, the spawned task is a complete independent task. However, it is still important to document in the design the fact that one task is responsible for creating (**pvm_spawn**) or killing (sending a termination signal to – **pvm_kill**) other tasks. A *directed dotted-line* from *Task 0* to *Task 2* means that *Task 0* creates (**pvm_spawn**) *Task 1* (Figure 2). A *directed dotted-line with a cross in the middle* from *Task 0* to *Task 1* means that *Task 0* may kill (**pvm_kill**) *Task 1*.

Tasks which have compatible inputs and outputs can be connected. Consistency checks are carried out when two tasks are connected. These checks follow the semantics of the PVM operations. An interaction is denoted by a *solid line* as illustrated in Figure 2. A connection is not like a channel in Occam, for example, as connections are not explicitly declared in PVM.

An important part of the design of a parallel program is *agglomeration* where task are grouped to reduce parallelism or to simply the communication structure [15]. The concept of group in PVM corresponds to a collection of processes that is seen as unit. The main advantage of defining a group is that certain operations

can be applied to all members of the group instead of being applied individually. A group is represented as a *blob* (Figure 2) that delimits the member tasks of the group. One task can be member of more than one group, therefore group objects can overlap.

As described above, every graphical object in our representation corresponds to some PVM segment of code. The reverse is not necessarily true as not every PVM text has an equivalent graphical representation. The segment of code associated with a certain graphical object is supposed to denote its semantics. In order to maintain consistency, checks are carried out to guarantee that any change in a graphical object should affect its corresponding segment of code and vice-versa. A program skeleton can, therefore, be automatically derived from the graphical representation.

Unfortunately, in this paper we are not able to give all the details of the EDPEPPS graphical representation but the description presented in this section outlines the expressiveness of the representation. The first version of the EDPEPPS graphical, called **PVM-Graph**, has been completed and tested.

4. SimPVM - A Simulation Oriented Language

PVMGraph allows PVM applications to be developed using a combination of graphical objects and text. From this description, executable PVM programs may be generated, but to simulate program execution, annotations must be inserted into the graphical/textual source to control the simulation. This allows both an executable and a "simulatable" version of the program to be generated from the same graphical/textual source. All simulation models in EDPEPPS are based on queueing networks. The "simulatable" code generated by PVMGraph is predominantly a description of the software rather than the execution platform. To simulate the application, a model of the intended platform must be available. Thus, a simulation model is fundamentally partitioned into two submodels: a dynamic model automatically generated from the PVM-Graph description, which is comprised of the application software description and some aspects of the platform (eg. number and type of hardware nodes); and a static model which represents the underlying parallel platform, to a suitable level of detail. By building the static descriptions into the simulation system itself, the service is transparent to the application designer, yet provides a virtual, simulation platform for the generated application.

SimPVM lies above the *libpvm* level of the simulation model but some special functions are also provided that direct interaction with the kernel model. A SimPVM program is translated into an SES/Workbench [8] simulation model where lines of the program are interpreted as simulation objects[2], which can be a *Reference* for a process, a *Call to a Reference* for the PVM functions, or a *Specific Node* for C instructions.

5. Simulation

Simulation in EDPEPPS is based on discrete-event modelling a technique well-proven in the simulation of computer hardware and software. Discrete-event models underpin Transim for example, which achieves a remarkable degree of accuracy. The technology is well-established, and sophisticated modelling tools are available commercially. EDPEPPS uses SES/Workbench^{TM} [8], which has wide functionality meeting the requirements of computer system modelling, a time-saving graphical design interface, and animation-based visualisation capabilities. Techniques for parallelising discrete-event simulation programs are well-established, thus providing a route for optimising the run-time performance of the simulator. The workbench is used both to develop, and simulate platform models. Thus the simulation engine in the workbench is an intrinsic part of the prototype EDPEPPS toolset. The design of the platform simulator is described in the following sections.

The EDPEPPS simulation model consists of the PVM platform model itself and the PVM programs for simulation. The PVM platform model is partitioned into three layers (Figure 3): the *message passing layer*, the *operating system layer* and the *hardware layer*. Modularity and extensibility are two key criteria in simulation modelling, therefore layers are decomposed into modules which permits a re-configuration of the entire PVM platform model. The initial modelled configuration consists of a PVM environment which uses the TCP/IP protocol, and a cluster of Sun/SPARC

---

[2]The SES/Workbench simulation model language is defined by graphical nodes

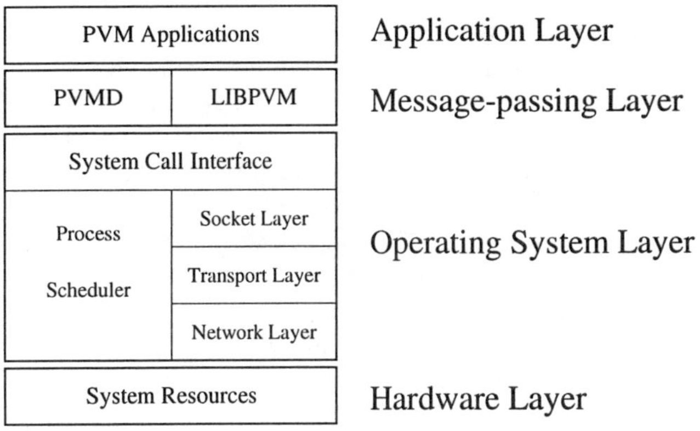

Figure 3. Simulation model architecture.

workstations connected to a single 10 Mbit/s Ethernet network.

A PVM program generated by the PVMGraph graphical design tool, is translated and passed to the workbench, where it is integrated with the platform model in readiness for simulation.

6. Visualisation

During the simulation, it is possible to generate (trace) information about the behaviour of the parallel application. This process is similar to the monitoring of an executing parallel application. However, it happens in a more controlled environment as the collection of information does not disturb the simulation in the same way as monitoring can affect the program execution.

In EDPEPPS, a trace file written in TAPE/PVM format [16] is generated during the simulation. This file contains the usual information (events) such as when the communication starts and ends but it also includes special tags which relate the events with the corresponding graphical objects of PVMGraph.

Our visualisation tool provides two views: a graphical animation of the design and a platform view of statistics. The graphical animation is useful to understand the behaviour of a parallel application. The platform view is useful for the optimisation of the system load balancing. The first version of the visualisation, which is part of PVMGraph is under development.

7. Conclusion

This paper has described a toolset, EDPEPPS, to support a performance-oriented parallel program design method. The toolset supports graphical design, performance prediction through modelling and simulation, and visualisation of predicted program behaviour. The designer is not required to leave the graphical design environment to view the program's behaviour, since the principal visualisation facility is an animation of the graphical program description, and the transition between design and visualisation viewpoints is virtually seamless. It is intended that this environment will encourage a philosophy of program *design*, based on a rapid synthesis-evaluation design cycle, in the emerging breed of parallel programmers.

Acknowledgement

Thierry Delaitre wishes to acknowledge the support and contributions of his supervisor, Dr. Stefan Poslad, in the simulation aspects of the work reported in this paper.

References

[1] C M Pancake. Software support for parallel computing: Where are we headed? *Comm. of the ACM*, 34(11):53–64, 1991.

[2] S. C. Winter and P. Kacsuk. Software engineering for parallel processing. In A. Pataricza, editor, *The Eight Symposium on Microcomputer and Microprocessor Applications*, volume 1, pages 285–293, Budapest Technical University, october 1994.

[3] E.R. Hart and S.J. Flavell. Prototyping transputer applications. In H.S.M. Zedan, editor, *Real-Time Systems with transputers*, pages 241–247. IOS Press: Amsterdam, 1990.

[4] P. Pouzet, J. Paris, and V. Jorrand. Parallel application design: The simulation approach with HASTE. In W. Gentzsch and U. Harms, editors, *High–Performance Computing and Networking*, volume 2, pages 379–393, International Conference and Exhibition, Munich, Germany, April 1994.

[5] A. Ferscha and J. Johnson. N-MAP: A virtual processor discrete event simulation tool for performance prediction in the CAPSE environment. In *28th Annual Hawaii International Conference on Systems Sciences*, pages 276–285. IEEE Computer Society Press, 1995.

[6] Joao Paulo Kitajima, Cécile Tron, and Brigitte Plateau. ALPES: a tool for the performance evaluation of parallel programs. In J. J. Dongarra and B. Tourancheau, editors, *Environments*

and Tools for Parallel Scientific Computing*, pages 213–228, Amsterdam, The Netherlands, 1993. North-Holland.

[7] V.S. Sunderam. PVM: A framework for parallel distributed computing. *Concurrency: Practice and Experience*, 2(4):315–339, December 1990.

[8] Scientific and Engineering Software Inc. *SES/ workbench Reference Manual, Release 2.1*. Scientific Engineering Software Inc., 4301 Westbank Drive, Austin TX 78746, February 1992.

[9] University of Westminster. Data processing and apparatus for parallel discrete event simulation. UK Patent Application No. 9419892.6 / US Patent Application No. 08/538248 (inventor: N. Kalantery), October 1994.

[10] P. Newton. A graphical retargetable parallel programming environment and its efficient implementation. Technical Report TR93-28, Dept. of Computer Sciences, University of Texas at Austin, 1993.

[11] K. Ng, J. Kramer, J. Magee, and N. Dulay. The software architect's assistant – a visual environment for distributed programming. In *28th Annual Hawaii International Conference on Systems Sciences*, pages 254–263. IEEE Computer Society Press, January 1995.

[12] M. R. Barbacci, C. B. Weinstock, D. L. Doubleday, M. J. Gardner, and R. Lichota. Durra: a structure description language for developing distributed applications. *Software Engineering Journal*, 8(2):83–94, March 1993.

[13] G. Dózsa, T. Fadgyas, and P. Kacsuk. GRAPNEL: A graphical programming language for parallel programs. In E. Selenyi A. Pataricza and A. Somogyi, editors, *Eighth Symposium on Microcomputer and Micropocessor Applications*, pages 285–293. IEEE Press, October 1994.

[14] G. Wirtz. Modularization, re-use and testing for parallel message-passing programs. In *28th Annual Hawaii International Conference on Systems Sciences*, pages 299–308. IEEE Computer Society Press, January 1995.

[15] Ian Foster. *Designing and Building Parallel Programs*. Addison-Wesley, 1995.

[16] E. Maillet. Tape/pvm an efficient performance monitor for pvm applications. Technical report, User guide LMC-IMAG technical report, 1993.

An Efficient Clustering-based Approach for Mapping Parallel Programs

M.A. Senar, A. Ripoll, A. Cortés and E. Luque
Departament d'Informàtica
Unitat d'Arquitectura d'Ordinadors i Sistemes Operatius
Universitat Autònoma de Barcelona
08193 - Bellaterra (Barcelona), SPAIN
e-mail: iinfd@cc.uab.es

Abstract[1]

An efficient task assignment scheme based on task clustering and task reassignment algorithms is proposed for the effective mapping of a parallel program onto a message-passing parallel computer. It is evaluated by comparison with various algorithms: Largest Processing Time First (LPTF), Largest Global Cost First(LGCF), Simulated Annealing (SA) and Tabu Search (TS). This strategy is suitable for applications which could be partitioned into parallel executable tasks without execution precedence limitation. It is shown to be very effective for computations whose communication topology matches some well-known regular graph families such as trees, rings and meshes, as well as for arbitrary computations with irregular communications patterns. Its solution quality is nearly as good as (and sometimes better) than that produced by Simulated Annealing and its computation time is several orders of magnitude less.

Keywords: Mapping, load balancing, task assignment, distributed-memory parallel machines, program graphs, heuristics.

1. Introduction

The mapping problem is one of assigning the tasks of a parallel program among the processors of a parallel computer in a way that minimises the total completion time of the program. In general, given a task graph modelling the parallel program, with vertex weights representing computational load of the tasks and edge weights reflecting the amount of data exchanged between tasks, the problem is that of assigning the vertices of the task graph onto processors in a way that minimises an objective function correlated with the program completion time [7].

This problem is known to be NP-complete [4] except in a few special situations with very unrealistic constraints that do not hold in practice. Hence, several heuristic algorithms capable of producing suboptimal solutions in a reasonable amount of computation time are proposed [1,2,3,5,8,9].

Heuristic methods fall into two main categories: greedy algorithms and iterative algorithms. First ones construct partially the solution and mapping is done without backtracking. The assignment of one task on one processor is based on a criterion that depends on the assignment of previously scanned tasks. In these algorithms the tasks are first sorted on a given criterion and then are mapped in that order on the processors.

Iterative algorithms start from an initial solution and try to improve it. Usually, this initial solution is found at random. Most iterative algorithms try to exchange tasks between processors to improve locally a solution and they also use random perturbations to leave local minima of the cost function and to obtain better solutions. These algorithms therefore have bigger complexity than greedy ones.

In this paper we propose a strategy based on the family of heuristic approaches that looks for a trade-off between the computational efficiency of the pure greedy methods and the solution quality of the pure iterative methods. This strategy is suitable for applications which could be partitioned into parallel executable tasks with negligible execution precedence limitation and mapped on message-passing parallel computers.

The heuristic is based on a task clustering algorithm (CA) that implicitly attempts to minimise the work load cost (execution time + communication time) for each

---

[1] *This work has been supported by the CYCYT under contract TIC 95-0868, and partially sponsored by the EU's Copernicus Programme under contract numbers CIPA CI-93-0251 and CIPA CP-93-5383.*

processor within which a task cluster is assigned. The assignment resulting from CA is further improved by task movements and task exchanges in an efficient way such that improves the assignment already found. A minimax cost function is formulated to evaluate the effectiveness of the mapping strategy.

The paper is organised as follows. Section 2 formally defines the mapping problem. Section 3 presents our new heuristic strategy based on clustering and reassignment algorithms. Section 4 presents experimental results and compares the performance of our strategy with other greedy and iterative methods when they are used to map some regular and irregular graphs that correspond to real parallel applications. Section 5 gives our final conclusions.

2. The mapping problem

In this section we formalise the mapping problem considered and describe the cost function that we attempt to minimise. The parallel program is modelled by a Task Interaction Graph (TIG), $G(V,E)$, whose vertices, $V = \{v_1, v_2, ..., v_N\}$ represent the tasks of a program, and vertices weights represent known or estimated computation cost of the tasks. The edges, $E = \{e_1, e_2, ..., e_M\}$, represent communication requirements between tasks, with edge weights reflecting the relative amounts of communication involved between tasks.

The TIG model can be used to approximately model the behaviour of complex parallel programs by lumping together all estimated communications between pair of tasks and ignoring the temporal execution dependencies [8]. It is used for modelling computations at a coarse granularity where tasks are persistent processes which exist for the duration of a computation and where there are stable communication patterns between them [3][10].

This model is capable of modelling computations of arbitrary granularity characterised by irregular and asynchronous communications as well as computations whose communication topology matches well-known graph families such as binary trees, rings, meshes, etc. We note that the TIG does not model non-deterministic computations and dynamically spanned tasks.

The parallel computer is assumed to be homogeneous, i.e. all the processors are equally powerful. Processors execute a computation or perform a communication at any given time, but they don't perform computation and communication simultaneously. The cost of a communication is assumed to depend only on the size of the message so that all processors are considered to be equidistant. This assumption is indeed true when considering commercially parallel architectures where either an specialised hardware or a software layer is responsible for routing messages between processors

achieving an homogeneous latency between all pairs of processors [6].

Formally defined, a mapping is an application called f: $V \rightarrow P$ which associates with each task v_i an unique cluster (or virtual processor) $\text{clust}_q = f(v_i)$. Assuming that there are K physical processors and every cluster will be finally mapped onto one physical processor, the number of all possible solutions is K^N. The cluster clust_q is defined as the group of tasks mapped onto it:

$$\text{clust}_q = \{ v_i \mid f(v_i) = \text{clust}_q \} \qquad q = 1,..,K$$

The Processing Cost (PC_q) of clust_q is the total computational weight of all tasks mapped onto it,

$$PC_q = \sum_{v_j \in \text{clust}_q} w_j, \quad q = 1..K$$

w_j being the computational weight of task v_j.

The Communication Set (CS_q) of clust_q is the set of edges of the Task Interaction Graph that go between it and some other clusters under the mapping f:

$$CS_q = \left\{ (v_i, v_j) \mid f(v_i) = \text{clust}_q, f(v_j) \neq \text{clust}_q \right\} q = 1..K$$

The Communication Cost (CC_q) of clust_q is the total weighted cost of the edges in its communication set:

$$CC_q = \sum_{(v_i, v_j) \in CS_q} c_{i,j} \qquad q = 1..K$$

c_{ij} denotes the communication weight for the edge that joins task v_i and task v_j.

The total cost for clust_q (cluster work load) is the sum of both PC_q and CC_q costs.

$$\text{cost}(\text{clust}_q) = PC_q + CC_q$$

If clust_q is assigned to a physical processor p, the total time spent by processor p will be $\text{cost}(\text{clust}_q)$. Then the total time required to complete the whole program under the assumption of negligible processor idleness will be $\max_{\forall q}\left(\text{cost}\left(\text{clust}_q\right)\right)$. Therefore, from the point of reducing the total processing time, the cost function used as a cost measure for the effectiveness of a mapping instance is:

$$\cos t\_\text{map}(f) = \max_{\forall q}\left(\text{cost}\left(\text{clust}_q\right)\right) \qquad \text{(Eq. 1)}$$

The smaller the cost_map(), the better the mapping f.

3. A clustering-based mapping strategy

In order to solve the mapping problem we propose a new heuristic that will produce good allocation instances without incurring a high algorithm complexity. For that purpose the objective of the algorithm is to form clusters with a minimum work load. It uses two phases. The first one starts by assuming that all graph tasks constitute independent unit clusters that can be assigned to different processors and performs a sequence of clustering refinement steps to eliminate communication costs and to balance the computational load among clusters. In general, the results of this greedy phase will not be optimal and, as a consequence, a second phase consisting of an iterative algorithm is used to improve the final mapping. The minimax cost function denoted as Eq.1 in Section 2 is used to guide the steps performed in the two phases of the algorithm.

An additional notation which reflects the elimination of communication costs when merging two clusters is indicated below. When merging two clusters $clust_i$ and $clust_j$ the cost for the new cluster will be:

$$c\_merg(clust_i, clust_j) = cost(clust_i) + cost(clust_j) - 2 * c_{i,j}$$

For each arc joining two tasks v_i, v_j in the original graph there is a $c\_merg(v_i, v_j)$ value associated.

Basically, the two phases can be formalised as follows,

3.1. Phase 1: Clustering Algorithm (CA)

The initial step assumes that each task is mapped onto a unit cluster. A clustering algorithm (CA) forms new clusters by fusing pairs of tasks into bigger ones. This greedy process ends when the number of clusters obtained is equal to the number of processors. At each step, the algorithm reduces by one the number of clusters by merging two of them. A merging operation implies zeroing an edge cost connecting two clusters. This algorithm is shown in Fig.1.

Although not indicated in the figure, this phase is slightly improved by an additional loop which continues the edge-zeroing while the cost_map() is reduced. This is done in such a way so as to remove the weightiest edges and possibly obtain fewer clusters than the number of processors.

3.2. Phase 2: Reassignment Algorithm

This algorithm looks for the most loaded cluster and tries to shift individual tasks from it to another cluster, in such a way that its work load is reduced and, as a consequence, the overall load is also reduced.

Compute cost($clust_i$) for each original task in the graph
Compute c_merg ($clust_i$, $clust_j$) for every edge in the graph
Sort c_merg ($clust_i$, $clust_j$) in increasing order
While number of clusters > number of processors **Do**
  Find $clust_k$ with biggest cost($clust_k$)
  If there exist a $clust_h$ such that
  c_merg($clust_k$, $clust_h$) < cost ($clust_k$) **then**
    Merge $clust_k$ and $clust_h$
  else
    Take the minimum c_merg ($clust_i$, $clust_j$) and
    merge $clust_i$ and $clust_j$.
  Update cost() value for the new cluster as well as
  c_merg() for all the edges of the new cluster
EndWhile

Fig.1. Clustering Algorithm

This process is repeated until no improvement is achieved in minimising the load of the most loaded cluster. When shifting tasks, two different strategies have been proposed: the first one (denoted as CRM algorithm: Clustering and Reassignment by Movements) only performs individual movements of tasks between clusters, and the second one (denoted as CRME: Clustering and Reassignment by Movements and Exchanges) exchanges also pairs of tasks between different clusters. The CRME algorithm works by iterating a sequence of task movements followed by an iteration of task exchanges. This sequence of movements and exchanges is performed until no improvement is obtained in the cost function, then the final assignment is obtained. Fig. 2 shows the task reassignment algorithm.

4. Experimental Study

To evaluate the performance of our mapping strategies (CA, CRM and CRME algorithms) in finding suboptimal task assignments which minimise the cost function, two experiments were developed. In the first one we used regular computation graphs and we compared the results obtained by our approach with the results obtained applying other mapping strategies. The comparison was performed considering several graphs of different sizes. For small graphs an optimal branch and bound algorithm was used to compare the effectiveness of each mapping strategy. Another set of tests were conducted to evaluate the relative performance of each strategy for mapping large graphs. The second experiment was done to evaluate the performance of the strategies for mapping irregular graphs. All the experiments were conducted on a Sun Sparcsation. A more detailed description of each experiment follows:

```
Repeat
  Set No_Improvement to TRUE
  Repeat (*)
    Set No_Move_Done to TRUE
    Let clust_k to be the most loaded cluster
    For all tasks v_i assigned to clust_k check the
      cost of moving v_i to any other cluster
    If there are moves that decrease the cost of
    clust_k then {
      Move v_j to clust_h, subject to being this
        movement the best one in decreasing
        cost_map()
      Set No_Move_Done to FALSE }
  Until No_Move_Done
  Repeat
    Set No_Exchange_Done to TRUE
    Let clust_k to be the most loaded cluster
    For all tasks v_i assigned to clust_k check the cost
      of changing v_i with any task of ALL the other
      clusters
    If there are exchanges that decrease the cost of
    clust_k then {
      Exchange task v_j from clust_k with task v_s from
        clust_l, subject to being this exchange the best one
        in decreasing cost_map()
      Set No_Exchange_Done to FALSE
      Set No_Improvement to FALSE }
  Until No_Exchange_Done
Until No_Improvement

(*) CRM algorithm consists only of this REPEAT loop.
```

Fig.2. Reassignment Algorithm

4.1. Experiment 1. Regular graphs

The set of mapping heuristics used in the comparison process were the following [2]:

Largest Processing Time First (LPTF): in this heuristic tasks are first sorted by decreasing order of their computation weight and then they are allocated following this order on the processors.

Largest Global Cost First (LGCF): this greedy heuristic is similar to LPTF but, in this case, tasks are sorted according to the sum of both computation and communication weights incurred by each task. They are then mapped on the processors following that order.

Simulated Annealing (SA): this is a widely used and well-known iterative heuristic which, starting from a randomly chosen initial mapping, improves this mapping using a probabilistic hill-climbing algorithm. The improvement method consists of elementary operations involving task exchanges.

Task exchanges are accepted if they lead to a new configuration where the cost function has decreased. If the exchange increases the cost function, then it is accepted with a probability which is controlled by a temperature parameter T that is decreased to zero during the execution of the algorithm using an annealing schedule.

Tabu Search (TS): this is an iterative heuristic that was recently adapted to solve the mapping problem [2]. It starts from a given solution and tries to improve it by pair-wise exchange of tasks. Accessible solutions using local moves are called neighbours of the current solution. At a given step, the best unexplored neighbour is chosen and information about the last explored neighbour is recorded in a 'tabu list' that it is used to reduce the possibilities of cycling.

Simulated Annealing and Tabu Search are algorithms very hard to use because there are several parameters that have to be tuned in practice and have to be done after many experiments. Since random numbers are used for generating initial assignments different runs on the same graph will generally produce different final assignments. Hence, an average-case speeds-up are reported for sets of five runs.

The set of regular graphs used in this experiment correspond to regular structures that usually appeared in real parallel applications. For instance, matrix-oriented algorithms have an organisation that is well suited for mesh graph structures (meshes, wrap-around meshes, etc.), divide and conquer algorithms, such as searching and sorting, usually have a tree topology graph (binary trees, binomial trees, in-out trees, etc.); and other applications that require data processing through a chain of processes have a ring-like topology (pipe, ring, n-body ring, etc.).

To take into account the influence of computation/communication ratio (denoted as CCR) in our study, different values of this ratio were considered and the regular graphs were classified into two main categories:

- CR: coarse grain graphs where the CCR range is between 5 and 15. Computation costs are substantially bigger than communication costs.
- MD: medium grain graphs where the CCR range is between 0.8 and 1.2. Computation costs are close to communication costs.

Fine grain graphs (CCR < 0.8) were not considered because optimal mappings for are obtained when all tasks are assigned to the same processor due to the high weight incurred by the communications.

For the small graphs the number of tasks ranged between 15 and 20, and each graph was mapped onto 4 processors. Large graphs varied between 255 and 400 tasks and were mapped to 32 processors. In both cases,

Table I: Mapping solution quality relative to optimal mapping (small graphs)										
Topology	TREES			MESHES			RINGS			
CCR	MD.	CR.	AVG.	MD.	CR.	AVG.	MD.	CR.	AVG.	Total
LPTF	61.4	90	76	60.7	88.3	74.5	61.6	91	76.2	75.56
LGCF	80.2	94.3	87.3	81.3	90.7	86	80.6	91.5	86.1	86.46
SA	98.3	100	99.1	100	99.1	99.6	100	100	100	99.56
TS	93.1	97	95	82.8	94.2	88.5	85.4	97.7	91.5	91.66
CA	94.6	78.6	86.6	88	95.2	91.6	99.7	100	99.8	92.66
CRM	98.6	98.4	98.5	95	95.2	95.1	100	100	100	97.86
CRME	98.6	100	99.3	95	98	96.4	100	100	100	98.56

Table II: Mapping improvement average relative to LPTF (large graphs)										
Topology	TREES			MESHES			RINGS			
CCR	MD.	CR.	AVG.	MD.	CR.	AVG.	MD.	CR.	AVG.	Total
LGCF	1.24	1.02	1.13	1.18	1.03	1.11	1.18	1.01	1.13	1.12
SA	1.91	1.10	1.51	1.94	1.14	1.54	2.26	1.09	1.64	1.56
TS	2.21	1.05	1.63	2.19	1.05	1.62	2.36	1.04	1.72	1.65
CA	1.68	0.76	1.22	1.88	1.01	1.44	2.35	1.00	1.69	1.45
CRM	2.02	1.13	1.57	2.11	1.22	1.66	2.50	1.15	1.85	1.69
CRME	2.02	1.14	1.58	2.12	1.22	1.67	2.50	1.21	1.88	1.71

task computational weights and communication weights were generated in the range [1,500] units. A total number (evenly distributed between mesh-like, tree-like and ring-like topologies) of 36 and 32 small and large graphs, respectively, were used in the simulation runs. Table I and table II summarise the results and illustrate the quality of the solutions obtained by the different heuristics.

Table I shows the average ratio R (in %) of the mapping costs obtained by each strategy relative to the optimal one. Optimal assignment are found when R = 100. The 'Total' column depicts the overall average ratio for each heuristic and the 'AVG.' column gives the average ratio for each topology group of graphs.

The results of these simulations show our strategies to be very successful in finding suboptimal assignments. Both strategies CRM and CRME provided nearly optimal assignment for practically all the cases and were very close to the results of SA algorithm. Note that for all the topologies and computation/communication ratios there were no substantial deviations, demonstrating its effectiveness. Table II illustrate the results obtained when the mapping heuristics were applied to the large graphs. Given that LPTF proved to be the worst mapping strategy, table II shows the average improvement achieved by each heuristic relative to LPTF. These values have been computed using T_{lptf}/T_p, where T_p is the

mapping cost found by each heuristic and T_{lptf} is the mapping cost for the LPTF heuristic.

As it is seen in table II, the qualities of solutions obtained by the CRM and CRME heuristics are superior to those of the TS and SA heuristics.

4.2. Experiment 2. Irregular graphs

The second experiment was conducted to evaluate the efficiency of all the mapping strategies when they were applied to irregular computation graphs for 8 processors. Instead of generating random graphs that do not represent any real application, we used a set of Directed Acyclic Graphs (DAGs) that were transformed to Task Interaction Graphs (TIGs) applying the DSC (Dominant Sequence Clustering) algorithm [21]. This algorithm maps a DAG onto an unbounded number of virtual processors, subject to minimise the parallel execution time of the DAG. The resulting graph from DSC is a TIG with a reduced number of vertices as the original DAG and without precedence relations between tasks. Therefore, it is a graph suitable for applying the mapping heuristics which this paper deals with.

Table III gives a brief description of each graph. and Table IV shows the average improvement achieved by each heuristic relative to LPTF when mapping those irregular graphs.

Table III. Graph description			
graph name	DAG size	TIG size	Application description
g1	365	46	Algorithm for searching minimum paths of a graph
g2	1002	100	generic time-space systolic algorithm
g3	1534	512	divide-and-conquer algorithm
g4	530	32	gauss elimination algorithm
g5	1026	62	transitive closure of a directed graph
g6	1483	573	Strassen algorithm for matrix multiplication

Table IV. Mapping improvement average relative to LPTF for irregular graphs							
	g1	g2	g3	g4	g5	g6	Total
LGCF	1.11	1.16	1.25	1.06	1.04	1.42	1.17
SA	1.25	1.44	1.31	1.09	1.07	1.81	1.33
TS	1.06	1.41	1.31	1.08	1.07	1.94	1.31
CA	1.03	1.40	1.25	0.9	1.02	1.80	1.23
CRM	1.12	1.46	1.31	1.02	1.07	2.15	1.35
CRME	1.19	1.54	1.31	1.08	1.07	2.29	1.41

These results confirm also the quality of solutions obtained by the CRM and CRME heuristics.

A new comparison was performed in order to analyse the real computation times spent by each strategy. The SA strategy, as expected, was the most computationally expensive one (2600 seconds on the average for all graphs with more than 100 vertices). On the other hand, the CRME strategy spent on the average 4,3 and 13,6 seconds for regular and irregular graphs, respectively.

5. Conclusions

We have presented a new task assignment strategy for solving the mapping problem in message-passing parallel computers where parallel applications are modelled by a Task Interaction Graph (TIG) without considering precedence relations between tasks. This strategy has been compared with several mapping heuristics (LPTF, LGCF, SA, and TS) using regular graphs such as trees, meshes and rings, as well as for arbitrary computations representing real parallel applications. The results indicate that the proposed heuristics (CRM and CRME) are very promising alternatives for solving the mapping problem. Their solution qualities are as good as those produced by some complex iterative methods like SA and TS but their computation time is several orders of magnitude less.

References

[1] S. H. Bokhari, "On the mapping problem", IEEE Trans on Computers, Vol. C-30 No. 3, March (1981), pp. 207-214.

[2] P. Bouvry, J. Chassin de Kergommeaux & D. Trystram, "Efficient solutions for mapping parallel programs". Proceedings of EuroPar'95. Springer-Verlag, August (1995), pp. 379-390.

[3] T. Bultan & C. Aykanat, "A new mapping heuristic based on mean field annealing". Journal of Parallel and Distributed Computing, Vol. 16, (1992), pp. 292-305.

[4] M.R. Garey and D.S. Johnson, "Computer and Intractability - A Guide to the Theory of NP-Completeness", (Freeman, New York, 1979).

[5] V. M. Lo et alter, "OREGAMI: Tools for mapping parallel computations to parallel architectures". Int. Journal of Parallel Programming, 20 (3) (1991), pp. 237-279.

[6] M. D. May, P. W. Thompson & P. H. Welch, "Networks, Routers & Transputers", IOS Press (1993).

[7] M. G. Norman & P. Thanish, "Models of machines and computation for mapping in multicomputers". ACM Computer Surveys, 25 (3) (1993), pp. 263-302.

[8] P. Sadayappan, F.Ercal and J. Ramanujam, "Cluster partitioning approaches to mapping parallel problems on to a hypercube", Parallel Computing, 13 (1) (1990), pp. 1-6.

[9] S. Selvakumar & C. Silva Ram Murthy, "An efficient heuristic algorithm for mapping parallel programs onto multicomputers". Microprocessing and Microprogramming 36 (1992/1993) pp 83-92.

[10] J. Shield, "Partitioning concurrent VLSI simulation programs onto a multiprocessor by simulated annealing", IEE Proc. Part G, (134) (1987), pp. 24-28.

[11] T. Yang and A. Gerasoulis, "DSC: scheduling parallel tasks on an unbounded number of processors", IEEE Trans. Parallel and Distributed Systems, 5 (9) (1994), pp. 951-967.

A Proposed Mobile Architecture
for
Distributed Database Environment

O. Bukhres, S. Morton, P. Zhang
Department of Computer Science
Purdue University
Indianapolis, IN

E. Vanderdijs
Systems Programming
Lucent Technologies
Naperville, IL

C. Crawley
Senior Project Engineer
Delco Electronics
Kokomo, IN

J. Platt
Software Engineer
IBM Corp
Austin, TX

M. Mossman
Senior Systems Programming
Polygram Holding Incorporated
Fishers, IN

Abstract

Much research has been devoted to mobile computing and database query management with the advent of portable computers and wireless communication systems. This paper proposes an architecture based on current mobile models, but with the addition of a mailbox, which serves as a storage area for the mobile hosts. Mobile Hosts (MHs) and Mobile Support Stations (MSSs) are connected over a wireless virtual subnet, and the MSSs are in turn connected to a wired static network. The architecture uses the TCP/IP protocol for communication in a mobile computing environment. Cellular providers (CP), the mobile network, and supporting hardware are defined and then assembled into a detailed example which traces the database query through the architecture.

1 Introduction

In the past, computer users would have to disconnect from the network every time they needed to travel, but with the emergence of wireless connections the user is able to maintain a connection to the network during movement. A mobile host capable of both communication and executing user-initiated computation, which differentiates the mobile host from communication-only devices such as pagers or portable terminals is described in [2]. The mobile host in the proposed architecture is a mobile computer that resides in a car, which is able to receive information from the distributed database.

Mobile computing presents new problems to database query management due to the mobility of users, power restrictions, and the limited bandwidth of the wireless connection. These challenges include the following: mobility, disconnection, data access modes, and scales [8]. Mobility involves the location of users, replicating information and queries on location dependent information. Disconnection covers the topics of cache consistency, hand-off and recovery. The wireless medium and efficient data management are a part of the data access method. In this paper, we discuss the mobility and disconnection issues, but we do not cover scale or data access modes.

Due to the fact that a mobile computer has a limited battery life, it needs to perform most of the query on the mobile host's base station, which is a specialized fixed host. When a mobile host disconnects from the network, it must be assured that the values of the data that it is using are valid, and that all the updates will be reflected in the database [20]. Also, the computation executing on a mobile host must not be interrupted when a mobile host no longer maintains a connection to the static portion of the network.

An architecture that supports database queries that are created by a mobile host is introduced in this paper. Discussed are the concepts, the requirements, and the limitations of the architecture in the mobile computing environment. The mobility issues of hand-off, zone crossing are also discussed. An IP-Addressing approach is selected, and a detailed example of a database query is presented.

The organization of the rest of the paper is as follows. Section 2 defines the mobile model and mobile queries. In section 3, the components of the architecture and the mobile issues are explained. Section 4 discusses an application of this architecture, an example and considers related work. Fi-

413

nally, section 5 concludes the paper with a summary of the presented material and a discussion of the future work.

2 Mobile Model

The term "mobile" implies the ability to move while retaining a network connection [2]. The mobile model consists of mobile hosts (MH) and mobile support stations (MSS). A mobile host is an intelligent computing device which can freely move while maintaining its connection to the network. The MSS, which is connected to the network via a wired medium, provides a wireless interface that allows the mobile host to interact with the static network. Each MSS is responsible for a geographical cellular region, called a cell, and is required to maintain the addresses of the MHs which are located within its cell. With the addition of mobile hosts to distributed systems, the model will involve a static network of fixed hosts, and a wireless network consisting of mobile hosts and the MSSs that communicate with the MHs. Figure 1 presents the system model of the mobile computing environment based on [2].

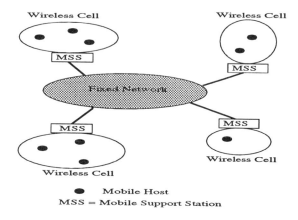

Figure 1. Model of a Distributed System with Mobile Hosts

Mobile computing is susceptible to environmental factors that can cause loss of communication or data. There are three types of failures in mobile computing: failure of the mobile host, disconnection of the mobile host, and message loss due to weak wireless links. Failure of a mobile host results in the loss of its volatile state. Disconnection of a mobile host is a consequence of a limited power source, which forces the host to be frequently powered off to conserve the battery. A disconnection can be treated as *planned* failures which can be anticipated and prepared for [9]. Mobile hosts and their local base stations are connected by slow, unreliable links that lead to message loss.

2.1 Mobile Queries

In [6], the mobile [query] as the basic unit of computation on the mobile environment is defined. In contrast to [6], the mobile host in this paper is identified by a home zone, which will be defined in the next section. A query initiated by a mobile host is similar in structure to that of a query in a static network. Queries may range from a simple query, "Where is the airport?," to a more difficult query, "Where is the nearest rest area from this current location?" Mobile computing involves location constraints - i.e., constraints which involve the individual location of users [7]. Mobile queries tend to be long in duration due to the wireless connection to the network. The mobile host may wish to disconnect from the network while the query is executed. These mobile characteristics lead to problems that are not present in a static network.

3 Architecture

Our proposed architecture uses the mobile model discussed above along with some crucial additions. Unlike the model in [2], our architecture subdivides MHs into two categories: nomadic and home. Each MH will be affiliated with a particular cell, and this cell will be governed by the MHs home MSS. Whenever a MH wishes to connect within this cell, it will be recognized as a home MH by the MSS. If the MH moves out of this cell, the MSS for the next cell will identify the MH as a nomadic MH. In addition, we introduce the idea of a mailbox for each mobile host. The mailbox will be the recipient of all the query messages/results from the network. The following is a description of the different components of the architecture:

- **Mailboxes**

  The key to successful implementation of the architecture is to have an easily accessible mailbox [9] available at all times. Mailboxes provide a central repository for all of the MH's query responses and logs. Since they must be available at all times and easily locatable, the user's primary cellular provider will maintain a mailbox for each subscriber. Each MH will have access to the mailbox that is created by the local cellular provider. The mailbox will be similar to the idea of voice-mail, but the memory location will contain all query information, such as completed queries, and logs. The MH will be able to access the mailbox by utilizing the current MSS, either local or remote, to connect with the home cellular provider. This mailbox could be the key to mobile transaction recovery, because all messages destined for the MH will be sent to the mailbox. Also, it can help reduce the load on the system if the MH decides to have the query results only sent to the mailbox as opposed to sending unnecessary messages on the network to find the location of the MH.

- **Mobile Support Stations(MSS)**

  The mobile support station is the physical and software component required to support a wireless connection from a MH to the static network. These components include the mobile support router (MSR), the query manager, and the network router. The mobile support router [11] is the unit which communicates with the mobile hosts by passing packets to and from the query manager. The network router communicates with the static network, and also returns query results from the static network back to the query manager.

- **Query Manager(QM)**

  A query manager is the coordinator of all queries initiated on a distributed system. It provides the application programming interface, creates query identifiers and tracks the participating resource manager [5]. Upon receiving a query, the QM decides if the request can be satisfied by the local cellular provider. If not, then the QM will begin a search for a location where the query can be completed. The QM will attempt to report the results back to the MH as well as the MHs mailbox.

- **Zones**

  Zones are defined to be the geographical area where one or more mobile support routers can supply a connection to the MHs. Generally, the zone will correspond to the cellular area of a cellular phone system. Two types of zones exist in the mobile architecture: local and remote. The local zone is defined to be the zone where an MH's primary cellular provider is located (i.e. the zone of coverage of a cellular provider for all MHs which have a mailbox with that cellular provider). A remote zone is defined to be any zone which is not a particular MH's local zone. Figure 2 represents the proposed architecture.

3.1 Mobility Issues

When dealing with mobile computing, there are two mobility issues which must be addressed: mobile support router hand-off and zone-crossing. Mobile support router hand-off occurs when a mobile computer moves within a given

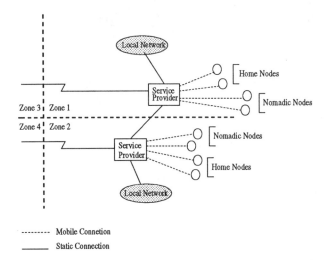

Figure 2. The Proposed Architecture

cellular zone. Zone-crossing occurs when a mobile computer moves between cellular zones. The mobile support router hand-off and zone-crossing problem are addressed using a mobile protocol adapted from the Columbia mobile host protocol proposal [11, 12, 10, 17].

3.2 MSR Hand-off

An MH makes the decision when an MSR hand-off should occur. The hand-off [14] criteria used is typically a physical layer issue and will not be discussed in this paper. When the MH decides to switch between MSRs, the Greeting packet sent to the target MSR must contain a list of MSR IP addresses which previously serviced the MH during its current connection within the mobile network. The target MSR must then send Forward-Pointer packets to the MSRs in the list to inform them of MH migration. The MSRs must then respond to the target MSRs with Forward-Acknowledgment packets and subsequently tunnel destination MH datagrams to the target MSR. When an MSR receives an MH datagram whose location is unknown, the MSR multi-casts Who-Has-MH packets to other MSRs. The participating MSRs must respond with I-Have packets indicating whether or not the MSR is servicing that particular MH. Confirming I-Have packets contain the MH IP address. Thus, the virtual subnet scheme scales well as long as the MH remains within the administrative domain of an CP.

3.3 Zone Crossing

When the MH migrates from one CP to another, i.e. crosses zones, the network and virtual subnet number of the mobile network may change as well. This situation is handled by the Mobile Inter-networking Control Protocol with

Pop-up packets [16]. After an MH has established a connection with a new remote CP's MSR, the MH must first obtain a temporary or "nonce" [12] IP address from the new remote CP's MSR. Since only routers can participate in datagram tunneling, the MH emulates a remote MSR by establishing a connection with one of its home MSRs by sending a Pop-up packet to that home MSR. The nonce address allows the MH to appear as a local MH in the remote CP's virtual subnet and the Pop-up packet allows the MH to appear as tunnel endpoint MSR to one of its home MSRs. When home MSRs receive datagrams destined for the Pop-up MH, a home MSR will tunnel the datagrams to the remote MH which is masked as a remote MSR.

3.4 Solutions

One of the problems that a mobile architecture must handle or solve is temporary loss of communication by the mobile support router to the MH as a consequence either of intentional or unintentional disconnection by the MH. One proposed solution to the problem is backtracking to find the location of the results by the mobile user. Backtracking consists of maintaining the link established before the disconnection occurred. The mobile user needs to remember the link where the query was initiated in order to be able to reestablish the connection and obtain any needed results. This is burdensome for the MH because it may have to remember many links for many queries.

This proposed architecture solves the above problem by incorporating the mailbox [9] feature. This feature consists of sending the query results to the MH's mailbox by the cellular provider's QM so that the mobile user can access the results at her leisure.

Since the cellular provider knows who the mobile user is (and, thus, who her primary cellular provider is), the proposed architecture can easily handle the billing process. The cellular provider with whom the MH is connected sends the billing information to the MH's primary cellular provider.

4 Applications

Now that the components of the model have been defined and the mobile issues discussed, the interaction between the MH and the network during a query will be shown. First, a detailed trace of a query will be presented followed by some examples.

The MH will initiate the connection with the network. Using the TCP/IP method discussed in [3] a wireless connection will be established between the MH and an MSR when the MH responds to an MSR's beacon with a GREETING packet. Once the network connection has been established, the CP must validate the MH's service authorization.

When handshaking at all levels has been successfully completed, the MH is free to make a query against any database to which the QM is linked. Logging of the request will be sent to both the MH's mailbox and to the MH's primary CP. Once the query has been submitted, the MH has several options: disconnection from the service provider, submission of additional queries, or retrieval of current or previous query results.

Assuming that the query completes successfully and the response is with the QM, the QM will post the results to the MH's mailbox, log the reply to both the MH's mailbox and to the MH's primary CP and automatically forward the results to the MH. If the MH is not connected, a host unreachable situation will occur. When the MH wishes to retrieve information from the mailbox, the MH submits a query to the QM to read the mailbox. This query is treated the same as any other query, except the QM forwards only the logging information since forwarding the results to the MH's mailbox would result in duplication.

4.1 Example

Consider a mobile user (Alex) who drives from Indianapolis to New York and who carries a computer capable of serving as a mobile host with her.

When Alex arrives in Columbus, Ohio, she wants to check her email. She powers up her computer and initiates a connection to the network. The mobile host broadcasts a beacon signal containing a Pop-up packet. A local MSR in Columbus receives the mobile host's beacon. Using the Pop-up information in the beacon, the local MSR recognizes the mobile host as alien to the Columbus district, and makes a connection with an MSR in the mobile host's home district.

When the connection is established, Alex's cellular provider initiates the authorization process, again using information from the Pop-up packet. Presuming an authorization will soon be received, Alex begins the query that retrieves whatever information may be in her mailbox. The authorization is granted, and the messages are forwarded from her mailbox. One of the messages she retrieves is a message from her colleague (Bob), who is also driving to New York, and who also is equipped with a mobile host computer. The message asks her to retrieve some items he left at his friend's (Carl's) house in Pittsburgh. Alex initiates a query for Carl's phone number and for the best route from Columbus to Pittsburgh. The local cellular provider in Columbus, having received authorization from Alex's Indianapolis provider, will handle the queries; the cellular provider's query manager now decides how best to respond to them. The information on the route can probably be retrieved locally, but the request for the Pittsburgh phone number will have to be forwarded to a cellular provider in the Pittsburgh area.

The Columbus cellular provider sends two messages to Alex: one contains information on the best route to Pittsburgh, which it has retrieved from its own databases; the other is a notice that the phone number information is not available locally and will be forwarded as soon as it is retrieved from the remote source. If the mobile host receives these messages, it will return acknowledgments. If the local provider does not receive acknowledgments, it assumes the mobile host has disconnected and echoes the unacknowledged messages to Alex's mailbox in Indianapolis. Here we suppose Alex receives the messages, disconnects, and drives to Pittsburgh on the given route. When she arrives in Pittsburgh, Alex turns on her computer and again initiates a connection to the network. As before, a local MSR hears the beacon, notes it as an alien host, and connects to Alex's home cellular provider. The cellular provider's last record of Alex is in Columbus, so in addition to establishing and authorizing a connection, the home cellular provider also initiates a hand-off, officially notifying the MSR in Columbus that it no longer has responsibility for tracking Alex's host. When it receives the hand-off request, the query manager in Columbus checks to see if the queries Alex initiated in Columbus have finished. If they have, and the results have been sent on to Alex's mailbox, the hand-off is acknowledged. If they haven't finished, there are two possibilities: (1) The Columbus query manager can wait; in the future, when it has received the result of Alex's query, it can forward the result to Alex's mailbox and then finish the hand-off. (2) The Columbus query manager is told by Alex's home query manager to cancel the query, which allows it to finish the hand-off.

No matter when the hand-off is finished, if Alex finds the query has yet to finish, she can choose either to continue the query or to notify her home query manager to abort the query. She can also choose to reissue it. Here, we suppose that Alex's query was successful and she is able to retrieve the message containing Carl's phone number from her home mailbox when she reconnects in Pittsburgh. Then, in more conventional ways, she finds her way to Carl's house. When Alex gets Bob's items from Carl, she reconnects to send Bob email confirming her success and telling him where she is staying in New York.

Again, this example illustrates how the mailbox serves the vital role of stationary proxy for the mobile host while it is disconnected from the network, and how the home cellular provider manages the mobile host's remote connections, including hand-offs and delayed query management.

4.2 Related Work

A transport-layer transparency architecture is described in [22]. The architecture is modularized into well-defined logical components that allow the architecture to be flexible and able to be introduced into existing infrastructures. In [28], an architecture that provides an autonomous query management strategy in a cooperative processing environment across heterogeneous database systems is used. The approach decomposes the operating environment into two parts: the mobile workstation level, and the stationary computer level.

The architecture proposed by [6] involves split queries and global queries in a multi-database environment. The architecture utilizes a Data Access Agent, which is located at each base station, to coordinate the mobile user's requests. In [13], a new wireless data networking architecture that integrates diverse wireless technologies into a seamless internetwork is described. By taking advantage of the overlaying of wireless networks, a wide-area coverage can be provided while achieving the best possible bandwidth and latency for mobile devices.

The presence of mobile computing units in a database environment introduces problems such as frequent disconnection and limited battery power. A model that localizes the communication and data structures necessary for an algorithm within the static portion of the network is discussed in [1]. A message and queuing facility to provide a common communication and data exchange protocol to manage a query submitted by an MH is introduced in [28].

The Columbia Mobile Host Protocol can be added to an existing IP networking protocol to allow mobile hosts to be integrated into the existing network infrastructure even if the mobile hosts move between different networks. This protocol provides a method, depending on the ancillary machines, to track the location of the mobile hosts. This protocol is discussed at length in [12, 10, 17].

5 Conclusion

A mobile architecture that utilizes a mailbox as a storage area for all queries created by the mobile host has been proposed. The mobile units attach to the network only when convenient, and these connections are subject to occasional involuntary losses of connectivity during sessions. To accommodate the restrictions that discontinuous connectivity imposes on the model, we have proposed that a mailbox stores all messages destined for a mobile user, which can be retrieved after a mobile host reconnects to the network.

We have also proposed that the principle underlying IP addressing approach is fundamentally in conflict with the idea of mobile computing. Using an IP address both as a distinguishing mark of an individual host and as a bearer of routing information for packets destined for that host is an idea that is untenable in a mobile computing environment. At present, no proposed protocol (that we know of) divorces these two functions in a way that effectively supports mobile computing. We endorse a solution similar to the Mobile

Host Protocol (MHP) developed at Columbia University, in which a certain set of IP addresses are assigned to the mobile hosts, which then compose a virtual subnet. The Columbia model could be enhanced so that rather than each network designating its own set of addresses to make up the mobile sub-net, and MSR's communicating only within each subnet, a network standard will designate the same range of addresses in each network to be associated with the mobile hosts. Thus any network will be able to recognize a packet as destined for an mobile host and route it to an MSR.

This architecture is designed to handle distributed queries created by a mobile user. The next logical step will be the use of distributed transactions to access local and non-local information. We are currently looking into transaction coordinator that will be manage transactions created by a mobile host while that mobile host is disconnected from the network.

References

[1] A. Acharya and B. Badrinath. Structuring Distributed Algorithms for Mobile Hosts. In *Proceedings of the 14th International Conference on Distributed Computing Systems*, 1994.

[2] B. Badrinath, A. Acharya, and T. Imielinski. Impact of Mobility on Distributed Computations. *Sigops Review*, 1993.

[3] H. Balakrishnan, S. Seshan, E. Amir, and R. Katz. Improving TCP/IP Performance over Wireless Networks. In *Proceedings of the 1st ACM Conference on Mobile Computing and Networking*, 1995.

[4] G.Forman and J. Zahorjan. The Challenges of Mobile Computing. Technical Report 93-11-03, University of Washington, 1994.

[5] J. Gray and A. Reuter. *Transaction Processing: Concepts and Techniques*. Morgan Kaufman, 1993.

[6] A. Helal and M. Eich. Supporting Mobile Transaction Processing in Database Systems. Technical Report TR-CSE-95-003, University of Texas at Arlington, 1995.

[7] T. Imielinski and B. Badrinath. Querying in a Highly Mobile Distributed Environment. In *Proceedings of the 18th Conference on Very Large Data Bases*, pages 41–52, 1992.

[8] T. Imielinski and B. Badrinath. Data Management for Mobile Computing. *SIGMOD Record*, 22(1):34–39, 1993.

[9] T. Imielinski and B. Badrinath. Mobile Wireless Computing: Solutions and Challenges in Data Management. Technical Report DCS-TR-296/ WINLAB TR-49, Rutgers University, 1993.

[10] J. Ioannidis and D. Duchamp. The Design and Implementation of a Mobile Internetworking Architecture. In *Winter USENIX*, 1993.

[11] J. Ioannidis, D. Duchamp, and G. Maguire. IP-based Protocols for Mobile Internetworking. In *SIGCOMM '91: Symposium on Communications Architectures and Protocols*, pages 235–245, 1991.

[12] J. Ioannidis, D. Duchamp, G. Maguire, and S. Deering. Protocols for Supporting Mobile IP Hosts, 1992. Mobile IP Working Group, Internet-Draft.

[13] R. H. Katz and E. A. B. et al. The Bay Area Research Wireless Access Network (BARWAN). In *Proceedings Spring COMPCON Conference*, 1996.

[14] P. Krishna, N. Vaidya, and D. Pradhan. Recovery in Distributed Mobile Environments. In *IEEE Workshop on Advances in Parallel and Distributed Systems*, pages 83–88, 1993.

[15] B. Marsh, F. Douglis, and R. Caceres. Systems Issues in Mobile Computing. Technical Report MITL-TR-50-93, Matsushita Information Technology Laboratory, 1993.

[16] J. Mogul and J. Postel. Internet Standard Subnetting Procedure. RFC 950, 1985.

[17] A. Myles and D. Skellern. Comparison of Mobile Host Protocols for IP. Mobile IP Working Group, Macquarie University, 1993.

[18] M. Özsu and P. Valduriez. *Principles of Distributed Database Systems*. Prentice-Hall, Inc, 1991.

[19] C. Perkins and Y. Rekhter. Short-cut Routing for Mobile Hosts. Draft RFC, T. J. Watson Research Center, 1992.

[20] E. Pitoura and B. Bhargava. Revising Transaction Concepts for Mobile Computing. In *Proceedings of the 1st IEEE Workshop on Mobile Computing Systems and Applications (MCSA94)*, pages 164–169, 1994.

[21] J. Postel. INTERNET PROTOCOL. RFC 791, 1981.

[22] F. Reichert. Integration of mobile communication into fixed networks. Royal Institute of Technolo Teleinformat s, 1993.

[23] W. Simpson. IP in IP Tunneling. RFC 1853, 1995.

[24] A. Tanenbaum. *Computer Networks*. Prentice Hall, 1989.

[25] F. Teraoka. VIP: IP Extensions for Host Migration Transparency. Draft RFC, 1992.

[26] F. Teraoka, K. Claffy, and M. Tokoro. Design Implementation and Evaluation of Virtual Internet Protocol. In *Proceedings of the 12th International Conf. on Distributed Computing Systems*, pages 170–177, 1992.

[27] F. Teraoka, Y. Yokote, and M. Tokoro. A Network Architecture Providing Host Migration Transparency. In *SIGCOMM '91 Proceedings, ACM*, 1991.

[28] L. Yeo and A. Zaslavsky. Submission of Transactions from Mobile Workstations in a Cooperative Multidatabase Processing Environment. In *Proceedings IEEE/CS 14th International Conference on Distributed Computing Systems*, pages 472–479, 1994.

Collection Types for Database Programming in the BSP Model

K Ronald Sujithan and Jonathan M D Hill
Programming Research Group
Oxford University Computing Laboratory
{Ronald.Sujithan,Jonathan.Hill}@comlab.ox.ac.uk

Abstract

We study the pragmatics of integrating collection types, that model a broad class of non-numerical applications, into the Bulk Synchronous Parallel (BSP) model which abstracts a diversity of parallel architectures using just four numerical parameters. We outline how the collection types have been built on-top of the direct BSP programming environment provided by BSPlib, give results on a SGI PowerChallenge and IBM SP2, and discuss how these types can help implement object databases.

1 Introduction

Parallel computers have been successfully deployed in many scientific and numerical application areas, but their use in commercial applications, which are often non-numerical in nature, has been scarce. One of the impediments in the long-term commercial uptake of parallel computing has been the proliferation of differing machine architectures and corresponding programming models. However, due to several technological and economic reasons, the various classes of parallel computers such as shared-memory machines, distributed-memory machines, and networks of workstations are beginning to acquire a familiar appearance: a workstation-like processor-memory pair at the node level, and a fast, robust interconnection network that provides node-to-node communication [11].

The aim of recent research into the Bulk Synchronous Parallel Model [12, 20] has been to take advantage of this architectural convergence. The central idea of BSP is to provide a high level abstraction of parallel computing hardware whilst providing a realisation of a parallel programming model that enables architecture independent programs to deliver scalable performance on diverse hardware platforms. Although BSP programming environments have been successfully utilised in several numerical applications, they provide little help in non-numeric applications as they are based upon an explicit distribution and manipulation of arrays among a number of processors.

Previous approaches to adding collection types to parallel languages were taken from a specific programming model viewpoint. Data-parallel approaches achieve parallelism by the wholesale manipulation of collection types such as arrays, sets, or lists. A general unifying approach to data-parallelism is exemplified by the work on data-parallel functional programming [8] in terms of the Bird-Meertens Formalism or Skeletons [3, 4, 16]. However, apart from a plethora of purely theoretical results, there have been few practical implementations of data-parallel functional languages other than the language NESL developed by Blelloch [1].

1.1 Contributions

The goal of this paper is to study the cost-effective realisation of a number of well known *collection types*, in order to provide higher-level programming abstractions within a BSP programming environment. Specifically, the work described in this paper considers the pragmatics of supporting the functional style of data-parallelism in the BSP model. We focus on the problem of uniting data-parallelism, data distribution and load balancing and accurate cost prediction within the BSP model. Our work is motivated by an object database case study, and the type system needed to model a broad class of database applications. We provide some encouraging results from a preliminary BSP implementation of the **select-from-where** form of a database query.

The rest of this paper is organised as follows. We conclude this section with an outline of the application case study. In section 2, we introduce the BSP model, performance prediction under the model, and the *BSPlib* programming environment. Section 3 introduces the *BSP-Collections* model of sets, lists, and bags, and section 4 present the BSP implementation of collections and a variety of operations on collections. Finally, in section 6 we provide results from the case study.

1.2 The case study

The Object Database Management Group (ODMG), as part of the OMG Organisation (an industrial consortium established to promote object technology) has proposed an industry standard for object databases [2]. The ODMG-93 standard defines an object model of data, and a companion object definition (ODL) and query languages (OQL). We work with the main elements of the data model, particularly the data types supported — the generalised collections data type and the specialised data types *sets, bags, lists* and *arrays*— and the operations defined for these types [17].

The utility of the collections datatypes considered in this paper will be demonstrated in the context of supporting elements of ODMG. Our example is essentially a database query based upon this standard, which forms an ideal, representative, non-numerical application, to evaluate the programming concepts under consideration.

2 The BSP model

Before collection types are considered, we give a brief introduction to the BSP model. A *BSP computer* is an abstraction of any real parallel computer, and can be decomposed into three parts: (1) a number of processor/memory components. Usually each consists of sequential processor with a block of local memory; (2) an interconnection network that delivers messages in a point-to-point manner among the processors; (3) a facility for globally synchronising *all* the processors by means of a barrier.

The *BSP model* defines the way in which programs are executed on the BSP computer. The model defines that a program consists of a sequence of *supersteps*. During a superstep, each processor-memory pair can perform a number of local computations on values held locally to each processors memory at the start of the superstep. During the superstep, each processor may also initiate communication with other processor-memory pairs. However, the model does not prescribe any particular style of communication, although it does require that at the end of a superstep there is a barrier synchronisation at which point any pending communications must be completed [19].

2.1 BSP cost model

For each of the algorithms we describe later, we analyse their computational and communication costs. The superstep methodology that forms the heart of the BSP model facilities cost analysis because the cost of a BSP program running on a number of processors is simply the sum of each separate superstep executed by the program. In turn, for each superstep, the costs can be decomposed into those attributed to purely local computation, global exchange of data, and barrier synchronisation. To ensure that cost analysis can be performed in an *architecture independent* way, cost formulas are parameterised by four *architecture dependent* constants:

p number of processor/memory pairs
s computation speed of a single processor (#flops)
l minimum time for barrier synchronisation (#flops)
g the ratio of local computational operations/second to the #words delivered by the network

Given these four constants, then the cost of a superstep is captured by the formulae $\alpha + \beta g + l$ [6]; where α is an *architecture independent cost* that models the maximum number of operations executed by *one* of the processes in the local computation phase of a superstep; and β is the largest accumulated size of all messages either entering or leaving a process within a superstep.

2.2 The Oxford BSP toolset

Two modes of BSP programming are possible: (1) in *automatic mode* [20] the run-time system hides memory distribution/management from the user (i.e., PRAM style of programming); (2) in *direct mode* the programmer retains control over data distribution and manipulation among the processors. The aim of this paper can be considered to provide an automatic mode for a variety of collection types on-top of a library of direct mode primitives outlined next.

A number of researchers are currently forming a World-Wide Standard BSP Library [7] by synthesising several low-level (direct mode) BSP programming approaches that have been pursued over the last few years. They propose a library called *BSPlib* to provide a parallel communication library based around a SPMD model of computation.

The main parts of *BSPlib* are: (1) routines to spawn a number of processes to be run in an SPMD manner; (2) an operation that synchronises all processes, and therefore identifies the end of one superstep and the start of the next; (3) Direct Remote Memory Access (DRMA) communication facilities that allow a process to manipulate the address space of remote processes *without the active participation of the remote process*; (4) Bulk Synchronous Message Passing (BSMP) operations that provide a non-blocking send operation that delivers messages to a system buffer associated with the destination process at the end of a superstep.

The results described in this paper have been obtained using the Oxford BSP toolset implementation of *BSPlib* [9], which also contains a profiling tool to help visualise the inter-process communication patterns occurring in each superstep. The profiling tool graphically exposes three important pieces of information: (a) the elapsed time taken to perform communication; (b) the pattern of communication; (c) the computational elapsed time. When discussing the results in section 6, we will highlight these three attributes.

3 BSP realisation of collections

We consider three particular kinds of collections, with different applications in mind: (1) *sets* are unordered collections that contains no duplicates; (2) *bags* are unordered collections that allow duplicates; (3) *lists* (or sequences) are ordered collections that allow duplicates; Sets and bags are fundamental types in database schema design, whereas lists play a dual role. Firstly lists act as a fundamental construct that represent several useful non-linear data structures, such as graphs, trees etc., in object databases. Secondly, we use sorted lists without duplicates as the central type in our parallel implementation.

A collection $collection\langle\tau\rangle$ containing n elements of type τ is initially distributed among p processors of a BSP machine in blocks of n/p elements (other distribution schemes such as, whole, cyclic and random, are also possible). We maintain the data-structure invariant using a parallel sorting algorithm, to be described next, which works upon an extra tag that we associate with each element of type τ in the collection $collection\langle\tau\rangle$. For a list based collection, the tag will be a simple boolean valued attribute that determines if a collection element is "active". However, for a set based collection the tag is the element itself of type τ, which ensures the data-structure invariance of sorted lists.

Sorting Several sorting methods have been devised for a variety of parallel architectures, including BSP sorting algorithms [6]. After careful consideration of these methods, we have selected and implemented a practical variant of the sample sort algorithm [13, 15]. Central to this method is the fact that runs of elements containing the same key will be distributed to the same processor – this property is utilised in the algorithms that follow.

Our implementation, (1) performs a local sort; (2) each processor selects p regular samples which are gathered onto processor zero; (3) these samples are sorted and p regular pivots are picked from the p^2 samples; (4) these pivot values are broadcast to all the processors; (5) each processor partitions its local block using the pivots; (6) each processor sends it's partition i to processor i; and finally (7) local merge of the sorted partitions produces the desired effect of a global sort.

Since the complexity of an optimal comparison-based sequential sort is $\text{SEQSORT}(n) = n\log n$, then the cost of locally sorting p processors chunks of data is $\text{SEQSORT}(n/p)$. The communication cost is gn/p for the permute (i.e., at most the entire segment needs to be transferred to a different processor), and therefore the upper-bound BSP cost for the parallel sort is $\text{PARSORT}(n) = \text{SEQSORT}(n/p) + gn/p + l$ (refined analysis, including the load balancing properties of this algorithm, can be found in [18]).

4 Collection operations

We first describe the fundamental collection operations expressed as the familiar higher-order functions (i.e. functions that take a function as an argument), *map*, *filter*, and *fold*. The BSP implementation of each of these operations is presented, in the context of the distributed collection types introduced above, along with their BSP costs. Where appropriate, we indicate alternative algorithms for these operations based on the parameters, c, p, l and g, where c is the maximum cost of applying the function f to a single element of the collection. We mention the database interpretations of these higher-order functions in section 7.

4.1 Single collection operations

Map We begin with the most basic collection operator *map* that applies a function $f : \tau \to \sigma$ to every element of a collection $collection\langle\tau\rangle$ to create a new collection $collection\langle\sigma\rangle$. It is the essence of the data-parallel paradigm as it models embarrassingly parallel computations because the application of f to each element in the collection can occur concurrently. If we ignore nesting, then the BSP cost is cn/p for this operation.

Fold Fold (or reduce) is a higher order function that given an associative and commutative (commutativity may be required to work with unordered set collections) operator $\otimes$ and a collection $[x_1, x_2, \ldots, x_n]$ computes the values $x_1 \otimes x_2 \otimes \ldots \otimes x_n$. The parallel interpretation of fold is that a sequential fold can be performed in parallel to each segment of the collection of size n/p in time proportional to cn/p. Depending on the relative values of c, p, l and g, each of the p results from the local computation can then be obtained by using either, (1) a divide-and-conquer technique to fold the p values held in each process in $\log p$ supersteps, or, (2) in just a single superstep. The BSP cost of the entire fold operation will be, (1) $cn/p + \log p \, (l+g+c)$, and, (2) $cn/p + cp + pg + l$, repetively.

Filter Given a collection $collection\langle\tau\rangle$, then a filtered version of the collection that satisfies a predicate $f : \tau \to \mathbb{B}$. In the context of collections distributed among p processors in n/p chunks, a global filter can be implemented in terms of p local filters with cost cn/p, but there are potential problems with data-skew as the filter may produce a new collection that is significantly smaller than the original. This potential skewing of data can be addressed by a rebalancing algorithm based on the parallel prefix technique [6]. Alternatively, the load balancing properties of the sorting routine can be employed *en route*, as demonstrated in our simulations (section 5).

4.2 Multiple collection operations

By using the type conversion rules discussed in [18], or using the ODMG-93 explicitly defined function **listtoset** for this purpose, any collection type can be converted into a *set* collection. Sets can therefore provide the basis for our implementation of multiple collection operations, without resorting to tailored implementations of each collection type.

Our task therefore reduces to one of implementing all the set-theoretic operations on set collections. As pointed out in [14], a fast sorting procedure can be used as the basis for the efficient processing of these operations. Given two sets S and T, we describe how to calculate the set theoretic operations $S - T$ (difference), $S \cup T$ (union), and $S \cap T$ (intersection) in BSP. We make a similar assumption to those in section 3 about the distribution of S and T; that is n elements of S and m elements of T are distributed across the p processors.

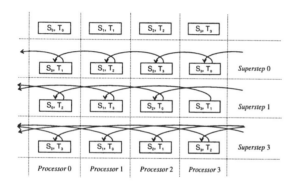

Figure 1. The cartesian product algorithm

Cartesian product Given two collections S of type $collection\langle\tau\rangle$ and T of type $collection\langle\sigma\rangle$, then the cartesian product $S \times T$ calculates the collection of all pairs from S and T of type $collection\langle\tau \times \sigma\rangle$. The BSP implementation works by transposing the data blocks of the smaller collection, say T, in successive supersteps, and then computing the local cartesian product. Clearly, this will bring every element s_i of S with every element t_i of T into the same processor, to form the pair (s_i, t_i) within $p - 1$ supersteps. The BSP cost of local computation is cnm/p^2 and communication gm/p, thus the total cost is (assuming $m \leq n$), $cmn/p^2 + gm/p + l$ for a single iteration. Thus the total cost is $cmn/p + (p - 1)(gm/p + l)$ for all $p - 1$ supersteps. Figure 1 shows this algorithm for 4-processors.

Difference To compute $S - T$ in BSP, we: (1) locally append the n/p and m/p list elements of the sorted list implementation of the sets together; (2) locally sort the appended list; (3) locally eliminate duplicates, as duplicates

are only introduced when an element from T is in S; (4) perform a global sort on the appended lists (as the sorting algorithm we use never causes sequences of similar valued elements to straddle processors); then (5) a final local elimination phase removes duplicates, which completes the implementation of set difference. The BSP cost of the algorithm is $c(n + m)/p + \text{SEQSORT}((n + m)/p) + \text{PARSORT}(n + m)$.

Union and Intersection Union is implemented in a manner similar to set difference. That is, to compute $S \cup T$: (1) the local blocks of S and T are appended, sorted, and then all-but-one duplicates eliminated; (2) a global sort is performed; (3) as sort does not cause "runs" to straddle processors, locally eliminating all-but-one duplicate completes set union. The BSP cost of this algorithm is also $(n + m)/p + \text{SEQSORT}((n + m)/p) + \text{PARSORT}(n + m)$. Using the same assumptions, $S \cap T$ can be implemented in terms of $S - (S - T)$.

5 An object database query

We synthesise the basic operations discussed so far into a case study of an object database query according to the ODMG-93 definition. The essence of the ODMG-93 standard is to extend the set-based relational model with collection types, and OQL which allows high-level expression of database query statements. As [10] observes, OQL is essentially an extension of SQL to deal with collection-valued fields instead of just set-valued fields. The most common form of a query in OQL is a select statement of the form:

> **select** e
> **from** x_1 **in** C_1, x_2 **in** C_2, ..., x_n **in** C_n
> **where** $pred$

Such statements translate into the following comprehension notation [5] $bag\{ e \mid x_1 \leftarrow C_1, x_2 \leftarrow C_2, ..., C_n \leftarrow C_n, pred \}$. Processing this query involves applying the filter predicate (i.e. selection) to the collections involved (to reduce the number of elements), taking the cartesian product (i.e. join) of the (filtered) collections, $C_1 \times C_2 \times \cdots \times C_n$, followed by a map function that selects the attributes specified by the expression e (i.e. projection).

We have simulated this OQL **select-from-where** construct using the *BSPlib*, and analysed the results using the Oxford BSP Toolset. Our simulation method is described next. Two collections C_1 and C_2 of 1024 keys each are defined to represent a database, and after the two collections are filtered, they are individually sorted to regain order and load balance. A cartesian product is formed next, which is followed by sorting and duplicate elimination. Finally the map function selects the desired attributes. The collection sizes we chose are small enough so that communication latencies are paramount in comparison to local computation.

6 Experimental results

Machine	p	s	l	g
Uniprocessor Sun	4	0.7	198000	68
SGI PowerChallenge	4	74	1902	9.3
IBM SP2 (switch)	8	26	5412	11.4

Table 1. BSP parameters

In this section, results are presented for our BSP simulation on a uniprocessor Sun workstation, a 4-processor shared-memory SGI Power Challenge, and an 8-processor distributed-memory (switch based) IBM SP/2. Table 1 shows the observed BSP parameter values (in #flops) for these machines, and profiling charts generated from execution of the simulation on each machine are discussed in the context of these values. They highlight the salient features of processing collections on real machines[1].

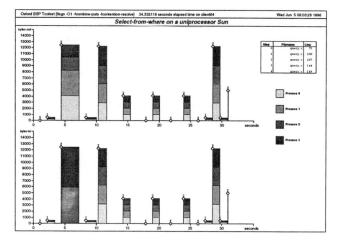

Figure 2. Sun Workstation profile

In the profiling charts, such as the one shown in figure 2, the top graph contains bars whose height identifies the amount of data leaving each process, whereas the lower graph shows the amount of data entering each processor during the superstep. The width of the bars indicate the elapsed time taken to perform communication and synchronisation within a superstep, whereas the "white spaces" or gaps between the bars indicate local computation within the specified superstep.

Figure 2 shows the profiling results from a Sun workstation. The bars marked with 1 relate to the communication involved in gathering the regular samples and then redistributing the pivot values to all the processors during the (sample)

[1]These simulations are run using the same program, without any machine specific optimisations, and using the native *BSPlib* implementation.

sorting phase, as described in section 4. The bars marked with 2 relate to the communication intensive data redistribution phase of sorting. Since this phase also restores load balance in our simulation, it could be viewed as the communication involved in load balancing intermediate results.

The $p - 1 = 3$ bars marked with 3 relate to the communication involved during the computation of cartesian product. As described in section 4 the algorithm uses $p - 1$ supersteps to permute the data blocks, to bring the blocks into the appropriate processors. The gaps in between the bars represent the time for computing the local cartesian product. Other gaps between the bars relate to the compute-bound map that performs projection and filter which performs the selection.

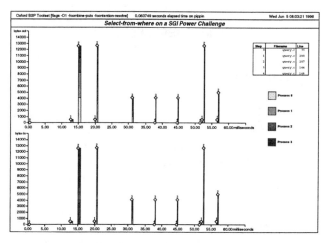

Figure 3. SGI PowerChallenge profile

In contrast, figure 3 shows the execution of the same program on a 4-processor SGI Power Challenge. Apart from the much reduced time for communication due to a much reduced value for g on an PowerChallenge (note the change of scale from seconds to milliseconds), processors also perform more balanced communication, although they exchange the same amount of information. The substantial reduction in the gap between the bars reflects the speedup obtained using four (faster) processors.

In figure 4, results are shown for the execution of the simulation on an 8-processor IBM SP/2. In this case, $p - 1 = 7$ supersteps are needed to complete the cartesian product, as the bars marked with 3 indicate, but the amount of data communicated during each superstep is reduced correspondingly. The slight difference in the width of the bars is due to the difference in the rate of communication on a distributed memory machine as compared to a shared memory based implementation, that is, the SP/2 has a higher value of g than the SGI. However the smaller gaps between the bars indicates the additional speedup attained due to the availability of extra processors in the embarrassingly parallel operations.

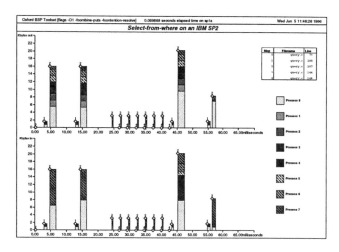

Figure 4. IBM SP2 profile

7 Conclusions

In this paper, we have investigated a way to provide high-level programming abstractions in terms of collection types for parallel database programming. In particular, the task of incorporating a representative group of collection types, that can model a broad class of non-numerical applications, into the BSP programming environment was considered.

We briefly introduced the ongoing work on *BSPlib*, and this paper has taken the first steps towards providing an automatic BSP programming environment, that provides a sufficient level of abstraction to tackle the challenges of non-numerical computations. Databases and database query processing, remains to be a challenging application in this class, and can benefit from the progress being made in general-purpose parallel computing. Finally, we have outlined how a BSP environment augmented with richer types can help to implement object database operations. Our experimental simulation on parallel machines show encouraging results for further work.

References

[1] G. Blelloch. NESL: A Nested Data-Parallel Language. Technical Report CMU-CS-93-129, Department of Computer Science, Carnegie Mellon University, April 1993.

[2] R. G. G. Cattell. *The Object Database Standard: ODMG-93*. Morgan Kaufmann, San Francisco, California, 1994.

[3] M. Cole. Parallel Programming, List Homomorphisms and the Maximum Segment Sum Problem. In G. Joubert, editor, *Parallel Computing: Trends and Applications*, pages 489–492. North-Holland, 1994.

[4] J. Darlington, A. J. Field, P. G. Harrison, P. H. J. Kelly, D. W. N. Sharp, Q. Wu, and R. L. While. Parallel Programming using Skeleton Functions. In *Parallel Architectures and Languages Europe*, 1993.

[5] L. Fegaras and D. Maier. Towards an Effective Calculus for Object Query Languages. In *ACM SIGMOD International Conference on Management of Data*, May 1995.

[6] A. V. Gerbessiotis and L. G. Valiant. Direct Bulk Synchronous Parallel Algorithms. *Journal of Parallel and Distributed Computing*, 22:251–267, 1994.

[7] M. W. Goudreau, J. M. D. Hill, K. Lang, W. F. McColl, S. B. Rao, D. C. Stefanescu, T. Suel, and T. Tsantilas. A Proposal for the BSP Worldwide Standard Library (Preliminary Version). Technical report, Oxford University Computing Laboratory, Apr. 1996. (see www.bsp-worldwide.org for more details).

[8] J. M. D. Hill. *Data-Parallel Lazy Functional Programming*. PhD thesis, Dept of Computer Science, Queen Mary & Westfield College, University of London, Sept. 1994.

[9] J. M. D. Hill, P. I. Crumpton, and D. A. Burgess. Theory, Practice, and a Tool for BSP Performance Prediction. In *EuroPar'96*, number 1124 in LNCS. Springer-Verlag, Aug. 1996.

[10] W. Kim. Observations on the ODMG-93 Proposal for an Object-Oriented Database Language. *SIGMOD Record*, 23(1):4–9, 1994.

[11] W. F. McColl. General Purpose Parallel Computing. In A. M. Gibbons and P. Spirakis, editors, *Lectures on Parallel Computation*, pages 337–391. Cambridge University Press, 1993.

[12] W. F. McColl. Scalable Computing. In J. van Leeuwen, editor, *Computer Science Today: Recent Trends and Developments*, number 1000 in LNCS, pages 46–61. Springer-Verlag, 1995.

[13] J. H. Reif and L. G. Valiant. Logarithmic Time Sort for Linear Size Networks. *Journal of the ACM*, 34(1):60–76, 1987.

[14] J. T. Schwartz. Ultracomputers. *ACM Transactions on Programming Languages and Systems*, 2(4):484–521, Oct. 1980.

[15] H. Shi and J. Schaeffer. Parallel Sorting by Regular Sampling. *Journal of Parallel and Distributed Computing*, 14(4):361–372, 1992.

[16] D. B. Skillicorn. *Foundations of Parallel Programming*. Cambridge University Press, 1994.

[17] K. R. Sujithan. An Object Model of Data, Based on the ODMG Industry Standard for Database Applications. In *IEE/BCS International Seminar on Client/Server Computing*, Oct. 1995.

[18] K. R. Sujithan. Towards a Scalable Parallel Object Database – The Bulk Synchronous Parallel Approach. Technical Report PRG-TR-17-96, Oxford University Computing Laboratory, Aug. 1996.

[19] L. G. Valiant. Bulk Synchronous Parallel Computers. In M. Reeve and S. E. Zenith, editors, *Parallel Processing and Artificial Intelligence*, pages 15–22. Wiley, Chichester, U.K., 1989.

[20] L. G. Valiant. A Bridging Model for Parallel Computation. *Communications of the ACM*, 33(8):103–111, Aug. 1990.

Distributed Computational Processes for Image Reconstruction in Massively Parallel Structure

Nadiya Gubareny, Aleksander Katkov
Technical University of Częstochowa
Institute of Mathematics & Computer Science
42-200 Częstochowa, Poland
Email: gubareni@matinf.pcz.czest.pl

Abstract

A new approach for organization of distributed computational processes in computing massively parallel homogeneous structures on the basis of principle of TTTS (True Time True Space) is considered. Each processor of such MPS (Massively Parallel Structure) executes its computations on the level of discrete mathematical model of real physical environment. It has a reduced instruction set, a small local memory and connected with only eight neighboured elements. Computational process in MPS is defined by chaotic interaction of connected processor elements. The mathematical model of chaotic computational processes in MPS for image reconstruction with limited projection data is built. A new chaotic iterative algorithm of modelling distributed computational processes in such MPS on the basis of asynchronous iterative methods is elaborated.

1. Introduction

The problem of investigating the internal structure of object without destroying it has arisen in a large number of scientific and practical areas. In recent years the technique of computerized tomography has found a wide application for solving such problems. This technique allows to reconstruct the internal structure of object from data collected outside the object. This data, usually called the projection data or projections for short, are represented mathematically as the Radon transform. Theoretically it is possible to reconstruct the internal structure of object uniquelly without errors by means of Radon's inversion formula. However in practice the projections have been obtained by physical measurement and so their number is limited and given with some errors. If the number of projections

may be obtained large enough then in such applications (in medicine, for example) it is more preferred to use the analytical methods based on the inverse Radon transform. However in other scientific fields (such as optical researches, geophysics, investigation of plasma, combustion problems) the number of the projection data is very limited as a rule. In these cases the use of analytical methods doesn't give enough good results of image reconstruction and for better reconstruction the iterative algebraic algorithms are usually used. However for solving the real practical problems the application of these algorithms has two main defects. One is the very long computation time required to converge to a satisfactory estimate. And the other is the very large memory space required to store the reconstruction image, projection data and necessary matrix coefficients.

In the recent time with the development of special-purpose parallel computer technique the interest to different iterative algebraic algorithms for image reconstruction was increased with possibility of their parallelizing to solve real problems in suitable time. One of the possible approach for their parallelizing is given by Y.Censor [1]. The implementation of parallel image reconstruction algorithms onto distributed memory parallel machines is considered in works [2], [3]. Another models of asynchronous parallel chaotic iteration methods are considered in work [4]. It is assumed that these models are fulfilled by computing structure consisted of independent processors connected with a shared memory. The number of all processors equals to the number of all equations in the solved system and each processor carries out its computations connected with corresponding equation. In this case each processor has to have enough large local memory to store the reconstruction data.

In this paper we consider some different parallel implementation of iterative algebraic algorithm for image

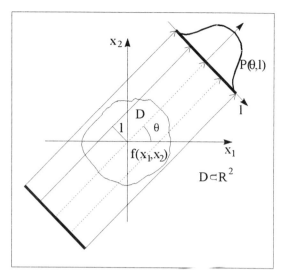

Figure 1.

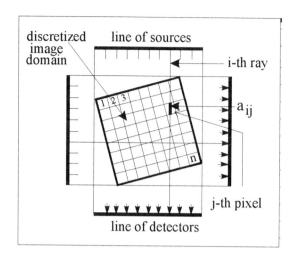

Figure 2.

reconstruction which may be realized CMPS (Computing Massively Parallel Structure) consisted of independent elementary processors the number of which equals to the number of all unknowns in the solved system. In such computing structure each elementary processor executes independently its calculations by means of the same simple algorithms. It has a reduced instruction set, a very small local memory and it is connected with only eight neighboured processors. After every its calculations the processor sends the necessary data to another one of its neighboured processor, the number of which it defines itself, and stores the computing data in its local memory.

We assume that each processor executes its calculations with its own pace and we allow the communication channels to deliver messages out of order. In this case we have the chaotic character of interactions in such CMPS which corresponds to some chaotic iterative algorithm. This algorithm realized on such CMPS is based on the asynchronous method [5].

The remainder of the paper is organized as follows: in section 2 we describe some methods to reconstruct 2D images from incomplete data. Section 3 is devoted to the parallelizing of these methods on CMPS. In section 4 we describe the parallel chaotic iterative algorithm arising in such computing structure.

2. Iterative algebraic algorithms

The main problem of 2D computerized tomography is to reconstruct a distribution function f from its known line integrals (or projection data).

Let an image function f be defined in some domain $D \subset R^2$. It needs to reconstruct the function f from given set of projection data which are its integrals over straight lines:

$$p(\theta, l) = \int_{-\infty}^{+\infty} f(l \cos \theta - t \sin \theta, l \sin \theta + t \cos \theta) dt, \quad (1)$$

where θ is the projection angle, l is the coordinate along the projection line (see fig.1). As a rule in practice we have only discrete set of projection data for finite number of θ and l. For some problems of physical sciences the number of θ may be very small, for example 3 or 5. So we have such reconstruction problem: it is given a set $p_{\theta_j}(l_i)$ for $j = 1, 2, ..., NA$; $i = 1, 2, ..., NR$; it needs to find an estimate $\tilde{f}$ of f.

One of the approach for solving this problem consists in discretizing the model and reducing it to solve the system of linear algebraic equations. For this purpose we construct the full discrete model of image object from its projections. First we divide reconstruction domain D into n small pixels and assume that image function f has constant uniform value x_j throughout the j-th pixel for $j = 1, 2, ..., n$. Secondly we assume that sources and detectors are points and the rays between them are lines. Then we denote by a_{ij} ($i = 1, 2, ..., m$; $j = 1, 2, ..., n$; $m = NA \times NR$) the length of intersection of i-th ray with j-th pixel (see fig.2). Let p_i be a physical measurement and represent the line integral (1) along the ith ray, which in this approximation replaced by a finite sum

$$p_i \simeq \sum_{j=1}^{n} a_{ij} x_j,$$

and at the result we obtain the full discrete model of image reconstruction in matrix form:

$$\mathbf{p} = \mathbf{A}\mathbf{x}, \qquad (2)$$

where $\mathbf{p} = (p_i) \in R^m$ is the measurement vector, $\mathbf{x} = (x_j) \in R^n$ is the image vector and $\mathbf{A} = (a_{ij}) \in R^{m,n}$ is the projection matrix.

This system of linear algebraic equation has some characteristic features: as a rule the matrix A isn't square and it has a large dimension (approximately $10^4 \times 10^5$), the matrix A is a very sparse (only 10% of all its coefficients don't equal to 0), the system is inconsistent and indeterminated.

For solving such systems of equations there are often used different kind of sequential iterative algebraic algorithms which are based on well-known Kaczmarz method [6], the most well-known from which are ART and MART algorithms [7], [8], [9]. They are generally simple, flexible and permit to use *a priori* knowledge of the object before its reconstruction that is very important in problems of physical sciences.

The basic idea of all ART methods is to run through all equations cyclically with modification of the present estimate $\mathbf{x}^{(k)}$ in such way that the present equation with index i is fulfilled. It can be expressed as follows [7]:

$$\mathbf{x}^{(k+1)} = \mathbf{x}^{(k)} + \omega_k \frac{p_{i(k)} - (\mathbf{a}^{i(k)}, \mathbf{x}^{(k)})}{\|\mathbf{a}^{i(k)}\|^2} \mathbf{a}^{i(k)} \qquad (3)$$

with an arbitrary vector $\mathbf{x}^{(0)}$ and $\mathbf{a}^{i(k)} = (a_{i1}, a_{i2}, ..., a_{in})^T$, where $i(k) = k \bmod m + 1$ and $0 < \omega_k < 2$ is a relaxation parameter.

The rate of convergence of this algorithm is very slow and so we have to fulfil a lot of iterations to obtain a satisfactory solution.

3. Massively parallel structure for image reconstruction

Refusing the sequential cyclical fulfilment of every iteration (3) we propose some model of parallel implementation of algorithm ART on CMPS. The organization of distributed computational processes in such CMPS is based on principle TTTS (True Time True Space). Such CMPS consists of independent elementary processors called PPs (Pixel Processors), the number of which equals to the number of all pixels in discrete reconstruction domain, or in other words the number of all unknowns in solved system. In CMPS each PP executes its calculations independently corresponding to the real domain of image space by the same

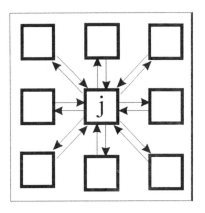

Figure 3.

algorithms. Every PP is connected with eight local neighboured PPs and has its own local small memory (see fig.3).

At the beginning of work each j-th PP loads its initial value $x_j^{(0)}$. After its calculations PP changes the value $x_j^{(k)}$ by new value $x_i^{(k+1)}$ stored in its local memory and sends the necessary computing data to one of its neighboured PP, the number of which it defines itself according to its input data. Each processor works locally independently and executes one of the two fixed algorithms:

1) modelling the process of spreading ray;
2) correction of values of image function.

After fulfilling each algorithm PP defines the direction of sending information, i.e. the number of neighboured PP which must receive the corresponding data, and waits the confirmation from this PP about receiving this information. Then PP turns into waiting mode untill receiving signals from the side of neighboured PPs.

Among all PP we mark out the special BP1s and BP2s (Boundary Processors of the 1-st type and the 2-nd type) which correspond to the boundary pixels of discrete reconstruction domain in which the rays input and from which the rays output correspondingly. We assume that every PP has so many input buffers as the number of all rays crossed the corresponding point of discrete domain and every input buffer corresponds to one of these rays. Each BP1 receives into its input the value of projection data p_i, the relaxation parameter ω, and the coordinates of the first intersection point of ray with corresponding boundary pixel for every input ray L_i crossed this point. For the first algorithm we set a flag $\alpha = 1$ and a flag $\alpha = 2$ for the second algorithm. Each PP always receives a value α which indicates it what algorithm must be fulfilled (at the first step $\alpha = 1$

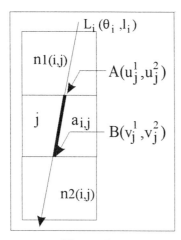

Figure 4.

and we solve the first problem of modelling the process of spreading ray).

If $\alpha = 1$ and the input data is received from the input buffer corresponding to i-th ray then j-th PP executes the next computing algorithm (see fig.4):

Algorithm 1

1) finding the coordinates v_j^1, v_j^2 of the second intersection point of ray with j-th pixel;

2) determination of number $n2(i,j)$ of the neighboured PP to which current data will be send;

3) calculation of the intersection length of ray L_i with j-th pixel, i.e. the coefficient a_{ij} of matrix A;

4) calculation of the product of coefficient a_{ij} by current value x_j which is stored at a time in the local memory of j-th PP;

5) calculation of differens:

$$S1_i := S1_i - a_{ij}x_j$$

(for BP1 $S1_i := p_i - a_{ij}x_j$);

6) calculation of sum:

$$S2_i := S2_i + a_{ij}^2$$

(for BP1 $S2_i := 0$).

After solving the first algorithm j-th PP sends to $n2(i,j)$-th neighboured processor the next data: θ_i, l_i, $S1_i$, $S2_i$, $\alpha = 1$, $u_{n2(i,j)}^1 = v_j^1$, $u_{n2(i,j)}^2 = v_j^2$, ω_i. After receiving this data from the j-th PP the neighboured $n2(i,j)$-th PP "conducts" ray further solving the analogous algorithm 1.

If j-th PP is BP2 then after fulfilling the algorithm 1 it calculates the value

$$\delta_i = \omega \frac{S1_i}{S2_i} = \omega \frac{p_i - \sum_j a_{ij}x_j}{\sum_j a_{ij}^2} = \omega \frac{p_i - (\mathbf{a}^i, \mathbf{x})}{\|\mathbf{a}^i\|^2},$$

changes flag $\alpha = 1$ to flag $\alpha = 2$ and at once begins to execute the algorithm 2.

If $\alpha = 2$, the input data is received from the input buffer corresponding to i-th ray and j-th PP isn't BP2 then PP executes the next computing algorithm.

Algorithm 2.

1), 3) are the same as in algorithm 1;

2) determination of number $n1(i,j)$ of the neighboured PP to which current data will be send;

4) fulfilling the correction of value of image function. During this fulfilment the current value x_j stored at a time in the local memory of the j-th PP is changed by value y according to formula:

$$y = \mathbf{F}_i(\mathbf{x}) = x_j + \delta_i a_{ij}. \tag{5}$$

After fulfilment this algorithm j-th PP sends to the neighboured $n1(i,j)$-th PP the next data: θ_i, l_i, $\alpha = 2$, $u_{n1(i,j)}^1 = v_j^1$, $u_{n1(i,j)}^2 = v_j^2$, δ_i.

If $n1(i,j)$-th PP is BP1 then after fulfilment of algorithm 2 it changes the flag $\alpha = 1$.

Each PP may have several loaded input buffers simultaneously. In this case in the first place it chooses the buffer with $\alpha = 2$. If the number of these buffers is more than 1 then PP chooses the need buffer among them at random. And if there are not such buffers then PP chooses the need buffer among the input buffers with $\alpha = 1$ at random as well. So each PP of such CMPS interacts with neighboured PPs following to the local strategy of behaviour at random. At the result we have chaotic computational processes in such CMPS.

4. Parallel chaotic iterative reconstruction algorithm

The realization of principle of TTTS in CMPS considered in previous section leads to arising chaotic computational processes in it. It is possible to describe the computational processes in such CMPS by means of chaotic iterative algorithm.

We use the basic notions of the theory of asynchronous iterative methods developing in works [5], [10],[11], [12], [13], [14], [15].

A sequence of nonempty subsets $I = \{I_k\}_{k=0}^{\infty}$ of set $\{1, 2, ..., n\}$ is a sequence of chaotic sets if

$$\limsup_{k \to \infty} I_k = \{1, 2, ..., n\} \tag{6}$$

(another words each of the integers $1, 2, ..., n$ appears in this sequence infinitely often).

A sequence $J = \{\sigma(k)\}_{k=1}^{\infty}$ of n-dimensional vectors $\sigma(k) = \{\sigma_1(k), \sigma_2(k), ..., \sigma_n(k)\}$ with integer coordinates satisfying for every $i = 1, 2, ..., n$ and $k \in N$ such properties:

$$0 \le \sigma_i(k) \le k;$$
$$\lim_{k \to \infty} \sigma_i(k) = \infty \qquad (7)$$

is called *a delay sequence*.

Consider chaotic iterative reconstruction algorithm which is fulfilled on such CMPS. Introduce discrete time $\{t_k\}_{k=0}^{\infty}$. We assume that at the initial time $t_0 = 0$ every i-th processor has initial value of image function $x_i^{(0)}$. Let $\mathbf{x}^{(k)}$ - value of image vector at the instante of time t_k. Now assume that change from state $\mathbf{x}^{(k)}$ to state $\mathbf{x}^{(k+1)}$ is fulfilled on MPS consisting of n PP by such iterative formula:

$$x_j^{(k)} = \mathbf{F}_{i(k)}(\mathbf{x}^{(k-1)}) \qquad (8)$$

for $j = 1, 2, ..., n$, where $\mathbf{F}_{i(k)}$ is the operator as in formula (5).

As every PP fulfils its calculations independently and for correction of its value each PP uses the previous values of another PP calculated for different steps of iteration the work of all CMPS may be defined by means of sequences of chaotic sets $I = \{I_k\}_{k=1}^{\infty}$, $I^j = \{I_k^j\}_{k=1}^{\infty}$ $(j = 1, 2, ..., n)$ and delay sequences $J_i = \{\sigma^i(k)\}_{k=1}^{\infty}$ $(i = 1, 2, ..., m)$, where subset I_k is the set of numbers of those PP, which take place really at the calculation of vector coordinates $\mathbf{x}^{(k)}$, subset I_k^j is the number of fulfilling operator and $\sigma_j^i(k)$ shows what previous iterations of vector $\mathbf{x}$ is used really on the k-th step of iteration by j-th processor from set I_k.

Now we will build the necessary sequences of chaotic sets I_k, I_k^j $(j = 1, 2, ..., n)$ and the delay sequences J_i $(i = 1, 2, ..., m)$.

For every j-th PP we consider the pixel set $PS_j = \{i_1, i_2, ..., i_{r(j)}\}$ consisted of those numbers of rays which crossed the j-th pixel. And for every time t_k and for every j-th PP we denote by $PS1_{jk}$ $(PS2_{jk})$ the set of loaded input buffers with $\alpha = 1$ $(\alpha = 2)$. For $k = 1$ $PS1_{j1}$ coincides with the set of all rays input to j-th pixel if $j \in BP1$ and $PS1_{j1} = \emptyset$ otherwise. And we assume that $PS2_{j1} = \emptyset$ for every j-th PP. Let $m_1(j, k)$ $(m_2(j, k))$ be the number of elements of set $PS1_{jk}$ $(PS2_{jk})$.

At time t_k the work of CMPS is defined by means of a sequence

$$\xi^k = \{\xi_1^k, \xi_2^k, ..., \xi_n^k\}$$

consisted from two-dimensional vectors $\xi_j^k = (\xi_j^k(1), \xi_j^k(2))$, where $\xi_j^k(1)$ and $\xi_j^k(2)$ may be built by such way.

If $m_2(j, k) = m_2 \ne 0$ then $\xi_j^k(2)$ is a random discrete variable chosen from the set $PS2_{jk}$ with some probability, for example $1/m_2$. If $m_2 = 0$ and $m_1(j, k) = $

$m_1 \ne 0$ then $\xi_j^k(2)$ is chosen from the set $PS1_{jk}$ with some probability, for example $1/m_1$. If $m_1 = m_2 = 0$ then $\xi_j^k(2) = 0$.

We assume that if j-th PP continues its work then $\xi_j^k(1) = 0$, otherwise numbers $\xi_j^k(1)$ may be defined according to such formula:

$$\xi_j^k = \begin{cases} 2 & \text{if } m_2(j, k) \ne 0 \\ 1 & \text{if } m_2(j, k) = 0, \ m_1(j, k) \ne 0 \\ 0 & \text{otherwise} \end{cases}$$

for $i = 1, 2, ..., n$.

At every time t_k the sequence ξ^k shows at what phase of work every PP is. If $\xi_j^k = (2, i)$ then new correction is fulfilled in j-th PP by means of operator $\mathbf{F}_i$. In other cases the j-th PP continues its work or is in the waiting mode and in both cases the corresponding pixel value isn't changed.

Computational process in each PP is defined by the sequence of chaotic sets $I = \{I_k\}_{k=1}^{\infty}$, $I^j = \{I_k^j\}_{k=1}^{\infty}$ $(j = 1, 2, ..., n)$ and delay sequences $J_i = \{\sigma^i(k)\}_{k=1}^{\infty}$ $(i = 1, 2, ..., m)$, which are built by means of sequence $\{\xi^k\}_{k=1}^{\infty}$. Chaotic set I_k is built by vector ξ^k in such way:

$$I_k = \{j \in (1, 2, ..., n) \mid \xi_j^k(1) = 2\} \qquad (9)$$

The set I_k^j may be built by such formula:

$$I_k^j = \begin{cases} i & \text{if } \xi_j^k(1) = 2, \ \xi_j^k(2) = i \\ \emptyset & \text{otherwise} \end{cases},$$

If $j \in I_k$ then $I_k^j \ne \emptyset$. In this case as $\xi_j^k(2)$ is chosen from the set $PS2_{jk} \subset PS_j$ then $I_k^j \subset \{i_1, i_2, ..., i_{r(j)}\}$.

The delay sequence $J_i = \{\sigma^i(k)\}_{k=1}^{\infty}$ may be built in such way:

1. $\sigma_j^i(1) = 0$, $s_j(1) = 0$;

2. if $k > 1$ then
$$\sigma_j^i(k) = \begin{cases} s_j(k-1) & \text{if } \xi_j^k(1) = 2, \xi_j^k(2) = i, \\ \sigma_j^i(k-1) & \text{otherwise} \end{cases}$$
$$(10)$$

where
$$s_j(k) = \begin{cases} s_j(k-1) + 1 & \text{if } j \in I_k \\ s_j(k-1) & \text{if } j \notin I_k \end{cases},$$

for $i = 1, 2, ..., m$, $j = 1, 2, ..., n$.

So change of value from $\mathbf{x}^{(k)}$ to $\mathbf{x}^{(k+1)}$ is calculated CMPS consisting of n PP by means of sequence of chaotic sets and the delay sequence by such formula:

$$x_j^{(k+1)} = x_j^{(k)} + \omega_k \frac{p_i - (\mathbf{a}^i, \mathbf{x}^{\sigma^i(k)})}{\|\mathbf{a}^i\|^2} \mathbf{a}^i$$

if $j \in I_k$, $\quad i \in I_k^j$
and
$$x_j^{(k+1)} = x_j^{(k)}$$
otherwise.

This algorithm is some generalization of asynchronous methods considered in works [5], [10], [11].

5. Conclusion

In this paper we propose the principle of TTTS for mapping of discrete mathematical model of distributed physical processes onto homogeneous computing environment. It is shown the possibility of realization of TTTS for modelling processes for image reconstruction with limited number of projection data of distributed objects by means of homogeneous MPS. The mathematical model of chaotic computational processes in such CMPS is built. Chaotic character of interaction in such CMPS corresponds to chaotic iterative algorithm. The corresponding chaotic iterative algorithm of modelling distributed computational processes in CMPS for image reconstruction is elaborated.

References

[1] Y.Censor, "Parallel application of block-iterative methods in medical imaging and radiation therapy," *Math. Programming*, Vol.42, pp.307-325, 1988.

[2] C. Chen, S. Lee, Z.Cho, "Parallelisation of EM Algorithm for a 3-D PET Image reconstruction," *IEEE Transactions on Medical Imaging*, Vol.10, pp.513-522, 1991.

[3] C. Chen, S. Lee, "On Parallelizing the EM Algorithm for PET Image Reconstruction," *IEEE Transactions on Parallel and Distributed Systems*, Vol.5, No.8, pp.860-873, 1994.

[4] R.Bru, L.Elsner, M.Neumann, "Models of Parallel Chaotic Iteration Methods," *Linear Algebra Appl.*, Vol.103, pp.175-192, 1988.

[5] D.P. Bertsekas and J.N. Tsitsiklis, *Parallel and Distributed Computation* Prentice-Hall, Englewood Cliffs, NJ, 1989.

[6] Kaczmarz S., "Angenäherte Auflösung von Systemen Lineare Gleichungen," *Bull. Acad. Polon. Sci. Lett. A*, vol.35, pp.355-357, 1937.

[7] G.T.Herman, *Image Reconstruction from Projections*, Academic, New York, 1980.

[8] G.T.Herman, "A relaxation method for reconstructing objects from noisy x-rays," *Math. Programming*, Vol.8, pp.1-19, 1975.

[9] G.T.Herman, A.Lent, S.Rowland, "ART: Mathematics and application (a report on the mathematical foundations and on the applicability to real data of the Algebraic Reconstruction Techniques)," *Journ. of Theoretica Biology*, Vol.43, pp.1-32, 1973.

[10] D.Chazan, W.Miranker, "Chaotic Relaxation," *Linear Algebra Appl.*, Vol.2, pp.199-222, 1969.

[11] G.M.Baudet, "Asynchronous iterative methods for multiprocessors," *J. Assoc. Comput. Mach.*, Vol.25, pp.226-244, 1978.

[12] J.C.Miellou, "Itérations chaotiques à retards," *Comptes Rendus. Acad. Sci. Paris*, Vol.278, série A, pp.957-960,1974.

[13] J.C.Miellou, "Algorithmes de relaxation chaotique à retards," *R.A.I.R.O., 9ème année*, R-1, pp.55-82, 1975.

[14] J.C.Miellou, "Itérations chaotiques à retards; études de la convergence dans le cas d'espaces partiellement ordonnés," *Comptes Rendus. Acad. Sci. Paris*, Vol.280, série A, pp.233-236,1975.

[15] F.Robert, M.Charnay, F.Musy, "Itérations chaotiques série-parallèle pour des équations non linéaires de point fixe," *Apl. Mat.*, Vol.20, pp.1-38, 1975.

Multilink extension to support deadlock-free adaptive non-minimal routing [1]

Antonio Robles, José Duato

Departamento de Ingeniería de Sistemas, Computadores y Automática

Universidad Politécnica de Valencia (Spain)

email : {arobles,jduato}@gap.upv.es

Abstract

In this paper, an extension of the multilink concept to non-minimal routing is proposed. The multilink concept is the basis of a new pipelined flow control technique for multicomputer networks. The multilink technique allows the design of deadlock-free adaptive, both minimal and non-minimal, routing algorithms. Through simulation, the performance of two families of routing strategies based on multilinks are investigated in the hypercube topology. All the proposed adaptive routing strategies outperform the deterministic one significantly. In turn, the proposed non-minimal routing strategies increase the performance with regard to minimal ones when messages are long, especially with local distribution of messages.

Keywords: Interconnection networks, adaptive routing, deadlock-free routing, wormhole, hypercube.

1. Introduction

Multicomputers, as massively parallel computers, provide an excellent cost/performance ratio. A key architectural issue is the interconnection network. Wormhole routing is the most widely used flow-control technique [6]. The particular behavior of this mechanism, very prone to deadlock, makes necessary the use of deadlock-free routing algorithms.

Several solutions have been developed for wormhole routing. The first approach is based on the assignment of an ordering to the channels and the restriction of routing to visit the channels in decreasing order to eliminate cycles in the channel dependency graph. It is based on Dally and Seitz's theorem [6], which established a necessary and sufficient condition for a deterministic routing function to be deadlock-free. Although this method avoids deadlock, it can increase traffic jams, specially in heavily loaded networks with long messages.

So, several adaptive algorithms have been developed for wormhole routing in order to obtain greater efficiency. These adaptive strategies are also based on Dally and Seitz's theorem, which becomes only a sufficient condition for deadlock-free adaptive routing. Some of these algorithms use virtual channels [4] to eliminate the cyclic dependencies between channels. Design methodologies like the one based on the virtual network concept [11,15] allow the development of fully adaptive routing algorithms. However, the use of virtual channels may produce a noticeable cost and an increase in the network latency. Thus, several partially adaptive algorithms have been proposed, either by using a moderate amount of virtual channels [2] or not using them at all [10].

A different approach consists of allowing the existence of cyclic dependencies between channels, providing fully adaptive routing with a modest number of virtual channels. According to Duato's theorem [7], cyclic dependencies between channels are allowed, provided that there exists a connected channel subset free of cyclic dependencies. Afterwards, others authors have proposed adaptive routing algorithms whose channel dependency graph is not necessarily acyclic [5,14]. Alternatively, other algorithms make use of different flow-control techniques, like circuit-switching [3,8] or deadlock recovery techniques [1,12,16], to guarantee deadlock freedom. Other strategies make use of misrouting to increase adaptivity [13]. Guaranteeing livelock and deadlock freedom involves routing restrictions. As a consequence, non-minimal partially adaptive algorithms have been proposed [10].

Circuit-switching [9] has been used to solve the deadlock problem. This strategy can provide fault-tolerant properties, especially when backtracking is used [9]. However, when it is applied to non faulty networks and depending on the network load, poor performance is obtained due to the higher setup time. Therefore, in non faulty networks, misrouting backtracking protocols must be used with some restrictions in order to improve performance.

1 This work was supported by Spanish CYCYT under Grant TIC94-0510-C02-01

This work analyzes two families of adaptive routing strategies, based on the *multilink* concept [17]. In order to improve performance, we propose an extension of the *multilink* concept to non-minimal routing in a particular case. An informal description of the *multilink* concept is made in section 2. Two families of deadlock-free partially adaptive minimal routing strategies based on *multilinks* together their extension to non-minimal routing are proposed in section 3. Section 4 shows a formal description of the *multilink* technique for both, minimal and non-minimal routing, and its application to the deadlock problem. Section 5 establishes the simulation conditions and performance measurements. A justification of the extension to non-minimal routing is made in section 6. The evaluation of the proposed routing strategies for hypercube network is made in section 7. Finally, some conclusions are drawn.

2. *Multilink* concept: Informal description

The *multilink* [17] concept is a new approach to the design of deadlock-free adaptive routing algorithms for multicomputers with direct interconnection networks. This technique can be considered as a new pipelined flow-control mechanism complementary to other ones such as wormhole routing and virtual channels. However, virtual channels are not necessary, thus avoiding the additional cost derived from using them. The *multilink* concept makes possible the routing of messages without visiting channels in order, taking adventage of both, minimal and non-minimal, alternative paths to route messages towards their destination.

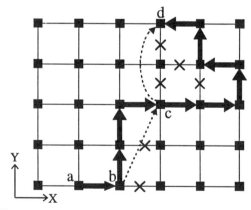

Figure 1. Physical channels valid for establishing a *multilink* in a 2D mesh. Minimal *multilink* between nodes 'b' and 'c'. Non-minimal *multilink* between nodes 'c' and 'd'. Routing in order: first X, after Y.

A *multilink* is a virtual link formed by two or more adjacent physical channels, which are reserved and freed

as a whole. This is ensured by the *multilink* searching protocol. A *multilink* establishes a virtual link between two non adjacent nodes. The *multilink size* is the number of physical channels that form the *multilink*. The maximum value is determined by the routing function used.

In the case of minimal routing, when the maximum *multilink* size is greater than or equal to the network diameter it will be possible to connect any couple of nodes in the network. In this case, the *multilink* technique would operate like the pipelined circuit switching flow-control mechanism [8]. However, there is a fundamental difference: the *multilink* technique does not need to establish a full path between source and destination nodes.

To reserve all the channels belonging to a *multilink*, a control flit, which we call *explorer*, is generated by the router and sent across a free channel to the next node. The *explorer* performs an exhaustive searching protocol with backtracking. The *explorer* only contains information about channels that need to be reserved along the next nodes to establish the *multilink*. The header size is the same as in *e-cube* routing with the addition of two bits. A control bit is needed to distinguish between a header and a *explorer*. The second one distinguishes between minimal and non-minimal *multilink*.

The router can make a single routing decision at a time. Each node has a crossbar, which connects input and output channels.

3. Routing strategies based on *multilinks*

In what follows, we propose two models of deadlock-free partially adaptive minimal routing strategies. These are valid for any interconnection network. The degree of adaptivity is determined by the routing strategy by means of the maximum *multilink* size. The *multilink* size is bounded by min(d,m), where d is the distance between nodes and m is the maximum *multilink* size. When m is equal to the diameter of the network, the routing strategy will be fully adaptive.

Model 1: It always tries to route across the next channel in the conventional path. If this channel is busy then it tries to obtain a *multilink* with maximum size. If this is not possible, it will search for the next shorter size and so on.

Model 2: It starts searching for a *multilink* with maximum size. If this is not possible, it will search for the next shorter size and so on. Finally, if the message has not been routed yet, the next channel in the conventional path is tried.

The conventional path is determined by the *e-cube* routing strategy.

The above models can be extended to non-minimal routing. We do it in the particular case that the message is stopped at a distance equal to one from its destination node. In this case, when the last channel for reaching the destination is busy, the only way to proceed forward is through a non-minimal *multilink*.

In the case of binary hypercube, the above models allow the definition of two families of deadlock-free partially adaptive minimal routing strategies: MR1-m (model 1) and MR2-m (model 2). Where m is the maximum *multilink* size. The extension to non-minimal routing is made by establishing a non-minimal *multilink* with size equal to three when a message is stopped at a distance equal to one from its destination node. In an *n-cube*, up to n-1 alternative paths are available to establish a non-minimal *multilink* with size equal to 3. Thus, the above strategies can be extended to define EMR1-m (model 1) and EMR2-m (model 2) on the established conditions. The parameter m only affects the establishment of minimal *multilinks*.

4. Formal aspects: Deadlock-free routing conditions

In this section we formally prove that the extended routing function based on *multilinks* is deadlock- and livelock-free.

Definition 1: An *interconnection network* is modeled by a graph $I=G(N,C)$, where N and C represent the sets of nodes and physical channels, respectively.

Definition 2: Given two channels $c_i, c_j \in C$, it said that they form a *pair of complementary channels* if both of them are associated with the same dimension but each one crosses it in different direction. By extension, two sequences of n channels $\{c_i\}_{i=1,n}$, $\{c_j\}_{j=1,n} \subset C$ are complementary if their channels form n pairs of complementary channels.

Definition 3: The addition of new channels or *multilinks* extends the set of channels $C=\{c_i\}$, defining the set $C_E = C \cup C_M^2 \cup C_M^3 \cup .... \cup C_M^t$, where $C_M^m = \{mc_i^m\}$ represents the *set of multilinks* with size m | m≤t, where t is the maximum allowed *multilink* size. This size can become greater than the network diameter. If non-minimal paths are allowed, the size m must be equal to s+2r, where s represents the minimum distance between the nodes linked by the *multilink*, and r represents the distance covered moving away from the destination node.

A *multilink* with size m, mc_i^m, will be formed by the sequence of physical channels $\{c_{ij}\}_{j=1,m} \subset C$, such that $\{c_{ij}\}_{j=1,m} = \{c^u_{ij}\}_{j=1,s} \cup \{c^a_{ij}\}_{j=1,r} \cup \{c^b_{ij}\}_{j=1,r}$, where $\{c^u_{ij}\}_{j=1,s}$ represent the s useful channels reserved by *multilink*, $\{c^a_{ij}\}_{j=1,r}$ and $\{c^b_{ij}\}_{j=1,r}$ are two complementary sequences of channels. $\{c^a_{ij}\}_{j=1,r}$ represent the r channels that move the message away from its destination. $\{c^b_{ij}\}_{j=1,r}$

represent the r channels that bring the message close to the destination. When r=0, the *multilink* will be minimal.

Definition 4: An *adaptive routing function* R: $C \times N \to \wp(C)$, where $\wp(C)$ is the power set of C, supplies a set of alternative output channels to send a message from the current channel c_i to destination node n_d, $R(c_i, n_d) = \{c_{i1}, c_{i2}, ..., c_{ip}\}$, $c_i \neq c_{ik}$ $\forall k \in [1..p]$.

Definition 5: Given an interconnection network I, a routing function R and a pair of channels $c_i, c_j \in C$, there is a *dependency* from c_i to c_j iff $\exists x \in N \mid c_j \in R(c_i, x)$. Dependencies define a relation between channels. If there is a dependency from c_i to c_j, then $c_i > c_j$. The relation between channels in C can be extended to C_E. Given $c_j \in C$ and $mc_i^m \in C_M^m$, $mc_i^m > c_j$ if $c^u_{ik} > c_j$ $\forall k \in [1..s]$ and $c^b_{ig} > c_j$ $\forall g \in [1..r]$. Also $c_j > mc_i^m$ if $c_j > c^u_{ik}$ $\forall k \in [1..s]$. Additionally, given $mc_i^p \in C_M^p$ and $mc_j^q \in C_M^q$ | p=s+2r and q=v+2t, $mc_i^p > mc_j^q$ if $c^u_{ik} > c^u_{jh}$ $\forall k \in [1..s]$ and $\forall h \in [1..v]$ and $c^b_{ig} > c^u_{jk}$ $\forall g \in [1..r]$ and $\forall h \in [1..v]$.

Definition 6: A *channel dependency graph D* for a given interconnection network I and routing function R, is a directed graph $D = G(C,E)$. The vertices of D are the channels of I. The arcs of D are the pairs of channels (c_i, c_j) such that there is a dependency from c_i to c_j.

Dally and Seitz showed that a routing function R is deadlock-free if the channel dependency graph D has no cycles [6]. They also showed that if D is acyclic, then it is possible to establish an order relation between channels.

The channel set can be extended by considering *multilinks* in addition to physical channels. The new set of channels C_E is given by definition 3. The routing function as well as the channel dependency graph can be extended by considering the new set of channels. However, we are interested on a restricted set of routing functions, as indicated in the following definition:

Definition 7: An *extended adaptive routing function* $R_E: C_E \times N \to \wp(C_E)$ is an extension of a routing function R, such that

$$R_E(c_i, n_d) = \{c_{j1}, .., c_{jp}, mc_{k1}^2, .., mc_{kq}^r\}$$
$$R_E(mc_i^s, n_d) = \{c_{j1}, .., c_{jp}, mc_{k1}^2, .., mc_{kq}^r\}$$

This routing function defines dependencies between channels in C_E, such that

$c_i > c_{jh}$ $\forall h \in [1..p]$, $c_i > mc_{kg}^f$ $\forall f \in [2..r]$ and $\forall g \in [1..q]$
$mc_i^s > c_{jh}$ $\forall h \in [1..p]$, $mc_i^s > mc_{kg}^r$ $\forall f \in [2..r]$ and $\forall g \in [1..q]$

r≤t, where t is the maximum allowed size of *multilink*. R_E is an adaptive routing function where each *multilink* mc_{kg}^f can be formed by several minimal and non-minimal physical paths. The routing function R can be considered as a subfunction of R_E on the set of physical channels C, that is,

$$R(c_i, n_d) = R_E(c_i, n_d) \cap C \quad \forall c_i \in C \wedge \forall n_d \in N. \quad (1)$$

Theorem 1: The routing function R_E does not have cycles in the channel dependency graph D_E if the channel *dependency graph D for a routing function R defined by expression (1) is acyclic.*

Proof: We will prove it by contradiction. There are two possible cases:

a) R_E is a minimal routing function. Let us suppose that there is a cycle in D_E. There are also two possible cases:

a.1) All the channels that form the cycle belong to the set of physical channels C. Then, they would form a cycle in D, contrary to the initial assumption.

a.2) There are one or more *multilinks* in the cycle. By splitting up each *multilink* into the physical channels that form it and taking into account the definition of R_E, cyclic dependencies would appear in D, which is again contrary to the initial assumption.

b) R_E is a non-minimal routing function. In this case, if there was a cycle in D_E, the useful channels would form a cycle in D, contrary to the initial assumption and definition 5.

Thus, R_E does not have cycles in D_E.■

Theorem 2: The routing function R_E is deadlock-free.

Proof: Taking into account that the searching *multilink* protocol guarantees that all the channels belonging to a *multilink* are reserved and freed as if they were a single channel, the Dally and Seitz's theorem can also be applied to networks containing *multilinks*. According to previous theorem 1 the channel dependency graph D_E for R_E is acyclic. Thus, applying Dally and Seitz's theorem, the routing function R_E is deadlock-free.■

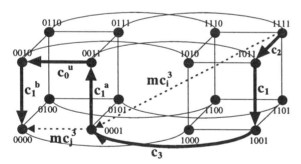

Figure 2. Establishing of a minimal *multilink* of size 3 between nodes 1111 and 0001, in addition to non-minimal one when the message is at a distance equal to one from the destination node and it cannot proceed forward because the physical channel is busy.

Theorem 3: The routing function R_E is livelock-free.

Proof: If R_E is a minimal routing function, it is obviously livelock-free. When R_E is non-minimal it is also livelock-free because the non-minimal *multilinks* always cross a useful channel at least. Hence, a message always comes closer to its destination node.■

Figure 2 shows an example of *multilinks* establishing on binary hypercube. In this case, the *e-cube* algorithm has be chosen as the deadlock-free routing function R, which restricts routing to cross dimensions only in decreasing order.

5. Simulation conditions and performance measures

We have considered that message generation rate is constant and the same for all the nodes. Each new message will be generated after a random number of clocks cycles. This amounts to fix the average number of flits/cycle/node generated. We have assumed that up to two outgoing messages per node are supported. Two distributions of message destinations have been proved: uniform and exponential.

Messages can be short or long. Short messages have a length uniformly distributed between 16 and 19 flits, while long messages are uniformly distributed between 31 and 510 flits in length.

We assumed that the reception bandwidth on each node is infinite and that the transmission time of a message through a channel and the routing time of headers and *explorers* are one clock cycle. The routing header and the *explorer* are one flit long. Also channel width is assumed to be one flit.

The most important performance measures are average delay and throughput. Average delay is the difference between average latency and average minimum latency. Latency is the time elapsed since data is available at the source node until the message is completely delivered at the destination node. Minimum latency is that of a network without message contention. Average delay is measured in clock cycles. Throughput is the maximum amount of information delivered per time unit (maximum traffic accepted by the network). Traffic is the flit reception rate, measured in flits per node per cycle.

6. Application of non-minimal *multilinks*: Justification

Establishing a non-minimal *multilink* when messages are stopped at a distance equal to one from their destination is due to the assumption that they contribute to the increase in overall average delay. The impossibility of obtaining an alternative path prevents messages from proceeding forward.

In this situation, an alternative path must be necessarily non-minimal. The idea is to avoid the busy channel by making a detour. It involves crossing one or more useless dimensions twice (a round trip), besides the useful remaining dimension. In this case, the routing would not be deadlock-free because dimension-order routing cannot be guaranteed, but establishing a non-minimal *multilink* to the destination node can resolve the deadlock problem.

However, we must be aware that this solution is proposed to improve network performance, and establishing a *multilink* has a noticeable cost, which depends on the *multilink* size. Thus, we propose to establish the shortest possible non-minimal *multilink*, its size will therfore be three.

7. Results

In what follows, the performance of new non-minimal adaptive routing algorithms based on *multilinks* is analyzed. In order to show the improvement with regard to deterministic routing, the *e-cube* strategy will be plotted on graphics.

the MR2-m strategy outperforms the MR1-m for a fixed *multilink* size m. Thus, only the best strategies are included in figure 3.

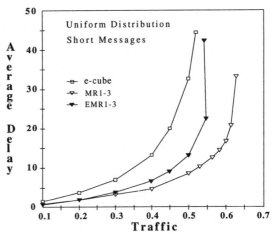

Figure 4. Average delay vs traffic with short messages

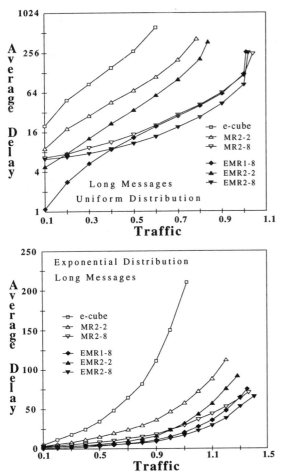

Figure 3. Average delay vs traffic with long messages

In [17] it was shown that when messages are long the larger the maximum *multilink* size, the higher the performance of the adaptive routing strategies. Moreover,

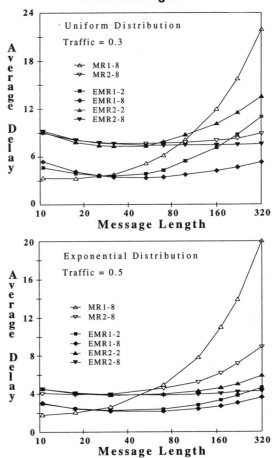

Figure 5. Average delay vs message length for small network load

In this case, EMR1-m and EMR2-m strategies improve performance, especially with local distribution. MR1-m strategies and those with a low value of m are those that benefit most from the extension to non-minimal routing. The advantage is greater with medium and low traffic in the network. With local distribution and traffic level lower than 0.9, non-minimal strategies outperform all minimal ones. The average delay decrease is roughly between 50% and 90% with regard to minimal routing strategies.

When messages are short, the MR1 adaptive strategies outperform the MR2 for any value of maximum *multilink* size. It has been found that the optimum maximum *multilink* size is three. This value represents the trade-off point between the advantages of establishing a greater *multilink* and the higher cost associated with it. For short messages, the grater influence of routing cost on latency justifies this behavior. In this case, non-minimal routing strategies do not outperform minimal strategies, even with local distribution, as is shown in figure 4. This behaviour can be explained by latency sensibility to the cost of establishing a *multilink*.

Figure 5 shows the influence of message length on performance with medium-low load. With message lengths above 30 flits, EMR1-m strategies outperform those based on minimal *multilinks*. As message length and network load increase, EMR2-m strategies yield better performance.

8. Conclusions

The non-minimal *multilink* concept has been proposed as an extension of the previous concept of *multilink*. The new concept is applied to resolve the deadlock problem in multicomputer networks, allowing the design of deadlock-free non-minimal adaptive routing strategies.

Two families of partially adaptive non-minimal routing algorithms based on *multilinks* have been proposed and analyzed on a hypercube topology. Each member of the family is distinguished by the maximum allowed size of minimal *multilink*. But all of them make use of a non-minimal *multilink* with size equal to three when messages are stopped at a distance equal to one from the destination node. In this case, the mean delay of such messages has a noticeable influence on the overall average delay, depending on the network load and messages distribution.

The proposed adaptive non-minimal strategies outperform the minimal strategies when messages are long and network load is medium or low, especially with local distribution of messages. When messages are short, non-minimal strategies obtain worse performance than minimal estrategies as a consequence of the cost of establishing a *multilink*. In this case, the best strategies are the minimal strategies, like MR1-m, that only make use of *multilinks* when it is necessary. Therefore, the *multilink* technique provides a deadlock-free adaptive routing

alternative that is less sensitive than circuit-switching to routing time.

References

[1] K.V. Anjan and T.M. Pinkston. DISHA: An efficient fully adaptive deadlock recovery scheme. *Proc. 9th Int. Symp. Parallel Processing*. April 1995.

[2] A.A. Chien and J.H. Kim. Planar-adaptive routing: low-cost adaptive networks for multiprocessors. *19th Int. Symp. on Computer Architecture*, 1992, pp. 268-277.

[3] E. Chow, H.Madan, J.Peterson, D. Grunwald and D.A. Reed. Hyperswitch network for the hypercube computer. *Proc. 15th Int. Symp. Computer Architecture*, June 1988, pp. 90-99.

[4] W.J. Dally. Virtual-channel flow control. *Proc. 17th Int. Symp. Computer Architecture*, May 1990, pp. 60-68.

[5] W.J. Dally and H. Aoki. Deadlock-free adaptive routing in multiprocessor networks using virtual channels. *IEEE Trans. on Parallel and Distributed Systems*, v. 4, n. 4 April 1993, pp. 466-474.

[6] W.J. Dally and C.L. Seitz. Deadlock-free message routing in multiprocessor interconnection networks. *IEEE Trans. on Computers*, v. C-36, n. 5, May 1987, pp.547-553.

[7] J. Duato. On the design of deadlock-free adaptive routing algorithms for multicomputers: design methodologies. *Proc. Parallel Architectures and Languages*, June 1991, pp. 234-243.

[8] P.T. Gaughan and S. Yalamanchili. Pipelined circuit-switching: A fault-tolerant variant of wormhole routing. *Proc. of IEEE Symp. on Parallel and Distributed Processing*, December 1992.

[9] P.T. Gaughan and S. Yalamanchili. A family of fault-tolerant routing protocols for direct multiprocessor network. *IEEE Trans. on Parallel and Distributed Systems*. May 1995, v. 6, n. 5, pp. 482-497.

[10] C.J. Glass and L.M. Ni. The turn model for adaptive routing. *19th Int. Symp. on Computer Architecture*, 1992, pp. 278-287.

[11] C.R. Jesshope, P.R. Miller and J.T. Yantchev. High performance communications in processor networks. *Proc. 16th Int. Symp. Computer Architecture*, June 1991.

[12] J.H. Kim, Z. Liu and A.A. Chien. Compression-less routing. *Proc. Int. Symp. Computer Architecture*, April 1994.

[13] S. Konstantinidou and L. Snyder. The Chaos router: A practical application of randomization in network routing. *2nd. Annu. Symp. on Parallel Algorithms and Architectures SPAA'1990*, pp. 21-30.

[14] X. Lin, P.K. McKinley and L.M. Ni. The message flow model for routing in wormhole-routed networks. *Proc. Int. Conf. Parallel Processing*, August 1993.

[15] D.H. Linder and J.C. Harden. An adaptive and fault tolerant wormhole routing strategy for k-ary n-cubes. *IEEE Trans. on Computers*, v. 40, n. 1, January 1991, pp. 2-12.

[16] D.S. Reeves, E.F. Genhringer and A. Chandiramani. Adaptive routing and deadlock recovery: a simulation study. *Proc. 4th Conf. on Hypercube Concurrent Computers & Applications*, March 1989, pp. 1-7.

[17] A. Robles and J. Duato. Deadlock-free adaptive routing based on multilinks. *Proc. 2nd Int. Conf. on Massivelly Parallel Computing Systems, MPCS'96*, May 1996.

Evaluating Latency of Distributed Algorithms
Using Petri Nets

Nicole Sergent

Département d'Informatique

Ecole Polytechnique Fédérale de Lausanne

CH - 1015 Lausanne (Switzerland)

sergent@lse.epfl.ch

Abstract

The time it takes to a distributed algorithm to finish (the distributed algorithm latency) cannot be directly measured in asynchronous systems if the algorithm starts and ends on different processors, since the system has no global time. A simple method to evaluate this latency is to build and simulate a unified model which includes the network and the distributed algorithm sub-models. In this paper we introduce a network model for UDP (User Datagram Protocol) which allows to establish a relationship between the number of messages exchanged in a distributed algorithm and the communication delays. As an application, we consider the two-phase commitment algorithm. Numerical results derived from simulating the model are compared with data obtained from performance measures.

1. Introduction

Usually, the performance of distributed algorithms is measured in terms of the number of messages exchanged during the execution. This is not the only relevant metric, assessing the algorithm latency may be also important, especially for real-time applications.

In distributed systems there is no shared memory nor global clock, so the communication and the synchronisation between processes on different nodes are done by message passing. The distributed algorithm latencies cannot be measured if computation begins and ends on different processors because processes do not have access to a global time. Another major impediment in the performance measures approach is that results are usually biased by unpredictable network and stations loads, not related to the studied algorithm. From these two reasons stems the interest in modelling the distributed algorithm and the underlying network using a formal description technique. By simulating this model it is possible to evaluate the algorithm latency with pretty good accuracy.

A distributed algorithm may be seen as an upper layer application based on a lower layer, the network. Between these two layers there is a strong interconnection. The number of messages generated by the algorithm has a direct influence on the end-to-end delay experienced by a message in the underlying network. This is particularly obvious in Ethernet based networks, where allocating the bus becomes a bottleneck, but this may be also true for networks capable of carrying several messages simultaneously, like FDDI. For some algorithms [3], the number of generated messages depends on the communication delays. This interrelation between the network and the algorithm makes it difficult to build an analytical model from which to derive the algorithm latency. An analytic modelling approach is presented in [10], for algorithms with a deterministic number of exchanged messages.

A more direct approach is to use a formal description technique, such as Petri nets[12], for modelling both the network and the distributed algorithm and then to derive the algorithm latency from simulations.

Since it is impossible to provide a universally valid network model, we focus on a very common network protocol, the User Datagram Protocol (UDP) [2]. First, a simple model for UDP in a LAN was built and validated through performance measures. The UDP model was translated into a Petri net model, which is reusable for all kinds of distributed algorithms based on exchanging messages.

As an application, we have chosen the two-phase commitment protocol [5]. The performance of any other distributed algorithm may be studied within this framework. Using the hierarchy concept of Petri nets, we build a unified model, which is simulated with a different number of participant processes. Approximate performance measures for the two-phase commitment protocol are used to validate the unified model.

The model is scalable with respect to the number of participant processes, i.e. we may increase the number of processes without modifying the model structure, which would be time-consuming. This is an important asset of our modelling approach over the more difficult performance measures.

2. Petri net model

The classical Petri net [11], [12] is a directed bipartite graph with two kinds of nodes, places and transitions. The nodes are connected by directed, weighted arcs. Arcs do not connect nodes of the same type. Places are graphically represented by circles and transitions by rectangles. Places may contain a number of tokens, drawn as black dots.

A place p is called an *input* place for a transition t if there exists a directed arc from p to t. A place p is called an *output* place of t if there exists a directed arc from t to p. The disposition of tokens on the places is called a *marking*. M(p) is the number of tokens on the place p. The initial marking of a net is the contents in tokens of each place before executing the net. During the execution the number of tokens may change.

A transition is *enabled* if each input place contains "enough" tokens, corresponding to the input arc weights. An enabled transition is eager to fire. When transition t fires, it removes the enabling tokens from the input places and produces new tokens for the output places. A transition t produces multiple tokens for an output place p if the weight of the arc connecting t to p is more than one (the number of produced tokens is the weight of the arc).

Petri nets have been used in many application areas, like communication protocols, distributed systems, flexible manufacturing systems, hardware design, information systems. Classical Petri nets describing real systems tend to be complex and extremely large. This leads to extensions of the initial Petri nets, like introducing "colour" and "hierarchy" [9]. Such extensions are necessary for modelling complex systems but are not sufficient for modelling time issues. The "time" extension was introduced in Petri nets to allow to use them in the area of the performance evaluation. We will informally present the three extensions (for more details see [9]).

Adding colour in Petri nets was a step comparable with the introduction of types in the programming languages. Each token may carry complex typed information and this information may influence the firing rule of transitions. Colours considerably reduce the size of Petri nets but preserve formal analysis possibilities.

The basic Petri nets are not suitable for timed applications, so several propositions were made to include time in the model [11]. We consider the model where each token has a timestamp which indicates when the token becomes available. The timestamp of an output token, produced by a transition t, is equal to the sum of the firing time and a *delay* specified by the transition t [13].

The introduction of hierarchical Petri nets [8] is comparable with the development of structural languages, where subroutines provide reusable code. In hierarchical Petri nets complex systems can be decomposed into subsystems, more easy to specify and design. The modeller may concentrate on the details of a subsystem, ignoring all the other aspects of a system.

3. The UDP/IP model

The UDP/IP protocol is widely used for message exchange between distant processes connected through a LAN (Local Area Network). The analysis presented in this paper considers that UDP/IP is built on top of an Ethernet (CSMA/CD) bus [2], so the protocol layers involved in a message exchange are as presented in Figure 1.

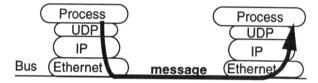

Figure 1 Communication between two processes

To simplify our analysis, we make several assumptions:
- the stations connected on the bus are identical
- there is at most one process running on a station
- the LAN is private, i.e. there is no other message passing on the network except those generated by the considered processes
- there is no message loss, nor transmission error
- at the process level, the instructions are executed in a null time delay.

The size of the messages at the process level is 4 bytes, the IP datagram size is 32 bytes and the Ethernet frame size is 64 bytes. We assume point-to-point communications, implemented via UDP sockets by datagrams. The network controller [2] has its own processor, which is responsible for implementing the Ethernet protocol.

Sending a message from the process level to the network controller requires the allocation of the station's CPU. If the operation succeeds, the CPU of the sending station will be unavailable for t_S time units, the delay for a send operation; t_S is a constant depending on the UDP/IP implementation and the operating system characteristics. If a process attempts to send a message while the CPU is busy, the message will have to wait until the CPU becomes idle. We denote this waiting time by t_{wS}.

For receiving a message, a process has to allocate the CPU of the host station for t_R time units, counted from the moment the last bit of the frame has been read by the network controller. If the CPU is busy, the message will wait t_{wR} time units before being received by the process. The network controller is available immediately after the last bit of a message has passed, so it can detect a new frame.

For sending the bits of a frame on the bus, the controller needs t_t time units, which represents the transmission time; t_t can be computed as L/D, where L is the frame length in bits and D is the number of bits which are transmitted in a second. For D=10 Mbits/s, we have t_t=52 μs. The propagation time t_p represents the time it takes for a bit to pass on the bus from one station to another. For a maximal distance of 500 meters on the bus between two stations, t_p is 2,5 μs. The time needed to send a frame on the bus is t_n, which is the sum of t_t, t_p and other memory access delays. This means t_n>54.5 μs. If the bus is busy, a frame will have to wait for t_{wn} time units, before being transmitted by the controller. Sending a message occupies the bus during t_t+t_p time units, in order to simplify the model we consider the bus unavailable for t_n time units.

The end-to-end communication delay T experienced by a message exchanged between two distant processes is $T=t_{wS}+t_S+t_{wn}+t_n+t_{wR}+t_R$. While t_S, t_n and t_R are constants, t_{wS}, t_{wn} and t_{wR} are variable delays depending on the network and stations loads [1].

4. Model validation

The model was validated against the performance results of a real system, consisting in a network of SUN stations (SS2-GX, 1 x CPU SPARC, 40 Mhz, 64MB RAM), interconnected over an Ethernet CSMA/CD bus (no repeaters) at 10 Mbits/s. We run several simple tests. The results of the first three tests are used to identify the t_S, t_n and t_R constants and the last test validates the model. The exchanged messages have a special identifier which makes sure there is no message loss during our performance measures.

4.1 Finding the constants

1) In the first test there are two processes, p_1 and p_2, running on different stations and exchanging the messages m_1 and m_2, as in Figure 2.

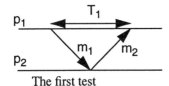

Figure 2   The first test

Process p_1 sends a message m_1 to p_2 and waits for a reply. After receiving the reply from p_2, p_1 records the elapsed

time T_1. This test is analysed using the UDP/IP model. Process p_1 sends m_1 at time $t=0$, so m_1 arrives at the controller at $t=t_S$, since the first station's CPU is available ($t_{wS}=0$). At this moment the bus is idle, so m_1 passes on the network ($t_{wn}=0$) and is received by the controller of the second station at $t=t_S+t_n$. The second station's CPU is idle, so m_1 will be received by p_2 at $t=t_S+t_n+t_R$. The reply m_2 is sent at $t=2t_S+t_n+t_R$ and received by the controller of the first station at $t=2t_S+2t_n+t_R$. Finally, p_2 receives m_2 at $t=2t_S+2t_n+2t_R$ ($t_{wR}=0$, since the first station's CPU is available). Figure 3 presents the results of this analysis.

	t_{wS}	t_S	t_{wn}	t_n	t_{wR}	t_R
m_1	0	t_S	0	t_n	0	t_R
m_2	0	t_S	0	t_n	0	t_R

Figure 3   Waiting times in the first test

The model gives $T_1=2t_S+2t_n+2t_R$ and the performance measures result is T_{1exp}=1.336 ms. The first equation is:
$$T_1=T_{1exp} \qquad (1)$$

2) In the second test there are three processes, p_1, p_2 and p_3, exchanging four messages, as in Figure 4.

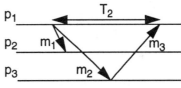

Figure 4   The second test

Process p_1 sends two messages, to p_2 and p_3 respectively, and waits for a reply from p_3. The analysis is similar to that performed for the first test, except for the message m_2 waiting times, t_{wS} and t_{wn}. The message m_2 arrives at the controller at $t=2t_S$, since it has to wait for m_1 to be sent. If $t_S>t_n$, m_1 has already passed on the bus and the bus is idle, so $t_{wn}=0$. If $t_S<t_n$, m_2 has to wait for the bus ($t_{wn}=t_n-t_S$). So $t_{wn}=max(0,t_n-t_S)$. These results are presented in Figure 5, where the constants t_S, t_n and t_R are omitted.

	t_{wS}	t_{wn}	t_{wR}
m_1	0	0	0
m_2	t_S	$max(0,t_n-t_S)$	0
m_3	0	0	0

Figure 5   Waiting times in the second test

We have $T_2=3t_S+2t_n+2t_R+max(0,t_n-t_S)$, or

$$T_2 = \begin{cases} 3t_S + 2t_n + 2t_R, & \text{if } t_S \geq t_n \\ 2t_S + 3t_n + 2t_R, & \text{if } t_S < t_n \end{cases}$$

Our performance measures provided $T_{2exp}=1.605$ ms. The second equation is: $\qquad T_2=T_{2exp}$ (2)

3) In the third test, two processes, p_1 and p_2, exchange the m_1, m_2, m_3 and m_4 messages, as depicted in Figure 6.

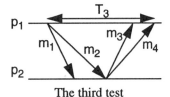

Figure 6 The third test

Process p_1 sends two messages to p_2 and waits for two replies. After receiving the second reply, p_1 records the elapsed time T_3. Analysing this test provides the results from Figure 7.

	t_{wS}	t_{wn}	t_{wR}
m_1	0	0	0
m_2	t_S	$max(0,t_n-t_S)$	t
m_3	0	0	0
m_4	t_S	$max(0,t_n-t_S)$	t

Figure 7 Waiting times in the third test

The message m_1 is received by p_2 at $t_1=t_S+t_n+t_R$. The message m_2 is received by the controller of the second station at $t_2=2t_S+t_n+max(0,t_n-t_S)$. If $t_1<t_2$ then m_2 is immediately received by p_2, otherwise it has to wait the reception of m_1 by p_2.
We have

$$t = max(0, t_1 - t_2) \Rightarrow t = \begin{cases} 0, & \text{if } t_1 \leq t_2 \\ t_1 - t_2, & \text{if } t_1 > t_2 \end{cases}$$

$$t = \begin{cases} 0, & \text{if } (t_S > t_n) \text{ and } (t_S > t_R) \\ 0, & \text{if } (t_n > t_S) \text{ and } (t_n > t_R) \\ t_R - t_S, & \text{if } (t_S > t_n) \text{ and } (t_R > t_S) \\ t_R - t_n, & \text{if } (t_n > t_S) \text{ and } (t_R > t_n) \end{cases}$$

From the model, $T_3=4t_S+2t_n+2t_R+2max(0,t_n-t_S)+2t$.
The performance measures result is $T_{3exp}=1.92$ ms. The third equation is $\qquad T_3=T_{3exp}$ (3)
The system of equations (1),(2) and (3) gives two solutions:

(i) $t_S=0.269$ ms, $t_n=0.107$ ms, $t_R=0.292$ ms   and
(ii) $t_S=0.107$ ms, $t_n=0.269$ ms, $t_R=0.292$ ms.
We expect $t_S \cong t_R$, which will be confirmed by the fourth test.

4.2. Validating the constants

4) In the fourth test there are six processes which exchange messages, as depicted in Figure 8.

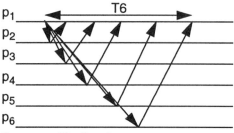

Figure 8 The fourth test

The performance measures give $T_{6exp}=2.928$ ms. The first solution of our model gives $T_6=2.805$ ms. The second solution gives $T_6=3.473$ms. We have to reject the second solution and validate only the first one. The relative error is 4.2%.

5. The UDP/IP Petri net model

We have built our Petri nets using EXSPECT, a software tool developed by the Eindhoven University of Technology [4], [6], [7], [13]. The language EXSPECT consists of two parts, a functional part and a dynamic part. The functional part is used to define types and functions. The dynamic part is used to specify the net. EXSPECT provides a hierarchy construct, called system. A system is an aggregate of transitions, places and (possibly) subsystems. Graphically, squares with a marked bottom right-hand corner denote transitions, rectangles denote systems, circles denote places, crossed circles denote one-capacity places (stores). Exspect allows interactive net simulation.

The UDP/IP Petri net model is presented in Figure 9. For readability reasons we do not include arc inscriptions,

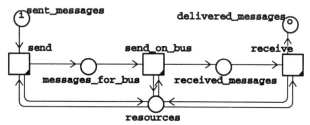

Figure 9 The UDP/IP model

written in a functional language, together with the nets.

440

Instead we present in detail the functioning of the net.

When a process sends a message to another process, it deposes a token in the «sent_messages» place. The token carries several data, such as the source and destination process identifiers, the message type and the message contents. The tokens from the «messages_for_bus» place model messages which are waiting for the bus at the sending controller level. If several messages are waiting for the bus, the one who will occupy the bus is chosen randomly (i.e. all the messages have the same priority). Messages received at the controller level but not yet received by the process are modelled as tokens in the «received_messages» place. Tokens in the «delivered_messages» place model messages received at the process level. The send and receive operations have the same priority on a station.

To arrive at the controller, a message from the «sent_messages» place needs the station's CPU, which is modelled as a token residing in the «resources» place. This place contains a token for each station CPU and a token which models the bus. Colours allow to distinguish the different resources. The «send» transition models a send operation from the process level to the controller level. It consumes two input tokens, from the «sent_messages» and «resources» places and produces two output tokens, delayed with t_S, for the «resources» and «messages_for_bus» places. The «send_on_bus» transition models the bus allocation and the message transmission. This transition may fire if it can consume the «bus» token (the bus is idle) and a message token from the «messages_for_bus» place. Firing will produce a message token, in the «received_messages» place, and the bus token, in the «resources» place, both delayed with t_n. The «receive» transition models the message reception and the station's CPU allocation during t_R time units.

6. The two phase-commitment algorithm

To ensure consistency in a distributed data base, transaction updates involving several sites must be integrated in the database by an atomic action. Protocols for ensuring transaction atomicity are called *commit protocols*.

The simplest commit protocol is proposed in [5]. This protocol uses a designated process, the coordinator. In the first step, the coordinator sends a «vote-request» message to all other participant processes and each process votes on whether to commit («yes») or to abort («no») the transaction (see Figure 10). In the second step, the coordinator gathers all the votes and informs each participant of the outcome. The protocol is not fault-tolerant, it blocks if one of the processes crashes. The *termination time* (latency) for this protocol is the time elapsed from the moment the coordinator sends the «vote-request» message to the first partic-

ipant until all the participants have received the coordinator's decision.

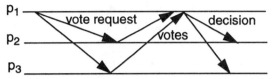

Figure 10 The two-phase commitment protocol with 3 processes

The performance measures we have made to evaluate this latency are approximate: we measure the time elapsed from the moment the coordinator sends the transaction to all the participants until the coordinator gathers all votes from the participants (this is possible since the measurements are made on the same station) and we add half of the round-trip time.

7. The unified model

The unified Petri net model for the two-phase commitment protocol is presented in Figure 11. The «network» system from Figure 11 is the Petri net from Figure 9 (we are using here the hierarchy concept [8] of Petri nets to hide the complexity of the UDP/IP model inside the unified model). The «sent_messages» and «delivered_messages» places are the connections between the two Petri nets.

Before executing the net, the *n* processes, modelled by *n* coloured tokens, are situated in the «start» place. Each token has a colour which models the *pid* of the corresponding process. One of the processes (for instance, the one which has the greatest pid) is the coordinator. The «vote_request» transition firing consumes the coordinator token and produces *n-1* token messages, one for each participant, in the «sent_messages» place. The coordinator token is put in the «waiting_replies» place, reflecting the new state of the coordinator process. Each participant waits in the «start» place until it detects a «vote request» message token in the «delivered_messages» place. Colours allow a participant to detect whether the message is addressed to him or not. Then the «send_vote» transaction fires and the vote token is put in the «sent_messages» place. A message token contains the same data as in the UDP/IP Petri net model, i.e. the source and destination identifiers, the message type and the message contents. After sending his vote, a participant proceeds to a new state, reflected by a token output in the «waiting_decision» place.

The coordinator stores the number of the votes he has currently received in a special place, «votes», represented as a crossed circle, which contains only one token. After receiving *n-1* votes, the «receive_votes» transaction will output *n-1* message tokens in the «sent_messages» place and a coordinator token in the «decided» place. The «finish» transition detects the algorithm end, when all the participants have decided, and records the current time in the «results» place, using the current time value from the «time» store, updated by the EXSPECT simulator.

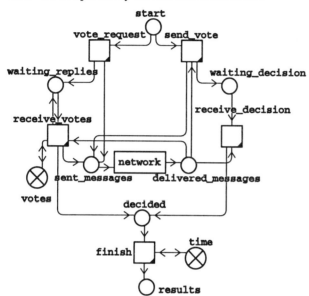

Figure 11   The two-phase commitment model

The model was validated by the invariant analysis technique [9],[12] and by performance measures, executed in the same environment as for the UDP/IP validation. A special analysis tool, the IAT, found the place invariant M(start)+M(waiting_replies)+M(waiting_decision)+M(decided)=constant [4]. This invariant proves that the number of processes does not change during the net execution. Figure 12 depicts the two-phase-commitment latency over the number of participant processes. To minimise the bias from extra-loads on stations and network, the approximate performance measures were done at unsocial hours. The simulation results correspond to the performance measures results within 6%.

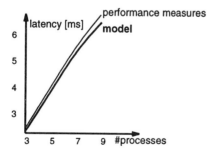

Figure 12   Simulation and performance measures results

8. Conclusions

This paper presents a modelling approach, based on

Petri nets, for the evaluation of the distributed algorithm latencies. As an application, we have chosen the two-phase commitment protocol, for which a Petri net model was developed. The performance results obtained by simulating this model were proved to be close enough to the performance measures derived from the real system. An accurate model of the UDP/IP protocol was developed using Petri nets and integrated into the two-phase commitment algorithm model. The advantage of using Hierarchical Coloured Timed Petri nets and the EXSPECT tool is the possibility to make a good trade-off between the size of the net and the length of the code. The model is scalable: while the size (the number of processes involved in the atomic commitment) of the modelled system increases substantially, the size of the model remains constant and the modelling time grows insignificantly. Simulating the model is more attractive than performance measures, since the results are not biased by unpredictable system loads or by approximations due to the lack of global time. The UDP/IP model may be reused for the evaluation of other distributed algorithms.

References:

[1] Cabrera L. F., Hunter E., Karels M. and D.Mosher.1988, User-Process Communication Performance in Networks of Computers, *IEEE Transactions on Software Engineering*, vol. 14, no.1.

[2] Comer D.E. and L.D. Stevens, *Internetworking with TCP/IP*, Volume II, 1991, Prentice-Hall.

[3] Chandra T. D. and S. Toueg. 1996. "Unreliable failure detectors for reliable distributed systems". *Journal of ACM*, 34(1), pp. 225-267.

[4] ExSpect Reference Manual - Release 5.0., Bakkenist ExSpect, Netherlands, november 1994.

[5] Gray J.N., Notes on Database Operating Systems, Operating Systems: An Advanced Course, Springer-Verlag, 1979.

[6] Hee K.M. Van, Somers L.J., Voorhoeve M., Executable Specifications for distributed information systems.. In Information System Concepts: An In-depth Analysis, North-Holland, 1989.

[7] Hee K.M. Van, Houben, Dietz J.L.G., Modeling of discrete dynamic systems-framework and examples, In Information Systems, Vol. 14, No.4, Pergamon Press, 1989, pp.277-289.

[8] Huber P., Jensen K., Shapiro R.M., Hierarchies in Coloured Petri Nets, In Advances in Petri Nets 1990, LNCS 483.

[9] Jensen K., Coloured Petri nets: basic concepts, analysis methods and practical use. , Springer 1994.

[10] Menascé D., Yesha Y., On a Unified Framework for the Evaluation of Distributed Quorum Attainment Protocols, IEEE Transactions on Software engineering, vol.20, no. 11, november 1994.

[11] Molloy M.K., Petri Net Modelling, The Past, the Present and the Future, International Conference on Petri Nets and Performance Models, 1989.

[12] Peterson J.L., Petri Nets Theory and the modelling of systems, Prentice Hall 1981.

[13] Voorhoeve M., Reus B.M. de, ExSpect Language Tutorial - Release 5.0, Bakkenist ExSpect, Netherlands, december 1994.

❖ SESSION 9 ❖

Numerical Algorithms

Chair

G. Sechi

A New Orthogonal Version of the Gauss-Jordan Algorithm and Its Parallel Implementation

Roman Wyrzykowski
Technical University of Czestochowa
Dept. Math. & Comp. Sci.
Dabrowskiego 73, Czestochowa, Poland
roman@matinf.pcz.czest.pl

Juri Kanevski, Oleg Maslennikov
Kiev Polytechnic Institute
Department of Computer Engineering
Pr. Peremogy 37, 252-056 Kiev, Ukraine
kanevski@parcos.kiev.ua

Abstract

A new orthogonal version of the Gauss-Jordan algorithm is proposed for the parallel solution of dense linear system. It is based on using a combination of Householder reflections and Gaussian eliminations in the two-stage orthogonal Faddeev algorithm. Preserving the advantages of the classical Gauss-Jordan elimination, the proposed algorithm allows us to solve additionally least squares problems and compute pseudoinverses, as well as to reduce the operation complexity in comparison with other orthogonal algorithms of a similar type. Using a systematic design methodology, this algorithm is mapped onto scalable, processor arrays with ring architectures. One of these arrays is implemented on a PC-based parallel system dedicated for signal processing and numerical applications.

1. Introduction

Gauss-Jordan algorithm [1] is an efficient alternative to classical Gauss elimination for the solution of dense linear systems

$$AX = B \qquad (1)$$

where $\mathbf{A} \in R^{N \times N}$, $\mathbf{X} \in R^{N \times R}$, $\mathbf{B} \in R^{N \times R}$. The main advantage [2] is that it gathers together the two phases: decomposition of the matrix into the triangular matrices and solution of the triangular system by substitution. Although the sequential cost of the algorithm overcomes that of the two phases, it is compensated in parallel by a more efficient use of the processors [2, 3].

However, the use of the classical, nonorthogonal version of the Gauss-Jordan algorithm allows operating only with square and nonsingular matrices $\mathbf{A} \in R^{n \times n}$. This limits the range of functionality of the algorithm. To extend this range, an orthogonal decomposition [1]

should be employed, providing the capabilities of operating with rectangular matrices $\mathbf{A} \in R^{M \times N}$, $M \geq N$, i.e. solving least squares and pseudoinverse problems.

Orthogonal versions [4, 5] of the Faddeev algorithm [6], which computes the matrix expression

$$\mathbf{X} = \mathbf{C}\mathbf{A}^{-1}\mathbf{B} + \mathbf{D} \qquad (2)$$

enable solving least squares problems and calculating pseudoinverses without the necessity to perform the back substitution. However, the disadvantage of such a direct approach is its large operation complexity.

In this paper, based on the orthogonal Faddeev algorithm [4], an orthogonal version of the Gauss-Jordan algorithm is proposed with a reduced operation complexity. This algorithm employs a composition of Gaussian eliminations and Householder reflections, and provides efficient parallel computations on systolic-type linear array architectures [7]. Unlike two-dimensional structures [8, 4], these one-dimensional (1-D) arrays provide, firstly, the minimization of the amount of I/O channels, which are connected only with the first or/and last processing element (PE). As a result, the memory bandwidth for a linear array is independent of the size of the array. Secondly, such arrays allows minimizing the required bandwidth for communications between PEs. Thirdly, linear structures provide a simple way of hardware scalability because a large structure can be constructed simply by concatenation of smaller arrays.

This papers is organized as follows. Section 2 presents briefly the Faddeev algorithm and its modifications. In Section 3, the proposed version of the Gauss-Jordan algorithm is described. Section 4 deals with the mapping of the proposed algorithm onto 1-D array architectures, while Section 5 presents some details of a practical implementation. The way of deriving parallel implementations of this algorithm is similar to that which has been used for the orthogonal Faddeev algorithm proposed by us in Ref.[5]. That is way, the related material is presented quite shortly in this paper.

2. Faddeev algorithm

Let $\mathbf{A}, \mathbf{B}, \mathbf{C}$ and $\mathbf{D}$ be input matrices of sizes $N \times N$, $N \times R$, $P \times N$ and $P \times R$, respectively. In the Faddeev algorithm [6] for computing the Schur complement (2), an $(N + P) \times (N + R)$ joint input matrix $\mathbf{H}$ is transformed in the following way:

$$\mathbf{H} = \begin{bmatrix} \mathbf{A} & \mathbf{B} \\ -\mathbf{C} & \mathbf{D} \end{bmatrix} \Rightarrow \mathbf{H}^* = \begin{bmatrix} \mathbf{R} & \mathbf{B}^* \\ \mathbf{0} & \mathbf{X} \end{bmatrix}$$

where $\mathbf{R}$ is the upper triangular matrix. To carry out these operations with nonsingular $\mathbf{A}$, Gaussian elimination is used. This approach allows us to solve a set of problems, including

- solving linear systems $\mathbf{AX} = \mathbf{B}$ (for $\mathbf{C} = \mathbf{I}, \mathbf{D} = \mathbf{0}$)

- matrix multiply-add operations $\mathbf{X} = \mathbf{CB} + \mathbf{D}$ (for $\mathbf{A} = \mathbf{I}$)

- matrix inversions $\mathbf{X} = \mathbf{A}^{-1}$ (for $\mathbf{C}, \mathbf{B} = \mathbf{I}$, $\mathbf{D} = \mathbf{0}$)

The use of Gaussian eliminations limits the range of functionality of the algorithm, which operates only with square matrices $\mathbf{A}$. To extend this range, the orthogonal decomposition based, for example, on Givens rotations can be employed together with Gaussian eliminations, providing processing rectangular $M \times N$ matrices $\mathbf{A}$, where $M \geq N$. Such a two-stage approach was originally proposed in Ref.[4]. According to it, first the matrix $\mathbf{A}$ is triangularized by Givens rotations, simultaneously applied to $\mathbf{B}$-matrix. As a result, after the first stage we obtain

$$\begin{bmatrix} \begin{bmatrix} \mathbf{R} \\ \mathbf{0} \end{bmatrix} & \begin{bmatrix} \mathbf{Q}_1^t \mathbf{B} \\ \mathbf{Q}_2^t \mathbf{B} \end{bmatrix} \\ \mathbf{C} & \mathbf{D} \end{bmatrix} \quad (3)$$

where $\mathbf{Q} = [\mathbf{Q}_1 : \mathbf{Q}_2]$ is an orthogonal matrix. Then the remainder of the process is accomplished by Gaussian eliminations using the diagonal elements of $\mathbf{R}$ as pivot elements. After this stage, the final form of the matrix $\mathbf{H}$ is

$$\begin{bmatrix} \begin{bmatrix} \mathbf{R} \\ \mathbf{0} \end{bmatrix} & \begin{bmatrix} \mathbf{Q}_1^t \mathbf{B} \\ \mathbf{Q}_2^t \mathbf{B} \end{bmatrix} \\ \mathbf{0} & \mathbf{CR}^{-1} \mathbf{Q}_1^t \mathbf{B} + \mathbf{D} \end{bmatrix} \quad (4)$$

As $\mathbf{R}^{-1} \mathbf{Q}_1^t = \mathbf{A}^{-1}$, the result $\mathbf{CA}^{-1} \mathbf{B} + \mathbf{D}$ will appear in the lower right quadrant.

The above-described orthogonal approach provides additional functional capabilities in comparison with the traditional Faddeev algorithm based entirely on Gaussian elimination. The most important among them are: matrix pseudoinverse, least squares solution (for both overdetermined and underdetermined systems), and generalized least squares [4].

3. Orthogonal Gauss-Jordan algorithm

To solve systems $\mathbf{AX} = \mathbf{B}$ with $\mathbf{A} \in R^{M \times N}$, $\mathbf{X} \in R^{N \times R}$, $\mathbf{B} \in R^{M \times R}$, it is sufficiently to assume $\mathbf{C} = \mathbf{I}$, $\mathbf{D} = \mathbf{0}$, and $P = N$, in equation (2). Consequently, when using the orthogonal Faddeev algorithm [4, 5] for solving such a system, we need to process additionally some auxiliary matrices $\mathbf{C} \in R^{N \times N}$ and $\mathbf{D} \in R^{N \times R}$. This leads to a considerable addition of the operation complexity. For example, in the case of the two-stage approach proposed by Nash et al. [4], the total operation complexity W_F of solving a linear system is

$$\begin{aligned} W_F &= 2N(N + 1)(2N + 1)/3 + 2N(N + 1) \times \\ &\quad (M - 3N/4 + R) + 4NR(M - 3N/4) \end{aligned}$$

A version of the orthogonal Faddeev algorithm, especially modified for solving systems of linear equations of the form:

$$\mathbf{Ax} = \mathbf{b}$$

with $\mathbf{A} \in R^{N \times N}$, was proposed in Ref.[9], where the following joint matrix $\mathbf{H}$ is formed:

$$\begin{bmatrix} \mathbf{A}^T & \mathbf{I} & \mathbf{0} \\ -\mathbf{b}^T & \mathbf{0}^T & 1 \end{bmatrix} \quad (5)$$

with $\mathbf{I} \in R^{N \times N}$, and $\mathbf{0} \in R^{N \times 1}$. The matrix $\mathbf{H}$ is triangularized by Givens rotations of a special kind. As a result, we have

$$\mathbf{QH} = \begin{bmatrix} \mathbf{R} & \mathbf{Q}_{11} & \mathbf{q}_{12} \\ \mathbf{0}^T & \mathbf{x}^T q_{22} & q_{22} \end{bmatrix}$$

where $\mathbf{R}$ is the upper triangular matrix, while $\mathbf{Q}_{11}$, $\mathbf{q}_{12}$, and q_{22} are submatrices of the orhogonal matrix $\mathbf{Q}$. The solution vector $\mathbf{x}$ is determined by

$$\mathbf{x}^T = \frac{1}{q_{22}} (\mathbf{x}^T q_{22})$$

As compared with the two-stage approach [4], such an algorithm allows simplifying the scheme of computations, since now only Givens rotations are performed. However, this advantage is obtained at the cost of increasing the operation complexity, which equals to

$$\begin{aligned} W_G &= 2N(N + 1)(2N + 1)/3 + 2NR(N + 1) + \\ &\quad 2N^2(N + 2R + 1) \end{aligned}$$

The large operation complexity of using the orthogonal Faddeev algorithm given by equations (3,4) for solving linear systems is a result of neglecting pecularities of processing matrices $\mathbf{C} = \mathbf{I}$ and $\mathbf{D} = \mathbf{0}$ at the second stage of the algorithm, which consists in performing Gaussian eliminations. To take into account these pecularities, we note that at the i-th step of carrying out Gaussian eliminations for matrices $\mathbf{C}$ and $\mathbf{D}$, where $i = 1, 2, \ldots, N$, only those elements of these matrices are modified which are located in rows from the first to the i-th. Morover, in the matrix $\mathbf{C}$, these modifications involve only columns from the i-th to the N-th, since the i-th column of $\mathbf{C}$ has a single nonzero element at this step (it is a diagonal element). Consequently, there is no need in processing the rest of elements of these two matrices.

Such an approach allows decreasing the number of multiply-add operations for the second stage of the orthogonal Faddeev algorithm [4] from $N^2(N + 1)/2 + N^2R$ to $N(N + 1)(N + R)/2 - N^3/3$, i.e. approximately three times for $R = 1$, while solving linear systems with a single right-hand vector, and more than twice for $R = N$. It should be noted that the use of this approach for the classical Faddeev algorithm [6] allows deriving the classical Gauss-Jordan algorithm [1], whose functional range is limited only to the solution of systems with nonsingular matrices $\mathbf{A}$.

Implementing the above-described approach for the two-stage orthogonal Faddeev algorithm proposed in Ref.[4], we can construct an orthogonal version of the Gauss-Jordan algorithm with capabilities of solving least squares problems and computing pseudoinverses. However, this advantage is obtained at the cost of the increased operation complexity of Givens rotations in comparison with Gaussian eliminations [1], and load imbalance which is a result of difference in operation complexities of Givens rotations and Gaussian eliminations.

The orthogonal decomposition based on Householder reflections [1] enables reducing the number of multiplications twice in comparison with Givens rotations. In addition, instead of $(N/2)(2M - N)$, only N square root operations are required now. That is why, by combining Householder reflections on the first stage of the two-stage orthogonal Faddeev algorithm (i.e. for matrices $\mathbf{A}$ and $\mathbf{B}$) with Gaussian eliminations on the second stage, and taking into account the pecularities of processing matrices $\mathbf{C}$ and $\mathbf{D}$ on the second stage, we work out a new orthogonal modification of the Gauss-Jordan algorithm with a reduced complexity and good load balancing.

This modification can be expressed in the following form:

```
for i:= 1 step 1 until N do
begin
{------ begin of pivot phase ------}
{-- only Householder reflections --}
  {computing the norm of the ith column of A}
  sigma[i]:= 0;
  for j:= i step 1 until M do
  sigma[i]:=sigma[i] + h[M-j+1,i]*h[M-j+1,i];
  if h[i,i]<0 then alpha[i]:=sqrt(sigma(i))
              else alpha[i]:=-sqrt(sigma(i));
  r[i,i]:= h[i,i] - alpha[i];
  beta[i]:= 1/(sigma[i] - h[i,i]*alpha[i]);
  h[i,i]:= r[i,i]
  {computing inner products of the i-th
   column of A with columns of A or B}
  for k:=i+1 step 1 until N+R do
  begin
    y[k,i]:= 0;
    for j:=i step 1 until M do
      y[k,i]:=y[k,i] + h[M-j+1,i]*h[M-j+1,k];
    y[k,i]:= y[k,i]*beta[i];
  end {k};
{------ end of pivot phase ------}
{------ begin of transformation phase ------}
  {---- calculation of multipliers m
        for Gaussian eliminations  ----}
  for j:= M+1 step 1 until M+i-1 do
    if r[i,i]=0 then m[j,i]:= 0
                else m[j,i]:=-h[j,i]/r[i,i];
  if r[i,i]=0 then m[M+i,i]:=0
              else m[M+i,i]:=1/r[i,i];
{transformations of rows of the joint matrix}
  for k:= i+1 step 1 until N+R do
  begin
  { using Householder reflections }
    for j:= i step 1 until M do
      h[M-j+1,k]:=h[M-j+1,k] + y[k,i]*h[i,k];
    { using Gaussian eliminations }
    for j:= M+1 step 1 until M+i-1 do
      h[j,k]:= h[j,k] + m[j,i]*h[i,k];
    h[M+i,k]:=m[M+i,i]*h[i,k];
  end {k}
{------ end of transformation phase -------}
end {i}
```

Its operation complexity W_{GJ} is given by

$$
\begin{aligned}
W_{GJ} = \ & N(N + 1)(N + R + 1)/2 + N(N + 1) \times \\
& (2N + 1)/6 + N(N + 1)(R + M - N) + \\
& N(N + 1)/2 + 2NR(M - N + 1/2)
\end{aligned}
$$

Hence, in comparison with the known algorithms [4, 9], the derived orthogonal version of the Gauss-Jordan algorithm allows us to minimize the amount of com-

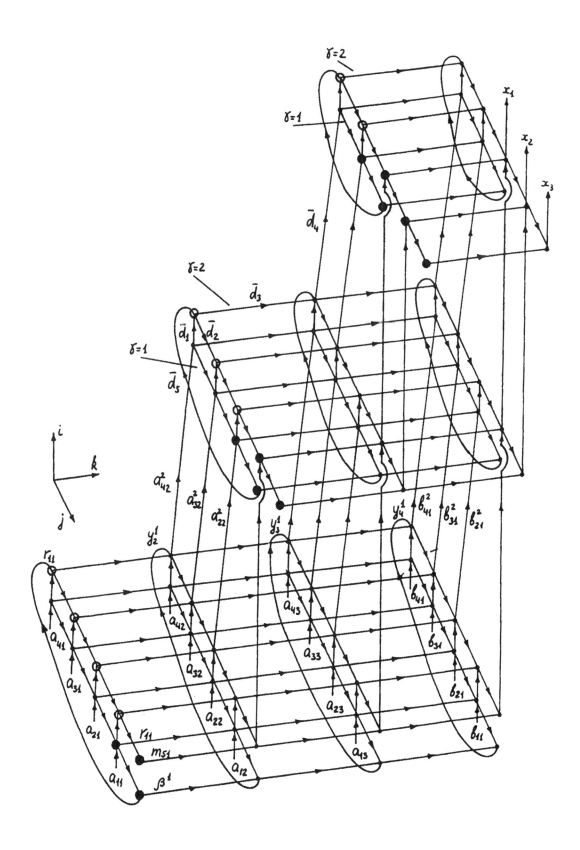

Figure 1. Dependence graph of the orthogonal Gauss-Jordan algorithm

putations, since for $R = 1$ and $R = N$ we obtain $W_F/W_{GJ} \approx 2.2$, $W_G/W_{GJ} \approx 4$, and $W_F/W_{GJ} \approx 2.3$, $W_G/W_{GJ} \approx 4.3$, respectively.

4. Mapping the algorithm into systolic-type arrays

Systolic-type arrays can be designed systematically by applying linear mappings to algorithms expressed by nested loops [10, 11]. Basically, the design is composed of the following components: an algorithm specifying computations; an allocation mapping that maps computations to PEs; a schedule mapping specifying the execution time for each computation.

Nested loops with regular data dependencies can be represented [12] by regular or quasi-regular dependence graphs (DGs) or a composition of them. Each node of such a DG corresponds to a certain iteration of the algorithm, and is associated with an integer vector $\mathbf{K} = (k_1, ..., k_n)'$ because all the nodes are located in vertices $\mathbf{K}$ of an integer lattice $K^n \subset \mathbf{Z}^n$. This lattice is called the iteration space. Arcs between nodes of the DG, or data dependencies between iterations of the algorithm, are represented by a dependence matrix $\mathbf{D}$, in which the i-th column is a dependence vector $\mathbf{d}_i$.

In Ref.[12], we presented a methodology for mapping an n-dimensional recursive algorithm into a variety of m-dimensional processor arrays, where $m < n$. This methodology is based on finding first the set of all nonequivalent allocation mappings $\mathbf{F}_S$ satisfying given constraints for the locality of links between PEs, which are located in vertices of an integer lattice $K^m \subset \mathbf{Z}^m$. For each of network topologies S corresponding to this set, we find then a schedule mapping $\mathbf{F}_T$, which preserves dependencies without computation conflicts, and is optimal with respect to chosen criteria (e.g., some performance criteria, complexity of local memories). The mapping $\mathbf{F}_T$ is constructed as a linear function with n unknown coefficients.

The basic DG $\mathbf{G}_B$ corresponds to the execution of the proposed Gauss-Jordan algorithm according to the given lexicographic order. This graph is shown in Fig.1, for $M = 4$, $N = 3$, $R = 1$. Nodes of $\mathbf{G}_B$ are located in vertices of the 3-D lattice $Q = \{\mathbf{K} = (i, j, k) : 1 \leq i \leq N, i \leq j \leq M + i, i \leq k \leq N + R\}$. The projection of $\mathbf{G}_B$ onto $(\mathbf{i}, \mathbf{k})$-plane is shown in Fig.2a, where $N = 6$, $R = 3$. Each node of $\mathbf{G}_B$ is composed of two subnodes corresponding to the pivot ($z = 1$) and transformation ($z = 2$) phases of the proposed algorithm. Hence, the subnodes of $\mathbf{G}_B$ are located in the 4-D extended lattice $Q_E = \{\mathbf{K}_E = (i, j, k, z)\}$.

For the graph $\mathbf{G}_B$, there are four possible 1-D topologies S_l with fully local links. The most promis-

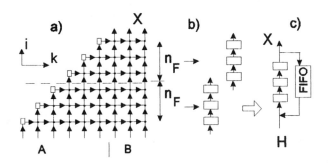

Figure 2. Design of fixed-size linear array.

sing is S_1 which corresponds to the projection of $\mathbf{G}_B$ onto $\mathbf{i}$-axis (see Fig.2b). This choice allows minimizing the number of PEs and I/O channels, as well as PE-to-PE communication bandwidth. The internal structure of any PE in the array given by S_1 and the schedule vector $\mathbf{F}_{T,1}^E = [M + 2 \;\; 1 \;\; 2M + 1 \;\; M + 1]$ is shown in Fig.3, where $M+1$ and $2M+1$ are FIFO buffers with corresponding lengths, AU denotes arithmetic unit, and R is a register.

4.1. Design of fixed-size arrays

A basic requirement in practical system designs for matrix problems is an ability to process large size matrices on processor arrays with a fixed number of PEs [7]. To provide this ability, two basic partitioning methods [7, 10] are usually used. Both of them are based on the decomposition of the DG of an algorithm into a set of regular subgraphs, but differ in the way how these subgraphs are mapped onto resulting arrays. In the block method, one subgraph is mapped to one PE, and each PE sequentially executes the nodes of the corresponding subgraph. Therefore, an additional local memory within each PE is needed. To avoid this disadvantage, one subgraph is mapped to one array in the cyclic method. All nodes within one subgraph

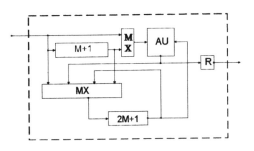

Figure 3. Internal structure of PEs.

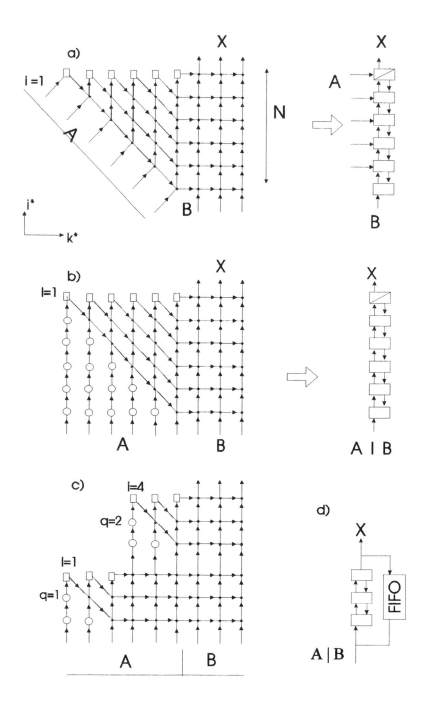

Figure 4. Design of linear arrays, using transformations of the basic DG: (a) intermediate DG and structure corresponding to it; (b) resulting DG and structure S corresponding to it; (c) DG partitioning; (d) fixed-size linear array for the Gauss-Jordan algorithm.

are processed concurrently, while all subgraphs are processed sequentially. As a result, all intermediate data which correspond to dependencies between subgraphs are stored in buffers outside the array.

In order to implement the proposed algorithm on a linear array with $n_F < N$ PEs, where $n_F = const$, we employ the cyclic method, which requires to decompose the graph $\mathbf{G}_B$ into a set of $s =]N/n_F[$ subgraphs with the "same" topology and without bidirectional data dependencies. Such a decomposition can be carried out only in one way, cutting $\mathbf{G}_B$ by a set of 2-D hyperplanes perpendicular to $\mathbf{i}$-axis (see Fig.2a). All the subgraphs are then mapped into one array with n_F PEs. This can be done only by projecting each subgraph onto $\mathbf{i}$-axis. Taking into account the way how the array corresponding to S_1 is derived from the DG $\mathbf{G}_B$, we conclude that a fixed-size linear architecture for the Gauss-Jordan algorithm will be obtained (see Fig.2c) by providing this array with an external FIFO buffer for the intermediate data.

4.2. Using graph transformations

To obtain such a structure S which minimizes not only the number of I/O channels, but also the amount of PEs with division and square root capabilities, we use a purposive transformation of each subgraph of the basic DG G_B before their space-time mapping onto an array. This transformation can be described informally as a rotation of the triangular part of each subgraph by an angle of 45° clockwise (see Fig.4a). After completing every subgraph with "empty" nodes which provide the suitable input of some elements of the matrix $\mathbf{A}$ through boundary nodes (see Fig.4b), we project each resulting subgraph onto $\mathbf{i}^*-$axis in order to obtain a fixed-size array architecture shown in Fig.4d. In this array, which is provided with an external FIFO buffer, only the last PE perform division and square-rooting, while the rest of PEs, which are of the same time, perform only multiplication-addition.

The important feature of this array is that all the complicated operations like square rooting and division are carried out by the same boundary PE, whereas other PEs perform only multiplication-additions. On the contrary, the array architecture corresponding to the structure S_1 requires to perform divisions and square-root operations in all the PEs, but it allows decreasing the number of communication channels between PEs. This advantage is important when implementing the Gauss-Jordan algorithm on modern programmable signal processors, for which the bandwidth of I/O paths is a limiting factor.

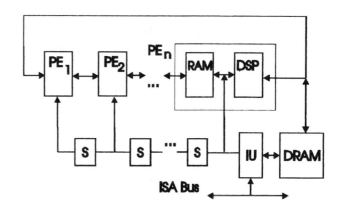

Figure 5. Parallel system architecture (S and IU denote switch and interface unit, respectively).

5. Implementation

The fixed-size architecture shown in Fig.2c has been programmed on a PC-based, low-cost parallel system dedicated for high-speed signal processing and numerical applications [13]. It has been designed at the Department of Computer Engineering of Kiev Polytechnic Institute. The kernel of this design is a plug-in supercomputer board with four Motorola DSPs 96002 running at 66MHz with the peak performance of 400 MFLOPs (one DSP can execute one floating-point multiplication and two additions every two clock periods). The system architecture represents (see Fig.5) a processor ring in which any DSP can access to the memories of its left and right neighbours. Such a solution allows scalability to 32 (or more) DSPs with the peak performance expandable to 3.200 MFLOPs. The ring architecture has been chosen among one and multidimensional variants because of its low cost/performance ratio. Moreover, in the area of signal processing and linear algebraic computations, as long as the number of PEs does not exceed the size of an algorithm, the linear array structure with a RAM buffer in the feedback is invariant to dimension and form of the iteration space K^n corresponding to the algorithm, as well as to structure of data dependencies in the algorithm graph [13].

The resulting implementation of the proposed algorithm makes it perfectly possible to match the limited Memory-to-DSP communication bandwidth in the system, This is illustrated in Fig.6, which presents four consecutive cycles of running the proposed algorithm on the first DSP. Note that values y_k^i are stored in on-chip register file of DSPs; only the elements of

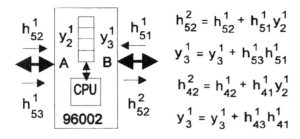

$$h_{52}^2 = h_{52}^1 + h_{51}^1 y_2^1$$

$$y_3^1 = y_3^1 + h_{53}^1 h_{51}^1$$

$$h_{42}^2 = h_{42}^1 + h_{41}^1 y_2^1$$

$$y_3^1 = y_3^1 + h_{43}^1 h_{41}^1$$

Figure 6. Running the Gauss-Jordan algorithm on DSP.

the joint matrix $\mathbf{H}^{i+1}$ derived at the i-th step of the algorithm and previously computed elements of $\mathbf{H}^i$ ($\mathbf{H}^1 = \mathbf{H} = [\mathbf{A}|\mathbf{B}]$), are passed between memories and DSPs. Consequently, there no idle DSP cycles due to memory-DSP transfers. However, some idle cycles appear due to the fact that the number of rows participating in the pivot phase of the algorithm decreases by one with each step. To match this decrease [14], lenghts of FIFO buffers in the array should be changed in the course of computations. Actually, we exploit the possibility of varying only the lenght of the external buffer, so the corresponding degradation in performance is no greater than 1/8.

The results of running the proposed algorithm on the simulator of the target system has shown that the ratio of real to peak perormance is no less than 0.58. The actual figures depend on relations between sizes M, N, and R of matrices, and agree with theoretical estimations.

References

[1] G.H. Golub and Ch.F. Van Loan, *Matrix Computations*, J. Hopkins Univ. Press, Baltimore, 1989.

[2] M. Cosnard, M. Tchuente and B. Tourancheau, Systolic Gauss-Jordan Elimination for Dense Linear Systems, *Parallel Computing*, Vol.9, pp.1-6, 1989.

[3] R. Melhem, Parallel Gauss-Jordan limination for the Solution of Dense Linear Systems, *Parallel Computing*, Vol.4, pp.339-343, 1987.

[4] J.G. Nash and S. Hansen, Modified Faddeev Algorithm for Concurrent Execution of Linear Algebraic Operations, *IEEE Trans. Comput.*, Vol.C-37, pp.129-137, 1988.

[5] J.Kanevski, O. Maslennikov and R. Wyrzykowski, VLSI Implementation of Linear Algebraic Operations Based on the Ortogonal Faddeev Algorithm, *Advances in Parallel Computing*, Vol.11, pp.641-644, 1996.

[6] D.K. Faddeev and V.N. Faddeeva, *Computational Methods of Linear Algebra*, W.H. Freeman and Company, 1963.

[7] T. Lang and J.H. Moreno, *Matrix Computations on Systolic-Type Meshes*, Kluwer, Boston, 1992.

[8] P. Quinton and Y. Robert, *Systolic Algorithms and Architectures*, Prentice Hall, Englewood Cliffs, 1991.

[9] J. Gotze, B. Bruckmeier and U. Schwiegelshohn, VLSI-Suited Solution of Linear Systems, *Proc. IEEE Int. Symp. Circuits and Syst.*, pp.187-190, 1989.

[10] S.Y. Kung, *VLSI Array Processors*, Prentice-Hall, Englewood Cliffs, 1988.

[11] H. Barada and A. El-Amawy, A Methodology for Algorithm Regularization and Mapping into Time-Optimal VLSI Arrays *Parallel Computing*, Vol.19, pp.33-61, 1993.

[12] R. Wyrzykowski and J.S. Kanevski, Mapping Recursive Algorithms into Processor Arrays, *Proc. Int. Workshop "Parallel Numerics 94"*, Smolenice (Slovakia), pp.169-191, 1994.

[13] J.S. Kanevski, A.M. Sergyienko and O.V. Maslennikov, Processor Array for Signal Computing and Numerical Applications, *Proc. Int. Conf. Signal Proc. Applicat. and Technol.*, Boston, pp.573-579, 1995.

[14] R. Wyrzykowski and J.S. Kanevski, Systolic-Type Implementation of Matrix Computations Based on the Faddeev Algorithm, *Proc. 1-st IEEE Conf. Massively Parallel Computing Systems*, Ischia (Italy), pp.31-42, 1994.

Solving Linear Systems of Equations Overlapping Communications and Computations in Torus Networks

C.N. Ojeda-Guerra*, Alvaro Suárez

Grupo de Arquitectura y Concurrencia (G.A.C.)
Dpto. de Electrónica, Telemática y Automática
Universidad de Las Palmas de Gran Canaria
Campus Universitario de Tafira (Pabellón A)
35017 - Las Palmas de G.C.
phone:+34 28 458987/451239
fax:+34 28 451243
e-mail: {cnieves,alvaro}@cic.teleco.ulpgc.es

Abstract

The problem of solving a linear system of equations ($A \times X = B$) is very important in scientific applications. In this paper, we present the factorization of the matrix A, dense and strictly diagonally dominant, according to $A = L \times U$, where L is a lower triangular matrix and U is an upper triangular matrix, and the solution of the triangular systems $L \times Y = B$ and $U \times X = Y$. We consider the sequential algorithms of the LU decomposition and the forward reduction and backsubstitution for performing the final parallel algorithm. We solve the linear system by linking these parallel algorithms without data redistribution, onto a torus multicomputer overlapping communications and computations.

1 Introduction

The implementation of any parallel algorithm on a multicomputer [1] with a certain interconnection topology is highly influenced by the characteristics of this algorithm. Characteristics such as the movement of data, the communication between processors, initial distribution of data, influence in the choosing of the topology used. On the other hand, the utilization of the processors and the communication time are two important considerations in designing parallel algorithms. Communication is one of the most expensive resources in a multicomputer and the efficient management of it, is important. The modelation of computations and communications with a graph G is important in order to study this communication. In a similar way, the parallel architecture (in which the parallel algorithm will be executed) can be modelled with another graph H [2].

In this paper, we present the LU factorization for a matrix A, dense and strictly diagonally dominant, and the solution of the triangular systems $L \times Y = B$ and $U \times X = Y$ in order to solve a linear system. Our main target is to obtain an initial data distribution that enables us to overlap communications and computations in order to hide the communication overhead. We use the sequential algorithms of the LU decomposition and the forward reduction and backsubstitution with some modifications due to every processor element (PE) of the arquitecture must solve a piece of the final problem. The steps of our method can be found in [5]. In this paper, we carry out a total embbeding and we include one step for optimizing the initial data distribution.

In [6] and in [7] two algorithms for solving a linear system onto a hypercube are presented and good results are obtained.

In section 2 we present the sequential algorithms for the matrix factorization and forward reduction and backsubstitution. In section 3 the embedding is defined and the initial data distribution is studied. In section 4 we discuss the computation distribution. In section 5 the implementation of the parallel algorithm in a torus multicomputer is presented. In section 6 the experimental results using a transputer based multicomputer are presented. Finally in section 7 we sum up some conclusions and future work.

2 Sequential algorithm

Let $X(x_j)$ and $B(b_i)$ be two vectors of n elements and $A(a_{i,j})$ be a dense and strictly diagonally dominant matrix [3], of $n \times n$ elements, where $A(a_{i,j})$ and $B(b_i)$ are given and $X(x_j)$ is a vector to be computed such that $A \times X = B$. For solving this system, some methods use the factorization

---

*Centre for Applied Microelectronic member

of the matrix A in two triangular matrices (lower triangular L and upper triangular U according to $A = L \times U$), which ease the computation of the vector X instead of computing the inverse of the matrix A which is a more costly computation. So, the solution to the original $A \times X = B$ problem is easily found by a two step triangular solve process (equations 1 and 2).

$$A \times X = B \quad \text{y} \quad A = L \times U \quad \Rightarrow \quad L \times U \times X = B$$

$$L \times y = B \tag{1}$$

$$U \times X = y \tag{2}$$

The solution of the system 1 is the vector of independent terms of the system 2. The solution of the system 2 is the final solution of the original problem $A \times X = B$. A sequential algorithm which computes the Doolittle factorization [3] is given in (3), where L is unit lower triangular and U is upper triangular. If $i > j$ then $a_{i,j}$ keeps $l_{i,j}$. If $i \leq j$ then $a_{i,j}$ keeps $u_{i,j}$. In this algorithm, the order of execution of computations in the matrices L and U is specified. Thus, their elements must be obtained before the computation of the elements of the matrix A (inner loop of the sequential algorithm).

$$
\begin{aligned}
&do \ \ k = 0, n-1 \\
&\quad do \ \ j = k, n-1 \\
&\qquad u_{k,j} = a_{k,j} \\
&\quad enddo \\
&\quad do \ \ i = k+1, n-1 \\
&\qquad l_{i,k} = a_{i,k}/a_{k,k} \\
&\quad enddo \\
&\quad do \ \ i = k+1, n-1 \\
&\qquad do \ \ j = k+1, n-1 \\
&\qquad\quad a_{i,j} = a_{i,j} - l_{i,k} \times u_{k,j} \\
&\qquad enddo \\
&\quad enddo \\
&enddo
\end{aligned}
\tag{3}
$$

In (4) and (5) the algorithms of forward reduction and back-substitution are presented. We suppose that the elements of the matrices L and U are stored in the matrix A. In the first sentence, the initial value of the solution vector in the i-th term is computed and in the inner loop the final value of the solution vector, depending on the i-1..0-th terms (i+1..n-1-th), is calculated.

$$
\begin{aligned}
&do \ \ i = 0, n-1 \\
&\quad y_i = b_i/a_{i,i} \\
&\quad do \ \ j = i-1, 0, -1 \\
&\qquad y_i = y_i - (a_{i,j}/a_{i,i}) \times y_j \\
&\quad enddo \\
&enddo
\end{aligned}
\tag{4}
$$

$$
\begin{aligned}
&do \ \ i = n-1, 0, -1 \\
&\quad x_i = y_i/a_{i,i} \\
&\quad do \ \ j = i+1, n-1 \\
&\qquad x_i = x_i - (a_{i,j}/a_{i,i}) \times x_j \\
&\quad enddo \\
&enddo
\end{aligned}
\tag{5}
$$

3 Embedding and initial data distribution

For solving the problem of the embedding of the graph G onto the graph H and the initial data distribution, we consider the sequential algorithms and the data dependencies in these algorithms.

3.1 Factorization

In the sequential algorithm there are three nested loops and three sentences that belong to the inner loops. The first sentence implements the computation of the elements in the matrix U, the second sentence computes the elements in the matrix L and the last sentence implements the computation of the elements in the matrix A, which will be used in the next iteration.

Given $k = k_1$ for all i and j such that $i = k_1+1..n-1$ and $j = k_1..n-1$, the elements in the matrix U are computed such that $u_{k_1,j} = a_{k_1,j}$ and the elements in the matrix L such that $l_{i,k_1} = a_{i,k_1}/a_{k_1,k_1}$. Once these elements have been calculated, the elements in the matrix A will be computed for $i = k_1 + 1..n-1$ and $j = k_1 + 1..n-1$, which will be used in the next iteration of the variable k (inner loop of the sequential algorithm). Every new element $a_{i,j}$ depends on its old value (in the iteration $k = k_1 - 1$), l_{i,k_1} and $u_{k_1,j}$.

The relationship among every element in the matrix A and the new elements in the factorization can be studied in the dependence graph (figure 1.b for $n = 4$) [8]. The coordinates in this space are the variables in the loops of the sequential algorithm. We can see there are dependencies in the dimensions i, j and k. Every point in this space represents a computation which is carried out in the sentences of the loops. We suppose that each point is a process that can be executed in parallel with other processes. The dependencies impose a partial order of execution that limits the parallelism. In this algorithm, the order of execution is very strict. Each process must have the elements of the matrices to be used in the represented point. It can be necessary an element of a matrix in more than one process. To take into account the relationship among the elements in the matrices is very important because it helps to realize us how the data must be distributed in the memories of the processors.

Every process in the $3 - D$ iteration space (IS) (figure 1.a) can be executed by one diferent processor. However, this implementation depends on the value of the variable n, so the number of processors must be very big. For decreasing the number of processors, we do a mapping of the data onto a plane of processes.

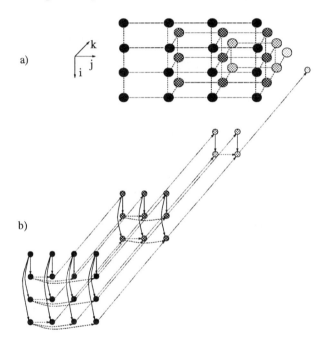

Figure 1: a) $3 - D$ IS for the LU factorization. b) Dependencies for $n = 4$

Figure 1.a shows that the matrix A initially is in the plane $\pi(i, j, k = 0)$. The elements in the matrix $L(l_{i,k})$ initially are in the plane $\pi(i, j, k)$, such that $j = k$ y $i > k$. This can be deduced from the sequential algorithm because of in every iteration $k = k_1$, the elements in L will be calculated for all i such that $i = k_1 + 1..n - 1$ and will be used for all j such that $j > k_1$. In the same way, the elements in the matrix $U(u_{k,j})$ initially are in the plane $\pi(i, j, k)$, such that $i = k$ y $j \geq k$. This can be deduced from the sequential algorithm because of in every iteration $k = k_1$, the elements in U will be calculated for all j such that $j = k_1..n - 1$ and will be used for all i such that $i > k_1$. There are dependencies among the calculated data in the matrices L and U (first

and second *do* sentences) and the used data in the inner loop.

In figure 1.b the dependencies are shown. There are three kinds of dependencies: two data dependencies are broadcast (in the dimensions i and j) and one data dependence is a data flow dependence (in the dimension k). The dependence vectors are: $\vec{d_1} = (0, 0, 1)$, $\vec{d_2} = (*, 0, 0)$ and $\vec{d_3} = (0, *, 0)$, where $\vec{d_1}$ is the data dependence in the dimension k. In this dimension, the execution of the iterations has strictly a sequential order of execution. However, in the dimensions i and j, this order of execution can be relaxed due to the broadcast dependencies. So, we do a mapping of the data onto the plane $\pi(i, j, k = 0)$, which allow to overlap communications (elements in L and U) and computations (elements in A). In this plane, the process (i, j) computes:

$$a_{i,j} \quad and \quad u_{i,j} \qquad i = i_1 \ and \ j \geq i_1$$

$$a_{i,j} \quad and \quad l_{i,j} \qquad j = j_1 \ and \ i > j_1$$

In this way, we can use the matrix A for storing the matrices L and U.

In [5] a partial embedding is studied in order to eliminate the data redundancy in the plane of processes, for the matrix by matrix algorithm. However, in the LU factorization, the data redundancy doesn't exist so we do a total embedding. Once the embedding has been performed, the embedding of the graph G onto the graph H is immediate. In figure 2, we present the mapped processes on the projection plane (in black shadow the processes which calculate the elements in U and in white shadow the processes which compute the elements in L). Other implementations with a diferent strategy, which compute the LU factorization can be found in [9], [10]. In [11] the overlapping of communications and computations is studied using one modification of a systolic algorithm.

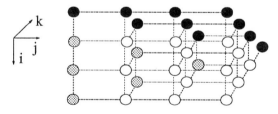

Figure 2: **Mapped processes on the plane** $\pi(i, j, k = 0)$ **for** $n = 4$

3.2 Triangular systems

In the sequential algorithms there are two nested loops and two sentences that belong to the inner loops. The first sentence implements the computation of the initial value in the solution vector and the second sentence implements the computation of the final value in the solution, which depends on the previous calculeted values.

Focus on the forward reduction. Given $i = i_1$, the initial value of the solution vector Y is obtained, such that $y_{i_1} = b_{i_1}/a_{i_1,i_1}$. The element y_{i_1} is recalculated for all j such that $j = i_1 - 1..0$ and depends on its previous value and y_j. The relationship among y_{i_1} in Y and the calculated elements in that vector can be studied in figure 3.b for $n = 4$. The coordinates in this IS are the variables in the loops of the sequential algorithm. We can see there are dependencies in the dimensions i, j. Every point in this IS represents a computation which is carried out in the sentences of the loops and we suppose that each point is a process that can be executed in parallel with other processes. Again, the parallelism strictly is limited by the dependencies. Each process must have the elements of the matrix and the elements of the independent terms vector to be used in the represented point. It can be necessary an element of the matrix (vector) in more than one process. The same as LU factorization, we have to do a mapping of the data onto a straight line of processes in order to reduce the number of processors.

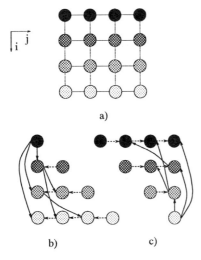

Figure 3: **a)** $2 - $D **IS for the triangular systems. b) Dependencies for** n $= 4$**, forward reduction. c) Dependencies for** n $= 4$**, backsubstitution**

Figure 3.a shows that the matrix A initially is in the plane $\pi(i, j)$ such that $j < i$ for the forward reduction. In the points $j = i$, lower triangular L stores the value 1. For the backsubstitution, the matrix A initially is in the plane $\pi(i, j)$ such that $j \geq i$. The elements in the vector Y initially are in the plane $\pi(i, j)$ such that $j = i$ because of the values b_i and $a_{i,i}$ are in those points (sequential algorithm). The computation of the elements in Y follows an specific order. In every iteration $i = i_1$, the element y_{i_1} will be recalculated for all y_j such that $j = i_1 - 1..0$ so there are data dependencies among the calculated values in every iteration of the variable j.

In figure 3.b the dependencies are shown. There are two kinds of dependencies: one data dependencies is broadcast (in the quadrant i, j) and one data dependence is a data flow dependence (in the dimension j). The dependence vectors are: $\vec{d_1} = (0, -1)$ and $\vec{d_2} = (1 \leq i \leq n-1, 0 \leq j \leq n-2)$, where $\vec{d_1}$ is the data dependence in the dimension j. In this dimension, the execution of the iterations has strictly a sequential order of execution (first the value of y_j, $j = i-1..0$, has to be calculated and then the value of y_i is computed). However, due to the broadcast dependence vectors don't became $(0, -1)$, the order of execution in the quadrant (i, j) such that $i \neq 0$ can be relaxed. Thus, we do a mapping of the data onto the straight line $\pi(i, j = 0)$, which allow to overlap communications (elements in Y) and computations (elements in Y in the present iteration). In this straight line, the process (i) computes y_i. The same is for the backsubstitution $U \times X = Y$, where Y is the solution vector in the forward reduction.

4 Distribution of computations in the PEs

After the distribution of data has been done, we distribute the computations guided by the data distribution. This computation distribution can be derived directly from the sequential algorithm.

Focus on the LU factorization. We suppose that $n \times n$ PEs exist. The $PE(i, j)$ stores the elements $a_{i,j}$, $l_{i,k}$ and $u_{k,j}$ in its local memory, and carries out the computations of the process (i, j). In the iteration $k = k_1$, the PE, which owns $a_{k_1,j}$, computes $u_{k_1,j}$ ($k_1 \leq j \leq n - 1$), and the PE, which owns a_{i,k_1} and a_{k_1,k_1}, computes l_{i,k_1} ($k_1 + 1 \leq i \leq n - 1$). But, the PE which computes l_{i,k_1} isn't the owner of a_{k_1,k_1}, so either this value has to be replicated in its local memory or has to be communicated to it. In the same way, the PE which has to compute $a_{i,j}$ ($k_1 + 1 \leq i, j \leq n - 1$), needs $u_{k_1,j}$ and l_{i,k_1} which have been calculated in this iteration. These elements have to be communicated to this PE.

In short, in the iteration k_1, the computation of the elements in the matrix U carried out by the PEs in the i-th row (such that $j \geq k_1$) can be made in parallel due to there aren't dependencies. The PEs in the j-th column (such that $i > k_1$) can make in parallel the computation of the elements in L if they store the elements a_{k_1,k_1}. However, the computation of the elements $a_{i,j}$ can't be made in parallel. Because of there are dependencies among the elements in L, U and A, it is neccesary to communicate the data in L and U and then the data in A can be computed using these values.

On the other hand, this mapping has one problem: the large amount of communications to be performed [7]. In addition of this, these communications can't be parallelized as a whole. In the practice, we have proved a low efficiency in a transputer based multicomputer.

Advised by these results, we have modified our embedding on the basis of this preliminary solution (optimizing of the initial data distribution). Now, we map the plane of processes onto a *ring* of m PEs, where $n = m$. In this way, the mapping for the LU factorization is similar to the mapping for the triangular systems. A PE z ($0 \leq z \leq m - 1$) has stored a group of elements of the matrix A (by rows) in its local memory and computes a group of elements in L and U. With this new mapping, we reduce the number of communications due to be the elements in L aren't comunicated.

In this case, every PE stores n/m rows of the matrix A, where every row has n elements. In the iteration $k = k_1$, the PE z ($z = k_1$) computes the elements $u_{k_1,j}$ ($k_1 \leq j \leq n - 1$). The rest of PEs, in the *ring*, have to wait for the elements $u_{k_1,j}$ for computing their elements of the matrix L and A. In figure 4 the initial data distribution after the factorization is presented. The elements in L and U for an specific PE are with the same shadow.

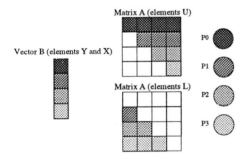

Figure 4: **Data distribution after the LU factorization**

Once the triangularization has been finished, the computation of the solution vector Y is begun, using the lower triangular matrix (L). In the iteration $i = i_1$, the PE z ($z = i_1$) computes y_{i_1} overwritting b_i. When the computation finishes, the PE z must communicate it to the rest of PEs in the *ring*. With this datum, these PEs can begin to calculate their pieces of the solution vector Y. Next, the backsubstitution is carried out for computing the solution vector (X) of the final problem using the upper triangular matrix (U). It's very important to notice that between the LU factorization and the solving of triangular systems the data redistribution is not neccesary.

5 Implementation onto torus multicomputer

In the torus topology, each processor has two neighbours in each dimension with direct independent links. In our case, the *ring* of processors can be seen like a torus multicomputer of $P_1 \times P_2$ PEs, where P_1 and P_2 can be greater or equal than 1.

The initial stored data in the PEs will go through the *ring* so that in one iteration, a PE (the generator PE $-GPE-$) computes a group of data in the matrix U (Y or X) and sends them to the rest of PEs in the whole dimensions in

the torus. When the data arrive at their destinations, the rest of PEs compute their own data and the process goes on until $k = n-1$ ($i = n-1$ or $i = 0$). In the following sections we will study the parallel algorithm for a number of PEs (m) less than the number of rows (columns) in the matrix (n).

5.1 Parallel algorithm for m < n

In order to design the parallel algorithm for a generic PE z, we take into account: the applied embedding, the optimization of the initial data distribution and the overlapping of communications and computations.

Initially, the matrix A is distributed in the PEs such that every PE stores n/m non-consecutive rows. The rows are divided into groups of size g, being g multiple of n/m. The distribution of these groups is made in a cyclical way onto the PEs in the *ring*.

P0 ⇒	$u_{0,0}$	$u_{0,1}$	$u_{0,2}$	$u_{0,3}$	$u_{0,4}$	$u_{0,5}$	$u_{0,6}$	$u_{0,7}$	y_0	x_0
	$l_{4,0}$	$l_{4,1}$	$l_{4,2}$	$l_{4,3}$	$u_{4,4}$	$u_{4,5}$	$u_{4,6}$	$u_{4,7}$	y_4	x_4
P1 ⇒	$l_{1,0}$	$u_{1,1}$	$u_{1,2}$	$u_{1,3}$	$u_{1,4}$	$u_{1,5}$	$u_{1,6}$	$u_{1,7}$	y_1	x_1
	$l_{5,0}$	$l_{5,1}$	$l_{5,2}$	$l_{5,3}$	$l_{5,4}$	$u_{5,5}$	$u_{5,6}$	$u_{5,7}$	y_5	x_5
P2 ⇒	$l_{2,0}$	$l_{2,1}$	$u_{2,2}$	$u_{2,3}$	$u_{2,4}$	$u_{2,5}$	$u_{2,6}$	$u_{2,7}$	y_2	x_2
	$l_{6,0}$	$l_{6,1}$	$l_{6,2}$	$l_{6,3}$	$l_{6,4}$	$l_{6,5}$	$u_{6,6}$	$u_{6,7}$	y_6	x_6
P3 ⇒	$l_{3,0}$	$l_{3,1}$	$l_{3,2}$	$u_{3,3}$	$u_{3,4}$	$u_{3,5}$	$u_{3,6}$	$u_{3,7}$	y_3	x_3
	$l_{7,0}$	$l_{7,1}$	$l_{7,2}$	$l_{7,3}$	$l_{7,4}$	$l_{7,5}$	$l_{7,6}$	$u_{7,7}$	y_7	x_7

Figure 5: **Data distribution after the LU factorization for n = 8, m = 4 and g = 1**

With this distribution, the GPE in the iteration $k = k_1$ calculates $u_{r,j}$ ($r = k_1..k_1 + g$, where $j = r..n - 1$), l_{i,k_1} ($i = k_1 + 1..k_1 + g - 1$) and the values $a_{i,j}$ belong to the rest of its group of rows such that the locations of these rows into the matrix A are greater than $k_1 + g - 1$. Moreover, with this distribution the parallelism can be incresed due to the GPE, at the same time can communicate the data, which have been computed previously and can calculate the values of the matrix A. In figure 5 the data distribution after the factorization for $m < n$ is presented.

At the beginning of the forward reduction, in the iteration $i = i_1$, the GPE has to compute y_r ($r = i_1..i_1 + g - 1$) and some terms of the elements y_j belong to its group of rows (being the locations of these rows into the lower triangular matrix L greater than $i_1 + g - 1$) using the previous values of Y. Again, we can communicate the calculated data and compute the next values of Y. The same can be considered for backsubstitution.

In figure 6 an scheme of overlapping of the communications and computations, for forward reduction and $m = 4$, is shown. We can see that the communications are overlapped perfectly with the computations except for the last iterations.

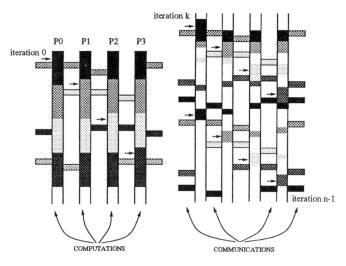

iteration k

P0 P1 P2 P3

iteration 0

iteration n-1

COMPUTATIONS   COMMUNICATIONS

Figure 6: **Overlapping communications and computations for m = 4 in the forward reduction**

This is due to the computation time is less than communication time (there are few data for computing). Initially, the PEs compute the initial values of their pieces of Y. In the iteration 0, the GPE (PE 0) communicates their pieces of Y to the rest of PEs after computing the first g (marked with the symbol $\rightarrow$). At the same time, the GPE goes on initializing the rest of elements of Y. In the iteration 1, the GPE (PE 1) has received the values of Y which were computed in the last iteration. With these new data, the GPE computes the next g values of the vector Y. When it finishes, GPE communicates them to the rest and computes other terms of their own elements of Y. The rest of PEs receive these new data of Y and at the same time compute the terms of their pieces of Y. The path of communication has a maximum size of $log_2 m$.

5.2 Parallel algorithm

The parallel algorithm is obtained from the results of the previous section. In this case, the PEs must index submatrices A of dimension $\frac{n}{m} \times n$ and subvectors B of dimension $\frac{n}{m}$ in their local memories. Furthermore, they must carry out computations on the matrices L, U and A and next on the vectors Y and X (in fact the matrix A and vector B are only used) and communicate the data of U, Y and X to the neighbour PEs. Once these values are produced by themselves and other time are produced by other PE. Following, we show the algorithms of LU factorization and forward reduction for a generic PE (z).

```
if z=0 then      {LU factorization}
    compute elements u_{r,j} (r = 0..g − 1, j = 0..n − 1)
    communicate block u_{r,j}
else
    communicate block u_{r,j}
endif
```

```
do k = 0, n − 1, g
    if (((k + g)/g)  mod  m)= z then
        compute elements l_{i,k}
        compute elements a_{i,j}
            (i = k + g..k + 2 × g − 1), (j = k + 1..n − 1)
        compute elements u_{r,j}
            (r = k + g..k + 2 × g − 1), (j = k + g..n − 1)
        par
            communicate block u_{r,j}
            compute elements l_{i,k}
            compute elements a_{i,j}
                (∀ its i >(k + g + mg))
                and (j = k + g..n − 1)
        endpar
    else
        par
            communicate block u_{r,j}
            compute elements l_{i,k}
            compute elements a_{i,j}
                (∀ its i >(k + g)), (j = k + 1..n − 1)
        endpar
    endif
enddo
```

```
if z=0 then       {forward reduction}
    compute y_i = b_r /a_{i,i}   (i = 0..g − 1)
    compute y_r(y_i)   (r = 1..g − 1), (i = 0..r − 1)
    par
        communicate y_r
        compute y_i = b_i /a_{i,i}   (∀ its i > 0)
    endpar
else
    par
        communicate y_r
        compute y_i = b_i /a_{i,i}   (∀ its i > 0)
    endpar
endif
do i = 0, n − 1, g
    if (((i + g)/g)  mod  m)= z then
        compute y_r(y_j)
            (r = i + g..i + 2 × g − 1), (j = i..r − 1)
        par
            communicate y_r
            compute y_l(y_j)
                (∀ its l >(i + g + mg))
                and (j = i + g..i + 2 × g − 1)
        endpar
    else
        par
            communicate y_r
            compute y_l(y_j)
                (∀ its l >(i + g)), (j = i..i + g − 1)
        endpar
    endif
enddo
```

Every PE has $\frac{n}{mg}$ groups of rows, where $mg = m \times g$. In this algorithm some auxiliar variables are used $(u(..), l(..), y(..))$ for clarifing, although only the matrix A and vector B are used. The *comunicate* sentence is the algorithm which carries out the sending and receipt of the data among PEs. The algorithm of the backsubstitution is similar to the algorithm of the forward reduction.

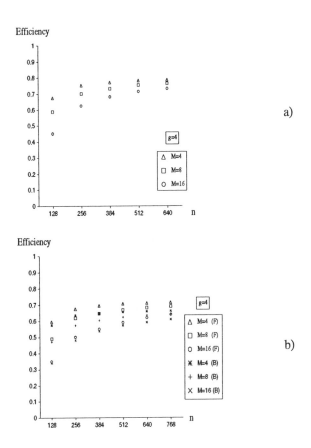

Figure 7: **Efficiency** *vs* **n for** g $=$ 4. **a) Factorization. b) Triangular systems**

6 Experimental results

We have implemented the parallel algorithm of last section in a SN-1000 transputer based multicomputer in the Centro Europeo de Paralelismo de Barcelona (C.E.P.B.A.) [12]. In this configuration, the transputers have 4Mbyte of local memory and a clock frequency of 20MHz. The data of the matrix A and the elements of the vector B originally are in the memory of the host (PC computer). We have used OCCAM2 parallel language for programming it with INMOS toolsets [13]. In figure 7 and 8 we can see the expirimental results (efficiency *vs* n) for 4 transputers (2×2), 8 transputers

(2×4) and 16 transputers (4×4), and 2 values of the variable g (number of consecutive rows per PE).

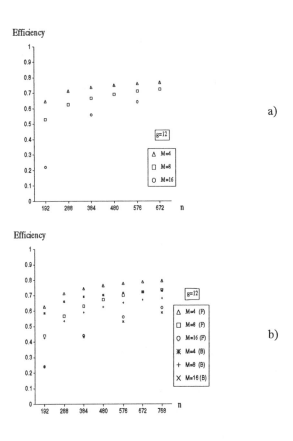

Figure 8: **Efficiency** *vs* **n for** g $=$ 12. **a) Factorization. b) Triangular systems**

For measuring the time of the parallel algorithm we have taken into account the time spent in distributing the data stored in the host computer memory into the local memories of tranputers. Moreover, we have included the time spent unloading the solution vector (X) back to the host computer memory. The ascendent slope of the efficiency curves must be observed. The saturation is around 75-80% for the LU factorization and around 70-75% for the triangular systems.

7 Conclusions and future work

In this paper we have studied the LU factorization for dense and strictly diagonally dominant matrices, and the solving of triangular systems for computing the solution of $A \times X = B$. The data distribution carried out in the PEs allows us the non-redistribution of the data after the factorization. The LU factorization and the computation of the vectors Y and X have been made overlapping communications and computations, so the time spent in the communication is minimized. We have considered the sequential algorithms of the LU factorization and the forward reduction and back-substitution adding the message passing primitives. In the measuring of the efficiency, we took into account the time spent in distributing the data to the PEs and in unloading the results. Guided by these results, we are implementing other algorithms like LU factorization with partial pivoting, QR factorization, computations of pseudoinverse, conjugate gradient, etc ... for dense and sparse matrices.

References

[1] Athas, W.C., Seitz C.L. *Multicomputer. Message passing concurrent computers. IEEE computer, August 1988, pp. 9-24.*

[2] Ho C., Jonhsson S.L. *On embedding of arbitrary meshes in boolean cubes with expansion two dilation two. Proc. international conf. Parallel processing, 1987, pp. 188-191.*

[3] Golub G.H., Van Loan C.F., *Matrix Computations. Second Edition. 1990, pp. 86-132.*

[4] Calvin C., Colombet L., Michallon P., *Overlapping Techniques of Communications. The International-Conference and Exhibition of High Performance Computing and Networking. (HPCN EUROPE 1995).*

[5] Suárez Alvaro, Ojeda-Guerra C.N., *Overlapping Computations and Communications on Torus Networks. Fourth Euromicro Workshop on Parallel and Distributed Processing, January 1996, pp. 162-169.*

[6] Chu E., George A., *Gaussian Elimination with Partial Pivoting and Load Balancing on a Multiprocessor. Parallel Computing 5, 1987, pp. 65-74.*

[7] Fox G., Johnson M., Lyzenga G., Otto S., Salmon J., Walker D., *Solving Problems on Concurrent Processors. Volume I. General Techniques and Regular Problems. Prentice Hall Inc. 1988, pp. 363-397.*

[8] Wolfe M.J., *Optimizing Supercompilers for Supercomputers, Ph.D. thesis, University of Illinois, 1982.*

[9] Hwang Kai, *Advanced Computer Arquitecture. Parallelism, Scalability, Programmability. McGraw-Hill Inc. 1993, pp. 650-652.*

[10] Dongarra J.J., Gustavson F.G., Karp A., *Implementing Linear Algebra Algorithms For Dense Matrices on a Vector Pipeline Machine. SIAM Vol. 26, No. 1, January, 1984.*

[11] Fernández A., Llabería J.M., Navarro J.J., Valero-García M., *Systematic Transformation of Systolic Algorithms for Distributed Memory Multiprocessors. UPC/DAC Report No. RR-90/20, September-90.*

[12] *Transputer. Occam 2 Toolset. User Manual. INMOS Limited, 1989.*

[13] Hoare C.A.R., *Occam 2. Reference Manual. INMOS Limited. Prentice Hall International Series in Computer Science, 1988.*

Boolean matrix exponentiation : a case story for scalable massively parallel matrix-machine with string architecture

György Vesztergombi
Research Institute for Particle Physics
P.O.Box 49 H-1525 Budapest, Hungary
veszter@rmki.kfki.hu

Francois Rohrbach
CERN
Genève 23, CH-1211, Switzerland
F.Rohrbach@cern.ch

Géza Ódor
Research Institute for Materials Science
P.O.Box 49 H-1525 Budapest, Hungary
odor@ra.atki.kfki.hu

Géza Varga and Ferenc Tátrai
Technical University of Budapest
Department of Chemical Technology
H-1521 Budapest, Hungary
fox@ch.bme.hu

Abstract

A scalable bit-matrix machine model is proposed relying on the so-called memory architecture. In the broader sense this architecture means that each line of the memory is equipped by a local primitive processor. These processors are communicating each other vertically along a string. The whole system is driven centrally in a SIMD like manner. The computational capabilities are demonstrated on matrix algorithms. Despite the simple string architecture the boolean matrix multiplication is executed in $O(n)$ time by n^2 processors. The scalability assumes simultaneous memory scaling, ensuring that the loading of $n \times n$ matrices becomes feasible in $O(n)$ time too. A 64×64 bit version is realized on a 4096 processor ASTRA machine.

1. Introduction

It is a general principle in biological computers (i.e. in living organisms): use (logically) simple elements but in large quantities. In computer industry one of the cheapest elements is the memory, especially, if one counts in bit/$, and it is produced really in enormous quantities. (Here we refer only to Si-based elements.) It is in the forefront of technological development,that even the density of Billionbit/chip is imaginable in the near future, see announcement of NEC [2]. In this respect a massively parallel machine, which is based on some *memory architecture,* can have rather sexy technological and/or biological appeal. Under memory architecture we understand that most part of the chip surface is occupied by repetitive copies of some basic cell.

In this paper we should like to present a case story on Boolean matrix manipulation to demonstrate how effectively can one use the memory architecture with minimal additional CPU logics relying on a string-like architecture. The paper is organised in the following way. In Section 2 the theoretical concept of the bit-matrix machine is presented. The general Boolean matrix manipulating algorithms will be discussed in Section 3. The origin of the Boolean matrix exponentiation problem is exposed in Section 4 by describing the role of the Boolean adjacency matrix in the chemical processing plant modelling. In Section 5 a prototype of the memory architecture massively parallel computer system, the ASTRA machine will be introduced. Historically the Associative String Processor (ASP) architecture applied in the ASTRA machine draw our attention to notice the similarities between massively parallelism and memory architecture. With simple hardware modifications in the ASP one can achieve $O(n)$ processing time in matrix operations (e.g. multiplication) despite the limitations of the string communication. That would enable, theoretically, to integrate 10^5 processing elements on a single chip.

Finally we discuss questions on scalability: in what sense can one "beat" (or at least saturate) Amdahl's law.

2. The Computer Model

The basic features of the proposed **matrix-machine** can be illustrated in the best way by defining a theoretical computer model. Thus the logical structure can be demonstrated without cumbersome technical details.

2.1. General features of the matrix-machine

The simultaneous requirement of massive parallelism and simplicity basically determines that one should adopt the so called SIMD (Single Instruction Multiple Data) architecture. This means that the **same** instruction, defined by the Central Controller, are executed by all the **selected** processor elements. This *restricted* SIMD definition with the word "selected" is very essential. Its meaning will be explained in the next.

As it is outlined in Fig. 1, one can regard the system from two different points of view depending on the purpose of the presentation. The standard one is the *horizontal* view, where each horizontal line represents one tiny "nano-computer" with its reduced CPU, registers etc.

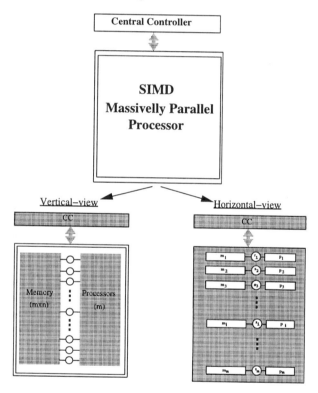

Figure 1. Different views on processor versus memory relation

In parallel computing the cardinal decision concerns the selection of the inter-processor communication system. In our spirit of simplicity we opt for the cheapest network, the string where the individual processing elements are communicating only with their nearest neighbour along a string, that is P_i has direct connection only to P_{i-1} and P_{i+1}. (Of course, beside this they are all connected to the Central Controller by the corresponding buses to be able to execute the common instructions broadcasted from there.) The flexibility in this seemingly rigid system is achieved by the

above emphasised "selectivity". The command, issued by the Central Controller will be executed only by those processors whose Selector-bit, S_i was set to 1. These Selector-bits are set *associatively* in a programmed way. The general philosophy of the **A**ssociative **S**tring **P**rocessor (ASP) is explained in ref. [3]. Later we will demonstrate on concrete examples, how this associative selection works.

Besides the standard horizontal view, here we should like to turn the attention towards the so called *memory aspect*, which can be characterised as the *vertical* viewpoint. Because by the same extremely simple processor chain (with eventual change of the string's length) one can serve completely different memory matrices. One can have, in one hand, tasks where 32-bit memory/processor may be enough. But one can, on the other hand, imagine situation, where 1 kbit per processor is the optimal. Assuming e.g. a memory-matrix of 1000×1000 bits having at one of the edges 1000 nano-processors, the system would look more like a *memory-* than a *processor-chip*.

2.2. Memory organisation

Corresponding to the above mentioned two aspects the in/out data transfer from the memory can happen in both, vertical and horizontal directions assuming that the memory is organised as an $m \times n$ bit-matrix. Data can be communicated on the n-bit data-bus between the Word-Buffer and Selected rows of memory, as it is shown in Fig.2. In case of "verti-

Vertical transfer

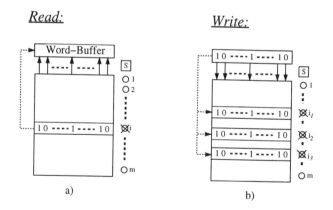

Figure 2. Input-Output procedures

cal READ" only one line out of the m total can be selected (Fig.2a). During this operation n-bits of the i-th row are read in parallel. The "vertical WRITE" operation is particular in the sense, that the content of the Word-Buffer is simultaneously copied (Fig.2b) to any subset of preselected memory rows whose Selection-Bit $S_i = 1$, $i \in \{i_1, i_2, \ldots, i_k\}$.

The vertical connection towards the outside world is maintained by the Central Controller through the Word-

Buffer. The data movement inside the processing elements is ensured by the "horizontal I/O" operation. It is governed by the global Bit-Pointer (BP) which is part of the Central Controller because in the SIMD machine each processor executes the same command, thus each will address the same bit in its "local" memory and this task can be accomplished by a single universal pointer. In horizontal operations the Selector-Bits (Fig.3) are defining those rows (i.e. processors), which are really active during execution, in similar way as for vertical WRITE.

Horizontal– transfer

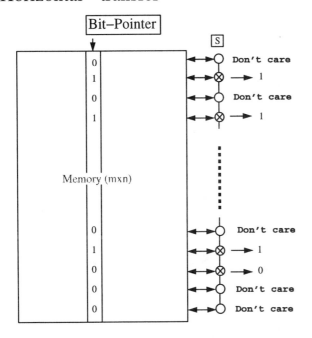

Figure 3. Horizontal I/O between memory and Activity Register

2.3. Processor elements

The individual processing elements, P_i have rather simple structure (see Fig.4). Additionally to the n-bit memory (M_i) and Selection Bit (S_i) described above they have a k-bit Activity Register (AR_i), a Tag-Bit(T_i) and some local CPU_i. The Control-Bus (C), Activity-Bus (A) and Data-Bus (D) connects the CPU, AR and Memory to the Central Controller, respectively. The processors communicate among each other by the TAG-SHIFT operation only through the Tag-Bit i.e. T_i: is connected only to T_{i-1} and T_{i+1}. If during a tagging operation at least one T_i is set then one gets a Match-Reply. The Activity Register consists of ternary-digits, which has 3 states "0","1" and "don't care" (of course, they are realized by 2 normal bits). Therefore in case of k-bit one needs $2k$ lines in the Activity-Bus

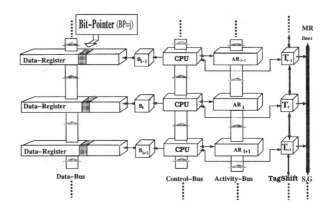

Figure 4. Structure of the processor string

to test its content. For short-hand notation one denotes by **A1,A2,...,Ak** the separate digits of AR.

The basic property of the ASP architecture is that the selection of the active subset of processors is divided in two steps : tagging and activation. **Tagging** means the setting T_i. Its value depends on the content of M_i, AR_i and the A,C buses. i.e. it is a *local* decision. (The meaning of double MR line will be explained in the next.) **Activation** (i.e. setting S_i), however can be influenced by the state of Tag Bits of other processors which means that they can be set "non-locally" by its tagged environment which turns out to be a very flexible programming tool.

2.4. String segments

An other powerful feature of the ASP architecture – which we want to incorporate in our model also – arises from the fact that the complete string of m processors can be divided into individual substrings by the running program itself during its execution. The separating switches between the segments are operated by the program running in the Central Controller. In practice, these switches just connect/disconnect the communication between the Tag-Bits in the corresponding places. In our model version, we assume that the Match-Reply line also have segment switches, which are simultenously controlled with the string switches. Thus one can have for each segment an individual Segment-Match-Reply (SMR) making them, in this sense also, to behave as functionally *complete* strings. It should be mentioned that in the present ASP realization there exists only the Global-Match-Reply. In our concrete model (Fig.5) we assume that we have $m = n^2$ processors, thus the string can be divided into n-segment by n switches (including the possibility of circular structure).

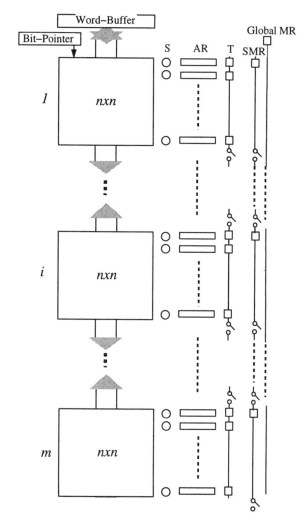

Figure 5. Schematic view of the n^2 processor string

3. Boolean matrix operation

As it was mentioned in the introduction here we concentrate on the manipulation of Boolean matrices in a massively parallel computer. The elements of the Boolean matrix has only two values **true(=1)** and **false(=0)** that can be stored by a simple bit in the memory. Thus the storage of $n \times n$ Boolean matrix requires $n \times n$ bits.

3.1. Matrix representations

In our computer model we have n^2 processors, thus we can put n copies of a matrix in the available n^3 bit volume. There are different possibilities. For our purposes we selected 3 main representations:

a) **Matrix-representation:** $n \times n$ bit-matrix (Fig.6a) in the substrings (in principle, different substrings can contain different matrices, but generally one uses n identical copies);

b) **String-representation:** n^2 bit-vector (Fig.6b) in one of the bit of AR along the total string (each AR column can contain a separate matrix);

b') Transposed vector representation (see in separate section);

c) **Dispersed row-representation:** subsequent rows of the matrix are stored segment by segment in the memory of the first processor (Fig.6c).

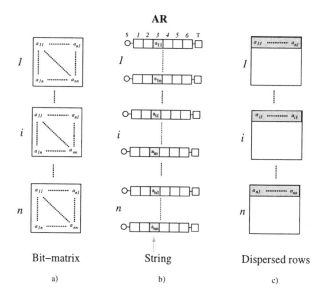

Figure 6. The basic matrix representation forms

The latest one requires some explanation. It turns out to be a very useful intermediate state. Because through this representation one can easily transform the matrices between the two previous ones.

Due to the parallel writing of n-bits all the n^2 bits of the total matrix are loaded in n-cycles. Thus the load procedure needs $O(n)$ execution time independently whether one produces n-fold matrix-representation or dispersed row representation.

3.2. Transition between different matrix representations

To make all transformations among representations it is enough to demonstrate the procedure by which the dispersed representation is transformed back and forth to the string and matrix representations, respectively. In order to be explicit we introduce the following notations: the bits of Word-Buffer and Memory-Words are numbered from right-to-left starting by 0, but the row index of matrix elements a_{ij} are numbered from left to right, thus a_{i1} will be stored in Bit_{n-1} a_{in} will be stored in Bit_0.

A. Transform dispersed row- to string-representation

The execution of this subroutine produces a copy of the matrix in one of the bit column of AR (eg. in **A2**, assuming that the segment starts are marked by **A1**). The first segment will contain the first row in vertical (column-like) position, the second segment will contain the second row and so on ...

During this procedure segments are separated and work in parallel: LOAD the next bit into the first processor's **A2** and move it down by TAG-SHIFT. The execution time goes as $O(n)$ because it is repeated for each bit. The reverse procedure uses TAG-SHIFT up-ward and STOREs the upper bit in the corresponding memory bit.

B. Transform dispersed image to n-fold matrix representation

As we will see later for matrix product calculations one requires n copy of the $n \times n$ bit matrix. The creation of the dispersed image seems to be superfluous if one is loading the data from outside source, but we need this intermediate image if we want to use the string-representation for input or output. As usual we assume that the **A1**-bits are masking the first processors in each virtual segments. (Segments are only "virtual" if the switches are closed.)

In the starting position different segments contains different rows. In the first step one reads out the last row and writes it back in n copies to the last line of each segment. This is repeated then for the other lines, too. As usual this procedure requires also $O(n)$ execution time. In the reverse procedure one should be careful to reset to zero the bits not used in the dispersed row representation.

3.3. Matrix transposition

In some applications the transposed matrix is required. Here we present the procedure, which fulfils this task starting from the n-fold matrix image creating the transposed matrix in string-representation. This is rather trivial because one should simply use columns instead of rows, which are automatically given if one regards the memory vertically. The trick is that one should copy the i-th column into the i-th segment, but i-th column stored at Bit-Pointer=$(n - i)$, which complicates a bit the tagging order, starting the copying of the columns from backward. This is also an $O(n)$ type problem.

3.4. Matrix "addition"

Let us have two Boolean matrix **A** and **B** stored in string representation in AR bits **A4** and **A5**, respectively. It is trivial to calculate:

$$\mathbf{A} \bigoplus \mathbf{B} = \mathbf{C}$$

in bit **A6**, also in string-representation simply executing in parallel n^2 times.

$$a_{ij} \bigoplus b_{ij} = c_{ij}$$

in each processor, where $\bigoplus$ can be :
   a) Boolean add (or) : $0+0 = 0, 0+1 = 1+0 = 1+1 = 1$
   b) Boolean product (and) : $0 \cdot 0 = 0 \cdot 1 = 1 \cdot 0 = 0, 1 \cdot 1 = 1$
   c) Exclusive or : $0 * 0 = 1 * 1 = 0, 1 * 0 = 0 * 1 = 1$
   Here we can use the full power of parallelism, therefore we have $O(1)$ execution time.

3.5. Matrix multiplication

Let us store matrix **A** in string representation in **A4** of AR and the matrix **B** as n-fold bit-matrix in the memory. One can observe that the scene is well set to calculate

$$c_{ij} = a_{i1} \cdot b_{1j} + a_{i2} \cdot b_{2j} + \ldots + a_{in} \cdot b_{nj}$$

if one takes segment $'i'$, then one finds in **A4** bit of AR column a_{ik} the values i-th row of matrix **A** and b_{kj} values in the memory column at Bit-Pointer=$(n - j)$ the j-th column of matrix **B**. Thus by fixing j it requires a SINGLE instruction to calculate all the n^2 combination of products $a_{ik} \cdot b_{kj}$ and store then in **A3** as it shown in Fig.7. For a given i the

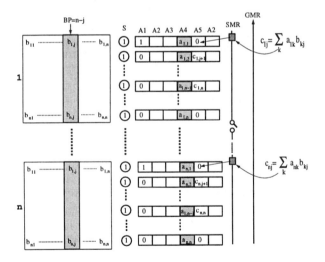

Figure 7. One step of the Boolean multiplication

sum of $a_{ik} \cdot b_{kj}$ is identical with the SEGMENT MATCH REPLY, thus a simple tagging automatically performs the summation along k, because due to the Boolean logics if any $a_{ik} \cdot b_{kj}$ is set to 1 the sum will be 1 . Copying the SEGMENT MATCH REPLY in the first processor's **A5** bit we can reach the same situation which occurred during the transformation of the dispersed image to string segmentation. Shifting the

A5 simultaneously with the Bit-Pointer we can put step by step the j-th element of each row of the **C** matrix in the corresponding segment. In essence the multiplication is not much more complicated than the vector loading, which well characterises the computing power of this architecture. In summary one can conclude that the matrix multiplication can be accomplished by $O(n)$ time. Which is optimal in the sense that $O(n^3)$ operation is performed O(n) time on n^2 processors.

4. Strongly connected component analysis in chemical process modelling

The idea for Boolean-matrix calculation is occurred to us following from some chemical studies.

In chemical plants the different processes are executed by interconnected parts of the system. Several equipments (reactors, distillation columns, splitters etc.) are connected to each other by stream pipes. The interconnectivity structure of the given chemical process network is frequently depicted by some flow-sheet in the form a directed graph in which the nodes represent the equipment units and the directed edges represent the flow streams of material and energy. These connection streams and the description of chemical units behaviour can be described usually by a nonlinear system of equations. To each node i one can assign a function f_i in analytical or numerical form, which depends on the x_i variables, denoting output values of the corresponding nodes. The connectivity information contained in the system of equations can be condensed in the adjacency matrix A, whose element $a_{ij} = 1$ if f_j is explicitly depending on x_i otherwise it is equal to zero, including $a_{ii} = 0$, because the i-th node is not "adjacent" to i-th node.

DEFINITION : The L-th reachability matrix R^L is defined such $r_{ij} = 1$ if there exists at least one path no longer than L from vertex v_i to v_j.

It is obvious that $r_{ij} = 1$ and $r_{ji} = 1$ conditions are defining the strongly connected parts. Mathematically this condition can be checked by composing the intersection of R and the transposed R^T matrix.

$$W = R \cap R^T$$

In order to calculate the matrix W, which provides the strongly connected part of the adjacency matrix A, the key step is to calculate the n-th power of $B = I + A$ because $R = B^n$.

For sake of simplicity we assume that :

$$n = 2^k \quad i.e. \quad k = log_2(n)$$

In this case of *pure* exponent the procedure is extremely simple. It starts with the loading of matrix B to the Data-Register memories through the Word-Buffer in dispersed-row-representation. Then by help of the standard transformation procedures one creates the string- and matrix-representations in the **A4** bit of the Activity-Register and the Data-Register memories, respectively. The result of the multiplication is accumulated in the **A5** bit in string-representation. Filling this back to **A4** and the memory, one repeats the procedure until one finds B^n in **A5**. In total, it means $k = log(n)$ matrix multiplication requiring each $O(n)$ processing time.

In case of *mixed* exponent one needs to store an intermediate mixed product in the **A6** string. Due to the fact, that the maximal number of intermediate multiplications is not more than $log(n)$, the exponentiation procedure can be finished in $O(n \cdot log(n))$ time even in the worst mixed case, too.

At the end of the exponentiation procedure one gets the result in string-representation in **A5**. The filling into memory and bringing back the transposed matrix into **A4** requires $O(n)$ time. By "AND"-ing bit by bit **A4** and **A5** one gets matrix W in **A6** as a result of a single step operation. Thus the completion of the full W-procedure including loading and transmission will require $O(n \cdot log(n))$ time, which is a real gain compared to the brute force $O(n^4)$ sequential algorithm.

5. The Associative String Processor (ASP)

Basically, the ASP has SIMD(Single Instruction with Multiple Data) architecture. A given instruction is executed, however, only by preselected subset of active APEs, where the activation process is steered by running program itself, exactly corresponding our computer model defined above.

In contrast to more traditional parallel computer architectures, ASP uses content-matching rather than location addressing techniques. ASP selects APE-s for subsequent parallel processing by comparing their 'Data-register' and 'Activity-registers' content with the states of the corresponding 'Data-' and 'Activity-buses'. Therefore the Comparator is an extremely important part of the single processor element. Each APE incorporates a n-bit 'Data-register' and a a-bit 'Activity-register', thus the required comparator length is $c = n + a$. In the following we assume $n = 64$ and $a = 6$.

Each APE is a mini-microcomputer with its own single-bit CPU performing four basic operations: match, add, read and write. As the structure of APE is very simple (they are "intelligent memory cells") many of them (up to 1024 in the near future) can be put on single VLSI chip. The speed is assured by the 20 MHz clock frequency.

Existing ASTRA machines have 4096 (or 8192) processors. It was built in four exemplars in the framework of the MPPC project [1]. They represent complete realisation of our model machine with $n = 64$ because it has 64 × 64 processor with 64 memory-bits per processor. Even it has a "superfluous" 32-bits content addressing capability through the data-bus, which is not used in our "model computer", because for the matrix operations one doesn't need this feature. The ASTRA machine doesn't have however SMR, the segment match reply, therefore it is realized with the help of a few software commands.

The Boolean matrix exponentiation algorithm was tested on the ASTRA machine within the above mentioned limitation: no SMR and maximum n=64. The $O(nlog(n))$ behaviour was reproduced, but the real interest would be in case of $n > 1000$ which would require at least one million processors. It is not realistic in the present technology but it would become easily available by a technical break-through toward the proposed memory architecture.

6. Performance scaling

The scaling property, that is e.g. the full strongly connected component analysis can be executed by the same procedure just setting the new value of n is valid in the sense that, simultaneously, the number of processors is increased to n^2 **and** the memory length in each processor will be increased to n. This is a relatively modest, but very essential ingredient, whose meaning will be discussed here in more details.

In order to concentrate the essentially parallel part of the algorithm let us deal only with the question of matrix multiplication. It is well known, that using a mesh with n^2 processors one can perform the matrix multiplication in $O(n)$ time. Here we demonstrated on Boolean-matrices that even a string with n^2 processors is able to achieve this speed. It means a theoretical speed up by a factor of n^2 relative to a sequential algorithm. But the calculation algorithm is only one part of the problem. The data for the processing should be present before the calculation. This loading procedure in general is a sequential process and in our case, if it is performed by the usual way, it requires $O(n^2)$ time. Thus f, the sequential to parallel ratio will be worsened by n and after some threshold the sequential part will overtake and there will not be any reason to increase the number of processors because according to the Amdahl's law, the maximal speed-up is

$$\frac{1}{(1-f)}$$

In our computer model with **scalable memory** this problem is circumvented in a balanced way. Assuming that we have parallel sources which are producing matrix-rows, that is really the case in CCD-image detectors, we can feed our system with a speed-up factor of n, and can perform the loading procedure in $O(n)$ time, as it was foreseen in our algorithm. This means though in matrix multiplication the value of f will be constant, one gets a "real speed-up" a factor of n due to the increased I/O bandwidth. In this sense our system is

"beating" the Amdahl's law, because the $O(n^3)$ problem will be solved together with loading in $O(n)$ time which represents an $O(n^2)$ speed-up.

All the above considerations can be generalised for numerical matrix calculations, but one should provide additional memory to store more than one bit per matrix element. Of course, the simplicity of Boolean operations will be overtaken by a more complicated procedure which still can be executed however in $O(n)$ steps.

7. Conclusions

The basic concepts of the bit-matrix machine are:

1. Memory (which is cheap) contains n-fold copies of the bit-matrix in n^3 bits. This provides *column-wise* vectorisation.

2. The content addressable Activity-Register (which is relatively expensive) contains the bit-matrix in n^2 bits providing *row-wise* vectorisation.

3. The n^2 processors assure n^2-fold parallelism in the matrix element a_{ij} level and n-fold parallelism on row/column level. This provides execution times $O(1)$ for addition, $O(n)$ for multiplication and transposition, $O(n \cdot log(n))$ for the calculation of n-th power.

4. The key element is the dispersed row representation by which all the other matrix representation are reachable in $O(n)$ steps.

5. According to our knowledge this is the first attempt to apply massively parallel processing techniques for chemical process modelling. Though the scope of the present problem does not require so enormous computing resources, it can serve as a precedent towards more sophisticated modelling problems.

6. Algorithms upto n=64 can be tested in real ASTRA machines whose architecture provides adequate model for the proposed bit-matrix machine.

If the technological progress is continuing with the present rate a chip with $n = 30000$ processor each equipped with 30000 bits memory should not be much larger than the present 1 Gigabit memory-chip prototype of NEC, which can bring our model machine concept closer to the reality .

References

[1] F. R. et al. The mppc project : final report. *CERN preprint*, 93-07, 1993.
[2] B. Holmes. *New Scientist*, 20:1966, 1995.
[3] R. M. Lea. A cost effective parallel microcomputer. *IEEE Micro*, October 1988.

Simulation of Poly-Electrolyte Solutions on a Parallel Dedicated System

G. Danese, I. De Lotto, D. Dotti, F. Leporati

Dipartimento di Informatica e Sistemistica - Via Ferrata, 1 - 27100 Pavia

Tel. 0382/505350 - Fax 0382/505373 - e-mail: gianni@ipvvis.unipv.it

Abstract

This paper compares the results obtained by simulating a particle system by a standard Monte Carlo algorithm, to those provided by an its modified version. The speed-up provided by the chosen parallel architecture is also given.

At first the analysis of the simulation is carried out by means of the PVM software package on a cluster of workstations HP-705; successively the modified algorithm is executed on a Special Purpose Computer (SPC).

Introduction

The study of the physical behaviour of interacting particle systems exhibits remarkable difficulties both in experiments and simulations through computers. In the former case problems arise regarding the reproducibility of the operating conditions and the measurement of the main parameters of the system; in the latter case, problems concern the synthesis of the models and the selection of simulation algorithms to provide reliable results within reasonable times.

The systems of colloidal particles include, in their classification, a quantity of substances very interesting in the Matter Physics field. The most remarkable features of these systems are to be found in the spatial distribution of the particles; experimentally, it is possible only in a few cases to obtain such measures through light diffraction techniques, however yielding low accuracy results.

This work has been developed in order to simulate a particular colloidal system made up of poly-electrolytes dispersed in a solution; poly-electrolytes are particles which, in contact with the solvent, create a constant number of monovalent counter-ions, so gaining a positive electric charge.

The physical interactions between the two kinds of particles (poly-electrolytes and counter-ions) makes preferable the use of Monte Carlo simulation methods, even if the resulting simulation process turns out to be slow. In order to overcome this drawback, two solutions have been envisaged:

- the former consists in a modification of the Monte Carlo-Metropolis algorithm, so that the convergency speed of the simulation for colloidal systems becomes remarkable faster;
- the latter concerns porting the algorithm on a parallel architecture, purposely designed for an efficient mapping of the algorithm itself.

The modification of the algorithm has been carried out exploiting the physical properties of the simulated system, while holding unchanged the originary features of the method.

The research activity carried out in the last times at the laboratory of Microcomputers at the University of Pavia, Italy, brought us to design and build a parallel machine, Special Purpose Computer (SPC), particularly well suited to the simulation of particles systems, through the Monte Carlo-Metropolis algorithm; in order to face the new problem, regarding the colloidal systems, a proper connection topology has been studied, while retaining the already available Processing Elements (PE).

The free selection of the connection architecture, aimed at the exploitation of each PE in the execution of the simulation algorithm, together with the low implementation cost and the access easiness to the processing facilities, makes the use of the SPC profitable in the approach to this new problem.

The results which will be obtained from the simulation of poly-electrolyte solutions will be used to validate the experimental studies about the diffraction properties on laser beams, performed by the Quantum Electronics Laboratory in our University.

The main steps needed to achieve the final results include:

- the study of the physical system, of its model and of the existing simulation algorithms;
- the choice of the model, of the simulation algorithm and their validation;
- the parallelisation of the implemented algorithm on a few virtual architectures, with relevant performance evaluation;

- the porting of the most promising algorithm/architecture into a specially conceived version of our SPC.

The Physical problem

When a substance (solute) dissolves into another (solvent) to create a solution, the chemical bounds among the solute molecules break and the particles distribute uniformly inside the solution.

However other classes of material exist where the solute does not really dissolve, but holds a certain aggregation degree like solid, liquid or gas; those materials are called *colloids*.

As an example, paints and some lubricants are suspensions of solids in liquids, fog and clouds are liquids in gases, and smoke and smog are solids in gases; finally alloyes and ceramics are solids in solids.

Colloidal solutions considered in this paper are solid-liquid featuring small free ions and bigger particles, micelles or poly-electrolytes, with a charge equivalent to some tens or hundreds of ions.

The colloidal solutions are two component systems made-up by micelles-ions or more generally poly-electrolytes-ions.

Simulation of interacting particles with coulombian model must reproduce a smooth decay with the distance (1/r). Furthermore, collisions between particles have to be considered.

Two models can be used to describe particle collisions: the former is the Hard Sphere model, which prevents any penetration of the particles; the latter is the Soft Sphere one, which allows a moderate amount of it [1].

Usually, the particle system is confined in a cubic box with stiff walls, but this is not always the correct approach to follow. In the simulation of bulk liquids, for example, problems arise due to the considerable number of particles on the surface of the simulated sample (in a 10x10x10 cube they are 488). If the sample is surrounded by a containing wall, the particles on the surface will show forces different from the real situation: to overcome these difficulties, periodic boundary conditions are implemented in the simulation model. The cubic box containing the particle system is replicated throughout space to form an infinite lattice. In the course of the simulation, as a molecule moves in the original box, its periodic image in each of the neighboring boxes moves in exactly the same direction. Thus, as a molecule leaves the central box, one of its images will enter through the opposite face. This correctly represents the topology of the system, if not its geometry.

The time it takes for the double loop used to evaluate the forces or potential energy is proportional to N^2. Special techniques may reduce this dependence on $O(N)$, for very large systems, but the force/energy loop still dictates the overall speed and, clearly, smaller systems will always be less expensive.

A further approximation significantly reduces the computations required, considering that the largest contribution to the potential and force comes from the neighbouring molecules. It is therefore possible to apply a spherical cut-off radius, setting the pair potential at zero for $r > r_c$, where r_c is the cut-off distance. The cut-off distance must be no greater than half the box side, for consistency with the periodic boundary conditions.

This approximation works well with short-range interactions or in the case of long-range interactions with a potential that rapidly decays with the distance (long-range forces are defined as forces in which the potential decay law is not faster than the dimension of the system).

In the case of charge-charge or dipole-dipole long-range interactions, the approach described above is inadequate because their range is greater than half a box side for typical simulations. Therefore, other solutions like the Ewald method (which takes into account the interactions between a particle and all its periodic images) or the Reaction field method are preferred [2].

The Simulation Algorithm

The algorithms for the simulation of particle systems are mainly divided into two categories: Molecular Dynamics and Monte Carlo.

Molecular Dynamics (MD) algorithms are based on the mechanics of the particle systems, and integrate the motion equation of each particle; each of them is featured by its own position and speed at every time instant; as a consequence each algorithm step corresponds to a time interval in the real system. At each step, the force field of the whole system is computed and all the particles are consequently moved [3].

On the contrary Monte Carlo-Metropolis algorithm is a non-deterministic method using random number generation to build probability distributions and to simulate statistical systems by computer.

The application of the Monte Carlo technique to particle system simulation was introduced by Metropolis in 1953 [4] and yields the average values of significant system parameters; the method identifies a high number of particle configurations representing the relative statistical behaviour.

The transition from one configuration to the next, usually called *move*, is carried out as follows:

1) one of the particles is randomly selected;
2) a random space displacement is attributed to that particle and the relative energy variation ΔW is evaluated;
3) the space displacement is accepted if ΔW is < 0 or if the quantity $\exp(-\beta \Delta W)$ is smaller than a randomly selected value uniformly distributed in $[0...1]$. (β is $K_b * T$, where K_b is the Boltzmann constant and T the temperature).

To accelerate the simulation convergency, the width of the space displacement is periodically adjusted so as to obtain a mean acceptance probability of 50%.

An initial set of *moves* carries the particle system from an arbitrary start configuration to an *equilibrium* status. The macroscopic matter properties are evaluated from the particle distances every 2N *moves,* that is, after a single mean displacement for each particle: this is usually called *macrostep.* Overall, for a thousand particles, 10^{12} to 10^{15} floating point operations are required, a hard task even for a supercomputer.

On literature [5] MD techniques are usually preferred to Monte Carlo-Metropolis (MM) algorithm since in the considered solutions most free ions surround the nearest poly-electrolyte. Ion accumulation around the micelle generates narrow and sharp potential holes and lowers acceptation probability for micelle *moves* since particle collisions are highly probable. However the MD simulations may be unprecise since the force field evaluation shows low accuracy due to the effect of the strong potential variation around the micelles.

MD simulation convergence turns out to be 4 times faster than the MM in a case described in literature [5], very similar to ours to be described later. However the MM method is the most natural approach when the particle force field varies rapidly in space as in our case; it is in fact based on the potential evaluation, whilst MD method considers interaction forces among the particles.

To avoid a slow convergence we modified the MM algorithm taking care of the physical features of the problem without affecting the statistical properties of the original method.

A modification to the simulation algorithm

The MM algorithm simulates two body systems: in the case of colloidal systems, they correspond to micelles and ions. Recalling that most problems with MM arise from the collisions between each micelle and the ions surrounding it, a new entity (*cluster*) has been introduced, which includes one micelle and the nearest ions (Fig. 1). The algorithm is then modified to be able to consider cluster-cluster, cluster-ion and ion-ion interactions and is called Cluster Move (CM).

In the proposed approach the set of ions surrounding a micelle undergoes its same displacement with much lower collision probability; the *moves* relative to the ions belonging to the cluster will be considered later with higher success probability.

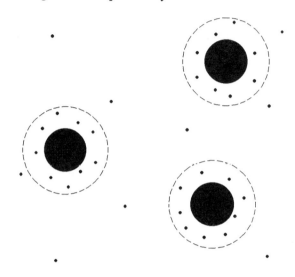

Fig. 1 - Poly-electrolytes with ions

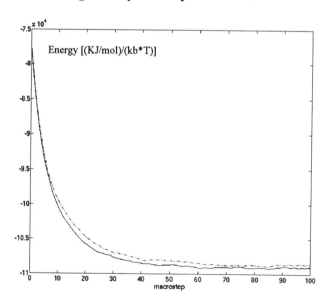

Fig. 2 - Energy during the first 100 macrostep

Since each cluster displacement is accepted on the basis of the global energy variation, the evaluation time is proportional to the number of the ions belonging to the cluster (cluster-ions), whose interactions with the remaining particles have to be calculated.

Then, the ions will be moved, following these steps:

1) if the cluster *move* has not been accepted, the same *move* is proposed for each cluster-ion;
2) otherwise, an opposite *move* is proposed for each cluster-ion.

These last *moves* are computationally cheap, because most of the computations required are already available from the processing of the cluster *move*.

To balance the rate of displacement for particles, also the ions not previously considered are moved.

The new displacement method is compatible with the original MM because it respects the following rules:
1) each particles configuration can be reached through a proper *move* succession;
2) the *move* acceptance is executed sequentially.

Instead there are no restrictions on the number of particles involved in one *move*, and in the extent of the displacement; the parameters only affect the acceptance probability which should be kept around 50%.

Considering that the *move* acceptance for polyelectrolytes is the critical stage in the MM method, the improvements provided by the proposed procedure mean that *move* acceptance probability is substantially greater. Conversely, they allow considerable extension of the *move* which in any case substantially reduces computing times.

Results of the simulation and improvements

The simulation environment mimics a salt-free aqueous solution of a sodium *n*-octylsulfonate with a micellar number density $\rho = 3 \cdot 10^{-6}$ Å^{-3}; the radius of micelles and ions is 15Å e di 2Å, respectively [5].

ij pairs	A_{ij} *(KJ/ Å)*	σ_{ij} *(Å)*
Micelle Micelle	7088.32	30
Ion Ion	17.7208	4
Micelle Ion	-354.416	17

Table 1- Parameters for the Hard Sphere model

The Hard Sphere Model model was chosen for the interactions between *i* and *j* particles, considering them like as spheres with an equal diameter σ and with pair potential V_{ij} expressed by:

$$V_{ij} = \begin{cases} \dfrac{A_{ij}}{r_{ij}} & r_{ij} \geq \sigma \\ \infty & r_{ij} < \sigma \end{cases}$$

Tab. 1 portrays the values used for the A_{ij}, Coulombian constant, and σ_{ij}, sum of the Hard Sphere radii of *i* and *j* particles.

A_{ij} constant is given by the product of the elementary charge numbers $(Z_i Z_j)$ by the Bjerrum length (L_B).

$$A_{i,j} = Z_i \cdot Z_j \cdot L_B \qquad L_B = \frac{e^2}{4 \cdot \pi \cdot \varepsilon_o \cdot \varepsilon_r \cdot k \cdot T}$$

where *e* is the electron charge, ε_0, ε_r are the dielectric constants in the vacuum and in the solution, *k* is the Boltzman constant and *T* is the absolute temperature. In the case we are considering, the coulombian constant A_{ij} has been evaluated with a 298° K absolute temperature and with the water relative dielectric constant equal to 78.

Simulation environment is made up by a *L* side computational cubic box with constant temperature and volume values. In this first approach we neglected the contribution of the duplicated computational boxes, considering rigid the walls of the main box.

The simulation program evaluates the Radial Distribution Function (RDF) considering the distances of all the possible micelle-micelle, ion-ion, micelle-ion pairs. Only the micelle-micelle RDF are here presented.

Figures 2, 3, 4 compare the two algorithm results; full lines refer to Metropolis method, while dashed lines refer to the Cluster Move algorithm.

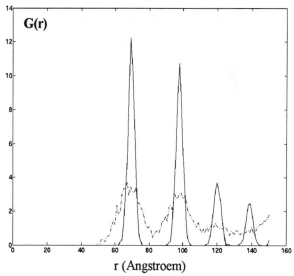

Figure 3 - RDF of micelle-micelle pairs after 100 microsteps

Figure 2 shows the energy trend as a function of the macrostep number; two different phases can be seen:
1) the first one (about 50 macrosteps), with an abrupt reduction of energy, corresponds to the migration of the ions around each micelle;

471

2) the second one, with a convergence to an asymptotic value, corresponds to the slow movements of the micelles which brings the system towards the equilibrium state.

The difference between the energy convergence rate of the two algorithms is minimal.

The RDF of micelle pairs makes possible the evaluation of the convergence speed-up for the inter-particle distance: Fig. 3 shows that after 100 macrosteps the Cluster Move algorithm is more departed from the initial site distribution than the classical algorithm implementation.

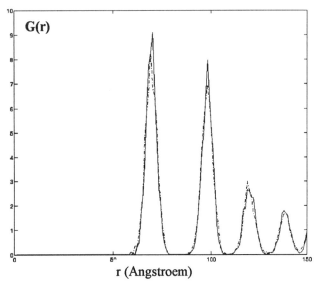

Figure 4 - Comparison between micelle-micelle pairs RDF distributions for the two algorithms

Fig. 4 shows the RDF of the original method (full line) after 200 macrosteps and of the Cluster Move method (dashed line) after 10 macrosteps: they are in practice equal, with a gain of 20 in terms of convergence velocity using the new algorithm: however, this is a favourable case; Fig. 5 portrays the trend of the gain considering different numbers of macrosteps with an asymptotic value equal to 15.

To develop a more rigorous model for the simulation we are implementing two modifications to the algorithm:

1) the first one is the introduction of the Ewald potentials to evaluate the interaction energy [6]; the Ewald method efficiently evaluates the electrostatic potential of a particle system by summing the interaction between each particle and the periodic images of all the others. It was originally developed in the course of research on ionic crystals, and successively extended to other systems. The Ewald method usually requires a substantial computing time, so slowing down the processing speed. However it allows to work on a reduced number of particles in the main box, retaining an equivalent accuracy level. Furthermore, we are developing an interpolation algorithm that allows to obtain the Ewald potentials from a 3D array with minimal computing times; of course the array is filled with values computed at the beginning of the operation;

2) in order to respect the microscopic reversibility issue [7], the *move* of a cluster is accepted only if does not involve a change in the number of ions contained. Of course, the *move* of the cluster-ions is not differentiated from that of all the free ions.

Even though the new algorithm speeds-up the calculations, simulations took tens of hours on a workstations HP-705 without reaching the convergence of the system: it is, thus, useful to develop and build a parallel system dedicated to this problem, capable to solve it in acceptable times.

Cluster Move algorithm parallelisation

We parallelised the algorithm subdiving portions of code and data among multiple Processing Elements.

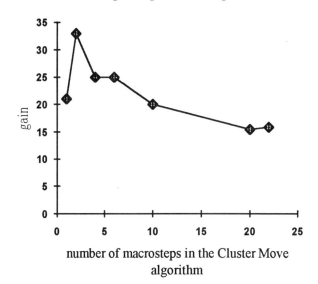

Fig. 5 - Gain of the convergence speed for the Cluster Move algorithm

The difference in the memory requirements and in computing times between micelles and ions brought us to fraction the elaboration in a first part regarding the micelles charged to a MASTER PE and more equal parts of the code regarding the ions charged on SLAVE PE's.

A number of SLAVE PE's equal to the charge asymmetry could give a good load balance in the simulation, because each node would store the same number of particles and the computing times relative to energy and RDF evaluations would be equally distributed.

The MASTER PE carries out the initialisation phase, the gathering of the results, the statistical evaluations and all the functions inherent to the user interface.

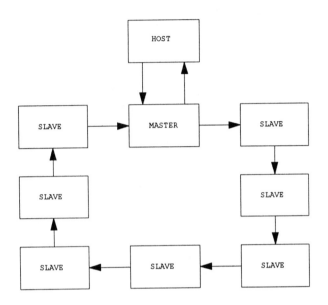

Fig. 6 - Parallel architecture proposed

During the cluster *move* the MASTER selects a micelle and evaluates a *move* for it, communicating to the SLAVE PE's the relevant coordinates; the selection of particle and *moves* are performed with a random procedure by the MASTER.

The energy variation due to the interactions between the selected micelle and all the others is evaluated by the MASTER, whilst the SLAVE PE's identify the ions belonging to the cluster associated to the extracted micelle and calculate the energy variation due to the interactions between the micelle and the ions not belonging to the cluster.

The SLAVE PE's communicate to the MASTER the composition of the cluster and compute the energy variation due to the interactions between the ions inside and outside the cluster, while the MASTER evaluates the interactions among the micelles and the ions external to the cluster.

Finally all partial results are dispatched from the SLAVE PE's to the MASTER, which carries on the *move* acceptation phase like as in the serial algorithm.

The accepted *moves* are then communicated to the SLAVE PE's for the updating of the coordinates of their ions.

Also the RDF evaluation phase is heavy from the computational point of view, since it computes the distances of all the particle pairs in the system. The parallelisation has been realised, communicating the coordinates of all the particles to all the PE's and calculating in each node their distances in an independent and concurrent way.

The parallel architecture implemented

The proposed parallel architecture implementing the Cluster Move algorithm follows from the previous considerations: one node acts as MASTER PE, while the remaining are the SLAVE PE's.

The connection topology chosen is a ring (Fig. 6), which presents three advantages:

- simplicity in the lay-out;
- easiness in the routing algorithm;
- minimization of PE idle times, since at each step of the program data arrive where they are processed.

The MASTER PE is inserted in the ring but communicates also with the user through a PC-Host Computer.

Software development environment and porting on SPC

To estimate the efficiency of the parallel version of the Cluster Move algorithm and the load balance among the PE's, a computational platform has been used. It is based on a network of HP-705 workstations clustered by PVM software package [8]

PVM transforms a network of computing machines into a parallel system, by means of system calls activating the processes on each CPU and managing data-communications among them; thus, it is possible to evaluate computing times, communication idle times and to test different architectures identifying the best suited to the algorithm implemented.

A dedicated SPC is convenient in this field of activity because it represents a desktop low-cost system available to the experimenter with a performance comparable to that of the supercomputers.

In the last years our group already developed and built a SPC dedicated to the simulation of long-range interacting spins on a 2D lattice, achieving performance similar to that of a two-unit Cray Ymp C90 [9][10].

The performance of the SPC was also tested in an application field different of that originated its development: we used it for implementing a parallel version of the Vortex Blob Model, simulating the impact of a uniform stream on a couple of circular cylinders (a classic problem of CFD). In this case the SPC performance resulted comparable to that of an

Exemplar SPP 1000 supercomputer with 8 HP 120 Mhz Risc processors [11].

The parallel architecture tested by means of PVM is ported on the SPC with the only cost of the substitution of the communication routines with those prepared for our system, referring to the existing hardware and to the required connections between the nodes. In our system this last operation corresponds to the realisation of a motherboard to which each PE has the access to communicate with each others.

Results and Conclusions

At present the following results has been assessed :
1) the simulation of the particle system presents a good agreement with the literature results about it.
To improve the adherence of the simulation results to the experimental data, we introduced the Ewald method in the evaluation of the potential instead of considering it as only due to coulombian forces.
2) the convergency of the Cluster Move algorithm is much faster than that of the original method;
3) a comparison between the network of HP-705 (*LAN*) and the *SPC* has been made considering the time to execute a macrostep. The gain results from the ratio between the resulting times expressed in seconds:

$$G_{LAN/SPC} = \frac{1676.06}{329.7} = 5.08 .$$

We have also evaluated the speedup and the efficiency of the parallelisation on a SPC with 8 PE's.
The results are:

speed-up=7.02   efficiency = 87.73%

for the simulation of a significative system of 512 micelles and 10280 ions.

From the simulations described and the executed experimentations, we can deduce that the joint use of the SPC and of the Cluster Move algorithm can give the same results obtained on a serial system, with a speed-up factor ranging from 70 to 100 times for the physical system considered.

Bibliography

[1] Luc Belloni. *Electrostatic interactions in colloidal solutions: Comparison between primitive and one component models*. J. Chem. Phys. vol. 85 - 1 July 1986.
[2] M. P. Allen, D. J. Tildesley. *Computer Simulation of Liquids*. Clarendon press - Oxford - 1987.
[3] R. W. Hockney, J. W. Eastwood. *Computer simulation using particles*. Adam Higler - 1989.
[4] N. Metropolis, A. Rosenbluth, M. Rosenbluth, A. Teller. *Equation of state calculations by fast computing methods*. J. Chem. Phys. vol. 21 - June 1953.
[5] Per Linse. *Accurate solution of a highly asymmetric electrolyte: Molecular dynamics simulation and integral equation*. J. Chem. Phys. vol. 93 - 15 July 1990.
[6] Ewald P., *Die Berechnung optischer und elektrostatischer Gitterpotentiale*, Ann. Phys. vol. 64, pp. 253-287, 1921.
[7] G. Orkoulas, A. Z. Panagiotopoulos, *Free energy and phase equilibria for the restricted primitive model of ionic fluids from Monte Carlo simulations*, J. Chem. Phys. January 1994.
[8] A. Geist, A.Beguelin, J. Dongarra, W. Jiang, R. Manchek, V. Sunderam. *PVM: Parallel Virtual Machine - A Users' Guide and Tutorial for Networked Parallel Computing*. The MIT Press Cambridge, Massachussets, London, England - 1994.
[9] G. Danese, I. De Lotto, D. Dotti, F. Leporati. *An instrument for Computational Physics*. INFM Institute Internal Report - November 1994.
[10]G. Danese, I. De Lotto, D. Dotti, D. Lanterna, F. Leporati, R. Lombardi, S. Lunghi, S. Romano. *A development environment for a parallel Special Purpose Computer (SPC)*. Annual Conference AICA '93 - Gallipoli, September 1993, pagg. 93-99.
[11]G. Braschi, G. Danese, I. De Lotto, D. Dotti, M. Gallati, F. Leporati, M. Mazzoleni, "Vortex blob models implemented on a Parallel Special Purpose Computer", Proceed. of PARCFD '96 - Parallel Computational Fluid Dynamics Conference, Capri, May 1996. To be printed.

❖ SESSION 10 ❖

Performance Analysis and Evaluation

Chair

S. Smith

The Controlled Logical Clock –
a Global Time for Trace Based Software Monitoring
of Parallel Applications in Workstation Clusters

Rolf Rabenseifner

Computing Center University of Stuttgart, Allmandring 30, D-70550 Stuttgart,
Germany, Tel. ++49 711 6855530, e-mail: rabenseifner@rus.uni-stuttgart.de

Abstract

Event tracing and monitoring of parallel applications are difficult if each processor has its own unsynchronized clock. A survey is given on several strategies to generate a global time, and their limits are discussed.

The controlled logical clock is a new method based on Lamport's logical clock and provides a method to modify inexact timestamps of tracefiles. The new timestamps guarantee the clock condition, i.e. that the receive event of a message has a later timestamp than the send event. The corrected timestamps can also be used for performance measurements with pairs of events in different processes.

The controlled logical clock is motivated and it is analyzed in detail by computer simulations. No additional protocol overhead is needed for the new method while tracing an application. It can be implemented as a filter for tracefiles or it can be integrated into monitor tools for parallel applications.

Keywords: Logical time, global time, clock, monitoring, clock synchronization, causality, distributed computing, parallel computing.

1. Introduction

With global time a correct representation of the time sequence of tracing information is possible. Parallel and distributed applications can be analyzed to obtain an insight into their behavior and their performance. On systems without global time there are different strategies of approximating a global time. This paper presents a new algorithm – the controlled logical clock. It was developed especially for workstation clusters or comparable systems and can be used as a filter for tracefiles. The processors' clocks used for generating timestamps are synchronized subsequently if the tracefile contains backward references. Backward references are messages with a timestamp of the send event that is later than the timestamp of the receive event. The controlled logical clock modifies the timestamps to fulfill the clock condition [18], i.e. the send event always has an earlier timestamp than the corresponding receive event. Besides the generation of the timestamps and their collection in the monitor tool there is no additional protocol effort. An exchange of the timestamps along with the messages is not necessary because those tools have complete insight into the trace information of the application.

The controlled logical clock requires clock differences to be limited to about 2 ms by a previous synchronization. This can be achieved by an explicit synchronization before and after the run of the application [20] and a linear interpolation – as done by several monitor tools –, or it can be done by a resources saving continuous synchronization, e. g. with xntp [22].

The controlled logical clock does not modify the timestamps of the original clocks C_i as long as the timestamp of a receive event is later than the timestamp of the corresponding send event plus the minimum message delay. The controlled logical clock is a modification of Lamport's piecewise differentiable logical clock LC_i with $dLC_i(t)/dt := dC_i(t)/dt$ as described also in [16]. Hence as opposed to this clock, the time difference $LC - C$ of the controlled logical clock is limited. It is well suited for visualizing the causal order. It can also be used for averaged time difference measurements between events in different processes. For such measurements within one process the original clock is more appropriate. But the timestamps of the controlled logical clock can be used also because, in general, its deviation is less than 5 %. The small deviation is evident because most monitor tools do not support more than one time scale.

2. Related Works

For monitoring and performance analysis of parallel and distributed applications there are different approaches to synchronizing local clocks. Lamport's discrete logical clock [18] can be used directly for monitoring [4, 31]. In addition to this Raynal [27] proposes an algorithm to prevent the drift between the logical clocks. The vector clock – an enhancement from Fidge [11, 12] and Mattern [21] – allows an equivalent representation of the causal order given by the send/receive event pairs. It is used in some monitor tools [5, 10, 19]. In [13] global events are introduced and in [25] spontaneous events (e.g. collisions on a network) are taken into account. In the summary in [29] the limits of the logical clock and the vector clock are illustrated.

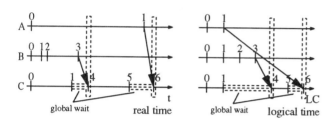

Figure 1. Global waits visualized in real time and in discrete logical time

A further limit of the usability of the logical clock is shown in Fig. 1. The example has two global waits. Process C waits until a message can be received from A or B. The time axis is dotted during periods of waiting. In the left picture the example is visualized by using a real time axis. In the right picture the logical time is used as time scale. This representation is only of limited value because it seems that process A has sent its message at $t = 1$, but this message is not taken into account in the global wait of process C also started at $t = 1$. The wait is not finished until process B sends its message at $t = 3$. This example shows that the logical clock is not sufficient for visualizing monitor information.

A representation without backward references can be achieved alternatively with a sufficiently exact synchronization of the local clocks [15, 18, 20]. Often used methods are an exact synchronization and drift estimation before the beginning of the application [8, 9] or better before and after the application [20] with a linear interpolation while the application is running. The exact synchronization can be done by deterministic [28] or probabilistic [2, 3] methods.

Continuous synchronization with little resource usage (e. g. xntp [22]) is normally not sufficiently exact due to the large jitter of the message delays in local area networks.

The trace based synchronization is another alternative. The differences between the clocks are computed by the rule that a receive event must not arrive before the send event plus the minimum transfer time. Duda [7] has developed two algorithms, one with a regression analysis, and another with a convex hull. Using a minimal spanning tree algorithm Jezequel [16] has adopted Duda's algorithm for any processor topologies. Hofmann [14] has improved Duda's algorithm by using a simple minimum/maximum strategy, and he has proposed dividing the execution time into several intervals to compensate different clock drifts in long running applications. Babaoglu and Drummond [1, 6] show that an almost no cost clock synchronization is possible if the application makes a full message exchange between all processors in sufficient short intervals. A survey of further work can be found in [30]. The limits of these methods are given by the message delay jitter, by the non linear relation of message delay and message length, and by a one-sided communication topology in some applications (e. g. producer/consumer scenarios).

The controlled logical clock is a novel development based on both Lamport's logical clocks, the discrete case and that with $dLC_i(t)/dt := dC_i(t)/dt$. It also contains components of the trace based synchronization because it does not need any further protocol overhead if it is used in monitor and debug tools. It implements a subsequent synchronization based on existing timestamps and their communication relations.

In contrary to the trace based synchronization, the controlled logical clock can also be used in systems with clock ticks longer than the minimum message delay. But the controlled logical clock needs a preceding synchronization that limits the differences between the original clocks to the fourfold of the minimum message delay.

3. The Clock Condition

For monitoring, clocks are needed which are sufficiently exact for performance measurements and which hold the clock condition defined below [18]. The clock condition must be held to enable the visualization of a program in a spacetime diagram.

Definition 1 n is the number of processes, e_i^j is the jth event in the process i, $E = \{e_i^j | i = 1..n, j = 0..j_{\max}(i)\}$ is the set of events, and $M = \{(e_k^l, e_i^j) | e_k^l$ is a send event, and e_i^j is its corresponding receive event$\}$ is the set of send/receive pairs. e_i^j is a internal event if it is not a send event and not a receive event.

For two events e_k^l, e_i^j the relation e_k^l *happened directly before* e_i^j, shortened by $e_k^l \vec{\rightarrow} e_i^j$, is held, if and only if
(a) $(e_k^l, e_i^j) \in M$, or (1)
(b) the events are in the same process and they succeed one another, i.e. $k = i \wedge l = j - 1$. (2)

478

The relation *happened before*, shortened by $\rightarrow$, is the transitive hull of the relation $\overset{.}{\rightarrow}$, i.e. the smallest relation that additionally satisfies

$$\text{(c)} \quad e_k^l \rightarrow e_i^j \wedge e_i^j \rightarrow e_n^m \implies e_k^l \rightarrow e_n^m \tag{3}$$

Definition 2 A clock $\mathcal{C} : E \mapsto \mathbf{R}$ satisfies the *Clock Condition* if and only if

$$\underset{e_k^l \in E, e_i^j \in E}{\forall} e_k^l \rightarrow e_i^j \implies \mathcal{C}(e_k^l) < \mathcal{C}(e_i^j) \tag{4}$$

Neglecting different clock drifts the following theorem can be simply shown:

Theorem 1 *If the differences between the processors' clocks are constantly less than the minimum message delay then the clock condition is held by the processors' clocks.*

A more precise theorem for theoretical continuous clocks with limited drifts can be found in [17, 20]. In [15] real clocks with discrete clock ticks are analyzed. This paper examines the case that the clock differences are in general longer than the minimum message delay, but limited by about the fourfold of the minimum message delay. This limit can be achived with low cpu and network costs by usual software synchronization tools. In this case the premise of Theorem 1 is not held.

4. The Simple Logical Clock

The simple logical clock is an enhancement of Lamport's logical clock. The name *simple* is chosen to distinguish clearly between it and the *controlled* logical clock that is itself based on the simple one.

First a *weak synchronization* must be done. There are different methods to achive clock errors less than about the fourfold of the minimum message delay, e.g. SBA – sampling before and after the application's run with a linear balancing in the meantime [20] or a low cost clock synchronization by software (timeslave, timed, xntp). Because these methods must not synchronize with the wall clock time (UTC), the synchronization is modeled with:

Definition 3 t is the wall clock time, $T(t)$ is the global time to which the process clocks $C_i(t)$ $(i = 1..n)$ are synchronized with limited errors, i.e. constants e_i^- and e_i^+ exist with $-e_i^- \leq C_i(t) - T(t) \leq e_i^+$.

Now for each process the logical clock LC_i will be defined: it nearly stops while $LC_i > C_i$ and else it equals C_i; at each receive event it is set on the maximum of its current value and of the sender's clock at the time of sending plus the minimum transfer delay μ. The minimum transfer delay should be estimated as a byproduct of the synchronization

at the beginning or at the end. This logical clock is a modification of Lamport's logical clock. In the following it is named the **simple logical clock**. In the next section it will be enhanced to the controlled logical clock.

Algorithm 1. The simple logical clock LC is exactly defined with

$$LC_i(e_i^j) := \begin{cases} \max(LC_k(e_k^l) + \mu_{k,i}, LC_i(e_i^{j-1}) + \delta_i, \\ \quad C_i(t(e_i^j))) \quad \text{if } \underset{e_k^l}{\exists} (e_k^l, e_i^j) \in M \quad (5) \\ \max(LC_i(e_i^{j-1}) + \delta_i, C_i(t(e_i^j))) \\ \quad \text{otherwise} \quad (6) \\ \text{and if } j = 0 \text{ then the terms} \\ \quad LC_i(e_i^{j-1}) + \delta_i \text{ must be omitted} \end{cases}$$

with

$\delta_i = $ minimal difference between two events in process i, i.e. δ_i are constants with

$$\delta_i > 0 \quad \wedge \quad \underset{i,j}{\forall} T(t(e_i^j)) - T(t(e_i^{j-1})) \geq \delta_i \tag{7}$$

$\mu_{k,i} = $ minimum message delay of messages from process k to process i, i.e. $\mu_{k,i}$ are constants with

$$\mu_{k,i} > 0 \quad \wedge \quad \underset{(e_k^l, e_i^j) \in M}{\forall} T(t(e_i^j)) - T(t(e_k^l)) \geq \mu_{k,i} \tag{8}$$

The global simple logical clock is then defined as

$$LC(e_i^j) := LC_i(e_i^j) \tag{9}$$

Theorem 2 *The simple logical clock LC satisfies the* **clock condition**.

Proof. The algorithm 1 satisfies Lamport's rules IR1 and IR2 in [18] and therefore holds the clock condition. $\quad\square$

In the following the error will be modeled based on C_i:

$$\underset{e_i^j}{\forall} t_0 < t(e_i^j) < t_e \quad \wedge$$

$$\underset{t : t_0 < t < t_e}{\forall} -e^- \leq -e_i^- \leq C_i(t) - T(t) \leq e_i^+ \leq e^+ \tag{10}$$

i.e. the corrected clocks C_i are at maximum e_i^+ fast and at minimum e_i^- slow in comparison with the global time T.

Theorem 3 *If all clocks C_i are not more than e^+ fast then the simple logical clock LC is also not more than e^+ fast, i.e.*

$$\underset{e_i^j}{\forall} C_i(t(e_i^j)) - T(t(e_i^j)) \leq e^+ \implies \underset{e_i^j}{\forall} LC(e_i^j) - T(t(e_i^j)) \leq e^+$$

Proof. Assuming there is a (i, j) with

$$LC(e_i^j) - T(t(e_i^j)) > e^+ \tag{11}$$

and without loss of generality e_i^j may be the earliest event satisfying (11) $\tag{12}$

479

Case a) $LC(e_i^j) = LC_i(e_i^j)$ is defined with (5). Then

$$
LC(e_i^j) - T(t(e_i^j)) \overset{(9)}{=} LC_i(e_i^j) - T(t(e_i^j))
$$
$$
\overset{(5)}{=} \max(LC_k(e_k^l) + \mu_{k,i},
$$
$$
LC_i(e_i^{j-1}) + \delta_i,
$$
$$
C_i(t(e_i^j))) - T(t(e_i^j))
$$

and (α) if in the maximum in (5) the first term is valid:

$$
\overset{(5,1^{st}\ term)}{=} LC_k(e_k^l) + \mu_{k,i} - T(t(e_i^j))
$$
$$
\overset{(8)}{\leq} LC_k(e_k^l) - T(t(e_k^l)) \overset{(12)}{\leq} e^+
$$

and (β) if in the maximum in (5) the second term is valid:

$$
\overset{(5,2^{nd}\ term)}{=} LC_i(e_i^{j-1}) + \delta_i - T(t(e_i^j))
$$
$$
\overset{(7)}{\leq} LC_i(e_i^{j-1}) - T(t(e_i^{j-1})) \overset{(12)}{\leq} e^+
$$

and (γ) if in the maximum in (5) the third term is valid:

$$
\overset{(5,3^{rd}\ term)}{=} C_i(t(e_i^j)) - T(t(e_i^j)) \overset{premise}{\leq} e^+
$$

Therefore in all three cases ($\alpha - \gamma$) there is a contradiction to the assumption (11).

Case b) $LC(e_i^j) = LC_i(e_i^j)$ is defined with (6). Then analog to the cases a) (β) and a) (γ) the contradiction can be shown.

Therefore in all possible cases a contradiction to the assumption (11) can be shown and therefore the theorem is proved. $\square$

Theorem 4 *If in a process i the clock C_i is never more than e_i^- slow then the simple logical clock LC_i in this process is also never more than e_i^- slow, i.e.*

$$
\underset{i}{\forall} \left[\underset{j}{\forall} \ T(t(e_i^j)) - C(e_i^j) \leq e_i^- \Longrightarrow \underset{j}{\forall} \ T(t(e_i^j)) - LC(e_i^j) \leq e_i^- \right]
$$

Proof. $T(t(e_i^j)) - LC(e_i^j) \overset{(9)}{=} T(t(e_i^j)) - LC_i(e_i^j))$

$$
\overset{(5,6)}{=} T(t(e_i^j)) - \left\{ \begin{matrix} \max(LC_k(e_k^l) + \mu_{k,i}, \ LC_i(e_i^{j-1}) + \delta_i, \\ C_i(t(e_i^j))) \quad \text{if} \dots \\ \max(LC_i(e_i^{j-1}) + \delta_i, \ C_i(t(e_i^j))) \text{ otherwise} \end{matrix} \right\}
$$
$$
\overset{-\max(\dots last\ term)}{\leq} T(t(e_i^j)) - \left\{ \begin{matrix} C_i(t(e_i^j)) \\ C_i(t(e_i^j)) \end{matrix} \right\} \overset{premise}{\leq} e_i^- \quad \square
$$

Observation 1 *There is no symmetry between Theorem 3 and Theorem 4: The being fast of the simple logical clock LC is limited only globally by the maximum of the being fast of all involved clocks, whereas the being slow of LC is limited in each process independently by the minimal being slow of the corresponding C_i.*

A modeling of the errors e_i^- and e^+ for continuous and discrete clocks can be seen in [26].

5. The Controlled Logical Clock

In the Algorithm 1 the term $LC_k(e_k^l) + \mu_{k,i}$ in (5) can cause the logical clock $LC(e_i^j)$ to be set forward compared to $C_i(t(e_i^j))$. At subsequent events in the same process the term $LC_i(e_i^{j-1}) + \delta_i$ in (6) causes that in principle LC **stops** (i.e. it advances only the small ticks δ_i) until it has **fallen back** to the value of $C_i(t(e_i^j))$ that is the last term in (5) and (6)).

Now the simple logical clock from Alg. 1 will be enhanced in two steps to the controlled logical clock in order to run more continuously and to prevent the alternate advancing and stopping.

Algorithm 2. LC' is the basis of the controlled logical clock:

$$
LC_i'(e_i^j) := \begin{cases} \max(LC_k'(e_k^l) + \mu_{k,i}, \ LC_i'(e_i^{j-1}) + \delta_i, \\ \quad LC_i'(e_i^{j-1}) + \gamma_i^j (C_i(t(e_i^j)) - C_i(t(e_i^{j-1}))), \\ \quad C_i(t(e_i^j))) \quad \text{if} \ \underset{e_k^l}{\exists} \ (e_k^l, e_i^j) \in M \quad (13) \\ \max(LC_i'(e_i^{j-1}) + \delta_i, \\ \quad LC_i'(e_i^{j-1}) + \gamma_i^j (C_i(t(e_i^j)) - C_i(t(e_i^{j-1}))), \\ \quad C_i(t(e_i^j))) \quad \text{otherwise} \quad (14) \\ \text{and if } j = 0 \text{ then the terms} \\ LC_i(e_i^{j-1}) + \delta_i \text{ must be omitted} \end{cases}
$$

with δ_i and $\mu_{k,i}$ defined as in Alg. 1 and with freely selectable $\gamma_i^j \in [0, 1]$. This algorithm will be completed later by the control unit in Alg. 3. The global logical clock is based on the logical clock of the individual processes

$$
LC'(e_i^j) := LC_i'(e_i^j) \quad (15)
$$

Obviously $LC_{\text{Alg.1}} = LC'_{\text{Alg.2}}$ for $\gamma_i^j \equiv 0$. For $\gamma_i^j \equiv 1$ the definition of LC' is identical with Lamport's piecewise differentiable logical clock LC with $d LC_i/dt = d C_i/dt$ for the time between receive events.

Theorem 4 – the limitation of being slow – is also valid for LC'. The proof is the same. However Theorem 3 – the limitation of being fast – is **not** valid for LC'. It is possible to construct examples for any large e and any positive lower limit γ_{min} that has for each choice of $\gamma_i^j \geq \gamma_{min}$ an event e_i^j with $LC'(e_i^j)$ being fast more than e, i.e. $LC'(e_i^j) - T(t(e_i^j)) > e$. The technical report [26] shows two examples with unlimited error increase.

In most cases – related to the distribution of the clock errors – and with normal applications, that not only communicate but also compute – one can assume that $\gamma_{min} > 0.5$, i.e. that for γ values less than 0.5 the logical clock LC' is limited in its being fast.

To limit the being fast of LC' it makes sense to control $\gamma_i^j \in [0, 1]$ by a control loop because normally γ values nearby 1 are desirable and also possible. Fig. 2 shows its

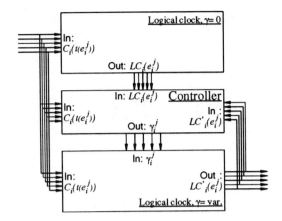

Figure 2. Control loop for γ_i^j

structure. The controller tries to limit the differences between LC' and T, i.e. it limits the output error $LC' - T$. The controller must estimate the output error indirectly because $T(t(e_i^j))$ is unknown. The input error $C - T$ can not be determined for the same reason. Provided that the errors of C_i are limited

$$\forall_{e_i^j} - e^- \leq -e_i^- \leq C_i(t(e_i^j)) - T(t(e_i^j)) \leq e_i^+ \leq e^+ \quad (10)$$

the Theorem 3 imply

$$\underbrace{LC_i - C_i}_{\text{measurable}} \leq e^+ + e_i^-$$

and the error of $LC' - T$ is limited by

$$\underbrace{(LC_i' - T)}_{\substack{\text{to be limited} \\ \text{by the controller}}} \leq e_i^+ + \underbrace{(LC_i' - C_i)}_{\text{measurable}}$$

This is the motivation for the following controller algorithm:

Algorithm 3. For this algorithm the logical clocks in the Alg. 1 and 2 are calculated stepwise. In each step s new values for $LC_i(e_i^j)$ and $LC_i'(e_i^j)$ are computed[1] for those processes $i \in P_s$ for which the input values are already determined (i.e. $i \notin P_s$, if $\exists_{e_k^l}(e_k^l, e_i^j) \in M$ and $LC_k(e_k^l)$ and $LC_k'(e_k^l)$ are not computed in a former step). After each step the control variables γ_i^j are calculated again for each $i \in P_s$ by the following algorithm:

$$D_{i,0} := q_{init} \quad (16)$$
$$D_{i,0}' := q_{init} \quad (17)$$

---

[1] j is an abbreviation of $j_{i,s}$ and $j_{i,s}$ is the index of that event, of which the logical clock is computed in process i in step s.

$$D_{i,s} := \max(LC_i(e_i^j) - C_i(t(e_i^j)),$$
$$q_{factor}(D_{i,s-1} - q_{min}) + q_{min}) \quad (18)$$
$$D_{i,s}' := \max(LC_i'(e_i^j) - C_i(t(e_i^j)),$$
$$q_{factor}(D_{i,s-1}' - q_{min}) + q_{min}) \quad (19)$$
$$\gamma_i^1 := \gamma_{max} \quad (20)$$

$$\gamma_i^{j+1} := \begin{cases} \gamma_i^j \cdot \gamma_{degress} \\ \quad \text{if } D_{i,s}' > l_{upper} \cdot D_{i,s} \quad (21) \\ \min(\gamma_i^j/\gamma_{degress}, \gamma_{max}) \\ \quad \text{if } D_{i,s}' < l_{lower} \cdot D_{i,s} \quad (22) \\ \gamma_i^j \quad \text{otherwise} \quad (23) \end{cases}$$

Explanations:

In each step, new logical clock values are computed for as many processes as possible. The proposed control mechanism computes γ_i^{j+1} only on the basis of data belonging to process i. Therefore the computation of the logical clock values can be partially parallelized and the computation of the controller can be fully parallelized.

With $q_{init}, q_{min}, q_{factor}, \gamma_{max}, \gamma_{degress}, l_{upper}$ and l_{lower} the controller must be adjusted. Based on the results in Section 6 the following values are recommended for Ethernet or FDDI based clusters: $q_{init} = 250\mu s$, $q_{min} = 250\mu s$, $q_{factor} = 0.9$, $\gamma_{max} = 0.95$, $\gamma_{degress} = 0.9$, $l_{upper} = 2.0$, $l_{lower} = 1.8$.

$D_{i,s}$ is a measurement for the deviation of the simple logical clocks LC_i from the system clocks C_i. $D_{i,s}$ computes the maximum of $LC - C$ under *forgetting* older values after some time. $q_{factor} \in (0,1)$ is the *forget-factor*, see (18). q_{min} in (18) is a lower limit for $D_{i,s}$. It says which clock errors should be tolerated. q_{min} should also be used as start value in q_{init} in (16). $D_{i,s}'$ is defined in the same way as $D_{i,s}$. It measures the deviation of the controlled logical clocks LC_i' from the system clocks C_i. $D_{i,s}'$ computes the maximum of $LC' - C$ (see (17) and (19)).

With (21) the controller tries to limit the deviation $D_{i,s}'$ as soon as it exceeds the upper limit ($l_{upper} \cdot D_{i,s}$). By the reduction of γ_i^j the behavior of the controlled logical clock becomes stepwise more alike the behavior of the simple logical clock. γ_i^j in (22) is stepwise increased as soon as $D_{i,s}'$ comes below the lower limit ($l_{lower} \cdot D_{i,s}$). The upper boundary for this increase is γ_{max}. $1 - \gamma_{max}$ determines how much the controlled logical clock is slowed down to compensate for being fast.

6. Simulation of the Controlled Logical Clock

The efficiency of the controlled logical clock defined by Alg. 2 and 3 was examined by computer simulations. The components of this computer simulation are the following:

481

(a) the simulated run of a parallel FE-computation on a regular grid produces the set of events $E = \{e_i^j\}$ with the wall clock timestamps $t(e_i^j)$, (b) simulated system clocks with a given error behavior are used to generate differences between $C(t(e_i^j))$ and $t(e_i^j)$, (c) the controlled logical clock computes the values of $LC'(e_i^j)$ and $LC(e_i^j)$, and (d) an analysis module evaluates the controlled logical clock. This section summarizes the most important results. Details can be found in the technical report [26].

6.1. The Set of Events

The base is a fictitious FE-computation with $n_1 \times n_2$ processes. Each iteration in each process consists of

1. computation of finite elements at the borders to the neighbors,
2. sending the new results to the neighbors,
3. computing the remaining finite elements,
4. and receiving the new values from the neighbors.

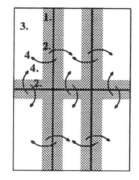

Figure 3. A fictitious parallel computation

Execution times and message delays were defined randomly between given limits. These limits were varied in different simulations.

6.2. Simulated Clock Errors

$T(t) := t$ can be chosen because the difference between T and t does not influence the outcome of the algorithms. The different clock errors used in the simulations are denoted by **pictograms**. They plot $C_i(t) - t$ against t.

Most types are continuous clocks with varying drift rates. The default maximum clock error is $\Delta = 1000\mu s$. And one type is a discrete clock with the tick length default $\tau_l = 1000\mu s$.

6.3. The Logical Clock Module

The logical clock module is an implementation of the Algorithms 1, 2 and 3. It needed approximately $\text{sizeof}(\text{void}*) \cdot n^2 + 100 \cdot n$ bytes of memory for its variables and about $\max(6.2/n^{0.0726}, 2.85n^{0.1911})\mu s$ execution time for each event on a R8000 processor, i.e. between 5 and 11 μs for each event if up to 1000 processors are producing the events.

6.4. The Analysis

Many observables were examined but only a few main results will be presented here. One advantage of computer simulations is that observables can be analyzed that are not usually accessible in real experiments. In our experiments this is the global time t and all derived observables as $LC' - T$.

For the evaluation the following observables of the controlled logical clock are used: $\overline{\mathcal{F}_{LC'}}$ the averaged being fast of LC', $\overline{\mathcal{S}_{LC'}}$ the averaged being slow of LC', and $\overline{\mathcal{A}_{LC'}}$ the averaged absolute deviation of LC'. $\overline{\mathcal{A}_{LC'}}$ is the average over all processes of the sum of $|\Delta LC' - \Delta T|$ for all the time intervals of two succeeding events and related to the whole execution time. All these observables were also examined for the simple logical clock: $\overline{\mathcal{F}_{LC}}$, $\overline{\mathcal{S}_{LC}}$, and $\overline{\mathcal{A}_{LC}}$. Then criteria for the evaluation were defined as:

- $\overline{\mathcal{F}_{LC'}}/\overline{\mathcal{F}_{LC}}$ should be less than 2, i.e. the controller should limit the being fast to the double of the being fast of the simple logical clock;

- $\overline{\mathcal{S}_{LC'}}/\overline{\mathcal{S}_{LC}}$ should be clearly less than 1, i.e. the controlled logical clock should clearly improve any being slow;

- $\overline{\mathcal{A}_{LC'}}$ is a measurement for the usefulness of the controlled logical clock for performance measurements. It should be less than 5 %.

6.5. The Results

Experiments with ⊥ and △ show that the results are fairly independent of the duration τ_{all} but strictly dependent on the clock error Δ. Experiments with different drift changing profiles like △, ◁, and ◁ show that the results are independent of these curves. Therefore the following experiment is representative of a lot of other experiments: One clock from 20 clocks is constantly 1000 μs fast.

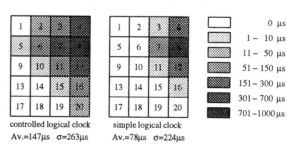

Figure 4. Average of being fast $\overline{\mathcal{F}_{LC'}}$ and $\overline{\mathcal{F}_{LC}}$

482

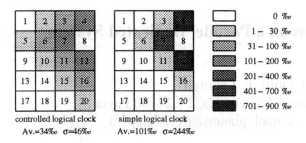

controlled logical clock
Av.=34‰ σ=46‰

simple logical clock
Av.=101‰ σ=244‰

0 ‰
1 – 30 ‰
31 – 100 ‰
101 – 200 ‰
201 – 400 ‰
401 – 700 ‰
701 – 900 ‰

Figure 5. Average of the absolute deviation $\overline{\mathcal{A}_{LC'}}$ and $\overline{\mathcal{A}_{LC}}$

Fig. 4 and Fig. 5 represent the absolute results for each process and the averages $\overline{\mathcal{F}}$ and $\overline{\mathcal{A}}$ for both logical clocks LC' and LC. Process No. 8 is fast by 1000 μs all the time. Fig. 4 shows that the controlled logical clock is not really more fast than the simple logical clock, however the controlled logical clock is fast in a wider neighborhood of process No. 8. This is a good sign because the controlled logical clock tries to bring all clocks to the fastest one. Fig. 5 shows that the absolute deviation of the controlled logical clock is clearly better than that of the simple logical clock. In the protocol of the experiment it can be seen that only in six processes $\mathcal{A}_{LC'}$ is greater than 5 % and that the maximum is 13 % whereas the simple logical clock has values of 40 - 82 % in three processes.

The criteria defined in the last section are fulfilled by the controlled logical clock in this experiment.

Another type of experiment is the usage of clocks that are slow. Here the controlled logical clock can compensate up to 65 % of the being slow. The absolute deviation of that process is reduced from $\mathcal{A}_{LC} = 96.1$ % to $\mathcal{A}_{LC'} = 13{,}2$ % ($\overline{\mathcal{A}_{LC'}} = 0.7$ %) and the critical observables are clearly less than the defined criteria.

Experiments with different height Δ of the clock error show that Δ should be limited by about the fourfold of the minimum message delay if local time differences in the area of the tenth of the minimum message delay should be measured with an error of less than 5 % in the average over all processes.

The variation of the controller parameters shows that the controller is very stable.

In the last experiment clocks with a clock tick of 1 ms are used. In this case the simple logical clock already provides all benefits. The controlled logical clock does not really improve the results but also does not make them worse.

7. Usage of the Controlled Logical Clock

The controlled logical clock is designed for *monitoring* distributed and parallel applications. The controlled logical clock can be used as a filter. A tracefile with backward references, i.e. with timestamps not fulfilling the clock condition, will be modified subsequently. Then the clock condition is guaranteed and in general performance measurements are possible with the new timestamps.

The controlled logical clock is designed primarily to work on events sequentially from the beginning. If it should be used inside of a monitor tool then there is a problem if the tool allows interactive repositioning with subsequent scrolling forward and backward. To solve this, the Algorithms 1, 2 and 3 can be started at each position in a tracefile. For scrolling backward one can use these algorithms but the sign of the timestamps must be changed and the role of the send and receive events must be exchanged. There is one disadvantage: the values of the modified timestamps depend on the choice of the start event, i.e. the user sees the same event with (slightly) different timestamp values.

By assigning two timestamps to each event the monitor can compensate for this disadvantage. The two values are

- the time of the system clocks, normally corrected by algorithms fulfilling Def. 3; it can be used for measurements of time differences inside a process or used to refer to an event;

- the time of the controlled logical clock; it can be used to visualize the events in spacetime diagrams and to measure time differences between two processes; the values depend on the start event chosen after the last repositioning.

It is recommended that an estimate of the minimum transfer delay is obtained as a byproduct of the used synchronization algorithm. The variance of the message delays has a significant region below the most frequent delay values. Our measurements in an Ethernet and an FDDI ring indicate that in general the minimum message delay is larger than a quarter of the most frequent round trip time of an empty remote procedure call.

Additional application areas are possible because the Alg. 1, 2 and 3 can be integrated into parallel applications in the same way as Lamport's logical clock. For this, only the already computed timestamps $LC_k(e_k^l)$ and $LC_k'(e_k^l)$ must be additionally transferred inside the messages $(e_k^l, e_i^j) \in M$. In this way all necessary data required to compute Alg. 1 and 2 is available in each process. The control operation can also be done locally, in which case the step index s must be substituted by the event index j.

8. Summary

The controlled logical clock is a method of correcting timestamps of a parallel application. It guarantees that the corrected timestamps fulfill the clock condition. Also the being fast of the new timestamps is bounded and the being slow is reduced. The new timestamps are suited for performance measuring and for event visualization in spacetime diagrams. Previously synchronized clocks with a maximum difference of about two milliseconds are necessary. Usually in workstation clusters such synchronization methods are already installed for other purposes. The controlled logical clock is insensitive to a drift jitter of a few percent sometimes used for synchronizing the system clocks. In combination with such synchronization methods an additional synchronization before and after the sampling can be dropped.

Mainly in the case of long execution times the controlled logical clock is better than other methods because these ones assume a little variance of the system clocks' speed.

9. Future Work

First tests of the controlled logical clock in practice as a filter for VAMPIR/PARvis [24] monitor tracefiles are done. They show that the γ reduction rule (21) can be weakened.

The principle of the current controller limits the value of γ to below 1, in the practice to 0.95. For this reason the controlled logical clock often falls back to the value of the system clock C_i. It is planed to allow $\gamma = 1$ or at least $\gamma = 1 - 10^{-5}$ with a modified controller. It is planned to modify the controller to achieve by the controlled logical clock LC' a better approximation of the maximum of all system clocks C_i.

The simulation has also shown that the clock errors should be limited to about the fourfold of the message passing delay. Reasons and more precise rules for that limitation must be examined.

Additional questions arise if one wants to use the controlled logical clock in systems combing message passing with one-sided communication, i.e. GET and PUT operations directly into the memory of a remote process. In [23] an ATM adapter is described in which the PUTs are implemented mainly in hardware. Besides the problem that normally it is not possible to record a trace event in the remote process, one must study the effects of the different latencies of the message passing and of the one-sided communication.

References

[1] O. Babaoglu and R. Drummond. (Almost) no cost clock synchronization. In *Proceedings of 7th International Symposium on Fault-Tolerant Computing*, pages 42–47. IEEE Computer Society Press, July 1987.

[2] F. Cristian and C. Fetzer. Probabilistic internal clock synchronization. In *Proceedings. 13th Symposium on Reliable Distributed Systems, Dana Point, CA, USA, Oct. 25-27, 1994*, pages 22–31. IEEE Computer Society Press, 1994.

[3] F. Cristian and C. Fetzer. Probabilistic internal clock synchronization. Technical Report CS94-367, University of California, San Diego, May 18 1995. ftp://cs.ucsd.edu/pub/team/internalProbClockSync.ps.Z, ftp://cs.ucsd.edu/pub/cfetzer/CS94-367.ps.Z.

[4] J. E. Cuny, A. A. Hough, and J. Kundu. Logical time in visualizations produced by parallel programs. In *Proceedings. Visualization '92, Boston, MA, USA, Oct. 19-23, 1992*, pages 186–193. IEEE Computer Society Press, 1992.

[5] G. v. Dijk and A. v. d. Wal. Partial ordering of sychronization events for distributed debugging in tightly-coupled multiprocessor systems. In A. Bode, editor, *Distributed Memory Computing, 2nd European Conference, EDMCC2,*

Munich, FRG, LNCS 487, pages 100–109. Springer-Verlag, April 22-24 1991.

[6] R. Drummond and O. Babaoglu. Low-cost clock synchronization. *Distributed Computing*, 6(4):193–203, July 1993.

[7] A. Duda, G. Harrus, Y. Haddad, and G. Bernard. Estimating global time in distributed systems. In *Proceedings of the 7th International Conference on Distributed Computing Systems, Berlin, September 21-25, 1987*, pages 299–306. IEEE Computer Society Press, 1987.

[8] T. H. Dunigan. Hypercube clock synchronization. Technical Report ORNL TM-11744, Oak Ridge National Laboratory, TN, February 1991.

[9] T. H. Dunigan. Hypercube clock synchronization. ORNL TM-11744 (updated), September 1994. http://www.epm.ornl.gov/~dunigan/clock.ps.

[10] D. Edwards and P. Kearns. DTVS: a distribute trace visualization system. In *Proceedings. Sixth IEEE Symposium on Parallel and Distributed Processing, Dallas, Oct. 26-29, 1994*, pages 281–288. IEEE Computer Society Press, 1994.

[11] C. J. Fidge. Timestamps in message-passing systems that preserve partial ordering. In *Proceedings of 11th Australian Computer Science Conference*, pages 56–66, February 1988.

[12] C. J. Fidge. Partial orders for parallel debugging. *ACM SIGPLAN Notices*, 24(1):183–194, January 1989.

[13] D. Haban and W. Weigel. Global events and global breakpoints in distributed systems. In *Proceedings of 21st Hawaii International Conference on System Sciences*, pages 166–175, vol. II, 1988.

[14] R. Hofmann. Gemeinsame Zeitskala für lokale Ereignisspuren. In B. Walke and O. Spaniol, editors, *Messung, Modellierung und Bewertung von Rechen- und Kommunikationssystemen, 7. GI/ITG-Fachtagung, Aachen, 21.-23. September 1993*. Springer-Verlag, Berlin, 1993. ftp://faui79.informatik.uni-erlangen.de/pub/doc/mmb93_globtime.ps.Z.

[15] R. Hofmann. Gesicherte Zeitbezüge für die Leistungsanalyse in parallelen und verteilten Systemen. Dissertation, Universität Erlangen-Nürnberg, Technische Fakultät, 1993. ftp://faui79.informatik.uni-erlangen.de/pub/doc/immd26#3.ps.Z.

[16] J.-M. Jézéquel. Building a global time on parallel machines. In J.-C. Bermond and M. Raynal, editors, *Proceedings of the 3rd International Workshop on Distributed Algorithms*, LNCS 392, pages 136–147. Springer-Verlag, 1989.

[17] J.-M. Jézéquel. *Outils pour l'expérimentation d'algorithmes distribués sur machines parallèles*. PhD thesis, Université de Rennes, 1. Oct. 1989.

[18] L. Lamport. Time, clocks, and the ordering of events in a distributed system. *Communications of the ACM*, 21(7):558–565, July 1978.

[19] W. S. Lloyd and P. Kearns. Tracing the execution of distributed programs. *Journal of Systems and Software*, 21(3):201–214, June 1993.

[20] E. Maillet and C. Tron. On efficiently implementing global time for performance evaluation on multiprocessor systems. *Journal of Parallel and Distributed Computing*, 28:84–93, 1995.

[21] F. Mattern. Virtual time and global states of distributed systems. In M. Cosnard and P. Quinton, editors, *Proceedings of International Workshop on Parallel and Distributed Algorithms, Chateau de Bonas, France, October 1988*, pages 215–226. Elsevier Science Publishers B. V., Amsterdam, 1989.

[22] D. L. Mills. Network time protocol (version 3), specification, implementation and analysis. RFC 1305, Request for Comments, March 1992.

[23] T. Mummert, C. Kosak, P. Steenkiste, and A. Fisher. Fine grain parallel communication on general purpose LANs. In *International Conference on Supercomputing, ACM, Philadelphia*, May 1996. http://www.cs.cmu.edu/afs/cs/project/iwarp/archive/nectar-papers/96ics.ps.

[24] W. E. Nagel and A. Arnold. Performance visualization of parallel programs: The parvis environment. Technical report, Forschungszentrum Jülich, 1995. http://www.kfa-juelich.de/zam/PT/ReDec/SoftTools/PARtools/PARvis.html.

[25] R. L. Probert, H. Yu, and K. Saleh. Relative-clock-based specification and test result analysis of distributed systems. In *Eleventh Annual International Phoenix Conference on Computers and Communications, Scottsdale, AZ, USA, April 1-3, 1992*, pages 687–694. IEEE, New York, 1992.

[26] R. Rabenseifner. Die geregelte logical Clock – Definition, Simulation und Anwendung. Technical Report RUS-30, Rechenzentrum, Universität Stuttgart, Germany, May 1996. http://www.uni-stuttgart.de/People/rabenseifner/log_clock_rus30.html.

[27] M. Raynal. A distributed algorithm to prevent mutual drift between n logical clocks. *Information Processing Letters*, 24:199–202, 1987.

[28] F. B. Schneider. Understanding protocols for byzantine clock synchronization. Technical Report 87-859, Department of Computer Science, Cornell University, August 1987. http://cs-tr.cs.cornell.edu/TR/CORNELLCS:TR87-859/Print.

[29] R. Schwarz and F. Mattern. Detecting causal relationships in distributed computations: in search of the holy grail. *Distributed Computing*, 7(3):149–174, 1994.

[30] Z. Yang and A. Marsland, T. Annotated bibliography on global states and times in distributed systems. *Operating Systems Review*, 27(3):55–74, July 1993.

[31] M. Zaki, M. El-Nahas, and H. Allam. DPDP: an interactive debugger for parallel and distributed processing. *Journal of Systems and Software*, 22(1):45–61, July 1993.

Machine independent Analytical models for cost evaluation of template–based programs

Davide Pasetto and Marco Vanneschi
Dipartimento di Informatica, Università di Pisa,
Corso Italia 40, 56125 Pisa, Italy,
tel +39 50 887228, fax +39 50 887226
e-mail: {davide,vannesch}@di.unipi.it

Abstract

Structured parallel programming is one of the possible solutions to exploit Programmability, Portability and Performance in the parallel programming world. The power of this approach stands in the possibility to build an optimizing template–based compiler using low time complexity algorithms. In order to optimize the code, the compiler needs formulas that describe the performance of language constructs over the target architecture. We propose a set of parameters able to describe current parallel systems and build deterministic performance models for basic forms of parallelism. This model describes construct performance in a parametric way.

1. Introduction

Parallel programming is a difficult task because the programmer should take into account a great number of problems, such as mapping, load balancing, resource usage and lots more. The major differences between existing parallel machine hardware make efficient programming a parallel application in a portable way a task even harder and often impossible. Tools should help programmers writing efficient and portable applications but unfortunately building a tool able to deal efficiently with general parallel programs is very hard due to the size and complexity of the problems involved [2]. A possible solution to this problem is the skeleton approach [12, 6, 11, 9]: restrict the program structure to basic forms of parallelism, called skeletons, composing and nesting them to build a parallel application. This approach is feasible because most parallel applications exhibit the same parallel structure exploiting the same *kind of parallelism*, such as data–parallel, pipeline and so on. Each skeleton refers to a specific form of parallelism. Having a restricted set of parallel process interaction graphs we can

devise good implementation templates, one or more for each form of parallelism, which take into account mapping, load balancing and so on, and solve the resulting problem for each architecture. It is also simpler to develop formulas which describe the performance of these templates for each machine and use these formulas to optimize both efficiency and performance.

2. Basic forms of parallelism

The parallel computation model we are interested in is **skeleton–based**: users are not allowed to use any parallel interaction structure except for a limited set of basic forms of parallelism [6]. Studying this approach we defined a structured parallel language, called P^3L [9], in which each construct denotes a specific form of parallelism, that is a single parallel interaction structure. Each construct can be istanciated using a limited set of parameters and the user builds a parallel application nesting and composing constructs. Structured parallel programs can be described using a **construct tree**, which shows how the programmer compose and nest the basic forms of parallelism. The language has a **macro dataflow semantic**: each construct is a pure functional module and data flow between constructs like a **stream of tasks**. Now we introduce the set of basic forms of parallelism (constructs) we consider in this document. Each skeleton can be implemented using several techniques and/or strategies which define **high-level templates**; in the following description we report one of these high level templates. We'll analyze the following forms:

Sequential constructs represent the leaves of the construct tree and contain the basic code blocks of the application. These constructs are pure functional modules: they receive input data from the input channel, execute their sequential algorithm and output the results to the output channel. Each data received is called **task**; successive tasks can be grouped into a **token** to

1066-6192/97 $10.00 © 1997 IEEE

reduce the overhead for sending and receiving messages. The number of tasks contained in a single token is called **task granularity**. Each sequential construct is implemented on a distinct processing element: no multitasking is allowed.

Pipe constructs express pipeline parallelism.

Farm constructs express the stream parallelism based on the independence of activation of pure functional modules on different input data.

Loop constructs are used to model parallel iterative computation of each element of the input stream.

Geometric constructs express geometric parallelism [12]: each input task is composed of an n dimensional array and we want to iterate the application of a convolution operator on each single array element. The input task can also contain data items that should be used in the computation of each update element of the array. The computation phase consists in a loop of steps; each step begins with a data gathering from a set of neighboring processors (the communication pattern is called the *stencil*) and is followed by a local computation. Both the number of iterations and the data access stencil must be known at compile time.

Map constructs denote a form of parallelism which is a special case of the geometric one. In map computations, a single function is applied to each element in the input array and the computations are all independent of each other [5, 11]. So, we do not need a data access stencil and we do not iterate.

3. Building an optimizing compiler for a structured parallel language

We developed an optimizing compiler for our structured parallel language. The compiler is based on libraries of implementation templates and on performance models for these templates on specific machines. The compilation algorithm used in our compiler is able to optimize both program performance and resource usage [3].

The compilation proceeds through the following stages:

1. Source program is analyzed and construct tree is build.

2. A first compilation is done without taking into account target machine size: the compiler examines each used construct and selects an implementation template. The selection is done computing template's maximum theoretical performance, using the template performance model, and choosing the one that obtains the best values.

3. The compiler tries to enhance program performance applying a set of rewriting rules studied to increase the parallelism exploited. All these rewriting rules maintain program semantic but modify the parallel structure in order to exploit more parallelism and obtain better performance. This phase can insert new constructs and can select smarter implementation templates that optimize specific construct compositions.

4. The compiler balances the load on all the pipelines of the program applying another set of rewriting rules, for example reducing construct performance reducing the number of workers, joining sequential stages, and so on. This phase uses the performance model to estimate the performance of each rewrite of the program.

5. At this stage the resulting program is well balanced and gets the best performance the optimizer is able to obtain on the current target system Now the compiler starts removing resources from the program in order to obtain an amount of resources small enough to run on a specific machine hardware. The resource removal process keeps the communication and computation load balanced between PEs using the performance model to compare different solutions.

6. When the amount of resources required by the program fits into the target system, an executable program is produced.

All the algorithms needed to implement such approach have a polynomial time complexity. Obviously the key point of this approach is to be able to predict program performance with a good approximation. If we devise a performance model able to describe the performance of basic forms of parallelism over all parallel machine hardware using a limited set of parameters, we will be able to port such a compiler onto different architecture just writing the physical implementation templates and adding the new machine description in the performance model. In the following sections we show how to build and use such a model for a **message passing style** implementation of the template library; we are also studying other implementation techniques like shared memory, collective operations and mixed implementations.

4. The architectural model

We are interested in MIMD architectures with distributed memory. A MIMD system is composed by a set of processing elements (PEs). Each PE is build out of one or more processors and some memory banks and is connected to one or more interconnection networks through a network interface. While the node processors are usually standard RISCs (as they come from the high speed workstation world), the network and its interface change from machine to machine. In this paper we model MIMD architecture by looking at their basic performance figures.

This approach has previously been used in other models, such as the LogP model [7]. Unfortunately this model is too restricted to predict performance with an high approximation: for example it does not include a support for special block transfer hardware (although this has been added in a successive revision), it cannot model important contention–free communication pattern, it's difficult to model situations with parallel input, output and computation, and has other severe limitation. These limits arise from the fact that LogP model has been studied to help *humans* to write applications, so it is simple enough to be used by hand.

The reference abstract architecture is standard: a set of computing elements, each with a number of network connections, and a global communication network that supports message routing. To model the performance we use the following parameters:

Processor speed. The processor must execute the sequential code that is part of the application as well as the run time support (RTS). We compute processor speed by benchmarking or simulating the time spent in executing both user and RTS code.

Network ports. Each processing element is connected to the communication network through one or more ports. The number of these ports pose an upper limit to the communications a PE can perform in parallel.

Node architecture. We must also take into account the special features allowed by a communication processor or by a specific node architecture. To obtain the better performance we wish to overlap communication and computation whenever is possible. We model overall node performance by using a function $\mathcal{P}$ which express the service time of a module that reads an input token, executes a local computation upon the received data and finally outputs a result token. If the architecture supports parallel input, output and computing, the implementation of this procedure should exploit pipeline parallelism in order to obtain better bandwidth. The function is defined as:

$$\mathcal{P}(T_{in}^c, T_{in}^o, T_{out}^c, T_{out}^o, T_t)$$

where T_t is the local task running time, T^c is the data communication time and T^o is the communication overhead, that is the time needed to setup the network interface. The model can be extended to use a family of functions indexed by the number of "simultaneous" input and output communications. This way we can model specific node architectures: for example

CM–5 nodes [13] cannot do computation and communication in parallel, so the definition of $\mathcal{P}$ is the sum of all the parameters. Transputer–based systems instead have a direct memory access engine for each communication channel and this translates in:

$$\max\{T_c + T_{in}^o + T_{out}^o, T_{in}^c, T_{out}^c\}$$

Network and interface speed. Network and interface performance can be modeled using the following parameters:

$$
\begin{array}{lcl}
T_s(len) & : & \text{send comm. time.} \\
T_r(len) & : & \text{receive comm. time.} \\
T_s^o(len) & : & \text{send overhead.} \\
T_r^o(len) & : & \text{receive overhead.}
\end{array}
$$

Grid mapping. Several basic forms of parallelism, especially data–parallel one like geometric or map constructs, operate on multi-dimensional vectors, so we must map a grid computation onto the target machine. To express the overheads of this operation we sum–up the relevant info from network type, topology, routing and flow control in two parameters. First of all we need to exchange data between logically neighboring processors one dimension at a time and (possibly) in both directions in parallel. To handle this we define the parameter g_d:

$$g_d = \begin{cases} 2 & \text{if must do one direction at a time} \\ 1 & \text{if can do both directions in parallel} \end{cases}$$

We must also know how many communications used to implement this data movement can be pipelined through the interconnection structure; to express this we define two functions, called **pipelinization factors**, the first relative to unidirectional communications and the second to bidirectional one:

$$g_p^u(\overline{D}, i)$$
$$g_p^b(\overline{D}, i)$$

where $\overline{D}$ is a vector of n elements (D_j is the number of PEs in dimension j) and i is the dimension through which we move data; this parameter heavily depends on network flow control and routing algorithm.

We don't explicit include contention in the network performance model because recent studies and experiments [4, 8, 1, 13] show that, if the communication pattern does not exhibit hot spots, message latency raises very slowly until a specific load level (dependent on routing and topological solutions) is reached. If the load increases above the threshold the network quickly saturates. This means that, if we can avoid hot spots at compile time, it is possible to use a network below his saturation point and so consider latency as a (small) constant. A structured parallel language compiler can use the available performance models, which describe the performance of each implementation template, to balance the communication and computation load of each processor and so completely avoid hot spots at compile time.

Please note that the parameters here introduced can be used to model the process networks we are interested in, that is those produced by the template based support of a structured parallel program, and do not represent a general parallel computation model.

5. Construct implementation models

Now we devise a performance model which describes the performance of each high level template described along with each language construct. This model defines the **mean service time** of each construct parametric with respect to the input task granularity (that is the number of task per input token). The inputs required by the performance model are the mean service time of the user and system sequential code and the sizes of the exchanged data. Along with each formula we briefly comment how the template must be implemented in order to perform as predicted and report some of the optimizations the compiler is able to perform.

Throughout the formulas we'll use the following parameters:

k : Input task granularity.
s_i : Size of input data.
s_o : Size of output data.
T_c : Seq. computation time.
T_o : RTS sequential code time.
n : Parallelism degree.
N : Number of array dim.
N_i : Card. of dim. i.
d_i : Size of input array elem.
d_o : Size of output array elem.
b_i : Size of input broadcasted data.
b_o : Size of output common data.

Sequential. The performance of a sequential code module derives directly from the node architecture (recall that each of them is mapped onto a different PE):

$$\mathcal{T}(k) = \mathcal{P}(T_r(ks_i), T_r^o(ks_i), T_s(ks_o), T_s^o(ks_o), kT_t)$$

Pipe. In an h stage pipeline we denote with $\mathcal{T}^i(k)$ the performance of stage i when used with input granularity k; the whole construct exhibits the following service time:

$$\mathcal{T}(k) = \max_{i=1..h} \{\mathcal{T}^i(k)\}$$

The optimization strategy must balance the load between stages to enhance resource usage; to do this it is possible to merge adjacent sequential stages that are too fast with respect to the others, to farm–out a slow stage and to insert a specific number of resources in a parallel stage to obtain a given performance.

Farm. The particular farm template we refer in this document has an emitter, a collector and some workers that run in parallel. The emitter exploits the load balancing strategy best suited for the machine architecture [10]. We call h the task granularity internally used by the construct (this granularity can be different from input task granularity) and $\mathcal{T}_w(h)$ the farm body service time. The performance of this high level template can be expressed as follows:

$$\mathcal{T}(k) = \max\{\tfrac{T_e(k,h)}{h}, \tfrac{T_c(k,h)}{h}, \tfrac{\mathcal{T}_w(h)}{n}\}$$
$$T_e(k,h) = \mathcal{P}(hT_r(ks_i), hT_r^o(ks_i), kT_s(hs_i), kT_s^o(hs_i), T_o)$$
$$T_c(k,h) = \mathcal{P}(kT_r(hs_o), kT_r^o(hs_o), hT_s(ks_o), hT_s^o(ks_o), T_o)$$

Loop construct implementation considered here uses an input process, which reads data from the input and the feedback channels and sends them to the loop body, and an output process, which computes the termination condition for each token. Construct overall performance can be defined in terms of the mean number of iterations (l) and construct internal task granularity (h):

$$\mathcal{T}(k) = l \max\{\tfrac{T_I(k,h)}{h}, \tfrac{T_O(k,h)}{h}, \mathcal{T}_{body}(h)\}$$
$$T_I(k,h) = \mathcal{P}(hT_r(ks_i), hT_r^o(ks_i), kT_s(hs_i), kT_s^o(hs_i), T_o)$$
$$T_O(k,h) = \mathcal{P}(kT_r(hs_o), kT_r^o(hs_o), hT_s(ks_o), hT_s^o(ks_o), T_o + T_{cond})$$

Geometric implementation template analyzed here uses an emitter, a collector and a set of workers logically arranged in a virtual topology like an n–dimensional grid. Data loading and collection is pipelined into the structure rows and columns. This template maps each array element on a single virtual processor in order to obtain the maximum degree of parallelism; having a bounded number of physical processors and non zero communication time, we'll need to map several virtual processors onto each physical processor. This grouping is represented by parameter d_i (data granularity for dimension i): if the i dimension of the grid has cardinality N_i, we allocate a grid with $\frac{N_i}{d_i}$ PEs in dimension i. The construct receives k requests within a token and sequentially executes them by distributing data to the available workers, computing the function in parallel on each worker and collecting the output data. Construct performance is:

$$\mathcal{T}(k) = k(T_{dis}() + T_{calc} + T_{col})$$

Data loading strategy examined here implements a pipelined distribution tree and proceeds one dimension at a time. Construct input task builds n_1 packets each consisting in a $n_2 \times n_3 \times \ldots \times n_n$ elements plus one copy of broadcasted data. The packets are loaded in the first row using a pipelined technique; then each worker in the first row builds n_2 packets splitting the data he received and adding one copy of broadcasted data and sends them down in pipeline along his column and so on until last dimension. Data collection works the reversed way. The performance of this data loading and collection strategy can be expressed as follows:

$$n_i = \frac{N_i}{d_i}$$

$$\overline{D} = [n_1, \ldots, n_N]$$

$$s_i^i = b_i + d_i d_i \prod_{j=i+1}^{N} N_j$$

$$
\begin{aligned}
T_{dis} = \; & \mathcal{P}(T_r(s_i), T_r^o(s_i), n_1 g_p^u(\overline{D}, 1) T_s(s_i^1), \\
& n_1 T_s^o(s_i^1), T_o) + \\
& \sum_{i=2}^{N} \mathcal{P}(g_p^u(\overline{D}, i-1) T_r(s_i^{i-1}), T_r^o(s_i^{i-1}), \\
& g_p^u(\overline{D}, i) n_i T_s(s_i^i), n_i T_s^o(s_i^i), T_o)
\end{aligned}
$$

$$s_o^i = b_o + d_o d_i \prod_{j=i+1}^{N} N_j$$

$$
\begin{aligned}
T_{coll} = \; & \mathcal{P}(T_r(s_o), T_r^o(s_o), n_1 g_p^u(\overline{D}, 1) T_s(s_o^1), \\
& n_1 T_s^o(s_o^1), T_o) + \\
& \sum_{i=2}^{N} \mathcal{P}(g_p^u(\overline{D}, i-1) T_r(s_o^{i-1}), T_r^o(s_o^{i-1}), \\
& g_p^u(\overline{D}, i) n_i T_s(s_o^i), n_i T_s^o(s_o^i), T_o)
\end{aligned}
$$

The pipelinization factor g_p^u is used to keep track of the conflicts that arise between different messages along the same dimension.

Finally we define the actual data access stencil as the smallest nD subcube that contains the elements referenced by a given logical processor. Data gathering operation is implemented through iterated data shift. With n data shift phases, phase i shifts data along dimension i doing $\lceil \frac{l_i}{d_i} \rceil$ communications in both directions between logically adjacent processing nodes. Each phase shift moves all the data moved by previous phases plus the local data. The number of vector elements exchanged in phase i (s_i) and the number of shifts to do in phase i (l_i') are:

$$l_i' = \left\lceil \frac{l_i}{d_i} \right\rceil$$

$$s_i = \begin{cases} 1 & \text{if } i = 1 \\ s_{i-1}(2l_{i-1}' + 1) & \text{if } i > 1 \end{cases}$$

Computation of gathering time of phase i (T_{gat}^i) depends heavily on node and network architecture: if the PE has at least 2 I/O network interfaces, to obtain a better performance we can map grid computation in such a way to do shifts in both directions in parallel (recall that the network ability to handle such a mapping is described by g_d parameter). Also we must use the pipelinization factor for data shifts, called g_p^b, to know how many communications of a particular data shift can happen in parallel.

$$
\begin{aligned}
T_{gat}^i = \; & g_d l_i' \mathcal{P}(g_p^b(\overline{D}, i) T_r(s_i d_i), \\
& T_r^o(s_i d_i), g_p^b(\overline{D}, i) T_s(s_i d_i), T_s^o(s_i d_i), T_o) \\
T_{gat} = \; & \sum_{i=1}^{n} T_{gat}^i
\end{aligned}
$$

The overall construct computation time, for an l loop computation, is:

$$T_{calc} = l\left(T_{gat} + T_c \prod_{i=1}^{N} d_i\right)$$

Obviously there are other implementation algorithms for the gather phase and they can also be modeled using the architectural parameters introduced here. The compiler should choose the algorithm which performs best for a given communication stencil. The proposed method is good if the stencil is very similar to a nD subcube centered around the requesting processor; if this is not the case other data gather strategy could move less redundant data than this one.

Map construct, as a sub-case of geometric one, can be implemented on a logical nD grid of processors and using the same data distribution and collection strategies. What changes is just the computation time because we do not iterate and don't need a data gathering phase. This leads to the following performance formula:

$$\mathcal{T}(k) = k(T_{dis}() + T_c \prod_{i=1}^{N} d_i + T_{col})$$

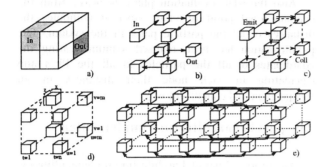

Figure 1. Templates for 3D mesh network with e–cube routing.

6. Template implementation onto real machines

Now we show how template implementors can use the high level implementation template to create process networks performing as predicted by the performance model. Process interaction structures must be defined according to network type, topology and features. Processing node architecture does not necessarily change the shape of a template for a construct but changes its performance and its speedup figures. Having a restricted and statically defined set of process graph to implement, compiler developers can map processes and communication channels aiming at reducing network contention. In order to be able to implement construct composition and nesting using simple mapping techniques, each template is defined as a process graph whose shape is a subset of the topology it is studied for.

6.1. Direct 3D mesh with e–cube routing

Several mapping strategies can be employed in 3D mesh based networks and most of them are just some kind of heuristic; in this work we report a methodology where each template is considered as a 3D cube with input and output nodes at opposite corners (see figure 1.a). The compiler should try out several different strategies in order obtain a better mapping of the program.

Pipe template is very simple and can be obtained just putting one stage after the other. This linear pipeline can be transformed in 3D by wrapping it two times. In figure 1.b we show a wrapping strategy that reduces link conflicts at minimum and works well when stages have about the same size.

Farm template is obtained by arranging all the workers plus an emitter process and a collector process in a 3D grid as shown in figure 1.c. Emitter and collector are positioned at opposite corners while workers run on every other node inside the cube; the figures show also how conflicts for link usage between emission and collection communications are reduced to a minimum.

Map Mapping a nD grid into a 3D grid is quite simple: if n is 1 (or 2) we just make a "segment" (or a plane) and wrap it up to obtain a 3D structure; if n is more than 3 we divide it in a number of 3D sub-cubes and put them one after the other (see figure 1.d). If $n > 3$ we have conflicts when doing parallel movements of data between different 3D sub-cubes. As we can see in figure 1.e, when shifting data along the fourth dimension we have link conflicts. This conflicts, whose number is equal to dimension cardinality, can result in a total communications serialization when pure wormhole flow control is used. The pipelinization factor for distribution with wormhole flow control is then equal to:

$$g_p^u(\overline{D}, i) = \begin{cases} 1 & \text{if } i < 4 \\ D_i & \text{otherwise} \end{cases}$$

while is always 1 when another flow control strategy is used.

Geometric template is the same as the map one. With this kind of topology data shifts can occur in parallel in both directions (obviously if links are bidirectional) so $g_d = 1$. As in map template wormhole flow control can reduce performance when $n > 3$. In such a machine we will map the structure in such a way that the last 3 shift phases, which move the largest amount of data, do not exhibit contention in the network. The pipelinization factor for data shifts on a wormhole network is then equal to:

$$g_p^b(\overline{D}, i) = \begin{cases} 1 & \text{if } \|\overline{D}\| - i < 3 \\ D_i & \text{otherwise} \end{cases}$$

while is always 1 with another flow control strategy.

6.2. Indirect dual generalized Fat–Tree

Generalized Fat–Tree networks are used by some commercial machine such as CM–5 and CS–2; in figure 2.a we can see the network topology for a generalized fat–tree build with 4 way by 4 way switches. Usually these networks use an adaptive or a random routing strategy and the existence of multiple paths between each pair of node makes them very powerful. The mapping strategy for this kind of systems is very simple: the process network shape is just a "segment" of processors with input from the leftmost one and output from the rightmost. *It is possible to prove that using the templates proposed here we are able to plan message routing at compile time in such a way to have no network conflicts.*

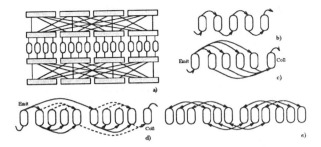

Figure 2. Templates for dual generalized Fat–Tree network.

single template and tested them extensively comparing measured and predicted times. Figure 3 reports example values obtained during single construct tests.

number of workers	predicted performance	measured performance	error
2	15239	14945	1%
4	7619	7373	3%
6	5079	4946	2%
10	3047	3070	0.7%
15	2435	2642	7%
20	2435	2658	7%

Figure 3. Comparison between predicted and measures service time for farm construct on Cray T3D.

program name	predicted performance	measured performance	error
DPR	23.5	26.5	11%
DFR	0.0012	0.0013	7%
CFL	0.068	0.07	2%
CAT	23.5	25	6%
DEL	19.2	20	4%

Figure 4. Comparison between predicted and measured service time for test applications (all times are in seconds).

Pipe mapping strategy is very simple: stages are putted one after the other and communication happens alternatively through the upper and the lower network. We can see the resulting shape in figure 2.b.

Farm template consists of a processing node that implements the emitter, one that implements the collector and a set of workers in the middle of these two processing nodes. Emission and collection communications happen on two different networks to avoid link conflicts between different message types (see figure 2.c).

Map implementation consists in a hierarchy of farm–like structure, one for each dimension (see figure 2.d for an example of 2D map). It is also simple to show that data distribution always happens in pipeline and so $g_p^b(\overline{D}, i) = 1$

Geometric workers are laid out one row after the other, one dimension after the other; during data loading phase communication happen like in map template while data shifts, used in stencil gather implementation, work as in the pipeline template with communication placed alternatively on the upper and on the lower net (see figure 2.e for a 2D geometric horizontal shift). With this kind of interconnection structure is possible to do data shifts in parallel in both directions, so g_d is 1, and is simple to show that different messages do not conflict due to network redundancy of paths and especially for the availability of two networks so also $g_p^u(\overline{D}, i)$ is 1.

7. The performance model validated

To validate the precision of this performance model we measured the parameters of some commercial parallel architectures and wrote a set of benchmarks composed of a

To validate the correctness of the model with construct composition and nesting we wrote a number of testing applications and compiled them with our compiler. The test programs are [14]:

DPR Data parallel ray-tracer, a simple parallelization of a sequential algorithm obtained mapping it onto every image pixel.

DFR Data flow ray-tracer, another parallel version obtained by a data flow analysis of the sequential code.

CFL Circuit fault list analysis, about 1000 gate circuit with 1600 possible faults.

CAT Computer aided thermography image analysis, 32 by 32 pixel images.

TDE Three dimensional delaunay triangulation, 1024 point dataset.

Figure 4 reports the results obtained from runs of the test applications and compares them with predicted performance values. The values are relative to process network service time. The absolute performance of all these programs is usually very high, for example to compute each image DPR takes 140 seconds of CPU time on an HP 9000/735 workstation with 64Mbytes of RAM and just 27 seconds with 40 T800. As we can see, the error in the analytical prediction of the service time is very low.

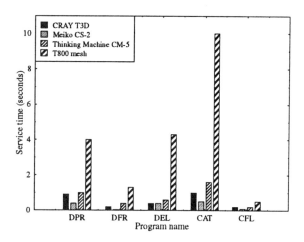

Figure 5. Testsuit programs minimum service time over different parallel architectures.

A comparison between the predicted service time of the various programs over some parallel architectures is reported in figure 5; note that circuit fault list service time is multiplied by 100 and dataflow ray-tracer by 1000 to make the graph visible.

8. Conclusions

In this paper we show a performance model that can be used during the development of a template–based compiler to build formulas that describe the performance of parallel construct in an architectural independent way. The performance model is complex and covers several aspects of machine hardware, such as network speed, coprocessor hardware, internal processing node parallelism, etc.. This model is not intended to be used directly by users but to be included in a template–based compiler for a structured parallel language. Its complexity, much higher that other performance models like LogP, can achieve a good degree of precision in predicting parallel structures performance and allows for several program optimizations.

References

[1] V. S. Adve and mary K. Vernon. Performance Analysis of Mesh Interconnection Networks with Deterministic Routing. Technical Report 1001b, University of Wisconsin–Madison, Computer Science Department, July 1993.

[2] S. Antonelli and S. Pelagatti. On the complexity of the mapping problem for massively parallel architectures. *International Journal of Foundations of Computer Science*, 3(3):379–387, Sept. 1992.

[3] B. Bacci, M. Danelutto, and S. Pelagatti. Resource optimization via structured parallel programming. In K. Decker and R. Rehmann, editors, *Programming Environments for Massively Parallel Distributed Systems*, pages 13–25. Birkhäuser Verlag, Basel, Switzerland, 1994.

[4] L. N. Bhuyan, Q. Yang, and D. P. Agrawal. Performance of Multiprocessor Interconnection Networks. *IEEE Computer*, pages 25–37, Feb. 1989.

[5] R. S. Bird. An introduction to the Theory of Lists. In M. Broy, editor, *Logic of programming and calculi of discrete design*, volume F36 of *NATO ASI*, pages 5–42. Springer-Verlag, 1987.

[6] M. Cole. *Algorithmic Skeletons: Structured Management of Parallel Computation*. The MIT Press, Cambridge, Massachusetts, 1989.

[7] D. E. Culler, R. Karp, D. Patterson, et al. Logp: Towards a realistic model of parallel computation. In *Proc. of Fourth ACM SIGPLAN Symp. on Principles and Practice of Parallel Programming*, San Diego, CA, May 1993.

[8] W. J. Dally. Performance Analysis of *k*–ary *n*–cube Interconnection Networks. *IEEE Transactions on Computers*, 39(6):775–785, June 1990.

[9] M. Danelutto, R. D. Meglio, S. Orlando, S. Pelagatti, and M. Vanneschi. A methodology for the development and the support of massively parallel programs. *Future Generation Computer Systems*, 8:205–220, Aug. 1992.

[10] M. Danelutto, S. Pelagatti, and M. Vanneschi. An analytic study of the processor farm paradigm. Technical Report TR–3/132, Progetto finalizzato C.N.R. "Sistemi Informatici e Calcolo Parallelo", sottoprogetto "Architetture Parallele", May 1994.

[11] J. Darlington, A. Field, P. Harrison, P. Kelly, R. While, and Q. Wu. Parallel Programming using Skeleton Functions. In A. B. M. Reeve and G. Wolf, editors, *Proc. of PARLE'93*, volume 694 of *LNCS*, pages 146–160. Springer-Verlag, 1993.

[12] H. Kung. Computational models for parallel computers. In R. J. Elliott and C. A. R. Hoare, editors, *Scientific Applications of Multiprocessors*, pages 1–17. Prentice Hall, 1989.

[13] T. T. Kwan, B. K. Tatty, and D. A. Reed. Communication and Computation Performance of the CM–5. In *Supercomputing '93*, pages 192–201, Nov. 1993.

[14] D. Pasetto and M. Vanneschi. Design and evaluation of parallel applications using a structured parallel language. In *International Conference on Parallel and Distributed Processing Techniques and Applications (PDPTA'96)*, Sunnyvale, CA, Aug. 1996.

Automatic Generation of GSPN Models for the Performance Evaluation of Heterogeneous Applications

Cosimo Anglano *
Dipartimento di Informatica, Università di Torino
email: mino@di.unito.it

Abstract

The allocation of the tasks of heterogeneous applications on the machines of the system is crucial to achieve adequate performance. The development of effective allocations is dependent upon the possibility of obtaining accurate predictions of the performance of the application. In this paper we present a technique for the automatic generation of performance models of heterogeneous applications starting from Zoom, a high-level graphical formalism for the representation of heterogeneous applications. Generalized Stochastic Petri Nets are used to specify these performance models. A testbed heterogeneous application is used to illustrate the proposed technique.

1. Introduction

In the last decade distributed heterogeneous systems, consisting of a collection of autonomous high-performance machines connected by a fast communication network, have emerged as a powerful and cost-effective platform for the execution of computationally intensive applications. The feasibility of the heterogeneous implementation of these applications, and the performance gains that is possible to achieve, have been demonstrated in the past [5, 7, 8, 10, 11, 13, 15]. Typical heterogeneous applications are composed of few coarse grained, resource intensive tasks, which are concurrently executed on the machines of a heterogeneous systems. By exploiting both parallelism and heterogeneity in their code, these applications may achieve higher performance than possible in a homogeneous system [9].

To effectively use the potentialities of heterogeneous systems, it is crucial to individuate potential affinities existing among the tasks of the application and the machines of the system, and to exploit them by means of task mappings which promote performance. To distinguish good mappings from ineffective ones, the performance of the application under the various task allocations must be evaluated. This evaluation is typically performed by using a performance model of the system, which is obtained by joining a model of the application with a model of the computing platform. This paper focuses on the construction of performance models of heterogeneous applications, while the construction of performance models of heterogeneous computing platforms is left for a further study

In this paper we shall use as modeling formalism Generalized Stochastic Petri Nets [1], a timed extension of Petri nets [1] in which transitions are associated either with a zero delay (*immediate transitions*) or with an exponentially distributed random delay (*timed transitions*). Our choice is motivated by the encouraging results obtained by using GSPN models for the performance evaluation of heterogeneous applications [3]. Preliminary results discussed in [3] show indeed that GSPN models may provide accurate predictions for the execution time of heterogeneous applications. Moreover, the small number of tasks typical of heterogeneous applications leads to models with modest size, which could be analyzed with a reasonable computational costs. However, despite these advantages, the practical applicability of GSPN models may be limited by the difficulty of building them, which is due to the fact that the level of abstraction more suited to describe the programs (and with which heterogeneous programmers are more familiar) is different from the one supported by Petri nets, where everything must be represented in terms of places, transitions, and tokens. Filling the gap between these two levels is often difficult and error-prone.

With the aim of alleviating this difficulty, in this paper we propose a technique for the automatic construction of GSPN models of heterogeneous applications. The main idea is to use a a high-level graphical language (Zoom [4]) to describe the characteristics of the application, and to automatically translate this description into a GSPN model. By separating

---

*This work has been partially supported by the EEC-HCM project No. CHRX-CT94-0452 "MATCH" and by the italian MURST under projects 40% and 60%

[1]In this paper we assume that the reader is familiar with GSPNs. The interested reader may refer to [2] for a presentation of the formalism.

the application specification from the model generation, heterogeneous programmers can exploit the benefits provided by GSPN models without having to deal directly with their construction.

The paper is organized as follows. Section 2 briefly introduces Zoom, while Section 3 describes the translation technique. Section 4 illustrates the use of this technique by applying it to a testbed heterogeneous application. Finally, Section 5 concludes the paper and outlines future research directions.

2. Zoom

Zoom is a graphical, hierarchical formalism for the representation of heterogeneous applications. Zoom provides a hierarchy of three levels to model applications: (a) The *structure level*, which represents an application in terms of its units of parallel execution and their data dependences; (b) The *implementation level*, which represents the information about the different implementation alternatives available for each application task; (c) The *resource level*, which represents the information about the computational and communication resource requirements of each of the above alternatives. For more details on Zoom, the interested reader may refer to [4].

Structure Level The structure level representation of a heterogeneous application H consists of a directed graph SG_H, called *structure graph*, whose nodes represent the application tasks and whose edges represent data dependencies among them. The nodes of SG_H are partitioned into two subsets, called *coupling nodes* and *structure nodes*. Coupling nodes represent the tasks of the application (named *coupling units* in the Zoom terminology), and are graphically depicted as boxes labeled with the name of the coupling units they represent. The data dependencies among coupling units are represented by means of *data flow edges*, graphically depicted as directed dashed arcs whose direction indicates the flow of data. Coupling nodes execute according to the *non-strict macro dataflow* paradigm [4], a variation of the dataflow paradigm in which nodes are allowed to start their computation using a subset of their input arcs. Consequently, data flow edges represent just dependencies, and not precedences among nodes.

Complex computation patterns involving several coupling nodes are represented by enclosing the above nodes into pairs of structure nodes. Structure nodes are of three types: *Phase nodes*, *iteration nodes*, and *terminal nodes*. Phase nodes allow to represent the computation phases [2] of an application. The first and the last phases are indicated

by means of terminal nodes (labelled respectively *INITIAL* and *FINAL*) [3]. Finally, iteration nodes enclose portions of the application whose execution is iteratively repeated for a fixed number of times or until a given condition is satisfied.

Implementation Level The implementation graph IG_H of application H is obtained by "expanding" the coupling nodes and the data flow edges of the structure graph SG_H. Each coupling node is associated with set of *instances*, representing the set of different implementations which are available for the corresponding coupling unit. Graphically, instances are represented as ovals, embedded into the corresponding coupling node and labeled with the name of their target machine. The instance of coupling node A with label X is denoted as A_X.

An *executable configuration* represents a mapping of the application tasks on the machines of the system. Graphically, an executable configuration is shown by lightly shading the ovals corresponding to the coupling unit instances used in the particular mapping, and by modifying the shape of data flow edges according to the interactions among the specified instances. In particular, if the execution of two communicating coupling units is pipelined, the edge connecting them is drawn as a *tube* (represented as two parallel lines terminating into an arrow), while if their execution is serialized the edge is drawn as a *wire* (depicted as a continuous line). Finally, if *data conversion routines* are necessary to convert the data exchanged between two instances, a square is drawn on the corresponding edge.

Resource Level The resource requirements of a given instance are specified by abstractly representing its execution as evolving through a sequence of *segments*, each of which is associated with the information concerning its resource requirements. Roughly speaking, a segment corresponds to a portion of the computation comprised between a "send" and a "receive" communication operation, that is to the processing of some input data and to the consequent communication of the produced results. The segments of an instance A_X are represented by means of the *segment table* $S[A_X]$, which contains an entry for each segment. Each entry contains three fields, named respectively *From*, *Time*, and *To*. *From* contains a pair $\langle X_i, w_{X_i} \rangle$ for each coupling unit X_i whose output is used as input by the segment; w_{X_i} is the number of data items (produced by X_i) needed by the segment in order to start its execution. The field *To* contains the list $\langle Z_1, \ldots, Z_m \rangle$ of the coupling nodes to which the data produced by the segment are sent. Finally, the field *Time* contains a pair $\langle K, T(x_1, \ldots, x_m) \rangle$, where K is the number of computation subdomains in which the segment computa-

---

[2] A phase is the coordinated execution of a subset of coupling units solving one of the subproblems in which the general problem addressed by the application can be decomposed.

[3] For the sake of the clarity of pictures, the terminal nodes are omitted whenever the application has a single phase

tion is subdivided and $T(x_1, \ldots, x_m)$ is a function expressing the duration of the above computation.

The last resource level entity is the *conversion matrix* $M_{A,B}$, which represents the information about the data conversions required by the communications between the (selected instances of) coupling nodes A and B. In particular, it contains the information concerning the machine on which the conversions are performed and their time durations.

3. Translating Zoom Models into GSPNs

The translation of a Zoom model into a GSPN is performed through a sequence of translation steps, in which an initial abstract GSPN model, representing the general structure of the application, is refined into the final model of the particular executable configuration under consideration. In the first step, for each phase a GSPN *template* (i.e. a GSPN in which timed transitions abstract complex computation patterns) is constructed. The second translation step consists in the replacement of the timed transitions of the phase templates with the GSPN models of the corresponding complex computations. Finally, all these GSPN submodels are composed, by superposition of places with equal name, to obtain the GSPN model of the entire application.

3.1. Generation of Phase Templates

The GSPN template of a generic phase is depicted in Fig. 1. Timed transitions $X1, \ldots, Xn$ correspond to the *macro*

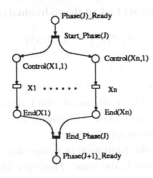

Figure 1. GSPN template of a generic phase

computations which is possible to form with nodes belonging to the phase. A macro computation is a set of nodes containing either (a) a single coupling node not belonging to any iteration body or (b) all the (coupling and structure) nodes belonging to an iteration body which is not nested into another iteration body.

The beginning of the phase execution is represented by the firing of transition *Start_Phase(J)*, occurring when place *Phase(J)_Ready* is marked (i.e. when the previous phase is terminated), which enables the transition $X1, \ldots, Xn$. The firings of the above transitions, which abstractly represent the termination of the corresponding macro computations,

enable the transition *End_Phase(J)*, which in turn represents the termination of the computation of phase J. Initially place *Phase(1)_Ready* is marked, indicating the phase from which the application computation starts.

3.2. Refinement of Phase Templates

After the GSPN templates of phases have been generated, each of them is considered in turn, and the timed transitions $X1, \ldots, Xn$ it contains are refined into the subnets $\tau(X1), \ldots, \tau(Xn)$ modeling the corresponding macro computations. The refinement process is accomplished by applying the procedure **refine()** shown in Fig. 2 to each transition Xi. This procedure works as follows: If Xi corre-

---

procedure refine(Xi):
if Xi **corresponds to a coupling node**
then generate $\tau(Xi)$;
else begin
    generate the template $IT(Xi)$;
    for each timed transition $B_i \in IT(Xi)$
    do refine(B_i);
end

Figure 2. Procedure for the refinement of timed transitions

sponds to a single coupling node, then $\tau(Xi)$ is generated directly from the corresponding resource level representation (see below). Conversely, if Xi corresponds to an iterative computation, a GSPN *iteration template* $IT(Xi)$ is generated and subsequently refined by the recursive invocation of **refine**.

GSPN templates of iterative computations The GSPN template of an iterative computation is generated analogously to phase templates. First, the nodes making up the iterative computations are grouped into macro computations (by using the same grouping rule described for phase templates). Subsequently, an iteration template $IT(Xi)$, whose generic structure is depicted in Fig. 3, is generated. The beginning of the iterative computation is represented by transition *Start(Xi)*, whose firing has the effect of marking places *Iter_Left(B1), \ldots, Iter_Left(Bn)* with N tokens, where N is the number of iterations which have to be performed (as specified in the structure graph of the application). The beginning of the execution of the $i - th$ macro computation is represented by the firing of transition *Next_Iter(Bi)*, while its termination is represented by the firing of transition Bi. The N repetitions of macro i computation are represented by repeating the firing sequence *Next_Iter(Bi)*-Bi N times, that is until place *Iter_Left(Bi)* is empty and place *End(Bi)* is marked. When all the above sequences

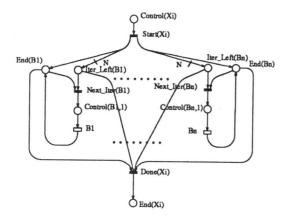

Figure 3. Skeleton of the generic iterative computation

have been fired, transition *Done(Xi)* is enabled and may fire (note the presence of the inhibitor arcs connecting places *Iter_Left(B1),...,Iter_Left(Bn)* to *Done(Xi)*).

GSPN models of instances. The GSPN model of a given instance A is constructed by composing the GSPN models of its segments. The GSPN model of the j-th segment of A, with input list $\langle X1, w_{X1} \rangle, \langle X2, w_{X2} \rangle, \ldots, \langle Xn, w_{Xn} \rangle$ and output list $\langle Z1, Z2, \ldots, Zm \rangle$, is shown in Fig. 4. Transition *Start(A,j)* represens the beginning of the segmen-

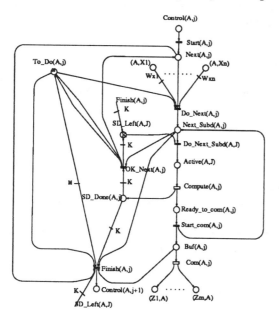

Figure 4. GSPN model of segment j of instance A_X

t's activity and fires when the computation of the previous segment is terminated (i.e. when place *Control(A,j)* is marked). The activity of the segment, which consists in the processing of the different computation subdomains, is repeated until all the input data items produced by the coupling nodes $X1, \ldots, Xn$ (represented by places *(A,X1),...,(A,Xn)*) have been processed. The beginning of each repetition is represented by transition *Do_Next(A,j)*. The number M of repetitions is represented by place *To_Do(A,j)*, which initially contains M tokens. This number depends on the total number of data items produced by each node Xi and on the value of w_{Xi}. In particular, if M_{X_i} is the number of times X_i's computation is repeated, and K_{X_i} is its number of subdomains, then $M = (M_{X_i} \cdot K_{X_i})/w_{Xi}$. Any pair $\langle X_i, w_{Xi} \rangle$ in the input list may be used in the above calculation, since in a correct Zoom model the relation $(M_{X_i} \cdot K_{X_i})/w_{Xi} = (M_{X_j} \cdot K_{X_j})/w_{Xj}$ must hold for each pair i, j.

Place *SD_Left(A,j)* keeps track of the number of subdomains that remain to be processed in order to complete the current repetition (it is initially marked with K tokens, where K is the number of computation subdomains of the segment). Transition *Do_Next_Subd(A,j)* represents the beginning of the processing of a subdomain, while its completion is represented by the timed transition *Compute(A,j)*, whose firing rate [4] is computed by using the function contained in the *Time* field of the corresponding segment table entry. After *Compute(A,j)* fires, transition *Start_com(A,j)*, representing the beginning of the communication operation, is enabled and may fire, enabling in turn transition *Com(A,j)*. This transition represents the completion of the above communication, and its rate is computed by dividing the size of the data items (produced by the segment) by the available network bandwidth. If the communication is asynchronous, that is the segment can start to process the next subdomain before the data items have been delivered to the corresponding segments, then – as indicated in Fig. 4 – place *Next_Subd(A,j)* is marked immediately after the firing of *Start_com(A,j)*. The case of synchronous communication is modeled by connecting transition *Com(A,j)* to place *Next_Subd(A,j)* and by removing the arc connecting this place with transition *Start_com(A,j)*.

Place *SD_Done(A,j)* keeps track of the number of subdomains already processed. When this place is marked with K tokens (i.e. all the subdomains have been processed), the current repetition terminates. If there are still repetitions to be performed (place *To_Do(A,j)* contains at least one token), then transition *OK_Next(A,j)* may fire, bringing the system back to a state in which a new repetition can start. If, conversely, all the repetitions have been completed (place

---

[4]Note that now, unlike the template case, timed transitions represent "basic" activities such as computations and communications which can be naturally associated with a delay.

To_Do(A,j) is empty), then transition *Finish(A,j)*, which represents the termination of the segment activity, may fire. If segment *j* is the last one of the corresponding instance, then the output place of *Finish(A,j)* is labeled *End(A)* rather than *Control(A,j+1)*.

Finally, the overhead due to the possible presence of data conversion routines is represented by composing the model of the related segment with one of the GSPN subnets depicted in Fig. 5(a)–(b). In the case of conversion performed

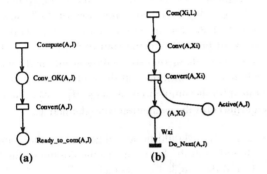

Figure 5. Conversion on (a) the sending (b) the receiving machine

on the sending machine (Fig. 5(a)), the timed transition *Convert(A,j)*, representing the completion of the conversion operation, fires after the subdomain has been processed and before the communication operation takes place. In the other case (Fig. 5(b)), the conversion operation is represented by transition *Convert(A,Xi)*, which fires before the destination coupling node *Xi* uses the data which have to be converted. Transition *Convert(A,Xi)* is replicated for each destination coupling unit. The rates of these transitions is are set according to the information contained in the conversion matrices.

3.3. Performance Indices

The GSPN models generated as discussed above allow to estimate several performance indices which may help programmers to assess and to predict the efficiency of heterogeneous applications. In this section we discuss how these indices, defined abstractly in terms of application entities (e.g. coupling units and communications) can be expressed in GSPN terms and computed by means of analysis techniques typical of this formalism.

The first performance index of interest is the average execution time *ET* of a given executable configuration. To compute a steady state estimate for *ET*, the GSPN model should account for infinite executions of the application. This is accomplished by adding to the model an immediate transition *END* which brings the system from the final state back to the initial one by "moving" the token from place *End_Comp* to place *Phase(1)_Ready* (this corresponds to restarting the ap-

plication an infinite number of times). *ET* is then computed as $1/X(END)$, where $X(t)$ denotes the throughput of transition *t* (i.e. its average number of firings in unit time.)

If the efficiency achieved by a given executable configuration is not satisfactory, then it is necessary to find and remove the sources of the inefficiency. To individuate these performance bottlenecks, it is sufficient to identify the coupling unit instances which do not produce their outputs fast enough to keep other instances busy, and that consequently slow down the entire execution of the application. The efficiency of a given instance A_X is estimated by evaluating the efficiency of each of its segments. Given the *j*-th segment of A_X, we compute the probability $P_S(A_X^j)$ that it is not ready to process immediately its inputs. In GSPN terms, $P_S(A_X^j)$ is defined as:

$$P_S(A_X^j) = \mathcal{P}\{\#Next(A_X, j) = 0 \bigwedge_{i=1}^{n} \#(A_X, Xi) \geq w_{Xi}\}$$

$$(1)$$

where $\mathcal{P}\{A\}$ and $\#p$ denote respectively the probability of event *A* and the number of tokens in place *p*. An high value of $P_S(A_X^j)$ means that the segment cannot process its inputs fast enough, so the instance to which it belongs may be a bottleneck. Conversely, a small value of $P_S(A_X^j)$ means that there are high chances that, when the inputs of the segment have been already delivered, it is ready to process them. However, this does not necessarily mean that the segment produces its output at its maximum speed, since it may be forced to wait a relatively long time before all its inputs become available. To find out if this is the case, we use the performance index $Wait(A_X^j)$, the fraction of time that the *j*-th segment of A_X spends idle waiting for input. In GSPN terms, $Wait(A_X^j)$ is defined as:

$$Wait(A_X^j) = \overline{M}[Next(A_X, j)] \qquad (2)$$

where $\overline{M}[p]$ denotes the average marking of place *p*. If $Wait(A_X^j)$ is close to 1, then the segment is slowed down by some "slow" input not produced fast enough. These "slow" inputs can be identified by computing, for each input coupling unit X_i, the probability $P_W(A_X^j, X_i)$ that the segment is waiting for the output produced by X_i. In GSPN terms, we have:

$$P_W(A_X^j, X_i) = \mathcal{P}\{\#Next(A_X, j) = 1 \wedge \#(A_X, Xi) < w_{Xi}\}$$

$$(3)$$

That is, $P_W(A_X^j, X_i)$ is computed as the probability that place $Next(A_X, j)$ is marked (i.e. the segment is ready to start another repetition of its computation) and that place (A_X, Xi) does not contain enough tokens to enable transition $Do\_Next(A_X, j)$.

4. An Example

To give an example of the application of the technique described in the previous section, let us consider the heterogeneous application whose Zoom representation is shown in

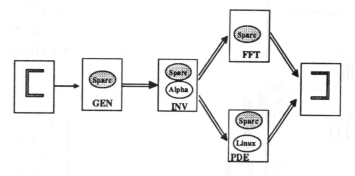

Instance	From	Time	To
GEN_{Sparc}	$\langle ENV, 1 \rangle$	$\langle 1, 23841.1 - 1835.53N + 26.1468N^2 + 1.10738N^3 \rangle$	$\langle INV \rangle$
INV_{Sparc}	$\langle GEN, 1 \rangle$	$\langle 1, -4774.29 + 1351.09N - 20.3145N^2 + 1.31916N^3 \rangle$	$\langle FFT, PDE \rangle$
INV_{Alpha}	$\langle GEN, 1 \rangle$	$\langle 1, -11272.6 + 1523.71N - 26.1471N^2 + 0.707264N^3 \rangle$	$\langle FFT, PDE \rangle$
FFT_{Sparc}	$\langle INV, 1 \rangle$	$\langle 1, 368 + 27.2552N + 18.2368N^2 + 0.0115458N^3 \rangle$,	$\langle ENV \rangle$
PDE_{Sparc}	$\langle INV, 1 \rangle$	$\langle 1, 10417 - 687.365N + 94.0127N^2 - 0.0699259N^3 \rangle$	$\langle ENV \rangle$
PDE_{Linux}	$\langle INV, 1 \rangle$	$\langle 1, -91771.4 + 12257.4N - 542.268N^2 + 15.5485N^3 \rangle$	$\langle ENV \rangle$

Figure 6. Zoom model of the example application

Fig. 6. This example program, developed to mimic the behavior of typical heterogeneous applications, has been implemented by coupling the executions of different scientific codes (taken from [12]) by means of PVM3.3 [14]. In this way, not only the behavior, but also the computation and communication requirements of the application are similar to those of real heterogeneous programs. The application is made up by four coupling units:

- **GEN**, which generates a set of K square matrices of floating point numbers and sends each of them to *INV*; a random number generator is used to generate the matrix entries. K and the order of the matrix (N) are provided as initial input (as indicated by the keyword *ENV* in the segment tables);

- **INV**, which computes the inverse of each matrix received from *GEN*, and sends it to both *FFT* and *PDE*. Two implementations are available: the first runs on Sun SPARC platforms, and uses an algorithm bases on LU decomposition and backsubstitution, while the second one runs on DEC-Alpha machines and employs the Gauss-Jordan algorithm;

- **FFT**, which computes the fast cosine transform of the N points corresponding to each column of the received matrix; consequently, N computations are performed on each matrix. The output of *FFT* is stored on disk (as indicated by the keyword *ENV* in the segment table);

- **PDE**, which computes the solution to the Poisson equation having as coefficients the values stored in the received matrix. Two implementations are available: the

first one runs on Sun SPARC platforms and uses a full multigrid algorithm, while the second one runs on machines running Linux and uses SOR with Chebyshev acceleration. As for *FFT*, the output of *PDE* is stored on disk.

In our example, the application is executed on a cluster of workstations which consists of two Sun SparcStation Classic respectively with 16 and 32 MBytes of main memory, one Sun SparcStation ELC with 16 MBytes of RAM, one Sun SparcStation 10 with 80 MBytes RAM, one DEC Alpha 3000 with 64 MBytes of RAM, and a PC based on an Intel Pentium 100Mhz. with 16 MBytes of RAM. These machines are connected by an Ethernet network, providing a bandwidth of 0.7 MBytes/sec. The codes have been run on the above machines for different input sizes in order to determine the execution time (expressed in μsec.) as function of N. In particular, we ran GEN on the Sparc ELC, INV on the DEC-Alpha 3000 and on the Sparc Classic with 32M, FFT on the other Sparc Classic, and PDE on the PC and on the Sparc 10. From the measured execution times, we have determined the functions reported in the **Time** fields of the segment tables (shown in Fig. 6) by curve fitting.

The translation technique applied to the Zoom model of Fig. 6, yields the GSPN model shown in Fig. 7. The application has only one phase, which does not contain iterative computations. Therefore, the resulting GSPN model is obtained by composing the submodels of the different coupling unit instances (enclosed into lightly-shaded frames) with the phase template. Note that, since all the instances have a single segment, the GSPN model depicted in Fig. 7

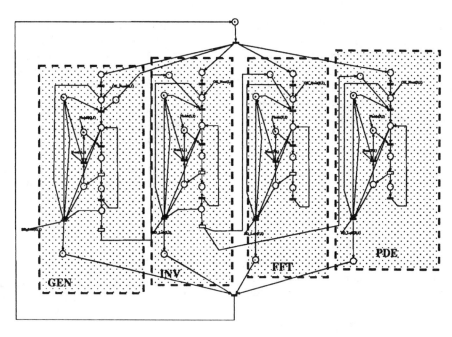

Figure 7. GSPN model of the example application

represents the structure of any possible executable configuration. The only modifications needed to model a particular executable configuration is to change the rates of the various timed transitions according to execution times of the selected instances.

Now, let us consider the executable configuration shown in Fig. 6, and suppose that we want to predict its execution time for $K = 5$ and $N = 64$. As discussed above, to obtain the GSPN model of this configuration it is sufficient to specify suitable values for the rates of the timed transitions and for the marking of some places. The execution times of GEN_{Sparc}, INV_{Sparc}, FFT_{Sparc}, and PDE_{Sparc}, computed by letting $N = 64$ in the function contained in the segment tables of the instances, are respectively 303757 μs, 344298 μs, 79837 μs, and 333171 μs. The transmission times (22322 μs) are computed by dividing the amount of data transmitted for each communication (0.015625 MBytes, corresponding to 64 × 64 4-bytes floating point numbers) by the network bandwidth (0.7 MBytes/sec.). The rates of transitions are computed as the reciprocal of the above times. Finally, place *(GEN,ENV)* (representing the initial value of K) is marked with 5 tokens, as well as places *To_Do(GEN,1)*, *To_Do(INV,1)*, *To_Do(FFT,1)*, *To_Do(PDE,1)*.

From the steady-state solution [5] of the GSPN model obtained as discussed above, we get $ET = 3.22$ sec. (3.08 sec. is instead the average execution time computed by using measurements gathered during several executions

of the program). Furthermore, the computation of the performance index P_S (Eq. (1)) yields the following values: $P_S(INV^1_{Sparc}) = 0.29$, $P_S(PDE^1_{Sparc}) = 0.20$, and $P_S(FFT^1_{Sparc}) = 0.015$. From these values, none of the instances appears to be too slow to process its inputs. However, the analysis of the performance index $Wait(.)$ (Eq. (2)) reveals that the efficiency of the application can be improved by replacing the instance INV_{Sparc}. As a matter of fact, we have that $Wait(INV^1_{Sparc}) = 0.24$, $Wait(PDE^1_{Sparc}) = 0.492$, and $Wait(FFT^1_{Sparc}) = 0.696$, which coincide with the values of $P_W(PDE^1_{Sparc})$ and $P_W(FFT^1_{Sparc})$ since each instance has only one single input. From these values we can deduce that INV_{Sparc} does not produce its outputs fast enough to keep PDE_{Sparc} and FFT_{Sparc} busy. Let us now consider the possibility of using the Alpha implementation rather than the Sparc one. For $N = 64$, the execution time of INV_{Alpha} is 164551 μs, so it is obvious that by using this instance the execution time of the application will decrease. However, in order to verify that the GSPN model correctly predicts the trend, let us solve it for this second executable configuration. From the steady-state solution, we obtain $ET = 2.7$ sec. (the actual execution time is 2.6 sec.), $Wait(PDE^1_{Sparc}) = 0.39$, and $Wait(FFT^1_{Sparc} = 0.6)$, so the GSPN model has been able to predict the trend.

5. Conclusions and Future Work

In this paper we have presented a technique, for the automatic generation of GSPN models of heterogeneous applications, which relies on the Zoom formalism for the speci-

---

[5] All the GSPN models presented in this paper have been drawn and analyzed by means of the GreatSPN[6] package.

fication of the application structure and of the performance indices to be evaluated. The coupling of Zoom with GSPNs allows one to envision an environment in which the application and the performance indices of interest are defined by means of a high-level, easy-to-use descriptive language (Zoom), while the performance evaluation is carried out by means of standard GSPN analysis techniques without the need for the user to deal directly with the GSPN model. It is our belief that an environment of this type would be helpful to the designers of heterogeneous applications.

A necessary step that needs to be further investigated in order to develop the above environment is the definition of GSPN models of the hardware resources that are used by the application. In the simple example presented in this paper we ran the application on a lightly loaded system, so the effects due to resource contention were negligible. However, in more realistic situations resource contention may greatly affect the behavior and the performance of the application. To take these effects into consideration it is necessary to explicitly model the resources of the heterogeneous computing system (e.g. cpus, network, etc.). However, the definition of these models is difficult because of the large number of different machines and networks that may be used in a heterogeneous system. Some preliminary work on the modeling of shared-medium communication network has been done in [3], but a more general solution still lacks.

Alternatively, this problem could be attacked by using suitable distributions for the execution times of the various components of the program, rather than the negative exponential one typical of GSPN models. As a matter of fact, the presence of resource contention introduces variability in the above execution times, which may not be suitably represented by the negative exponential distribution. However, using a distribution different from the negative exponential one for the firing delays of timed transitions yields to models which are not analytically tractable with standard Markovian techniques, so in this case alternative solution techniques have to be sought.

Acknowledgements

The author whishes to thank the technical staff of the Dipartimento di Informatica of the University of Torino for their support in the setup of the computing platform used in the experiments.

References

[1] M. Ajmone Marsan, G. Balbo, and G. Conte. A class of generalized stochastic Petri nets for the performance analysis of multiprocessor systems. *ACM Transactions on Computer Systems*, 2(1), May 1984.

[2] M. Ajmone Marsan, G. Balbo, G. Conte, S. Donatelli, and G. Franceschinis. *Modelling with Generalized Stochastic Petri Nets*. J. Wiley, 1995.

[3] C. Anglano. Performance Modeling of Heterogeneous Distributed Applications. In *Proceedings of the fourth International Workshop on Modeling and Analysis of Computer and Telecommunication Systems (MASCOTS 96)*. IEEE CS Press, February 1996.

[4] C. Anglano, J. Schopf, R. Wolski, and F. Berman. Representing Heterogeneous Applications with Zoom. Unpublished manuscript (http://www.di.unito.it/WWW/PEgroup/persons/mino.html), March 1996.

[5] J. Becker and L. Dagum. Particle Simulation on Heterogeneous Distributed Supercomputers. *Concurrency: Practice and Experience*, 5(4):367–377, June 1993.

[6] G. Chiola, G. Franceschinis, R. Gaeta, and M. Ribaudo. GreatSPN1.7: GRaphical Editor and Analyzer for Timed and Stochastic Petri Nets. *Performance Evaluation*, 24, 1995. Special Issues on Performance Modelling Tools.

[7] R. Clay and P. Steenkiste. Distributing a Chemical Process Optimization Application over a Gigabit Network. In *Proceedings of Supercomputing '95*, December 1995. http://scxy.tc.cornell.edu/sc95/proceedings.

[8] P. Homer and R. Schlichting. Using Schooner to support distribution and heterogeneity in the Numerical Propulsion System Simulation project. *Concurrency: Practice and Experience*, 6(4):271–287, June 1994. Special Issue on High-Performance Distributed Computing.

[9] A. Khokhar, V. Prasanna, M. Shaaban, and C. Wang. Heterogeneous Computing: Challenges and Opportunities. *IEEE Computer*, June 1993.

[10] A. Klietz, A. Malevsky, and K. Chin-Purcell. A Case Study in Metacomputing: Distributed Simulations of Mixing in Turbulent Convection. In *Proceedings of the 2nd. Workshop on Heterogeneous Processing*, pages 101–106. IEEE-CS Press, 1993.

[11] C. R. Mechoso, C.-C. Ma, J. D. Farrara, J. A. Spahr, and R. W. Moore. Parallelization and Distribution of a Coupled Atmosphere-Ocean general Circulation Model. *Monthly Weather Review*, 121(7):2062–76, July 1993.

[12] W. Press, W. Vetterling, S. Teukolsky, and B. Flannery. *Numerical Recipes in C – The Art of Scientific Computing, 2nd Ed.* Cambridge University Press, 1992.

[13] D. W. Robertson, V. Jacobson, W. Johnston, S. Loken, E. Theil, and B. Thierney. Distributed Visualization Using Workstations, Supercomputers, and High Speed Networks. In *Proceedings of Visualization 91*, San Diego, CA, 1991. IEEE-CS Press.

[14] V. S. Sunderam, G. A. Geist, J. Dongarra, and R. Manchek. The PVM concurrent computing system: evolution, experiences, and trends. *Parallel Computing*, 20(4):531–45, April 1994.

[15] M. Wu and A. Kupperman. CASA Quantum Chemical Reaction Dynamics. In *1994 CASA Gigabit Network Testbed Annual Report*. 1994.

Author Index

Notes

Notes

Notes